e SAGE
book *of*

nental

Disorders

The SAGE
Handbook *of*

Developmental Disorders

Edited by
Patricia Howlin,
Tony Charman,
& Mohammad Ghaziuddin

Los Angeles | London | New Delhi
Singapore | Washington DC

SAGE Publications Ltd
1 Oliver's Yard 55 City Road
London EC1Y 1SP

SAGE Publications Inc.
2455 Teller Road
Thousand Oaks, California 91320

SAGE Publications India Pvt Ltd
B 1/I 1 Mohan Cooperative Industrial Area
Mathura Road
New Delhi 110 044

SAGE Publications Asia-Pacific Pte Ltd
33 Pekin Street #02-01
Far East Square
Singapore 048763

Library of Congress Control Number: 2010940447

British Library Cataloguing in Publication data

A catalogue record for this book is available from the
British Library

ISBN 978-1-4129-4486-1
ISBN 978-1-4462-9582-3 (pb)

Typeset by Cenveo Publisher Services
Printed in Great Britain by Henry Ling Limited, Dorchester
Printed on paper from sustainable resources

Contents

Contributors

Adriana Di Martino, M.D., is a Leon Levy Assistant Professor of Child and Adolescent Psychiatry at the Phyllis Green and Randolph C wen Institute for Pediatric Neuroscience at the NYU Child Study Center. Dr. Di Martino graduated magna cum laude from the University of Cagliari School of Medicine in Italy. Following a five-year residency training in pediatric neurology and child and adolescent psychiatry, Dr. Di Martino joined the NYU Child Study Center where she conducts research focuses on functional neuroimaging studies to reveal the physiopathological mechanisms underlying of Autism and related neurodevelopment disorders. Dr. Di Martino's work has been published in several peer-reviewed journals including *Biological Psychiatry, and* the *American Journal of Psychiatry*. Dr. Di Martino has been invited to present her research results at national and international scientific conferences in the U.S., Italy, Germany, Belgium and Spain.

Alison Kerr qualified in Medicine at Edinburgh Medical School and Edinburgh University in 1963 and then specialized in Paediatric Medicine, working in Edinburgh, Sheffield, Aberdeen, Cambridge and finally Glasgow University and Royal Hospital for Sick Children, becoming a Senior Lecturer and Honorary Consultant in Paediatrics and Chronic Neurological Disability. An interest in the recently described Rett syndrome began in 1982 while she was working in the Fraser of Allander Assessment Unit with Professor John Stephenson and together they identified the first group of Scottish cases. A major research interest developed in the subtle early infancy signs and the striking paroxysmal disturbances of consciousness, respiration and movement characteristic of the disorder. Funding for a senior lectureship was provided by Quarrier's Homes and the Scottish and English Rett Syndrome Associations. In 1991, Dr Kerr was invited to provide advice at 2-day clinics organized by the Rett Syndrome Associations throughout the British Isles and from that experience of the disorder she developed a national longitudinal health survey that led to a series of research collaborations and many publications and national and international recognition. Contributions to research included elucidation of the fundamental characteristics of the disorder across a wide range of severities, the earliest signs of the disorder, the electroencephalographic, respiratory and brainstem disturbances and the long-term outlook for sufferers. Dr Kerr was made a Fellow of the Royal College of Medicine of Edinburgh, awarded an OBE by the Queen for services to paediatrics in 2003 and received an MD with distinction for her doctoral thesis on Rett disorder in 2006. On her retirement in 2005 the British Isles Rett Survey became based at the University of Wales with Professor Angus Clarke. The non-invasive methods developed for central autonomic monitoring in Rett and other brainstem disorders continue in service and research in Britain and Sweden led by Dr Peter Julu and Dr Ingegerd Witt Engerstrom. The detailed study of infants with Rett disorder is now conducted by Dr Christa Einspieler in Austria.

Andrea Eugenio Cavanna MD is a Consultant in Behavioral Neurology at the Department of Neuropsychiatry, Birmingham, Honorary Senior Clinical Lecturer in Neuroscience at the University of Birmingham, and Honorary Senior Research Fellow at the Institute of Neurology, University College London, United Kingdom. He currently is leading consultant for the

Tourette Clinic at the Department of Neuropsychiatry, Birmingham. He has published extensively in the field of behavioral neurology and neuropsychiatry, with special focus on the behavioral aspects of Tourette syndrome and epilepsy. His other research areas include the neural correlates of altered conscious states in neuropsychiatric/neurodegenerative conditions. In 2010 he received the American Neuropsychiatric Association Career Development Award.

Andrea Schneider PhD is a postdoctoral research scholar at the University of California at Davis, M.I.N.D. Institute, USA. From early on in her academic career, she focused on the connection between basic psychophysiology and behavior. In her doctoral dissertation, she studied the neurophysiological bases of ADHD (attention-deficit/hyperactivity disorder) and dyslexia. Being also a clinical psychologist, her other area of interest is intervention research. She completed a small study of a phytopharmacological intervention (*Ginkgo biloba*) in dyslexia, and a study about the efficacy of neurofeedback in ADHD. Currently, her main research interest is the association between genetic and brain abnormalities underlying the neuropsychopathology, behavioral, and psychiatric symptoms in carriers with the fragile X mutation. She is also an affiliate of the ARTP (Autism Research and Treatment) program at the M.I.N.D. Institute, and a member of the FENS (Federation of European Neuroscience Society), and the Center for Cognitive Studies, University of Potsdam, Germany.

Anna Mandalis is a paediatric neuropsychologist with 16 years of clinical experience. She started her career at Sydney Children's Hospital Randwick as a clinician for the Brain Injury Rehabilitation Program. Her clinical expertise is in the area of paediatric rehabilitation. She was appointed Head of Psychology at Sydney Children's Hospital from 2001 to 2005 before taking up a position as a Senior Neuropsychologist on the newly developed state-wide Victorian Paediatric Rehabilitation Service in Victoria. During this time she was employed as a Clinical Researcher by the Australian Centre Centre for Child Neuropsychological Studies (ACCNS) at Royal Children's Hospital Melbourne. She returned to Sydney Children's Hospital in 2008 and was re-appointed to the Head of Psychology position in 2009. She routinely lectures to postgraduates enrolled in the Clinical Neuropsychology course and supervises their students at Sydney Children's Hospital. She is a reviewer for international peer-reviewed journals.

Anthony Holland holds the health Foundation Chair in the Psychiatry of Learning Disabilities in the Department of Psychiatry at the University of Cambridge and he is a Consultant Psychiatrist in the Cambridgeshire and Peterborough Foundation Trust.

Bernard Dan did most of his training in neurology, paediatric neurology and rehabilitation medicine at the Université Libre de Bruxelles (ULB), Brussels, Belgium. He is now Professor of Neurophysiology and Neurobiology and Developmental Neurology at the ULB, Head of the Department of Neurology at the Hôpital Universitaire des Enfants Reine Fabiola (ULB) and Medical Director of one of Belgium's five reference centres for cerebral palsy, the Centre Interuniversitaire de Référence pour l'Infirmité Motrice Cérébrale ULB-VUB-ULg (CIRICU). His research interests include motor control and neurophysiology in typical development and a number of neurodevelopmental conditions. He wrote more than 150 scientific articles and several books, including *Handicaps et Déficiences de l'Enfant* (with S. Dalla Piazza; De Boeck Université, 2001) and *Angelman Syndrome* (Wiley, 2008).

Camilla Azis-Clauson ran her own successful business for many years before spending time at home with her family. During that period she trained and practiced as a counsellor for abused children and obtained a BSc in psychology. She now works as a research assistant at the Social Genetic & Developmental Psychiatry Centre at the Institute of Psychiatry, King's College, London. Her particular area of interest is the long-term sequelae of, and treatment possibilities for, severe deprivation occurring in infancy.

Catherine Lord PhD is the Director of the University of Michigan Autism and Communication Disorders Center (UMACC) and a professor of psychology, psychiatry and pediatrics. She is a clinical psychologist who has worked in Canada and the UK and at various universities in the USA, including the TEACCH program. She was involved in developing standardized diagnostic instruments for ASD (the Autism Diagnostic Observation Schedule (ADOS), an observational scale, and the Autism Diagnostic Interview—Revised (ADI-R), a parent interview, considered the gold standard for research diagnoses. She was the Chair of the Committee on Effectiveness of Early Intervention in Autism for the National Research Council.

As Director of UMACC, she provides clinical evaluations and consultations and trains university students and professionals in the diagnosis of ASD. Current projects include the development of a toddler module for the ADOS and use of it in longitudinal follow-up of very young children with possible ASD; organization of the Simons Simplex Collection, a repository of cell lines and phenotypic data for families with a child with autism and a typical child; the development of a measure of spontaneous, functional language in children with ASD; two studies of different interventions with very young children; and a longitudinal study of children followed from age 2 who are now in their teens. The UMACC website is www.umaccweb.com

Chris Oliver BSc, MPhil, PhD, AFBPsS is Professor of Neurodevelopmental Disorders at the University of Birmingham and director of the Cerebra Centre for Neurodevelopmental Disorders. He trained as a clinical psychologist at Edinburgh University before completing a PhD on self-injurious behavior in people with intellectual disability at the Institute of Psychiatry, London. He is currently researching early intervention, behavior disorders in people with severe intellectual disability, behavioral phenotypes in genetic syndromes, neuropsychological and behavioral assessment for people with severe intellectual disability and Alzheimer's disease in adults with Down syndrome. Sadly, he supports Luton Town Football Club.

Cory Shulman is a senior lecturer in the Paul Baerwald School of Social Work and Social Welfare at the Hebrew University of Jerusalem, specializing in research in autism and other intellectual and developmental disabilities. By combining research involving individuals with disabilities and their families with consultative services to Hadassah Hospital and the Ministries of Health, Education and Welfare, Dr Shulman is committed to applying research results in the development of services and policy decisions which will improve the lives of individuals with disabilities.

Courtenay Frazier Norbury is an RCUK Research Fellow in Cognitive Science in the Psychology Department of Royal Holloway, University of London. Before embarking on a research career, she was a practising speech-language therapist in Hackney, East London. She completed her DPhil with Dorothy Bishop at the University of Oxford, exploring the nature of pragmatic language impairment and the overlap between autistic spectrum disorders and specific language impairment. Her current research programme utilizes eye-tracking technology to investigate language and social processing in real time. She is also interested in understanding comorbidity and what makes language particularly vulnerable across developmental disorders. She is an Associate Editor for the *Journal of Speech, Language and Hearing Research* and has recently co-edited the book *Understanding Developmental Language Disorders*, with Dorothy Bishop and Bruce Tomblin.

Daniela Plesa Skwerer PhD is a developmental psychologist in the Laboratory of Developmental Cognitive Neuroscience at Boston University School of Medicine, where she conducts research on behavioral phenotypes in Williams syndrome and other neurodevelopmental disorders. She is currently a co-investigator on a research project focused on social cognition and perception in adolescents and adults with Williams syndrome and has been principal investigator on a research project on social-emotional development in children with Williams syndrome and children with Down syndrome, projects funded by the National Institutes of Health. The domain of social and psychological understanding has been the main focus of her developmental work for almost a decade. In her recent work she has been employing a combination of behavioral observations, computerized behavioral experiments, psychophysiological measures, eye-tracking technology, and developmental/cognitive assessments to investigate the social-cognitive phenotype associated with Williams syndrome. She is particularly interested in the developmental aspects of social cognition, communication, and emotional functioning in typical and atypical development.

David Hessl PhD is Associate Professor for Psychiatry and Behavioral Sciences at the University of California at Davis, M.I.N.D. Institute. Dr. Hessl's clinical interests involve cognitive, emotional, and behavioral evaluation of children, adolescents, and adults with neurodevelopmental disorders, especially those with fragile X syndrome, autism spectrum disorders, ADHD, and learning disabilities. He also has expertise in developmental psychopathology, particularly mood and anxiety disorders, in infants and young children. He has focused his recent research on genetic, environmental, and hormonal contributions to cognition and behavior in children with fragile X syndrome. Dr Hessl has developed a laboratory to investigate the emotional psychophysiology of children with neurodevelopmental disorders at the UC Davis M.I.N.D. Institute, where his work currently concentrates on autism, fragile X syndrome, and most recently individuals who are carriers of the fragile X gene. He also conducts collaborative studies with other researchers, investigating brain imaging, molecular genetics, and neuropsychology in an effort to understand links between genetics, brain function, and behavior.

Deborah J. Fidler is an Associated Professor in the Department of Human Development and Family Studies at Colorado State University. She received her PhD from UCLA in the Graduate School of Education and Information Studies. Dr Fidler conducts research on behavioral phenotypes in children with genetic disorders associated with intellectual disabilities. Most recently, she has been examining how phenotypic profiles emerge in early childhood, and how to use this information for effective intervention planning.

Dieter Wolke PhD is Professor of Developmental Psychology and Individual Differences at the Department of Psychology (Faculty of Science) and at Warwick Medical School, University of Warwick, Coventry. He has held positions in Germany (Munich), Switzerland (Zurich) and the UK (London, Hatfield, Bristol). His teaching of undergraduates and clinical psychologists is in the field of Developmental Psychopathology. His major research areas are the study of (a) the effects of preterm birth (as a natural experiment) on brain development and functional outcome; (b) early regulatory problems and developmental outcomes and (c) peer and sibling bullying – their origins and longterm consequences. He is involved in several large scale whole population studies including the Bavarian Longitudinal Study, the EPICure Study , The Avon Longitudinal Study and Understanding Society: the UK Household Longitudinal Survey that assess both, psychological factors and biomarkers.

Frank Muscara is a pediatric clinical neuropsychologist who has a number of years experience working with children with various forms of acquired brain injury and neurological disorders. In addition to his clinical work, he has developed his research career at the Murdoch Childrens Research Institute, where his expertise lies in tracking long-term social outcomes following pediatric acquired brain injury. Dr Muscara coordinates research projects within his team, and has recently expanded his research interests to include the intervention and rehabilitation of children with acquired brain injuries, and their families. He is a longstanding member of the Australian Centre for Child Neuropsychological Studies (ACCNS), at the Royal Children's Hospital, Melbourne, Australia.

Frederick Sundram is currently a clinical senior registrar in Psychiatry at Connolly Hospital, Dublin and a lecturer at the Royal College of Surgeons in Ireland (RCSI). He is also a research fellow at both the Institute of psychiatry, King's College London and RCSI. He graduated with a medical degree in 2000 from University College Cork followed by training in psychiatry at St John of God Hospital, Dublin and is a member of the Royal College of Psychiatrists (UK). He has also completed a masters degree in healthcare management from the Institute of Public Administration, Dublin in 2009. His research interests include neuroimaging, neurodevelopmental disorders, epilepsy, and psychopathy.

Fred R. Volkmar, BS, MA, MD is Director of Yale Child Study Center. His main research interests have centered on several aspects of autism and related disorders including issues of diagnosis, longitudinal studies of development, and the nature of social difficulties (including brain related) difficulties in autism. Hc also has a long standing interest in facilitating the entry of new investigators, from various disciplines, in the field. In addition to his research interests he currently serves as chairperson of his department and is editor of the Journal of Autism and Developmental Disorders.

Grace Iarocci is an Associate Professor of Psychology, a Michael Smith Foundation for Health Research Scholar and Director of the Autism and Developmental Disorders Lab (ADDL) at Simon Fraser University in British Columbia. Dr Iarocci and her team at ADDL investigate the basic processes of attention and perception that are involved in the social-cognitive development of individuals with an autism spectrum disorder (ASD) and how families and communities may support the development of social competence. Dr Iarocci works closely with government and community agencies in British Columbia to disseminate research information on ASD and influence policy on ASD and other developmental disabilities.

Hayley Archer is a Consultant in Clinical Genetics in the University Hospital of Wales in Cardiff and a NISCHR Research Fellow. She undertook an MD investigating the clinical and molecular basis of Rett syndrome and related disorders from 2003 to 2006. The Cardiff research group was involved in a successful collaboration, presenting a key paper on the identification of CDKL5 mutations in patients with early onset of severe epilepsy and Rett-like features. She has an ongoing research interest in Rett syndrome and related disorders.

Heidi Flores is an MA student in the Department of Educational and Counselling Psychology at McGill University specializing in human development and is the research coordinator of the McGill Youth Study Team.

Helen Tager-Flusberg is Professor of Psychology at Boston University and of Anatomy & Neurobiology and Pediatrics at Boston University School of Medicine. She began her career as a developmental psycholinguist, studying language acquisition in children with autism. Her work has expanded to encompass other neurodevelopmental disorders, including Williams syndrome, Down syndrome, and specific language impairment, as well as other developmental domains, especially social cognition. She is particularly interested in the interconnections between language and social cognition and uses behavioral, psychophysiological, and neuroimaging methods to investigate neurocognitive phenotypes associated with different disorders. More recently she has now embarked on a large-scale longitudinal study exploring the origins of language and social impairments associated with autism and SLI in infants defined as at genetic risk for these complex disorders.

Ian Miller MD is a pediatric epileptologist at Miami Children's Hospital, where he is the Director of Neuroinformatics. He has special interest in surgically treatable epilepsy, genetic epilepsy syndromes, and image processing. He helped establish the Tuberous Sclerosis Program and the Ion Channel Epilepsy Program at Miami Children's Hospital, and performs research in clinical outcomes in epilepsy.

Jacob A. (Jake) Burack is Professor of Human Development and School Applied Child Psychology in the Department of Educational and Counselling Psychology at McGill University, founder and Director of the McGill Youth Study Team (MYST), and a research consultant at Hôpital Rivière des Prairies. Jake and his students work within the MYST motto of 'a commitment to excellence in the study and education of all children'. Their theoretical framework is that of developmental psychopathology, the interface of typical and atypical development and developmental histories. Their primary focus of study is the development of attention and cognition among typically developing children, persons with autism, and persons with specific syndromes associated with intellectual disabilities. In a second area of research, they study the academic, social, and emotional well-being of First Nations adolescents who live in northern communities.

Jane McCarthy is Consultant Psychiatrist for the Mental Health in Learning Disability Service, South London & Maudsley NHS Foundation Trust based at Guy's Hospital, London, UK and Lead for Research & Development, Estia Centre, Health Service and Population Research Department, Institute of Psychiatry, King's College London. She has worked as a senior clinician in intellectual disability and mental health services across England including child, adolescent and adult services. She has taught at a number of academic centres including University College London and University of Cambridge. Her main areas of research are the mental health needs of people with intellectual disability, specifically people with Down syndrome and those with autism spectrum conditions. She is secretary to the European Association for Mental Health in Intellectual Disability and co-editor of the *Advances in Mental Health and Learning Disabilities Journal*.

Janet Carr qualified as a clinical psychologist in 1950 and worked in adult and child psychiatry. She later specialized in learning disability, and was until her retirement in 1992 Regional Tutor in the Psychology of Learning Disability at St George's Hospital, London. Her principal research interest has concerned a longitudinal study of a cohort of children with Down syndrome and their families, and a matched comparison group of non-disabled babies and their families, beginning when the children were 6 weeks old and continuing (so far) until 45 years old. The study has generated 28 papers and book chapters, and two books, *Young Children with Down's Syndrome* (Butterworth, 1975) and *Down's Syndrome: Children Growing Up* (Cambridge University Press, 1995).

Jenny Sloneem BSc, PhD, DClinPsy, CPsychol is a highly specialist clinical psychologist working in West London Mental Health NHS Trust. She works with children and adolescents diagnosed with learning difficulties and/or autistic spectrum disorders who have emotional and behavioral difficulties. She is also an honorary member of the research team at University of Birmingham's Cerebra Centre for Neurodevelopmental Disorders. In 2003, she completed a PhD at the University of Birmingham, where her research focused on self-injurious behavior in Cornelia de Lange syndrome. This research shaped her career and, when she later trained as a clinical psychologist at the Institute of Psychiatry, London, her doctoral thesis concentrated on the challenging behavior shown by children and adults with Smith–Magenis syndrome. She remains involved with the parent support groups for both Cornelia de Lange syndrome and Smith–Magenis syndrome and continues to be interested in the field of behavioral phenotypes. She aims to use research findings in this area to inform the clinical interventions that she undertakes with families.

Jeremy Turk MD is Professor of Developmental Psychiatry at St George's, University of London, and Consultant Child and Adolescent Psychiatrist in the South West London and St George's Mental Health NHS Trust where he is Clinical Team Leader in the CAMHS–LD service. His main clinical and academic interests and expertise relate to the mental health issues experienced by children and young people with intellectual disability. He is also Consultant Psychiatrist to the National Autistic Society and Council Member of the Royal Society of Medicine Intellectual Disability Forum.

Joyce Whittington was a Senior Research Associate at the University of Cambridge prior to her retirement last year. Originally a mathematician, she later trained in psychology followed by a PhD on the topic of dyscalculia. Moving to Cambridge in 1988, she worked on human–computer interaction with the Medical Research Council, then as a psychologist on the Health and Lifestyle Survey at the University of Cambridge, before joining Tony Holland in 1998 to work on Prader–Willi syndrome. Their collaboration, together with colleagues in Cambridge and Birmingham, led to several research grants, some important original findings, a wealth of published papers, and a book on Prader–Willi syndrome published in 2004.

Karine Pelc is a paediatric neurologist. She is an Associate Chief of the Neurology Clinic at the Hôpital Universitaire des Enfants Reine Fabiola of the Université Libre de Bruxelles (ULB), Brussels, Belgium. Her clinical interests include a wide range of conditions, such as ADHD, cerebral palsy, Rett syndrome and Angelman syndrome. Her research is mainly in clinical neurophysiology.

Kate Arron BSc, MPhil, ClinPsyD is a clinical psychologist working in the National Health Service in the UK and an honorary Research Fellow at the Cerebra Centre for Neurodevelopmental Disorders at the University of Birmingham. She completed her clinical psychology doctorate on self-injurious and aggressive behavior in genetic disorders in 2005 following her research into the behavioral phenotype of Cornelia de Lange syndrome.

Kieran C. Murphy initially trained in internal medicine at the Mater Misericordiae University Hospital, Dublin after graduating from University College Dublin in 1987. Subsequently, Professor Murphy trained in psychiatry at St John of God Hospital, Dublin where he also obtained a masters degree in psychoanalytical psychotherapy from UCD. He moved to Cardiff University in 1994 where he completed his higher clinical training in psychiatry, undertook two research fellowships and obtained a PhD in psychiatric genetics. In 1999, he was appointed senior lecturer in behavioral genetics at the Institute of Psychiatry, King's College London and in 2002, took up his current appointment as professor and chairman of the Academic Department of Psychiatry, Royal College of Surgeons in Ireland and consultant psychiatrist at

Beaumont Hospital, Dublin. He is a Fellow of the Royal College of Physicians of Ireland and a Fellow of the Royal College of Psychiatrists (UK) and was appointed President of the Irish Medical Council in July 2008. He has published in excess of 130 publications and his research interests include the genetics of psychiatric disorders and the assessment and neurobiology of behavioral phenotypes in genetic disorders.

Kieran D. O'Malley was born in Belfast, Northern Ireland and went to Clongowes Wood College School in Co. Kildare. Dr O'Malley qualified in medicine from University College Dublin in 1972. He has trained in public health in London, UK, and completed a Family Medicine Residency Training in Edmonton, Canada, where he practiced as a family physician for 5 years. He completed adult psychiatric training at McGill University, Montreal and University of Alberta, Edmonton, Canada. He completed child psychiatry training at Cornell Medical School, New York, and Alberta Children's Hospital, Calgary, Canada. He is a Board Certified Psychiatrist and Board Eligible Child Psychiatrist. His academic interest is in developmental disability and neuropsychiatric disorders, especially fetal alcohol spectrum disorders and he has worked in this area for 20 years, initially starting an FAS clinic in Glenrose Hospital, Edmonton in 1991. Later he joined the academic faculty of the University of Washington, Seattle, 1998–2006 and worked with Professor Ann Streissgiuth, a pioneer in the field of FAS/FASD research. He has written 50 papers, nine book chapters, and two books. He has presented plenary sessions, papers, and posters, and lectured in the USA, Canada, Australia, the UK, Ireland, Belgium, France, Italy, and Finland. He recently was a consultant adolescent psychiatrist in the Belfast Trust, 2006–2009, and worked at The Young Peoples Centre and Royal Victoria Hospital. Currently, he is working as a child and adolescent psychiatrist in Dublin, Ireland, based at the Charlemont Clinic, and is involved in teaching and research on FASD at Lucena Clinic, Rathgar, Dublin.

Kimberly Gilbert PhD is an Assistant Professor at Hofstra University with primary responsibility in the PsyD program in school/community psychology. She is the founder and Director of the Diagnostic and Research Institute for Autism Spectrum Disorders, a specialty clinic of the Psychological Evaluation and Research Center at Hofstra University. Dr Gilbert supervises and trains doctoral students in the techniques of applied behavior analysis, as well as in various interventions for children with ASD, such as milieu communication training, and in ASD diagnostic evaluations utilizing such instruments as the Autism Diagnostic Observation Schedule (ADOS) and the Autism Diagnostic Interview-Revised (ADI-R). Dr Gilbert's areas of expertise are in the area of developmental disabilities, particularly autism spectrum disorders, and special needs assessment. Her current research interests include exploration of the phenotypic expression of children along the autism spectrum to further delineate early-onset predictive behaviors of autism spectrum disorders and in the efficacy of language interventions, such as milieu communication treatment. Dr Gilbert has explored the efficacy of behavior, language, and prelinguistic interventions for children with special needs at Vanderbilt University and as a consultant for the intervention, milieu communication training, at Yale University. Dr Gilbert is a licensed clinical psychologist and certified school psychologist, and has published articles in various journals, such as the *Journal of Higher Education, Bulletin of the Psychonomic Society, Journal of Autism and Developmental Disorders, Perspectives on Early Language Learning*, as well as chapters on language development for children with ASDs such as in the *Textbook of Autism Spectrum Disorders* published by the American Psychiatric Publishing, Inc. Dr Gilbert has presented her research at numerous national and international conferences.

Laurie Powis BSc graduated with a BSc in Psychology in 2007 and is currently a PhD student at the University of Birmingham. Her work at the Cerebra centre for neurodevelopmental

Disorders is co-supervised by Professor Chris and Dr Ian Apperly. Following the completion of her PhD, Laurie hopes to train as a clinical psychologist.

Lisa A. Daunhauer is an Assistant Professor in the Department of Occupational Therapy at Colorado State University. She received her ScD from Boston University, Sargent College of Rehabilitation Science. In addition to her empirical work in the field of occupational therapy, she has published several recent manuscripts regarding Down syndrome. Her current research interests include systematically exploring the relationship of executive functioning to both developmental and functional outcomes in individuals with Down syndrome.

Mary May Robertson graduated from the University of Cape Town, South Africa, with her medical degree (MBChB) in 1971, thereafter training in the UK and obtaining her psychiatric qualification (MRCPsych) in 1979, which was followed by the Fellowship of the Royal College of Psychiatrists (FRCPsych) in 1991. She also undertook a 3-year MD doctoral research thesis (PhD in USA and Europe) at the National Hospital for Neurology and Neurosurgery, Queen Square, London entitled 'Depression in People with Epilepsy'. She was made a professor at UCL in 1998. She was subsequently awarded the Fellowships of both the Royal College of Physicians (UK) as well as the Royal College of Paediatrics and Child Health. In 2006 she was awarded a DSc (Med) in Neuropsychiatry entitled 'What makes us Tic?' For her travelling in 1976 (transatlantic on a yacht, circumnavigating under square rig, undertaking solo expeditions up-river and living with the Ibans in the Borneo jungle), she was elected a Fellow of the Royal Geographical Society.

She has over 320 medical and scientific publications (198 peer reviewed). She has authored papers on depression and epilepsy, depressive illness, unusual psychiatric syndromes and numerous aspects of Tourette syndrome, many appearing in high-impact factor journals: she has been cited numerous times. She has co-authored four and edited two books. Her books have been translated into 10 foreign languages. Three of the authored books have been on Tourette syndrome. She has 11 national and international awards, has delivered over a dozen keynote international lectures, and has been awarded over 20 competitive grants supporting research staff. She has been an advisor to the World Health Organization twice, including once on dysthymia in epilepsy and once on Tourette syndrome, was an Executive Committee Member of the International Neuropsychiatric Association, was Foundation Treasurer of the British Neuropsychiatry Association for 12 years, an Elected Fellow on Council and was also Sub-Dean for Examinations, of The Royal College of Psychiatrists.

She is currently Emeritus Professor of Neuropsychiatry at the University College London and Visiting Professor and Honorary Consultant to the Tourette Clinic at St George's Hospital and Medical School, London. She is a member of the American Tourette Syndrome Association International Consortium for Genetics. In 2008, she was elected Honorary Life President of ESSTS (European Society for the Study of Tourette Syndrome).

She has three prizes and a scholarship named after her at the University of Cape Town in South Africa and two prizes have been instituted in both the United Kingdom and Canada. Her biography has been published in Marquis Whose Who in 2010 (International). She has been commissioned to write in the health section of *The Daily Telegraph*, for a section of articles devoted to the UK NHS.

Mohammad Ghaziuddin is Professor of Psychiatry at the University of Michigan, Ann Arbor, USA. He is also the Director of the Autism Spectrum Disorders Program and the Child Psychiatry Fellowship Training Program at the University of Michigan. His main areas of research and clinical interests are the comorbidity and classification of autism spectrum disorders. He has published widely in the areas of developmental disorders and has served as an expert consultant to funding agencies in the US and elsewhere. He is also a member of the editorial boards of several professional journals.

Nick Bouras is Professor Emeritus of Psychiatry at the Institute of Psychiatry, King's College London. He is currently Director of Maudsley International. He has also been a lead clinician and he trained several doctors who now run clinical services, including specialist mental health services for people with intellectual disabilities. His research interests have focused on health service research and population studies, including evaluation of clinical effectiveness of mental health interventions, quality of life and bio-psychosocial determinants of behavior mostly for people with intellectual disabilities and mental health problems. He has published widely, including research and scientific papers, review articles, chapters in books and edited or written several books on mental health aspects. A number of his publications have been translated into different languages.

Orlee Udwin is a consultant clinical psychologist and child clinical psychology lead in West London Mental Health Trust's Child and Adolescent Mental Health Services in Ealing and Hounslow. She is also an honorary senior lecturer at the Institute of Psychiatry, Kings College, London. She has worked with children and young people with learning difficulties and other developmental disorders for many years, originally in South London in Lambeth and at the Maudsley Hospital, and more recently in West London in the boroughs of Ealing and Hounslow. Her research interests focus on the study of behavioral phenotypes in genetically determined syndromes which result in learning difficulties, and she has undertaken extensive studies of the cognitive and behavioral characteristics and difficulties in children and adults with Williams syndrome and Smith–Magenis syndrome. She has written a number of papers and book chapters in this field, co-edited a book with Professor Patricia Howlin on '*Outcomes in Neurodevelopmental and Genetic Disorders*' (Cambridge University Press, 2002), and produced guidelines for parents, teachers and other professionals on the management of children and adults with rare genetic syndromes.

Patricia Howlin PhD is Professor of Clinical Child Psychology at the Institute of Psychiatry, King's College, London. She is a chartered clinical psychologist with a PhD in Psychology and a Fellow of the British Psychological Society. Her principal research interests focus on autism and other developmental disorders. She has conducted evaluations of a variety of different intervention programmes, including comparative studies of home and school-based treatments; control trials of communication training programmes, and longer-term studies of the impact of early interventions. She has also been involved in research on the transition to adulthood by people with autism and individuals with Williams syndrome, developmental language disorders and fragile X syndrome. She was a founding editor of the journal *Autism: The International Journal of Research and Practice*; currently, she is associate editor of the *Journal of Applied Research in Intellectual Disabilities* and is on the editorial board of a number of other journals, including *Journal of Child Psychology and Psychiatry*; *Journal of Autism and Developmental Disorders*; *Child Psychology and Psychiatry Review*; *Focus on Autism and Developmental Disabilities*, *International Journal of Language and Communication Disorders* and *International Journal of Pediatrics*. Her books and articles on autism and Asperger syndrome have been translated into a number of different languages, including Japanese, Spanish, Hungarian, Italian, Romanian, Swedish and Korean.

Paul J. Hagerman MD is a Professor in the Department of Biochemistry and Molecular Medicine, and a M.I.N.D. Institute Investigator at the University of California, Davis, School of Medicine. He is a molecular biologist with a passionate interest in understanding the basis for specific neurodevelopmental and neurodegenerative diseases, particularly with respect to the fragile X (*FMR1*) gene. The Hagerman lab is currently using the fragile X gene as a model system for understanding the molecular basis of neurodegenerative disorders like Parkinson's disease and Alzheimer's disease through the rapidly expanding knowledge on fragile X-associated tremor/ataxia syndrome (FXTAS). He is the director of the UC Davis NeuroTherapeutics Research Institute (NTRI), an international consortium dedicated to inter-disciplinary research on the FXTAS model of neurodegeneration which began in 2007. Dr Hagerman is currently on the scientific advisory board of the National Fragile X Foundation, and is on the editorial boards of several journals.

Penny Tunnicliffe BSc, PhD is a trainee clinical psychologist at Staffordshire University and an honorary Research Associate at the Cerebra Centre for Neurodevelopmental Disorders at the University of Birmingham. In 2009, she completed her PhD at the University of Birmingham (supervised by Professor Chris Oliver) on self-injurious and aggressive behavior in Angelman, cri du chat and Cornelia de Lange syndromes. She is currently researching aspects of the behavioral phenotype of Prader–Willi syndrome. Penny is member of the Cornelia de Lange syndrome Scientific and Clinical Advisory Team in the UK.

Petrus de Vries MBChB, MRCPsych, PhD Consultant in Developmental Neuropsychiatry, Cambridgeshire & Peterborough NHS Foundation Trust, Cambridge, UK. Dr de Vries is a child and adolescent psychiatrist and is the clinical lead for a multi-agency, multi-disciplinary service for school-aged children with neurodevelopmental disorders. He has a particular clinical interest in assessment and intervention for young people with very complex neurodevelopmental and mental health needs. His research interests include autism spectrum disorders, tuberous sclerosis complex and the application of neuropsychological assessments in the clinical and educational setting. Petrus has a particular interest in the molecular mechanisms underlying neurocognitive and neurodevelopmental deficits associated with the TSC1/2-mTOR signalling pathway.

Dr de Vries is a Medical Advisor to the Tuberous Sclerosis Association (UK), a member of the Professional Advisory Board and International Scientific Advisory Panel of the Tuberous Sclerosis Alliance (USA) and a Specialist Advisor to TSDeutschland. He is also chairperson of the Society for the Study of Behavioral Phenotypes (SSBP), an international interdisciplinary research society for studying the learning and behavioral problems of individuals with genetic disorders.

Randi J. Hagerman MD is a developmental and behavioral pediatrician and Medical Director of the M.I.N.D. Institute at the University of California at Davis Medical Center, USA. She also holds an Endowed Chair in Fragile X Research and she is a Professor of Pediatrics at UC Davis. Her research has focused on genotype–phenotype correlations in those with mutations in the *FMR1* or fragile X gene. She and her colleagues discovered the late-onset neurodegenerative disorder in premutation carriers termed the fragile X-associated tremor/ataxia syndrome (FXTAS) in 2001. She has described a broad spectrum of clinical involvement in premutation carriers including ADHD, anxiety and autism spectrum disorders in children and psychopathology, neu-ropathy, hypothyroidism and fibromyalgia in adults in addition to FXTAS. Her current work also includes targeted treatments for both fragile X syndrome and premutation involvement including FXTAS. These targeted treatments include memantine for FXTAS and mGluR5 antagonists, minocycline, and R-Baclofen for those with fragile X syndrome. Targeted treatments are also being studied in combination with cognitive and educational programmes to enhance cognition in those with fragile X mutations. The screening of patients at high risk for fragile X mutations and newborns is also being carried out so that interventions can begin as soon as possible.

Rhea Paul PhD, CCC-SLP is Professor and Director of the Communication Disorders Section and Laboratory of Developmental Communication Disorders at the Yale Child Study Center. Research interests include the acquisition of speech, language, prosody, and reading comprehension in children with autism spectrum disorders, and the enhancement of preliteracy skills in at-risk pre-schoolers.

Dr Paul received her BA from Brandeis University in 1971, her master degree in Reading and Learning Disabilities from the Harvard Graduate School of Education in 1974 and her PhD in Communication Disorders from the University of Wisconsin-Madison in 1981. She is author of over 70 refereed journal articles, 30 book chapters, and seven books. She has been Principal Investigator on research projects on language disorders and autism funded by the National Institutes of Health as well as private foundations. Dr Paul has participated in a variety of expert panels and boards, has served as Vice President of both the Oregon and Connecticut State Speech-Language-Hearing Associations, and is currently President of the Connecticut Speech-Language-Hearing Association. Winner of the National 1996 Editor's Award of the AJSLP, Dr Paul is a Fellow of ASHA.

Roberto Tuchman MD, FAAP, FAAN is the Director of the Autism and Neurodevelopment Program at Miami Children's Hospital Dan Marino Center. He is an Associate Professor of Neurology at University of Miami Miller School of Medicine. He is Consulting Medical Director of the Center for Autism and Related Disorders at University of Miami-Nova Southeastern University (UM-NSU CARD). He was co-editor, with Isabelle Rapin, of *Autism: A Neurological Disorder of Early Brain Development*. He is on the Scientific Advisory Committee for Autism Speaks and on the Pediatric Commission for the International League against Epilepsy. He presently serves as the Chair of the Autism-Epilepsy Task Force, a collaborative international consortium of clinicians and scientists from the International League against Epilepsy and Autism Speaks.

Sir Michael Rutter is Professor of Developmental Psychopathology at the Institute of Psychiatry, King's College, London. His research interests span a wide field, covering studies of both school and family influences on children's behavior; assessment of the effects of maternal deprivation; and, more recently, resilience and the developmental interplay between nature and nurture and the use of natural experiments to test causal hypotheses about genetic and environmental mediation of risk in relation to normal and abnormal psychological development. He has also led a major study into the effect of early severe institutional deprivation on Romanian children adopted into the UK, the most recent phase of which was the follow-up of the children at age 15.

So Hyun 'Sophy' Kim is currently a doctoral candidate in clinical psychology at the University of Michigan. Sophy received a BA in Psychology from Ewha University, South Korea, and studied at Mount Holyoke College, Massachusetts, as an exchange student. Her research interests include developing and refining diagnostic instruments for autistic spectrum disorders and evidence-based treatment of core deficits of autism. At present, she continues to receive intensive clinical training at the University of Michigan Autism and Communication Disorders Center (UMACC) on the various diagnostic measures, including Autism Diagnostic Interview—Revised (ADI-R) and Autism Diagnostic Observation Schedule (ADOS), as well as on multiple intervention protocols.

Thomas J. Spencer MD is Associate Professor of Psychiatry at Harvard Medical School and Associate Chief of the Clinical and Research Program in Pediatric Psychopharmacology at Massachusetts General Hospital, both in Boston, Massachusetts. Before joining Massachusetts

General Hospital, he was Head of the Clinical Team for the Child and Adolescent Division of the Massachusetts Department of Mental Health.

Dr Spencer's research and clinical interests have focused on the effectiveness and safety of standard and novel pharmacologic treatments of attention-deficit/hyperactivity disorder (ADHD) throughout the life cycle. Dr Spencer has been a co-investigator in Dr Biederman's longitudinal and family-genetic studies of ADHD. Dr Spencer is the Principal Investigator in an NIMH-funded project that examines the translation of improvement of ADHD symptoms into increased cognitive and functional capacities as well as quality of life in adults with ADHD. Dr Spencer is also the principal investigator in a large; NIMH-funded PET study examining dopamine transporter binding and genetic markers in adults with ADHD. He has also edited a book on adult ADHD, published more than 200 scientific articles and over 35 book chapters, and serves on the editorial boards of a number of journals.

Timothy Edwin Wilens MD is Associate Professor of Psychiatry at Harvard Medical School. Additionally, he is Director of Adolescent Substance Abuse Services and Fellowship Director in Pediatric Psychopharmacology in the Pediatric Psychopharmacology Clinic and Research Program at the Massachusetts General Hospital in Boston, Massachusetts.

Dr Wilens earned his medical degree from the University of Michigan Medical School in Ann Arbor. He went on to complete his residency in psychiatry at Massachusetts General Hospital. He is certified by the American Board of Psychiatry and Neurology in General Psychiatry, Child and Adolescent Psychiatry, and Addiction Psychiatry.

Specializing in the diagnosis and pharmacological treatment of children and adults with ADHD, bipolar, substance abuse, and other psychopathological conditions, Dr Wilens cares for patients, supervises clinical trials, and consults on difficult cases. His expertise is sought both nationally and internationally.

Widely published, Dr Wilens has more than 300 original articles, reviews, chapters, and editorials to his credit. He is a regular presenter at national and international meetings and is sought as a speaker outside his academic responsibilities. He serves on the editorial boards of several journals and is a reviewer for many other journals. He is a distinguished fellow in the American Psychiatric Association, a fellow in the American Academy of Child and Adolescent Psychiatry, and a member of the College of Problems on Drug Dependence and the World Psychiatric Association and serves on several committees within these organizations.

Dr Wilens is a consultant on substance abuse to both the National Football League and Major League Baseball and is consistently named one of the Best Doctors in America for psychiatry.

Tony Charman is Chair in Clinical Child Psychology at the Institute of Psychiatry, King's College London. Professor Charman holds an honorary contract at Great Ormond Street Hospital for Children NHS Trust where he works in a diagnostic service for children with complex neurodevelopmental conditions. His main research interest is the investigation of early social cognitive development in children with autism and the clinical application of this work via screening, epidemiological, outcome, early intervention and 'at risk' studies. He has published more than 125 peer-reviewed papers and is the author of over 25 book chapters. He is former Editor-in-Chief of the *Journal of Child Psychology and Psychiatry*; an Associate Editor of the *Journal of Autism and Developmental Disorders* and is on the Editorial/Advisory Boards of a number of other journals. He has served on a number of expert panels for the Medical Research Council in the UK and the National Institutes of Health in the USA. He is the current Chair of the Advisory Group to the UK All Party Parliamentary Group on Autism.

PART 1

Overview

Introduction

Profound changes have occurred in the science and practice of intellectual disability over the past two decades. Apart from the change in terminology from 'mental retardation' to 'intellectual disability' (Schalock et al., 2007), progress in basic science and clinical practice has shifted the landscape— motivating us to commission leading scholars worldwide to contribute to this volume in order to capture the current state of knowledge and point to new areas of enquiry in the decades ahead.

GENETICS

The last decade has seen a revolution in our knowledge about the genetic basis of intellectual and neurodevelopmental disorders. From the discovery in the late 1950s that trisomy of chromosome 21 was the cause of Down syndrome (Fidler & Daunhauer, Chapter 1), through the knowledge that fragile X syndrome is nearly always caused by expansions of a CGG repeat in the 5′ untranslated region (5′UTR) of the fragile X mental retardation 1 (*FMR1*) gene (Hagerman, Turk, Schneider & Hagerman, Chapter 3), to the discovery in 1999 that mutations in the X-linked gene for the methyl CpG binding protein (*MECP2*) were the cause of Rett syndrome (Kerr, Chapter 8), it is now understood that most neurodevelopmental conditions have a genetic basis. However, despite much progress, the underlying genetic basis of other disorders, such as developmental language disorder (Norbury, Chapter 16) and autism spectrum disorders (Lord, Kim & DiMartino, Chapter 14) has remained more elusive. In other cases, genetic subtyping has led to important discoveries, for example, the realization that Prader–Willi syndrome had two different genetic causes: deletion involving the PWSCR of chromosome 15 of paternal origin or the inheritance of two maternally derived, but no paternally derived, chromosome 15s—referred to as maternal uniparental disomy (mUPD) (Whittington & Holland, Chapter 6). This has also led to important clinical observations, with the latter mUPD subtype but not the deletion subtype being highly associated with adult psychosis.

BASIC SCIENCE IMPROVEMENTS

Improvements in perinatal and post-traumatic medicine mean that intellectual disability and other medical sequelae are found in increasing numbers of individuals who are born very preterm (Wolke, Chapter 25) or who have suffered traumatic brain injury (Mandalis, Muscara & Anderson, Chapter 23). Other neurodevelopmental disorders result from different environmental factors such the fetal alcohol spectrum disorders (O'Malley, Chapter 24) and extreme environmental deprivation (Rutter & Azis-Clauson, Chapter 26). In both the latter examples, longitudinal studies have begun to tease out the organic effects of such insults, for example, microcephaly from the post-insult environmental circumstances that may provide protection.

NEUROPSYCHOLOGY

Other important breakthroughs have come from detailed neuropsychological study of profiles on different sets of cognitive skills, despite the presence of low IQ. For example, in individuals with Williams syndrome there is a relative weakness in visuospatial construction (assessed by the pattern construction subtest) and relative strengths in auditory short-term memory and language, even in low-functioning individuals (Plesa Skwerer & Tager-Flusberg, Chapter 5). Individuals with Velo-cardio-facial syndrome also tend to show an uneven neuropsychological profile with a discrepancy between verbal and performance IQ in 22q11DS, whereby verbal IQ (VIQ) exceeds performance IQ (PIQ) (Sundram & Murphy, Chapter 11).

COMORBIDITY

Another important clinical realization has been the recognition that neurodevelopmental disorders show high levels of comorbidities. For example, epileptic disorders are associated with intellectual disability, autism and psychiatric disorders (Miller & Tuchman, Chapter 21); attention-deficit/hyperactivity disorder (ADHD) is seen at high rates in many other neurodevelopmental conditions, including tuberous sclerosis (de Vries, Chapter 10), fragile X syndrome, autism spectrum disorders and developmental language disorders. It has also been recognized that, while specific genetic mutations account for only a minority of cases of autism spectrum disorders, autistic symptoms are very prevalent in individuals with severe intellectual disability with known genetic causes, including Cornelia de Lange syndrome and cri du chat syndrome (Oliver, Arron, Powis & Tunnicliffe, Chapter 12). However, severe intellectual disability is not universally associated with impaired social interest, as shown by the characteristic social engagement and social interest seen in Rubinstein–Taybi syndrome and Angelman syndrome (Dan & Pelc, Chapter 7). Other behavioural problems are commonly seen in individuals with intellectual disability; for example, sleep disorders are often present in children with epileptic disorders, particularly in individuals with Smith–Magenis syndrome (Sloneem & Udwin, Chapter 9).

INTERVENTION

Across the spectrum of neurodevelopmental disorders, approaches to intervention are very varied. For some disorders, such as developmental language disorder, these are solely psychoeducational (Paul & Gilbert, Chapter 17), while for others, such as Tourette syndrome (Robertson & Cavanna, Chapter 22) and ADHD (Wilens & Spencer, Chapter 13), the primary intervention is pharmacological, albeit increasingly in combination with cognitive behavioural approaches. Generic approaches that support cognitive and adaptive functioning, as well as the facility to communicate wishes and needs, are often used for individuals with global intellectual disability (Shulman, Flores, Iarocci & Burack, Chapter 18) as well as for children with disintegrative disorders (Volkmar, Chapter 20).

ADULT OUTCOMES

Until the last few decades the focus of a volume such as the present one would have been on children with developmental disorders. However, over the past few decades, as increasing numbers of children with the neurodevelopmental disorders covered in this handbook have been followed into adulthood and middle age, we now know more about outcomes than previously. For some conditions, such as autism spectrum disorders (Howlin & Charman, Chapter 15) prognosis is more variable than previously thought and is often highly dependent on environmental factors. It has also become apparent that mental health problems are common in adults with neurodevelopmental disorders, for example, in adults with fragile X syndrome (Schneider & Hessl, Chapter 4) as well as in individuals with intellectual disability of unknown origin (McCarthy & Bouras, Chapter 19). For other disorders particular

issues arise, such as the well-established vulnerability to Alzheimer's disease for people with Down syndrome (Carr, Chapter 2).

CONCLUSIONS

In most developed countries, the philosophy and organization of services has also changed so that the ambition is for individuals with neurodevelopmental disorders to live healthy and happy lives as part of a diverse and inclusive society. Over the next decades further discoveries in basic science, as well as clinical practice, will push forward the development of new interventions to ameliorate the medical, physical and behavioural sequelae that are commonly associated with intellectual disability and will further allow this ambition to be fulfilled.

REFERENCES

Schalock, R.L., Luckasson, R.A., Shogren, K.A., Borthwick-Duffy, S., Bradley, V., Buntinx, W.H.E., et al. (2007) 'The renaming of mental retardation: understanding the change to the term intellectual disability', *Intellectual and Developmental Disabilities*, 45: 116–124.

PART 2

Disorders with a Known Genetic Cause

Down Syndrome: General Overview

Deborah J. Fidler, & Lisa A. Daunhauer

BRIEF HISTORICAL PERSPECTIVE

It is difficult to identify when the physical and psychological features associated with Down syndrome were identified as constituting a specific phenomenon. Archeological evidence of the remains of a person with Down syndrome dates back to the seventh century (Roizen, 2007). Some posit that artistic renderings of individuals with Down syndrome can be found in paintings produced as far back as the 1600s (Volpe, 1986). But it is clear that by the middle part of the nineteenth century, recognition of the disorder had entered into the scientific literature. John Langdon Down (1866/1995) and Edouard Seguin (1866) each published work describing a cluster of symptoms associated with intellectual impairments in their patient populations. Down (1866/1995), for example, argued that the unique physical (mainly craniofacial) appearance of the cheeks, eyes, lips, and tongue was so distinct as to be caused by a common cause. He noted that '[s]o marked is this, that when placed side by side, it is difficult to believe that the speci-

mens compared are not children of the same parents (p. 55).' By 1877, the textbook *On Idiocy and Imbecility* was the first to include a special category on what was then termed 'Mongolian idiocy' (Ireland, 1877).

The subsequent search for the underlying etiology of these physical and psychological symptoms continued during the early part of the twentieth century and into the 1950s. Along the way, numerous erroneous etiologies for Down syndrome were put forth in the literature, including maternal tuberculosis during pregnancy and thyroid dysfunction (Clark, 1933; Muir, 1903). Other discoveries that have been borne out were made during this process, such as the recognition that advanced maternal age was a critical contributing factor in Down syndrome (Penrose, 1933, 1934).

There is a historical footnote to the discovery of Down syndrome that includes an unfortunate racial element to the earliest scientific work with this population. John Langdon Down's original observations in 1866 placed the disorder within an ethnicity-related classification system, wherein the regrettable term

'Mongolism' was originated. Though this terminology left a legacy of derogatory racial connotations, Down's views on ethnicity were actually enlightened for his time, as he argued that if a child with cognitive impairments of one race could show the 'racial features' of another race, it 'proved that racial differences were not specific' (Brain, 1967: p. 4). Down's observations regarding the universality of such characteristics even led him to argue against the institution of slavery in the United States during the time of the US Civil War (Brain, 1967). The ethnic classification of such impairments was later publicly refuted by Down's son, Reginald, a physician who worked in a home established by John Langdon Down for individuals with disabilities (Brain, 1967).

By 1959, Lejeune and his team had linked the disorder via karyotyping to the presence of an extra chromosome 21 (Lejeune et al., 1959). The following year, Polani and colleagues identified a case of Down syndrome caused by the translocation of material from chromosomes 15 and 21 (Polani et al., 1960). Mosaic Down syndrome was subsequently described in the literature in 1961 (Clarke et al., 1961).

EPIDEMIOLOGY

According to the most recent analysis of data from the US-based National Birth Defects Prevention Network, the prevalence of Down syndrome is 1 in every 732 live births when averaged across all maternal ages (Canfield et al., 2006). There is some evidence that the vast majority (80%) of trisomy 21 pregnancies result in miscarriage (Hook et al., 1995). Canfield et al. (2006) found a higher prevalence of Down syndrome in Hispanic families in the United States (prevalence ratio compared to non-Hispanic white families = 1.12) when compared to non-Hispanic white (prevalence ratio = 1.00) and non-Hispanic black families (prevalence ratio = 0.77). Possible explanations for this finding include differential use of prenatal health care, termination rates, and genetic or environmental factors, as well as artifacts of the research methodology

employed in the Canfield et al. (2006) study (see Sherman et al., 2007 for a discussion).

Causation

The vast majority of cases of Down syndrome (90–95%) are caused by non-disjunction involving chromosome 21 during meiosis (oogenesis and spermatogenesis). The National Down Syndrome Project, a large-scale US-based epidemiological study of Down syndrome, reported that 93.2% of observed cases were caused by maternal non-disjunction and 4.1% were caused by paternal non-disjunction (Freeman et al., 2007). In a Spanish population-based study of the etiology of Down syndrome, Gomez et al. (2000) found that 88% of observed cases had maternal meiotic origin and 5.6% of the cases observed were of paternal meiotic origin. Of the maternal cases in the Gomez et al. (2000) study, 90.6% occurred in during the first meiotic division and 6.2% occurred during the second meiotic division. In the paternal cases, half occurred during meiosis I and half occurred during meiosis II. There is some suggestion, however, that some meiosis II errors may actually originate in meiosis I (Sherman et al., 2005).

Though non-disjunction during meiosis is the main cause of Down syndrome, accounting for the vast majority of cases, there are two other etiological mechanisms. Roughly 1% of cases of Down syndrome are mosaic in nature (Connor & Ferguson-Smith, 1997). Mosaicism results from errors in mitosis following fertilization, leading to two different cell lines in a developing zygote/embryo (Connor & Ferguson-Smith, 1997). One cell line contains the normal 46 chromosomes and a second cell line contains the additional chromosome 21. In the majority of cases (80%), mosaicism resulted from non-disjunction in mitosis in a zygote that already had trisomy 21. In the remaining cases (20%), mosaicism occurred in a euploid zygote (Connor & Ferguson-Smith, 1997).

Down syndrome can be caused by a translocation of genetic material between chromosome 21 and another chromosome (Connor & Ferguson-Smith, 1997). This is the cause of roughly 4% of cases of Down syndrome. Translocation leading to Down syndrome can either be passed on from a parent who is carrying a balanced translocation, or it can occur de novo. Parental translocations leading to Down syndrome are considered 'balanced', in that the exchange of information from one chromosome to another did not lead to overall loss or gain of chromosomal material in the parent. However, the offspring of a parent who carries a balanced translocation often does show chromosomal imbalances due to further complications during meiosis (Connor & Ferguson-Smith, 1997). When the offspring imbalance is observed to involve chromosome 21, this causes translocation leading to Down syndrome.

Though the genetic causes of Down syndrome are relatively well-researched, the pathway from gene overexpression on chromosome 21 to the observed phenotypic outcomes in Down syndrome remains poorly understood at present. Silverman (2007) notes that the complexity of this gene overexpression includes the potential interaction between proteins produced by these genes as well as the potential interaction between these proteins and other genes on other chromosomes beyond chromosome 21. It also appears that a wide range of genes on chromosome 21 may contribute to the cognitive phenotype in Down syndrome, and thus, research will need to take a broader approach beyond identifying a small critical region responsible for the majority of outcomes in this disorder (Olson, et al., 2007; Silverman, 2007).

Risk factors

Advanced maternal age is associated with only one cause of Down syndrome, maternal non-disjunction. The link between advanced maternal age and non-disjunction is attributed to the extended nature of meiosis and the generation of ovum in human females, which can last between 10 and 50 years (Sherman et al., 2005, 2007). Risk for errors in first meiosis and second meiosis are both associated with maternal age (Sherman et al., 2005). The mechanism that causes non-disjunction to become likelier

in older females is unclear, though competing hypotheses include hormonal changes leading to poorer performance of the ovaries, exposure to toxins over time, and the compromising effect of suspended and then resumed meiosis over several decades (Sherman et al., 2007). Advanced maternal age is not associated with other etiologies of Down syndrome, including paternal non-disjunction, translocations, and mosaicism (see Sherman et al., 2005).

Another factor that increases the risk of maternal non-disjunction is atypical recombination during meiosis (Sherman et al., 2005). During the phase of meiosis when exchange of genetic information across sister chromosomes takes place, there are patterns that can increase the risk of non-disjunction occurring (Sherman et al., 2005). Sherman et al. (2005) describe that this can include a lack of information exchanged or exchanges at either the far end of the chromosomes (telomeres) or in the center of the chromosome (centromere). It is unclear whether maternal age is associated with alterations in the recombination phase of meiosis.

Possible environmental causes have been discussed in the literature on the etiology of Down syndrome as well. Smoking at the time of conception has been examined as a potential cause of non-disjunction errors leading to trisomy 21 (Sherman et al., 2005; Yang et al., 1999). In particular, Yang et al. (1999) found that younger mothers of individuals with Down syndrome who were found to both take oral contraceptives and smoke cigarettes at the time of conception were more likely to have had errors in meiosis II rather than meiosis I. Other potential environmental causes may be identified in the future, though none are supported by substantial scientific evidence to date (Sherman et al., 2005).

CORE CHARACTERISTICS

Cognition

Most individuals with Down syndrome fall into the mild to moderate range of intellectual disability, with IQs spanning between 40 and 70 (Hodapp et al., 1999). The trajectory of intelligence quotient (IQ) scores in Down syndrome involves a distinctive deceleration after the first few years of life, which leads to a decline in IQ scores during this period (Hodapp et al., 1999). This pattern appears to be unique to Down syndrome and not observed in children with intellectual disability, in general.

One area of cognitive development that is of critical importance in this population is the development of executive functioning. Executive function (EF) is an umbrella term used to describe the cognitive processes integral to adaptive, goal-directed actions, including working memory, inhibition, shifting, and planning (Blair et al., 2005; Carlson, 2005; Fletcher, 1996). Though more research is needed on the topic, there is some evidence that individuals with Down syndrome demonstrate deficits in these adaptive, goal-directed behaviors (Dawson et al., 1998; Kittler et al., 2008; Pennington et al., 2003; Rowe et al., 2006). Consequently, researchers have begun studying Down syndrome with neuropsychological tasks in addition to developmental activities (Edgin, 2003; Pennington et al., 2003).

Working memory

Working memory is the process of storing and manipulating information for complex tasks such as learning and reasoning (Baddeley, 1992). Upon discovering deficits in verbal short-term memory in individuals with Down syndrome, Jarrold and Baddeley (1997) began investigating how individuals with Down syndrome simultaneously store and use information. Research from this team and others indicates that working memory deficits have been observed in this population (Jarrold Baddeley et al., 2000; 2002; Lanfranchi et al., 2004). However, this impairment seems to be more pronounced with verbal information, as impairments are minimal in visuospatial domains. The deficit appears to be neither a motor nor an articulatory problem (Kanno & Ikeda, 2002) and

may relate to the phonological loop (Laws, 2002; Jarrold & Baddeley, 2007).

Interestingly, Pennington and colleagues (2003) studied working memory in school-aged children and adolescents with Down syndrome and initially found no impairments when using a counting activity. Baddeley and Jarrold (2007) noted that this finding was inconsistent with expectations for the population based on multiple studies indicating individuals with Down syndrome have difficulty with tasks such as remembering lists. Indeed, subsequent research by Pennington and colleagues, as well as others (Lanfranchi et al., 2004; Visu-Petra et al., 2007), indicated that verbal tasks and tasks requiring higher executive load elicited more difficulties in Down syndrome groups as opposed to comparison groups (see Nadel, 2003 for a review).

Inhibition

Through inhibition, also referred to as response inhibition, individuals exert control over their own behavior to override automatic, or prepotent, responses (Carlson, 2005; Diamond et al., 2007; Pennington, 1997). Studies of early emotion regulation and delay of gratification in preschool-aged children with Down syndrome suggest that poor inhibition contributes to poor performance on instrumental thinking tasks (Kopp et al., 1983). In one study, 3–4-year-old children with Down syndrome showed significantly shorter latency to touch a prohibited target toy than mental age (MA)- or language age-matched children (Kopp et al., 1983). In addition, young children with Down syndrome in this study generated fewer and less effective strategies for delaying gratification, including directing more of their time and attention to the prohibited target object than comparison group children. Another line of research suggests that when faced with cognitive challenges, children with Down syndrome are more likely than developmentally matched children to avoid the tasks with both positive and negative behaviors (Wishart, 1996). Along these lines, preschoolers with Down syndrome show lower levels of task persistence and higher levels of off-task behavior during simple play tasks than MA-matched comparison group children (Landry & Chapieski, 1990; Pitcairn & Wishart, 1994; Ruskin et al., 1994; Vlachou & Farrell, 2000).

Shifting

Evidence regarding the ability for children with Down syndrome to determine new rules and apply them, called shifting or cognitive flexibility, comes primarily from one published study. This study focused on components of EF and autism that employed a Down syndrome comparison group. Dawson and colleagues (1998) found that a modest-sized group of 5 year olds with Down syndrome was able to perform a delayed non-matching to object task (after being reinforced for searching for a reward hidden under one of two objects, the child must locate a new reward when it is hidden) significantly better than matched peers with autism. Also, the Down syndrome group was able to perform a simple rule-learning game significantly better than the autism group. However, the authors did not compare the performance of the Down syndrome group children with disabilities other than autism, a group known to show pronounced deficits in EF (Hill, 2004).

Conversely, in an unpublished dissertation thesis, a cross-sectional study of adolescents and young adults with Down syndrome indicated that shifting may actually be difficult for this population. Using a task, the dimensional card sort, participants had to determine the rule by which target cards are sorted (e.g. dimensions of shape, color, or number) and then when the rule changed the participant had to discover the new rule and sort accordingly (Edgin, 2003). Almost 41% of the individuals with Down syndrome in this study could not shift on the dimensional card sorting task. In contrast, only 8% of the comparison group with Williams syndrome could not shift correctly. Importantly, the Down syndrome group with an MA equivalent to 7 years of age would have been expected to ceiling out of the card sorting task (ceiling

age 4 years in typical development) if their shifting abilities had met MA level, therefore, the Down syndrome group in this study performed shifting tasks well below MA expectations. More evidence is needed to better understand cognitive flexibility in individuals with Down syndrome. Also, this informative study found that participants' in *both* groups had no change in performance when Edgin manipulated the task from including explicit verbal instructions for the preswitch rule to having no explicitly stated rules. However, verbal IQ did predict switching performance. It is possible that language processing in conjunction with other components may underlie shifting abilities.

Planning

Planning, or problem-solving, is an aspect of executive functioning requiring the generation of appropriate steps needed to reach a goal. Individuals with Down syndrome have been shown to take longer to complete problem-solving tasks, are more likely to abandon problem-solving tasks, and perform more poorly than developmentally-matched children on problem-solving tasks (Fidler et al., 2005b; Kasari & Freeman, 2001; Pitcairn & Wishart, 1994). In contrast, in the unpublished dissertation thesis of adolescents and young adults with Down syndrome described above, Edgin (2003) found that in contrast to their shifting performance, the individuals with Down syndrome performed a single planning task (Tower of London) at approximately MA level. However, the work of others (e.g. Fidler and colleagues) examined problem solving with more depth and found more problems in this population.

Poor problem-solving skills may impact academic performance. For example, on a novel counting task, older children with Down syndrome (9–13 years) showed fewer self-corrections than their typically developing classmates, an important indicator of goal monitoring (Gelman & Cohen, 1988). They also failed to generate new strategies when faced with a new goal, evidence of deficits in the use of analogous problem solving (Gelman

& Cohen, 1988). Evidence of an emerging deficit in problem solving can be traced back to the earliest stages of development in children with Down syndrome, as difficulties in the development of means-end thinking become evident (Cicchetti & Mans-Wagener, 1987; Dunst, 1988).

There is also evidence that young children with Down syndrome show impairments in the related area of goal-directed behavior. Ruskin et al. (1994) found that 22-month-old children with Down syndrome showed significantly shorter chains of continuous goal-directed mastery behaviors (e.g. fitting blocks through corresponding holes) than developmentally-matched typically developing children with a cause-and-effect toy. Along these lines, another study demonstrated that toddlers with Down syndrome show less optimal strategies on an object retrieval instrumental thinking task than developmentally-matched typically developing toddlers and toddlers with other developmental disabilities (Fidler et al., 2005b).

Language development

Language delays are common in individuals with Down syndrome, with receptive language and comprehension often outstripping expressive capabilities throughout development (Chapman, 1999; Fabretti et al., 1997; Sigman & Ruskin, 1999). The majority of children with Down syndrome begin to demonstrate this profile before the age of 5 years (Miller, 1999), with some showing impairments beginning at the stage of first words and others showing the onset of impairments as more advanced morphological and syntactic skills emerge (Miller, 1999).

The expressive language deficit is both a function of deficits in the motoric components of speech as well as the acquisition of more complex expressive language forms. Atypical development of the vocal cords, oral cavity, palate, and muscle tone all contribute to articulation and intelligibility issues in many individuals with Down syndrome

(Miller & Leddy, 1999; Stoel-Gammon, 2003), and a low estimate of at least 15% of individuals show evidence of verbal apraxia (Kumin, 2006). A pronounced deficit in grammar is frequently observed in individuals with Down syndrome, and many adults do not progress beyond the early stages of morphological and syntactic development (Fowler, 1990). In fact, it has been argued that many individuals with Down syndrome show a profile similar to that which is observed in specific language impairment (SLI; Chapman et al., 1998; Eadie et al., 2002). Even within receptive language, receptive vocabulary tends to develop with greater competence while comprehension of syntax lags behind (Abbeduto et al., 2003; Chapman et al., 1991).

Though expressive language development tends to pose challenges to many individuals with Down syndrome, non-verbal communication skills tend to emerge competently and facilitate the social relatedness strength often observed in individuals with Down syndrome. For example, young children with Down syndrome show MA-appropriate levels of non-verbal joint attention, a critical early developmental milestone that is evidence of triadic relating (Mundy et al., 1988, 1995; Fidler et al., 2005c; Wetherby et al., 1989). However, it is also notable that non-verbal requesting, another critical early communicative skill that involves triadic relating, appears to be impaired in many young children with Down syndrome (Fidler et al., 2005; Mundy et al., 1988, 1995; Wetherby et al., 1989). Other examples of communicative competence can be found in descriptions of a 'gesture advantage' in young children with Down syndrome compared with controls matched for word comprehension (Caselli et al., 1998).

Social-emotional functioning

Social relatedness is an area of relative strength for many individuals with Down syndrome, though a small percentage of individuals with Down syndrome show evidence of autism or autism spectrum disorder and do not show this area of strength. In this section, we discuss findings that pertain to the majority of individuals with Down syndrome who do not show comorbid autism. In early childhood, this strength involves the competent development of visual imitative skills (Heiman & Ullstadius, 1999) and social communicative signaling (see Fidler, 2006 for a review). In later childhood, this strength involves the presence of prosocial behaviors (Kasari et al., 2003) and the competent formation of friendships (Freeman & Kasari, 2002). It has been hypothesized that social relatedness emerges in childhood as such a pronounced area of strength that children with Down syndrome may also 'overuse' their social skills to compensate for other weaker domains of functioning (Fidler, 2006; Kasari & Freeman, 2002). High rates of off-task social behavior has been reported in several studies when children with Down syndrome are presented with challenging cognitive tasks (Kasari & Freeman, 2002; Pitcairn & Wishart, 1994).

In early development, there is some evidence that children with Down syndrome reach milestones associated with early social relatedness with competence. Primary intersubjective competence is evident in studies of early looking behavior, where infants with Down syndrome look longer at their mothers than typically developing infants (Crown et al., 1992; Gunn et al., 1982; Kasari et al., 1995), as well as findings of increased melodic sounds, vocalic sounds, and emotional sounds in infants with Down syndrome when interacting with people rather than objects (Legerstee et al., 1992). Toddlers with Down syndrome also achieve competence in the area of secondary intersubjective milestones, such as joint attention, showing objects, and other social initiations (Mundy et al., 1988; Sigman & Ruskin, 1999).

Studies of emotional development and emotional signaling have demonstrated increased positive affect signaling in individuals with Down syndrome. Though early studies reported more muted emotion expression in infants with Down syndrome (Berger & Cunningham, 1986; Buckhalt et al., 1978; Cicchetti & Sroufe, 1976; Emde & Brown, 1978; Rothbart & Hanson, 1983) subsequent work did not support this finding. Studies conducted with more objective coding systems found frequent low-intensity smiling in young children with Down syndrome, but this was in addition to frequent high-intensity smiling (Kasari et al., 1990; Knieps et al., 1994). Older children with Down syndrome have also been shown to smile more frequently than children at similar developmental ages, though this finding decreases as children approach adolescence and adulthood (Fidler et al., 2005a).

Motor functioning

Motor delays are commonly observed in infants and young children with Down syndrome (Chen & Woolley, 1978; Dunst, 1988), including the presence of abnormal movement patterns, hypotonia, and hyperflexibility (Harris & Shea, 1991). In addition, delays in the emergence and termination of reflexes are prevalent in early motor development in this population (Block, 1991; Harris & Shea, 1991). In older individuals with Down syndrome, Jobling (1998) reports specific motor impairments, including difficulty with precise movements of limbs (e.g. stepping over a stick while on a balance beam) and fingers (e.g. pivoting thumb and index finger) as well as gross motor tasks such as sit-ups and push-ups. However, in other domains such as running speed and agility and visual-motor control, Jobling (1998) reports that child performance in Down syndrome can be at chronological-age (CA)-levels.

Similar relative weaknesses have been demonstrated in motor planning, or praxis (Mon-Williams, et al., 2001). Infants with Down syndrome show more deviation from straight lines and changes in plane of motion during reaching behavior than typically developing infants, evidence of a deficit in the organization of reaching movement (Cadoret & Beuter, 1994). Fidler et al. (2005b) found that toddlers with Down syndrome performed significantly worse on a battery of motor planning tasks, including reaching into a jar to grasp a Nerf ball, and stringing beads. These findings have important implications for practice in this population, as partial correlations demonstrated a strong association between adaptive behavior skills and motor planning performance.

NEUROBEHAVIORAL FUNCTIONING

Behavioral and psychiatric disorders

The social relatedness strengths described in individuals with Down syndrome above may potentially be one of many protective factors against psychiatric disorders and behavioral problems in this population (Dykens, 2007). Dykens emphasized that while individuals with intellectual disabilities like Down syndrome are likely to experience more behavioral and psychiatric problems than the general population, at present many mental health professionals are unaware of the high co-occurrence of intellectual disability with psychiatric disorders. Misinterpreting indicators of psychiatric or behavioral disorders such as depression or aggression as part of an intellectual disability is known as *diagnostic overshadowing* (Reiss et al., 1982).

Researchers have found that children with Down syndrome actually display fewer behavioral problems in childhood than individuals with other intellectual disabilities, but more than those observed in typically developing children (see Dykens, 2007 for a review). For example, researches following through an outpatient clinic found more than 50% of them demonstrated hyperactivity (Pueschel et al., 1991), while other researchers studying children with Down syndrome in the general community found that 32% of them had behavioral problems including inattention, disobedience, and psychiatric behavior (Coe et al., 1999). In another study, Dykens and colleagues (2002) found low rates of severe aggression (6%) and high rates of low-level aggression, such as being disobedient (73%), as measured by the Childhood Behavior Checklist in children and adolescents with Down syndrome. The majority of the study participants were recruited from a community, as opposed to a clinical population. In the community sample, 20% had clinical-level behavioral problems, 15% were borderline for clinical behavioral problems, and 65% scored below the clinical range. In this same study, a subsample of adolescents ($n = 37$) exhibited less externalizing behaviors and more internalizing behaviors compared to the younger children. Similarly, in another cross-sectional study, Patti and Tsiouris (2006) found fewer challenging behaviors in adults with Down syndrome as age increased. They also found that mood and anxiety disorders were more prevalent than other psychiatric diagnoses in this sample of adults.

Dykens (2007) emphasized that further research, particularly longitudinal research, is needed on behavioral and psychiatric disorders in adolescents with Down syndrome. This information will be important to understand which symptoms may indicate clinical-level problems in contrast to behaviors that may not necessarily indicate a disorder (e.g. agitation in response to transition to high school). Additionally, this research may identify whether the observed mood changes in adults are a prodrome to the onset of Alzheimer's disease (AD).

Autism

Incidence in Down syndrome

Despite the relative strengths in core social relatedness associated with the Down syndrome behavioral phenotype, an increasing incidence of children with Down syndrome and comorbid autism has been reported in the literature (Dykens, 2007; Hepburn et al., 2008;

Kent et al., 1999). Autism is a neurodevelopmental disorder distinguished by difficulties in language, social relatedness, and by restricted and repetitive interests as well as unusual responses to sensory stimulation. While once thought to occur at low rates in the Down syndrome population (1–2%, see Dykens, 2007 for a review), improved diagnosis criteria for autism has indicated that this indeed is not the case. Currently, between 5 and 10% of children with Down syndrome also meet the criteria for autistic disorder (Hepburn et al., 2008; Kent et al., 1999; Lowenthal et al., 2007). By comparison, in the general population autism occurs less frequently (Gurney et al., 2003). Despite the improved diagnostic criteria, researchers (Castillo et al., 2008; Hepburn et al., 2008) have cautioned that diagnoses must be made carefully. Hepburn and colleagues pointed out that the Autism Diagnostic Observation Schedule-General used alone over-identified comorbid autism in toddlers with Down syndrome as compared to the Autism Diagnostic Interview-Revised and ratings of experienced clinical psychologists. Others (Castillo et al., 2008; Starr et al., 2005) highlighted that is difficult to determine whether individuals with Down syndrome who have profound cognitive difficulties truly had autism spectrum disorder or were exhibiting symptoms related to their intellectual disability.

Delayed diagnosis and regression

Children with a dual diagnosis of Down syndrome and autism often receive the autism diagnosis at an older age than children who have autism without a dual diagnosis (Rasmussen et al., 2001). Rasmussen and colleagues found in a small group of children and adults with Down syndrome that the mean age at time of diagnosis was 14 years of age. Additionally, they identified four possible factors related to the dual occurrence of Down syndrome with autism: having a first- or second-degree relative with autism; infantile spasms (a type of epilepsy); hypothyroidism; and potential brain-damaging events during birth or afterwards. Furthermore, a loss of previously acquired developmental skills or

regression occurs in approximately a quarter of the individuals with autism with no Down syndrome from 18 to 21 months of age (Lainhart et al., 2002). Researchers have observed similar types of regression in skills such as language, social engagement, and responsiveness in children with Down syndrome and comorbid autism compared to children with autism and no Down syndrome; however, the *timing* of regression is significantly different. For example, Castillo and colleagues (2008) found that children with autism and no Down syndrome experienced language regression at an average age of 19.7 months compared to 61.8 months in children with Down syndrome and comorbid autism. The authors reported that the children with Down syndrome continued to slowly acquire skills until regression started. Also, the researchers found the average age of acquiring single-word use was significantly older (40.6 months) for children with a dual diagnosis compared to 14.9 months for the children with autism and no Down syndrome. Consequently, the authors suggested that the delay of regression observed in the dual diagnosis group may be reflective of the general developmental delay associated with the behavioral phenotype of Down syndrome. The mechanisms of regression are unknown in both autism and Down syndrome with comorbid autism. The researchers noted that two parents of the children with Down syndrome and comorbid autism in that study reported that their children developed language through the use of signs followed by the mastery of spoken words. The children then lost their skills in the inverse order that they were attained, losing spoken words first and then the ability to use signs meaningfully.

Autism symptoms

In a small study including six participants with Down syndrome who met or nearly met the lifetime criteria for autistic disorder, researchers noted that almost half of the participants were reported to present with more autistic-like features in early childhood than as pre-adolescents or adults (Starr et al.,

2005). At the time of the study, some of the participants were unable to maintain social eye contact, while others were able to be socially responsive. This small group represented a wide variety of autistic and non-autistic behaviors. Predictably, researchers using a behavioral assessment and the Childhood Autism Rating Scale have found that a modestly sized group of children with this dual diagnosis exhibit poorer communication and social skills and more stereotypical behavior than children with Down syndrome without autism (Ghosh et al., 2008). Hepburn and colleagues (2008) found in a small sample that of the 20 children with Down syndrome, the three children identified as having autism or autism spectrum disorder also met the same diagnostic criteria used 2 years later. Finally, Capone and colleagues (2005) found that children with comorbid Down syndrome and autism had scores on the Aberrant Behavior Checklist that highly correlated with DSM-IV (Diagnostic and Statistical Manual of Mental Disorders 4th ed) criteria for autism.

Neuroanatomical correlates

Recently, Carter et al. (2008) used magnetic resonance imaging (MRI) to examine brain structures and their relationship to behavior in children with Down syndrome, those with comorbid autism, and controls. They found that hyperplasia of white matter in the cerebellum was positively associated with the stereotypic behaviors observed in children and adolescents with comorbid autism spectrum disorder (Carter et al., 2008).

In summary, these findings highlight the need for further research on assessment, regression, and mechanisms of the co-occurrence of Down syndrome and autism. Until more data are available, clinicians and early interventionists should be aware that a regression in skills for preschoolers and kindergartners with Down syndrome may indicate comorbid autism (Castillo et al., 2008). Furthermore, both researchers and clinicians need to use care in diagnosing comorbid autism with Down syndrome because behaviors related to profound cognitive delays may appear similar to those related to autism (e.g. stereotypies). Researchers also need to consider the role of the environment and intellectual ability in the expression of autistic symptoms in children with Down syndrome (Capone et al., 2005; Starr et al., 2005).

AGING, ALZHEIMER'S AND DOWN SYNDROME

'Mr C' is a 70-year-old male with a complete triplication of chromosome 21 who has become the face for successful aging for individuals with Down syndrome (Krinsky-McHale et al., 2008a). Mr C was born in 1936. He lived with his family until age 5, when he was institutionalized. Mr C spent the next 36 years of his life residing in institutions, punctuated by regular 2-month vacations at home. His family remained involved in his life. He now lives in the community and continues to work 5 days a week. He is independent in most daily activities.

Krinsky-McHale and colleagues reported that he has no heart defects, no thyroid problems, and remarkably, no Alzheimer's related dementia. Mr C's full-scale Wechsler IQ has ranged from 52 to 60. His performance on mental status evaluations has been stable for the past 16 years, as has his behavior. Mr. C does demonstrate difficulty with concentration and fine motor coordination (writing, copying shapes) and sometimes exhibits behavior problems – lying or cursing – but the former is attributed to a lack of formal education and the latter to a stable characteristic. None of these traits have changed since Kittler and colleagues (2008) began following him. He has, however, shown great variability in episodic memory – at times, meeting possible criteria for Alzheimer's disease. However, he recently obtained his second highest score on this task. He has also demonstrated diminishing visuospatial skills. The researchers suggested that his performance on memory and visuospatial skills indicate age-related changes in cognition, but not clinical dementia.

Krinsky-McHale and her colleagues considered both genetic and environmental reasons for Mr C's successful aging. Genetically, Mr C has complete triplication of chromosome 21, no mosaicism, no partial trisomy, and has the neutral apolipoprotein E (APOE) allele that neither protects against Alzheimer's disease nor promotes longevity. They suggested that perhaps his parents conferred an element of healthy aging, given that they both lived into their 80s with no dementia. The authors also suggested that his family's involvement may have moderated the effects of institutionalization. The researchers concluded that many still unknown factors contribute to phenotypic variability and further research is needed to understand phenotypic expression and successful aging in this population.

While aging in Down syndrome is characterized by great individual variability, most adults in this population do not age as well as Mr C. According to research, adults with Down syndrome are at risk for developing early-onset Alzheimer's disease (Lott & Head, 2001). This is hypothesized to be caused, in part, by the fact that trisomy 21 is associated with overexpression for amyloid precursor protein (APP), which contributes to the deposit of B-amyloid proteins and fibrillar plaques associated with AD (see Zana ct al., 2007 for a review). Another hypothesis, the 'two-hit' hypothesis for AD, proposes either oxidative stress 'or alterations in mitotic signaling' can start the onset of AD, but both must be present for AD to develop (Zana et al., 2007: p. 650). Therefore, in a neurodevelopmental disorder like Down syndrome, neurons that have been stressed (having mutations) ' . . . devote their compensatory potential to adjusting to current stimuli and thereby lose the capability of further adaption needed to respond to other insults in the future' (p. 650).

Research indicates that the symptoms of Alzheimer's disease in adults with Down syndrome may differ from those observed in the general population (Lott & Head, 2001). For example, Ball and colleagues (2006) found in

a follow-up to a previously studied group of adults with Down syndrome that (a) personality and behavior changes and (b) executive dysfunction are early indicators of AD in people with Down syndrome. This contrasts with the memory changes that are associated with AD in the general population. Adults with Down syndrome in the early stages of AD also exhibit diminished selective attention (multitrial cancellation task) and increased variability in their performance compared to a control group of healthy participants (Krinsky-McHale et al., 2008b). The investigators of this study noted that the multitrial cancellation task may be a valuable asset to include in a neuropsychological battery to assess AD in adults with Down syndrome. Also, recently, Ball and her colleagues (2008) provided further evidence for frontal lobe functioning impairments in early or preclinical stages of AD in adults with Down syndrome. They found adults with Down syndrome and diagnosed AD had more problems in personality/behavior and in measures of executive function than the group with Down syndrome and no diagnosed AD.

Furthermore, researchers using MRI have detected early brain changes related to dementia in adults with Down syndrome before symptoms of AD are present. Researchers have found evidence of increased glucose metabolic rates combined with less gray matter in specific areas (temporal cortex including the parahippocampus and hippocampus, thalamus, caudate, and frontal lobe; Haier et al., 2008). This finding may support the hypothesis that the brain responds by compensating for loss of gray matter during early stages of AD.

Finally, it is helpful to remember that there is considerable variability in aging outcomes in Down syndrome, and dementia is not universal in this population. For example, Esbensen and colleagues (2008) studied how adults with Down syndrome changed in functional abilities, health, and behavior with age. They found that, compared to other adults with intellectual disabilities, adults under 40 years of age with Down syndrome maintained functional abilities better than the comparison group and had less behavioral problems. The health status in the Down syndrome group declined at a slightly faster rate than the comparison group. Importantly, poor family relationships were associated with more problems in health, behavior, and personal care skills. Relatedly, parental death was also associated with more behavioral problems.

IMPLICATIONS FOR CLINICAL PRACTICE

Historical background

In quite possibly the most poignant drama that occurred in his own life, it was publicly disclosed recently that the late playwright Arthur Miller and his third wife Inge Morath had a son with Down syndrome in 1966 (Andrews, 2007). Their son, Daniel Miller, was institutionalized as a toddler. Almost unbelievably in the late 1960s, that's just about a generation ago, it was still common for doctors to recommend that parents institutionalize a child with Down syndrome. In fact, it's only been since the mid 1970s that children with Down syndrome and other disabilities were guaranteed a public education through federal legislation. At that point, a move was made away from institutionalization.

Currently in the United States, early interventionists and other professionals serving children with special education needs provide their services following guidelines delineated in the Individuals with Disabilities Education Act of 2004 (IDEA; Trohanis, 2008). Part C of this legislation specifies how early intervention meets the family's and child's (newborn through 3 years of age) needs and how these needs are documented through Individual Family Service Plans. From age 3, the right to a free and appropriate public education and related services are guaranteed through Part B of this same legislation. In this setting, the Individual Education Plan is the primary means of documenting

any special education needs, baseline performance, goals, and services the child/student needs to participate in learning. Daniel Miller did not have the benefit of this educational legislation and Arthur Miller did not publicly acknowledge his son until much later in life. Despite institutionalization, Daniel Miller is living an exceptional life – he served as an advocate for deinstitutionalization, maintains a job, and lives with a couple who have functioned as his extended family (Andrews, 2007).

How does nature versus nurture play out in phenotypes?

Dykens (2007) highlighted potential protective and risk factors associated with Down syndrome that may have affected both Mr C's and Daniel Miller's outcomes. Emphasizing that there is considerable individual variability in the expression of the Down syndrome behavioral phenotype, Dykens suggested protective factors in addition to relative strengths in sociability include potentially more positive interactions due to a 'babyfaced' craniofacial appearance. She also pointed out known and potential risk factors including stigma related to cranio-facial features, sleep problems, low serotonin, obesity, hypothyroidism, and cardiac complications, to name a few.

In addition to individual variation in genetic and biological endowment, the environmental context must also be examined in considering the outcomes for individuals with Down syndrome. From the onset of life, our brains constantly register information whether we are crying, laughing, exploring, throwing a tantrum, or just holding it together. Consequently, how children with Down syndrome and other disabilities are cared for in early life may significantly affect patterns of learning and interactions. The effects enriched environments (EEs) have on both behavior and neural structures have been well-documented in typically developing children (for a review, see Huttenlocher, 2002). However, the extent neural plasticity exists in individuals with Down syndrome still remains somewhat of a question (Dierssen et al., 2006).

Currently, two studies using mouse models of Down syndrome inform our understanding. Mice models allow the study of behavior and neuroanatomy using methods that are not possible in human research. In one study (Martinéz-Cué et al., 2002), researchers examined whether raising newly weaned mice bred to represent the genetic and behavioral aspects of the Down syndrome phenotype Ts65Dn benefitted from 7 weeks in an enriched environment. The enriched environment condition included greater mouse social contact, a variety of objects to explore, and a variety of food. The TS65Dn mice in the EE condition demonstrated higher visual spatial learning than the non-EE mice. Notably, the female TS65Dn mice made significant improvements, while the males did not. In fact, the males *regressed.* While the EE condition led to improved learning, the findings may also indicate that gender moderates the effects of the EE condition. In another study, Dierrsen et al. (2003) used older (1-year-old) TS65Dn mice to examine the effects of an EE on neural structures. In this study, the researchers found no significant changes in dendrites of pyramidal cells in the frontal cortex of the TS65Dn mice after the EE condition, but found larger, more branched, and more spinous dendrites in the controlled mice. This finding suggests that mechanisms that control neural plasticity may be affected in this syndrome; however, further research is needed.

In examining the environment and the Down syndrome behavioral phenotype in humans, Buckley and colleagues (2006) demonstrated that British children with Down syndrome who attended a school with an 'inclusive' educational model actually demonstrated non-adaptive communication deficits relative to social and daily living skills in contrast to adolescents with Down syndrome who attended special education without inclusion. Therefore, the researchers suggested that they were able to demonstrate that an approach could indeed *modify* the Down syndrome behavioral phenotype.

Researchers have begun considering the effects of the caregiving (parenting) environment on the developmental outcomes of individuals with Down syndrome. After determining two major motor interventions were not effective for children with Down syndrome, Mahoney and Perales (2006) reconsidered their findings. They noted that while therapists saw children for 1-hour weekly sessions for about 35 sessions, annually this accounted for a small fraction of a child's interactions during the course of a year. By comparison, using a conservative estimate, the authors emphasized that parents could potentially interact with their children for 2–3 hours a day and thereby *hundreds* of hours a year. Given the potentially profound influence parents can have on their child's interactions, it's not surprising that Head and Abbeduto (2007) recommended taking into account the family environment and caregiving in addition to the child's developmental status when treating children with developmental disabilities. In fact, qualitative differences in interactions have been found between parents and their children with Down syndrome (Spiker et al., 2002). More specifically, researchers have found that mothers of children with Down syndrome tend to adjust their language to give instruction or use more physical guidance to engage their children in learning (Kim & Mahoney, 2004; Marfo, 1990). A vital issue fundamental to this body of inquiry is how and when parent–child interactions promote development in children with behavioral phenotypes associated with intellectual disabilities such as Down syndrome (Hodapp, 2004).

What do we currently know about intervention specifically for individuals with Down syndrome?

In his vision for early intervention science, Guralnick (2005) urged researchers to use *specificity* in developmental disabilities research in addition to examining biological risk, environment, and general early intervention. He argued that examining carefully defined subgroups of children and families as well as specified outcomes and specific components of intervention will further our understanding of individual variability and responsiveness. Potentially, in populations like Down syndrome, specific challenges linked to phenotypic characteristics (such as challenges in syntax) could be addressed through both intervention and educational approaches. There is a paucity of evidence demonstrating syndrome-specific intervention success for individuals with Down syndrome; however, research in this area is growing (for a review see Fidler and Nadel, 2007).

Some researchers have begun to explore intervention research just as Guralnick (2005) suggested. For example, researchers have begun targeting exacting components of the Down syndrome behavioral phenotype in their intervention research such as reading instruction (Cupples & Iacono, 2002; van Brysterveldt et al., 2006). Additionally, to validate the investment in both time and resources in providing specific interventions, more data are needed regarding whether individuals with Down syndrome or other developmental disabilities respond differentially to techniques. One study lending evidence in this direction found that goal-directed behaviors in children with Down syndrome did not show improvements after a maternal play/support intervention, while a control group of developmentally-matched children demonstrated such gains (Landry et al., 1998). This suggests that it may be important to identify approaches that are uniquely effective for children in this population.

CONCLUSION

When considering the potential for interventions to improve outcomes for individuals with Down syndrome, Fidler and Nadel (2007) emphasized that individuals with Down syndrome do not just simply materialize at age 8 or 9 or 10. Therefore, these patterns of relative strengths and challenges may play out entirely differently if targeted at an early age. Early development may be a crucial window of opportunity for intervention, as emerging characteristics have not yet snowballed into pronounced areas of strength and weakness. Finally, collaborative work between developmentalists, educators, behavioral scientists, neurobiologists, and animal model researchers will be needed to coordinate knowledge gains that will guide future research and intervention.

REFERENCES

Abbeduto, L., Murphy, M.M., Cawthon, S.W., Richmond, E.K., Weissman, M.D., Karadottir, S. et al. (2003) 'Receptive language skills of adolescents and young adults with Down or fragile X syndrome', *American Journal on Mental Retardation*, 108: 149–160.

Andrews, S. (2007) 'Arthur miller's missing act', *Vanity Fair*. Retrieved October 24, 2008 from http://www.vanityfair.com/

Baddeley, A. (1992) 'Working memory', *Science*, 255: 556–559.

Baddeley A. & Jarrold, C. (2007) 'Working memory and Down syndrome', *Journal of Intellectual Disability Research*, 51: 925–931.

Ball, S.L., Holland, A.J., Hon, J., Huppert, F.A., Treppner, P., & Watson P.C. (2006) 'Personality and behavior changes mark the early stages of Alzheimer's disease in adults with Down's syndrome: Findings from a prospective population-based study', *International Journal of Geriatric Psychiatry*, 21: 661–673.

Ball, S.L., Holland, A., Treppner, P., Watson, P.C., & Huppert, F.A. (2008) 'Executive dysfunction and its association with personality and behavior changes in the development of Alzheimer's disease in adults with Down syndrome and mild to moderate learning disabilities', *British Journal of Clinical Psychology*, 47: 1–29.

Berger, J. & Cunningham, C.C. (1986) 'Aspects of early social smiling by infants with Down's syndrome', *Child: Care, Health and Development*, 12: 13–24.

Blair, C., Zelazo, P.D., & Greenberg, M.T. (2005) 'The measurement of executive function in early childhood', *Developmental Neuropsychology*, 28: 561–571.

Block, M.E. (1991) 'Motor development in children with Down syndrome: a review of the literature', *Adapted Physical Activity Quarterly*, 8: 179–209.

Brain, L. (1967) 'Chairman's opening remarks: a historical introduction', in G.E.W. Wolstenhome (ed.), *Mongolism*. Boston: Little Brown, pp.1–5.

Buckhalt, J.A., Rutherford, R.B. & Goldberg, K.E. (1978) 'Verbal and nonverbal interaction of mothers with their Down's syndrome and nonretarded infants', *American Journal on Mental Deficiency,* 82: 337–343.

Buckley S., Bird G., & Sacks B. (2006) 'Evidence that we can change the profile from a study of inclusive education', *Down Syndrome: Research and Practice,* 9: 51–53.

Cadoret, G. & Beuter, A. (1994) 'Early development of reaching in Down syndrome infants', *Early Human Development,* 36: 157–173.

Canfield, M.A., Honein, M.A., Yuskiv, N., Xing, J., Mai, C.T., Collins, J.S. et al. (2006) 'National estimates and race/ethnic-specific variation of selected birth defects in the United States, 1999–2001', *Birth Defects Research Part A: Clinical and Molecular Teratology,* 76: 747–756.

Capone, G.T., Grados, M.A., Kaufman, W.E., Bernad-Ripoll, S., & Jewell, A. (2005) 'Down syndrome and co-morbid autism spectrum disorder: Characterization using the aberrant behavior checklist', *American Journal of Medical Genetics,* 143: 373–380.

Carlson, S. (2005) 'Developmental sensitive measures of executive function in preschool children', *Developmental Neuropsychology,* 28: 595–616.

Carter, J.C., Capone, G.T., & Kaurmann, W.E. (2008) 'Neuroanatomic correlates of autism and stereotypy in children with Down Syndrome', *Clinical Neuroscience and Neuropathology: Neuroreport,* 19: 653–656.

Caselli, M.C., Vicari, S., Longobardi, E., Lami, L., Pizzoli, C., & Stella, G. (1998) 'Gestures and words in early development of children with Down syndrome', *Journal of Speech, Language, and Hearing Research,* 41: 1125 1135.

Castillo, H., Patterson, B., Hickey, F., Kinsman, A., Howard, J.M., Mitchell, T. et al. (2008) 'Difference in age at regression in children with autism with and without Down syndrome', *Journal of Developmental & Behavioral Pediatrics,* 29: 89–93.

Chapman, R., Seung, H., Schwartz, S., & Bird, E. (1998) 'Language skills of children and adolescents with Down syndrome: II. Production deficits', *Journal of Speech, Language, and Hearing Research,* 41: 861–873.

Chapman, R.S. (1999) 'Language development in children and adolescents with Down syndrome', in J. Miller, M. Leddy, & L.A. Leavitt (eds), *Improving the Communication of People with Down Syndrome.* Baltimore: Brookes Publishing Inc., pp. 41–60.

Chapman, R.S. & Hesketh, L.J. (1998) 'Behavioral phenotype of individuals with Down syndrome', *Mental Retardation and Developmental Disabilities Research Reviews,* 6: 84–95.

Chapman, R.S., Schwartz, S.E., & Raining Bird, E.K. (1991) 'Language skills of children and adolescents with Down syndrome I. Comprehension', *Journal of Speech and Hearing Research,* 34: 1106–1120.

Chen, H. & Woolley, P.V. (1978) 'A developmental assessment chart for non-institutionalized Down syndrome children', *Growth,* 42: 157–165.

Cicchetti, D. & Mans-Wagener, L. (1987) 'Sequences, stages, and structures in the organization of cognitive development in infants with Down syndrome', in I.C. Uzgiris & J.M. Hunt (eds), *Infant Performance and Experience: New Findings with the Ordinal Scales.* Champaign, IL: University of Illinois Press, pp. 281–310.

Cicchetti, D. & Sroufe, L.A. (1978) 'An organizational view of affect: illustration from the study of Down's syndrome infants', in M. Lewis & L.A. Rosenbaum (eds), *The development of Affect.* New York: Plenum Press.

Clark, R. (1933) 'The mongol: a new explanation', *The Journal of Mental Science,* 328–335.

Clarke, C.M., Edwards, J.H., & Smallpiece, V. (1961) '21-trisomy/normal mosaicism in an intelligent child with some mongoloid characters', *Lancet,* May 13: 1028–1030.

Coe, D., Matson, J., Russell, D.W., Slifer, K. J., Capone, G. T., Baglio, C., & Stallings, S. (1999) 'Behavior problems of children with Down syndrome and life events', *Journal of Autism and Developmental Disorders,* 29: 149–156.

Connor, M. & Ferguson-Smith, M. (1997) *Essential Medical Genetics.* Oxford: Blackwell.

Crown, C.L., Feldstein, S., Jasnow, M.D., & Beebe, B. (1992) 'Down's syndrome and infant gaze: gaze behavior of Down's syndrome and nondelayed infants In Interactions with their mothers', *European Journal of Child and Adolescent Psychiatry: Acta Paedopsychiatrica,* 55: 51–55.

Cupples, L. & Iacono, T. (2000) 'The efficacy of "whole word" versus "analytic" reading instruction for children with Down Syndrome', *Reading and Writing,* 15: 549–574.

Dawson, G., Meltzoff, A.N., Osterling, J., & Rinaldi, J. (1998) 'Neuropsychological correlates of early symptoms of autism', *Child Development,* 69: 1276–1285.

Diamond, A., Barnett, W.S., Thomas, J., & Munro, S. (2007) 'Preschool program improves cognitive control', *Science,* 318: 1387–1388.

Dierssen, M., Ortiz-Abalia, J., Arque, G., Martínez de Lágran, M., & Fillart, C. (2006) 'Pitfalls and hopes in Down syndrome therapeutic approaches: in the search for evidence-based treatments', *Behavior Genetics,* 36: 454–468.

Down, J.L. (1866/1995) 'Observations on an ethnic classification of idiots', *Mental Retardation,* 33: 54–56.

Dunst, C. (1988) 'Stage transitioning in the sensorimotor development of Down's syndrome infants', *Journal of Mental Deficiency Research,* 32: 405–410.

Dykens, E.M. (2007) 'Psychiatric and behavioral disorders in persons with Down syndrome', *Mental Retardation and Developmental Disabilities Research Reviews,* 13: 272–278.

Dykens, E.M., Shah, B., Sagun, J., Beck, T., & King, B.H. (2002) 'Maladaptive behavior in children and adolescents with Down's syndrome', *Journal of Intellectual Disability Research,* 46: 484–492.

Eadie, P.A., Fey, M.E., Douglas, J.M., & Parsons, C.L. (2002) 'Profiles of grammatical morphology and sentence imitation in children with specific language impairment and Down syndrome', *Journal of Speech Language Hearing Research,* 45: 720–732.

Edgin, J.O. (2003). *A neuropsychological model for the development of the cognitive profiles in mental retardation syndromes: evidence from Down syndrome and Williams syndrome.* Unpublished dissertation. Denver, CO: Denver University.

Emde, R.N. & Brown, C. (1978) 'Adaptation to the birth of a Down's syndrome infant: grieving and maternal attachment', *Journal of the American Academy of Child Psychiatry,* 17: 299–323.

Esbensen, A.J., Seltzer, M.M., & Krauss, M.W. (2008) 'Stability and change in health, functional abilities, and behavior problems among adults with and without Down syndrome', *American Journal on Mental Retardation,* 113: 263–277.

Fabretti, D., Pizzuto, E., Vicari, S., & Voterra, V. (1997) 'A story description task in children with Down's syndrome: lexical and morphosyntatic abilities', *Journal of Intellectual Disability Research,* 41: 165–179.

Fidler, D.J. (2006) 'The emergence of a syndrome-specific personality-motivation profile in young children with Down syndrome', in J.A. Rondal & J. Perera (eds), *Down Syndrome Neurobehavioral Specificity.* Chichester, UK: John Wiley and Sons.

Fidler, D.J. & Nadel, L. (2007) 'Educating children with Down syndrome: neuroscience, development, and intervention', *Mental Retardation and Developmental Disabilities Research Reviews,* 13: 262–271.

Fidler, D.J., Barrett, K.C., & Most, D.E. (2005a) 'Age related differences in smiling and personality in Down syndrome', *Journal of Developmental and Physical Disabilities,* 17: 263–280.

Fidler, D.J., Hepburn, S., Mankin, G., & Rogers, S. (2005b) 'Praxis skills in young children with Down syndrome, other developmental disabilities, and

typically developing children', *American Journal of Occupational Therapy,* 59: 129–138.

Fidler, D.J., Philofsky, A., Hepburn, S., & Rogers, S. (2005c) 'Nonverbal requesting and problem solving in toddlers with Down syndrome', *American Journal on Mental Retardation,* 110: 312–322.

Fletcher, J.M. (1996) 'Executive functions in children: introduction to the special series', *Developmental Neuropsychology,* 12: 1–4.

Fowler, A. (1990) 'Language abilities in children with Down syndrome: evidence for a specific syntactic delay', in D. Cicchetti & M. Beeghly (eds), *Children with Down Syndrome: A Developmental Perspective.* Cambridge: Cambridge University Press, pp. 302–328.

Freeman, S.B., Allen, E.G., Oxford-Wright, C.L., Tinker, S.W., Druschel, C., Hobbs, C.A. et al (2007) 'The National Down Syndrome Project: design and implementation', *Public Health Reports,* 122: 62–72.

Freeman, S.F.N. & Kasari, C. (2002) 'Characteristics and qualities of the play dates of children with Down syndrome: emerging or true friendships?', *American Journal on Mental Retardation,* 107: 16–31.

Gelman, R. & Cohen, M. (1988) 'Qualitative differences in the way Down syndrome and normal children solve a novel counting problem', in L. Nadel (ed.), *The Psychobiology of Down Syndrome: Issues in the Biology of Language and Cognition.* Cambridge, MA: MIT Press, pp. 51–99.

Ghosh, M., Shah, A., Dhir, K., & Merchant, K.F. (2008) 'Behavior in children with Down syndrome', *Indian Journal of Pediatrics,* 75: 685–689.

Gomez, D., Solsona, E., Guitart, M., Baena, N., Gabau, E., Egozcue, J., & Caballin, M.R. (2000) 'Origin of trisomy 21 in Down syndrome cases from a Spanish population registry', *Annales de Genetique,* 43: 23–28.

Gunn, P., Berry, P., & Andrews, R.J. (1982) 'Looking behavior of Down syndrome infants', *American Journal of Mental Deficiency,* 87: 344–347.

Guralnick, M.J. (2005) 'Early intervention for children with intellectual disabilities: current knowledge and future prospects', *Journal of Applied Research in Intellectual Disabilities,* 18: 313–324.

Gurney J., Fritz M., Ness K., Sievers P., Newschaffer C., Shapiro E. (2003) 'Analysis of prevalence trends of autism spectrum disorder in Minnesota', *Arch Pediatr Adolesc Med,* 157(7): 622–627.

Haier, R.J., Head, K., Head, E., & Lott, I.T. (2008) 'Neuroimaging of individuals with Down's syndrome at-risk for dementia: evidence for possible compensatory events', *Neuroimage,* 39: 1324–1332.

Harris, S.R. & Shea, A.M. (1991) 'Down syndrome' in S.K. Campbell (ed.), *Pediatric Neurologic Physical*

Therapy (2nd edn). Melbourne, Australia: Churchill Livingstone, pp. 131–168.

Head, L.S. & Abbeduto, L. (2007) 'Recognizing the role of parents in developmental outcomes: a systems approach to evaluating the child with developmental disabilities', *Mental Retardation and Developmental Disabilities,* 13: 293–301.

Heiman, M. & Ullstadius, E. (1999) 'Neonatal imitation and imitation among children with autism and Down's syndrome', in J. Nadel & G. Butterworth (eds), *Imitation in Infancy.* Cambridge: Cambridge University Press, pp. 235–253.

Hepburn, S., Philofsky, A., Fidler, D.J., & Rogers, S. (2008) 'Autism symptoms in toddlers with Down syndrome: a descriptive study', *Journal of Applied Research in Intellectual Disabilities,* 21: 48–57.

Hill, E.L. (2004) 'Executive dysfunction in autism', *TRENDS in Cognitive Sciences,* 8: 26–32.

Hodapp, R.M. (2004) 'Behavioral phenotypes: going beyond the two-group approach', *International Review of Research in Mental Retardation,* 29: 1–30.

Hodapp, R.M., Evans, D., & Gray, F.L. (1999) 'Intellectual development in children with Down syndrome', in *Down Syndrome: A Review of Current Knowledge.* London: Whurr Publishers, pp. 124–132.

Hook, E.B., Mutton, D.E., Ide, R., Alberman, E., & Bobrow, M. (1995) 'The natural history of Down syndrome concept uses diagnosed prenatally that are not electively terminated', *American Journal of Human Genetics,* 57: 875–881.

Huttenlocher, P.R. (2002) *Neural Plasticity: The Effects of Environment on the Development of the Cerebral Cortex.* Cambridge, MA: Harvard University Press.

Ireland, W.W. (1877) *On Idiocy and Imbecility.* London: Churchill.

Jarrold, C. & Baddeley, A.D. (1997). 'Short-term memory for verbal and visuospatial information in Down's syndrome', *Cognitive Neuropsychiatry,* 2: 101–122.

Jarrold, C., Baddeley, A.D., & Hewes, A.K. (2000) 'Verbal short-term memory deficits in Down syndrome: a consequence of problems in rehearsal?', *Journal of Child Psychology and Psychiatry,* 41: 233–244.

Jarrold, C., Baddeley, A., & Phillips, C.E. (2002) 'Verbal short-term memory in Down syndrome: a problem of memory, audition, or speech?', *Journal of Speech, Language and Hearing Research,* 45: 531–544.

Jobling, A. (1998) 'Motor development in school-aged children with Down syndrome: a longitudinal perspective', *International Journal of Disability, Development, and Education,* 45: 283–293.

Kanno, K. & Ikeda, Y. (2002) 'Word-length effect in verbal short-term memory in individuals with Down's syndrome', *Journal of Intellectual Disability Research,* 46: 613–618.

Kasari, C. & Freeman, S.F.N. (2002) 'Task-related social behavior in children with Down syndrome', *American Journal on Mental Retardation,* 106: 253–264.

Kasari, C., Mundy, P., Yirmiya, N., & Sigman, M. (1990) 'Affect and attention in children with Down syndrome', *American Journal of Mental Retardation,* 95: 55–67.

Kasari, C., Freeman, S., Mundy, P., & Sigman, M.D. (1995) 'Attention regulation by children with Down syndrome: coordinated joint attention and social referencing looks', *American Journal on Mental Retardation,* 100: 128–136.

Kasari, C., Freeman, S.F.N., & Bass, W. (2003) 'Empathy and responses to distress in children with Down syndrome', *Journal of Child Psychology and Psychiatry and Allied Disciplines,* 44: 424–431.

Kent, L., Evans, J., Paul, M., & Sharp, M. (1999) 'Comorbidity of autistic spectrum disorders in children with Down syndrome', *Developmental Medicine and Child Neurology,* 41: 153–158.

Kim, J-M. & Mahoney, G. (2004) 'The effects of mother's style of interaction on children's engagement: implications for using responsive intervention with parents', *Topics in Early Childhood Education,* 24: 31–38.

Kittler, P.M., Krinsky-McHale, S.J., & Devenny, D.A. (2008) 'Dual-task processing as a measure of executive function: a comparison between adults with Williams and Down syndromes', *American Journal on Mental Retardation,* 113: 117–132.

Knieps, L.J., Walden, T.A., & Baxter, A. (1994) 'Affective expressions of toddlers with and without Down syndrome in a social referencing context', *American Journal on Mental Retardation,* 99: 301–312.

Kopp, C.B., Krakow, J.B., & Johnson, K.L. (1983) 'Strategy production by young Down syndrome children', *American Journal of Mental Deficiency,* 88: 164–169.

Krinsky-McHale, S.J., Devenny, D.A., Hong, G. et al. (2008a) 'Successful aging in a 70-year-old man with Down syndrome: a case study', *Intellectual and Developmental Disabilities,* 46: 215–228.

Krinsky-McHale, S.J., Devenny, D., Kittler, P., & Silverman, W. (2008b) 'Selective attention deficits associated with mild cognitive impairment and early stage Alzheimer's disease in adults with Down syndrome', *American Journal of Mental Retardation,* 113: 369–386.

Kumin, L. (2006) 'Speech intelligibility and childhood verbal apraxia in children with Down syndrome', *Down's Syndrome, Research and Practice,* 10: 10–22.

Lainhart, J.E., Ozonoff, S., Coon, H., Krasny, L., Dinh, E., Nice, J., & McMahon, W. (2002) 'Autism, regression and genetics', *American Journal of Medical Genetics,* 113: 231–237.

Landry, S., Smith, K.E., Miller-Loncar, C.L., & Swank, P.R. (1998) 'The relation of change in maternal interactive styles to the developing social competence of full-term and preterm children', *Child Development,* 69: 105–123.

Landry, S.H. & Chapieski, M.L. (1990) 'Joint attention and infant toy exploration: effects of Down syndrome and prematurity', *Child Development,* 60: 103–118.

Lanfranchi, S., Cornoldi, C. & Vianello, R. (2004) 'Verbal and visuospatial working memory deficits in children with Down syndrome', *American Journal on Mental Retardation,* 109: 456–466.

Laws, G. (2002) 'Working memory in children and adolescents with Down syndrome: evidence from a colour memory experiment', *Journal of Child Psychology and Psychiatry,* 43: 353–364.

Legerstee, M., Bowman, T.G., & Fels, S. (1992) 'People and objects affect the quality of vocalizations in infants with Down syndrome', *Early Development and Parenting,* 1: 149–156.

Lejeune, J., Turpin, R., & Gautier, M. (1959) [Mongolism; a chromosomal disease (trisomy)]. *Bulletin of the Academy of National Medicine,* 143: 256–265. [in French].

Lott, I.T. & Head, E. (2001) 'Down syndrome and Alzheimer's disease: a link between development and aging', *Mental Retardation and Developmental Disabilities,* 7: 172–178.

Lowenthal, R., Paula, C.S., Schwartzman, J.S., Brunoni, D., Mercadante, M.T. (2007) 'Prevalence of Pervasive Developmental Disorder in Down's syndrome', *Journal of Autism and Developmental Disorders,* 37: 1394–1395.

Mahoney, G. & Perales, F. (2006) 'The role of parents in early motor intervention', *Down's Syndrome, Research and Practice,* 10: 67–73.

Marfo, K. (1990) 'Maternal directiveness in interactions with handicapped children: an analytical commentary', *Journal of Child Psychology and Psychiatry,* 31: 531–549.

Martinéz-Cué, C., Baamonde, B., Lumbreras, M., Paz, J., Davisson, M.T., Schmidt, C., Dierssen, M., Flórez, J. (2002) 'Differential effects of environmental enrichment on behavior and learning of male and female Ts65Dn mice, a model for Down syndrome', *Behavioural Brain Research,* 134: 185–200.

Miller, J.F. (1999) 'Profiles of language development in children with Down syndrome', in J. Miller, M. Leddy, & L.A. Leavitt (eds), *Improving the Communication of People with Down Syndrome.* Baltimore: Brookes Publishing, pp. 11–40.

Miller, J.F. & Leddy, M. (1999) 'Verbal fluency, speech intelligibility, and communicative effectiveness', in J.F Miller, M. Leddy, & L.A. Leavitt (eds), *Improving the Communication of People with Down Syndrome.* Baltimore: Brookes Publishing, pp. 81–91.

Mon-Williams, M., Tresilian, J.R., Bell, V.E. et al. (2001) 'The preparation of reach to grasp movements in adults with Down syndrome', *Human Movement Science,* 20: 587–602.

Muir, J. (1903) 'An analysis of twenty-six cases of mongolism', *Archives of Pediatrics,* 161–169.

Mundy, P., Sigman, M., Kasari, C., & Yirmiya, N. (1988) 'Nonverbal communication skills in Down syndrome children', *Child Development,* 59: 235–249.

Mundy, P., Kasari, C., Sigman, M., & Ruskin, E. (1995) 'Nonverbal communication and early language acquisition in children with Down syndrome and normally developing children', *Journal of Speech and Hearing Research,* 38: 157–167.

Nadel, L. (2003) 'Down's syndrome: a genetic disorder in biobehavioral perspective', *Genes, Brain and Behavior,* 2: 156–166.

Olson, L.E., Roper, R.J., Sengstaken, C.L., Peterson, E.A., Aquino, V., Galdzicki, Z. et al. (2007) 'Trisomy for the Down syndrome "critical region" is necessary but not sufficient for brain phenotypes of trisomic mice', *Human Molecular Genetics,* 16: 774–782.

Patti, P.J. & Tsiouris, J.A. (2006) 'Psychopathology in adults with Down syndrome: clinical findings from an outpatient clinic', *International Journal on Disability and Human Development,* 5: 357–364.

Pennington, B.F. (1997) 'Dimensions of executive functions in normal and abnormal development', in N.A. Krasnegor, G.R. Lyon, & P.S. Goldman-Rakic (eds), *Development of the Prefrontal Cortex: Evolution, Neurobiology, and Behavior.* Baltimore: Paul H. Brookes Publishing Co., pp. 265–281.

Pennington, B.F., Moon, J., Edgin, J., Stedron, J., & Nadel, L. (2003) 'The neuropsychology of Down syndrome: Evidence for hippocampal dysfunction', *Child Development,* 74: 75–93.

Penrose, L.S. (1933) 'The relative effects of paternal and maternal age in mongolism', *Journal of Genetics,* 27: 219–224.

Penrose, L.S. (1934) 'The relative aetiological importance of birth order and maternal age in mongolism', *Proceedings of the Royal Society of London,* 115: 431–450.

Pitcairn, T.K. & Wishart, J.G. (1994) 'Reactions of young children with Down's syndrome to an impossible task', *British Journal of Developmental Psychology,* 12: 485–489.

Polani, P.E., Briggs, J.H., Ford, C.E., Clarke, C.M., & Berg, J.M. (1960) 'A Mongol girl with 46 chromosomes', *Lancet,* April 2: 721–724.

Pueschel, S.M., Bernier, J.C., & Pezzullo, J.C. (1991) 'Behavioral observations in children with Down's syndrome', *Journal of Mental Deficiency Research,* 35: 502–511.

Rasmussen, P., Börjesson, O., Wentz, E., & Gillberg, C. (2001) 'Autistic disorders in Down syndrome: background factors and clinical correlates', *Developmental Medicine and Child Neurology,* 43: 750–754.

Reiss, S.S., Levitan, G.W., & Szyszko J. (1982) 'Emotional disturbance and mental retardation: diagnostic overshadowing. *American Journal of Mental Deficiency,* 86: 567–574.

Roizen, N.J. (2007) 'Down syndrome', in M. Batshaw, L. Pellegrino, & N.J. Roizen, (eds), *Children with Disabilities.* Baltimore: Brookes Publishing, pp. 263–273.

Rothbart, M.K. & Hanson, M.J. (1983) 'A caregiver report comparison of temperamental characteristics of Down syndrome and normal infants', *Developmental Psychology,* 19: 766–769.

Rowe, J., Lavender, A., & Turk, V. (2006) 'Cognitive executive function in Down's syndrome', *British Journal of Clinical Psychology,* 45: 5–17.

Ruskin, E.M., Kasari, C., Mundy, P., & Sigman, M. (1994) 'Attention to people and toys during social and object mastery in children with Down syndrome', *American Journal on Mental Retardation,* 99: 103–111.

Seguin, E.O. (1866) *Idiocy and Its Treatment by the Physiological Method.* New York: Wood.

Sherman, S.L., Freeman, S.B., Allen, E.G., & Lamb, N.E. (2005) 'Risk factors for nondisjunction of trisomy 21', *Cytogenetic Genome Research,* 111: 273–280.

Sherman, S.L., Allen, E.G., Bean, L.H., & Freeman, S.B. (2007) 'Epidemiology of Down syndrome', *Mental Retardation and Developmental Disabilities Research Reviews,* 13: 221–227.

Sigman, M. & Ruskin, E. (1999) 'Continuity and change in the social competence of children with autism, Down syndrome, and developmental delays', *Monographs of the Society for Research in Child Development,* 64: v-114.

Silverman, W. (2007) 'Down syndrome: cognitive phenotype', *Mental Retardation and Developmental Disabilities Research Reviews,* 13: 228–236.

Spiker, D., Boyce, G.C., & Boyce, L.K. (2002) 'Parent–child interactions when young children have disabilities', *International Review of Research in Mental Retardation,* 25: 35–70.

Starr, E.M., Berument, S.K., Tomlins, M., Papnikolaou, K., & Rutter, M. (2005) 'Brief report: autism in individuals with Down syndrome', *Journal of Autism and Developmental Disorders,* 35: 665–673.

Stoel-Gammon, C. (2003) 'Speech acquisition and approaches to intervention', in J. Rondal & S. Buckley (eds), *Speech and Language Intervention in Down Syndrome.* London: Whurr, pp. 49–62.

Trohanis, P.L. (2008) 'Progress in providing services to young children with special needs and their families—an overview to and update on the implementation of the Individuals with Disabilities Education Act', *Journal of Early Intervention,* 30: 140–151.

Van Bysterveldt, A.K., Gillon, G.T., & Moran, C. (2006) 'Enhancing phonological awareness and letter knowledge in preschool children with Down syndrome', *International Journal of Disabilities and Developmental Education,* 53: 301–329.

Visu-Petra, L. Benga, O., Tincas, I., & Miclea, M. (2007) 'Visual-spatial processing in children and adolescents with Down's syndrome: a computerized assessment of memory skills', *Journal of Intellectual Disability Research,* 51: 942–952.

Vlachou, M. & Farrell, P. (2000) 'Object mastery motivation in pre-school children with and without disabilities', *Educational Psychology,* 20: 167–176.

Volpe, E.P. (1986) 'Is Down syndrome a modern disease', *Perspectives in Biology and Medicine,* 29: 423–436.

Wetherby, A.M., Yonclas, D.G., & Bryan, A.A. (1989) 'Communicative profiles of preschool children with handicaps: implications for early identification', *Journal of Speech and Hearing Disorders,* 54: 148–158.

Wishart, J.G. (1996) 'Avoidant learning styles and cognitive development in young children', in B. Stratford & P. Gunn (eds). *New Approaches to Down Syndrome,* London: Cassell, pp. 157–172.

Yang, Q., Sherman, S.L., Hassold, T.J., Allran K., Taft L., Pettay D., Khoury M. J., Erickson J. D., Freeman S. B. (1999) 'Risk factors for trisomy 21: maternal cigarette smoking and oral contraceptive use in a population-based case-control study', *Genetics in Medicine,* 1: 80–88.

Zana, M., Jánka, Z., & Kálmán, J. (2007) 'Oxidative stress: a bridge between Down's syndrome and Alzheimer's disease', *Neurobiology of Aging,* 28: 648–676.

2

Down Syndrome: Lifetime Course and Strategies for Intervention

Janet Carr

The last 60 years have seen significant changes – educational, medical and social – in the lives of people with Down syndrome. In parallel with these changes has been the increase in life expectancy, from 12 years in 1929 (Penrose & Smith, 1966) to approaching 60 (Glasson et al., 2002). Longevity, too, has risen, with people over the age of 60 now 'not exceptional' (Dupont, 1986). Over 30 years ago the oldest person who could be traced at that time was aged 73 (Carr, 1975) while more recently people aged 74, 75 and 86 have been reported as 'leading healthy lives with no apparent evidence of impairment or deterioration' (Dalton & Wisniewski, 1990). This enhanced life span, welcome as it is, brings in its train fresh concerns. Parents who previously comforted themselves with the likelihood that they would be able to care for this child throughout his/her lifetime now have to accept that this may not be the case,

and that they may have to make provision for the time when they are unable to continue caring. Moreover, increasing numbers of the surviving people with Down syndrome are now vulnerable in their later years to Alzheimer's disease.

INTELLECTUAL DEVELOPMENT AND ACADEMIC ACHIEVEMENT

Developmental tests given to infants with Down syndrome commonly show mean scores somewhat lower than the general population average; then, with succeeding months, the gap between the two sets of scores widens. Thus, in one study (Carr, 1975) the mean mental age (MA) at chronological age (CA) 1.5 months was 1 month, whereas at CA 48 months it was under 22 months. (Both groups

Table 2.1   Mean IQs, 4 Years to 40 Years (n = 34)

Age, years	4	11	21	30	35	40
Mean IQ	40.8	35.6	44.9	43.4	43.0	41.5
SD		11.1	10.8	14.0	14.5	13.5	12.9

of babies were living in their own homes; mean MAs for the six babies living out of their own homes were 1.4 and 17 months, respectively.). This pattern – of scores declining over the early years – has been found in numerous studies (Cunningham, 1987; Ludlow & Allen, 1979; Share et al., 1961). In middle childhood, CA 10–11 years, mean IQs of 44 (Ludlow & Allen, 1979) and 37 (Carr, 1995) have been reported, while in early adulthood (CA 18–21), these two groups of researchers found mean MAs of 66 months and 59 months, respectively (Carr, 1995; Cunningham, 2006). In Carr's group the equivalent IQ was 42, and further follow-up to age 40 showed little change (see Table 2.1)

It is also important to note the considerable differences in ability between individuals with Down syndrome. About a third have scores in the low-average to mild intellectual disability range (IQ (70–52)); a minority, 10–15%, scores in the profoundly intellectually disabled range (IQ <20) and the remainder, about half, have scores in the range of moderate to severe intellectual disability. Despite high correlations between scores at the various ages (from age 4 years to 40 years, between 0.57 and 0.93) individuals also show considerable score variation. Almost half (42%) of IQ scores obtained from 4 to 40 years varied between ages by between 13 and 30 points (Carr, 2009). Scores at the extremes were more stable, particularly those at the lower extreme (IQ <20), but in general reliable prediction of later from earlier scores cannot be made (Carr, 2008b).

Two variables have been considered in relation to their effect on the IQ of people with Down syndrome. Higher parental IQ and education level have been found to be associated with higher IQ in offspring with Down syndrome in some studies (Cunningham, 1987; Fraser & Sadovnick, 1976; Golden & Pashayan, 1976) but not in others (Bennett et al., 1979; Carr, 1995; Irwin, 1989). There is greater consensus for the effect of gender, females being found almost invariably to have higher mean scores, at least until the menopause (Carr, 1995, 2003; Patel et al., 2001) while Carr (1995) also found a preponderance of females in the upper and of males in the lower IQ ranges.

In adults beyond the fourth decade of life cognitive ability generally declines. This is similar to, but earlier than, the decline seen in individuals with intellectual disabilities due to other causes, and in the general population. This may be due to the onset of Alzheimer's disease, but some decline may be expected as part of the normal ageing process (Devenny et al., 2000). Contrary to the findings at earlier ages, scores for older women were lower than those for men (Burt et al., 2005) which may be attributable to the menopause and consequent oestrogen deficiency in females (Patel et al., 2001). A review of studies of tests of both verbal and performance intelligence suggested that the trajectory of these with age in people with Down syndrome differs from that in the general population, in whom verbal (crystallized) intelligence holds up and performance (fluid) intelligence declines: in the 11 studies reviewed, with one exception, the reverse was seen in people with Down syndrome (Carr, 2005).

The development of academic skills such as reading and number work in children with Down syndrome has been documented in several research reports (Buckley, 1985; Pieterse & Treloar, 1981). Lorenz et al. (1985) studied reading ability in 115 five to seven year olds and found 31% were able to read five or more words, similar to the proportion found in an earlier study of children given intensive reading teaching (Buckley & Wood, 1983). Turner and Alborz (2003) found teachers' estimates of reading to increase over three time points (mean ages 9, 14 and 21 years) at all ability levels, though, after adjustments for IQ, with some tailing off after age 16. Children attending mainstream schools have been found to make better progress, independent of level of intellectual disability, than those attending special schools (Philps, 1995; Turner et al., 2008).

Young adults tested at age 18–20 years obtained a mean reading age of 7 years 10 months, and 21–24 year olds one of 8 years 8 months, with higher scores for those in integrated schools (Bochner et al., 2001). In another study of 21 year olds, most of whom had attended special schools, mean reading age was 7.8 years (Carr, 1995). Despite the 'tailing off' observed by Turner and Alborz (2003), the mean reading age of Carr's group continued to rise, albeit slowly, over the next 20 years, to means of 8 years at age 30, 8.1 years at age 35 and 8.3 years at age 40 (Carr, 2000, 2003, 2009).

Number work has received less attention, and is almost invariably found to be more problematical for people with Down syndrome than reading. Dunsdon's (1960) group were reported to have arithmetic ages 4 years below their reading ages, and similar findings have been reported by others (Buckley, 1985; Irwin, 1989). There are anecdotal reports of 20 year olds succeeding with three-place addition and a few with long multiplication (Pototzky & Grigg, 1942), though Gibson (1978: p. 78) finds these figures 'difficult to credit'. Neither was achieved by any of Carr's 21 year olds (Carr, 1995) and this remained the case at every stage to age 40 with two exceptions: one woman at 30 years succeeded with simple division (12 ÷ 4) and another at 40 years with simple multiplication (3 × 2). Buckley (1985) suggests that number may be more difficult for people with Down syndrome because they appear to take an essentially concrete approach and abstract concepts may be more difficult to grasp, though she cautions that this may also be due to the limitations of the teaching they have experienced.

LANGUAGE

The speech of children with Down syndrome is commonly impaired, especially where verbal expression is concerned (Clausen, 1968), compounded by physical features such as a protruding and furrowed tongue. Rondal (1996) noted delays, in many individuals, in the consistent use of conventional words before age 3. This was supported by Carr (1975: p. 35) in whose cohort two-word use was seen by that age in only 57%. Facility in language, as measured by mean length of utterance, progresses slowly but steadily until about mid-adolescence, when it reaches a plateaux at about six words, a level reached by non-disabled children soon after the age of 6 (Rondal, 1996). Language skills, especially expressive language, lag behind cognitive development, and this gap increases with age (Gunn & Crombie, 1996). Hearing problems, common in children with Down syndrome, may also lead to language difficulties. Interestingly, children who had been treated for a hearing problem (otitis media) had significantly higher language scores than those who had not been treated, although this did not apply to those who had never suffered from the condition (Whiteman et al., 1986). In adulthood, mean scores on both expressive and receptive language increased slightly from age 21 to 30, then declined marginally to 35 and again to 40 years (Carr, 2000, 2008b). For those included in Carr's study continuously to age 40, means for receptive language age were about 5 months ahead of means for expressive language. In older age, adults with Down syndrome have been found to have poorer scores on receptive, but not on expressive, language with increasing age (Carter-Young & Kramer, 1991; Cooper & Collacott, 1995) although this was not confirmed by Prasher (1996). Cooper and Collacott (1995) showed that, in people aged between 20 and 30 years, expressive language correlated highly with general ability (both measures derived from the ABS and Vineland Scale), and suggested that, as expressive language holds up well in older age, this could be used as a proxy measure of previous ability levels.

Self-help and independence

As do those of non-disabled children, parents of children with Down syndrome concentrate a good deal of effort in helping them to attain the basic skills of self-care: feeding, washing, dressing and toiletting. Feeding their babies with Down syndrome, who were sleepy and undemanding, caused many mothers anxiety in the early months, the babies needing to be woken for feeds and, with a poor sucking reflex, taking a long time over them (Carr, 1975). By 4 years old, although still behind developmentally, two-thirds could now feed themselves competently, took ordinary (not minced) foods, and could drink alone, and feeding was no longer a major problem for their mothers. Toilet training took longer and by 4 years the children with Down syndrome were noticeably behind their non-disabled contemporaries. Nevertheless, by this time over a third (38%) were virtually clean and dry by day, and nearly half (46%) managed their own toiletting with little or no help.

Further progress is made in adolescence. Table 2.2 shows the percentages from three studies of 11–17 year olds said to be independent in each area (Buckley & Sacks, 1987; Carr, 1995; Shepperdson, 1992).

As Table 2.2 indicates the majority of adolescents were able to feed themselves and over half were reliably toilet trained. Apart from those reported by Buckley, only a quarter to a third could manage bathing and dressing independently. (Where differences between results from different studies are concerned, allowance needs to be made for different populations, and, perhaps, different interpretations of terms such as 'independent'.) In later life, skills were further consolidated, with latterly some decline in competence, as evidenced by Carr's cohort at ages 21, 30, 35 and 40 (Table 2.3).

A large study of nearly 23,000 older people has found skills such as eating, toilet-

Table 2.2 Percentages of Adolescents in Three Studies Described as Independent in Self-Help

	Carr (1995)	Buckley & Sacks (1987)	Shepperdson (1992)
Age (years)	11	11–17	15–17
Independent % in			
Feeding	74	62	83
Dressing	33	62	23
Bathing	30	61	28
Toilet	60	81	55

ting and ambulation to decline in people with Down syndrome earlier than they do in those with intellectual disabilities due to other causes (Strauss & Zigman, 1996). Other research has been broadly consistent in finding significant age-related deficits after the age of 49–50 (Roeden & Zitman, 1997); these deficits become 'pronounced' after age 60 (Collacott, 1992; Zigman et al., 1989). Zigman et al. (1987) propose that changes in daily living skills provide 'the most sensitive manifestation of regression in a population whose cognitive skills are relatively limited'.

The relationship of self-help to chronological and mental age has been examined throughout the life span. Ross (1971) reported on an institutional population aged from 5 to 55 years, and, in a severely disabled sample, found self-help to be independent of chronological age across the entire age range. Others, however, have found both chronological and IQ/mental age to be significantly related in

Table 2.3 Percentages Of Adults Described as Independent in Self-Help (Skills) (Carr Longitudinal Cohort)

Independent % in	Age			
	21	30	35	40
Feeding	92	82	76	70
Dressing	76	77	67	79
Bathing	41	68	62	59
Toilet (dry day/night)	73	85	88	73
Total self-help	41	35	23	23

young children, mean CA 4½ years (Loveland & Kelley, 1991), and in adolescents, mean CA 14 years (Loveland & Kelley, 1988); similar findings are reported by Turner et al. (1991). In Carr's (1995) study, total self-help scores were highly significantly related to IQ at both 11 and 21 years, and at age 30 (Carr, 2000), 35 (Carr, 2003) and 40 (Carr, 2009). Other research on older people has also found CA to be negatively related to self-help (Collacott, 1992; Hawkins et al., 2003; Silverstein et al., 1986). Thus, while IQ/MA is positively related to self-help competence throughout the life span, in childhood chronological age is positively related but in old age the reverse is found, with the skills of older people falling below those of the younger.

Allowing independence to a child – the freedom to go out and about or to be left alone in the home – can be a difficult area to negotiate for families of children without disabilities, and the difficulties are greater where the children have learning disabilities. Table 2.4 gives the findings from three studies (Buckley & Sacks, 1987; Carr, 1995; Shepperdson, 1992), showing that around half the children and adolescents were never left alone in the house. This proportion diminished to about one-tenth in adulthood, when over two-thirds were now left for 1 hour or more, although from age 30 onwards over half of these would be left for no more than 1 hour.

Over half the children and adolescents were never allowed out alone, and this proportion also declined to about a tenth in adulthood. Perhaps surprisingly, around a third were allowed out beyond the garden alone, more than those in Shepperdson's and Carr's 21 year old groups who would be left alone in the house. Mothers in both Shepperdson's and Carr's studies expressed concerns about the possibility of strangers coming to the door, or of fire, if their sons or daughters with Down syndrome were alone in the house.

PERSONALITY

The popular image of people with Down syndrome as happy, loving and fond of music was challenged by Blacketer-Simmonds (1953), who found them to be less docile and more mischievous than were people with other forms of intellectual disability. There was no difference between the two groups in their responsiveness to music. This stereotype, however, still persists with much of the general population, and there has been some research support for it (Johnson & Abelson, 1969; Silverstein et al., 1985). The last-named authors suggest that, as the stereotype is so well known, carers may expect pleasant behaviours from people with Down syndrome and this in turn may lead them to interact with them in such a way as to elicit these behaviours.

A less positive personality trait is obstinacy, or stubbornness, often remarked on and notably by Langdon Down: 'Another feature is their great obstinacy .... No amount of coercion will induce them to do that which they have made up their minds not to do' (Down, 1887). In Carr's group almost half (48%) of the 11 year olds and over two-thirds (68%) of 21 year olds were said to be stubborn, although the proportion declined in older age to about a third (36%) at age 40 (Carr, unpublished work). It may be significant that Down was apparently discussing

Table 2.4 Independence – Going Out and Staying at Home Alone

		Stay Home Alone		Go Out Alone	
Study	Age	Never	1hour+	Never	Beyond Garden
Carr (1995)	11	43	17	62	38
Buckley & Sacks (1987)	11–17	59	14	66	31*
Shepperdson (1992)	15–17	62	0	55	32
Carr (1995)	21	12	26	47	53
Carr (2000)	30	9	70	6	41
Carr (2003)	35	12	77	15	45
Carr (2008b)	40	12	66	15	48

* Were said to be able to 'go to a shop alone', Buckley & Sacks (1987).

younger rather than older people. Zihni (1994) has suggested that 'obstinacy' may result from a deficiency in myelin ('long observed in Down syndrome') and other physical conditions such as heart defects, which may lead to tiredness, 'and then to a disinclination to carry out required tasks'. As far as is known this suggestion has not been pursued.

LIVING SITUATION

The majority, over 80%, of small children in two studies (Carr, 1975; Pueschel, 1984) lived in their own homes, and for two-thirds of Carr's group this still applied at age 11 years. This was not a new phenomenon: popular beliefs notwithstanding, in the 1950s 74% of children and young adults grew up in their own homes (Graliker et al., 1965; Tizard & Grad, 1961). Two-thirds to four-fifths of young adults in two later studies were at home, most of the remainder living in hostels (Shepperdson, 1992), and a small number, 10%, in hospitals (Carr, 1995). With increasing age the proportion at home in the latter study dropped from 71% at age 21 to 60% at age 30, 54% at age 35 and 50% at age 40, when 25% were in small group homes and 25% in larger facilities; none lived in hospital after age 21 (Carr, 2008a). Whether this will continue to be the case remains to be seen: Collacott (1992) reported that the proportion living in hospital rose from 17% of 40–49 year olds to 42% of those aged 60+. However, with the current emphasis on community living as the preferred option for people with intellectual disabilities, this pattern may change in the future.

DAYTIME OCCUPATION AND EMPLOYMENT

At 4 years of age, over half the children studied by Carr (1975) attended a school of some kind, three-quarters of these, compared with only one control child, attending full time (Carr, 1975). In the 1970s and 1980s three-quarters of teenagers attended schools for the severely intellectually disabled (Carr, 1995; Shepperdson, 1992), most of the remainder attending schools for the mildly intellectually disabled. Two in Shepperdson's but none in Carr's studies attended mainstream schools. These children were at school in the 1970s and early 1980s, and the situation is different now. In 2004, 51% of children with Down syndrome were found to be in mainstream, compared with 34% in special schools (Down Syndrome Association, 2004), while in 2008 a review of calls to the DSA behavioural advice line found 72% to be in mainstream and 24% in special schools (Carr, unpublished work). The proportion of children in primary was consistently far higher than in secondary schools: 67% of the DSA and 86% of Carr's samples were in primary schools, whereas at secondary level the proportions were 27% and 42%, respectively.

Data from 20 years ago show that, for the majority (70–90%) of adults with Down syndrome, daytime occupation was provided at an adult day centre (Social Education Centre), with only a small number (2–15%) attending further education courses (Holmes, 1988; Lane, 1985; Shepperdson, 1992). More recently, such data as are available suggest that this has changed, with full-time attendance at Social Education Centres dropping to 21% and at least part-time attendance at further education colleges rising to 36% by age 40 (Carr, 2008a). Similarly, in 1985, not one person with Down syndrome could be found in employment (Innes et al., 1978); by 1994, 29 people with Down syndrome were known by the Mencap Pathways Employment Service in the south of England and New to be employed. In 2004, nine people (26% of the cohort) were employed (Carr, 2008a), albeit all of them part time. More impressive figures come from Australia, where a questionnaire survey of 110 adults with Down syndrome, mean age 28 years, showed that over half attended further study courses, and 65% were employed, most in sheltered workshops, but over a third in outside employment (Jobling & Cuskelly, 2002).

SOCIAL RELATIONSHIPS

In early childhood most of the social contacts that children with Down syndrome had was with friends of their brothers and sisters. Ninety one percent met their siblings' friends, and almost all of these welcomed the child, two-thirds including him or her in their games, when they played games of school or of hospital, where the Down syndrome child filled the role of pupil or patient (Carr, 1975). Only a third (33%) of the children with Down syndrome had a friend of their own (all but one non-disabled children) compared with three-quarters of the controls. By age 11, 88% of the children had at least one friend, over half had a non-disabled friend (most of them relatives or family friends), often in addition to a friend with disabilities. Shepperdson's (1992) group had fewer friends: both as young children (6–8 year olds) and as teenagers, two-thirds had no friend. Shepperdson details the difficulties experienced by the children – that their school friends were often not from the same locality, or if they were, they might be of different age, sex or ability, so the friendships did not flourish. Similar problems were described by mothers in Carr's (1995) study, while Buckley and Sacks (1987) found that while the children had friends and played with them, for the majority this occurred less than once a week.

In Carr's study (1995) more significant friendships featured. Three-quarters of the 11 year olds had a best friend, usually a child with disabilities of the same sex, although for 18% the best friend was a non-disabled child. At age 21, nearly 80% had a friend, but now only just over a third had a best friend, only one of these being non-disabled, and the figures for the 30–40 year cohort were very similar. Friends also tended to be seen rather infrequently, and interactions with friends

diminished with increasing age. Interest in people of the opposite sex is common and this was shown by over half the adolescents in Pueschel and Scola's (1988) study, of whom 17% had a boy or girl friend and over a third said they would like to marry. Similarly, between a fifth and a quarter of 30–40 year olds in Carr's study had a boy or girl friend, about half of these being judged to be in serious relationships and three men having gone as far as getting engaged, although none had married (Carr, 2008a). Marriage is relatively unusual for people with Down syndrome. Thirty-eight marriages (35 women and three men with Down syndrome) were reported by Edwards (1988), and although anecdotal accounts of individual marriages are found (e.g. Cable, 2006) and the numbers are said to be increasing (Brown, 1996), a literature search has not produced any further reference relating to marriages of people with Down syndrome.

AGEING AND ALZHEIMER'S DISEASE

Ageing brings about some changes and declines in performance in all populations, and some characteristic patterns have been observed as part of normal ageing in people with Down syndrome. Their relative difference on verbal and performance tests, and the contrast with that seen in the general population, has been described already. Two studies have found the scores of premenopausal women to be higher than those of age-matched males, but postmenopausal women performed less well than did their male contemporaries (Burt et al., 2005, Patel et al., 2001). Patel et al. suggest that cognitive decline in postmenopausal women with Down syndrome may be associated with oestrogen deficiency rather than with age, and that hormone replacement therapy could be valuable in countering dementia in these people.

The increase in longevity in people with Down syndrome has brought to greater prominence in their vulnerability to Alzheimer's disease. Neuropathological signs of the disease have been found in the brains of all people with Down syndrome dying over the age of 40 (Thase, 1982). The clinical signs, however, summarized by Oliver and Holland (1986) as comprising a loss of self-care skills, deterioration of language, apathy, and becoming unmanageable or withdrawn, occur much less frequently, not in substantial numbers until after age 50 and increasingly after age 60. Research on the psychological indicators of the disease in people with Down syndrome have focused on three main areas: general ability (IQ), memory, and daily living skills. Most studies of intelligence in old age agree that raw scores decline with age in people with Down syndrome as they do in the non-disabled population. Declines were more frequent in those over age 45 but were mostly small and of doubtful significance (Devenny et al., 1996; Fenner et al., 1987; Haxby, 1989). Small declines in IQ are likely to be part of the normal ageing process and any decline needs to be considerable to be seen as indicating dementia. In any case such an approach may be applicable to only a proportion of the population: those with severe and profound intellectual disabilities could not be diagnosed through the use of cognitive tests, because of floor effects (Margello-Lana et al., 2007).

The scores of people with Down syndrome on memory tests decrease with increasing age (Thase, 1982). Decline in memory function begins at an average age of 49 years (Dalton & Crapper-McLaughlan, 1984) and affects both auditory and visual skills (Marcell & Weeks, 1988). In longitudinal studies, decline in memory has been shown to be an early indication of deterioration in people with Down syndrome, occurring before aphasia, apraxia or agnosia became apparent (Dalton et al., 1999; Oliver et al., 1998). Other approaches, too, have been used to identify early-stage dementia. Devenny et al. (2002) used a modified version of the Cued Recall Test and were able to identify eight people who were not suspected of but later went on

to develop dementia. Oliver et al. (2005) showed that, even in older (40+) adults with Down syndrome who did not show signs of dementia on other criteria, increasing the task load (increasing the number of items to be recalled from two to three) revealed deficits when their performance was compared to that of younger participants.

A large study of nearly 23,000 older people has found skills such as eating, toileting and ambulation to decline in people with Down syndrome earlier than they do in those with intellectual disabilities due to other causes (Strauss & Zigman, 1996). Other research has been broadly consistent in finding significant age-related deficits in self-help skills after the age of 50 (Roeden & Zitman, 1997), these deficits becoming 'pronounced' after age 60 (Collacott, 1992; Zigman et al., 1989).

APPROACHES TO INTERVENTION, AND CHALLENGES FOR THE FUTURE

These may be discussed in four areas: cognitive, educational, occupational and social.

Cognitive approaches

Efforts to ameliorate the cognitive deficits of children with Down syndrome proliferated in the 1960s to 1980s (see Carr, 2002). In summary, programmes were set up in which young children with Down syndrome were given special teaching and stimulation, either by professionals or, increasingly, by their parents (usually the mothers), who were trained by the professionals. Early studies showed the children making significant advances in comparison with children who had not taken part in such programmes (e.g., Hanson & Schwartz, 1978; Ludlow & Allen, 1979) but longer-term follow-up showed that these advances were not sustained (Cunningham, 1987; Gibson & Harris, 1988). Once the intensive teaching was discontinued, the level of the targeted children gradually returned to that of the comparison groups. Despite this research evidence, the Portage model of intervention continues to be provided, in the UK at least. While parents are often undoubtedly glad to be involved in working with their children, in having something they can do for them, it is questionable whether they are aware of the limited value of this work to the children themselves. Other forms of help have been advocated, and could be researched. Gibson and Harris (1998) point out that much is known now about how children with Down syndrome learn, which could be incorporated into the curriculum, while they also make the, perhaps controversial, suggestion that teaching should be concentrated on late rather than early childhood, and on adulthood. Cunningham (1987) stresses the importance of social-interactive models, and, especially, of enhanced support for parents, crucially around the time when they are told of the diagnosis. Cunningham also highlights the need to focus on practical topics, such as transport, respite care, etc., and of encouraging the parents' confidence in their own parenting skills. These are as yet untried strategies, and as Gibson and Harris (1998) emphasise, if they were to be adopted they should be scrutinised in 'well designed longitudinal comparison studies'. There is, however, little sign of this actually occurring.

Educational approaches

Increasingly, it is taken as self-evident that children with Down syndrome should attend mainstream schools, that this constitutes the optimum setting for them both educationally and socially. It is also, in the writer's experience, almost invariably the parents' preferred option. Evidence on the point is, however, sparse and conflicting. Sloper et al. (1990) found support for mainstream schools as far as educational achievement is concerned, while Fewell and Oelwein (1990) did not. Socially, several studies have shown that real

integration and the development of close friendships between those in mainstream schools with and without Down syndrome are limited (Ashman & Elkins, 1996; Sinson & Wetherick, 1981). Sloper et al. (1990) also failed to find increased social contacts in out-of-school hours for those at mainstream schools. There is a pressing need for research into how this situation could be improved. Serafica (1990) has shown that, given the choice, children with Down syndrome sought out other children with Down syndrome as playmates, rather than typically developing children. Thus, in mainstream schools they may need to have access to larger numbers of other children with intellectual disabilities with whom they can establish genuine relationships. It has to be admitted that it is not easy to see how, given the relatively small proportion of children with intellectual disabilities in mainstream schools, this could be accomplished.

As Gibson and Harris (1988) proposed, education for people with Down syndrome should not end when they leave school, and indeed it does not. Although practical life skills may seem to be more important for adults than literacy and numeracy, both for their own pleasure and to help them manage their lives, the teaching of basic educational skills needs to be continued into adulthood; Faragher and Brown (2005) also suggested that this could contribute positively to their quality of life. Van Kraayenoord et al. (2002) describe a literacy programme, including 'shared' and 'purposeful' reading and writing – engaging in these activities in conjunction with a teacher, and focussing on a relevant task, such as writing a letter to a friend. At the completion of a 2-year mixed full- and part-time course, the first six graduates of the programme had made gains of an average of 14 months in reading accuracy and nearly 9 months in comprehension. While it may be uncertain whether this particular regime, or simply the length and intensity of the course, was responsible for the gains made, the approach is an interesting one that merits further research.

Occupation and employment

Many (though not all) people with Down syndrome want to work; those who do find employment obtain much satisfaction from it, and it seems likely that many more could work than is currently the case (Carr, 2009). Programmes to help people with Down syndrome to get and keep jobs have been described, including identifying and analysing the requirements for a particular job, designing a work schedule for the individual, and providing a job coach who monitors the worker's progress and prompts appropriate actions where necessary (Perera, 1996). Contardi (2002) emphasises the need to teach associated skills, such as grooming and cleanliness (essential if the work is in a food complex), travelling independently, asking for help in difficulty, etc. The same report describes eight young people with Down syndrome who gained jobs in a MacDonald's restaurant, which, 4–8 years later, they still held. Perera (1996) also notes that attention must be paid to the worker's personality. Wheeler et al. (1988) and Renzaglia et al. (1991) describe in detail how a combination of these approaches enabled a moderately intellectually disabled young man with Down syndrome to succeed as an animal caretaker in a university laboratory. Perera believes that 'people with Down syndrome of any age or condition can work', given sufficient support and attention to their needs. This is a large claim that still needs to be thoroughly explored in practice.

Social relationships

Despite the exodus from institutions to the community, most children—and more particularly adults—with Down syndrome continue to be limited in their social relationships, whether they live in their own families or in community facilities (Emerson & McVilly, 2004; Holmes, 1988; Putnam et al., 1988). Putnam et al. note that this comes about even where the young person has had a good social life as a child, when their childhood

friends start work or move away. They advocate the provision of a greater variety of leisure options, the pairing of disabled and non-disabled adults for recreational purposes, and programmes that provide training alongside integrated community activities. Emerson and McVilly (2004) take a rather different line. They noted that those in one particular locality (identified as 'locality B') were more than 70% more likely to be involved with friends than those in any other locality. They suggest that 'the setting in which a person lives is a more significant determinant ... of activities with their friends than the characteristics of participants'. The crucial characteristics of the setting that promote the friendships still need to be identified.

One final factor for consideration is the preferences that people with Down syndrome have in their choice of friends. Research suggests that people with intellectual disabilities tend to choose other people with intellectual disabilities, rather than non-disabled people, as friends (Emerson & McVilly, 2004). Children and adults with Down syndrome also prefer activities with other people with Down syndrome rather than with non-disabled peers (Neumayer et al., 1993; Serafica, 1990). Along with the numerous benefits that have accrued from the move away from the institutions, it may also have entailed the loss to people with intellectual disabilities, including those with Down syndrome, of a sizeable population of potential friends. How to make good that loss, without a return to the institutions, will be one of the major challenges for the future.

REFERENCES

Ashman, A.E. & Elkins, S. (1996) 'School and integration', in B. Stratford & P. Gunn (eds), *New Approaches to Down Syndrome,* London: Cassell, pp. 341–357.
Bennett, F.C., Sells, C.J., & Brand, C. (1979) 'Influences on measured intelligence in Down's syndrome', *American Journal of Diseases of Childhood,* 133: 700–703.

Blacketer-Simmonds, D.A. (1953) 'An investigation into the supposed difference existing between mongols and other mentally defective subjects with regard to certain psychological traits', *Journal of Mental Science,* 99: 709–719.

Bochner, S., Outhred, L., & Pieterse, M. (2001) 'A study of functional literacy skills in young adults with Down syndrome', *International Journal of Disability, Development and Education,* 48: 67–90.

Brown, R.I. (1996) 'Growing older: challenges and opportunities', in B. Stratford & P. Gunn (eds), *New Approaches to Down Syndrome.* London: Cassell, pp. 249–267.

Buckley, S. (1985) 'Attaining basic educational skills: reading, writing and number', in D. Lane & B. Stratford (eds), *Current Approaches to Down's Syndrome.* London: Holt, Rinehart and Winston, pp. 315–343.

Buckley, S. & Sacks, B. (1987) *The Adolescent with Down's Syndrome.* Portsmouth Polytechnic.

Buckley, S. & Wood, E. (1983) 'The extent and significance of reading skills in pre-school children with Down's syndrome'. Paper presented at conference of British Psychological Society, London. (Cited in Buckley, S. (1985) 'Attaining basic educational skills: reading, writing and number', in D. Lane & B. Stratford (eds), *Current Approaches to Down's Syndrome.* London: Holt, Rinehart and Winston, pp. 315–343.

Burt, D.B., Primeaux-Hart, S., Loveland, K.A., Cleveland, L.A., Lewis, K.R., Lesser, J., & Pearson, P.L. (2005) 'Aging in adults with intellectual disabilities', *American Journal on Mental Retardation,* 110: 268–284.

Cable, A. (2006) 'A marriage to lift the heart', *Daily Mail,* 6 June.

Carr, J. (1975) *Young Children with Down's Syndrome: Their Development, Upbringing and Effect on their Families.* London: Butterworth.

Carr, J. (1995) *Down's Syndrome: Children Growing Up.* Cambridge: Cambridge University Press.

Carr, J. (2000) '30 year olds with Down's syndrome: continuation of a longitudinal study', *Journal of Applied Research in Intellectual Disabilities,* 13: 1–16.

Carr, J. (2002) 'Down's syndrome', in P. Howlin & O. Udwin (eds), *Outcomes in Neurodevelopmental Disorders.* Cambridge: Cambridge University Press.

Carr, J. (2003) 'Patterns of ageing in 30–35-year-olds with Down's syndrome', *Journal of Applied Research in Intellectual Disability,* 16: 29–40.

Carr, J. (2005) 'Stability and change in cognitive ability over the life span: a comparison of populations with and without Down's syndrome', *Journal of Intellectual Disability Research,* 49: 915–928.

Carr, J. (2008a) 'The everyday life of adults with Down's syndrome', *Journal of Applied Research in Intellectual Disability,* 21: 389–397.

Carr, J. (2008b) 'Four to forty years: the pattern of development of abilities in a cohort with Down's Syndrome', Paper presented at the 13th World Congress, IASSID, Cape Town.

Carr, J. (2009) '40 years of life with Down syndrome', *Down Syndrome Quarterly,* 18–25.

Carter-Young, E. & Kramer, B. (1991) 'Characteristics of age-related language decline in adults with Down syndrome', *Mental Retardation,* 29: 75.

Clausen, J. (1968) 'Behavioural characteristics of Down's syndrome subjects', *American Journal of Mental Deficiency,* 73: 118–126.

Collacott, R. (1992) 'The effect of age and residential placement on adaptive behaviour of adults with Down's syndrome', *British Journal of Psychiatry,* 161: 675–679.

Contardi, A. (2002) 'From autonomy to work placement' in M. Cuskelly, A. Jobling, & S. Buckley (eds), *Down Syndrome Across the Life Span.* London. Whurr Publishers.

Cooper, S-A. & Collacott, R.A. (1995). 'The effect of age on language in people with Down's syndrome', *Journal of Intellectual Disability Research,* 39: 197–200.

Cunningham, C.C. (1987) 'Early intervention in Down's syndrome', in G. Hosking & G. Murphy (eds), *Prevention of Mental Handicap: A World View.* RSM Services International Congress and Symposium Series No.112. London: Royal Society of Medicine Services Ltd, pp. 169–182.

Cunningham, C.C. (2006) *Down's Syndrome: An Introduction for Parents.* Souvenir Press, Human Horizon Series. 3rd edn. (Reporting follow-up data from Ludlow, J.)

Dalton, A. & Crapper-McLaughlan, D.R. (1984) 'Incidence of memory deterioration in ageing persons with Down's syndrome', in J.M. Berg (ed.), *Perspectives and Progress in Mental Retardation,* Vol. 2. Baltimore, MD: University Park Press, pp. 55–62.

Dalton, A.J. & Wisniewski, H.M. (1990) 'Down's syndrome and the dementia of Alzheimer disease', *International Review of Psychiatry,* 2: 43–52.

Dalton, A.J., Mehta, P.D., Fedor, B.L., & Patti, P.J. (1999) 'Cognitive changes in memory precede those in praxis in persons with Down's syndrome', *Journal of Intellectual and Developmental Disability,* 24: 169–187.

Devenny, D.A., Silverman, W.P., Hill, A.L., Jenkins, E., Sersen, E.A., & Wisniewski, K.E. (1996) 'Normal ageing in adults with Down's syndrome: a longitudinal study', *Journal of Intellectual Disability Research,* 40: 208–221.

Devenny, D.A., Krinsky-McHale, S.J., Sersen, G., & Silverman, W.P. (2000) 'Sequence of cognitive decline in dementia in adults with Down's syndrome', *Journal of Intellectual Disability Research,* 44: 654–665.

Devenny, D.A., Zimmerli, E.J., Kittler, P., & Krinsky-McHale, S.J. (2002) 'Cued recall in early-dementia in adults with Down's syndrome', *Journal of Intellectual Disability Research,* 46: 472–483.

Down, J.L.H. (1887) *Mental Affections of Childhood and Youth.* London: J. & A. Churchill. Quoted by Penrose, L.S. & Smith, G.F. (1966) *Down's Anomaly.* London: J. & A. Churchill, p. 54.

Down Syndrome Association (2004) *Access to Education—A Report on the Barriers to Education for Children with Down's syndrome.* London: DSA Publications.

Dunsdon, M.I., Carter, C.O., & Huntley, R.M.C. (1960) 'Upper end of range of intelligence in mongolism,' *Lancet,* i: 565–568.

Dupont, A. (1986) 'Non-psychiatric aspects of the young severely mentally retarded and the family', *British Journal of Psychiatry,* 148: 227–234.

Edwards, J. (1988) 'Sexuality, marriage and parenting for persons with Down syndrome', in S.M. Pueschel (ed.), *The Young Person with Down Syndrome.* Baltimore: Brookes, pp. 187–204.

Emerson, E. & McVilly, K. (2004) 'Friendship activities of adults with intellectual disabilities in supported accommodation in Northern England', *Journal of Applied Research in Intellectual Disability,* 17: 191–197.

Faragher, R. & Brown, R.I. (2005) 'Numeracy for adults with Down syndrome: it's a matter of quality of life', *Journal of Intellectual Disability Research,* 49: 761–765.

Fenner, M.E., Hewitt, K.E., & Torpy, M. (1987) 'Down's syndrome: intellectual and behavioural functioning during adulthood', *Journal of Mental Deficiency Research,* 31: 241–246.

Fewell, R.R. & Oelwein, P.L. (1990) 'The relationship between time in integrated environments and developmental gains in young children with special needs', *Topics in Early Childhood Special Education,* 10: 104–116.

Fraser, F.C. & Sadovnick, A.D. (1976) 'Correlation of IQ in subjects with Down syndrome and their parents and sibs', *Journal of Mental Deficiency Research,* 20: 179–182.

Gibson, D. (1978) 'The foundations of intelligence', in *Down's Syndrome: The Psychology of Mongolism.* Cambridge, England: Cambridge University Press, pp. 78–110.

Gibson, D. & Harris, A. (1988) 'Aggregated early intervention effects for Down syndrome persons: patterning and longevity of benefits', *Journal of Mental Deficiency Research,* 32: 1–17.

Glasson, E.J., Sullivan, S.G., Hussain, R., Petterson, B.A., Bittles, A.H. (2002) 'The changing profile of people with Down syndrome', *Clinical Genetics,* 62: 390–393.

Golden, W. & Pashayan, H.M. (1976) 'The effect of parental education on the eventual mental development of non-institutionalized children with Down syndrome', *Journal of Pediatrics,* 89: 403–407.

Graliker, B.V., Koch, R., & Henderson, R.A. (1965) 'A study of factors influencing the placement of retarded children in a residential institution', *American Journal of Mental Deficiency,* 69: 553–559.

Gunn, P. & Crombie, M. (1996) 'Language and speech', in: B. Stratford & P. Gunn (eds), *New Approaches to Down Syndrome.* London: Cassell, pp. 249–267.

Hanson, M. & Schwartz, R.H. (1978) 'Result of a longitudinal intervention program for Down's syndrome infants and their families', *Education and Training of the Mentally Retarded,* 13: 403–407.

Hawkins, B.A., Eklund, S.J., James, D.R., & Foose, A.K. (2003) 'Adaptive behaviour of adults with Down Syndrome: modeling change with age', *Mental Retardation,* 41: 7–28.

Haxby, J.V. (1989) 'Neuropsychological evaluation of adults with Down's syndrome: patterns of selective impairment in non-demented old adults', *Journal of Mental Deficiency Research,* 33: 193–210.

Holmes, N. (1988) 'The quality of life of mentally handicapped adults and their parents'. PhD thesis, University of London.

Innes, G., Johnson, A.W., & Miller, M.W. (1978) *Mental Subnormality in N.E. Scotland.* Scottish Home and Health Department.

Irwin, K.C. (1989) 'The school achievement of children with Down's syndrome', *New Zealand Medical Journal,* 102: 11–13.

Jobling A. & Cuskelly, M. (2002) 'Life styles of adults with Down syndrome living at home', in M. Cuskelly, A. Jobling, & S. Buckley (eds), *Down Syndrome Across the Life Span.* London: Whurr Publishers.

Johnson, A.W. & Abelson, R.W. (1969) 'The behavioural competence of mongoloid and non-mongoloid retardates', *American Journal of Mental Deficiency,* 73: 856–857.

Lane, D. (1985) 'After school: work and employment for adults with Down's syndrome?', in D. Lane & B. Stratford (eds), *Current Approaches to Down's Syndrome.* London: Holt, Rinehart and Winston, pp. 386–400.

Lorenz, S., Sloper, T., & Cunningham, C. (1985) 'Reading and Down's syndrome', *British Journal of Special Education,* 12: 65–67.

Loveland, K.A. & Kelly, M.L. (1988) 'Development of adaptive behavior in adolescents and young adults with autism and Down syndrome', *American Journal on Mental Retardation,* 96: 13–20.

Loveland, K.A. & Kelly, M.L. (1991) 'Development of adaptive behavior in preschoolers with autism and Down syndrome', *American Journal on Mental Retardation,* 93: 84–92.

Ludlow, J.R. & Allen, L.M. (1979) 'The effect of early intervention and pre-school stimulus on the development of the Down's syndrome child', *Journal of Mental Deficiency Research,* 23: 29–44.

Marcell, M.M. & Weeks, S.L. (1988) 'Short-term memory difficulties and Down's syndrome', *Journal of Mental Deficiency Research,* 32: 153–162.

Margello-Lana, M.L., Moore, P.B., Kay, D.W., Perry, R.H., Reid, B.E., Berney, T.P. et al. (2007) 'Fifteen-year follow-up of 92 hospitalized adults with Down's syndrome: incidence of cognitive decline, its relation to age and neuropathology', *Journal of Applied Research in Intellectual Disability,* 51: 463–477.

Neumayer, R., Smith, R.W., & Lundgren, H.M. (1993) 'Leisure-related peer preference choices of individuals with Down syndrome', Mental Retardation, 31: 396–402.

Oliver, C. & Holland A.J. (1986) 'Down's syndrome and Alzheimer's disease: a review', *Psychological Medicine,* 16: 307–322.

Oliver, C., Crayton, L., Holland, A.J., Hall, S., & Bradbury, J. (1998) 'A four-year prospective study of age-related cognitive change in adults with Down's syndrome', *Psychological Medicine,* 28: 1365–1377.

Oliver, C., Holland A.J., Hall, S., & Crayton, L. (2005) 'Effects of increasing task load on memory impairment in adults with Down syndrome', *American Journal on Mental Retardation,* 110: 339–345.

Patel, B.N., Seltzer, G.B., Wu, H.S., & Schupf, N. (2001) 'Effect of menopause on cognitive performance in women with Down syndrome', *Cognitive Neuroscience and Neuropsychology,* 12: 2659–2662.

Penrose, L.S. & Smith, G.F. (1966) *Down's Anomaly.* London: J. & A. Churchill.

Perera, J. (1996) 'Social and labour integration of people with Down's syndrome', in J.A. Rondal, J. Perera, L. Nadel, & A. Comblain (eds), *Down's Syndrome: Psychological, Psychobiological and Socio-educational Perspectives.* London: Whurr Press.

Philps, C. (1995) 'Research into academic attainments and language development of children with Down's syndrome', *Down's Syndrome Association Newsletter,* No. 77.

Pieterse, M. & Treloar, R. (1981) *The Down's Syndrome Program.* Progress Report, 1981, MacQuarie University. (Cited by Buckley, S. (1985) 'Attaining basic educational skills: reading, writing and number', in D. Lane & B. Stratford (eds), *Current Approaches to Down's Syndrome,* London: Holt, Rinehart and Winston, pp. 315–343.

Pototzky, C. & Grigg, A.E. (1942) 'A revision of the prognosis in mongolism', *American Journal of Orthopsychiatry,* 12: 503–510.

Prasher, V.P. (1996) 'The effect of age on language in people with Down's syndrome', *Journal of Intellectual Disability Research,* 40: 484–485. [Letter]

Pueschel, S.M. (ed.) (1984) *The Young Child with Down's Syndrome.* New York: Human Sciences Press.

Pueschel, S.M. & Scola, P.S. (1988) 'Parents' perceptions of social and sexual functions of adolescents with Down syndrome', *Journal of Mental Deficiency Research,* 32: 215–220.

Putnam, J.W., Pueschel, S.M., & Holman, J.G. (1988) 'Community activities of youths and adults with Down's syndrome', *British Journal of Mental Subnormality,* 34: 47–53.

Renzaglia, P., Wheeler, J.J., Hanson, H.B., & Miller, S.R. (1991) 'The use of extended follow-along procedures in a supported employment setting', *Education and Training in Mental Retardation,* 20: 64–69.

Roeden, J.M. & Zitman, F.G. (1997) 'A longitudinal comparison of cognitive and adaptive changes in subjects with Down's syndrome and an intellectually disabled control group', *Journal of Applied Research in Intellectual Disabilities,* 4: 289–302.

Rondal, J.A. (1996) 'Oral language in Down's syndrome' in J.A. Rondal, J. Perera, L. Nadel & A. Comblain (eds), *Down's Syndrome: Psychological, Psychobiological and Socio-educational Perspectives.* London: Whurr Publishers.

Ross, T. (1971) 'A preliminary study of self-help skills and age in hospitalized Down's syndrome patients', *American Journal of Mental Deficiency,* 76: 373–377.

Serafica, F.C. (1990) 'Peer relations of children with Down syndrome', in D. Cicchetti & M. Beeghly (eds), *Children with Down Syndrome: a Developmental Perspective,* Cambridge: Cambridge University Press, pp. 369–398.

Share, J., Webb, A., & Koch, R. (1961) 'A preliminary investigation of the early developmental status of mongoloid infants', *American Journal of Mental Deficiency,* 66: 238–241.

Shepperdson, B. (1992) *A Longitudinal Study of Down Syndrome Adults.* End of award report. Economic and Research Council, Swindon.

Silverstein, A.B., Ageno, D., Alleman, A.C., Derecho, K.T., & Gray, S.B. (1985) 'Adaptive behavior of institutionalized individuals with Down syndrome', *American Journal of Mental Deficiency,* 89: 555–558.

Silverstein, A.B., Herbs, D., Nasuta, R., & White, J. (1986) 'Effects of age on the adaptive behavior of institutionalized individuals with Down syndrome', *American Journal of Mental Deficiency,* 90: 659–662.

Sinson, J. & Wetherick, N.E. (1981) 'The behaviour of children with Down's syndrome in normal playgroups', *Journal of Mental Deficiency Research,* 25: 113–120.

Sloper, P., Cunningham, C., Turner, S., & Knussen, C. (1990) 'Factors related to the academic attainments of children with Down's syndrome', *British Journal of Educational Psychology,* 60: 284–298.

Strauss, D. & Zigman, W.B. (1996) 'Behavioral capabilities and mortality risk in adults with and without Down syndrome', *American Journal on Mental Retardation,* 101: 269–281.

Thase, M.E. (1982) 'The relationship between Down syndrome and Alzheimer's disease', in L. Nadal (ed.) *The Psychobiology of Down Syndrome.* Cambridge, MA: MIT Press, pp. 345–368.

Tizard, J. & Grad, J. (1961) *The Mentally Handicapped and Their Families.* London: Oxford University Press.

Turner, S. & Alborz, A. (2003) 'Academic attainments of children with Down's Syndrome: a longitudinal study', *British Journal of Educational Psychology,* 73: 563–583.

Turner, S., Sloper, P., Knussen, C., & Cunningham, C. (1991) 'Factors relating to self-sufficiency in children with Down's syndrome', *Journal of Mental Deficiency Research,* 35: 13–24.

Turner, S., Alborz, A., & Gayle, V. (2008) 'Predictors of academic attainments of young people with Down's syndrome', *Journal of Intellectual Disability Research,* 52: 380–392.

Van Kraayenoord, C., Moni, K.B., Jobling, A., & Ziebarth, K. (2002) 'Broadening approaches to literacy development for young adults with Down syndrome', in M. Cuskelly, A. Jobling & S. Buckley (eds), *Down Syndrome Across the Life Span.* London: Whurr Publishers.

Wheeler, J.J., Bates, P., Marshall, K.J., & Miller, S.R. (1988) 'Teaching appropriate social behaviours to a young man with moderate mental retardation in a supported competitive employment setting', *Education and Training in Mental Retardation.* 23: 105–116.

Whiteman, B.C., Simpson, G.B., & Compton, W.C. (1986) 'Relationship of otitis media and language impairment in adolescents with Down syndrome', *Mental Retardation,* 6: 353–356.

Zigman, W.B., Schupf, N., Lubin, R.A., & Silverman, W.P. (1987) 'Premature regression of adults with Down syndrome', *American Journal of Mental Deficiency,* 92: 161–168.

Zigman, W.B., Schupf, N., Silverman, W.P., & Sterling, R.C. (1989) 'Changes in adaptive functioning of adults with developmental disabilities', *Australia and New Zealand Journal of Developmental Disabilities,* 15: 277–287.

Zihni, L. (1994) 'Obstinacy and Down's syndrome: a misunderstanding of behaviour in the past', *History and Philosophy of Psychology Newsletter,* 18: 10–16.

3

Fragile X Syndrome: Medical and Genetic Aspects

R.J. Hagerman, J. Turk, A. Schneider, & P.J. Hagerman

GENERAL OVERVIEW

Fragile X syndrome (FXS) is the most common identifiable inherited cause of intellectual disability and the most common known single-gene mutation leading to autism. FXS is nearly always caused by expansions of a CGG repeat in the 5′ untranslated region (5′UTR) of the fragile X mental retardation 1 (*FMR1*) gene (Verkerk et al., 1991), which is located in the terminal portion (Xq27.3) of the long arm of the X chromosome. FXS is established on the basis of genotyping of the *FMR1* gene, which includes both polymerase chain reaction (PCR) and Southern blot analyses. The normal range of the CGG repeat element is 5 to 44 CGG repeats, with repeat expansions classified as *gray zone* (45 to 54 CGG repeats), *premutation* (55 to 200 CGG repeats), and *full mutation* (>200 CGG repeats) (Maddalena et al., 2001). Full mutation alleles give rise to FXS due to methylation-coupled gene silenc-

ing, leading to a lack of the *FMR1* protein, FMRP (Loesch et al., 2004).

Although most individuals with premutation alleles have normal cognitive abilities, those with >150 repeats may have features of FXS due to reduced levels of FMRP at the upper end of the premutation range (Tassone et al., 2000b). However, in contrast to the gene silencing observed for full mutation alleles, premutation alleles give rise to elevated levels of *FMR1* mRNA, ranging from 2 to 8 times normal (Tassone et al., 2000b). It is currently believed that the excess, expanded-repeat RNA leads to an RNA gain-of-function-toxicity causing premutation specific disorders in aging, including primary ovarian insufficiency (POI) in approximately 16–20% of female carriers (A.K. Sullivan et al., 2005) and the fragile X-associated tremor/ataxia syndrome (FXTAS) in 40% of male carriers (Jacquemont et al., 2004) and 8% of female carriers (Coffey et al., 2008) ascertained through families with a fragile

X syndrome proband. There is also evidence that premutation alleles can cause a neurodevelopmental disorder manifesting as attention-deficit/hyperactivity disorder (ADHD) and/or autism spectrum disorder (A.R. Cummings & Carr, 2009; D.E. Cummings et al., 2002; Moss & Howlin, 2009) in children (Aziz et al., 2003; Farzin et al., 2006; Goodlin-Jones et al., 2004), and working memory problems in adults (Cornish et al., 2009). Therefore, expanded *FMR1* alleles can affect all generations and all ages in a fragile X family.

HISTORICAL PERSPECTIVE

Martin and Bell published the initial report of a family with intellectual disability and associated characteristic physical features which were transmitted transgenerationally in an X-linked fashion (Martin & Bell, 1943). The first report of the marker X chromosome in 1969 described two brothers with intellectual disability (Lubs, 1969). The marker X chromosome was later consistently described as the fragile X chromosome, which was observed in culture only when folate-deficient tissue culture media were used (Sutherland, 1977). In retrospect, the first report of X-linked mental impairment, the Martin Bell pedigree with 11 males with cognitive disability (Martin & Bell, 1943), was later found to have the fragile X chromosome. Throughout the 1980s individuals were diagnosed with FXS by cytogenetic testing until the *FMR1* gene was discovered in 1991 (Oberle et al., 1991; Verkerk et al., 1991), leading to utilization of *FMR1* DNA testing. The FXS physical phenotype was characterized as involving a connective tissue dysplasia leading to soft velvet-like skin, hyperextensible joints, and prominent ears (R.J. Hagerman & McBogg, 1983) as well as a range of other physical features including a long face, large head, prominent chin, high-arched palate, single palmar crease, testicular enlargement during and after puberty,

and epilepsy (Turk & Patton, 2000). In 1982, the presence of autism in some individuals with FXS was first reported by Brown et al. (1982). The presence of genetic anticipation – increasing penetrance and/or severity of the phenotype – was first described by Stephanie Sherman and has been referred to as 'Sherman's paradox' (Sherman et al., 1985).

Characterization of molecular clinical correlations accelerated during the 1990s, with the development of a consensus that approximately 15% of males with FXS are high functioning (IQ ≥ 70), an observation that is now regarded as being due to the presence of size- and/or methylation-mosaicism (R.J. Hagerman et al., 1994), the former referring to the presence of both premutation and full mutation alleles, and the latter indicating that a portion of *FMR1* alleles in a given individual have at least partially escaped methylation and silencing. These individuals are expected to have somewhat higher FMRP levels (Tassone et al., 1999) than for those individuals whose alleles are fully methylated.

Premutation involvement leading to POI was first described by Cronister et al. (1991). More recent reports have demonstrated that the penetrance of POI is dependent on the size of the CGG repeat (A.K. Sullivan et al., 2005). Although larger CGG repeats are associated with a greater prevalence of POI, individuals with alleles having more than 120 repeats appear to have a lower prevalence of POI for reasons that are not understood at present.

The discovery of elevated *FMR1* mRNA in premutation carriers was made by Tassone et al. (2000b). For alleles in the premutation range, there is a strong positive correlation of mRNA level with increasing repeat number. Somewhat paradoxically, FMRP levels trend to somewhat lower levels with increasing repeat size in the same range (Tassone et al., 2000b), owing to reduced translational efficiency of the mRNAs with the larger CGG repeat (Feng et al., 1995; Primerano et al., 2002).

The finding of a molecular phenotype in the premutation range helped to establish the clinical phenotype of FXTAS (R.J. Hagerman et al., 2001) with associated age-related cognitive changes in premutation carriers (Cornish et al., 2009). FXTAS was discovered because the mothers of children with FXS were concerned about the neurological problems of their fathers who were carriers. These fathers had never had developmental problems, but they were experiencing a progressive tremor and ataxia in addition to cognitive decline in their later years. The prevalence of FXTAS was found to be 17% in the male carriers in their 50s, 38% in their 60s, 47% in their 70s, and 75% in their 80s (Jacquemont et al., 2004) among families with known FXS probands. Although FXTAS also affects female carriers (R.J. Hagerman et al., 2004), its prevalence (~8%) is less than in males (Berry-Kravis et al., 2007; Coffey et al., 2008).

EPIDEMIOLOGY

The prevalence figures for FXS have varied depending on the population being ascertained and how FXS has been defined. If intellectual disability is included in the diagnosis, the prevalence is considered to be 1 in 3600 in the general population (Crawford et al., 2002). However, many individuals with FXS, particularly females, have an IQ> 70. Only about 25% of females with the full mutation have an IQ <70 (Bennetto & Pennington, 2002). Instead, if we consider that all individuals with full mutation alleles will have some form of social, behavioral, or intellectual impairment, then the prevalence of the disorder will approach the allele frequency of approximately 1 per 2500 (P.J. Hagerman, 2008).

Premutation alleles are much more common than full mutation alleles, with approximately 1 in 130 to 250 females and 1 per 250 to 813 males in the general population harboring such alleles (Dombrowski et al., 2002; P.J. Hagerman, 2008; Pesso et al., 2000; Rousseau et al., 1996; Song et al., 2003). Therefore, premutation involvement is expected to be much more frequent than FXS, although

onset of clinical involvement extends from childhood through late adulthood.

CAUSATION

Full mutation *FMR1* alleles are generally hypermethylated, leading to a lack of transcription and consequently of translation, resulting in the absence or near-absence of FMRP. It is the lack of FMRP that leads to FXS, characterized by physical features noted above, along with cognitive deficits and behavioral problems including hyperactivity, attention problems, anxiety, and mood instability. Females with full mutation alleles are generally less affected than males due to the presence of a second, normal X chromosome. Therefore, the amount of FMRP will depend on the percentage of cells with the normal X as the active X chromosome (activation ratio). The level of FMRP correlates with the IQ in individuals with the full mutation (Loesch et al., 2004).

Premutation involvement involves two distinct mechanisms for phenotypic involvement – RNA 'toxicity' and diminished FMRP, the latter becoming more important at the upper end of the premutation range. These mechanisms are likely to be working both in early development and in adulthood, although the relative importance of each has yet to be precisely defined. However, for the premutation-specific disorders such as FXTAS, the RNA toxicity is likely to be the dominant pathogenic mechanism (Amiri et al., 2008; Arocena et al., 2005; Iwahashi et al., 2006). Within the upper portion of the premutation range (~120 to 200 CGG repeats), the mild deficits in FMRP (~30–50% reductions) (Tassone et al., 2000b) are thought to be a major factor leading to both the physical and cognitive/behavioral features of FXS (Aziz et al., 2003; Goodlin-Jones et al., 2004; R.J. Hagerman, 2006). Additionally, the high level of mRNA could also contribute to phenotypic changes in early development (Chen, 2008; Hagerman & Hagerman, 2004).

DIAGNOSTIC CRITERIA AND CORE CHARACTERISTICS

For individuals who have physical and/or cognitive/behavioral features of FXS, the singular diagnostic requirement for FXS is the presence of a full mutation allele of the *FMR1* gene, based on molecular assessment of the CGG repeat size. However, it should be noted that about 1% of *FMR1* mutations are not repeat expansions, but point mutations or deletions, which must be established for the FXS diagnosis in the absence of evident allele expansion. This molecular assessment is essential because many children with FXS may have very few, if any, evident physical features and may also be high functioning intellectually without obvious cognitive deficits, particularly among females with a full mutation allele. The clinical features of FXS range from mild emotional or learning problems to severe intellectual disabilities with autism. The degree of clinical involvement generally correlates with the level of FMRP present in peripheral blood lymphocytes (Loesch et al., 2004; Tassone et al., 1999). As noted above, molecular assessment is carried out with both a PCR and a Southern blot (Maddalena et al., 2001; Saluto et al., 2005). These studies provide the CGG repeat number, the activation ratio, and the degree of methylation present in the full mutation. Although assessment of FMRP levels is currently available in at least one clinical laboratory, the method is only semi-quantitative at present and has not been established as a diagnostic criterion in the absence of genotyping.

CORE PSYCHOLOGICAL CHARACTERISTICS

Intellectually, individuals with full mutation alleles usually function in the mild to moderate intellectual disability range, with a verbal-performance discrepancy favoring language skills over mathematical and visuospatial abilities (Kogan et al., 2004; Roberts et al., 2005b). Cognitive abilities tend to plateau in their development towards adolescence because of particular difficulties in sequential information processing, as opposed to the easier and more basic simultaneous information processing that predominates in childhood (Bennetto & Pennington, 2002). There is typically a steady decline in IQ, particularly in males, although the Leiter-R growth scores continue to increase throughout childhood, demonstrating a steady but suboptimal intellectual growth instead of deterioration (Skinner et al., 2005). Speech and language are usually highly characteristic with jocular litanic phraseology, perseverativeness, repetitions, echolalia, palilalia, rapid utterances and dysrhythmias (Abbeduto et al., 2003; Belser & Sudhalter, 2001; Cornish et al., 2004a; Roberts et al., 2005a). Young boys with FXS acquire expressive language skills at one-third the rate of normally developing children and receptive language skills at half the rate of normal (Roberts et al., 2001).

Social impairments are pervasive and include high degrees of social anxiety, gaze aversion in association with a range of other visual, auditory, tactile, olfactory, and gustatory sensitivities; self-injury (Hall et al., 2008b; Symons et al., 2003), usually in the form of hand-biting in response to anxiety or excitement; and marked stereotypic repetitive behaviors including hand flapping, rocking, jumping, and running round in circles (Turk & Graham, 1997). The association between the *etiological* diagnosis of FXS and the *clinical-phenomenological* diagnosis of autism is well-evidenced yet complex (Cornish et al., 2007; Hatton et al., 2006; Kaufmann et al., 2004). Approximately 26% of people with autism have FXS (R.J. Hagerman et al., 2008b; Reddy, 2005), and approximately a third of boys with FXS have autism (Harris et al., 2008; Rogers et al., 2001). This proportion rises to almost two-thirds in young men (Das & Turk, 2002). However, a far higher proportion of individuals with FXS manifest the paradoxical juxtaposition of a friendly and sociable (albeit often shy and socially anxious) personality in the presence of multiple autistic-like communicatory and ritualistic qualitative impairments. In addition there is usually a good understanding of facial expression (Turk & Cornish, 1998) and theory of mind abilities are as expected for an individual's general cognitive ability levels (Garner et al., 1999). Kaufmann et al. (2004) have pointed out that the finding of autism in FXS depends on the severity of the social and communication deficits, not the severity of poor eye contact or unusual hand mannerisms. However, in a comparison study with an intellectual disabled control group without fragile X, Grant et al. (2007) point out that the theory of mind difficulties are an important aspect of the FXS clinical profile, but are most likely based on a more basic difficulty with working memory.

In a comprehensive literature review, Moss and Howlin (2009) compared autism spectrum disorders(ASD) in different genetic syndromes. They point out that the diagnosis can be overshadowed with the intellectual disability, but is crucial for appropriate behavioral management and educational placement.

Attention deficits and hyperactivity are extremely common and are aggravated by the high levels of anxiety (Turk, 1998), sometimes of a degree sufficient to warrant a diagnostic label of post-traumatic stress disorder (Turk et al., 2005). Inattentiveness, restlessness, fidgetiness, impulsiveness, and distractibility, as well as inability to sustain attention are all frequent, common, and usually severe disabilities. Sullivan et al. compared 63 children with FXS, and 56 age-matched control children. The prevalence rate for ADHD symptoms varied depending on the type of measure, scoring method, and parent vs teacher report (K. Sullivan et al., 2006). Overall, 54 59% of boys with FXS met the DSM-IV (Diagnostic and Statistical Manual of Mental Disorders, 4th edn) criteria for ADHD-inattentive type, ADHD-hyperactive type, or ADHD-combined type. These numbers are higher than expected for the general population and their age-matched peers. However, gross motor activity levels may not be greater than those of similarly intellectually disabled non-fragile X peers, suggesting that the most appropriate diagnostic neuropsychiatric label for children with FXS without hyperactivity may often be that of ADHD, predominantly inattentive type. There is also some evidence that these debilitating features do not spontaneously improve with development as they often do for non-fragile X individuals. However, they do respond very well to medical as well as psychological approaches (R.J. Hagerman et al., 1988; Ingrassia & Turk, 2005; Turk, 2003a, 2004). Sleep disorders are also common (Gould et al., 2000) and often respond well to melatonin for sleep induction difficulties (Turk, 2003b) and clonidine for sleep maintenance problems (Ingrassia & Turk, 2005).

Boys with premutation alleles have been reported as having similarly raised rates of delayed development of adaptive behavior, autism spectrum and attention-deficit disorders, and speech and language difficulties, notably relating to social use of language, speech intelligibility, and expressive language (Aziz et al., 2003; Farzin et al., 2006). Females with FXS also often show intellectual impairments, autism spectrum and attention-deficit disorders, and executive function problems, irrespective of CGG expansion size (R.J. Hagerman et al., 1992).

In a study on social/emotional skills in high-function female carriers and FXS, Mazzocco et al. found no significant worse performance in this group if executive function or non-verbal deficits are taken into account. The emerging group differences could be explained by the influence of full-scale IQ (Mazzocco et al., 1992, 1993, 1994). The research on neuropsychological correlations in female premutation carriers is confounded by the random activation of either the affected X-chromosome, or the unaffected. Also, there is a great variance in activation ratios, making it difficult to find distinct genotype phenotype correlations (Tassone et al., 2000c).

Neuropsychological impairments mediating the above challenging developmental and behavioral features include memory access and retention problems, impaired inhibitory control and cognitive switching abilities, impaired sequential information processing, and impaired arousal modulation (Cornish et al., 2004b). These phenomena have been identified in individuals with premutation as well as full mutation alleles (Cornish et al., 2005; Grigsby et al., 2007). However, Rivera & Reiss (2009) describe the heterogeneous association of cognitive and behavioral dysfunction with molecular findings in the premutation as a 'continuum', which is also influenced by environmental factors—for example, the psychological and psychiatric outcome in female premutation carriers is significantly influenced by raising a child with the full mutation *FMR1* allele (D.B. Bailey Jr. et al., 2008).

CURRENT RESEARCH ON NEUROBIOLOGICAL CORRELATES AND APPLICATION IN CURRENT PRACTICE

The advances in neurobiology relate to our understanding of the role of FMRP in synaptic plasticity and regulation of translation of many messages at the synapse (Bagni & Greenough, 2005; Bassell & Warren, 2008). In the absence of FMRP there is significant upregulation of the metabotropic glutamate receptor 5 (mGluR5) pathway, because FMRP is an inhibitor of translation of proteins that internalize the AMPA receptors. Excess upregulation in the absence of FMRP leads to long-term depression (LTD) at synapses, causing weak synaptic connections and intellectual disability (Bear et al., 2004). The advent of mGluR5 antagonists that can reverse the upregulation of this pathway has spurred treatment studies in the fragile X animal models. Treatment of mice or *Drosophila*, as animal models of FXS, with mGluR5 antagonists have led to reversal of seizures, behavior problems, and cognitive

deficits (de Vrij et al., 2008; Dolen et al., 2007; McBride et al., 2005; Yan et al., 2005). The first mGluR5 antagonist available for clinical trials in adults with FXS is fenobam, and early pharmacokinetics and toxicity studies have demonstrated that this medication is well tolerated in adults with FXS (Berry-Kravis et al., 2009). Fenobam and other new mGluR5 antagonists are currently tried in controlled trials in adults and teenagers with FXS. If these trials are beneficial without significant toxicity, children with FXS will be included. Because of the similarities in the neurobiology between FXS and autism, it is likely that mGluR5 antagonists will be helpful in some patients with autism without FXS. Since 2009, the treatment with R-Baclofen is studied in individuals with autism in parallel to trials in FXS, because it is likely to downregulate glutamate systems.

A recent paper by Bilousova et al. (2009) found that minocycline treatment in newborn fragile X knockout mice reversed the synaptic phenotype in FXS. One month of treatment normalized the long thin and weak synaptic connections in these baby mice. The mechanism for normalizing the synaptic connections was shown to be related to lowering the matrix metalloproteinase 9 (MMP9) levels (Bilousova et al., 2009). The MMP9 level is also thought to be controlled by the mGluR5 pathway and the levels of MMP9 are high in FXS compared to controls. MMP9 is important for synaptic plasticity and minocycline normalizes these levels. Since minocycline is a tetracycline antibiotic that is currently widely available, it represents a potential agent for targeted treatment of FXS. However, the use of minocycline can cause tooth graying when used in children younger than 7 years of age. Therefore, current trials of minocycline in children are being initiated in children older than 7 to avoid this complication. Additional side effects of minocycline include increased sun sensitivity, the occasional occurrence of pseudotumor cerebri, and the rare occurrence of a positive antinuclear antibody (ANA) or drug-induced lupus.

Preliminary anecdotal results have shown subtle but clear benefits of minocycline in approximately 70% of families whose older children are treated with minocycline in doses ranging from 50 to 200 mg per day. Comments regarding improvement in articulation, attention, and mood stabilization are compelling but only controlled trials will tell if these effects are from a placebo response or from an improvement in brain functioning with minocycline (Utari et al., 2010).

A parallel research program is building on the increasing evidence for psychologically stabilizing qualities of traditional anticonvulsants such as sodium valproate, carbamazepine, and lamotrigine. Early clinical studies suggest promising cognitive, emotional, behavioral, social, communicatory, and attentional improvements with these long-established, relatively safe, and inexpensive agents (Mahadevappa & Turk, 2008).

Lithium is another relatively inexpensive agent that is used in the treatment of bipolar disorder and mood stabilization. Lithium also can downregulate the mGluR5 system and it has been studied in a small open trial in individuals with FXS and found to be efficacious for behavior and perhaps beneficial for some aspects of cognition (Berry-Kravis et al., 2008). Further studies are warranted regarding this medication in long-term use in fragile X because of beneficial effects in aging and neuroprotection.

LIFETIME COURSE OF MEDICAL SYMPTOMS

Infants with FXS are often hypotonic and irritable, with frequent vomiting after feedings related to gastroesophageal reflux (R.J. Hagerman, 2002b). However, the diagnosis of FXS is usually not considered until they demonstrate some developmental delays, most commonly in language around 2 years of age (Bailey et al., 1998, 2003). The first 3 years of life are often marked by recurrent ear infections (R.J. Hagerman et al., 1987) and frequent visual issues, including refractory errors, strabismus, and ptosis (Maino et al., 1991), which can further delay language and social development. Therefore, early placement of PE tubes is recommended for children with recurrent otitis media infections (R.J. Hagerman, 2002a). Close attention to visual development and functioning is crucial, requiring an eye examination by an ophthalmologist or optometrist.

Longitudinal cognitive studies demonstrate IQ decline over time in most males and some females with FXS (Bennetto & Pennington, 2002). This is thought to relate to the deficits in abstract reasoning, with lowering of IQ over time (Skinner et al., 2005; Wright-Talamante et al., 1996). However, mental age continues to increase throughout childhood and into adolescence, indicating that there is not a true loss of cognitive abilities (Skinner et al., 2005). Individuals with the lowest IQ are usually those who also have autism (Hatton et al., 2006; Kaufmann et al., 2004; Rogers et al., 2001). Therefore, medical intervention, including screening for seizures with an EEG, should be aggressively undertaken in those who have both autism and FXS (Garcia-Nonell et al., 2008). There is also evidence that autism may be more common with aging in those with FXS (Das & Turk, 2002; Hatton et al., 2006). Individuals may become more reclusive with age and this can lead to a lack of cognitive stimulation over time and a decline in IQ.

Recent molecular studies suggest cause for concern regarding the deleterious effects of a lack of FMRP over a lifetime. There are a number of reasons to expect problems in aging in individuals with FXS, although follow-up studies have not been carried out in those over 40 years with FXS. FMRP regulates the translation of many proteins, including the amyloid precursor protein (APP) that is associated with Alzheimer's disease (Westmark & Malter, 2007). Because of the elevation in APP in those with FXS, there may be a higher rate of Alzheimer's disease in FXS; however, this has not been assessed. In addition, a recent report documented that FMRP also regulates adult neurogenesis (Shan et al., 2008), so that a lack of FMRP may compromise neurogenesis, perhaps leading to cognitive decline and brain atrophy in aging. Lastly, those individuals who are high functioning with FXS because of mosaicism or a lack of methylation typically have high levels of *FMR1* mRNA (Tassone et al., 2000a); thus, they are theoretically at risk for neurodegeneration related to RNA toxicity in aging, although no individual with FXS and harboring a full mutation allele FXS has ever been reported to have FXTAS. In aggregate, these molecular findings demonstrate that aging studies are needed among those with FXS.

APPROACHES TO MEDICAL INTERVENTION

A variety of currently available medications can be given to treat behavioral problems, particularly mood instability, hyperactivity, and anxiety, in children with FXS (Hills-Epstein et al., 2002). Stimulants work well for hyperactivity and attention problems for children 5 years of age and older, although only one controlled trial has been carried out (demonstrated efficacy compared to placebo) (R.J. Hagerman et al., 1988). α2-Agonists such as guanfacine (Amaria et al., 2001) and clonidine (Ingrassia & Turk, 2005) can also have a calming effect for hyperactivity, as well as alleviating attentional deficits and enhancing concentration and attentional skills. Most recently, aripiprazole (Abilify) has demonstrated efficacy in treatment of not only hyperactivity but also mood instability, aggression, and irritability (Erickson, 2008; R.J. Hagerman et al., 2009).

Anxiety is another key behavior problem in those with FXS and in many with the premutation allele. This symptom typically responds well to a selective serotonin reuptake inhibitor (SSRI) such as sertraline, fluoxetine or citalopram (Amaria et al., 2001; Berry-Kravis & Potanos, 2004). Although all of the currently available medications for behavioral problems can be helpful in patients with FXS, none of these medications can reverse the cognitive deficits of FXS. Therefore, the advent of new targeted treatments that hold hope of reversing the neurobiological abnormalities in FXS hold promise of reversing the cognitive and behavioral problems.

Unquestionably the most critical early and later interventions to maximize potential and quality of life in individuals with FXS are the educational ones (Dew-Hughes, 2004). High-quality speech and language therapy is also crucial to helping individuals with developmental disabilities, including those with FXS (Fidler et al., 2007), as is occupational therapy, particularly in the form of sensory integration approaches (Braden, 2002; Scharfenaker et al., 2002). Psychological programs, particularly those based on cognitive/behavioral principles, are a further component of a comprehensive, multimodal interagency therapeutic and support package; these approaches have recently been reviewed (R.J. Hagerman et al., 2009; Hall et al., 2008a).

CONCLUSION—CHALLENGES FOR THE FUTURE

The use of targeted medical and psychological treatments for FXS will dominate intervention research through the next decade, with the exciting potential of reversing cognitive, emotional, and behavioral problems of FXS. This disorder is leading the way for treatment of related conditions, such as autism and ADHD, and these novel treatments will encourage new screening studies for FXS, particularly in the newborn period and even in adulthood. These studies are facilitated by new screening techniques, such as the blood spot methodology, reported by Tassone and colleagues, which can lower the cost of screening to less than $5 per sample (Tassone et al., 2008).

Although newborn screening is controversial for some (Bailey et al., 2008), it holds the promise of early identification of children with both the premutation and full mutation alleles who may have significant developmental delays warranting early medical and educational interventions. Furthermore, surveys of families with FXS members demonstrate the widespread desire for the earliest possible identification of those with expanded alleles. Development of optimal early intervention programs for infants with FXS is critical to improving their long-term outcome. The identification of a child with the premutation is controversial because this individual may develop neurological problems in late adulthood (e.g. FXTAS). However, children, particularly boys with a premutation allele, are at risk for early developmental delays that can benefit from early intervention (Farzin et al., 2006). In addition, their aging problems appear to be improved by early treatment of their psychiatric problems and medical issues, such as hypertension, migraine, depression, and anxiety, so prevention and early intervention are facilitated by an early diagnosis (R.J. Hagerman et al., 2008a).

The development of the blood spot screening test will also facilitate high-risk screening among individuals with autism or other psychiatric diagnoses that are comorbid with FXS or premutation involvement, and such screening efforts will lead to enhanced identification of those affected and in need of treatment, including newer targeted treatments. The benefit to the family of knowledge brought by genetic counseling and the understanding of involvement of others in multiple generations can lead to a greater appreciation for the treatment possibilities and the end to their odyssey of finding a cause for their difficulties (Bailey et al., 2008; Cornish et al., 2008; R.J. Hagerman et al., 2009; McConkie-Rosell et al., 2007).

ACKNOWLEDGMENTS

This work was supported by NIH grants HD036071, HD02274, DE19583, AG032119, AG032115; and 90DD0596 from the Health and Human Services Administration on Developmental Disabilities.

REFERENCES

Abbeduto, L., Murphy, M.M., Cawthon, S.W., Richmond, E.K., Weissman, M.D., Karadottir, S. et al. (2003) 'Receptive language skills of adolescents and young adults with Down or fragile X syndrome', *Am J Ment Retard,* 108(3): 149–160.

Amaria, R.N., Billeisen, L.L., & Hagerman, R.J. (2001) 'Medication use in fragile X syndrome', *Mental Health Aspects of Developmental Disabilities,* 4(4): 143–147.

Amiri, K., Hagerman, R.J., & Hagerman, P.J. (2008) 'Fragile X-associated tremor/ataxia syndrome: an aging face of the fragile X gene', *Arch Neurol,* 65(1): 19–25.

Arocena, D.G., Iwahashi, C.K., Won, N., Beilina, A., Ludwig, A.L., Tassone, F. et al. (2005) 'Induction of inclusion formation and disruption of lamin A/C structure by premutation CGG-repeat RNA in human cultured neural cells', *Hum Mol Genet,* 14(23): 3661–3671.

Aziz, M., Stathopulu, E., Callias, M., Taylor, C., Turk, J., Oostra, B. et al. (2003) 'Clinical features of boys with fragile X premutations and intermediate alleles', *Am J Med Genet,* 121B(1): 119–127.

Bagni, C. & Greenough, W.T. (2005) 'From mRNP trafficking to spine dysmorphogenesis: the roots of fragile X syndrome', *Nat Rev Neurosci,* 6(5): 376–387.

Bailey, D.B., Jr, Hatton, D.D., & Skinner, M. (1998) 'Early developmental trajectories of males with fragile X syndrome', *Am J Ment Retard,* 103(1): 29–39.

Bailey, D.B., Jr, Skinner, D., & Sparkman, K.L. (2003) 'Discovering fragile X syndrome: family experiences and perceptions', *Pediatrics,* 111(2): 407–416.

Bailey, D.B., Jr, Skinner, D., Davis, A.M., Whitmarsh, I., & Powell, C. (2008) 'Ethical, legal, and social concerns about expanded newborn screening: fragile X syndrome as a prototype for emerging issues', *Pediatrics,* 121(3): e693–704.

Bailey, D.B., Jr, Sideris, J., Roberts, J.E. et al. (2008). Child and genetic variables associated with maternal adaptation to fragile X syndrome: a multidimensional analysis. *Am J Med Genet A,* 146(6): 720–9.

Bassell, G.J. & Warren, S.T. (2008) 'Fragile X syndrome: loss of local mRNA regulation alters synaptic development and function', *Neuron,* 60(2): 201–214.

Bear, M.F., Huber, K.M., & Warren, S.T. (2004) 'The mGluR theory of fragile X mental retardation', *Trends Neurosci,* 27(7): 370–377.

Belser, R.C. & Sudhalter, V. (2001) 'Conversational characteristics of children with fragile X syndrome: repetitive speech', *Am J Ment Retard,* 106(1): 28–38.

Bennetto, L. & Pennington, B.F. (2002) 'Neuropsychology', in R.J. Hagerman & P.J. Hagerman (eds), *Fragile X Syndrome: Diagnosis, Treatment, and Research,* 3rd edn. Baltimore: Johns Hopkins University Press, pp. 206–248.

Berry-Kravis, E. & Potanos, K. (2004) 'Psychopharmacology in fragile X syndrome—present and future', *Ment Retard Dev Disabil Res Rev,* 10(1): 42–48.

Berry-Kravis, E., Abrams, L., Coffey, S.M., Hall, D.A., Greco, C., Gane, L.W. et al. (2007) 'Fragile X-associated tremor/ataxia syndrome: clinical features, genetics, and testing guidelines', *Mov Disord,* 22(14): 2018–2030.

Berry-Kravis, E., Sumis, A., Hervey, C., Nelson, M., Porges, S.W., Weng, N. et al. (2008) 'Open-label treatment trial of lithium to target the underlying defect in fragile X syndrome', *J Dev Behav Pediatr,* 29(4): 293–302.

Berry-Kravis, E.M., Hessl, D., Coffey, S., Hervey, C., Schneider, A., Yuhas, J. et al. (2009) 'A pilot open label, single dose trial of fenobam in adults with fragile X syndrome', *J Med Genet,* 46(4): 266–271.

Bilousova, T., Dansie, L., Ngo, M., Aye, J., Charles, J.R., Ethell, D.W. et al. (2009). 'Minocycline promotes dendritic spine maturation and improves behavioral performance in the fragile X mouse model', *J Med Genet,* 46(2): 94–102.

Braden, M. (2002) 'Academic interventions in fragile X', in R.J. Hagerman & P.J. Hagerman (eds), *Fragile X Syndrome: Diagnosis, Treatment and Research,* 3rd edn. Baltimore: Johns Hopkins University Press, pp. 428–464.

Brown, W.T., Jenkins, E.C., Friedman, E., Brooks, J., Wisniewski, K., Raguthu, S. et al. (1982) 'Autism is associated with the fragile-X syndrome', *J Autism Dev Disord,* 12(3): 303–308.

Chen, Y. (2008). 'Abnormal growth and synaptic architecture in hippocampal neurons cultured from a mouse model of FXTAS'. Paper Presented at the 11th International Fragile X Conference, July 23–27, St. Louis, MO.

Coffey, S.M., Cook, K., Tartaglia, N., Tassone, F., Nguyen, D.V., Pan, R. et al. (2008) 'Expanded clinical phenotype of women with the FMR1 premutation', *Am J Med Genet A,* 146(8): 1009–1016.

Cornish, K.M., Sudhalter, V., & Turk, J. (2004a) 'Attention and language in fragile X', *Ment Retard Dev Disabil Res Rev,* 10(1): 11–16.

Cornish, K.M., Turk, J., Wilding, J., Sudhalter, V., Munir, F., Kooy, F. et al. (2004b) 'Annotation:

deconstructing the attention deficit in fragile X syndrome: a developmental neuropsychological approach', *J Child Psychol Psychiatry,* 45(6): 1042–1053.

Cornish, K.M., Kogan, C., Turk, J., Manly, T., James, N., Mills, A. et al. (2005) 'The emerging fragile X premutation phenotype: evidence from the domain of social cognition', *Brain Cogn,* 57(1): 53–60.

Cornish, K.M., Turk, J., & Levitas, A. (2007) 'Fragile X syndrome & autism: common developmental pathways?', *Curr Pediatr Rev,* 3: 61–68.

Cornish, K.M., Turk, J., & Hagerman, R. (2008) 'The fragile X continuum: new advances and perspectives', *J Intellect Disabil Res,* 52(Pt 6): 469–482.

Cornish, K.M., Kogan, C.S., Li, L., Turk, J., Jacquemont, S., & Hagerman, R.J. (2009) 'Lifespan changes in working memory in fragile X premutation males', *Brain Cogn,* 69(3): 551–558.

Crawford, D.C., Meadows, K.L., Newman, J.L., Taft, L.F., Scott, E., Leslie, M., et al. (2002) 'Prevalence of the fragile X syndrome in African-Americans', *Am J Med Genet,* 110(3): 226–233.

Cronister, A., Schreiner, R., Wittenberger, M., Amiri, K., Harris, K., & Hagerman, R.J. (1991) 'Heterozygous fragile X female: historical, physical, cognitive, and cytogenetic features', *Am J Med Genet,* 38(2–3): 269–274.

Cummings, A.R. & Carr, J.E. (2009) 'Evaluating progress in behavioral programs for children with autism spectrum disorders via continuous and discontinuous measurement', *J Appl Behav Anal,* 42(1): 57–71.

Cummings, D.E., Clement, K., Purnell, J.Q., Vaisse, C., Foster, K.E., Frayo, R.S. et al. (2002) 'Elevated plasma ghrelin levels in Prader–Willi syndrome', *Nature Medicine,* 8(7): 643–644.

Das, D. & Turk, J. (2002) 'The development of social and communicatory functioning in boys with fragile X syndrome'. Paper presented at the National Fragile X Conference, Chicago, IL.

de Vrij, F.M., Levenga, J., van der Linde, H.C., Koekkoek, S.K., De Zeeuw, C.I., Nelson, D.L. et al. (2008) 'Rescue of behavioral phenotype and neuronal protrusion morphology in Fmr1 KO mice', *Neurobiol Dis,* 31(1): 127–132.

Dew-Hughes, D. (2004) *Educating Children with Fragile X Syndrome: A Multi-Professional View.* New York: RoutledgeFalmer.

Dolen, G., Osterweil, E., Rao, B.S., Smith, G.B., Auerbach, B.D., Chattarji, S. et al. (2007) 'Correction of fragile X syndrome in mice', *Neuron,* 56(6): 955–962.

Dombrowski, C., Levesque, M.L., Morel, M.L., Rouillard, P., Morgan, K., & Rousseau, F. (2002)

'Premutation and intermediate-size FMR1 alleles in 10572 males from the general population: loss of an AGG interruption is a late event in the generation of fragile X syndrome alleles', *Hum Mol Genet*, 11(4): 371–378.

Erickson, C. (2008) 'A prospective, 12-week open-label study of aripiprazole in fragile X syndrome'. Paper presented at the 11th International Fragile X Conference, July 23–27, St. Louis, MO.

Farzin, F., Perry, H., Hessl, D., Loesch, D., Cohen, J., Bacalman, S. et al. (2006) 'Autism spectrum disorders and attention-deficit/hyperactivity disorder in boys with the fragile X premutation', *J Dev Behav Pediatr*, 27(2 Suppl): S137–144.

Feng, Y., Zhang, F., Lokey, L.K., Chastain, J.L., Lakkis, L., Eberhart, D. et al. (1995) 'Translational suppression by trinucleotide repeat expansion at FMR1', *Science*, 268(5211): 731–734.

Fidler, D.J., Philofsky, A., & Hepburn, S.L. (2007) 'Language phenotypes and intervention planning: bridging research and practice', *Ment Retard Dev Disabil Res Rev.* 2007; 13(1):47–57. Review.

Garcia-Nonell, C., Ratera, E.R., Harris, S., Hessl, D., Ono, M.Y., Tartaglia, N. et al. (2008) 'Secondary medical diagnosis in fragile X syndrome with and without autism spectrum disorder', *Am J Med Genet A*, 146A(15): 1911–1916.

Garner, C., Callias, M., & Turk, J. (1999) 'Executive function and theory of mind performance of boys with fragile-X syndrome', *J Intellect Disabil Res*, 43(Pt 6): 466–474.

Goodlin-Jones, B., Tassone, F., Gane, L.W., & Hagerman, R.J. (2004) 'Autistic spectrum disorder and the fragile X premutation', *J Dev Behav Pediatr*, 25(6): 392–398.

Gould, E.L., Loesch, D.Z., Martin, M.J., Hagerman, R.J., Armstrong, S.M., & Huggins, R.M. (2000) 'Melatonin profiles and sleep characteristics in boys with fragile X syndrome: a preliminary study', *Am J Med Genet*, 95(4): 307–315.

Grant, C.M., Apperly, I., & Oliver, C. (2007) 'Is theory of mind understanding impaired in males with fragile X syndrome?', *Journal of Abnormal Child Psychology*, 35(1): 17–28.

Grigsby, J., Brega, A.G., Leehey, M.A., Goodrich, G.K., Jacquemont, S., Loesch, D.Z. et al. (2007) 'Impairment of executive cognitive functioning in males with fragile X-associated tremor/ataxia syndrome', *Mov Disord*, 22(5): 645–650.

Hagerman, P.J. (2008) 'The fragile X prevalence paradox', *J Med Genet*, 45(8): 498–499.

Hagerman, P.J. & Hagerman, R.J. (2004) 'The fragile-X premutation: a maturing perspective', *Am J Hum Genet*, 74(5): 805–816.

Hagerman, R.J. (2002a) 'Medical follow-up and pharmacotherapy', in R.J. Hagerman & P.J. Hagerman (eds), *Fragile X Syndrome: Diagnosis, Treatment and Research*, 3rd edn. Baltimore: Johns Hopkins University Press, pp. 287–338.

Hagerman, R.J. (2002b) 'Physical and behavioral phenotype' in R.J. Hagerman & P.J. Hagerman (eds), *Fragile X syndrome: Diagnosis, Treatment and Research*, 3rd edn. Baltimore: The Johns Hopkins University Press, pp. 3–109.

Hagerman, R.J. (2006) 'Lessons from fragile X regarding neurobiology, autism, and neurodegeneration', *J Dev Behav Pediatr*, 27(1): 63–74.

Hagerman, R.J. & McBogg, P.M. (eds) (1983) *The Fragile X Syndrome: Diagnosis, Biochemistry, and Intervention*. Dillon, CO: Spectra Publishing Co.

Hagerman, R.J., Altshul-Stark, D., & McBogg, P. (1987) 'Recurrent otitis media in boys with the fragile X syndrome', *American Journal of Diseases of Children*, 141: 184–187.

Hagerman, R.J., Murphy, M.A., & Wittenberger, M.D. (1988) 'A controlled trial of stimulant medication in children with the fragile X syndrome', *Am J Med Genet*, 30(1–2): 377–392.

Hagerman, R.J., Jackson, C., Amiri, K., Silverman, A.C., O'Connor, R., & Sobesky, W. (1992) 'Girls with fragile X syndrome: physical and neurocognitive status and outcome', *Pediatrics*, 89(3): 395–400.

Hagerman, R.J., Hull, C.E., Safanda, J.F., Carpenter, I., Staley, L.W., O'Connor, R.A. et al. (1994) 'High functioning fragile X males: demonstration of an unmethylated fully expanded FMR-1 mutation associated with protein expression', *Am J Med Genet*, 51(4): 298–308.

Hagerman, R.J., Leehey, M., Heinrichs, W., Tassone, F., Wilson, R., Hills, J., et al. (2001) 'Intention tremor, parkinsonism, and generalized brain atrophy in male carriers of fragile X', *Neurology*, 57: 127–130.

Hagerman, R.J., Leavitt, B.R., Farzin, F., Jacquemont, S., Greco, C.M., Brunberg, J.A. et al. (2004) 'Fragile-X-associated tremor/ataxia syndrome (FXTAS) in females with the *FMR1* premutation', *Am J Hum Genet*, 74(5): 1051–1056.

Hagerman, R.J., Hall, D.A., Coffey, S., Leehey, M., Bourgeois, J., Gould, J. et al. (2008a) 'Treatment of fragile X-associated tremor ataxia syndrome (FXTAS) and related neurological problems', *Clin Interv Aging*, 3(2): 251–262.

Hagerman, R.J., Rivera, S.M., & Hagerman, P.J. (2008b) 'The fragile X family of disorders: a model for autism and targeted treatments', *Current Pediatric Reviews*, 4: 40–52.

Hagerman, R.J., Berry-Kravis, E., Kaufmann, W.E., Ono, M.Y., Tartaglia, N., Lachiewicz, A. et al. (2009) 'Advances in the treatment of fragile X syndrome', *Pediatrics,* 123(1): 378–390.

Hall, S.S., Burns, D.D., Lightbody, A.A., & Reiss, A.L. (2008a) 'Longitudinal changes in intellectual development in children with fragile X syndrome', *J Abnorm Child Psychol,* 36(6): 927–939.

Hall, S.S., Lightbody, A.A., & Reiss, A.L. (2008b) 'Compulsive, self-injurious, and autistic behavior in children and adolescents with fragile X syndrome', *Am J Ment Retard,* 113(1): 44–53.

Harris, S.W., Hessl, D., Goodlin-Jones, B. et al. (2008) 'Autism profiles in males with fragile X syndrome', *Am J Ment Retard,* 113(6): 427–438.

Hatton, D.D., Sideris, J., Skinner, M., Mankowski, J., Bailey, D.B., Jr., Roberts, J.E. et al. (2006) 'Autistic behavior in children with fragile X syndrome: prevalence, stability, and the impact of FMRP', *Am J Med Genet A,* 140(17): 1804–1813.

Hills-Epstein, J., Riley, K., & Sobesky, W. (2002) 'The treatment of emotional and behavioral problems', in R.J. Hagerman & P.J. Hagerman (eds), *Fragile X Syndrome: Diagnosis, Treatment, and Research,* 3rd edn. Baltimore: Johns Hopkins University Press, pp. 339–362.

Ingrassia, A. & Turk, J. (2005) 'The use of clonidine for severe and intractable sleep problems in children with neurodevelopmental disorders—a case series', *Eur Child Adolesc Psychiatry,* 14(1): 34–40.

Iwahashi, C.K., Yasui, D.H., An, H.J., Greco, C.M., Tassone, F., Nannen, K. et al. (2006) 'Protein composition of the intranuclear inclusions of FXTAS', *Brain,* 129(Pt 1): 256–271.

Jacquemont, S., Hagerman, R.J., Leehey, M.A., Hall, D.A., Levine, R.A., Brunberg, J.A. et al. (2004) 'Penetrance of the fragile X-associated tremor/ataxia syndrome in a premutation carrier population', *JAMA,* 291(4): 460–469.

Kaufmann, W.E., Cortell, R., Kau, A.S., Bukelis, I., Tierney, E., Gray, R.M. et al. (2004) 'Autism spectrum disorder in fragile X syndrome: communication, social interaction, and specific behaviors', *Am J Med Genet,* 129A(3): 225–234.

Kogan, C.S., Boutet, I., Cornish, K.M., Zangenehpour, S., Mullen, K.T., Holden, J.J. et al. (2004) 'Differential impact of the FMR1 gene on visual processing in fragile X syndrome', *Brain,* 127(Pt 3): 591–601.

Loesch, D.Z., Huggins, R.M., & Hagerman, R.J. (2004) 'Phenotypic variation and FMRP levels in fragile X', *Ment Retard Dev Disabil Res Rev,* 10(1): 31–41.

Lubs, H.A. (1969) 'A marker X chromosome', *Am J Hum Genet,* 21(3): 231–244.

McBride, S.M., Choi, C.H., Wang, Y., Liebelt, D., Braunstein, E., Ferreiro, D. et al. (2005) 'Pharmacological rescue of synaptic plasticity, courtship behavior, and mushroom body defects in a *Drosophila* model of fragile X syndrome', *Neuron,* 45(5): 753–764.

McConkie-Rosell, A., Abrams, L., Finucane, B., Cronister, A., Gane, L.W., Coffey, S.M. et al. (2007) 'Recommendations from multi-disciplinary focus groups on cascade testing and genetic counseling for fragile X-associated disorders', *J Genet Couns,* 16(5): 593–606.

Maddalena, A., Richards, C.S., McGinniss, M.J., Brothman, A., Desnick, R.J., Grier, R.E. et al. (2001) 'Technical standards and guidelines for fragile X: the first of a series of disease-specific supplements to the Standards and Guidelines for Clinical Genetics Laboratories of the American College of Medical Genetics. Quality Assurance Subcommittee of the Laboratory Practice Committee. *Genet Med,* 3(3): 200–205.

Mahadevappa, H. & Turk, J. (2008) 'Carbamazepine improves social and communicatory functioning in full mutation fragile X syndrome', Paper presented at the 11th International Fragile X Conference, July 23–27, St. Louis, MO.

Maino, D.M., Wesson, M., Schlange, D., Cibis, G., & Maino, J.H. (1991) 'Optometric findings in the fragile X syndrome', *Optom Vis Sci,* 68(8): 634–640.

Martin, J.P. & Bell, J. (1943) 'A pedigree of mental defect showing sex linkage', *J Neur Psychiatry,* 6: 154–157.

Mazzocco, M.M., Hagerman, R.J., Cronister Silverman, A., & Pennington, B.F. (1992) 'Specific frontal lobe deficits among women with the fragile X gene', *J Am Acad Child Adolesc Psychiatry,* 31(6): 1141–1148.

Mazzocco, M.M., Pennington, B.F., & Hagerman, R.J. (1993) 'The neurocognitive phenotype of female carriers of fragile X: additional evidence for specificity', *J Dev Behav Pediatr,* 14(5): 328–335.

Mazzocco, M.M., Pennington, B.F., & Hagerman, R.J. (1994) 'Social cognition skills among females with fragile X', *J Autism Dev Disord,* 24(4): 473–485.

Moss, J. & Howlin, P. (2009) 'Autism spectrum disorders in genetic syndromes: implications for diagnosis, intervention and understanding the wider autism spectrum disorder population', *J Intellect Disabil Res,* 53(10): 852–873.

Oberle, I., Rousseau, F., Heitz, D., Kretz, C., Devys, D., Hanauer, A. et al. (1991) 'Instability of a 550-base pair DNA segment and abnormal methylation in fragile X syndrome', *Science,* 252(5010): 1097–1102.

Pesso, R., Berkenstadt, M., Cuckle, H., Gak, E., Peleg, L., Frydman, M. et al. (2000) 'Screening for fragile X syndrome in women of reproductive age', *Prenat Diagn,* 20(8): 611–614.

Primerano, B., Tassone, F., Hagerman, R.J., Hagerman, P.J., Amaldi, F., & Bagni, C. (2002) 'Reduced FMR1 mRNA translation efficiency in Fragile X patients with premutations', *RNA,* 8(12): 1482–1488.

Reddy, K.S. (2005) 'Cytogenetic abnormalities and fragile-X syndrome in Autism Spectrum Disorder', *BMC Med Genet,* 6(1): 3.

Rivera, S.R. & Reiss, A.L. (2009) 'From genes to behavior: the case of fragile X syndrome', in J.M. Rumsey & M. Ernst (eds), *Neuroimaging in Developmental Clinical Neuroscience.* Cambridge: Cambridge University Press.

Roberts, J.E., Mirrett, P., & Burchinal, M. (2001) 'Receptive and expressive communication development of young males with fragile X syndrome', *Am J Ment Retard,* 106(3): 216–230.

Roberts, J.E., Long, S.H., Malkin, C., Barnes, E., Skinner, M., Hennon, E.A. et al. (2005a) 'A comparison of phonological skills of boys with fragile X syndrome and Down syndrome', *J Speech Lang Hear Res,* 48(5): 980–995.

Roberts, J.E., Schaaf, J.M., Skinner, M., Wheeler, A., Hooper, S., Hatton, D.D. et al. (2005b) 'Academic skills of boys with fragile X syndrome: profiles and predictors', *Am J Ment Retard,* 110(2): 107–120.

Rogers, S.J., Wehner, E.A., & Hagerman, R.J. (2001) 'The behavioral phenotype in fragile X: symptoms of autism in very young children with fragile X syndrome, idiopathic autism, and other developmental disorders', *J Dev Behav Pediatr,* 22(6): 409–417.

Rousseau, F., Morel, M.-L., Rouillard, P., Khandjian, E.W., & Morgan, K. (1996) 'Surprisingly low prevalence of FMR1 premutation among males from the general population', *Am J Hum Genet,* 59(Suppl): A188–1069.

Saluto, A., Brussino, A., Tassone, F., Pappi, P., Arduino, C., Hagerman, P.J. et al. (2005) 'An enhanced polymerase chain reaction assay to detect pre- and full mutation alleles of the fragile X mental retardation 1 gene', *J Mol Diagn,* 7(5): 605–612.

Scharfenaker, S., O'Connor, R., Stackhouse, T., & Noble, L. (2002) 'An integrated approach to intervention' in R.J. Hagerman & P.J. Hagerman (eds), *Fragile X Syndrome: Diagnosis, Treatment and Research,* 3rd edn, Baltimore: Johns Hopkins University Press, pp. 363–427.

Shan, G., Luo, Y., Smrt, R., Li, X., Duan, R., Barkho, B. et al. (2008) 'Fragile X mental retardation protein regulates adult neurogenesis'. Paper presented at the American Society of Human Genetics 58th Annual Meeting, November 11–15, Philadelphia, PA.

Sherman, S.L., Jacobs, P.A., Morton, N.E., Froster-Iskenius, U., Howard-Peebles, P.N., Nielsen, K.B. et al. (1985) 'Further segregation analysis of the fragile X syndrome with special reference to transmitting males', *Hum Genet,* 69(4): 289–299.

Skinner, M., Hooper, S., Hatton, D.D., Roberts, J.E., Mirrett, P., Schaaf, J. et al. (2005) 'Mapping nonverbal IQ in young boys with fragile X syndrome', *Am J Med Genet A,* 132(1): 25–32.

Song, F.J., Barton, P., Sleightholme, V., Yao, G.L., & Fry-Smith, A. (2003) 'Screening for fragile X syndrome: a literature review and modelling study', *Health Technol Assess,* 7(16): 1–106.

Sullivan, A.K., Marcus, M., Epstein, M.P., Allen, E.G., Anido, A.E., Paquin, J.J. et al. (2005) 'Association of FMR1 repeat size with ovarian dysfunction', *Hum Reprod,* 20(2): 402–412.

Sullivan, K., Hatton, D., Hammer, J., Sideris, J., Hooper, S., Ornstein, P. et al. (2006) 'ADHD symptoms in children with FXS', *Am J Med Genet A,* 140(21): 2275–2288.

Sutherland, G.R. (1977) 'Fragile sites on human chromosomes: demonstration of their dependence of the type of tissue culture medium', *Science,* 197: 265–266.

Symons, F.J., Clark, R.D., Hatton, D.D., Skinner, M., & Bailey, D.B., Jr (2003) 'Self-injurious behavior in young boys with fragile X syndrome', *Am J Med Genet A,* 118(2): 115–121.

Tassone, F., Hagerman, R.J., Iklé, D.N., Dyer, P.N., Lampe, M., Willemsen, R. et al. (1999) 'FMRP expression as a potential prognostic indicator in fragile X syndrome', *Am J Med Genet,* 84(3): 250–261.

Tassone, F., Hagerman, R.J., Loesch, D.Z., Lachiewicz, A., Taylor, A.K., & Hagerman, P.J. (2000a) 'Fragile X males with unmethylated, full mutation trinucleotide repeat expansions have elevated levels of FMR1 messenger RNA', *Am J Med Genet,* 94(3): 232–236.

Tassone, F., Hagerman, R.J., Taylor, A.K., Gane, L.W., Godfrey, T.E., & Hagerman, P.J. (2000b) 'Elevated levels of FMR1 mRNA in carrier males: a new mechanism of involvement in the fragile-X syndrome', *Am J Hum Genet,* 66(1): 6–15.

Tassone, F., Hagerman, R.J., Taylor, A.K., Mills, J.B., Harris, S.W., Gane, L.W. et al. (2000c) 'Clinical involvement and protein expression in individuals with the FMR1 premutation', *Am J Med Genet,* 91(2): 144–152.

Tassone, F., Pan, R., Amiri, K., Taylor, A.K., & Hagerman, P.J. (2008) 'A rapid polymerase chain reaction-based screening method for identification of all expanded alleles of the fragile X (FMR1) gene in newborn and high-risk populations', *J Mol Diagn,* 10(1): 43–49.

Turk, J. (1998) 'Fragile X syndrome and attentional deficits', *Journal of Applied Research in Intellectual Disabilities,* 11: 175–191.

Turk, J. (2003a) 'Medication matters, in D. Dew-Hughes (ed.), *Educating Children with Fragile X Syndrome.* London: Routledge Falmer, pp. 149–155.

Turk, J. (2003b) 'Melatonin supplementation for severe and intractable sleep disturbance in young people with genetically determined developmental disabilities: short review and commentary', *J Med Genet,* 40(11): 793–796.

Turk, J. (2004) 'Children with developmental disabilities and their parents', in P. Graham (ed.), *Cognitive Behaviour Therapy for Children and Families,* 2nd edn, Cambridge: Cambridge University Press, pp. 244–262.

Turk, J. & Cornish, K.M. (1998) 'Face recognition and emotion perception in boys with fragile-X syndrome', *J Intellect Disabil Res,* 42 (Pt 6): 490–499.

Turk, J. & Graham, P. (1997) 'Fragile X syndrome, autism, and autistic features', *Autism,* 1(2): 175–197.

Turk, J. & Patton, M. (2000) 'Sensory impairment and head circumference in fragile X syndrome, Down syndrome and idiopathic intellectual disability', *J Intellect Dev Disabil,* 25(1): 59–68.

Turk, J., Robbins, I., & Woodhead, M. (2005) 'Post-traumatic stress disorder in young people with intellectual disability', *J Intellect Disabil Res,* 49(Pt 11): 872–875.

Utari, A., Chonchaiya, W., Rivera, S., Schneider, A., Hagerman, R.J., Faradz, S.M.H., Ethell, I.M., Nguyen, D.V. (2010). Side Effects of Minocycline Treatment in Patients With Fragile X Syndrome and Exploration of Outcome Measures. American Journal on Intellectual and Developmental Disabilities: September 2010, Vol. 115, No. 5, pp. 433–443.

Verkerk, A.J., Pieretti, M., Sutcliffe, J.S., Fu, Y.H., Kuhl, D.P., Pizzuti, A. et al. (1991) 'Identification of a gene (FMR-1) containing a CGG repeat coincident with a breakpoint cluster region exhibiting length variation in fragile X syndrome', *Cell,* 65(5): 905–914.

Westmark, C.J. & Malter, J.S. (2007) 'FMRP mediates mGluR5-dependent translation of amyloid precursor protein', *PLoS Biol,* 5(3): e52.

Wright-Talamante, C., Cheema, A., Riddle, J.E., Luckey, D.W., Taylor, A.K., & Hagerman, R.J. (1996) 'A controlled study of longitudinal IQ changes in females and males with fragile X syndrome', *Am J Med Genet,* 64(2): 350–355.

Yan, Q.J., Rammal, M., Tranfaglia, M., & Bauchwitz, R.P. (2005) 'Suppression of two major fragile X syndrome mouse model phenotypes by the mGluR5 antagonist MPEP', *Neuropharmacology,* 49(7): 1053–1066.

4

Fragile X Syndrome: Life Course and Strategies for Intervention

Andrea Schneider & David Hessl

INTRODUCTION

In Chapter 3, the authors gave a detailed insight into the medical background, epidemiology, and pharmacotherapy of fragile X syndrome (FXS), the most common inherited cause of intellectual and learning disability.

This chapter provides an overview about the life course in carriers with full FXS mutation alleles and also for carriers of the premutation alleles, and non-medical interventions. However, only a small number of controlled intervention studies have been published in the field so far, and the description of the interventional approaches are derived from the general research in intellectual disability, the clinical experience of the authors, and the clinical reports of colleagues.

Presently, although the knowledge about the neurobiological and neurogenetic causes

for fragile X grows exponentially, and recent animal studies documenting rescue of FXS features, there is no cure or proven targeted intervention for humans yet. For better care and behavioral management, a team approach is needed. It usually includes the physician for medical and pharmaceutical care, a special educational teacher, a speech and language pathologist, an occupational therapist, a psychologist, and a genetic counselor.

BEHAVIORAL PHENOTYPE

The fragile X mental retardation protein (FMRP) abnormalities in the fragile X mutations influence the developmental trajectories in several areas such as physical symptoms, cognitive ability, emotional status, and adaptive behaviors. As pointed out in Chapter 3, patients with FXS show distinct behavioral features (R.J. Hagerman, 2002; Reiss & Dant, 2003; Sabaratnam, 2006):

- Cognitive delay and intellectual disability
- Hyperarousal and hyperactivity, especially impulsivity and short attention span
- Autism or autistic features, avoiding eye-contact, hand-flapping and hand-biting, sensory defensiveness, and poor adaption to changes in routine
- Shyness and social anxiety
- Stereotypies and tics
- Aggressive outbursts
- Enuresis, encopresis

Reiss and Dant emphasize the variability of behavioral and cognitive symptoms in FXS between males and females with the explanation of a complex interaction of genetic, environmental, and biological risk factors. The developmental trajectory and the changes throughout the life span are similar to those with typical developmental trajectories (Reiss & Dant, 2003).

A common finding in FXS is a comorbidity with psychiatric symptoms that is often overlooked because of diagnostic overshadowing. However, the diagnosis of psychiatric problems in the intellectually disabled individual is challenging for the mental health practitioner (Kwok & Cheung, 2007). Generally, there is a higher rate of psychiatric disorders in people with learning disabilities than in the general population, with the prevalence estimated at 30–75% (Borthwick-Duffy, 1994; Rojahn et al., 1993). In FXS, an increased rate of bipolar affective disorders, psychosis, and mood instability with aggression and depression have been reported. In some cases, the psychiatric symptoms are masked with developmental-level appropriate behaviors: for example, psychosis can present as perseverative mumbling, self-talk or verbalization of experiences, and other stereotypic behaviors (Sabaratnam, 2006). An adult with fragile X may engage in self-talk and imaginary play; however, if this person's mental age is 3 years, the behavior would be considered developmentally within normal expectations.

A review by Grossman and colleagues indicates the tremendous influence of the environment and experience on the psychopathological outcomes in both genetic and developmental disorders like FXS, fetal alcohol syndrome, depression, and schizophrenia (Grossman et al., 2003).

Life course of FXS—the early years

The developmental course of FXS in childhood, adolescence, and young adulthood has been extensively reported and shows a wide spectrum of distinct symptoms (Einfeld et al., 1999; R.J. Hagerman & P.J. Hagerman, 2002; Jakala et al., 1997). Reiss and Dant (2003) give a comprehensive overview about genetic influences, trajectories of cognition and behavior, variation in brain structure and function, and biological and environmental factors that influence developmental and cognitive outcomes of children with fragile X.

In general, a developmental delay can be identified in male FXS infants as early as 9–12 months of age by a low muscle tone, motor problems, hyperactivity and irritability; furthermore, there is a delay in reaching other developmental milestones such as speech, crawling or walking (Bailey et al., 2000). The identification of developmental delays in female FXS infants and toddlers remains challenging because of the milder phenotype (Borghgraef et al., 1996; Loesch & Hay, 1988).

A study in toddlers with FXS showed the difficulties in executive control that are typical for older children and adults with FXS (Scerif et al., 2004). The experimental design included a touch-screen-based task that required searching for targets amongst a random number of distractors that were similar to the targets in size. Showing problems in inhibiting prior to successful responses, the toddlers with FXS repeatedly touched targets from previous trials. This reaction pattern has been shown in older children with FXS (Wilding et al., 2002). Deficits in inhibiting inappropriate eye movements in an analogue of the antisaccade task were also demonstrated in infants with FXS as young as 12 months old (Scerif et al., 2005). Based on findings by Kogan et al. (2004a, 2004b), who showed a specific impairment in the precortical magnocellular visual pathway in older children and adolescents with FXS and Flanagan et al. (2007), who reported the relation to visual orientation and attention, Farzin et al. (2008, 2009) reported deficits in the dorsal or magnocellular visual pathway, the ventral or parvocellular pathway already in infants and toddlers with FXS.

The most common behavioral problems in both male and female preschoolers with FXS are temper tantrums, hyperactivity, aggression, attention deficits, and mood instability (D. Hatton et al., 2002; Mazzocco et al., 1998). Especially in male FXS, several symptoms of the problematic behaviors overlap with the DSM-IV (Diagnostic and Statistical Manual of Mental Disorders, 4th edn) criteria for PDD-NOS (pervasive developmental disorder), or ASD (autism spectrum disorder) (Bailey et al., 2001; D.D. Hatton et al., 2006). Effectively, autism is one of the most common comorbid diagnoses in FXS and affects approximately 30% of the individuals (Rogers et al., 2001b). Autistic-like features in FXS include hand-flapping, hand-biting, perseverative speech, social anxiety, and poor eye contact (Garcia-Nonell et al., 2008; Rogers et al., 2001b). Generally, individuals with FXS are interested in social relationships, and do not meet the social deficit criteria of autism. However, the relationship between molecular measures (FMRP, *FMR1* mRNA, CGG repeat number) and the symptoms of autism on conventional assessments (ADOS, ADI-R, DSM-IV checklist) has shown no significant correlations (Harris et al., 2008), pointing to other genetic and/or environmental factors.

FXS at school age

Over 90% of males and 50% females have intellectual disability by the school-age years

(D. Hessl et al., 2009). A gradual decline in IQ occurs as the gap between the child's lower rates of cognitive growth widens relative to the development of typical peers. The rate of cognitive growth in children with FXS is approximately half of normal (Hall et al., 2008). Neuropsychological testing shows a distinct cognitive profile in school-age children with FXS, including difficulties in visual-motor coordination, sequential processing, short-term memory deficits and arithmetic problems (Freund & Reiss, 1991; Rivera et al., 2002; Tamm et al., 2002), attention and inhibitory control problems (Cornish et al., 2004; R.J. Hagerman et al., 1985), fine and gross motor delay, and problems with coordination (Bailey et al., 1998; Zingerevich et al., 2008). The development of language, especially in males, is closely linked to the IQ level, and includes distinct speech abnormalities: delayed and distorted speech, perseveration, delayed echolalia, and cluttering of speech. In a longitudinal study by Fisch and colleagues, the language domain and communication skills were the most affected adaptive behavior domains, compared to socialization or daily living skills (Fisch et al., 1996, 2002).

In school-age children with FXS, the deficit in executive control, already seen in toddlers with FXS, continues to be the most common finding. The deficit involves goal-directed behavior, working memory, planning, and inhibitory control that persist over the life span (Cornish et al., 2001, 2009; Garner et al., 1999; Munir et al., 2000; Sobesky et al., 1994; Wilding et al., 2002).

Adolescence and young adulthood

Einfeld and colleagues (Einfeld et al., 1999) carried out a 7-year follow-up study of 46 individuals with FXS from adolescence into young adulthood (mean age-22.4, SD-5.47 years), and found reductions in disruptive behavior (similar to patients with autism) but an increase in antisocial behavior. Declines in IQ scores have been documented in many males and females with FXS throughout childhood and into adolescence (Fisch et al., 1992, 1994, 2002; R.J. Hagerman et al., 1989; Hodapp et al., 1991; Lachiewicz et al., 1987; Wright-Talamante et al., 1996). Clinicians have reported stability of IQ measures throughout adulthood.

The social interactions for male and female FXS adolescents remain challenging; in particular, women with FXS and social anxiety are at risk for developing symptoms of major depression (Angkustsiri et al., 2008; Hagan et al., 2008; Reiss et al., 1989; Tranebjaerg & Orum, 1991), which could be a secondary effect of the social neglect by peers or of growing self-awareness of having a disability.

Similar to females with fragile X, male adolescents with FXS show social anxiety symptoms that impair their social interactions. A major indicator of the social anxiety is the gaze avoidance, especially in males with fragile X (Cohen et al., 1988; Dalton et al., 2008; Farzin et al., 2009; Garrett et al., 2004; D. Hessl et al., 2006; Holsen et al., 2008; Simon & Finucane, 1996; Watson et al., 2008).

Aggression is a common problem for males with FXS. A study by Hessl and colleagues (D. Hessl et al., 2008) reported that the most common aggressive behaviors in a sample of males with FXS between 8 and 24 years were hitting others (49% of the sample) and kicking others (30%), with 75% demonstrating some aggression toward others during the 2-month reporting period. This study also discovered that variation in the serotonin transporter gene polymorphism was related to the severity of aggression, suggesting that background genes regulating mood moderate expression of the behavioral phenotype, which may have implications regarding which patients best respond to the selective serotonin reuptake inhibitors (SSRIs) commonly prescribed. Clinical experience suggests that aggression and irritability increase and reach a peak during late adolescence and early adulthood, perhaps as a result of central nervous system (CNS) changes related to puberty and stresses asso-

ciated with leaving the stability and structure of the school system. Also, aggressive behaviors are perceived as more serious during this time as the increased size and strength of patients makes their behaviors more threatening and potentially dangerous.

Managing aggression is a top priority for families during this time. While no interventions have been systematically tested, it is important to identify triggers for heightened arousal and anxiety, as these often lead to the aggressive outbursts. Once identified, the individual may be more easily calmed or distracted with another activity and given an opportunity to self-regulate by removing himself from the triggering situation and rewarded for inhibiting the aggressive impulse.

Sexual development

Masturbation and other forms of self-stimulatory behavior are common, and it is not unusual for sexual behaviors to take on an obsessive nature, or for the individual to engage in such behaviors in public. Usually counseling aimed at clarifying the appropriate time and place for sexual gratification is helpful. Fertility is usually normal in men with FXS, although it is very unusual for fully affected males with FXS to father a child. Females with FXS who are higher functioning often have children. These children may have the full mutation or they may be normal with regard to fragile X by transmission of the normal X chromosome. Genetic counseling is strongly advised for any female with FXS of reproductive age who may be or will soon become sexually active.

Aging in FXS

The development of FXS in adulthood has not received much attention in research studies, and only a few case reports mostly relying on anecdotal clinical experience, have been published.

Aging research in normal mice showed that the expression of the fragile X mental retardation gene (*FMR1*) changes across the life span (Singh et al., 2007). FMRP levels were highest in young male mice and lowest in aging mice. Since FMRP has been shown to be important for regulating learning, memory, and cognition (Zalfa et al., 2006), the normative age-related decrease in those cognitive processes could be closely linked with FMRP.

Recent neurophysiological evidence in the mouse models has linked the fragile X mental retardation protein (FMRP) to Alzheimer's disease (AD) (Westmark & Malter, 2007). The authors reported that in normal mice, FMRP downregulates amyloid precursor protein (APP) by binding to the coding region of the APP mRNA, which then decreases the level of beta amyloids (Aβ). In the FXS knockout (KO) mice, FMRP was absent, which in turn increased levels of Aβ. The deposition of Aβ in the brain is a principal mechanism of AD (Gatz, 2007). It is not known whether the lack of FMRP in humans with FXS leads to Aβ deposition or cognitive changes with aging.

Studies on IQ decline showed a diverse pattern in FXS (Brun et al., 1995; R.J. Hagerman et al., 1983, 1989; Wright-Talamante et al., 1996). For example, one male FXS subgroup showed a significant IQ decline during childhood, whereas the IQ of females remained relatively stable. Those with the highest IQs often experienced the greatest decline, suggesting that high-functioning males may be most at risk (R.J. Hagerman et al., 1989). In retrospect this may be related to early toxicity from elevated mRNA (see studies of fragile X-associated tremor/ataxia syndrome (FXTAS)). The developmental trajectory of children with FXS remains at approximately half the rate of typically developing children (Cornish et al., 2008; Hall et al., 2008). Therefore the gap in cognitive and adaptive performance increases over time, accounting for the declines in IQ and other scores standardized by age. The IQ decline typically does not represent any type of cognitive regression.

Medical research on aging in older adults with FXS shows increased rates of mitral valve prolapse, musculoskeletal disorders (early menopause has not been reported in full mutation carriers), epilepsy, and visual impairments (WHO Report on Healthy Ageing – Adults with Intellectual Disabilities).

Only limited information is available regarding the behavioral and neuropsychological profile in older individuals with FXS. Borghgraef et al. (2002) presented a 10-year follow-up study of 10 males with FXS, with ages ranging from 33 years to 65 years. A significant overall IQ decline was documented on the McCarthy scales: a significant decline in verbal abilities in five subjects, and a significant decline in performance abilities in two subjects.

To the authors' knowledge, there have been no studies so far on aging in FXS individuals older than 50 years. Even aging studies in autism without FXS are scarce. In a study by Piven et al., 1996, the Autism Diagnostic Interview Revised (ADI-R) (Lord et al., 1994) was given to the parents of 38 high-functioning adolescents and adults with autism aged 13 to 28 years. The ratings of current behavior were significantly less abnormal on all three domains than the retrospectively assessed lifetime scores from age 4. Similar results were replicated by Bolte et al. (2000) in 93 individuals with autism aged 15 to 37 years, and by Gilchrist et al. (2001). Other studies of aging in individuals with autistic features or autism have also focused on adolescence to early or (at most) mid adulthood. Gillberg and Steffenburg (1987) found that behavioral problems increased in adolescence, similar to FXS (R.J. Hagerman et al., 2002), but that considerable improvement occurs in early adulthood. However, significant adaptive and social problems persist lifelong (Kobayashi & Murata, 1998; Rumsey et al., 1985; Seltzer et al., 2004; Venter et al., 1992). An additional study of Beadle-Brown and colleagues followed a cohort of patients over 11 years and found improvements in self-care skills, communication skills, and educational achievements (Beadle-Brown et al., 2000). The overall picture into mid adulthood in individuals with autism spectrum disorders (ASD) is one of gradual improvement, although there is significant stress in the family home where approximately 50% of the adults live (Seltzer et al., 2001). The effects of aging on the brains of individuals with autism or FXS (or both conditions) are unknown. As the rate of autism diagnosis increases in the general population, there has been increased concern about how to best diagnose and treat autism in aging or elderly individuals. Because FXS is associated with high rates of autism, it provides a unique opportunity to study how the aging process manifests itself in autism and mental impairment, the services individuals require, and how to help family members assist these patients.

DIAGNOSTICS OF FXS

So far, there are no practice guidelines available for the initial diagnosis of FXS. However, the American Academy of Pediatrics recommends fragile X testing in males and females with intellectual disability (ID), ASD or hyperactivity combined with behavioral problems of unknown etiology (Moeschler & Shevell, 2006). Figure 4.1 summarizes the diagnostic and treatment algorithm in FXS.

The assessment of a patient with a developmental delay in cognitive, social, and motor function of unknown origin should include a complete medical and family history review. If the pedigree shows family members with intellectual disability and/or autistic symptoms, premature ovarian failure, or neurodegenerative symptoms of unknown origin, FXS should be considered. The diagnosis of fragile X syndrome is confirmed by molecular genetic testing of the X-linked *FMR1* gene. The 5′ *FMR1* locus is characterized by a repetitive CGG trinucleotide sequence, which is repeated approximately 6–40 times in unaffected individuals. A repeat size between 55 and 200 CGG is referred to as premutation. A full mutation consists of more than 200 CGG repeats in the *FMR1* gene, causing hypermethylation (methyl groups attach to the CGG triplets), which leads to an inability to produce the *FMR1* protein, FMRP.

The physical phenotype and the intellectual impairment are closely correlated with the extent of the FMRP deficit (Kaufmann et al., 1999; Loesch et al., 2004). The physical examination shows the FXS phenotype with a broad forehead, elongated face, large prominent ears, and other physical features in adults (Sabaratnam, 2006), whereas the behavioral phenotype is more prominent in children. Common neurologic findings in children with FXS are electroencephalography (EEG) abnormalities and seizures (Berry-Kravis, 2002). If seizures are suspected, or the child has staring spells or 'zoning out', a clinical EEG is advised. A speech and language assessment shows typical impairments such as tangential language, perseverative and repetitive speech, and delayed echolalia in most males with FXS (Belser & Sudhalter, 2001; Cornish et al., 2004; Sudhalter et al., 1990, 1991, 1992). The ID in FXS is the predominant finding of the cognitive profile in a neuropsychological assessment. Typically, males with FXS are mildly to moderately affected, and show a distinct pattern of cognitive functioning, with weaknesses in visual-motor coordination, spatial memory, and arithmetic. The strengths are verbal labeling and comprehension (Freund & Reiss, 1991). In female carriers of FXS, only half are affected by a cognitive impairment, depending on the activation of the mutated X-chromosome in the cell. Based on the outcome of the assessments, a profile of strengths and weaknesses can be helpful to distinguish the severity of impairment in the FXS individual, and the sequence of treatment possibilities. Also, this profile can be helpful in guiding educational placement and behavioral therapy. A psychologist can be especially helpful with the management of behavior problems, such as aggression and attention deficits. However, a multiprofessional

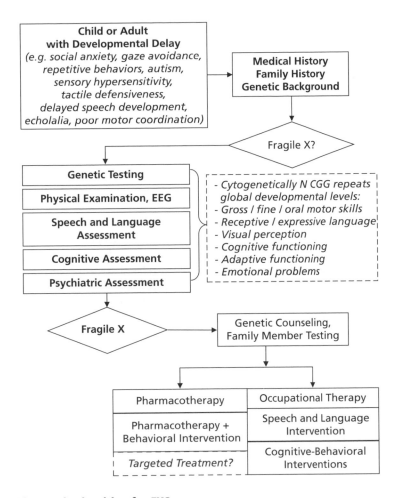

Figure 4.1   Diagnostic algorithm for FXS

approach for the treatment of FXS, including pharmacotherapy, speech and language, occupational, and cognitive-behavioral approaches can facilitate the integration of calmer behavior, cognitive skills, language, and sensory integration (Scharfenaker et al., 2002).

LIFE COURSE OF PREMUTATION CARRIERS

Individuals with a *FMR1* CGG allele size between 55 and 200 repeats are fragile X premutation carriers. Those individuals are at risk for transmission of the gene in its expanded full mutation form in subsequent generations.

Neurodegenerative disease arising in later life, the fragile X-associated tremor/ataxia syndrome (FXTAS) (R.J. Hagerman et al., 2001b), and POI (primary ovarian insufficiency) (Sullivan et al., 2005) are now established disorders associated with the fragile X premutation that are not observed in those with the full mutation. The pathogenetic mechanism is considered to be an overexpression of *FMR1* mRNA, which has been detected in premutation alleles (Allen et al., 2004; Kenneson et al., 2001; Tassone et al., 2000c), resulting in an RNA toxic gain of function that is directly related to CGG repeat size (P.J. Hagerman & R.J. Hagerman, 2004; Tassone et al., 2000b). Although many children with the premutation are unaffected, a subgroup demonstrates significant clinical symptoms of hyperactivity, social deficits and ASD (Aziz et al., 2003; Cornish et al., 2005b; Farzin et al., 2006; Goodlin-Jones et al., 2004). Some of these individuals with the premutation and neurodevelopmental problems have a mild to moderate deficit of FMRP (Tassone et al., 2000c). The level of FMRP decreases with increased CGG repeat number and is more evident in the upper end of the premutation range, leading to physical and behavioral features similar to fragile X syndrome (P.J. Hagerman & R.J. Hagerman, 2007; Tassone et al., 1999). The gradual lowering of FMRP in the premutation has also been documented in the knock-in mouse model of the premutation (Brouwer et al., 2007; Entezam et al., 2007).

Most studies about the neuropsychological and neuropsychiatric involvement in the fragile X premutation focus primarily on males, who are expected to be more affected because of the X chromosome locus of *FMR1*. British researchers examined *FMR1* function and neuropsychological performance in 20 males with the premutation and an age- and IQ-matched comparison group of healthy men (Moore et al., 2004). Male carriers had significant deficits in several domains of memory on the Wechsler Memory Scales (Wechsler, 1997), and also poorer executive functions. In a neuroimaging study, Koldewyn et al. (2008) showed a possible correlation to functional neuroanatomy: men with the premutation had reduced hippocampal activation during a memory retrieval task that was associated with elevated *FMR1* mRNA. Another study by Cornish and colleagues reported that men with the premutation, as compared to matched family and non-family controls, display a neurocognitive pattern similar, albeit milder in presentation, to that of the fragile X full mutation, including impairment in social cognition (Hessl et al., 2007), the Reading the Mind in the Eyes task (Baron-Cohen et al., 2001),

obsessive-compulsive traits, and executive function problems including inhibitory control (Cornish et al., 2005a, 2005b; Hessl et al., 2007). In a more recent study, Cornish et al. (2008) updated the neurocognitive differences between carriers and non-carriers under the age of 50. Both Cornish and Grigsby reported no significant differences in the more general measures of intelligence, sustained attention, visual spatial function, and visual memory (Grigsby et al., 2008). In these studies, the specific deficits in premutation carriers were in the area of executive functioning, response inhibition, and some aspects of verbal learning and memory that were related to CGG repeat size and age. However, a comprehensive study by Hunter and colleagues with a considerably large sample size (30 male premutation carriers, 75 male controls, 293 female premutation carriers, 117 female controls) from 18 to 50 years of age, found no differences in executive functioning, nor a correlation of neurocognitive differences with CGG repeat length (Hunter et al., 2008b). Interestingly, Hunter found a significantly large number of self-reported attention problems in female premutation carriers, especially on the inattention/memory, impulsivity/emotional lability, and problems with self-concept subscales of the Conners Adult ADHD Rating Scales (CAARS) (Conners et al., 1999) that were not related to the psychosocial stress of raising a child with FXS. The finding of problems with self-concept in female premutation carriers, and a general negative affect has been replicated in different studies (Hunter et al., 2008a; McConkie-Rosell et al., 2000, 2001). Most of the female study participants are adult women with the premutation who typically have one or more significantly impaired children with FXS. This makes it difficult to separate direct genetic effects from the associated environmental stress of having children with significant behavioral and cognitive difficulties (Abbeduto et al., 2004; Johnston et al., 2003; Lewis et al., 2006). Considering that bias, Franke et al. (1998) studied mothers with the premutation to determine whether psychological problems were related to the premutation itself or to the stress of raising a developmentally impaired child. They compared 13 mothers with the full mutation, 61 mothers with the premutation, 17 women with the premutation who were siblings of the first two groups but did not have children with FXS, and 18 women siblings without the *FMR1* mutation and without children, and 42 mothers without the *FMR1* mutation who had children with autism. The study used a psychiatric interview to obtain DSM-IV diagnoses and to assess personality disorders. Mothers with a premutation, as well as their siblings with the premutation but without affected children, were more likely to be diagnosed with social phobia than a control group of mothers of children with autism. The authors concluded that social avoidance, as expressed by social phobia or avoidant personality disorder, has been underestimated in previous studies. Unfortunately, the awareness of psychiatric disability in the fragile X premutation is lower because these problems are not as common and not as obvious as in the full mutation (Cornish et al., 2005b; Farzin et al., 2006; Hessl et al., 2005; Johnston et al., 2001; Roberts et al., 2009). In a literature review of clinical articles referring to psychiatric clinical manifestations in fragile X-associated conditions, Bourgeois and colleagues reported an increased rate of psychiatric comorbidity, especially mood and anxiety disorders. Male premutation carriers without FXTAS are at risk for social avoidance disorders (Bourgeois et al., 2009).

In our clinical experience we have encountered several patients who have demonstrated both an elevated mRNA level (at least twice normal) and a lowered FMRP level (below 70% of normal). These individuals typically have an unmethylated full mutation or a high-end premutation (>150 CGG repeats). Therefore, they experience a dual mechanism of involvement including the toxicity of the elevated mRNA in addition to the upregulation of protein expression related to the lowering of FMRP, a modulator of translation (Qin et al., 2005). This phenotype could be referred to as 'double hit', and combines elements of FXS and premutation involvement. However, the research data and diagnostic approaches remain unclear and should be focus of future studies.

Fragile X-associated tremor/ataxia syndrome

Much of the experience with aging in fragile X has been with premutation carriers looking at the physical, behavioral, and cognitive phenotype of FXTAS, a progressive neurodegenerative disorder affecting males who carry the *FMR1* gene premutation with CGG repeats ranging from 55 to 200 (Amiri et al., 2008; Jacquemont et al., 2003). In an initial study, Hagerman and colleagues reported on five elderly men with the fragile X premutation and FXTAS (R.J. Hagerman et al., 2001a). These individuals presented with executive function deficits and generalized brain atrophy. All of these men had elevated mRNA levels and relatively normal levels of FMRP. In a subsequent study, a group of 26 male subjects over 50 years of age with the premutation (Jacquemont et al., 2003) presented with short-term memory loss, executive function deficits, Parkinsonism, and general cognitive decline. These findings have been confirmed in a larger data set of 93 subjects (Tassone et al., 2007). FXTAS affects 17% of male carriers in their 50s and up to 75% of males in their 80s (Jacquemont et al., 2004b). Onset of neurological symptoms is between 50 and 70 years of age, with a variable time interval between occurrence of motor features and cognitive changes (Jacquemont et al., 2004a; Leehey et al., 2007). FXTAS has also been identified in female premutation carriers (R.J. Hagerman et al., 2004) and is associated with intentional tremor, gait difficulties, peripheral neuropathy, POI, thyroid disorders, mood swings, depression, vertigo, and immune dysregulation (Coffey et al., 2008). The psychiatric comorbidities in FXTAS include agitation, disinhibition, and anxiety (Bacalman et al., 2006). The neurobiological base for the neurodegeneration in premutation carriers has been proposed as a 'toxic gain-of-function' mechanism (Amiri et al., 2008; R.J. Hagerman et al., 2001b; Tassone et al., 2000a). The excess mRNA leads to eosinophilic inclusions in astrocytes and neurons and eventually leads to cell death (C. Greco et al., 2003; C.M. Greco et al., 2006). In adult male carriers, the CGG repeat number correlates with the number of inclusions as well as the age of onset of tremor/ataxia and inversely correlates with the age of death (C.M. Greco et al., 2006).

While there have been anecdotal clinical reports of tremor or other motor problems in FXS full mutation individuals, there has never been documentation of FXTAS in those with the full mutation. Certainly, individuals with repeat-size mosaicism who have full mutation and premutation alleles could have both a significant FMRP deficit as well as abnormal elevation of mRNA. If the elevated mRNA is a cause of the tremor/ataxia symptoms in premutation carriers, then an individual with mosaicism could theoretically present with both FXS and FXTAS symptoms; however, FXTAS is rare or nonexistent in the upper premutation range and it is likely that a deficit of FMRP in this range is protective and decreases the prevalence of FXTAS with higher CGG repeats. Westmark and Malter (2007) found that a lack of FMRP could be causative of neurodegeneration similar to AD in the full mutation. Longitudinal and cross-sectional aging studies of individuals with FXS are needed to better understand the natural progression of the condition throughout adulthood as well as how the FMRP deficit affects brain function, cognition, and behavior over time.

The high prevalence of premutation alleles of approximately 1 in 250–800 males and 1 in 130–250 females in the general population (Fernandez-Carvajal et al., 2009; P.J. Hagerman, 2008) should increase the awareness toward possible medical and emotional problems in this population. The advent of newborn screening will increase the number identified with FXS and the premutation (R.J. Hagerman et al., 2009). Newly diagnosed carriers, through newborn screening, clinical assessment of an FXS child, or pedigree analysis, may experience guilt at having transmitted a genetic disorder. Additional to the coping with possible psychiatric symptoms in younger premutation carriers, or the cognitive decline and motor impairment in FXTAS, the psychotherapeutic treatment should focus on a gentle confrontation of distortional beliefs, and a supportive cognitive-behavioral approach (Bacalman et al., 2006; Bourgeois et al., 2007, 2009; R.J. Hagerman et al., 2008). However, the psychiatric symptoms in premutation carriers could also be determined by other stressors, and are not solely attributable to the psychiatric vulnerability of the molecular status.

GENETIC COUNSELING

Genetic counseling is important for educating families with carriers of the fragile X gene mutation about the heritability, the implications, and prognosis. In working on the pedigree, the genetic counselor identifies other possible carriers of the fragile X gene mutation who could be alerted by the family. Furthermore, the genetic counselor can provide information about the availability of testing and administrative help.

A typical transmission pedigree of the female X-linked mutation is shown in Figure 4.2. In females with the premutation, the CGG trinucleotide expansion in the *FMR1* gene is hereditarily unstable. There is a high risk of the premutation expanding to a full mutation when it is transmitted from a woman to her children (black box). If the mutated X chromosome does not expand, there is a 50% chance of transmitting the affected X to both male and female offspring, causing them to be carriers of the premutation. However, both men and women can

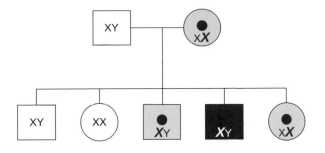

Figure 4.2   Female X-linked pedigree

pass the premutation to their offspring, but in males, it does not significantly increase in size (see Figure 4.3).

The sons of a male premutation carrier do not receive the X chromosome and are not affected. His daughters receive the premutation and are obligate premutation carriers. Their children are at risk of inheriting the full mutation. Heterozygous females who receive the full mutation from their mothers may have clinical features of fragile X syndrome. The transmission of the mutation through phenotypically normal daughters to their grandchildren (the so-called Sherman paradox or 'genetic anticipation') occurs when the disease severity increases through successive generations. About 30–35% of female premutation carriers have learning disabilities and emotional problems, and they are more likely to have similarly affected offspring than are intellectually normal carrier females.

NON-PHARMACEUTICAL INTERVENTIONS

General overview

So far, there is no cure available for the treatment of FXS. Although a multidisciplinary approach has been identified to be most helpful for the improvement of educational and behavioral problems in FXS, the scientific background for those interventions is still not satisfying. Despite the wealth of knowledge regarding the behavioral phenotype of FXS, there are almost no empirical studies on the effectiveness of behavioral treatments in patients with FXS (Reiss & Hall, 2007). Obviously, the lack of treatment studies severely restricts the specificity of treatment recommendations that can be made to patients with FXS and their families. Providers have therefore generally relied on their own clinical experience, in combination with an understanding of the above-mentioned factors shown to be associated with behavioral

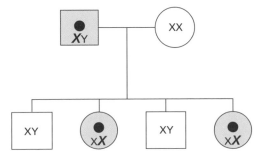

Figure 4.3   Male X-linked pedigree

problems in phenotype studies, to guide treatment approach. Clinical reports show that individuals with FXS benefit from medication therapy, speech and language intervention, behavioral approaches, and special education. Especially in the early years, the interventions appear to be most efficient for FXS children, including physical, speech, and sensory training, and the promotion of a routine for the child, which helps to reduce anxiety. Supporting parents and siblings with family education and genetic counseling is important to facilitate the acceptance and understanding of individuals with FXS. In older individuals, a cognitive-behavioral approach can be used for treatment of anxiety and depression. Banks (2006) describes the adjustment of classical psychotherapeutic approaches to people with learning disabilities (LD) and intellectual disabilities (ID). Dagnan et al. (2000) identify two distinct approaches to cognitive therapy that have been used with people with ID. The first is based on a 'deficit' model which assumes that emotional and behavioral difficulties are due to a lack of cognitive skills and process. The second approach is concerned with 'cognitive distortion' and has been developed from a psychotherapeutic tradition. In the classical cognitive-behavioral approaches, the cognitive processes are important in behavior modification, even in patients with ID. People with LD and ID have problems recognizing and labeling emotional states in themselves and others. Any treatment should be modified to suit the individual's level of functioning, using non-verbal materials, visual aids such as drawings, symbols, videos, photographs, and dolls, and role play.

Impact of the environment on development

Animal studies have shown that FMRP levels in rat brain regions undergoing active synaptogenesis can increase following exposure to a complex environment, such as exposure to various toys and objects (in comparison to standard housing) (Irwin et al., 2000). Restivo et al. (2005) later showed that *FMR1*-KO mice kept in standard cages were hyperactive, displayed an altered pattern of open-field exploration, and did not show habituation, whereas those in enriched environmental conditions rescued the behavioral abnormalities, as well as neuronal abnormalities in the hippocampus, selectively increasing AMPA activity and gene expression of GluR1 (glutamate receptor subunit 1).

The animal work and a motivation to discover environmental factors contributing to more favorable outcomes in children with fragile X syndrome led to a series of studies by Reiss and colleagues at the Behavioral Neurogenetic Research Center at Stanford (Dyer-Friedman et al., 2002; Glaser et al., 2003; Hessl et al., 2001, 2002, 2006). This group examined a large cohort of 120 sibling pairs (one with FXS and one normal with regard to *FMR1*) by visiting each family's home to collect data on the children, both parents, and the family environment using standardized tests as well as neuroendocrine measures related to stress, clinician interviews, and home observations. This program of research led to a number of important findings related to children with FXS and their families, having implications for intervention. First, the quality of the home environment (e.g. learning materials, exposure to culture and the arts, organization, parenting approaches, availability of materials, and space for play) was associated with both cognitive and behavioral outcomes, independent of FMRP, parental cognitive and psychiatric factors, and socioeconomic status (SES). Specifically, children with FXS living in a higher-quality home environment had higher IQ scores, better adaptive behavior and independence in daily-living skills, and less severe autistic symptoms. Secondly, children with fragile X syndrome, especially males, were found to have elevated levels of cortisol, a stress hormone regulated by the hypothalamic–pituitary–adrenal (HPA) axis. This elevation of cortisol was associated with more severe behavioral problems, especially internalizing symptoms and social problems. In a subsequent analysis, it was shown that cortisol reactivity was specifically related to gaze avoidance, one of the most common behavioral features of FXS. Thirdly, the quality of school interventions, as rated by the parents, was associated with severity of internalizing, externalizing, and autistic behaviors. Together, these studies suggest that interventions designed to support families in the home and to reduce stress-inducing stimuli might lead to positive developmental trajectories in children with FXS. In combination with the animal studies described above, the research studies to date suggest that improvements in behavior and brain morphology can result from environmental manipulation. Unfortunately, recent treatment efforts have focused primarily on psychopharmacological intervention. While these biologically based treatments are critical and carry a strong rationale, it seems likely that they would be significantly enhanced by also utilizing environmental interventions and behavioral techniques to optimize outcomes and facilitate further any CNS improvement that the drugs may provide.

Interventions for FXS with anxiety

As mentioned earlier, anxiety is very common in FXS. In a behavioral approach, the therapist can apply the techniques of systematic desensitization, fading, prompting, or chaining to reduce anxiety. However, researchers have suggested that it is necessary to modify the diagnostic criteria used to identify anxiety in people with intellectual disabilities (Bailey et al., 2000) and have highlighted that the cognitive and self-report elements of the diagnostic criteria can be hard to identify in people with more severe disabilities. Clinical guidelines clearly identify cognitive-behavioral interventions as the most effective psychological intervention to treat anxiety for people without intellectual disabilities. Anxiety is typically under-diagnosed in those

with FXS and the great majority of patients have more than one anxiety disorder when a standardized tool for measuring anxiety is used (Cordeiro et al., 2009).

The finding that children with FXS have heightened electrodermal responses to sensory stimuli (Miller et al., 1999) and elevated stress hormone levels which are related to severity of behavioral and social problems (Hessl et al., 2002, 2006) suggests that interventions aimed at reducing and better coping with stress and sensory input should result in better outcomes, but again, no treatment studies have been done to document this. Reiss and Hall (2007), in their review of assessment and treatment of FXS, provide examples of novel behavior modification interventions aimed at improving social eye contact and stress reduction, and have supported treatment models which combine behavioral intervention with experimental pharmacological or hormonal treatments which are supported by laboratory data. Studies comparing behavioral, targeted pharmacological and combined approaches are needed.

Some studies suggest an emphasis on the face-to-face contact in FXS, and try to force eye contact between the FXS individual and the teacher. However, studies linking social gaze abnormalities to elevated stress hormone levels and autonomic system reactivity suggest that direct eye gaze is experienced as aversive for individuals with FXS. Therefore, increasing direct eye gaze through behavioral intervention may need to be paired with stress- and anxiety-reduction training. Advantageous in a behavioral intervention in FXS are a good long-term memory, good imitation skills, and daily living skills, if acquired.

Interventions for FXS with autism symptoms

The state of the science in psychosocial treatment through behavioral interventions in autism has been comprehensively reviewed by an NIH-sponsored panel of national experts (Lord et al., 2005). This review offers important insights and recommendations that are applicable to behavioral treatment of individuals with FXS, because of the very high rates of autism and autistic-like behaviors. The authors emphasize that the traditional 1 hour per week treatments for language, social skills, or behavior, used in the US mental health and educational systems, are rarely sufficient to lead to generalized improvements in children with autism. This statement is probably reflective of the needs of FXS children with autism as well, although no empirical data are currently available to support this conclusion. The unique factors likely to be contributing to maladaptive behaviors in FXS— that is, anxiety, sensory overload, and inattention/impulsivity—would need to be fully appreciated by an equivalently trained behavioral intervention team. Lastly, there are several treatment models, including the Treatment and Education of Autistic and related Communication Handicapped Children (TEACCH) (Schopler et al., 1984) and the Denver models (Rogers et al., 2001a), Pivotal Response Training (Koegel et al., 2001), and Applied Behavior Analysis (ABA) (Smith et al., 2007) that are well-established in autism treatment (www.autismspeaks.org). These models, or aspects of these models, should be applied to groups of individuals with FXS, or perhaps more ideally those with FXS and autism to test their efficacy. In our clinical experience, these treatment programs have been helpful for many children with FXS and ASD.

Psychotherapy and counseling

Higher-functioning individuals with FXS can benefit from psychotherapy or counseling (Braden, 2000b; Hills-Epstein et al., 2002), although it should be noted that even many higher-functioning individuals may lack the insight, social skill, or executive function necessary to fully benefit from this type of treatment. This work can focus on anxiety reduction through desensitization, sexuality issues, management of depression usually through structured cognitive-behavioral approaches, and socialization issues. It is likely that structured and behavioral, or cognitive-behavioral approaches would lead to better outcomes than exploratory, patient-guided, or psychodynamic approaches. Many individuals with FXS who have autistic symptoms and social anxiety can also benefit from social skills-oriented group therapy (Braden, 2000a). A recent program to help behavioral problems and sexuality issues in adolescence and young adulthood was developed by the National Fragile X Foundation (NFXF) to guide professionals and the family and can be found at www.fragileX.org.

Most people with LD and ID live with their families, or in family-type groups, group homes or larger institutions. As with the other intervention approaches, only very little has been published about family therapy and systemic work, although these models are influential. Especially the concept of loss in various types needs to be addressed through the family life cycle. Most adults with FXS have problems with depression over the loss of their parents when they die. Loss is a frequent theme, with transitions such as graduating from high school or changing placements in adult life.

Intervention for FXS with aggression

Aggressive behavior in FXS is related to impulsivity, over-reactivity to stimuli, and mood instability. The individual appears to be uncontrollable, unpredictable, and violent. Often, their behavior may represent a desire to be left alone or to escape a threatening situation (Sabaratnam, 2006). In an overview by Epstein and colleagues (Epstein et al., 2002), behavior modification with counseling is suggested to manage aggression.

In every behavioral intervention, the short attention span and intellectual disability in FXS should be taken into account, and the special needs education should provide a structured environment with no distractions, a limited number of choices, and a developmental-age-appropriate learning schedule to reduce anxiety.

Adaptive skills

Usually, the interventional approaches in FXS focus on the development of academic skills such as reading, writing, and mathematics, but the resources may be needed to target behavioral disturbances, autism or limitations in independent daily living skills, and need to be shifted toward development of vocational skills, management of money, transportation, and other skills required for independent living, especially as the individual begins the transition from adolescence to adulthood. During that transition, individuals with FXS shift from a daily life typically structured by school and therapeutic services to a routine that varies widely across individuals. When school attendance is no longer required, and if there are few structured activities such as work or regular recreation, many individuals with FXS become more socially withdrawn, anxious, and isolated. Clinical experience suggests that continuing to provide a range of structured recreational, work, and social activities may protect the individual from a tendency toward social withdrawal or repetitive behaviors.

In a recent cross-sectional study, Bailey and colleagues described the functional skills of 981 individuals with FXS from birth to young adulthood (Bailey et al., 2009). The eating behavior shows a steady increase of skills with age. About 97% of males were using a spoon or fork by adulthood. More than 90% of males could remove their clothing and dress independently, but one-third were not able to tie their own shoelaces by adulthood. In general, females achieved the developmental milestones earlier. It was found that 93% of adults were able to use the toilet independently; however, only two-thirds of males could wipe themselves independently. Three-quarters of adult males were able to bath independently, and two-

thirds were able to use a toothbrush, compared with 94% and 86% of females, respectively. While 86% of males could speak in two- or three-word phrases, only 62% could speak fluently with complex sentences and only 59% could manage a conversation by adulthood. It was found that 89% of females could use complex sentences and 91% had conversational skills. Only 44% of males attained the ability to read simple picture books and just 19% could read books with new concepts and words, in contrast to 76% of females. Regression analyses showed that a number of different characteristics— including thinking, reasoning, and learning ability; ability to pay attention; and total number of co-occurring conditions—were associated with functional skill attainment for males and females. Rates and trajectories of the achievement of skills in each of these areas can be found in Bailey et al. (2009).

A study by Mirrett and Roberts gives an excellent overview of adaptive functioning and early interventions in boys with FXS, interviewing 51 speech and language therapists who provide services for FXS (Mirrett et al., 2003). They emphasize the necessity of environmental accommodations for interventions, taking into account the limited attention span, difficulties with topic and activity transitions, sensory deficits, and low threshold for anxiety in FXS.

CONCLUSION

There has been rapid advancement in the understanding of the neurobiology, genetics, and behavioral and cognitive phenotype of FXS, and only recently have targeted treatments been initiated. Unfortunately, the state of the science in behavioral treatment, or non-pharmacological treatment of FXS across the life span, is weak, and little empirical information exists to confidently guide treatment and inform families and educational professionals. Even when medications are eventually proven to help normalize brain function in patients with FXS, there will be a need for effective behavioral or environmental interventions to help translate the normalized brain function into positive cognitive and behavioral outcomes, especially in older individuals who have already had many years of altered sensory, cognitive, and social experiences. As with the targeted pharmacological trials now underway, in the near future it will be necessary to conduct collaborative multisite studies to carry out the standardized behavioral treatments of individuals with FXS.

Although large behavioral treatment studies of individuals with FXS are difficult, well-designed multiple baseline individual subject studies are quite feasible and can yield convincing accounts of efficacy with relatively few participants. Weiskop et al. (2005) used such a design to investigate a parent training program to reduce sleep problems in children with autism ($n = 6$) and FXS ($n = 5$). Although the study was small, the program appeared generally successful and provides a good model for other multiple baseline studies that could be accomplished to focus on aggression, self-injury, and other maladaptive behaviors.

There is currently a strong push to develop and test novel psychopharmacological agents such as metabotropic glutamate receptor 5 (mGluR5) antagonists and γ-aminobutyric acid (GABA) agonists in patients with FXS, and several mainline medications such as atypical antipsychotics, stimulants and SSRIs are, or will be, tested in the near future. However, it is our impression that successful treatment of individuals with FXS will also depend on well-designed behavioral interventions or environmental manipulations or teaching approaches that can be used both independently and in concert with proven psychopharmacological agents. Indeed, effective learning and management of behaviors could work synergistically with medications that normalize brain function and lead to the most optimal outcomes. Therefore, carefully designed studies to evaluate these behaviorally- and environmentally-based interventions are urgently needed.

ACKNOWLEDGMENTS

This work was supported by National Institute of Health Grants MH 078041, HD 036071, HD02274, and MH 77554; National Institute on Aging grants AG032119 and AG032115 90DD05969; and support from the Health and Human Services Administration of Developmental Disabilities. We also thank Randi Hagerman MD and the UC Davis M.I.N.D. Institute.

REFERENCES

Abbeduto, L., Seltzer, M.M., Shattuck, P., Krauss, M.W., Orsmond, G., & Murphy, M.M. (2004) 'Psychological well-being and coping in mothers of youths with autism, Down syndrome, or fragile X syndrome', *Am J Ment Retard,* 109(3): 237–254.

Allen, E.G., He, W., Yadav-Shah, M., & Sherman, S.L. (2004) 'A study of the distributional characteristics of FMR1 transcript levels in 238 individuals', *Hum Genet,* 114(5): 439–447.

Amiri, K., Hagerman, R.J., & Hagerman, P.J. (2008) 'Fragile X-associated tremor/ataxia syndrome: an aging face of the fragile X gene', *Arch Neurol,* 65(1): 19–25.

Angkustsiri, K., Wirojanan, J., Deprey, L.J., Gane, L.W., & Hagerman, R.J. (2008) 'Fragile X syndrome with anxiety disorder and exceptional verbal intelligence', *Am J Med Genet A,* 146(3): 376–379.

Aziz, M., Stathopulu, E., Callias, M., Taylor, C., Turk, J., Oostra, B. et al. (2003) 'Clinical features of boys with fragile X premutations and intermediate alleles', *Am J Med Genet,* 121B(1): 119–127.

Bacalman, S., Farzin, F., Bourgeois, J.A., Cogswell, J., Goodlin-Jones, B.L., Gane, L.W. et al. (2006) 'Psychiatric phenotype of the fragile X-associated tremor/ataxia syndrome (FXTAS) in males: newly described fronto-subcortical dementia', *J Clin Psychiatry,* 67(1): 87–94.

Bailey, D.B., Jr, Hatton, D.D., & Skinner, M. (1998) 'Early developmental trajectories of males with fragile X syndrome', *Am J Ment Retard,* 103(1): 29–39.

Bailey, D.B., Jr, Hatton, D.D., Mesibov, G.B., Ament, N., & Skinner, M. (2000) 'Early development, temperament and functional impairment in autism and fragile X syndrome', *J Autism Dev Disord,* 30(1): 49–59.

Bailey, D.B., Jr, Hatton, D.D., Skinner, M., & Mesibov, G.B. (2001) 'Autistic behavior, FMR1 protein, and developmental trajectories in young males with fragile X syndrome', *J Autism Dev Disord,* 31(2): 165–174.

Bailey, D.B., Raspa, M., Holiday, D., Bishop, E., & Olmsted, M. (2009) 'Functional skills of individuals with fragile X syndrome: a lifespan cross-sectional analysis', *Am J Intellect Dev Disabil,* 114(4): 289–303.

Banks, R. (2006) 'Psychotherapeutic interventions for people with learning disabilities—learning disability. Part 2 of 2. *Psychiatry,* 5(10): 363–367.

Baron-Cohen, S., Wheelwright, S., Hill, J., Raste, Y., & Plumb, I. (2001) 'The 'Reading the mind in the eyes' Test revised version: a study with normal adults, and adults with Asperger syndrome or high-functioning autism', *J Child Psychol Psychiatry,* 42(2): 241–251.

Beadle-Brown, J., Murphy, G., Wing, L., Gould, J., Shah, A., & Holmes, N. (2000) 'Changes in skills for people with intellectual disability: a follow-up of the Camberwell Cohort', *J Intellect Disabil Res,* 44(Pt 1): 12–24.

Belser, R.C. & Sudhalter, V. (2001) 'Conversational characteristics of children with fragile X syndrome: repetitive speech', *Am J Ment Retard,* 106(1): 28–38.

Berry-Kravis, E. (2002) 'Epilepsy in fragile X syndrome', *Developmental Medicine and Child Neurology,* 44(11): 724–728.

Bolte, S., Adam-Schwebe, S., Englert, E., Schmeck, K., & Poustka, F. (2000) [Utilization of psychological tests for diagnosis in German child and adolescent psychiatry: results of a survey]. *Z Kinder Jugendpsychiatr Psychother,* 28(3): 151–161. [in German]

Borghgraef, M., Umans, S., Steyaert, J., Legius, E., & Fryns, J.P. (1996) 'New findings in the behavioral profile of young FraX females', *Am J Med Genet,* 64(2), 346–349.

Borghgraef, M., Van Buggenhout, G., Volcke, P., De Vos, B., Steyaert, J., Maes, B. et al. (2002) 'Aging in fragile X: followup data in adult fragile X males'. The National Fragile X Foundation's 8th International Fragile X Conference, Hosted by The Fragile X Resource Group of Greater Chicago, Chicago, Illinois, July 17–21, 2002, Conference Proceedings, p. 123.

Borthwick-Duffy, S.A. (1994) 'Epidemiology and prevalence of psychopathology in people with mental retardation', *J Consult Clin Psychol,* 62(1), 17–27.

Bourgeois, J.A., Cogswell, J.B., Hessl, D., Zhang, L., Ono, M.Y., Tassone, F. et al. (2007) 'Cognitive, anxiety and mood disorders in the fragile X-associated tremor/ataxia syndrome', *Gen Hosp Psychiatry,* 29(4): 349–356.

Bourgeois, J.A., Coffey, S.M., Rivera, S.M., Hessl, D., Gane, L.W., Tassone, F. et al. (2009) 'A review of fragile X premutation disorders: expanding the psychiatric perspective', *J Clin Psychiatry,* 70(6), 852–862.

Braden, M.L. (2000a) 'Education', in J. Weber (ed.), *Children with Fragile X Syndrome: A Parent's Guide.* Bethesda, MD: Woodbine House, pp. 243–305.

Braden, M.L. (2000b) *Fragile, Handle with Care: More about Fragile X Syndrome, Adolescents and Adults.* Dillon, Co: Spectra Publishing Co.

Brouwer, J.R., Mientjes, E.J., Bakker, C.E., Nieuwenhuizen, I.M., Severijnen, L.A., Van der Linde, H.C. et al. (2007) 'Elevated Fmr1 mRNA levels and reduced protein expression in a mouse model with an unmethylated Fragile X full mutation', *Exp Cell Res,* 313(2): 244–253.

Brun, C., Obiols, J.E., Cheema, A., O'Connor, R., & Hagerman, R.J. (1995) 'Longitudinal IQ changes in fragile X females', *Developmental Brain Dysfunction,* 8: 280–292.

Coffey, S.M., Cook, K., Tartaglia, N., Tassone, F., Nguyen, D.V., Pan, R. et al. (2008) 'Expanded clinical phenotype of women with the FMR1 premutation', *Am J Med Genet A,* 146(8): 1009–1016.

Cohen, I.L., Fisch, G.S., Sudhalter, V., Wolf-Schein, E.G., Hanson, D., Hagerman, R.J. et al. (1988) 'Social gaze, social avoidance, and repetitive behavior in fragile X males: a controlled study', *Am J Ment Retard,* 92(5): 436–446.

Conners, C.K., Erhardt, D., & Sparrow, E. (1999) *Conners' Adult ADHD Rating Scales (CAARS) Technical Manual.* North Tonawanda, NY: Multi-Health Systems, Inc.

Cordeiro, L., Ballinger, E., Hagerman, R.J., & Hessl, D. (2009) 'Anxiety in fragile X syndrome: clinical assessment, characterization and prevalence'. Paper presented at the 14th International Workshop on Fragile X and X-Linked Mental Retardation Praia do Forte, September 15–19, 2009, Bahia, Brazil.

Cornish, K.M., Munir, F., & Cross, G. (2001) 'Differential impact of the FMR-1 full mutation on memory and attention functioning: a neuropsychological perspective', *J Cogn Neurosci,* 13(1): 144–150.

Cornish, K.M., Sudhalter, V., & Turk, J. (2004) 'Attention and language in fragile X', *Ment Retard Dev Disabil Res Rev,* 10(1): 11–16.

Cornish, K.M., Burack, J.A., Rahman, A., Munir, F., Russo, N., & Grant, C. (2005a). 'Theory of mind deficits in children with fragile X syndrome', *J Intellect Disabil Res,* 49(Pt 5): 372–378.

Cornish, K.M., Kogan, C., Turk, J., Manly, T., James, N., Mills, A. et al. (2005b) 'The emerging fragile X premutation phenotype: evidence from the domain of social cognition', *Brain Cogn,* 57(1): 53–60.

Cornish, K.M., Li, L., Kogan, C.S., Jacquemont, S., Turk, J., Dalton, A. et al. (2008) 'Age-dependent cognitive changes in carriers of the fragile X syndrome', *Cortex,* 44(6): 628–636.

Cornish, K.M., Kogan, C.S., Li, L., Turk, J., Jacquemont, S., & Hagerman, R.J. (2009) 'Lifespan changes in working memory in fragile X premutation males', *Brain Cogn,* 69(3): 551–558.

Dagnan, D., Chadwick P., & Proudlove, J. (2000) 'Toward an assessment of suitability of people with mental retardation for cognitive therapy', *Cognitive Therapy and Research,* 24(6): 627–636.

Dalton, K.M., Holsen, L., Abbeduto, L., & Davidson, R.J. (2008) 'Brain function and gaze fixation during facial-emotional processing in fragile X and autism', *Autism Research,* 1: 231–239.

Dyer-Friedman, J., Glaser, B., Hessl, D., Johnston, C., Huffman, L.C., Taylor, A. et al. (2002) 'Genetic and environmental influences on the cognitive outcomes of children with fragile X syndrome', *J Am Acad Child Adolesc Psychiatry,* 41(3): 237–244.

Einfeld, S., Tonge, B., & Turner, G. (1999) 'Longitudinal course of behavioral and emotional problems in fragile X syndrome', *Am J Med Genet,* 87(5), 436–439.

Entezam, A., Biacsi, R., Orrison, B., Saha, T., Hoffman, G.E., Grabczyk, E. et al. (2007) 'Regional FMRP deficits and large repeat expansions into the full mutation range in a new Fragile X premutation mouse model', *Gene,* 395(1–2): 125–134.

Epstein, J., Riley, K., & Sobesky, W. (2002) 'The treatment of emotional and behavioral problems', in R. Hagerman & P. Hagerman (eds), *Fragile X Syndrome: Diagnosis, Treatment, and Research,* 3rd edn. Baltimore: Johns Hopkins University Press, pp. 339–362.

Farzin, F., Perry, H., Hessl, D., Loesch, D., Cohen, J., Bacalman, S. et al. (2006) 'Autism spectrum disorders and attention-deficit/hyperactivity disorder in boys with the fragile X premutation', *J Dev Behav Pediatr,* 27(2 Suppl): S137–144.

Farzin, F., Whitney, D., Hagerman, R.J., & Rivera, S.M. (2008) 'Contrast detection in infants with fragile X syndrome', *Vision Res,* 48(13): 1471–1478.

Farzin, F., Rivera, S.M., & Hessl, D. (2009) 'Brief report: visual processing of faces in individuals with fragile X syndrome: an eye tracking study', *J Autism Dev Disord,* 39(6): 946–952.

Fernandez-Carvajal, I., Walichiewicz, P., Xiaosen, X., Pan, R., Hagerman, P.J., & Tassone, F. (2009) 'Screening for expanded alleles of the FMR1 gene in blood spots from newborn males in a Spanish population', *J Mol Diagn,* 11(4): 324–329.

Fisch, G.S., Shapiro, L.R., Simensen, R., Schwartz, C.E., Fryns, J.P., Borghgraef, M. et al. (1992) 'Longitudinal changes in IQ among fragile X males: clinical evidence of more than one mutation?', *Am J Med Genet,* 43(1–2): 28–34.

Fisch, G.S., Simensen, R., Arinami, T., Borghgraef, M., & Fryns, J.P. (1994) 'Longitudinal changes in IQ among fragile X females: a preliminary multicenter analysis', *Am J Med Genet,* 51(4): 353–357.

Fisch, G.S., Simensen, R., Tarleton, J., Chalifoux, M., Holden, J.J., Carpenter, N. et al. (1996) 'Longitudinal study of cognitive abilities and adaptive behavior levels in fragile X males: a prospective multicenter analysis', *Am J Med Genet,* 64(2): 356–361.

Fisch, G.S., Simensen, R.J., & Schroer, R.J. (2002) 'Longitudinal changes in cognitive and adaptive behavior scores in children and adolescents with the fragile X mutation or autism', *J Autism Dev Disord,* 32(2): 107–114.

Flanagan, T., Enns, J.T., Murphy, M.M., Russo, N., Abbeduto, L., Randolph, B. et al. (2007) 'Differences in visual orienting between persons with Down or fragile X syndrome', *Brain Cogn,* 65(1), 128–134.

Franke, P., Leboyer, M., Gansicke, M., Weiffenbach, O., Biancalana, V., Cornillet-Lefebre, P. et al. (1998) 'Genotype–phenotype relationship in female carriers of the premutation and full mutation of FMR-1', *Psychiatry Res,* 80(2): 113–127.

Freund, L.S. & Reiss, A.L. (1991) 'Cognitive profiles associated with the fra(X) syndrome in males and females', *Am J Med Genet,* 38(4): 542–547.

Garcia-Nonell, C., Ratera, E.R., Harris, S., Hessl, D., Ono, M.Y., Tartaglia, N. et al. (2008) 'Secondary medical diagnosis in fragile X syndrome with and without autism spectrum disorder', *Am J Med Genet A,* 146A(15): 1911–1916.

Garner, C., Callias, M., & Turk, J. (1999) 'Executive function and theory of mind performance of boys with fragile-X syndrome', *J Intellect Disabil Res,* 43(Pt 6): 466–474.

Garrett, A.S., Menon, V., MacKenzie, K., & Reiss, A.L. (2004) 'Here's looking at you, kid: neural systems underlying face and gaze processing in fragile X syndrome', *Arch Gen Psychiatry,* 61(3): 281–288.

Gatz, M. (2007) 'Genetics, dementia, and the elderly', *Curr Direct Psychol Sci,* 16(3): 123–127.

Gilchrist, A., Green, J., Cox, A., Burton, D., Rutter, M., & Le Couteur, A. (2001) 'Development and current functioning in adolescents with Asperger syndrome: a comparative study', *J Child Psychol Psychiatry,* 42(2): 227–240.

Gillberg, C. & Steffenburg, S. (1987) 'Outcome and prognostic factors in infantile autism and similar conditions: a population-based study of 46 cases followed through puberty', *J Autism Dev Disord*, 17(2): 273–287.

Glaser, B., Hessl, D., Dyer-Friedman, J., Johnston, C., Wisbeck, J., Taylor, A. et al. (2003) 'Biological and environmental contributions to adaptive behavior in fragile X syndrome', *Am J Med Genet A*, 117(1): 21–29.

Goodlin-Jones, B., Tassone, F., Gane, L.W., & Hagerman, R.J. (2004) 'Autistic spectrum disorder and the fragile X premutation', *J Dev Behav Pediatr*, 25(6): 392–398.

Greco, C., Tassone, F., Jacquemont, S., Hagerman, R.J., Sahota, P.K., Delacourte, A. et al. (2003) 'Intranuclear neuronal inclusions in two female carriers of the fragile X premutation', 53rd Annual Meeting, Los Angeles, CA., *Am J Hum Genetics*. 73(Suppl) (5):A2452:586.

Greco, C.M., Berman, R.F., Martin, R.M., Tassone, F., Schwartz, P.H., Chang, A. et al. (2006) 'Neuropathology of fragile X-associated tremor/ataxia syndrome (FXTAS)', *Brain*, 129(Pt 1): 243–255.

Grigsby, J., Brega, A.G., Engle, K., Leehey, M.A., Hagerman, R.J., Tassone, F., et al. (2008) 'Cognitive profile of fragile X premutation carriers with and without fragile X-associated tremor/ataxia syndrome', *Neuropsychology*, 22(1): 48–60.

Grossman, A.W., Churchill, J.D., McKinney, B.C., Kodish, I.M., Otte, S.L., & Greenough, W.T. (2003) 'Experience effects on brain development: possible contributions to psychopathology', *J Child Psychol Psychiatry*, 44(1): 33–63.

Hagan, C.C., Hoeft, F., Mackey, A., Mobbs, D., & Reiss, A.L. (2008) 'Aberrant neural function during emotion attribution in female subjects with fragile X syndrome', *J Am Acad Child Adolesc Psychiatry*, 47(12): 1443–1354.

Hagerman, P.J. (2008) 'The fragile X prevalence paradox', *J Med Genet*, 45(8): 498–499.

Hagerman, P.J. & Hagerman, R.J. (2004) 'The fragile-X premutation: a maturing perspective', *Am J Hum Genet*, 74(5): 805–816.

Hagerman, P.J. & Hagerman, R.J. (2007) 'Fragile X-associated tremor/ataxia syndrome—an older face of the fragile X gene', *Nat Clin Pract Neurol*, 3(2): 107–112.

Hagerman, R.J. (2002) 'Physical and behavioral phenotype', in R.J. Hagerman & P.J. Hagerman (eds), *Fragile X Syndrome: Diagnosis, Treatment and Research*, 3rd edn. Baltimore: Johns Hopkins University Press, pp. 3–109.

Hagerman, R.J. & Hagerman, P.J. (2002) *Fragile X Syndrome: Diagnosis, Treatment, and Research, 3rd edn*. Baltimore: Johns Hopkins University Press.

Hagerman, R.J., McBogg, P., & Hagerman, P.J. (1983) 'The fragile X syndrome: history, diagnosis, and treatment', *J Developmental & Behavioral Pediatrics*, 4(2): 122–130.

Hagerman, R.J., Kemper, M., & Hudson, M. (1985) 'Learning disabilities and attentional problems in boys with the fragile X syndrome', *Am J Dis Child*, 139(7): 674–678.

Hagerman, R.J., Schreiner, R.A., Kemper, M.B., Wittenberger, M.D., Zahn, B., & Habicht, K. (1989) 'Longitudinal IQ changes in fragile X males', *Am J Med Genet A*, 33(4): 513–518.

Hagerman, R.J., Greco, C., Chudley, A., Leehey, M., Tassone, F., Grigsby, J. et al. (2001a). 'Neuropathology and neurodegenerative features in some older male premutation carriers'. Paper presented at the 10th International Workshop on Fragile X Syndrome and X Linked Mental Retardation, Frascati, Italy, September 19–22.

Hagerman, R.J., Leehey, M., Heinrichs, W., Tassone, F., Wilson, R., Hills, J. et al. (2001b) 'Intention tremor, parkinsonism, and generalized brain atrophy in male carriers of fragile X', *Neurology*, 57: 127–130.

Hagerman, R.J., Goodlin-Jones, B.L., Spence, S., Albrect, L., Bacalman, S., Tassone, F. et al. (2002) 'The fragile X premutation and autistic spectrum disorders', *Am J Hum Genet*, *Suppl 71* A679(4): 287.

Hagerman, R.J., Leavitt, B.R., Farzin, F., Jacquemont, S., Greco, C.M., Brunberg, J.A., et al. (2004) 'Fragile-X-associated tremor/ataxia syndrome (FXTAS) in females with the *FMR1* premutation', *Am J Hum Genet*, 74(5): 1051–1056.

Hagerman, R.J., Hall, D.A., Coffey, S., Leehey, M., Bourgeois, J., Gould, J. et al. (2008) 'Treatment of fragile X-associated tremor ataxia syndrome (FXTAS) and related neurological problems', *Clin Interv Aging*, 3(2): 251–262.

Hagerman, R.J., Berry-Kravis, E., Kaufmann, W.E., Ono, M.Y., Tartaglia, N., Lachiewicz, A. et al. (2009) 'Advances in the treatment of fragile X syndrome', *Pediatrics*, 123(1): 378–390.

Hall, S.S., Burns, D.D., Lightbody, A.A., & Reiss, A.L. (2008) 'Longitudinal changes in intellectual development in children with fragile X syndrome, '*J Abnorm Child Psychol*, 36(6): 927–939.

Harris SW, Hessl D, Goodlin-Jones B, Ferranti J, Bacalman S, Barbato I, Tassone F, Hagerman PJ, Herman H, Hagerman RJ. (2008). 'Autism profiles of males with fragile X syndrome', *Am J Ment Retard*.;113 (6):427–38.

Hatton, D., Hooper, S.R., Bailey, D.B., Skinner, M.L., Sullivan, K.M., & Wheeler, A. (2002) 'Problem behavior in boys with fragile X syndrome', *Am J Med Genet,* 108(2): 105–116.

Hatton, D.D., Sideris, J., Skinner, M., Mankowski, J., Bailey, D.B., Jr., Roberts, J.E. et al. (2006) 'Autistic behavior in children with fragile X syndrome: prevalence, stability, and the impact of FMRP', *Am J Med Genet A,* 140(17): 1804–1813.

Hessl, D., Dyer-Friedman, J., Glaser, B., Wisbeck, J., Barajas, R.G., Taylor, A. et al. (2001) 'The influence of environmental and genetic factors on behavior problems and autistic symptoms in boys and girls with fragile X syndrome', *Pediatrics,* 108(5): E88.

Hessl, D., Glaser, B., Dyer-Friedman, J., Blasey, C., Hastie, T., Gunnar, M. et al. (2002) 'Cortisol and behavior in fragile X syndrome,' *Psychoneuroendocrinology,* 27(7): 855–872.

Hessl, D., Tassone, F., Loesch, D.Z., Berry-Kravis, E., Leehey, M.A., Gane, L.W. et al. (2005) 'Abnormal elevation of FMR1 mRNA is associated with psychological symptoms in individuals with the fragile X premutation', *Am J Med Genet B Neuropsychiatr Genet,* 139(1): 115–121.

Hessl, D., Glaser, B., Dyer-Friedman, J., & Reiss, A.L. (2006) 'Social behavior and cortisol reactivity in children with fragile X syndrome', *J Child Psychol Psychiatry,* 47(6): 602–610.

Hessl, D., Rivera, S., Koldewyn, K., Cordeiro, L., Adams, J., Tassone, F. et al. (2007) 'Amygdala dysfunction in men with the fragile X premutation', *Brain,* 130(Pt 2): 404–416.

Hessl, D., Tassone, F., Cordeiro, L., Koldewyn, K., McCormick, C., Green, C. et al. (2009) 'Brief report: aggression and stereotypic behavior in males with fragile X syndrome—moderating secondary genes in a "single gene" disorder', *J Autism Dev Disord,* 38(1): 184–189.

Hessl, D., Nguyen, D., Green, C., Chavez, A., Tassone, F., Hagerman, R. et al. (2009) 'A solution to limitations of cognitive testing in children with intellectual disabilities: the case of fragile X syndrome', *J Neurodev Disord,* 1(1): 33–45.

Hills-Epstein, J., Riley, K., & Sobesky, W. (2002) 'The treatment of emotional and behavioral problems', in R.J. Hagerman & P.J. Hagerman (eds), *Fragile X Syndrome: Diagnosis, Treatment, and Research, 3rd edn.* Baltimore: Johns Hopkins University Press, pp. 339–362.

Hodapp, R.M., Dykens, E.M., Ort, S.I., Zelinsky, D.G., & Leckman, J.F. (1991) 'Changing patterns of intellectual strengths and weaknesses in males with fragile X syndrome', *J Autism Dev Disord,* 21(4): 503–516.

Holsen, L.M., Dalton, K.M., Johnstone, T., & Davidson, R.J. (2008) 'Prefrontal social cognition network dysfunction underlying face encoding and social anxiety in fragile X syndrome', *Neuroimage,* 43(3): 592–604.

Hunter, J.E., Allen, E.G., Abramowitz, A., Rusin, M., Leslie, M., Novak, G. et al. (2008a) 'Investigation of phenotypes associated with mood and anxiety among male and female fragile X premutation carriers', *Behav Genet,* 38(5): 493–502.

Hunter, J.E., Allen, E.G., Abramowitz, A., Rusin, M., Leslie, M., Novak, G. et al. (2008b) 'No evidence for a difference in neuropsychological profile among carriers and noncarriers of the FMR1 premutation in adults under the age of 50', *Am J Hum Genet,* 83(6): 692–702.

Irwin, S.A., Swain, R.A., Christmon, C.A., Chakravarti, A., Weiler, I.J., & Greenough, W.T. (2000) 'Evidence for altered Fragile-X mental retardation protein expression in response to behavioral stimulation [corrected and republished with original paging, article originally printed in *Neurobiol Learn Mem* 2000; 73(1): 87–93]. *Neurobiol Learn Mem,* 74(1): 87–93.

Jacquemont, S., Hagerman, R.J., Leehey, M., Grigsby, J., Zhang, L., Brunberg, J.A. et al. (2003) 'Fragile X premutation tremor/ataxia syndrome: molecular, clinical, and neuroimaging correlates', *Am J Hum Genet,* 72(4): 869–878.

Jacquemont, S., Farzin, F., Hall, D., Leehey, M., Tassone, F., Gane, L. et al. (2004a) 'Aging in individuals with the FMR1 mutation', *Am J Ment Retard,* 109(2): 154–164.

Jacquemont, S., Hagerman, R.J., Leehey, M.A., Hall, D.A., Levine, R.A., Brunberg, J.A. et al. (2004b) 'Penetrance of the fragile X-associated tremor/ataxia syndrome in a premutation carrier population', *JAMA,* 291(4): 460–469.

Jakala, P., Hanninen, T., Ryynanen, M., Laakso, M., Partanen, K., Mannermaa, A. et al. (1997) 'Fragile-X: neuropsychological test performance, CGG triplet repeat lengths, and hippocampal volumes', *J Clin Invest,* 100(2): 331–338.

Johnston, C., Eliez, S., Dyer-Friedman, J., Hessl, D., Glaser, B., Blasey, C. et al. (2001) 'Neurobehavioral phenotype in carriers of the fragile X premutation', *Am J Med Genet,* 103(4): 314–319.

Johnston, C., Hessl, D., Blasey, C., Eliez, S., Erba, H., Dyer-Friedman, J. et al. (2003) 'Factors associated with parenting stress in mothers of children with fragile X syndrome', *J Dev Behav Pediatr,* 24(4): 267–275.

Kaufmann, W.E., Abrams, M.T., Chen, W., & Reiss, A.L. (1999) 'Genotype, molecular phenotype, and cognitive phenotype: correlations in fragile X syndrome', *Am J Med Genet,* 83(4): 286–295.

Kenneson, A., Zhang, F., Hagedorn, C.H., & Warren, S.T. (2001) 'Reduced FMRP and increased FMR1 transcription is proportionally associated with CGG repeat number in intermediate-length and premutation carriers', *Hum Mol Genet,* 10(14): 1449–1454.

Kobayashi, R. & Murata, T. (1998) 'Behavioral characteristics of 187 young adults with autism', *Psychiatry Clin Neurosci,* 52(4): 383–390.

Koegel, R.L., Koegel, L.K., & McNerney, E.K. (2001) 'Pivotal areas in intervention for autism', *J Clin Child Psychol,* 30(1): 19–32.

Kogan, C.S., Bertone, A., Cornish, K.M., Boutet, I., Der Kaloustian, V.M., Andermann, E. et al. (2004a) 'Integrative cortical dysfunction and pervasive motion perception deficit in fragile X syndrome', *Neurology,* 63(9): 1634–1639.

Kogan, C.S., Boutet, I., Cornish, K.M., Zangenehpour, S., Mullen, K.T., Holden, J.J. et al. (2004b), 'Differential impact of the FMR1 gene on visual processing in fragile X syndrome', *Brain,* 127(Pt 3): 591–601.

Koldewyn, K., Hessl, D., Adams, J., Tassone, F., Hagerman, R.J., Hagerman, P.J. et al. (2008) 'Reduced hippocampal activation during recall is associated with elevated FMR1 mRNA and psychiatric symptoms in men with the fragile X premutation', *Brain Imaging Behav,* 2(2): 105–116.

Kwok, H. & Cheung, P.W. (2007) 'Co-morbidity of psychiatric disorder and medical illness in people with intellectual disabilities', *Curr Opin Psychiatry,* 20(5): 443–449.

Lachiewicz, A.M., Gullion, C., Spiridigliozzi, G., & Aylsworth, A. (1987) 'Declining IQs of young males with the fragile X syndrome', *Am J Ment Retard,* 92: 272–278.

Leehey, M.A., Berry-Kravis, E., Goetz, C.G., Zhang, L., Hall, D.A., Li, L. et al. (2007) 'FMR1 CGG repeat length predicts motor dysfunction in premutation carriers', *Neurology,* 70(16 Pt 2): 1397–1402.

Lewis, P., Abbeduto, L., Murphy, M., Richmond, E., Giles, N., Bruno, L. et al. (2006) 'Psychological well-being of mothers of youth with fragile X syndrome: syndrome specificity and within-syndrome variability', *J Intellect Disabil Res,* 50(Pt 12): 894–904.

Loesch, D.Z. & Hay, D.A. (1988) 'Clinical features and reproductive patterns in fragile X female heterozygotes', *J Med Genet,* 25: 407–414.

Loesch, D.Z., Huggins, R.M., & Hagerman, R.J. (2004) 'Phenotypic variation and FMRP levels in fragile X', *Ment Retard Dev Disabil Res Rev,* 10(1): 31–41.

Lord, C., Rutter, M., & Le Couteur, A. (1994) 'Autism Diagnostic Interview-Revised: a revised version of a diagnostic interview for caregivers of individuals with possible pervasive developmental disorders', *J Autism Dev Disord,* 24(5): 659–685.

Lord, C., Wagner, A., Rogers, S., Szatmari, P., Aman, M., Charman, T. et al. (2005) 'Challenges in evaluating psychosocial interventions for Autistic Spectrum Disorders', *J Autism Dev Disord,* 35(6): 695–708; discussion 709–611.

McConkie-Rosell, A., Spiridigliozzi, G.A., Sullivan, J.A., Dawson, D.V., & Lachiewicz, A.M. (2000) 'Carrier testing in fragile X syndrome: effect on self-concept', *Am J Med Genet,* 92(5): 336–342.

McConkie-Rosell, A., Spiridigliozzi, G.A., Sullivan, J.A., Dawson, D.V., & Lachiewicz, A.M. (2001) 'Longitudinal study of the carrier testing process for fragile X syndrome: perceptions and coping', *Am J Med Genet,* 98(1), 37–45.

Mazzocco, M.M.M., Myers, G.F., Hamner, J.L., Panoscha, R., Shapiro, B.K., & Reiss, A.L. (1998) 'The prevalence of the FMR1 and FMR2 mutations amoung preschool children with language delay', *J Pediatr,* 132: 795–801.

Miller, L.J., McIntosh, D.N., McGrath, J., Shyu, V., Lampe, M., Taylor, A.K. et al. (1999) 'Electrodermal responses to sensory stimuli in individuals with fragile X syndrome: a preliminary report', *Am J Med Genet,* 83(4): 268–279.

Mirrett, P.L., Roberts, J.E., & Price, J. (2003) 'Early intervention practices and communication intervention strategies for young males with fragile X syndrome', *Lang Speech Hear Serv Sch,* 34(4): 320–331.

Moeschler, J.B. & Shevell, M. (2006) 'Clinical genetic evaluation of the child with mental retardation or developmental delays', *Pediatrics,* 117(6): 2304–2316.

Moore, C.J., Daly, E.M., Schmitz, N., Tassone, F., Tysoe, C., Hagerman, R.J. et al. (2004) 'A neuropsychological investigation of male premutation carriers of fragile X syndrome', *Neuropsychologia,* 42(14): 1934–1947.

Munir, F., Cornish, K.M., & Wilding, J. (2000) 'A neuropsychological profile of attention deficits in young males with fragile X syndrome', *Neuropsychologia,* 38(9): 1261–1270.

Piven, J., Harper, J., Palmer, P., & Arndt, S. (1996) 'Course of behavioral change in autism: a retrospective study of high-IQ adolescents and adults', *J Am Acad Child Adolesc Psychiatry,* 35(4): 523–529.

Qin, M., Kang, J., Burlin, T.V., Jiang, C., & Smith, C.B. (2005) 'Postadolescent changes in regional cerebral protein synthesis: an in vivo study in the FMR1 null mouse', *J Neurosci,* 25(20): 5087–5095.

Reiss, A.L. & Dant, C.C. (2003) 'The behavioral neurogenetics of fragile X syndrome: analyzing gene–brain–behavior relationships in child developmental psychopathologies', *Dev Psychopathol,* 15(4): 927–968.

Reiss, A.L. & Hall, S.S. (2007) 'Fragile X syndrome: assessment and treatment implications', *Child Adolesc Psychiatr Clin N Am,* 16(3): 663–675.

Reiss, A.L., Freund, L., Vinogradov, S., Hagerman, R.J., & Cronister, A. (1989) 'Parental inheritance and psychological disability in fragile X females', *Am J Hum Genet,* 45(5): 697–705.

Restivo, L., Ferrari, F., Passino, E., Sgobio, C., Bock, J., Oostra, B.A. et al. (2005) 'Enriched environment promotes behavioral and morphological recovery in a mouse model for the fragile X syndrome', *Proc Natl Acad Sci U S A,* 102(32): 11557–11562.

Rivera, S.M., Menon, V., White, C.D., Glaser, B., & Reiss, A.L. (2002) 'Functional brain activation during arithmetic processing in females with fragile X syndrome is related to FMR1 protein expression', *Hum Brain Mapp,* 16: 206–218.

Roberts, J.E., Bailey, D.B., Jr, Mankowski, J., Ford, A., Sideris, J., Weisenfeld, L.A. et al. (2009) 'Mood and anxiety disorders in females with the FMR1 premutation', *Am J Med Genet B Neuropsychiatr Genet,* 150B(1): 130–139.

Rogers, S.J., Hall, T., Osaki, D., Reaven, J., & Herbison, J. (2001a) 'The Denver model: a comprehensive, integrated educational approach to young children with autism and their families', in J.S. Handelman & S.L. Harris (eds), *Preschool Education Programs for Children with Autism,* 2nd edn. Austin: Pro-ed, pp. 95–134.

Rogers, S.J., Wehner, E.A., & Hagerman, R.J. (2001b). 'The behavioral phenotype in fragile X: symptoms of autism in very young children with fragile X syndrome, idiopathic autism, and other developmental disorders', *J Dev Behav Pediatr,* 22(6): 409–417.

Rojahn, J., Borthwick-Duffy, S.A., & Jacobson, J.W. (1993) 'The association between psychiatric diagnoses and severe behavior problems in mental retardation', *Ann Clin Psychiatry,* 5(3): 163–170.

Rumsey, J.M., Rapoport, J.L., & Sceery, W.R. (1985) 'Autistic children as adults: psychiatric, social, and behavioral outcomes', *J Am Acad Child Psychiatry,* 24(4): 465–473.

Sabaratnam, M. (2006) 'Fragile-X syndrome', *Psychiatry,* 5(9): 325–330.

Scerif, G., Cornish, K.M., Wilding, J., Driver, J., & Karmiloff-Smith, A. (2004) 'Visual search in typically developing toddlers and toddlers with Fragile X or Williams syndrome', *Dev Sci,* 7(1): 116–130.

Scerif, G., Karmiloff-Smith, A., Campos, R., Elsabbagh, M., Driver, J., & Cornish, K.M. (2005) 'To look or not to look? Typical and atypical development of oculomotor control', *J Cogn Neurosci,* 17(4): 591–604.

Scharfenaker, S., O'Connor, R., Stackhouse, T., & Noble, L. (2002) 'An integrated approach to intervention', in R.J. Hagerman & P.J. Hagerman (eds), *Fragile X Syndrome: Diagnosis, Treatment and Research,* 3rd edn. Baltimore: Johns Hopkins University Press, pp. 363–427.

Schopler, E., Mesibov, G., Shigley, R., & Bashford, A. (1984) 'Helping autistic children through their parents: the TEACCH model', in C.R. Reynolds & T.R. Gutkin (eds), *The Handbook of School Psychology.* New York: Wiley, pp. 629–643.

Seltzer, M.M., Krauss, M.W., Orsmond, G., & Vestal, C. (2001) 'Families of adolescents and adults with autism: uncharted territory'. Unpublished manuscript.

Seltzer, M.M., Abbeduto, L., Krauss, M.W., Greenberg, J., & Swe, A. (2004) 'Comparison groups in autism family research: Down syndrome, fragile X syndrome, and schizophrenia', *J Autism Dev Disord,* 34(1): 41–48.

Simon, E.W. & Finucane, B.M. (1996) 'Facial emotion identification in males with fragile X syndrome', *Am J Med Genet,* 67(1): 77–80.

Singh, K., Gaur, P., & Prasad, S. (2007) 'Fragile X mental retardation (Fmr-1) gene expression is down regulated in brain of mice during aging', *Mol Biol Rep,* 34(3): 173–181.

Smith, T., Mozingo, D., Mruzek, D.W., & Zarcone, J.R. (2007) 'Applied behavior analysis in the treatment of autism', in E. Hollander & E. Anagnostou (eds), *Clinical Manual for the Treatment of Autism.* Washington, DC: American Psychiatric Publishing, pp. 153–177.

Sobesky, W.E., Pennington, B.F., Porter, D., Hull, C.E., & Hagerman, R.J. (1994) 'Emotional and neurocognitive deficits in fragile X', *Am J Med Genet,* 51(4): 378–385.

Sudhalter, V., Cohen, I.L., Silverman, W., & Wolf-Schein, E.G. (1990) 'Conversational analyses of males with fragile X, Down syndrome, and autism: comparison of the emergence of deviant language', *Am J Ment Retard,* 94(4): 431–441.

Sudhalter, V., Scarborough, H.S., & Cohen, I.L. (1991) 'Syntactic delay and pragmatic deviance in the language of fragile X males', *Am J Med Genet,* 38(2–3): 493–497.

Sudhalter, V., Maranion, M., & Brooks, P. (1992) 'Expressive semantic deficit in the productive language of males with fragile X syndrome', *Am J Med Genet,* 43(1–2): 65–71.

Sullivan, A.K., Marcus, M., Epstein, M.P., Allen, E.G., Anido, A.E., Paquin, J.J. et al. (2005) 'Association of FMR1 repeat size with ovarian dysfunction', *Hum Reprod,* 20(2): 402–412.

Tamm, L., Menon, V., Johnston, C.K., Hessl, D.R., & Reiss, A.L. (2002) 'fMRI study of cognitive interference processing in females with fragile X syndrome', *J Cogn Neurosci,* 14(2): 160–171.

Tassone, F., Adams, J., Berry-Kravis, E.M., Cohen, S.S., Brusco, A., Leehey, M.A. et al. (2007) 'CGG repeat length correlates with age of onset of motor signs of the fragile X-associated tremor/ataxia syndrome (FXTAS)', *Am J Med Genet B Neuropsychiatr Genet,* 144(4): 566–569.

Tassone, F., Hagerman, R.J., Iklé, D.N., Dyer, P.N., Lampe, M., Willemsen, R. et al. (1999) 'FMRP expression as a potential prognostic indicator in fragile X syndrome', *Am J Med Genet,* 84(3): 250–261.

Tassone, F., Hagerman, R.J., Chamberlain, W.D., & Hagerman, P.J. (2000a) 'Transcription of the FMR1 gene in individuals with fragile X syndrome', *Am J Med Genet (Semin Med Genet),* 97(3): 195–203.

Tassone, F., Hagerman, R.J., Loesch, D.Z., Lachiewicz, A., Taylor, A.K., & Hagerman, P.J. (2000b) 'Fragile X males with unmethylated, full mutation trinucleotide repeat expansions have elevated levels of FMR1 messenger RNA', *Am J Med Genet,* 94(3): 232–236.

Tassone, F., Hagerman, R.J., Taylor, A.K., Gane, L.W., Godfrey, T.E., & Hagerman, P.J. (2000c) 'Elevated levels of FMR1 mRNA in carrier males: a new mechanism of involvement in the fragile-X syndrome', *Am J Hum Genet,* 66(1): 6–15.

Tranebjaerg, L. & Orum, A. (1991) 'Major depressive disorder as a prominent but underestimated feature of fragile X syndrome', *Compr Psychiatry,* 32(1): 83–87.

Venter, A., Lord, C., & Schopler, E. (1992) 'A follow-up study of high-functioning autistic children', *J Child Psychol Psychiatry,* 33(3): 489–507.

Watson, C., Hoeft, F., Garrett, A.S., Hall, S.S., & Reiss, A.L. (2008) 'Aberrant brain activation during gaze processing in boys with fragile X syndrome', *Arch Gen Psychiatry,* 65(11): 1315–1323.

Wechsler, D. (1997) *Wechsler Memory Scale,* 3rd edn (WMS-III). San Antonio, TX: Harcourt Assessment, Inc.

Weiskop, S., Richdale, A., & Matthews, J. (2005) 'Behavioural treatment to reduce sleep problems in children with autism or fragile X syndrome', *Dev Med Child Neurol,* 47(2): 94–104.

Westmark, C.J. & Malter, J.S. (2007) 'FMRP mediates mGluR5-dependent translation of amyloid precursor protein', *PLoS Biol,* 5(3): e52.

Wilding, J., Cornish, K., & Munir, F. (2002) 'Further delineation of the executive deficit in males with fragile-X syndrome', *Neuropsychologia,* 40(8): 1343–1349.

Wright-Talamante, C., Cheema, A., Riddle, J.E., Luckey, D.W., Taylor, A.K., & Hagerman, R.J. (1996) 'A controlled study of longitudinal IQ changes in females and males with fragile X syndrome', *Am J Med Genet,* 64(2): 350–355.

Zalfa, F., Achsel, T., & Bagni, C. (2006) 'mRNPs, polysomes or granules: FMRP in neuronal protein synthesis', *Curr Opin Neurobiol,* 16(3): 265–269.

Zingerevich, C., Greiss-Hess, L., Lemons-Chitwood, K., Harris, S.W., Hessl, D., Cook, K. et al. (2009) 'Motor abilities of children diagnosed with fragile X syndrome with and without autism', *J Intellect Disabil Res,* 53(1): 11–18.

5

Williams Syndrome: Overview and Recent Advances in Research

Daniela Plesa Skwerer & Helen Tager-Flusberg

OVERVIEW

Williams syndrome (WS) was first discovered in the early 1960s by Williams et al. (1961) and Beuren et al. (1962), who independently described patients with cardiac problems, hypercalcemia, developmental delay, and unusual but striking facial characteristics. Children with some of these symptoms had previously been referred to as having 'idiopathic hypercalcemia of infancy' (Bongiovanni et al., 1957) but the link to cardiac abnormalities had not been recognized. Although it was initially thought to be an extremely rare condition, current estimates range from 1 in 7500 (Stromme et al., 2002) to 1 in 20,000 (Morris et al., 1988). It is now known that WS is caused by a heterozygous deletion of about 1.6 Mb on the long arm of chromosome 7 (7q11.23), which encompasses about 25–28 genes (Francke, 1999). The deletions are identical in length across the vast majority of individuals; they are the result of crossover events in misaligned duplicated regions of high sequence identity that flank the deletion (Osborne & Mervis, 2007).

Diagnosis of WS is typically confirmed using FISH (fluorescent in situ hybridization) to detect the absence of one of the critical genes, *ELN*, which lies in the middle of the deleted region. This gene is responsible for the cardiac symptoms in WS and led to the discovery of the genetic basis of the disorder (Ewart et al., 1993). Although there is variability in the phenotype of WS, clinical diagnoses are based on a range of physical, medical, and behavioral characteristics, some of which show age-related changes (Mervis et al., 1999). These characteristics include 'elfin' faces, growth delay, supravalvular aortic stenosis, connective tissue features such as hoarse voice or premature skin aging, failure to thrive, hypercalcemia, learning or intellectual disability, attention deficit disorder, anxiety, and striking cognitive and social-personality profiles.

Over the past two decades research studies on WS have yielded a wealth of information about the core behavioral features of this unique syndrome. Individuals with WS generally have intellectual disability in the mild to moderate range. Bellugi and her colleagues were the first to describe the cognitive strengths and weaknesses that are a stable feature of the phenotype (Bellugi et al., 1988). These include relatively strong language and auditory memory skills but extremely impaired visuospatial abilities. The cognitive profile for WS was operationalized by Mervis and her colleagues, based on relatively large-scale studies that included individuals spanning a wide age range (Mervis et al., 2000). The profile is defined on the basis of assessments using the Differential Abilities Scales (DAS; Elliott, 1990) on the basis of the following criteria: pattern construction standard score in the lowest 20th percentile, and lower than other core tests and digit recall; standard score on digit recall, naming/definitions or similarities above the first percentile. The profile thus reflects the relative weakness in visuospatial construction (assessed by the pattern construction subtest) and relative strengths in auditory short-term memory and language, even in low-functioning individuals (Mervis et al., 1999).

The profile of social-personality characteristics is also unusual among children and adults with WS. Based on parent report measures and other assessment tools, individuals with WS have been shown to be unusually interested in and friendly toward strangers, socially engaging, empathic, and outgoing (e.g. Gosch & Pankau, 1997; Klein-Tasman & Mervis, 2003). At the same time, these positive features are often accompanied by problem behaviors that can be picked up by checklists or other assessments. Difficulties with attention, distractibility, and hyperactivity are quite prevalent among younger children with WS (Dilts et al., 1990). Psychiatric interviews highlight comorbid diagnoses of attention-deficit/hyperactivity disorder (ADHD), specific phobias, and generalized anxiety disorder, which tends to emerge during adolescence (Leyfer et al., 2006; Stinton et al., 2010). And, finally, despite their gregarious outgoing personality profile, by middle childhood many children with WS begin to experience difficulties with peer relationships (e.g. Davies et al., 1998). The presence of these problem behaviors and comorbid conditions

are similar to those experienced by individuals with other genetic syndromes.

In sum, the profile of people with WS includes both unusual relative strengths coupled with significant weaknesses, which can be readily evaluated during clinical observation and standardized assessments. This descriptive profile serves as a backdrop to the exponential growth in research on WS that has taken place especially in the past decade (see Figure 5.1), which we summarize in the following sections.

CURRENT RESEARCH

Genetic research

Recent advances in investigating the molecular basis of WS have underscored the intricate interplay between specific genetic abnormalities and the developmental processes they disrupt, resulting in syndrome-specific phenotypic outcomes (Osborne & Pober, 2001). However, to date, only the role of the elastin (ELN) gene is relatively well understood in the causation of certain physical features associated with WS (i.e. cardiovascular and connective tissue abnormalities), whereas the functional contributions of the other genes in the common WS deletion region to specific phenotypic traits of the syndrome remain unclear or disputed (Osborne, 2006).

Two main methodological approaches have been used in efforts to link the action of individual genes to specific phenotypic traits. One is the comprehensive study of individuals with atypical deletions or other chromosomal rearrangements of the WS locus. The second approach involves the generation of animal models with genetically engineered deficiencies in specific genes or deletions of choice (e.g. knockout mice). Using both these approaches, the contributions of several genes within the deletion region on 7q that are highly expressed in the brain (e.g. LIMK1, CYLN2, FZD9, STXIA, GTF2I, and GTF2IRD1) and constitute prime functional candidates for

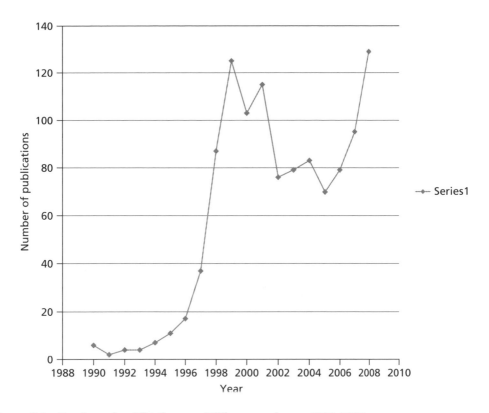

Figure 5.1 Number of publications on Williams syndrome 1990–2009

involvement in aspects of the WS neurobehavioral phenotype, have been extensively studied, so far with controversial results.

One example is research on the function of LIM-kinase 1 (LIMK1). Initial findings implicating LIMK1 hemizygosity in the visuospatial constructive impairment characteristic of WS (Frangiskakis et al., 1996) have been challenged by the discovery that some individuals with atypical deletions including LIMK1 did not show severe visuospatial deficits (Tassabehji et al., 1996). At the same time, LIMK1 knockout mice show abnormalities in the dendritic spine structure of neurons in the hippocampus, associated with impaired spatial learning (Meng et al., 2002), suggesting that LIMK1 hemizygosity may play a role in some aspects of the WS cognitive profile, but is not solely responsible for visuospatial deficits.

Young and colleagues (2008) generated GTF2IRD1 mutant mice that showed responses strikingly similar to aspects of the behavioral phenotype associated with WS. They were less aggressive and engaged more with an unknown intruder compared to the wild-type mice; they showed decreased fear response and increased social activity, combined with impaired amygdala-based learning. But, unlike individuals with WS, they also demonstrated normal spatial learning and memory. Dai et al. (2009) reported on a case study of a young girl with an atypical deletion including hemizygosity for all the genes in the classic WS region except for GTF2I. This girl did not display the typical hypersociability of WS individuals with full deletions, thus implicating the involvement of GTF2I in aspects of social behavior. However, she also had relatively higher IQ and no language delay, in contrast to children with WS.

Another interesting set of findings comes from the identification of individuals with duplications of the WS locus (Somerville et al., 2005). The phenotype described for these individuals contrasts in several essential aspects with the WS phenotype: they show severe delay in speech and expressive language, but have visuospatial construction abilities at the level of other unaffected family members (Berg et al., 2007; Meyer-Lindenberg et al., 2006; Osborne & Mervis, 2007). These findings indicate that 'specific genes at 7q11.23 are exquisitely sensitive to dosage alterations that can influence human language and visuospatial abilities' (Sommerville et al., 2005: 1694).

Even as our understanding of the molecular genomic bases of WS progresses, the specific contributions of various genes to aspects of the cognitive and behavioral profile remain uncertain. It is becoming increasingly clear that the unusual constellation of WS phenotypes is a product of the combinatorial effect of the deletion of multiple genes (Osborne, 2006). Some of these genes are involved in the regulation of pathways for brain development and function, showing dosage-sensitive effects and complex interactions that affect the regulation of gene expression over time. As Karmiloff-Smith and her colleagues have repeatedly cautioned (Karmiloff-Smith et al., 2006), any efforts to clarify genotype–phenotype relations should take into account the process of ontogenetic development that crucially affects adult phenotypic outcomes, which are always the result of a complex interplay between genetic, maturational, and experiential factors.

Neuroanatomical research

At least half the genes within the WS deletion are expressed in the brain and clearly play critical roles during early development. Studies of postmortem tissue specimens and in vivo methods, using magnetic resonance imaging (MRI), have provided a wealth of information about how the brains of people with WS differ from typically developing individuals, and have illuminated the brain abnormalities that underlie the key behavioral characteristics of WS, with particular emphasis on the dorsal pathways and their association with visuospatial impairments.

People with WS have brains that are significantly smaller than age-matched typical controls (Chiang et al., 2007; Jernigan & Bellugi, 1994). There are regional differences in gray matter volume, with the most consistent findings relating to reductions in posterior areas, particularly in parietal-occipital zones, including the intraparietal sulcus (Meyer-Lindenberg et al., 2004; Reiss et al., 2004). These findings were confirmed in a study of children with WS (Campbell et al., 2009). Additional areas showing relative reductions include the posterior corpus callosum, thalamus, and basal ganglia (Chiang et al., 2007), the third ventricle, and orbito-frontal cortex (Meyer-Lindenberg et al., 2006). These reductions have been related to the visuo-spatial impairments, performance IQ scores (measuring nonverbal abilities such as perceptual organization and processing speed), and unusual responses to social stimuli that are all part of the WS phenotype. In contrast, other areas of the frontal lobes, superior temporal gyrus, amygdala, fusiform gyrus, anterior cingulate, and cerebellum are all relatively preserved in size (Chiang et al. 2007; but see Sampaio et al., 2008). These regions are conjectured to be associated with the language, face processing, and social components of the WS phenotype (Gothelf et al., 2005; Reiss et al., 2004). Postmortem studies have found that there are smaller neurons in several layers of primary visual cortex (Galaburda et al., 2002), consistent with abnormalities in the dorsal pathway, but larger neurons bilaterally in layer II and in layer VI in the left hemisphere in the auditory cortex, which may be associated with language and musical interests in WS (Holinger et al., 2005).

Studies of cortical shape and thickness have also revealed interesting differences in individuals with WS. Meyer-Lindenberg and his colleagues (2006) found decreased curvature of the brain and increased gyrification in occipital and parietal cortices as well as in the temporal-parietal areas. Thompson et al. (2005) found increases in cortical thickness in the right perisylvian and inferior temporal regions, which they associated with failures in cortical maturation. Differences in sulcal patterns have also been found, including bilateral reductions in sulcal depth in the intraparietal/occipitoparietal sulcus and in the left orbitofrontal region (Kippenhan et al., 2005). Only one study, by Meyer-Lindenberg and colleagues (2005a), investigated the hippocampus in adults with WS. Although there were no differences in size, there were subtle alterations in the shape, and MR spectroscopy revealed reductions in N-acetylaspartate, which is a marker of synaptic activity. All these differences are consistent with neuroanatomical abnormalities associated with severe deficits in visuospatial functioning.

Finally, a number of recent studies have used diffusion tensor imaging to investigate white matter tracts in WS. Hoeft et al. (2007) found increased fractional anisotropy (FA), a measure of microstructural integrity, in the superior longitudinal fasciculus, especially in the right hemisphere, which was associated with deficits in visuospatial functioning. Elevations in FA could reflect increases in myelination or deficits in axonal structure or packing density. Marenco et al. (2007) found alterations in the posterior fiber tracts and decreased lateralization of fiber coherence that may signify alterations in later stages of neuronal migration and differences in the timing of hemispheric development. Together, these studies reveal several significant differences in the brains of children and adults with WS that are consistent with the behavioral phenotype of WS. Future research will begin to tie these atypical brain patterns to specific genetic influences using both human and animal models.

Neuropsychological and cognitive neuroscience research

Early studies of the neuropsychological profile of individuals with WS emphasized the presence of 'peaks and valleys' of abilities, which were taken as evidence for clear-cut dissociations between broad cognitive domains, such as language and cognition (Bellugi et al., 1988). These studies energized theoretical debates about the genetic bases of human cognitive architecture and the 'modularity of mind' and were instrumental in attracting other behavioral and neuroscientists to the field. As research advanced, the picture of the cognitive and behavioral profile of WS became significantly more complex, revealing sometimes surprising mixtures of relative strengths and weaknesses *within* cognitive domains, underscoring the need for clear and objective definitions of the phenotype, as well as the need to trace the developmental trajectories of well-characterized phenotypic outcomes to understand how genomic variations and ontogenetic processes bring about this unusual profile. Considerable progress has been made in the last decade in achieving detailed phenotypic descriptions confirming the distinctiveness of the cognitive behavioral profile of WS, despite considerable individual variability in its expression (Mervis et al., 2000; Porter & Colheart, 2005). In the following sections we review the current research on cognitive domains that are central to the WS phenotype.

General intelligence

Because WS is generally associated with mental retardation, almost all studies including individuals with WS incorporate standardized assessments of IQ as part of the investigative measures used. The majority of studies report mean IQ scores between 50 and 60, but across studies scores range from severe mental retardation to average intelligence (< 40 to >100). This wide range reflects not only the cognitive variability found within the WS population but also discrepancies in scores related to the characteristics of the instruments used to assess IQ. On several widely used IQ tests (e.g. the Wechsler Scales) many individuals with WS obtain higher scores on verbal (VIQ) than on non-verbal tests (PIQ), but this difference is not always statistically significant (see Martens et al., 2008a for a review). Larger discrepancies are more common among individuals with relatively high VIQ (Jarrold et al., 1998). If the PIQ measure includes tests of visuospatial abilities, then greater discrepancies are found. To avoid penalizing participants with WS for their specific visuospatial deficit, many researchers have used the Kaufman Brief Intelligence Test (Kaufman & Kaufman, 2004) to assess IQ, because this test consists of a verbal and a non-verbal reasoning scale, without a component testing spatial constructive ability.

Visuospatial cognition

One of the most consistent findings across studies of people with WS is their extremely poor performance on tests of visuospatial construction, such as block design or pattern construction, or on drawing and copying tasks (see Farran & Jarrold, 2003 for review). These tasks entail the ability to visualize an object as a set of parts and then construct a replica from those parts. Significant progress has been made in the last decade in clarifying the nature of the visuospatial deficit in WS because this particular topic has been systematically investigated with multiple methodologies in an effort to achieve a systems-level characterization of genetically mediated abnormalities in neural circuits that could provide 'unique opportunities to investigate genetic influences on complex brain functions in a "bottom-up" way' (Meyer-Lindenberg et al., 2006: 380).

The first step in clarifying the causes of impairment in visuospatial cognition in WS is to examine its possible relations to basic sensory visual functions. Atkinson and colleagues (2001) conducted comprehensive assessments of functional vision in children with WS. Despite a high incidence of basic sensory visual and oculomotor problems, these were not causally related to children's

performance on visuospatial tasks, leading Atkinson and colleagues (2003) to conclude that higher-order cortical or subcortical neural mechanisms involved in processing and transforming spatial information were likely to be the main source of the visuospatial deficit.

A number of researchers have explained the visuospatial impairments in WS by invoking an atypical processing style, characterized as a bias toward featural analysis, whereby individuals with WS focus on the local details of an image, failing to adequately process its global configuration (e.g. Wang et al., 1995). This interpretation was initially based on analyses of the qualitative differences in the types of errors made on block design tasks (Bellugi et al., 1988). Children with WS tended to choose the correct parts but placed them incorrectly, producing broken configurations. A similar processing style was demonstrated on other tests of spatial organization, such as drawing tasks (Farran & Jarrold, 2003).

Farran and her colleagues (2003) argued that a local bias is shown only when the task involves *constructional* demands, because reproducing a model entails integrating form and location information, working memory, planning, and execution of motor sequences, all of which could play a role in performance on such tasks even if the perception of global structure is unimpaired. Indeed, performance consistent with their mental age level has been reported for WS individuals on perceptual tasks of face and object recognition (Landau et al., 2006), visual closure (Deruelle et al., 2006), perceptual grouping (Pani et al., 1999), and detection of biological motion (Jordan et al., 2002), all of which require the ability to integrate fragmentary information into a global percept. Farran et al. (2003) demonstrated that people with WS could process visual information at both global and local levels when primed to do so. Moreover, close inspection of their performance suggests a pattern of performance similar to the 'broken configurations' produced by typically developing children younger than 6 years (Akshoomoff & Stiles, 1996), thus indicating a delayed rather than deviant visual processing style. Longitudinal analyses of drawing abilities in WS found improvements with age in the global organization of drawings (Bertrand et al., 1997), suggesting that developmental models are more appropriate for characterizing the deficits evidenced by people with WS on a range of visual-construction tasks.

To disentangle the possible sources of difficulty shown by older children with WS on visuospatial tasks that go beyond the preschool years, Hoffman and his colleagues (2003) conducted a detailed componential analysis of performance on a computerized block design task, examining eye fixations and error patterns. The main findings were that on simple problems children with WS and mental age matched controls were comparable in performance and showed similar eye-fixation patterns, whereas on more complex block designs the performance of the WS children dropped abruptly, as they fixated models and checked partial solutions less often than the controls and attempted fewer repairs when detecting errors. The authors concluded that basic executive processes and some aspects of perceptual organization were intact in WS, but that the children with WS showed a persistent deficit in *representing the spatial relationships*. For the complex problems the deficit in representing spatial relationships impacted how executive processes were deployed. A deficit in spatial representational processes is consistent with poor performance by individuals with WS on tasks involving mental imagery, mental rotation, even in the absence of any motor component demands (Farran & Jarrold, 2003) and have been linked to poor planning and control of saccadic eye movements in children and adults with WS (Brown et al., 2003; Montfoort et al., 2007). Atkinson et al. (2003) also found that young children with WS show 'sticky fixation' when presented with competing visual targets, suggesting that the inadequate development of the saccadic system could have a cascade of effects

on more complex action systems based on spatial representations, such as those involved in visuospatial construction tasks.

The performance profiles on visuospatial tasks in WS have been linked to functional abnormalities in several neural systems, including the dorsal stream of visual cortical processing (Atkinson et al., 1997; Paul et al., 2002), which encodes information about spatial relations and the visual control of action; frontoparietal circuits involved in visual spatial working memory and executive control processes required for spatially directed responses (Atkinson et al., 2003; Mobbs et al., 2007; Vicari et al., 2003); and the oculomotor vermis of the cerebellum involved in the control of saccade accuracy (Montfoort et al., 2007). While the particular relationships between these abnormalities and aspects of visuospatial cognition in WS remain unclear, researchers have begun to hone in on the neural correlates of the visuospatial construction deficit.

Meyer-Lindenberg and collaborators (2004) conducted a series of functional MRI (fMRI) experiments with adults with WS who had normal-range intelligence scores, and matched typical controls. Results showed consistent hypoactivation of the dorsal stream areas in the WS group compared with controls, but normal activation of the ventral stream. Path analyses used to model the interregional flow of information in the visual system indicated that part of the mechanism for the dorsal stream dysfunction found in WS could be the deficient input from the intraparietal sulcus (IPS) into the later dorsal stream. Sarpal and colleagues (2008) probed the neural interactions of the ventral visual stream with brain regions that further process object information using a passive face- and house-viewing paradigm with normal IQ adults with WS and matched controls. When looking at houses, specific abnormalities were revealed in activation in the IPS. Among the WS individuals, functional connectivity analyses showed significant decreases in connectivity between the 'parahippocampal place area' (PPA) and the parietal cortex, including the IPS, indicating abnormalities in the PPA-IPS circuit, which supports topographic representation of space and thus plays a critical role in visuospatial function.

In summary, visuospatial cognition in WS presents a complex picture of selective impairments, developmental delay, and typical performance across various aspects of visual processing. Careful analyses of behavioral performance in conjunction with analyses of eye movements and of patterns of brain activation relative to specific task demands have enabled researchers to identify specialized neurocognitive mechanisms underlying the distinctive performance profiles shown by individuals with WS on visuospatial tasks and may provide the appropriate framework for identifying genetic contributions to complex behavior such as visuospatial cognition in humans.

Face processing

In contrast to the extreme weakness in visuospatial construction skills, face recognition abilities have frequently been cited as a strength for people with WS (e.g. Bellugi et al., 1988; Tager-Flusberg et al., 2003; Wang et al., 1995) because they obtain scores within or near age norms on standardized measures of face identity recognition such as the Benton Facial Recognition test (Benton et al., 1983). This strength has been related to the unusually high interest in faces shown by individuals with WS from infancy. However, the neurocognitive processes underlying performance in face recognition in WS are still under debate.

The remarkable expertise that all people have in recognizing faces depends on holistic and configural processing, which refer to encoding and recognizing faces in terms of a template-like representation of the gestalt, and distinguishing faces based on the relative positioning and spatial distances amongst internal features. These processes are disrupted when faces are shown upside-down, leading to increased reliance on featural

processing for identification. Early studies, based on small samples of individuals with WS of widely varying ages and ability levels, claimed that people with WS process faces by relying on features because they did not show the inversion effect (e.g. Elgar & Campbell, 2001). However, normal face inversion effects have been reported in several more recent studies that included larger samples of adolescents and adults with WS using more sensitive experimental paradigms (Mills et al., 2000; Rose et al., 2007; Tager-Flusberg et al., 2003). There is still a debate over whether people with WS are impaired in configural processing of higher-order relations in faces (Karmiloff-Smith et al., 2004), an ability that undergoes developmental changes in later childhood in typical development, and whether a configural processing deficit represents delay or deviance in the developmental trajectory of face processing skills in people with WS.

Atypical electrophysiological responses on face processing tasks have been reported in adults with WS. Mills and her colleagues (2000) recoded event-related potentials (ERPs) during a face identity match paradigm and found unusually small early ERP components, the N100 and P170, but large N200 peaks in WS, the latter reflecting the increased attention that people with WS pay to faces. On the later N320 component, which is linked to face recognition processes, the ERP patterns found among the adults with WS were similar to those seen in younger controls, but were somewhat larger and delayed relative to the age-matched adults. The authors concluded that 'in WS, the brain systems that mediate face recognition might be normally organized but developmentally delayed', (Mills et al., 2000: 59). Studies using fMRI methods have generally shown similar patterns of activation in the 'face fusiform area' (FFA) (a functionally distinct subregion in the parahippocampal gyrus that responds) in adults with WS and control groups when viewing faces (Meyer-Lindenberg et al., 2004; Mobbs et al., 2004; Sarpal et al., 2008). So far most of the evidence points to generally similar neuro-cognitive mechanisms underlying processing of facial identity in WS as in normal populations, but little is known about the development of face recognition strategies in relation to the distinctive social phenotype.

Social cognition

Social cognition is another domain that, in light of new research, has undergone a dramatic shift in our understanding of the profile of abilities of people with WS. No doubt some of the most endearing aspects of the behavioral phenotype of people with WS, including their gregariousness, heightened sociability, keen interest and affection for people, empathy, friendliness, and eagerness to initiate social interactions, are consistently revealed in parental reports as well as in observational laboratory-based behavioral assessments (Doyle et al., 2004; Jarvinen-Paysley et al., 2008; Plesa Skwerer et al., 2008). These aspects of the profile of children and adults with WS distinguish them from people with other developmental disorders (Klein-Tasman & Mervis, 2003) and initially led researchers to hypothesize that people with WS might have a good understanding of the social world, showing domain-specific sparing in social cognition or theory of mind (Karmiloff-Smith et al., 1995; Tager-Flusberg et al., 1998).

Theory of mind refers to reasoning about people's actions based on inferences about their mental states, such as intentions, knowledge, or beliefs. Tests of 'false belief' understanding, which require participants to discount their own knowledge of the true situation and infer the beliefs and actions of an uninformed character, are passed by typically developing children at age 4 or 5. Karmiloff-Smith and colleagues (1995) administered a number of theory of mind tasks to a small group of children and adults with WS. The majority of the WS participants passed these tasks, leading these authors to conclude that theory of mind may be an

'islet of preserved ability' (Karmiloff-Smith et al., 1995: 202). This interpretation of the findings, however, might be misleading given that their WS participants were much older than the age at which typical children pass such tests (Brock et al., 2008). Later studies of children and adolescents with WS found that their performance was no better than that of other participants with intellectual disability on false belief tasks (Porter et al., 2007; Tager-Flusberg & Sullivan, 2000), second-order belief reasoning (Sullivan & Tager-Flusberg, 1999), distinguishing between lies and jokes (Sullivan et al., 2003), and using trait information to attribute intentionality (Plesa Skwerer & Tager-Flusberg, 2006). Thus, studies on theory of mind in WS provide no evidence of relative sparing in this domain of social reasoning.

Researchers have also investigated 'on-line', perceptually-based judgments of mental states based on cues available in people's faces, voices, and body movements. In contrast to their strong face recognition skills, on explicit measures of emotion processing, children and adults with WS perform no better than comparison groups matched on mental age. Several different paradigms yielded similar findings when probing the ability to discriminate, match or label facial emotional expression using static images (Meyer-Lindenberg et al., 2005b; Porter et al., 2007; Tager-Flusberg & Sullivan, 2000) or dynamic videos (Gagliardi et al., 2003; Plesa Skwerer et al., 2006). Several research teams reported similar findings using the Diagnostic Analysis of Nonverbal Accuracy test (DANVA-2; Nowicki & Duke, 1994), which probes the ability to label basic emotions based on cues from facial, vocal, and body expressions (Plesa Skwerer et al., 2006; Porter et al., 2007). Participants with WS made errors differentiating among negative emotions, whereas their recognition of happy expressions was almost at the level of accuracy of typical controls, suggesting a relatively unimpaired ability to distinguish emotional valence in WS (see also Plesa Skwerer et al., 2007).

Although one early study reported relative sparing in the ability to identify mental states from the eye region of the face (Tager-Flusberg et al., 1998), a later study which used a more stringent 'eyes task' (Baron-Cohen et al., 2001) found that adults with WS performed no better than a comparison group with intellectual disabilities (Plesa Skwerer et al., 2005). Another social-perceptual task that has been used in several studies on WS taps the ability to infer trustworthiness of strangers from photographs of faces. These tasks are of particular interest because of anecdotal reports about the indiscriminant friendliness of people with WS toward strangers. Bellugi et al. (1999) found that adults with WS gave more positive ratings across all photographs on an adapted version of the Approachability/Trustworthiness task (Adolphs et al., 1998). Frigerio et al. (2006) used a set of emotionally expressive faces and found that the group with WS rated only the *happy* faces as more approachable than the matched controls. In contrast, faces expressing negative emotions were rated as even less approachable compared to controls. Porter and her colleagues (2007) also obtained ratings for a set of emotionally expressive faces and found that approachability ratings were related to performance on the facial emotion recognition measure: for those expressions that were correctly recognized, the WS group displayed the same rank order of approachability judgments as the typical controls. These authors interpret their findings as consistent with the hypothesis of a frontal lobe dysfunction in WS, on which the tendency of WS individuals to approach strangers in real life is viewed as an impairment in response inhibition, leading to a dissociation between 'knowing' that strangers should not be approached and 'doing', their inability to inhibit their social approach tendency (cf. Frigerio et al., 2006).

Martens and colleagues (2008b) proposed a developmental explanation for the inconsistencies in the findings from these studies. They also used the Adolphs task with a group spanning a wide age range. Overall, participants with WS rated both positive and negative faces as more approachable than controls, replicating Bellugi's findings (Bellugi et al., 1999). However, when the sample was divided by age, they found that children rated both the negative and positive faces with a more positive bias; the adolescents rated only the positive faces as more approachable than similar-aged controls; and the adults continued to rate the positive faces as more approachable than controls, but rated the negative faces with a more negative bias, similar to the results reported by Frigerio et al. (2006).

Taken together, these experimental results largely complement findings from studies that used parent report measures (Davies et al., 1998; Klein-Tasman & Mervis, 2003). These studies offer a framework for understanding the paradox of parental reports of high sociability but poor social adjustment and social competence seen in people with WS, by providing a systematic characterization of their social cognitive abilities, which undergo developmental changes in light of accumulating social experiences. Longitudinal studies are needed to understand the roots of the unique social phenotype associated with WS. For instance, is the indiscriminate friendliness toward strangers showed by children with WS related to dysfunctions in the attachment system, in the process of forming preferential emotional bonds early in life (Plesa Skwerer et al., 2008)? Or is it related to more general impairments in inhibitory control that affect both social and nonsocial domains (Mobbs et al., 2007)?

In the search for developmental precursors of hypersociability in WS one of the most striking features is a fascination with faces, which begins in infancy. Toddlers with WS look significantly longer and with greater intensity at social partners than other toddlers (Doyle et al., 2004; Mervis et al., 2003). Experimental evidence of prolonged face gaze in adolescents and adults with WS was reported by Riby and Hancock (2008, 2009) using eye tracking methods. These findings are consistent with reports of the tendency of people with WS to hold direct eye contact with another person for longer than is usually comfortable in face-to-face interactions. Interestingly, when viewing scenes with embedded faces or scrambled images, the WS individuals showed less scene scanning and were slower to detect faces than controls, but once they discovered the faces, the WS participants spent significantly more time fixating, suggesting that people with WS have attention disengagement difficulties in conditions of relatively typical attention capture by faces (Riby & Hancock, 2008).

There are likely to be significant consequences of this unusual attentional behavior for the development of social-communicative capacities in children with WS, and several researchers have found overlapping phenotypic expression with aspects of autism spectrum disorders (ASD). Laing and her colleagues (2002) administered the Early Social Communication Scales to toddlers with WS and developmentally matched controls. The toddlers with WS showed fewer object-related joint attention behaviors and more social interactive behaviors than the comparison group, confirming earlier findings by Mervis and Bertrand (1997). Klein-Tasman and colleagues (2007) found that on the Autism Diagnostic Observation Schedule (ADOS) – an instrument used to diagnose ASD through assessments of play, interaction, and social communication – about half of young children with WS met criteria for ASD. Lincoln and his colleagues (2007) directly compared young children with WS and ASD on the ADOS. Many of the children with WS showed one or more ASD symptoms in social-communication behaviors; however, most of the WS children did make social overtures and efforts to capture the attention of others, showing relatively few problems on items related to reciprocal social engagement. It remains unclear whether the symptoms common to both disorders reflect true comorbidity or simply represent the result of risk factors afforded by mental retardation (Klein-Tasman et al., 2007).

Anecdotal reports, as well as several recent experimental investigations, have called attention to the emotional responsiveness of children with WS toward others as a highly distinctive personality characteristic manifested from an early age. Using a simulated distress paradigm, several studies found that toddlers with WS showed significantly more comforting behavior, expressions of sympathy and overall concern than control groups (Ciciolla et al., 2007; Thomas et al., 2002). In contrast, ratings of empathic responsiveness toward a person expressing joy for having received good news or eagerness to help a person in need did not differentiate between children with WS and comparison groups with and without developmental disabilities (Plesa Skwerer et al., 2008). Fidler and colleagues (2007) found that, compared to children with other developmental delays, children with WS demonstrated heightened emotional responsivity manifested in increased mimicry of the experimenter's facial and vocal affect when expressing likes or dislikes for certain food items. However, the children with WS were similar to the comparison group in the proportion of correct responses to the researcher's request for more food, with less than half of participants taking into account the experimenter's expressed food likes and dislikes in their social decision making. This poor performance on the measure of interpersonal perspective taking shows that emotional responsivity 'docs not automatically enable one to extract the underlying meaning of others' behavior' (Fidler et al., 2007:16). Taken together these studies demonstrate that aspects of emotional responsiveness may signal a developmental precursor to social disinhibition in WS (Fidler et al., 2007). Children with WS, while hypersocial and empathic, have difficulties linking their affective responsiveness to appropriate social behavior, and may also have difficulties learning social norms.

Significant advances have been made in identifying the neural mechanisms underlying the social phenotype in adults with WS. The role of the amygdala in the atypical social responsiveness of people with WS has been a focus of interest in several studies.

Meyer-Lindenberg and colleagues (2005b) used fMRI to investigate amygdala function in response to threatening social (angry/fearful faces) and non-social photographs. In contrast to the activation patterns of the control participants, they found significantly lower amygdala activation to the faces among the WS adults, but significantly higher amygdala activation to the nonsocial scenes. They also found differences in prefrontal regions, which are densely connected to the amygdala. In contrast to the controls, the WS group did not activate the orbito-frontal cortex to the face stimuli. Instead these participants showed equivalent activation to the social and nonsocial stimuli in medial and dorso-lateral prefrontal regions, suggesting that the neurobiological substrate for the atypical social phenotype in WS lies in the abnormal regulation or modulation of amygdala function by the orbito-frontal cortex (Meyer-Lindenberg et al., 2005b).

Sarpal and colleagues (2008) investigated the functional connectivity between regions of the ventral stream in adults with WS and controls when looking at faces. They found significantly reduced functional connectivity between the FFA and amygdala and prefrontal cortex, suggesting that in adults with WS social information has less access to amygdala and regulatory prefrontal areas from the ventral stream. This finding suggests another mechanism that could account for reduced amygdala activation to threat-related facial expressions and may account for the lack of social fear seen in WS.

Recently Haas et al. (2009) used a combined fMRI and event-related potential (ERP) approach to investigate neural responses to emotional facial expressions in a sample of adults with WS compared to typical and intellectually disabled controls. They found a unique pattern of brain responses in the WS group, with heightened right amygdala activation to *happy* faces, but not to fearful or neutral faces, suggesting that in WS amygdala activation indexes increased emotional salience of positive expressions. The diminished amygdala reactivity to fearful expres-

sions in the WS group was also seen in the ERP data, indexed by decreases in the mean amplitudes of the N200, a component linked to attention and arousal. Interestingly, in a behavioral study of working memory in WS, O'Hearn and colleagues (2008) found a selective advantage in memory for smiling faces, suggesting that enhanced attention to positive expressions may have increased activation in ventral stream areas in the temporal lobe and fronto-parietal areas, compensating for the abnormalities in functional connectivity between these areas and the amygdala.

Current research on social attention, social engagement and social cognition in WS provides a mixed and complex picture of the strengths and weaknesses that define the phenotype. Although across all ages people with WS are hypersociable, this does not translate into relatively spared emotion processing or theory of mind abilities, as initially hypothesized. The consequences of this unusual and uneven social profile may be difficulties with peer relations and a relatively high rate of emotional and behavioral adaptive problems (Dykens & Rosner, 1999). Higher levels of anxiety compared to the general population are common in people with WS, many of whom develop depression as adults. These mood disorders may, in part, be related to the accumulation of unsuccessful social experiences (Gosch & Pankau, 1997), although other authors have found no association between the presence of mental health problems and external, life events variables (Stinton et al., 2010).

Language

Despite early reports of remarkable sparing of linguistic abilities in WS, which were based on small numbers of subjects compared mainly with individuals with Down syndrome (Bellugi et al., 1992), current research suggests that, for the most part, language abilities are commensurate with mental age levels in both children and adults (Brock, 2007). In addition, within language, there is an uneven profile of relative strengths (e.g. receptive vocabulary) and weaknesses (e.g. discourse skills) highlighting a more complex picture of this component of the WS phenotype. Much of the research is based on performance on standardized language tests or psycholinguistic tasks using cross-sectional research designs, and most studies have focused on English (but see Bartke & Siegmuller, 2004). Few longitudinal studies have been conducted so relatively little is known about the developmental course, especially during the preschool years. There have also been no functional imaging studies that have explored the biological foundations for language processing in WS. Still, behavioral studies conducted in recent years that have included well-matched control groups and relatively large numbers of participants have provided a wealth of information about language skills and use in this population.

All children with WS are delayed in the onset of language milestones in the first two years, the timing of which is in line with their mental age level (Mervis & Beccera, 2007). In typically developing children early language is closely connected to specific motor, cognitive and social-communicative developments, however, the pattern of these interconnections is somewhat different among toddlers with WS. Like typically developing children and children with other developmental disabilities, in WS early babbling is closely connected to the onset of rhythmic hand banging (Masataka, 2001) and early vocabulary is tied to categorization skills (Mervis, 2006) and phonological short-term memory (Brock et al., 2005). However, the acquisition of new words is not tied to joint attention, particularly referential pointing, or to object sorting skills, both of which are rarely observed in young children with WS (Mervis & Bertrand, 1997). Other aspects of early language, particularly the development of phonological knowledge and phonological short-term memory are relative strengths in WS when compared to children with other disabilities, particularly Down syndrome (Brock et al., 2007; Udwin & Yule, 1990).

Once children with WS begin developing vocabulary, their knowledge of words is a clear strength. Receptive vocabulary scores are generally higher than expected for mental age, though this does not extend to performance on expressive vocabulary measures (Brock et al., 2007). An early study, based on only a handful of children, suggested that they had unusual vocabularies composed of a relatively large number of low frequency words that reflected atypical semantic organization (Bellugi et al., 1992). Later, more comprehensive investigations failed to replicate this finding for English-speaking (Mervis et al., 1999), Italian-speaking (Volterra et al., 1996) or Hebrew-speaking (Levy & Bechar, 2003) children.

Recent studies have highlighted specific deficits that children with WS have with abstract relational vocabulary, including spatial descriptions (Laing & Jarrold, 2007) or, more generally, words encoding abstract relational concepts (Mervis & John, 2008). Landau and Zukowski (2003) asked children to summarize events depicted in videos. While the children were able to provide basic descriptions of the events, they had difficulty with path descriptions, reflecting problems integrating abstract relational vocabulary with spatial memory. Landau and Zukowski (2003) concluded that these language difficulties reflect the significant deficits in visuospatial skills that are the hallmark of the WS phenotype. Lukacs et al. (2004) also found that spatial morphology was specifically impaired in Hungarian-speaking children with WS. Brock (2007) argues that children with WS have difficulty mapping language onto mental models, however, Mervis and Becerra (2007) suggest that because the deficits encompass other abstract vocabulary, including temporal and quantitative relational terms, the problem in WS involves the broader "magnitude system" which is based in inferior parietal cortex (Meyer-Lindenberg et al., 2006). It would be interesting to explore further the neurobiological basis of relational language impairments in WS using functional imaging methods.

The development of syntactic and morphological skills follows a typical pathway in WS. Children with WS show close connections between grammar, vocabulary and mental age, unlike children with other disorders such as Down syndrome, fragile X or specific language impairment (Brock, 2007; Mervis et al., 2003). Despite the unusually strong relationship between language and verbal memory in WS (Mervis et al., 2003), careful experimental studies using elicited production methods have shown that children with WS are not acquiring morphosyntactic skills by relying on rote learning (Zukowski, 2004). Clahsen and Almazan (1998) claimed that children with WS were relatively impaired in acquiring irregular morphology in English, including irregular past tense (e.g. go–went) and plurals (e.g. mouse–mice), but other studies have not replicated their findings (Thomas et al., 2001). A few studies have explored comprehension and production of grammatical structures that are usually not mastered until middle childhood, including complex syntax such as relative clauses (Zukowski, 2009) and passives (Joffe & Varlokosta, 2007), as well as pronominal reference (Perovic & Wexler, 2007). Children with WS continue to make errors on these more advanced constructions, reflecting developmental delays that are commensurate with their general cognitive abilities.

Children and adults with WS particularly enjoy engaging in conversation with both familiar and unfamiliar people (Semel & Rosner, 2003). Despite this desire to communicate with others, parents report deficits in pragmatic skills on the Children's Communication Checklist, including problems in coherence, over-reliance on context, inappropriate initiations and conversational rapport (Laws & Bishop, 2004), although they are not as severely impaired as children with ASD (Philofsky et al., 2007). Analyses of conversations between children with WS and an experimenter also revealed problems in providing adequate responses to questions, offering too little information and difficulty maintaining topic (Stojanovik, 2006).

Conflicting findings have been reported on the narrative skills of children and adults with WS. Several studies highlighted the rich narratives produced by children with WS, which included evaluative devices, audience "hookers" and affective expressive prosody (Reilly et al., 1990, 2004). But, again, other studies have not replicated these findings with adults or using slightly different methods (Crawford et al., 2008; Stojanovik et al., 2004). One important factor appears to be age: Crawford and her colleagues (2008) found a decline in expressive prosody between adolescence and adulthood and concluded that the earlier studies found the most striking narrative features primarily in younger children. Little is known about developmental changes in pragmatic and discourse skills in WS as no longitudinal studies have been conducted.

Future research should investigate social and cognitive factors that predict the different strengths and weaknesses in this important domain. For example, are early joint attention skills related to later discourse impairments? Does empathy correlate with the unusual expressive language style that is so striking in younger children with WS? And what are the connections between theory of mind and pragmatics in this population? Answers to these questions will lead to the development of novel interventions for children and adolescents with WS that may have important consequences for their social adaptation.

Music

The 'musicality' of people with WS has been a widely reported but poorly defined distinctive feature of the phenotype. Unusual acoustical and musical sensitivities manifested in strong attraction or aversion for certain sounds are commonplace among individuals with WS, who spend more time listening to music and certain noises and show stronger emotional reactions to music compared to typical individuals (Lenhoff et al., 1997; Levitin &

Bellugi, 2006). However, results concerning the musical abilities of individuals with WS have been mixed (Don et al., 1999; Levitin et al., 2004) and true musical giftedness is rare. Children and adults with WS eagerly engage in playing music or singing, and some have a great memory for songs and an uncanny sense of rhythm and perfect pitch, although these are not universal characteristics of the syndrome (Carrasco et al., 2005).

Levitin et al. (2003) conducted the only fMRI study examining brain activation to music in adults with WS. Among the controls there was a well-defined activation pattern in the superior and middle temporal gyrus and superior temporal sulcus to music vs noise. In contrast, the activation patterns were more widespread for the WS group, involving both cortical and subcortical regions, especially the amygdaloid complex, as well as regions of the cerebellum and brain stem. The authors suggested that the additional brain areas recruited in WS form the functional basis for their increased orientation toward and emotional salience of acoustic stimuli and may also account for their heightened emotional responsiveness to music.

LIFETIME COURSE

Few studies have focused on the adult population with WS despite increasing evidence that 'WS is a multisystem disorder throughout the lifecycle' (Cherniske et al, 2004: 255). Cherniske and colleagues (2004) performed a multisystem assessment of adults with WS. According to caregiver reports, almost all the WS individuals had clinically significant problems with anxiety and/or depression, which were confirmed by psychiatric evaluations. About half of the sample used medication to treat these problems. There was some evidence for selective mild accelerated aging in WS, mainly for physical characteristics, hearing loss, and episodic memory. In one of the few investigations of the trajectory of adult life-span changes in

specific cognitive abilities, Devenny and colleagues (2004) found premature decline in performance on selected measures of episodic memory in a relatively small group of older adults with WS compared to adults with unspecified mental retardation, but longitudinal IQ data generally do not show decline over time in people with WS (see also Searcy et al., 2004). Using both cross-sectional and longitudinal research designs Howlin and her collaborators (2010) examined age-related changes in cognitive, linguistic, and adaptive functioning in a large sample of adults with WS ranging from 19 to 55 years. Both approaches revealed a pattern of relative stability in cognitive and language abilities as measured by standardized tests, and relative gains in adaptive behavior with age, as assessed by the Vineland Adaptive Behavior Scales. Improvements with age in adaptive functioning skills were found in the Daily Living and Social domains of the Vineland, together with significant decreases in Maladaptive scores. The findings indicate that there is no evidence of decline in cognitive ability in people with WS from the early adult years to the mid 1950s, while adaptive behaviors continue to improve over time (Howlin et al., 2010).

Changes in social understanding, such as a more mature conception of self, encompassing psychological and social dimensions, emerge by early adulthood, as reflected in extensive interviews with individuals with WS about how they view themselves (Plesa Skwerer et al., 2004). For adults, their syndrome often plays a significant role in self-definition and their own attitude about 'having WS' appears to be related to the accumulation of social experiences that do not always turn out to be as rewarding as they expect. With age, many of the individuals with WS come to view their syndrome as socially disabling, or limiting their prospects and hopes for social integration, an attitude rarely seen in younger children and that may have important consequences for the mental well-being of people with WS as they mature. Developmental changes in temperament and personality were explored by Gosch and Pankau (1997). They found relative stability in personality characteristics, but adults with WS were rated by their parents as calmer, more inhibited, and less quarrelsome or over-friendly than the children.

Researchers in the UK (Howlin & Udwin, 2006; Howlin et al., 2010) and Australia (Einfeld et al., 2001) followed relatively large cohorts of individuals with WS over time, collecting caregiver reports on adaptive behavior skills. These studies found that many of the behavioral and emotional difficulties identified in studies of children with WS (e.g. social disinhibition, attention problems, impulsivity, anxiety, over-friendliness, inappropriate in conversations, and too trusting of others) persist into adulthood and some become more apparent and pervasive with age. Among the most prevalent social difficulties reported by parents and caregivers were problems in establishing and maintaining friendships, with almost three-quarters of the people with WS described as socially isolated, despite their persistent efforts toward social contact. Given their high drive toward social engagement, trusting nature, and often indiscriminate social behavior, there is a relatively heightened risk for sexual exploitation and abuse of children and young adults, especially girls with WS (Hodapp & Dykens, 2005), but the prevalence of sexual abuse in this population is currently unknown. One troubling finding reported in the follow-up study in UK was an increase in mental health problems with age, some 'serious, such as depression, withdrawal, severe phobias and even suicide attempts' (Howlin & Udwin, 2006: 152). Rates of social, emotional, and behavioral difficulties remained high in the entire cohort, as did the families' concerns about living arrangements, social, educational, and medical support and care, independence, and employment prospects for their adult children with WS. Longitudinal follow-up findings in the Australian cohort yielded similar findings (Einfeld et al., 2001), underscoring the need for early and continuing intervention with individuals with WS, especially to help them deal with anxiety and

social-emotional difficulties. In a recent large-scale study of the mental health problems of adults with WS in the UK (Stinton, et al., 2010), the investigators used an assessment measure designed specifically for individuals with intellectual disabilities: the Psychiatric Assessment Schedule for Adults with Developmental Disabilities (PAS-ADD; Moss et al., 1996) in addition to parent/caregiver interviews. They found mental health problems meeting psychiatric diagnostic criteria in 29% of the sample. The most common diagnoses were anxiety (16.5%) and specific phobia (12%), often associated with depression (9%), which were present at higher rates than in individuals with intellectual disabilities of unknown etiology. Although only about a quarter of the sample of adults with WS met criteria for a diagnosable psychiatric disturbance on the PAS-ADD, according to parent/caregiver interviews, about 80% of the adults experienced emotional/behavioral difficulties (e.g. distractibility, changeable mood, preoccupations, and compulsive behavior) consistent with previous reports in the literature (Gosch & Pankau, 1997; Udwin et al., 1987). Thus, there is now a wealth of research into the emotional/behavioral difficulties and potential for psychopathology in both children and adults with WS, which can inform and guide the design of appropriate interventions and treatment options, including pharmacological treatments, which should be used in conjunction with psychoeducational interventions.

APPROACHES TO INTERVENTION

In contrast to the remarkable quantity of neurobehavioral, genetic, and cognitive research on WS over the past decade, there is a striking scarcity of treatment and intervention research targeting this unusual population/condition. In their seminal book Semel and Rosner (2003) provide a wealth of practical information illustrating how the explosion of research in the field of Williams syndrome could lead to the development of relevant interventions for people with WS, creating bridges between research and clinical practice. In their view, the fundamental strategy for interventions should rely on using the strengths shown by most people with WS as mediation tools for supporting and enhancing learning of new skills and adaptive behaviors, including, for example, love of performing, receptiveness to social interaction, empathy, socially engaging use of narrative devices and other aspects of language and memory skills, and musical interests.

Morris (2006) notes that currently used treatments comprise early intervention programs, special education in school and vocational training programs, as well as more specific speech and language, physical, occupational, and sensory integration therapies. The choice of therapy should be based on comprehensive individual evaluations, and may also include behavioral counseling and psychotropic medications, which are often used to manage behavior problems, especially attentional difficulties and anxiety. Parents, teachers, and other people involved with children and adults with WS need to develop strategies to ward off anticipatory anxiety by explaining the reasons for change and realistic outcomes of novel situations they encounter.

Various forms of psychotherapy could be beneficial for individuals with WS throughout their life span, such as family and group therapy, which might be facilitated by the sociability, verbal fluency, eagerness to talk and share personal information of many people with WS. Several therapeutic approaches that could effectively draw on the cognitive-behavioral phenotype of people with WS, according to Semel and Rosner (2003), are play-therapy, socio-drama, bibliotherapy, assertiveness training and, more generally, art and/or music therapy, which need to be flexibly tailored to the specific difficulties and personality characteristics of the individuals treated.

Most people with WS show significant difficulties with motor activities requiring visuospatial guidance, such as walking down steps or on uneven surfaces (Atkinson et al., 2001), spatial navigation, as well as with fine-motor skills, such as handwriting or tying shoelaces. Semel and Rosner (2003) describe several forms of intervention that may be suited for improving perceptual and motor skills in WS. Early intervention and rehabilitation programs targeting specific aspects of psychomotor development are important to help children deal with such problems related to their specific visuospatial impairment. Distinguishing between aspects of visuospatial cognition that are severely impaired and those that are relatively spared could lead to finding strategies for helping people with WS compensate for their impairments by building on their relatively spared abilities. For instance, one approach involves the guided use of compensatory strategies, especially verbal mediation, thus building on the relative strength in verbal abilities and the spontaneous tendency of children with WS to 'talk themselves through activities' (Mervis et al., 1999). Using verbal instructions and teaching individuals with WS to use verbal self-direction and words to remember places or the succession of steps in completing activities that involve spatial and temporal components can encourage finding alternative ways to overcome difficulties in areas of weakness, such as motor tasks and spatial memory (Tager-Flusberg & Plesa Skwerer, 2007).

More research is needed on how syndrome-specific outcomes emerge and develop over time in order to find windows of opportunity for interventions. For instance, a particular concern with people with WS is that their superficially fluent social language and communication behavior and high sociability can be misleading and give the impression that they are more able than they actually are. This appearance masks both general intellectual disability as well as more significant deficits in many areas of social cognition, which could lead to misguided educational expectations or misunderstandings and upsetting social experiences. Interventions to promote social reasoning skills are needed, which could focus on creating opportunities to practice solving basic social problems through role-play and social scripts. Activities such as 'Circle of Friends' may be useful to deliberately teach who is a friend, an acquaintance, or a stranger, and what are the appropriate rules of behavior in a variety of common social situations. Rehearsing social situations in role-play and providing appropriate models could also lead to improvements in social skills. Teachers and parents can discourage excessive chatter and inappropriate speech about favorite topics or preoccupations by insisting that children with WS answer their own repetitive questions, thus promoting pragmatic conversational skills (Semel & Rosner, 2003). Drawing on verbal mediation techniques, the accurate use of verbal labels for emotional expressions or other subtle social cues could be taught and then used to compensate for the deficits in social cognition in children and adults with WS. Another approach is to design task-specific interventions, which involve targeted training and guided learning experiences in a particular area of weakness. This type of intervention might build on the plasticity of brain connections and potentially lead to a gradual improvement in those brain circuits deficient in WS (cf. Meyer-Lindenberg et al., 2006).

Williams syndrome is associated with a complex array of medical problems, some of which manifest in infancy (e.g. growth deficiency, feeding difficulties, gastroesophageal reflux, idiopathic hypercalcemia that causes vomiting, constipation, and extreme irritability) and may improve or resolve with age, while others persist into adulthood, or develop later in life (Kaplan, 2006; Pober, 2006). Proper medical monitoring that starts as early as a diagnosis is made and continues throughout the life span is important for improving the quality of life of individuals with WS and for preventing the possible worsening over time of their medical complications. For instance, the majority of children with WS have cardiovascular abnormalities, the most common of which is supravalvar aortic sten-

osis, a condition that may progress in severity and often requires surgical repair (Lacro & Smoot, 2006). Cardiology evaluations are recommended annually until the age of 5 years and should be repeated periodically, depending on previous clinical findings through adulthood (American Academy of Pediatrics Committee on Genetics, 2001). Other common medical problems that require periodical assessments and monitoring beyond childhood include hypertension, gastrointestinal problems (e.g. constipation, diverticular disease), renal abnormalities (e.g. recurrent infections, renal artery stenosis), musculoskeletal problems (e.g. progressive joint limitations, contractures involving lower extremities, spinal abnormalities), elevated blood calcium levels and abnormal glucose tolerance, weight gain, dental problems (e.g. increased frequency of malocclusion, cavities, and gum disease), ophthalmologic problems (e.g. strabismus, presbyopia, cataracts), mild to moderate hearing loss, neurologic problems (e.g. hypertonia, hyperreflexia, gait and fine motor abnormalities), as well as mental health problems noted in the previous section (Plissart et al., 1994; see Pober, 2006 for recommendations for medical monitoring of adults with WS). However, not all these medical problems are experienced by every person with WS and most children and adults with WS, with adequate health management and regular monitoring for potential complications in any of the areas of concern described, can lead active, full lives.

Available data from the few longitudinal studies conducted with people with WS underscore the need for continuing medical supervision and social support throughout adulthood, and point to the need to involve mental health professionals in the support system of people with WS given the increased frequency of psychiatric problems with age. The complex nature of many of the problems found in individuals with WS requires the involvement of many health and educational professionals in collaboration with families, to ensure not only adequate care but also a good quality of life for people with WS.

CONCLUSION

Williams syndrome is one of the most striking genetically based neurodevelopmental disorders. Children and adults with WS are warm, endearing, and always a joy to be around – they have clearly captured the hearts and minds of researchers from around the world. Over two decades of research has provided us with detailed descriptions of the unusual phenotype that is seen in most individuals with WS, though it is no longer viewed as a syndrome that offers clear support for dissociations between different cognitive domains. Despite advances made in identifying the genes that are within the deletion region, it has clearly proven to be more challenging than initially expected to link most of these genes directly to features of the WS phenotype. There has been greater success in unraveling the neurobiological mechanisms and pathways that underlie behavioral and cognitive characteristics of WS, particularly those associated with visuospatial and social components. But there is still much to be learned, and we hope that future researchers undertake longitudinal investigations that integrate more comprehensive genetic, neurobiological, and environmental predictors of development. These approaches may lead to innovative ways to provide support and interventions for people with WS who experience lifelong difficulties in social communication and visuospatial functioning as well as more severe challenges with anxiety and other forms of psychopathology.

ACKNOWLEDGMENTS

Preparation of this chapter was supported by a grant from the National Institute on Child Health and Human Development (R01 HD 33470). We thank Marie Christine Andre and Emily Ammerman for their help.

REFERENCES

Adolphs, R., Tranel, D., & Damasio, A.R. (1998) 'The human amygdala in social judgment', *Nature*, 393: 470–475.

Akshoomoff, N. & Stiles, J. (1996) 'The influence of pattern type on children's block design performance', *Journal of the International Neuropsychological Society*, 2: 392–402.

American Academy of Pediatrics Committee on Genetics (2001) 'Health care supervision for children with Williams syndrome', *Pediatrics*, 107: 1192–1204.

Atkinson, J., King., Braddick, O., Nokes, L., Anker, S., & Braddick, F. (1997) 'A specific deficit of dorsal stream function in Williams syndrome', *Neuroreport: Cognitive Neuroscience and Neuropsychology*, 8: 1919–1922.

Atkinson, J., Anker S., Braddick, O., Nokes, L., Mason, A. & Braddick, F. (2001) 'Visual and visuospatial development in young children with Williams syndrome', *Developmental Medicine and Child Neurology*, 43: 330–337.

Atkinson, J., Braddick, O., Anker, S., Curran, W., Andrew, R., Wattam-Bell, J., & Braddick, F. (2003) 'Neurobiological models of visuospatial cognition in children with Williams syndrome: measures of dorsal stream and frontal function', *Developmental Neuropsychology*, 23: 139–172.

Baron-Cohen, S., Wheelwright, S., Hill, J., Raste, Y., & Plumb, I. (2001) 'The "Reading the Mind in the Eyes" Test revised version: a study with normal adults, and adults with Asperger syndrome or high-functioning autism', *Journal of Child Psychology and Psychiatry*, 42: 241–251.

Bartke, S. & Siegmuller, J. (eds) (2004) *Williams Syndrome Across Languages*. Philadelphia: John Benjamins.

Bellugi, U., Marks, S., Bihrle, A., & Sabo, H. (1988) 'Dissociation between language and cognitive functions in Williams syndrome', in D. Bishop & K. Mogford (eds), *Language Development in Exceptional Circumstances*. London: Churchill Livingstone, pp. 177–189.

Bellugi, U., Bihrle, A., Neville, H., Jernigan, T., & Doherty, S. (1992) 'Language, cognition, and brain organization in a neurodevelopmental disorder', in M. Gunnar & C. Nelson (eds), *Developmental Behavioral Neuroscience: The Minnesota Symposium*. Hillsdale, NJ: LEA, pp. 201–232.

Bellugi, U., Adolphs, R., Cassady, C., & Chiles M. (1999) 'Towards the neural basis for hypersociability in a genetic syndrome', *Neuroreport*, 10: 1653–1657.

Benton, A.L., Hamsher, K. de S., Varney, N.R., & Spreen, O. (1983) *Contributions to Neuropsychological Assessment*. New York: Oxford University Press.

Berg, J.S., Brunetti-Pierri, N., Peters, S.U., Kang, S.L., Fong, C., Salamone, J. et al. (2007) 'Speech delay and autism spectrum behaviors are frequently associated with duplication of the 7q11.23 Williams–Beuren syndrome region', *Genetics in Medicine*, 9(7): 427–441.

Bertrand, J., Mervis, C.B., & Eisenberg, J.D. (1997) 'Drawing by children with Williams syndrome: a developmental perspective', *Developmental Neuropsychology*, 13: 41–67.

Beuren, A., Apitz, J., & Harmanz, D. (1962) 'Supravalvular aortic stenosis in association with mental retardation and a certain facial appearance', *Circulation*, 26: 1235–1240.

Bongiovanni, A., Eberlein, W., & Jones, I. (1957) 'Idiopathic hypercalcemia of infancy, with failure to thrive: report of three cases, with a consideration of the possible etiology', *New England Journal of Medicine*, 257: 951–958.

Brock, J. (2007) 'Language abilities in Williams syndrome: a critical review', *Development and Psychopathology*, 19: 97–127.

Brock, J., McCormack, T., & Boucher, J. (2005) 'Probed serial recall in Williams syndrome: lexical influences on phonological short-term memory', *Journal of Speech Language and Hearing Research*, 48: 360–371.

Brock, J., Jarrold, C., Farran, E., Laws, G., & Riby, D. (2007) 'Do children with Williams syndrome really have good vocabulary knowledge? Methods for comparing cognitive and linguistic abilities in developmental disorders', *Clinical Linguistics and Phonetics*, 21: 673–688.

Brock, J., Einav, S., & Riby, D. (2008) 'The other end of the spectrum? Social cognition in Williams syndrome', in T. Striano & V. Reid (eds), *Social Cognition: Development, Neuroscience and Autism*. Oxford: Blackwell, pp. 281–300.

Brown, J., Johnson, M.H., Paterson, S., Gilmore, R.O, Gsödl, M, Longhi, E., & Karmiloff-Smith, A. (2003) 'Spatial representation and attention in toddlers with Williams syndrome and Down syndrome', *Neuropsychologia*, 41: 1037–1046.

Campbell, L., Daly, E., Toal, F., Stevens, A., Azuma, R., Karmiloff-Smith, A., Murphy, D., & Murphy, K. (2009) 'Brain structural differences associated with the behavioral phenotype in children with Williams syndrome', *Brain Research*, 1258: 96–107.

Carrasco, X., Castillo, S., Aravena, T., Rothhammer, P., & Aboitiz, F. (2005) 'Williams syndrome: pediatric, neurologic, and cognitive development', *Pediatric Neurology*, 32: 166–172.

Cherniske, E., Carpenter, T., Klaiman, C., Young, R., Bregman, J., Insogna, K., Schultz, R., & Pober, B. (2004) 'Multisystem study of 20 older adults with Williams syndrome', *American Journal of Medical Genetics*, 131A: 255–264.

Chiang, M-C., Reiss, A., Lee, A., Bellugi, U., Galaburda, A., Kroenberg, J., Mills, D., Toga, A., & Thompson, P. (2007) '3D pattern of brain abnormalities in Williams syndrome visualized using tensor-based morphometry', *Neuroimage*, 36: 1096–1109.

Ciciolla, L., Plesa Skwerer, D., & Katz, R. (2007). *Exploring Helping Behaviors and Empathy in Young Children with Williams Syndrome*. Boston, MA: Society for Research in Child Development.

Clahsen, H. & Almazan, M. (1998) 'Syntax and morphology in Williams syndrome', *Cognition*, 68: 167–198.

Crawford, N., Edelson, L., Plesa Skwerer, D., & Tager-Flusberg, H. (2008) 'Expressive language style among adolescents and adults with Williams syndrome', *Applied Psycholinguistics*, 29: 585–602.

Dai, L., Bellugi, U., Chen, X-N., Pulst-Korenberg, A.M., Järvinen-Pasley, A., Tirosh-Wagner, T., Eis, P.S., Graham, J., Mills, D., Searcy, Y., & Korenberg, J.R. (2009) 'Is it Williams syndrome? GTF2IRD1 implicated in visual–spatial construction and GTF2I in sociability revealed by high resolution arrays', *American Journal of Medical Genetics*, 149A: 302–314.

Davies, M., Udwin, O., & Howlin, P. (1998) 'Adults with Williams syndrome', *British Journal of Psychiatry*, 172: 273–274.

Deruelle, C., Rondan, C., Mancini, J., & Livet, M.O. (2006) 'Do children with Williams syndrome fail to process visual configural information?', *Research in Developmental Disabilities*, 27: 243–253.

Devenny, D.A., Krinsky-McHale, S.J., Kittler, P., Flory, M., Jenkins, E., & Brown, W.T. (2004) 'Age- associated memory changes in adults with Williams syndrome', *Developmental Neuropsychology*, 26: 691–706.

Dilts, C., Morris, C., & Leonard, C. (1990) 'Hypothesis for development of a behavioral phenotype in Williams syndrome', *American Journal of Medical Genetics, Supplement*, 6: 126–131.

Don, A., Schellenberg, E., & Rourke, B. (1999) 'Music and language skills in children with Williams syndrome', *Child Neuropsychology*, 5: 154–170.

Doyle, T.F., Bellugi, U., Korenberg, J.R., & Graham, J. (2004) '"Everybody in the world is my friend": Hyperso ciability in young children with Williams syndrome', *American Journal of Medical Genetics,* 124A: 263–273.

Dykens, E.M. & Rosner, B. (1999) 'Refining behavioral phenotypes: personality-motivation in Williams and Prader–Willi syndromes', *American Journal on Mental Retardation,* 104: 158–169.

Einfeld, S., Tonge, B., & Rees, V. (2001) 'Longitudinal course of behavioral and emotional problems in Williams syndrome', *American Journal of Mental Retardation,* 106: 73–81.

Elgar, K. & Campbell, R. (2001) 'Annotation: the cognitive neuroscience of face recognition: implications for developmental disorders', *Journal of Child Psychology and Psychiatry,* 42: 705–717.

Elliott, C.D. (1990) *Differential Ability Scales: Introductory and Technical Handbook.* New York: The Psychological Corporation.

Ewart, A.K., Morris, C.A., Atkinson, D., Jin, W., Sternes, K., Spallone, P., Stock, A.D., Leppert, M., & Keating, M.T. (1993) 'Hemizygosity at the elastin locus in a developmental disorder, Williams syndrome', *Nature Genetics,* 5: 11–16.

Farran, E.K. & Jarrold, C. (2003) 'Visuospatial cognition in Williams syndrome: reviewing and accounting for the strengths and weaknesses in performance', *Developmental Neuropsychology,* 23: 173–200.

Farran, E.K., Jarrold, C., & Gathercole, S.E. (2003) 'Divided attention, selective attention and drawing: processing preferences in Williams syndrome are dependent on the task administered', *Neuropsychologia,* 4: 676–687.

Fidler, D.J., Hepburn, S.L., Most, D.E., Philofsky, A., & Rogers, S.J. (2007) 'Emotional responsivity in young children with Williams syndrome', *American Journal on Mental Retardation,* 112: 194–206.

Francke U. (1999) 'Williams–Beuren syndrome: genes and mechanisms', *Human Molecular Genetics,* 8: 1947–1954.

Frangiskakis, J.M., Ewart, A., Morris, C.A., Mervis, C.B., Bertrand, J., Robinson, B.F. et al. (1996) 'LIM-kinase1 hemizygosity implicated in impaired visuospatial constructive cognition', *Cell,* 86: 59–69.

Frigerio, E., Burt, D.M., Gagliardi,C., Cioffi, G., Martelli, S., Perrett, D.I., & Borgatti, R. (2006) 'Is everybody always my friend? Perception of approachability in Williams syndrome', *Neuropsychologia,* 44: 254–259.

Gagliardi, C., Frigerio, E., Burt, D.M., Cazzaniga, I., Perrett, D., & Borgatti, R. (2003) 'Facial expression recognition in Williams syndrome', *Neuropsychologia* 41: 733–738.

Galaburda, A., Holinger, D., Bellugi, U., & Sherman, G. (2002) 'Williams syndrome: neuronal size and neuronal-packing density in primary visual cortex', *Archives of Neurology,* 59: 1461–1467.

Gosch, A. & Pankau, R. (1997) 'Personality characteristics and behavior problems in individuals of different ages with Williams syndrome', *Developmental Medicine and Child Neurology,* 39: 327–533.

Gothelf, D., Furfaro, J., Penniman, L., Glover, G., & Reiss, A. (2005) 'The contribution of novel brain imaging techniques to understanding the neurobiology of mental retardation and developmental disabilities', *Mental Retardation and Developmental Disabilities Research Review,* 11: 331–339.

Haas, B., Mills, D., Yam, A., Hoeft, F., Bellugi, U., & Reiss, A. (2009) 'Genetic influences on sociability: heightened amygdala reactivity and event-related responses to positive social stimuli in Williams syndrome', *Journal of Neuroscience,* 29: 1132–1139.

Hodapp, R.M. & Dykens, E. (2005) 'Problems of girls and young women with mental retardation (intellectual disabilities)', in D.J. Bell, S.L. Foster, & E.J. Mash (eds), *Handbook of Behavioral and Emotional Problems in Girls,* New York: Springer, pp. 239–262.

Hoeft, F., Barnea-Goraly, N., Haas, B.W., Golarai, G., Ng, D., Mills, D., Korenberg, J., Bellugi, U., Galaburda, A., & Reiss, A.L. (2007) 'More is not always better: increased fractional anisotropy of superior longitudinal fasciculus associated with poor visuospatial abilities in Williams syndrome', *The Journal of Neuroscience,* 27: 11960 –11965.

Hoffman, J.E., Landau, B., & Pagani, B. (2003) 'Spatial breakdown in spatial construction: evidence from eye fixations in children with Williams syndrome', *Cognitive Psychology,* 46: 260–301.

Holinger, D.P., Bellugi, U., Mills, D.L., Korenberg, J.R. Reiss, A.L., Sherman, G.F., & Galaburda, A.M. (2005) 'Relative sparing of primary auditory cortex in Williams syndrome', *Brain Research,* 1037: 35–42.

Howlin, P. & Udwin, O. (2006) 'Outcome in adult life for people with Williams syndrome—results from a survey of 239 families', *Journal of Intellectual Disability Research,* 50: 151–160.

Howlin, P., Elison, S., Udwin, O., & Stinton, C. (2010) 'Cognitive, linguistic and adaptive functioning in Williams syndrome: Trajectories from early to middle adulthood', *Journal of Applied Research in Intellectual Disabilities,* 23(4): 322–336.

Jarrold, C., Baddeley, A., & Hewes, A.K. (1998) 'Verbal and nonverbal abilities in the Williams syndrome phenotype: evidence for diverging developmental trajectories', *Journal of Child Psychology and Psychiatry,* 39: 511–523.

Jarvinen-Pasley, A., Bellugi, U., Reilly, J., Mills, D.L., Galaburda, A., Reiss, A.L., & Korenberg, J.R. (2008) 'Defining the social phenotype in Williams syndrome: a model for linking gene, the brain, and behavior', *Development and Psychopathology,* 20: 1–35.

Jernigan, T.L. & Bellugi, U. (1994) 'Neuroanatomical distinctions between Williams and Down syndromes', in S. Broman & J. Grafman (eds), *Atypical Cognitive Deficits in Developmental Disorders: Implications in Brain Function.* Hillsdale, NJ: Lawrence Erlbaum Associates. pp. 57–66.

Joffe, V. & Varlokosta, S. (2007) 'Patterns of syntactic development in children with Williams syndrome and Down's syndrome: evidence from passives and Wh-questions', *Clinical Linguistics and Phonetics,* 21: 705–727.

Jordan, H., Reiss, J.E., Hoffman, J.E., & Landau, B. (2002) 'Intact perception of biological motion in the face of profound spatial deficits: Williams syndrome', *Psychological Science,* 13: 162–167.

Kaplan, P. (2006) 'The medical management of children with Williams–Beuren syndrome', in C.A. Morris, H.M. Lenhoff, and P. Wang (eds), *Williams–Beuren Syndrome: Research and Clinical Perspectives.* Baltimore, MD: Johns Hopkins University Press. pp. 83–106.

Karmiloff-Smith, A., Klima, E., Bellugi, U., Grant, J., & Baron-Cohen, S. (1995) 'Is there a social module? Language, face processing and theory of mind in individuals with Williams syndrome', *Journal of Cognitive Neuroscience,* 7: 196–208.

Karmiloff-Smith, A., Thomas, M., Annaz, D., Humphreys, K., Ewing, S., Brace, N., Van Duuren, M., Pike, G., Grice, S., & Campbell, R. (2004) 'Exploring the Williams syndrome face-processing debate: the importance of building developmental trajectories', *Journal of Child Psychology and Psychiatry,* 45: 1258–1274.

Karmiloff-Smith, A., Ansari, D., Campbell, L., Scerif, G., & Thomas, M. (2006) 'Theoretical implications of studying cognitive development in genetic disorders: the case of Williams–Beuren syndrome', in C.A. Morris, H.M. Lenhoff & P. Wang (eds), *Williams–Beuren Syndrome: Research and Clinical Perspectives.* Baltimore, MD: Johns Hopkins University Press. pp. 254–273.

Kaufman, A. & Kaufman, N. (2004) *Manual for the Kaufman Brief Test of Intelligence,* 2nd edn, Circle Pines, MN: American Guidance Service.

Kippenhan, J., Olsen, R., Mervis, C., Morris, C., Kohn, P., Meyer-Lindenberg, A., & Berman, K. (2005) 'Genetic contributions to human gyrification: sulcal morphometry in Williams syndrome', *Journal of Neuroscience,* 25: 7840–7846.

Klein-Tasman, B.P. & Mervis, C.B. (2003) 'Distinctive personality characteristics of 8-, 9-, and 10-year-olds with Williams syndrome, *Developmental Neuropsychology,* 23: 269–290.

Klein-Tasman, B.P. Mervis, C.B., Lord, C., & Phillips, K. (2007) 'Socio-communicative deficits in young children with Williams syndrome: performance on the Autism Diagnostic Observation Schedule', *Child Neuropsychology,* 13: 444–467.

Lacro, R.V. & Smoot, L.B. (2006) 'Cardiovascular disease in Williams–Beuren syndrome', in C.A. Morris, H.M. Lenhoff, & P. Wang (eds), *Williams–Beuren syndrome: Research and Clinical Perspectives.* Baltimore, MD: Johns Hopkins University Press, pp. 107–124.

Laing, E. & Jarrold, C. (2007) 'Comprehension of spatial language in Williams syndrome: evidence for impaired spatial representation of verbal descriptions', *Clinical Linguistics and Phonetics,* 21: 689–704.

Laing, E., Butterworth, G., Ansari, D., Gsodl, M., Longhi, E., Panagiotaki, G., Paterson, S., & Karmiloff-Smith, A. (2002) 'Atypical development of language and social communication in toddlers with Williams Syndrome', *Developmental Science,* 5: 233–246.

Landau, B. & Zukowski, A. (2003) 'Objects, motions and paths: spatial language in children with Williams syndrome', *Developmental Neuropsychology,* 23: 105–137.

Landau, B., Hoffman, J.E., & Kurz, N. (2006) 'Object recognition with severe spatial deficits in Williams Syndrome: sparing and breakdown', *Cognition,* 100: 483–510.

Laws, G. & Bishop, D. (2004) 'Pragmatic language impairment and social deficits in Williams syndrome: a comparison with Down's syndrome and specific language impairment', *International Journal of Language and Communication Disorders,* 39: 45–64.

Lenhoff, H.M., Wang, P.P., Greenberg, F., & Bellugi, U. (1997) 'Williams syndrome and the brain', *Scientific American,* 277: 68–73.

Levitin, D. & Bellugi, U. (2006) 'Rhythm, timbre and hyperacusis in Williams–Beuren syndrome', in C.A. Morris, H.M. Lenhoff, & P. Wang (eds), *Williams Beuren Syndrome: Research and Clinical Perspectives.* Baltimore, MD: Johns Hopkins University Press, pp. 343–358.

Levitin, D., Menon, V., Schmitt, J., Eliez, S., White, C., Glover, G., Kadis, J., Korenberg, J., Bellugi, U., & Reiss, A. (2003) 'Neural correlates of auditory perception in Williams syndrome: An fMRI study', *Neuroimage,* 18: 74–82.

Levitin, D., Cole, K., Chiles, M., Lai, Z., Lincoln, A., & Bellugi, U. (2004) 'Characterizing the musical phenotype in individuals with Williams syndrome', *Child Neuropsychology,* 10: 223–247.

Levy, Y. & Bechar, T. (2003) 'Cognitive, lexical and morpho-syntactic profiles of Israeli children with Williams syndrome', *Cortex,* 39: 255–271.

Leyfer, O., Woodruff-Borden, J., Klein-Tasman, B., Fricke, J., & Mervis, C. (2006) 'Prevalence of psychiatric disorders in 4 to 16-year-olds with Williams syndrome', *American Journal of Medical Genetics, Part B: Neuropsychiatric Genetics,* 141B: 615–622.

Lincoln, A.J., Searcy, Y.M., Jones, W., & Lord, C. (2007) 'Social interaction behaviors discriminate young children with autism and Williams syndrome', *Journal of the American Academy of Child and Adolescent Psychiatry,* 46: 323–331.

Lukacs, A., Pleh, C., & Racsmany, M. (2004) 'Language in Hungarian children with Williams syndrome', in S. Bartke & J. Siegmuller (eds), *Williams Syndrome across Language.* Philadelphia: John Benjamins, pp. 187–220.

Marenco, S., Siuta, M., Kippenhan, J., Grodofsky, S., Chang, W-L., Kohn, P. et al. (2007) 'Genetic contributions to white matter architecture revealed by diffusion tensor imaging in Williams syndrome', *Proceedings of the National Academy of Science,* 104: 15117–15122.

Martens, M.A., Wilson, S.J., & Reutens, D.C. (2008a) 'Williams syndrome: a critical review of the cognitive, behavioral, and neuroanatomical phenotype', *Journal of Child Psychology and Psychiatry,* 49: 576–608.

Martens, M.A., Wilson, S.J., & Reutens, D.C. (2008b) 'Cognitive and behavioral profile of Australian individuals with Williams syndrome'. The 12th International Professional Conference on Williams Syndrome, Orange County, CA.

Masataka, N. (2001) 'Why early linguistic milestones are delayed in children with Williams syndrome: late onset of hand banging as a possible rate-limiting constraint on the emergence of canonical babbling', *Developmental Science,* 4: 158–164.

Meng, Y., Zhang, Y., Tregoubov, V., Janus, C., Cruz, L., Jackson, M., Lu, W.Y., MacDonald, J.F., Wang, J.Y., Falls, D.L., & Jia, Z. (2002) 'Abnormal spine morphology and enhanced LTP in LIMK-1 knockout mice', *Neuron,* 35: 121–33.

Mervis, C. & Becerra, A. (2007) 'Language and communicative development in Williams syndrome', *Mental Retardation and Developmental Disabilities Research Reviews,* 13: 3–15.

Mervis, C.B. (2006) 'Language abilities in Williams–Beuren syndrome', in C. Morris, H. Lenhoff, & P. Wang (eds), *Williams–Beuren syndrome: Research, Evaluation, and Treatment.* Baltimore, MD: Johns Hopkins University Press, pp. 159–206.

Mervis, C.B. & Bertrand, J. (1997) 'Developmental relations between cognition and language: evidence from Williams Syndrome', in L.B. Adamson & M.A. Romski (eds), *Research on Communication and Language Disorders: Contributions to Theories of Language Development.* New York: Brookes. pp. 75–106.

Mervis, C.B. & John, A. (2008) 'Vocabulary abilities of children with Williams syndrome: strengths, weaknesses, and relation to visuospatial construction ability', *Journal of Speech Language and Hearing Research,* 51: 967–982.

Mervis, C.B., Morris, C.A., Bertrand, J., & Robinson, B.F. (1999) 'Williams syndrome: findings from an integrated program of research', in H. Tager-Flusberg (ed), *Neurodevelopmental Disorders.* Cambridge, MA: MIT Press, pp. 65–110.

Mervis, C.B., Robinson, B.F., Bertrand, J., Morris C.A., Klein-Tasman, B.P., & Armstrong, S.C. (2000) 'The Williams syndrome cognitive profile', *Brain and Cognition,* 44: 604–628.

Mervis, C., Morris, C.A., Klein-Tasman, B.P., Bertrand, J., Kwitny, S., Appelbaum, L.G., & Rice, C.E. (2003) 'Attentional characteristics of infants and toddlers with Williams syndrome during triadic interactions', *Developmental Neuropsychology,* 2: 243–268.

Meyer-Lindenberg, A., Kohn, P., Mervis, C.B., Kippenhan, J.S., Olsen, R.K., Morris, C.A., & Berman, K.F. (2004) 'Neural basis of genetically determined visuospatial construction deficit in Williams syndrome', *Neuron,* 43: 623–631.

Meyer-Lindenberg, A., Mervis, C.B., Sarpal, D., Koch, P., Steele, S., Kohn, P. et al. (2005a) 'Functional, structural, and metabolic abnormalities of the hippocampal formation in Williams syndrome', *The Journal of Clinical Investigation,* 115: 1888–1895.

Meyer-Lindenberg, A., Hariri, A.R., Munoz, K.E., Mervis, C.B., Mattay, V.S., Morris, C.A., & Berman, K.F. (2005b) 'Neural correlates of genetically abnormal social cognition in Williams syndrome', *Nature Neuroscience,* 8: 991–993.

Meyer-Lindenberg, A., Mervis, C.B., & Berman, K.F. (2006) 'Neural mechanisms in Williams syndrome: a unique window to genetic influences on cognition and behavior', *Nature Reviews: Neuroscience,* 7: 380–393.

Mills, D.L., Alvarez, T.D., St. George, M., Appelbaum, L.G., Bellugi, U., & Neville, H. (2000) 'Electrophysiological studies of face processing in

Williams syndrome', *Journal of Cognitive Neuroscience,* 12 (Suppl): 47–64.

Mobbs, D., Garrett, A.S., Menon, V., Rose, F.E., Bellugi, U., & Reiss, A.L. (2004) 'Anomalous brain activation during face and gaze processing in Williams syndrome', *Neurology,* 62: 2070–2076.

Mobbs, D., Eckert, M.A., Mills, D., Korenberg, J., Bellugi, U., Galaburda, A.M., & Reiss, A.L. (2007) 'Frontostriatal dysfunction during response inhibition in Williams syndrome', *Biological Psychiatry,* 62: 256–261.

Montfoort, I., Frens, M.A., Hooge, I.T., Haselen, G.C., & van der Geest, J.N. (2007) 'Visual search deficits in Williams–Beuren syndrome', *Neuropsychologia,* 45: 931–938.

Morris, C. (2006) 'The dysmorphology, genetics, and natural history of Williams–Beuren syndrome', in C.A. Morris, H.M. Lenhoff, & P. Wang (eds), *Williams–Beuren Syndrome: Research and Clinical Perspectives.* Baltimore, MD: Johns Hopkins University Press, pp. 3–17.

Morris, C., Dilts, C., Demsey, S., Leonard, C., & Blackburn, B. (1988) 'The natural history of Williams syndrome: physical characteristics', *Journal of Pediatrics,* 113: 318–326.

Moss, S., Goldberg, D., Patel, P., Prosser, H., Ibbotson, B., Simpson, N. et al. (1996) 'The Psychiatric Assessment Schedule for Adults with Developmental Disabilities'. Manchester: Hester Adrian Research Centre.

Nowicki, S., Jr. & Duke, M.P. (1994) 'Individual differences in the nonverbal communication of affect: the Diagnostic Analysis of Nonverbal Accuracy Scale', *Journal of Nonverbal Behavior,* 18: 9–35.

O'Hearn, K., Courtney, S., Street, W., & Landau, B. (2008) 'Working memory impairment in people with Williams syndrome: effects of delay, task and stimulus', *Brain and Cognition,* 69(3): 495–503.

Osborne, L.R. (2006) 'The molecular basis of a multisystem disorder', in C.A. Morris, H.M. Lenhoff, & P. Wang (eds), *Williams–Beuren Syndrome: Research and Clinical Perspectives.* Baltimore, MD: Johns Hopkins University Press, pp. 18–58.

Osborne, L.R. & Mervis, C.B. (2007) 'Rearrangements of the Williams–Beuren syndrome locus: molecular basis and implications for speech and language development', *Expert Reviews in Molecular Medicine,* 9(15): 1–16.

Osborne, L.R. & Pober, B. (2001) 'Genetics of childhood disorders: XXVII. Genes and cognition in Williams syndrome', *Journal of the American Academy of Child & Adolescent Psychiatry,* 40: 732–735.

Pani, J., Mervis, C.B., & Robinson, B.F. (1999) 'Global spatial organization by individuals with Williams syndrome', *Psychological Science,* 10: 453–458.

Paul, B.M., Stiles, J., Passarotti, A., Bavar, N., & Bellugi, U. (2002) 'Face and place processing in Williams syndrome: evidence for a dorsal-ventral dissociation', *Neuroreport* 13: 1115–1119.

Perovic, A. & Wexler, K. (2007) 'Complex grammar in Williams syndrome', *Clinical Linguistics and Phonetics,* 21: 729–745.

Philofsky, A., Fidler, D., & Hepburn, S. (2007) 'Pragmatic language profiles of school-age children with autism spectrum disorders and Williams syndrome', *American Journal of Speech-Language Pathology,* 16: 368–380.

Plesa Skwerer, D. & Tager-Flusberg, H. (2006) 'Social cognition in Williams-Beuren syndrome', in C.A. Morris, H.M. Lenhoff, & P. Wang (eds), *Williams–Beuren Syndrome: Research and Clinical Perspectives.* Baltimore, MD: Johns Hopkins University Press, pp. 237–253.

Plesa Skwerer, D., Sullivan, K., Joffre, K., & Tager-Flusberg, H. (2004) 'Self concept in people with Williams syndrome and Prader–Willi syndrome', *Research in Developmental Disabilities,* 25: 119–138.

Plesa Skwerer, D., Verbalis, A., Schofield, C., Faja, S., & Tager-Flusberg, H. (2005) 'Social-perceptual abilities in adolescents and adults with Williams syndrome', *Cognitive Neuropsychology* 22: 1–12.

Plesa Skwerer, D., Faja, S., Schofield, C., Verbalis, A., & Tager-Flusberg, H. (2006) 'Perceiving facial and vocal expression of emotion in Williams syndrome', *American Journal on Mental Retardation,* 111: 15–26.

Plesa Skwerer, D., Schofield, C., Verbalis, A., Faja, S., & Tager-Flusberg, H. (2007) 'Receptive prosody in adolescents and adults with Williams syndrome', *Language and Cognitive Processes,* 22: 247–271.

Plesa Skwerer, D., Lindeke, M., Ogrodnik, K., & Tager-Flusberg, H. (2008) 'Observational assessments of attachment and temperament in young children with Williams syndrome: toward a profile of early socio-emotional functioning', The 12th International Professional Conference on Williams Syndrome, Orange County, CA.

Plissart, L., Borghgraef, M., Volcke, P., Van den Berghe, H., & Fryns, J.P. (1994) 'Adults with Williams–Beuren syndrome: evaluation of the medical, psychological and behavioral aspects', *Clinical Genetics,* 46(2): 161–167.

Pober, B. (2006) 'Evidence-based medical management of adults with Williams–Beuren syndrome', in C.A. Morris, H.M. Lenhoff, & P. Wang (eds), *Williams–Beuren Syndrome: Research and Clinical Perspectives.* Baltimore, MD: Johns Hopkins University Press, pp. 125–143.

Porter, M. & Coltheart, M. (2005) 'Cognitive heterogeneity in Williams syndrome', *Developmental Neuropsychology,* 27(2): 275–306.

Porter, M., Coltheart, M., & Langdon, R. (2007) 'The neuropsychological basis of hypersociability in Williams and Down syndrome', *Neuropsychologia,* 45: 2839–2849.

Reilly, J., Klima, E., & Bellugi, U. (1990) 'Once more with feeling: affect and language in atypical populations', *Development and Psychopathology,* 2: 367–391.

Reilly, J., Losh, M., Bellugi, U., & Wulfeck, B. (2004) '"Frog, where are you?" Narratives in children with specific language impairment, early focal brain injury and Williams syndrome', *Brain and Language,* 88: 229–247.

Reiss, A., Eckert, M., Rose, F., Karchemskiy, A., Kesler, S., Chang, M., Reynolds, Kwon, H., & Galaburda, A. (2004) 'An experiment of nature: brain anatomy parallels cognition and behavior in Williams syndrome', *Journal of Neuroscience,* 24: 5009–5015.

Riby, D.M. & Hancock, P.J. (2008) 'Viewing it differently: social scene perception in Williams syndrome and autism,' *Neuropsychologia,* 46(11): 2855–2860

Riby, D.M. & Hancock, P.J. (2009) 'Do faces capture the attention of individuals with Williams syndrome or autism? Evidence from tracking eye movements?', *Journal of Autism and Developmental Disorders,* 39(3): 421–431.

Rose, F.E., Lincoln, A.J., Lai, Z., Ene, M., Searcy, Y.M., & Bellugi, U. (2007) 'Orientation and affective expression effects on face recognition in Williams syndrome and autism', *Journal of Autism and Developmental Disorders,* 37(3): 513–522.

Sampaio, A., Sousa, N., Fernandez, M., Vasconcelos, C., Shenton, M., & Goncalves, O. (2008) 'MRI assessment of superior temporal gyrus in Williams syndrome', *Cognitive and Behavioral Neurology,* 21: 150–156.

Sarpal, D., Buchsbaum, B.R., Kohn, P.D., Kippenhan, J.S., Mervis, C.B., Meyer-Lindenberg, A., & Berman, K.F. (2008) 'A genetic model for understanding higher order visual processing: functional interactions of the ventral stream in Williams syndrome', *Cerebral Cortex,* 18: 2402–2409.

Searcy, Y.M., Lincoln, A.J., Rose, F.E., Klima, E.S., & Bavar, N. (2004) 'The relationship between age and IQ in adults with Williams syndrome', *American Journal on Mental Retardation,* 109: 231–236.

Semel, E. & Rosner, S. (2003) *Understanding Williams Syndrome.* Hillsdale, NJ: Lawrence Erlbaum Associates.

Somerville, M.J., Mervis, C.B., Young, E.J., Seo, E.-J., del Campo, M., Bamforth, S., Peregrine, E., Lilley, M., Pérez-Jurado, L., Morris, C.A., Scherer, S.W., & Osborne, L.R. (2005) 'Severe expressive language delay related to duplication of the Williams–Beuren locus', *New England Journal of Medicine,* 353: 1694–1701.

Stinton, C., Elison, S., & Howlin, P. (2010) 'Mental health in Williams syndrome', *American Journal on Mental Retardation,* 115(1): 3–18.

Stojanovik, V. (2006) 'Social interaction deficits and conversational inadequacy in Williams syndrome', *Journal of Neurolinguistics,* 19: 157–173.

Stojanovik, V., Perkins, M.R., & Howard, S. (2004) 'Williams Syndrome and Specific Language Impairment do not support claims for developmental double dissociations and innate modularity', *Journal of Neurolinguistics,* 17: 403–424.

Stromme, P., Bjornstad, P., & Ramstad, K. (2002) 'Prevalence estimation of Williams syndrome', *Journal of Child Neurology,* 17: 269–271.

Sullivan, K. & Tager-Flusberg, H. (1999) 'Second-order belief attribution in Williams syndrome: intact or impaired?', *American Journal on Mental Retardation,* 104: 523–532.

Sullivan, K., Winner, E., & Tager-Flusberg, H. (2003) 'Can adolescents with Williams syndrome tell the difference between lies and jokes?', *Developmental Neuropsychology,* 23: 87–105.

Tager-Flusberg, H. & Plesa Skwerer, D. (2007) 'Williams syndrome: a model developmental syndrome for exploring brain-behavior relationships', in D. Coch, G. Dawson, & K. Fischer (eds), *Human Behavior and the Developing Brain: Volume 2: Atypical Development.* New York: Guilford, pp. 87–116.

Tager-Flusberg, H. & Sullivan, K. (2000) 'A componential view of theory of mind: evidence from Williams syndrome', *Cognition,* 76: 59–89.

Tager-Flusberg, H., Boshart, J., & Baron-Cohen, S. (1998) 'Reading the windows to the soul: evidence of domain-specific sparing in Williams syndrome', *Journal of Cognitive Neuroscience,* 10(5): 631–639.

Tager-Flusberg, H., Plesa Skwerer, D., Faja, S., & Joseph, R.M. (2003) 'People with Williams syndrome process faces holistically', *Cognition,* 89: 11–24.

Tassabehji, M., Metcalfe, K., Fergusson, W.D., Carette, M.J.A., Dore, J.K., Donnai, D., Read, A.P., Proschel, C., Gutowski, N.J., Mao, X., & Sheer, D. (1996) 'LIM-kinase deleted in Williams syndrome', *Nature Genetics,* 13: 272–273.

Thomas, M., Grant, J., Barnham, Z., Gsodl, M., Laing, E., Lakusta, L., Tyler, L.K., Grice, S., Paterson, S., & Karmiloff-Smith, A. (2001) 'Past tense formation in Williams syndrome', *Language and Cognitive Processes,* 16: 143–176.

Thomas, M.L., Beccera, A.M., & Mervis, C.B. (2002) 'The development of empathy in 4-year-old children with Williams syndrome'. 9th International Professional Conference on Williams Syndrome, Long Beach, CA.

Thompson, P., Lee, A., Dutton, R., Geaga, J., Hayashi, K., Bellugi, U., Galaburda, A., Korenberg, J., Mills, D., Toga, A., & Reiss, A. (2005) 'Abnormal cortical complexity and thickness profiles mapped in Williams syndrome', *Journal of Neuroscience,* 25: 4146–4158.

Udwin, O. & Yule, W. (1990) 'Expressive language of children with Williams syndrome', *American Journal of Medical Genetics,* 6 (Suppl): 108–114.

Udwin, O., Yule, W., & Martin, N. (1987) 'Cognitive abilities and behavioural characteristics of children with idiopathic infantile hypercalcaemia', *Journal of Child Psychology and Psychiatry,* 28: 297–309.

Vicari, S., Bellucci, S., & Carlesimo, G.A. (2003) 'Visual and spatial working memory dissociation: evidence from Williams syndrome', *Developmental Medicine & Child Neurology,* 45: 269–273.

Volterra, V., Capirci, O., Pezzini, G., Sabbadini, L., & Vicari, S. (1996) 'Linguistic abilities in Italian children with Williams syndrome', *Cortex,* 32: 663–677.

Wang, P.P., Doherty, S., Rourke, S.B., & Bellugi, U. (1995) 'Unique profile of visuo-perceptual skills in a genetic syndrome', *Brain and Cognition,* 29: 54–65.

Williams, J., Barrett-Boyes, B. & Lowe, J. (1961) 'Supravalvular aortic stenosis', *Circulation,* 24: 1311–1318.

Young, E.J., Lipina, T., Tam, E., Mandel, A., Clapcote, S.J., Bechard, A.R., Chambers, J., Mount, H.T., Fletcher, P.J., Roder, J.C., & Osborne, L.R. (2008) 'Reduced fear and aggression and altered serotonin metabolism in Gtf2ird1-targeted mice', *Genes, Brain and Behavior,* 7: 224–234.

Zukowski, A. (2004) 'Investigating knowledge of complex syntax: insights from experimental studies of Williams syndrome', in M. Rice & S. Warren (eds), *Developmental Language Disorders: From Phenotypes to Etiologies.* Mahwah, NJ: Erlbaum, pp. 97–117.

Zukowski, A. (2009) 'Elicited production of relative clauses in children with Williams syndrome', *Language and Cognitive Processes,* 24: 1–43.

6

Prader-Willi Syndrome

Joyce Whittington & Anthony Holland

INTRODUCTION

Prader–Willi syndrome (PWS) is now recognized as a genetically determined complex neurodevelopmental syndrome with distinct characteristics that evolve during early development and result in the physical and behavioural phenotype of the syndrome. In this chapter we review some of the recent advances that have helped both to reframe the way we think about PWS and have also led to interventions and support strategies that can improve the lives of those with the syndrome and of their families. We briefly review the advances in our understanding of the PWS genotype and phenotype and then focus specifically on those areas of clinical research and practice that have advanced in the last 5–10 years. These include our understanding of the eating disorder, endocrinology, and mental health.

GENETICS OF PWS

When the syndrome was first described in 1956 by endocrinologists, hypotonia, hypog-onadism, hyperphagia and obesity were considered the defining features (Prader et al., 1956). Whereas a genetic basis was suspected, it was not until later that it was noticed that in some cases there was a small deletion in one chromosome 15, but this was not apparent in all those who clinically had the syndrome. Advances in genetics in the late 1980s eventually led to the present view of PWS being caused by the lack of expression of maternally imprinted/paternally expressed genes in the region q11-q13 of the paternally inherited chromosome 15 (Nicholls, 1993). This region is known as the Prader–Willi syndrome critical region (PWSCR). The two main mechanisms resulting in PWS are a deletion involving the PWSCR of chromosome 15 of paternal origin or the inheritance of two maternally derived, but not paternally derived, chromosome 15s – referred to as maternal uniparental disomy (mUPD). The chromosomal deletions usually have one of two fixed pairs of endpoints, denoted as breakpoint 1 (BP1), breakpoint 2 (BP2) and breakpoint 3 (BP3), the larger deletions running from BP1 to BP3 and the smaller from BP2 to BP3. Much more rarely, an unbalanced translocation with a break point in the critical region or a defect of imprinting such that the maternal imprint fails to be reset on the paternally inherited chromosome can also give rise to the syndrome.

Genes that are imprinted depending on the gender of the parent of origin are therefore expressed only from one chromosome being 'switched off' on the other analogous chromosome. For example, maternally imprinted genes are expressed only from the paternally derived chromosome and paternally imprinted genes are expressed only from the maternally derived chromosome. The significance of imprinting can be seen in the fact that a similar deletion occurring on the maternally derived chromosome 15, so that the genes that are paternally imprinted/maternally expressed are deleted, resulting in a totally different syndrome (Angelman syndrome). It is not known how many imprinted genes there are in the PWSCR or the absence of how many of them contribute to the syndrome. It is to be noted that non-imprinted genes can be expressed from either the maternally derived or the paternally derived chromosome and hence expression of non-imprinted genes is not lost in PWS. However, in the deletion phenotype there is the possibility that a non-dominant allele is expressed more often than in the general population. Thus, the phenotypic characteristic 'fair for family background' of the deletion subtype arises from the pigmentation gene found in the PWSCR.

The general consensus is that PWS is polygenic in origin, but a 2003 hypothesis paper in the *Lancet* (Holland et al., 2003) argued that it could be explained by a single gene, as yet unidentified, with certain properties relating to energy balance. However, neither the number or identities of the genes involved in the polygenic hypothesis nor any single gene matching the single gene hypothesis have yet been found. Recently, researchers claimed that a deletion in the C/D box snoRNAs HBll-85 caused PWS (Sahoo et al., 2008). This was based on a single case study and the diagnosis

of PWS is somewhat controversial, although these snoRNAs have been implicated in some of the phenotypic features of PWS (see next paragraph). If this claim is valid, then any missing phenotypic features in this case, such as small stature, could be explained by the presence and expression of other imprinted genes that are usually also not expressed in people with PWS – the report mentioned only the absence of necdin – so this remains speculation.

Most of the recent work on PWS genetics has been on mouse models, relating the absence of one or more of the imprinted genes of the PWSCR to one or more phenotypic features or ruling them out as candidate genes for PWS. Thus, HBll-52 (Runte et al., 2005) and the cluster MKRN3, MAGEL2 and NDN (Kanber et al., 2009) have been ruled out as candidate genes. MBll-85 snoRNA was found to be critical for neonatal lethality in the PWS mouse (Ding et al., 2005), to cause postnatal growth retardation (Skryabin et al., 2007), to cause growth deficiency and hyperphagia (Ding et al., 2008), and to cause hyperphagia, obesity and hypogonadism (de Smith et al., 2009). Necdin was found to be involved in respiratory regulation (Camfferman et al., 2008; Zanella et al., 2008), to be associated with alterations in a number of 5HT2CR-related behaviours including impulsive responding, locomotor activity and reactivity to palatable food (Doe et al., 2009), and to regulate gonadotropin-releasing hormone neurons during development. Loss of MAGEL2 in mice causes reduced fertility; females show extended and irregular oestrous cycles and males show reduced testosterone levels and reduced preferences for female odours (Mercer & Wevrick, 2009). They also display hypoactivity and increased adiposity (Mercer et al., 2009). A transgenic deletion PWS mouse model showed foetal and neonatal growth retardation, lethality that appeared to result from severe hypoglycaemia, and in these mice ghrelin levels rose with falling glucose levels (Stefan et al., 2005).

One exception to mouse model work is a report of nine cases of people with a microdeletion between breakpoints 1 and 2 of the PWSCR, which is known to include maternally imprinted genes (Doornbos et al., 2009). Shared clinical features of these cases included delayed motor and speech development, dysmorphisms and behaviour problems such as attention-daficit/hyperactivity disorder(ADHD), autism and obsessive-compulsive behaviour. These features should therefore be expected to be more prominent in type 1 deletions if the genes are not imprinted or in both type 1 deletions and in mUPD if the genes are imprinted (see section on genetic subtype differences).

BIRTH INCIDENCE AND MORTALITY

Prior to the advent of reliable genetic tests for PWS, when diagnosis was based on characteristic clinical features, birth incidence estimates ranged from 1:8000 to 1:25,000, with a widely quoted mode of 1:16,000. This is still found in articles published recently. The birth incidence of 1:22,000 to 1:25,000 estimated from a population study of PWS and based on genetic confirmation (Whittington et al., 2001) has been supported by genetic records studies in Australia (Smith et al., 2003) and in Flanders (Vogels et al., 2003). There is some evidence that birth incidence could be rising in countries such as the UK and France where families are being started later in life, the increase being in the mUPD genetic subtype where the risk rises almost exponentially with increasing maternal age (Whittington et al., 2006). Concern about deaths in PWS appears to have been stimulated by the controversy over the possibility of sudden death following commencement of growth hormone (GH) therapy and by previous findings of high mortality rates inferred from the age profiles of PWS populations. In the above-mentioned population study of PWS, the death rate was estimated from the age structure of the population to be about 3% per annum, linearly across all ages. Mortality rates in PWS have

been estimated to be six times higher than in other people with different causes for their learning disabilities (Einfeld et al., 2006).

Four studies looked at causes of death in a series of cases (Nagai et al., 2005; Schrander-Stumpel et al., 2004; Stevenson et al., 2004; Vogels et al., 2003) and arrived at a consensus that causes of death are similar in GH-treated and in non-treated groups and that in children sudden death is associated with respiratory infection and high temperature and in adults with circulatory or respiratory problems. Other studies examined cardiac and vascular structure and function (Patel et al., 2007) and central adrenal insufficiency (de Lind van Wijngaarden et al., 2008) and suggested that these may be causally linked to deaths in PWS. Recommendations are that signs of illness in PWS should be treated as serious in all cases and that people with PWS with central adrenal insufficiency should be treated with hydrocortisone during acute illness.

THE PHENOTYPES OF PRADER–WILLI SYNDROME

The primary, secondary and supportive diagnostic criteria for PWS were first described by Holm et al. (1993). Since then it has been established that there are certain core characteristics that, if absent, predict a normal methylation test, which is regarded as the definitive genetic test (Whittington et al., 2002). Core characteristics include marked hypotonia at birth and failure to thrive, with the later emergence of the overeating behaviour and evident short stature. Males also have undescended testes and females have absent or sporadic menstruation (Whittington & Holland, 2004).

It is clear that the phenotype of PWS has at least two distinct stages. The first phenotypic stage is evident from birth, and may in fact be present prenatally. This early stage is dominated by a lack of suck, severe hypotonia and a disinterest in food. A recent study shows that 100% of the sample of children under 5 with PWS had sucking problems from birth and 87% had at some point been tube-fed (Butler et al., 2009). However, difficulty in persuading the child to eat is a transient stage and generally disappears in the earliest years of the child's life. The study suggests that the transition between phenotypic stages is gradual, rather than a distinct switch between food disinterest and food preoccupation. This change involves a period of normalization of eating behaviour, reported to occur around the end of the first year (Butler et al., 2009). Unexpectedly, there is also evidence to suggest that the propensity to obesity may develop before the onset of hyperphagia, with a parentally reported increase in food interest developing after the first escalation in body mass index(BMI) (Butler et al., 2009; Goldstone et al., 2008; McCune & Driscoll, 2005). This would suggest that in PWS there is an underlying metabolic or endocrine deficiency that leads to obesity, and is further aggravated by the ensuing overeating behaviour.

The older phenotype is characterized by an abnormal interest in food, ranging from obsessions with food subjects in speech, play and reading materials to compulsive active foraging; mild to moderate intellectual disabilities; reduced hypotonia; hypogonadism; small stature; and behavioural difficulties, especially repetitive and ritualistic behaviours (Whittington & Holland, 2004). Although varying in severity, these characteristics seem to be universal in children and adults with PWS. A range of other characteristics have been described – such as daytime sleepiness, sleep apnoea, skin picking, and lowered sensitivity to temperature and pain – all of which are more prevalent than in the general population but are not inevitable. In the earlier literature these characteristics were described as present or absent in a given individual but, in view of their varying severity in the PWS population, are perhaps more appropriately conceived as having a distribution in PWS that is shifted towards the more severe extreme relative to their distribution in the general population. These characteristics of the PWS

phenotype have in common a deficiency of regulatory mechanisms which have been ascribed to a disorder of the hypothalamus. With subsequent research into later life, a third phenotypic phase has been suggested in which comorbid affective disorder or affective illness becomes apparent (see below).

Table 6.1 lists the generally accepted characteristics and how they emerge across time.

EATING DISORDER

One of the most distinguishing features of PWS is the eating disorder. Early descriptions of the syndrome depicted it as an insatiable appetite driven by hunger and, in some cases, including the eating of non-food items (pica), and inevitably leading to obesity. Although this description does appear to fit the stereotype, research shows that, while there are some individuals who steal food, or money to buy food, and actively forage, others exhibit only obsessions with food subjects in their speech, play or reading materials. As long as this group are in supported settings with parents or carers it is possible to limit the availability of and access to food, and obesity can thus be prevented. Any attempt at independent living always seems to lead to loss of control. It is not clear whether these variations in

Table 6.1   Characteristics and Development of PWS

Infancy
- Extreme hypotonia
- Failure to thrive
- Undescended testes in males

Childhood
- Developmental delay – intellectual disabilities
- Short stature – relative growth hormone deficiency
- Sexual immaturity – sex hormone deficiencies
- Overeating – risk of severe obesity and its complications
- Scoliosis, respiratory disorders, maladaptive behaviours

Adulthood
- Increased risk of obesity (with greater independence)
- Age-related physical and psychiatric morbidity

severity are innate or shaped by the early management by parents. It will be interesting to see if the current early diagnosis and the advice on management given to parents will result in less severe eating problems as this generation matures. For many parents the eating behaviour is the most distressing symptom of PWS, requiring, at least, daily vigilance, food items kept out of sight or under lock and key, and restriction of social life. To date, appetite reducing drugs have proved ineffectual (Goldstone, 2004; Shapira et al., 2004), as have surgical procedures.

The view that abnormally acute feelings of hunger were driving the urge to eat have been largely discounted, and it is now generally agreed that the disorder arises from defective satiety mechanisms (Holland et al., 1993). A number of researchers have confirmed this by comparing the brain regions activated by various stimuli when hungry (fasted) and the brain regions activated following various-sized meals both in controls and those with PWS. In the earliest report, fasted subjects were given a glucose drink while in the scanner, and time to activation of known satiety regions (insula, ventromedial prefrontal cortex, nucleus accumbens) was measured; there was a distinct lag in response time in PWS subjects (Shapira et al., 2005). A similar neural representation of hunger (fasting) was found in PWS and non-PWS participants, but the normal representation of satiety (i.e. that observed in the control group) was not found in the PWS group, even after a triple food load (Hinton et al., 2006a). In this study the role of food preferences was also studied via pictures of previously ascertained, high- and low-preference foods tailored to each individual. Food preferences were not reflected in brain activation (Hinton et al., 2006b). Pictures of food, animals and blurred images were shown before and after a meal to PWS and healthy-weight control participants. Greater activation to food pictures in food motivation brain networks was shown before the meal in the control group but after the meal in the PWS group (Holsen et al., 2006). In another brain scan study, food pictures were found to enhance activation of reward centres, suggesting a motivation for increased food consumption (Miller et al., 2007a), while a further report found that this was particularly true of high calorie foods (Dimitropoulos & Schultz, 2008).

ENDOCRINOLOGY

Growth hormone

Growth hormone treatment was originally prescribed about 20 years ago in a few cases of children with PWS in order to counter the small stature that is a feature of the syndrome. As the treatment became more widely used, about 10 years later, it was found that moderate increases in height were achieved but that the most beneficial effects were the improved body composition, especially increased muscle mass that led to increased physical activity.

Following numerous case study reports of sudden death after commencing growth hormone (GH) treatment, which began to appear when GH treatment became more widespread, two studies reported on the causes of death in treated versus untreated groups; neither found group differences in causes (Nagai et al., 2005; Tauber et al., 2008). The more recent report found that most deaths in the GH-treated group occurred within the first 9 months of treatment and both reports recommend careful monitoring early in GH treatment.

Previously, it was considered that scoliosis was a contraindication for GH treatment, but two studies found no difference in scoliosis prevalence between GH-treated and untreated groups (De Lind van Wijngaarden et al., 2009a; Nakamura et al., 2009). Progression of scoliosis was similar in the two groups (De Lind van Wijngaarden et al., 2009a); and progression was worse in those patients with a double curve (Nakamura et al., 2009).

The advantages of GH treatment were noted in a series of reports:

- It helps body composition and dietary fat intake, depending on developmental stage (Galassetti et al., 2007).

- It improves development, both physical and mental, in infants and toddlers (Festen et al., 2008).
- It normalizes height and improves body composition (Lindgren & Lindberg, 2008).
- It improves physical activity (Gondoni et al., 2008).
- It increases bone mineral density (de Lind van Wijngaarden et al., 2009b).

It is particularly recommended in cases where there is early diet control, where it appears that less obesity later in life is bought at the expense of decreased stature (Schmidt et al., 2008).

Fertility

Because of the hypogonadism, people with PWS were considered to be infertile until the first report of a woman with confirmed PWS giving birth appeared in 1999, followed by a second case in 2001. To date, no reports of male fertility have appeared. The possibility that people with PWS can be fertile has led to increased prescription of birth control pills and investigation of probability of fertility in PWS. Two recent papers on hypogonadism in males with PWS have concluded that it is a combination of hypothalamic and peripheral hypogonadism (Eiholzer et al., 2006) and that primary testicular dysfunction is a major component of hypogonadism in PWS (Hirsch et al., 2009). The probability of male fertility was examined by analysing testicular histology in boys; the results were heterogeneous, with two out of eight found to be normal (Vogels et al., 2008). Primary ovarian dysfunction was found to contribute to the hypogonadism in women with PWS (Eldar-Geva et al., 2009).

In a study of hormone levels in PWS adults, oestradiol levels in females were below normal, equivalent to normal postmenopausal levels, and testosterone levels in males were below the normal range in 19 of 23 cases (Brandau et al., 2008).

Ghrelin and other peptides

A decade ago there was great interest in the newly discovered gut hormone ghrelin, which is an appetite stimulant, when it was found that PWS adults had abnormally high levels. High levels had also been found in people with anorexia nervosa. In 2004 it was reported that levels in PWS children were higher than in BMI-matched controls (Butler et al., 2004b; Paik et al., 2004) and that in people with PWS ghrelin levels were inversely correlated with age, BMI and BMI percentile (Paik et al., 2004), while peptide YY (PYY) levels in youngsters with PWS were lower than in those without PWS (Butler et al., 2004b). However, another report on younger children with PWS (0–5 years), who had not yet developed hyperphagia or obesity, found that ghrelin, insulin and glucose levels were similar to BMI-, age- and sex-matched controls. Ghrelin levels correlated inversely with BMI in controls but not in the PWS group (Erdie-Lalena et al., 2006). On the other hand, a more recent report found that ghrelin levels were elevated in PWS both in children younger than 3 years and in those aged 3–17 years (Feigerlova et al., 2008). This study found an inverse relationship between ghrelin levels and age in both PWS and controls, and between ghrelin and BMI Z-score, insulin, leptin and lean mass. A partial reconciliation between these two reports is suggested in a more recent finding that young infants with PWS who have not yet developed hyperphagia or obesity have median fasting ghrelin levels similar to controls, while a subset of youngsters with PWS have high ghrelin levels despite BMI Z-scores below zero in about half of this subset (Haqq et al., 2008). This report also found that the age-related decline in ghrelin levels is blunted in PWS.

Two recent studies have reported on ghrelin level changes in response to food and to octreotide treatment, respectively. In the former, PWS and control subjects were monitored over 24 hours; insulin levels decreased and cholecystokinin (CCK) and ghrelin increased in PWS over 24 hours. The response pattern of these hormones to meals in PWS paralleled that of the controls (Paik et al., 2007). In the other study, octreotide treatment caused a decrease in ghrelin in adolescents with PWS but did not improve BMI or decrease appetite (De Waele et al., 2008).

Two investigations of adiponectin levels in PWS have also been reported. The first found adiponectin levels higher in PWS and less insulin resistance relative to their obesity levels than in non-PWS obesity; this was true for both major genetic subtypes (Kennedy et al., 2006). The later study confirmed higher adiponectin levels in PWS children and adolescents relative to age- and BMI-matched controls (Haqq et al., 2007).

GENETIC SUBTYPE DIFFERENCES

Although the genetic subtypes of PWS share common 'core' characteristics – namely, the abnormal interest in food, mild to moderate intellectual disabilities, hypotonia, hypogonadism, small stature and compulsive behaviour – the subtypes also show consistent differences. The consistency of findings rule out sampling differences due to aggregation of individual differences and suggest genetic influences arising from the consistent differences in gene expression in the PWSCR. No other explanation has been proposed for subtype differences. Thus, the mUPD and imprinting defect subtypes will have two active copies of paternally imprinted genes in this region, unlike the deletion subtype and the general population, who each have a single copy. Again, type 1 and type 2 deletions will differ with respect to expression of maternally imprinted genes between break points 1 and 2.

Two major genetic subtype differences had been acknowledged prior to 2004: the superior verbal IQ (VIQ), inferior performance IQ (PIQ) of the mUPD subtype and the vastly higher prevalence of psychosis in this subtype, relative to the deletion subtype (see Mental health section). A study published in 2004 found subtype differences in cognitive profiles using the Wechsler intelligence scales; the deletion subtype had a similar profile to that of a mixed aetiology intellectu-

ally disabled comparison group, whereas the mUPD subtype had a quite different profile (Whittington et al., 2004). It was also known that mother's age at conception was linked to genetic subtype, older mothers giving birth to more mUPD babies. The importance of these findings for future provision of services to people with PWS has further been underlined by the suggestion in the UK and France that the tendency to have children later in life is leading to an increase in the relative proportion of the mUPD subtype in PWS births (Whittington et al., 2006). Another development has been the splitting of the deletion subtype into Type 1 and Type 2, depending on the size of the deletion.

Two European studies have reported high rates of problems in pregnancy, neonatal and early postnatal periods in both the major genetic subtypes (Dudley & Muscatelli, 2007; Whittington et al., 2008) but few differences between the subtypes except for more induction of labour and more prematurity in mUPD and lower birth weight in deletions. Two South American studies have found more seizures (Varela et al., 2005) and more need for special feeding techniques (Torrado et al., 2007) in the deletion subtype. The latter study also reported more articulation defects, fewer IQ scores above 70 and more sleep disorders in the deletion group. The finding of more seizures in the deletion subtype has also been reported in a study of seizures in PWS (Fan et al., 2009).

More autistic symptomatology was reported in the mUPD subtype relative to the deletion subtype (Veltman et al., 2004), and this was also found by other researchers, who further reported no differences in autistic traits or behavioural phenotype between type 1 and type 2 deletions (Milner et al., 2005). A more recent study also found no deletion subtype differences in their measures of problem behaviour, compulsivity, hyperphagia and adaptive skills (Dykens & Roof, 2008) but found favourable changes with age in type 1 deletions only. However, other researchers have reported subtype differences in measures of behaviour, typically finding type 1 deletions to have more problems with maladaptive behaviours (Hartley et al., 2005); different and stronger compulsions than type 2 deletions or mUPD (Zarcone et al., 2007); lower adaptive behaviour scores; more specific obsessive-compulsive behaviours compared with mUPD; poorer attainment scores, and poorer visual-motor integration (Butler et al., 2004a). The researchers in the latter study also examined differences between type 1 and type 2 and mRNA measures of the four genes identified in the BP1 to BP2 region and showed positive correlations between mRNA and better assessment scores (Bittel et al., 2006).

Differences between the subtypes in cognitive measures have included a speed of processing deficit shown by delayed response times, as measured by event-related potential (ERP) on an inhibition task in the mUPD group (Stauder et al., 2005), which gives support to the finding of a significantly lower average score on the Coding subtest of the Wechsler IQ battery (Whittington et al., 2004). There also seems to be a difference in familial cognitive inheritance, with mUPD IQ correlated as usual with sibling IQ but deletion IQ not correlated with sibling IQ (Whittington et al., 2009). The deletion subtype was found to show a relative strength in visual processing of shape identity and a relative deficit in visual processing of location (Woodcock et al., 2009a). A behavioural and ERP study of face and gaze processing found no differences between deletion and mUPD groups on the behavioural measures of face processing and autistic symptoms but face orientation and gaze direction discriminated between the subtypes in the amplitude of the n170 component (Halit et al., 2008).

Two studies have explored brain activation in response to food images. The first, an ERP study, measuring perceptual categorization and motivational relevance, found that the deletion group categorized the food stimuli in terms of composition while the mUPD group focused on suitability for consumption (Holsen et al., 2009). The other was a functional magnetic resonance imaging (fMRI) study in which food images were viewed before and after a standard meal. Both subtypes reacted to food images more than controls; the deletion group showed greater food motivation network activation both pre- and post-meal, while the mUPD group showed greater activation post-meal in higher-order cognitive regions (Key & Dykens, 2008).

MENTAL HEALTH

Reports of mental illness in PWS began to occur soon after the condition was first diagnosed. However, diagnosis of PWS was then based on clinical criteria and we cannot be certain that all of these reports were on genuine cases of PWS. Also, the illnesses described were given various diagnoses, depending on the particular clinician and the school of psychiatry in which s/he had trained. Thus, it is not surprising that the relationship between mUPD and psychosis was not noticed until genetic testing for PWS was firmly established and a population sample was examined for mental illness.

The first paper to report the genetic subtype differences in the prevalence of psychosis in PWS appeared in 2002 (Boer et al., 2002). The 100% prevalence rate in non-deletion PWS over the age of 28 reported in this study suggested that a single maternally expressed imprinted gene was responsible. Three follow-up papers have confirmed the high prevalence rate in non-deletion PWS, described the course and outcome of the illness (Skryabin et al., 2007) and the phenomenology (Soni et al., 2008), and, in genetic studies of deletion PWS with psychosis found supportive evidence for the genetic hypothesis and delineated the region in which such a causative gene must lie (Webb et al., 2008). The study of the phenomenology of mental illness in PWS suggests that depressive illness is more prevalent in deletion subtypes and an atypical affective psychosis in the non-deletion subtypes. This latter description does not fit comfortably into standard classifications and probably explains the variety of diagnoses found in the literature. These conditions are presently treated by medication, the type and dosage varying according to the psychiatrist in charge. It is hoped that finding a causative gene will lead to more consistent, targeted treatment.

In other literature on psychiatric and emotional disorders in PWS, psychotic disorders in PWS were discussed and support for the genetic subtype differences was given (Vogels et al., 2004), the nature of the psychosis seen in PWS was described (Verhoeven & Tuinier, 2006) and emotional disturbances in children were reported (Reddy & Pfeiffer, 2007). An investigation of pervasive developmental disorders using DSM-III-R criteria found that 19% of the PWS sample met criteria, compared with 15% of other intellectually disabled people and that the PWS group displayed an autistic-like phenotype, more prevalent in the mUPD subtype (Descheemaeker et al., 2006).

In a study of quality of life in PWS, self-esteem was found to be lower in people with a lower score on the mini mental state examination (MMSE) and mental problems were found to be greater in people with characteristic facial features (Caliandro et al., 2007).

COGNITION AND BEHAVIOUR

People with PWS lack social skills; typically, they do not get on with their peers, expressive language is problematic (Van Borsel et al., 2007) and Vineland socialization domain scores are low. Cognitive scores depend on the particular samples assessed; probably the best estimate comes from the UK population sample, where the mean IQ was 62 (Whittington & Holland, 2004). The behaviour profile includes features of obsessive-compulsive (O-C) behaviour and autism, but only rarely do cases meet full diagnostic criteria for either of these disorders. The O-C behaviours are generally similar to those found in typically developing children and load on the general factor found in a factor analysis of behaviours in O-C disorder (Baer, 1993). Similarly, autistic traits are confined to a subset (mainly O-C behaviour) of those found in autism. Research has recently been concerned with similarities and differences between PWS and other disorders and with examining the correlates between behaviour and brain mechanisms, as indicated below.

A study in which a PWS group was compared with an IQ-matched control group and a group with pervasive developmental disorder (PDD) on the Social Attribution Task (a measure of ability to make appropriate social attributions from an ambiguous visual display) found that the PWS group performed significantly worse than controls and not significantly different from the PDD group (Koenig et al., 2004). Two studies have suggested that behaviour problems might be associated with dopamine levels in γ-aminobutic acid PWS and with GABA(A) receptor abnormalities, respectively. Compulsive behaviour was related to eye blink rate, which was taken as an indirect measure of dopamine (Holsen & Thompson, 2004). Cerebral GABA(A) receptors were assessed using positron emission tomography of the benzodiazepine binding site, employing [^{11}C]flumazenil, and a reduction in binding was found in the brains of people with PWS relative to controls (Lucignani et al., 2004).

Three more recent reports have dealt with repetitive behaviour. Compared with children with autism, those with PWS had similar scores on the Childhood Routines Inventory, but high scoring items differed (Greaves et al., 2006). The Repetitive Behaviour Questionnaire was administered to groups representing seven different genetic syndromes; profiles of scores differed for each of the syndromes, suggesting that they have different characteristic repetitive behaviours (Moss et al., 2009). One such characteristic in PWS is a strong preference for routine and this was shown to be associated with task-switching (between target identity and target location) deficits on an adapted Simon spatial interference task. In this task, the participant responds to one of two images in one of two locations as quickly as possible (Woodcock et al. 2009b). This finding suggests that executive function might be impaired in PWS but an investigation of executive function in PWS adults found no significant differences between their performance and that of controls matched for age and verbal ability (Walley & Donaldson, 2005). On the other hand, when compared with a normal population on standard tests of attention, memory and executive functions, almost all scores were significantly lower (Jauregi et al., 2007).

Maths skills were investigated in two studies; the first study concluded that maths skills and short-term memory were more impaired than other cognitive functions and that the maths deficit was not confined to specific maths domains (Bertella et al., 2005). The second study examined genetic subtype differences as well as particular maths domains and concluded that mUPD is less affected in transcoding and comparison of number of tasks and that people with PWS perform normally in analogue number scale tasks (Semenza et al., 2008).

Jigsaw puzzle strategies were investigated in people with PWS and mental age-matched controls; the PWS group used shape as a guide, whereas the control group used picture details. Group performances were similar on standard interlocking puzzles and standard straight edge puzzles, but superior in the PWS group on blank interlocking puzzles (Verdine et al., 2008).

SENSORY, PHYSICAL IMPAIRMENTS AND SLEEP

The phenotype of older people with PWS includes disorders of regulatory mechanisms, including regulation of temperature, sleep and pain. Abnormalities of body temperature, as well as perception of temperature, have been recorded in adults: hypothermia with no precipitating factors and water temperatures needing to be set by carers. Abnormally high

and low temperatures have been recorded in babies with PWS. Daytime sleepiness is commonly reported, even overtaking people in the middle of work activities. The high pain threshold can be extreme: a man with PWS going to work with a broken ankle, a child not complaining when he had a perforated bowel. These regulatory mechanisms continue to be addressed. Attention has been drawn to the risk of hyperthermia in infants with PWS and the need for careful monitoring of such occurrences was stressed (Ince et al., 2005).

A review of daytime sleepiness in PWS concluded that this is not only associated with obstructive sleep apnoea syndrome but also with hypothalamic dysfunction (Camfferman et al., 2008). Another study of sleep disorders confirmed a relationship between central adrenal insufficiency and sleep apnoea and showed that the latter increased under stress (Dewan & Chanoine, 2009). Daytime sleepiness and narcolepsy-like symptoms in PWS were assessed relative to narcoleptic patients with cataplexy who have a general loss of hypocretin (orexin) in the lateral hypothalamus. The total number of hypocretin-containing neurons in hypothalamic material in PWS was not significantly different from normal and it was concluded that such neurons are not responsible for daytime sleepiness in PWS (Fronczek et al., 2005).

Thermal and pain thresholds but not vibratory were found to be higher in PWS than in healthy and obese controls. It was concluded that altered perception in PWS does not seem attributable to a peripheral nerve derangement but that impairment of the small nociceptive neurons of dorsal root ganglia or of the hypothalamus region cannot be excluded (Priano et al., 2009).

As already noted, the physical features of PWS include small stature, typical facies, scoliosis and fragile bones. The small stature and typical facies can be ameliorated by growth hormone therapy. Scoliosis is treated in childhood with braces or, in severe cases, by surgery. Fractures are quite common in PWS and have been attributed to low bone density as well as poor balance control, probably linked to poor muscle tone. A study of bone mineral density in PWS, compared with age- sex- and BMI-matched controls, concluded that the PWS group had low bone mineral density due to a high bone turnover and that the latter was probably linked to sex steroid deficiency (Vestergaard et al., 2004).

BRAIN MORPHOLOGY

Advances in scanning techniques have made the study of brain morphology more reliable and accurate and studies of brain morphology are appearing more frequently in the literature. Three such studies have recently been reported. One found differences in PWS brains in left frontal white matter and left dorsomedial thalamus, and in the posterior limb of the internal capsule bilaterally, the right frontal white matter and the splenium of the corpus callosum and related these to the clinical features of PWS (Yamada ct al., 2006). White matter lesions were found in six of 17 people with PWS and also in five of 18 people with early-onset morbid obesity in a study that also measured cognitive, achievement and behavioural problems (Miller et al., 2006). The third study compared brains in three groups of people: PWS, early-onset morbid obesity and normal weight controls. Only the PWS group showed brain abnormalities, including ventriculomegaly (in 100%), decreased brain tissue volume in the parietal-occipital lobe (in 50%), sylvan fissure polymicrogyria (in 60%) and incomplete insular closure (in 65%) (Miller et al., 2007b).

AGEING

Because of the high mortality rate in PWS in the past, few people with PWS have been found in older age groups. The UK population study found only three people over age 40, the oldest 47, in a population of five million (Whittington et al., 2001). However, the earlier diagnosis, more available information and better management techniques mean that people are expected to survive longer in future and this seems to have prompted research into ageing in PWS.

Maladaptive and compulsive behaviour problems were reported to decline in older (30+ years) adults compared with younger (<30 years) people with PWS (Dykens, 2004). In another study, the age-related decline in behaviour problems was found significant only in people with type 1 deletions (Dykens & Roof, 2008). Behavioural and emotional disturbances were found to be increased in adolescence and young adulthood compared with younger and older age groups (Steinhausen et al., 2004). Rates of obesity and morbidity were found to be higher in adults with PWS than in those aged 18 or younger and were ascribed to late diagnosis and lack of early diet control in the older group (Vogels & Fryns, 2004).

FUTURE DIRECTIONS

The number of publications on PWS research is growing fast, partly due to the higher profile associated with concerns about obesity, partly due to research being undertaken in more countries and more institutions within countries, and partly due to more knowledge leading to more questions. The fascination of PWS is that, although we know so much about people with the syndrome, the fundamental questions are still unanswered. The unknowns include knowledge about the exact genes involved, the relationships between genotype and phenotype, and how to explain individual differences. These present continuing challenges. Likely areas of growth include further advances in genetics, continuing interest in genetic subtype differences, more interest in ageing, and the effects of early diagnosis and advice to new parents on outcomes in later life.

Advances in PWS genetics are likely to be based on knockout mouse models, possibly based around the snoRNAs HBII-85, which look the most likely source of most of the core phenotypic features if the research summarized above can be replicated. Another possible advance in genetics would be the identification of the 'psychosis gene', leading to targeted treatment of the atypical affective psychosis seen in people with PWS. Interest in genetics more generally is likely to arise from continuing research into genetic subtype differences, linking phenotypic differences to genetic differences. This might eventually lead to the identification of links between cognitive and behavioural characteristics and brain networks.

In the more distant future we predict that there will be more interest in ageing as people with PWS live longer and increased numbers of people in the older age groups make more detailed, statistical analyses possible. Already there are interesting questions being raised by studies that have found trends in samples too small to provide significant results; for example, do older adults become less obsessive, have fewer behaviour problems, or develop early-onset dementia?

IMPLICATIONS FOR SUPPORT

From the perspective of providing support to people with PWS, the most significant advances that have arisen from the research are in three broad areas. First, from an endocrinological perspective, GH is now established as an appropriate treatment and, in an increasing number of countries, its use is accepted. The questions that remain include its use in the very young infant and its continuation into adult life. Secondly, although there is still no treatment for the eating disorder, the pathophysiological basis is better illuminated and the need to control the eating environment now well established and accepted. Early diagnosis enables parents to be prepared for and supported to manage the onset of the overeating. Thus, at least in childhood, severe obesity and its consequences can

be prevented. In the absence of treatment for the overeating, supervision and management of the food environment remain the primary approaches in adult life. Thirdly, there is a better understanding of the profile of maladaptive behaviours that commonly occur in people with PWS. Importantly, the recognition that affective disorder and affective psychosis are serious risks in the teenage years and in adult life emphasizes the importance of clinical assessment. The important clinical issue is the distinction between the presence of repetitive and ritualistic behaviours as part of the syndrome (best managed by psychological means) and the potential for the development of a comorbid mental illness that may present as a deterioration in behaviour. Here the careful use of antidepressant and/or antipsychotic medication, initially at low doses, may be of value together with other environmental approaches such as consistency and reducing the level of emotional demands.

Although these three areas have perhaps seen the most significant increase in understanding, the recognition of other potential health risks and their prevention and management remains very important. These include the management of scoliosis; detecting and treating sleep apnoea; good dental care; and being sensitive to the possibility of potentially fatal illnesses such as gastric paresis following overeating, peritonitis following appendicitis, respiratory illness, obesity-related diabetes mellitus, and adrenal insufficiency in cases of acute illness. People with PWS may carry medical alert information booklets for these reasons.

REFERENCES

Baer, L. (1993) 'Factor analysis of symptom subtypes of obsessive-compulsive disorder and their relation to personality and tic disorders', *J Clin Psychiatry*, 55: 18–23.

Bertella, L., Girelli, L., Grugni, G., Marchi, S., Molinari, E., & Semenza, C. (2005) 'Mathematical skills in Prader–Willi syndrome', *J Intellect Disabil Res*, 49(2): 159–169.

Bittel, D.C., Kibiryeva, N., & Butler, M.G. (2006) 'Expression of 4 genes between chromosome 15 breakpoints 1 and 2 and behavioral outcomes in Prader–Willi syndrome', *Pediatrics,* 118(4): e1276–1283.

Boer, H., Holland, A.J., Whittington, J.E., Butler, J.V., Webb, T., & Clarke, D. J. (2002) 'Psychotic illness in people with Prader–Willi syndrome due to chromosome 15 maternal uniparental disomy', *Lancet,* 359: 135–136.

Brandau, D.T., Theodoro, M., Garg, U., & Butler, M.G. (2008) 'Follicle stimulating and leutinizing hormones, estradiol and testosterone in Prader–Willi syndrome', *Am J Med Genet, Part A,* 146(5): 665.

Butler, J.V., Whittington, J.E, Holland, A.J., McAllister, C.J., & Goldstone, A.P. (2009) 'The transition between the phenotypes of Prader–Willi syndrome during infancy and early childhood', *Dev Med Child Neurol.* e-published Dec 23

Butler, M.G., Bittel, D.C., Kibiryeva, N., Talebizadeh, Z., & Thompson, T. (2004a) 'Behavioral differences among subjects with Prader–Willi syndrome and type I or type II deletion and maternal disomy', *Pediatrics,* 113(3): 565.

Butler, M.G., Bittel, D.C., & Talebizadeh, Z. (2004b) 'Plasma peptide YY and ghrelin levels in infants and children with Prader–Willi syndrome', *J Pediatri Endocrinol Metab,* 17: 1177–1184.

Caliandro, P., Grugni, G., Padua, L., Kodra, Y., Tonali, P., Gargantini, L., et al. (2007) 'Quality of life assessment in a sample of patients affected by Prader–Willi syndrome', *J Paediatr Child Health,* 43(12): 826–830.

Camfferman, D., McEvoy, R.D., O'Donoghue, F., & Lushington, K. (2008) 'Prader Willi Syndrome and excessive daytime sleepiness', *Sleep Med Revi,* 12(1): 65–75.

de Lind van Wijngaarden, R.F., Otten, B.J., Festen, D.A., Joosten, K.F., de Jong, F.H., Sweep, F.C., et al. (2008). 'High prevalence of central adrenal insufficiency in patients with Prader–Willi syndrome', *J Clin Endocrinol Metab,* 93(5): 1649–1654.

De Lind van Wijngaarden, R.F., de Klerk, L.W., Festen, D.A., Duivenvoorden, H.J., Otten, B.J., & Hokken-Koelega, A.C. (2009a) 'Randomized controlled trial to investigate the effects of growth hormone treatment on scoliosis in children with Prader–Willi syndrome', *J Clin Endocrinol Metab,* 94(4): 1274–1280.

de Lind van Wijngaarden, R.F., Festen, D.A., Otten, B.J., van Mil, E.G., Rotteveel, J., Odink, R.J., et al. (2009b) 'Bone mineral density and effects of growth hormone treatment in prepubertal children with Prader–Willi syndrome: a randomized controlled trial', *J Clin Endocrinol. Metab,* 94(10): 3763–3771.

Descheemaeker, M.J., Govers, V., Vermeulen, P., & Fryns, J.P. (2006) 'Pervasive developmental disorders in Prader–Willi syndrome: the Leuven experience in 59 subjects and controls', *Am J Med Genet, Part A,* 140(11): 1136.

de Smith, A.J., Purmann, C., Walters, R.G., Ellis, R.J., Holder, S.E., Van Haelst, M.M., et al. (2009) 'A deletion of the HBII-85 class of small nucleolar RNAs (snoRNAs) is associated with hyperphagia, obesity and hypogonadism', *Hum Mol Genet,* 18(17): 3257–3265.

De Waele, K., Ishkanian, S.L., Bogarin, R., Miranda, C.A., Ghatei, M.A., Bloom, S.R., et al. (2008) 'Long-acting octreotide treatment causes a sustained decrease in ghrelin concentrations but does not affect weight, behaviour and appetite in subjects with Prader–Willi syndrome', *Eur J Endocrinol,* 159: 381–388.

Dewan, T. & Chanoine, J.P. (2009) 'Body mass index in children with Prader–Willi Syndrome during human growth hormone therapy: a real world situation', *J Clin Endocrinol Metab,* 94(7): 2387–2393.

Dimitropoulos, A. & Schultz, R.T. (2008) 'Food-related neural circuitry in Prader–Willi syndrome: response to high- versus low-calorie foods', *J Autism Dev Disord,* 38(9): 1642–1653.

Ding, F., Prints, Y., Dhar, M.S., Johnson, D.K., Garnacho–Montero, C., Nicholls, R.D., et al. (2005) 'Lack of Pwcr1/MBII-85 snoRNA is critical for neonatal lethality in Prader–Willi syndrome mouse models', *Mamm Genome,* 16(6): 424–431.

Ding, F., Li, H.H., Zhang, S., Solomon, N.M., Camper, S.A., Cohen, P., et al. (2008) 'SnoRNA Snord116 (Pwcr1/MBII-85) deletion causes growth deficiency and hyperphagia in mice', *PLoS One,* 3(3): e1709.

Doe, C.M., Relkovic, D., Garfield, A.S., Dalley, J.W., Theobald, D.E., Humby, T., et al. (2009) 'Loss of the imprinted snoRNA mbii-52 leads to increased 5htr2c pre-RNA editing and altered 5HT2CR-mediated behaviour', *Hum Mol Genet,* 18(12): 2140–2148.

Doornbos, M., Sikkema-Raddatz, B., Ruijvenkamp, C.A., Dijkhuizen, T., Bijlsma, E.K.,Gijsbers, A. C., et al. (2009) 'Nine patients with a microdeletion 15q11.2 between breakpoints 1 and 2 of the Prader–Willi critical region, possibly associated with behavioural disturbances', *Eur J Med Genet,* 52: 108–15.

Dudley, O. & Muscatelli, F. (2007) 'Clinical evidence of intrauterine disturbance in Prader–Willi syndrome, a genetically imprinted neurodevelopmental disorder', *Early Hum Dev,* 83(7): 471–478.

Dykens, E.M. (2004) 'Maladaptive and compulsive behavior in Prader–Willi syndrome: new insights from older adults', *Am J Ment Retard,* 109(2): 142–153.

Dykens, E.M., & Roof, E. (2008) 'Behavior in Prader–Willi syndrome: relationship to genetic subtypes and age', *J Child Psychol Psychiatry,* 49(9): 1001–1008.

Eiholzer, U., l'Allemand, D., Rousson, V., Schlumpf, M., Gasser, T., Girard, J., et al. (2006) 'Hypothalamic and gonadal components of hypogonadism in boys with Prader–Labhart–Willi syndrome', *J Clin Endocrinol Metab,* 91(3): 892.

Eldar-Geva, T., Hirsch, H.J., Rabinowitz, R., Benarroch, F., Rubinstein, O., & Gross-Tsur, V. (2009) 'Primary ovarian dysfunction contributes to the hypogonadism in women with Prader–Willi Syndrome', *Horm Res,* 72(3): 153–159.

Erdie-Lalena, C.R., Holm, V.A., Kelly, P.C., Frayo, R.S., & Cummings, D.E. (2006) 'Ghrelin levels in young children with Prader–Willi syndrome', *J Pediatr,* 149(2): 199–204.

Fan, Z., Greenwood, R., Fisher, A., Pendyal, S., & Powell, C.M. (2009) 'Characteristics and frequency of seizure disorder in 56 patients with Prader–Willi syndrome', *Am J Med Genet, Part A,* 149A(7): 1581–1584.

Feigerlova, E., Diene, G., Conte-Auriol, F., Molinas, C., Gennero, I., Salles, J.P., et al. (2008) 'Hyperghrelinemia precedes obesity in Prader–Willi syndrome', *J Clin Endocrinol Metab,* 93(7): 2800.

Festen, D.A., Wevers, M., Lindgren, A.C., Bohm, B., Otten, B.J., Wit, J.M., et al. (2008) 'Mental and motor development before and during growth hormone treatment in infants and toddlers with Prader–Willi syndrome', *Clini Endocrinol (Oxf),* 68(6): 919.

Fronczek, R., Lammers, G.J., Balesar, R., Unmehopa, U.A., & Swaab, D.F. (2005) 'The number of hypothalamic hypocretin (orexin) neurons is not affected in Prader–Willi syndrome', *J of Clin Endocrinol Metab,* 90(9): 5466.

Galassetti, P., Saetrum Opgaard, O., Cassidy, S.B., & Pontello, A. (2007) 'Nutrient intake and body composition variables in Prader–Willi syndrome – effect of growth hormone supplementation and genetic subtype', *J Pediatr Endocrinol Metab,* 20: 491–500.

Goldstone, A.P. (2004) 'Prader–Willi syndrome: advances in genetics, pathophysiology and treatment', *Trends Endocrinol Metab,* 15: 12–20

Goldstone, A.P., Holland, A.J., Hauffa, B.P., Hokken-Koelega, A.C., & Tauber, M. (2008) 'Recommendations for the diagnosis and management of Prader–Willi syndrome', *J Clin Endocrinol Metab,* 93: 4183–4197.

Gondoni, L.A., Vismara, L., Marzullo, P., Vettor, R., Liuzzi, A., & Grugni, G. (2008) 'Growth hormone therapy improves exercise capacity in adult patients with Prader–Willi syndrome', *J Endocrinol Invest,* 31(9): 765–772.

Greaves, N., Prince, E., Evans, D.W., & Charman, T. (2006) 'Repetitive and ritualistic behaviour in children with Prader-Willi syndrome and children with autism', *J Intellect Disabil Res,* 50(2): 92–100.

Halit, H., Grice, S.J., Bolton, P., & Johnson, M.H. (2008) 'Face and gaze processing in Prader–Willi syndrome', *J Neuropsychol,* 2(1): 65–77.

Haqq, A.M., Muehlbauer, M., Svetkey, L.P., Newgard, C.B., Purnell, J.Q., Grambow, S.C., et al. (2007) 'Altered distribution of adiponectin isoforms in children with Prader–Willi syndrome (PWS): association with insulin sensitivity and circulating satiety peptide hormones', *Clin Endocrinol,* 67(6): 944.

Haqq, A.M., Grambow, S.C., Muehlbauer, M., Newgard, C.B., Svetkey, L.P., Carrel, A.L., et al. (2008) 'Ghrelin concentrations in Prader–Willi syndrome (PWS) infants and children: changes during development', *Clin Endocrinol,* 69(6): 911.

Hartley, S.L., MacLean Jr, W.E., Butler, M.G., Zarcone, J., & Thompson, T. (2005) 'Maladaptive behaviors and risk factors among the genetic subtypes of Prader–Willi syndrome', *Am J Medi Genet, Part A,* 136(2): 140.

Hinton, E.C., Holland, A.J., Gellatly, M.S., Soni, S., Patterson, M., Ghatei, M.A., et al. (2006a) 'Neural representations of hunger and satiety in Prader–Willi syndrome', *Int J Obes,* 30(2): 313.

Hinton, E.C., Holland, A.J., Gellatly, M.S.N., Soni, S., & Owen, A.M. (2006b) 'An investigation into food preferences and the neural basis of food-related incentive motivation in Prader-Willi syndrome', *J Intellect Disabil Res,* 50(9): 633–642.

Hirsch, H.J., Eldar-Geva, T., Benarroch, F., Rubinstein, O., & Gross-Tsur, V. (2009) 'Primary testicular dysfunction is a major contributor to abnormal pubertal development in males with Prader–Willi syndrome', *J Clin Endocrinol Metab,* 94(7): 2262–2268.

Holland, A., Whittington, J., & Hinton, E. (2003) 'The paradox of Prader–Willi syndrome: a genetic model of starvation', *Lancet,* 362(9388): 989–991.

Holland, A.J., Treasure, J., Coskeran, P., Dallow, J., Milton, M., & Hillhouse, E. (1993) 'Measurement of excessive appetite and metabolic changes in Prader–Willi syndrome', *Int J Obes Relat Metab Disord,* 17: 527–532.

Holm, V.A., Cassidy, S.B., & Butler, M.G. (1993) 'Prader–Willi syndrome: consensus diagnostic criteria', *Pediatrics,* 91: 398–402.

Holsen, L. & Thompson, T. (2004) 'Compulsive behavior and eye blink in Prader–Willi syndrome:

neurochemical implications', *Am J Ment Retard,* 109(3): 197–207.

Holsen, L.M., Zarcone, J.R., Brooks, W.M., Butler, M.G., Thompson, T.I., Ahluwalia, J.S., et al. (2006) 'Neural mechanisms underlying hyperphagia in Prader–Willi syndrome', *Obesity (Silver Spring, Md.),* 14(6): 1028.

Holsen, L.M., Zarcone, J.R., Chambers, R., Butler, M.G., Bittel, D.C., Brooks, W.M., et al. (2009) 'Genetic subtype differences in neural circuitry of food motivation in Prader–Willi syndrome', *Int J Obes (Lond)* 33: 273–283.

Ince, E., Ciftci, E., Tekin, M., Kendirli, T.I., Tutar, E., Dalglc, N., et al. (2005) 'Characteristics of hyperthermia and its complications in patients with Prader – Willi syndrome', *Pediatr Int,* 47(5): 550–553.

Jauregi, J., Arias, C., Vegas, O., Alen, F., Martinez, S., Copet, P., et al. (2007) 'A neuropsychological assessment of frontal cognitive functions in Prader–Willi syndrome', *J Intellect Disabil Res,* 51(5): 350–365.

Kanber, D., Giltay, J., Wieczorek, D., Zogel, C., Hochstenbach, R., Caliebe, A., et al. (2009) 'A paternal deletion of MKRN3, MAGEL2 and NDN does not result in Prader–Willi syndrome', *Eur J Hum Genet,* 17(5), 582–590.

Kennedy, L., Bittel, D.C., Kibiryeva, N., Kalra, S.P., Torto, R., & Butler, M.G. (2006) 'Circulating adiponectin levels, body composition and obesity-related variables in Prader–Willi syndrome: comparison with obese subjects', *Int J Obes (Lond),* 30(2): 382–387.

Key, A.P., & Dykens, E.M. (2008) ' "Hungry eyes": visual processing of food images in adults with Prader–Willi syndrome', *J Intellect Disabil Res,* 52: 536–546

Koenig, K., Klin, A., & Schultz, R. (2004) 'Deficits in social attribution ability in Prader–Willi syndrome', *J Autism Dev Disord,* 34(5): 573–582.

Lindgren, A.C., & Lindberg, A. (2008). 'Growth hormone treatment completely normalizes adult height and improves body composition in Prader–Willi syndrome: experience from KIGS (Pfizer International Growth Database)', *Horm Res,* 70(3): 182–187.

Lucignani, G., Panzacchi, A., Bosio, L., Moresco, R.M., Ravasi, L., Coppa, I., et al. (2004) 'GABAA receptor abnormalities in Prader–Willi syndrome assessed with positron emission tomography and [^{11}C] flumazenil', *Neuroimage,* 22(1): 22–28.

McCune, H. & Driscoll, D.J. (2005) 'Prader–Willi syndrome', in S.W., Efvall, & V.K. Efvall, (eds), *Paediatric Nutrition in Chronic Diseases and Developmental Disorders,* 2nd edn. New York: Oxford University Press.

Mercer, R.E., & Wevrick, R. (2009) 'Loss of magel2, a candidate gene for features of Prader–Willi syndrome, impairs reproductive function in mice', *PLoS One,* 4(1): e4291.

Mercer, R.E., Kwolek, E.M., Bischof, J.M., van Ede, M., Henkelman, R.M., & Wevrick, R. (2009) 'Regionally reduced brain volume, altered serotonin neurochemistry, and abnormal behavior in mice null for the circadian rhythm output gene Magel2', *Am J Med Genet, B Neuropsychiatr Genet,* 150B(8): 1085–1099.

Miller, J., Kranzler, J., Liu, Y., Schmalfuss, I., Theriaque, D.W., Shuster, J.J., et al. (2006) 'Neurocognitive findings in Prader–Willi syndrome and early-onset morbid obesity', *J Pediatr,* 149(2): 192–198.

Miller, J.L., James, G.A., Goldstone, A.P., Couch, J.A., He, G., Driscoll, D.J., et al. (2007a) 'Enhanced activation of reward mediating prefrontal regions in response to food stimuli in Prader–Willi syndrome,' *J Neurol Neurosurg Psychiatry,* 78(6): 615–619.

Miller, J.L., Couch, J.A., Schmalfuss, I., He, G., Liu, Y., & Driscoll, D. J. (2007b) 'Intracranial abnormalities detected by three-dimensional magnetic resonance imaging in Prader–Willi syndrome', *Am J Med Genet , Part A,* 143: 476–483.

Milner, K.M., Craig, E.E., Thompson, R.J., Veltman, M.W., Thomas, N.S., Roberts, S., et al. (2005) 'Prader–Willi syndrome: intellectual abilities and behavioural features by genetic subtype', *J Child Psychol Psychiatry,* 46(10): 1089–1096.

Moss, J., Oliver, C., Arron, K., Burbidge, C., & Berg, K. (2009) 'The prevalence and phenomenology of repetitive behavior in genetic syndromes', *J Autism Dev Disord,* 39(4): 572–588.

Nagai, T., Obata, K., Tonoki, H., Temma, S., Murakami, N., Katada, Y., et al. (2005) 'Cause of sudden, unexpected death of Prader–Willi syndrome patients with or without growth hormone treatment', *Am J Med Genet, Part A,* 136(1): 45.

Nakamura, Y., Nagai, T., Iida, T., Ozeki, S., & Nohara, Y. (2009) 'Epidemiological aspects of scoliosis in a cohort of Japanese patients with Prader–Willi syndrome', *Spine J,* 9(10): 809–816.

Nicholls, R.D. (1993) 'Genomic imprinting and candidate genes in the Prader-Willi and Angelman syndromes', *Curr Opin Genet Dev,* 3: 445–456.

Paik, K.H., Jin, D.K., Song, S.Y., Lee, J.E., Ko, S.H., Song, S.M., et al. (2004) 'Correlation between fasting plasma ghrelin levels and age, body mass index (BMI), BMI percentiles, and 24-hour plasma ghrelin profiles in Prader–Willi syndrome', *J Clin Endocrinol Metab,* 89(8): 3885.

Paik, K.H., Jin, D.K., Lee, K.H., Armstrong, L., Lee, J.E., Oh, Y.J., et al. (2007) 'Peptide YY, cholecystokinin, insulin and ghrelin response to meal did not change, but mean serum levels of insulin is reduced in children with Prader–Willi syndrome', *J Korean Med Sci,* 22(3): 436.

Patel, S., Harmer, J.A., Loughnan, G., Skilton, M.R., Steinbeck, K., & Celermajer, D.S. (2007) 'Characteristics of cardiac and vascular structure and function in Prader–Willi syndrome', *Clin Endocrinol (Oxf)* 66(6): 771.

Peery, E.G., Elmore, M.D., Resnick, J.L., Brannan, C.I., & Johnstone, K.A. (2007) 'A targeted deletion upstream of Snrpn does not result in an imprinting defect', *Mamm Genome,* 18(4): 255–262.

Prader, A., Labhart, A., & Willi, H. (1956) 'Ein syndrom von adipositas, kleinwuchs, kryptorchismus und oligophrenie nach myatonieartigem zustand in neugeborenenalter', *Schweizerische Medizinische Wochenschrift,* 86:1260–1261

Priano, L., Miscio, G., Grugni, G., Milano, E., Baudo, S., Sellitti, L., et al. (2009) 'On the origin of sensory impairment and altered pain perception in Prader–Willi syndrome: a neurophysiological study', *Eur J Pain,* 13(8): 829–835.

Reddy, L.A., & Pfeiffer, S.I. (2007) 'Behavioral and emotional symptoms of children and adolescents with Prader–Willi Syndrome', *J Autism Dev Disord,* 37(5): 830–839.

Runte, M., Varon, R., Horn, D., Horsthemke, B., & Buiting, K. (2005). Exclusion of the C/D box snoRNA gene cluster HBII-52 from a major role in Prader–Willi syndrome. *Hum Genet,* 116(3): 228–230.

Sahoo, T., del Gaudio, D., German, J.R., Shinawi, M., Peters, S.U., Person, R.E., et al. (2008) 'Prader–Willi phenotype caused by paternal deficiency for the HBII-85 C/D box small nucleolar RNA cluster', *Nature Genet,* 40(6): 719.

Schmidt, H., Pozza, S.B., Bonfig, W., Schwarz, H.P., & Dokoupil, K. (2008) 'Successful early dietary intervention avoids obesity in patients with Prader–Willi syndrome: a ten-year follow-up', *J Pediatr Endocrinol Metab,* 21(7): 651.

Schrander-Stumpel, C.T., Curfs, L.M., Sastrowijoto, P., Cassidy, S.B., Schrander, J.J., & Fryns, J.P. (2004) 'Prader–Willi syndrome: causes of death in an international series of 27 cases', *Am J Med Genet,* 124(4): 333–338.

Semenza, C., Pignatti, R., Bertella, L., Ceriani, F., Mori, I., Molinari, E., et al. (2008) 'Genetics and mathematics: evidence from Prader–Willi syndrome', *Neuropsychologia,* 46(1): 206–212.

Shapira, N.A., Lessig, M.C., Lewis, M.H., Goodman, W.K., & Driscoll, D.J. (2004) 'Effects of topiramate in adults with Prader–Willi syndrome', *Am J Ment Retard* 109: 301–309.

Shapira, N.A., Lessig, M.C., He, A.G., James, G.A., Driscoll, D.J., & Liu, Y.(2005) 'Satiety dysfunction in Prader–Willi syndrome demonstrated by fMRI', *Br Med J,* 76(2): 260.

Skryabin, B.V., Gubar, L.V., Seeger, B., Pfeiffer, J., Handel, S., Robeck, T., et al. (2007) 'Deletion of the MBII-85 snoRNA gene cluster in mice results in postnatal growth retardation', *PLoS Genet,* 3(12): e235.

Smith A., Egan J., Ridley G., Haan E., Montgomery P., Williams K., Elliott E. (2003) Birth prevalence of Prader-Willi syndrome in Australia. *Arch Dis child* 88:263–264.

Soni, S., Whittington, J., Holland, A.J., Webb, T., Maina, E.N., Boer, H., et al. (2008) 'The phenomenology and diagnosis of psychiatric illness in people with Prader–Willi syndrome', *Psycho Medi,* 38(10): 1505–1514.

Stauder, J.E., Boer, H., Gerits, R.H., Tummers, A., Whittington, J., & Curfs, L. M. (2005) 'Differences in behavioural phenotype between parental deletion and maternal uniparental disomy in Prader–Willi syndrome: an ERP study', *Clin Neurophysiol,* 116(6): 1464–1470.

Stefan, M., Ji, H., Simmons, R.A., Cummings, D.E., Ahima, R.S., Friedman, M. I., et al. (2005) 'Hormonal and metabolic defects in a Prader–Willi syndrome mouse model with neonatal failure to thrive', *Endocrinology,* 146(10): 4377.

Steinhausen, H.C., Eiholzer, U., Hauffa, B.P., & Malin, Z. (2004) 'Behavioural and emotional disturbances in people with Prader–Willi Syndrome', *J Intellect Disabil Res,* 48(1): 47–52.

Stevenson, D.A., Anaya, T.M., Clayton-Smith, J., Hall, B.D., Van Allen, M.I., Zori, R.T., et al. (2004) 'Unexpected death and critical illness in Prader–Willi syndrome: report of ten individuals', *Am J Med Genet,* 124(2): 158–164.

Tauber, M., Diene, G., Molinas, C., & Hébert, M. (2008) 'Review of 64 cases of death in children with Prader-Willi syndrome (PWS)', *Am J Med Genet, Part A,* 146(7): 881.

Torrado, M., Araoz, V., Baialardo, E., Abraldes, K., Mazza, C., Krochik, G., et al. (2007) 'Clinical–etiologic correlation in children with Prader–Willi syndrome (PWS): an interdisciplinary study', *Am J Med Genet, Part A,* 143(5): 460.

Van Borsel, J., Defloor, T., & Curfs, L.M. (2007) 'Expressive language in persons with Prader–Willi syndrome', *Genet Couns,* 18(1): 17–28.

Varela, M.C., Kok, F., Setian, N., Kim, C.A., & Koiffmann, C.P. (2005) 'Impact of molecular mechanisms, including deletion size, on Prader–Willi syndrome phenotype: study of 75 patients', *Clin Genet,* 67(1): 47–52.

Veltman, M.W., Thompson, R.J., Roberts, S.E., Thomas, N.S., Whittington, J., & Bolton, P.F. (2004) 'Prader–Willi syndrome a study comparing deletion and uniparental disomy cases with reference to autism spectrum disorders', *Eur Child Adolesc Psychiatry,* 13(1): 42–50.

Verdine, B.N., Troseth, G.L., Hodapp, R.M., & Dykens, E.M. (2008) 'Strategies and correlates of jigsaw puzzle and visuospatial performance by persons with Prader–Willi syndrome', *Am J Ment Retard,* 113(5): 343–355.

Verhoeven, W.M. & Tuinier, S. (2006) 'Prader–Willi syndrome: atypical psychoses and motor dysfunctions', *Int Rev Neurobiol,* 72: 119.

Vestergaard, P., Kristensen, K., Bruun, J.M., Østergaard, J.R., Heickendorff, L., Mosekilde, L., et al. (2004) 'Reduced bone mineral density and increased bone turnover in Prader–Willi syndrome compared with controls matched for sex and body mass index – a cross-sectional study', *J Pediatr,* 144(5): 614–619.

Vogels, A., & Fryns, J.P. (2004) 'Age at diagnosis, body mass index and physical morbidity in children and adults with the Prader–Willi syndrome', *Genet Couns,* 15(4): 397–404.

Vogels, A., Van Den Ende, J., Keymolen, K., Mortier, G., Devriendt, K., Legius, E., et al. (2003) 'Minimum prevalence, birth incidence and cause of death for Prader–Willi syndrome in Flanders', *Eur J Hum Genet,* 12(3): 238–240.

Vogels, A., De Hert, M., Descheemaeker, M.J., Govers, V., Devriendt, K., Legius, E., et al. (2004) 'Psychotic disorders in Prader–Willi syndrome', *Am J Med Genet,* 127(3): 238–243.

Vogels, A., Moerman, P., Frijns, J.P., & Bogaert, G.A. (2008) 'Testicular histology in boys with Prader–Willi syndrome: fertile or infertile?', *J Urol,* 180: 1800–1804.

Walley, R.M., & Donaldson, M.D. (2005) 'An investigation of executive function abilities in adults with Prader–Willi syndrome', *J Intellect Disabil Res,* 49(8): 613–625.

Webb, T., Maina, E.N., Soni, S., Whittington, J., Boer, H., Clarke, D., et al. (2008) 'In search of the psychosis gene in people with Prader-Willi syndrome', *Am J Med Genet, Part A,* 146(7): 843.

Whittington, J.E. & Holland, A.J. (2004) *Prader–Willi Syndrome: Development and Manifestations.* Cambridge, UK: Cambridge University Press.

Whittington, J.E., Holland, A.J., Webb, T., Butler, J.V., Clarke, D.J., Boer, H. (2001) 'Population prevalence and estimated birth incidence and mortality rate for people with Prader–Willi Syndrome in one UK Health Region', *J Med Genet,* 38: 792–798.

Whittington, J.E., Holland, A.J., Webb, T., Butler, J.V., Clarke, D.J., Boer, H. (2002) 'Relationship between clinical and genetic diagnosis of Prader–Willi syndrome', *J Med Genet,* 38: 926–932.

Whittington, J.E., Holland, A.J., Webb, T., Butler, J.V., Clarke, D.J., Boer, H. (2004) 'Cognitive abilities and genotype in a population-based sample of people with Prader–Willi syndrome', *J Intellect Disabil Res,* 48: 172–187

Whittington, J.E., Butler, J.V., & Holland, A.J. (2006) 'Changing rates of genetic subtypes of Prader–Willi syndrome in the UK', *Eur J Hum Genet,* 15(1): 127–130.

Whittington, J.E., Butler, J.V., & Holland, A.J. (2008) 'Pre-, peri- and postnatal complications in Prader–Willi syndrome in a UK sample', *Early Hum Dev,* 84(5): 331–336.

Whittington, J., Holland, A., & Webb, T. (2009) 'Relationship between the IQ of people with Prader–Willi syndrome and that of their siblings: evidence for imprinted gene effects', *J Intellect Disabil, Res,* 53(5): 411–418.

Woodcock, K.A., Humphreys, G.W., & Oliver, C. (2009a) 'Dorsal and ventral stream mediated visual processing in genetic subtypes of Prader–Willi syndrome', *Neuropsychologia,* 47(12): 2367–2373.

Woodcock, K.A., Oliver, C., & Humphreys, G.W. (2009b) 'Task-switching deficits and repetitive behaviour in genetic neurodevelopmental disorders: data from children with Prader–Willi syndrome chromosome 15 q11-q13 deletion and boys with Fragile X syndrome', *Cogn Neuropsychol,* 26(2): 172–194.

Yamada, K., Matsuzawa, H., Uchiyama, M., Kwee, I.L., & Nakada, T. (2006) 'Brain developmental abnormalities in Prader–Willi syndrome detected by diffusion tensor imaging', *Pediatrics,* 118(2): e442.

Zanella, S., Watrin, F., Mebarek, S., Marly, F., Roussel, M., Gire, C., et al. (2008) 'Necdin plays a role in the serotonergic modulation of the mouse respiratory network: implication for Prader–Willi syndrome', *J Neurosci,* 28(7): 1745.

Zarcone, J., Napolitano, D., Peterson, C., Breidbord, J., Ferraioli, S., Caruso-Anderson, M., et al. (2007) 'The relationship between compulsive behaviour and academic achievement across the three genetic subtypes of Prader–Willi syndrome', *J Intellect Disabil Res,* 51(6): 478.

7

Angelman Syndrome

Bernard Dan & Karine Pelc

INTRODUCTION

Angelman syndrome is a neurogenetic condition clinically characterized by a constellation of features that comprise a specific behavioural phenotype (Table 7.1). This behavioural uniqueness includes prominent smiling laughter, marked hyperactivity, an unusual communication pattern with absent speech contrasting with eagerness for social interaction, mouthing of objects and motor stereotypes. It is caused by lack of the product of a gene that is normally expressed in the brain from the chromosome 15 inherited from the mother. Given its multifaceted implications, which range from molecular biology to developmental neuropsychology, it has been argued that Angelman syndrome can serve as a disease model, opening broad questioning of genetic and epigenetic influences in neurology, as well as of several concepts such as psychomotor development, cerebral palsy, behavioural phenotypes and epileptic syndromes. Readers with specific interest in Angelman syndrome can be referred to a comprehensive review of the many aspects of the syndrome recently published as a monograph (Dan, 2008). This integrates current knowledge on clinical and genetic diagnostic issues, natural history, possible pathophysiological pathways, specific clinical problems (motor impairment, behaviour, learning difficulties, communication, sleep, epilepsy), clinical neurophysiology, neuropathology, rehabilitation and basic research.

BRIEF HISTORICAL PERSPECTIVE

In 1965, a British paediatrician named Harry Angelman described three children with severe intellectual disability, frequent, easily provoked bouts of laughter, no speech, physical features including micro-brachycephaly and tongue protrusion, and neurological manifestations, such as hypotonia, increased knee jerks, ataxia and epilepsy (Angelman, 1965). Laboratory investigations available at the time, including chromosome examination, were normal except for electroencephalograms, which showed epileptiform discharges, and air encephalogram, which showed mild dilatation of the ventricular system. Angelman commented that the children described in his paper 'possess[ed] such similarities as to

Table 7.1   Clinical Diagnostic Criteria for Angelman Syndrome

A. Consistent features (100%)

Developmental delay: functionally severe

Motor disorder: usually ataxia of gait, and/or tremulous movement of limbs; the movement disorder can be mild

Behavioural uniqueness: any combination of frequent laughter/smiling; apparent happy demeanour; easily excitable personality, often with uplifted hand-flapping, or waving movements; hypermotor behaviour

Speech impairment: none or minimal use of words; receptive and non-verbal communication skills higher than verbal ones

B. Frequent features (more than 80%)

Relative microcephaly: delayed, disproportionate growth in head circumference, usually resulting in microcephaly (−2 standard deviations of normal head circumference) by age 2 years; microcephaly is more pronounced in individuals with 15q11-q13 deletions

Epilepsy: seizures onset usually before 3 years of age; severity usually decreases with age but the seizure disorder lasts throughout adulthood

Abnormal electroencephalogram: characteristic rhythmic patterns (described and categorized in Dan & Boyd, 2003); the electroencephalographic abnormalities can occur in the first 2 years of life, can precede clinical features, and are often not correlated to clinical seizure events

C. Associated features (20–80%)

Flat occiput

Occipital groove

Protruding tongue

Tongue thrusting; sucking/swallowing disorders

Feeding problems and/or truncal hypotonia during infancy

Prognathia

Wide mouth, wide-spaced teeth

Frequent drooling

Excessive chewing/mouthing behaviours

Strabismus

Hypopigmented skin, light hair, and eye colour compared to family, seen only in those with 15q11-q13 deletions

Hyperactive lower extremity deep tendon reflexes

Uplifted, flexed arm position especially during ambulation

Wide-based gait with pronated or valgus-positioned ankles

Increased sensitivity to heat

Abnormal sleep–wake cycles and diminished need for sleep

Attraction to/fascination with water; fascination with crinkly items such as certain papers and plastics

Abnormal food-related behaviours

Obesity (in the older child)

Scoliosis

Constipation

Adapted from Williams et al. (2006).

justify combining them into a specific group, as yet of unknown cause'. In the 10 years that followed the original description, only 11 additional individuals were recorded in the international literature. However, interest in the syndrome increased dramatically from the mid 1980s, particularly after reports of chromosome 15 abnormalities in a region otherwise implicated in Prader–Willi syndrome (see Chapter 6). It was demonstrated that these two disorders illustrate the phenomenon of genomic imprinting, characterized by differential expression of genes according to their maternal or paternal origin. Several mechanisms leading to the absence of maternal imprinting of chromosome 15 were shown to cause Angelman syndrome. In 1995, a group of clinicians and scientists involved in the study of the syndrome, including Harry Angelman, published a consensus for clinical diagnostic criteria (Williams et al., 1995). The criteria were based on the clinical profile of individuals with Angelman syndrome. At the time, genetic testing could confirm the diagnosis in about 80% of individuals. In 1997, two independent teams (Kishino et al., 1997; Matsuura et al., 1997) identified specific lack of expression of the *UBE3A* gene as responsible for the phenotype. Advances in molecular research and genetic engineering led to the possibility of designing animal models of Angelman syndrome. There are now five main mouse models based on the genetic homology between human chromosome

15q11-q13 and murine chromosome 7C (Cattanach et al., 1997; Gabriel et al., 1999; Homanics et al., 1997; Jiang et al., 1998; Miura et al., 2002). There is also a drosophila model of knockout *Dube3a* (Wu et al., 2008). The clinical diagnostic criteria were updated in 2005, taking into account increased knowledge about the molecular and clinical features of the syndrome (Williams et al., 2006).

EPIDEMIOLOGY

Prevalence of Angelman syndrome has been estimated to be between 1:10,000 and 1:40,000 (Petersen et al., 1995; Steffenburg et al., 1996; Thomson et al., 2006). The syndrome is equally represented in both genders and is assumed to be uniformly distributed in all populations (Clayton-Smith & Laan, 2003). The vast majority of cases are sporadic. The incidence of familial recurrence (about 7%) depends on the underlying molecular mechanism. The recurrence risk is very low (<1%) in case of de novo 15q11-13 deletion or uniparental disomy. Situations involving *UBE3A* gene mutations or imprinting defects may be more complex, as members of the mother's extended family are also at increased risk. Most mutations occur de novo and are associated with a very low recurrence risk, but mutations inherited from the mother are associated with a 50% recurrence risk.

CAUSATION

Angelman syndrome is a genetic condition but its pattern of inheritance is not typically Mendelian. It illustrates the physiological process of genomic imprinting, where expression of 'imprinted' genes is effectively monoallelic and dependent on the parental origin (Horsthemke & Wagstaff, 2008). Angelman syndrome is inherited down the maternal line and it can 'skip' generations. It

must be noted that, while the parental origin of the allele is determinant, the effects of genomic imprinting are indifferent to the actual gender of the offspring. Angelman syndrome is thus caused by lack of expression of the imprinted *UBE3A* gene, located on the long arm of chromosome 15. This gene is specifically imprinted in the brain, where it is expressed from the allele inherited from the mother with silencing of the paternal allele. In different mouse models, evidence of expression has been found predominantly in the hippocampus, olfactory bulbs and the cerebellar Purkinje cell layer (Albrecht et al., 1997; Jiang et al., 1998; Miura et al., 2002). The role of *UBE3A* in the pathophysiology of the Angelman syndrome phenotype is currently unclear. The gene product *(UBE3A)* is a ubiquitin-ligase involved in labelling protein for selective destruction along the ubiquitin-proteasome pathway, but relevant substrates are yet to be discovered. In addition, other functions of *UBE3A* cannot be ruled out. According to one hypothesis, *UBE3A* plays a central role in regulating the number of functional γ-aminobutyric acid $GABA_A$ receptors at the synaptic level (Dan & Boyd, 2003). Recent findings of possible interaction between *UBE3A* and calcium/calmodulin-dependent protein kinase II and of localizing of *UBE3A* at the postsynaptic density (van Woerden et al., 2007; Weeber et al., 2003) suggest that *UBE3A* may have roles in glutamatergic neurotransmission.

Molecular classes

Lack of *UBE3A* expression can result from different molecular mechanisms (Clayton-Smith & Laan, 2003). In about 70% of individuals, it is due to an interstitial loss of a segment of the long arm of the chromosome 15 inherited from the mother. Most deletions occur de novo. In the vast majority of cases, they cannot be detected by a routine chromosome study but are detectable by fluorescence in situ hybridization (FISH) analysis with specific probes or by comparative genomic hybridization (CGH) analysis. The most critical gene involved in this deletion of the maternal chromosome 15q11-q13 appears to be *UBE3A*, though other genes are implicated in the deletion. For example, the 'pink-eyed dilution' or *P* gene, which is not imprinted, is thought to be responsible for the hypopigmentation seen in individuals with a deletion, which is similar to that found in Prader–Willi syndrome (see Chapter 6). Absence of a copy of several genes which code for subunits of the $GABA_A$ receptor has tentatively been related to abnormalities in GABAergic neurotransmission (Olsen & Avoli, 1997). Statistically, individuals who have a deletion have a more severe phenotype than those in other molecular classes. For example, they tend to have more severe microcephaly, a complete absence of speech and more severely impaired receptive communication; they also tend to sit and walk later, have more severe seizures and show more hypopigmentation (Lossie et al., 2001).

Approximately 2–3% of individuals have inherited both copies of chromosome 15 from the father and none from the mother, i.e. paternal uniparental disomy. As a result, no functional copy of the *UBE3A* gene is inherited from the mother. Uniparental disomy can be detected using DNA methylation analysis or DNA polymorphism testing.

About 3–5% of individuals have an imprinting defect resulting in a lack of the typical maternal pattern of DNA methylation. Imprinting defects may be due to microdeletions or point mutations of the 'imprinting centre', a small region in chromosome 15q11-q13 that regulates gene expression. A significant proportion of imprinting defects are inherited. Imprinting defects may be detected by DNA methylation analysis, but additional testing (FISH) is required to exclude a deletion.

In another 5–10% of individuals, there is a mutation in the maternal *UBE3A* gene. The majority of *UBE3A* gene mutations occur de novo but around 20% are carried by the mother. They can be detected by *UBE3A* gene sequence analysis. The phenotype of individuals with a *UBE3A* gene mutation is similar to that of those with a deletion with respect to microcephaly, seizure disorder and absence of speech. In contrast, pigmentation, development of motor skills and ability to follow simple commands appear to be similar to individuals with uniparental disomy or imprinting defect (Lossie et al., 2001). In 1–2% of cases, inactivation of the maternal *UBE3A* gene may rarely result from rearrangements of chromosome 15. Finally, in less than 10% with a typical phenotype for Angelman syndrome, no genetic abnormalities can be found.

DIAGNOSTIC CRITERIA AND CORE CHARACTERISTICS

The clinical diagnosis of Angelman syndrome is based on a set of physical and behavioural features (Williams et al., 2006) (Table 7.1). The main craniofacial signs are illustrated in Figure 7.1. All individuals have developmental delay with severely impaired cognitive skills, though accurate assessment is often difficult. There is a specific speech impairment: about one-third of individuals speak no words at all; the remainder rarely use more than 5 words. This contrasts with better verbal understanding and relatively good communication using spontaneous or learned signs. Behaviour is characteristically overactive, happy and sociable. Muscle tone abnormalities include axial hypotonia, present from birth, and spastic hypertonia of the limbs that becomes apparent during the first year of life. Despite varying degrees of ataxia, most children develop independent walking. Gait is distinctive, with a wide base, lower limb extension and lateral rotation, and associated elbow flexion and wrist supination. More than 80% of individuals have epileptic seizures. The interictal electroencephalogram shows three typical rhythmic patterns (Dan & Boyd, 2003).

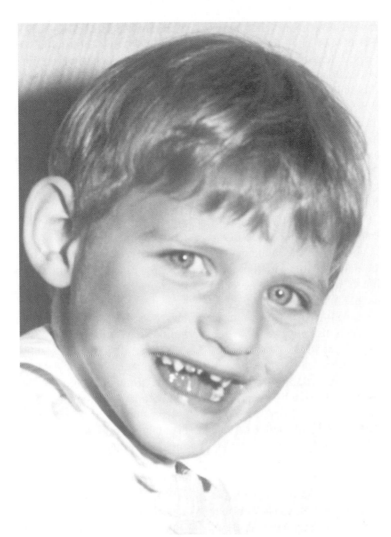

Figure 7.1   Facial characteristics of a child with Angelman syndrome. Note visual contact, fair eyes, pointed nose, wide smiling mouth, prognathism and drooling

Cognitive abilities

Intellectual impairment is one of the consistent features of Angelman syndrome but is difficult to evaluate because of the variable impact of confounding factors, including adaptive skills, behavioural and motor features. Most individuals are regarded by professionals as having severe to profound intellectual disability. It must be noted that parental perception of intellectual disability may differ greatly from professional evalua-

tion. In a study involving 179 families of children with Angelman syndrome, fewer than 50% of parents regarded their child as having severe or profound intellectual disability, whereas professionals considered that more than 70% of the children did (Miller, 1995). Formal psychometric evaluation in children and adolescents with Angelman syndrome commonly relies on scales that were originally designed for assessing the development of infants and very young children. As a result, the developmental profile in individuals with Angelman syndrome is sometimes described as 'cognitive arrest' at 24 months of age (Handforth et al., 2005), which does not account for clinical complexity and continuing learning (Clayton-Smith, 2001). Several studies conducted in children and adolescents have found consistent cognitive impairment, with scores below those expected for typically developing 2-year-old children (Andersen et al., 2001; Peters et al., 2004a; Trillingsgaard & Østergaard, 2004). In several recent series, however, the distribution or IQ (or analogous measurements) was found to be in the severe range in about 50% and in the moderate range in about 40%, with a small proportion of individuals in the mild or profound range (Beckung et al., 2004; Thomson et al., 2006), contrasting with 100% of severe or profound intellectual disability suggested in earlier reports (Laan et al., 1999; Leitner & Smith, 1996). There is currently limited information on the cognitive profile. Executive attention seems to be markedly impaired. Among other factors, attention may be disrupted by seizure activity (Pelc et al., 2008a). Anecdotally, individuals may exhibit relatively good skills in spatial navigation and long-term memory, particularly in the spatial domain, contrasting with the severity of learning difficulties. Intellectual disability may be statistically more severe in individuals with a chromosome 15q11-q13 deletion, but cognitive abilities show great overlap across the different molecular classes (Lossie et al., 2001).

Communication

Communicative functioning is reduced because of specific dysphasic problems that may involve oral dyspraxia, pragmatic factors and intellectual disability. Speech impairment is consistently severe; even the rare individuals who can say more than a few words do not use speech as their primary means of communication (Alvares & Downing, 1998; Andersen et al., 2001; Jolleff

& Ryan, 1993; Lossie et al., 2001; Penner et al., 1993). In contrast, individuals typically show spontaneous interest for more or less refined non-verbal language and relative preservation of receptive verbal language (Clayton-Smith, 1993; Trillingsgaard & Østergaard, 2004; Williams et al., 2006). Most individuals develop some degree of visual-manual expressive communication (Alvares & Downing, 1998; Clayton-Smith, 1993; Duker et al., 2002; Miller, 1995). Many individuals spontaneously develop pointing towards objects, which they use a lot in communication. Many can consistently nod for 'yes', shake their head for 'no' or wave their hand. In addition to pointing, nodding and other gestures, expressive skills typically include facial expression, though a bias towards positive expressions is possible, limiting expressive selectivity.

Almost all individuals show a desire for social interaction. They commonly tend to initiate communication but they often show significant deficits in several pragmatic aspects that are important for promoting and maintaining communication, including orientation to the speaker, stability of eye contact, joint attention and communicative sharing (Didden et al., 2004a; Duker et al., 2002). The typically prominent smiling is a major signal in social interaction (Horsler & Oliver, 2006a; Oliver et al., 2002). Communication may be enhanced by optimizing interaction contexts by means of predictability, visual cues, facilitation of turn-taking and the use of non-verbal signals that may include spontaneous or learned gestures, pictograms or other communication devices (Alvares & Downing, 1998; Miller, 1995).

Happy conduct

An apparently happy demeanour is among the cardinal features of the 'behavioural uniqueness' that characterizes Angelman syndrome (Table 7.1). Frequent smiling and laughing have been regarded as a hallmark of the Angelman syndrome since the original description and served to label the condition ('happy puppet syndrome') for many years. Some authors have suggested that bouts of laughter were inappropriate, whether context-inappropriate or unrelated to context (Williams & Frias, 1982). Alternatively, it has been suggested that laughter was independent of happy or sad environments and not associated with any emotional change. In fact, there has been mounting evidence showing that laughter is very often clearly related to context (Horsler & Oliver, 2006a; Oliver et al., 2002), though it may occur in situations that are not thought to be pleasant, such as blood sampling (Dooley et al., 1981; Kibel & Burness, 1973; Pelc et al., 2008b). Laughing and smiling may increase markedly with anxiety and some individuals appear to be in discomfort during pervasive bouts of laughter (Oliver et al., 2007). In the original report, Angelman (1965) noted that laughter could often occur as 'an almost convulsive state' and that 'spike and wave forms were present during the period of laughter'. However, there has been no further evidence of gelastic seizures in Angelman syndrome (Pelc et al., 2008a). Extremely rarely, laughing can provoke potentially dangerous syncope (which is amenable to pharmacological treatment) (Vanagt et al., 2005). More often, smiling and laughing appear to be appropriate, appearing expressly in social contexts, enhanced by adult speech, touch, smiling, laughing and eye contact (Horsler & Oliver, 2006a). Laughter may become less frequent with advancing age (Buntinx et al., 1995; Laan et al., 1996). We have seen several adolescents and adults who appeared miserable for prolonged periods of time; in some cases, this was accompanied by medical problems such as severe gastro-oesophageal reflux.

Emotion

Despite the prominence of apparent happy demeanour, little is known about emotions in this condition although absence of strong expressions of negative emotion has been suggested to be typical. Children with Angelman syndrome have been reported to appear less overly sensitive, to cry less and argue less with children or adults than children with other forms of intellectual disability (Walz & Benson, 2002). They often show difficulties with processing and recognizing expressions of partners' emotions, though this seems to be more marked for emotional facial expressions than for hand gestures. This problem contributes to difficulties with sensitivity to social feedback, which may cause social maladaptiveness.

Hyperactivity

Hypermotor, exuberant behaviour is almost persistent, at least in childhood. Comparisons with non-syndromic developmental disabilities or other specific syndromes have yielded discrepant results (Pelc et al., 2008b). Hyperactivity appears to decrease with age (Buntinx et al., 1995; Clarke & Marston, 2002), possibly giving way to reluctance to exercise in adolescence and adulthood (Clayton-Smith, 2001). Impulsivity, distractibility and short attention span occur at similar frequencies to other conditions with moderate to profound intellectual disability (Barry et al., 2005; Walz & Benson, 2002) and attention span increases with age (Clayton-Smith, 2001). It must be stressed that clinical characteristics of the DSM-IV-defined attention-deficit/ hyperactivity disorder (ADHD) are not discriminating features of Angelman syndrome (Barry et al., 2005) and this label is misleading in this context for counselling, management and research issues (Pelc & Dan, 2008).

Stereotypies and other autistic features

Motor stereotypies are very frequent (Summers et al., 1992; Walz, 2006). No single pattern appears to be specific, or even evocative, despite classical emphasis on hand-flapping and waving (Table 7.1). It must be noted that hand-flapping is also frequent in other syndromes (e.g. fragile X syndrome; see Chapter 3) as well as in non-syndromic intellectual disability and autism spectrum disorders, not to mention typically developing infants, toddlers and children. Stereotypies also often involve the mouth, with mouthing or chewing of non-edible objects. Compulsive eye-rubbing, which may become prominent in adolescence or adulthood, can result in keratoconus. Although these stereotypies may appear similar to those seen in the autistic spectrum, they were found to correlate with a low developmental profile rather than being specific to autism in a study addressing autistic traits in children with Angelman syndrome (Bonati et al., 2007).

In addition to these stereotypies, several characteristic features of Angelman syndrome may be seen in the context of the autistic spectrum, including virtual absence of speech, impaired use of non-verbal communicative behaviours, attention deficits, hyperactivity, feeding and sleeping problems, and delays in motor development. As a result, autistic features have been regarded as characteristic of the syndrome by some authors (Steffenburg et al., 1996) and as comorbidity by others (Williams et al., 2001). However, systematic studies of the incidence of autistic features in children with Angelman syndrome have yielded discrepant results. Several authors have reported a low incidence of autistic features (Cohen et al., 2005; Veltman et al., 2005), emphasizing appropriate social reciprocity as a distinctive feature (Saitoh et al., 1994; Smith et al., 1996). This is in contrast to other recent studies on relatively small groups, which reported a high incidence of DSM-IV-based diagnoses of autistic disorder (10 in 16 in Trillingsgaard & Østergaard, 2004; 8 in 19 in Peters et al., 2004b). These discrepancies may relate to differences in studied populations and in study design. Subjective interpretation of the symptomatology may also be an important factor, even in studies based on validated evaluation scales. It must be stressed that incorrect diagnosis of

autistic spectrum may result in misinterpretation of behavioural features and in overlooking the social and communication potential of individuals with Angelman syndrome.

Social interaction

In contrast to the autistic-like features, the conviviality of most individuals with Angelman syndrome is particularly striking. Interest in social interaction seems to be prominent from early infancy. Most are eager to communicate despite their verbal impairments, although, as noted above, non-verbal behaviours, such as facial expressions, body postures, and gestures regulating social interaction, may lack accuracy and be difficult to interpret. The 'happy' disposition is accompanied by a markedly positive interpersonal bias and social disinhibition, which persists in adulthood. However, despite their sociability and gregariousness, individuals often encounter problems in everyday interaction because of poor understanding of and inappropriate responses to others' emotional and social signals. Fear of strangers is often diminished but there may be specific phobias, for example, fear of crowds or of noise.

All individuals require supervision, including as adults. In general, young adults are described as fitting well into their local communities and as being very sociable. There is, however, wide variation in self-help skills. The main problems appear to be related to difficulties in remaining focused on an activity and impaired recognition of danger.

Aggressiveness

Aggression and other challenging behaviours have been differently emphasized in various reports (Clayton-Smith, 2001; Summers et al., 1995; Zori et al., 1992). Problem behaviours include excessive laughter, overactivity and restlessness, short attention span, problems with sleeping and eating, pica, attraction to water and repetitive and stereotyped behaviours. Lack of compliance to instructions or more generally to social rules can also be problematic (Summers et al., 1995), although behavioural flexibility in individuals with Angelman syndrome has been found to be relatively high compared to individuals with non-specific intellectual disability (Didden et al., 2008). In addition, temper tantrums and aggression have been reported. An extensive literature review suggested a 6% overall occurrence of aggressive behaviour in children and adults, but there is marked variability (Horsler & Oliver, 2006b), with some reports of up to 80% (Oliver et al., 2005). It must be recognized that aggression in individuals with Angelman syndrome may take the form of grabs or rough hugs and thus the phenomenology differs from other conditions (Summers & Feldman, 1999). Excessive sociability may have a role in the development and maintenance of these behaviours through proactive attention-seeking. This has significant implications for clinical practice and behavioural intervention.

Sleep problems

Sleep problems are frequently encountered, with prevalence figures reaching 90% (Clayton-Smith, 1993). Until recently, emphasis was placed exclusively on parental reports of clinically apparent sleep disturbances (Bruni et al., 2004; Didden et al., 2004b; Walz et al., 2005) rather than on polysomnographic documentation (Miano et al., 2004). The observed sleep abnormalities are multiple, none being distinctively characteristic of Angelman syndrome. The emerging pattern involves a combination of difficulties in initiating or maintaining sleep (i.e. dyssomnias), irregular sleep–wake cycles, sometimes aggravated by inappropriate nocturnal behaviours, such as screaming or laughing, sleep-related seizure disorder or sleep-related movement disorder (Pelc et al., 2008b).

As in other neurodevelopmental conditions, sleep problems appear to be more severe in early childhood, being maximal between 2 and 6 years of age (Clayton-Smith, 1993). Some authors have suggested that they commonly diminish or disappear altogether by late childhood (Bruni et al., 2004; Didden et al., 2004b; Smith et al., 1996), with continuing improvement through adolescence and adulthood (Clayton-Smith, 2001). In some individuals with Angelman syndrome, however, sleep problems persist in adulthood (Bruni et al., 2004; Didden et al., 2004b).

Unstable, very variable circadian cycles in young children with Angelman syndrome may impede physiological readiness to follow a regular sleep schedule. It has been hypothesized, but not confirmed, that this might be due to decreased production of melatonin, decreased expression of its receptors or other factors determining sensitivity to this hormone (Zhdanova et al., 1999).

However severe the sleep problems may be, they do not usually affect individuals' alertness or activity level when awake or even their personal quality of life. Indeed, it has been suggested that children with Angelman syndrome have a 'diminished need for sleep' as compared with other children (Clayton-Smith, 1993; Williams et al., 2006). It must be stressed, though, that the sleep problems of the individual with Angelman syndrome commonly affect the entire family. Parents in particular may experience more marked effects of sleep deprivation than the child who shows the primary problem. In addition to the anxiety, anger and feelings of helplessness that family members may experience in relation to the child's sleeplessness, they may suffer from fatigue, irritability, limitation of activities and other disturbances as a result of their own lack of sleep.

ASSESSMENT AND DIFFERENTIAL DIAGNOSIS

The diagnosis of Angelman syndrome is rarely made in the first months of life, despite early medical attention, because the presentation (typically developmental delay or seizures) lacks specificity and/or because many clinicians are unfamiliar with the condition. As already emphasized, the clinical diagnosis relies on recognition of the association of typical clinical features (see Table 7.1). Genetic confirmation can be obtained following an algorithm suggested by Clayton-Smith and Laan (2003). It is of utmost importance for adequate counselling, as the recurrence risk depends essentially on the genetic mechanism that gives rise to Angelman syndrome.

The differential diagnoses considered will depend on the clinical context. In the neonatal period and early infancy, signs are so mild or non-specific that no specific aetiological diagnosis may be suspected and symptoms may be attributed to failure to thrive or gastro-oesophageal reflux. Later in infancy, the developmental delay may appear as non-specific, although the social aspects, in particular prominent smiling, may be suggestive of Angelman syndrome. The association of epilepsy and developmental delay may prompt a medical work-up for developmental encephalopathy (see Chapter 18) or even a metabolic encephalopathy. Lennox–Gastaut syndrome is a common misdiagnosis with reference to epilepsy, vague electroencephalographic similarities and developmental delay (see Chapter 21). The delay in acquiring motor skills, the lack of selectivity in motor organization and eventual muscle tone abnormality may suggest cerebral palsy (e.g. attributed to early anoxic-ischaemic insult) (see Chapter 25), while stereotyped behaviours may suggest autism (see Chapters 14 and 15).

All current definitions of the autistic spectrum concept (whether under the labels of pervasive developmental disorders, autistic spectrum disorders or other terms) include impaired social interaction, impaired communication and stereotypies. Therefore, the clinical presentation of individuals with Angelman syndrome can be indicative of this heterogeneous diagnostic label. The estimated prevalence of Angelman syndrome in autism is 1% (Cohen et al., 2005). Conversely,

reports of the incidence of autistic disorder diagnosis in individuals with Angelman syndrome has been variable (Bonati et al., 2007; Peters et al., 2004b; Trillingsgaard & Østergaard, 2004), but in some studies all participants were considered to have autism (Barry et al., 2005; Steffenburg et al., 1996). Differential diagnosis thus appears difficult. However, many individuals with Angelman syndrome are highly sociable, which contrasts markedly with autism, in which the core problem is the impairment in reciprocal social interaction. Other features common in Angelman syndrome that are unusual in autism include the facial features, the happy disposition, some of the motor characteristics and the electroencephalographic findings (Tuchman & Rapin, 2006). A distinction has been made between 'syndromic autism' and 'idiopathic' (or 'primary') autism. In line with this view, we suggest that individuals with Angelman syndrome and a sound diagnosis of autism (i.e. a diagnosis made on the basis of expert clinical judgement and standardized assessments) should be regarded as having syndromic autism. It must be stressed that erroneous diagnosis of autistic spectrum in individuals with Angelman syndrome may result in misinterpretation of behavioural features and in overlooking the social and communication potential of those with this condition.

Another diagnostic label sometimes considered in individuals with Angelman syndrome is ADHD. However, we consider that attempts to single out the cognitive and behavioural features of these individuals as corresponding to ADHD are inappropriate (Pelc & Dan, 2008). Admittedly, this view might render symptoms less unusual and more acceptable to parents in the general context of disability. However, more importantly, it often calls for prescription of 'ADHD drugs'. As regards the current accent on pharmacological treatment of ADHD, there has been limited indication of effectiveness of psychostimulant drugs in various neurogenetic disorders (Bawden et al., 1997; Gothelf et al., 2003; Hagerman et al., 1988). Particular caution is needed when prescribing for this group considering the very small number of studies that have been conducted. These have involved relatively small numbers of participants, have not covered the range of drugs prescribed in ADHD and have given little if any attention to safety. In a 7-year-old boy with Angelman syndrome, methylphenidate precipitated a state of lethargy associated with generalized fast, presumably non-epileptic electroencephalographic activity ('mu rhythm status') (Dan & Boyd, 2005).

Other conditions, such as Rett syndrome, may be specifically considered in children and several other chromosomal disorders have overlapping features with Angelman syndrome (Table 7.2). Rett syndrome is another neurogenetic condition, due to mutations in the X-linked *MECP2* gene (see Chapter 8). It almost exclusively affects girls, who present with early neurological regression of motor, cognitive and communication skills accompanied by progressive microcephaly. There is some degree of phenotypic overlap with Angelman syndrome, particularly with regard to the severe developmental delay, motor impairment, stereotyped movements, absence of speech and epilepsy (Dan & Cheron, 2008; Ellaway et al., 1998; Scheffer et al., 1990). Episodic laughter is not uncommon in Rett syndrome and is considered among the supportive diagnostic criteria for this condition (Hagberg et al., 2002). Features that distinguish it from Angelman syndrome include a history of early regression in Rett syndrome, but this may not be obvious in children in whom regression begins early in life. Electroencephalographic features may be helpful in the differential diagnosis, and of course, genetic testing is discriminating.

In older individuals, a specific diagnosis may be sought less often and clinicians involved in intellectual disability services for adults are usually less familiar with Angelman syndrome. Adults with undiagnosed Angelman syndrome are often considered to have non-specific intellectual disability, cerebral palsy or sequelae from infantile epilep-

tic encephalopathy or from other early insult (e.g. meningitis).

Table 7.2 Conditions that can Mimic Angelman Syndrome and Relevant Discriminating Investigations

Heterogeneous generic neurodevelopmental disorders

Cerebral palsy	Motor pattern, history, MRI
Autistic spectrum	Behavioural features, history
Lennox–Gastaut syndrome	Seizure characterization, EEG
Other non-progressive encephalopathies	Extensive work-up

Monogenic disorders

Rett syndrome	*MECP2* gene, *CDKL5* gene
Untreated phenylketonuria	Amino acid chromatography
MTHFR deficiency	Plasma homocysteine level
ATR-X syndrome	Hb electrophoresis, *ATR-X* gene

Chromosome disorders

22q13.3 terminal deletions	Cytogenetic study
Mowat–Wilson syndrome	Cytogenetic study
inv dup(15)	Cytogenetic study

Adapted from Dan (2008). MRI, magnetic resonance imaging; EEG, electroencephalogram; Hb, haemoglobin.

LIFETIME COURSE AND INTERVENTIONS

Available data on the natural history of Angelman syndrome are mostly retrospective. As most reports have concerned children, relatively little is known about adults, particularly older ones. Sample selection biases may also occur. For example, it is not clear to what extent samples recruited in institutions or through support and advocacy groups are representative of the general adult population with Angelman syndrome. Moreover, as observed in conditions such as cerebral palsy or Down syndrome, levels of functional competence and participation may have increased over the last few decades. This is probably due to improvements in management and diagnosis, as genetic confirmation has become possible in individuals with milder phenotypes who might not have been recognized as having Angelman syndrome before non-deletion causes could be identified.

Neonatal period

Retrospectively, parents may report mild to moderate neonatal hypotonia and feeding difficulties, with weak sucking and prominent regurgitation (Clayton-Smith, 1993; Smith et al., 1996; Zori et al., 1992). This presentation is not unusual in neonates with other conditions and it may also occur transiently in babies who are otherwise normal. As a result, it does not point to the diagnosis of Angelman syndrome. Weight loss or growth stagnation may occur. Affected newborn babies are often described as placid and hypoactive. Hypotonia seems to have a predominantly axial distribution, but it is much less marked than the neonatal presentation of Prader–Willi syndrome or other conditions with neonatal hypotonia.

Infancy

The diagnosis of Angelman syndrome is rarely evoked in infancy, although developmental delay gradually becomes more evident. Young infants are retrospectively reported to show less motor activity than siblings and to cry less often than other infants. In contrast, social smiling often emerges early or at a normal age, i.e. between 4 and 6 weeks (Clayton-Smith, 1993). Smiling may be prominent, constituting early evidence of the distinctive happy disposition. It is soon accompanied by reflexive laughter and giggling, which can occur as early as the first weeks of life (Clayton-Smith & Laan, 2003). In a number of individuals, this may promote early social interaction and overshadow intellectual disability. Strabismus, whether convergent or divergent, is common. Infants typically show decreased or delayed cooing and babbling.

Feeding problems are common in infancy (Buntinx et al., 1995; Smith et al., 1996; Zori et al., 1992). They mostly include slow feeding, poor sucking, regurgitation or vomiting and may result in failure to thrive, which may be another reason for seeking medical help (Thomson et al., 2006). Gastro-oesophageal reflux may further enhance the feeding difficulties. Feeding difficulties, failure to thrive and gastro-oesophageal reflux can usually be managed with conservative measures. Constipation is also common and may be related to hypotonia.

Gross motor milestones are delayed. For example, independent sitting rarely appears before the age of 12 months. Muscle tone regulation is impaired. Sleep–wake cycles are often perturbed and infants may also have difficulties in initiating or maintaining sleep. Whereas epilepsy is often a problem in childhood, seizure onset occurs during infancy in a minority of individuals, mostly in a febrile context. Infants may show a propensity to develop recurrent mild upper respiratory tract infections and otitis media.

Childhood

Medical attention is commonly sought during childhood because of the developmental delay, which is evident in all areas. In early childhood the characteristic features, and in particular the typical behavioural aspects and lack of speech, become clear enough for most clinicians who are familiar with

Angelman syndrome to consider this diagnosis by the age of 3. Smiling and laughing become prominent and often in response to many different stimuli so that they appear to be non-specific (rather than 'inappropriate', see above). Children appear to understand contextual information and follow commands and they can indicate their needs. Social interaction may be poorly differentiated (i.e. with little partner-specificity) and attention span is short. Some degree of motor hyperactivity is seen in virtually all affected children, without any gender predominance (Buntinx et al., 1995). Some children may show virtually ceaseless activity, often with repetitive, purposeless hand movements, including flapping. Many individuals, particularly those who have severe seizures or extreme hyperactivity, cannot attend long enough to establish sufficiently sustained eye contact or other prerequisites that are important for communication and learning. Play is also limited by cognitive and fine motor problems. It is mostly exploratory (through manipulation as well as chewing) and tends to be repetitive. There is a marked delay in the emergence of presymbolic play (e.g. empty/fill up containers, hide/uncover objects) and symbolic play (e.g. make-believe, regarding toys as characters) rarely emerges.

Mouthing behaviours, including sucking and chewing, may become more pronounced as children grow older. About half of the children show persistent tongue protrusion and drooling; otherwise, tongue protrusion is often associated with laughter. Feeding difficulties tend to improve markedly or resolve altogether in early childhood.

As regards motor development, low, horizontal postures may be preferred for long periods before an interest for vertical postures emerges. For movement, asymmetric bottom-shuffle is common. Children usually start to walk independently after 3 or 4 years of age (Buntinx et al., 1995; Zori et al., 1992), but about 10% never achieve independent walking (Lossie et al., 2001). Spasticity may develop from childhood, with a lower extremity predominance. Physical therapy may be indicated to facilitate variability and selectivity in motor control and to prevent muscle contracture that may result from sustained hypertonia (Dan & Cheron, 2008). During childhood, sleep disturbances can be severe, although there is often some improvement in later childhood. Most children have seizure onset between 18 months and 4 years (Buntinx et al., 1995; Clayton-Smith, 1993; Saitoh et al., 1994).

Children require an individually adapted educational approach, which is commonly organized within a multidisciplinary setting.

Adolescence

Puberty occurs at a normal age or with a mild to moderate delay (up to 3 years), with development of normal secondary sexual characteristics. The face tends to be less round than in childhood, with deep-set eyes and enlarged mandible. The adolescent growth spurt may be accompanied by the development of scoliosis (Clayton-Smith, 2001; Thomson et al., 2006). There may be a tendency towards bulimia or pica (Barry et al., 2005) and weight gain can be evident in this period, occasionally leading to obesity, with a marked female predominance. Motivation for physical activities may decrease dramatically, including reluctance to walk.

In many individuals, hyperactivity and bursts of laughter decrease significantly, though the sociability and happy disposition remain (Buntinx et al., 1995, Clayton-Smith, 2001). In parallel, attention span increases, leading to somewhat improved learning and communication skills. Some adolescents tend to become placid and seem to enjoy staying immobile and watching their surroundings. In some individuals, stereotypies decrease, but other behaviours including eye-rubbing and masturbation may become prominent. Sleep quality usually improves and the seizure disorder, too, improves markedly in teenage years.

Adulthood

Most of the available reports of adults have described individuals who had been long-standing residents in large institutions (Buntinx et al., 1995; Laan et al., 1996). One study focused on individuals who had lived with their family or in small-group homes for most of their life (Clayton-Smith, 2001), and this is likely to represent an increasing proportion of adults. General health is usually good, although in some individuals, epilepsy, gastrointestinal or other problems may be severe. Life span has been described as normal in several reviews. However, this notion is not researched-based and would be inconsistent with shortening of life expectancy commonly associated with immobility, severe scoliosis, dysphagia, aspiration or severe epilepsy that may affect a significant proportion of individuals.

Facial traits become more marked, especially prognathism (i.e. projecting jaws). The intensity of hyperactivity continues to diminish in adulthood, with some adults becoming rather tranquil and/or stubborn (Buntinx et al., 1995; Clayton-Smith, 2001). The frequency of laughing may decrease. Concentration sometimes improves markedly, including in complex activities, and interest for objects may become more sustained. Improved communicative skills may be seen, with increased expressive gestures and better comprehension. In parallel, learning may be successfully pursued in a proportion of individuals. In contrast, progressive deterioration of mobility can occur due to ataxia, spasticity, tremor, dystonia, muscle contracture, skeletal deformity including scoliosis and lack of motivation (Dan & Cheron, 2008).

A proportion of adults may experience sleep problems, such as difficulties in initiating and maintaining sleep, paroxysmal movements, obstructive sleep apnoea and excessive daytime somnolence. However, in her study of adults with Angelman syndrome, Clayton-Smith (2001) commented that they did not have the poor sleep pattern seen in younger children. Although epilepsy often diminishes in adolescence, seizure frequency may increase in adults. Non-convulsive status epilepticus may interfere with normal activities and may account for motor or behavioural deterioration.

APPROACHES TO INTERVENTION

Management of individuals with Angelman syndrome rests essentially on (re)habilitation programmes aimed at optimizing cognitive, communication and motor development and functioning. Such programmes are tailored individually, based on the specific needs of patients rather than on the aetiological diagnosis. All individuals require special education. As a number of clinical problems, including inattention and hyperactivity, tend to improve with age, the potential for continued learning extends well beyond the usual school-leaving age. Communication ability may be enhanced through specific teaching programmes to facilitate interaction with people and objects, and to encourage skills such as turn-taking. For expressive communication, most individuals use spontaneous or learned signs and gestures (Alvares & Downing, 1998; Clayton-Smith, 1993; Duker et al., 2002; Miller, 1995). Many older individuals also possess adequate levels of abstraction skills to enable them to use symbols or more figurative drawings (pictograms). Communication cards, picture charts and electronic communication devices may also be used to facilitate understanding and communicative competence.

Management of problem behaviours is primarily based on behavioural approaches, though psychoactive medication (e.g. neuroleptics or antidepressants) may be required. It must be recognized that so-called 'challenging behaviours' may serve a communication function, for example, to obtain attention. Counselling and direct behavioural advice can help carers to develop more effective management skills (van den Borne et al., 1999).

In most individuals, stereotypies do not cause discomfort or significant social impairment, and thus, no treatment is required. However, if management is indicated, non-pharmacological approaches often have little effect. Pharmacological treatment may also be limited, both by lack of efficacy and adverse effect. Possible options include risperidone and fluoxetine. Some stereotyped behaviours can result in self-injury, such as compulsive eye-rubbing, which may become prominent in adolescence or adulthood and can cause keratoconus. Again, non-pharmacological management appears limited, though enhanced variability in sensorimotor experiences may have more effect.

As regards sleeping difficulties, there has also been a lack of systematic evaluation of intervention approaches and stabilization of sleep problems is difficult to achieve. Behavioural management, following general principles of sleep hygiene, is recommended, although pharmacological treatment with sedative and hypnotic drugs may also be required (Walz et al., 2005). There have been a few reports of improvement of sleep problems with administration of melatonin (Braam et al., 2008; Zhdanova et al., 1999) but more studies are required in order to know if this hormone can be safely recommended, what types of sleep problems it might help, in which individuals it might be considered (e.g. according to age, basal melatonin production levels, etc.) and what dosage would be optimal.

Physical therapy can facilitate the emergence of more selective or varied movement patterns. It can also prevent the development of muscle contracture and joint deformity to some extent. Postural stabilization is often important, with particular emphasis on axial righting of the trunk and visual–manual–oral coordination. Hydrotherapy can be considered, given the characteristic fascination with water. This has the additional advantages of offering particular sensory stimulation and facilitating gravitational control. Specifically adapted orthoses (e.g. ankle–foot orthoses in case of equinus or ankle instability) in combination with physical therapy may be required to prevent muscle contracture, facilitate balance or promote selective movement at the level of other joints.

Behavioural approaches can help to improve social skills and reduce socially inappropriate behaviour as well as developing adaptive skills. In a study evaluating the effect of a 'backward chaining' procedure in establishing daytime continence in six children with Angelman syndrome aged 6–19 years, Didden et al. (2001) found not only long-lasting improvement in toileting but also increased independence with dressing and undressing. Educational and cultural factors may also have a major impact on social interaction. It must be noted that participation in life events and society at large is often limited by a form of cultural prescription which may need to be overcome at many levels. Efforts to increase participation of individuals with Angelman syndrome or other disabling conditions should be directed as much at changing environmental factors as improving adaptive skills.

CURRENT RESEARCH

Since the original account of Angelman in 1965, several hundred individuals with Angelman syndrome have been described in the scientific literature. The clinical picture has been broadly documented, principally in children but with an increasing emphasis on adolescents and adults. Given the unusual and multifaceted aspects of its biology and clinical presentation, the syndrome has become emblematic of a number of different topics, ranging from genomic imprinting to behavioural phenotypes, genetic epilepsies or neurodevelopmental disorders. However, much uncertainty remains because available information appears to be fragmentary and anecdotal with regard to many specific points, perhaps because data collection is often not standardized. Published evaluation of clinical problems has often been based on reported impressions obtained from clinicians or parents. On occasion, assessment has been performed using tests that were used or designed ad hoc by individual teams. The samples from which data are drawn are not necessarily representative, given the clinical heterogeneity of Angelman syndrome.

In contrast, the genetic complexity of the condition has been studied thoroughly over the last 20 years. Diagnostic techniques have become more reliable and their availability is increasing. Advances have been made in the understanding of various molecular mechanisms giving rise to Angelman syndrome and many issues that are important for genetic counselling have been clarified. However, the mechanisms linking the genetic defect with the manifestations of the syndrome are still largely unexplored. There are currently no satisfactory pathophysiological explanations for any of the major features. As a result, no specific management approaches can be proposed at present.

Molecular biology and genetics

A large number of current studies involve molecular biology, including investigation of the mechanisms of imprinting and the possible roles of *UBE3A*. These studies are extremely important for achieving a better understanding of the processes involved. Based on this understanding, appropriate modulation might be proposed to improve neurological functioning in individuals with Angelman syndrome. Some studies concentrate on the possible relationship between genes implicated in Angelman syndrome and other conditions, such as Rett syndrome, autism or epileptic syndromes. In particular, there seems to be some crucial interactions in the regulation of *MECP2* and *UBE3A* expression (Samaco et al., 2005).

Active research is dedicated to designing animal models of Angelman syndrome (Cattanach et al., 1997; Gabriel et al., 1999; Homanics et al., 1997; Jiang et al., 1998; Miura et al., 2002; Wu et al., 2006; Wu et al.,

2008). Although, some of these models have not been studied beyond preliminary description, others have been successfully used for testing hypotheses that might be relevant to human patients.

Neurological issues

As regards the neurology of Angelman syndrome, epilepsy has been the most studied subject (Pelc et al., 2008a) although other neurological features also deserve special attention. With respect to motor control, for example, dysfunctions of various components of the motor system, including the motor cortex, cerebellum and basal ganglia, have been hypothesized, but more studies are required to test the hypotheses. Similarly, almost all electrophysiological studies conducted previously were limited to electroencephalography. The methods that have been recently developed to address internal brain dynamics and how they modulate neural processing can probably yield invaluable information in Angelman syndrome. The typical rhythmic electroencephalographic activities probably reflect dynamic states of neural circuits (Dan & Boyd, 2003). Neuroimaging should also provide more insights into Angelman syndrome (Dan et al., 2009) and functional imaging can address a number of highly relevant issues, including speech processing. Moreover, given the extreme paucity of neuropathological material (only two published autopsies!), awareness of the potential progress that can be made from direct brain observation should be encouraged.

Neuropsychological issues

Much of the current debate on the psychological and behavioural features of Angelman syndrome has concentrated on whether or not it is appropriate to consider affected individuals as falling within the autistic spectrum, or whether their frequent smiling and laughing consistently reflect mirth (Oliver et al., 2007). The studies that fuel these debates are interesting as they provide systematically collected data. However, due to methodological difficulties inherent to both the subject and limitations related to behaviour and communication, they are unlikely to settle these questions unequivocally. In contrast, the domain of cognition seems important to investigate further. Neuropsychological studies of well-defined subgroups of participants are still much needed in order to shed more light on cognitive processing and learning strategies. This might have important implications for the development of more effective, syndrome-specific educational approaches. More pragmatic studies of behavioural and other teaching programmes are also required. In particular, behavioural approaches aimed at teaching notions of behavioural limits, social rules, sleep routines, etc., need to be designed and better evaluated.

CONCLUSION

Great challenges remain to be met. They mainly concern evidence-based management of the clinical problems and understanding of their pathophysiology for designing specific therapeutic approaches. Clinical problems that appear to be most at the forefront include severe developmental delay (and in particular learning difficulties), seizure disorder, sleep problems and lack of autonomy and participation in society in relation to intellectual disability, communication impairment, behavioural adaptation and motor problems. There is an urgent need for well-designed studies of the effects of management strategies. As regards the relationship between the genetic abnormalities and the manifestations of Angelman syndrome, no definite functional links have yet been established. However, a few notions have emerged. Specific lack of *UBE3A* production in certain brain cell populations (and perhaps during certain periods in development) is central to the expression of Angelman syndrome. Studies of the regulation of *UBE3A* expression are likely to prove extremely important, as they may point to possibilities of upregulation. Possible roles in specific protein degradation, specific intracellular trafficking and regulation of transcription should be studied in order to gain understanding of relevant effects of *UBE3A* that might lead to targeted intervention. Moreover, the physiological phenotype involving cortical networks (with particular emphasis on the hippocampus), thalamocortical networks and cerebellar networks should be documented more extensively, including in a developmental perspective. Abnormal neuronal functioning related to excessive rhythmic, synchronous electrophysiological activities probably interferes with physiological neural processing of information necessary for a number of integrative functions, including cognitive functions, behavioural adaptation, communication, motor control and some aspects of sleep. Progress in neuromodulation approaches—including pharmacology, specific stimulation or inhibition—might, hopefully, result in improved neurological function.

REFERENCES

Albrecht, U., Sutcliffe, J.S., Cattanach, B.M., Beechey, C.V., Armstrong, D., Eichele, G., & Beaudet, A.L. (1997) 'Imprinted expression of the murine Angelman syndrome gene, *Ube3a*, in hippocampal and Purkinje neurons', *Nat Genet*, 17: 75–78.

Alvares, R.L. & Downing, S.F. (1998) 'A survey of expressive communication skills in children with Angelman syndrome', *Am J Speech Lang Pathology*, 7: 14–24.

Andersen, W.H., Rasmussen, R.K., Strømme, P. (2001) 'Levels of cognitive and linguistic development in Angelman syndrome: a study of 20 children,' *Logoped Phoniatr Vocol*, 26: 2–9.

Angelman, H. (1965) '"Puppet" children: a report on three cases,' *Dev Med Child Neurol*, 7: 681–688.

Barry R.J., Leitner, R.P., Clarke, A.R., & Einfeld, S.L. (2005) 'Behavioral aspects of Angelman syndrome: a case control study', *Am J Med Genet*, 132: 8–12.

Bawden, H.N., MacDonald, G.W., & Shea, S. (1997) 'Treatment of children with Williams syndrome with methylphenidate,' *J Child Neurol*, 12: 248–252.

Beckung, E., Steffenburg, S., & Kyllerman, M. (2004) 'Motor impairments, neurological signs, and developmental level in individuals with Angelman syndrome', *Dev Med Child Neurol*, 46: 239–243.

Bonati, M.T., Russo, S., Finelli, P., Valsecchi, M.R., Cogliati, F., Cavalleri, F., Robert, W., Elia, M., & Larizza, L. (2007) 'Evaluation of autism traits in Angelman syndrome: a resource to unfold autism genes', *Neurogenetics*, 8: 169–178.

Braam, W., Didden, R., Smits, M.G., & Curfs, L.M. (2008) 'Melatonin for chronic insomnia in Angelman syndrome: a randomized placebo-controlled trial', *J Child Neurol*, 23: 649–654.

Bruni, O., Ferri, R., D'Agostino, G., Miano, S., Roccella, M., & Elia, M. (2004) 'Sleep disturbances in Angelman syndrome: a questionnaire study', *Brain Dev*, 26: 233–240.

Buntinx, I.M., Hennekam, R.C.M., Brouwer, O.F., Stroink, H., Beuten, J., Mangelschots, K., & Fryns, J.P. (1995) 'Clinical profile of Angelman syndrome at different ages', *Am J Med Genet*, 56: 176–183.

Cattanach, B.M., Barr, J.A., Beechey, C.V., Martin, J., Noebels, J., & Jones, J. (1997) 'A candidate model for Angelman syndrome in the mouse', *Mamm Genome*, 8: 472–478.

Clarke, D.J. & Marston, G. (2002) 'Problem behaviors associated with 15q-Angelman syndrome', *Am J Ment Retard*, 105: 25–31.

Clayton-Smith, J. (1993) 'Clinical research on Angelman syndrome in the United Kingdom: observations on 82 affected individuals', *Am J Med Genet*, 46: 12–15.

Clayton-Smith, J. (2001) 'Angelman syndrome: evolution of the phenotype in adolescents and adults', *Dev Med Child Neurol*, 43: 476–480.

Clayton-Smith, J. & Laan, L. (2003) 'Angelman syndrome: a review of the clinical and genetic aspects', *J Med Genet*, 40: 87–95.

Cohen, D., Pichard, N., Tordjman, S., Baumann, C., Burglen, L., Excoffier, E., Lazar, G., Mazet, P., Pinquier, C., Verloes, A., & Heron, D. (2005) 'Specific genetic disorders and autism: clinical contribution towards their identification', *J Autism Dev Disord*, 35: 103–116.

Dan, B. (2008) *Angelman Syndrome.* London: Mac Keith Press, Blackwell Publishing.

Dan, B. & Boyd, S.G. (2003) 'Angelman syndrome reviewed from a neurophysiological perspective. The *UBE3A-GABRB3* hypothesis', *Neuropediatrics*, 34: 169–176.

Dan, B. & Boyd, S.G. (2005) Nonconvulsive (dialeptic) status epilepticus in children', *Curr Pediatr Rev*, 1: 7–16.

Dan, B. & Cheron, G. (2008) 'Postural control in children with Rett syndrome or Angelman syndrome' in M. Hadders-Algra, E. Brogren Carlberg (eds), *Posture: A Key Issue in Developmental Disorders.* London: Mac Keith Press, pp. 148–169.

Dan, B., Pelc, K., & Christophe, C. (2009) 'What would the brain look like in Angelman syndrome?' *Eur J Paediatr Neurol*, 13(3): 269–270.

Didden, R., Sikkema, S.P.E., Bosman, I.T.M., Ducker, P.C. (2001) 'Use of a modified Azrin-Foxx toilet training procedure with individuals with Angelman syndrome', *J Appl Res Intellect Dis*, 14: 64–70.

Didden, R., Korzilius, H., Duker, P., & Curfs, L.M.G. (2004a) 'Communicative functioning in individuals with Angelman syndrome: a comparative study', *Disabil Rehabil*, 26: 1263–1267.

Didden, R., Korzilius, H., Smits, M.G., & Curfs, L.M.G. (2004b) 'Sleep problems in individuals with Angelman syndrome', *Am J Ment Retard*, 109: 275–284.

Didden, R., Sigafoos, J., Green, V.A., Korzilius, H., Mouws, C., Lancioni, G.E., O'Reilly, M.F., & Curfs, L.M. (2008) 'Behavioural flexibility in individuals with Angelman syndrome, Down syndrome, non-specific intellectual disability and Autism spectrum disorder', *J Intellect Disabil Res*, 52: 503–509.

Dooley, J.M., Berg, J.M., Pakula, Z., & MacGregor, D.L. (1981) 'The puppet-like syndrome of Angelman', *Am J Dis Child*, 135: 621–624.

Duker, P.C., van Driel, S., & van de Bercken J. (2002) 'Communication profiles of individuals with Down syndrome, Angelman syndrome, and pervasive developmental disorder', *J Intellect Disabil Res*, 46: 35–40.

Ellaway, C., Buchholz, T., Smith, A., Leonard, H., & Christodoulou J. (1998) 'Rett syndrome: significant clinical overlap with Angelman syndrome but not with methylation status', *J Child Neurol*, 13: 448–451.

Gabriel, J.M., Merchant, M., Ohta, T., Ji, Y., Caldwell, R.G., Ramsey, M.J., Tucker, J.D., Longnecker, R., & Nicholls, R.D. (1999) 'A transgene insertion creating a heritable chromosome deletion mouse model of Prader–Willi and Angelman syndromes', *Proc Natl Acad Sci USA*, 96: 9258–9263.

Gothelf, D., Gruber, R., Presburger, G., Dotan, I., Brand-Gothelf, A., Burg, M., Inbar, D., Steinberg, T., Frisch, A., Apter, A., & Weizman, A. (2003) 'Methylphenidate treatment for attention-deficit/hyperactivity disorder in children and adolescents with velocardiofacial syndrome: an open-label study', *J Clin Psychiatry*, 64: 1163–1169.

Hagberg, B., Hanefeld, F., Percy, A., & Skjeldal, O. (2002) 'An update on clinically applicable diagnostic criteria in Rett syndrome', *Eur J Paediatr Neurol*, 6: 293–297.

Hagerman, R.J, Murphy, M.A., & Wittenberger, M.D. (1988) 'A controlled trial of stimulant medication in children with the fragile X syndrome', *Am J Med Genet*, 30: 377–392.

Handforth, A., Delorey, T.M., Homanics, G.E., & Olsen, R.W. (2005) 'Pharmacologic evidence for abnormal thalamocortical functioning in GABA receptor β3 subunit-deficient mice, a model of Angelman syndrome', *Epilepsia*, 46: 1860–1870.

Homanics, G.E., DeLorey, T.M., Firestone, L.L., Quinlan, J.J., Handforth, A., Harrison, N.L., et al. (1997) 'Mice devoid of gamma-aminobutyrate type A receptor beta3 subunit have epilepsy, cleft palate, and hypersensitive behavior', *Proc Natl Acad Sci USA*, 94: 4143–4148.

Horsler, K. & Oliver, C. (2006a) 'Environmental influences on the behavioral phenotype of Angelman syndrome', *Am J Ment Retard*, 111: 311–321.

Horsler, K. & Oliver, C. (2006b) 'The behavioural phenotype of Angelman syndrome', *J Intellect Disabil Res*, 50: 33–53.

Horsthemke, B. & Wagstaff, J. (2008) 'Mechanisms of imprinting of the Prader–Willi/Angelman region', *Am J Med Genet A*, 146: 2041–2052.

Jiang, Y.H., Armstrong, D., Albrecht, U., Atkins, C.M., Noebels, J.L., Eichele, G., Sweatt, J.D., & Beaudet, A.L. (1998) 'Mutation of the Angelman ubiquitin ligase in mice causes increased cytoplasmic p53 and deficits of contextual learning and long-term potentiation', *Neuron*, 21: 799–811.

Jolleff, N. & Ryan, M. (1993) 'Communication development in Angelman's syndrome', *Arch Dis Child*, 69: 148–158.

Kibel, M.A. & Burness, F.R. (1973) 'The 'Happy Puppet' syndrome', *Centr Afr J Med*, 19: 91–93.

Kishino, T., Lalande, M., & Wagstaff, J. (1997) '*UBE3A/E6-AP* mutations cause Angelman syndrome', *Nat Genet*, 15: 70–73.

Laan, L.A.E.M., den Boer, A.T.H., Hennekam, R.C.M., Renier, W.O., & Brouwer, O.F. (1996) 'Angelman syndrome in adulthood', *Am J Med Genet*, 66(3): 356–360.

Laan, L.A.E.M., van Haeringen, A., & Brouwer, O.F. (1999) 'Angelman syndrome: a review of clinical and genetic aspects', *Clin Neurol Neurosurg*, 101: 161–170.

Leitner, R.P. & Smith A. (1996) 'An Angelman syndrome clinic: report on 24 patients', *J Paed Child Health*, 32: 94–98.

Lossie, A.C., Whitney, M.M., Amidon, D., Dong, H.J., Chen, P., Theriaque, D., Hutson, A., Nicholls, R.D., Zori, R.T., Williams, C.A., & Driscoll, D.J. (2001) 'Distinct phenotypes distinguish the molecular classes of Angelman syndrome', *J Med Genet*, 38: 834–845.

Matsuura, T., Sutcliffe, J.S., Fang, P., Galjaard, R.J., Jiang, Y.H., Benton, C.S., Rommens, J.M., & Beaudet, A.L. (1997) 'De novo truncating mutations in E6-AP ubiquitin-protein ligase gene (*UBE3A*) in Angelman syndrome', *Nat Genet*, 15: 74–77.

Miano, S., Bruni, O., Leuzzi, V., Elia, M., Verrillo, E., & Ferri, R. (2004) 'Sleep polygraphy in Angelman syndrome', *Clin Neurophysiol*, 115: 938–945.

Miller, L.W. (1995) *Angelman Syndrome: A Parent's Guide Survey: 179 Returned Surveys from Parents Caring for Children Diagnosed with AS*. Fredericksburg: Mary Washington College, Masters of Arts in Liberal Studies Program.

Miura, K., Kishino, T., Li, E., Webber, H., Dikkes, P., Holmes, G.L., & Wagstaff, J. (2002) 'Neurobehavioral and electroencephalographic abnormalities in Ube 3a maternal-deficient mice' *Neurobiol Dis*, 9: 149–159.

Oliver, C., Demeetriades, L., & Hall, S. (2002) 'Effects of environmental events on smiling and laughing behavior in Angelman syndrome', *Am J Ment Retard*, 107: 194–200.

Oliver, C., Arron, K., Berg, K., Burbidge, C., Caley, A., Duffay, S., Hooker, M., & Moss, J. (2005) 'A comparison of Cornelia de Lange, cri du chat, Prader–Willi, Smith–Magenis, Lowe, Angelman and fragile X syndromes', *Genet Counsel*, 13: 363–381.

Oliver, C., Horsler, K., Berg, K., Bellamy, G., Dick, K., & Griffiths, E. (2007) 'Genomic imprinting and the expression of affect in Angelman syndrome: what's in the smile?' *J Child Psychol Psychiatry*, 48: 571–579.

Olsen, R.W. & Avoli, M. (1997) 'GABA and epileptogenesis', *Epilepsia*, 38: 399–407.

Pelc, K. & Dan, B. (2008) 'The ADHD Tetragrammaton taken in vain in neurogenetic disorders?', *Acta Paediatr*, 97: 2–4.

Pelc, K., Boyd, S.G., Cheron, G., & Dan, B. (2008a) 'Epilepsy in Angelman syndrome', *Seizure*, 17: 211–217.

Pelc, K., Cheron, G., & Dan, B. (2008b) 'Behavior and neuropsychiatric manifestations in Angelman syndrome', *Neuropsychiatr Dis Treat*, 4: 577–584.

Penner, K.A., Johnston, J., Faircloth, B.H., Irish, P., & Williams, C.A. (1993) 'Communication, cognition and social interaction in the Angelman Syndrome', *Am J Med Genet*, 46: 34–39.

Peters, S.U., Goddard-Finegold, J., Beaudet, A.L., Madduri, N., Turcich, M., & Bacino, C.A. (2004a) 'Cognitive and adaptive behavior profiles of children with Angelman syndrome', *Am J Med Genet*, 128: 110–113.

Peters, S.U., Beaudet, A.L., Madduri, N., Bacino, C.A. (2004b) 'Autism in Angelman's syndrome: implications for autism research', *Clin Genet*, 66: 530–536.

Petersen, M.B., Brondum-Nielsen, K., Hansen, L.K., & Wulff, K. (1995) 'Clinical, cytogenetic, and molecular diagnosis of Angelman syndrome: estimated prevalence rate in a Danish county', *Am J Med Genet*, 60: 261–262.

Samaco, R.C., Hogart, A., & LaSalle, J.M. (2005) 'Epigenetic overlap in autism-spectrum neurodevelopmental disorders: MECP2 deficiency causes reduced expression of *UBE3A* and *GABRB3*', *Hum Mol Genet*, 14: 483–492.

Saitoh, S., Harada, N., Jinno, Y., Hashimoto, K., Imaizumi, K., Kuroki, Y., et al. (1994) 'Molecular and clinical study of 61 Angelman syndrome patients', *Am J Med Genet*, 52: 158–163.

Scheffer, I., Brett, E.M., Wilson, J., & Baraitser, M. (1990) 'Angelman's syndrome', *J Med Genet*, 27: 275–277.

Smith, A., Wiles, C., Haan, E., McGill, J., Wallace, G., Dixon, J., Selby, R., Colley, A., Marks, R., & Trent, R.J. (1996) 'Clinical features in 27 patients with Angelman syndrome resulting from DNA deletion', *J Med Genet*, 33: 107–112.

Steffenburg, S., Gillberg, C.L., Steffenburg, U., & Kyllerman, M. (1996) 'Autism in Angelman syndrome: a population-based study', *Pediatr Neurol*, 14: 131–136.

Summer, J.A., Allison, D.B., Lynch, P.S., & Sandler, L. (1995) 'Behaviour problems in Angelman syndrome', *J Intellect Disabil Res*, 39: 97–106.

Summers, J.A. & Feldman, M.A. (1999) 'Distinctive pattern of behavioural functioning in Angelman syndrome', *Am J Ment Retard*, 104: 376–384.

Summers, J.A., Lynch, P.S., Harris, J.C., Burke, J.C., Allison, D.B., & Sandler, L. (1992) 'A combined behavioral/pharmacological treatment of sleep-wake schedule disorder in Angelman syndrome', *J Dev Behav Pediatr*, 13: 284–287.

Thomson, A.K., Glasson, E.J, & Bittles, A.H. (2006) 'A long-term population-based clinical and morbidity profile of Angelman syndrome in Western Australia: 1953–2003', *Disabil Rehabil*, 28: 299–305.

Trillingsgaard, A. & Østergaard, J.R. (2004) 'Autism in Angelman syndrome: an exploration of comorbidity', *Autism*, 8: 163–174.

Tuchman, R. & Rapin, I. (eds) (2006) *Autism: a Neurological Disorder of Early Brain Development*. London: Mac Keith Press.

Vanagt, W.Y., Pulles-Heintzberger, C.F., Vernooy, K., Cornelussen, R.N., & Delhaas, T. (2005) 'Asystole during outbursts of laughing in a child with Angelman syndrome', *Pediatr Cardiol*, 26: 866–868.

van den Borne, H.W., van Hooren, R.H., van Gestel, M., Rienmeijer, P., Fryns, J.P., & Curfs, L.M.G. (1999) 'Psychosocial problems, coping strategies, and the need for information of parents of children with Prader–Willi syndrome and Angelman syndrome', *Patient Educ Couns,* 38: 205–216.

van Woerden, G.M., Harris, K.D., Hojjati, M.R., Gustin, R.M., de Avila Freire, R., Jiang, Y.H., Elgersma, Y., & Weeber, E.J. (2007) 'Rescue of neurological deficits in a mouse model for Angelman syndrome by reduction of CaMKII inhibitory phosphorylation', *Nat Neurosci*, 10: 280–282.

Veltman, M.W.M., Craig, E.E., & Bolton, P. (2006) 'Autism spectrum disorders in Prader–Willi and Angelman syndromes: a systematic review', *Psychiatric Genetics*, 15: 243–254.

Walz, N.C. (2006) 'Parent report of stereotyped behaviors, social interaction, and developmental disturbances in individuals with Angelman syndrome', *J Autism Dev Disord*, 36: 472–479.

Walz, N.C. & Benson, B.A. (2002) 'Behavioral phenotypes in children with Down syndrome, Prader–Willi syndrome, and Angelman syndrome', *J Dev Phys Disabil,* 14: 307–321.

Walz, N.C., Beebe, D., & Byars, K. (2005) 'Sleep in individuals with Angelman syndrome: parent perceptions of patterns and problems', *Am J Ment Retard*, 110: 243–252.

Weeber, E.J., Jiang, Y.H., Elgersma, Y., Varga, A.W., Carrasquillo, Y., Brown, S.E., Christian, J.M., Mirnikjoo, B., Silva, A., Beaudet, A.L., & Sweatt, J.D. (2003) 'Derangements of hippocampal calcium/calmodulin-dependent protein kinase II in a mouse model for Angelman mental retardation syndrome', *J Neurosci*, 23: 2634–2644.

Williams, C.A. & Frias, J.L. (1982) 'The Angelman ("happy puppet") syndrome' *Am J Med Genet*, 11: 453–460.

Williams, C.A., Angelman, H., Clayton-Smith, J., Driscoll, D.J., Hendrickson, J.E., Knoll, J.H.M., Magenis, R.E., Schinzel, A., Wagstaff, J., Whidden, E.M., & Zori, R.T. (1995) 'Angelman syndrome: consensus for diagnostic criteria. Angelman Syndrome Foundation', *Am J Med Genet*, 56: 237–238.

Williams, C.A., Lossie, A., Driscoll, D., & R.C. Philips Unit. (2001) 'Angelman syndrome: mimicking conditions and phenotypes', *Am J Med Genet*, 101: 59–64.

Williams, C.A., Beaudet, A.L., Clayton-Smith, J., Knoll, J.H., Kyllerman, M., Laan, L.A., Magenis, R.E., Moncla, A., Schinzel, A.A., Summers, J.A., & Wagstaff, J. (2006) 'Angelman syndrome 2005: updated consensus for diagnostic criteria', *Am J Med Genet*, 140: 413–418.

Wu, Y., Bolduc, F.V., Bell, K., Tully, T., Fang, Y., Sehgal, A., & Fischer, J.A. (2008) 'A Drosophila model for Angelman syndrome', *Proc Natl Acad Sci USA*, 105: 12399–12404.

Wu, M.Y., Chen, K.S., Bressler, J., Hou, A., Tsai, T.F., & 'Beaudet, A.L. (2006) 'Mouse imprinting defect mutations that model Angelman syndrome', *Genesis*, 44: 12–22.

Zhdanova, I.V., Wurtman, R.J., & Wagstaff, J. (1999) 'Effects of a low dose of melatonin on sleep in children with Angelman syndrome', *J Pediatr Endocrinol Metab*, 12: 57–67.

Zori, R.T., Hendrickson, J., Woolven, S., Whidden, E.M., Gray, B., & Williams, C.A. (1992) 'Angelman syndrome: clinical profile', *J Child Neurol*, 7: 270–280.

8

Rett Disorder

Alison Kerr & Hayley Archer

Our aim in this chapter is to describe the clinical features of the Rett disorder (RD), to indicate the associated genetic, anatomical and physiological disturbances that underlie its problems and to discuss some interventions that have been found effective and recent initiatives that may lead to more radical treatment. Figure 8.1 shows one person with RD as a child and as an adult.

This predominantly female, profoundly disabling developmental neurological disorder results from mutations in the X-linked gene for the methyl CpG binding protein (*MECP2*) (Amir et al., 1999) and is called after Andreas Rett, the Austrian neurologist who described it (Rett, 1966). The prevalence has been estimated at 1 in 10,000 females under 14 years (Hagberg, 1993; Hagberg & Hagberg, 1997; Kerr, 1991). Although they are usually severely neurologically disabled, people with the condition may survive into middle age with good general health. A highly characteristic presentation, variable in severity, allows clinical recognition (Table 8.1) and upon suspicion of the diagnosis, genetic testing confirms the disorder in many cases. Much can be done to support the affected person and there is

substantial hope that more specific intervention will be developed in future. This chapter is chiefly based on the author's personal experience during the provision of advice for affected people of all ages at clinics throughout the British Isles, upon data from the longitudinal British Isles Survey for Rett (*n* = 1295) that grew out of that experience and upon engagement in clinical, neurophysiological and genetic research throughout the period 1982–2008.

HISTORICAL REVIEW

Andreas Rett published his first observations of the disorder in German-language journals and used cine-film of his first cases to demonstrate the characteristic appearance and behaviour of affected girls, raising awareness of the condition (Rett, 1966). The Swedish paediatric neurologist Bengt Hagberg with colleagues from France, Portugal and Switzerland published a description in English of a group of cases and at a presentation of these cases met Andreas Rett (Hagberg et al., 1983). This led to a firm friendship and

Figure 8.1 Photograph of the same individual with Rett disorder as a child (9 years old) and adult (24 years old)

Table 8.1 Characteristic Clinical Signs in Rett Disorder

Apparently normal gestation and birth

Appearance and head circumference within normal limits at birth

Head circumference falling below expected growth lines, often in the first months

Some developmental progress occurs but is suboptimal

Disturbed early spontaneous movements, lack of 3-month 'fidgety' movements.

Reduction in skills around 1–2 years of age (especially communication and hand skills)

Stereotyped hand movements, twisting, patting, or rubbing at the face, hair, together or apart

Disturbed muscle tone—hypotonia commonly gives way to hypertonia and dystonia

Failure to walk or dyspraxic gait

Irregular respiratory rhythm, deep or shallow with breath-holding, forced expiration and non-epileptic vacant spells.

Scoliosis usually develops with growth in height

Constipation is very common, not invariable

Reduction in final height is usual

Epilepsy is common but not invariably present

These signs appear with growth and, although present in virtually all cases, the severity varies from very severe with early death to near normal.

international scientific collaboration. Strong support for the research effort and for families was provided by the founding of an International Rett Syndrome Association by Mrs Kathy Hunter in the USA, soon to be followed by the founding of similar parents' associations throughout the world. International meetings were planned to discuss the disorder and to support research. These events brought together clinical and laboratory-based researchers with the affected girls and their parents, a strategy that has fostered broad collaboration and ensured that the needs of the affected child and adult remain central to the research effort. National clinical surveys are now conducted in Sweden, Britain, the USA, Australia and, increasingly, throughout the world.

Since the cause of the condition was not initially known the descriptive term 'Rett syndrome' was adopted and criteria were proposed (Hagberg et al., 1985; Rett, 1966). These early criteria were based on the assumption that the disease was limited to females, had its onset some months after birth and was degenerative. The early behaviour of affected children was described as autistic. Modification of these initial criteria became necessary as the course of the disorder and its underlying pathology became known. It became clear that the disorder was not degenerative but developmental (Armstrong, 1995), was already detectable at birth (Burford et al., 2003; Einspieler et al., 2005a, 2005b) and was compatible with long life (Hagberg, 1993; Kerr & Stephenson, 1986). The repetitive behaviours were seen to be involuntary (Kerr et al., 1987). After the initial months of life it became clear that the affected people made good social contact and were not autistic (Kerr, 1995). In addition to the female majority, male cases were diagnosed (Chahrour & Zoghbi, 2007).

Before discovery of the genetic basis for the Rett disorder, people with similar problems but differing in minor respects from the well-recognized 'classic' syndrome were described as presenting 'atypical' or 'variant' Rett syndrome (Hagberg & Rasmussen, 1986; Hagberg & Skjeldal, 1994; Zappella et al., 1992). Some of these 'variants', including the milder 'forme fruste' or 'preserved speech' and severe 'male' variants have been found to have the Rett disorder with different levels of severity. Other 'variant' forms have been found to be due to distinct, previously unrecognized disorders (Chahrour & Zoghbi, 2007). Gradually, the underlying pathogenesis in these disorders is coming to light, indicating the bases for their similarities and differences from Rett disorder. Some of these differential diagnoses of Rett disorder will be discussed below. Here we use the term Rett disorder (RD) to include the situation whenever a *MECP2* mutation is associated with the characteristic signs. Geneticists have adopted the symbol RTT to indicate cases with a mutation in the *MECP2* gene.

THE UNDERLYING PROBLEMS

The genetic basis

The *MECP2* gene is located on the X chromosome and produces the MeCP2 protein. The reader will recall that male cells contain the mother's X and the father's Y chromosome, whereas female cells contain two X chromosomes, one from each parent. In the healthy female embryo, one of these is routinely and randomly inactivated so that only one is used in daughter cells. In RD approximately half of all the cells use the mutated protein and half use the healthy protein. It follows that females are usually less severely affected than XY males, in whom the single X with the mutation is active in each cell. In a severe dominant X-linked condition, such as RD, males are unlikely to survive early childhood.

Most people who have a mutation in the *MECP2* gene have severe learning disability and are unlikely to reproduce. For this reason, although the condition is dominant it is not usually seen in more than one generation in a family and most mutations that come to light are those that arise de novo (sporadic events).

Since sperm undergo more cell divisions than ova, the X chromosome of the male is more liable to develop mutations than in the female ova. These factors help to explain the female preponderance of RD. It is also possible that the cells in the testis that form sperm may have a survival advantage if they have a *MECP2* mutation.

A mutation may also occur in one cell of the newly formed zygote, destined to become the embryo, thus affecting only a proportion of cells in the developing child. Such a 'mosaic' case may be male or female and so few cells may be affected that there is little or no sign of the disease although the individual may have an affected child. A male with Klinefelter syndrome, having more than one X chromosome in each cell, may show RD in the same way as a female (Schwartzman et al., 1999).

In the laboratory of Adrian Bird it was discovered that the protein *mecp2* produced by the *MECP2* gene binds to methylated CpG islands on the promoters of other genes, thus regulating their activity (Nan et al., 1996). After the importance of the mutations was recognized in RD (Amir et al., 1999), mouse models were developed in the laboratories of Bird and Jaenisch, with different mutations in *Mecp2* (Chen et al., 2001, Guy et al., 2001). The mice have proved useful animal models for the disease, making it possible to investigate the normal activities of the MeCp2 protein and the deficits resulting from a mutation. This has greatly extended the possibilities for future therapeutic intervention.

Understanding of the key functions of the MeCP2 protein has grown rapidly in recent years. It regulates the relative expression of different forms of many proteins during critical phases of development (Armstrong, 2005). In the mature brain it functions to 'switch off' and 'switch on' the expression of a large number of other genes, many of which have a key role in normal brain development (Chahrour et al., 2008). It also fine tunes the production of different forms of proteins which have an important role in normal neuronal and neurochemical function: for example, the NMDA receptor (Young et al., 2005). MeCP2 is also bound to imprinted regions, such as the critical locus on chromosome 15 for Prader–Willi and Angelman syndromes (Samaco et al., 2005).

In the mouse hypothalamus, an *Mecp2* mutation has been shown to affect the levels of expression of thousands of genes, including CREB1 and many others with roles in brain development and function (Chahrour et al., 2008). Thus, gradually, the extensive influence of *MECP2* in the brain is beginning to explain why other genetic conditions lead to some features that overlap with those in RD.

Mutations can arise throughout the *MECP2* gene but eight common mutations account for 70% of recognizable RD (Kerr & Prescott, 2005). The exact position and type of mutation carries some significance for the severity of the resulting disease. For example, those with mutations at pR133C and pR306C generally have a milder disease course, whereas those at pR255X and pT158M tend to run a more severe course (Kerr & Prescott, 2005). However, these general observations cannot be assumed to apply automatically to individual cases because other factors, some of which are barely understood, also influence severity. One factor is the variable proportion of normal and mutated MeCP2 protein used in the brain. Alterations in other genes, such as *BDNF*, also may affect clinical severity (Nextoux et al., 2008). The clinical signs still undoubtedly constitute the most reliable means of diagnosis and provide the best indication of severity and prognosis (Kerr & Prescott, 2005).

Pathophysiological defects

Stature and the size of all the organs is reduced in RD (Armstrong, 2005), reflecting the widespread effects of the *MECP2* mutation. The chief pathological impact appears to be on the neurons, initially in the brainstem during embryonic development and later in the maturing cortical neurons (Armstrong, 2005). No degeneration has been demonstrated in the brain (Armstrong, 2005). It does not grow to the expected size, although in most cases it does continue to grow, remaining near the 5th centile (2nd standard deviation (SD)) (Hagberg et al., 2000; Kerr, 2002). The cortical neurons are smaller and closer together than normal (Armstrong, 2005, Baumann et al., 1995) and the minicolumns of the Cortex also lie more closely together than in the normal brain, indicating reduction in the space normally occupied by the interneuronal connections, upon which much complex neural activity depends (Casanova et al., 2003). There is particular involvement of the inferior temporal and parietal regions, with relative sparing of the visual cortex (Armstrong, 2005). From study of the affected mice with *Mecp2* mutations it

has been found that during development of the embryo, the brainstem nuclei responsible for regulation of cardiorespiratory rhythm are among the first to be affected (Armstrong, 2001). This early defect presumably underlies the impaired control of heart rate, blood pressure and breathing found in affected people (Julu et al., 2001) and contributes to the early neonatal deaths that occur in the most severe cases (Kerr et al., 1997).

There is severe disturbance of the normal complex balance of neurotransmitters in the cortex. Blue and colleagues demonstrated greatly increased density of glutamate receptors, the main excitatory neurotransmitter, in the 2-year-old Rett brain, as compared with the normal brain and greatly diminished levels by 10 years (Blue and Johnston, 2001). Serotonin receptors appear to be particularly affected in the brainstem (Armstrong, 2001).

EPIDEMIOLOGY

The prevalence of 1 in 10,000 females has been generally agreed (Hagberg, 1993; Kerr, 1991). Males have been so seldom detected that a reliable male incidence cannot yet be given (Schüle et al., 2008). Among severely mentally and physically disabled women, RD probably accounts for at least 1 in 10 (Kerr et al., 1995). Although the disorder does not appear to progress, clinically or pathologically, the problems do change, new difficulties emerging with growth and ageing and survival is markedly reduced in the most severely affected people (Kerr et al., 1997). The severely affected boys may not survive beyond infancy and the few cases that have been documented seem to indicate that this early death is due to failure of cardiorespiratory control by the affected neurons of the brainstem (Julu et al., 2001). Cardiorespiratory failure is probably also a factor in those who die during adolescence or early adult life (Kerr et al., 1997). Approximately one-fifth of deaths at those ages are sudden and essentially unexplained, sometimes following minor respiratory infections (Kerr et al., 1997). Epilepsy has also been implicated in some deaths (Kerr et al., 1997). A small proportion die from causes unrelated to their RD (Kerr et al., 1997). Poor nutrition, due to the difficulties in feeding, is probably a factor in premature death (Kerr et al., 1997). Recurring aspiration pneumonia contributes to some deaths (Kerr et al., 1997). However, if nutritional state and posture are well managed, even severely affected people may survive into adult life and mildly affected people who can walk, may live into old age in good health (Kerr & Burford, 2001, Kerr et al., 1997). A simple severity estimate, based on clinical and parental reports, was developed in the UK for retrospective and prospective use and this does provide useful prognostic indications (Table 8.2) (Kerr et al., 2001).

CLINICAL FEATURES

The clinical signs of the disease are the key to diagnosis and since the disorder usually occurs sporadically, clinical suspicion must precede genetic diagnosis. It is essential to appreciate that while the clinical signs of the condition are readily recognized in most cases, due to the nature of the genetic abnormality the clinical severity of RD varies greatly from very severe (causing neonatal death) to very mild (compatible with a normal lifespan) (Kerr & Witt Engerström, 2001). It is also important for the clinician to appreciate that although the disorder is present from birth the early signs are subtle and the full constellation of signs appears only gradually with growth (Table 8.3).

Table 8.2   Severity Score in Rett Disorder Developed for the British Survey

Item	Score 0	Score 1	Score 2
Muscle tone	Near normal	Dystonic	Hypo- or hypertonic
Locomotor skill	Walks solo	Has walked solo	Never walked solo
Scoliosis	None	Slight scoliosis	Marked scoliosis
Epilepsy	None (to date)	Epilepsy (past)	Epilepsy (currently)
Feeding difficulty	None/slight (1–2)	Moderate (3–8)	Severe (9+)

Feeding difficulty score. This provides a score out of 20 that is included in the Severity score.

Shape or posture	No problem	Some problem	Severe problem
Mouth closure	No problem	Some problem	Severe problem
Chews	No problem	Poor chewing	Not chewing
Swallows	No problem	Some problem	Severe problem
Obstructing movement	No problem	Some problem	Severe problem
Vomits/regurgitates	No problem	Some problem	Severe problem
Secretions	No problem	Some problem	Severe problem
Appetite	No problem	Some problem	Severe problem
Drinking	No problem	Some problem	Severe problem
Selffeeding	No problem	Constant supervision	Totally dependent

Modified from Kerr et al. (1996).

The simplicity of this system makes it possible to combine information from parents, clinical reports and direct examination from the period before regression and each 5-year period thereafter, in order to provide a useful prognostic indicator. Due to the evolving signs, the severity score rises in all cases until 15 years and then levels off (Kerr & Prescott, 2005).

Table 8.3   Expected Presentation at Different Ages and Levels of Severity in Rhett Disorder

	Infancy	Mid-childhood	Adolescence and adulthood
Severe	Severe hypotonia and cardiorespiratory dysregulation little or no progress may prove lethal	Regression is early severe hypotonia/hypertonia no walking, hand use or speech cardiorespiratory dysregulation early progressive scoliosis limb contractures common weak hand stereotypy epilepsy common feeding difficulties common	Few survive to adult life severe hypo- or hypertonia variable feeding difficulties prone to aspiration prone to hypoxia
Typical 'classical'	Normal appearance usually placid disturbed spontaneous movements development suboptimal fall-off in OFC	About 60% walk little or no speech little or no hand use marked cardiorespiratory dysregulation marked hand stereotypy mean OFC at 2SD below norm epilepsy in about 60% dystonic/hypertonic	About half survive to adulthood about 40% walk independently speech may diminish hand use may improve hand movements reduced amplitude 'Valsalva' breathing may develop feeding difficulties may increase epilepsy may remit
Mildest	Normal appearance signs present but more subtle progress to self-feeding walking and speech	Regression mild, late or none respiration irregular when agitated hand stereotypy when agitated scoliosis often milder and later slight dystonia and dyspraxia epilepsy uncommon	Over 70% survive feeding problems uncommon hand stereotypy when agitated scoliosis often mild if present slight dystonia and dyspraxia epilepsy uncommon

From the British Isles Rett Survey. OFC, occipitofrontal head circumference, SD, standard deviation.

Before regression

The gestation period and birth of the affected child are usually unexceptional and the newborn looks normal although in large Rett population studies the mean head circumference is suboptimal (Kerr, 2002; Leonard & Bower, 1998; Naidu, 1997). Studies employing early family videos of these babies have shown disorganization of the normal spontaneous limb and trunk movements that should be present before 3 months of age (Einspieler et al., 2005a) and reduction or absence of the small circular movements ('fidgety move-

Failure to recognize the disorder is very common during the first months of life because no problem is expected and the child looks attractive and makes some, albeit slow, developmental progress.

ments') of the hands and feet that are normally generated in the healthy brainstem and are prominent at 4–9 months. Even at this early stage, muscle tone is often altered, either abnormally increased or reduced (Kerr et al., 1987). Although some developmental progress is made, this is suboptimal. Standing and walking are generally delayed or absent and this is often the first concern leading to referral for paediatric advice. Hand use is often poor. Pointing and finger-thumb apposition may fail to develop. However, many children do begin to use the hands for self-feeding and some progress to using a spoon. Stereotyped patting or twisting finger movements become increasingly prominent. During this early period the child is characteristically placid and inexperienced parents may think that all is well until they begin to compare with other children. In the British survey an older relative or home visiting nurse has often been the first to suspect a problem in cognitive development (Burford, et al., 2003).

Regression

Typically, around 12–24 months, or sometimes earlier or later, the child's developmental progress arrests and skills are lost. This has come to be known as the 'regression period' and it commonly lasts for several months. Particularly noticeable is a reduction in speech and hand use, with increasingly stereotyped hand movements. Walking may become less steady and interpersonal contact is interrupted. Many children become agitated or distressed, with sudden attacks of crying, and sleep may be disturbed. This change from a placid to an agitated child is very distressing for parents and doubtless for the child also, disrupting the previous easy relationships among members of the family. Parents often feel that they have 'lost' their child, who has become a different person. This is the period during which the diagnosis of autism may be suggested because the child appears to have become absorbed in her stereotyped movement patterns (Kerr & Witt Engerström, 2001). Short episodes of interrupted awareness may occur. Initially, the electroencephalogram (EEG) may be reported as normal or immature (Cooper et al., 1998). In some cases centrotemporal spikes have been seen (Hagne et al., 1989). By the end of the regression period, bursts of slow waves may appear on all leads and epileptic seizures sometimes occur (Cooper et al., 1998). Towards the end of the regression, periods of breath-holding and rapid and/or deep breathing may be detected and, in those who can walk, the gait may become unsteady.

In the mildest cases this regression period may occur much later in childhood or may be absent. In such people, skills fail to develop normally. In the most severe cases, skills may not have developed sufficiently for a regression to be noticed. In that situation the deficient cardiorespiratory control may prove

lethal before the other features have fully emerged (Kerr et al., 1997).

Following regression

The end of the regression period is less abrupt than its onset and it is often marked by an improvement in mood and renewed readiness to learn and to relate to other people. Most children emerge into a more stable condition in which, however, their severe mental and physical problems are evident. The disorder primarily impacts on the developing central nervous system, affecting thinking, memory and mood, but also growth, posture and movement, cardiac and respiratory control, eating and digestion.

The same pattern of involvement and therefore of clinical signs, emerging in each case with growth, aids recognition and diagnosis. However, after regression, the cohort of cases can be broadly divided into groups according to severity (Kerr & Stephenson, 1986) (see Table 8.3). Muscle tone is a useful indicator of severity (Kerr & Stephenson, 1986; Kerr & Prescott, 2005). The persistently hypotonic frequently fail to achieve walking and may become overweight. In this group there is a tendency for respiratory movement to be poor, with reduced gas exchange, permitting severe drops in oxygen level. A second group whose early hypotonia gives way to increased, sometimes dystonic muscle tone, may achieve independent walking and become very active and agitated. These children are inclined to be thin. In this group, alternate hyperventilation and breath-holding are commonly striking. A third group, after severe early hypotonia, become severely hypertonic. Contractures of hips, knees, ankles and feet develop readily and may prevent walking. In general, the least-affected individuals have the least hypotonia in the first months and mildest increase in muscle tone later. The following description applies to the commonly encountered 'classic' cases but it must be kept in mind that while the same areas of difficulty occur in virtually every case, the level of severity varies very widely (Kerr & Witt Engerström 2001).

Movement and posture

Muscle tone, the precisely balanced tension in the skeletal muscles, allows posture to be maintained and movements to be controlled. In RD it is virtually always affected to a greater or lesser extent. In the infant it is often reduced (hypotonia), when the child appears floppy, slow to sit unsupported and to move about. In some, however, it is even then increased (hypertonia or dystonia) when the infant may appear rather stiff. By the end of the first year it is usual in RD for the muscle tone in the lower limbs to increase and the deep tendon reflexes to become abnormally brisk. With increasing age, muscle tone tends to increase in the back and limbs, and without regular physiotherapy this leads to limitation of movement with contractures at the ankles, knees, hips, shoulders, elbows, wrists and hands. With growth of the spine, scoliosis develops in all but a few and may become very severe, interfering with sitting, breathing and digestion, and necessitating surgical correction (Kerr et al., 2003). Dystonic muscle spasms may interrupt movement and may even be mistaken for epileptic seizures. It is characteristic of the most severely affected to fail to walk (Kerr & Witt Engerström, 2001) (see Table 8.3).

Hand use and stereotypies

The hands are specifically and severely disabled in RD. Even in early infancy postures and movements of affected individuals indicate disturbed control (Einspieler et al., 2005a, 2005b) and their use is often poor. With the onset of regression, even the simplest actions—such as grasping or self-feeding—become impossible for many. Typically, the hands are engaged in small patting, squeezing or twisting actions together or at the face. Each hand develops its own pattern of movement that is so invariable that injury may occur to the skin of the hands or the area where they are active, such as the skin of the face or the hair. When voluntary action is possible it may be seen after considerable delay while the child appears to be contemplating action. Finally, the act is then quick and well directed, as if snatched from the obligatory repetitive cycle. In the most severe cases of RD, weakness may prevent all but the feeblest twitching of the fingers (Kerr et al., 2001). In contrast, in the mildest cases for whom fine movements such as writing are possible, the characteristic repetitive movement may be seen only when the individual is agitated (Kerr et al., 2005).

Growth and nutrition

Growth is affected by RD and adult height is almost always reduced (Holm, 1986). Among 239 measured individuals over 18 years in the British Survey, mean height was 143.3 cm. The hands and feet are often narrow and relatively short 4th digits have been reported in a proportion of cases (Kerr et al., 1995; Leonard et al., 1999b). Head circumference commonly falls below the original centiles during infancy and comes to lie around the 5th centile (2nd SD below the mean), although there is a range in severity as with all other clinical signs (Kerr, 2002). Feeding difficulties are common and certainly affect growth. Many factors contribute to the difficulty in feeding, including the problems of finding a suitable posture when contractures have developed, poor retention of food in the mouth, reduced movement of food within the mouth, limited chewing, defective swallowing and probably also poor digestion. An assessment of feeding difficulty is a useful part of an overall assessment of severity of the condition and an indicator of prognosis (see Table 8.2) (Kerr et al., 1997). Gastro-oesophageal reflux and aerophagy are very common and a frequent cause of distress. In some less-affected people, and in some severe, hypotonic but placid people, feeding may be easy and obesity can readily develop. Periodic food refusal is a problem in a minority and we have encountered this in adults, raising the question of coexisting depression (Kerr, 2002). Constipation is very common and is compounded by physical inactivity, poor diet and difficulty in accepting fluids. Since the autonomic system is involved in the regulation of peristalsis in the gut, it seems likely that the known defects of parasympathetic function also affect the bowel. Osteoporosis has been reported even in those who remain mobile (Leonard et al., 1999a).

Central autonomic problems

The early involvement of the brainstem in RD has severe implications for the autonomic system, upon which the spontaneous activities of the healthy body—heart rate, blood pressure and breathing—depend. Non-invasive monitoring of these functions has shown that the sympathetic activity ('fight or flight' response) is relatively normal, whereas the parasympathetic activities, which should act reciprocally with the sympathetic system, fail to do so (Julu et al., 2001). The parasympathetic system appears to be immature (Julu, 2001; Julu et al., 1997, 2001). The appearance of the young child may indicate the unopposed sympathetic influence, with flushing of the face, dilatation of the pupils and agitation. Heart rate is normally monitored by the nucleus ambiguus (NA) in the brainstem, in order to keep the blood pressure steady and appropriate for the needs of the circulation. Sensors in the aorta transmit to the NA and axons carry the instruction to the sinoatrial node to adjust the heart rate and stabilize the blood pressure. In Rett disorder, this feedback mechanism is deficient, with the result that the blood pressure is not well controlled (Julu, 2001; Julu et al., 2001). This is apparent even at rest, but becomes very marked during the bizarre breathing rhythms of RD. The respiratory neurons in the brainstem similarly fail in their task of maintaining the respiratory rate, affecting the exchange of carbon dioxide for oxygen. Thus, oxygen levels may fall and carbon dioxide levels may fall or rise beyond healthy physiological limits (Julu, 2001; Julu et al., 2001).

In most cases, it is at the end of the regression period that breathing rhythm is noticed to be irregular with long breath-holds and periods of rapid or deep or very shallow breathing. The abnormality is particularly marked during waking periods and when the individual is alert. Attacks occur in which the individual seems to be interrupted in her activities or transiently loses consciousness (Southall et al., 1988). These very common events in RD have been named 'non-epileptic vacant spells' as they are not accompanied by epileptic discharges on the EEG (Kerr, 1995).

Several types of vacant spell have been described and researched (Julu et al., 2001). In the most severely and persistently hypotonic people, who may appear rather quiet and placid, ventilation is often inadequate and hypoxia may develop due to poor gas exchange (Julu & Witt Engerstrom, 2005). On the other hand, in the very agitated people, deep and rapid breathing amounting to hyperventilation leads to hypocarbia. In such cases hypocalcaemic tetany has been recorded (Julu et al., 2001; Southall et al., 1988). Either type of breathing may evolve into a style best described as 'Valsalva breathing' (Julu et al., 2001; Southall et al., 1988) in which normal expiration is replaced by forced expiration against a closed glottis. The build-up of air in the lungs leads to extreme fluctuations in blood pressure and brief episodes during which central autonomic regulation by the cardiorespiratory brainstem nuclei is suspended (Julu, 2001; Julu et al., 2001).

These autonomic abnormalities are often very striking, disturbing to the individual and alarming to carers. They probably contribute to some early deaths (Kerr et al., 1997; Schüle et al., 2008). In those people with poor nutrition who have died after recurrent aspiration and pneumonia, autonomic failure is suspected to play some part (Kerr et al., 1997).

However, many people live into adult life in spite of this bizarre cardiorespiratory dysfunction and enjoy good health in other respects.

The peripheral circulation is also affected in RD, presumably due to the same imbalance between low parasympathetic tone and normal but unopposed sympathetic tone. The skin of the lower legs is commonly blue and in a few cases cold injury develops in winter. It has been noticed that division of the sympathetic neural chain during scoliosis surgery leads to temporarily improved growth and warmth in the foot on the same side (Kerr, 2002).

Epilepsy

Generalized or focal cortical motor epilepsy occurs in around 75% but persists in fewer (Kerr, 2002) and is usually responsive to anticonvulsant therapy. If epilepsy occurs it usually begins after the regression period, often during an intercurrent febrile illness. Both generalized and focal epilepsies have been described but not '3-per-second' petit mal epilepsy. A major problem in management is distinction between attacks of epilepsy and brainstem attacks, the vacant spells described above. The same child is likely to have both types of attack, the non-epileptic attacks being much more frequent than the epileptic ones. The distinction is very important as the brainstem attacks do not respond to anticonvulsant medication and if a correct diagnosis is not made, overdosage of anticonvulsant medication is apt to occur (Julu et al., 2001).

Emotional disturbances

In the weeks after birth most infants with RD appear placid unless they are in pain. Typically, they are described as 'very good' babies: that is, quiet and uncomplaining. It is usual for parent–child bonding to be successful. With the onset of regression, mood may change dramatically, sometimes quite suddenly, with agitation and spells of intense unhappiness. Sleep is commonly disrupted, with failure in going to sleep or waking during the night in distress. Although there is improvement after regression, mood swings remain a problem for many. Sudden switches from laughing to apparent deep unhappiness are common and the absence of speech and apparent understanding in all but a few can makes this behaviour hard to interpret. In spite of mood swings, most people with Rett disorder are usually happy and enjoy quiet company. In contrast to autistic people, they appear to enjoy gazing at a human face. The few people with speech seem to enjoy using it and are sociable (Kerr et al., 2001, 2005). Families often assert that their affected daughter understands more speech than she can produce. Against the background of their very abnormal profile of neurotransmitter activity, it is difficult to judge if psychosis or depression have developed in people with RD (Sansom et al., 1993). Signs of unhappiness can often be traced by the family or regular carers of an individual to a cause of pain or distress, and removing that relieves the distress. Many parents become expert at reading the signs that indicate particular pains even though the person cannot speak or even point to the source (Lindberg, 2006). Common causes of discomfort include toothache, muscle cramps, urinary and skin infections, reflux oesophagitis, constipation and aerophagy with distension. Cholelithiasis has occurred in a number of people. Frustration, inactivity and boredom certainly contribute to unhappiness.

Sleep

Disturbance of sleep rhythm has been described in young children with RD (McArthur & Budden, 1998) and may indeed herald regression. Later in life it still affects a number of people who may refuse to go to sleep, awaken with distress or rise long before others wish to do so. McArthur and Budden found melanin levels to be low and the normal night-time peak reduced (McArthur & Budden, 1998). A detailed analysis of the sleep structure is provided by Nomura and Segawa (2001).

Understanding, communication and learning

Cerebral activity is greatly affected in RD. Even those who are mildly affected appear to encounter severe difficulties in understanding (Kerr et al., 2001). Acquisition of speech before regression is limited and in most cases it is lost at regression, although in less-severe cases words may be retained and new words learned after regression and in the least-affected people speech is well developed to the extent of engaging in conversation (Kerr et al., 2001, 2005). The lack of speech and hand use are great impediments to assessing the intelligence of people with RD and yet anyone working with these people finds that there is undoubted learning potential and that new skills can be acquired and retained at every age (Lindberg, 2006). There have been several studies demonstrating active choice and preferences regarding music, food, company and activities (Elefant, 2002). This sensitivity and involvement is a source of delight but also of frustration when desires are thwarted. Music plays an exceptionally important part in the life of most people with Rett disorder. It clearly provides pleasure and many people demonstrate quite individual taste that matures with age (Elefant, 2002). Through participation in music-making, people with RD can learn to express themselves and interact meaningfully with others (Elefant, 2002). Music has therefore come to occupy a highly valued role in Rett centres.

DIAGNOSIS AND DIFFERENTIAL DIAGNOSIS

Diagnosis

The clinical history and signs of RD are clearly paramount in its diagnosis. In early infancy it should be suspected that if a child who looks normal and seems healthy is failing to make satisfactory developmental progress or losing skills, especially if the head circumference is lagging behind other growth measures or abnormal movements are seen. In older children the characteristic history and the emergence of those age-related signs, described above, usually puts the diagnosis beyond doubt. However, in every case, genetic testing should be carried out, not only to confirm the diagnosis for that child but also so that screening can be made available to the family.

All patients with the suspected Rett diagnosis require both sequencing of the *MECP2* gene and screening for large deletions. However, in about 10% of cases with all the typical clinical signs of RD it has not been possible to demonstrate a mutation. This does not invalidate the diagnosis, since the current technologies do not detect all possible mutation types within the gene. Failure of expression of the gene may also be due to factors other than a mutation in the gene itself.

Of those individuals with signs less typical of RD, about half do have an identified change in the *MECP2* gene and it is to be expected that in some of the remaining cases without a *MECP2* mutation, a variety of underlying aetiologies will be found. There are also reports of a few cases with neurological or psychiatric problems quite different from those seen in RD and changes in *MECP2* that have not been associated with RD.

Differential diagnosis

As in the diagnosis of RD, so also in considering its differential diagnosis, the clinical history and signs are paramount and the age of the individual must be taken into account, There are several conditions with similarities to RD that lead to mistaken diagnosis.

Prader–Willi syndrome, Angelman syndrome and cerebral palsy due to prenatal or birth injury may be confused with RD in early infancy and childhood, when the child is placid, hypotonic and poorly mobile with generally delayed development but no evident illness. Serial head circumference measurements are helpful in RD, often demonstrating a fall-off after the first few weeks. To an experienced examiner the particular disturbed spontaneous general movements in RD may indicate the correct diagnosis (Einspieler et al., 2005a).

The infantile lysosomal storage diseases (especially Batten disease) may present with regression and hand clapping or flapping in the first or second year. The affected child may have previously achieved better skills and at the time of regression may appear more unwell than the child with RD. Later, retinal changes appear and the downward course of the disease and its pathology make the distinction clear (Hagberg & Witt Engerström, 1990). At this stage although the child with Rett is often distressed she does not appear to be ill but rather agitated and typical finger twisting, patting, rubbing or clasping stereotypies may be seen. In severe RD, respiratory rhythm may already be abnormal.

The diagnosis of autism is commonly considered when the regression period is clearly established in RD, because there is withdrawal from interpersonal contact and the repetitive hand movements become very marked. However, the abnormal breathing pattern in Rett disorder is not seen in autism and, as the regression period passes, the Rett child usually regains social awareness and clearly enjoys face-to-face contact.

In Pitt–Hopkins syndrome, children may show some signs suggestive of RD, including hyperventilation. However, that usually appears later than in RD. There is severe epilepsy in some and the appearance coarsens with increasing age. There are long slender hands and feet and clubbing may be present. Abnormalities of the corpus callosum and/or thalamus may be seen on scanning (Peippo et al., 2006).

The onset of a number of severe infantile epilepsies may also lead to confusion with Rett disorder if these produce regression in infancy. One such is the CDKL5 disorder, which is characterized by the onset of epilepsy by 3–8 months, with infantile spasms in half (Bahi-Buisson et al., 2008).

Although some of these individuals have a seizure-free period, and in some the seizures can be controlled or remit (Bahi-Buisson et al., 2008), many of the individuals develop an intractable seizure disorder that evolves into a myoclonic encephalopathy (Archer et al., 2006). The electroencephalographic changes are usually generalized and may include focal discharges, especially frontal and hypsarrhythmia.

By contrast, epilepsy in RD rarely begins before 6 months of age and usually after regression. Repeated bursts of slow waves commonly appear towards the end of the regression period and regular theta waves often predominate in later childhood. The abnormal brainstem control of breathing and cardiac rhythm also helps to distinguish RD.

Mutations in the *FOXG1* autosomal gene are described with abnormal development from birth, post natal microcephaly, hypotonia, hand stereotypy, full lips, depressed nasal bridge and simplified frontal cortex and corpus callosum hypoplasia on MRI (Mencarelli et al., 2009).

ASSESSMENT AND INTERVENTION

Assessment and monitoring of care

The complexity of the Rett disorder necessitates a team approach involving specialists in several disciplines for diagnosis, assessment and the provision of care at every age (Kerr, 2003). Although a general (family) practitioner will be able to meet many of the day-to-day medical needs, we strongly recommend the provision of a regional specialist paediatric and adult clinic to meet the more complex needs requiring specialist supervision including the difficult distinction between epilepsy and brainstem attacks, the development of scoliosis and contractures, intractable nutritional problems, severe sleeping difficulties and the need for genetic guidance. For example, such a specialist Rett clinic will have direct access to neurology, genetics, orthopaedics, physiotherapy, dietetic, occupational, communication and music therapy. Such an arrangement allows a family to meet each of the relevant specialists and the specialists to discuss joint management during a single clinic appointment. For the medical team involved, such a clinic also provides a wealth of experience and therefore develops expertise. The report from such a clinic session provides a valuable summary for carers and colleagues.

The areas of function to be assessed and monitored include all those known to be compromised by the disorder, in addition to the normal screening procedures required for any healthy individual. In RD, that invariable requires assessment of posture, mobility and range of movement at all the joints including the spine, nutritional state and the ability to eat and drink in comfort without aspiration, actual and potential abilities to understand and communicate and to use the hands. Routine dental care may require hospital admission in some cases. Regular tests of vision and hearing are very important, as these senses are relatively unaffected by the disorder and they provide interest and allow engagement in activities with others.

A routine is outlined in Table 8.4 (Kerr, 2003). The assessment of central autonomic control of cardiorespiratory function is described in the section on intervention below.

Intervention

With discovery of the causative mutations and development of mouse models for the disorder, the prospect of effective treatment has greatly improved; however, for the affected individual the physical therapies remain the mainstay of good management. Any intervention must be directed by thorough and regular assessment of the needs of the person as described above. This regular reassessment and supervision must be continued lifelong.

Nutrition

Good nutrition is fundamental to satisfactory care and healthy survival. A dietician should be involved in the care of every case and the aim should be to maintain the weight within the normal centiles for height (Oddy et al., 2007). We have used the simple set of questions in Table 8.2, the answers to which indicate the level of feeding difficulty experienced by the chief carer assisting the person with RD. If there are difficulties, it is advisable to carry out a full clinical and radiological feeding assessment (Morton et al., 1997; Oddy et al., 2007). Adjustment of the seating position, food textures and implements should be considered. When aspiration is taking place or the intake of food is insufficient to maintain the appropriate weight for height, transcutaneous insertion of a feeding tube into the stomach may be the best solution. About 6% of people in the UK survey have benefited from this (Kerr, 2002). In such cases it is essential for the gastroenterological unit responsible for the operation to continue to monitor care of the stoma and provide ready advice to the carer. Very active and agitated young people require more calories than expected for their height in order to maintain a satisfactory weight (Motil et al., 1994). The least-affected people with RD may have no difficulties. In the least-active people, who are often in the persistently hypotonic group with severe disability, obesity may become a major problem. Constipation is common, due not only to parasympathetic deficiency but also to poor diet and inactivity. It is often possible to avoid medication by increasing physical activities—supported swimming and horse riding and improving the intake of high-residue foods and fluids. Gentle abdominal massage under the guidance of a physiotherapist may be helpful.

Mobility

Physical activity is an essential part of satisfactory care, without which wasting and

Table 8.4   Routine Clinic Assessment in Individuals with Rett Disorder

Make the diagnosis, primarily from the developmental history and clinical examination, confirming if possible by genetic analysis and arrange for genetic advice to be offered

Explain the nature of the condition and invite questions—offering an early appointment for further questions to be aired

Ensure that parents, educators and therapists are invited to contribute to assessments

Consider the needs of the family or carer for physical support and advice, household aids, additional day and night assistance, day-centre availability for adults

The parent or carer should be provided with a home-held progress record with the results of all investigations and decisions, in terms that he/she can understand. This should be brought to the clinic and updated at each visit

Overmedication is common in RD. The requirement, dosage and compatibility of all medications, including herbal remedies, should be checked. Avoid sedatives as far as possible

Referral to a specialist centre will be appropriate for advice and treatment of complex problems. These may include epilepsy that fails to respond to a single medication and attacks of uncertain origin for neurological assessment with central autonomic monitoring, the development and progression of scoliosis or limb contractures for orthopaedic advice and intractable nutritional difficulties for gastro-enterological assessment. A thorough reassessment is advised at least every 3 years

At every clinic appearance the following areas should be checked

Posture and joint positions. Regular physiotherapy advice should be available to the carer. Check the suitability of chairs and wheelchairs and other transport

Scoliosis commonly develops with growth and may progress rapidly. Light bracing may be helpful but corrective surgery is usually indicated if the curve threatens to exceed 40%

Mobililty, locomotion and hand use, actual and potential. Are suitable opportunities being given to maintain the skills and to increase the range? Walking, swimming, riding and other protected movement activities are essential

Repetitive movements: Are these causing injury to the individual or to others? Are they being appropriately managed?

Epilepsy. A careful history and electroencephalography are required to distinguish epilepsy from non-epileptic autonomic attacks and dystonic spasms. In epilepsy the choice of medication should be determined by the type of seizure. Lamotrigine and carbamazepine have been most prescribed in the UK. If epilepsy is infrequent, the individual may be better off without medication

The central autonomic disturbance results in irregular breathing and fluctuating oxygen, carbon dioxide, blood pressure and heart rate. When severe, with vacant spells, central autonomic monitoring should be carried out. This non-invasive outpatient neurophysiological assessment indicates brainstem control of cardiorespiratory function. This helps to direct management, particularly when surgery is contemplated

Cold hands and feet are a consequence of the sympathetic/parasympathetic imbalance and may need extra protection in cold weather.

Feeding difficulty. Simple questions to the chief carer (see Table 8.2) indicate the level of difficulty. If this is severe, videofluoroscopic feeding assessment should be arranged. In the UK, this involves dietician, physiotherapist and speech therapist

Constipation, gastro-oesophageal reflux, aspiration and distension due to air forced into the stomach during Valsalva's manoeuvres common problems

Communication, actual and potential. Although speech is often absent, some people can speak, read and write. All can demonstrate choice and many show strong preferences. It is essential to ensure the provision of appropriate opportunities and encouragement to interact and be creative. Music therapy has been found to be particularly valuable

Vision and hearing should be reassessed by an optometrist or audiologist every 3–5 years. Sight and hearing are very important sources of pleasure when other means are denied

(continued)

Table 8.4 Routine Clinic Assessment in Individuals with Rett Disorder (Continued)

In some cases dental care requires hospital admission and general anaesthetic for some procedures. Advise careful regular use of an electric toothbrush from an early age

Of course people with RD are at risk from the same diseases as the healthy population. They also seem prone to urinary infections and gallstones. Well-woman checks for breast and cervical cancer should be offered, as in healthy women

Modified after Kerr (2003) 'Clinical Checklist for patients with Rett Disorder', *Primary Psychiatry*, 10(2): 32–33.

contractures readily develop, even in mildly affected people (Lotan & Hanks, 2006). When walking is possible, that should be encouraged and supported in adults, as in children, and regular activities in a warmed pool activities are most valuable. Active movement should also be encouraged on a soft surface. Pool and play activities are particularly essential to those who are unable to walk. Carers and teachers can learn the correct handling techniques from the physiotherapist to avoid injury and obtain most benefit. Gentle massage can encourage active movement and maintain skin health. Attention must be given to the position of the spine, shoulders and upper body joints as much as to the lower limbs. Long periods sitting with the feet down inevitably leads to contracture and dependent oedema, with the risks of venous thromboses and breakdown of the skin.

Scoliosis develops in all but a few people, the first signs often being rotation in the lower lumbar spine. The routine advice now is to consider surgery in any rapidly progressing curve at any age and to operate if the curve seems likely to exceed a Cobb angle of 40% (Kerr et al., 2003). With careful one-to-one physiotherapy supervision, swimming or exercise in a pool and riding can help to maintain freedom and flexibility of movement in the spine and limbs.

Epilepsy and autonomic disturbances

When true epilepsy occurs in RD it is usually responsive to the standard medication for the type of seizure. If it cannot be controlled with one anticonvulsant, then ambulatory EEG with video should establish the presence and type of event and monitor progress. If this demonstrates that the attacks are not epileptic, then full autonomic assessment should be carried out to characterize the non-epileptic vacant spells. These take different forms and the management of each is likely to be different. The procedure for brainstem monitoring involves a simple non-invasive outpatient procedure lasting 1 hour, using the computer-based equipment developed by Julu and co-workers (Julu, 2001; Julu et al., 2001). It does require neurophysiological expertise. In this method of autonomic monitoring, there is continuous video recording of the individual, who sits in a chair beside her parent or carer (Julu et al., 2001). The EEG trace, respiratory movement, transcutaneous oxygen and carbon dioxide, heart rate and blood pressure are all continuously monitored and the data are displayed on monitors and stored in the computer. The vagal tone and baroreflex sensitivity are calculated automatically and also displayed. Since all the recordings are seen simultaneously on monitors, the exact sequences of events can be seen and everyone learns from the event. Because of the frequency of the brainstem vacant spells, and continuous evidence of the cardiorespiratory irregularities, 1 hour is almost always sufficient to capture the evidence for the nature of the disturbance.

Several types of vacant spell have been successfully managed pharmacologically (Julu, 2001; Julu & Witt Engerström, 2005). Such treatment is symptomatic and not curative. In every case it is important to undertake full autonomic monitoring, before and after the start of therapy, and to be prepared to stop if the medication is not effective. The several different types of non-epileptic vacant spell are described above in the section on clinical features.

Intense hyperventilation has responded in some cases to administration of buspirone (Julu, 2001). Hypoventilation may respond to treatment with a respiratory stimulant such as theophylline (Julu & Witt Engerström, 2005). The Valsalva type of breathing has not been found to respond to any medication so far.

Hand use and stereotypies

It is important to appreciate that the hand activities in RD are largely involuntary, with rather stable tremor-like amplitudes, accelerations and frequencies (Wright et al., 2003), and efforts to induce the individual to stop them are generally futile. However, they may be interrupted when the attention is strongly focused. The aim in RD should be to ignore or accommodate these movements and to engage the individual directly and appropriately, capturing her interest and encouraging her to use the skills of which she is capable. This is helped by a quiet non-threatening environment, a close one-to-one relationship and exploration of the areas that seem to afford most interest to her. Holding one hand sometimes enables the other to be used more effectively. If injury is occurring to the hands or the areas where they are active, then some protection will be necessary in the form of a mitten or even a light elbow splint; however, this should be no more than enough to prevent the damaging contact. As with all the clinical features in RD, the hand use and stereotypies range in severity with the overall severity of the condition. In the most severe infants they are hardly seen because of extreme hypotonia, in classic cases they are vigorous and in the mildest cases they may appear only when the individual is agitated (Kerr et al., 2001).

Emotional health and communication

Speech is present in mildly affected people and develops further after regression in some (Kerr et al., 2001). Many parents report that their children understand speech even when they cannot use it. The speech we have witnessed appears to reflect a severely limited understanding but a real enjoyment of social contact (Kerr et al., 2001, 2005). In contrast to the major difficulties with speech, music appears to have an enormous appeal to

virtually all people with RD and should have a central place in provision for them. Medication has little place in the management of behaviour in people with RD. Selective serotonin reuptake inhibitors have been used with some reported temporary benefit in some older people who appear to be depressed, but a formal trial of medication has not been carried out.

Because of its appeal, capturing attention and encouraging active participation, individual music therapy has found a special place as the key communication therapy for people with RD. There are good reasons why this might be expected to be helpful. People with RD are socially aware, enjoy contact and exhibit individual preferences. Their hearing is generally good, yet speech and use of the hands, the major means of human contact and self-expression, are severely disabled and the cortical areas associated with their use are specifically affected by the disease. The reception and enjoyment of music, on the other hand, accesses and involves a very much wider area of the brain (Merker & Wallin, 2001). The recent literature on the neurophysiology of music and its value in disabling neurological disease strongly supports its use in this therapeutic role. Music as therapy has been shown similarly to facilitate, encourage and enable response, enjoyment and participation in a number of severely disabling neurological conditions, impressively illustrated by Oliver Sack's *Musicophilia* (2007). Parents often find that singing or playing music will still a fretting child. Given the opportunity, people with RD will demonstrate a decided taste, preferring the music that suits their mood at the time and developing favourites that change with age.

In order to develop the potential of this most powerful therapy the therapist must not only be skilled in her craft but also sensitive to the needs and limitations of her client. We would stress, that as in all therapy, a careful initial assessment and the establishment of a good relationship between the therapist and client are essential to a good outcome.

Educational and daytime activity

It has long been accepted in the UK that every child, however disabled, should be provided with a suitable school place and should be encouraged and supported so as to develop his or her full educational potential. When a child is mildly affected by RD it may be satisfactory for educational facilities to be shared within a normal play group and later a normal school. However, for most, the need to be active but protected and to receive specific one-to-one therapies makes provision of a special school with all these facilities at hand a more satisfactory alternative.

In adulthood, it is equally important to provide continuing day-time activity outside the home or residence, with provision for and in expectation of continued learning. This provides varied company, activities and environments for the affected individuals and allows respite for carers. A warm, protected and not too lengthy means of transport (preferably under half an hour) from home to day centre should be provided.

Support for the family

At diagnosis, expert genetic guidance should be offered to the family. The mother and sisters of the affected person are usually offered genetic testing and prenatal screening may be offered if the risk of recurrence is high. As siblings reach adulthood, further questions usually arise and access to genetic advice should be readily available.

When the affected person lives at home, support for the family is of great importance because the burden of care is huge. This provision should be planned in full consultation with the family, as needs will alter with time and changing conditions. Household adaptations are likely to be necessary, such as suitable seating and lifting devices, wheelchair access into and around the home and showering or bathing arrangements. In some families there will be a need for night-time relief, daytime shopping breaks and holiday breaks when the rest of the family can spend time together. Respite care must be at least equivalent in quality to home care, with one-to-one supervision or the trust of the family will be lost. Loving families provide a remarkable level of care and commitment to their affected members and save the country a huge expenditure. To fail to meet their needs would be an economic folly as well as inhumane.

Many families prefer to care for their children at home but as the person with RD grows older and the natural family is less able to provide care, a move to a small supported home environment should be carefully planned. This should be near the family home so that frequent visiting is possible. It is important to ensure that the behaviour of any other residents is compatible with the comfort, safety and continued mobility of the person with RD. Provision for walking is essential for those who can walk and physical activities such as closely supervised swimming, exercise in water and riding should be part of every day. In our experience a small home environment with no more than 4–6 people of compatible temperaments and full-time staffing work best. Staff require specific training and ready access to advice for themselves and medical services for their clients. Such homes require frequent unannounced visits to monitor standards.

NEW RESEARCH AND FUTURE PROSPECTS

Developmental genetic disorders are not to be regarded as inevitably irreversible. Nor are genes mere recipes for the development of the brain and body. They are highly active agents that may respond, by the millisecond, in response to internal controls. A recent milestone in research has been the discovery that RD can be reversed in the affected mice, even after the clinical defects have appeared (Guy et al., 2007; Luikenhuis et al., 2004). This gives hope for families whose member has already been diagnosed with the condition; however, it must be kept in mind that this experiment was conducted in mice whose mutation was designed to be reversible.

A better understanding of the role of *MECP2* in the normal brain is also beginning to explain the symptomatology of RD (Fyffe et al., 2008; Nuber et al., 2005).

The existence of the mouse model has been an important step in developing potential therapeutic interventions. Future possibilities include that of switching the use in the female cell from the mutated *MECP2* gene to the normal gene that lies inactivated in each cell. At present it is not known whether this can be done and whether it can be done without adverse effects. Introduction of the healthy gene or its protein product also offers possibilities currently under investigation. However, an excess of *MECP2* can be as damaging as a deficit as has already been demonstrated in a case of natural duplication of the *MECP2* gene (Moretti & Zoghbi, 2006). Progress in this field will require immense care and expertise.

Trials of pharmacological interventions are currently undergoing trials in the affected mice, and human clinical trials may soon be justified (e.g. Jugloff et al., 2008; Nag et al., 2008). A practical difficulty in such trials will be to establish stable, objective and practicable measures of outcome. At present encephalographic recordings and wellstandardized measures of the central autonomic disturbance seem suitable candidates.

Further investigation is clearly required to reach an understanding of the several conditions, some only recently discovered, that have led to confusion with RD. The fact that *MECP2* influences the expression of many other genes has provided fresh impetus for this research and will doubtless lead to elucidation of other pervasive developmental disorders such as autism, Angelman syndrome, 'nonsyndromic learning disability' and CDKL5.

The contribution of Rett Associations

Families and their affected children and the Rett Associations worldwide have become central to the research effort, through inviting research scientists and clinicians to come together to share their knowledge and to collaborate.

CONCLUSION

The Rett investigation over the past 50 years highlights certain principles of effective clinical medical research. We suggest that these include:

- The fundamental place of accurate clinical observation in such research.
- The importance of the family's contribution to a detailed history and disease description.
- The particular importance of the very early signs of the disease, however subtle.
- The need to look beyond the clinical impression and nomenclature to the underlying cause at genetic, anatomical and physiological levels.
- The importance of cross-specialty sharing and collaboration.
- The need to understand the organic bases for the retained abilities as well as the deficits.
- Appreciation that a wide range in severities is compatible with consistent diagnostic signs.

Challenges

Challenges that remain for the future include:

- To prevent and cure this disease by genetic or pharmacological means
- To develop treatment for the specific problems associated with the disease
- To enrich the lives of those affected and their families
- To understand the several developmental disorders, currently unrecognized and confused with Rett disorder due to overlapping symptomatology
- To assess and support the mental and physical potential of people with RD
- To develop the use of music in assessment, treatment and research in RD
- To allow insight from the use of music in RD to illuminate understanding of what music does and may do in the healthy brain and in disease states.

We have attempted here briefly to describe what is currently known about the Rett disorder. This is work in progress. A developmental brain disorder that may be cured by genetic means, RD leads the way for others to follow.

ACKNOWLEDGEMENTS

We gratefully acknowledge the many colleagues and collaborators whose papers we have quoted, the institutions that have supported our work and the Rett Associations and families that have made it possible to study people with Rett disorder. Dr Ania Jaworska supplied the recent figures from the British Survey. Dr Archer is employed by Cardiff and Vale NHS Trust as a Consultant in Clinical Genetics.

Dr Kerr is retired and was previously employed by the University of Glasgow funded by a grant from the Scottish and the UK Rett Associations.

REFERENCES

Amir, R.E., Van Den Veyver, I.B., Wan, M., Tran, C.Q., Franke, U., & Zoghbi, H. (1999) 'Rett Syndrome is caused by mutations in X-linked MECP2, encoding methyl CpG binding protein 2'. *Nature Genetics*, 23: 185–188.

Archer, H.L., Evans, J., Edwards, S., Colley, J., Newabur-Ecob, R., O'Callaghan, F., Huyton, M., O'Regan, M., Tolmie, J., Sampson, J., Clarke, A., & Osborne, J. (2006) 'CDKL5 mutations cause infantile spasms, early onset seizures and severe mental retardation in female patients', *Journal of Medical Genetics,* 43(9): 729–734.

Ariani, F., Hayek, G., Rondinella, D., Artuso, R., Mencrelli, M.A., Spanho-Rosseto, A., et al. (2008) 'FOXG1 is responsible for the congenital variant of Rett syndrome'. *American Journal of Human Genetics* 83(1): 89–93.

Armstrong, D.D. (1995) 'The neuropathology of Rett Syndrome—overview 1994', *Neuropediatrics,* 26: 100–104.

Armstrong, D.D. (2001) 'The neuropathology of Rett syndrome', in A.M. Kerr and I. Witt Engerström (eds), *Rett Disorder and the Developing Brain.* Oxford: Oxford University Press, pp. 349–359.

Armstrong, D.D. (2005) 'Can we relate MeCP2 deficiency to the structural and chemical abnormalities in the Rett brain?', *Brain and Development,* 27: S72–76.

Bahi-Buisson, N., Nectoux, J., Rosas-Vargas, H., Milh, M., Boddaert, N., Girard, B., Cances, C., Ville, D., Afenjar, A., Rio, M., Heron, D., Nguiyen, M.M.A., Arximanoglou, A., Philippe, C., Jonveaux, P., Chelly, J., & Bienvenue, T. (2008) 'Key features to identify girls with CDKL5 mutations', *Brain,* 131(10): 2647–2661.

Bauman, M.L., Kemper, T.L., & Arin, D.M. (1995) 'Microscopic observations of the brain in Rett syndrome', *Neuropediatrics,* 26: 105–108.

Blue, M.E. & Johnston, M.V. (2001) 'Amino acid receptor studies in Rett syndrome', in A.M. Kerr and I. Witt Engerstrom (eds), *Rett Disorder and the Developing Brain.* Oxford: Oxford University Press, pp. 85–110.

Burford, B., Kerr, A.M., & Macleod, H.A. (2003) 'Nurse recognition of early deviation in development in home videos of infants with Rett disorder', *Journal of Intellectual Disability Research,* 47(8): 588–596.

Casanova, M.F., Buxhoeveden, D., Switala, A., & Roy, E. (2003) 'Rett syndrome as a mini-columnopathy', *Clinical Neuropathology,* 22(4): 163–168.

Chahrour, M. & Zoghbi, H.Y. (2007) 'The story of Rett syndrome from clinic to neurobiology', *Neuron,* 56(3): 422–437.

Chahrour, M., Jung, S.Y., Shaw, C., Zhou, X., Wong, S.T.C., Qin, J., & Zoghbi, H.Y. (2008) 'MeCP2, a key contributor to neurological disease, activates and represses transcription', *Science,* 320(5880): 1224–1229.

Chen, R.Z., Akbarian, S., Tudor, M. & Jaenisch, R. (2001) 'Deficiency of methyl-CpG binding protein-2 in CNS neurons results in a Rett-like phenotype in mice', *Nature Genetics,* 27:327–333.

Cooper, R.A., Kerr, A.M., & Amos, P.M. (1998) 'Rett syndrome: critical examination of clinical features, serial EEG and video-monitoring in understanding and management', *European Journal of Paediatric Neurology,* 2: 127–135.

Einspieler, C., Kerr, A.M., & Prechtl, H.F.R. (2005a) 'Abnormal general movements of girls with Rett disorder: the first 4 months of life', *Brain and Development,* 27: S8–13.

Einspieler, C., Kerr, A.M., & Prechtl, H.F.R. (2005b) 'Is the development of girls with Rett Disorder really normal?', *Pediatric Research,* 57: 1–5.

Elefant, C. (2002) 'Speechless yet communicative: revealing the person behind the disability of Rett syndrome through clinical research on songs in music therapy', in G. Aldridge, G. Di Franco, E. Ruud & T. Wigram (eds), *Music Therapy in Europe*. Rome: Ismez.

Fyffe, S.L., Jeff, L., Neul, R., Samaco, C., Chao, H-T., Ben-Shachar, S., Moretti, P., McGill, B.E., Goulding E.H., Sullivan, E., Tecott, L.H., et al. (2008) 'Deletion of Mecp2 in Sim1-expressing neurons reveals a critical role for MeCP2 in feeding behavior, aggression, and the response to stress', *Neuron*, 59: 947–958.

Guy, J., Hendrich, B., Holmes, M., Martin, J.E., & Bird, A. (2001) 'A mouse Mecp2-null mutation causes neurological symptoms that mimic Rett syndrome', *American Journal of Medical Genetics* 27: 322–326.

Guy, J., Gan, J., Selfridge, J. Cobb, S., Bird, & A. (2007) 'Reversal of neurological defects in a mouse model of Rett syndrome', *Science,* 315(5815): 1143–1147.

Hagberg, B. (1993) 'Clinical criteria, stages and natural history'. in B. Hagberg, M. Anvret, and J. Wahlstrom (eds), *Rett Syndrome—Clinical and Biological Aspects. Clinics in Developmental Medicine 127.* Cambridge: MacKeith Cambridge University Press, pp. 4–20.

Hagberg, B., & Hagberg, G. (1997), 'Rett syndrome: epidemiology and geographical variability', *European Child and Adolescent Psychiatry*, 6: 5–7.

Hagberg, B., & Rasmussen, P. (1986). "Forme fruste" of Rett syndrome—a case report,' *American Journal of Medical Genetics*, 24: 175–181.

Hagberg, B., & Skjeldal, O. (1994) 'Rett variants: a suggested model for inclusion criteria,' *Pediatric Neurology*, 11: 5–11.

Hagberg, B., & Witt Engerström, I. (1990) 'Early stages Rett syndrome and infantile neuronal ceroid lipfucsinosis—a difficult differential diagnosis', *Brain and Development*, 12: 20–22.

Hagberg, B., Aicardi, J., Dias, K., & Ramos, O. (1983). 'A progressive syndrome of autism, dementia, ataxia and loss of purposeful hand use in girls: Rett's syndrome—report of 35 cases', *Annals of Neurology*, 14: 471–479.

Hagberg, B., Goutieres, F., Hanefeld, F., Rett, A., & Wilson, J. (1985), 'Rett syndrome—criteria for inclusion and exclusion,' *Brain and Development*, 7: 372–373.

Hagberg, G., Stenbom, Y., & Witt Engerström. (2000) 'Head growth in Rett syndrome', *Acta Paediatrica,* 89: 198–202.

Hagne, I., Witt-Engerström, I., & Hagberg, B. (1989) 'EEG development in Rett syndrome. A study of 30 cases', *Electroencephalograpy and Neurophysiology,* 72: 1–6.

Holm, V.A. (1986) 'Physical growth and development in patients with Rett syndrome', *American Journal of Medical Genetics*, 24: 119–126.

Jugloff, D.G., Vandamme, K., Logan, R., Visanji, M.P., Brotchie, J.M., & Eubanks, J.H. (2008) 'Targeted delivery of an Mecp2 transgene to forebrain neurons improves the behavior of female Mecp2-deficient mice', *Human Molecular Genetics*, 17(10): 1386–1396.

Julu, P.O.O. (2001) 'The central autonomic disturbance in Rett syndrome', in A.M. Kerr, I. Witt Engerström (eds), *Rett Disorder and the Developing Brain.* Oxford: Oxford University Press, pp. 131–182.

Julu, P.O.O. & Witt Engerström, I. (2005) 'Assessment of the maturity related brainstem functions reveals the heterogeneous phenotypes and facilitates clinical management of Rett syndrome', *Brain and Development,* 27: S43–53.

Julu, P.O., Kerr, A.M., Hansen, S., Apartopoulos, F., & Jamal, G.A. (1997) 'Functional evidence of brain stem immaturity in Rett syndrome', *European Child and Adolescent Psychiatry*, 6(1): 47–54.

Julu, P.O.O., Kerr, A.M., Apartopoulos, F., Al-Rawas, S., Witt Engerström, I., Engerström, L., Jamal, G.A., & Hansen, S. (2001) 'Characterisation of breathing and associated autonomic dysfunction in the Rett disorder', *Archives of Disease in Childhood,* 85: 29–37.

Kerr, A.M. (1991) 'Rett syndrome British Longitudinal Study 1982–1990', in J.J. Roosendaal (ed.), *Mental Retardation and Medical Care.* Zeist: Uitgeverij Kerckbosch, pp. 143–145.

Kerr, A.M. (1995) 'Early clinical signs in the Rett disorder', *Neuropediatrics,* 26: 67–71.

Kerr, A.M. (2002) 'Rett syndrome', in I. Goodyer and P. Howlin (eds) *Outcomes in Neuro-Developmental and Genetic Disorders,* Cambridge: Cambridge University Press, pp. 241–271.

Kerr, A.M. (2003) 'Clinical checklist for patients with Rett disorder', *Primary Psychiatry*, 10(2): 32–33.

Kerr, A.M. & Burford, B. (2001) 'Towards a full life with Rett disorder', *Paediatric Rehabilitation*, 4(4): 157–168.

Kerr, A.M. & Prescott, R. (2005) 'Predictive value of the early clinical signs in Rett disorder', *Brain and Development*, 27: S20–24.

Kerr, A.M. & Stephenson, J. B. P. (1986) 'A study of the natural history of Rett syndrome in 23 girls', *American Journal of Medical Genetics*, 24: 77–83.

Kerr, A.M. & Witt Engerström, I. (2001) 'The clinical background' and 'The developmental perspective', in A.M. Kerr and I. Witt Engerström (eds), *Rett Disorder and the Developing Brain*. Oxford: Oxford University Press, pp. 1–26 and 349–359.

Kerr, A.M., Montague, J., & Stephenson, J.B.P. (1987) 'The hands, and the mind, pre- and post-regression, in Rett syndrome', *Brain and Development*, 9: 487–490.

Kerr, A.M., Mitchell, J.M, & Robertson, P. (1995) 'Short fourth toes in Rett syndrome: a biological indicator', *Neuropediatrics*, 26: 72–74.

Kerr, A.M., Armstrong, D.D., Prescott, R.J., Doyle, D., & Kearney, D.L. (1997) 'Analysis of deaths in the British Rett Survey', *European Child and Adolescent Psychiatry*, 6: 71–74.

Kerr, A.M., Belichenko, P., Woodcock, T., & Woodcock, M. (2001) 'Mind and brain in Rett disorder', *Brain and Development*, 23: S44–449.

Kerr, A.M., Webb, P., Prescott, R., & Milne, Y. (2003) 'Results of surgery for scoliosis in Rett syndrome', *Journal of Child Neurology*, 18(10): 703–708.

Kerr, A.M., Archer, H.L., Evans, J., & Gibbon, F. (2005) 'People with mutation positive Rett disorder who converse', *Journal of Intellectual Disability Research*, 50 (5): 386–394.

Leonard, H. & Bower, C. (1998) 'Is the girl with Rett syndrome normal at birth?' *Developmental Medicine and Child Neurology*, 40: 115–121.

Leonard, H., Thomson, M.R., Glasson, E., Fyfe, S., Leonard, S., Bower, C., & Ellaway, C. (1999a) 'A population based approach to the investigation of osteopenia in Rett syndrome', *Developmental Medicine and Child Neurology*, 41: 323–328.

Leonard, H., Thomson, M.M., Lasson, E., Fyfe, S., Leonard, S., Ellaway, C., Christodoulou, J., & Bower, C. (1999b) 'Metacarpophalangeal pattern profile and bone age in Rett syndrome: further radiological clues to the diagnosis', *American Journal of Medical Genetics*, 83: 88–95.

Lindberg, B. (2006) *Understanding Rett Syndrome* . Cambridge, MA: Hogrefe and Huber.

Lotan, M. & Hanks, S. (2006) 'Physical therapy intervention for individuals with Rett syndrome', *The Scientific World Journal*, 6: 1314–1338.

Luikenhuis, S., Giacometti, E., Beard, C.F., & Jaenisch, R. (2004) 'Expression of MeCP2 in postmitotic neurons rescues Rett syndrome in mice', *Proceedings of the National Academy of Sciences of the USA*, 101(16): 6033–6038.

McArthur, A. & Budden, S.S. (1998) 'Sleep dysfunction in Rett syndrome: a trial of exogenous melatonin treatment', *Developmental Medicine and Child Neurology*, 40: 186–192.

Mencarelli, M.A., Spanhol-Rosseto, A., Artuso, R., Rondinella, D., De Filippis, R., Bahi-Buisson, N., Nectoux, J., Rubinsztajn, R., Bienvenu, T., Moncla, A., Chabro, B., Villard, L., Krumina, Z., Armstrong, J.,

Roche, A., Pineda, M., Gak, E., Mari, F., Ariani, F., Renieri, A. (2010) 'Novel FOXG1 mutations associated with the congenital variant of Rett syndrome', *J Med Genet*, 47:49–53.

Merker, B. & Wallin, N.L. (2001) 'Musical responsiveness in the Rett disorder', in A.M. Kerr and I. Witt Engerström (eds), *Rett Disorder and the Developing Brain*. Oxford: Oxford University Press, pp. 327–338.

Moretti, P. & Zoghbi, H.Y. (2006) 'MeCP2 dysfunction in Rett syndrome and related disorders', *Current Opinion in Genetic Development*, 16(3): 276–281.

Morton, R.E., Bonas, R., Minford, J., Kerr, A., & Ellis, R.E. (1997) 'Feeding ability in Rett syndrome', *Developmental Medicine and Child Neurology*, 39: 331–335.

Motil, K.J., Schultz, R., Brown, B., Glaze, D.G., & Percy, A.K. (1994) 'Altered energy balance may account for growth failure in Rett syndrome', *Journal of Child Neurology*, 9: 315–319.

Nag, N., Mellott, T.J., & Berger-Sweeney, J.E. (2008) 'Effects of postnatal dietary choline supplementation on motor regional brain volume and growth factor expression in a mouse model of Rett syndrome', *Brain Research* 27(1237): 101–109.

Naidu, S. (1997) 'Rett syndrome: a disorder affecting early brain growth', *Annals of Neurology*, 42(1): 3–10.

Nan, X., Tate, P., Li, E., & Bird, A. (1996) 'DNA methylation specifies chromosomal localization of MeCP2', *Molecular Cell Biology*, 16(1): 414–421.

Nan, X., Campoy, F.J., & Bird, A. (1997) 'MeCP2 is a transcriptional repressor with abundant binding sites in genomic chromatin', *Cell*, 88(4):471–481.

Neul, J.L., Fang, P., Barrish, J., Lane, J., Caeg, E.B., Smith, E.O., Zoghbi, H., Percy, A., & Glaze, D.G. (2008) 'Specific mutations in methyl-CpG-binding protein 2 confer different severity in Rett syndrome', *Neurology*, 70(16): 1313–1321.

Nextoux, J., Bahi-Buisson, N., Gurellec, I., Coste, J., De Roux, N., Rosas, H., Tardieu, M., Chelly, J., & Bienvenue, T. (2008) 'The p.Val66Met polymorphism in the BDNF gene protects against early seizures in Rett syndrome', *Neurology*, 70(22. 2): 2145–2151.

Nomura, Y. & Segawa, M. (2001) 'The monoamine hypothesis in Rett syndrome', in A.M. Kerr and I. Witt Engerström (eds), *Rett Disorder and the Developing Brain*. Oxford: Oxford University Press, pp. 183–204.

Nuber, U.A., Kriaucionis, S., Roloff, T.C., Guy, J., Selfridge, J., Steinhoff, C., Schulz, R., Lipkowitz, B., Ropers, H.H., Holmes, M.C., & Bird, A. (2005) 'Up-regulation of glucocorticoid-regulated genes in a mouse model of Rett Syndrome', *Human Molecular Genetics*, 14(15): 2247–2256.

Oddy, W.H., Webb, K.G., Baikie, G., Thompson, S.M., Reilly, S., Fyfe, S.D., Young, D., Anderson, A.M., & Leonard, H. (2007) 'Feeding experiences and growth status in a Rett syndrome population', *Journal of Paediatric Gastroenterology and Nutrition,* 45(5): 582–590.

Peippo, M.M., Simola, K.O., Valaanne, L.K., Lasen, A.T., Kahkonen, M., Auranen, M.P., & Ignatius, J. (2006) 'Pitt–Hopkins syndrome in two patients and further definition of the phenotype', *Clinical Dysmorphology,* 15(2): 47–54.

Rett, A. (1966) 'Uber ein eigenartiges hirnatrophisches Syndrome bei hyperammonamie im Kindsalter', *Wiener Medizinische Wochenschrift,* 116: 723–726.

Sacks, O. (2007) *Musicophilia,* Kent: Pan Macmillan.

Samaco, R.C., Hogart, A., & Lasalle, J.M. (2005) 'Epigenetic overlap in autism-spectrum disorders: MECP2 deficiency causes reduced expression of UBE3A and GABRB3', *American Journal of Medical Genetics,* 132A(2): 117–120.

Sansom, D., Krishnan, V.H.R., Corbett, J., & Kerr, A.M. (1993) 'Emotional and behavioural aspects of Rett syndrome', *Developmental Medicine and Child Neurology,* 35: 340–345.

Schüle, B., Armstrong, D.D., Vogel, H., Oviedo, A., & Franke, U. (2008) 'Severe congenital encephalopathy caused by MECP2 null mutations in males: central hypoxia and reduced neuronal dendritic structure', *Clinical Genetics,* 74(2): 116–126.

Schwartzman, J.S., Zatz, M., Vasquez, L.D.R., Gomez, R.R., Koiffmann, C.P., Fridman, C.P., & Otto, P.G. (1999) 'Rett syndrome in a boy with 47 XXY karyotype', *American Journal of Medical Genetics,* 64: 1781–1785.

Southall, D., Kerr, A.M., Tirosh, E., Amos, P., Lang, M., & Stephenson, J.B.P. (1988) 'Hyperventilation in the awake state, potentially treatable component of Rett syndrome', *Archives of Disease in Childhood,* 63: 1039–1048.

Wright, M., Van der Linden, M.L., Kerr, A.M., Burford, B., Arrowsmith, G., & Middleton, R.L. (2003) 'Motion analysis of stereotyped hand movements in Rett syndrome', *Journal of Intellectual Disability Research,* 47(2): 85–89.

Young, J.I., Hong, E.P., Castle, J.C., Crespo-Barreto, J., Bowman, A.B., Rose, M.F., Kang, D., Richman, R., Johnson, J.M., Berget, S., & Zoghbi, H. Y. (2005) 'Regulation of RNA splicing by the methylation-dependent transcriptional repressor methyl-CpG binding protein 2', *Proceedings of the National Academy of Sciences of the USA.,* 102(49): 17551–17558.

Zappella, M. (1992) 'The Rett girls with preserved speech', *Brain and Development,* 14: 998–1001.

9

Smith–Magenis Syndrome

Jenny Sloneem & Orlee Udwin

INTRODUCTION

Smith–Magenis syndrome (SMS) is a rare, genetically determined disorder characterized by a constellation of specific physical features, together with intellectual disability and a range of distinctive behavioural and cognitive characteristics. Although rare, this syndrome is becoming better known amongst health professionals, and more and more affected individuals are being identified.

This chapter summarizes the information that is currently available about the syndrome. Epidemiology, aetiology and core characteristics of SMS are outlined and interventions that have been reported as helpful are described. We then address the long-term course of the syndrome and the adjustment of individuals into adulthood to help plan for later life.

HISTORICAL PERSPECTIVE

In 1982, Anne Smith and her colleagues (Smith et al., 1982) published a short abstract describing the unique finding of two unrelated males with the same chromosomal abnormality and similar physical anomalies. Soon after, two case reports were published describing three further individuals with the same physical and chromosomal features (Patil & Bartley, 1984; Stallard et al., 1984). Four years later the clinical features of the syndrome were delineated (Smith et al., 1986; Stratton et al., 1986), and since then the condition has taken the name of the main authors who described the disorder: 'Smith–Magenis syndrome'.

EPIDEMIOLOGY AND CAUSATION

Smith–Magenis syndrome affects both males and females equally and occurs in all ethnic groups. Prevalence estimates for the disorder range from 1 per 50,000 (Colley et al., 1990) to the more frequently cited figure of 1 per 25,000 (Greenberg et al., 1991; Smith et al., 1998a). Owing to a combination of lack of awareness of the syndrome and the subtle presentation of phenotypic features in early childhood, there are likely to be many people with the condition who remain undiagnosed. As awareness increases and diagnostic tools improve, reported prevalence is expected to increase (Gropman et al., 2007). Greenberg et al. (1991) claim that SMS may be as common as Prader–Willi syndrome (1 per 16,000; Burd et al., 1990).

The diagnosis of SMS is not usually immediately apparent in infants and is therefore more likely to occur in early to mid-childhood, when the clinical features of the syndrome are most striking (Gropman et al., 2006). It is not uncommon for a diagnosis of autism, Prader–Willi syndrome, DiGeorge syndrome, Down syndrome, velocardiofacial syndrome, fragile X syndrome or Angelman syndrome to be considered initially, before a diagnosis of SMS is investigated (Gropman et al., 2007; Santhosh et al., 2006).

It has long been known that SMS is associated with an interstitial deletion of the short arm of chromosome 17, specifically band 17(p11.2p11.2) (Smith et al., 1986). However, more recently, a single candidate gene has been identified for SMS: the retinoic acid induced 1(*RAI1*) gene. The syndrome is caused by either a deletion at 17p11.2 encompassing the *RAI1* gene, as seen in 90% of people with SMS, or it is caused by a heterozygous point mutation in the gene itself within the SMS critical region (Girirajan et al., 2005; Slager et al., 2003). Such mutations account for 10% of people with SMS (Elsea & Girirajan, 2008). Cytogenetics labs have historically diagnosed SMS by performing blood tests using the FISH technique (fluorescence in situ hybridization). FISH is a process that paints specific portions of chromosomes with fluorescent molecules and identifies deletions in the SMS critical region. Seventy per cent of the individuals with interstitial deletions of chromosome 17 have a common 3.5 Mb deletion, whereas 30% have smaller or larger deletions. Small deletions (<2 Mb) sometimes go undetected because of the limits of the resolution of the cytogenic analysis. Two newer, more cost-effective technologies than FISH may also be used (multiplex litigation-dependent prob amplification and real-time quantitive polymerase chain reaction (PCR) (Elsea & Girirajan, 2008). Whereas the single *RAI1* gene is thought to be responsible for the main features of the SMS phenotype, Girirajan et al. (2006) suggest that other systematic manifestations seen in people with the syndrome, as well as the severity and variability of features seen in individuals with SMS, are attributed to other genes in 17p11.2.

The cause of deletion and gene mutation remains unknown and there is no evidence to suggest a parental age contribution. With few exceptions, occurrences of SMS are de novo. Consequently, the recurrence risk for parents whose chromosomes are normal is reported as low (less than 1%) (Elsea & Girirajan, 2008; Gropman et al., 2006). However, it should be noted that parental mosaicism has been found (Elsea, unpublished data, in Gropman et al., 2007). Zori et al. (1993) reported a case of a vertical transmission of the deleted chromosome to a daughter from a mosaic mother who had only very mild phenotypic findings.

There have been two cases described of prenatally diagnosed Smith–Magenis syndrome. Thomas et al. (2000) described a fetus in which the diagnosis of Smith–Magenis syndrome was made at 16 weeks of gestation following amniocentesis for increased risk for Down syndrome. Ultrasound evaluation revealed multiple fetal anomalies. The authors describe how molecular genetic techniques in the diagnosis of the Smith–Magenis syndrome and other small deletions are becoming an important tool in the genetic evaluation of ultrasound abnormalities.

DIAGNOSTIC CRITERIA AND CORE CHARACTERISTICS

Clinical characteristics and comorbid conditions

Physical characteristics associated with SMS have been reported at length in the literature and are described briefly below.

Individuals affected by the syndrome have characteristic facial features that are subtle in infancy and that become more pronounced as the child grows (Allanson et al., 1999). Infants with SMS present with a mild facial dysmorphism and a 'cherubic' appearance. However, the faces of older children with SMS arc often clearly square in shape, with a flattened mid-face. They frequently have broad mouths, with full lips (the upper said to be shaped like a 'cupid's bow'). Additionally, individuals commonly have heavy brows with deep-set eyes and a short nose with a broad base and a full tip. Brachycephaly (a short broad head) is also frequently seen. Other physical characteristics associated with the syndrome include short, broad hands and feet, small toes and in-bent fingers.

Infants with SMS often have a weak, hoarse cry, decreased vocalization and babbling, infantile hypotonia, feeding difficulties and lethargy. Gross and fine motor skills are also delayed (Gropman et al., 2007). Older children, adolescents and adults usually have short stature, fair hair compared to the rest of the family, an unusual gait, are prone to obesity and have a hoarse deep voice (Colley et al., 1990; Greenberg et al., 1991; Lockwood et al., 1988). The latter may be related to features such as laryngeal anomalies, including polyps, nodules, oedema, paralysis of the vocal chords and structural vocal-fold abnormalities which have commonly been reported in individuals with Smith–Magenis syndrome (Greenberg et al., 1996).

Common medical difficulties include feeding difficulties and failure to thrive in infancy, hypercholesterolaemia, frequent ear infections, conductive and/or sensorineural hearing loss and eye abnormalities including iris anomalies, microcornea, strabismus, cataracts and myopia (Chen et al., 1996a; Finucane et al., 1993; Smith et al., 2002). A high prevalence of dental anomalies (> 90%) has also been reported (Tomona et al., 2006). Other difficulties include, scoliosis (in at least 24%), cardiac defects (in 37% of cases), renal abnormalities (in 35%) and thyroid abnormalities (29% of cases) (Barnicoat et al., 1996; Drouin-Garraud et al., 2002; Finucane et al., 1993; Goldman, 2006). Cleft palate in SMS is associated with larger chromosomal deletions (<4 Mb) at the 17p11.2 locus.

Evidence also exists that both the central and peripheral nervous systems are affected in SMS. Central nervous system difficulties include hypotonia, seizures (in 11–30%), and epileptiform abnormalities (abnormal EEGs) without a clinical history of overt seizures. Additionally, up to 75% of individuals with SMS have been reported to show signs of peripheral neuropathy, resulting in delayed nerve conduction velocities, decreased tendon reflexes, insensitivity to pain and temperature, reduced leg muscle mass, gait disturbances and muscle weakness (Greenberg et al., 1996; Webber, 1999). Indeed, the genetic locus of SMS, at 17p (near 17p12), is associated with peripheral neuropathies including Charcot–Marie–Tooth disease (type 1A) (the most common inherited peripheral neuropathy) characterized by a slowly progressive degeneration of the muscles in the foot, lower leg, hand and forearm, and a mild loss of sensation in the limbs, fingers and toes.

Reports to date indicate that people with both aetiologies of SMS (deletion versus mutation in *RAI1* gene) have most of the clinical phenotypic features of SMS and differ only with regard to minor features. As seen in Table 9.1, those people with deletions are more likely to have a more severe phenotype, with a higher prevalence of speech and motor

Table 9.1 Summary of the Difficulties Found with Increased Prevalence in the Different SMS Genotypes

RAI1 Gene Deletion	Point Mutation in the RAI1 Gene
A more severe phenotype	Less severe phenotype
Speech delay	Muscle cramping
Motor delay	Overeating
Cardiovascular anomalies	Dry skin and skin picking
Renal anomalies	
Short stature	
Smaller head circumference	
Ear infections and hearing loss	
Hypotonia	

delay, cardiovascular and renal anomalies, short stature, smaller head circumference, hearing loss, ear infections and hypotonia (Edelman et al., 2007; Santhosh et al., 2006). Those with the *RAI1* point mutation have also been found to have more muscle cramping and dry skin and greater levels of overeating (Edelman et al., 2007). Edelman et al. (2007) compared individuals with different types of deletions and found that patients with smaller deletions were less likely to have dental and iris anomalies compared to people with common deletions, and were less likely to be obese than those with a *RAI1* mutation.

Interventions for physical and medical characteristics

Given the multisystemic involvement and physical and medical problems associated with Smith–Magenis syndrome, newly diagnosed patients should be screened for heart and kidney anomalies with renal ultrasonography and an echocardiogram, together with assessment for velopharyngeal incompetence and quantitative immunoglobin and lipid quantification (Edelman et al., 2007; Shelley & Robertson, 2001). There is a need for regular medical checks, including eye examinations, ear, nose and throat examinations, as well as endocrine, scoliosis and thyroid evaluations. An increase in dental caries observed in older individuals with SMS (Tomona et al., 2006) suggests a need for more dental care in the adolescent years. In view of a recent case report of a young woman who underwent repeat cardiac surgery and suffered a postoperative stroke (Chaudhry et al., 2007), it has been recommended that all patients who require open heart surgery should be evaluated for premature cerebrovascular disease.

Feeding difficulties in children with the syndrome are common, in particular with chewing solid foods. In childhood, oral motor and feeding training are important. Speech and language therapists can assist with these difficulties.

Table 9.2   Prevalence of Behavioural difficulties and Characteristics Found in Individuals with Smith–Magenis Syndrome

Difficulty or Characteristic	Prevalence Reported in Individuals With SMS
Intellectual disability	Affects the majority of individuals (>75%)
Sleep disturbance	65–100%
Impulsivity	80% or higher
Autistic-type behaviour	70–93%
Self-hugging	'highly characteristic'
Hyperactivity and distractibility	Over 80%
Physical aggression	38–93% (mainly over 70%)
Destructive behaviour	81%
Self-injury	38–97% (mainly over 70%)

In addition to the clinical characteristics and comorbid medical conditions associated with Smith–Magenis syndrome, individuals with the condition are more likely to be affected by a range of other impairments and difficulties. These are summarized in Table 9.2 and are described in more detail below.

Cognitive and adaptive skills

Cognitive and adaptive deficits in people with SMS become apparent in late infancy and early childhood and last throughout the life span (Martin et al., 2006). The level of intellectual disability in SMS is extremely variable but mainly falls in the moderate to severe range of cognitive impairment (Greenberg et al., 1991; Madduri et al., 2006; Udwin et al., 2001). Indeed, only 3 of the 29 schoolchildren in Udwin et al.'s sample attended mainstream schools (one in a remedial class), while the rest attended special schools or units.

However, it is possible that the more able individuals with SMS have been underrepresented in research samples because of the lack of awareness of the syndrome amongst health professionals and a bias to diagnosing those with more severe disabilities. Indeed, whereas moderate to severe delays are common in people with SMS, several cases of individuals functioning in the low-average range have also been reported (Crumley, 1998; Martin et al., 2006). Additionally, two recent studies have described participants as falling mainly in the mild to moderate range of intellectual disability. Madduri et al. (2006) assessed 57 participants and found that the mean IQ or developmental quotient was 50 (range 19–78, SD 12.9). Martin et al. (2006) reported a mean IQ score of 62.5 in 18 children with SMS (± 14.4), with 67% in the mild to moderate range. Differences in cognitive abilities between those with point *RAI1* mutations and deletions have not yet been evaluated. However, it has been suggested that those with the point mutation may also have a lesser degree of cognitive impairment (Edelman et al., 2007).

In terms of neuropsychological profile, Madduri et al. (2006) found no difference between verbal and performance IQ in participants with SMS. Studies have also shown that long-term memory, perceptual closure skills, alertness to the environment, attention to meaningful visual detail, and computer skills are areas of strength in this group (Dykens et al., 1997; Udwin et al., 2001). Individuals with SMS tend to be visual learners and have an affinity for computers and electronics. Relative weaknesses have been reported in sequential processing and short-term memory (Dykens et al., 1997).

Deficits in adaptive behaviour are also evident in children with SMS and continue into adolescence and throughout adulthood, where occupational attainment is low. Several studies have measured adaptive behaviour in people with SMS using the Vineland Adaptive Behavior Scales (Dykens et al., 1997; Madduri et al., 2006; Martin et al., 2006; Taylor & Oliver, 2008). They all found significant delays in the three domains that are measured by the interview (daily living skills, socialization and communication skills) and suggest that, on average, individuals show moderate deficits in adaptive ability. Martin et al. (2006) found that proficiency with daily

living skills appeared to worsen in comparison to age-related peers as chronological age increased, and Udwin et al. (2001) found that adults with SMS were more dependent than might be expected given their level of intellectual functioning. They suggest that this is related to the behavioural disturbance seen in this group. In terms of strengths and weaknesses, using the Vineland Adaptive Behavior Scales, Dykens et al. (1997) found no differences in the three domains that comprise adaptive behaviour. However, Madduri et al. (2006) found daily living skills to be a relative weakness compared to communication and socialization skills, whereas both Taylor and Oliver (2008) and Martin et al. (2006) found that their participants scored lower in both communication and daily living skills than in socialization skills.

Studies are beginning to explore behaviours and skills in the context of deletion size. Madduri et al. (2006) found that cognition and adaptive function were related to the size of the chromosomal deletion in participants, with those who had larger deletions, more likely to have lower scores.

Interventions to improve cognitive and adaptive skills

Dykens et al. (1997) stressed the need for teaching strategies for people with SMS that take account of their weaknesses in sequential processing and take advantage of their strengths in visual reasoning and other nonverbal areas. Udwin (2003) reported that the use of visual cues in the form of pictures and symbols can aid recall of more complex sequential tasks and generally help with comprehension. She stated that the particular interest in computers shown by people with SMS can also be used in teaching pre-reading and reading skills and promoting visuospatial skills. Individuals with Smith–Magenis syndrome tend to be eager to please and very responsive to adult attention; hence, praise and attention from teachers and other adults, if used judiciously, can serve as useful reinforcers. Occupational therapy is also recommended to help in difficulties with visuospatial skills, sequencing and coordination.

Linguistic skills

Speech and language development is markedly delayed in individuals with Smith–Magenis syndrome. As noted above, scores derived from studies using the Vineland Adaptive Behavior Scales all show communication as significantly delayed (Dykens et al., 1997; Madduri et al., 2006; Martin et al, 2006; Taylor & Oliver, 2008). Martin et al. (2006) found that communication was significantly associated with cognitive level and expressive language abilities are generally more impaired than receptive language skills (Chen et al., 1996a; Greenberg et al., 1991; Moncla et al., 1991; Udwin et al., 2001).

Linguistic intervention

Udwin (2003) suggests that using speech and language therapy and a total communication approach (including the use of sign and symbol systems) is likely to be helpful in promoting speech development and comprehension, and in alleviating frustration associated with poor expressive language skills (Smith et al., 1998a).

Sleep disturbance

Severe sleep disturbance is believed to be a hallmark of SMS, beginning in infancy and continuing into adulthood. It is thought to be caused by a shift in the circadian rhythm of melatonin (De Leersnyder et al., 2001a; De Leersnyder et al., 2001b). Individuals have an inverted melatonin secretion pattern, in which melatonin levels are low at night and high during the day, which is opposite to the patterns seen in the general population. Use of polysomnography, wrist actigraphy and sleep diaries have confirmed that the problem is widespread (Greenberg et al., 1996; Smith et al., 1998b; Webber, 1999). Estimates vary,

but it is thought that between 65 and 100% of individuals with SMS have symptoms of a sleep disorder with a chronic sleep debt.

The sleep disturbance commonly takes the form of reduced sleep in infants, followed by difficulties falling asleep, reduced rapid eye movement (REM) sleep, shortened sleep cycles, frequent or prolonged night waking, early morning waking, excessive daytime sleepiness and daytime napping in older individuals (De Leersnyder et al., 2001a; Smith et al., 1998b). Reduced sleep time has been most commonly documented, with children generally sleeping 1–2 hours less per 24-hour period than healthy, age-matched controls. In Webber's sample of 29 children aged 6–16 years old, 25 (86%) exhibited early waking (5.00 a.m. or earlier); 59% did this on a daily basis and about half of the total sample regularly slept during the day. Specific sleep stage anomalies have also been identified. Abnormalities of REM sleep and slow-wave sleep have been reported in over half of those studied with polysomnography (De Leersnyder et al., 2001b; Greenberg et al., 1991; Potocki et al., 2000). Night-time sleep patterns change between childhood and adolescence. Night-time arousal is more elevated in the second half of the night in children under 10, whereas arousal is increased during the first half of the night in individuals over 10, affecting settling in the evening and initiation of sleep (Gropman et al., 2007).

Intervention for sleep disorders

To date, parents' interventions have focused on keeping their children safe at night and attempting to minimize the disruption caused by night waking (Udwin, 2003). Implementing a firm and consistent approach, removing all small objects and breakables from the bedroom, locking the bedroom door or other doors in the house, use of blackout curtains to minimize light, firm and consistent instructions to return to bed, and providing soft toys, magazines, a tape recorder or television (in the case of older individuals), have all been reported to be helpful in minimizing night-time disruption in at least some cases, although not necessarily in increasing the amount of sleep (Horn, 1999; Smith et al., 1998b; Webber, 1999). Reducing daytime sleep is also effective for some individuals, although it can result in a worsening in behaviour in other cases.

There are many anecdotal reports of improvements in sleep disturbance in SMS with the administration of melatonin. Others feel that melatonin administration is not warranted because it is the kinetics of the hormone that is erratic rather than the amount of hormone being abnormal (Shelley & Robertson, 2005). Formal attempts to correct night-time sleep problems with melatonin or beta blockers to prevent daytime elevation of melatonin have had variable success. Other medications for sleep have anecdotally shown mixed responses, with many individuals finding them ineffective (Horn, 1999; Webber, 1999). De Leersnyder et al. (2001b) examined the effects of the beta-1-adrenergic blocker acebutolol (10 mg/kg) as a single morning dose. They noticed that this led to the suppression of diurnal secretion of melatonin and a significant improvement was reported in terms of delayed sleep onset, increased hours of sleep and delayed waking. Controlled treatment trials are required before any recommendations can be made in this regard and trials using a combination of evening melatonin together with various beta-adrenergic antagonists are underway.

Impulsivity

Since the early reports describing SMS, a wealth of research has indicated that impulsivity is highly associated with the syndrome. Prevalence for impulsivity has generally been reported as 80% or higher (Dykens et al., 1997, 2000) and impulsivity is one of several characteristics that has successfully been used to distinguish a group of people with SMS from groups with other intellectual disabilities (Clarke & Boer, 1998; Dykens et al., 2000; Oliver, 2005a, 2005b). Studies also show that when it does manifest, impulsive

behaviour is particularly problematic (Clarke & Boer, 1998). Sloneem et al. (in review) found that individuals with Smith–Magenis syndrome scored significantly higher on a informant questionnaire measure of impulsivity (the DEX, Wilson et al., 1996) than the other groups using the same measure reported in the literature. Interestingly, Martin et al. (2006) reported a gender difference in impulsivity scores, with girls showing higher scores than boys.

Indeed, impulsivity is so striking in SMS that many reviews have indicated that this is a key feature of the syndrome (Allanson et al., 1999; Chen et al., 1996b; Dykens & Rosner, 1999, Dykens & Smith, 1998; Dykens et al., 2000; Haas-Givler & Finucane, 2000; Hagerman, 1999; Moldavsky et al., 2001; Smith & Gropman, 2001; Smith, et al. 1998a; Webber, 1999). Given that impulsivity is bound to interfere with learning and daily activities, Udwin et al. (2001) suggest that dependence in daily living skills may be related, amongst other things, to impulsivity.

Social skills and autistic-type behaviour

Several single case reports describing children with Smith–Magenis syndrome who fulfil the diagnostic criteria for autism have been published (Smith et al., 1986; Stratton et al., 1986; Vostanis et al., 1994). As described above, people with SMS typically have speech and language delay and non-verbal communication is also affected. Additionally, over half of adults with SMS show marked repetitive and stereotypic behaviours, including repetitive questioning, insistence on sameness, a limited pattern of self-chosen activities, a tendency to communicate around repetitive themes, and routine and stereotypical hand movements. Few show appropriate emotional responses, and social approaches are described as one-sided and on their own terms. Feinstein and Singh (2007) also refer to an 'intense egocentrism' (p. 638) and an 'inability to see the perspective or subjective needs of others' (p. 639). They hypothesize that individuals with SMS therefore have deficits in theory of mind.

Webber (1999) conducted the first systematic investigation of the association between autism and SMS. She found that 93% of a sample of 29 children qualified for a diagnosis of autism using Wing's (1980) Schedule of Handicaps, Behaviour and Skills. Although this instrument is sometimes considered to overdiagnose autism, Webber's findings highlight the association with autistic-type behaviours. Horn (1999) used the Diagnostic Interview for Social and Communication Disorders (Wing & Gould, 1994) to examine autistic features in adults with SMS. Seventy per cent of her sample fulfilled diagnostic criteria for autism according to ICD-10 and DSM-IV criteria. This rate is considerably higher than the rates reported in the general population (Fombonne, 1999), in populations of adults with moderate learning disabilities (Callacott et al., 1992) and in other genetic syndromes, including fragile X syndrome (Bailey et al., 1993). Martin et al. (2006), using the Childhood Autism Rating Scale, found that children with SMS fell at the low end of the mild classification of autism.

However, as Horn (1999) points out, while the behavioural characteristics associated with the syndrome might qualify for a diagnosis of autism on a standard diagnostic measure, they are quite distinct in a number of ways. Most affected individuals show some social awareness, are able to maintain eye contact, greet people appropriately and seek social and physical comfort from others. Indeed, Martin et al. (2006) describe children with SMS as friendly, affectionate and outgoing. They found that children's socialization scores were significantly higher than their IQ scores and reported that socialization was actually a relative strength in participants. Sarimski (2004) also found that children with SMS showed a strong desire to interact socially with people and to maintain conversations in spite of their limited cognitive processing. It has also been commonly reported that individuals with Smith–Magenis syndrome are very adult-oriented and particularly 'crave'

adult attention or have an 'insatiable' need for individualized attention (e.g., Feinstein & Singh, 2007; Smith et al., 1998a). Dykens and Smith (1998) found that individuals with SMS showed a stronger demand for adult attention than individuals with Prader–Willi syndrome or those with mixed aetiology intellectual disability.

Social skills intervention

In view of the prevalence of autistic-type behaviours in individuals with Smith–Magenis syndrome, Udwin (2003) recommends that multidisciplinary assessment for autistic spectrum disorder is undertaken. She argues that this would allow for a greater understanding of their communication difficulties and needs by parents and professionals, and could facilitate access to appropriate educational and mental health services. Strategies that are useful in working with individuals with autism may then be usefully implemented in this group.

Parents and teachers may need specifically to teach social skills, including turn-taking and sharing. Some parents recommend 'scripting', whereby the child is taught appropriate social phrases to use. Some children with SMS are able to integrate successfully into more organized and supervised activities such as Scouts or Guides and social and sports activities.

Additional behavioural and personality characteristics

Unusual behaviours

A benign, yet unusual behaviour that has been described in SMS is 'self-hugging'. Individuals have frequently been reported to engage in tic-like tensing of the upper body, for a few seconds at a time, with hand-squeezing or arm-hugging motions. They may also clasp the hands at chest level or under the chin with fingers interlocked, while squeezing their arms tightly against their sides. Sometimes referred to as the 'spasmodic upper-body squeeze', this behaviour is now thought to be highly characteristic of SMS and has been seen as a major clinical clue to diagnosis (Shelley & Robertson, 2005). This behaviour is reported to be commonly elicited by excitement, happiness or positive stimuli (Dykens & Smith, 1998; Finucane et al., 1994; Horne, 1999; Webber, 1999). In their meta-analysis of 105 cases, Edelman et al. (2007) found that people whose SMS was caused by a *RAI1* point mutation exhibited more self-hugging than those for whom the syndrome was caused by a deletion at 17p11.2. This may be partly explained by the decreased hypotonia in the latter group. Dykens and Smith (1998) reported that a repetitive 'lick and flip' behaviour was also frequently observed in people with SMS. However, there are no other reports of this behaviour in the literature.

Mood and personality

There are anecdotal descriptions of babies with SMS as placid (Colley et al., 1990) and complacent (Gropman et al., 2007). Children are also described as loving and caring, with a good sense of humour. Many are reported to love music, which can be used as a reinforcer, as well as helping to calm children down. Individuals with SMS are further described as reacting well to consistency, structure and routine (Udwin, 2003).

A recent paper has described a woman with SMS who, as a result of symptoms such as sudden dysphoric shifts in mood and lack of impulse control, has also been diagnosed with mood disorder not otherwise specified and intermittent explosive disorder (Bersani et al., 2007).

Hyperactivity and distractibility

In addition to impulsivity, a relatively large number of case studies and research papers have described children and adults with SMS as showing hyperactive behaviours and/or distractibility (Behjati et al., 1997; Clarke & Boer, 1998; Colley et al., 1990; De Rijk-van Ande et al., 1991; Drouin-Garraud et al., 2002; Dykens & Smith, 1998; Finucane et al., 1993, 1994; Greenberg et al., 1991; Kondo et al., 1991; Lockwood et al., 1988;

Martin et al., 2006; Popp, 1987; Potocki et al., 2000; Smith et al., 1986; Stratton, et al., 1986; Webber, 1999). Greenberg et al. (1991) and Chen et al., (1996b), reported prevalence figures for hyperactivity of 82% and 83% respectively. Dykens and Smith (1998) demonstrated that hyperactivity was 1 of 12 behaviours that distinguished individuals with SMS from two comparison groups (of people with Prader–Willi syndrome and heterogeneous intellectual disabilities) with 100% accuracy. Webber (1999) found that although no children in her study fulfilled the three main features for a diagnosis of hyperkinetic disorder, there was an association between SMS and difficulties with concentration and movement. Martin et al. (2006) used the Connor's Parent Rating Scale and showed that the mean hyperactivity score for their SMS sample was significantly elevated. De Leersnyder et al. *(*2001b) hypothesize that the hyperactivity may result, in part, from increases in daytime levels of melatonin, with individuals struggling against falling asleep. Edelman et al. (2007) found that individuals with smaller deletions were less likely to show hyperactive behaviours compared to those with common deletions and *RAI1* mutations.

Physical aggression

One of the most challenging behaviours reported in people with SMS is the aggression that they show towards others: figures vary between 38% (Madduri et al., 2002) and 93% (Webber, 1999), due at least in part to the varied parameters used to define the behaviour. If Webber (1999) had included tissue damage criterion, the prevalence in her sample would have fallen, but still remained relatively high at 59%. However, other studies suggest that the prevalence is likely to be over 70% (Dykens et al., 1993, 1997; Oliver 2005a, 2005b; Sloneem et al., in review). Sloneem et al.'s study compared the prevalence to the figures reported for individuals with mixed aetiological intellectual disability and found that aggressive behaviour was significantly more prevalent in SMS, and that it occurred on average on a daily basis in this group.

Reported topographies of physical aggression include behaviours commonly seen in other groups, such as hitting (Hagerman, 1999) and punching (Colley et al., 1990). However, people with SMS have also been noted to show less common behaviours, including pinching, biting, hitting, grabbing, kicking, head-butting, hair-pulling, choking, using objects as weapons (Sloneem et al., in review) and other behaviours such as poking at other people's eyes (Finucane et al., 1994) and 'strangling' family pets (Smith et al., 1998a).

Destructive behaviour

Destructive behaviour is also commonly reported in SMS and prevalence is estimated to be as high as 81% (Sloneem et al., in review). This is more frequent than in other conditions, such as Prader-Willi syndrome (Dykens & Smith, 1998) or non-specific intellectual disabilities (Dykens & Smith, 1998; Sloneem et al., in review). Amongst anecdotal descriptions, Colley et al. (1990) noted that one individual destroyed home furnishings, whereas Hagerman (1999) described how a child destroyed family property and cut his clothes. The American SMS support group PRISMS (Parents and Researchers Interested in Smith–Magenis Syndrome) (2004) noted that they received telephone calls from parents whose children have punched their fists through walls, doors or windows during rages. More systematic investigations into these behaviours are required.

Self-injury

The prevalence of self-injury is also believed to be extremely high in people with SMS, ranging from 38% (Madduri et al., 2002) to 97% (Finucane et al., 2001; Sloneem et al., in review). Most studies place the figure at above 70% (e.g. Dykens & Smith, 1998; Greenberg et al., 1993; Oliver, 2005a, 2005b). Martin et al. (2006) report that parents rated these behaviours as interfering 'mildly' in the child's life, whereas Shelley and Robertson (2005) describe the behaviours as posing severe management difficulties, inflicting a very stressful burden on parents. Sloneem et al. (in review) found that individuals showed self-injury, on average, on at least a daily basis.

Many of the self-injurious behaviours commonly seen in SMS are similar to those observed in people with intellectual disabilities of mixed aetiology (e.g. head-banging, self-biting, skin-picking and self-hitting) (Dykens & Smith, 1998; Finucane et al., 2001; Greenberg et al., 1991). Interestingly, there are differences in the phenomenology of self-injury both within the syndrome and between syndrome groups. Individuals with *RAI1* point mutation exhibit more skin-picking than those with SMS caused by a deletion (Edelman et al., 2007). However, what may distinguish people with Smith–Magenis syndrome from those without the syndrome is not the form of injury but the location. In SMS, a significant proportion of the self-injury appears to be directed to the hands and, in particular, the nails (Finucane et al., 2001; Greenberg et al., 1991).

Many individuals with SMS have also been reported to display a form of self-injury rarely seen in onychotillomania (pulling finger and toe nails out). Onychotillomania has been noted in several case reports of individuals with SMS and has also been described by authors of larger-scale studies (Dykens & Smith, 1998; Finucane et al., 2001; Greenberg et al., 1991). Because of its unusual nature, much interest has arisen around this topography of self-injury, and it has been suggested that it forms part of the behavioural phenotype of the syndrome. Finucane et al. (2001) suggested that approximately half of people with SMS display onychotillomania. Similarly, Horn (1999) found that 62% of her sample of adults with SMS removed their nails. Webber (1999) considered a number of self-injurious behaviours related to hands and toes (nail removal, picking at the dry/loose skin on hands and feet, biting nails and tearing nails off), and found that 69% of the children in her sample engaged in these behaviours. Greenberg et al. (1991) stated that onychotillomania is present in older children, but rare in children aged below 5 years. The removal of the nails may be an extension of the hand-directed picking and biting described above.

Another form of self-injurious behaviour rarely seen elsewhere but that has been reported as relatively frequent in SMS is polyembolokoilamania (insertion of foreign bodies into bodily orifices). Dykens et al. (2000) noted that 25% of people with SMS displayed this behaviour (Dykens & Smith, 1998). Horn (1999) found that 19% of an adult sample inserted objects into bodily orifices, but Webber (1999) reported that only two participants (7%) in her sample of children with SMS displayed this behaviour. According to Edelman et al. (2007), this behaviour is seen more frequently in people with an *RAI1* point mutation compared to those with deletions. It is possible that the unusual nature of the behaviours has caused the reviews of SMS to overestimate the association between SMS and unusual forms of self-injury. However, because these behaviours are so rarely seen elsewhere, they still may be closely associated with the syndrome. Unfortunately, it is not possible to confirm this claim. Given that most standardized measures and checklists of topographies of self-injury do not include such rare forms of the behaviour, it is not possible to determine whether these behaviours occur in other individuals and are simply not reported, or whether they do not occur at all.

Causes of challenging behaviour and interventions

Controlled treatment trials using either medication or behavioural interventions are sparse and urgently needed. However, anecdotal and descriptive information gathered through observation and from parents, teachers and other carers have been useful in indicating that many of the behavioural difficulties described above may be modifiable. They have also helped to identify helpful interventions and educational strategies for this population (Haas-Givler & Finucane, 1996; Horn, 1999; Smith et al., 1998a, 1998b; Taylor & Oliver, 2008; Webber, 1999).

In order to intervene with the behaviours, we need to understand why they occur. A number of explanations exists to account for the high prevalence of aggressive behaviours in SMS. Biological theories suggest that aggressive behaviours are a product of aberrant internal processes that are dictated by specific genes, physiological drives or are caused by disturbances in the production of organic agents (King, 1993). There is often an implicit assumption when people with genetic syndromes display unusual behaviours, that their genotype is directly responsible. Slager et al. (2003) exemplify this by claiming that in SMS: 'Haploinsufficiency of *RAI1* is probably responsible for the behavioural, neurological, otolaryngological and craniofacial aspects of the syndrome' (p. 467). Additionally, Shelley and Robertson (2005) claim that people with SMS have 'genetically driven behaviours' (p. 92) and state that people add to their repertoire of self-injurious behaviour as they grow older due to age-dependent gene expression. However, direct gene to behaviour relationships and relationships between gene, biochemical abnormality and behaviour have not yet been confirmed. Hicks et al. (2008) describe 3½-year-old monozygotic twins with SMS who displayed clear behavioural differences. One twin showed very significant head-banging, self-biting, outbursts and property destruction, whereas the other showed only minor disturbances in terms of these behaviours. This suggests that such behaviours are affected by more than genes alone.

A range of medications have been tried in an attempt to reduce the characteristic aggressive outbursts of people with SMS, with varying results (Gropman et al., 2006; Horn, 1999; Webber, 1999). Unfortunately, medication has only successfully reduced aggressive behaviours in a minority of people with the syndrome and there have been no controlled trials of effectiveness. Anecdotally, some medications have proven ineffective; others have been beneficial in some cases, but resulted in a worsening of behaviour for other individuals. Several reports have suggested that selective serotonin reuptake inhibitors (SSRIs) may be helpful in managing aggression in SMS (Hagerman, 1999; Smith et al., 1998a), and antipsychotics such as risperidone have also been reported as being helpful in treating aggression (Hagerman, 1999; Niederhofer, 2007). Crumley (1998) reported that a girl with SMS responded to lithium when prescribed the drug for mood lability, aggression and anger. However, the mechanisms that underlie the efficacy have not been reported. Clearly, if medication is going to be introduced, side effects and efficacy will need to be carefully monitored.

It is possible that, rather than a direct gene–behaviour link, the biological factors interact with a constellation of clinical characteristics commonly seen in people with SMS and give rise to an increased risk of exhibiting the behavioural difficulties. Although challenging behaviour has not been found to be associated with either adaptive behaviour or cognitive functioning, the phenotype of SMS is related to a number of other high-risk characteristics associated with challenging behaviour in people without the syndrome. These include communication impairment (including a receptive-expressive language discrepancy), health difficulties, sensory problems (hearing and visual impairment), sleep problems, hyperactivity and impulsivity. The cumulative effect of all of these risk markers together may increase the probability of individuals with the syndrome engaging in problem behaviour. There is evidence that some of the risk markers associated with challenging behaviour in people with mixed aetiological learning disabilities are also associated with challenging behaviour in SMS, including sleep disturbance, health problems, communication disturbance, impulsivity, hyperactivity and peripheral sensory neuropathy.

Sleep disturbances (factors such as melatonin rise, nap length and snoring) have been found to be associated with the exhibition of aggression in SMS (De Leersnyder et al., 2001a; Dykens & Smith, 1998; Horn, 1999; Smith & Gropman, 2001; Webber, 1999). The characteristically high levels of impulsivity and hyperactivity may also have an impact on challenging behaviour and tantrums. Both Smith and Gropman (2001) and Haas-Givler and Finucapdane (2005) express the opinion that although people with SMS have some degree of control over their behaviours, many of the negative behaviours originate from *internally driven impulses*. Supporting this, Sloneem et al. (in review) found that the severity of aggression in their sample of participants with SMS was significantly associated with higher levels of hyperactivity, autistic-type behaviours and impulsivity.

Peripheral sensory neuropathy is a characteristic frequently seen in SMS and this may relate specifically to the high prevalence of self-injury. Peripheral neuropathy may allow the individual to engage in persistent self-injurious action, with a number of benefits (enabling individuals to access a preferred environmental state such as gaining attention/ tangible items/ escaping demands), but with little perceived cost (pain). It is, therefore, important not to neglect these additional factors when attempting to address the challenging behaviour displayed by individuals with SMS. For example, increasing sleep, medicating an ear infection and teaching communication strategies may have a significant impact on behaviour. Expert opinion suggests that total communication approaches (e.g. sign language), early intervention therapies (speech and language therapy (SLT), occupational therapy (OT) and sensory integration), special education and medication approaches have been useful (Udwin, 2003).

Operant models of aggression have been amongst the most influential explanations of challenging behaviour in groups of people with mixed aetiological intellectual disabilities. The key assumption of operant theories is that aggression is a learned behaviour that is shaped and maintained through socially and/or sensory-mediated processes. It is likely that in addition to behaviour being affected by underlying biological factors and risk markers for aggression, operant processes are also at play, shaping the behaviours that enter individuals' repertoires. Desire for adult attention is reported to be a characteristic of SMS and individuals with SMS may be expected to engage in challenging behaviour when there is a decrease in the amount of adult attention they receive (Smith et al., 1998a). Taylor and Oliver (2008) used observational analysis on a small sample of people with SMS and found that aggressive behaviours were associated with a decrease in adult attention. Other environmental factors affecting behaviour include transitioning from one activity or setting to another, unexpected changes in routine, frustration, being reprimanded and not getting their own way. It may therefore be useful to try to anticipate and avoid aversive situations, for example, by preparing the child for a change of routine well ahead of time; clear instructions, rewards and distraction techniques (music, for example) are also often effective in diffusing the situation (Udwin, 2003).

Sloneem et al. (in review) investigated the function of aggression in SMS using the 'Questions About Behavioral Function' (QABF) questionnaire (Matson & Vollmer, 1995). This questionnaire associates challenging behaviours with different environmental factors and functions. The highest scores for physical and verbal aggression were associated with 'attention', followed by 'escape' (from aversive events), then access to 'tangible rewards'. In contrast, for both self-injury and destructive behaviour, 'self-stimulation' yielded the highest totals followed by 'attention', then 'escape'. The range of triggers for aggressive behaviours highlights the importance of carrying out a thorough functional analysis in each case so that appropriate interventions can be introduced. Strategies in line with behavioural models may then be used to stop any inadvertent reinforcement of the behaviour. For example, ignoring aggressive behaviours or removing the child to another room and let-

ting outbursts run their course may be helpful if the behaviour is thought to be maintained by adult attention (Udwin, 2003).

Finucane et al. (2001) have hypothesized that self-injury first occurs as a result of gene expression—for example, unusual sensations due to peripheral neuropathy—and this behaviour becomes reinforced by social consequences. Bass and Speak's work (2005) illustrates this in their assessment and treatment of severe self-injury in a woman with SMS. They suggest that decreased sensitivity to pain meant there was a low response cost for the behaviour. Functional assessment suggested that positive and negative social reinforcement was maintaining the self-injury. An intervention with differential reinforcement of other behavior (DRO) using social reinforcement, successfully yielded a marked reduction in self-injury and physical aggression.

The high prevalence rates of aggressive and self-injurious behaviours in both children and adults with Smith–Magenis syndrome and the burden that these behaviours place on families underline the urgent need for research into effective management techniques, and for appropriate and accessible mental health and social services provision for this population.

LIFE EXPECTANCY AND LIFETIME COURSE

Although several cases of premature deaths have been noted in the literature, Smith–Magenis syndrome has not generally been associated with a reduced life span and individuals with the syndrome are thought to have a normal life expectancy (Smith & Gropman, 2001). Indeed, several people in their 60s and 70s have been described in the literature (e.g. Greenberg et al., 1991) and Chaudhry et al. (2007) report that the oldest known person with SMS was 80 years old. However, to date, no-one has conducted a detailed study investigating life expectancy and cause of death in individuals with SMS, and families may benefit from research in this area.

Furthermore, little is known about the natural history of Smith–Magenis syndrome and the persistence of characteristic behavioural features into adulthood. The information currently available about the natural history of individuals with SMS comes from a handful of descriptive studies of small, mixed samples of affected children and adults, and from one more systematic study of a sample of 21 adults aged 16–51 years (Udwin et al., 2001). Udwin et al. completed psychometric assessments on 19 affected adults; one adult scored at the floor of the test, a quarter had full scale IQs below 50, while just under three-quarters had IQs within the mild learning disability range (IQ 50–69). Adult IQs were, on average, somewhat higher than those reported for affected children. While this may be a result of the different cognitive tests that were used, it does suggest that adults with Smith–Magenis syndrome, at least those aged up to 50 years old, do not show a decline in cognitive abilities over time.

As is the case for children with the syndrome, long-term memory (for past events and routes), computing and perceptual skills are areas of strength, while visuomotor coordination, sequencing and response speed tend to be areas of weakness. Despite their intellectual abilities falling largely in the mild learning disabilities range, the attainments of the adults in Udwin et al.'s (2001) sample in reading and spelling were on average only at a 6–7–year level. Moreover, they showed little independence in daily living skills and were more dependent on carers than might be expected from their level of intellectual functioning. About 70% were unable to dress independently, while 85–90% could not cook a meal or undertake other household chores without supervision. No adults were able to travel any considerable distance on their own; 86% of the sample could only be left on their own for short periods of time, while 57% could only be left alone for a matter of minutes. No adult lived

independently; around half lived with their families, while the remainder lived in residential communities or group homes. Only one adult worked in sheltered employment; the remainder attended day centres, adult training centres or college courses for people with learning disabilities. A few had work placements on day release programmes; in almost all cases these adults were reported by carers to require either substantial or continuous supervision.

A study by Horn (1999) confirmed previous reports of the persistence into adulthood of the severe behaviour difficulties associated with the syndrome. Most of the adults continued to show marked impulsivity and distractibility, although the rate of over-activity appeared to decline in adolescence and adulthood. Over 80% were reported to exhibit high rates of verbal and physical aggression, and self-injurious behaviours were reported in 100% of cases. The behaviours had very similar triggers and typologies to those described in children. The trajectory from childhood to adulthood was variable, with some showing improvement in adulthood, but others showing a worsening of the aggression and self-injury, or no change. These findings are consistent with previous reports based on smaller samples of children and adults (Dykens et al., 1997; Greenberg et al., 1991).

Horn (1999) highlighted the violent and alarming nature of the aggressive outbursts exhibited by some affected adults. In some cases, the outbursts were of such severity that the police had to be called. Three of the sample of adults had been admitted to hospital under a section of the Mental Health Act, and another two were placed in regional secure units for people with learning disabilities. Five carers reported that adults had attempted to 'strangle' them on occasions when they were angry. Strangulation of pets was reported in two cases. As noted earlier, strangulation may be related to the self-hug that is characteristic of the syndrome, which in turn may be related to another characteristic of the syndrome, peripheral neuropathy

(Greenberg et al., 1996). If so, it is possible that this behaviour is not necessarily intentional, but rather that individuals with Smith–Magenis syndrome have difficulties gauging their own strength due to reduced sensation in their hands and arms.

Sleep disturbance continues to be a prominent feature of Smith-Magenis syndrome into adulthood (Greenberg et al., 1996; Horn, 1999; Smith et al., 1998b). The rates reported in these studies are significantly higher than rates for adults with general learning disabilities (Espie & Tweedie, 1991). The adults investigated by Horn (1999) woke an average of once or twice a night and took a mean time of 46 minutes to return to sleep. Their mean morning wake-up time was 6.00 a.m., though the majority woke at 5.00 a.m., and they slept for an average of 6 hours 40 minutes. Smith et al. (1998b) reported very similar findings, and also found that increased age was related to earlier wake-up times, shorter duration of sleep and an increased number of wakings in the night. Interestingly, carers reported that in most cases adults' sleep problems had shown some improvement over time (Horn, 1999). Horn concluded that this was not because adults slept for longer or woke less in the night but because, with age, individuals became less disruptive during periods of wakefulness and were more able to occupy themselves. Behaviours reported to have occurred in childhood, such as climbing out of windows, attempting to cook breakfast, or rearranging bedroom furniture, were replaced by more adaptive behaviours such as listening to tapes and watching television.

As noted above, there are few studies that have specifically researched the long-term course of Smith–Magenis syndrome and thus conclusions drawn should be regarded as tentative. Further research in this area is warranted. Additionally, caution should be exercised when drawing comparisons between groups of younger and older people with SMS to determine lifetime course. Because of the lack of awareness of Smith–Magenis syndrome and the less-sensitive diagnostic tools that had been used until relatively recently, many adults with a subtle presentation of phenotypic features would not have been diagnosed as children and therefore would remain undiagnosed today. As a result, the groups of adults involved in published research to date may not be representative of the total population of adults with SMS. It is easy to see how this could lead to a cohort effect whereby adults with SMS may appear to have more severe difficulties than samples of children, which include those with more subtle features of the SMS phenotype. Additionally, as interventions for sleep and challenging behaviours improve and specifically target younger people with the syndrome whose difficulties are not so entrenched, this cohort effect may be compounded. This is likely to change in the future as children with the more subtle phenotype are diagnosed and become adults. In the meantime, longitudinal studies of individuals with SMS are required to overcome the difficulties in comparing groups of different ages.

CONCLUSION

Researchers and clinicians have come a long way in terms of their understanding of Smith–Magenis syndrome since it was first reported in 1982 (Smith et al., 1982). There is considerable information about the clinical characteristics and medical complications associated with SMS and greater understanding about the behaviours that are commonly exhibited by affected individuals. However, further work is required in order to help individuals with the syndrome and their families. Although we now understand the genetic anomalies that cause the syndrome, we do not know why these anomalies arise. Such research would help in the prevention of the disorder. Although we are better aware of the clinical characteristics that define the syndrome, it is clear that this information needs to be disseminated to relevant health professionals to help facilitate more timely diagnosis of SMS. Moreover, although much more is now known about the prevalence and phenomenology of the difficulties associated with SMS, controlled trials are needed to provide families with effective interventions to help with the problems. Also, more research is required better to understand the lifetime course of the syndrome and to improve management and adjustment of individuals later in life.

REFERENCES

Allanson, J.E, Greenberg, F., & Smith, A.C.M. (1999) 'The face of Smith–Magenis syndrome: a subjective and objective study', *Journal of Medical Genetics,* 36: 394–397.

Bailey, A., Bolton, P., Butler, L. Lecouter, A., Murphy, M., Scott, S., Webb, T., & Rutter, M., (1993) 'Prevalence of the Fragile X Anomaly amongst autistic twins and singletons', *Journal of Child Psychology and Psychiatry and Allied Disciplines,* 34(5): 673–688.

Barnicoat, A.J., Moller, H.U., Palmer, R.W., Russell-Eggitt, I., & Winter, R.M. (1996) 'An unusual presentation of Smith–Magenis syndrome with iris dysgenesis', *Clinical Dysmorphology,* 5: 153–158.

Bass, M.N. & Speak, B.L. (2005) 'A behavioural approach to the assessment and treatment of severe self-injury in a woman with Smith–Magenis syndrome: a single case study', *Behavioural and Cognitive Psychotherapy,* 33: 361–368.

Behjati, F. Mullarkey, M., Bergbaum, A., Berry, A.C., & Docherty (1997) 'Chromosome deletion 17p11.2 (Smith–Magenis syndrome) in seven new participants, four of whom had been referred for Fragile-X investigation', *Clinical Genetics,* 51: 71–74.

Bersani, G., Russo, D., Limpido, L., & Marconi, D. (2007) 'Mood disorder in a patient with Smith–Magenis syndrome; a case report', *Neuroendocrinology Letters,* 28(1): 7–10.

Burd, L., Vesely, B., Martsolf, J., & Kerbeshian, J. (1990) 'Prevalence study of Prader–Willi syndrome in North Dakota', *American Journal of Medical Genetics,* 37: 97–99.

Chaudhry, A.P., Schwartz, C., & Singh, A.K. (2007) 'Stroke after cardiac surgery in a patient with Smith–Magenis syndrome', *Texas Heart Institute Journal,* 34: 247–249.

Chen, K.S., Lupski, J.R., Greenberg, F., & Lewis, R.A. (1996a) 'Ophthalmic manifestations of Smith–Magenis syndrome', *Ophthalmology,* 103: 1084–1091.

Chen, K.S., Potocki, L., & Lupski, J.R. (1996b) 'The Smith–Magenis syndrome [del(17)p11.2]: clinical review and molecular advances', *Mental Retardation and Developmental Disability Research Review,* 2: 122–129.

Clarke, D.J. & Boer, H. (1998) 'Problem behaviors associated with deletion Prader–Willi, Smith–Magenis and cri du chat syndromes', *American Journal of Mental Retardation,* 103: 246–271.

Collacott, R.A., Cooper, S.A. & McGrother, C. (1992) 'Differential rates of psychiatric disorders in adults with Downs-syndrome compared with other mentally-handicapped adults', *British Journal of Psychiatry,* 161: 671–674.

Colley, A.F., Leversha, M.A., Voullaire, L.E. & Rogers, J.G. (1990) 'Five cases demonstrating the distinctive behavioural features of chromosome deletion 17 (p11.2 p11.2) (Smith–Magenis syndrome)', *Journal of Paediatrics and Child Health,* 26: 17–21.

Crumley, F.E. (1998) 'Smith–Magenis syndrome', *Journal of the American Academy of Child and Adolescent Psychiatry,* 37: 1131–1132.

De Leersnyder, H., Blois, M.C., Claustrat, B., Romana, U.A., Kleist-Retzow, J-C., Delobel, B., Viot, G., Lyonnet, S., Vekemans, M., & Munnich, A. (2001a) 'Inversion of the circadian rhythm of melatonin in the Smith–Magenis syndrome', *Journal of Pediatrics,* 139(1): 111–116.

De Leersnyder, H., Blois, M.C., Vekemans, M., Sidi, D., Villian, E., Kindermans, C., & Munnich, A. (2001b). 'Beta 1-adrenergic antagonists improve sleep and behavioural disturbances in a circadian disorder, Smith–Magenis syndrome', *Journal of Medical Genetics,* 38: 568–590.

de Rijk-van Andel, J.F., Catsman-Berrevoets, van Hemel, J.O., & Hamers, A.J.H. (1991) 'Clinical and chromosome studies of three patients with Smith–Magenis syndrome', *Developmental Medicine and Child Neurology,* 33: 343–355.

Drouin-Garraud, V., Brossard, V., Obstoy, M.F., Marie, J.P., Monroc, M., & Frebourg, T. (2002). 'Abnormal trajectory of the internal carotid within the middle ear in a patient with Smith–Magenis syndrome', *American Journal of Human Genetics,* 71(4): 608.

Dykens, E.M., Finucane, B.M., & Gayley, C. (1997) 'Cognitive and behavioural profiles in persons with Smith–Magenis syndrome', *Journal of Autism and Developmental Disorders,* 27: 203–211.

Dykens E.M., Hodapp R.M., & Finucane, B.M. (2000) *Genetics and Mental Retardation Syndromes: A New Look at Behavior and Interventions.* Baltimore, MD: Paul H Brookes Publishing Co.

Dykens, E.M. & Smith, A.C.M. (1998) 'Distinctiveness and correlates of maladaptive behaviour in children and adolescents with Smith–Magenis syndrome', *Journal of Intellectual Disability Research,* 42: 481–489.

Dykens, E.M., Finucane, B., & Gayley, C. (1993) 'Neuropsychological and behavioral profiles in individuals with Smith-Magenis syndrome', *American Journal of Human Genetics,* 53: 425.

Dykens, E.M. & Smith, A.C.M. (1998) 'Distinctiveness and correlates of maladaptive behaviour in children and adolescents with Smith–Magenis syndrome', *Journal of Intellectual Disability Research,* 42: 481–489.

Dykens. E.M., (1999) 'Direct Effects Genetic Mental Retardation Syndromes: Maladaptive Behavior and Psychopathology', *International Review of Research in Mental Retardation,* 22: 1–26.

Dykens, M.D. & Rosner, B.A. (1999) 'Refining behavioural phenotypes: personality-motivation in Williams and Prader–Willi syndromes', *American Journal of Mental Retardation,* 104: 158–169.

Edelman, E.A., Girirajan, S., Finucane, B., Patel, P.L., Lupski, J.R., Smithy, A.C.M., & Elsea, S.H. (2007) 'Gender and genotype differences in Smith–Magenis syndrome: a meta-analysis of 105 cases', *Clinical Genetics,* 71: 540–550.

Elsea, S. & Girirajan, S. (2008) 'Smith–Magenis syndrome', *European Journal of Human Genetics,* 16: 412–421.

Espie, C.A. & Tweedie, F.M. (1991) 'Sleep patterns and sleep problems amongst people with mental handicap', *Journal of Mental Deficiency Research,* 35: 25–36.

Feinstein, C. & Singh, S. (2007) 'Social phenotypes in neurogenetic syndromes', *Child and Adolescent Psychiatric Clinics of North America,* 16: 631–647.

Finucane, B.M., Jaeger, E.R., Kurtz, M.B., Weinstein, M., & Scott, C.I. (1993) 'Eye abnormalities in the Smith–Magenis contiguous gene deletion syndrome', *American Journal of Medical Genetics,* 45: 443–446.

Finucane, B.M., Konar, D., Haas-Givler, B., Kurtz, M.B., & Scott, C.I. (1994) 'The spasmodic upper-body squeeze: a characteristic behaviour in Smith–Magenis syndrome', *Developmental Medicine and Child Neurology,* 36: 70–83.

Finucane, B.M., Dirrigl, K.H., & Simon, E.W. (2001) 'Characterisation of self-injurious behaviors in children and adults with Smith–Magenis syndrome', *American Journal of Mental Retardation,* 106: 52–58.

Fombonne, E., (1999) 'The epidemiology of autism: a review', *Psychological Medicine,* 29(4): 769–786

Goldman, A.M. (2006) 'Topical review: epilepsy and chromosomal rearrangements in Smith–Magenis syndrome [del(17)(p11.2p11.2)]', *Journal of Child Neurology,* 21(2): 93–98.

Girirajan, S., Elsas, L.J., Devriendt, K., & Elsea, S.H. (2005). 'RAI1 variations in Smith–Magenis syndrome patients without 17p11.2 deletions', *Journal of Medical Genetics,* 42: 820–828.

Girirajan, S., Vlangos, C.N., Szomju, B.B., Edelman, E., Trevors, C.D., Dupuis, L., Nezerati, M., Bunyan, D.J., & Elsea, S.H. (2006) 'Genotype–phenotype correlation in Smith–Magenis syndrome: evidence that multiple genes in 17p11.2 contribute to the clinical spectrum', *Genetics in Medicine,* 8: 417–427.

Greenberg, F., Guzzetta, V., de Oca-Luna, R.M., Magenis, R.E., Smith, A.C.M., Richter, S.F., Kondo, I., Dobyns, W.B., Patel, P.I., & Lupski, J.R. (1991) 'Molecular analysis of the Smith–Magenis syndrome: a possible contiguous gene syndrome associated with del (17)(p11.2)', *American Journal of Human Genetics,* 49: 1207–1218.

Greenberg, F., Lewis, R. A., Killian, J., Glaze, D.G., Williamson, W.G., Patel, Q., & Lupski, J. R. (1993) 'Updated clinical findings in Smith-Magenis syndrome', *American Journal of Human Genetics,* 53: 110.

Greenberg, F., Lewis, R.A., Potocki, L., Glaze, D., Parkem J., Killian, J., Murphy, M.A., Williamson, D., Brown, F., Dutton, R., McCluggage, C., Friedman, E., Sulek, M., & Lupski, J.R. (1996) 'Multi-disciplinary clinical study of Smith–Magenis syndrome (deletion 17p11.2)', *American Journal of Medical Genetics,* 62: 247–254.

Gropman, A.L., Duncan, W.C., & Smith, A.C. (2006) 'Neurologic and developmental features of the Smith–Magenis syndrome (del 17p11.2)', *Pediatric Neurology,* 34: 337–350.

Gropman, A.L., Elsea, S., Duncan, W.C., & Smith, A.C.M. (2007) 'New developments in Smith–Magenis syndrome (del 17p11.2)', *Current Opinion in Neurology,* 20: 125–134.

Haas-Givler, B. & Finucane, B. (1996) '''What's a teacher to do?'': classroom strategies that enhance learning for children with Smith–Magenis syndrome', *Spectrum (Newsletter of PRISMS),* 2(1): 6–8.

Haas-Givler, B. & Finucane, B. (2000) *Educational considerations and classroom strategies: children with SMS.* 'Parents and Researchers interested in Smith–Magenis syndrome, second National Conference on Smith–Magenis syndrome', September 21(24): 2000, Arlington, Virginia.

Haas-Givler, B., & Finucane, B. (2005) 'Classroom Strategies That Enhance Learning For Children with Smith–Magenis syndrome', reprinted *Spectrum* newsletter, Volume 2, 1, Winter/Spring 1995.

Hagerman, R.J. (1999) 'Psychopharmacological inter-ventions in Fragile X syndrome, fetal alcohol syndrome, Prader–Willi syndrome, Angelman syndrome, Smith–Magenis syndrome, and velocardiofacial syndrome', *Mental Retardation & Developmental Disabilities Research Reviews,* 5: 305–313.

Hicks, M., Ferguson, S., Bernier, F., & Lemay, J. (2008) 'A case of monozygotic twins with Smith–Magenis syndrome', *Journal of Developmental Behavioral Pediatrics,* 29(1): 42–46.

Horn, I. (1999) 'The cognitive and behavioural phenotype of Smith–Magenis syndrome'. Unpublished doctoral thesis, University of London.

King, B.H., (1993) 'Self-injury by people with mental retardation: a compulsive behavior hypothesis', *American Journal of Mental Retardation,* 98: 93–112.

Kondo, I., Matsuura, S., Kuwajima, K., Tokashiki, M., Izumikawa, Y., Naritomi, K., Niikawa, N., & Kajii, T. (1991) 'Diagnostic hand anomalies in Smith–Magenis syndrome: four new participants with del (17)(p11.2p11.2)', *American Journal of Medical Genetics,* 41: 225–229.

Lockwood, D., Hecht, F., Dowman, C., Hecht, B.K., Rizkallahm T.H., Goodwin, T.M., & Allanson, J. (1988) 'Chromosomal sub band 17p11.2 deletion: a minute deletion syndrome', *American Journal of Medical Genetics,* 25: 732–737.

Madduri, N., Peters, S.U., Voigt, G.G., Llorente, A.M., Lupski, J.R., & Potocki, L. (2006) 'Cognitive and adaptive behavior profiles in Smith–Magenis syndrome', *Journal of Developmental and Behavioral Pediatrics,* 27(3): 188–192.

Madduri, N.S., Turcich, M., & Lupski, J.R. (2002) 'Low adaptive behavior and cognitive functioning in patients with Smith–Magenis syndrome [del(17)(p11.2p11.2)]', *American Journal of Human Genetics,* 17: 109.

Martin, S.C., Wolters, P.L., & Smith, A.C.M. (2006) 'Adaptive and maladaptive behaviour in Smith–Magenis syndrome', *Journal of Autism and Developmental Disorders,* 36(4): 541–552.

Matson, J.L. & Vollmer, T.R. (1995) *Users Guide: Questions About Behavioural Function (QABF).* Baton Rouge, LA: Scientific Publishers, Inc.

Moldavsky, M., Lev, D., & Lergman-Sagie, T. (2001) 'Behavioral phenotypes of genetic syndromes: a reference guide for psychiatrists'. *Journal of the American Academy of Child and Adolescent Psychiatry,* 40(7): 749–761.

Moncla, A., Livet, M.O., Auger, M., Mattei, J.F., Mattei, M.G., & Firaud, F. (1991) 'Smith–Magenis syndrome: a new contiguous gene syndrome. Report of three new cases', *Journal of Medical Genetics,* 28: 627–632.

Niederhofer, H. (2007) 'Efficacy of risperidone treatment in Smith–Magenis syndrome (del 17p11.2)', *Psychiatria Danubina,* 19(3): 189–192.

Oliver C. (2005a) 'The nature of self-injurious behaviour in individuals with genetic syndromes', Understanding the Genetic Causes of Learning Disability. Royal Society of Medicine Intellectual Disability Forum. Belfast, May 2005.

Oliver, C. (2005b) 'Behaviour problems in children and adults with Smith–Magenis Syndrome', Presentation at the Smith–Magenis syndrome Foundation AGM and Family Conference, April 2005.

Patil, S.R. & Bartley, J.A. (1984) 'Interstitial deletion of the short arm of chromosome 17', *Human Genetics,* 67: 237–238.

Popp, D. (1987) 'Letter to the editor; an additional case of deletion 17p11.2', *American Journal of Medical Genetics,* 26: 493–495.

Potocki, L., Chen, K-S., Park, S-S., Osterholm, D.E., Withers, M.A., Kimonis, V., et al. (2000) 'Molecular mechanism for duplication 17p11.2—the homologous recombination reciprocal of the Smith–Magenis microdeletion', *Nature Genetics,* 24: 84–87.

PRISMS (2004) PRISMS—Parents and Researchers Interested in Smith–Magenis Syndrome Overview page [on-line]. Available at: http://www.smithmagenis.org/overview.htm Retrieved September 24, 2004.

Santhosh, G., Vlangos, C.N., Szomju, B.B., Edelman, E., Trevors, C.D., Dupuis, L., Nezarati, M., Bunyan, D.J., & Elsea, S.H. (2006) 'Genotype–phenotype correlation in Smith–Magenis syndrome: evidence that multiple genes in 17p11.2 contribute to the clinical spectrum', *Genetics in Medicine,* 8(7): 417–427.

Sarimski, K. (2004) 'Communicative competence and behavioural phenotype in children with Smith–Magenis syndrome', *Genetic Counseling,* 15(3): 347–355.

Shelley, B.P. & Robertson, M.M. (2005) 'The neuropsychiatry and multisystem features of the Smith–Magenis syndrome: a review', *Journal of Neuropsychiatry and Clinical Neuroscience,* 17(1): 91–97.

Slager, R.E., Lynn, T., Newton, T.L., Vlangos, C.N., Finucane, B., & Elsea, S.H. (2003) 'Mutations in RAI1 associated with Smith–Magenis syndrome', *Nature Genetics,* 33(4): 466–468.

Sloneem, J., Udwin, O., & Oliver, C. (In review) 'Aggressive and impulsive behavior in Smith–Magenis syndrome'.

Smith, A.C.M. & Gropman A. (2001) 'Smith–Magenis syndrome', in S.B. Cassidy & J.E. Allanson (eds), *Management of Genetic Syndromes.* New York: John Wiley and Sons, pp. 363–387.

Smith, A.C.M., McGavran, L., & Waldstein, G. (1982) 'Deletion of the 17 short arm in two patients with facial clefts', *American Journal of Human Genetics,* 34(Suppl): A410.

Smith, A.C.M., McGavran, L., Robinson, J., Waldstein, G., Macfarlane, J., Zonona, J., Reiss, J., Lahr, M., Allen, L., & Magenis, E. (1986) 'Interstitial deletion of (17)(p11.2p11.2) in nine participants', *American Journal of Medical Genetics,* 24: 393–414.

Smith, A.C.M., Dykens, E., & Greenberg, F. (1998a) 'Behavioral phenotype of Smith–Magenis syndrome (del 17 p11.2)', *American Journal of Medical Genetics,* 81: 179–185.

Smith, A.C.M., Dykens, E., & Greenberg, F. (1998b) 'Sleep disturbance in Smith–Magenis syndrome (del 17 p11.2)', *American Journal of Medical Genetics,* 81: 186–191.

Smith, A.C., Gropman, A.L., Bailey-Wilson, J.E., Goker-Alpan, O., Elsea, S.H., & Blancato, J. (2002) 'Hypercholesterolemia in children with Smith–Magenis syndrome: del (17)(p11.2p11.2)', *Genetic Medicine,* 4: 118–125.

Stallard, R., Dubin, A., & Coury, D. (1984) 'Monosomy of 17p11.2 in two unrelated infants with developmental delay', *American Journal of Human Genetics,* 46: 115s.

Stratton, R.F., Dobyns, W.B., Greenberg, F., DeSana, J.B., Moore, C., Fidone, G., Runge, G.H. Feldman, P., Sekhon, G.S., Pauli, R.M. & Ledbetter, D.H. (1986) 'Interstitial deletion of (17) (p11.2p11.2): report of six additional patients with a new chromosome deletion syndrome', *American Journal of Medical Genetics,* 24: 421–432.

Taylor, L. & Oliver, C. (2008) 'The behavioural phenotype of Smith–Magenis syndrome; evidence for gene–environment interaction', *Journal of Intellectual Disability Research,* 52(10): 830–841.

Thomas, D.G., Jacques, S.M., Flore, L.A., Feldman, B., Evans, M.I., & Qureshi, F. (2000) 'Prenatal diagnosis of Smith–Magenis syndrome (del 17p11.2)', *Fetal Diagnosis and Therapy,* 15(6): 335–337.

Tomona, N., Smith, A.C.M., Guadagnini, J.P., & Hart, T.C. (2006) 'Craniofacial and dental phenotype of Smith–Magenis syndrome', *American Journal of Medical Genetics,* 140: 2256–2261.

Udwin, O. (2003) 'Williams syndrome and Smith–Magenis syndrome: outcomes in adulthood and implications for intervention', in P., Howlin, & O., Udwin, (eds), *Outcomes in Children with Specific Neurodevelopmental Disorders: A Guide for Practice and Research.* Cambridge: Cambridge University Press.

Udwin, O., Webber, C., & Horn, I. (2001) 'Abilities and attainment in Smith–Magenis syndrome', *Developmental Medicine and Child Neurology,* 43: 823–828.

Vostanis, P., Harrington, R., Prendergast, M., & Farndon, P. (1994) 'Case reports of autism with interstitial deletion of chromosome 17 (p11.2p11.2) and monosomy of chromosome 5 (5pter .5p15.3)'. *Psychiatric Genetics,* 4: 109–111.

Webber, C. (1999) 'Cognitive and behavioural phenotype of children with Smith–Magenis syndrome'. Unpublished doctoral dissertation, University of Leicester.

Wilson, B.A., Alderman, N., Burgess, P.W., Emslie, H. & Evans, J.J. (1996) 'Behavioural Assessment of the Dysexecutive Syndrome', *Thames Valley Test Company: Bury St Edmunds,* (England).

Wing, L. (1980) 'The MRC Handicaps, Behaviour and Skills (HBS) Schedule'. *Acta Psychiatrica Scandinavica,* 62: 241–248.

Wing, L. & Gould, J. (1994) *Diagnostic Interview for Social and Communication Disorders (DISCO).* London: National Autistic Society Centre for Social and Communication Disorders.

Zori, R.T., Lupski, J.R., Heju, Z., Greenberg, F., Killin, J.M., Gray, B.A., Driscoll, D.J., Patel, P.I. & Zackowski, J.L. (1993) 'Clinical, cytogenic, and molecular evidence for an infant with Smith–Magenis syndrome born from a mother having a mosaic 17p11.2p12 deletion', *American Journal of Medical Genetics,* 47: 504–511.

10

Tuberous Sclerosis Complex

Petrus J. de Vries

GENERAL OVERVIEW

Brief historical perspective

Tuberous sclerosis complex (TSC) is a multi-system genetic disorder, inherited in autosomal dominant fashion, and is caused by mutations in one of the two genes, the *TSC1* gene on chromosome 9q34 or the *TSC2* gene on chromosome 16p13.3 (Crino et al., 2006; Curatolo, 2003; Curatolo et al., 2008; Povey et al., 1994). The disorder is associated with an enormous range of neurodevelopmental difficulties ranging from profound intellectual disability and clear-cut developmental disorders to subtle neuropsychological deficits (de Vries et al., 2007; Prather & de Vries, 2004).

The term 'tuberous sclerosis' was first coined by Desire-Magloire Bourneville, a French physician, in 1880. Bourneville published the case of a 15-year-old girl, referred to as L. Marie, who had a history of intractable epilepsy, intellectual disability (mental retardation) and had a 'confluent vesiculo-papular eruption on her nose, cheeks and forehead' (Bourneville, 1880). Post-mortem examination of her brain showed white, hard lesions in the cerebral cortex and small, white tumours in the corpus striatum protruding into the lat-

eral ventricles. Bourneville used the term '*tuberous* (potato-like) *sclerosis* (white lesions) *of the cerebral convolutions*' to describe the condition (Bourneville, 1880).

In 1881, Bourneville and Brissaud described the second case of tuberous sclerosis in the *Archives of Neurology* (*Paris*). Further cases were described over the following 10 years in Europe. For a detailed historical account, see Gomez et al. (1999). The first published case of tuberous sclerosis in the English language was by Pringle in the *British Journal of Dermatology* (1890) where he described the case of a young adult woman with mild intellectual disability who presented with a very unusual facial rash, referred to by Pringle and others as 'adenoma sebaceum'. By 1908, Vogt, a German physician, proposed a diagnostic triad for tuberous sclerosis consisting of seizures, intellectual disability (mental retardation) and 'adenoma sebaceum' as indicative of cerebral tuberous sclerosis. During the first half of the twentieth century other organ systems were gradually identified in association with cerebral tuberous sclerosis, including kidney and heart pathology in 1905, lung involvement in 1918 and retinal phacomas in 1920 (Gomez et al., 1999). As early as 1910 tuberous sclerosis was recognized as having a hereditary nature. In 1942, Moolten, an American physician, suggested the use of the term 'tuberous sclerosis complex' to indicate the coexistence of pathological changes in peripheral organ systems alongside the cerebral tuberous sclerosis (Moolten, 1942). Today, tuberous sclerosis complex (abbreviation 'TSC') is the preferred term for the condition.

The diagnostic triad introduced by Vogt in 1908 was used for clinical purposes until 1979 when Manuel Gomez, an American neurologist, drew up a comprehensive set of diagnostic criteria based on a large case series of patients with TSC at the Mayo Clinic in Rochester, Minnesota. Gomez showed that 45% of his patients with TSC had normal intellectual ability, that only 29% had the complete 'Vogt triad', and that 6% had none of the features in the triad (Gomez et al., 1999).

Developmental and intellectual disabilities were identified and described in TSC from the very first cases. Bourneville and Brissaud's cases had severe intellectual disability. Pringle's case was a 25-year-old married woman who was described (in characteristic late nineteenth-century terminology) as having 'intelligence decidedly under par; her answers to questions are hesitating and unreliable' (Pringle, 1890: p. 2). One of the best early descriptions of neurodevelopmental and behavioural issues in individuals with TSC was published by Critchley and Earl in the journal *Brain* in 1932. Critchley and Earl presented a case series of 29 inpatients at four 'Mental Hospitals' in and around London. The authors described developmental delay of motor and language milestones in many of their patients and the absence of language development in eight of their patients. They described a wide range of intellectual ability, a range of challenging behaviours and a number of behaviours that may have been pre-Kanner descriptions of autism or autism-related behaviours. These included 'solitary, silent and apathetic' behaviour, ' echolalia and short perseverative repetition of phrases', 'secret speech', 'hand-and-finger play' and 'bizarre attitudes and stereotyped movements' (Critchley & Earl, 1932: pp. 318–322).

No systematic studies of neurocognitive or behavioural problems in TSC were performed until the 1980s when Ann Hunt, the parent of a son with TSC and co-founder of the UK Tuberous Sclerosis Association, started the first postal surveys, case-control studies and epidemiological investigations focusing on neurodevelopment and behaviour in the disorder (Hunt, 1983, 1993; Hunt & Shepherd, 1993). Since the 1980s, and very much under the inspiration of Ann Hunt, there has been a gradual increase in the research activity relating to the neurocognitive and behavioural aspects of TSC in the UK and elsewhere.

Epidemiology

Earlier population-based prevalence studies suggested widely different prevalence rates for TSC ranging from 1:14,000 to 1:150,000. More recent epidemiological studies utilizing better neuroimaging and physical work-up suggest prevalence rates in the order of 1:10,000 and a birth incidence of 1:5800 (Osborne et al., 1991).

All epidemiological studies to date have been based on the identification of clinical criteria for TSC. Given the increasing awareness of TSC and the improved molecular diagnostic tools, the prevalence rates of TSC are likely to increase over the coming decades.

There is an equal gender distribution of TSC across all aspects of the physical phenotype, with the exception of lung manifestations, which occur almost exclusively in females with the disorder. In contrast to the gender distribution in the general population where there is a male preponderance, intellectual disability, autism spectrum disorders (ASD) and attention-deficit/hyperactivity disorder (ADHD) in TSC show an equal gender distribution (de Vries et al., 2007). Similarly, mood disorders, typically overrepresented in females, also do not show any gender differences in TSC (de Vries et al., 2007).

Causation

Tuberous sclerosis complex is caused by a pathogenic mutation affecting either the *TSC1* gene located on chromosome 9q34 or the *TSC2* gene located on chromosome 16p13.3 (Povey et al., 1994). Thousands of different disease-causing mutations have been identified in *TSC1* and *TSC2* so far, including missense and nonsense mutations. An international database of mutations is curated by Sue Povey and Rosemary Ekong through the University of Leiden (http://chromium.liacs.nl/LOVD2/*Tsc*/home.php). In the majority of cases (~70%), mutations occur spontaneously and are referred to as sporadic or *de novo* mutations. In the remaining 30% of cases, mutations are familial and are inherited in autosomal dominant fashion. Even though there is a 100% penetrance of the mutation, there is widely variable expression of the phenotype: that is, some individuals with TSC will be mildly affected by physical and neurocognitive manifestations, whereas others may have very severe and functionally impairing manifestations. There is well-documented, age-related expression of many features of TSC. Cardiac rhabdomyomas, for instance, are typically detectable prenatally and reduce or disappear by the age of 5 years. In contrast, facial angiofibromas (previously referred to as 'adenoma sebaceum') and renal angiomyolipomas tend to have low rates in the first few years of life, but become more prominent into adolescence. Ungual fibromas typically present in early adulthood, while LAM (lymphangioleiomyomatosis of the lung) usually presents in females aged 30–50 years old (Curatolo et al., 2008).

TSC1 and *TSC2* both encode large proteins. The TSC1 protein, hamartin, consists of 1164 amino acids and the TSC2 protein, tuberin, consists of 1807 amino acids. The TSC1 and TSC2 proteins form a heterodimeric complex (referred to here as TSC1-2) in the cell and acts as a central regulator and integrator of a range of extracellular and intracellular signals to regulate cell physiology, growth and proliferation (Crino et al., 2006; de Vries & Howe, 2007).

Figure 10.1 shows how the TSC1-2 complex receives 'upstream' input signals from AMPK (adenosine monophosphate-activated protein kinase), ERK1/2 (extracellular signal-regulated kinase 1 and 2), MK2 (p38 mitogen-activated protein kinase-activated kinase 2), AKT (protein kinase B) and GSK3β (glycogen synthase kinase 3 beta). The best understood 'downstream' or output pathway is from the GTPase-activating protein (GAP) domain of TSC2, although several other downstream pathways are also likely to play a role. The TSC1 and TSC2 proteins each contain several activating or inhibitory phosphorylation sites. Inhibition of the GAP function of TSC2 leads to the activation of mTOR (mammalian target of rapamycin) complex 1 (mTORC1) by Rheb (Ras homologue enriched in brain) and ultimately leads to the phosphorylation of ribosomal proteins S6 and 4E-BP. These events lead to increased protein synthesis and cell proliferation (Crino et al., 2006; de Vries & Howe, 2007).

So, what happens in TSC? Given the advances in knowledge of the putative structure and signalling roles of TSC1-2, it has become relatively easy to understand how the peripheral manifestations of TSC occur. As shown in Figure 10.1, it is proposed that, in the kidney for instance, loss of one functional copy of the *TSC1* or *TSC2* gene through either a spontaneous or an inherited mutation is followed by a 'second hit' event that leads to the inactivation or loss of the remaining allele that was still functional. This is referred to as loss of heterozygosity (LOH). The LOH disrupts the signalling balance inside the cell, and leads to overactivation of mTOR and thus dysregulated cell growth of fat cells, blood vessels and muscle cells, leading to an angiomyolipoma (AML) – angio (blood vessel) + myo (smooth muscle) + lipoma (fat cell) – in the kidney (Crino et al., 2006).

In contrast to the causal model for AML and other peripheral features of TSC, it is still not clear what the most appropriate causal model for the central nervous system and neurodevelopmental manifestations of TSC might be. There is, for instance, almost

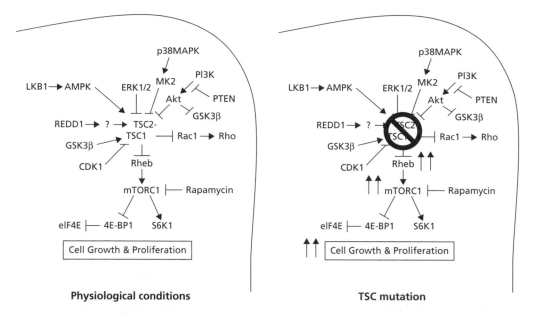

Figure 10.1   Intracellular signalling in tuberous sclerosis complex. Under physiological conditions, the TSC1 and TSC2 proteins act as a heterodimeric complex at the centre of a number of cell signalling cascades. The TSC1-2 complex receives direct input signals from AMPK, ERK1/2, MK2, AKT and GSK3β. The main output signal pathway known to date is through Rheb and mTORC1. Under physiological conditions, the TSC1-2 proteins controls mTOR complex 1 through inhibition of Rheb. When a *TSC* mutation occurs, the TSC1-2 complex loses its ability to inhibit Rheb. The high levels of Rheb activity lead to overactivation of mTORC1 signalling, resulting in enhanced and dysregulated protein synthesis, cell growth and proliferation.

no evidence of LOH in the brain. One proposal suggests that haploinsufficiency (loss of one functional copy of a gene, leading to reduction in the amount of protein produced), rather than total loss of protein (through LOH), may be sufficient to lead to the neurocognitive and behavioural abnormalities observed in TSC (de Vries & Howe, 2007). From a developmental disorder perspective it is of great importance to reach a clear understanding of the mechanisms underlying the neurocognitive and behavioural manifestations in TSC. The recent progress in understanding the molecular neurobiology of TSC may provide fundamental information to refine causal models of neurodevelopmental disorders in TSC and other disorders involved in the TSC1-2–mTOR signalling pathways. These possibilities will be discussed further under the section on current research.

DIAGNOSTIC CRITERIA AND CORE CHARACTERISTICS (COGNITIVE, LINGUISTIC, SOCIAL, BEHAVIOURAL AND EMOTIONAL)

The physical phenotype of TSC

The revised diagnostic criteria for TSC are listed in Table 10.1. For a diagnosis of 'definite' TSC, two major criteria or one major criterion plus two minor criteria are required. For a diagnosis of 'probable' TSC, one major criterion and one minor criterion are required. The criteria, as revised by an expert panel in 1998, remain the internationally accepted criteria (Roach et al., 1998) and should be used for clinical diagnostic purposes. A clinical diagnosis can be confirmed by genetic testing for a mutation in the *TSC1* or *TSC2* genes. Disease-associated mutations are identified in 80–90% of individuals who meet clinical criteria for

Table 10.1   Diagnostic Criteria for Tuberous Sclerosis Complex

Criteria	Description	Typical Age of Onset
Major criteria		
Facial angiofibroma	Red, raised facial rash in butterfly distribution over nose and cheeks, sparing the upper lip. May be confused with acne vulgaris	Early childhood to adulthood, often increases during adolescence
Ungual fibroma	Growths in nail groove on hands and/or feet	Adolescence to adulthood
Shagreen patch	Coarse, thickened skin, typically in sacro-iliac region	Childhood
Hypomelanotic macules (3 or more)	White patches on skin, often only visible under Woods lamp	Infancy to childhood
Cortical tuber (CT)	Potato-like white lesions in cerebral cortex or subcortical regions. Best detectable on FLAIR MRI as hyperintense areas	Prenatally
Subependymal nodule (SEN)	Small, hard growths in brain ventricles and adjacent subcortical matter. Typically appear in the thalamo-striatal region and close to foramen of Munro. If calcified, detectable on CT scan of brain	Presents prenatally. May calcify in childhood to adolescence
Subependymal giant cell astrocytoma (SEGA)	SEN that show serial growth on MRI. Can become very large and lead to obstruction of cerebrospinal fluid with resultant raised intracranial pressure (RICP), hydrocephalus and papilloedema. SEGA may not show RICP until large in size	Childhood to adolescence
Retinal hamartomas	Hamartomatous growths in retina	Throughout life
Cardiac rhabdomyoma	Benign tumours in cardiac muscle, sometimes protruding into ventricles	Prenatally
Renal angiomyolipoma (AML)*	Benign tumours of fat, smooth muscle and blood vessels in kidneys. Can be single or multiple	Childhood to adulthood. May increase during adolescence
Lymphangioleiomyomatosis (LAM)*	Progressive cystic lesions of the lung. Leads to gradual deterioration in lung function, patient may become oxygen-dependent	Adulthood. Almost exclusively seen in females
Minor criteria		
Multiple pits in dental enamel		
Hamartomatous rectal polyps		
Bone cysts		
Cerebral white matter radial migration lines		
Gingival fibromas		
Retina achromic patch		
'Confetti' skin lesions (groups of small, lightly pigmented spots)		
Multiple renal cysts		

'Definite' TSC = two major criteria **or** one major **plus** two minor criteria.

'Probable' TSC = one major criterion **plus** one minor criterion.

'Possible" TSC = one major criterion **or** two or more minor criteria.

*Current diagnostic criteria suggest that where patients have AML and LAM, a third major criterion is required for 'definite TSC'.

definite TSC. For more detail of diagnostic criteria including colour photographs of the multi-organ involvement, please refer to Kwiatkowski et al., 2010.

There is a general agreement that *TSC1* and *TSC2* mutations are associated with the same physical features, but that *TSC2* mutations are more likely to be associated with a more severe physical phenotype (Curatolo, 2003; Lewis et al., 2004). The same also applies to the neurodevelopmental and neurocognitive features of TSC. The rates of intellectual disability and other developmental disorders have been reported to be higher in association with a *TSC2* mutation (Lewis et al., 2004). However, the clinical value of these findings is doubtful. There are many individuals with *TSC2* mutations who have entirely normal intellectual ability, and there are multiple examples of *TSC1* mutations associated with severe to profound intellectual disability (de Vries & Howe, 2007). Genotype should not be used to predict the likely outcome of any individual with TSC. Instead, individuals should be assessed and monitored as outlined in TSC guidelines (de Vries et al., 2005; Roach et al., 1999).

The neurodevelopmental phenotype of TSC (cognitive, linguistic, social, behavioural and emotional)

TSC is associated with a vast range of neurodevelopmental difficulties across many levels of investigation (Prather & de Vries, 2004; de Vries et al., 2005, 2007, 2010a). One of the most striking characteristics of the neurodevelopmental phenotype in TSC is the variability of patterns and profiles seen in individuals with the disorder. Whereas one individual with TSC may have profound intellectual disability, severe epilepsy and high levels of challenging behaviours, another may have above-average or superior intellectual ability with only subtle specific neuropsychological deficits. Here, the most likely presenting problems across the levels of behavioural, psychiatric, intellectual, aca-

demic, neuropsychological, psychosocial and biological presentation are described.

Behavioural

TSC is associated with many problem behaviours. These include social-communication behaviours (such as poor eye contact, repetitive and ritualistic behaviours, delayed or absent language), attention-related behaviours (such as impulsivity, restlessness, overactivity, inattention and distractibility), mood-related problems (with depressed mood, anxiety, specific phobias), self-injury and sleep problems (de Vries et al., 2007; Prather & de Vries, 2004). Some of these behavioural manifestations are associated with the degree of intellectual disability. These include social-communication, attention-related and self-injurious behaviours. However, in a pattern similar to the early Isle of Wight studies of Rutter and colleagues, aggression, anxiety, depressed mood and extreme levels of shyness appear to be independent of the level of intellectual disability in individuals with TSC (de Vries et al., 2007). These observations suggest that there may be shared and non-shared pathways between psychopathology and intellectual ability in TSC.

At a clinical level, results suggest that all children and adults with TSC, including those with normal intellectual abilities, are at an increased risk of a range of behavioural problems that may cross thresholds to meet criteria for psychiatric and developmental disorders as defined in the World Health Organization International Classification of Diseases (ICD-10) (1993) and the American Psychiatric Association's *Diagnostic and Statistical Manual of Mental Disorders* (DSM-IV) (1994).

Psychiatric and developmental disorders

In the general population the rates of ASD may be as high as 1% (Baird et al., 2006) and severe ADHD is reported in at least 3–5% of the childhood population (Taylor et al., 2004). Between 5 and 10% of adults may meet criteria for a depressive or anxiety disorder, while the lifetime prevalence of psychotic disorders are around 1% (DSM-IV, 1994; ICD-10, 1993).

Various studies have suggested that 30–50% of individuals with TSC meet criteria for autism or an autism spectrum disorder (Gillberg et al., 1994; Hunt & Shepherd, 1993; Smalley et al., 1992). The most robust study of ASD in TSC to date identified core autism in 24% of those with TSC, with a total of 41% meeting criteria for an ASD (Bolton et al., 2002). Even though no systematic studies have been performed to date to confirm whether there may be qualitative differences between autism in association with TSC versus idiopathic autism, expert clinical consensus suggests that autism in TSC is indistinguishable from idiopathic autism.

With regard to the rates of TSC in autism population-based studies, meta-analysis by Fombonne (1999, 2003) showed that at least 1% of individuals with ASD will have TSC as an associated medical condition. Fombonne therefore suggested that TSC is about 100 times more common in those with autism, than in the non-autistic population. Tuberous sclerosis complex is therefore now clearly acknowledged as one of the medical conditions most highly associated with autism. The rate of a diagnosis of ASD in TSC individuals with intellectual disability is around 66% (de Vries et al., 2007). Strikingly, the most recently reported rate of ASD in normally intelligent individuals with TSC was 17%, a 10–20-fold overrepresentation in comparison to general population expectations (de Vries et al., 2007).

In spite of the absence of robust, high-quality studies of ADHD in TSC, the best-available data suggest that more than 50% of children and adolescents with TSC may meet criteria for ADHD (de Vries, 2002; de Vries et al., 2007; Gillberg et al., 1994). Even in the group with normal intellectual ability, rates are around 30%, 10 times higher than expected in the general population. There have been no studies of pharmacological or non-pharmacological interventions for ADHD or related disorders in TSC to date.

In adults with TSC, the rates of depressive disorders are around 30%, while the rates of anxiety disorders are over 50% (Lewis et al., 2004; Smalley et al., 1994). These rates, particularly those for anxiety disorders, are significantly higher than expected in the general population. There have been no recent studies with careful characterization of the mood and anxiety profiles in individuals with TSC. Whereas many have suggested that it is not surprising to have high levels of depressed mood and anxiety, given the complexity and chronicity of the disorder, others have suggested that there might be specific neurobiological effects of the genetic mutations that may increase the vulnerability to a mood or anxiety disorder (Smalley et al., 1994).

Psychotic disorders in TSC are typically seen in association with epilepsy, particularly of the temporal lobes. The reported rates of psychotic disorders in TSC are around 1%, which is similar to general population rates (Raznahan et al., 2006). There have been some reports of obsessive compulsive disorder (OCD) and Tourette's syndrome in TSC (Raznahan et al., 2006). It is, however, important to acknowledge that there has to date been very few rigorous, systematic studies of major mental illness in TSC.

Based on current best estimates, children and adolescents with TSC seem to be at a very high risk of developmental disorders such as ASD and ADHD. Adults with TSC are at high risk of mood and anxiety disorders, but not of psychotic disorders. A psychotic presentation should always raise the suspicion of seizures or other physical abnormalities.

Intellectual abilities

In the general population, intellectual ability, as measured on IQ-type tests, shows a normal distribution, with a mean of ~100. In TSC, at least two intellectual subgroups are seen. About 30% of individuals with TSC cannot be assessed using standardized direct measures of intelligence. Using indirect measures of adaptive behaviours, such as the Vineland Adaptive Behaviour Scales (Sparrow et al., 2006), they show developmental levels in the profoundly impaired range. As shown in Figure 10.2, we have suggested referring to this intellectual subgroup as the 'profound' or 'P' phenotype to

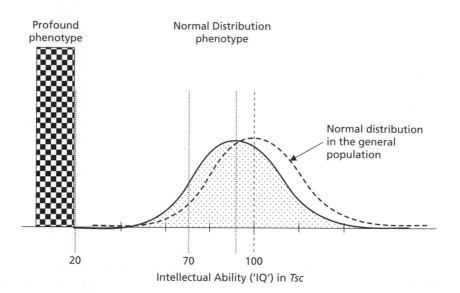

Figure 10.2   Intellectual phenotypes in tuberous sclerosis complex. A clear bimodal distribution is seen in TSC. About 30% of individuals with TSC have profound intellectual disability and cannot be assessed directly with formal measures. This group is referred to as the profound phenotype. The remaining 70% of individuals with TSC can be assessed directly and fall on a normal distribution of intellectual ability, slightly shifted to the left. This group is referred to as the normal distribution phenotype. At least 50% of individual with TSC have normal intellectual ability (IQ > 80).

indicate that these individuals represent a distinct subphenotype of TSC (de Vries & Prather, 2007). Individuals within the P phenotype typically have multiple and complex neurodevelopmental and physical needs.

The remaining 70% of individuals can be assessed directly using IQ-type measures. They fall on a normal distribution of intelligence, with the mean IQ shifted slightly downwards to ~93 (Joinson et al., 2003). We suggested referring to this intellectual subgroup as the 'normal distribution' or 'ND' phenotype (de Vries & Prather, 2007). About 50% of all individuals with TSC have intellectual abilities in the normal range (IQ > 80), some in the superior to very superior range (IQ = 120 and above).

Until the most recent versions of IQ-type measures, IQ scores were divided into verbal IQ (VIQ) and performance IQ (PIQ). In contrast to a number of other genetic and neurodevelopmental disorders, there is no evidence of a specific pattern of relative strength in either VIQ or PIQ in TSC. In a sequential case series

at a Boston TSC clinic, Prather and colleagues showed that there was a very variable pattern among the 43 children and adolescents, with many showing significant discrepancies of more than 15 IQ points between VIQ and PIQ (Prather et al., 2006). Of those, some had a pattern where VIQ > PIQ, while others showed the opposite pattern of significantly stronger performance skills. The most striking feature of Prather's findings was the highly variable pattern of strengths and weaknesses seen on subtest scores between individuals.

In terms of the developmental trajectory of intellectual abilities, Humphrey described how infants with TSC gradually fell further behind the expectations of their age, due to a developmental gradient that was less than the pattern seen in the general population (Humphrey et al., 2004). At 12 months of age, Humphrey's sample were 4.7 months behind age expectations on the *Mullen Scales of Early Learning* (1995); by 24 months, they were 10 months behind, and by 36 months, they were 12.8 months behind (Humphrey et al., 2004).

The 30% of individuals with the P phenotype show very little developmental gain over time. Individuals in the ND phenotypic group do show developmental gain over time, albeit at a rate that is less than expected for their age. It is important to ensure that the different gradient of development (which may lead to a gradual reduction in age-standardized IQ scores) in TSC is clearly distinguished from a *loss* of intellectual skills, which is not expected in TSC. Any loss of intellectual abilities should immediately lead to a physical and neurological work-up to identify the underlying medical or neurological cause. Possible causes may include renal failure, seizures, effects of antiepilepsy medication and development of a subependymal giant cell astrocytoma (SEGA).

Academic/scholastic skills

To date, there have unfortunately not been any systematic studies of the academic, scholastic or learning disorders seen in TSC. At an anecdotal level and on informal survey of families, high rates of reading, writing, spelling and mathematical difficulties are reported. Even in children with entirely normal intellectual abilities, specific difficulties in scholastic skills are frequently seen.

Neuropsychological skills

As discussed above, 'IQ' refers to a derived score or set of scores designed to measure what is conceptualized as the unitary 'general intellectual ability' of an individual. Although IQ-type tests may have many strengths, one of their key weaknesses is that IQ does not provide a 'brain-referenced' approach to learning and behaviour that is, neither summative nor specific aspects of IQ measures are very helpful to dissect brain–behaviour relationships. A neuropsychological approach to learning and behaviour is a brain-referenced approach, where observation, specific tools and experiments are used to diagnose or localize a specific brain-based deficit, in order to understand the observed behaviour and to implement a rehabilitation or skill-building strategy for that specific brain function (Lezak et al., 2004).

The first neuropsychological investigation in TSC was performed by Jambaque and colleagues (1991). In the study of 23 children and adolescents with TSC, they used a range of measures to evaluate IQ and neuropsychological skills. Seven of the 23 individuals (30%) showed profoundly impaired abilities, so much so that no subscale scores could be derived on direct testing. This proportion is identical to the population-derived rate of profound intellectual disability identified more recently by Joinson and colleagues (2003). A further seven children showed normal intellectual abilities. In those seven children, the investigators identified developmental coordination disorder (dyspraxia), speech delay, visuospatial deficits, memory impairment and dyscalculia (Jambaque et al., 1991).

The most comprehensive neuropsychological study to date was performed by Prather and colleagues in Boston. Prather, a developmental neuropsychologist, evaluated the neuropsychological skills in 43 children and adolescents at their TSC clinic. Specific neuropsychological tools were used to evaluate language skills, spatial skills, memory, attentional, executive and visuoconstructional skills. Deficits were defined as a score below the 5th percentile of expected performance on a particular test. Of the children with normal intellectual ability 19% had spatial deficits, 24% had language deficits, 38% had memory deficits, 54% had visuoconstruction deficits and 66% had executive deficits (Prather et al., 2006).

Given the high rates of ADHD and attention-related behaviours, de Vries and colleagues studied neuropsychological attention skills in children with TSC and their unaffected siblings. The study showed that, even when controlling the effect of age, gender, IQ and familial status, children and adolescents with TSC had significantly lower selective attention, sustained attention, response inhibition, attentional switching and dual-tasking abilities. In particular, the study showed that 17/20 children with TSC had impaired performance (defined as scores below the 2nd percentile) on one or both of the dual tasks and that only 2/20 (10%) of the children had no deficits on any of the attentional tasks in the battery used (de Vries & Watson, 2008; de Vries et al., 2009).

Significant neuropsychological deficits have now also been confirmed on tasks of memory in normally intelligent adults with TSC. Ridler and colleagues showed significantly lower performance ($p \leq 0.002$) by those with TSC on tasks of verbal working memory (digits backward), spatial working memory (spatial span), story recall (immediate), paired associates learning and complex self-ordered working memory, in comparison to age-, sex- and IQ-matched controls (Ridler et al., 2007).

Recent studies have started to explore visuospatial skills in TSC, both to describe the pattern of neuropsychological strengths and weaknesses and to identify neural correlates of these skills. These will be discussed further under current neuropsychological research.

Psychosocial and emotional characteristics

TSC is a disorder that typically presents with long-term and changeable multisystem physical manifestations. Some of those can be life-threatening, such as giant cell astrocytomas or status epilepticus; others are highly visible, such as the facial angiofibromas; many of the features are chronic and require regular medical follow-up, such as the AML and epilepsy. Even just having the physical features of the disorder would have a profound impact on the psychosocial and emotional well-being of those with the condition and on their families. Once the neuropsychiatric manifestations of TSC are added to the peripheral system manifestations, TSC presents a real challenge to individuals, families, carers and professionals.

It is not uncommon to see the impact of TSC on self-esteem and on self-efficacy in families and individuals. Parental stress levels are often very high. It is not uncommon to see one parent withdrawing from a caring role to their child, leaving the other parent, typically the mother, to manage all aspects of care. Another problematic familial maladaptive pattern is seen when parents and grandparents adopt an overprotective and overcaring role towards an affected family member. This can be particularly challenging where the individual has normal intellectual ability, but presents with mild–moderate anxiety symptoms and may have some difficulties with executive skills, such as self-organizing, planning and emotional dysregulation.

Adolescents and adults with normal intellectual abilities have very specific challenges at the psychosocial and emotional level. They have typically attended mainstream schools and have the potential to progress towards college and occupational and personal independence. However, making this transition to an independent adult life is very difficult for most, and impossible for some. It is likely that many layers may contribute to this dilemma. At the behavioural and psychiatric level, many may have mild–moderate anxiety features and may avoid social situations, or stick to 'safe' environments such as home. At the neuropsychological and intellectual level, they may have real weaknesses that may not have been identified, such as in emotional regulation and response inhibition, in their ability to organize and plan their activities and in their ability to maintain a long-term perspective on their personal goals without being unrealistic or unable to change plans when they don't work out.

Parents, family members and friends are often uncertain to what extent they should 'push' or 'protect' the young adult. Some of the key elements in managing this challenging life phase include having access to good and up-to-date evaluation of the individual, establishing collaborative working between families and professionals and developing a clear, realistic future plan in partnership with the intellectually able individual with TSC with ongoing support, monitoring and coaching (de Vries, 2010a).

Biological characteristics

Epilepsy is seen in 70–80% of individuals with TSC (Crino et al., 2006; Curatolo, 2003; Curatolo et al., 2008). Almost all types of seizures are seen, including tonic-clonic, simple and complex partial and absence seizures. Very often seizures are hard to treat and resistant to medications. Alternative strategies used in seizure management include epilepsy surgery, vagal nerve stimulation and the ketogenic diet.

Infantile spasms (IS) is a seizure type very typically associated with TSC. Also referred to as 'salaam spasms', between 20 and 30% of those with TSC have a lifetime history of IS. More than 60% of individuals with a history of IS have significant intellectual disability (Crino et al., 2006). It is not known whether the association between IS and intellectual disability is attributable to the effect of the early seizures or to an independent mechanism. Clinically, IS usually appear in the first year of life, and can be quite subtle in TSC. Clinicians should have a very high index of suspicion for infantile spasms in the first year of any child with TSC. Vigabatrin, a γ-aminobutyric acid (GABA) transaminase, is often used as first-line treatment of IS in TSC (Crino et al., 2006).

Renal AML can be associated with renal failure, hypertension and bleeding, and can cause significant flank pain (Curatolo, 2003). Renal cancer develops in 2–3% of individuals with TSC (Curatolo, 2003). The growth of SEGA can be associated with overt neurological signs of raised intracranial pressure, including headache, vomiting and visual disturbance. However, both renal AML and SEGA can lead to subtle physical manifestations. Renal failure leads to electrolyte disturbances that can present with tiredness, weakness and other non-specific neuropsychiatric features. Sometimes the first symptoms of SEGA may be deterioration in behaviour, in intellectual or scholastic performance (Goh et al., 2004). It is crucial to remember that at least 30% of individuals with TSC have profound intellectual disability

and may not have any communicative language to express their physical symptoms.

Of the cardiac abnormalities associated with TSC, rhythm disturbances, including Wolff–Parkinson–White syndrome, is seen in up to 10% of children (Curatolo, 2003). Arrhythmias, associated with palpitations and tachycardia, can be misinterpreted by the child and others as features of anxiety.

These are just some of the many physical manifestations of TSC that can present with neuropsychiatric features or that can be confused with mental health problems. It is essential that all professionals maintain a high index of suspicion for physical abnormalities in TSC, and that these are evaluated and treated as a priority.

ASSESSMENT, DIFFERENTIAL DIAGNOSIS AND COMORBID CONDITIONS

Assessment and diagnosis of the physical features of TSC

The initial diagnostic assessment for TSC is typically done by paediatricians and paediatric neurologists when an infant or child presents with seizures. In some instances, TSC can be identified prenatally when structural abnormalities such as cardiac rhabdomyomas or cortical tubers are identified on fetal ultrasound. Where an adult is known to have TSC, they have a 50% chance of having a child with TSC (Roach et al., 1999). Particularly careful monitoring during pregnancy and postpartum will be required to identify clinical manifestations of TSC as soon as possible, and to treat them swiftly.

When individuals with TSC are more mildly affected, an initial diagnosis may be made by a range of professionals, such as dermatologists, renal physicians or lung physicians. Mental health and developmental professionals may also be the first to encounter a child or adult with as-yet undiagnosed TSC. In any individual who presents with neurodevelopmental or behavioural difficulties who also has an unusual facial rash or epilepsy, TSC should be considered as a possible medical condition. Whenever a child has a diagnosis of autism and epilepsy, physical examination for TSC has to be performed by an appropriate clinician or clinical team.

Given the complexities and age-related expression of the physical features, TSC clearly requires assessment at diagnosis and at various points throughout life. Consensus guidelines were drawn up in 1998 by an expert panel to guide work-up for newly diagnosed patients with TSC, for the follow-up and monitoring of diagnosed patients and for the evaluation of family members who may potentially be affected by TSC. The guidelines were published by Roach et al., in 1999. Table 10.2 summarizes the recommendations for physical work-up and monitoring.

A sudden change in physical status, such as a rapid change in seizure control, headaches, vomiting and photophobia, should always lead to a rapid physical work-up to identify the underlying cause of such a physical change. Key conditions to consider are development of a SEGA, renal failure, electrolyte status and side effects of medications.

Assessment of the neurocognitive and behavioural features of TSC

It is clear that the neuropsychiatric manifestations of TSC are complex, variable and may change, develop or emerge over time. Some of the neurocognitive, behavioural and psychiatric problems may manifest clearly, such as classic autism, overt intellectual disabilities or major psychiatric disorders. However, many of the neurodevelopmental features of TSC are not easily identified. Failure to identify and treat these difficulties can result in severe challenges in education, at work and in daily life.

Previous guidelines recommended neurodevelopmental assessment at diagnosis and school entry (Roach et al, 1999). In 2003, an international consensus panel with multidisciplinary and parent representation was convened in Cambridge to draw up revised clinical guidelines for assessment of the cognitive and behavioural problems associated with TSC (de Vries et al., 2005). The consensus rationale stated that it can never be good clinical practice to wait until a child or adult with TSC has failed before assessment and interventions are offered. Given the high

Table 10.2   Consensus Recommendations for Physical Investigations in TSC at Initial Diagnosis and for Monitoring

Investigation	At Initial Diagnosis	Monitoring
Brain MRI	✓	Every 1–3 years from childhood until early adulthood
Renal ultrasound	✓	Every 1–3 years
Electroencephalography (EEG)	If seizures occur or are suspected	As indicated for seizure management
Electrocardiography (ECG)	✓	As indicated for management
Echocardiography	If cardiac symptoms are present	If cardiac dysfunction is present
Opthalmological examination	✓	As clinically indicated
Chest CT scan	In adulthood (women only)	If pulmonary dysfunction occurs

MRI, magnetic resonance imaging. CT, computed tomography.

Modified from Roach et al., (1999).

rates, the range and variability of neurocognitive and behavioural features seen in TSC, it is important to perform regular and appropriate monitoring of all individuals with TSC to identify the emerging problems known to be associated with the disorder. The second recommendation was to perform a comprehensive assessment in response to sudden or unexpected changes in cognitive development or behaviour to identify and treat the underlying causes of the neurobehavioural change.

Table 10.3 provides a summary of the time points recommended for evaluation, and the goals of evaluations, and lists specific areas of concern for each age group.

It is clear from Tables 10.2 and 10.3 that assessment and intervention in TSC requires multiple professionals to work as a team in collaboration with families in order to perform comprehensive assessments, to formulate the needs of that individual and to implement, coordinate and monitor the progress of that individual appropriately.

There are an increasing number of specialist TSC clinics around the world, where a team of expert professionals are drawn together around families and individuals with TSC. Multi-agency teamwork has clear challenges, but there is no doubt that this is the most helpful approach from the perspective of the individual with TSC.

TSC is not associated with inevitable decline. Sudden educational deterioration, behavioural disturbance or loss of neuropsychological skills may be a marker of the development of a SEGA, associated with loss of seizure control or non-convulsive status epilepticus, or be secondary to physical illness, renal failure or medication side-effects. A sudden change in any of the neuropsychiatric manifestations of an individual with TSC should always lead to a rapid physical work-up to rule out any underlying physical cause of such a change rather than to assume a mental health or behavioural explanation.

CURRENT RESEARCH

Recent studies of neurological, biochemical and genetic correlates

Neurological correlates of learning and behaviour

Research in the twentieth century focused predominantly on describing, surveying and characterizing the physical, neurodevelopmental and behavioural features of TSC. With the advent of neuroimaging technology interest grew in the neural correlates of the neurocognitive and neurodevelopmental phenomena observed in the disorder. By the end of the twentieth century, two main causal models had emerged to explain the neurocognitive features.

First, structural brain models suggested that intellectual disability in TSC was caused by the number, location or 'load' of cortical tubers in the brain (O'Callaghan et al., 2004; Raznahan et al., 2007). A meta-analysis in 1997 suggested that an individual with more than seven cortical tubers was at high risk of intellectual disability (Goodman et al., 1997) and suggested tubers as 'biomarkers' of intellectual ability. Other authors made similar suggestions. On closer inspection of studies, there were, however, many weaknesses. Few studies used standardized measures of intellectual abilities, many studies did not replicate previous findings, and even where studies used relatively good measures, tubers only explained a relatively small proportion of variance seen in IQ (O'Callaghan et al., 2004; Raznahan et al., 2007). Ridler reviewed many of these studies (Ridler et al. 2004) and performed an elegant study using standardized tools and computational morphometric analysis to show that tubers did not correlate with intellectual ability or with specific memory skills (Ridler et al., 2007). However, Ridler identified fine-grained grey and white matter abnormalities in normal-appearing brain regions (Ridler et al., 2001), and showed that some aspects of memory correlated with

Table 10.3 The Consensus Clinical Guidelines for the Assessment of Behavioural, Psychiatric, Intellectual, Academic and Neuropsychological Skills in TSC*

Assessment Stage	Age Range for Assessment	General Purpose of Assessment	General Areas to Assess	Areas of Particular Concern in TSC†	Behavioural, Psychiatric And Academic Disorders of Particular Concern in TSC†
At diagnosis		Initial assessment of cognitive and behavioural profile	As listed for chronological age		
Infancy	Birth to 12 months	To perform a baseline assessment for regular monitoring of development	Global standardized assessment of infant development	Impact of seizure onset and treatment on development	
Toddler	1 year to 2 year 11 month	To identify early developmental delay or developmental disorders	Global intellectual ability and adaptive behaviours Specific skills: • gross and fine motor skills • social-communication skills	Quality of eye contact, joint attention, reciprocity	Autism and autism spectrum disorders (ASD) Severe aggressive outbursts Severe sleep problems
Pre-school	3 year to school entry	Evaluation of cognitive and behavioural profile to ensure the provision of appropriate educational programmes	Global intellectual ability Specific neuropsychological skills: • receptive and expressive language • social-communication skills • attentional and executive skills • visuospatial skills • motor skills	Uneven profile of abilities Poor expressive language Poor reciprocity, peer interaction Poor regulation of affect and impulse Poor bilateral coordination	Autism and ASD ADHD and related disorders Self-injurious behaviour
Early school years	6–8 years	Monitoring the child's ability to make appropriate educational progress	Global intellectual abilities Specific neuropsychological skills: • receptive and expressive language • social-communication skills	Best time to establish baseline to assess whether specific cognitive skills and academic performance is discrepant from global intellectual abilities Poor expressive language and word retrieval	Academic difficulties (reading, writing, spelling, mathematics) ADHD and related disorders Peer problems Aggressive behaviours

Stage	Age	Goal of the evaluation	Evaluation	Specific areas of concern*	Associated disorders‡
Middle school years	9–12 years	Comprehensive review of child's abilities, specific learning difficulties and behavioural problems in preparation for the transition to secondary education	Global intellectual abilities Specific neuropsychological skills: • receptive and expressive language • social-communication skills • memory skills • attentional and executive skills • visuospatial skills • motor skills	Rote learning difficulties Selective attention, sustained attention difficulties	Asperger's syndrome Peer problems Academic difficulties (reading, writing, spelling, mathematics)
Adolescence	13–16 years	Determining individual needs and the support required for transition into adult life	Global intellectual abilities Specific neuropsychological skills • attentional and executive skills Vocational assessment with knowledge of cognitive strengths and weaknesses Adaptive behaviour and daily living skills	Subtle deficits of social-communication, unusual interests Poor working memory, episodic memory Planning, organizational abilities, multi-tasking difficulties Poor judgement, decision-making	Depressive disorders Anxiety disorders Peer problems Epilepsy-related psychotic disorders
Adults	18+ years	Newly diagnosed adults: assessment of cognitive, behavioural and vocational profile, determining bio-psycho-social needs	Global intellectual abilities Specific neuropsychological skills: • attentional and executive skills • memory skills	Difficulty with integrational skills Working memory, episodic memory problems	Depressive disorders Anxiety disorders Epilepsy-related psychotic disorders
Adults (follow-up)	18+ years	Monitoring for emergence of psychiatric problems or changes in existing cognitive and behavioural profile	*Dependent adults:* Annual review of social care needs and support *Independent adults:* Vocational advice Genetic counselling as appropriate Review if problems arise	Pay particular attention to *change* in cognitive abilities or behaviour Pay particular attention to *change* in cognitive abilities, vocational performance and behaviour	Depressive disorders Anxiety disorders Epilepsy-related psychotic disorders

ASD, autism spectrum disorders; ADHD, attention-deficit hyperactivity disorder.

* The table shows the time points recommended for evaluation, the goals of evaluations and lists specific areas of concern for each age group

(Table reproduced and modified with permission from de Vries et al., (2005)).

‡ Many features listed in these columns can present at any age, but are listed here at stages most commonly associated with the emergence of such difficulties in TSC.

these fine-grained deficits in the basal ganglia (Ridler et al., 2007). There is therefore increasing evidence that tubers are neither necessary nor sufficient to explain the intellectual and neuropsychological deficits observed in TSC (de Vries & Howe, 2007; de Vries & Prather, 2007).

The second main causal model was an electrophysiological one. Given the known association between epilepsy and learning, a number of authors suggested that seizure parameters (such as type, age of onset or duration) were the determinants of intellectual outcome (Crino et al., 2006; O'Callaghan et al., 2004; Raznahan et al., 2007). However, only a small proportion of the variance in IQ is attributable to seizures, as shown by O'Callaghan and Raznahan, and many exceptions to the rule are seen in clinical practice. Individuals with hard-to-treat epilepsy may have normal intellectual abilities, while there are some profoundly impaired individuals with TSC who have no or very minor seizures. Recent neuropsychological studies showed that seizures are a poor predictor of specific neuropsychological deficits (de Vries et al., 2009; Ridler et al., 2007). It has become clear that electrophysiological and seizure-based models are also neither necessary nor sufficient to explain the observed learning or behavioural phenotypes in TSC.

A combination of the structural and electrophysiological models was also used to propose an aetiological model of autism in TSC. Bolton and colleagues suggested that temporal lobe tubers and early-onset (particularly temporal) seizures, were strong predictors of autism or autism spectrum disorders (Bolton & Griffiths, 1998; Bolton et al., 2002). However, these findings have not been replicated to date by the authors or by others. Weber and colleagues reported that ASD correlated with cerebellar tubers (Weber et al., 2000). Asano and colleagues proposed a more complex model where functional deficits in the temporal lobes were associated with communication deficits while subcortical abnormalities were associated with the stereotyped and repetitive behaviours and reciprocal social interaction difficulties (Asano et al., 2001).

Biochemical and genetic correlates of learning and behaviour

The first decade of the twenty-first century has been characterised by rapid developments in understanding the molecular biology of TSC. By the end of the twentieth century the TSC1 and TSC2 proteins had been identified and it was known that they acted as a heterodimeric complex and were thought to be tumour suppressor proteins. Experimental work using *Drosophila* (the fruit fly) showed that TSC1 and TSC2 were signalling proteins in the PI3K-mTOR (insulin signalling) pathway (Potter et al., 2001). This finding led to significant subsequent advances.

The recognition of the molecular pathways involved in the pathophysiology of the peripheral features of TSC directly allowed for pre-clinical and subsequent clinical trials aimed at reversing the molecular deficit caused in the disorder (Bissler et al., 2008; Crino et al., 2006; Davies et al., 2008; de Vries, 2010b). Rapamycin, a macrolide that has been isolated from a strain of *Streptomyces hygroscopicus*, indigenous to the Easter Island, is a direct inhibitor of mTOR (see Figure 10.1). Clinical trials using rapamycin and other mTOR inhibitors have shown positive early results in the ability to shrink renal AML (Bissler et al., 2008; Davies et al., 2008), brain giant cell astrocytomas (SEGA) (Franz et al., 2006) and reduce the skin manifestations of TSC (Hofbauer et al., 2008). The use of rapamycin in this way is one of the first examples of a molecularly targeted treatment for any genetic disorder.

The fundamental molecular advances also stimulated interest in a search for direct molecular contributions to neurocognition and neurodevelopment. De Vries and Prather (2007) had criticized the existing 'tuber' and 'seizure' models as oversimplistic and suggested that molecular models were required. Later in 2007, de Vries and Howe published the first molecular aetiological model for the neurocognitive and neurodevelopmental abnormalities of TSC (de Vries & Howe, 2007). The authors reviewed the neurobiological literature of the PI3K–TSC–mTOR, AMPK and MAPK pathways, and pointed out that many of the signalling proteins in these pathways had independently been shown to be involved in neurobiological processes such as neuronal migration, myelination, forebrain development, neuronal polarity, cytoskeletal integrity and long-term potentiation (LTP). They proposed that, given that the TSC1-2 complex acts as a **G**lobal **R**egulator and **I**ntegrator of this range of **P**hysiological **P**rocesses (**GRIPP**), mutations in the *TSC1* or *TSC2* gene would be sufficient to disrupt these crucial pathways and lead directly to neurocognitive and neurodevelopmental abnormalities (de Vries & Howe, 2007).

The GRIPP hypothesis had two components. GRIPP-I stated that tubers and seizures were neither necessary nor sufficient to explain the neurocognitive and neuro developmental phenotype in TSC, which instead resulted from direct disruption of the signalling pathways. GRIPP-I therefore suggested that haploinsufficiency for TSC1 or TSC2 would be sufficient to lead to upstream and downstream signalling defects. The GRIPP-I hypothesis was predicted to be supported by evidence of neurocognitive deficits in the absence of structural brain abnormalities and seizures and by the ability to reverse such deficits through mTOR inhibition.

De Vries and Howe also pointed out that the biochemical literature was showing increasing evidence that different TSC mutations were associated with different functional consequences, both in terms of the ability of the TSC1-2 complex to receive upstream signals from targets such as AKT, ERK1/2 or p38MAPK and in terms of signalling to downstream effectors such as mTOR and S6K. The second part of the hypothesis (GRIPP-II) therefore proposed that the variability of neurocognitive manifestations observed in TSC would be explained, at least in part, by the differential functional effects of different mutations and consequent signal-

ling effects on input and output pathways. The hypothesis therefore suggested that the TSC1-2 complex acts as a 'molecular switchboard' that can have multiple combinations and permutations of upstream and downstream effects, rather than a simple 'on/off' or switch effect. A prediction of GRIPP-II would be that different animal models of TSC would show different phenotypic manifestations, and that these differences would be explained by the functional consequences of mutations rather than by background or environmental factors (de Vries & Howe, 2007).

Animal models in TSC

A further advance in TSC has been the development of a number of animal models for various aspects of the disorder. The first study of neurocognition using a TSC animal model was performed by Waltereit and colleagues (2006), using the Eker rat, a naturally occurring $Tsc2^{+/-}$ rodent model. The rats had no seizures or structural brain abnormalities. On behavioural experiments the authors did not identify any deficits but, instead, found suggestions of 'enhanced episodic memory' in the $Tsc2^{+/-}$ rats. There is no satisfactory explanation for these findings to date. Interestingly, Waltereit also reported impaired synaptic plasticity in LTP and long-term depression (von der Brelie et al., 2006).

In 2007, a Dutch group under the direction of Elgersma, studied a $Tsc1^{+/-}$ mouse free from seizures and structural brain abnormalities (Goorden et al., 2007). The $Tsc1^{+/-}$ mice showed clear deficits on spatial learning, conditioning and social interaction tasks. Wong and colleagues developed a different $Tsc1$ conditional knockout mouse. Behavioural tests before the onset of seizures showed significant learning deficits in spatial learning and conditioning, with associated abnormalities in hippocampal LTP (Zeng et al., 2008).

Using a $Tsc2^{+/-}$ mouse, also free from seizures and cerebral lesions, Silva and colleagues performed similar behavioural experiments (Ehninger et al., 2008). They reported conditioning abnormalities and spatial learning deficits, but found normal socialization behaviours in their mice. They showed direct evidence of abnormal LTP in the hippocampus and showed that intraperitoneal administration of rapamycin for 5 days reversed the abnormal LTP and the learning and conditioning deficits in the $Tsc2^{+/-}$ mice (Ehninger et al., 2008).

Unpublished data from the USA suggested that rapamycin and other mTOR inhibitors may also reverse some of the socialization deficits seen in Tsc mice. Many other mouse models are currently under development and many further behavioural experiments will add to the study of the molecular basis of neurocognitive and neurodevelopmental deficits. The emerging data are beginning to provide empirical evidence that at least some aspects of neurocognition and development can be understood and manipulated directly at the molecular level. There is great potential for mouse models to increase our understanding of the mechanisms of disorders and to contribute to the development of novel molecularly targeted treatment strategies.

Neuropsychological research

In recent years some work has continued in basic descriptive neuropsychological research, particularly of neuropsychological aspects that had not been studied to date. These include further characterization of attentional and executive skills in adults and children with TSC, differentiation of neuropsychological skills associated with specific developmental and psychiatric disorders and in the documentation of standardized clinic-based work-up (de Vries et al., 2009; Pulsifer et al., 2007).

One interesting area of current investigation is the study of cognitive development of infants with TSC. Ayla Humphrey, a psychologist from Cambridge, UK, has been interested in the association between seizures and development. Given the debate about the contribution of seizures to cognitive development, Humphrey set out to study longitudinal

development of infants prior to the onset of their first seizure. Results were quite interesting. The 11 infants with diagnosed TSC showed very different patterns. Some showed the predicted pattern of deterioration after the onset of seizures; others, however, continued to show normal or above-normal development in spite of the onset of seizures. Her case series also included children who showed significant delay in cognitive development, even without the onset of any seizures. Humphrey interpreted her elegant and detailed data as suggesting that seizures are not necessary or sufficient to cause intellectual disability in TSC (Humphrey et al., 2008).

This study is perhaps of greater clinical significance than the modest sample size may suggest. Given the prevailing view that seizures lead to intellectual deficits, there have been proponents of prophylactic antiepilepsy medication (Jozwiak et al., 2007). The rationale is that antiepilepsy medication from birth will prevent the onset of seizures and therefore prevent intellectual disability. Humphrey's data clearly suggested that the link between intellectual ability and seizure is not an inevitable one. She warned that prophylactic antiepilepsy drugs may have significant side effects that may affect cognitive development adversely. A recent anecdote from parents of a child with TSC was a case in point. A baby was diagnosed with TSC prenatally. Given that the parents were professionals with good access to medical care and to the scientific literature, they insisted on prophylactic antiepilepsy medication. At about 9 months of age, their child, however, developed infantile spasms that became very hard to control. A few years later, the child was confirmed to have severe intellectual disability and autism. There is no doubt that the debate around seizures and neurocognition in TSC will continue for some time.

A second area of current investigation is in the integration of neuroimaging and neuropsychology in an attempt to answer questions about the neural substrates of neuropsychological skills. A good example here is the work of Deborah McCartney done in collaboration with Petrus de Vries and Ed Bullmore, in Cambridge, UK. During a visual search eye-tracking task in children with TSC, McCartney observed that children attended to more targets on the right side of the screen than on the left. The search patterns reminded McCartney of the search patterns in patients with unilateral neglect after right hemisphere brain lesions. This led to a study of spatial attention and unilateral neglect in normally intelligent adults with TSC. McCartney used standard line bisection and cancellation tasks of neglect and showed that adults with TSC had rightward line bisection patterns when bisecting with their dominant hands, similar to the pattern seen in patients with unilateral neglect. Given that the TSC literature had reported frequent executive deficits in adults with TSC, McCartney next asked whether spatial attention deficits may have contributed to executive task performance, given that most executive tasks had strong visual and spatial components. Results showed that individuals with TSC made significantly more errors on the right side of the executive tasks, suggesting that biased spatial attention was indeed contributory to so-called executive deficits (McCartney, 2008).

One of the outstanding questions in the spatial attention literature is about the relative contribution of intrahemispheric and interhemispheric white matter tracks (Bartolomeo et al., 2007). The head injury literature has identified evidence of intra- but not of interhemispheric contributions. McCartney, de Vries and Bullmore performed DTI (diffusion tensor imaging) MRI on study participants, and, through the use of computational analysis and structure–function correlations, showed that spatial attention in TSC required contributions from both intrahemispheric and interhemispheric white matter pathways. Very significant contributions to spatial attention was seen in the splenium of the corpus callosum, the first in vivo evidence from any neurological disorder (McCartney, 2008; unpublished results). Studies like these show that TSC and other genetic disorders can also be helpful to answer questions of relevance to the wider neuroscience community.

A third line of current investigation in the neuropsychology of TSC is to ask whether targeted molecular approaches may be able to improve neurocognitive and neurodevelopmental outcome in TSC (de Vries, 2010b). In de Vries and Howe's (2007) molecular hypothesis of neurocognition in TSC, they proposed that inhibition of mTOR will lead to improvement in aspects of neurocognition such as memory skills that were dependent on a balance between protein synthesis and breakdown. De Vries proposed an inverted U-shaped curve relationship between mTOR activity and cognitive task performance: that is, he proposed that for optimal task performance mTOR needs an optimal level. Levels that are too high (as in TSC), or too low (as in wild-type animals given rapamycin) will lead to cognitive deficits. The hypothesis therefore was that rapamycin would improve performance on 'mTOR-dependent' neurocognitive tasks in TSC.

In 2004, de Vries had persuaded colleagues to add neuropsychological measures as exploratory variables in a phase II trial of the efficacy of rapamycin on renal AML (Davies et al., 2008). The trial had a small sample size ($n = 14$) and was not powered for the purpose of the neurocognitive component. However, results showed a significant improvement ($P < 0.05$) in self-ordered spatial working memory and planning between baseline and 4 months, and in attentional set-shifting between baseline and 12 months on rapamycin (de Vries et al., 2008). These results were very encouraging and were highly consistent with the initial results on *Tsc* mice (Ehninger et al., 2008). However, caution is required. Case-by-case examination of results showed that, while the majority of subjects showed positive change of 20% or more from their baseline scores, one subject showed negative change, or reduction, on memory scores from baseline. These findings suggested that the neurocognitive effects of mTOR inhibitors may not be uniform and may, in some cases, lead to adverse effects on neurocognition.

These and the animal findings were used to motivate for phase II and phase III trials of neurocognition that are underway. Many questions remain:

• Will larger-scale studies show clear clinical neurocognitive benefits of mTOR inhibitors?
• Will these drugs also impact on neurodevelopmental disorders such as ASD or ADHD? Will it improve anxiety and depressive disorders in TSC?
• What will the impact of such drugs be on the severely to profoundly impaired group of those with TSC?
• Why do some individuals benefit while others deteriorate?

Implications of current research for clinical practice

TSC research is at a remarkable time in its history. The phenomena described by Bourneville and others in the late nineteenth century are still used to diagnose TSC in clinics around the world. Yet, remarkably, the genes have been identified and the proteins placed at the centre of a number of fundamental signalling pathways. Animal models of TSC are being used to elucidate molecular mechanisms and molecularly targeted treatments are in clinical trials for various aspects of the multisystem disorder, including renal AML, SEGA, epilepsy and neurocognitive and developmental disorders.

Current research at the neurological, biochemical and neurocognitive level are likely to have a profound impact on clinical practice in TSC. It is not inconceivable that there will be international approval for the use of mTOR inhibitors to treat aspects of TSC in the near future. It is likely that drugs such as rapamycin will be approved for some but not all indications under current investigation. It will be remarkable if an understanding of the molecular causes of the disorder will have led to ways of shrinking tumours, reducing

seizures and improving neurodevelopmental outcomes for individuals with TSC.

So, how may of these advances influence day-to-day clinical practice? All professionals who work with individuals with developmental disorders will still need to identify TSC and know how to diagnose and evaluate all the complex and multilayered aspects of the condition. Special investigations and careful neurodevelopmental and neurocognitive work-up will still be required to diagnose and monitor outcome. Educational and life needs will still require a careful formulation and, without any doubt, non-pharmacological interventions and support will remain an essential component of management for individuals with TSC and their families.

If clinical trials continue to show positive outcomes, new questions will emerge. Some may relate to the variability of treatment response and lead to a search for biomarkers. The realization that mTOR inhibitors may only be helpful for some aspects of TSC is likely to lead to studies into other molecular mechanisms as well as in gene–environment interactions.

Infant studies may help to guide treatment decisions such as the use of non-molecularly targeted prophylactic drugs. Where studies of TSC can shed light on neuroscience mechanisms of relevance to other disorders, the implication of findings for clinical practice in TSC may become relevant also to other disorders that may share similar neurobiological and molecular mechanisms (de Vries, 2010b).

LIFETIME COURSE AND INTERVENTIONS

Lifetime trajectory from infancy to adulthood, with focus on issues related to social integration and physical and mental health

There are surprisingly few studies of the lifetime trajectory in TSC. As discussed above, Humphrey examined the development of infants over the first 3 years of life (Humphrey et al., 2004), while Hunt followed up 23 individuals from childhood into adulthood (Ferguson et al., 2002). A large-scale natural history database has been set up by the TS Alliance in the USA, but no publications have emerged from the database to date.

Infants often come to professional attention due to the onset of seizures or due to developmental delays. It can be difficult to diagnose subtle infantile spasms, and for many families the first year or two of the life of their child with TSC can be very challenging at many levels. This may include the challenges of diagnostic confirmation, seizure control and coming to terms with a genetic diagnosis. The typical goals in infancy are to determine an early baseline of development and to examine the impact of early seizures and their treatment on the infant's development. Some parents seek support from parent organizations such as the UK Tuberous Sclerosis Association (www. tuberous-sclerosis.org) or the US-based TS Alliance (www.tsalliance.org) early on; others do not yet feel able to share their story with other families.

By the toddler years, the early developmental trajectory of the child becomes clearer. If seizures are controlled, the global intellectual abilities, motor skills and social-communication skills start to emerge. This is the stage where typical prosocial behaviours and social-communication skills are expected, and this is therefore when some families may start to notice unusual eye contact, unusual or absent play, and delayed onset of language. Many children with TSC present with social-communication difficulties, even when they do not meet criteria for an ASD. The combination of ongoing physical health and developmental delays may impact the child and family's capacity for social integration significantly.

In the preschool years parents often become aware of the fact that their child is failing to keep up with their peers. This may be associated with global intellectual disability, with specific language delays, be related to social-communication difficulties or be due to significant attention-related and disruptive behaviours. Depending on a child's developmental profile, many children will require specialist assessment to plan educational provisions.

During the pre-adolescent years many children with TSC will have ongoing physical difficulties. The likelihood of facial angiofibromas, renal AML and SEGA increase during this time. Generally speaking, this is a good time to reassess the overall baseline and to reconsider the profile of a child to determine their biological, psychological and social needs. An intellectually able child with TSC will now be at risk of specific scholastic difficulties and peer problems and may increasingly become aware of their genetic disorder and difference. A more impaired child with TSC may continue to present with significant challenging behaviours, or may have settled well into a special school placement.

Adolescence is associated with a range of challenges. Many of the physical features of TSC become more prominent into adolescence, such as the facial angiofibromas, the renal AML and the risk of SEGA. Seizure disorders may change or become less well controlled due to physical growth and hormonal effects. The typical physical, neurocognitive, psychological and social changes of adolescence also occur in TSC. A small proportion of individuals with TSC have precocious puberty, but the majority have typical patterns of adolescent development. Adolescence is, however, clearly complicated by the presence of TSC. An already self-conscious adolescent girl may be much more affected by the presence of a prominent skin condition or seizure disorder. In the severely to profoundly impaired individual with TSC, adolescence can bring physical urges and behaviours that may pose challenges for parents, carers and others. These may include masturbation, dealing with menstruation, and keeping safe from sexual harm or risk.

Changing from primary to secondary school in early adolescence bring additional challenges. It is crucial that every young adolescent with TSC has a clear transitional plan in place with liaison between professionals and the family. For this reason, it is important to perform a good review of the needs of the young adolescent in preparation for secondary transfer.

By adolescence, major mental health problems are likely to start to emerge. High levels of anxiety, depression and social shyness may impact adversely on the young person's ability to attend school or to make good progress. Particular neuropsychological problems in the intellectually able group at this stage relate to poor judgement and decision-making skills, poor planning and self-organization, and, often to poor emotional regulation. Adolescents with TSC are at risk of simply being thought of as 'typical teenagers'. However, they have a complex interaction between 'typical' and many neurocognitive and behavioural challenges from which they will be at high risk.

The transition from adolescence to adulthood is a very problematic time for the majority of intellectually able individuals with TSC. Vocational skills, adaptive behaviours and daily living skills can pose a problem for many. Ongoing executive difficulties in planning, organization, self-regulation and emerging mental health problems can have a significant impact on a young adult's ability to make a transition into independent living. In many countries, mental health and developmental services change from 'child and adolescent' to 'adult' services around the age of 18 years. Families and professionals should work collaboratively to bridge this gap and ensure seamless support towards increased independence for all those with TSC.

For young adults with normal intellectual abilities, additional tasks will include genetic counselling about the possibility of having a child with TSC. For many adults it is not easy to identify with a particular peer group. In the UK and USA, the TSC non-profit organizations have developed specific peer support groups for able adults with TSC. For many, these are very powerful and hugely positive groups.

Adults with severe to profound intellectual disability are highly likely to be in specialist group homes or residential units. In a small proportion of cases, adults remain at home with their parents or carers. It is important to ensure that annual reviews are performed of the physical, mental, social care and support needs of the individual with TSC and of their family. It is also important to be respectful to the needs and preferences of families with a disabled adult at home. Particular care should be taken to ensure that the likely physical complications of TSC are considered, and that regular appropriate special investigations are done. Great care should be taken when change is observed in cognitive skills, behaviour, sleep patterns or seizures. Change may be a key marker for an underlying physical or psychiatric disorder.

Very little is known about the needs and challenges of older adults with TSC. There are currently no data on the rates of physical illness, dementia or other disorders specifically associated with older adults.

Approaches to intervention: psychological, medical, educational, social and occupational

TSC requires a multilevel, multidisciplinary approach to intervention (de Vries et al., 2005; Prather & de Vries, 2004; de Vries, 2010a). There is no single professional group that can meet all the needs of those with TSC. The needs of individuals with TSC change over time, and one level of difficulty may impact on others.

Apart from the experimental molecular interventions, there are currently no TSC-specific treatments for any of the physical or neurodevelopmental aspects of the disorder. It is therefore impossible to provide a comprehensive manual for interventions. Table 10.4 lists some principles in the approach to intervention.

Table 10.4   Approaches to Intervention in Tuberous Sclerosis Complex

Neuropsychiatric

- Perform regular assessments across all levels of investigation (behavioural, psychiatric, intellectual, academic, neuropsychological, psychosocial) to identify emerging problems and to treat them quickly and effectively using best-practice clinical guidelines
- Maintain a low index of suspicion for the neuropsychiatric features that are high risk for individuals with TSC
- If ASD is identified, start early intervention programmes
- Treat psychiatric illnesses and developmental disorders with non-pharmacological and pharmacological treatments as set out in evidence-based treatment guidelines for each disorder
- Remain mindful of the physical features of the disorder when pharmacological treatments are considered
- Where sudden change is reported or observed in any aspects of an individual's neuropsychiatric profile, perform urgent physical and neurological work-up to rule out serious physical abnormalities or complications

Medical

- Know which physical manifestations and complications to expect and maintain a low threshold to identify these. If they occur, treat quickly and effectively. If you are uncertain or in doubt, seek support or consultation from colleagues who have more expertise in TSC
- Manage and monitor seizures carefully and vigorously. Good seizure control can be achieved, and vagal nerve stimulation (VNS), epilepsy surgery and ketogenic diets can be very helpful
- Watch out for SEGA throughout childhood and into adulthood by performing serial MRI scans every 1–3 years. Neurological symptoms of a SEGA may include headaches, vomiting, photophobia and papilloedema, but may not emerge until a SEGA is large. Early signs of a SEGA may be neurocognitive and/or behavioural change
- Perform regular ultrasound of the kidneys, as recommended in clinical guidelines
- Be mindful of LAM in women over the age of 30

Educational

- Children and adolescents with TSC have complex needs and uneven educational and learning profiles
- Anticipate academic and educational challenges, even in those individuals with normal intellectual abilities
- Assess and reassess using standardized and formal measures, rather than just through classroom observation
- Anticipate and plan transitions from primary to secondary education, and from secondary education into adult life
- Ensure that a thorough vocational evaluation has been performed before a young person with TSC leaves school
- Join collaboratively with parents to advocate for the educational needs of every child
- Almost all children and adolescents with TSC will have some degree of special educational need

Social

- Families with TSC will have high psychosocial needs that will vary enormously between families. The combination of a physical and developmental disorder will have a significant impact on the social care needs of the whole family
- TSC runs in families, so more than one family member may be affected, whether diagnosed or not. Levels of family stress are high, there is a big impact on self-esteem and self-efficacy and need for support
- Statutory social organizations should engage with families to identify respite, groups, home-based and financial support to meet the needs of the family
- Voluntary organizations have access to family support workers, advocates and other specialists and can be an extremely valuable resource to families. These include the Tuberous Sclerosis Association, UK (www.tuberous-sclerosis.org) and the TS Alliance, USA (www.tsalliance.org)

Occupational

- Individuals with severe-profound intellectual abilities will require high levels of care
- It is important to remain mindful that those with normal intellectual abilities may have high levels of need for support in occupational settings. Getting and keeping jobs may be hard

CONCLUSION

TSC is in a very exciting phase of translational research. Current research efforts are seeking real translations from the underlying molecular biology to physical and neurodevelopmental manifestations and treatments for the condition. There is no doubt that there are many challenges ahead, but TSC has emerged as a powerful example in the study of gene–protein–brain–neurodevelopmental connections. Further research is required at almost every level of investigation. And, given the multisystem nature of the disorder, one of the key future challenges will also be in the careful integration of findings and interpretations across levels.

There is real potential for molecularly targeted treatments for some of the physical aspects of TSC. Equally exciting is the possibility of molecularly targeted treatments for aspects of neurocognition and development in the disorder.

The recent realization that the PI3K–TSC–mTOR signalling pathway also directly involves disorders such as fragile X, neurofibromatosis type 1 and PTEN suggests that the commonalities in the underlying neurobiological mechanisms of these conditions may point to shared molecular interventions for a range of genetic syndromes associated with neurodevelopmental and neurocognitive abnormalities (de Vries, 2010b).

At the time of writing there was not yet evidence that 'idiopathic' autism or ADHD was associated with signalling aberrations in the TSC1-2–mTOR pathways, but these are questions that should be explored. The rapid advances in tuberous sclerosis will increasingly help us to learn not only about TSC but also to gain new insights into other fundamental aspects of neurodevelopment and neuroscience.

REFERENCES

American Psychiatric Association (1994) *Diagnostic and Statistical Manual of Mental Disorders*, 4th edn. Washington, DC: APA.

Asano, E., Chugani, D.C., Muzik, O., Behen, M., Janisse, J., Rothermel, R., Mangner, T.J., Chakraborty, P.K., et al. (2001) 'Autism in tuberous sclerosis complex is related to both cortical and subcortical dysfunction', *Neurology*, 57: 1269–1277.

Baird, G., Simonoff, E., Pickles, A., Chandler, S., Loucas, T., Meldrum, D., & Charman, T. (2006) 'Prevalence of disorders of the autism spectrum in a population cohort of children in South Thames: the Special Needs and Autism Project (SNAP)', *Lancet*, 368: 210–215.

Bartolomeo, P., de Schotten, M.T., & Doricchi, F. (2007) 'Left neglect as a disconnection syndrome', *Cerebral Cortex*, 17: 2479–2490.

Bissler J.J., McCormack, F.X., Young, L.R., Elwing, J.M., Chuck, G., Leonard, J.M. et al. (2008) 'Sirolimus for angiomyolipoma in tuberous sclerosis complex or lymphangioleiomyomatosis', *New England Journal of Medicine*, 258(2): 140–151.

Bolton, P.F. & Griffiths, P.D. (1998) 'Association of tuberous sclerosis of temporal lobes with autism and atypical autism', *Lancet*, 349(9049): 392–395.

Bolton, P.F., Park, R.J., Higgins, J.N., Griffiths, P.D., & Pickles, A. (2002) 'Neuro-epileptic determinants of autism spectrum disorders in tuberous sclerosis complex', *Brain*, 125: 1247–1255.

Bourneville, D.M. (1880) 'Sclerose tubereuse des circonvolutions cerebrales: idiotie et epilepsie hemiplegique', *Archives of Neurology (Paris)*, 1: 81–91.

Bourneville, D.M. & Brissaud, E. (1881) 'Encephalite ou sclerose tubereuse de circonvolutions cerebrales', *Archives of Neurology (Paris)*, 1: 390–412.

Crino, P.B., Nathanson, K.L., & Henske, E.P. (2006) 'The tuberous sclerosis complex', *New England Journal of Medicine*, 355(13): 1345–1356.

Critchley, M. & Earl, C.J.C. (1932) 'Tuberous sclerosis and allied conditions', *Brain*, 55: 311–346.

Curatolo, P. (2003) *Tuberous Sclerosis Complex: From Basic Science to Clinical Phenotype*. London: MacKeith Press.

Curatolo, P., Bombardieri, R. & Jozwiak, S. (2008) 'Tuberous sclerosis', *Lancet*, 372: 657–668.

Davies, D.M., Johnson, S.R., Tattersfield, A.E., Kingswood, J.C., Cox, J.A., McCartney, D.L., Doyle, T., Elmslie, F., Saggar, A., de Vries, P.J., & Sampson, J.R. (2008) 'Sirolimus therapy in tuberous sclerosis or sporadic lymphangioleiomyomatosis', *New England Journal of Medicine*, 358(2): 200–203.

de Vries, P.J. (2002) 'The psychopathologies of attention in tuberous sclerosis'. PhD dissertation, University of Cambridge, Cambridge, UK.

de Vries, P.J. & Bolton, P.F. (2003) 'Tuberous sclerosis', in P. Howlin and O. Udwin (eds), *Outcome in Neurodevelopmental and Genetic Disorders.* Cambridge: Cambridge University Press.

de Vries, P.J. & Howe, C.J. (2007) 'The tuberous sclerosis complex proteins—a GRIPP on cognition and neurodevelopment', *Trends in Molecular Medicine,* 13(8): 319–326.

de Vries, P.J. & Prather, P. (2007) 'The tuberous sclerosis complex', *New England Journal of Medicine,* 356(1): 92.

de Vries, P.J. & Watson, P. (2008) 'Attention deficits in tuberous sclerosis complex (TSC): rethinking the pathways to the endstate', *Journal of Intellectual Disability Research,* 52: 348–357.

de Vries, P., Humphrey, A., McCartney, D., Prather, P., Bolton, P., Hunt, A., & the TSC Behaviour Consensus Panel (2005) 'Consensus clinical guidelines for the assessment of cognitive and behavioural problems in tuberous sclerosis', *European Child and Adolescent Psychiatry,* 14(4): 183–190.

de Vries, P.J., Hunt, A., & Bolton P.F. (2007) 'The psychopathologies of children and adolescents with tuberous sclerosis complex (TSC): a postal survey of UK families', *European Child and Adolescent Psychiatry,* 16: 16–24.

de Vries, P.J., McCartney, D.L., & the TESSTAL Trial Group (2008) 'Molecularly targeted intervention for cognition in Tuberous Sclerosis Complex (TSC)', *Journal of Intellectual Disability Research,* 52: 656.

de Vries, P.J., Gardiner, J., & Bolton, P.F. (2009) 'Neuropsychological attention deficits in tuberous sclerosis complex (TSC)', *American Journal of Medical Genetics Part A,* 149A(3): 387–395.

de Vries P.J. (2010a) 'Neurodevelopmental, Psychiatric and Cognitive Aspects of Tuberous Sclerosis Complex', in D.J. Kwiatkowski, V.H. Whittemore & E.T. Thiele (eds), *Tuberous Sclerosis Complex: Genes, Clinical Features, and Therapeutics.* Weinheim: Wiley-Blackwell.

de Vries, P.J. (2010b) 'Targeted Treatments for Cognitive and Neurodevelopmental Disorders in Tuberous Sclerosis Complex', *Neurotherapeutics,* 7: 275–282.

Ehninger, D., Han, S., Shilyansky, C., Shou, Y., Li, W., Kwiatkowski, D.J., Ramesh, V., & Silva, A.J. (2008) 'Reversal of learning deficits in a *Tsc2+/-* mouse model of tuberous sclerosis', *Nature Medicine,* 14(8): 843–848.

Ferguson, A.P., McKinlay, I.A., & Hunt, A. (2002) 'Care of adolescents with severe learning disability from tuberous sclerosis', *Developmental Medicine Child Neurology,* 44(4): 256–262.

Fombonne, E. (1999) 'The epidemiology of autism: a review', *Psychological Medicine,* 29(4): 769–786.

Fombonne, E. (2003) 'Epidemiological surveys of autism and other pervasive developmental disorders: an update', *Journal of Autism and Developmental Disorders,* 33(4): 365–382.

Franz, D.N., Leonard, J., Tudor, C., Chuck, G., Care, M., Sethuraman, G., Dinopoulos, A., Thomas, G., & Crone, K.R. (2006) 'Rapamycin causes regression of astrocytomas in tuberous sclerosis complex', *Annals of Neurology,* 59(3): 490–498.

Gillberg, I.C., Gillberg, C., & Ahlsen, G. (1994) 'Autistic behaviour and attention deficits in tuberous sclerosis: a population-based study', *Developmental Medicine Child Neurology,* 36: 50–56.

Goh, S., Butler, W., & Thiele, E.A. (2004) 'Subependymal giant cell tumors in tuberous sclerosis complex', *Neurology,* 63: 1457–1461.

Gomez, M.R., Sampson, J.R., Whittemore, V.H. (1999) *Tuberous Sclerosis Complex,* 3rd edn. New York: Oxford University Press. (1st edn, 1979.)

Goodman, M., Lamm, S.H., Engel, A., Shepherd, C.W., Houser, O.W., & Gomez, M.R. (1997) 'Cortical tuber count: a biomarker indicating neurologic severity of tuberous sclerosis complex', *Journal of Child Neurology,* 12: 85–90.

Goorden, S.M., van Woerden G.M., van der Weerd, L., Cheadle, J.P. & Elgersma, Y. (2007) 'Cognitive deficits in *Tsc1+/-* mice in the absence of cerebral lesions and seizures', *Annals of Neurology,* 62: 648–655.

Hofbauer, G.F., Marcollo-Pini, A., Corsenca, A., Kistler, A.D., French, L.E., Wuthrich, R.P. & Serra, A.L. (2008) 'The mTOR inhibitor rapamycin significantly improves facial angiofibroma lesions in a patient with tuberous sclerosis', *British Journal of Dermatology,* 159(2): 473–475.

Humphrey, A., Higgins, J.N., Pinto, E., & Bolton, P.F. (2004) 'A prospective longitudinal study of early cognitive development in tuberous sclerosis—a clinic based study', *European Child and Adolescent Psychiatry,* 13(3): 159–165.

Humphrey, A., Ploubidis, G., Haslop, M., Granader, Y., Clifford, M., MacLean, C., Bolton, P.F., & Yates, J.R.W. (2008) 'Pre-post seizure onset: cognitive development in infants with TS'. Paper presented at the TSC International Research Conference, Brighton, UK.

Hunt, A. (1983) 'Tuberous sclerosis: a survey of 97 cases. III. Family aspects', *Developmental Medicine Child Neurology,* 25: 353–357.

Hunt, A. (1993) 'Development, behaviour and seizures in 300 cases of tuberous sclerosis', *Journal of Intellectual Disability Research,* 37: 41–51.

Hunt, A. & Shepherd, C. (1993) 'A prevalence study of autism in tuberous sclerosis', *Journal of Autism and Developmental Disorders,* 23: 323–339.

Jambaque, I., Cusmai, R., Curatolo, P., Cortesi, F., Perrot, C., & Dulac, O. (1991) 'Neuropsychological aspects of tuberous sclerosis in relation to epilepsy and MRI findings', *Developmental Medicine Child Neurology,* 33: 698–705.

Joinson, C., O'Callaghan, F.J., Osborne, J.P., Martyn, C., Harris, T., & Bolton, P.F. (2003) 'Learning disability and epilepsy in an epidemiological sample of individuals with tuberous sclerosis complex', *Psychological Medicine,* 33: 335–344.

Jozwiak, S., Domanska-Pakiela, D., Kotulska, K., & Kaczorowska, M. (2007) 'Treatment before seizures: new indications for antiepilepsy therapy in children with tuberous sclerosis complex', *Epilepsia,* 48(8): 1632.

Kwiatkowski, D.J., Whittemore, V.H. & Thiele, E.A. (2010) *Tuberous Sclerosis Complex: Genes, Clinical Features, and Therapeutics.* Weinheim: Wiley-Blackwell.

Lewis, J.C., Thomas, H.V., Murphy, K.C., & Sampson, J.R. (2004) 'Genotype and psychological phenotype in tuberous sclerosis', *Journal of Medical Genetics,* 41: 203–207.

Lezak, M.D., Howieson, D.B., & Loring, D.W. (eds) (2004) *Neuropsychological Assessment,* 4th edn. New York: Oxford University Press. (1st edn, 1976.)

McCartney, D.L. (2008) 'Spatial attention in tuberous sclerosis complex'. PhD dissertation, University of Cambridge, Cambridge, UK.

Moolten, S.E. (1942) 'Hamartial nature of the tuberous sclerosis complex and its bearing on the tumor problem', *Archives of Internal Medicine,* 69: 589–623.

Mullen, E.M. (1995) *Mullen Scales of Early Learning.* Circle Pines, MN: American Guidance Service.

O'Callaghan, F.J., Harris, T., Joinson, C., Bolton, P., Noakes, M., Presdee, D., Renowden, S., Shiell, A., Martyn, C.N., & Osborne, J.P. (2004) 'The relation of infantile spasms, tubers, and intelligence in tuberous sclerosis complex', *Archives of Diseases in Childhood,* 89(6): 530–533.

Osborne, J.O., Fryer, A., & Webb, D. (1991) 'Epidemiology of tuberous sclerosis', *Annals New York Academy of Sciences,* 615: 125–127.

Potter, C.J., Huang, H., & Xu, T. (2001) 'Drosophila Tsc1 functions with Tsc2 to antagonize insulin signalling in regulating cell growth, cell proliferation, and organ size', *Cell,* 105(3): 357–368.

Povey, S., Burley, M.W., Attwood, J., Benham, F., Hunt, D., Jeremiah, S.J., Franklin, D., Gillett, G., Malas, S., Robson, E.B., et al. (1994) 'Two loci for tuberous

sclerosis: one on 9q34 and one on 16p13', *Annals of Human Genetics,* 58(2): 107–127.

Prather, P. & de Vries, P.J. (2004) 'Behavioral and cognitive aspects of tuberous sclerosis complex', *Journal of Child Neurology,* 19(9): 666–674.

Prather, P., Thiele, E., & de Vries, P.J. (2006) 'Neuropsychological profiling in tuberous sclerosis complex (TSC): implications for neurobiology and clinical interventions', *Journal of Intellectual Disability Research,* 50: 788.

Pringle, J.J. (1890) 'A case of congenital adenoma sebaceum', *British Journal of Dermatology,* 2: 1–14.

Pulsifer, M.B., Winterkorn, E.B., & Thiele, E.A. (2007) 'Psychological profile of adults with tuberous sclerosis complex', *Epilepsy & Behavior,* 10: 402–406.

Raznahan, A., Joinson, C., O'Callaghan, F., Osborne, J., & Bolton P.F. (2006) 'Psychopathology of tuberous sclerosis: an overview and findings in a population-based sample of adults with tuberous sclerosis', *Journal of Intellectual Disability Research,* 50: 561–569.

Raznahan, A., Higgins, N.P., Griffiths, P.D., Humphrey, A., Yates, J.R., & Bolton, P.F. (2007) 'Biological markers of intellectual disability in tuberous sclerosis', *Psychological Medicine,* 37: 1293–1304.

Ridler, K., Bullmore, E.T., de Vries, P.J., Suckling, J., Barker, G.J., Meara, S.J., Williams, S.C., & Bolton P.F. (2001) 'Widespread anatomical abnormalities of grey and white matter structure in tuberous sclerosis', *Psychological Medicine,* 31(8): 1437–1446.

Ridler, K., Suckling, J., Higgins, N., Bolton, P., & Bullmore, E. (2004) 'Standardised whole brain mapping of tubers and subependymal nodules in tuberous sclerosis complex', *Journal of Child Neurology,* 19: 658–665.

Ridler, K., Suckling, J., Higgins, N.J., de Vries, P.J., Stephenson, C.M., Bolton, P.F., & Bullmore, E.T. (2007) 'Neuroanatomical correlates of memory deficits in tuberous sclerosis complex', *Cerebral Cortex,* 17(2): 261–271.

Roach, E.S., Gomez, M.R., & Northrup, H. (1998) 'Tuberous sclerosis complex consensus conference: revised clinical diagnostic criteria', *Journal of Child Neurology,* 13: 624–628.

Roach, E.S., DiMario F.J., Kandt R.S., & Northrup H. (1999) 'Tuberous Sclerosis Consensus Conference: recommendations for diagnostic evaluation', *Journal of Child Neurology,* 14: 401–407.

Smalley, S.L., Tanguay, P.E., Smith, M., & Gutierrez, G. (1992) 'Autism and tuberous sclerosis', *Journal of Autism and Developmental Disorders,* 22: 339–355.

Smalley, S.L., Burger, F., & Smith M. (1994) 'Phenotypic variation of tuberous sclerosis in a single extended kindred', *Journal of Medical Genetics,* 31: 761–765.

Sparrow, S.S., Cicchetti, D.V., & Balla, D. (2006) *Vineland Adaptive Behavior Scales, Second Edition (Vineland-II)*. Circle Pines, MN: American Guidance Service. (1st edn, 1984.)

Taylor, E., Dopfner, M., Sergeant, J., Asherson, P., Banaschewski, T., Buitelaar, J., Coghill, D., Danckarets, M., et al. (2004) 'European clinical guidelines for hyperkinetic disorder—first upgrade', *European Child and Adolescent Psychiatry*, 13(S1): 7–30.

Von der Brelie, C., Waltereit, R., Zhang, L., Beck, H., & Kirschstein, T. (2006) 'Impaired synaptic plasticity in a rat model of tuberous sclerosis', *European Journal of Neuroscience*, 23: 686–692.

Waltereit, R., Welzl, H., Dichgans, J., Lipp, H-P., Schmidt, W.J., & Weller, M. (2006) 'Enhanced episodic-like memory and kindling epilepsy in a rat model of tuberous sclerosis', *Journal of Neurochemistry*, 96: 407–413.

Weber, A.M., Egelhoff, J.C., McKellop, J.M., & Franz, D.N. (2000) 'Autism and the cerebellum: evidence from tuberous sclerosis', *Journal of Autism and Developmental Disorders*, 30: 511–517.

World Health Organization (1993) *The ICD-10 Classification of Mental and Behavioural Disorders. Diagnostic Criteria for Research*. Geneva: WHO.

Zeng, L.H., Xu, L., Gutmann, D.H., & Wong, M. (2008) 'Rapamycin prevents epilepsy in a mouse model of tuberous sclerosis complex', *Annals of Neurology*, 63(4): 444–453.

11

Velo-Cardio-Facial Syndrome/ 22q11 Deletion Syndrome

Frederick Sundram & Kieran C. Murphy

BRIEF HISTORICAL PERSPECTIVE

Velocardiofacial syndrome (VCFS) is the most common human genetic deletion syndrome and is associated with deletions in chromosome 22. VCFS was once considered a rare congenital disorder but since the advent of molecular genetics, this view has now been countered. In 1992, a major breakthrough occurred in the study of VCFS and disorders related to chromosome 22 when deletions were specifically localized to the long arm of chromosome 22 (22q11) (Scambler et al., 1992). Subsequently, several reports followed which confirmed the microdeletion in chromosome 22 (Driscoll et al., 1992; Kelly et al., 1993). Tremendous interest in the syndrome still continues today as it is a complex disorder that affects essentially every organ system in the body and psychiatric disturbance is prominent.

Individuals with clinical symptoms of VCFS were described some 50 years agoby Sedlackova (Sedlackova, 1955) in Czechoslovakia and later by Strong (Strong, 1968). However, the earliest use of the term VCFS

and categorization as a syndrome did not occur until the 1970s (Shprintzen et al., 1978) and it was not until the early 1990s that research interest in the disorder really emerged. It is possible that VCFS was not formally categorized as a distinct syndrome even earlier because children with the disorder experienced multiple physical complications such as congenital heart defects that resulted in early death. Also, a syndrome is defined as a condition with multiple anomalies, all of which originate from a single cause and it was not until 1992 that the genetic deletion was identified at the 22q11.2 band. Furthermore, individuals with VCFS often presented to a variety of therapeutic disciplines, with each focusing on their own explicit area of expertise rather than the integrated approach that is currently practiced.

Though the syndrome is widely known as VCFS, it is also known as 22q11 deletion syndrome, Sedlackova syndrome, DiGeorge syndrome, Shprintzen syndrome, Cayler syndrome, Takao syndrome and conotruncal anomaly face syndrome amongst others. These nosologic labels represent not only the extensive variety of academic disciplines involved in the study of VCFS but also the possibility that competing research teams have each advocated the use of their preferred titles. As some of these nosologic labels have been provided by specialists in their own circumscribed field of study, they may not be entirely reflective of the full spectrum of the syndrome. Consequently, researchers and clinicians may have mistakenly believed that these labels represent discrete syndromes that are each caused by the same underlying deletion of chromosome 22 (Robin & Shprintzen, 2005). For the rest of the chapter, the syndrome will be referred to by its current description of 22q11 deletion syndrome (22q11DS).

EPIDEMIOLOGY

Owing to the wide phenotypic expression in 22q11DS, it was difficult precisely to quantify the incidence and prevalence rates prior to genetic study of the disorder. However, since genetic testing has become widely available, the incidence of 22q11DS has been estimated to be at between 1:4000 and 1:7000 live births (Botto et al., 2003; Oskarsdottir et al., 2004). These figures should be regarded as the absolute minimum as individuals with more subtle forms of 22q11DS may only be diagnosed at a later stage in life. Individuals with classical forms of the disorder, such as palatal defects and congenital heart anomalies, are typically detected early on while those with a milder phenotype may only be diagnosed when they present in late childhood with behavioral, learning or psychiatric disturbance, usually between 7 and 9 years of age. A further factor that determines the diagnosis of 22q11DS is clinician experience in developmental disorders, while undetected pregnancy losses or stillbirths may account for additional underreporting of the disorder.

Although 22q11DS appears to affect both genders equally (Botto et al., 2003), it is likely that the population prevalence of 22q11DS varies with place of birth (Shprintzen, 2008). This is a consequence of the high frequency of severe and life-threatening congenital heart defects associated with 22q11DS, and mortality rates may be higher during the neonatal period for those born in areas where there is poorer access to specialist surgical care or neonatal intensive care units.

CAUSATION

The majority of cases of 22q11DS are associated with an interstitial deletion of chromosome 22q11 (Carey et al., 1992). However, other genetic abnormalities involving chromosome 22q11, such as balanced translocations, terminal deletions, non-random rearrangements and mosaicism have been reported in a minority to contribute to the disorder. While the majority of deletions occur de novo, 5–10% of 22q11DS probands show an autosomal dominant pattern of inheritance for the deletion (Shprintzen et al., 1981; Ryan et al., 1997). There are also rare instances when individuals may possess the typical 22q11DS phenotype but lack chromosome 22 deletions.

22q11DS is regarded as a gene haploinsufficiency syndrome as a result of the deletion being carried in only one arm of chromosome 22 (Lindsay, 2001). Of the 22q11DS cases with chromosome 22 deletion, 90% have a 3 Mb interstitial deletion, known as the typically deleted region, while the remainder has a smaller or 'nested' deletion (1.5 to 2 Mb). Though chromosome 22 is regarded as one of the smallest autosomes in the human genome, the long arm of chromosome 22 contains a large number of genes (of the order of 40 genes). However, no specific gene has been identified as the causative mechanism that may fully explain all the features of the disorder (Scambler, 2000).

The genes in the typically deleted region are thought to play a critical role in neural crest development and migration and therefore in the formation of the third and fourth pharyngeal arches/pouches and cardiac outflow tract. Thus, the structures predominantly affected in 22q11DS are to some extent derived from the branchial arch/pharyngeal pouch structures for example the thymus gland, parathyroids and face.

DIAGNOSTIC CRITERIA

22q11DS has an extremely broad phenotypic spectrum, with more than 180 clinical characteristics encompassing both physical and behavioral attributes (Robin & Shprintzen, 2005; Shprintzen et al., 2005). Furthermore, as no single clinical feature occurs in all 22q11DS cases and there are no reported cases of the syndrome that have all or even most of the clinical findings, diagnosis through clinical criteria alone has proven unreliable. Therefore, as the syndrome shows marked variability in phenotypic expression, recent advances in molecular genetics have permitted a more robust identification of 22q11DS probands.

As 22q11DS is caused by a microdeletion of chromosome 22 at the q11.2 band, it is possible to detect this genetic deletion through a variety of cytogenetic laboratory techniques. Karyotyping is a method that assesses the physical structure of all chromosomes and has the potential to detect large chromosomal rearrangements or deletions. However, the majority of deletions that cause 22q11DS are too small to be assessed by karyotyping alone. Therefore, fluorescence in situ hybridization (FISH) or multiplex ligation-dependent probe amplification (MLPA) may be better suited for accurate diagnosis. Although FISH is commonly used for diagnosis (Robin & Shprintzen, 2005), chromosomal microarray analysis is gradually replacing FISH as the first line diagnostic tool for genomic disorders in general.

FISH directly assesses the area on chromosome 22 that is related to 22q11DS namely the 3 Mb typically deleted region (TDR).

With FISH, chromosome preparations are obtained from peripheral blood samples that have been denatured to allow hybridization of a probe specific to the TDR. Probes are stained with a dye and under proper laboratory conditions these fluorescent probes will bind to the corresponding area of chromosome 22q11. For persons having two normal (non-deleted) chromosome 22s, two stained probes appear with fluorescence microscopy. However, if there is a deletion on one of the chromosome 22s, there is lack of a substrate for the probe to adhere to and therefore only one probe appears (which is the case in 22q11DS).

The decision to perform genomic testing for the diagnosis of 22q11DS depends on clinical suspicion and the degree of clinical experience in developmental disorders. When major congenital heart anomalies are present, especially in the form of conotruncal anomalies and ventricular septal defects (VSDs), the likelihood of diagnosing 22q11DS is much higher.

The large majority of individuals with 22q11DS (90%) have de novo mutations where neither parent is affected. However, if a couple already has one child with 22q11DS or a parent is a known carrier of a 22q11 deletion, they may wish to know if a future pregnancy may be affected. Therefore testing can be performed during the pregnancy to assess for the presence of deletion through chorionic villus sampling (CVS) or amniocentesis. CVS is performed at an earlier stage than amniocentesis and usually at weeks 10 to 12 of gestation. With CVS, a sample of the placenta is taken either through the abdomen or cervix and is associated with approximately 1% chance of miscarriage. Amniocentesis is a more commonly performed procedure after 15 weeks gestation whereby amniotic fluid is obtained through the abdomen and is associated with a lower miscarriage rate. However, prenatal testing can only distinguish whether a deletion is present or absent and not the degree to which a fetus may be affected. A further option for a suspected pregnancy with 22q11DS is a fetal ultrasound/echocardiogram, which assesses the structure and the circulatory flow of and through the heart. As cardiac defects are found in a substantial proportion of people with 22q11DS (70–80%), a fetal echocardiogram can be performed after 18 weeks gestation, when the cardiac structures have been formed.

CORE CHARACTERISTICS

Physical

The description of the 22q11DS clinical phenotype has undergone an evolution ever since 22q11DS was classified as a syndrome. Currently, 22q11DS is recognized to demonstrate an expansive phenotype with more than 180 clinical features that affect practically every organ and system (Robin & Shprintzen, 2005). As the phenotypic expression shows high variability, some individuals at the mildest end of the spectrum are indistinguishable from normal while the most severe cases can experience life-threatening disorders. The most commonly occurring physical characteristics are palatal anomalies, pharyngeal insufficiency, congenital cardiac defects, vascular abnormalities, immunodeficiency, thymic hypoplasia and renal anomalies. These defects are often associated with small stature, hypotonia, facial dysmorphology and slender hands and digits (Goldberg et al., 1993).

The facial dysmorphology in 22q11DS is typically characterized by a long face with upslanting eyes, widened nasal bridge with a prominent nasal tip, small ears with overfurled helices and a small mouth associated with cleft lip and/or palate (Shprintzen, 2000a). Palatal abnormalities are common and the most frequently occurring are submucous cleft palate and occult submucous cleft palate (Shprintzen, 2000b).

Another striking feature is the presence of cardiac anomalies and after Down syndrome, 22q11DS is the commonest cause of heart defects (Glover, 1995). These are related to

the maldevelopment of the conotruncus, embryonic aortic arch structures and the ventricular septum (Goldmuntz et al., 1998) and include such defects as tetralogy of Fallot, interrupted aortic arch, truncus arteriosus, aortic arch anomalies and VSDs. Congenital heart disease is present in approximately 70% of cases and the type of heart anomaly may lead to stronger suspicion of 22q11DS than any other diagnosis (Shprintzen, 2008) as the cardiac phenotypes in 22q11DS are associated with hemizygosity of the gene *TBX1* that is expressed on chromosome 22 (Merscher et al., 2001). Approximately a quarter of people with 22q11DS also display abnormalities of the internal carotid arteries such as enlargement, medial displacement or tortuosity (Goldberg et al., 1993).

Immunodeficiency is also very common in 22q11DS (60–77%) and was observed as a component of the disorder as early as the 1960s. Although a proportion of children with 22q11DS have an absent thymus, most individuals have thymic tissue located in aberrant locations. This results in a lower number of T cells than normal but not complete aplasia and often leads to an increased prevalence of serious infections such as recurrent bronchitis or sinusitis. Furthermore, 22q11DS was recently found to be significantly associated with eczema and asthma but not with allergic rhinitis (Staple et al., 2005).

Other systems affected in 22q11DS include nephro-urologic, gastrointestinal and ophthalmologic with abnormalities such as multicystic renal dysplasia, renal agenesis, anal stenosis or intestinal malrotation. Tortuosity of the vessels in the retina has also been reported but may not be related to the presence of cardiac anomalies (Abel & O'Leary, 1997).

Cognition

General intellectual impairment is common in 22q11DS, with full-scale IQ (FSIQ) scores usually lying within the moderate intellectually disabled to the normal range with a mean of 70 (Swillen et al., 1997). Also, 22q11DS individuals with a familial deletion are found to have a lower mean FSIQ than individuals with a de novo deletion (Swillen et al., 1997; Gerdes et al., 1999). Cardiac defects, vascular abnormalities and physical comorbidities have been postulated as a causative mechanism for lower IQ in 22q11DS. However, there does not appear to be a well established association between such lesions and intellectual ability (Swillen et al., 1997; De Smedt et al., 2003).

There are also reports of a discrepancy between verbal and performance IQ in 22q11DS where verbal IQ (VIQ) exceeds performance IQ (PIQ) and therefore the intellectual disability has been described as a non-verbal learning disability (NVLD) (Swillen et al., 1997; Gerdes et al., 1999; Moss et al., 1999). Such NVLD may include significant deficits in visuospatial skills and non-verbal memory functioning (Lajiness-O'Neill et al., 2006). Some of the visuospatial memory deficits that are described have been in the domains of immediate and delayed memory which contrast with relatively preserved object memory and rote verbal memory (Bearden et al., 2001). Children with 22q11DS are also observed to perform less well in tasks that involve arithmetic in comparison to reading and spelling (Swillen et al., 1999a; Wang et al., 2000). Visual object perception and spatial cognition are other non-verbal abilities that are impaired in 22q11DS and the latter has been found to be related to impaired mathematical abilities.

In one report on educational attainments, Moss and colleagues (1999) excluded individuals with an FSIQ below 70 from the analysis, so as to avoid the potential confounding of intellectual disability. However, the same psychoeducational patterns emerged in this more homogenous group where VIQ > PIQ and additionally, reading and spelling > maths abilities suggesting that this profile is indeed characteristic of a 22q11 deletion rather than a consequence of a more general intellectual disability. Following comprehensive neuropsychological assessments of 22q11DS adults with schizophrenia and those without the psychiatric disorder, van Amelsvoort et al. (2004a) suggested that developmental brain abnormalities, for instance in the frontal lobe, may predispose to the development of schizophrenia in 22q11DS individuals.

As the frontal lobe is extensively involved in executive function (the coordination of cognitive processes involved in the execution of complex tasks), it has been proposed that abnormalities in the frontal lobe lead to difficulties in, for example, inhibiting inappropriate responses, generating novel responses or devising problem-solving strategies. In 22q11DS, deficits have also been found in planning that have been associated with increased impulsivity and poorer problem-solving skills (Henry et al., 2002).

Attention, concentration and tracking deficits have also been implicated in the behavioral profile of individuals with 22q11DS in a number of studies (Gerdes et al., 1999; Woodin et al., 2001). In particular, the behavioral pattern of children and adolescents is suggestive of impaired attentional networks. It is possible that significant deficits affecting these attentional networks may consequently lead to marked behavioral problems. However, most studies so far have used different tasks to assess attentional abilities, which makes it difficult to ascertain the exact nature of these impairments.

There are, however, also areas of relative strength in the 22q11DS cognitive profile. For example, auditory/verbal rote memory skills are usually relatively preserved in 22q11DS (Wang et al., 2000; Bearden et al., 2001). Other domains that are relatively preserved are reading (decoding), spelling and phonological processing skills (Moss et al., 1999; Woodin et al., 2001). Overall, an understanding of the neurocognitive processes characterizing 22q11DS and the associated behavioral outcomes is essential in order for clinicians to implement early, appropriate and targeted interventions.

Linguistic

Delayed speech and language development is characteristic of 22q11DS. Receptive language ability often exceeds expressive language ability and pose a significant concern for parents (Golding-Kushner et al., 1985; Gerdes et al., 1999). Although early development in 22q11DS is often characterized by mild delay in most areas, expressive language is often specifically delayed compared with other milestones. Speech impairments are very likely multifactorial in origin and linked to factors such as velopharyngeal insufficiency and developmental delay. Children with 22q11DS also demonstrate associated speech abnormalities such as hoarseness, compensatory articulation errors and a high-pitched voice.

Furthermore, language development in 22q11DS is thought to follow a different developmental trajectory compared with other groups of children. For instance, when 22q11DS children are compared to children with cleft lip/palate, increasing severity of impairments can be seen up to three years of age (Scherer et al., 1999) and these children can be non-verbal up to 30 months of age. Subsequently, 22q11DS children often show dramatic improvement between three and four years of age (Solot et al., 2001) and by school age, expressive language and speech improve (perhaps as a result of intervention) although specific language impairment persists. In addition, higher-order receptive language skills involving abstract thinking remain poorly developed, thereby affecting both communication and academic skills.

The process by which one's voice is produced is termed phonation and also appears to be abnormal in 22q11DS. Phonation is normally characterized by volume, quality and pitch and is dependent on the articulatory apparatus and respiration. In 22q11DS there is a larger prevalence of laryngeal webs, which shortens the length of the vibratory component of the vocal cords and impairs movement of the vocal folds and thereby results in hoarseness and an increased vocal pitch. A large majority of 22q11DS individuals (75%) are also hypernasal owing to velopharyngeal insufficiency despite palatal repair, which may be perhaps accounted for

by shrunken or absent adenoids (Havkin et al., 2000).

Behavioral and psychiatric disorder

Although the variety of psychiatric presentations in 22q11DS is heterogeneous, high rates of psychiatric morbidity have been reported ever since it was described as a genetic disorder (Shprintzen et al., 1992). Early studies of children with 22q11DS reported a characteristic personality with poor social interaction, both quantitatively and qualitatively, that was associated with a bland affect with minimal facial expression. It was also reported that children often exhibited extremes of behavior: notably, behavior that was disinhibited/impulsive or serious/shy (Golding-Kushner et al., 1985; Swillen et al., 1997). Parents of 22q11DS children up to the age of three years have often reported that their children present with somatic complaints, for example, eating difficulties or withdrawn behavior. This social withdrawal often persists into adolescence and is compounded by attentional deficits and poor social skills, which may be accounted for by impaired communication abilities. Additional temperamental features described in children and adolescents with 22q11DS include an exaggerated response to threatening stimuli, and an enduring fearfulness of painful situations (Golding-Kushner et al., 1985). While only a limited number of studies have assessed the psychiatric profile in 22q11DS children, these have reported high rates of comorbid psychiatric disorder (Arnold et al., 2001; Feinstein et al., 2002; Baker & Skuse, 2005).

Children with 22q11DS are reported to have high levels of anxiety and depression (Golding-Kushner et al., 1985; Swillen et al., 1997) and to display a diverse range of psychiatric symptoms, the most prevalent of which are mood disruptions, attention deficits and psychotic phenomena that appear to be independent of intellectual impairment (Baker & Skuse, 2005). To exclude the potential confounding effects of intellectual disability on mood and anxiety measures, primary school children with 22q11DS were compared to a group of children matched for intellectual ability and speech and language impairment (children with IQ < 70 were excluded from both groups) (Swillen et al., 2001). While both groups behaved similarly with respect to problematic social interaction, poor attention and anxiety, 22q11DS children were found to be more withdrawn and less aggressive compared to controls. This finding may suggest that 22q11DS children are more likely to show internalizing behaviors when compared to children at a similar developmental level but without the 22q11 deletion.

Mood disorder is common in 22q11DS children and adults and rates between 12 and 47% have been reported in the literature (Papolos et al., 1996; Carlson et al., 1997; Murphy et al., 1999; Arnold et al., 2001). Although an increased rate of bipolar affective disorder (BPAD) was initially reported (Papolos et al., 1996), subsequent studies have described an unstable mood disorder instead of BPAD (Vogels et al., 2002). It is possible that pubertal changes, increased social demands and genetic predisposition may place 22q11DS individuals at a heightened risk of developing anxiety and depressive disorders (Swillen et al., 1999b).

Attention-deficit hyperactivity disorder (ADHD) is common, with rates between 35 and 46% in children and young adults (Niklasson et al., 2001; Feinstein et al., 2002; Gothelf et al., 2004a) and perhaps is the most common psychiatric disorder in 22q11DS (Antshel et al., 2006; Zagursky et al., 2006). This is in marked contrast to an estimated prevalence of between 3 and 7% for non-deleted school-aged children (Polanczyk et al., 2007).

Rates of psychotic disorders such as schizophrenia and schizotypy are also significantly increased, at between 20 and 30% in 22q11DS, a rate approximately 25 times greater than that in the general population (Pulver et al., 1994; Murphy et al., 1999).

Deletion of 22q11.2 is the third highest risk factor for the development of schizophrenia, with only a greater risk conferred by being the child of two parents with schizophrenia or the monozygotic co-twin of an affected individual. More recently, a report suggested that the development of psychotic disorders in 22q11DS is a gradual process, with an initial presentation of subthreshold psychotic symptoms in childhood (Gothelf et al., 2007a). Furthermore, 22q11DS children display more serious psychiatric symptoms as they go through adolescence compared to children with idiopathic learning disability.

Higher rates of autism spectrum disorder in 22q11DS have also been reported at between 14 and 50% (Niklasson et al., 2001; Fine et al., 2005; Vorstman et al., 2006). Vorstman and colleagues suggest that autistic and psychotic disorders are major features of the behavioral phenotype in children with 22q11DS. The authors also suggested that the autistic symptoms identified in their study may be a reflection of the neurodevelopmental abnormalities in individuals with schizophrenia where autistic symptoms may represent prodromal features of psychosis rather than exclusively an autism spectrum disorder. Finally, other disorders, such as obsessive-compulsive disorder (OCD), have been described in several studies, with rates ranging from 8 to 33% (Papolos et al., 1996; Gothelf et al., 2004b).

DIFFERENTIAL DIAGNOSIS AND ASSOCIATIONS

Although 22q11DS shows broad phenotypic expression, some clinicians adopt a minimal diagnostic criteria or a probability approach to diagnosing genetic syndromes (Shprintzen, 2008). If this approach is employed in the absence of genetic confirmation, it is possible to diagnose someone who has cleft palate, intellectual disability, congenital heart defects, immunodeficiency, hypotonia, developmental delay, and small ears with overfurled helices with 22q11DS while these clinical criteria may be equally applicable to trisomy 21/Down syndrome (see Chapter 1).

Some patients with 22q11DS may also be incorrectly diagnosed as having the CHARGE syndrome (i.e. coloboma of the eye, heart defects, atresia of the nasal choanae, retardation of growth and/or development, genital and/or urinary abnormalities, and ear abnormalities and deafness). Although CHARGE is related to a mutation or deletion in the chromodomain helicase DNA-binding protein-7 (CHD7) gene located on chromosome 8 (Vissers et al., 2004) and genetic testing available for this disorder, it is still a largely clinical diagnosis as only 60% of patients tested have the CHD7 mutation (Lalani et al., 2006).

A further differential diagnosis to consider is another chromosome 22q deletion syndrome, that is, the 22q13.3 syndrome (Phelan-McDermid syndrome or deletion 22q13 syndrome). This syndrome is a chromosome microdeletion syndrome, also on the long arm of chromosome 22 but in the 13.3 band. It is characterized by neonatal hypotonia, global developmental delay, normal to accelerated growth, absent to severely delayed speech and minor dysmorphic features. Although this syndrome is not routinely tested for, it can be confirmed via FISH or array comparative genomic hybridization (CGH) and should be considered in all cases of hypotonia of unknown etiology and in individuals with absent speech (Phelan, 2008).

Partial monosomy of chromosome 10p is a rare genetic disorder where a significant proportion of individuals with the disorder demonstrate features of 22q11DS. Its main characteristics are hypoparathyroidism, deafness and renal dysplasia; hence, it is also known as the HDR syndrome (Lichtner et al., 2000). However, those with HDR lack the cardiac, palatal and T cell abnormalities that are present in 22q11DS.

An environmental disorder which causes impairment in neural crest development and branchial arch abnormalities is isotretinoin treatment for acne. As a result of increased use of isotretinoin, there has been a concomitant increase of associated birth defects. Isotretinoin embryopathy produces a phenocopy of 22q11DS (Coberly et al., 1996; Aggarwal & Morrow, 2008) and may be related to downregulation of *TBX1* (Zhang et al., 2005).

CURRENT RESEARCH

Genetic

The chromosome 22q11.2 locus is rich in genes including those that are involved in neurotransmission and neurodevelopment. As the large majority of individuals with 22q11DS have approximately 40 genes deleted in the TDR, the process of determining the specific factors involved in the causation of both physical and psychiatric/behavioral disorders i(Murphy & Owen, 2001; Prasad et al., 2008).2q11DS is highly variable and there is no evidence presently to suggest that the size of the underlying deletion has any influence on the physical or behavioral phenotype. However, given that 22q11DS is a genetic disorder with a high prevalence of psychiatric disorders, identification of susceptibility genes that may contribute to psychiatric disorders in individuals with 22q11DS, may be relevant to the non-deleted general population (Murphy & Owen, 2001; Prasad et al., 2008).

Although there is also accumulating evidence that the genetic basis of psychiatric disorders is heterogeneous, several promising genes that may have implications for the general population have been highlighted in recent studies.

Catechol-O-methyltransferase (COMT)

The gene for catechol-*O*-methyltransferase (COMT), an enzyme that degrades dopamine, and COMT deletion can be mapped to the 22q11 region (Grossman et al., 1992). COMT also appears to be a candidate gene that accounts for the higher levels of psychiatric morbidity seen in 22q11DS (Dunham et al., 1992; Craddock et al., 2006).

The gene coding for COMT encodes two distinct COMT isoenzymes: the membrane bound COMT (MB-COMT) and soluble COMT (S-COMT) (Bertocci et al., 1991). MB-COMT is primarily found in the brain, whereas S-COMT is found predominantly in peripheral tissue (Chen et al., 2004). The MB-COMT gene undergoes a naturally occurring polymorphism which has been reported to affect dopamine regulation (Akil et al., 2003). The polymorphism leads to an amino acid substitution (valine(Val) to methionine(Met)) at codon 158, whereas S-COMT has the same polymorphism at codon 108 (Lachman et al., 1996) and results in decreased thermostability and variable enzymatic activity. The Met allele of COMT has a lower activity compared with the Val allele, which results in the Met/Met variant of COMT displaying approximately 40% less enzymatic activity than the Val homozygote, whereas heterozygotes possess intermediate levels of activity (Chen et al., 2004). As a consequence of chromosomal deletion, 22q11DS individuals possess only one working copy of the COMT gene (i.e. they are haploin sufficient), which results in either a high-activity Val or low-activity Met isoform of the COMT enzyme.

Dopamine degradation in the prefrontal cortex (PFC) is mediated primarily through COMT activity (Tunbridge et al., 2004) while monoamine oxidase (MAO) and the dopamine transporter (DAT) are largely responsible for dopamine degradation in brain regions elsewhere (Chen et al., 2004). COMT activity attains maximal levels in early adulthood, especially in the PFC region, and COMT is also thought to modulate brain development and function (Hoglinger et al., 2004; Zinkstok et al., 2006). Indeed, disrupted dopaminergic neurotransmission has been reported in adults with 22q11DS but without a psychiatric history (Boot et al., 2008) and this may explain their vulnerability for psychiatric disorders.

However, recent evidence suggests that the association between COMT and the risk of schizophrenia may be more complex than Met/Val polymorphism alone and may involve an association with other loci within COMT, a gene-gene interaction or an environmental interaction (Caspi et al., 2005; Williams et al., 2007).

TBX1

The *TBX1* gene is a member of the T-box gene family of transcription factors with more than 20 genes identified in humans (Packham & Brook, 2003). It maps to chromosome 22q11.2 and is recognized to contribute to regulation of developmental processes and has a role in modulating defects arising from the pharyngeal apparatus (Stoller & Epstein, 2005; Aggarwal & Morrow, 2008).

In murine studies, *TBX1* mutations can cause gene-dosage-dependent pharyngeal arch and pouch abnormalities, particularly affecting the cardiac and vascular structures (Vitelli et al., 2002). *TBX1* may also contribute to brain development as it has been found to be expressed in the mouse brain, although this expression is limited to the vasculature in term embryos and adult mice (Paylor et al., 2006). This study further reported that *TBX1* also contributes to prepulse inhibition deficits in 22q11DS, which is considered an endophenotype of schizophrenia (Braff & Light, 2005).

Proline Dehydrogenase

Proline Dehydrogenase (PRODH) is a mitochondrial membrane enzyme that catalyses the first step in the proline degradation pathway (Bender et al., 2005). Proline is a non-essential amino-acid and may have a modulatory role in both glutaminergic and acetylcholinergic activity (Delwing et al., 2003). Hyperprolinemia has not only been documented in individuals with 22q11DS (McDermid & Morrow, 2002) but also in some individuals with schizophrenia (Liu et al., 2002).

As discussed above, in 22q11DS, there is an increased risk for psychosis and learning disability and recently, it has been shown in a hyperprolinemic mouse model, that an interaction between proline dehydrogenase and COMT could be involved in this phenotype (Raux et al., 2007). The authors characterized eight children with type I hyperprolinemia (HPI), an autosomal recessive disorder associated with reduced proline dehydrogenase activity and as a result, raised plasma proline levels. The children under investigation presented with learning disability and epilepsy and, in some cases, psychiatric features. Within the same study, the authors subsequently examined a cohort of 92 adults and adolescents with 22q11DS, of whom a subset had severe hyperprolinemia and demonstrated a phenotype distinguishable from that of other 22q11DS individuals and reminiscent of HPI. They conducted a forward stepwise multiple regression analysis and selected hyperprolinemia, psychosis and COMT genotype as independent variables influencing IQ; they found an inverse correlation between plasma proline level and IQ in the 22q11DS sample.

Neuropsychological

There is much inter-subject variability in 22q11DS cognitive functioning and most studies performed so far have been cross-sectional (Murphy & Scambler, 2005). Currently, work is underway to understand the process of cognitive development within the syndrome longitudinally. With regard to IQ, there is a discrepancy between VIQ and PIQ whereby VIQ exceeds the latter (Swillen et al., 1997). However, the degree of the discrepancy may not only predispose to learning difficulty but also to the development of psychosis. It has been reported that 22q11DS children and adolescents with significantly reduced adaptive skills and decreased VIQ are at higher risk for psychosis compared to their counterparts without psychotic symptoms (Debbane et al., 2006). Additionally, in the same study, psychotic probands were perceived by their parents as being more withdrawn and anxious/depressed, and psychotic manifestations were postulated to present earlier than typically reported in the literature.

School-aged children with 22q11DS have also been reported to demonstrate marked deficits in mathematics while showing normal scores for reading (decoding) and spelling (Moss et al., 1999; Woodin et al., 2001) and a similar profile has also been reported, as already established, in pre-school children (De Smedt et al., 2003). A more recent study (De Smedt et al., 2007) suggested that children with 22q11DS had preserved number reading abilities and retrieval of arithmetic facts, which, in combination, indicate that the verbal subsystem is not impaired in 22q11DS. It was further reported that 22q11DS children, by contrast, showed difficulties in number comparison, execution of a calculation strategy and word problem solving which all involve the semantic manipulation of quantities. The authors concluded that there is evidence for a specific deficit in the quantity subsystem in children with 22q11DS, which neuroanatomically suggests underlying abnormalities in the intraparietal sulcus.

Although reading decoding abilities are preserved in 22q11DS, reading comprehension skills are far less well developed (Antshel et al., 2005a; Antshel et al., 2008). Overall, mathematical abilities and reading comprehension and visuospatial, attention and executive function skills have all been reported to be well below average for age (Antshel et al., 2008).

There have been no studies comparing the cognitive and neuroanatomical characteristics of 22q11DS with other syndromes to determine if the cognitive strengths and difficulties and neuroanatomical differences associated with 22q11DS are specific to the syndrome. In view of this, we recently compared cognition and brain anatomy in 12 children with 22q11DS to 12 age-, gender- and FSIQ-matched children with Williams syndrome in order to investigate which cognitive and neuroanatomical features are specific to 22q11DS (Campbell et al., 2009). Williams syndrome was chosen as a comparator group since the literature suggests that both groups have areas of physical/cognitive/behavioral overlap but there has yet to be any direct comparison between the two groups. Despite being matched on FSIQ, the 22q11DS group showed significantly less impairment than those with Williams syndrome on tests of PIQ, while performing significantly worse on tasks measuring verbal, social and facial processing skills. Therefore, different neuropsychological profiles need to be considered when designing educational frameworks for working with such children.

Neuroimaging

The very high prevalence of cognitive, behavioral and psychiatric disorders in people with 22q11DS is likely to be caused by haploinsufficiency of one or more genes deleted on chromosome 22q11.2 and subsequent differences in brain maturation and neurotransmitter systems. Thus, 22q11DS provides a unique neurobiological template for understanding the evolution of such disorders through the assessment of influences on brain anatomy (Murphy & Owen, 2001).

Early neuroimaging studies in subjects with 22q11DS were mostly qualitative, and differences reported include an increased incidence of midline abnormalities such as white matter (WM) hyperintensities and septum pellucidum defects (Mitnick et al., 1994; van Amelsvoort et al., 2001) and there were additional reports of severe cerebral malformation (Kraynack et al., 1999; Bolland et al., 2000). Cortical malformations manifesting with polymicrogyria have also been found in individuals with 22q11DS (Robin et al., 2006) that is characterized by a thick cortex in association with shallow sulci, which is usually caused by ischemic injury during a critical period of embryonic brain maturation (Barkovich et al., 1995). Qualitative studies were an important first step and

subsequently led to quantitative studiesthat examined both gross anatomical changes and subtle cerebral anatomy differences.

Quantitative studies have found a significant reduction in total brain volume in children and adolescents with 22q11DS relative to normally developing subjects (of the order of 8.5–11%). The posterior brain structures in particular, such as the cerebellum, temporal and parietal lobes, are the main structures affected, with volume reduction being largely accounted for by decreased WM volume, with relatively preserved or enlarged frontal lobe tissue (Eliez et al., 2000; Kates et al., 2001; van Amelsvoort et al., 2001; van Amelsvoort et al., 2004b; Bish et al., 2006). In addition, in a study of 22q11DS children using a combination of automated voxel-based morphometry (VBM) and manual (hand tracing) magnetic resonance imaging (MRI) analytical techniques (Campbell et al., 2006), specific vulnerability of the cerebellar-cortical and fronto-striatal networks was reported.

Region-of-interest (ROI) studies have further supported a rostro-caudal gradient in volume reduction, whereby anterior regions are relatively preserved/enlarged while the structures in more posterior regions undergo volumetric reduction. Several structures exhibit such a gradient and include both WM and grey matter areas such as the caudate nucleus (Eliez et al., 2002; Kates et al., 2004; Campbell et al., 2006), corpus callosum (Antshel et al., 2005b; Machado et al., 2007), thalamus (Bish et al., 2004) and fusiform gyrus (Glaser et al., 2007).

In order to investigate neuroanatomical features that may be specific to 22q11DS, we recently compared the brain anatomy of 12 children with 22q11DS to 12 age-, gender- and FSIQ-matched children with Williams syndrome (Campbell et al., 2009). Despite similar overall brain volumes, there were significant differences in 22q11DS brain anatomy as reflected by regional differences where for instance, increased striatal volumes and reduced cerebellar volumes that may be specific to 22q11DS. Although quantitative neuroimaging studies have been carried out to identify cerebral volume alterations underlying the cognitive, behavioral, and psychiatric impairments associated with 22q11DS, only a limited number have focused on functional MRI (fMRI).

fMRI studies so far have targeted four areas recognized to be impaired in 22q11DS: arithmetic processing, face processing, executive function and working memory (Gothelf et al., 2008). In an fMRI study exploring the neural substrate underlying deficiencies in arithmetic reasoning using mathematical tasks of increasing difficulty (Eliez et al., 2001), the authors reported that children with 22q11DS showed more intensive and diffuse activity in the inferior parietal regions only during performance of difficult three-operand equations, whereas controls showed a similar pattern of parietal activation both during easy and difficult tasks. With regard to facial processing, two fMRI reports have been completed so far, with one study reporting less activation in both the right insula and frontal regions while increased activation was found in occipital regions (van Amelsvoort et al., 2006). However, when corrected for multiple comparisons, these results did not remain significant. A further study on facial processing which also assessed emotional processing in 22q11DS relative to healthy controls reported impaired face selectivity in the fusiform gyrus in the 22q11DS group but responses were intact to houses in both groups, with preserved selectivity in the parahippocampal gyrus (Andersson et al., 2008). The study also reported an abnormal repetition-suppression effect for fearful faces in the right amygdala, suggesting a lack of amygdala modulation by fear expression in 22q11DS.

In an fMRI study which assessed response inhibition with a Go/NoGo task, adolescents with 22q11DS were able to perform as well as typically developing controls and matched controls with developmental disability, although individuals with 22q11DS demonstrated more activation of the left inferior parietal regions (Gothelf et al., 2007b). Based

on their findings, the authors suggested that adolescents with 22q11DS compensate for executive dysfunction via recruitment of parietal regions.

Although there is increasing evidence that people with 22q11DS have regionally specific differences in brain anatomy, supra-regional brain systems often share common developmental influences (Cheverud, 1984) and perhaps especially affecting WM. If so, this suggests that people with 22q11DS may have differences in both brain 'connectivity' and in the microstructure of WM (Kiehl et al., 2009). Hence, interest has recently turned from assessing simple 'lesion of a region' to complementary approaches that investigate abnormalities in the 'connectivity' of neural systems using proxy measures of microstructural integrity acquired using diffusion tensor MRI (DT-MRI) (Basser et al., 1994a).

DT-MRI permits assessment of WM through a directional dependence of diffusion of water molecules termed anisotropy and is usually quantified through the calculation of fractional anisotropy (FA) (Pierpaoli & Basser, 1996). In the first DT-MRI study of people with 22q11DS (Barnea-Goraly et al., 2003), significantly reduced FA of WM was reported in frontal, parietal and temporal regions; and in WM tracts connecting the frontal and temporal lobes. This study was a valuable first step. However, both adults and children were combined as one group, and most of the cerebellum and brainstem was excluded from the analysis. A subsequent DT-MRI study of 22q11DS children and adolescents (Simon et al., 2005) replicated the earlier findings but additionally reported that the corpus callosum was posteriorly displaced in young people with 22q11DS. However, a healthy pediatric brain template was used for spatial normalization in this study which may present as a potential cause of misregistration. Given that the cerebellum and posterior brain structures have been previously implicated in volumetric MRI studies of 22q11DS, and that age and choice of brain template may confound measures of brain anatomy, it is important to examine WM anatomy in a relatively homogeneous group of children and adolescents with no clinically detectable comorbid psychiatric disorder and to include the posterior brain structures. Therefore, we recently examined the DT-MRI data of children and adolescents with 22q11DS but without psychiatric disorder relative to healthy controls. A customized brain template derived from all participants in the study was used for registration of FA maps and included the brainstem and cerebellum; after controlling for IQ, significantly lower FA was localized to interhemispheric and brainstem areas in addition to FA deficits in frontal, parietal and temporal lobe regions (Sundram et al., 2010).

In summary, while there is mounting evidence that people with 22q11DS have significant differences in the development of certain brain regions, 'connectivity' between specific brain regions may have a significant contribution to the evolution of the behavioral, psychiatric and cognitive deficits seen in 22q11DS; however, relatively few studies have directly examined the anatomy and microstructural integrity of WM.

TREATMENT AND INTERVENTION

There is currently no genetic cure for 22q11DS and treatment will be dependent on the underlying impairments or associated symptoms. As 22q11DS individuals have a variety of abnormalities in many organ systems, a multidisciplinary approach is required. A range of clinical assessments is required to identify areas of disability and subsequently, a treatment plan formulated to address these needs within the framework of a multidisciplinary team. Early identification of the syndrome (ideally genetic testing) is crucial to the institution of appropriate intervention.

A range of clinical specialties including psychiatry, psychology, speech and language therapy, cardiology, immunology, otolaryngology and clinical genetics should be involved in assessment and treatment

(Murphy, 2005). As a minimum, all suspected 22q11DS individuals should have detailed genetic, neuropsychological, psychiatric and speech and language assessments. Furthermore, educational provision is essential not only for the parents of children with 22q11DS but also mental health professionals working with such children, and children with the syndrome.

Physical

As cardiac abnormalities are common in 22q11DS, newborns will need to be evaluated by a cardiologist in the immediate postnatal phase. Newborns with the deletion may sometimes require early cardiac intervention for congenital heart anomalies due to the potentially life-threatening nature of such defects. Subsequently, a plastic surgeon and a speech therapist will need to evaluate cleft lip and/or palate and children will benefit from early intervention to aid with muscle strength and articulatory difficulties.

Additionally, it is vital that problems with the immune system are identified early so that special precautions may be taken with regard to blood transfusions or immunization with live vaccines. Thymus transplantation may also be considered to address absence of the thymus gland while bacterial infections are treated with antibiotics. In severe cases where immune system function is absent, bone marrow transplantation may be required. In the setting of hypoparathyroidism, which causes hypocalcaemia, this often requires lifelong vitamin D and calcium supplements.

Cognitive, linguistic, behavioral and psychiatric disorder

Given that the understanding of neuropsychological abnormalities in children with 22q11DS is gradually improving and that children with the syndrome continue to develop over the course of their lifetime, it is important that a dynamic approach is utilized to assess their abilities longitudinally. Some of the cognitive difficulties evident in 22q11DS include poor attentional and executive functioning, academic achievement and visuospatial skills which may manifest in disturbed behavior at home or at the school setting.

Difficult behaviors seen in children with 22q11DS (e.g. aggression, poor sleep patterns, temper outbursts) can be addressed with behavioral modification techniques, including the use of token economies and reward schemes (Murphy, 2005). Additionally, anger management programs and social skills training may also be effective. The majority of children with 22q11DS will be able to attend mainstream school, with varying degrees of additional intervention in the classroom. However, depending on their level of intellectual ability, a minority of children with 22q11DS will benefit by attending a school specializing in education for children with special needs, both in terms of their academic needs and their behavioral difficulties.

22q11DS is associated with high comorbidity with psychiatric disorders that are responsive to standard treatment protocols. Schizophrenia can be treated using conventional antipsychotic medication (Murphy et al., 1999; Bassett et al., 2003) while ADHD can be addressed by the use of psychostimulant medication such as methylphenidate. In future, larger controlled clinical trials are required to determine the relative efficacies of both pharmacological and psychological interventions in the treatment of schizophrenia, ADHD and other psychiatric disorders associated with 22q11DS.

of definitive predictive precursors to the subsequent development of prominent psychiatric disorders such as psychosis will help ensure the implementation of effective early interventions in such individuals.

Currently there is an increasing number of studies that have investigated the behavioral and psychiatric morbidity in either children or adults with 22q11DS. However, recruiting suitable control groups has always posed a challenge for researchers investigating syndromes associated with intellectual disability and developmental delays. Many studies have used normally developing children as control samples and, more recently, attempts have been made to use comparison samples that are functioning in the same general range of cognitive ability; however, even the latter practice may confound results, as the etiology of the intellectual disability may have an influence, for example, fetal alcohol syndrome vs more appropriate control samples such as Williams or Turner syndrome (Murphy et al., 2006).

Moreover, some of the completed studies have been hampered by methodological constraints such as sample heterogeneity, limited sample sizes and the lack of operationalized criteria for psychiatric diagnoses. Also, most of the research conducted in 22q11DS so far has relied on cross-sectional samples. The cross-sectional design of such studies may not have been able to detect within-individual change and thus may have inaccurately reported a more temporally stable developmental trajectory than is really occurring (Antshel et al., 2008). Therefore, future research will need to adopt a longitudinal design to assess not only variability within but also between subjects.

CONCLUSION

The key challenges for the future include identification of the neuroanatomical and genetic basis underlying the cognitive, psychiatric and behavioral disorders associated with 22q11DS. Furthermore, identification

REFERENCES

Abel, H.P. & O'Leary, D.J. (1997). 'Optometric findings in velocardiofacial syndrome' Optom Vis Sci 74(12): 1007–1010.

Aggarwal, V.S. & Morrow, B.E. (2008). 'Genetic modifiers of the physical malformations in velo-cardio-facial syndrome/DiGeorge syndrome' Dev Disabil Res Rev 14(1): 19–25.

Akil, M., Kolachana, B.S., Rothmond, D.A., Hyde, T.M., Weinberger, D.R. & Kleinman, J.E. (2003). 'Catechol-O-methyltransferase genotype and dopamine regulation in the human brain' J Neurosci 23(6): 2008–2013.

Andersson, F., Glaser, B., Spiridon, M., Debbane, M., Vuilleumier, P. & Eliez, S. (2008). 'Impaired activation of face processing networks revealed by functional magnetic resonance imaging in 22q11.2 deletion syndrome' Biol Psychiatry 63(1): 49–57.

Antshel, K.M., AbdulSabur, N., Roizen, N., Fremont, W. & Kates, W.R. (2005a). 'Sex differences in cognitive functioning in velocardiofacial syndrome (VCFS)' Dev Neuropsychol 28(3): 849–869.

Antshel, K.M., Conchelos, J., Lanzetta, G., Fremont, W. & Kates, W.R. (2005b). 'Behavior and corpus callosum morphology relationships in velocardiofacial syndrome (22q11.2 deletion syndrome)' Psychiatry Res 138(3): 235–245.

Antshel, K.M., Fremont, W. & Kates, W.R. (2008). 'The neurocognitive phenotype in velo-cardio-facial syndrome: a developmental perspective' Dev Disabil Res Rev 14(1): 43–51.

Antshel, K.M., Fremont, W., Roizen, N.J., Shprintzen, R., Higgins, A.M., Dhamoon, A. & Kates, W.R. (2006). 'ADHD, major depressive disorder, and simple phobias are prevalent psychiatric conditions in youth with velocardiofacial syndrome' J Am Acad Child Adolesc Psychiatry 45(5): 596–603.

Arnold, P.D., Siegel-Bartelt, J., Cytrynbaum, C., Teshima, I. & Schachar, R. (2001). 'Velo-cardio-facial syndrome: Implications of microdeletion 22q11 for schizophrenia and mood disorders' Am J Med Genet 105(4): 354–362.

Baker, K.D. & Skuse, D.H. (2005). 'Adolescents and young adults with 22q11 deletion syndrome: psychopathology in an at-risk group' Br J Psychiatry 186: 115–120.

Barkovich, A.J., Rowley, H. & Bollen, A. (1995). 'Correlation of prenatal events with the development of polymicrogyria' AJNR Am J Neuroradiol 16(4 Suppl): 822–827.

Barnea-Goraly, N., Menon, V., Krasnow, B., Ko, A., Reiss, A. & Eliez, S. (2003). 'Investigation of white matter structure in velocardiofacial syndrome: a diffusion tensor imaging study' Am J Psychiatry 160(10): 1863–1869.

Basser, P.J., Mattiello, J. & LeBihan, D. (1994a). 'Estimation of the effective self-diffusion tensor from the NMR spin echo' J Magn Reson B 103(3): 247–254.

Bassett, A.S., Chow, E.W., AbdelMalik, P., Gheorghiu, M., Husted, J., & Weksberg, R. (2003). 'The schizophrenia phenotype in 22q11 deletion syndrome' Am J Psychiatry 160(9): 1580–1586.

Bearden, C.E., Woodin, M.F., Wang, P.P., Moss, E., McDonald-McGinn, D., Zackai, E., Emannuel, B. & Cannon, T.D. (2001). 'The neurocognitive phenotype of the 22q11.2 deletion syndrome: selective deficit in visual-spatial memory' J Clin Exp Neuropsychol 23(4): 447–464.

Bender, H.U., Almashanu, S., Steel, G., Hu, C.A., Lin, W.W., Willis, A., Pulver, A. & Valle, D. (2005). 'Functional consequences of PRODH missense mutations' Am J Hum Genet 76(3): 409–420.

Bertocci, B., Miggiano, V., Da Prada, M., Dembic, Z., Lahm, H.W. & Malherbe, P. (1991). 'Human catechol-O-methyltransferase: cloning and expression of the membrane-associated form' Proc Natl Acad Sci U S A 88(4): 1416–1420.

Bish, J.P., Nguyen, V., Ding, L., Ferrante, S. & Simon, T.J. (2004). 'Thalamic reductions in children with chromosome 22q11.2 deletion syndrome' Neuroreport 15(9): 1413–1415.

Bish, J.P., Pendyal, A., Ding, L., Ferrante, H., Nguyen, V., McDonald-McGinn, D., Zackai, E. & Simon, T.J. (2006). 'Specific cerebellar reductions in children with chromosome 22q11.2 deletion syndrome' Neurosci Lett 399(3): 245–248.

Bolland, E., Manzur, A.Y., Milward, T.M. & Muntoni, F. (2000). 'Velocardiofacial syndrome associated with atrophy of the shoulder girdle muscles and cervicomedullary narrowing' Eur J Paediatr Neurol 4(2): 73–76.

Boot, E., Booij, J., Zinkstok, J., Abeling, N., de Haan, L., Baas, F., Linszen, D. & van Amelsvoort, T. (2008). 'Disrupted dopaminergic neurotransmission in 22q11 deletion syndrome' Neuropsychopharmacology 33(6): 1252–1258.

Botto, L.D., May, K., Fernhoff, P.M., Correa, A., Coleman, K., Rasmussen, S.A., Merritt, R.K., O'Leary, L.A., Wong, L.Y., Elixson, E.M., Mahle, W.T., & Campbell, R.M. (2003). 'A population-based study of the 22q11.2 deletion: phenotype, incidence, and contribution to major birth defects in the population' Pediatrics 112(1 Pt 1): 101–107.

Braff, D.L. & Light, G.A. (2005). 'The use of neurophysiological endophenotypes to understand the genetic basis of schizophrenia' Dialogues Clin Neurosci 7(2): 125–135.

Campbell, L.E., Daly, E., Toal, F., Stevens, A., Azuma, R., Catani, M. et al. (2006). 'Brain and behaviour in children with 22q11.2 deletion syndrome: a volumetric and voxel-based morphometry MRI study' Brain 129(Pt 5): 1218–1228.

Campbell, L.E., Stevens, A., Daly, E., Toal, F., Azuma, R., Karmiloff-Smith, A., Murphy, D.G. & Murphy, K.C. (2009). 'A comparative study of cognition and brain anatomy between two neurodevelopmental disorders: 22q11.2 deletion syndrome and Williams syndrome' Neuropsychologia 47(4): 1034–1044.

Carey, A.H., Kelly, D., Halford, S., Wadey, R., Wilson, D., Goodship J. et al. (1992). 'Molecular genetic study of the frequency of monosomy 22q11 in DiGeorge syndrome' Am J Hum Genet 51(5): 964–970.

Carlson, C., Papolos, D., Pandita, R.K., Faedda, G.L., Veit, S., Goldberg, R., Shprintzen, R., Kucherlapati, R. & Morrow, B. (1997). 'Molecular analysis of velo-cardio-facial syndrome patients with psychiatric disorders' Am J Hum Genet 60(4): 851–859.

Caspi, A., Moffitt, T.E., Cannon, M., McClay, J., Murray, R., Harrington, H., Taylor, A., Arseneault, L., Williams, B., Braithwaite, A., Poulton, R. & Craig, I.W. (2005). 'Moderation of the effect of adolescent-onset cannabis use on adult psychosis by a functional polymorphism in the catechol-O-methyltransferase gene: longitudinal evidence of a gene X environment interaction' Biol Psychiatry 57(10): 1117–1127.

Chen, J., Lipska, B.K., Halim, N., Ma, Q.D., Matsumoto, M., Melhem, S., Kolachana, B.S., Hyde, T.M., Herman, M.M., Apud, J., Egan, M. F., Kleinman, J.E. & Weinberger, D.R. (2004). 'Functional analysis of genetic variation in catechol-O-methyltransferase (COMT): effects on mRNA, protein, and enzyme activity in postmortem human brain' Am J Hum Genet 75(5): 807–821.

Cheverud, J.M. (1984). 'Quantitative genetics and developmental constraints on evolution by selection' J Theor Biol 110(2): 155–171.

Coberly, S., Lammer, E. & Alashari, M. (1996). 'Retinoic acid embryopathy: case report and review of literature' Pediatr Pathol Lab Med 16(5): 823–836.

Craddock, N., Owen, M.J. & O'Donovan, M.C. (2006). 'The catechol-O-methyl transferase (COMT) gene as a candidate for psychiatric phenotypes: evidence and lessons' Mol Psychiatry 11(5): 446–458.

De Smedt, B., Swillen, A., Devriendt, K., Fryns, J.P., Verschaffel, L. & Ghesquiere, P. (2007). 'Mathematical disabilities in children with velo-cardio-facial syndrome' Neuropsychologia 45(5): 885–895.

De Smedt, B., Swillen, A., Ghesquiere, P., Devriendt, K. & Fryns, J.P. (2003). 'Pre-academic and early academic achievement in children with velocardiofacial syndrome (del22q11.2) of borderline or normal intelligence' Genet Couns 14(1): 15–29.

Debbane, M., Glaser, B., David, M.K., Feinstein, C. & Eliez, S. (2006). 'Psychotic symptoms in children and adolescents with 22q11.2 deletion syndrome: Neuropsychological and behavioral implications' Schizophr Res 84(2–3): 187–193.

Delwing, D., Chiarani, F., Bavaresco, C.S., Wannmacher, C.M., Wajner, M. & Wyse, A.T. (2003). 'Proline reduces acetylcholinesterase activity in cerebral cortex of rats' Metab Brain Dis 18(1): 79–86.

Driscoll, D.A., Spinner, N.B., Budarf, M.L., McDonald-McGinn, D.M., Zackai, E.H., Goldberg, R.B., Shprintzen, R.J., Saal, H.M., Zonana, J., Jones, M.C. et al. (1992). 'Deletions and microdeletions of 22q11.2 in velo-cardio-facial syndrome' Am J Med Genet 44(2): 261–268.

Dunham, I., Collins, J., Wadey, R. & Scambler, P. (1992). 'Possible role for COMT in psychosis associated with velo-cardio-facial syndrome' Lancet 340(8831): 1361–1362.

Eliez, S., Barnea-Goraly, N., Schmitt, J.E., Liu, Y. & Reiss, A.L. (2002). 'Increased basal ganglia volumes in velo-cardio-facial syndrome (deletion 22q11.2)' Biol Psychiatry 52(1): 68–70.

Eliez, S., Blasey, C.M., Menon, V., White, C.D., Schmitt, J.E. & Reiss, A.L. (2001). 'Functional brain imaging study of mathematical reasoning abilities in velocardiofacial syndrome (del22q11.2)' Genet Med 3(1): 49–55.

Eliez, S., Schmitt, J.E., White, C.D. & Reiss, A.L. (2000). 'Children and adolescents with velocardiofacial syndrome: a volumetric MRI study' Am J Psychiatry 157(3): 409–415.

Feinstein, C., Eliez, S., Blasey, C. & Reiss, A.L. (2002). 'Psychiatric disorders and behavioral problems in children with velocardiofacial syndrome: usefulness as phenotypic indicators of schizophrenia risk' Biol Psychiatry 51(4): 312–318.

Fine, S.E., Weissman, A., Gerdes, M., Pinto-Martin, J., Zackai, E.H., McDonald-McGinn, D.M. & Emanuel, B.S. (2005). 'Autism spectrum disorders and symptoms in children with molecularly confirmed 22q11.2 deletion syndrome' J Autism Dev Disord 35(4): 461–470.

Gerdes, M., Solot, C., Wang, P.P., Moss, E., LaRossa, D., Randall, P., Goldmuntz, E., Clark, B.J., 3rd, Driscoll, D.A., Jawad, A., Emanuel, B.S., McDonald-McGinn, D.M., Batshaw, M.L. & Zackai, E.H. (1999). 'Cognitive and behavior profile of preschool children with chromosome 22q11.2 deletion' Am J Med Genet 85(2): 127–133.

Glaser, B., Schaer, M., Berney, S., Debbane, M., Vuilleumier, P. & Eliez, S. (2007). 'Structural changes to the fusiform gyrus: a cerebral marker for social impairments in 22q11.2 deletion syndrome?' Schizophr Res 96(1–3): 82–86.

Glover, T.W. (1995). 'CATCHing a break on 22' Nat Genet 10(3): 257–258.

Goldberg, R., Motzkin, B., Marion, R., Scambler, P.J. & Shprintzen, R.J. (1993). 'Velo-cardio-facial syndrome: a review of 120 patients' Am J Med Genet 45(3): 313–319.

Golding-Kushner, K.J., Weller, G. & Shprintzen, R.J. (1985). 'Velo-cardio-facial syndrome: language and psychological profiles' J Craniofac Genet Dev Biol 5(3): 259–266.

Goldmuntz, E., Clark, B.J., Mitchell, L.E., Jawad, A.F., Cuneo, B.F., Reed, L., McDonald-McGinn, D., Chien, P., Feuer, J., Zackai, E.H., Emanuel, B.S. & Driscoll, D.A. (1998). 'Frequency of 22q11 deletions in patients with conotruncal defects' J Am Coll Cardiol 32(2): 492–498.

Gothelf, D., Feinstein, C., Thompson, T., Gu, E., Penniman, L., Van Stone, E., Kwon, H., Eliez, S. & Reiss, A.L. (2007a). 'Risk factors for the emergence of psychotic disorders in adolescents with 22q11.2 deletion syndrome' Am J Psychiatry 164(4): 663–669.

Gothelf, D., Hoeft, F., Hinard, C., Hallmayer, J.F., Stoecker, J.V., Antonarakis, S.E., Morris, M.A. & Reiss, A.L. (2007b). 'Abnormal cortical activation during response inhibition in 22q11.2 deletion syndrome' Hum Brain Mapp 28(6): 533–542.

Gothelf, D., Presburger, G., Levy, D., Nahmani, A., Burg, M., Berant, M., Blieden, L.C., Finkelstein, Y., Frisch, A., Apter, A. & Weizman, A. (2004a). 'Genetic, developmental, and physical factors associated with attention deficit hyperactivity disorder in patients with velocardiofacial syndrome' Am J Med Genet B Neuropsychiatr Genet 126B(1): 116–121.

Gothelf, D., Presburger, G., Zohar, A.H., Burg, M., Nahmani, A., Frydman, M., Shohat, M., Inbar, D., Aviram-Goldring, A., Yeshaya, J., Steinberg, T., Finkelstein, Y., Frisch, A., Weizman, A. & Apter, A. (2004b). 'Obsessive-compulsive disorder in patients with velocardiofacial (22q11 deletion) syndrome' Am J Med Genet B Neuropsychiatr Genet 126B(1): 99–105.

Gothelf, D., Schaer, M. & Eliez, S. (2008). 'Genes, brain development and psychiatric phenotypes in velo-cardio-facial syndrome' Dev Disabil Res Rev 14(1): 59–68.

Grossman, M.H., Emanuel, B.S. & Budarf, M.L. (1992). 'Chromosomal mapping of the human catechol-O-methyltransferase gene to 22q11.1----q11.2' Genomics 12(4): 822–825.

Havkin, N., Tatum, S.A. & Shprintzen, R.J. (2000). 'Velopharyngeal insufficiency and articulation impair-ment in velo-cardio-facial syndrome: the influence of adenoids on phonemic development' Int J Pediatr Otorhinolaryngol 54(2–3): 103–110.

Henry, J.C., van Amelsvoort, T., Morris, R.G., Owen, M.J., Murphy, D.G. & Murphy, K.C. (2002). 'An investigation of the neuropsychological profile in adults with velo-cardio-facial syndrome (VCFS)' Neuropsychologia 40(5): 471–478.

Hoglinger, G.U., Rizk, P., Muriel, M.P., Duyckaerts, C., Oertel, W.H., Caille, I. & Hirsch, E.C. (2004). 'Dopamine depletion impairs precursor cell proliferation in Parkinson disease' Nat Neurosci 7(7): 726–735.

Kates, W.R., Burnette, C.P., Bessette, B.A., Folley, B.S., Strunge, L., Jabs, E.W. & Pearlson, G.D. (2004). 'Frontal and caudate alterations in velocardiofacial syndrome (deletion at chromosome 22q11.2)' J Child Neurol 19(5): 337–342.

Kates, W.R., Burnette, C.P., Jabs, E.W., Rutberg, J., Murphy, A.M., Grados, M., Geraghty, M., Kaufmann, W.E. & Pearlson, G.D. (2001). 'Regional cortical white matter reductions in velocardiofacial syndrome: a volumetric MRI analysis' Biol Psychiatry 49(8): 677–684.

Kelly, D., Goldberg, R., Wilson, D., Lindsay, E., Carey, A., Goodship, J., Burn, J., Cross, I., Shprintzen, R.J. & Scambler, P.J. (1993). 'Confirmation that the velo-cardio-facial syndrome is associated with haplo-insufficiency of genes at chromosome 22q11' Am J Med Genet 45(3): 308–312.

Kiehl, T.R., Chow, E.W., Mikulis, D.J., George, S.R. & Bassett, A.S. (2009). 'Neuropathologic features in adults with 22q11.2 deletion syndrome' Cereb Cortex 19(1): 153–164.

Kraynack, N.C., Hostoffer, R.W. & Robin, N.H. (1999). 'Agenesis of the corpus callosum associated with DiGeorge-velocardiofacial syndrome: a case report and review of the literature' J Child Neurol 14(11): 754–756.

Lachman, H.M., Papolos, D.F., Saito, T., Yu, Y.M., Szumlanski, C.L. & Weinshilboum, R.M. (1996). 'Human catechol-O-methyltransferase pharmacogenetics: description of a functional polymorphism and its potential application to neuropsychiatric disorders' Pharmacogenetics 6(3): 243–250.

Lajiness-O'Neill, R., Beaulieu, I., Asamoah, A., Titus, J.B., Bawle, E., Ahmad, S., Kirk, J.W. & Pollack, R. (2006). 'The neuropsychological phenotype of velocardiofacial syndrome (VCFS): relationship to psychopathology' Arch Clin Neuropsychol 21(2): 175–184.

Lalani, S.R., Safiullah, A.M., Fernbach, S.D., Harutyunyan, K.G., Thaller, C., Peterson, L.E., McPherson, J.D.

Gibbs, R.A., White, L.D., Hefner, M., Davenport, S.L., Graham, J.M., Bacino, C.A., Glass, N.L., Towbin, J.A., Craigen, W.J., Neish, S.R., Lin, A.E. & Belmont, J.W. (2006). 'Spectrum of CHD7 mutations in 110 individuals with CHARGE syndrome and genotype-phenotype correlation' Am J Hum Genet 78(2): 303–314.

Lichtner, P., Konig, R., Hasegawa, T., Van Esch, H., Meitinger, T. & Schuffenhauer, S. (2000). 'An HDR (hypoparathyroidism, deafness, renal dysplasia) syndrome locus maps distal to the DiGeorge syndrome region on 10p13/14' J Med Genet 37(1): 33–37.

Lindsay, E.A. (2001). 'Chromosomal microdeletions: dissecting del22q11 syndrome' Nat Rev Genet 2(11): 858–868.

Liu, H., Heath, S.C., Sobin, C., Roos, J.L., Galke, B.L., Blundell, M.L., Lenane, M., Robertson, B., Wijsman, E.M., Rapoport, J.L., Gogos, J.A. & Karayiorgou, M. (2002). 'Genetic variation at the 22q11 PRODH2/DGCR6 locus presents an unusual pattern and increases susceptibility to schizophrenia' Proc Natl Acad Sci U S A 99(6): 3717–3722.

Machado, A.M., Simon, T.J., Nguyen, V., McDonald-McGinn, D.M., Zackai, E.H. & Gee, J.C. (2007). 'Corpus callosum morphology and ventricular size in chromosome 22q11.2 deletion syndrome' Brain Res 1131(1): 197–210.

McDermid, H.E. & Morrow, B.E. (2002). 'Genomic disorders on 22q11' Am J Hum Genet 70(5): 1077–1088.

Merscher, S., Funke, B., Epstein, J.A., Heyer, J., Puech, A., Lu, M.M., Xavier, R.J., Demay, M.B., Russell, R.G., Factor, S., Tokooya, K., Jore, B.S., Lopez, M., Pandita, R.K., Lia, M., Carrion, D., Xu, H., Schorle, H., Kobler, J.B., Scambler, P., Wynshaw-Boris, A., Skoultchi, A.I., Morrow, B.E. & Kucherlapati, R. (2001). 'TBX1 is responsible for cardiovascular defects in velo-cardio-facial/DiGeorge syndrome' Cell 104(4): 619–629.

Mitnick, R.J., Bello, J.A. & Shprintzen, R.J. (1994). 'Brain anomalies in velo-cardio-facial syndrome' Am J Med Genet 54(2): 100–106.

Moss, E.M., Batshaw, M.L., Solot, C.B., Gerdes, M., McDonald-McGinn, D.M., Driscoll, D.A., Emanuel, B.S., Zackai, E.H. & Wang, P.P. (1999). 'Psychoeducational profile of the 22q11.2 microdeletion: A complex pattern' J Pediatr 134(2): 193–198.

Murphy, K.C. (2005). 'Annotation: velo-cardio-facial syndrome' J Child Psychol Psychiatry 46(6): 563–571.

Murphy, K.C., Jones, L.A. & Owen, M.J. (1999). 'High rates of schizophrenia in adults with velo-cardio-facial syndrome' Arch Gen Psychiatry 56(10): 940–945.

Murphy, K.C. & Owen, M.J. (2001). 'Velo-cardio-facial syndrome: a model for understanding the genetics and pathogenesis of schizophrenia' Br J Psychiatry 179: 397–402.

Murphy, K.C. & Scambler, P.J. (Eds) (2005). Velo-cardio-facial Syndrome: A Model for Understanding Microdeletion Disorders, Cambridge University Press.

Murphy, M.M., Mazzocco, M.M., Gerner, G. & Henry, A.E. (2006). 'Mathematics learning disability in girls with Turner syndrome or fragile X syndrome' Brain Cogn 61(2): 195–210.

Niklasson, L., Rasmussen, P., Oskarsdottir, S. & Gillberg, C. (2001). 'Neuropsychiatric disorders in the 22q11 deletion syndrome' Genet Med 3(1): 79–84.

Oskarsdottir, S., Vujic, M. & Fasth, A. (2004). 'Incidence and prevalence of the 22q11 deletion syndrome: a population-based study in Western Sweden' Arch Dis Child 89(2): 148–151.

Packham, E.A. & Brook, J.D. (2003). 'T-box genes in human disorders' Hum Mol Genet 12 Spec No 1: R37–44.

Papolos, D.F., Faedda, G.L., Veit, S., Goldberg, R., Morrow, B., Kucherlapati, R. & Shprintzen, R.J. (1996). 'Bipolar spectrum disorders in patients diagnosed with velo-cardio-facial syndrome: does a hemizygous deletion of chromosome 22q11 result in bipolar affective disorder?' Am J Psychiatry 153(12): 1541–1547.

Paylor, R., Glaser, B., Mupo, A., Ataliotis, P., Spencer, C., Sobotka, A., Sparks, C., Choi, C.H., Oghalai, J., Curran, S., Murphy, K.C., Monks, S., Williams, N., O'Donovan, M.C., Owen, M.J., Scambler, P.J. & Lindsay, E. (2006). 'Tbx1 haploinsufficiency is linked to behavioral disorders in mice and humans: implications for 22q11 deletion syndrome' Proc Natl Acad Sci U S A 103(20): 7729–7734.

Phelan, M.C. (2008). 'Deletion 22q13.3 syndrome' Orphanet J Rare Dis 3: 14.

Pierpaoli, C. & Basser, P.J. (1996). 'Toward a quantitative assessment of diffusion anisotropy' Magn Reson Med 36(6): 893–906.

Polanczyk, G., de Lima, M.S., Horta, B.L., Biederman, J. & Rohde, L.A. (2007). 'The worldwide prevalence of ADHD: a systematic review and metaregression analysis' Am J Psychiatry 164(6): 942–948.

Prasad, S.E., Howley, S. & Murphy, K.C. (2008). 'Candidate genes and the behavioral phenotype in 22q11.2 deletion syndrome' Dev Disabil Res Rev 14(1): 26–34.

Pulver, A.E., Nestadt, G., Goldberg, R., Shprintzen, R.J., Lamacz, M., Wolyniec, P.S., Morrow, B., Karayiorgou, M., Antonarakis, S.E., Housman, D. et al. (1994).

'Psychotic illness in patients diagnosed with velo-cardio-facial syndrome and their relatives' J Nerv Ment Dis 182(8): 476–478.

Raux, G., Bumsel, E., Hecketsweiler, B., van Amelsvoort, T., Zinkstok, J., Manouvrier-Hanu, S., Fantini, C., Breviere, G.M., Di Rosa, G., Pustorino, G., Vogels, A., Swillen, A., Legallic, S., Bou, J., Opolczynski, G., Drouin-Garraud, V., Lemarchand, M., Philip, N., Gerard-Desplanches, A., Carlier, M., Philippe, A., Nolen, M.C., Heron, D., Sarda, P., Lacombe, D., Coizet, C., Alembik, Y., Layet, V., Afenjar, A., Hannequin, D., Demily, C., Petit, M., Thibaut, F., Frebourg, T. & Campion, D. (2007). 'Involvement of hyperprolinemia in cognitive and psychiatric features of the 22q11 deletion syndrome' Hum Mol Genet 16(1): 83–91.

Robin, N.H. & Shprintzen, R.J. (2005). 'Defining the clinical spectrum of deletion 22q11.2' J Pediatr 147(1): 90–96.

Robin, N.H., Taylor, C.J., McDonald-McGinn, D.M., Zackai, E.H., Bingham, P., Collins, K.J., Earl, D., Gill, D., Granata, T., Guerrini, R., Katz, N., Kimonis, V., Lin, J. P., Lynch, D.R., Mohammed, S.N., Massey, R.F., McDonald, M., Rogers, R.C., Splitt, M., Stevens, C.A., Tischkowitz, M.D., Stoodley, N., Leventer, R.J., Pilz, D.T. & Dobyns, W.B. (2006). 'Polymicrogyria and deletion 22q11.2 syndrome: window to the etiology of a common cortical malformation' Am J Med Genet A 140(22): 2416–2425.

Ryan, A.K., Goodship, J.A., Wilson, D.I., Philip, N., Levy, A., Seidel, H., Schuffenhauer, S., Oechsler, H., Belohradsky, B., Prieur, M., Aurias, A., Raymond, F.L., Clayton-Smith, J., Hatchwell, E., McKeown, C., Beemer, F.A., Dallapiccola, B., Novelli, G., Hurst, J.A., Ignatius, J., Green, A.J., Winter, R.M., Brueton, L., Brondum-Nielsen, K., Scambler, P.J. et al. (1997). 'Spectrum of clinical features associated with interstitial chromosome 22q11 deletions: a European collaborative study' J Med Genet 34(10): 798–804.

Scambler, P.J. (2000). 'The 22q11 deletion syndromes' Hum Mol Genet 9(16): 2421–2426.

Scambler, P.J., Kelly, D., Lindsay, E., Williamson, R., Goldberg, R., Shprintzen, R., Wilson, D.I., Goodship, J.A., Cross, I.E. & Burn, J. (1992). 'Velo-cardio-facial syndrome associated with chromosome 22 deletions encompassing the DiGeorge locus' Lancet 339(8802): 1138–1139.

Scherer, N.J., D'Antonio, L.L. & Kalbfleisch, J.H. (1999). 'Early speech and language development in children with velocardiofacial syndrome' Am J Med Genet 88(6): 714–723.

Sedlackova, E. (1955). '[Insufficiency of palato laryngeal passage as a developmental disorder.]' Cas Lek Cesk 94(47–48): 1304–1307.

Shprintzen, R.J. (2000a). 'Velo-cardio-facial syndrome: a distinctive behavioral phenotype' Ment Retard Dev Disabil Res Rev 6(2): 142–147.

Shprintzen, R.J. (2000b). 'Velocardiofacial syndrome' Otolaryngol Clin North Am 33(6): 1217–1240, vi.

Shprintzen, R.J. (2008). 'Velo-cardio-facial syndrome: 30 Years of study' Dev Disabil Res Rev 14(1): 3–10.

Shprintzen, R., Goldberg, R., Golding-Kushner, K.J. & Marion, R.W. (1992). 'Late-onset psychosis in the velo-cardio-facial syndrome' Am J Med Genet 42(1): 141–142.

Shprintzen, R.J., Goldberg, R.B., Lewin, M.L., Sidoti, E.J., Berkman, M.D., Argamaso, R.V. & Young, D. (1978). 'A new syndrome involving cleft palate, cardiac anomalies, typical facies, and learning disabilities: velo-cardio-facial syndrome' Cleft Palate J 15(1): 56–62.

Shprintzen, R.J., Goldberg, R.B., Young, D. & Wolford, L. (1981). 'The velo-cardio-facial syndrome: a clinical and genetic analysis' Pediatrics 67(2): 167–172.

Shprintzen, R.J., Higgins, A.M., Antshel, K., Fremont, W., Roizen, N. & Kates, W. (2005). 'Velo-cardio-facial syndrome' Curr Opin Pediatr 17(6): 725–730.

Simon, T.J., Ding, L., Bish, J.P., McDonald-McGinn, D.M., Zackai, E.H. & Gee, J. (2005). 'Volumetric, connective, and morphologic changes in the brains of children with chromosome 22q11.2 deletion syndrome: an integrative study' Neuroimage 25(1): 169–180.

Solot, C.B., Gerdes, M., Kirschner, R.E., McDonald-McGinn, D.M., Moss, E., Woodin, M., Aleman, D., Zackai, E.H. & Wang, P.P. (2001). 'Communication issues in 22q11.2 deletion syndrome: children at risk' Genet Med 3(1): 67–71.

Staple, L., Andrews, T., McDonald-McGinn, D., Zackai, E. & Sullivan, K.E. (2005). 'Allergies in patients with chromosome 22q11.2 deletion syndrome (DiGeorge syndrome/velocardiofacial syndrome) and patients with chronic granulomatous disease' Pediatr Allergy Immunol 16(3): 226–230.

Stoller, J.Z. & Epstein, J.A. (2005). 'Identification of a novel nuclear localization signal in Tbx1 that is deleted in DiGeorge syndrome patients harboring the 1223delC mutation' Hum Mol Genet 14(7): 885–892.

Strong, W.B. (1968). 'Familial syndrome of right-sided aortic arch, mental deficiency, and facial dysmorphism' J Pediatr 73(6): 882–888.

Sundram, F., Campbell, L.E., Azuma, R., Daly, E., Bloemen, O.J.N., Barker, G.J., Chitnis, X., Jones, D.K., van Amelsvoort, T. & Murphy, K.C. (2010). 'White matter microstructure in 22q11 deletion syndrome: a pilot diffusion tensor imaging and voxel-based morphometry study of children and adolescents' Journal of Neurodevelopmental Disorders 2(2): 77–92.

Swillen, A., Devriendt, K., Ghesquiere, P. & Fryns, J.P. (2001). 'Children with a 22q11 deletion versus children with a speech-language impairment and learning disability: behavior during primary school age' Genet Couns 12(4): 309–317.

Swillen, A., Devriendt, K., Legius, E., Eyskens, B., Dumoulin, M., Gewillig, M. & Fryns, J.P. (1997). 'Intelligence and psychosocial adjustment in velocardiofacial syndrome: a study of 37 children and adolescents with VCFS' J Med Genet 34(6): 453–458.

Swillen, A., Devriendt, K., Legius, E., Prinzie, P., Vogels, A., Ghesquiere, P. & Fryns, J.P. (1999a). 'The behavioural phenotype in velo-cardio-facial syndrome (VCFS): from infancy to adolescence' Genet Couns 10(1): 79–88.

Swillen, A., Vandeputte, L., Cracco, J., Maes, B., Ghesquiere, P., Devriendt, K. & Fryns, J.P. (1999b). 'Neuropsychological, learning and psychosocial profile of primary school aged children with the velo-cardio-facial syndrome (22q11 deletion): evidence for a nonverbal learning disability?' Child Neuropsychol 5(4): 230–241.

Tunbridge, E.M., Bannerman, D.M., Sharp, T. & Harrison, P.J. (2004). 'Catechol-o-methyltransferase inhibition improves set-shifting performance and elevates stimulated dopamine release in the rat prefrontal cortex' J Neurosci 24(23): 5331–5335.

van Amelsvoort, T., Daly, E., Henry, J., Robertson, D., Ng, V., Owen, M., Murphy, K.C. & Murphy, D.G. (2004b). 'Brain anatomy in adults with velocardiofacial syndrome with and without schizophrenia: preliminary results of a structural magnetic resonance imaging study' Arch Gen Psychiatry 61(11): 1085–1096.

van Amelsvoort, T., Daly, E., Robertson, D., Suckling, J., Ng, V., Critchley, H., Owen, M.J., Henry, J., Murphy, K.C. & Murphy, D.G. (2001). 'Structural brain abnormalities associated with deletion at chromosome 22q11: quantitative neuroimaging study of adults with velo-cardio-facial syndrome' Br J Psychiatry 178: 412–419.

van Amelsvoort, T., Schmitz, N., Daly, E., Deeley, Q., Critchley, H., Henry, J., Robertson, D., Owen, M., Murphy, K.C. & Murphy, D.G. (2006). 'Processing facial emotions in adults with velo-cardio-facial syndrome: functional magnetic resonance imaging' Br J Psychiatry 189: 560–561.

Vissers, L.E., van Ravenswaaij, C.M., Admiraal, R., Hurst, J.A., de Vries, B.B., Janssen, I.M., van der Vliet, W.A., Huys, E.H., de Jong, P.J., Hamel, B.C., Schoenmakers, E.F., Brunner, H.G., Veltman, J.A. & van Kessel, A.G. (2004). 'Mutations in a new member of the chromodomain gene family cause CHARGE syndrome' Nat Genet 36(9): 955–957.

Vitelli, F., Morishima, M., Taddei, I., Lindsay, E.A. & Baldini, A. (2002). 'Tbx1 mutation causes multiple cardiovascular defects and disrupts neural crest and cranial nerve migratory pathways' Hum Mol Genet 11(8): 915–922.

Vogels, A., Verhoeven, W.M., Tuinier, S., DeVriendt, K., Swillen, A., Curfs, L.M. & Frijns, J.P. (2002). 'The psychopathological phenotype of velo-cardio-facial syndrome' Ann Genet 45(2): 89–95.

Vorstman, J.A., Morcus, M.E., Duijff, S.N., Klaassen, P.W., Heineman-de Boer, J. A., Beemer, F.A., Swaab, H., Kahn, R.S. & van Engeland, H. (2006). 'The 22q11.2 deletion in children: high rate of autistic disorders and early onset of psychotic symptoms' J Am Acad Child Adolesc Psychiatry 45(9): 1104–1113.

Wang, P.P., Woodin, M.F., Kreps-Falk, R. & Moss, E.M. (2000). 'Research on behavioral phenotypes: velo-cardiofacial syndrome (deletion 22q11.2)' Dev Med Child Neurol 42(6): 422–427.

Williams, H.J., Owen, M.J. & O'Donovan, M.C. (2007). 'Is COMT a susceptibility gene for schizophrenia?' Schizophr Bull 33(3): 635–641.

Woodin, M., Wang, P.P., Aleman, D., McDonald-McGinn, D., Zackai, E. & Moss, E. (2001). 'Neuropsychological profile of children and adolescents with the 22q11.2 microdeletion' Genet Med 3(1): 34–39.

Zagursky, K., Weller, R.A., Jessani, N., Abbas, J. & Weller, E.B. (2006). 'Prevalence of ADHD in children with velocardiofacial syndrome: a preliminary report' Curr Psychiatry Rep 8(2): 102–107.

Zhang, Z., Cerrato, F., Xu, H., Vitelli, F., Morishima, M., Vincentz, J., Furuta, Y., Ma, L., Martin, J.F., Baldini, A. & Lindsay, E. (2005). 'Tbx1 expression in pharyngeal epithelia is necessary for pharyngeal arch artery development' Development 132(23): 5307–5315.

Zinkstok, J., Schmitz, N., van Amelsvoort, T., de Win, M., van den Brink, W., Baas, F. & Linszen, D. (2006). 'The COMT val158met polymorphism and brain morphometry in healthy young adults' Neurosci Lett 405(1–2): 34–39.

12

Cornelia de Lange, Cri du Chat, and Rubinstein–Taybi Syndromes

Chris Oliver, Kate Arron, Laurie Powis, & Penny Tunnicliffe

INTRODUCTION

In this chapter we describe three comparatively rare genetic syndromes associated with
intellectual disability. The rarity of genetic
syndromes impacts significantly on the
amount of information that is available, the
likelihood that clinicians will have experience of a syndrome and the quality of advice
and intervention that may be offered. This is
perhaps unsurprising given the number of
genetic syndromes associated with intellectual disability but is nevertheless of concern.
This problem is mirrored in the volume of
research on individual rare syndromes. In
this respect many rare syndromes acquire the
status of orphan diseases, with little or no
information on cognitive and behavioural
phenomenology and even less on interventions. However, this does not mean that study
of these rare syndromes will not be as revealing as research into more common conditions
such as autism spectrum disorders (ASD).
Demonstrations of associations between specific cognitive impairments and social or

behavioural difference and disorder in rare
syndromes can usefully inform the conceptualization of gene–brain–behaviour–environment pathways, regardless of which syndrome
the pathway was identified in.

The syndromes selected for review in this
chapter have been chosen because, although
they are rare, they demonstrate different
pathways to behavioural outcomes, how different domains of behavioural phenotypes
may be dissociated within syndromes and
variability of behavioural outcome within
broad classes of behaviour. The three syndromes show striking differences in their
phenomenology and in doing so demonstrate
the importance of careful description and
conceptualization of cognitive and behavioural features. Levels of repetitive behaviours differ across the three syndromes, as
does the specificity of these behaviours.
Social impairment at either end of a sociability continuum is evident when comparing
Cornelia de Lange and Rubinstein–Taybi
syndromes, with equally important clinical
implications. An expressive communication

deficit is shared by those with cri du chat and Cornelia de Lange syndromes but the cause appears quite different. Cornelia de Lange and Rubinstein–Taybi syndromes both evidence age-related change but in different ways. Finally, in each syndrome genetic variability of differing forms is associated with a physical and behavioural phenotype to differing degrees. These shared and unique patterns of characteristics illustrate why the study of syndromes, regardless of their rarity, is of importance.

CORNELIA DE LANGE SYNDROME

Prevalence

Cornelia de Lange syndrome (CdLS) was first described by Brachmann in 1916 and subsequently by Cornelia de Lange in 1933. Beck (1976), investigating CdLS in a Danish population, found a prevalence rate of 0.5 per 100,000 with no gender differences, an estimate confirmed by Beck and Fenger (1985) for the years 1967–1982. Beck suggests that the findings are likely to demonstrate minimum figures due to problems associated with diagnosis and Opitz (1985) has proposed that a birth prevalence of approximately 1 per 10,000 is more accurate. With the identification of a more mild phenotype it is increasingly likely that the prevalence will be higher than 1 per 50,000.

Physical characteristics

Common physical characteristics of people with CdLS include low birth weight, growth retardation, upper limb abnormalities, excessive hair growth and a small head circumference (Ireland et al., 1993; Jackson et al., 1993; Kline et al., 1993, 2007a). Distinctive facial characteristics, considered important diagnostic features, include confluent, archshaped eyebrows, thin down-turned lips, long eyelashes, a

low hair line, low-set ears and a long philtrum (Ireland et al., 1993; Jackson et al., 1993; Kline et al., 1993, 2007a).

Health problems and sensory deficits are common in people with CdLS. Gastrooesophageal reflux and other gastrointestinal disorders are prominent (Hall et al., 2008; Luzanni et al., 2003) with reports of an association between reflux and behavioural disorder including self-injury (Luzanni et al., 2003; Moss et al., 2005). Other health problems include heart and kidney malformations in approximately 40% (Selicorni et al., 2005), dental problems, otitis media (Hall et al., 2008; Kline et al., 2007b; Marchisio et al., 2008) and ophthalmic and orthopaedic disorders (Levin et al., 1990; Nallasamy et al., 2006; Roposch et al., 2004; Wygnanski-Jaffe et al., 2005). Health problems are related to low mood (Berg et al., 2007) and warrant repeated assessment with aggressive intervention. Sensorineural hearing loss is reported with loss of or compromised neural function evident in 20%; conductive hearing loss due to middle ear effusion is also reported in 60% of individuals. This hearing loss may contribute to the delayed onset of speech and is correlated with severity of intellectual disability (Marchisio et al., 2008). Slow peripheral nerve transmission speeds have been recorded (Oliver et al., 2007) and may be related to anecdotally reported high pain thresholds.

Diagnosis and genetic studies

The first genetic mutation was mapped to 5p13.1, the site of the *NIPBL* gene (Krantz et al., 2004; Tonkin et al., 2004). *NIPBL* is the human homolog of the *Drosophila Nipped-B* gene. The exact function of the human *NIPBL* gene product, delangin, is unknown. To date, *NIPBL* mutations have been identified in between 20 and 50% of individuals diagnosed with CdLS (Krantz et al., 2004; Miyake et al., 2005; Tonkin et al., 2004). Some studies have identified a difference between those individuals with and those without the mutation with regard to stature, degree of disability and presence of limb abnormalities (Miyake et al., 2005). However, these findings need to be confirmed.

Subsequent to the discovery of the mutation of the *NIPBL* gene, additional mutations of the *SMC3* gene on chromosome 10 (Deardorff et al., 2007) and X-linked *SMC1* gene (Musio et al., 2006) have been identified and are reported to account for 5% of cases. All three genes are involved in the structure and regulation of the cohesion complex (Lui & Krantz, 2008). In total these three gene mutations still only account for approximately 55% of those diagnosed with CdLS; consequently, it is likely that further gene mutations will be discovered. Recently, a knockout mouse model of the *NIPBL* mutation has been described with features similar to those observed in CdLS, including small size, craniofacial anomalies, heart defects, hearing abnormalities, microbrachycephaly and behavioural disturbances, particularly stereotyped circling behaviour (Kawauchi et al., 2009).

INTELLECTUAL DISABILITY

CdLS was thought initially to be always associated with severe intellectual disability. However, a number of case studies report intelligence scores in the mild intellectual disability and normal range (Moeschler & Graham, 1993; Stefanatos & Musikoff, 1994). It is now recognized that the range of IQ scores seen in CdLS is wide, although most individuals diagnosed with CdLS do have intellectual disabilities.

Surveys of the range of intellectual disability indicate that most individuals have moderate to profound intellectual disabilities. Beck (1987) used the Vineland Social Maturity Scale to assess psychosocial skills in 36 individuals with CdLS. Social Quotients indicated that 50% of participants had profound disabilities, 14% had severe, 17%

moderate, 6% had mild intellectual disabilities and 14% of participants scored within the borderline or normal range. These figures are supported by a postal survey of 49 children and adults with CdLS, with 43% of participants showing profound intellectual disabilities, 20% severe, 18% moderate, 8% mild and 10% borderline disabilities (Berney et al., 1999). Oliver et al. (2008), using the Vineland Adaptive Behavior Scales, reported 50% of individuals with CdLS as having a profound intellectual disability; this figure was 24, 15 and 11 for severe, moderate and mild, respectively. An extensive study of development in CdLS using formal IQ testing has shown that the mean intelligence test score in people with CdLS falls within the moderate intellectual disability range (Kline et al., 1993). Results from the standardized tests indicated within-participant strengths in the areas of perceptual organization and visuospatial memory, recorded by scores of up to three standard deviations (SDS) higher than in other domains. The cognitive profile of CdLS warrants further research.

Communication

Prevalence figures of individuals with CdLS who do not develop speech are highly variable across a number of studies, with reports ranging from 30 to 85% (Beck, 1987; Goodban, 1993; Johnson et al., 1976; Sarimski, 1997). This variability is likely to reflect an increase in the number of mildly affected individuals being identified. Approximately 70% of individuals with CdLS display communication skills under the age equivalent of 3 years, 44% of individuals aged over 2 years are able to combine two or more words and only 4% develop language skills in the normal range (Beck, 1987; Goodban, 1993). These findings indicate that speech is compromised and, when evident, might develop later than expected. Using the Pre-Verbal Communication Scale (PVCS; Kiernan & Reid, 1987) Sarimski

(1997) reports that only 11% of 27 individuals used conventional words, suggesting that Goodban's findings might be an overestimate of the frequency of verbal communication. In addition to a delay in expressive communication, Goodban (1993) also states that expressive communication is notably inferior to the comprehension of language. Kline et al. (1993) report similar results, and this observation was confirmed in a case-control study by Oliver et al. (2008) using the communication subdomain scores of the Vineland Adaptive Behavior Scale.

Interestingly, Sarimski (2002) has demonstrated that the mean frequency of nonverbal communicative acts is significantly lower in individuals with CdLS compared to individuals with cri du chat and Down syndromes. According to Basile et al. (2007), 14 out of 56 individuals with CdLS aged between 1 and 31 years showed no verbal or non-verbal acts of intentional communication. These findings suggest that *both* verbal and non-verbal communication skills are compromised in CdLS. However, non-verbal communication is not completely absent. Sarimski (1997) reported the use of non-verbal communication to get other people's attention and to indicate needs. Similar results are described by Oliver et al. (2006). These findings suggest that rather than demonstrating socially directed communication, communication in CdLS is largely restricted to personal demands. This lack of socially directed communication is also evident in individuals who do develop expressive communication skills. Anecdotally, it has been reported that those individuals who do develop speech are often reluctant to use their communication (Goodban, 1993). Johnson et al. (1976) reported that although two out of nine participants had developed speech, both of them were quiet and spoke very little. Moss et al. (2008) anecdotally report a reluctance to communicate in their study. Selective mutism appears to be common and an experimental study by Richards et al. (2009) has demonstrated anxiety-related behaviours at the point

of social engagement in ongoing social interactions.

Social interaction

Johnson et al. (1976) describe a 'paucity of social response' in seven out of nine participants with CdLS. More recently, several studies have provided evidence to suggest that Johnson et al.'s (1976) proposal of compromised social interaction skills in CdLS may have been accurate. According to Sarimski (1997), 50% of individuals with CdLS have 'abnormal' eye contact and 54% were described by parents as being 'isolated as if in their own world'. Sarimski also described a lack of appropriate facial expression, with 48.1% of parents reporting difficulty in recognizing their child's feelings. Collis et al. (2008) report lower levels of facial expression of positive affect in CdLS. Oliver et al. (2006) also described a high prevalence of socially avoidant behaviors such as 'wriggling out of physical contact' and 'attempting to move away during an interaction' in 14 out of 16 individuals with CdLS. Further detailed study of early social interaction skills has demonstrated that poor eye contact in the first year of life may be predictive of social relatedness in later years (Sarimski, 2007). Interestingly, Sarmiski reported that 46.2% of individuals with CdLS were overfriendly with strangers. This indicates that some individuals with CdLS do engage in social interaction, although their understanding of what this involves might be limited.

Autism spectrum disorders

A number of studies have demonstrated that CdLS is associated with autism spectrum disorder-like impairments, including poor expressive communication skills, social deficits, repetitive behaviours and a preference for rigid routines (Bay et al., 1993; Beck, 1987; Goodban, 1993; Hyman et al., 2002; Johnson et al., 1976;

Sarimski, 1997). Several studies have reported a heightened probability of autism in affected individuals. A revised version of the Autism Behavior Checklist (Krug et al., 1980), Berney et al. (1999) report that 53% of 49 participants with CdLS showed the combination of impaired social interaction and communication skills and the presence of repetitive behaviour to a degree that might suggest the presence of autism (pronounced in 37% and mild in 16%). Similar findings are reported by Bhuiyan et al. (2006), who demonstrate that 17 out of 19 individuals with CdLS scored at a similar level to that expected in individuals with autistic spectrum disorders on the Diagnostic Interview for Social and Communication Disorders (Wing, 2002). On the autistic-relating subscale of the Developmental Behaviour Checklist (Einfield & Tonge, 1995), 15 of the 19 participants scored at a similar level to that expected in individuals with autistic spectrum disorder. Using the Autism Diagnostic Observation Schedule (ADOS), Moss et al. (2008) demonstrated that 61.8% of individuals with CdLS score above the cut-off for autism compared to 39.7% of individuals with cri du chat syndrome (CdCS). These groups were comparable for degree of disability and receptive language skills. Specifically, the CdLS group evidenced a greater level of impairment on the communication domain of the assessment in comparison to the CdCS group. This difference was replicated using the Social Communication Questionnaire, and was not accounted for by degree of disability, receptive language skills or the difficulties of identifying autism in individuals with profound intellectual disability. Finally, Oliver et al. (2008) reported that 32.1% of 54 individuals with CdLS scored within the 'severe autism' category of the CARS (Childhood Autism Rating Scale), compared to only 7.1% of a matched control group of individuals with intellectual disability, suggesting that the relationship between CdLS and ASD is not solely accounted for by associated degree of disability. Oliver et al. (2005)

also report that those with CdLS scored significantly higher on the Autism Screening Questionnaire (Berument et al., 1999) than individuals with cri du chat and Prader–Willi syndromes, with a mean score comparable to that of a group with fragile X syndrome. In combination, these findings indicate that features of ASD are evident in CdLS at a level similar to that seen in a syndrome considered high risk for ASD and that these features are independent of degree of intellectual disability.

Repetitive behaviour and restricted interests

Johnson et al. (1976) found seven out of nine (78%) individuals with CdLS to show stereotyped behaviour, with topographies including hand posturing, hand regard, body twirling and body turning. In a postal survey of 88 individuals with CdLS, 57% had shown stereotyped behaviour in the last month (Hyman et al., 2002) and Sarimski (1997) used the Behavior Problems Inventory to assess the presence of five topographies of stereotyped behaviour in 27 individuals with CdLS. The most common topographies included body rocking (56% of participants), bizarre body positioning (52%) and turning objects (44%). Comparative figures for individuals with intellectual disability range from 54 to 80%, suggesting that the prevalence of stereotyped behaviour in general intellectual disability populations is similar to those seen in CdLS. In a detailed study of repetitive behaviour across syndromes, Moss et al. (2009) showed that individuals with CdLS demonstrate significantly more tidying-up and lining-up behaviours than at least two other syndrome groups.

Hyman et al. (2002) report that 87.5% of affected individuals engage in at least one form of compulsive-like behaviour. Ordering and checking compulsions were the most common forms and a greater number of compulsive behaviours were reported within older participants. Comparative figures for individuals with severe and profound intellectual disabilities using the same measure have demonstrated that compulsions are shown by 40% of individuals in this population. Oliver et al. (2008) demonstrated that individuals with CdLS display significantly more compulsive behaviour than a comparison group of individuals matched on a number of demographic variables, including degree of disability, and that this difference could not be accounted for by the presence of ASD.

Self-injurious behaviour

Although results have varied, research examining self-injury in children and adults with CdLS suggests higher prevalence rates (ranging from 16 to 64%) for self-injurious behaviour (SIB) within CdLS (Beck, 1987; Berney et al., 1999; Gualtieri, 1990; Hyman et al., 2002; Sarimski, 1997). In a case-control study, Oliver et al. (2009) reported a prevalence of 55.6%, which was not statistically significantly higher than that for a matched contrast group (41.3%). This suggests that while the prevalence of SIB is high in CdLS, it does not fulfil the definition of a component of a behavioural phenotype.

Topographies of SIB reported in the early literature did not indicate a distinct topography associated with CdLS. Gualtieri (1990) reported that the most common topographies of self-injury include biting (shown by 27% of individuals), hitting (20%), hair pulling (15%), head banging (11%) and picking (10%). Berney et al. (1999) also found that finger biting and head banging was common in CdLS. In a recent case-control study, Oliver et al. (2009) described higher levels of more mild forms of self-injury. During natural observations, Sloneem et al. (2009) report higher levels of biting and more self-injury directed towards the hands.

Self-injurious behaviour within CdLS has often been described as severe. Bryson et al. (1971) and Dosseter et al. (1991) presented case studies on individuals with CdLS causing significant injury to themselves, resulting in repeated infections, excessive bleeding and loss of tissue and requiring stitching and hospitalization. Restraints and protective devices are also commonly required to manage self-injury in CdLS and the 38–40% prevalence rate for the use of restraints reported in the literature (Berney et al., 1999; Gualtieri, 1990) is three times that seen in general intellectual disability populations (Oliver et al., 1987). Individuals also express a preference for wearing restraints and a fear of being without restraints (Dossetor et al., 1991; Shear et al., 1971). Incorporating a measure of self-restraint, Hyman et al. (2002) found that 53% of participants displayed at least one form of self-restraint, with a significant association between self-injury and self-restraint. A number of authors have also suggested that self-injurious behaviour in CdLS has a 'compulsive quality' (Bryson et al., 1971; Shear et al., 1971). Hyman et al. (2002) demonstrated that compulsive behaviour was associated with self-injury and self-restraint.

Intervention, experimental and natural observation studies on self-injury in CdLS have shown that the environment can influence and shape behaviour in CdLS. Three separate studies have demonstrated the effect of environmental variables such as adult attention on the expression of self-injury and the effectiveness of behavioural treatment programmes in reducing the self-injury shown by three children with CdLS (Bay et al., 1993; Menolascino et al., 1982; Singh & Pulman, 1979). The data from these three studies support the notion that self-injury in individuals with CdLS can be influenced by factors in the environment. However, common problems observed with each of these studies are the use of small sample sizes and the reporting of only positive cases. Using larger samples of individuals with CdLS, Moss et al. (2005), Oliver et al. (2006) and Sloneem et al. (2009) all showed an association between environmental events and self-injury in a proportion of participants with CdLS.

Detailed observations of individuals with CdLS have shown that those who self-injure may seek restraint and that distress is evident when physical restraints are removed (Shear et al., 1971). Hyman et al. (2002) found that 53% of individuals with CdLS showed at least one form of self-restraint. The most common forms included holding onto other people to seek restraint, holding or squeezing objects, wrapping in clothing and holding hands together. The association between SIB and self-restraint was significant and those individuals showing SIB and self-restraint were also significantly more likely to display compulsions, which suggested that for some individuals with CdLS, self-injurious behaviour may become difficult to control and regulate.

Physical aggression

Hyman et al. (2002) found that 43% of individuals with CdLS had shown physical aggression in the last month and, in a study by Gualtieri (1990), 41% of 138 participants had shown physical aggression during the course of their lives. Berney et al. (1999) found a prevalence rate of 10% in a sample of 49 individuals for daily physical aggression. Hyman et al. (2002) report prevalence figures of 53% for destruction of property, Berney et al. (1999) found 33% of participants to show aggression towards objects, and Gualtieri (1990) reports destructiveness in 10% of individuals with CdLS. In the observational case-control study by Sloneem et al. (2009), aggregated 'other challenging behaviour', which included aggression and destruction of the environment, was reported to be significantly lower in the CdLS group than that seen in a matched contrast group.

Hyperactivity

Berney et al. (1999) found that 74% of children and adults with CdLS displayed at least one of four symptoms of hyperactivity,

including having an attention span of less than 10 minutes, 'fidgetiness', 'chaos creating' activity and overactivity. Gualtieri (1990) reported hyperactivity in 13% and non-compliance in 10% of individuals with CdLS. In a clinical sample of individuals with CdLS, Greenberg and Coleman (1973) found hyperactivity in 64% of participants, although it is not clear how behaviour was measured in the study. In the Luzanni et al. (2003) study, hyperactivity was reported to be related to gastro-oesophageal reflux.

Conclusion

Health problems are very common in CdLS and impact significantly on well-being and behaviour. Regular assessment with appropriate intervention should be of high priority. The majority of individuals with CdLS fall within the mild to profound range of intellectual disability. There are deficits evident in communication skills compared to overall ability, with a discrepancy between expressive and receptive language skills. Expressive language delay is common and hearing impairments should be treated at the earliest opportunity.

An increasing number of studies have investigated the association between CdLS and autism spectrum disorders. Individuals with CdLS are often described as showing poor social skills and 'disliking' social contact, showing communication deficits, excessive shyness and selective mutism and displaying specific forms of repetitive behaviour. More recent studies have highlighted that a heightened probability of ASD is evident, but the nature of the impairments and the relationship with ASD warrants further research.

Prevalence rates for topographies of challenging behaviour, including self-injury, aggression and hyperactivity, in CdLS are high but case-control studies reveal that SIB is no more common than might be expected when degree of intellectual and physical disability are controlled for, and aggression and destruction of the environment are less common than expected. Several studies of the severity of self-injurious behaviour have indicated that when individuals with CdLS show self-injury, they can cause significant harm. This observation is supported by data that show that self-injury is associated with self-restraint and compulsive behaviour. Additionally, self-injury appears to be associated with pain and discomfort that result from the health conditions associated with CdLS. Observational and intervention studies have shown that self-injury can be associated with environmental events, suggesting that for a proportion of people behavioural approaches might be effective. Assessment and intervention protocols for self-injury and other challenging behaviours in CdLS are available in Oliver et al. (2003) and Oliver et al. (2009a).

CRI DU CHAT SYNDROME (5P DELETION SYNDROME)

Prevalence

First described by Lejeune in 1963, cri du chat syndrome (CdCS), which takes its name from the 'cat-like cry', is often referred to as 5p deletion syndrome and chromosome 5 short-arm deletion. The prevalence has been estimated at 1 in 50,000 live births and although the exact gender ratio is unknown, the syndrome is thought to be approximately twice as prevalent in females as in males (Dykens et al., 2000; Niebuhr, 1978; Van Buggenhout et al., 2000).

Physical characteristics

The distinctive cat cry is a core feature of the syndrome and is still regarded as an important early clinical diagnostic feature in most but not all individuals (Mainardi et al., 2006). The cry is thought to be caused by anomalies of the larynx (small, narrow and diamond-shaped) and of the epiglottis, which is usually small and hypotonic (Niebuhr, 1978). Many infants tend to be of low birth weight, and low weight usually persists in the first 2 years of life for both sexes (Marinescu et al., 2000). Feeding difficulties are common and the associated failure to thrive may be the initial clinical presentation. Some infants may require tube feeding, a process which may have to continue for several years. Gastro-oesophageal reflux is common in CdCS during the first years of life (Collins & Eaton-Evans, 2001). Other health problems include respiratory tract infections, otitis media and dental problems. Many individuals with CdCS are prone to developing a curvature of the spine (congenital scoliosis) and this can become more apparent with advancing age. Some of the most frequently cited physically defining features of CdCS are facial characteristics, including microcephaly, rounded face, widely spaced eyes, downward slanting of palpebral fissures, low-set ears, broad nasal ridge and short neck (Dykens et al., 2000; Marinescu et al., 1999). Studies indicate that facial features change over time: specifically, lengthening of the face and coarsening of features (Mainardi et al., 2006).

Diagnosis and genetic studies

CdCS is predominantly caused by a partial deletion on the tip of the short arm of chromosome 5 (with a critical region of 5p15). The size of the deletion ranges from the entire short arm to the region 5p15 (Overhauser et al., 1994). A de novo deletion is present in 85% of cases; 10–15% are familial, with more than 90% due to a parental translocation and 5% due to an inversion of 5p (Van Buggenhout et al., 2000). Niebuhr first identified the specific chromosomal region implicated in the syndrome as 5p15.1-5p15.3, using cytogenetic analysis (Niebuhr, 1978). More recent work has mapped specific critical areas within this region as being responsible for the expression of the core clinical features of the syndrome. For example, the characteristic high-pitched 'cat-like' cry from which the syndrome derives its name has been mapped to the proximal part of 5p15.3, the speech delay to the distal part of 5p15.3 and severe intellectual impairment to 5p15.2 (Overhauser et al., 1994). This distinctive cry is considered the most prominent clinical diagnostic feature of the syndrome (Mainardi et al., 2006). Although relatively rare, CdCS represents the most common deletion syndrome in humans (Cornish et al., 2001).

Intellectual disability

Early reports on CdCS suggested that profound intellectual disability was a common feature of the syndrome (Niebuhr, 1978). More recent, albeit limited, research data indicate that there is a wider range of cognitive ability (Cornish, 1996; Cornish et al., 1999). Progression in motor development is delayed and adaptive behaviour within the domains of socialization, communication, daily living skills and motor skills does not appear to show any significant strengths or weakness, although no contrast groups have been employed in research studies (Cornish et al., 1998). Marinescu et al. (1999) found no association between the size of the genetic deletion on 5p and scores on the Vineland Adaptive Behavior Scales. However, individuals with translocations have been found to have a more severe developmental delay, heightened social withdrawal and more autistic-like features than those with deletions (Dykens & Clarke, 1997; Mainardi et al., 2006; Sarimski, 2003).

Communication

Most individuals with CdCS have minimal or no speech (Cornish et al., 1999), whereas receptive language tends to be significantly more developed than expressive and written skills. According to Sohner and Mitchell (1991), indicators of compromised expressive communication are present prior to speech development and can be evidenced by a delayed pattern of babbling development during infancy. Some researchers have suggested that the delay in the development of verbal communication is a result of congenital abnormalities of the larynx and delay in motor skills. It seems likely that problems in expressive language in CdCS are related to the physical abnormalities in the larynx and delayed motor skill development (Manning, 1977; Niehbur, 1978; Sohner & Mitchell, 1991). Receptive language skills are considered a marked strength within the cognitive profile of CdCS (Cornish & Munir, 1998; Cornish et al, 1998).

Although language development is significantly delayed, a number of studies have demonstrated that there is potential for verbal and non-verbal communication to develop in affected individuals. Wilkins et al. (1980) reported that of 65 individuals with CdCS, 16.9% had a vocabulary of more than 100 words and were able to form sentences of three or more words. A further 36.9% had limited but useful single-word vocabularies. According to Cornish and Pigram (1996), only 25.9% of 27 individuals with CdCS used speech to communicate their needs, whereas 55% were able to communicate using non-verbal methods. Importantly, Sarimski (2002) has demonstrated that in addition to using verbal and non-verbal communication to indicate their needs, individuals with CdCS engage in significantly more *socially directed* communication than individuals with Cornelia de Lange syndrome, performing at a level that is similar to individuals with Down syndrome. However, Cornish and Pigram (1996) report that only 7.4% of individuals use any formal signs, the majority (48.1%) using idiosyncratic gestures. These findings demonstrate a clear capacity and motivation to engage in communication in individuals with CdCS, and stress the importance of early intervention and introduction of sign language in order to further encourage the development of communication in individuals with CdCS.

Social interaction

Social interaction skills are considered to be a relative strength of individuals with CdCS (Carlin, 1983), who are often noted to have a 'friendly and happy' demeanour. However, empirical evidence for this is inconsistent. In a sample of 20 individuals with CdCS, no significant differences were identified between scores on the socialization domain of the Vineland Adaptive Behavior Scales compared to communication, motor and self-help domains (Cornish et al., 1998). These scores were in line with global mental age equivalence scores. Using the same assessment with a larger sample of 100 individuals with CdCS, Dykens, Hodapp and Rosner (1999; cited in Dykens et al., 2000) demonstrated that scores on the socialization domain were significantly higher than those on the remaining three domains. Specifically, Dykens et al. (1999) report that over 80% of individuals with the syndrome show an interest in their peers and the actions of other people.

Autism spectrum disorders

ASD-like behaviours are not commonly reported in CdCS. Moss et al. (2008) used the ADOS to assess 23 children and found a prevalence rate of 31.4% for autism and 60.7% for ASD. These rates were 0 and 8.7%, respectively, for scores on the Social Communication Questionnaire (Rutter et al., 2003). The prevalence of autism in CdCS reported in this study is well within the range reported for the wider intellectual disability population (up to 40%), suggesting that there is not a strong association between autism and CdCS. The heightened proportion of individuals scoring above the cut-off for ASD is likely to be accounted for by the associated intellectual disability and the difficulties in identifying ASD in individuals with severe to profound intellectual disability (Moss & Howlin, 2009).

Sleep problems

Few studies have extensively evaluated sleep problems in CdCS; however, a small number of research studies and anecdotal reports suggest that sleep difficulties are a significant problem in this group. Cornish and Pigram (1996) reported that 30% of 20 children with CdCS had an irregular sleep pattern. In a larger study, Cornish et al. (2003) reported that sleep problems were reported by parents to be a severe cause of concern in 50% of individuals. More recently, Maas et al. (2009) reported that nine out of 30 (30%) individuals with CdCS fulfilled criteria for either a mild or a severe sleep problem. Analysis of specific behaviours related to sleep disturbance demonstrated that 'head banging during sleep or when going off to sleep', 'needs security object', 'gagging or choking' and 'appears more active during daytime than other individuals' occurred significantly more often in the CdCS group compared to individuals with Down syndrome.

Repetitive behaviour and restricted interests

Repetitive behaviours are generally less common in CdCS than in other genetic syndromes. However, Moss et al. (2009) report that an attachment to specific objects is a marked characteristic of the syndrome. Occurring at a clinically significant level in over 67% of individuals, the frequency of this behaviour is significantly higher in CdCS than in four other genetic syndromes, comprising Angelman, Cornelia de Lange, fragile X and Prader–Willi syndromes, and in comparison to individuals with intellectual disability of heterogeneous cause. This behaviour differs from that commonly seen in ASD as it is usually focused on one specific item (as opposed to a class of items) and the item may change over time. Additionally, the behaviour tends to become less marked with age.

Self-injurious behaviour

Although self-injurious and aggressive behaviour appear to be common behavioural features of CdCS (Collins & Cornish, 2002; Cornish & Pigram, 1996; Cornish et al., 1998; Dykens & Clarke, 1997), there are very few studies examining prevalence and phenomenology. Using a questionnaire study to examine the prevalence of self-injury in children and young adults, Collins and Cornish (2002) found that 92% of the sample (n = 66) exhibited some form of SIB. Other questionnaire studies have found prevalence rates of self-injury to be approximately 70% (Cornish & Pigram, 1996; Dykens & Clarke, 1997). Collins and Cornish (2002) found the most common forms of SIB to be head banging, hitting the head against body parts and self-biting. In a recent questionnaire study, Arron et al. (in review) found SIB to be present in 76.8% of their sample and common topographies included pulling self, hitting self with objects, hitting self with body and rubbing or scratching self.

Physical aggression

Cornish and Pigram (1996) found the prevalence of aggressive behaviour in a sample of 27 individuals with CdCS to be 52%. Collins and Cornish (2002) found a higher occurrence, with 88% of the sample exhibiting aggressive behaviour and the most common topographies were hitting, pulling hair, biting and pinching. Arron et al. (in review) found aggressive behaviour to be present in 70% of the sample, with an odds ratio of 2.7 compared to a matched contrast group. Currently, there are no observational studies that have examined challenging behaviour in CdCS. In addition, there are no studies that have examined the correlates of challenging behaviour in CdCS, even though the syndrome is known to be associated with some risk markers for the development of challenging behaviour (e.g. severe level of intellectual disability, expressive communication impairments).

Hyperactivity

Hyperactivity is a commonly reported feature of CdCS. Findings vary from reports of no increase in level of activity (Baird et al., 2001) to 90% prevalence rates of hyperactivity (Cornish et al., 1998), with clinical hyperactivity (attention-deficit/hyperactivity disorder; ADHD) reported to be more prevalent in CdCS than in an intellectual disability comparison group (Cornish & Bramble, 2002). Of the studies assessing behaviour empirically, only two studies incorporated rating scales (Aberrant Behavior Checklist) normed on a population of people with intellectual disabilities (Clarke & Boer, 1998; Dykens & Clarke, 1997) and the most frequently used measure, although not consistently (in its entirety), was the Vineland Adaptive Behavior Scales (VABS), on which 'overly active', 'poor concentration and attention' and 'too impulsive' are individual items within the Externalizing Behavior factor. Only two studies have included comparison groups of different genetic syndromes and data from other studies of community and institutionally residing individuals (Clarke & Boer, 1998) and published normative data from two heterogeneous groups (Dykens & Clarke, 1997), reducing comparable data.

The available literature documents the contrast between the high prevalence of ADHD and the commonly identified immobility and severe motor delay (Cornish & Bramble, 2002). The reported high prevalence of ADHD-like phenomena has raised concerns regarding both the restrictions that may place on cognitive and emotional development (Cornish et al., 1998) and its role in determining familial stress (Cornish & Bramble, 2002). This highlights a need to clarify prevalence, as recommendations are being made for a relatively low threshold for medication in treating hyperactivity in these individuals (Dykens & Clarke, 1997), even though there is some evidence identifying intensive behaviour modification as the most effective intervention (Wilkins et al., 1980).

Conclusion

CdCS is characterized by notable variability, largely determined by the position and size of the deletion on the short arm of chromosome 5. There are a number of physical disorders and health problems that impinge on speech production and early feeding problems that warrant investigation and treatment. Scoliosis may increase with age.

Self-injurious and aggressive behaviour can be problematic and the prevalence is high for both these behaviours. There is anecdotal evidence that these behaviours may be related to an interaction between the compromised expressive language and impulsivity (Oliver et al., 2009b). An inability to produce speech clear enough to be understood may combine with an aversion to delay for reinforcement to evoke episodes of self-injurious or aggressive behaviour. If this analysis is correct, then a combination of implementing augmentative communication systems and behavioural management might be effective. Sleep problems in CdCS also warrant investigation, as this can act as a significant source of stress for families and can also impinge on daytime alertness and thus compromise educational opportunities.

The attachment to objects seen in CdCS is striking because the level of other repetitive behaviours is generally low. This profile of an isolated form of repetitive behaviour is unusual and warrants more detailed description and analysis.

RUBINSTEIN–TAYBI SYNDROME

Prevalence and diagnosis

Rubinstein–Taybi syndrome (RTS) was first described by Rubinstein and Taybi in 1963. Although prevalence estimates have varied, it is thought that the most accurate estimate is approximately 1 in 125,000 live births (Hennekam et al., 1990a). However, as the syndrome is diagnosed primarily by clinical characteristics, it is possible that a mild presentation may be undiagnosed. The syndrome affects males and females equally (Hennekam et al., 1990a) and has been reported in all racial groups, although diagnosis may be more difficult when the individual is non- Caucasian due to a less-marked facial expression (Rubinstein, 1990).

Genetic studies

RTS is a multiple congenital anomaly syndrome. The first genetic anomaly identified comprised break points, mutations and microdeletions within chromosome 16p13.3 (Lacombe et al., 1992). Following this discovery, Petrij et al. (1995) reported a molecular analysis that highlighted a gene located on chromosome 16p13.3 that coded for the cyclic AMP response element binding protein (CBP). It was shown subsequently that, in addition to the chromosomal rearrangements of chromosome 16, RTS can also arise from heterozygous point mutations in the CBP gene itself. More recently, the E1A binding protein p300 has also implicated in the syndrome (Roelfsema et al., 2005). The p300 is located at 22q13.2 and is a homolog of CBP. Both are highly related in both structure and function and, consequently, mutations in p300 can also result in RTS.

Despite these findings, chromosomal or molecular abnormalities are only found in around 55% of those diagnosed (Hennekam, 2006) and diagnosis is still based largely on the identification of clinical characteristics. At present, reports suggest that clinical differences between those diagnosed with the syndrome with and without deletions are minimal (Bartsch et al., 1999).

Physical characteristics

The physical characteristics associated with RTS have been well-documented and include broad thumbs and toes, postnatal growth retardation, small head, excessive hair growth and dental abnormalities (Hennekam & Van Doorne, 1990; Hennekam et al., 1990; Partington, 1990; Rubinstein, 1990; Stevens 1990a, 1990b).

The classical facial appearance in RTS is also well-documented. Descriptions typically include a prominent 'beaked' nose, eyes with downward slanting palpebral fissures, long eyelashes, thick eyebrows, and a small mouth (Hennekam, 2006; Hennekam et al., 1990b; Rubinstein, 1990; Stevens et al., 1990a; Wiley et al., 1990). Allanson (1990) reviewed those with the diagnosis of various ages and provided evidence for a changing facial phenotype. In newborns, characteristics include a prominent forehead, upward slanting palpebral fissures and a straight nose with upturned tip and fleshy bridge. Over time, palpebral fissures change to a downward slant, the nose becomes more prominent, narrow and sharp and facial asymmetry becomes more common.

Health and medical difficulties are common in RTS. Feeding and related weight difficulties have been reported repeatedly in the literature. During infancy, feeding difficulties include poor appetite, vomiting and failure to thrive (Hennekam et al. 1990b). However, a study by Stevens et al. (1990b) shows poor weight gain does not persist and reports that school-age boys and adolescent girls tend to be overweight for their height. Furthermore, they noted that several individuals had vigorous appetites. Consequently, comparisons regarding weight gain have recently been made between some individuals with RTS and individuals who have Prader–Willi syndrome (Hennekam, 2006).

Other health problems include renal abnormalities, constipation, vertebral anomalies, recurrent upper respiratory infections, undescended testes in males, and keloids (Rubinstein, 1990). Importantly, it has been documented that individuals with RTS may suffer an increased risk of developing cancer (Hennekam, 2006). Therefore, attention to early symptoms indicative of tumours is important to ensure early intervention. In addition, studies have reported a high incidence of bone fractures in the group (Hennekam et al., 1990b; Rubinstein, 1990). It has been suggested that the cause of this may be the combination of slender bones and hypotonia with the unsteady stiff gait common in the syndrome (Hennekam et al., 1990b).

Cognitive and adaptive ability

Intellectual disability is an associated characteristic of RTS. However, estimates made regarding the degree of intellectual disability have varied across studies. An early study of those with the diagnosis who were institutionalized suggested an average IQ of 36, with a range of 15–59 (Padfield et al., 1968). However, more recently, an IQ estimate of 51, with a range of 30–79, in those who are not institutionalized has been suggested (Stevens et al., 1990a). It is thought that most individuals lie within the mild to moderate range.

At present, a limited number of studies have documented cognitive or adaptive development in this syndrome. One questionnaire study by Stevens et al. (1990a) involving 50 individuals with RTS outlined difficulties with speech and reading skills. Speech difficulties were found in 90% of individuals and included problems such as speech delay and articulation difficulties. Reading ability was documented in 28 of the individuals and 67% could read. However, in all but three of these individuals reading was at an age equivalent level of only 7 years or younger. A later description of the syndrome by Baxter and Beer (1992) made the suggestion that 'speech is one of the slowest developmental areas for the child with this syndrome' (Baxter & Beer, 1992: p. 453). The authors also made the suggestion that receptive language may be superior to expressive language in the syndrome and highlighted the possibility that some individuals may not develop speech.

A number of studies have demonstrated a short attention span in individuals with RTS.

Stevens et al (1990a) conducted a questionnaire study and showed that 'poor concentration' was one of the most frequently reported problems, occurring in 76% of the individuals. Similarly, a survey conducted by Hennekam et al. (1992) using the Child Behaviour Checklist (CBCL) showed that 76% of individuals 'can't concentrate', one of the most frequently reported problems. Interestingly, problems with attention measured by the CBCL have recently been replicated in a questionnaire study by Galéra et al. (2009). Individuals with RTS were scored significantly higher on the item 'can't concentrate/pay attention for long' than a control group matched for age, gender and developmental level. Such findings warrant consideration, given the possible impact on educational and behavioural interventions.

Descriptions outlining the level of self-help skills possessed by individuals with RTS are limited. However, Baxter and Beer (1992) mention that individuals will require assistance with their skills but 'can become self sufficient in most self help areas, for example, feeding, dressing, toileting etc' (Baxter & Beer, 1992: p. 454). It may, however, be important to note that self-help ability may be affected by the tendency for individuals with RTS to experience motor difficulties. Goots and Liemohn (1977) assessed three children with RTS and described them as having more difficulties in planning motor acts and executing locomotor and oculomotor acts compared to individuals with nonspecific intellectual disability. Similarly, studies using the CBCL found individuals with RTS were frequently reported as 'poorly coordinated' and 'clumsy' (Galéra et al., 2009; Hennekam et al., 1992)

Although research outlining the cognitive ability of RTS is limited, it has begun to make links between the molecular abnormalities and cognitive dysfunction found in RTS. The CREB binding protein implicated in RTS has been shown to underlie long-term memory formation (Bartsch et al., 1995;

Bourtchuladze et al. 1994; Yin et al, 1994) and consequently it has been suggested that cognitive deficits may occur as a result of impaired long-term memory formation (D'Arcangelo & Curran, 1995; Weeber & Sweatt, 2002).

Social behaviour

One of the most frequently documented characteristics in RTS is the ability to initiate and maintain social contact despite cognitive delay (Hennekam, 2006). Reports have described repeatedly those with RTS as 'happy', 'loving', 'friendly' individuals who 'know no strangers' and 'love adult attention' (Baxter & Beer, 1992; Hennekam, 2006; Padfield et al., 1968; Rubinstein & Taybi, 1963; Stevens et al., 1990a). Importantly, in one follow-up study of eight individuals with RTS it was documented that 'all individuals had social behaviour that allowed them to live in small group homes or their parents' home' (Partington, 1990: p. 67).

More recently it has been suggested that the social communication and social competency skills shown in RTS are higher than in those with other causes of intellectual disability (Hennekam et al., 1992). Findings from comparison studies appear to support this assertion. Gotts and Liemohn (1977) compared three children with RTS to others with non-specific intellectual disability and found that children with RTS were friendlier and more readily accepted social contacts. Similarly, a recent questionnaire study found that individuals with RTS scored significantly lower on a scale assessing 'reduced contact or social interest' than a matched control group. Findings indicated better social contact and social interest along several items, including quality of eye contact, acceptance of physical contact, initiating play with other children, and looking up when spoken to (Galéra et al, 2009).

Repetitive behaviour

Reports have indicated that individuals with RTS often show stereotyped movements such as spinning, rocking, and hand flapping. It has also been reported that approximately three-quarters of children with RTS show behaviours such as insistence on sameness and adherence to routine (Hennekam et al., 1992; Stevens et al., 1990a). Furthermore, in a recent comparison study using a matched control group, it was reported that individuals with RTS displayed significantly higher levels of repetitive behaviours. More specifically, individuals with RTS were scored higher on questionnaire items assessing 'flaps arms/hands when excited', 'makes odd/fast movements with fingers/hands' and 'extremely pleased by certain movements/ keeps doing them' (Galéra et al., 2009).

In addition to the social behaviour and repetitive behaviours noted as part of the syndrome, other behaviours have also been documented. Studies have highlighted stubbornness, impulsivity, hyperactivity and sleeping difficulties (Gotts & Liemohn, 1977; Hennekam et al., 1992, Rubinstein & Taybi, 1963; Stevens, 2007; Stevens et al., 1990a). Other findings include a tendency for individuals to be 'more emotional', excitable and show a dislike for loud noises (Gotts & Liemohn, 1977; Stevens et al., 1990a).

Although the majority of reports describe children as generally happy and friendly, it has been suggested that individuals with RTS may experience behaviour change with age. Sudden mood changes, temper tantrums, uncertain behaviours and aggression have been identified in individuals during early adulthood (Hennekam, 2006). Case studies of older individuals appear to support this assertion. Verhoeven et al. (2008) described the case of a male aged 35 who was referred due to lowered mood, temper tantrums, anxieties and worrying. Similarly, Hellings et al. (2002) described a 39-year-old female who presented with mood lability and aggressive outbursts.

Conclusion

Rubinstein–Tabyi syndrome (RTS) is characterized by a distinct profile of physical, cognitive and behavioural features. Physical difficulties include failure to thrive in infancy, heightened risk of obesity in adolescence, heightened risk of cancer, respiratory infections, renal abnormalities and constipation. Furthermore, motor difficulties in this syndrome may impact on individuals' self-help abilities; however, with the right support and training, individuals with RTS usually become sufficient in most self-help areas.

In terms of cognitive ability, individuals with RTS generally have a mild to moderate intellectual disability, and are likely to have slower development of speech relative to other abilities. Short attention span, impulsivity and hyperactivity are likely to impact on an individual's ability to perform successfully both inside and outside of educational settings, and this should be taken into account when planning educational and behavioural strategies. Long-term memory may also be impaired in individuals with RTS, so the use of strategies to help overcome memory difficulties (e.g. visual timetables, repeated exposure to information) may be essential in this syndrome.

A behavioural characteristic that is common in RTS is that individuals are more likely to want to engage in social communication than those with other syndromes. One danger is that this desire for social contact coupled with intellectual disability may leave an individual vulnerable to social exploitation. It may be important to monitor the types of social interaction that an individual with RTS engages in, especially in the case of those individuals who are older and more independent. Individuals with RTS are also likely to engage in a range of repetitive behaviours and are likely to prefer predictable routines. Parents and clinicians should be aware that changes with age are reported in RTS such as increased mood swings, temper tantrums and aggressive outbursts and prepare for these changes. Future research should focus on why these changes with age occur.

ACKNOWLEDGEMENTS

Jane Waite, Jo Moss and Cheryl Burbidge each made a significant contribution to the material in this chapter via their doctoral work. Funding for work on the syndromes, including review of the literature, was provided by Cerebra, The Big Lottery and The Cornelia de Lange Syndrome Foundation (UK and Ireland).

REFERENCES

Allanson, J.E. (1990) 'Rubinstein-Taybi syndrome: the changing face', *American Journal of Medical Genetics, Supplement*, 6: 38–41.

Arron, K., Oliver, C., Berg, K., Moss, J., & Burbidge, C. (in review) 'Delineation of behavioural phenotypes in genetic syndromes. 2. Prevalence, phenomenology and correlates of self-injurious and aggressive behaviour', *Journal of Intellectual Disability Research*.

Baird, S.M., Campbell, D., Ingram, R., & Gomez, C. (2001) 'Young children with cri du chat: genetic, developmental and behavioral profiles' *Infant-Toddler Intervention: The Transdisciplinary Journal*, 11: 1–14.

Bartsch, D., Ghirardi, M., Skehel, P.A., Karl, K.A., Herder, S.P., Chen, M., Bailey, C.H., & Kandel, E.R. (1995) 'Aplysia CREB2 represses long term facilitation: relief of repression converts transient facilitation into long-term functional and structural change', *Cellular and Molecular Life Sciences*, 83: 979–992.

Bartsch, O., Wagner, A., Hinkel, G.K., Krebs, P., Stumm, M., Schmalenberger, B., Böhm, S., Balci, S., & Majewskiv., F. (1999) 'FISH studies in 45 patients with Rubinstein–Taybi syndrome: deletions associated with polysplenia, hypoplastic left heart and death in infancy', *European Journal of Human Genetics*, 7: 748–756.

Basile, E., Villa, L., Selicorni, A., & Molteni, M. (2007) 'The behavioural phenotype of Cornelia de Lange syndrome: a study of 56 individuals', *Journal of Intellectual Disability Research*, 51: 671–681.

Baxter, G. & Beer, J. (1992) 'Rubinstein Taybi syndrome', *Psychological Reports*, 70: 451–456.

Bay, C., Mauk, J., Radcliffe, J., & Kaplan, P. (1993) 'Mild Brachmann–Delange syndrome—delineation of the clinical phenotype, and characteristic behaviors in a 6-year-old boy', *American Journal of Medical Genetics*, 47(7): 965–968.

Beck, B. (1976) 'Epidemiology of Cornelia de Lange's syndrome', *Acta Paediatrica Scandinavia*, 65: 631–638.

Beck, B. (1987) 'Psycho-social assessment of 36 de Lange patients', *Journal of Mental Deficiency Research*, 31: 251–257.

Beck, B. & Fenger, K. (1985) 'Mortality, pathological findings and causes of death in the de Lange syndrome', *Acta Paediatrica Scandinavia*, 74: 765–769.

Berg, K., Arron, K., Burbidge, C., Moss, J. & Oliver, C. (2007) 'Carer reported contemporary health problems in people with severe learning disability and genetic syndromes', *Journal of Policy and Practice in Intellectual Disabilities*, 4: 120–128.

Berney, T. P., Ireland, M., & Burn, J. (1999) 'Behavioural phenotype of Cornelia de Lange syndrome', *Archives of Disease in Childhood*, 81(4): 333–336.

Berument, S.K., Rutter, M., Lord, C., Pickles, A., & Bailey, A. (1999) 'Autism Screening Questionnaire: diagnostic validity', *British Journal of Psychiatry*, 175: 444–451.

Bhuiyan, Z., Klien, M., Hammond, P., Mannens, M., Van Haeringen, A., Van Berckelaer-Onnes, I., & Hennekam, R.C. (2006) 'Genotype–phenotype correlations of 39 patients with Cornelia de Lange syndrome: the Dutch experience', *Journal of Medical Genetics*, 43: 568–575.

Bourtchuladze, R., Frenguelli, B., Blendy, J., Cioffi, D., Schutz, G, & Silva, A.J. (1994) 'Deficient long-term memory in mice with a targeted mutation of the cAMP-responsive element-binding protein', *Cellular and Molecular Life Sciences*, 79: 59–68.

Bryson, Y., Sakati, N., Nyhan, W., & Fish, C. (1971) 'Self-mutilative behavior in the Cornelia de Lange syndrome', *American Journal of Mental Deficiency*, 76: 319–324.

Carlin, M.E. (1983) 'The improved prognosis in cri-du-chat (5-p) syndrome, in W.I. Fraser (ed.), *Key Issues in Mental Retardation*. London: Routledge, pp. 65–73.

Clarke, D. & Boer, H. (1998) 'Problem behaviors associated with deletion Prader–Willi, Smith–Magenis and cri du chat syndromes', *American Journal on Mental Retardation*, 103: 264–271.

Collins, M.S. & Cornish, K. (2002) 'A survey of the prevalence of stereotypy, selfinjury and aggression in children and young adults with cri du chat syndrome', *Journal of Intellectual Disability Research*, 46: 133–140.

Collins, M. & Eaton-Evans, G. (2001) 'Growth study of cri du chat syndrome', *Archives of Diseases in Childhood*, 85: 337–338.

Collis, L., Moss, J., Jutley, J., Cornish, K., & Oliver, C. (2008) 'Facial expression of affect in Cornelia de Lange syndrome', *Journal of Intellectual Disability Research*, 52: 207–215.

Cornish, K.M. (1996) 'The neuropsychological profile of cri-du-chat syndrome without significant learning disability', *Developmental Medicine and Child Neurology*, 38: 941–944.

Cornish, K. & Bramble, D. (2002) 'Cri du chat syndrome: genotype–phenotype correlations and recommendations for clinical management', *Developmental Medicine and Child Neurology*, 44: 494–497.

Cornish, K. & Munir, F. (1998) 'Receptive and expressive language skills in children with cri-du chat syndrome', *Journal of Communication Disorders*, 31: 73–81.

Cornish, K. & Pigram, J. (1996) 'Developmental and behavioural characteristics of cri du chat syndrome', *Archives of Diseases in Childhood*, 75: 448–450.

Cornish, K., Munir, F., & Bramble, D. (1998) 'Adaptive and maladaptive behaviour in children with cri-du-chat syndrome', *Journal of Applied Research in Intellectual Disabilities*, 11: 239–246.

Cornish, K.M., Bramble, D., Munir, F., & Pigram, J. (1999) 'Cognitive functioning in children with typical cri du chat (5p-) syndrome', *Developmental Medicine and Child Neurology*, 41: 263–266.

Cornish, K., Bramble, D., & Standen, P. (2001) 'Cri du chat syndrome: toward a behavioral phenotype', *Mental Health Aspects of Developmental Disabilities*, 4: 156–160.

Cornish K., Oliver C., Standen P., Bramble D., & Collins M. (2003) *Cri-du-Chat Syndrome: Handbook for Parents and Professionals*, 2nd edn. CdCS Support Group, Earl Shilton.

D' Arcangelo, G. & Curran, T. (1995) 'Smart transcription factors. *Nature*, 376: 292–293.

Deardorff, M.A., Kaur, M., Yaeger, D., Rampuria, A., Korolev, S., Pie, J. et al. (2007) 'Mutations in cohesion complex members SMC3 and SMC1A cause a mild variant of Cornelia de Lange syndrome with predominant mental retardation', *American Journal of Human Genetics*, 80: 485–494.

Dossetor, D.R., Couryer, S., & Nicol, A.R. (1991) 'Massage for very severe self-injurious-behavior in a girl with cornelia-De-Lange-syndrome', *Developmental Medicine and Child Neurology*, 33: 636–640.

Dykens, E.M. & Clarke, D.J. (1997) 'Correlates of maladaptive behavior in individuals with 5p- (cri du chat) syndrome', *Developmental Medicine and Child Neurology*, 39: 752–756.

Dykens, E.M., Hodapp, R.M., & Finucane, B.M. (2000) *Genetics and Mental* Retardation Syndromes. Baltimore, MD: Paul H Brookes Publishing Co.

Einfeld, S.L. & Tonge, B.J. (1995) 'The developmental behavior checklist-the development and validation of an instrument to assess behavioral and emotional disturbance in children and adolescents with mental retardation', *Journal of Autism and Developmental Disorders*, 25: 81–104.

Goodban, M.T. (1993) 'Survey of speech and language-skills with prognostic indicators in 116 patients with de Lange, Cornelia syndrome', *American Journal of Medical Genetics*, 47: 1059–1063.

Gualtieri, C.T. (1990) *Neuropsychiatry and Behavioral Pharmacology* Springer Verlag.

Greenberg A. & Coleman, M. (1973) 'Depressed whole blood serotonin levels associated with behavioural abnormalities in the de', *Lange Syndrome. Pediatrics*, 52: 720–724.

Galéra, C., Taupiac, E., Fraisse, S., Naudion, S., Toussaint, E., Rooryck-Thambo, C., Delrue, M., Arveiler, B., Lacombe, D., & Bouvard, M. (2009) 'Socio-Behavioral Characteristics of Children with Rubinstein- Taybi Syndrome', *Journal of Autism and Developmental Disorders*. 7.

Goodban, M. T. (1993). Survey of speech and language-skills with prognostic indicators in 116 patients with de Lange, Cornelia syndrome. American Journal of Medical Genetics, 47, 1059–1063.

Goots, E.E. & Liemohn, W.P. (1977) 'Behavioral characteristics of three children with the broad thumb-hallux (Rubinstein-Tavhi) syndrome', *Biological Psychiatry*, 12: 413–423.

Hall, S.S., Arron, K., Sloneem, J., & Oliver, C. (2008) Health and sleep problems in Cornelia de Lange syndrome: a case controlled study', *Journal of Intellectual Disability Research*, 52: 458–468.

Hellings, J.A., Hossain, S., Martin, J.K., & Baratang, R.R. (2002) 'Psychopathology and the Rubinstein–Taybi syndrome: a review and case study', *American Journal of Medical Genetics*, 114C: 190–195.

Hennekam, R.M., Van Den Boogaard, M., Dijkstra, P.F., & Van de Kamp, J.J.P. (1990) 'Metacarpophalangeal Pattern Profile Analysis in Rubinstein-Taybi Syndrome', *American Journal of Medical Genetics. Supplement,* 6: 48–50.

Hennekam, R.M. (2006) 'Rubinstein–Taybi syndrome', *European Journal of Human Genetics*, 14: 981–985.

Hennekam, R.M. & Van Doorne, J.M. (1990) 'Oral aspects of Rubinstein–Taybi syndrome', *American Journal of Medical Genetics, Supplement*, 6: 42–47.

Hennekam, R.M., Stevens, CA., & Van de Kamp, J.J.P. (1990a) 'Etiology and recurrence risk in Rubinstein–Taybi syndrome', *American Journal of Medical Genetics, Supplement*, 6: 56–64.

Hennekam, R.M., Van Den Boogaard, M., Sibbles, B.J., & Van Spijker, H.G. (1990b) 'Rubinstein–Taybi syndrome in the Netherlands', *American Journal of Medical Genetics, Supplement*, 6: 17–29.

Hennekam, R.M., Baselier, A.C., Beyaert, E., Bos, A., Blok, J.B., Jansma, H.B., Thorbecke-Nilson, V.V., & Veerman, H. (1992) 'Psychological and speech studies in Rubinstein–Taybi syndrome', *American Journal of Mental Retardation*, 66: 645–660.

Hyman, P., Oliver, C., & Hall, S. (2002) 'Self-injurious behavior, self-restraint, and compulsive Behaviors in Cornelia de Lange syndrome', *American Journal on Mental Retardation*, 107: 146–154.

Ireland, M., Donnai, D., & Burn, J. (1993) 'Brachmann-deLange syndrome. Delineation of the clinical phenotype', *American Journal of Medical Genetics*, 47: 959–964.

Jackson, L., Kline, A.D., Barr, M.A., & Koch, S. (1993) 'De Lange syndrome: a clinical review of 310 individuals', *American Journal of Medical Genetics*, 47: 940–946.

Johnson, H., Ekman, P., Friesen, W., Nyhan, W., & Shear, C. (1976) 'A behavioral phenotype in the de Lange syndrome', *Pediatric Research*, 10: 843–850.

Kawauchi, S., Calof, A.L., Santos, R., Lopez-Burks, M.E., Young, C.M., Hoang, M.P., Chua, A., Lao, T., Lechner, M.S., Daniel, J.A., Nussenzweig, A. et al. (2009) 'Multiple organ system defects and transcriptional dysregulation in the Nipbl+/2 Mouse, a model of Cornelia de Lange syndrome' Open Access: Public Library of Science Genetics, September 2009, doi:10.1371/journal.pgen.1000650

Kiernan, C. & Reid, B. (1987) *Pre-verbal Communication Schedule*. Windsor: Nfer-Nelson.

Kline, A.D., Stanley, C., Belevich, J., Brodsky, K., Barr, M., & Jackson, L.G. (1993) 'Developmental data on individuals with the Brachmann–de Lange syndrome', *American Journal of Medical Genetics*, 47: 1053–1058.

Kline, A,D., Krantz, I,D., Sommer, A., Kliewer, M., Jackson, L.G., FitzPatrick, D.R., Levin, A.V., & Selicorni, A. (2007a) 'Cornelia de Lange syndrome: clinical review, diagnostic and scoring systems, and anticipatory guidance', *American Journal of Medical Genetics*, 143A: 1287–1296.

Kline, A.D., Grados, M., Sponseller, P., Levy, H.P., Blagowidow, N., Schoedel, S. et al. (2007b). 'Natural history of aging in Cornelia de Lange syndrome', *American Journal of Medical Genetics (Seminars in Medical Genetics)*, 145C: 248–260.

Krantz, I.D., McCallum, J., DeScripio, C., Kaur, M., Gillis, L.A., Yaeger, D., Jukofsky, L., Wasserman, N., Bottani, A., Morris, C.A., Nowaczyk, M.J. et al. (2004) 'Cornelia de Lange syndrome is caused by mutations in NIPBL, the human homolog of *Drosophilia melanogaster* Nipped-B', *Nature Genetics*, 36: 631–635.

Krug, D.A., Arick, J., & Almond, P. (1980) 'Behavior checklist for identifying severely handicapped individuals with high levels of autistic behavior', *Journal of Child Psychology and Psychiatry*: 21: 221–229.

Lacombe, D., Saura, R., Taine, L., & Battin, J. (1992) 'Confirmation of assignment of a locus for Rubinstein–Taybi syndrome gene to 16p13.3', *American Journal of Medical Genetics*, 44: 126–128.

Lejeune, J., Lafourcade, J., Berger, R., Vialatte, J., Boeswillwald, M., Seringe, P., & Turpin, R. (1963), 'Three cases of partial deletion of the short arm of a 5 chromosome', *Comptes Rendus Hebdomadaires des Seances de l'Academie des Sciences*, 257: 3098–3102. [in French].

Levin, A.V., Seidman, D.J., Nelson, L.B., & Jackson, L.G. (1990) 'Ophthalmologic findings in the Cornelia de Lange syndrome', *Journal of Pediatric Ophthalmology and Strabismus*, 27: 94–102.

Lui, J. & Krantz, I. (2008) 'Cohesin and human disease', *Annual Review of Genomics and Human Genetics*, 9: 303–320.

Luzzani, S., Macchini, F., Valade.A, Milani, D., & Selicorni, A. (2003) 'Gastroesophagel reflux in Cornelia de Lange syndrome', *American Journal of Medical Genetics*, 119A: 283–287.

Maas, A.P.H.M., Didden, R., Korzilius, H., Braam, W., Smits, M.G., & Curfs, L.M.G. (2009). 'Sleep in individuals with CdCS: a comparative study', *Journal of Intellectual Disability Research*, 53: 704–715.

Mainardi, P.C., Pastore, G., Castronovo, C., Godi, M., Guala, A., Tamiazzo, S., Provera, S., Pierluigi, M., & Bricarelli, F.D. (2006) 'The natural history of CdCS: a report from the Italian register', *European Journal of Medical Genetics*, 49: 363–383.

Manning, K.P. (1977) 'Larynx in cri du chat syndrome', *Journal of Laryngology and Otology*, 91: 887–892.

Marchisio, P., Selicorni, A., Pignataro, L., Milani, D., Baggi, E., Lambertini, L. et al. (2008) 'Otitis media with effusion and hearing loss in children with Cornelia de Lange syndrome', *American Journal of Medical Genetics*, 146A: 426–432.

Marinescu C., Johnson E., Dykens E., Hodapp R., & Overhauser J. (1999) 'No relationship between the size of the deletion and the level of developmental delay in cri-du-chat syndrome', *American Journal of Medical Genetics*, 86: 66–70.

Marinescu, R.C., Mainardi, P.C., Collins, M. R., Kouahou, M., Coucourde, G., Pastore, G., Eaton-Evans, J., & Overhauser, J. (2000) 'Growth charts for Cri-du-chat syndrome: an international collaborative study', *American Journal of Medical Genetics*, 94A: 153–162.

Menolascino, F., McGee, J., & Swanson, D. (1982) 'Behavioural dimensions of the de Lange syndrome', *Journal of Mental Deficiency Research*, 26: 259–261.

Miyake, N., Visser, R., Kinoshita, A., Yoshiura, K.I., Niikawa, N., Kondoh, T. et al. (2005) 'Four novel NIPBL mutations in Japanese patients with Cornelia de Lange syndrome', *American Journal of Medical Genetics*, 135: 103–105.

Moeschler, J.B. & Graham, J.M. (1993) 'mild Brachmann–de Lange syndrome. Phenotypic and developmental characteristics of mildly affected individuals', *American Journal of Medical Genetics* 47: 969–976.

Moss, J. & Howlin, P. (2009) 'Invited annotation – autism spectrum disorders in genetic syndromes: implications for diagnosis, intervention and understanding the wider ASD population', *Journal of Intellectual Disability Research*, 53: 852–872.

Moss, J., Oliver, C., Hall, S., Arron, K., Sloneem, J., & Petty, J. (2005) 'The association between environmental events and self-injurious behaviour in Cornelia de Lange syndrome', *Journal of Intellectual Disability Research*, 49: 269–277.

Moss, J., Oliver, C., Wilkie, L., Berg, K., Kaur, G., & Cornish, K. (2008) 'Prevalence of autism spectrum phenomenology in Cornelia de Lange and cri du chat syndromes', *American Journal of Mental Retardation*, 113: 278–291.

Moss, J., Oliver C., Arron, K., Burbidge, C., & Berg, K. (2009) 'The prevalence and phenomenology of repetitive behaviour in genetic syndromes', *Journal of Autism and Developmental Disorders*, 39: 572–588.

Musio, A., Selicorni, A., Focarelli, M.L., Gervsini, C., Milani, D., Russo, S., Vezzoni, P., & Larizza, L. (2006) 'X-linked Cornelia de Lange syndrome owing to SMC1L1 mutations', *Nature Genetics*, 38: 528–530.

Nallasamy, S., Kherani, F., Yaeger, D., McCallum, J., Kaur, M., Devoto, M., Jackson, L.G., Krantz, I.D., & Young, T.L. (2006) 'Opthalmologic findings in Cornelia de Lange syndrome: a genotype–phenotype correlation study', *Archives of Opthalmology*, 124: 552–557.

Niebuhr, E. (1978) 'The cri-du-chat syndrome', *Human Genetics*, 42: 143–156.

Oliver, C., Murphy, G., & Corbett, J. A. (1987) 'Self-injurious behaviour in people with mental handicap: a total population study', *Journal of Mental Deficiency Research*, 31: 147–162.

Oliver, C., Moss, J., Petty, J., Arron, K., Sloneem, J., & Hall, S. (2003). *Self-Injurious Behaviour in Cornelia de Lange Syndrome: A Guide for Parents and Carers*. London: Trident.

Oliver, C., Arron, K., Berg, K., Burbidge, C., Caley, A., Duffay, S., Hooker, M., & Moss, J. (2005) 'A comparison of Cornelia de Lange, cri du chat, Prader–Willi, Smith–Magenis, Lowe, Angelman and fragile X syndromes', *Genetic Counseling*, 13: 363–381.

Oliver, C., Arron, K., Hall, S., Sloneem, J., Forman, D., & McClintock, K. (2006) 'Effects of social context on social interaction and self-injurious behavior in Cornelia de Lange syndrome', *American Journal on Mental Retardation*, 111: 184–192.

Oliver, C., Jephcott, L., Seri, S., Friess, S., Kline, A., & Moss, J. (2007) 'Self-injurious behavior in Cornelia de Lange and cri du chat syndromes: associations with peripheral sensory neuropathy and social interactions', *American Journal of Medical Genetics*, 9999A: 1–9.

Oliver, C., Arron, K., Sloneem, J., & Hall, S. (2008) 'The behavioral phenotype of Cornelia de Lange syndrome: a case control study', *British Journal of Psychiatry*, 193: 466–470.

Oliver, C., Moss, J., Petty, J., Tunnicliffe, P., Hastings, R., Howlin, P., Griffith, G., Bull, L., Villa, D., & Yip, M. (2009a) '*Understanding and Changing Challenging Behaviour in Cornelia de Lange Syndrome*. Essex: Aerocom Ltd.

Oliver, C., Moss, J., Petty, J., Tunnicliffe, P., Hastings, R., Howlin, P., Griffith, G., Bull, L., Villa, D., & Yip, M. (2009b). *Understanding and Changing Challenging Behaviour in Cri du Chat Syndrome. Essex: Aerocom Ltd.*

Oliver, C., Sloneem, J., Arron, K. & Hall, S. (2009c) 'Self-injurious behaviour in Cornelia de Lange syndrome: prevalence and phenomenology', *Journal of Intellectual Disability Research*, 53: 575–589.

Opitz, J.M. (1985) 'The Brachmann–de Lange syndrome', *American Journal of Medical Genetics*, 22: 89–102.

Overhauser, J., Huang, X., Gersch, M., Wilson, W., McMahon, J., Bengtsson, U., Rojas, K., Meyer, M., & Wasmuth, J.J. (1994) 'Molecular and phenotypic mapping of the short arm of chromosome 5:

sublocalization of the critical region of the cri du chat syndrome', *Human Molecular Genetics*, 3: 247–252.

Padfield, C.J., Partington, M.W., & Simpson, N.E. (1968) 'The Rubinstein–Taybi Syndrome', *Archives of Disease in Childhood*, 43: 94–101.

Partington, M.W. (1990) 'Rubinstein–Taybi syndrome: a follow-up study', *American Journal of Medical Genetics, Supplement*, 6: 65–68.

Petrij, F., Giles, R.H., Dauwerse, H.G., Saris, J.J., Hennekam, R.C., Masuno, M., Tommerup, N., Van Ommen, G.B., Goodman, R.H., Peters, D.J.M., & Breuning, M.H. (1995) 'Rubinstein–Taybi syndrome caused by mutations in the transcriptional co-activator CBP', *Nature*, 376: 348–351.

Richards, C., Moss, J., O'Farrell. L, Kaur, G. & Oliver, C. (2009) 'Social anxiety in Cornelia de Lange syndrome', *Journal of Autism and Developmental Disorders*, 39: 1155–1162.

Roelfsema, J.H., White, S.J., Ariyurek, Y., Bartholdi, D., Niedrist, D., Papadia, F. et al. (2005) 'Genetic heterogeneity in Rubinstein–Taybi syndrome: mutations in both the CBP and EP300 genes cause disease', *American Journal of Human Genetics*, 76: 572–580.

Roposch, A., Bhaskar, A.R., Lee, F., Adedapo S., Mousny, M., & Alman, B.A. (2004) 'Orthopaedic manifestations of Brachmann–de Lange syndrome: a report of 34 patients', *Journal of Pediatric Orthopedics*, 13: 118–122.

Rubinstein, J.H. (1990). Broad thumb-hallux (Rubinstein–Taybi) syndrome 1957–1988', *American Journal of Medical Genetics, Supplement*, 6: 3–16.

Rubinstein, J.H. & Taybi, H. (1963) 'Broad thumbs and toes and facial abnormalities. A possible mental retardation syndrome', *American Journal of Diseases of Children* 105: 588–608.

Rutter, M., Bailey, A., Lord. C., & Berument, S.K. (2003) *The Social Communication Questionnaire*. Los Angeles: Western Psychological Services.

Sarimski, K. (1997) 'Communication, social-emotional development and parenting stress in Cornelia-de-Lange syndrome', *Journal of Intellectual Disability Research*, 41: 70–75.

Sarimski, K. (2002). 'Analysis of intentional communication in severely handicapped children with Cornelia-de-Lange syndrome', *Journal of Communication Disorders*, 35: 483–500.

Sarimski, K. (2003) 'Early play behaviour in children with 5p- (cri du chat) syndrome', *Journal of Intellectual Disability Research*, 47: 113–120.

Sarimski, K. (2007) 'Infant attentional behaviours as prognostic indicators in Cornelia de Lange syndrome', *Journal of Intellectual Disability Research*, 51: 697–701.

Selicorni, A., Sforzini, C., Milani, D., Cagnoli, G., Fossali, E., & Bianchetti, M.G. (2005) 'Anomalies of the kidney and urinary tract are common in de Lange syndrome', *American Journal of Medical Genetics*, 132A: 395–397.

Shear, C., Nyhan, W., Kirman, B., & Stern, J. (1971) 'Self-mutilative behavior as a feature of the de Lange Syndrome', *Journal of Pediatrics*, 78: 506–508.

Singh, N. & Pulman, R. (1979) 'Self-injury in the de Lange Syndrome', *Journal of Mental Deficiency Research*, 23: 79.

Sloneem, J., Arron, K., Hall, S.S., & Oliver, C. (2009) 'Self-injurious behaviour in Cornelia de Lange syndrome 2: association with environmental events', *Journal of Intellectual Disability Research*, 53: 590–603.

Sohner, L. & Mitchell, P. (1991) 'Phonatory and phonetic characteristics of prelinguistic vocal development in Cri du Chat syndrome,' *Journal of Communication Disorders*, 24: 13–20.

Stefanatos, G.A. & Musikoff, H. (1994) 'Specific neurocognitive deficits in Cornelia de Lange syndrome', *Developmental and Behavioral Pediatrics*, 15: 39–42.

Stevens, C.A. (2007) *GeneReviews: Rubinstein–Taybi syndrome*. Seattle: University of Washington. www.genetests.org.

Stevens, C.A., Carey, J.C., & Blackburn, B.L. (1990a) 'Rubinstein–Taybi syndrome: a natural history study', *American Journal of Medical Genetics, Supplement*, 6: 30–37.

Stevens, C.A., Hennekam, R.M, & Blackburn, B.L. (1990b) 'Growth in the Rubinstein–Taybi syndrome', *American Journal of Medical Genetics, Supplement*: 6: 51–55.

Tonkin, E., Wang, T.J., Lisgo, S., Bamshad, M.J., & Strachan, T. (2004) 'NIPBL, encoding a homolog of fungal Scc2-type sister chromatid cohesion proteins and fly Nipped-B, is mutated in Cornelia de Lange syndrome', *Nature Genetics*, 36: 636–641.

Van Buggenhout, G.J. C.M., Pijkels, E., Holyoet, M., Schaap, C., Hamel, B.C.J., & Fryns, J.P. (2000), 'Cri du chat syndrome: changing phenotype in older patients', *American Journal of Medical Genetics*, 90A: 203–215.

Verhoeven, W.M., Kuijpers, H.J., Wingbermühle, E., Egger, J.I., & Tuinier, S. (2008) 'Impulsivity as a major complaint in Rubinstein–Taybi syndrome', *European Psychiatry*, 23: P0102, S304–S409.

Weeber, E.J. & Sweatt, J.D. (2002) 'Molecular neurobiology of human cognition', *Neuron*, 33: 845–848.

Wing, L., Leekham, S.R., Libby, S.J., Gould, J. & Larcombe, M. (2002) 'The Diagnostic Interview for Social and Communication Disorders: background, inter-rater reliability and clinical use', *Journal of Child Psychology and Psychiatry*, 43: 307–325.

Wiley, S., Swayne, S., Rubinstein, J.H., Lanphear, N.E., & Stevens, C.A. (1990) 'Rubinstein–Taybi syndrome medical guidelines', *American Journal of Medical Genetics, Supplement,* 6: 101–110.

Wilkins, L.E., Brown, J.A., & Wolf, B (1980) 'Psycho-motor development in 65 home-reared children with cri du chat syndrome', *Journal of Pediatrics,* 97: 401–405.

Wygnanski-Jaffe, T., Shin, J., Perruzza, E., Abdolell, M., Jackson, L.G., & Levin, A.V. (2005) 'Ophthalmologic findings in the Cornelia de Lange syndrome', *Journal of the American Association for Pediatric Ophthalmology and Strabismus,* 9: 407–415.

Yin, J.C., Wallach, J.S., Del Vecchio, M., Wilder, E.L., Zhou, H., Quinn, W.G., & Tully, T. (1994) 'Induction of a dominant negative CREB transgene specifically blocks long-term memory in', *Drosphilia Cell,* 79: 49–58.

PART 3

Disorders with Complex or as yet Unknown Causes

13

Attention-Deficit/Hyperactivity Disorder

Timothy E. Wilens & Thomas J. Spencer

INTRODUCTION AND OVERVIEW

Attention-deficit/hyperactivity disorder (ADHD) is the most common emotional, cognitive, and neurobehavioral disorder treated in children (American Academy of Pediatrics, 2001; American Academy of Child and Adolescent Psychiatry, 2002). It carries a high rate of psychiatric comorbidity, notably oppositional defiant disorder (ODD), conduct disorder, mood and anxiety disorders, and cigarette and substance use disorders (Biederman, Monuteaux et al., 2006a). Across the life span, the social and societal costs of untreated ADHD are considerable, including academic underachievement, conducting problems, underemployment, motor vehicle safety, and difficulties with personal relationships (Barkley, 2002; Barkley, Murphy et al., 2002; Biederman, Monuteaux et al., 2006a; Swanson, Lerner et al., 2003). Current and developing treatment strategies involving cognitive/behavioral and pharmacologic interventions often help patients overcome the obstacles to normal functioning.

ADHD is more prevalent than schizophrenia, obsessive-compulsive disorder (OCD), and panic disorder, affecting an estimated 4–12% of school-aged children in the world (Polanczyk, de Lima et al., 2007) with survey and recent epidemiologically derived data showing that 4–5% of college-aged students and adults have ADHD (Kessler, Adler et al., 2006). In recent years, the recognition and diagnosis of ADHD in adults have been increasing, although treatment of adults with ADHD continues to lag substantially behind that of children (Centers for Disease Control and Prevention (CDC), 2005; Kessler, Adler et al., 2006). Data also indicate that, in contrast to a high rate of boys to girls with ADHD presenting for treatment, in adults, the gender ratio is about 1:1 (Biederman, Faraone et al., 2004).

DIAGNOSING ADHD

Although the validity of the ADHD diagnosis continues to be debated in the media, the scientific community has accepted the existence of the disorder, even in adulthood, for a number of years. ADHD can be reliably diagnosed in both children and adults (Barkley & Biederman, 1997). Using the current guidelines, the child or adult patient must meet the criteria in the *Diagnostic and Statistical Manual of Mental Disorders, 4th edn* (DSM-IV) (APA, 1994). It is important to note, however, that the DSM-IV criteria for ADHD symptoms were derived from field trials in youth to age 17 years and therefore were not specifically tailored to adults; hence, they may not always 'fit' adults with the disorder (APA, 1994; Barkley & Biederman, 1997). The symptoms of the disorder are categorized as follows:

- Inattention—difficulty sustaining attention and mental effort, forgetfulness, and distractibility
- Hyperactivity—fidgeting, excessive talking, and restlessness
- Impulsivity—difficulty waiting one's turn and frequent interruption of others

The DSM-IV criteria also include onset by age 7, impaired functioning in at least two settings (home, work, school, job), and more than 6 months of duration (APA, 1994). Three subtypes of the syndrome are currently recognized: predominantly inattentive; predominantly hyperactive/impulsive; and the combined type, which is the most common and typically more severe and with more comorbidity. Between 90 and 95% of adolescents and adults with ADHD manifest the inattention cluster of symptoms at least as a component of their disorder (Millstein, Wilens et al., 1997; Wilens, Biederman et al., 2009). Of interest, current speculation is that the combined subtype of ADHD may simply represent a more severe and debilitating presentation of ADHD (e.g. more symptoms) and that there is relatively more stability of the subtype with development (Lahey, Pelham et al., 2005; Millstein, Wilens et al., 1997). Similarly, some clinicians believe the inattentive subtype has been underdiagnosed— particularly in girls.

To meet the diagnostic criteria for the inattentive or hyperactive—impulsive subtypes, an individual must have six or more of the nine symptoms from either group of criteria (18 possible traits in all) (APA, 1994). For the combined subtype, an individual must have six or more inattentive symptoms and six or more hyperactive/impulsive symptoms. To warrant the ADHD diagnosis, symptoms must cause significant impairment. Adults diagnosed with the disorder must have had childhood onset and persistent and current symptoms, although allowance is made for incomplete persistence of full criteria (ADHD in partial remission).

There has been much debate on the age-of-onset criteria currently used for diagnosing adults with ADHD. Barkley has proposed that requiring child-based symptoms for adults to make the diagnosis of ADHD is too stringent (Barkley & Biederman, 1997). Recently, Faraone, Biederman et al., (2006) have examined differences between groups of adults with ADHD based on age of onset of symptoms of ADHD. In this study, these researchers explored if differences existed between 79 adults who had full current criteria for ADHD but did not have a clear track of symptoms prior to age 7 years to 127 adults who had their ADHD onset at < 7 years (Faraone, Biederman et al., 2006). Interestingly, no differences in rates of psychiatric comorbidity, family history of ADHD, or impairment were found between groups of adults with full-criteria ADHD and those who had a longitudinal track of ADHD without clear onset in youth, supporting the growing contention of problems with using the current onset of symptoms prior to age 7 years stringently (Barkley & Biederman, 1997). Clinical diagnosis is made through a combination of a careful clinical history and ancillary evidence, such as past records, teacher and/or family reports, and rating scales. For adolescents, ancillary information is necessary (e.g. parent report), whereas self-report in adults with ADHD has been shown valid and reliable (Murphy & Schachar, 2000; Stein, Sandoval et al., 1995). Of interest, whereas clinicians are concerned as to the possibility of scamming or over-reporting of ADHD symptoms by adults, data suggest the opposite may be operant. Mannuzza, Klein et al. (2002) in a prospective 16-year follow-up of children with ADHD, now at a mean age of 25, found that of the 176 individuals with a well-characterized past history of ADHD, only 28% of the adults through direct interviews were identified as having childhood ADHD. These data further highlight issues around the relatively poor sensitivity of recalling symptoms (and establishing the diagnosis of ADHD) by adult self-report—particularly when not anchoring symptoms in childhood.

The patient's symptoms, severity of impairment, possible comorbidity, family history, and psychosocial stressors may be determined during the patient and/or parent interview. In pediatric evaluations, the adolescent's behavior and parent–child interaction are observed, and the child's school, medical, and neurological status are evaluated (Anon, 2001).

Several diagnostic tools are employed with the child: the Conners Parent and Teacher Questionnaires, the ADHD Rating Scale-IV, the Achenbach Behavioral Checklist, the ADD-II Comprehensive Teacher Rating Scale, Vanderbilt scale, the Child Behavior Rating Scale and the Copeland Symptom Checklist for ADD. Symptom scales used with all age groups (to assess home, school, and job performance) include the ADHD Symptom Checklist, SNAP-IV Teacher and Parent Rating Scale, Conners Rating Scales—Revised, Brown Attention-Deficit Disorder Scales, Brown Attention-Deficit Disorder Scales for Children, and the ADHD Symptoms Rating Scale (Adler & Cohen, 2004). Although these tools quantify behavior deviating from norms, they should not be used alone to make or refute the diagnosis. In some instances, the scales are employed to assess and monitor the patient's response to treatment.

Diagnosing adults involves careful querying for developmentally appropriate criteria from the DSM IV concerning the childhood onset, persistence, and current presence of symptoms. With the caveat of under-reporting (Mannuzza, Klein et al., 2002), the diagnostic reliability of reporting adult ADHD symptoms retrospectively from childhood has been validated. For example, Murphy and Schachar (2000) found a high correlation (R's > 0.75) between reports of childhood ADHD made by adults with the disorder and their parents, and ratings of current symptoms made by adults with ADHD and their partners. Self-report forms such as the Wender, ADHD Rating Scale—Adult, Adult Diagnostic Self-Report Scale, Brown-ADD, and Conners Rating Scales have all been psychometrically evaluated and found valid and reliable as diagnostic aids for adult ADHD (Adler & Cohen, 2004; Sandra Kooij, Marije Boonstra et al., 2008). For a briefer screening of adults, the World Health Organization (WHO) Adult ADHD Self-Report Scale (Figure 13.1) has been validated as a means of identifying those at risk for ADHD who necessitate further investigation (Kessler, Adler et al., 2005).

Follow-up studies show that prominent symptoms and impairment related to the disorder persist into adulthood in approximately one-half of cases (Biederman, Faraone et al., 2000; Mick, Faraone et al., 2004). Beginning in adolescence, ADHD symptoms decline and change their presentation (Barkley, Fischer et al., 1990; Hart, Lahey et al., 1995). A majority of youth will lose full *syndromatic* criteria for ADHD as they grow up: they will no longer present with the full criteria. However, an even larger number will manifest *symptomatic* persistence (e.g. partial diagnostic criteria) of the disorder into adulthood: they will present with most of the symptoms and other criteria and with ADHD-related impairments (Biederman, Faraone, et al., 2000).

There appears to be developmental variance in the ADHD symptom profile across the life span (Biederman, Faraone et al., 2000; Hart, Lahey et al., 1995; Millstein, Wilens et al., 1997; Mick, Faraone et al., 2004; Wilens, Biederman et al., 2009). Longitudinally derived data in ADHD youth growing up indicate that the symptom cluster of hyperactivity and impulsivity decays over time, while the symptoms of inattention

Are you living with Adult ADHD?

The questions below can help you find out.

Many adults have been living with Adult Attention-Deficit/Hyperactivity Disorder (Adult ADHD) and don't recognize it. Why? Because its symptoms are often mistaken for a stressful life. If you've felt this type of frustration most of your life, you may have Adult ADHD – a condition your doctor can help diagnose and treat.

The following questionnaire can be used as a starting point to help you recognize the signs/symptoms of Adult ADHD but is not meant to replace consultation with a trained healthcare professional. **An accurate diagnosis can only be made through a clinical evaluation.** Regardless of the questionnaire results, if you have concerns about diagnosis and treatment of Adult ADHD, please discuss your concerns with your physician.

This Adult Self-Report Scale-V1.1 (ASRS-V1.1) Screener is intended for people aged 18 years or older.

Adult Self-Report Scale-V1.1 (ASRS-V1.1) Screener
from WHO Composite International Diagnostic Interview
© World Health Organization

	Date					
		Never	Rarely	Sometimes	Often	Very Often
Check the box that best describes how you have felt and conducted yourself over the past 6 months. Please give the completed questionnaire to your healthcare professional during your next appointment to discuss the results.						
1. How often do you have trouble wrapping up the final details of a project, once the challenging parts have been done?						
2. How often do you have difficulty getting things in order when you have to do a task that requires organization?						
3. How often do you have problems remembering appointments or obligations?						
4. When you have a task that requires a lot of thought, how often do you avoid or delay getting started?						
5. How often do you fidget or squirm with your hands or feet when you have to sit down for a long time?						
6. How often do you feel overly active and compelled to do things, like you were driven by a motor?						

Add the number of checkmarks that appear in the darkly shaded area. Four (4) or more checkmarks indicate that your symptoms may be consistent with Adult ADHD. It may be beneficial for you to talk with your healthcare provider about an evaluation.

The 6-question Adult Self-Report Scale-Version1.1 (ASRS-V1.1) Screener is a subset of the WHO's 18-question Adult ADHD Self-Report Scale-Version1.1 (Adult ASRS-V1.1) Symptom Checklist.

ASRS-V1.1 Screener COPYRIGHT © 2003 World Health Organization (WHO). Reprinted with permission of WHO. All rights reserved.

Figure 13.1 The WHO adult ADHD self-report scale

largely persist (Biederman, Faraone et al., 2000; Hart, Lahey et al., 1995; Mick, Faraone et al., 2004; Millstein, Wilens et al., 1997; Wilens, Biederman et al., 2009). In support of this notion, data derived from a group of clinically referred adults with ADHD indicate that approximately half of adults endorse clinically significant levels of hyperactivity/impulsivity, but 90% endorse prominent attentional symptoms (Millstein, Wilens et al., 1997; Wilens, Biederman et al., 2009).

Hyperactivity in children may morph into a sense of inner restlessness in adolescents and adults, accompanied by poor concentration, daydreaming, and forgetfulness. Childhood impulsivity symptoms can lead to low frustration tolerance, explosive emotional episodes, and reckless driving in adulthood. Presenting adults typically have poor self-discipline, short temper, difficulty establishing and keeping a routine, and difficulty thinking clearly (Millstein, Wilens et al., 1997; Wilens, Biederman et al., 2009).

A substantial body of literature implicates abnormalities of brain structure and function in the pathophysiology of both childhood and adult ADHD (Barkley, 1997; de Zeeuw, Aarnoudse-Moens et al., 2008; Martinussen, Hayden et al., 2005; Seidman, 2006; Sergeant, Geurts et al., 2002; Sonuga-Barke, Dalen et al., 2003). We have known for decades that ADHD youth show impaired performance on tasks assessing vigilance, motoric inhibition, organization, planning, complex problem solving, and verbal learning and memory. Prominent neuropsychologically derived executive dysfunction is associated with learning disabilities and poorer overall prognosis over time in ADHD youth (Biederman, Monuteaux et al., 2004). A smaller but substantial literature shows similar problems also impairing adults with ADHD (Hervey Epstein et al., 2004).

Consistent neuropsychological deficits have been documented in studies of adults with ADHD (Hervey, Epstein et al., 2004; Seidman, Doyle et al., 2004). These adults tend to have impaired performance on tasks assessing vigilance, motoric speed, response inhibition, verbal learning, and working memory (Hervey, Epstein et al., 2004; Seidman, Doyle et al., 2004). Age, learning disabilities, psychiatric comorbidity, and gender do not account for these impairments. Whereas neuropsychological testing is not used clinically to diagnose ADHD in adults, such testing aids in identifying learning disabilities, sub-average intelligence, and specific information-processing deficits.

Despite known neuropsychological differences between children and adults with ADHD and non-ADHD controls (Barkley, 1997; de Zeeuw, Aarnoudse-Moens et al., 2008; Martinussen, Hayden et al., 2005; Seidman, 2006; Sergeant, Geurts et al., 2002; Sonuga-Barke, Dalen et al., 2003), the role of neuropsychological testing in all age groups with the disorder remains unclear. Current consensus is that neuropsychological testing is used not to *diagnose* ADHD, but to better understand the extent of learning disabilities and learning dysfunction in affected individuals.

PSYCHIATRIC COMORBIDITY

During the past decade, epidemiological studies have documented high rates of concurrent psychiatric and learning disorders among individuals with ADHD (Anderson, Williams et al., 1987; Bird, Gould et al., 1993; Biederman, Monuteaux et al., 2006a). Most commonly, comorbidity with ADHD in youth includes oppositional, conduct, mood, and anxiety disorders (Biederman, Newcorn et al., 1991).

Conduct disorder

Conduct disorder is the best-established comorbid condition of childhood ADHD, and has been widely reported in epidemiological

(Bird, Gould et al., 1993), clinical (Biederman, Newcorn et al., 1991), follow-up (Biederman, Faraone et al., 1996; Gittelman, Mannuzza et al., 1985; Hechtman & Weiss, 1986; Loney, Kramer et al., 1981), and family genetic studies. Consistent with childhood studies, studies of referred and non-referred ADHD adults have found high rates of childhood conduct disorder as well as adult antisocial disorders in these subjects (Biederman, Monuteaux et al., 2006a).

Depression

Unlike the acceptance of comorbidity of ADHD with disruptive disorders, its comorbidity with mood disorders remains controversial. However, reviews of ADHD studies (Biederman, Newcorn et al., 1991) and reviews of depression studies (Angold & Costello, 1993) agree that ADHD and depression co-occur beyond what one would expect by chance alone. Follow-up studies provide additional evidence for major depression as an outcome of childhood hyperactivity. For example, Mannuzza, Klein et al. (1993) found that 23% of their hyperkinetic children had a lifetime diagnosis of depression in adulthood. This rate is similar to that reported among ADHD children and adults (Biederman, Monuteaux et al., 2006a). Similarly, epidemiological evidence in children (Jensen, Shervette et al., 1993) and adults (Kessler, Adler et al., 2006) have shown that ADHD increases the likelihood of having a depressive disorder by at least twofold. To what extent depression develops as a result of ADHD or independently remains to be seen.

Bipolar disorder

The overlap of ADHD and bipolar disorder is of recent clinical and scientific interest. Winokur, Coryell et al. (1993) showed that traits of hyperactivity in childhood were elevated among bipolar adults and their bipolar relatives. Similarly, many reports of bipolar children have noted the co-occurrence of mania and ADHD and case reports of hyperactive children developing manic-depressive illness have been reported (Geller, Zimerman et al., 2000; Wozniak, Biederman et al., 1995). Prior systematic studies of children and adolescents found rates of ADHD ranging from 57 to 98% in bipolar children and rates of bipolar disorder of 22% in ADHD inpatients (Faraone, Biederman et al., 1997). Family studies suggest a familial link between ADHD and bipolar disorder. Using pooled data from five studies, Faraone, Biederman et al. (1997) showed significantly elevated rates of ADHD in children of bipolar parents and significantly elevated rates of bipolar disorder among families of ADHD children.

Despite emerging literature from convergent sources, there continues to be much controversy about the validity of the concurrent diagnoses of ADHD and bipolar disorder. Overlap of symptoms does not account for spurious diagnosis of either bipolar or ADHD (Milberger, Biederman et al., 1995). Whereas ADHD is characterized by the typical cognitive and hyperactive/impulsive features of the disorder, bipolar disorder is characterized by mood instability, pervasive irritability, grandiosity, psychosis, cyclicity, and lack of response to structure (Wilens, Biederman et al., 2003). When individuals experience both sets of symptoms, they may suffer from both ADHD and bipolar disorder (Wilens, Biederman et al., 2003).

Substance use disorders

Combined data from retrospective accounts of adults and prospective observations of youth indicates that juveniles with ADHD are at increased risk for cigarette smoking and substance abuse (SA) during adolescence. In particular, ADHD youth with bipolar or conduct disorder are at risk for very early cigarette use and substance use disorder (SUD) (i.e. < 16 years of age), whereas the typical age of risk for the onset of SA accounted for by ADHD itself is probably between 17 and 22 years of age (Wilens & Biederman, 2006). ADHD adolescents and adults become addicted to cigarette smoking at twice the rate compared to non-ADHD individuals. ADHD youth disproportionately become involved with cigarettes (Wilens, Vitulano et al., 2008), which increases the risk for subsequent alcohol and drugs (Biederman, Monuteaux et al., 2006b). Moreover, ADHD substance abusers tend to prefer the class of drugs over alcohol with no evidence of a preference for specific types of drugs (Biederman, Wilens et al., 1995). Data indicate that cocaine and stimulant abuse are not over-represented in ADHD; in fact, as is the case in non-ADHD abusers, marijuana continues to be the most commonly abused agent (Biederman, Wilens et al., 1995). Individuals with ADHD, independent of comorbidity, tend to maintain their addiction longer compared to their non-ADHD peers (Levin & Evans, 2001; Wilens, Biederman et al., 1998).

Whereas concerns of the abuse liability and potential kindling of specific types of abuse secondary to early stimulant exposure in ADHD children have been raised largely in animal studies (Vitiello, 2001), the preponderance of clinical data and consensus in the field do not appear to support such a contention. For example, in a prospective study of ADHD girls followed into adolescence, a significant reduction in the risk for SA was reported in treated compared to untreated ADHD youth (Wilens, Adamson et al., 2008), with no increase (or decreased) SUD risk associated with stimulant treatment into adulthood (Biederman, Monuteaux et al., 2008). Furthermore, meta-analytic examination of this issue seems to suggest that treatment of ADHD reduces cigarette smoking and SUD into adolescence but that effect is lost in adulthood (Wilens, Faraone et al., 2003), most likely due to the lack of adherence to treatment. Clearly, further work in this important area needs be completed.

PATHOPHYSIOLOGY AND GENETICS

Neurobiology

ADHD has been viewed as a 'frontal' disorder due to associated deficits in executive function. Executive function deficits include problems with planning and organization, cognitive flexibility, working memory, and response inhibition/impulse control. Individuals with ADHD often have impaired performance on one or more tasks of vigilance, search, and attention; working memory (ability to retain information while processing new information); response inhibition (ability to juggle competing or distracting tasks); verbal learning (encoding); and delay aversion (the need to have immediate gratification).

Structural imaging studies have documented diffuse abnormalities in children and adults with ADHD. A large study by Castellanos, Lee et al. (2002) reported smaller total cerebrum, cerebellum, and the four cerebral lobes that did not change over time. Developmental trajectories of these structures paralleled that of the controls from age 5 to 18 years old. Of note, ADHD patients who were prescribed medication had larger (more normal) brain volumes than those who were not medicated.

A structural magnetic resonance imaging (MRI) study (Seidman, Valera et al., 2006) in adults with and without ADHD also revealed a smaller dorsolateral prefrontal cortex (DLPFC) and the anterior cingulate cortex (ACC). The DLPFC controls working memory, which involves the ability to retain information while processing new information. These differences are thought to account for deficits in goal-directed and task behavior in ADHD. The ACC is involved with rapidly choosing between competing or distracting tasks and is thought to be a key region of regulation involving the ability to focus on one task and choose between options. Furthermore, the nucleus accumbens, which is a key part of the reward motivational system, was somewhat larger (trend) in adults with ADHD compared to controls.

In addition to structure, others have looked at the developmental pattern of cortical maturation in ADHD. Shaw, Eckstrand et al. (2007) reported a delay in cortical thickness among ADHD patients. The pattern of brain development, from sensorimotor to associative areas, was similar in children with and without ADHD. However, the age of peak development was delayed in those with ADHD. Whereas some interpreted this finding to mean that the brain abnormalities associated with ADHD eventually normalized, that conclusion is not justified by these data. Adult data (Makris, Biederman et al., 2007), using the same measure of cortical thickness, have shown that cortical thickness is not normalized and that the areas of the brain that are affected in children with ADHD remain affected in adulthood. In this study, cortical thickness in the dorsolateral prefrontal cortex, parietal areas and anterior cingulate cortex is thinner in adults with ADHD than in normal controls.

Functional magnetic resonance imaging (fMRI) has been used to examine brain activity during selective cognitive challenges in individuals with ADHD. A recent study (Epstein, Casey et al., 2007) measured the amount of brain activity when the go/no go task was utilized. Both youths and adults with ADHD showed attenuated activity in the frontostriatal regions of the brain that are key for attention and inhibitory control (prefrontal cortex and caudate). In addition, adults with ADHD appeared to activate nonfrontostriatal regions (ACC, parietal areas) more than normals. The amount of brain activation observed correlated closely with the degree of efficiency on the task in both children and adults with ADHD.

Valera, Faraone et al. (2005) did an fMRI study using a different cognitive task (working memory) in adults with ADHD and controls. In this study the cerebellum was activated more in adult controls than adults with ADHD during the task. There are increasing data indicating that the cerebellum is a key regulator of cognition in normal individuals.

Casey and Durston (2006) summarized the results of fMRI studies and hypothesized that top-down and bottom-up control systems were affected in ADHD. They hypothesized that bottom-up neural systems detect the regularities and irregularities in the environment to alert the frontal brain systems to alter or adjust behavior. These systems are key regulators of maintaining sustained attention vs shifting attention due to sensory input. Casey and Durston (2006) posited that the striatum regulates *what* to expect (type of task), the cerebellum regulates *when* to expect it (timing of task), and the parietal lobe alerts one to novel or newer competing stimuli.

Sonuga-Barke (2003) also articulated an integrative theory of ADHD. He described a dual pathway model consisting of an executive circuit and a reward circuit. The reward circuit involves maintaining interest in a task and the ability to tolerate delayed rewards. The executive, cognitive, circuit involves directed attention and the ability to keep innate goals in mind long term while working on the details of a task. In concert with these tasks are different, parallel feedback control loops that regulate executive control; inhibition and emotional regulation; and motivation and reward (Cummings, 1993).

Additionally, medication may normalize some of these functional deficits. Bush et al. (2008) published a study showing that 7 weeks of treatment with methylphenidate normalized activation in the ACC. Individuals receiving medication showed increases in activation of the ACC and DLPFC at follow-up as compared to baseline and to those receiving placebo treatment. Hence, those areas of the brain that were underactive in adults without treatment normalized with treatment.

The neurobiology of ADHD is strongly influenced by genetic factors. As highlighted in a special issue of *Science* dedicated to the Human Genome Project, ADHD is among the most recognized genetic-based disorders in psychiatry (McGuffin, Riley et al., 2001).

Family studies of ADHD have shown that the relatives of ADHD children are at high risk for ADHD, comorbid psychiatric disorders, school failure, learning disability, and impairments in intellectual functioning (Faraone & Biederman, 1994). Additional lines of evidence from twin, adoption, and segregation analysis studies suggest that the familial aggregation of ADHD has a substantial genetic component. Twin studies find greater similarity for ADHD and components of the syndrome between monozygotic twins compared with dizygotic twins (Goodman & Stevenson, 1989; Levy, Hay et al., 1997). In a meta-analysis of the various studies, Faraone and Mick reported on the mean heritability of ADHD. Heritability refers to the amount of genetic influence for a particular condition. A coefficient of 1 indicates an entirely genetically influenced phenomenon, while a 0 indicates no genetic influence. Asthma, panic disorder, depression, and anxiety had mean heritability rates below 50%. Schizophrenia and autism, two of the most biologically driven medical psychiatric conditions, are heritable at ~75%. ADHD falls in this higher range as well, at a mean heritability rate of 75%.

As with many complex neuropsychiatric conditions, multifactorial causation is thought to be involved in ADHD: an additive affect of multiple vulnerability genes interacting with environmental influences. Pooled odds ratios from meta-analyses of candidate genes reveals that there is not one single gene associated with ADHD. Rather, the disorder is thought to result from a combination of small effects from a number of genes (polygenetic). Although there is no one gene for ADHD, there are a finite number of genes that must interact in order to produce a risk for this disorder. The candidate genes that have been identified thus far relate to synthesis, packaging, release, detection and recycling of dopamine or catecholamines, and other related neurotransmitters such as serotonin. These genes of small effect that confer additive susceptibility are *DRD4*, *DAT*, *DRD5*, and *SNAP-25*. Clearly, more work is necessary in disentangling the relationship of candidate genes in producing specific phenocopies of ADHD, as well as response prediction to pharmacological and non-pharmacological intervention.

TREATMENT

The management of ADHD includes consideration of two major areas: non-pharmacological (educational remediation and individual and family psychotherapy) and pharmacotherapy (Anon, 2001). Support groups for children and adolescents and their families, as well as adults with ADHD, are an invaluable and inexpensive manner for individuals to learn about ADHD and the resources available for their children or themselves. Support groups can be accessed by calling an ADHD hotline, a large support group organization (such as CHADD, ADDA, AddIN), or by using the internet.

Specialized educational planning based on the child's difficulties is necessary in a majority of cases (Pelham, Wheeler et al., 1998). Since learning disorders co-occur in one-third of ADHD youth, ADHD individuals should be screened and appropriate remediation plans developed. Parents should be encouraged to work closely with the child's school guidance counselor who can provide direct contact with the child as well as valuable liaison with teachers and school administration. The school's psychologist can be helpful in providing cognitive testing as well as assisting in the development and implementation of the individualized education plan. Educational adjustments should be considered in individuals with ADHD with difficulties in behavioral or academic performance. Increased structure, predictable routine, learning aids, resource room time, and checked homework are among typical educational considerations in these individuals. Similar modifications in the home environment should be undertaken to optimize the ability to complete homework. For youth, frequent parental communication with the school about the child's progress is essential.

Psychosocial treatments: cognitive-behavioral interventions

Clinicians have at their disposal a variety of psychosocial interventions for ADHD (for review see Chronis, Jones et al., 2006; Pelham, Wheeler et al., 1998. Apart from traditional psychotherapy, which addresses underlying emotions, tutors are available to help children develop strategies for improving academic performance and interpersonal relations. Tutors can assist the child with skills in organization and prioritization, as well as acting as mentors, advocates, and motivational figures. Family interactions between youngsters with ADHD and their parents and siblings are often problematic. Behavioral therapy is frequently recommended to address such problems (Chronis, Jones et al., 2006; Pelham, Wheeler et al., 1998). Behavioral approaches include parent training, behavioral family therapy, and parent–child interaction therapy. Parent training is often conducted using the antecedent behavior consequence model, and is implemented using various methods, including small and large parent training groups, parent training with individual families, videotapes, and behavioral sessions that include children. There has been some systematic study of the relative efficacy of these methods over time (van den Hoofdakker, van der Veen-Mulders et al., 2007). In the academic setting, virtually all children with ADHD must cope with organizational and behavioral demands and expectations. Classroom behavioral interventions often involve training the teacher in the use of these methods. Specialized parent programs can be highly beneficial for preschoolers (Sonuga-Barke, Daley et al., 2001; Sonuga-Barke, Thompson et al., 2006). Teachers can conduct individual and class-wide interventions using antecedents and/or consequence methods (Barkley, 2005). Antecedent interventions are based on an understanding of the range of antecedents (e.g. boredom, peer provocation, unclear inconsistent rules) that precipitate behavioral problems. Antecedent/consequence interventions involve understanding antecedents to inappropriate behavior and reinforcing appropriate behavior with rewards. Consequence interventions involve the judicious use of punishment to encourage appropriate classroom behavior.

Other behavioral strategies are used in the classroom setting to facilitate attention (Abikoff, 1991). These include placing the child with ADHD in proximity to the teacher, eliminating environmental distractions, and arranging seating in traditional rows rather than clusters. Lessons that involve novelty and stimulation in easy and repetitive tasks rather than new or difficult ones have been shown to benefit the child with ADHD. Additional interventions shown to be effective in the academic setting include peer-mediated interventions and token economies.

Exciting new work has shown that cognitive therapies (McDermott & Wilens, 2000) and cognitive behavioral therapy have been shown to be effective in adults with ADHD treated with medication who manifest residual ADHD symptoms (Safren et al., 2010; Solanto et al., 2010). Social skills remediation for improving interpersonal interactions, and coaching for improving organization and study skills, may be useful adjuncts to treatment although their generalizability remains debated. Few data exist for the use of neurofeedback, cerebellar training, attention or memory training, or ophthalmic manipulation (Barkley, 2005).

Results from studies suggest that non-pharmacologic treatment modalities, including types of cognitive behavioral therapy, are less effective over 1–2 years than the use of psychostimulants in treating ADHD (Hechtman, Abikoff et al., 2004; MTA Cooperative Group 1999a, 1999b). However, cognitive and behavioral therapies remain an important part of ADHD treatment, especially since a number of children are non-responsive to medication, experience adverse side effects that limit the use of medication, manifest residual symptoms, are not interested in medications, and have comorbid behavior problems that warrant additional treatment (Swanson, Kraemer et al., 2001; Wilens & Spencer, 2000).

Pharmacotherapy

Medications remain a mainstay of treatment for children, adolescents, and adults with ADHD. In fact, National Institutes of Health (NIH)-funded multisite studies support that medication management of ADHD is the most important variable in outcome in context to multimodal (Hechtman, Abikoff et al., 2004; MTA Cooperative Group, 1999a, 1999b) treatment. For example, in the largest prospective and randomized long-term trial of ADHD youth, those receiving stimulants alone were observed to have similar improvement in multiple domains at 14 months follow-up compared to those randomized to receive stimulants plus psychotherapy (MTA Cooperative Group, 1999a). Similarly, these data replicate an older similar study demonstrating the utility of medication in the treatment of ADHD (Abikoff, Hechtman et al., 2004). Of interest, medicated groups had a better overall outcome than those receiving extensive psychotherapy without stimulants. Some subgroups of youth manifest more improvement at 14 months with the combination compared to medication or psychotherapy alone. The stimulants, noradrenergic agents, antidepressants, and antihypertensives comprise the available agents for ADHD. The medications used in ADHD have been observed to have similar pharmacological responsivity across the life span, including school-aged children, adolescents, and adult groups with ADHD (Table 13.1).

Stimulants

Stimulants are among first-line agents for pediatric and adult groups with ADHD based on their extensive efficacy and safety data (Greenhill, Pliszka et al., 2002). Although there are more than 300 controlled studies of stimulants with more than 6000 children, adolescents, and adults, the vast majority of the studies are limited to latency age and Caucasian boys treated for no longer than 2 months (Spencer, Biederman et al., 1998b). The most commonly used compounds in this class are methylphenidate (Ritalin, Concerta, Metadate,

Daytrana and others) and amphetamine (Adderall, Dexedrine, Vyvanse). Stimulants are sympathomimetic drugs which increase intrasynaptic catecholamines (mainly dopamine and norepinephrine) by inhibiting the presynaptic reuptake mechanism and releasing presynaptic catecholamines (Wilens, 2006). Whereas methylphenidate is specific for blockade of the dopamine and noradrenergic transporter proteins, amphetamines (in addition to blocking the dopamine and noradrenergic transporter protein) also release catecholaminergic stores and cytoplasmic dopamine and norepinephrine directly into the synaptic cleft (for review, see Greenhill, Pliszka et al., 2002; Wilens, 2006). Moreover, amphetamines release serotonin to a greater extent than other stimulants.

Immediate-release methylphenidate and D-amphetamine are both short-acting compounds, with an onset of action within 30–60 minutes and a peak clinical effect usually seen between 1 and 2 hours after administration and lasting 2–5 hours. The amphetamine compounds (Adderall) and some sustained-release preparations of methylphenidate are intermediate-acting compounds with an onset of action within 60 minutes and a duration of 6–8 hours (Greenhill, Pliszka et al., 2002).

Given the need to additionally treat ADHD outside of academic settings (i.e. social, homework) and to reduce the need for in-school dosing and likelihood for diversion, there has been a shift to the extended-release preparations of the stimulants. Extended-release preparations diminish afternoon wearoff and rebound and appear to manifest less abuse liability compared to their immediate-release counterparts (Parasrampuria, Schoedel et al., 2007; Spencer, Biederman et al., 2006). In general, the extended-release preparations are distinguished from one another based on the release mechanisms (osmotic release, transdermal patch, beads), amount of medication released through the day (more in a.m. vs p.m.), and duration of action (8–12 hours).

The literature suggests more similarities than differences in response to the various available stimulants (Greenhill & Osman, 1999; Greenhill, Pliszka et al., 2002). However,

Table 13.1   Medications Used in the Treatment of ADHD

Generic Class (Brand Name)	Daily Dose (mg/kg)**	Daily Dosage Schedule	Typical Dosing Schedule**	Common Adverse Effects
Stimulants				
Amphetamine	0.3–1.5			Insomnia
Short-acting		Twice or three	5–30 mg BID	Decreased appetite, weight loss
(Dexedrine—tablets)		times	to TID	Tic exacerbation
				Depression, anxiety
Intermediate-acting		Once or twice	5–30 mg BID	Rebound phenomena (short-acting preparations)
(Adderall, Dexedrine spansules)				Increased blood pressure/ pulse
Extended-release				
(Adderall XR; Vyvanse)		Once	10–70 mg QD	
Methylphenidate				
Short-acting	0.5–2.0	Twice to	5–40 mg BID	Insomnia
(Ritalin, Metadate; Focalin)	(< 1 mg	four times	to QID	Decreased appetite, weight loss
Intermediate-acting	d-MPH or patch)			Tic exacerbation
(Ritalin SR, Metadate SR)		Once or twice	10–60 mg QD	Depression, anxiety
			to BID	Rebound phenomena (short-acting preparations)
				Increased blood pressure/pulse
Extended-release				
(Concerta; Metadate CD; Focalin XR; Daytrana patch)		Once	10–90 mg QD	
Noradrenergic Agents				
Atomoxetine (Strattera)	1.0–2.0	Once or twice	25–140 mg QD	GI upset, nausea
				Sedation, insomnia
				Agitation
Arousal Agents				
Modafinil*		Once or twice	100–400 mg QD	Insomnia
				Weight loss
				Increased blood pressure/pulse
				Skw RASH
Antidepressants				
Tricyclics (TCAs)*	2.0–5.0	Once or twice	25–300 mg QD	Dry mouth, constipation
e.g. imipramine,	(1.0–3.0 for NT)		(25–150 mg QD	Weight loss
desipramine, nortriptyline (NT)			for NT)	Vital sign and ECG changes

(*continued*)

Table 13.1 Medications Used in the Treatment of ADHD (Continued)

Generic Class (Brand Name)	Daily Dose (mg/kg)**	Daily Dosage Schedule	Typical Dosing Schedule**	Common Adverse Effects
Bupropion*				
(Wellbutrin short-acting and sustained-release—SR, XL)	1.0–6.0	Once to three times	75–100 mg TID	Irritability, insomnia
			150–200 BID	Risk of seizures
			(SR); 150–450 XL	Contraindicated in bulimics
Antihypertensives				
Clonidine				
Kapvay	3-10 µg/kg	twice	0.1mg - .4mg BID	
(Catapres)*	3–10 µg/kg	Twice or three times	0.05–0.1 mg TID	Sedation, dry mouth, depression
				Confusion (with high dose)
				Bradycardias, syncope
				Rebound hypertension
Guanfacine (Intuniv [extended-release]; Tenex*)	30–100 µg/kg	Twice	0.5–1 mg TID 1–4 mg daily	Similar to clonidine but less sedation

*Not FDA-approved at time of publication.

**Denotes typical clinical dosing of these compounds; not reflective of FDA-approved indications or dosing.

based on marginally different mechanisms of action, some patients who lack a satisfactory response or manifest adverse effects to one stimulant may respond favorably to another. Stimulants should be initiated at the lowest available dosing once daily and increased every 3–7 days until a response is noted or adverse effects emerge. Typically, parameters for upward daily dosing of the stimulants that may exceed FDA approved dosing are 1 mg/kg/day for the amphetamines and 2 mg/kg/day for racemic oral methylphenidate (Wilens & Spencer, 2000).

Stimulants appear to work in all age groups of individuals with ADHD. For instance, a recent controlled multisite study in preschoolers showed improvement in ADHD symptoms, and structured tasks; however, the response was less robust with a higher side-effect burden compared to other age groups (Greenhill, Kollins et al., 2006). Similarly, in adolescents, response has been reported as moderate to robust, with no abuse or tolerance noted (Greenhill, Kollins et al., 2006); of interest, in adolescents, self-report can be more relied upon to at least punctuate the clinical picture of response. There has been a great interest in the use of stimulant treatment in adults with ADHD. There have been approximately 40 studies of stimulants demonstrating moderate efficacy, particularly when aggressive dosing—i.e. 20 mg TID (twice a day) of methylphenidate (Spencer, Wilens et al., 1995) or 30 mg BID (three times a day) of Adderall—is employed. Currently, Food and Drug Administration (FDA) approval is only for the extended-release preparation of stimulants in adults.

Predictable short-term adverse effects include reduced appetite, insomnia, edginess, and gastrointestinal (GI) upset (Barkley, McMurray et al., 1990). Elevated vital signs may emerge, necessitating baseline and on-drug monitoring. There are a number of controversial issues related to chronic stimulant use. Although stimulants may produce anorexia and weight loss, their effect on ultimate height remains less certain. Whereas some reports suggest that there is a stimulant-associated decrease in growth in height in children (Safer, Allen et al., 1972; MTA Cooperative Group, 2004), particularly preschoolers (Swanson, Greenhill et al., 2006), other reports have failed to substantiate this finding (Kramer, Loney et al., 2000), and still others question the possibility that growth deficits may represent maturational delays related to ADHD itself rather than to stimulant treatment (Spencer, Biederman et al., 1998a). Whereas a number of studies have indicated potential growth delay earlier in treatment, normalization appears to occur with chronic treatment. Stimulants may precipitate or exacerbate tic symptoms in ADHD children. Longitudinal studies suggest that the majority of ADHD youth with tics can tolerate stimulant medications (Gadow, Sverd et al., 1999); however, up to one-third of children with tics may have worsening of their tics with stimulant exposure (Castellanos, Giedd et al., 1997). Current consensus suggests that stimulants can be used in youth with comorbid ADHD plus tics with careful monitoring for stimulant-induced tic exacerbation.

Recent warnings have also highlighted potential cardiovascular adverse events. Data suggest that rates of sudden and catastrophic adverse cardiovascular effects are no higher on stimulants and non-stimulants to treat ADHD compared to the general population (Rappley, Moore et al., 2006). Based on older guidelines from the American Heart Association, history and symptoms referable to structural heart disease should be queried prior to starting and during treatment with medications, including family history of premature death, congenital heart disease, palpitations, syncopal episodes, dizziness, or chest pain (Gutgesell, Atkins et al., 1999). Blood pressure and pulse monitoring at baseline and periodically thereafter are recommended, whereas ECG (electrocardiogram) monitoring is optional (Gutgesell, Atkins et al., 1999; Perrin, Friedman et al., 2008).

Despite lingering concerns of stimulant abuse, there is a paucity of scientific data supporting the concern that stimulant-treated ADHD individuals systematically abuse their medication (Wilens, Gignac et al., 2006). However, data suggest that diversion of stimulants to non-ADHD youth continues to be a concern (McCabe, Knight et al., 2005; Wilens, Adler et al., 2008). Families should closely monitor stimulant medication and college students receiving stimulants should be advised to carefully store their medication (Wilens, Adler et al., 2008). One study has shown less abuse liability associated with extended-release relative to immediate-release MPH (Spencer, Biederman et al., 2006).

Atomoxetine

Atomoxetine is a potent norepinephrine-specific reuptake inhibitor that has been studied in over 1800 youths with ADHD. Encouraging results from adult studies led to efforts to develop atomoxetine for use in children. Multiple controlled studies have demonstrated the efficacy of atomoxetine in ADHD in children and adolescents (Michelson, Allen et al., 2002; Michelson, Faries et al., 2001). Atomoxetine has also been shown to be effective in long-term use. A multicenter, randomized, placebo-controlled study conducted in 416 children and adolescents with ADHD found that atomoxetine was superior to placebo in preventing relapse—defined as a return to 90% of baseline symptom severity—at 9-month follow-up (Michelson, Buitelaar et al., 2004). In clinical trials, atomoxetine was well tolerated with nausea, GI distress, and sedation most commonly reported. Rarely, patients may have hostility, irritability, and/or suicidality. Rare hepatitis has been reported, although routine liver function monitoring is not recommended.

Atomoxetine has also been shown to be particularly useful in comorbid ADHD. In a non-inferiority study in children with ADHD and tic disorder, atomoxetine did not exacerbate tics, but, instead, reduced tic severity while improving ADHD symptoms. Similarly, analyses of prior studies showed that atomoxetine reduced oppositionality within ADHD significantly greater than placebo (Newcorn, Spencer et al., 2005). More recently, presented data indicate that children with ADHD and clinically significant anxiety responded more favorably to atomoxetine than placebo, with reductions in both anxiety and ADHD scores (Geller, Donnelly et al., 2007). Likewise, recent data in young adults with ADHD have shown that 12-week treatment with atomoxetine in recently abstinent alcoholics (4–30 days) was associated with significant reductions in ADHD and heavy drinking (not relapse) compared to placebo (Wilens et al., 2008).

Several additional medications have demonstrated benefit in controlled trials, but have not been approved by the FDA for the treatment of ADHD.

Antidepressants

Bupropion (Wellbutrin, Zyban) is an antidepressant with indirect dopamine and noradrenergic effects. Bupropion has been shown effective for ADHD in controlled trials of children (Conners, Casat et al., 1996) and adults (Wilens, Haight et al., 2005; Wilens, Spencer et al., 2001). Additionally, open trials in adolescents with ADHD and depression (Daviss, Bentivoglio et al., 2001) and adults with ADHD and bipolar disorder (Wilens, Prince et al., 2003) have suggested a further utility for this agent. Given its utility in reducing cigarette smoking, improving mood, lack of monitoring requirements, and paucity of adverse effects, bupropion is often used as an agent for complex ADHD patients with substance abuse or a mood disorder. It is recommended that the treatment be initiated at 75–100 mg and titrated upward every week up to 300 mg in children and 450 mg (XL preparation) in older children or adults. Adverse events include activation, irritability, insomnia, and (rarely) seizures.

The tricyclic antidepressants (TCAs)— imipramine (Tofranil), desipramine (Norpramin), and nortriptyline (Pamelor, Aventyl)—block the reuptake of neurotransmitters including norepinephrine. TCAs are effective in controlling abnormal behaviors and improving cognitive impairments associated with ADHD, but less so than the majority of stimulants (Spencer, Biederman et al., 1998b). The TCAs are particularly useful in stimulant failures, or when oppositionality, anxiety, tics, or depressive symptoms co-occur within ADHD. Dosing of the TCAs start with 25 mg daily, titrated upward slowly to a maximum of 5 mg/kg/day (2 mg/kg/day for nortriptyline) (Prince, Wilens et al., 2000). Although immediate relief can be seen, a lag of 2–4 weeks to maximal effect is common (Spencer, Biederman et al., 1998b). Unwanted side effects may emerge from activity at histaminic sites (sedation, weight gain), cholinergic sites (dry mouth, constipation), alpha-adrenergic sites (postural hypotension), and serotonergic sites (sexual dysfunction). In general, the secondary amines are more selective (noradrenergic) and have fewer side effects, an important consideration in sensitive juvenile populations. As minor increases in heart rate and the ECG intervals are predictable with TCAs, ECG monitoring at baseline and at therapeutic dose is suggested, but not mandatory.

Although the serotonin reuptake inhibitors (i.e. fluoxetine; Prozac) are not useful for ADHD, venlafaxine (Effexor), because of its noradrenergic reuptake inhibition, may have mild efficacy for ADHD (Reimherr, Hedges et al., 1995). Monoamine oxidase inhibitors (MAOIs) have been shown effective in juvenile and adult ADHD. The response to treatment is rapid, and standard antidepressant dosing is often necessary. A major limitation to the use of MAOIs is the potential for hypertensive crisis associated with dietetic transgressions with tyramine-containing foods (such as most cheeses) and interactions with prescribed, illicit, and over-the-counter drugs (pressor amines, most cold medicines, and amphetamines).

Antihypertensives/alpha agonists

The antihypertensives clonidine (Catapres) and guanfacine (Tenex) are alpha-adrenergic agonists which have been primarily used in the treatment of hypertension. Whereas clonidine affects alpha receptors more broadly, guanfacine appears to be more selective for the alpha 2a receptor. Clonidine is a relatively short-acting compound with a plasma half-life ranging from approximately 6 hours (in children) to 9 hours (in adults) (Connor, Fletcher et al., 1999; Hunt, Minderaa et al., 1985). Usual daily dose ranges from 0.05 mg to 0.4 mg.

Guanfacine is a longer-acting and less-potent-drug than clonidine, with usual daily dose ranges from 0.5 mg to 3 mg. Recently, once-daily preparations of guanfacine (Intuniv) and Clonidine (Kapvay) has been developed with a dose–response improvement in ADHD reported in children (Biederman, Melmed et al., 2008). Improvements in both attentional and hyperactivity/impulsivity have been demonstrated with the Alpha agonists. The alpha agonists have been used for the treatment of ADHD as well as associated tics, aggression, and sleep disturbances, particularly in younger children. Although sedation is more commonly seen with clonidine, both agents may cause depression and rebound hypertension.

Multisite combination studies using clonidine and methylphenidate have been conducted in youth with ADHD plus tics. Interestingly, the combination was more effective than either agent alone in improving both tics and for ADHD control (Hazell & Stuart, 2003; Kurlan, 2002; Palumbo et al., 2008). Although older reports have implicated the combination of clonidine plus methylphenidate in the deaths of four children, many mitigating and extenuating circumstances were operative, making these cases uninterpretable (Wilens, Spencer et al., 1999). In the multisite studies of clonidine and methylphenidate, no adverse cardiovascular events were observed (Hazell & Stuart, 2003; Kurlan, 2002). Cardiovascular monitoring by ECG remains optional.

Modafinil is currently approved as treatment for narcolepsy and has been tested in adults and children with ADHD (Biederman, Swanson et al., 2005). Modafinil has demonstrated efficacy in three double-blind, placebo-controlled studies in pediatric ADHD, but was not approved by the FDA for the treatment of ADHD due to safety concerns (erythema multiforme). Data in adolescents are lacking and studies in adults are negative. Modafinil may be particularly useful for enhancing attention, motivation, and general arousal.

Treatment refractory and complex cases

A number of individuals either do not respond to, or are intolerant of, the adverse effects of medications used to treat their ADHD. Youth who are non-responders to one stimulant should be considered for another stimulant (Bukstein). If two stimulant trials are unsuccessful, bupropion and the TCAs are reasonable second-line agents. Antihypertensives may be useful for younger children or those intolerant of stimulants. Alpha agonists may also be particularly useful for prominent hyperactivity, impulsivity, tics, and aggressiveness. Combined pharmacological approaches can be used for the treatment of comorbid ADHD, as augmentation strategies for patients with insufficient response to a single agent, pharmacokinetic synergism, and for the management of treatment-emergent adverse effects. Examples include the use of an antidepressant plus a stimulant for ADHD and comorbid depression (fluoxetine (Prozac) plus methylphenidate) (Gammon and Brown, 1993) or anxiety (Weiss & Hechtman, 2006), bupropion plus a stimulant for ADHD individuals with moodiness, the use of clonidine to ameliorate stimulant-induced insomnia (Prince, Wilens et al., 1996), atomoxetine plus a stimulant for refractory ADHD (Wilens et al., 2009), and the use of a mood stabilizer plus an anti-ADHD agent to treat ADHD comorbid with bipolar disorder (Findling, Short et al., 2007). While less articulated, medical comorbidities need to be considered. For instance, one small study has reported that the use of stimulants along with antihypertensives in adults with pre-existing hypertension appeared well tolerated (Wilens, Zusman et al., 2006).

SUMMARY

In summary, ADHD is a prevalent world-wide, heterogeneous disorder that frequently persists into adult years. The diagnosis of ADHD continues to be by careful history with an understanding of the developmental presentation of the disorder. The course of ADHD appears to be more chronic, with approximately one-half of children continuing to manifest symptoms and impairment of the disorder into adulthood. The scope of co-occurring disorders has expanded to include not only conduct and ODDs but also mood, anxiety, and SUDs. Girls and those with the inattentive subtype of ADHD are increasingly observed to manifest ADHD. In addition, ADHD in adults carries with it significant impairment in occupational, academic, social, and intrapersonal domains and necessitates treatment. Converging data strongly support a neurobiological and genetic basis for ADHD, with catecholaminergic dysfunction as a central finding.

Psychosocial interventions such as educational remediation, structure/routine, and cognitive-behavioral approaches should be considered in the management of ADHD. Recent work demonstrating improved outcomes associated with specific cognitive therapies in adults with ADHD have been shown. An extensive literature review supports the effectiveness of pharmacotherapy not only for the core behavioral symptoms of ADHD but also for improvement in linked impairments such as cognition, social skills, and family function. ADHD treatment may translate into reduced risk for the development of sequela such as substance abuse. Data suggest a similar positive response of individuals with ADHD to treatment from age 6 to 60 years. Similarities between juveniles and adults in the presentation, characteristics, neurobiology, and pharmacological responsivity of

ADHD support the continuity of the disorder across the life span.

ACKNOWLEDGMENTS

This chapter was in part underwritten by K24 DA016264 to T.E.W. Dr. Timothy Wilens receives or has received grant support from the following sources: Abbott, McNeil, Lilly, NIH(NIDA), Merck, and Shire. Dr. Timothy Wilens has been a speaker for the following: Lilly, McNeil, Novartis, and Shire. Dr. Timothy Wilens is or has been a consultant for: Abbott, Astra-Zeneca, McNeil, Lilly, NIH, Novartis, Merck, Shire. Dr. Timothy Wilens has a published book with Guilford Press. *Straight Talk About Psychiatric Medications for Kids.*

We would like to thank Sergio Aguilar-Gaxiola, Saena Arbadzadeh-Bouchez, Ron de Graaf, Josep Maria Haro, Norito Kawakami, Viviane Kovess, Jean-Pierre Lepine, Sing Lee, Daphna Levinson, Hans Ormel, Svetlana Stepukhovich, Maria Carmen Viana, Chuck Webb, Hans-Ulrich Wittchen, and Victoria Zakhozha for their comments on prior versions of the translations.

REFERENCES

Abikoff, H. (1991) 'Cognitive training in ADHD children; Less to it than meets the eye', *Journal of Learning Disabilities*, 24: 205–209.

Abikoff, H., Hechtman, L. et al. (2004) 'Symptomatic improvement in children with ADHD treated with long-term methylphenidate and multimodal psychosocial treatment', *Journal of the American Academy of Child and Adolescent Psychiatry*, 43(7): 802–811.

Adler, L. & Cohen, J. (2004) 'Diagnosis and evaluation of adults with ADHD', *Psychiatric Clinics of North America*, 27: 187–201.

American Academy of Child and Adolescent Psychiatry (2002) 'Practice parameter for the use of stimulant medications in the treatment of children, adolescents, and adults', *Journal of the American Academy of Child and Adolescent Psychiatry*, 41(2 Suppl): 26S–49S.

American Academy of Pediatrics (2001) 'Clinical practice guideline: treatment of the school-aged child with attention-deficit/hyperactivity disorder', *Pediatrics,* 108(4): 1033–1044.

Anderson, J.C., Williams, S. et al. (1987) 'DSM-III disorders in preadolescent children: prevalence in a large sample from the general population', *Archives of General Psychiatry,* 44: 69–76.

Angold, A. & Costello, E.J. (1993) 'Depressive comorbidity in children and adolescents: empirical, theoretical and methodological issues', *American Journal of Psychiatry,* 150(12): 1779–1791.

Anon (2001) 'Clinical practice guideline: treatment of the school-aged child with attention-deficit/hyperactivity disorder', *Pediatrics,* 108(4): 1033–1044.

APA (1994) *Diagnostic and Statistical Manual of Mental Disorders IV.* Washington, DC: American Psychiatric Association Press.

Barkley, R. (2002) 'Major life activity and health outcomes associated with attention-deficit hyperactivity disorder', *Journal of Clinical Psychiatry,* 63(Supp 12): 10–15.

Barkley, R. (2005) *Attention-Deficit/Hyperactivity Disorder: A Handbook for Diagnosis and Treatment.* New York: Guilford Press.

Barkley, R. & Biederman, J. (1997) 'The case against a specific age of onset criterion for attention deficit hyperactivity disorder', *American Journal of Psychiatry,* 36(9): 1204–1210.

Barkley, R.A. (1997) 'Behavioral inhibition, sustained attention, and executive functions: Constructing a unifying theory of ADHD', *Psychological Bulletin,* 121(1): 65–94.

Barkley, R.A., Fischer, M. et al. (1990) 'The adolescent outcome of hyperactive children diagnosed by research criteria: I. an 8-year prospective followup study', *Journal of the American Academy of Child and Adolescent Psychiatry,* 29: 546–557.

Barkley, R.A., McMurray, M.B. et al. (1990) 'Side effects of methylphenidate in children with attention deficit hyperactivity disorder: a systemic, placebo-controlled evaluation', *Pediatrics* 86(2): 184–192.

Barkley, R.A., Murphy, K.R. et al. (2002) 'Driving in young adults with attention deficit hyperactivity disorder: knowledge, performance, adverse outcomes, and the role of executive functioning', *Journal of the International Neuropsychological Society,* 8(5): 655–672.

Biederman, J., Faraone, S. et al. (1996) 'Comorbidity in outcome of attention-deficit hyperactivity disorder', in L. Hechtman (ed), *Do They Grow Out of It? Long Term Outcome of Childhood Disorders.* Washington, DC: American Psychiatric Press, pp. 39–76.

Biederman, J., Faraone, S. et al. (2000) 'Age dependent decline of ADHD symptoms revisited: impact of remission definition and symptom subtype', *American Journal of Psychiatry,* 157: 816–817.

Biederman, J., Faraone, S.V. et al. (2004) 'Gender effects of attention deficit hyperactivity disorder in adults, revisited', *Biological Psychiatry,* 55(7): 692–700.

Biederman, J., Melmed, R.D. et al. (2008) 'A randomized, double-blind, placebo-controlled study of guanfacine extended release in children and adolescents with attention-deficit/hyperactivity disorder', *Pediatrics* 121(1): e73–84.

Biederman, J., Monuteaux, M. et al. (2004) 'Impact of executive function deficits and ADHD on academic outcomes in children', *Journal of Consulting and Clinical Psychology* 72(5): 757–766.

Biederman, J., Monuteaux, M. et al. (2006a) 'Young adult outcome of attention deficit hyperactivity disorder: a controlled 10 year follow-up study', *Psychological Medicine,* 36: 167–179.

Biederman, J., Monuteaux, M. et al. (2006b). 'Is cigarette smoking a gateway drug to subsequent alcohol and illicit drug use disorders? A controlled study of youths with and without ADHD', *Biological Psychiatry* 59: 258–264.

Biederman, J., Monuteaux, M.C. et al. (2008) 'Stimulant therapy and risk for subsequent substance use disorders in male adults with ADHD: a naturalistic controlled 10-year follow-up study', *The American Journal of Psychiatry,* 165(5): 597–603.

Biederman, J., Newcorn, J. et al. (1991) 'Comorbidity of attention deficit hyperactivity disorder with conduct, depressive, anxiety, and other disorders', *American Journal of Psychiatry,* 148: 564–577.

Biederman, J., Swanson, J. et al. (2005) 'Efficacy and safety of modafinil film-coated tablets in children and adolescents with attention-deficit/hyperactivity disorder: results of a randomized, double-blind, placebo-controlled, flexible-dose study', *Pediatrics* 116: e777–784.

Biederman, J., Wilens, T. et al. (1995). 'Psychoactive substance use disorder in adults with attention deficit hyperactivity disorder: effects of ADHD and psychiatric comorbidity', *American Journal of Psychiatry* 152(11): 1652–1658.

Bird, H.R., Gould, M.S. et al. (1993) 'Patterns of diagnostic comorbidity in a community sample of children aged 9 through 16 years', *Journal of the American Academy of Child and Adolescent Psychiatry,* 32(2): 361–368.

Bush, G., Frazier, J.A. et al. (1999) 'Anterior cingulate cortex dysfunction in attention- deficit/hyperactivity disorder revealed by fMRI and the Counting Stroop', *Biological Psychiatry*, 45(12): 1542–1552.

Bush G, Spencer TJ, Holmes J, et al. (2008) 'Functional magnetic resonance imaging of methylphenidate and placebo in attention-deficit/hyperactivity disorder during the multi-source interference task', *Arch Gen Psychiatry*. Jan 2008;65(1): 102–114.

Bukstein OG. Clinical practice guidelines for attention-deficit/hyperactivity disorder: a review. *Postgrad Med*. Sep;122(5): 69–77.

Casey, B.J. & Durston S. (2006) 'From behavior to cognition to the brain and back: what have we learned from functional imaging studies of attention deficit hyperactivity disorder?' *The American Journal of Psychiatry*, 163(6): 957–960.

Castellanos, F.X., Giedd, J. N. et al. (1997) 'Controlled stimulant treatment of ADHD and comorbid Tourette's syndrome: effects of stimulant and dose', *Journal of the American Academy of Child and Adolescent Psychiatry*, 36(5): 589–596.

Castellanos, F.X., Lee, P.P. et al. (2002) 'Developmental trajectories of brain volume abnormalities in children and adolescents with attention-deficit/hyperactivity disorder', *The Journal of the American Medical Association*, 288(14): 1740–1748.

Centers for Disease Control and Prevention (CDC) (2005) 'Mental health in the United States. Prevalence of diagnosis and medication treatment for attention-deficit/hyperactivity disorder—United States, 2003', *Morbidity and Mortality Weekly Report*, 54: 842–847.

Chronis, A.M., Jones, H.A. et al. (2006) 'Evidence-based psychosocial treatments for children and adolescents with attention-deficit/hyperactivity disorder', *Clinical Psychology Review*, 26(4): 486–502.

Conners, C.K., Casat, C.D. et al. (1996) 'Bupropion hydrochloride in attention deficit disorder with hyperactivity', *Journal of the American Academy of Child and Adolescent Psychiatry*, 35(10): 1314–1321.

Connor, D.F., Fletcher, K.E. et al. (1999) 'A meta-analysis of clonidine for symptoms of attention-deficit hyperactivity disorder', *Journal of the American Academy of Child and Adolescent Psychiatry*, 38(12): 1551–1559.

Cummings, J.L. (1993) 'Frontal-subcortical circuits and human behavior', *Arch Neurol*, 50(8): 873–880.

Daviss, W.B., Bentivoglio, P. et al. (2001) 'Bupropion SR in adolescents with combined attention-deficit/hyperactivity disorder and depression', *Journal of the American Academy of Child and Adolescent Psychiatry*, 40: 307–314.

de Zeeuw, P., Aarnoudse-Moens, C. et al. (2008) 'Inhibitory performance, response speed, intraindividual variability, and response accuracy in ADHD', *Journal of the American Academy of Child and Adolescent Psychiatry*, 47(7): 808–816.

Epstein, J.N., Casey, B.J. et al. (2007). 'ADHD- and medication-related brain activation effects in concordantly affected parent–child dyads with ADHD', *Journal of Child Psychology and Psychiatry*, 48(9): 899–913.

Faraone, S. & Biederman, J. (1994) 'Genetics of attention-deficit hyperactivity disorder', *Child and Adolescent Psychiatric Clinics of North America*, 3(2): 285–302.

Faraone, S.V., Biederman, J. et al. (1997) 'Is comorbidity with ADHD a marker for juvenile onset mania?' *Journal of the American Academy of Child and Adolescent Psychiatry*, 36(8): 1046–1055.

Faraone, S.V. & Doyle, A.E. (2001) 'The nature and heritability of attention-deficit/hyperactivity disorder', Child and Adolescent Psychiatric Clinics of North America 10(2): 299–316, viii-ix.

Faraone S.V. & Mick E. (2010) Molecular Genetics of Attention Deficit Hyperactivity Disorder. Psychiatry Clinics of North America;33(1): 159–180.

Faraone, S.V., Biederman, J. et al. (2006) 'Diagnosing adult attention deficit hyperactivity disorder: are late onset and subthreshold diagnoses valid?', *American Journal of Psychiatry*, 163(10): 1720–1729.

Findling, R.L., Short, E.J. et al. (2007) 'Methylphenidate in the treatment of children and adolescents with bipolar disorder and attention-deficit/hyperactivity disorder', *Journal of the American Academy of Child and Adolescent Psychiatry*, 46(11): 1445–1453.

Gadow, K., Sverd, J. et al. (1999) 'Long-term methylphenidate therapy in children with comorbid attention-deficit hyperactivity disorder and chronic multiple tic disorder', *Archives of General Psychiatry*, 56(4): 330–336.

Gammon, G.D. & Brown, T.E. (1993) 'Fluoxetine and methylphenidate in combination for treatment of attention deficit disorder and comorbid depressive disorder', *Journal of Child and Adolescent Psychopharmacology*, 3(1): 1–10.

Geller, B., Zimerman, B. et al. (2000) 'Diagnostic characteristics of 93 cases of a prepubertal and early adolescent bipolar disorder phenotype by gender, puberty and comorbid attention deficit hyperactivity disorder', *Journal of Child and Adolescent Psychopharmacology*, 10(3): 157–164.

Geller, D., Donnelly, C. et al. (2007) 'Atomoxetine treatment for pediatric patients with attention-deficit/hyperactivity disorder with comorbid anxiety disorder', *Journal of the American Academy of Child and Adolescent Psychiatry*, 46(9): 1119–1127.

Gittelman, R., Mannuzza, S. et al. (1985) 'Hyperactive boys almost grown up. I. Psychiatric status', *Archives of General Psychiatry*, 42: 937–947.

Goodman, R. & Stevenson, J. (1989) 'A twin study of hyperactivity—I. An examination of hyperactivity scores and categories derived from Rutter teacher and parent questionnaires', *Journal of Child Psychology and Psychiatry*, 30(5): 671–689.

Greenhill, L. & Osman, B. (1999) *Ritalin: Theory and Practice*. New York: Mary Ann Liebert.

Greenhill, L., Kollins, S. et al. (2006) 'Efficacy and safety of immediate-release methylphenidate treatment for preschoolers with ADHD', *Journal of the American Academy of Child and Adolescent Psychiatry*, 45(11): 1284–1293.

Greenhill, L.L., Pliszka, S. et al. (2002) 'Practice parameter for the use of stimulant medications in the treatment of children, adolescents, and adults', *Journal of the American Academy of Child and Adolescent Psychiatry*, 41(2 Suppl): 26S–49S.

Gutgesell, H., Atkins, D. et al. (1999) 'Cardiovascular monitoring of children and adolescents receiving psychotropic drugs: A statement for healthcare professionals from the Committee on Congenital Cardiac Defects, Council on Cardiovascular Disease in the Young', *American Heart Association Circulation*, 99(7): 979–982.

Hammerness, P., Georgiopoulos, A. et al. (2009) 'An open study of adjunct OROS–methyophenidate in children who are atomoxetine partial responders: II. Tolerability and Pharmacoinetics', *J Child Adolesc Psychopharmacol*, 19(5): 493–499.

Hart, E.L., Lahey, B.B. et al. (1995) 'Developmental change in attention-deficit hyperactivity disorder in boys: a four-year longitudinal study', *Journal of Abnormal Child Psychology*, 23(6): 729–749.

Hazell, P.L. & Stuart, J.E. (2003) 'A randomized controlled trial of clonidine added to psychostimulant medication for hyperactive and aggressive children', *Journal of the American Academy of Child and Adolescent Psychiatry*, 42(8): 886–894.

Hechtman, L. & Weiss, G. (1986) 'Controlled prospective fifteen year follow-up of hyperactives as adults: non-medical drug and alcohol use and anti-social behaviour', *Canadian Journal of Psychiatry*, 31: 557–567.

Hechtman, L., Abikoff, H. et al. (2004) 'Academic achievement and emotional status of children with ADHD treated with long-term methylphenidate and multimodal psychosocial treatment', *Journal of the American Academy of Child and Adolescent Psychiatry*, 43(7): 812–819.

Hervey, A.S., Epstein, J. et al. (2004) 'The neuropsychology of adults with attention deficit hyperactivity disorder: a meta-analytic review', *Neuropsychology*, 18(3): 485–503.

Hunt, R.D., Minderaa, R.B. et al. (1985) 'Clonidine benefits children with attention deficit disorder and hyperactivity: report of a double-blind placebo-crossover therapeutic trial', *Journal of the American Academy of Child and Adolescent Psychiatry*, 24: 617–629.

Jensen, P.S., Shervette, R.E. et al. (1993) 'Anxiety and depressive disorders in attention deficit hyperactivity disorder with hyperactivity: new findings', *American Journal of Psychiatry*, 150: 1203–1209.

Kessler, R.C., Adler, L. et al. (2005) 'The World Health Organization Adult ADHD Self-Report Scale (ASRS): a short screening scale for use in the general population', *Psychological Medicine*, 35(2): 245–256.

Kessler, R.C., Adler, L. et al. (2006) 'The prevalence and correlates of adult ADHD in the United States: results from the national comorbidity survey replication', *American Journal of Psychiatry*, 163(4): 716–723.

Kramer, J.R., Loney, J. et al. (2000) 'Predictors of adult height and weight in boys treated with methylphenidate for childhood behavior problems', *Journal of the American Academy of Child and Adolescent Psychiatry*, 39(4): 517–524.

Kurlan, R. (2002) 'Methylphenidate to treat ADHD is not contraindicated in children with tics', *Movement Disorders* 17(1): 5–6.

Lahey, B.B., Pelham, W.E. et al. (2005) 'Instability of the DSM-IV Subtypes of ADHD from preschool through elementary school', *Archives of General Psychiatry*, 62(8): 896–902.

Levin, F.R. & Evans, S.M. (2001) 'Diagnostic and treatment issues in comorbid substance abuse and adult attention-deficit hyperactivity disorder', *Psychiatric Annals*, 31(5): 303–312.

Levy, F., Hay, D. et al. (1997) 'Attention-deficit hyperactivity disorder: a category or a continuum? Genetic analysis of a large-scale twin study', *Journal of the American Academy of Child and Adolescent Psychiatry* 36(6): 737–744.

Loney, J., Kramer, J. e t al. (1981) 'The hyperactive child grows up: predictors of symptoms, delinquency and achievement at follow-up', in K.D. Gadow & J. Loney (eds), *Psychosocial Aspects of Drug Treatment for Hyperactivity*. Boulder, CO: Westview Press, pp. 381–416.

McCabe, S.E., Knight, J.R. et al. (2005) 'Non-medical use of prescription stimulants among US college students: prevalence and correlates from a national survey', *Addiction*, 99(1): 96–106.

McDermott, S.P. & Wilens, T.E. (2000) 'Cognitive therapy for adults with ADHD', in T. Brown (ed.), *Subtypes of Attention Deficit Disorders in Children, Adolescents, and Adults*. Washington, DC: American Psychiatric Press, pp. 569–606.

McGuffin, P., Riley, B. et al. (2001) 'Toward behavioral genomics', *Science* 291: 1232–1249.

Makris, N., Biederman, J. et al. (2007) 'Cortical thinning of the attention and executive function networks in adults with attention-deficit/hyperactivity disorder', *Cerebral Cortex*, 17(6): 1364–1375.

Mannuzza, S., Klein, R.G. et al. (1993) 'Adult outcome of hyperactive boys: educational achievement, occupational rank and psychiatric status', *Archives of General Psychiatry*, 50: 565–576.

Mannuzza, S., Klein, R.G. et al. (2002) 'Young adult outcome of children with "situational" hyperactivity: a prospective, controlled follow-up study', *Journal of Abnormal Child Psychology*, 30(2): 191–198.

Martinussen, R., Hayden, J. et al. (2005) 'A meta-analysis of working memory impairments in children with attention-deficit/hyperactivity disorder', *Journal of the American Academy of Child and Adolescent Psychiatry*, 44(4): 377–384.

Michelson, D., Allen, A.J. et al. (2002) 'Once-daily atomoxetine treatment for children and adolescents with ADHD: a randomized, placebo-controlled study', *American Journal of Psychiatry*, 159: 1896–1901.

Michelson, D., Buitelaar, J.K. et al. (2004) 'Relapse prevention in pediatric patients with ADHD treated with atomoxetine: a randomized, double-blind, placebo-controlled study', *Journal of the American Academy of Child and Adolescent Psychiatry*, 43(7): 896–904.

Michelson, D., Faries, D. et al. (2001) 'Atomoxetine in the treatment of children and adolescents with attention-deficit/hyperactivity disorder: a randomized, placebo-controlled, dose-response study', *Pediatrics*, 108(5): E83.

Mick, E., Faraone, S.V. et al. (2004) 'The course and outcome of ADHD', *Primary Psychiatry*, 11(7): 42–48.

Milberger, S., Biederman, J. et al. (1995) 'Attention deficit hyperactivity disorder and comorbid disorders: issues of overlapping symptoms', *American Journal of Psychiatry*, 152(12): 1793–1799.

Millstein, R.B., Wilens, T.E. et al. (1997) 'Presenting ADHD symptoms and subtypes in clinically referred adults with ADHD', *Journal of Attention Disorders*, 2(3): 159–166.

MTA Cooperative Group (1999a) 'A 14-month randomized clinical trial of treatment strategies for attention-deficit/hyperactivity disorder. The MTA Cooperative Group. Multimodal Treatment Study of Children with ADHD [see comments]', *Archives of General Psychiatry*, 56(12): 1073–1086.

MTA Cooperative Group (1999b) 'Moderators and mediators of treatment response for children with attention-deficit/hyperactivity disorder: the Multimodal Treatment Study of Children with Attention-Deficit/Hyperactivity Disorder', *Archives of General Psychiatry*, 56(12): 1088–1096.

MTA Cooperative Group (1999c) 'A 14-month randomized clinical trial of treatment strategies for attention-deficit/hyperactivity disorder. The MTA Cooperative Group. Multimodal Treatment Study of Children with ADHD', *Archives of General Psychiatry*, 56(12): 1073–1086.

MTA Cooperative Group (2004) 'National Institute of Mental Health Multimodal Treatment Study of ADHD follow-up: changes in effectiveness and growth after the end of treatment', *Pediatrics* 113: 762–769.

Murphy, P. & Schachar, R. (2000) 'Use of self-ratings in the assessment of symptoms of attention deficit hyperactivity disorder in adults', *American Journal of Psychiatry*, 157(7): 1156–1159.

Newcorn, J.H., Spencer, T.J. et al. (2005) 'Atomoxetine treatment in children and adolescents with attention-deficit/hyperactivity disorder and comorbid oppositional defiant disorder', *Journal of the American Academy of Child and Adolescent Psychiatry*, 44(3): 240–248.

Palumbo, D.R., Sallee, F.R. et al. (2008) 'Clonidine for attention-deficit/hyperactivity disorder: I. Efficacy and tolerability outcomes', *Journal of the American Academy of Child and Adolescent Psychiatry*, 47(2): 180–188.

Parasrampuria, D.A., Schoedel, K.A. et al. (2007) 'Do formulation differences alter abuse liability of methylphenidate? A placebo-controlled, randomized, double-blind, crossover study in recreational drug users', *Journal of Clinical Psychopharmacology*, 27(5): 459–467.

Pelham, W., Wheeler, T. et al. (1998) 'Empirically supported psychosocial treatments for attention deficit hyperactivity disorder', *Journal of Clinical Child Psychology*, 27(2): 190–205.

Perrin, J.M., Friedman, R.A. et al. (2008) 'Cardiovascular monitoring and stimulant drugs for attention-deficit/hyperactivity disorder', *Pediatrics*, 122(2): 451–453.

Polanczyk, G., de Lima, M.S. et al. (2007) 'The worldwide prevalence of ADHD: a systematic review and metaregression analysis', *American Journal of Psychiatry*, 164(6): 942–948.

Prince, J., Wilens, T. et al. (1996) 'Clonidine for sleep disturbances associated with attention-deficit hyperactivity disorder: a systematic chart review of 62 cases', *Journal of the American Academy of Child and Adolescent Psychiatry*, 35(5): 599–605.

Prince, J.B., Wilens, T.E. et al. (2000) 'A controlled study of nortriptyline in children and adolescents with attention deficit hyperactivity disorder', *Journal of Child and Adolescent Psychopharmacology*, 10(3): 193–204.

Rappley, M.D., Moore, J.W. et al. (2006) 'ADHD drugs and cardiovascular risk', *New England Journal of Medicine*, 354(21): 2296–2298. author reply 2296–2298.

Reimherr, F.W., Hedges, D.W. et al. (1995) '*An open trial of venlafaxine in adult patients with attention deficit hyperactivity disorder*', 35th, Annual Meeting New Clinical Drug Evaluation Unit Program, Orlando, Florida.

Safer, D., Allen, R. et al. (1972) 'Depression of growth in hyperactive children on stimulant drugs', *New England Journal of Medicine*, 287(5): 217–220.

Safren SA, Sprich S, Mimiaga MJ, et al. Cognitive behavioral therapy vs relaxation with educational support for medication-treated adults with ADHD and persistent symptoms: a randomized controlled trial. *JAMA*. Aug 25 2010; 304(8): 875–880.

Sandra Kooij, J.J., Marije Boonstra, A. et al. (2008) 'Reliability, validity, and utility of instruments for self-report and informant report concerning symptoms of ADHD in adult patients', *Journal of Attention Disorders*, 11(4): 445–458.

Seidman, L., Doyle, A. et al. (2004) 'Neuropsychological functioning in adults with attention-deficit/hyperactivity disorder', *Psychiatric Clinics of North America*, 27: 261–282.

Seidman, L.J. (2006) 'Neuropsychological functioning in people with ADHD across the lifespan', *Clinical Psychology Review*, 26(4): 466–485.

Seidman, L.J., Valera, E.M. et al. (2006) 'Dorsolateral prefrontal and anterior cingulate cortex volumetric abnormalities in adults with attention-deficit/hyperactivity disorder identified by magnetic resonance imaging', *Biological Psychiatry*, 60(10): 1071–1080.

Sergeant, J.A., Geurts, H. et al. (2002) 'How specific is a deficit of executive functioning for attention-deficit/hyperactivity disorder?', *Behavioural Brain Research*, 130(1–2): 3–28.

Shaw, P., Eckstrand, K. et al. (2007) 'Attention-deficit/hyperactivity disorder is characterized by a delay in cortical maturation', *Proceedings of the National Academy of Sciences*, 104(49): 19649–19654.

Solanto MV, Marks DJ, Wasserstein J, et al. Efficacy of Meta-Cognitive Therapy for Adult ADHD. *Am J Psychiatry*. Aug 2010; 167(8): 958–968.

Sonuga-Barke, E., Dalen, L. et al. (2003) 'Do executive deficits and delay aversion make independent contributions to preschool attention-deficit/hyperactivity disorder symptoms', *Journal of the American Academy of Child and Adolescent Psychiatry*, 42(11): 1335–1342.

Sonuga-Barke, E., Daley, D. et al. (2001) 'Parent-based therapies for preschool ADHD; a randomized, controlled trial with a community sample', *Journal of the American Academy of Child and Adolescent Psychiatry*, 40(4): 402–408.

Sonuga-Barke, E., Thompson, M. et al. (2006) 'Nonpharmacological interventions for preschoolers with ADHD: the case for specialized parent training', *Infants & Young Children*, 19(2): 142–153.

Sonuga-Barke, E.J. (2003) 'The dual pathway model of AD/HD: an elaboration of neuro-developmental characteristics', *Neuroscience & Biobehavioral Reviews*, 27(7): 593–604.

Spencer, T., Biederman, J. et al. (1998a) 'Growth deficits in ADHD children', *Pediatrics,* 102(Suppl 2): 501–506.

Spencer, T., Biederman, J. et al. (1998b). 'Pharmacotherapy of attention-deficit/hyperactivity disorder: a life span perspective', in L. Dickstein, M. Riba, & J. Oldham (eds), *Review of Psychiatry*. Washington, DC: American Psychiatric Press, 16: IV-87–IV-127.

Spencer, T., Biederman, J. et al. (2006) 'A PET study examining pharmacokinetics, detection and likeability, and dopamine transporter receptor occupancy of short and long-acting orally administered formulations of methylphenidate in adults', *American Journal of Psychiatry*, 163(3): 387–395.

Spencer, T., Wilens, T.E. et al. (1995) 'A double blind, crossover comparison of methylphenidate and placebo in adults with childhood onset attention deficit hyperactivity disorder', *Archives of General Psychiatry*, 52: 434–443.

Stein, M.A., Sandoval, R. et al. (1995) 'Psychometric characteristics of the Wender Utah Rating Scale (WURS) reliability and factor structure for men and women', *Psychopharmacology Bulletin*, 31: 423–431.

Swanson, J., Greenhill, L. et al. (2006) 'Stimulant-related reductions of growth rates in the PATS', *Journal of the American Academy of Child and Adolescent Psychiatry*, 45(11): 1304–1313.

Swanson, J.M., Kraemer, H.C. et al. (2001) 'Clinical relevance of the primary findings of the MTA: success rates based on severity of ADHD and ODD symptoms at the end of treatment', *Journal of the American Academy of Child and Adolescent Psychiatry*, 40(2): 168–179.

Swanson, J., Lerner, M. et al. (2003) 'Development of a new once-a-day formulation of methylphenidate for the treatment of ADHD: proof of concept and proof of product studies', *Archives of General Psychiatry*, 60(2): 204–211.

Valera, E.M., Faraone, S.V. et al. (2005) 'Functional neuroanatomy of working memory in adults with attention-deficit/hyperactivity disorder', *Biological Psychiatry*, 57(5): 439–447.

van den Hoofdakker, B.J., van der Veen-Mulders, L. et al. (2007) 'Effectiveness of behavioral parent training for children with ADHD in routine clinical practice: a randomized controlled study', *Journal of the American Academy of Child and Adolescent Psychiatry*, 46(10): 1263–1271.

Vitiello, B. (2001) 'Long-term effects of stimulant medications on the brain: possible relevance to the treatment of attention deficit hyperactivity disorder', *Journal of Child and Adolescent Psychopharmacology*, 11(1): 25–34.

Weiss, M. & Hechtman, L. (2006) 'A randomized double-blind trial of paroxetine and/or dextroamphetamine and problem-focused therapy for attention-deficit/hyperactivity disorder in adults', *Journal of Clinical Psychiatry*, 67(4): 611–619.

Wilens, T. (2006) 'Mechanism of action of agents used in ADHD', *Journal of Clinical Psychiatry*, 67(Suppl 8): 32–37.

Wilens, T., Biederman, J. et al. (1998) 'Does ADHD affect the course of substance abuse? Findings from a sample of adults with and without ADHD', *American Journal on Addictions*, 7: 156–163.

Wilens, T., Biederman, J. et al. (2003) 'Can adults with attention-deficit hyperactivity disorder be distinguished from those with comorbid bipolar disorder: findings from a sample of clinically referred adults', *Biological Psychiatry*, 54(1): 1–8.

Wilens T.E., Adler L.A., Weiss M.D., et al. Atomoxetine treatment of adults with ADHD and comorbid alcohol use disorders. Drug *Alcohol Depend*. Jul 1 2008;96(1–2):145–154.

Wilens, T. & Biederman, J. (2006) 'Alcohol, drugs, and attention-deficit/hyperactivity disorder: a model for the study of addictions in youth', *Journal of Psychopharmacology*, 20(4): 580–588.

Wilens, T., Biederman, J. et al. (2009) 'Presenting ADHD symptoms, subtypes, and comorbid disorders in clinically referred adults with ADHD', *Journal of Clinical Psychiatry*, 70(11): 1557–1562.

Wilens, T., Faraone, S. et al. (2003) 'Does stimulant therapy of attention-deficit/hyperactivity disorder beget later substance abuse? A metaanalytic review of the literature', *Pediatrics*, 11(1): 179–185.

Wilens, T., Haight, B.R. et al. (2005) 'Bupropion XL in adults with ADHD: a randomized, placebo-controlled study', *Biological Psychiatry*, 57(7): 793–801.

Wilens, T., Prince, J. et al. (2003) 'An open trial of bupropion for the treatment of adults with attention deficit hyperactivity disorder and bipolar disorder', *Biological Psychiatry*, 54(1): 9–16.

Wilens, T., Zusman, R.M. et al. (2006) 'An open-label study of the tolerability of mixed amphetamine salts in adults with ADHD and treated primary essential hypertension', *Journal of Clinical Psychiatry*, 67(5): 696–702.

Wilens, T.E., Hammerness, P. et al. (2009) 'An Open Study of Adjunct OROS-Methylphenidate in Children and Adolescents who are a tomoxetine Partial Responders: I. Effectiveness', *J Child Adolesc Psychopharmacol*, 19(5): 485–492.

Wilens, T.E., Adamson, J. et al. (2008) 'Effect of prior stimulant treatment for attention-deficit/hyperactivity disorder on subsequent risk for cigarette smoking and alcohol and drug use disorders in adolescents', *Archives of Pediatric and Adolescent Medicine*, 162(10): 916–921.

Wilens, T.E., Adler, L.A. et al. (2008) 'Misuse and diversion of stimulants prescribed for ADHD: a systematic review of the literature', *Journal of the American Academy of Child and Adolescent Psychiatry*, 47(1): 21–31.

Wilens, T.E., Gignac, M. et al. (2006) 'Characteristics of adolescents and young adults with ADHD who divert or misuse their prescribed medications', *Journal of the American Academy of Child and Adolescent Psychiatry*, 45(4): 408–414.

Wilens, T.E. and Spencer, T. (2000) 'The stimulants revisited', *Child and Adolescent Psychiatric Clinics of North America*, 9: 573–603.

Wilens, T.E., Spencer, T.J. et al. (1999) 'Combining methylphenidate and clonidine: a clinically sound medication option', *Journal of the American Academy of Child and Adolescent Psychiatry*, 38(5): 614–619; discussion 619–622.

Wilens, T.E., Spencer, T.J. et al. (2001) 'A controlled clinical trial of bupropion for attention deficit hyperactivity disorder in adults', *American Journal of Psychiatry*, 158(2): 282–288.

Wilens, T.E., Vitulano, M. et al. (2008) 'Cigarette smoking associated with attention deficit hyperactivity disorder', *Journal of Pediatrics*, 153(3): 414–419.

Wilens T.E., Adler L.A, Weiss M.D., et al. Atomoxetine treatment of adults with ADHD and comorbid alcohol use disorders. Drug Alcohol Depend. Jul 1 2008; 96(1–2): 145–154.

Winokur, G., Coryell, W. et al. (1993) 'Further distinctions between manic-depressive illness (bipolar disorder) and primary depressive disorder (unipolar depression)', American Journal of Psychiatry, 150(8): 1176–1181.

Wozniak, J., Biederman, J. et al. (1995) 'Mania-like symptoms suggestive of childhood-onset bipolar disorder in clinically referred children', Journal of the American Academy of Child and Adolescent Psychiatry, 34: 867–876.

14

Autism Spectrum Disorders: General Overview

Catherine Lord, So Hyun Kim & Adriana Dimartino

HISTORICAL PERSPECTIVE

The history of research on autism spectrum disorders (ASD) is an intriguing example of the value of multidisciplinary and interdisciplinary approaches to developmental disorders. Though it is likely that autism has existed for a very long time (Lane, 1979), the first documentations of it as a syndrome were made in the early1940 in parallel by a psychiatrist and a pediatrician in different countries, in very different situations. Leo Kanner (1943) provided detailed descriptions of 11 children seen in his psychiatric clinic in Baltimore who shared qualities of social aloofness, insistence on sameness and language delays or oddities. At about the same time, Hans Asperger (1944), a pediatrician, described four "little professors" who shared qualities of social awkwardness and circumscribed interests, but who had strengths in vocabulary and syntactic aspects of language. Although these descriptions were not compared to each other until many years later (Frith, 1989), the behaviors described in these children form the base of conceptualizations of autism spectrum disorders even today.

Both Kanner and Asperger saw vestiges of the behaviors that defined their new syndromes in the parents of their child patients. These comments are now primarily interpreted as suggesting that a broader autism phenotype may run in some families. However, at the time, given the popularity of psychodynamic and psychoanalytic theory in the USA and Germany, interest developed in autism as a result of social deprivation and/or poor parenting (Bettelheim, 1967) and autism was believed to be a childhood form of schizophrenia (which was also believed to be psychogenic).

A number of clinical researchers began to question this approach in the late 1960 from several perspectives. Rutter and Lockyer (1967) argued that the associations between autism and seizures and intellectual disability were evidence that it was a neurologically based disorder. Rutter and Schopler (1978) also began to argue that language deficits were an integral part of autism. Rimland (1964), the scientist parent of a boy with autism, developed one of the first models of autism as a cognitive deficit arising from attentional difficulties. Ornitz and Ritvo (1968), two American psychiatrists, focused on sensory and vestibular systems in some of the first observational studies. Hermelin and O'Connor (1970), research psychologists in the UK, carried out some of the first systematic experiments on cognitive processing in children with autism, showing that this mysterious condition could be beginning to be understood by systematic testing of hypotheses about cognitive processes.

Finally, Schopler (1971) wrote a seminal paper, also working from the assumption that autism is a neurobiological disorder. Schopler proposed that parents were blamed for causing autism in the same way that other minorities are scapegoated for events that are not understood. Schopler also argued that, from a treatment perspective, a useful focus was the identification of emerging skills that could be facilitated and extended, presaging the more developmental approaches to therapy that have been proposed by others (Greenspan & Wieder, 1997).

At about the same time, Lovaas (1966) and other behaviorists came to autism with the belief that standard operant-learning principles could be employed to teach anyone anything, including teaching language and social skills to this unique group of children. This was the beginning of what is now the most well-documented treatment for autism, applied behavioral analysis (ABA).

In the late 1970, two other lines of research in autism emerged which have significantly changed our approaches to the disorder. One began with Folstein and Rutter's (1978) twin study comparing identical and fraternal twins with autism. This study pulled autism into the world of genetics, with the finding of much greater concordance for autism in monozygotic than dizygotic twins. However, another finding of the study proved equally important. This was the fact that while concordant for autism and autism-related behaviors, identical twins with autism-related symptoms were not *identical* in these symptoms, often showing very large discrepancies

in intellectual levels, severity of autism symptoms and levels of impairment. What was transmitted familially was not classical autism, a finding that underlies conceptualization of autism as a spectrum of disorders, even within the restricted range of identical genotypes in identical twins.

Another line of research that also has led to the concept of autism spectrum disorders came from an epidemiological study of children in London, led by Wing and Gould (1979). These authors described a triad of impairments in social reciprocity, language comprehension, and play. These deficits, in their most extreme, characterize autism but also occur in many individuals with other developmental disorders. Out of these findings came broader definitions of autism and the term pervasive developmental disorders used in the American Psychiatric Association manuals (APA, 1987), which determine diagnostic categorizations (and billing for services) in the USA. Other areas of research in autism that have dramatically changed our understanding of the disorder and clinical and educational practice are follow-up and treatment studies, described in Chapter 15.

Finally, one of the most important aspects of the history of autism research and practice has been the significant contribution of parent advocacy organizations. This began with the founding of the Autism Society of America and the British National Autism Society in the 1960. Pressed by parent-founded research advocacy programs (Cure Autism Now, National Alliance for Autism Research, both now merged into Autism Speaks, as well as others), foundations, and federal institutes in different countries, research groups across continents have begun to work together to create networks with access to large populations of individuals with autism. This, together with the availability of standardized diagnostic instruments in many languages, has led to much more sophisticated analyses and opportunities better to address individual differences. Public awareness, research funding, and sometimes, services, have benefited greatly from these parent-initiated efforts.

EPIDEMIOLOGY OF ASD

Epidemiology has played a major role in autism research, from the early studies of Wing and Gould (1979) to recent studies in Europe responding to claims that vaccines in various forms may play a causal role in autism spectrum disorders. The earliest studies of ASD in the 1960 indicated a prevalence rate for relatively narrowly defined autism of 4~5 in 10,000 (Fombonne, 2007). Autism was estimated to be about four times more common in males than females. Only about 20% of children with autism were estimated to have IQs outside the range of intellectual disability, though with large variation across studies.

These figures began to change, first in the late 1980, with reports from Japan, Canada, the UK and Sweden, of higher prevalence rates (above 10 in 10,000; Fombonne, 2009). Smaller studies found the highest rates of autism, suggesting that ascertainment affected estimate rates (Fombonne, 2009). By the late 1980, a high proportion of studies began to find these or even higher prevalence rates: Fombonne estimates 13~16 in 10,000 for autism, with even higher rates of the more broadly defined pervasive developmental disorders — not otherwise specified (PDD-NOS) of up to 20 — 21/10,000. Out of these figures, the typical estimate used by autism societies and public health agencies in the USA is that approximately 1 in 150 children have an ASD (CDC, 2007), although in the UK for example, the figure of 1 in 100 is used (Baird et al., 2006).

Proposals have been made that ASDs are more common in certain segments of Western countries, including families of higher socioeconomic status and families of immigrants, but these findings have not generally been confirmed. In the USA, there are clear discrepancies in when children of less well-educated parents are diagnosed (i.e. later) and there appear to be differences in the extent to which children of minority ethnic groups receive formal diagnoses of ASD (Rice et al.,

2004). Almost all recent studies have found smaller proportions of children with ASD to have intellectual disabilities (from 30 to 60%) than did earlier estimates (Baird et al., 2006; Chakrabarti & Fombonne, 2005).

Many claims have been made about the increasing prevalence of ASD. Links between these changes in prevalence and vaccination patterns have been consistently refuted (Offit, 2008). Other hypotheses to account for the increases that have received some support are the broader definitions (Kielinen et al., 2000), increased community awareness (Fombonne, 2007), and better ascertainment (Rice et al., 2004). Surveillance studies will be crucial to answer these questions. Studies in which broadly defined populations are very carefully described using standardized instruments would help to delineate the possible effects of changing diagnostic criteria. More epidemiological and case-control studies that address specific hypotheses about risk factors in different populations will also be critical.

CAUSES OF AUTISM SPECTRUM DISORDERS

By definition, autism spectrum disorders are not the result of known trauma or injury. By far the greatest emphasis on etiology of ASD in the last 20 years has been genetics. Advocacy groups have called for more studies of environmental factors but, on the whole, such research has not yet been very fruitful. In fact, to date, even though there have been a number of interesting findings and "leads" in the genetics of autism, there have been only a few findings with replications across samples, and these findings have accounted for only a small proportion of cases (see Bill & Geschwind, 2009; see Weiss et al., 2008 for an alternative point of view). As a clearer picture of the genetics of ASD emerges, the newer hope is to tell a story or stories about different points along the lines of brain development and function at which genetics could affect learning in order to yield the behavior patterns we characterize as ASD.

There are several known genetic syndromes in which a substantial minority of patients meets diagnostic criteria for ASD. These include tuberous sclerosis (TSC1; TSC2; Bolton et al., 2002), 15q11-13 (Schanen, 2006), and fragile X syndrome (Kaufmann et al., 2008). In these cases, children with the genetic syndromes who meet criteria for autism or ASD appear indistinguishable from other children with autism; other children with the syndrome have some characteristics (e.g. poor eye contact in fragile X), but not others. In general, within groups of children defined by these genetic tests, the children with autism are often more intellectually disabled (Rogers et al., 2001) and more likely to have seizures (Smalley, 1998) or clear neurological abnormalities as measured in magnetic resonance imaging (MRI) or functional MRI (fMRI) (Bolton, 2007). In addition, girls with Rett syndrome (MECP2; Neul et al., 2008) share a number of features with children with autism, including regression in the first or second year of life, repetitive hand movements and minimal communication skills, though as the girls with Rett syndrome get older, they have additional symptoms not associated with autism (e.g. spasticity) and may not have the specific social deficits that define ASD. Nevertheless, the overlaps in symptoms between ASD and these well-characterized genetic syndromes is a further argument in favor of autism, even with all its heterogeneity, being a genetic condition.

As discussed earlier, the concordance for ASD, and especially for ASD-related difficulties, is very high in identical twins (60~90%; Bailey et al., 1995) and also higher for siblings, including fraternal twins (5~10% for ASD; even greater for related difficulties; Piven et al., 1997). Based on these findings, some researchers have argued that autism is polygenic (Pickles et al., 1995), meaning that multiple genes must be involved in each individual case, estimating that from 3 to 20 genes contribute to a particular pattern.

Research aimed at discovering such genes has taken place from a number of perspectives. Linkage and association studies have found loci on chromosomes 1, 2, 3, 5, 6, 7, 11, 13, 15, 17, 19, and 22, as well as the X chromosome (Bill & Geschwind, 2009). Other research programs have attempted, through the use of broad questions about the three areas that define autism in DSM-IV (APA, 1994) and ICD-10 (World Health Organization, 1992) (communication, social skills, and repetitive behaviors) to look for patterns in families and non-autistic twins to assess the degree with which these general areas of behavior are familial (Ronald et al., 2008). In another study using an instrument that measures autism symptoms, including social deficits and repetitive behaviors and interests, the Social Responsiveness Scale (SRS), two differing patterns have been obtained (Constantino et al., 2006). The findings suggest a continuous distribution in the population of these characteristics when "unaffected" siblings in families of two or more children with autism were studied and in the general population and, more lately, a bimodal distribution with only a small number of cases of high scores in siblings of "singleton" children with autism (Constantino et al., 2004).

Most recently, intriguing findings have emerged about spontaneous mutations, called copy number variations (CNVs), in which the number of copies in a particular stretch of DNA is either increased (duplications) or decreased (deletions) during epigenesis (Cook & Scherer, 2008). A high number of different CNVs associated with autism would suggest an epigenetic origin or risk for autism that is not transmitted familially: i.e. there are genetic forms of autism that are not inherited.

NEUROLOGICAL AND BIOCHEMICAL STUDIES

Neuroanatomical and imaging studies

Though much indirect evidence (e.g. increased prevalence of seizures, and intellectual disabilities, and strong genetic component) supported the model of autism as a neurobiological disorder, only in the last 15~20 years has the search for biological markers taken hold. This change has largely been related to the broader availability of non-invasive MRI approaches. Previously available brain imaging techniques were limited by poor spatial resolution and the risks of the substantial radiation exposure associated with computed axial tomography or the radioactive ligands used for position emission tomography (PET) and single-photon emission computed tomography (SPECT). More direct approaches such as postmortem studies in ASD have raised many important questions. However, the small and likely unrepresentative samples of individuals with ASD have also limited their results (Bauman & Kemper, 2005). These postmortem studies have been carried out with a few adult brains from individuals with a high prevalence of epilepsy and/or profound intellectual disability. Nevertheless, findings of reduced cell size, increased cell packing density in the amygdala and other medial temporal regions, as well as reduced number of Purkinje cells in the posterior inferior cerebellar hemispheres, have been useful in providing leads to researchers. Additional research with larger samples and more advanced technology is eagerly awaited (Bauman & Kemper, 2005).

Small sample sizes and heterogeneity (e.g. age, symptom severity, IQ, and comorbidity differences) also constrained the first generation of brain imaging results in ASD, which can be summarized as a series of disappointingly unreplicated results (Minshew et al., 2006). Nevertheless, recent findings of increased white and gray matter volumes during the first years of life have been consistently replicated by independent cross-sectional and longitudinal studies (Courchesne et al., 2001). These findings are also consistent with longstanding reports of increased head circumference and brain weight in children with ASD (Bauman & Kemper, 2005). In pre-schoolers with ASD, gray and white matter enlargements have been found in the

frontal, temporal, and parietal lobes, all areas related to higher-order cognitive functions, which are among the slowest to develop ontogenetically. Though it appears that the brain overgrowth reaches a plateau or decreases during late childhood and adolescence, findings are not yet consistent about the exact timing and trajectories of growth, as some authors have reported increased volumes up to early adulthood (Carper et al., 2006).

Another replicated morphological finding is the enlargement of the cerebellar hemispheres, reported in several well-designed studies in children and adults (see Brambilla et al., 2003). In contrast, both increased and decreased volumes of hippocampus and amygdala have been reported in individuals with ASD (Munson et al., 2006). Such inconsistency has been attributed to age effects. Amygdala volume differences have been recently investigated in a longitudinal study of toddlers with autism from 2 to 4 years old (Mosconi et al., 2009). The authors found that enlargement of the right amygdala persisted from age 2 to 4 and correlated with joint attention deficits at age 4. This recent study is among the few that found a correlation between structural findings and clinical or functional measures in ASD (see also Juranek et al., 2006).

A more direct measure of the brain-behavior relationship can be attained with functional imaging studies. Currently, the gold standard approach is fMRI, which has focused predominantly, but not exclusively, on adults with ASD. Working from the hypothesis that social cognitive deficits are the defining features of autism, researchers have used social cognition-based paradigms to demarcate differences in the social brain of individuals with ASD. Among these, functional imaging studies examining face recognition and facial expression perception have consistently found diagnostic differences in activation of the fusiform gyrus, in response to faces compared to complex objects (e.g. Schultz et al., 2000). However, the direct role of hypoactivation of the fusiform area in

ASD remains unclear and recent findings suggest a lack of ASD differences in general after controlling for fixation or time of eye gaze, as well as during processing of familiar faces (Sterling et al., 2008). Studies of gaze-following and processing of biological motion have revealed a reduction in activation of the posterior component of the superior temporal sulcus (Pelphrey & Carter, 2008). This increasingly more sophisticated research is promising in its effort to disentangle different aspects of perception of social stimuli (e.g. face, eye gaze, and other biological agents) (Pelphrey & Carter, 2008).

Beyond these specific investigations, the most consistently replicated finding in the functional imaging literature of social cognition of ASD is the hypoactivation of rostral medial prefrontal cortex (MPFC) and adjacent pregenual anterior cingulate cortex (ACC). This pattern emerged very robustly in a meta-analysis of 39 functional imaging studies of social cognition in ASD published up to 2008 (Di Martino et al., 2009). In typical controls MPFC and pregenual ACC have been associated with social cognition (Amodio & Frith, 2006). Another recurrent, but more confusing theme has been the exploration of social motivation, with an emphasis on hypoactivation of the amygdala (Baron-Cohen et al., 2000). Amygdala dysfunction was initially linked to ASD due to the region's proposed role in evaluating facial expression and representing affective salience. The nature of amygdala functional abnormalities in autism-related symptoms needs further examinations. Recently, amygdala hyperactivity was noted in ASD, and related to ASD related phenomena such as diminished eye-gaze fixation (Dalton et al., 2005). Literature discrepancies may reflect functional and structural complexities of the characteristics of a small region such as amygdala, or possible differences in specific paradigms employed for the examinations of amygdala activation.

An increasing number of studies have focused on brain correlates of non-social cognitive profiles such as executive function-ing, motor, language, and auditory processing in ASD. A recurrent finding across studies, regardless of the specific paradigm implemented, is hypoactivation in task-targeted regions, accompanied by increased function in areas implicated in more basic sensory processing, such as the primary visual cortex. This finding has been regarded as an indirect evidence of top-down deregulation underlined by disconnections between brain regions (Minshew & Williams, 2007). Direct examination of functional connectivity (FC; defined as the temporal correlations between remote neurophysiological events; Friston, 1994) is provided by several task based fMRI studies (e.g. Just et al., 2004). An alternative approach that bypasses potential confounds of tasks is resting state fMRI. To date, only a few studies have examined intrinsic brain activity at rest in ASD. Results support the model of compromised long-range cortico-cortical connectivity (Kennedy & Courchesne, 2008). The dysconnection model of autism has been also supported by structural studies implementing diffusion tensor imaging (DTI), revealing diffuse patterns of decreased white integrity (e.g. Sundaram et al., 2008) with widely distributed loci. Though structural and functional neuroimaging studies have been the core of neurological research in autism, yielding many exciting research leads, no findings have had sufficient sensitivity or specificity that would allow neuroimaging to support diagnosis yet.

Neurochemical studies

Until recently, neurochemical research in autism has focused on three major neurotransmitters: norepinephrine, dopamine and serotonin (5-HT, 5-hydroxytryptamine); with some emerging interest in acetylcholine (Bauman et al., 2006). Findings have been inconsistent regarding dopamine. While there has been interest in norepinephrine as an indication of apparent increased response to stressors, these results could be due to a difference in level of perceived stress, a difference in physiological response, or in more general underlying abnormalities in stress and arousal.

Serotonin is the most well-studied neurotransmitter in autism. Links between serotonin and autism have been found on a number of levels. PET studies found lower serotonin in the thalamus and frontal cortex in young boys with autism compared to controls (Chugani et al, 1999); other studies found higher mean levels of serotonin in blood (which is congruent with less in brain) (Anderson et al., 2002). Some recent studies have suggested that the distribution of platelet 5-HT concentration is bimodal (Mulder et al., 2004). Cerebrospinal fluid (CSF) studies of serotonin levels have not found differences between individuals with autism and controls (Cook, 1990). Associations have been found between autism and particular polymorphisms of the serotonin transporter gene (Raznahan et al., 2009). Serotonin drugs (5-HT reuptake inhibitors) are often used to ameliorate mood-related symptoms in autism. Thus, the evidence supports the hypothesis that serotonin contributes somehow to the etiology of autism.

Another research area of much interest is the study of possible indicators of neuroinflammation, both in postmortem tissue and in CSF samples from living patients with autism (Vargas et al., 2005). The possibility that autism is like neurogenerative disorders and reflects an ongoing process is very promising in terms of an improved basic science understanding, but also very preliminary. At this point, findings have not yet been replicated nor led directly to treatments, though possibilities are being considered.

Animal models for autism are also beginning to be developed. Although the direct relationship between behaviors in rodents, primates and other animals, and in humans with autism will never be completely clear, there are a number of very carefully thought-out models for social and repetitive behaviors in mice (Crawley, 2007) and for affective behaviors in primates (Amaral et al., 2003).

The availability of these models and the emerging protocols for identifying layers of control tasks, such as measuring general activity level, memory, and health are important steps in the neuroscience of autism.

ENVIRONMENTAL HYPOTHESES

Although the increased prevalence of ASDs has led many parents and professionals to raise the possibility of environmental contributions to the etiology of autism, there is relatively little evidence yet that this is the case. The most common evidence used for an environmental approach to autism, besides the rising prevalence rates, is evidence that toxins ingested by mothers can result in autism in their children. Maternal exposures to valproic acid (an anticonvulsant sometimes used as a mood stabilizer or to treat migraines), thalidomide, and rubella have been linked to autistic behaviors in small samples of not particularly well-characterized children (Chess, 1971; Miller et al., 1998; Moore et al., 2000). In general, these studies have not been replicated using standard diagnostic criteria for autism (in part because, hopefully, few pregnant women are now exposed to these drugs and/or diseases), nor have the contributions of general intellectual disability, sensory impairments, and motor difficulties been carefully separated from deficits specific to autism. Children with ASD have a higher rate of non-optimal prenatal complications than their siblings and matched controls, also suggesting that factors during pregnancy may contribute to risk for autism (Gillberg & Gillberg, 1983). Recently, a relatively high proportion of low or very low birthweight children in a neonatal intensive care follow-up study were found to have ASD (Schendel & Bhasin, 2008), seconding this concern. A few studies have looked at "clusters" of autism in relation to environmental exposures, but none have been conclusive (Bertrand et al., 2001). Not much beyond these very general risk factors are known.

The most controversial and hence, well-studied, environmental risk has been vaccinations. Historically, concern was first raised in 1980 about the diphtheria pertussis typhoid vaccination and its link with autism (Jick & Kaye, 2004). In part, the recurring concern emerges because of the onset of autistic symptoms at the beginning or middle of the second year of life, a time when many children are receiving vaccines. In the mid-1990, a gastroenterologist in the UK, Andrew Wakefield, published a paper in which he claimed that children with autism had active measles virus in their guts and the onset of behavioral problems of those children was linked with measles, mumps, and rubella (MMR) vaccination (Wakefield et al., 1998). He suggested that the virus affected their immune systems, and then brain function, causing autism (Wakefield et al., 2000). These papers received an enormous amount of press and attention, resulting in a decrease in the MMR immunization rate in the UK of nearly 10% (Offit, 2008).

It has since been revealed that, before he wrote the paper, Wakefield had received a retaining fee from attorneys suing the government on behalf of these children. Some of Wakefield's co-authors have withdrawn their names from the paper and Wakefield has been charged in court. However, in the meanwhile, a very vocal antivaccine lobby has developed in the USA and UK. The arguments are that the increase in the number of early childhood vaccines accounts for the increase in prevalence of ASD, that reactions to vaccines can explain behavioral regressions that occur in a significant minority of children with ASD, and that there is a particular "autistic regression" phenotype characterized by gastrointestinal (GI) disturbances and regression (see Richler et al., 2006). After the specifics of the MMR argument were repeatedly refuted, antivaccine advocates turned their attention to thimerosal, the preservative which allowed MMR vaccines to be stored together. Thimerosal is a mercury-based compound, and it was pointed out that the amount of mercury in a typical vaccine exceeded federal limits for other kinds of mercury in food (see Fombonne, 2008). This argument resulted in thimerosal being removed from all vaccines routinely administered to young children in the USA.

None of the logical or empirical arguments supporting a connection between vaccines and autism has turned out to be valid. Increases in measured prevalence have continued even in the face of the absence of thimerosal and falling vaccination rates, including, for example, withdrawal of the MMR vaccination in Japan (Honda et al., 2005). There is not a link between regression and vaccinations. Although the parents of children with autism report a slightly higher rate of GI complaints, there does not seem to be any relation between major GI disorders and autism, and there is no relation between even the milder GI problems and vaccination history (Richler et al., 2006). Thus, the concerns about associations between vaccinations and autism have been shown to be unfounded on every single dimension studied. Nevertheless, celebrities and very committed parents continue to demand more research in this specific area.

Other attempts to link autism and environmental factors, from pet shampoos to carpet cleaners to parental exposure to chemicals, have so far been unsuccessful. A number of large-scale prospective surveillance studies, which have recently been funded by the US National Institutes of Health (NIH) using careful environmental measures to follow pregnant mothers, may help shed more light on these questions.

DIAGNOSIS AND CLASSIFICATION OF AUTISM SPECTRUM DISORDERS

As the new Diagnostic and Statistical Manual of the American Psychiatric Association (DSM-V) and the new International Classification of Diseases Code (ICD-11) are being formulated, many issues in the classification of children and adults with ASD are under consideration. Currently (APA, 1994; WHO, 1990), ASDs are formally referred to as pervasive developmental disorders (PDD). However, parent and professional advocacy groups have strongly argued for its replacement by *Autism Spectrum Disorders* on the grounds that ASD is a better understood term that reflects *autism* as the best-characterized core syndrome, with a *spectrum* of other disorders, distinguished from autism by several factors as well as severity within those factors, thus constituting a spectrum.

ASD is a diagnosis made purely on the basis of behavior. For a number of years, the hope was that a single biological marker would emerge from genetics or other neuroscientific research that would mean that behavioral diagnoses would no longer be necessary. However, given the extraordinary heterogeneity in genetics and other neurobiological research, it seems likely that behavioral diagnoses will be an important part of understanding and treating these disorders for many years. This is the case because, not only have many different genetic, neuroanatomic, and brain function findings been linked with ASD but also many of these biological findings are also associated with other psychological and psychiatric disorders with quite different trajectories and different symptoms. This suggests that it is not just that we have many types of ASD, but that the biological pathogenesis of ASD can also lead to other disorders.

Generally, the syndrome of *autism* is considered the most clearly defined of all the ASDs and also one of the most reliably, if not the most reliably, defined psychiatric disorder emerging in childhood (Volkmar et al., 1997). In the DSM-IV, three domains that determine autism are specified: social reciprocity, communication, and restricted and repetitive behaviors (RRBs) and interests. In addition, symptoms in at least one of the areas that define autism (social development, communication, and play) must be present before 36 months. Within each domain, subdomains are delineated (e.g. under social

reciprocity, non-verbal behaviors comprise one domain, peer interactions comprise another).

Probably most striking in the social domain are difficulties that individuals with autism have in using eye contact to communicate intention. People with autism also tend to have fewer and less interpretable socially directed facial expressions and gestures than others (Yirmiya et al., 2006). Higher-order aspects of social development are also affected including both response to specific contexts (such as comforting someone who is hurt or offering to share with someone), understanding of others' thoughts (i.e. theory of mind) and relationships, particularly friendships. Many children are first identified because of language delays, but language delay is not a requirement for autism and increasingly, children with normal language milestones (e.g. first words, first phrases) are being diagnosed with autism. Again, as with the social behaviors, there are specific aspects of communication and language with which many children with autism and sometimes adults have difficulty, including intonation and use of stereotyped or idiosyncratic phrases. Higher-order aspects of language, including the ability to hold a conversation and other aspects of pragmatics, as well as imaginative play, are also affected in most individuals.

Repetitive and restricted behaviors and interests include a wide gamut of behaviors, from repeated actions, such as spinning objects, to preoccupations with schedules or plumbing or appliances, to circumscribed interests, which may be similar to those of other children (e.g. Disney movies; Thomas the Tank Engine) but which reach a level of intensity that interferes with a child or family's ability to carry out ordinary activities.

In order to meet diagnostic criteria for autism, individuals must show behaviors that fall into at least two subdomains in the area of social reciprocity and one subdomain in communication and one subdomain of RRBs. A number of analyses of large datasets of standardized instruments, both caregiver reports and direct observations, have suggested that two domains: social communication and RRBs (including repetitive language); may better represent the clusters of behaviors that describe autism (Lecavalier et al., 2006) than the three domains (see also Gotham et al., 2007). On the other hand, language level (e.g. how well an individual can talk) is an extremely important factor in interpreting different behaviors and predicting outcome, so studies where communication abnormalities specific to autism are lumped with general language competence have continued to yield a separate language factor (Tadevosyan-Leyfer et al., 2003).

In addition, a number of studies have suggested that different aspects of RRBs are associated with different trajectories and other features in ASD (Richler et al., 2007). Most commonly, these studies have found that repetitive movements, simple repetitive behaviors (e.g. lining up objects), and behaviors likely derived from seeking of specific sensations (e.g. smelling objects, peering) appear more often in children with autism with intellectual disabilities than children without additional general delays. They decrease in frequency and severity with age. In contrast, insistence on sameness, compulsive behaviors, and rituals are less associated with intellectual disabilities and tend to show less change with age (Bishop et al., 2006). A recent study has suggested that circumscribed interests in age-appropriate topics (but of unusual intensity) form a third factor within RRBs (Lam et al., 2008). Similarly, preoccupations (which are usually defined in different ways for individuals of different ages and different levels of functioning) have been associated with all of the above factors in different studies. The general trend in diagnosis is to try to dimensionalize these different characteristics, but to do so requires standards for measurement and norms, which will need to be different depending on age, language skill and functional level.

In addition to autism, other syndromes are included in the formal diagnostic category of PDD. Rett syndrome, mentioned earlier, is one disorder that may or may not remain in the general category of ASD. Though most girls with Rett syndrome have symptoms that overlap with autism only during a relatively brief period of development, advocates have argued that individuals with Rett syndrome should not be excluded from ASD due to the identified genetic cause of the disorder, because eventually many individuals with ASD will have known genetic etiologies. Childhood disintegrative disorder (known as CDD) is a very rare condition, in which children have normal development until at least age 2, followed by marked deterioration in social behavior and communication, often accompanied by the development of RRBs and loss of motor and/or adaptive (e.g. toilet training, self-feeding) skills (Volkmar et al., 2005). Few recent studies of CDD are available which would allow up-to-date behavioral and neurological assessments. Questions have been raised whether at least some of the children who receive these diagnoses are no different from children with autism who experience regressions, except for the later timing and greater breadth of loss of skills. Loss of social skills, and sometimes words, occurs in a significant proportion of children with autism (and other ASD) diagnoses in the second year of life, but is not generally accompanied by loss of other kinds of skills. Currently, CDD (which according to DSM-IV precedence rules is supposed to be diagnosed "first," before autism) overlaps with autism in that a child who has a very marked loss of skills between ages 2 and 3 could receive either diagnosis. However, most children with autism who have regressions have not shown completely normal development up to 2 years (Werner & Dawson, 2005). Because children with CDD, in the end, look no different than children with autism and comparable levels of intellectual disability, in terms of services and prognosis, many end up with autism diagnoses.

The most controversial category within PDD is Asperger syndrome. In both of the sets of formal diagnostic criteria (DSM-IV and ICD-10), Asperger syndrome is differentiated from autism by the absence of language delay. Because language delay is not a criterion for autism (so an individual is not required to have a language delay to have autism), this differentiation also results in substantial overlap. Both DSM-IV and ICD-10 require that autism is diagnosed first, and thus, an individual who meets diagnostic criteria for autism cannot have Asperger syndrome. However, many parents, professionals, and individuals with the disorder have found it worthwhile to use the term Asperger syndrome in order to differentiate individuals with fluent language and autistic behaviors from other individuals with more general disabilities and autism. Most research has failed to find differences between individuals with Asperger syndrome and autism, when language level and IQ are equivalent, except on measures that likely affected recruiting into the specific groups (Klin et al., 2005; Miller & Ozonoff, 2000). For example, some groups have emphasized neuropsychological profiles in Asperger syndrome, such as high verbal and lower visual spatial skills; others have emphasized greater motor problems; others have emphasized empathy (Ghaziuddin & Butler, 1998; Gillberg, 1993). In these cases, differences are found in whatever factor is the focus in that study, but not those highlighted in other studies. This accumulation of findings has led many researchers to argue that Asperger syndrome is not a separate form of disorder, but is a term used in a variety of ways to describe individuals with autism who are less impaired in some way (Prior et al., 1998). Clarifying how to describe this phenomenon and how to provide consumers with accurate information about when it may be helpful to use a term like Asperger syndrome is a challenge for those working on new classification systems.

Less in the public eye, but equally problematic, is the term PDD-NOS, which is the term that is applied to an individual who has social deficits that are similar to those in autism and difficulties in either communication or RRBs or both (but a mild level). There is also no age-of-onset requirement for PDD-NOS, so the classification may be used for children where earlier symptoms are not detected, though prospective research suggests that, in most of these cases, the issue is the recognition of the problems, not really their onset.

PDD-NOS is an important concept because it acknowledges that there are many children (who constitute the bulk of research) and adults who have some symptoms of autism without meeting the full criteria. In some epidemiological studies with careful diagnoses, there have been more children with PDD-NOS than with autism (Fombonne, 2007). Thus, these children represent a very important group in terms of services. However, the diagnosis of PDD-NOS is so vague that it has left many parents and researchers quite frustrated. Research on PDD-NOS, which in itself is rare, has suggested that there is no single behavior or factor that differentiates it from autism or Asperger syndrome except that often, at least in the USA, PDD-NOS is frequently used to describe children of higher intelligence who may have had an early language delay (Klin et al., 2005). In other cases, PDD-NOS may be used to describe intellectually impaired children with some RRBs and some social awkwardness, but less severe social impairment (Kraijer & De Bildt, 2005). PDD-NOS is a less stable diagnosis over time than autism, with earlier studies showing many children with early diagnoses of PDD-NOS later receiving diagnoses of autism, and more recent studies, with less impaired children, showing more children with early diagnoses of PDD-NOS moving "out of the spectrum" as they get older (Turner & Stone, 2007).

ASSESSMENT, DIFFERENTIAL DIAGNOSES, AND COMORBIDITIES

There is a great deal of evidence to show the diagnosis of autism can be made with excellent sensitivity (the ability to identify successfully all the people with a disorder) and specificity (the ability to identify only persons with the disorder and not persons with other disorders). Sensitivity and specificity are higher for children and adolescents with moderate to no intellectual disabilities and when trained examiners use combinations of standardized instruments, most commonly the Autism Diagnostic Interview-Review (ADI-R; Lord et al., 1994; Rutter et al., 2003) and Autism Diagnostic Observation Schedule (ADOS; Risi et al., 2006). The combination of the ADOS and a parent screening questionnaire, the Social Communication Questionnaire (SCQ) yields almost as good results for school-age children as the ADOS and ADI-R (Corsello et al., 2007). It is possible that other combinations of observational measures (such as the Screening Test for Autism in 2 year olds; Stone et al., 2000) and parent interviews and/or well-studied questionnaires, such as the Social Responsiveness Scale (SRS; Constantino, 2002) or the Diagnostic Interview for Social and Communication Disorders (DISCO; Wing et al., 2002) may be similarly effective, but these have not yet been studied together. It seems clear that parent informant measures provide complementary information to examiner-based ratings of observations, and both are critical. In addition, Constantino et al. (2007) showed in one study that a combination of a parent and teacher questionnaire had excellent specificity in identifying children with ASD and fairly good sensitivity, although the correspondence with more comprehensive diagnoses is not yet well-understood. A number of very frequently used clinical instruments; e.g. the Gilliam Autism Rating Scale (Gilliam, 1995) and the Childhood Autism Rating Scale (Schopler et al., 2002); do not yield diagnoses that are comparable to research diagnoses, so examiners must be careful in reaching conclusions based on instruments normed on the basis of educational classifications (Sikora et al., 2008).

There has been intense interest in screening for autism in very young children for many years. To date, one-stage screening questionnaires identify so many children as positive that they are not useful and primarily then only seem to work if used with children

who have already been identified as having some kind of delay or if followed by a phone interview (Robins et al., 2001). However, more accurate quick screening may be possible with children at 24 months or older (Robins & Dumont-Mathieu, 2006); much work is in progress in this area (Bryson et al., 2007).

In general, diagnoses are less reliable for extremes of ages, very young children (30 months or younger) and adults, and for extremes of cognitive function, individuals with low developmental levels (under 15~18 months) and profound intellectual disabilities or individuals with average or greater intelligence (Risi et al., 2006). "Autism" diagnoses are also more stable than diagnoses of other types of ASD such as PDD-NOS and Asperger syndrome (Lord et al., 2006), which is one of the reasons why it has been proposed that DSM-IV adopts a single category for ASD with dimensions of severity and impairment within it.

The most common differential diagnoses for ASD vary by the age of child or adult. For young children, many of whom are referred because of language delays, and a subset who are referred because of non-specific behavior problems, the most common differential diagnoses are language delay or general developmental delay. Thus, the differentiating behaviors are specific social deficits, including the interest and ability to share attention, and repetitive or unusual sensory or motor behaviors (Chawarska et al., 2007). Children with ASD also often have more severe receptive language deficits than children who have comparable expressive language delays (Philofsky et al., 2004) and may, but not always, have more severe intellectual disabilities.

When older children or adolescents are referred for possible ASD, usually they are less severely language delayed or intellectually disabled, and the differential diagnoses are more likely to be attention-deficit/hyperactivity disorder (ADHD) or anxiety disorders, often coupled with other difficulties such as oppositional behavior or learning difficulties (Matson & Nebel-Schwalm, 2007). In these cases, basic social deficits (e.g. eye contact, facial expressions) may be more critical for diagnoses than peer interactions.

For first diagnoses in adulthood, the differential diagnoses for ASD are even more complicated and less well-studied, and include personality disorders, schizophrenia, and obsessive-compulsive disorder (OCD). The rate of comorbidities in ASD is high, with anxiety and possibly depression common in adolescents and adults, and hyperactivity common in younger ages (Ghaziuddin et al., 2002; Simonoff et al., 2008). Differentiating the repetitive interests associated with ASD from those that warrant an additional diagnosis of OCD is not a straightforward matter.

NEUROPSYCHOLOGICAL RESEARCH

For many years, estimates were that most children with autism tested within the range of intellectual disabilities. However, in recent years, epidemiological studies have suggested that, at least for ASD, more broadly defined, this may no longer be the case. This is probably largely because diagnosis of milder cases has become so much more common, but also calls attention to the enormous heterogeneity of ASD. When a child has autism and an intellectual disability, the intellectual disability can be as impairing as the ASD. On the other hand, an increasing proportion of individuals with ASD have at least non-verbal skills, if not verbal skills, in the typical range. Thus, assumptions about cognitive level cannot be made on the basis of autistic symptoms. Intellectual and language assessments are as crucial as diagnostic assessment for individuals with ASD. Although many individuals with ASD have relative strengths in visual-spatial skills compared to language (Thurm at al., 2007), as full-scale IQ approaches or surpasses 100 (average), individuals are as likely to show equal or superior verbal skills as they are a visuospatial advantage (William et al., 2005).

Two major perspectives on neuropsychological deficits in ASD can be contrasted. One perspective argues that there is a basic deficit in a primary aspect of cognition that has many downstream consequences for multiple systems of cognition. What is proposed as the central deficit differs across theorists, ranging from Theory of Mind (Baron-Cohen, 1989) to social motivation (Webbet al., 2006), to various aspects of attention (Landray & Bryson, 2004) and imitation (Rogers et al., 1996). The theories also differ in terms of whether they see deficits in social understanding or response as primary and specific (such as in a "gaze module;" Batkia et al., 2000) or as part of a broader cognitive deficit that has particularly strong effects on social development. For example, as a group, individuals with autism clearly have different strategies when looking at faces than persons without ASD. The strategies associated with ASD involve more attention to the lower half of the face and less attention to the eyes, less skill in interpreting social implications of eye direction, and more skill at recognizing inverted faces (so presumably less reliance on the visual gestalt of a face; Golarai et al., 2006). Differences in responding to the efforts of others to direct attention, particularly in young children, and differences in initiating joint attention, through pointing, showing, and social conversation, also characterize ASD. Neurophysiological studies, such as event-related potentials (ERP) studies, support differences in underlying brain function during similar tasks.

An alternative perspective, for which the most outspoken proponents are Minshew and her colleagues (2006), is that ASD is defined by a constellation of co-occurring deficits and intact abilities that are the outcome of abnormal development of the brain. These deficits include recall memory for complex material, organizational and problem-solving aspects of executive functioning, self-initiated concept formation, skilled motor movements, and processing capacity. What is striking, however, and emphasized in this theory is that simpler cognitive skills such as many aspects of sensory perception, working memory, and concept acquisition are unimpaired (compared to overall cognitive level). This model incorporates Frith's concept of deficits in central coherence (Happé & Frith, 2006) in that it would account for relative strengths in local processing due to equal or enhanced more basic cognitive skills, with greater deficits in global processing as integrative conceptualization and processing capacity demands increase.

CLINICAL IMPLICATIONS

Autism has gone from being viewed as a rare disorder, most commonly associated with moderate to severe intellectual disabilities, to a much more commonly acknowledged spectrum of difficulties that affect individuals from superior intelligence to profound delays, with a concomitantly large range of defining and associated difficulties. Although there is still no good biological marker, autism remains a category in the sense that the behaviors that define it result in impairments that are greater than the sum of the defining parts: i.e. someone with significant deficits in basic social-communicative behaviors, understanding of human actions and who has restricted interests and/or repetitive behaviors or interests is very likely to have long-standing difficulties that affect independence, health, and well-being. Although there is much evidence that autism has neurological roots, clear etiologies remain relatively rare and often, even when a genetic basis for autism can be determined, the genetic pattern is not in fact specific to autism, so the final pathway is not obvious.

Despite the lack of clear neurobiological causes or markers, neurobiological research offers hope for both treatments and perhaps prevention. It is helping us to understand the different ways in which children with autism spectrum disorders learn and ways in which we may facilitate this learning given the neuroplasticity of the developing brain. Our goal as clinicians is to identify both the strengths in a child and the deficits within the spectrum and within other areas (e.g. language, attention, motor development) that may in turn be strengthened through education, therapy, and family support.

Clinicians now have many tools available for diagnosis of autism spectrum disorders. It seems critical that information be obtained both through caregiver reports and direct clinician observation, and considered in the light of development (e.g. the child's language level and non-verbal problem-solving abilities). There is a trade-off between efficiency and accuracy, but diagnostic instruments are improving, particularly as they become more tailored to children and adults of different ages and language levels, which may allow for increased specificity (better differentiation between ASD and other disorders) while maintaining good sensitivity (not missing children who should be diagnosed). Dimensional measures, particularly where they can more efficiently lead to appropriate treatment goals and methods, may also be a step forward.

The now 65-year-old history of ASD reveals major shifts in understanding and conceptualizations of the condition, yet fairly remarkable consistency in the clinical characteristics that define the disorder. There is great hope that, in even less time, we will come to understand better the origins of ASD and, particularly with more collaboration among researchers and clinicians, become better able to help all affected individuals reach the best outcomes possible.

REFERENCES

Amaral, D.G., Bauman, M.D. & Schumann, C.M. (2003) 'The amygdala and autism: implications from non-human primate studies', *Genes, Brain, and Behavior*, 2(5): 295–302.

Amodio, D.M. & Frith, C.D. (2006) 'Meeting of minds: the medial frontal cortex and social cognition', *Nature Reviews Neuroscience*, 7: 268–277.

Anderson, G.M., Gutknecht, L., Cohen, D.J., Brailly-Tabard, S., Cohen, J.H., Ferrari, P., et al. (2002) 'Serotonin transporter promoter variants in autism: functional effects and relationship to platelet hyper-serotonemia', *Molecular Psychiatry*, 7(8): 831–836.

APA (1994) *Diagnostic and Statistical Manual of Mental Disorders*. 4th ed. Washington, DC: American Psychiatric Association.

Bailey, A., Le Couteur, A., Gottesman, I., Bolton, P., Simonoff, E., Yuzda, E., et al. (1995) 'Autism as a strongly genetic disorder: evidence from a British twin study', *Psychological Medicine*, 25(1): 63–78.

Baird, G., Simonoff, E., Pickles, A., Chandler, S., Loucas, T., Meldrum, D., et al. (2006) 'Prevalence of disorders of the autism spectrum in a population cohort of children in South Thames: the Special Needs and Autism Project (SNAP)', *Lancet*, 368(9531): 210–5.

Baron-Cohen, S. (1989) 'The autistic child's theory of mind: a case of specific developmental delay', *Journal of Child Psychology and Psychiatry*, 30: 285–297.

Baron-Cohen, S., Ring, H.A., Bullmore, E.T., Wheelwright, S., Ashwin, C. & Williams, S.C. (2000) 'The amygdala theory of autism', *Neuroscience and Biobehavioral Reviews*, 24: 355–364.

Batkia, A., Baron-Cohen, S., Wheelwright, S., Connellana, J. & Ahluwalia, J. (2000) 'Is there an innate gaze module? Evidence from human neonates', *Infant Behavior and Development*, 23(2): 223–229.

Bauman, M.L. & Kemper, T.L. (2005) 'Neuroanatomic observations of the brain in autism: a review and future directions', *International Journal of Developmental Neuroscience*, 23: 183–87.

Bauman, M.L., Anderson, G., Perry, E. & Ray, M. (2006) 'Neuroanatomical and neurochemical studies of the autistic brain: current thought and future directions', in S.O. Moldin and J.R. Rubenstein (eds), *Understanding Autism*. Boca Raton, FL: CRC Press. pp. 277–302.

Bertrand, J., Mars, A., Boyle, C., Bove, F., Yeargin-Allsopp, M., & Decoufle, P. (2001) 'Prevalence of autism in a United States population: the Brick Township, New Jersey, investigation', *Pediatrics*, 108(5): 1155–1161.

Bettelheim, B. (1967) *The Empty Fortress: Infantile Autism and the Birth of the Self*. New York: Free Press.

Bill, B.R. & Geschwind, D.H. (2009) 'Genetic advances in autism: heterogeneity and convergence on shared pathways', *Current Opinion in Genetics and Development*, 19(3): 271–278.

Bishop, S.L., Richler, J. & Lord, C. (2006) 'Association between restricted and repetitive behaviors and nonverbal IQ in children with autism spectrum disorders', *Child Neuropsychology*, 12: 247–267.

Bolton, P. (2007) 'Neuroepileptic correlates of autistic symtamatology in tuberous sclerosis', *Mental Retardation and Developmental Disabilities Research Reviews*, 10: 126–131.

Bolton, P.F., Park, R.J., Higgins, J.N., Griffiths, P.D., & Pickles, A. (2002) 'Neuro-epileptic determinants of autism spectrum disorders in tuberous sclerosis complex', *Brain*, 125: 1247–1255.

Brambilla, P., Hardan, A., DiNemi, S.U., Perez, J., Soares, J.C. & Barale, F. (2003) 'Brain anatomy and development in autism: review of structural MRI studies', *Brain Research Bulletin*, 61: 557–569.

Bryson, S.E., Zwaigenbaum, L., McDermott, C., Rombough, V. & Brian, J. (2007) 'The Autism Observation Scale for Infants: scale development and reliability data', *Journal of Autism and Developmental Disorders*, 38(4): 731–78.

Carper, R.A., Wideman, G.M. & Courchesne, E. (2006) 'Structural neuroimaging', in S.O. Moldin & J.R. Rubenstein (eds), *Understanding Autism,* Boca Rato, FL: CRC Press, pp. 349–373.

Center for Disease Control and Prevention (CDC) (2007) 'Prevalence of autism spectrum disorders; Autism and Developmental Disabilities Monitoring Network, 14 sites, United States, 2002', *MMWR Surveillance Summary*, 56: 1–28.

Chakrabarti, S. & Fombonne, E. (2005) 'Pervasive developmental disorders in preschool children: confirmation of high prevalence', *American Journal of Psychiatry*, 162(6): 1133–1141.

Chawarska, K., Klin, A., Paul, R. & Volkmar, F. (2007) 'Autism spectrum disorder in the second year: stability and change in syndrome expression', *Journal of Child Psychology and Psychiatry*, 48(2): 128–138.

Chess, S. (1971) 'Autism in children with congenital rubella', *Journal of Autism and Developmental Disorders*, 1(1): 33–47.

Chugani, D.C., Muzik, O., Behen, M., Rothermel, R., Janisse, J.J., Lee, J., et al. (1999) 'Developmental changes in brain serotonin synthesis capacity in autistic and nonautistic children', *Annual Neurology*, 45(3): 287–295.

Constantino, J.N. (2002) *The Social Responsiveness Scale*. Los Angeles: Western Psychological Services.

Constantino, J.N., Grober, C.P., Davis, S., Hayes, S., Passanante, N. & Przybeck, T. (2004) 'The factor structure of autistic traits', *Journal of Child Psychology and Psychiatry*, 45(4): 719–726.

Constantino, J., LaVesser, P., Zhang, Y., Abbacchi, A., Gray, T. & Todd, R. (2007) 'Rapid quantitative assessment of autistic social impairment by classroom teachers', *Journal of the American Academy of Child and Adolescent Psychiatry*, 46(12): 1668–1676.

Constantino, J.N., Lajonchere, C., Lutz, M, Gray, T., Abbacchi, A., McKenna, K., et al. (2006) 'Autistic social impairment in the siblings of children with pervasive developmental disorders', *American Journal of Psychiatry*, 163: 294–296.

Cook, E.H. (1990) 'Autism: review of neurochemical investigation', *Synapse*, 6(3): 292–308.

Cook, E.H. & Scherer, S.W. (2008) 'Review Article Copy-number variations associated with neuropsychiatric conditions', *Nature*, 455: 919–23.

Corsello, C., Hus, V., Pickles, A., Risi, S., Cook, E., Leventhal, B., et al. (2007) 'Between a ROC and a hard place: decision making and making decisions about using the SCQ', *Journal of Child Psychology and Psychiatry*, 48(9): 932–940.

Courchesne, E., Karns, C.M., Davis, H.R., Ziccardi, R., Carper, R.A., Tigue, Z.D., et al. (2001) 'Unusual brain growth patterns in early life in patients with autistic disorder: an MRI study', *Neurology*, 57: 245–254.

Crawley, J.N. (2007) 'Mouse behavioral assays relevant to the symptoms of autism', *Brain Pathology*, 17(4): 448–459.

Dalton, K.M., Nacewicz, B.M., Johnstone, T., Schaefer, H.S., Gernsbacher, M.A., Goldsmith, H.H., et al. (2005) 'Gaze fixation and the neural circuitry of face processing in autism', *Nature Neuroscience*, 8: 519–526.

Di Martino, A., Ross, K., Uddin, L.Q., Sklar, A.B., Castellanos, F.X. & Milham, M.P. (2009) 'Functional brain correlates of social and nonsocial processes in autism spectrum disorders: an activation likelihood estimation meta-analysis', *Biological Psychiatry*, 65: 63–74.

Folstein, S. & Rutter, M. (1978) 'A twin study of individuals with infantile autism', in M. Rutter and E. Schopler (eds), *Autism: A Reappraisal of Concepts and Treatment*. New York: Plenum, pp. 219–242.

Fombonne, E. (2007) 'Epidemiological surveys of pervasive developmental disorders', in F. Volkmar (ed), *Autism and Pervasive Developmental Disorders*, 2nd ed. New York: Cambridge University Press, pp. 33–68.

Fombonne, E. (2008) 'Thimerosal disappears but autism remains', *Archive of General Psychiatry*, 65(1): 15–16.

Fombonne E. (2009) 'Epidemiology of pervasive developmental disorders', *Pediatric Research*, 65(6): 591–598.

Friston, K. (1994) 'Functional and effective connectivity in neuroimaging: a synthesis', *Human Brain Mapping*, 2: 56–68.

Frith, U. (1989). *Autism: Explaining the Enigma*. Oxford: Basil Blackwell.

Ghaziuddin, M. & Butler, E. (1998) 'Clumsiness in autism and Asperger syndrome: a further report', *Journal of Intellectual Disability Research*, 42(1): 43–48.

Ghaziuddin M., Ghaziuddin, N. & Greden, J. (2002) 'Depression in persons with autism: implications for research and clinical care', *Journal of Autism and Developmental Disorders*, 32(4): 299–306.

Gillberg, C. & Gillberg C.I. (1983) 'Infantile autism: a total population study of reduced optimality in the pre-, peri-, and neonatal period', *Journal of Autism and Developmental Disorders*, 13(2): 153–166.

Gillberg, C. (1993) 'Autism and related behaviors', *Journal of Intellectual Disability Research*, 37(4): 343–372.

Gilliam, J.E. (1995). *Gilliam Autism Rating Scale (GARS)*. Austin, Texas: Pro-Ed.

Golarai, G., Grill-Spector, K. & Reiss, A.L. (2006) 'Autism and the development of face processing', *Clinical Neuroscience Research*, 6(3): 145–160.

Gotham, K., Risi, S., Pickles, A., & Lord, C. (2007). 'The autism diagnostic observation schedule (ADOS): revised algorithms for improved diagnostic validity. *Journal of Autism and Developmental Disorders'*, 37(4): 613–627.

Greenspan, S. & Wieder, S (1997) 'An integrated developmental approach to interventions for young children with severe difficulties in relating and communicating', *Zero the Three*, 18: 5–17.

Happé, F. & Frith, U. (2006) 'The weak coherence account: detail-focused cognitive style in autism spectrum disorders', *Journal of Autism and Developmental Disorders*, 36(1): 5–25.

Hermelin, B. & O'Connor, N. (1970) *Psychological Experiments with Autistic Children*. New York, Pergamon.

Honda, H., Shimizu, Y., & Rutter, M. (2005) 'No effect of MMR withdrawal on the incidence of autism: a total population study', *Journal of Child Psychology and Psychiatry*, 46(6): 572–579.

Jick, H. & Kaye J.A. (2004) 'Autism and DPT vaccination in the United Kingdom', New *England Journal of Medicine*, 350(26): 2722–2723.

Juranek, J., Filipek, P.A., Berenji, G.R., Modahl, C., Osann, K. & Spence, M.A. (2006) 'Association between amygdala volume and anxiety level: magnetic resonance imaging (MRI) study in autistic children', *Journal of Child Neurology*, 21(12): 1058–1068.

Just, M.A., Cherkassky, V.L., Keller, T.A., & Minshew, N.J. (2004) 'Cortical activation and synchronization during sentence comprehension in high-functioning autism: evidence of underconnectivity', *Brain,* 127: 1811–1821.

Kaufmann, W.E., Capone, G.T., Clarke, M., & Budimirovic, D.B. (2008) 'Autism in genetic intellectual disability: insights into idiopathic autism', in A.W. Zimmerman, (ed.), *Autism: Current Theories and Evidence.* Totowa, NJ: Humana Press. pp. 81–108.

Kennedy, D.P. & Courchesne, E. (2008) 'The intrinsic functional organization of the brain is altered in autism', *Neuroimage,* 39: 1877–1885.

Klin, A., Pauls, D., Schultz, R., & Volkmar, F. (2005) 'Three diagnostic approaches to Asperger syndrome: implications for research', *Journal of Autism and Developmental Disorders,* 35(2): 221–234.

Kielinen, M., Linna, S.L., & Moilanen, I. (2000) 'Autism in Northern Finland', *European Child & Adolescent Psychiatry,* 9(3): 162–167.

Kraijer, D. & De Bildt, A. (2005) The PDD-MRS: an instrument for identification of autism spectrum disorders in persons with mental retardation'. *Journal of Autism and Developmental Disorders,* 35(4): 499–513.

Lam, K., Bodfish, J., & Piven, J. (2008) 'Evidence of three subtypes of repetitive behavior in autism that differ in familiarity and association with other symptoms', *Journal of Child Psychology and Psychiatry,* 49(11): 1193–1200.

Landry, R. & Bryson, S. (2004) 'Impaired disengagement of attention in young children with autism', *Journal of Child Psychology and Psychiatry,* 45(6): 1115–1122.

Lane, H. (1979) *The Wild Boy of Aveyron.* Cambridge, MA: Harvard University Press.

Lecavalier, L., Aman, G., Scahill, L., McDougle, C., McCracken, J., Bitiello, B., et al. (2006) 'Validity of the Autism Diagnostic Interview-Revised', American *Journal on Mental Retardation,* 111(3): 199–215.

Lord, C., Risi, S., DiLavore, P., Shulman, C., Thurm, A., & Pickles, A. (2006) 'Autism from 2 to 9 years of age', *Archives of General Psychiatry,* 63(6): 694–701.

Lord, C., Rutter, M., & Le Couteur, A. (1994) 'Autism Diagnostic Interview-Revised: a revised version of a diagnostic interview for caregivers of individuals with possible pervasive developmental disorder, *Journal of Autism and Developmental Disorder,* 24(5): 659–685.

Lovaas, O.I. (1966) 'A program for the establishment of speech in psychotic children', *Early Childhood Autism.* Oxford: Pergamon, pp. 115–144.

Matson, J.L. & Nebel-Schwalm, M.S. (2007) 'Comorbid psychopathology with autism spectrum disorder in children: an overview,' *Research in Developmental Disabilities,* 28(4): 341–352.

Miller, M.T., Strömland, K., Gillberg, C. Johansson, M. & Nilsson, E.W. (1998) 'The puzzle of autism: an ophthalmologic contribution', *Trans American Ophthalmology Society,* 96: 369–387.

Miller, J.N. & Ozonoff, S. (2000) 'The external validity of Asperger disorder: lack of evidence from the domain of neuropsychology', *Journal of Abnormal Psychology,* 109(2): 227–238.

Minshew, N.J., Webb, S.J., Williams, D.L., & Dawson, G. (2006) 'Neuro psychology and neuro physiology of Autism Spectrum Disorders', in S.O. Moldin and J.R. Rubenstein, (eds.), *Understanding Autism.* Boca Raton, FL: CRC Press, pp. 379–416.

Minshew, N.J & Williams D.L. (2007) 'The new neurobiology of autism: cortex, connectivity, and neuronal organization', *Archives of Neurology,* 64(7): 945–950.

Moore, S.J., Turnpenny, P., Quinn, A., Glover, S., Lloyd, D.J., Montgomery, T., & Dean, J.S. (2000) 'A clinical study of 57 children with fetal anticonvulsant syndromes', *Journal of Medical Genetics,* 37(7): 489–497.

Mosconi, M.W., Cody-Hazlett, H., Poe, M.D., Gerig, G., Gimpel-Smith, R., & Piven, J. (2009) 'Longitudinal study of amygdala volume and joint attention in 2- to 4-year-old children with autism', *Archives of General Psychiatry,* 66, 509–516.

Mulder, E.J., Anderson, G.M., Kema, I.P., De Bildt, A., Van Lang, N.D., Den Boer, J.A. et al. (2004) 'Platelet serotonin levels in pervasive developmental disorders and mental retardation: diagnostic group differences, within-group distribution, and behavioral correlates', *Journal of American Academy of Child and Adolescent Psychiatry,* 43(4): 491–499.

Munson, J., Dawson, G., Abbott, R., Faja, S., Webb, S. J., Friedman, S.D., et al. (2006) 'Amygdala volume and behavioral development in autism', *Archives of General Psychiatry,* 63(6): 686–693.

Neul, J.L., Fang, P., Barrish, J., Lane, J., Caeg, E.B., Smith, E.O., et al. (2008) 'Specific mutations in methyl-CpG-binding protein 2 confer different severity in Rett syndrome', *Neurology,* 70(16): 1313–1321

Offit, P. (2008) *Autism's False Prophets: Bad Science, Risky Medicine, and the Search for a Cure.* New York: Columbia University Press.

Ornitz, M. & Ritvo, R. (1968) 'Perceptual inconstancy in early infantile autism', *Archives of General Psychiatry,* 18: 76–98.

Pelphrey, K.A. & Carter, E.J. (2008) 'Charting the typical and atypical development of the social brain', *Developmental Psychopathology,* 20: 1081–1102.

Philofsky, A., Hepburn, S.L., Hayes, A., Hagerman, R. & Rogers, S.J. (2004) 'Linguistic and cognitive functioning and autism symptoms in young children with fragile X syndrome', American *Journal of Mental Retardation,* 109(3): 208–218.

Pickles, A., Bolton, P., Macdonald, H. et al. (1995) 'Latent-class analysis of recurrence risks for complex phenotypes with selection and measurement error: a twin and family history study of autism', *American Journal of Human Genetics,* 57: 717–726.

Piven, J., Palmer, P., Jacobi, D., Childress, D. & Arndt, S. (1997) 'Broader autism phenotype: evidence from a family history study of multiple-incidence autism families', *American Journal of Psychiatry,* 154: 185–190.

Prior, M., Eisenmajer, R., Leekam, S., Wing, L., Gould, J., Ong, B., et al. (1998) 'Are there subgroups within the autistic spectrum? A cluster analysis of a group of children with autistic spectrum disorders', *Journal of Child Psychology and Psychiatry,* 39(6): 893–902.

Raznahan, A., Pugliese, L., Barker, G.J., Daly, E., Powell, J., Bolton, P.F., et al. (2009) 'Serotonin transporter genotype and neuroanatomy in autism spectrum disorders', *Psychiatric Genetics,* 19(3): 147–150.

Rice, C., Schendel, D., Cunniff, C., & Doernberg, N. (2004) 'Public health monitoring of developmental disabilities with a focus on the autism spectrum disorders', *American Journal of Medical Genetics,* 125(1): 22–27.

Richler, J., Luyster, R., Risi, S., Hsu, W., Dawson, G., Bernier, R., et al. (2006) 'Is there a 'regressive phenotype' of autism spectrum disorder associated with the measles-mumps-rubella vaccine? A CPEA study', *Journal of Autism and Developmental Disorders,* 36(3): 299–316.

Richler, J., Bishop, S.L., Kleinke, J.R., & Lord, C. (2007) 'Restricted and repetitive behaviors in young children with autism spectrum disorders', *Journal of Autism and Developmental Disorders,* 37: 73–85.

Rimland, B. (1964) *Infantile Autism: The Syndrome and Its Implications for a Neural Theory of Behavior.* East Norwalk, CT: Appleton-Century-Crofts.

Risi, S., Lord, C., Gotham, K., Corsello, C., Chrysler, C., Szatmari, P., et al. (2006) 'Combining information from multiple sources in the diagnosis of autism spectrum disorders', *Journal of the American Academy of Child and Adolescent Psychiatry,* 45(9): 1094–1103.

Robins, D. & Dumont-Mathieu, T. (2006) 'Early screening for autism spectrum disorders: update on the modified checklist for autism in toddlers and other measures', *Journal of Developmental & Behavioral Pediatrics,* 27(2): 111–119.

Robins, D.L., Fein, D., Barton, M.L., & Green, J.A. (2001) 'The Modified Checklist for Autism in Toddlers: an initial study investigating the early detection of autism and pervasive developmental disorders', *Journal of Autism and Developmental Disorders,* 31(2): 131–44.

Rogers, S.J., Bennetto, L., McEvoy, R., & Pennington, B.F. (1996). 'Imitation and pantomime in high-functioning adolescents with autism spectrum disorders', *Child Development,* 67(5): 2060–2073.

Rogers, S.J., Wehner, E.A., & Hagerman, R. (2001) 'The behavioral phenotype in fragile X: symptoms of autism in very young children with fragile X syndrome, idiopathic autism, and other developmental disorders', *Journal of Developmental and Behavioral Pediatrics,* 22(6): 409–17.

Ronald, A., Happé, F., & Plomin, R. (2008) 'A twin study investigating the genetic and environmental etiologies of parent, teacher and child ratings of autistic-like traits and their overlap', *European Child and Adolescent Psychiatry,* 17(8): 473–83.

Rutter, M. & Lockyer, L. (1967) 'A five to fifteen year follow-up study of infantile psychosis. I. Description of sample', *British Journal of Psychiatry,* 113(504): 1169–1182.

Rutter, M. & Schopler, E. (1978) *Autism: A Reappraisal of Concepts and Treatment.* New York: Plenum.

Rutter, M., Le Couteur, A., & Lord, C. (2003) *Autism Diagnostic Interview- Revised.* Los Angeles: Western Psychological Services.

Schanen, C.N. (2006) 'Epigenetics of autism spectrum disorders', *Human Molecular Genetics,* 15(2): 138–150.

Schendel, D. & Bhasin, T.K. (2008) 'Birth weight and gestational age characteristics of children with autism, including a comparison with other developmental disabilities', *Pediatrics,* 121(6): 1155–1164.

Schopler, E. (1971) 'Parents of psychotic children as scapegoats', *Journal of Contemporary Psychotherapy,* 4(1): 17–22.

Schopler, E., Reichler, R.J., & Renner, B.R. (2002*) The Childhood Autism Rating Scale (CARS).* Los Angeles: Western Psychological Services.

Schultz, R.T., Gauthier, I., Klin, A., Fulbright, R.K., Anderson, A.W., Volkmar, F., et al. (2000) 'Abnormal ventral temporal cortical activity during face discrimination among individuals with autism and

Asperger syndrome', *Archives of General Psychiatry*, 57(4): 331–340.

Sikora, D., Hall, T., Hartley, S., Gerrard-Morris, A., & Cagle, S. (2008) 'Does parent report of behavior differ across ADOS-G classifications: analysis of scores from the CBCL and GARS', *Journal of Autism and Developmental Disorders*, 3: 440–448.

Simonoff, E., Pickles, A., Charman, T., Chandler, S., Loucas, T., & Baird, L. (2008) 'Psychiatric disorders in children with autism spectrum disorders: prevalence, comorbidity, and associated factors in a population-derived sample', *Journal of the American Academy of Child and Adolescent Psychiatry*, 47(8): 921–929.

Smalley, S.L. (1998) 'Autism and tuberous sclerosis. Preview', *Journal of Autism and Developmental Disorders*, 28(5): 407–414.

Sterling, L., Dawson, G., Webb, S., Murias, M., Munson, J., Panagiotides, H., et al. (2008) 'The role of face familiarity in eye tracking of faces by individuals with autism spectrum disorders', *Journal of Autism and Developmental Disorders*, 38(9): 1666–1675.

Stone, W.L., Coonrod, E. and Ousley, O.Y. (2000) 'Brief report: screening tool for autism in two-year-olds (STAT): development and preliminary data', *Journal of Autism and Developmental Disorders*, 30(6): 607–612.

Sundaram, S.K., Sivaswamy, L., Makki, M.I., Behen, M.E., & Chugani, H.T. (2008) 'Absence of arcuate fasciculus in children with global developmental delay of unknown etiology: a diffusion tensor imaging study', Journal *of Pediatrics*, 152: 250–255.

Tadevosyan-Leyfer, O., Dowd, M., Mankoski, R., Winklosky, B., Putnam, S., McGrath, M., et al. (2003) 'Λ principal components analysis of the Autism Diagnostic Interview-Revised', *Journal of American Academy of Child and Adolescent Psychiatry*, 42(7): 864–872.

Thurm, A., Lord, C., Lee, L., & Newschaffer, C. (2007) 'Predictors of language acquisition in preschool children with autism spectrum disorders', *Journal of Autism and Developmental Disorders*, 37(9): 1721–1734.

Turner, M. & Stone, W. (2007) 'Variability in outcome for children with an ASD diagnosis at age 2', *Journal of Child Psychology and Psychiatry*, 48(8): 793–802.

Vargas, D.L., Nascimbene, C., Krishnan, C., Zimmerman, A.W., & Pardo, C.A. (2005) 'Neuroglial activation and neuroinflammation in the brain of patients with autism', *Annals of Neurology, 57*, 67–81.

Volkmar, F.R., Klin, A., & Cohen, D. (1997) 'Diagnosis and classification of autism and related conditions: consensus and issues', in F.R. Volkmar, R. Paul., A. Klin, and D. Cohen, (eds), *Handbook of Autism and Pervasive Developmental Disorders, Vol. 1: Diagnosis, Development, Neurobiology, and Behavior.* 3rd ed. Hoboken, NJ: John Wiley & Sons, pp. 5–40.

Volkmar, F.R., Koenig, K., & State, M. (2005) 'Childhood disintegrative disorder', in F.R. Volkmar, R. Paul., A. Klin, and D. Cohen, (eds), *Handbook of Autism and Pervasive Developmental Disorders, Vol. 1: Diagnosis, Development, Neurobiology, and Behavior.* 3rd edn. Hoboken, NJ: John Wiley & Sons, pp. 70–87.

Wakefield, A., Murch, S., Anthony, A., Linnell, J., Casson, D., Malik, M., et al. (1998) 'Ileal-lymphoid-nodular hyperplasia, non-specific colitis, and pervasive developmental disorder in children', Lancet, 351: 637–641.

Wakefield, A., Anthony, A., Murch, S., Thomson M, Montgomery, S., Davies, S., et al. (2000) 'Enterocolitis in children with developmental disorders', *American Journal of Gastroenterology*, 95: 2285–2295.

Webb, S.J., Dawson, G., Bernier, R., & Panagiotides, H. (2006) 'ERP evidence of atypical face processing in young children with autism', *Journal of Autism and Developmental Disorders*, 36(7): 881–890.

Weiss L.A., Shen, Y., Korn, J.M, Arking, D.E., Miller, D.T., Fossdal R, et al. (2008) 'Association between microdeletion and microduplication at 16p11.2 and autism', *New England Journal of Medicine*, 358(7): 667–675.

Werner, E. & Dawson, G. (2005) 'Validation of the phenomenon of autistic regression using home videotapes', *Archives of General Psychiatry*, 62(8): 889–895.

Williams, D.L., Goldstein, G., Carpenter, P.A., & Minshew, N.J. (2005) 'Verbal and spatial working memory in autism', *Journal of Autism and Developmental Disorders*, 35(6): 747–756.

Wing, L. & Gould, J. (1979) 'Severe impairments of social interaction and associated abnormalities in children: epidemiology and classification', *Journal of Autism and Developmental Disorders*, 9: 11–29.

Wing, L., Leekam, S.R., Libby, S.J., Gould, J., & Larcombe, M. (2002) 'The diagnostic interview for social and communication disorders: background, inter-rater reliability and clinical use', *Journal of Child Psychology and Psychiatry*, 43(3): 307–325.

World Health Organization (1990) *International Classification of Diseases* (10th revision). Geneva: World Health Organization.

Yirmiya, N., Kasari, C., Sigman, M., & Mundy, P. (2006) 'Facial expressions of affect in autistic, mentally retarded and normal children', *Journal of Child Psychology and Psychiatry*, 30(5): 725–735.

15

Autism Spectrum Disorders: Interventions and Outcome

Patricia Howlin & Tony Charman

INTERVENTION PROGRAMMES FOR INDIVIDUALS WITH AUTISM SPECTRUM DISORDERS

Historical background

In the years immediately following Kanner's initial descriptions of autism, many psychiatrists, including Kanner himself (1943), assumed the condition was an early form of schizophrenia with a psychogenic basis. Consequently, psychoanalysis, together with the drugs and other treatments used at the time for schizophrenia, including electroconvalsive therapy (ECT), were widely used. In adulthood, long-term placement in psychiatric hospitals or institutions for the 'mentally retarded' was the most likely outcome. However, in the mid to late 1960s, studies began to emerge documenting how operant approaches could be successfully used to modify many of the behaviours shown by children with autism (see Howlin & Rutter, 1987 for a review). Although certainly an improvement on psychoanalysis, the behavioural procedures used were often rigid and

prescriptive; reinforcement was predominantly food based, and there was a focus on the elimination of 'undesirable' behaviours, such as tantrums, aggression or self-injury, with frequent use of aversive procedures, including shouting, slapping and even electric shock. Most treatment was conducted on an inpatient, hospital basis with very little involvement of the child's family. Little attention was paid to factors such as the child's cognitive or linguistic level or the family situation, and therapy tended to lack any sound developmental or educational underpinnings.

In the 1970s, recognition of the fundamental cognitive, social and communication deficits underlying the disorder (Rutter, 1972) led to a move to more individually based treatments. Lovaas, one of the pioneers of behaviour therapy for autism, concluded that, unless parents were actively involved in therapy, hospital treatment had very limited long-term impact (Lovaas, 1987). Thus, home-based interventions, with parents playing an active role as co-therapists, began to replace inpatient programmes and there was much wider use of naturalistic teaching and reinforcement strategies. This trend continued throughout the 1980s, with increasing integration of home- and school-based programmes, greater involvement of typically developing peers in therapy and a steady movement towards more inclusive education. There was growing recognition, too, of the need for early, pre-school intervention and of the role played by communication deficits in causing many of the 'challenging behaviours' frequently associated with autism. Reactions against abuses arising from the use of aversive procedures led to a focus on the development of more positive treatment strategies.

More recent advances in research have also influenced approaches to intervention. First, it is now known that autism can occur in individuals of all cognitive and linguistic levels, not just in those of low IQ. Consequently, the terms 'autism spectrum disorders' (ASD) or 'autism spectrum conditions' (ASC) are now increasingly used to reflect the great variation in presentation Secondly, far from being a rare condition, it is now generally accepted that children with ASD probably constitute around 1% of the school-age population (Baird et al., 2006). Thirdly, the development of diagnostic instruments of established reliability and validity such as the Autism Diagnostic Observation Schedule (ADOS; Lord et al., 2000) and Autism Diagnostic Interview-Revised (ADI-R; Lord et al., 2000; Rutter et al., 2003), which can be used with even very young children, has meant that children can now be reliably identified by 2–3 years of age (Charman & Baird, 2002). Recognition of the wider prevalence of ASD has resulted in growing acknowledgement of the need for effective interventions, with a particular focus on developing programmes for newly diagnosed, pre-school children (Lord et al., 2005). There has also been an increasing focus on developmentally based approaches and much greater awareness of the importance of enhancing social and communication skills from the earliest years (Charman & Stone, 2006).

ASD has also attracted attention within the fields of "alternative" or "complementary" therapies. These cover a vast range, including pet therapies, psycho-educational therapies, such as the Waldon or Son-Rise programmes, facilitated communication, cranial osteopathy, special diets, vitamin supplements, wearing tinted spectacles or listening to tapes of filtered sounds, clay baths, hyperbaric oxygen tents and salt crystal lamps to name but a few. Some treatments, such as chelation therapy, serotonin, endocrine, gamma-globulin and other injections, and testosterone regulation treatments are potentially hazardous. Few have any valid theoretical underpinnings, and for most the evidence base is non-existent (see www.researchautism.net). Understandably, however, many parents find it very difficult to ignore the claims of 'cures' or 'miracles', with some studies reporting that 50–75% of families with a child with ASD use such therapies (Hanson et al., 2007; Levy & Hyman, 2008; Wong & Smith, 2006). The challenge for professionals is to help parents look beyond the enthusiastic claims and glossy brochures, and to support them in identifying treatments that may best suit, not only their child but also their own needs as a family. Fortunately, over the last few years, there has been a steady increase in well-conducted treatment trials, including a number of randomized controlled trials (RCTs), and the evidence base on which to recommend treatments to families is steadily improving (Rogers & Vismara, 2008).

Behavioural programmes

Applied behavioural analysis (ABA) refers to a particular way of analysing the possible cause(s) of—and developing specific, behaviourally based strategies for the treatment of—behavioural deficits or excesses. In contrast to early operant approaches, current behavioural interventions typically involve a range of different strategies. 'Discrete trial training' focuses specifically on developing skills in a hierarchical manner (using chaining, shaping and fading techniques), systematic identification of reinforcers, continuous monitoring of progress, and generalization to progressively less structured and more natural environments. Pivotal response training (PRT) is also used to foster motivation by including components such as child choice; turn-taking and maintenance strategies; and has been used to enhance language, play and social behaviours in naturalistic settings (Bauminger, 2002; Koegel et al., 1999; Schreibman & Koegel, 2005). A recent meta-analysis of interventions for autism (Ma, 2009) confirms the effectiveness of many behaviourally based procedures, such as systematic desensitization, positive reinforcement, priming and self-control training.

The most thoroughly evaluated behavioural programmes are based on the UCLA 'Young Autism' model of early intensive (home-based) behavioural intervention (EIBI), originally developed by Lovaas and his colleagues (Lovaas, 1987; McEachin et al., 1993; Maurice et al., 1996). The main tenets of the EIBI approach are that therapy should begin as early as possible, preferably before the age of 3 years, should take place for approximately 40 hours per week and last at least 2 years. Detailed manuals are provided to guide and monitor treatment, and therapists work under the supervision of qualified behavioural consultants. There have now been a number of replications or partial replications of Lovaas' original programme. On the whole, systematic reviews and meta-analyses have concluded that EIBI is very effective for some, *but by no means all* children with ASD, and in every study evaluated there have been children who fail to improve, and others who regress during the course of intervention (see Eikeseth, 2009; Howlin et al., 2009; Krebs-Seida et al., 2009; Odom et al., 2010; Reichow & Wolery, 2009; Rogers & Vismara, 2007; Spreckley & Boyd, 2009). Moreover, the reported gains in IQ scores are not always paralleled by improvements in other areas of functioning, especially in core autism symptoms (Dawson et al., 2010). Individual variability in outcomes has led to attempts to

identify the characteristics of the children who do or do not respond to early intensive intervention, but although initial IQ and language ability (especially receptive language) show some relationship with outcome, the impact of other variables (such as age of onset of treatment and severity of autism) is much less consistent (Howlin et al., 2009).

Despite the benefits that EIBI may provide, the costs, both financial and in terms of the amount of time and commitment required, are considerable. There is no strong evidence that these highly intensive behavioural programmes offer significant advantages, *in the longer term*, over programmes of equal quality but of lesser intensity and/or of shorter duration. For example, the Early Start Denver Model (Dawson et al., 2010) which combines behavioural and developmental approaches, resulted in significant changes in IQ, language and adaptive behaviour after 20 hours per week of therapist input over 2 years (i.e. 50% of the intensity of the Lovaas programme). The effectiveness of teaching parents how to apply more general behavioural techniques in the home setting, without necessarily involving many hours and years of intervention, has been evaluated in two RCTs (Jocelyn et al., 1998; Tonge et al., 2006), which report significant improvements in parents' mental health, knowledge of autism and perception of control, together with language gains in the children involved.

Educational programmes

The importance of structured educational programmes for children of elementary school age and above has been recognized for many years. Over 30 years ago, Rutter and Bartak (1973) confirmed that children with autism exposed to structured, task-oriented, teaching made significantly better educational and social progress than children in less structured environments. The TEACCH programme (Teaching and

Education of Autistic and related Communication-handicapped CHildren) of Eric Schopler and colleagues (see Mesibov et al., 2005) provides a framework for teaching that incorporates an individualized developmental and behavioural approach, but specifically emphasizes the need for structure, appropriate environmental organization and the use of clear visual cues. The programme also takes account of developmental levels and the importance of individually based teaching, as well as incorporating behavioural and cognitive approaches. Although improvements have been reported in child behaviour, adaptive skills and cognitive ability, and in parent satisfaction, with some generalization to non-treatment settings, comparative studies are few, sample size is generally small and the results tend to be somewhat inconsistent (cf. Tsang et al., 2007).

Although the term EIBI is often used interchangeably with ABA, the latter refers to a much broader approach to behavioural assessment and analysis and is fundamental to many autism-specific educational programmes. Koegel and Koegel (1995), for example, have demonstrated how traditional behavioural techniques can be successfully adapted for use in more naturalistic school settings. Other specific programmes with an underlying behavioural focus, although also incorporating educational and developmental approaches, include the 'Bright Start Program' (Butera & Haywood, 1995), the Denver model (Rogers et al., 2006) and the Douglass Center programme (Handleman et al., 2006). However, many other models exist and, in the USA, often involve staged integration into inclusive schooling, together with training and support for mainstream class teachers (see Howlin, 2008 for review). The potential value of computer-based teaching has also been demonstrated in a number of small-scale projects (Bernard-Opitz et al., 1999; Bosseler & Massaro; 2003; Moore & Calvert, 2000; Tjus et al., 2001). Harris et al. (2005) conclude that, as there is no good evidence in favour of any one specific model, choice of programme

needs to be based on the needs of the individual child and his or her family.

Only a minority of children with ASD will, of course, have access to any of the highly specific, research-based programmes described above and, indeed, for some children, high-quality, autism-focused, generic school placements may be just as effective (Magiati et al., 2007; Spreckley & Boyd, 2009). The crucial components for educational success include a high degree of structure, optimal use of visual teaching strategies, staff with specialist knowledge of and expertise in dealing with the problems associated with ASD and close liaison between home and school to ensure generalization of skills taught (Howlin, 2008).

Communication-based programmes

In recent years, intervention programmes have tended to shift from a focus on overt behavioural problems to exploration of the underlying causes of such difficulties, particularly the role played by communication deficits. Analysis of the underlying function of many so-called 'challenging' behaviours of children with ASD indicates that these are frequently a reflection of their very limited communication skills. Failure to understand what is going on around them, and inability to express their needs and feelings verbally, means that many children have no effective means of communicating other than by actions—which may be of an aggressive or disruptive nature. Systematic analysis of the *communicative function* of such behaviours and teaching the child to communicate the same needs, but in a different and more acceptable *communicative form* (e.g. signs, gestures, electronic aids or other alternative means) has been shown in many single case/ case series studies to reduce disruptive behaviours while at the same time establishing more effective communication skills (Durand & Merges, 2001; Prizant & Wetherby, 2005). At the same time, intervention approaches predicated on developmental evidence of the emergence of early social and communication abilities in typically developing infants and toddlers have been developed (see next section). These aim, alongside reducing maladaptive behavioural responses, to enhance and scaffold social interaction and (verbal and non-verbal) communication abilities in young pre-school children, thus targeting the 'core' autism symptoms.

Over the years it has become increasingly evident that programmes with a specific emphasis on teaching *speech* have little impact, particularly for children with more severe receptive and expressive impairments (Howlin, 2006). Recent intervention approaches therefore have focused on approaches to enhance broader communicative abilities.

PECS (Picture Exchange Communication System; Bondy & Frost, 1998) is a systematic, picture-based approach to enhancing communication, specifically developed for children with autism. The programme utilizes a behavioural approach to teaching and follows a set sequence of stages, from prompting the child to make requests to developing spontaneous verbal comments. Although small-scale studies have reported improvements in both social interaction and spoken language, RCTs suggest rather more limited effects. For example, Howlin et al. (2007) found that immediately following PECS training, the frequency of initiations and pupils' use of PECS in the classroom significantly increased. However, these increases were not paralleled by improvements in spoken language, formal language test scores, or changes in autism symptomatology, and treatment effects were not maintained when intervention ceased. Yoder and Stone (2006a, 2006b) have also reported some positive although limited effects of PECS on spontaneous communication.

The TEACCH programme (see above) is another widely used educational programme with a focus on using non-verbal cues to help circumvent the communication and comprehension difficulties of children with ASD.

There are also reports of success using a variety of alternative or augmentative communication systems, ranging from symbol and signing programmes such as Makaton (Grove & Walker, 1990) to sophisticated computerized devices (e.g. Bosseler & Massaro, 2003). However, most such studies rely on single case or case series reports, and systematic evaluation of their effectiveness is generally lacking (see Howlin, 2006).

Enhancing parent–child interaction

Another development in recent years has been the switch of focus to interventions that concentrate on the precursors to spoken language, such as joint attention and parent–child synchrony. One well-publicized programme is the DIR method (Developmental Individual Difference Relationship-Based Floortime model; Wieder & Greenspan, 2003). This focuses on helping children to master the basic skills required for relating and communicating by means of 'Floortime' exercises in which the parent takes an active, developmental role in spontaneous and play activities that are directed by the child's interests and actions. Although the model is suggested as a cost-effective intervention for young children with ASD (Solomon et al., 2007) adequate controlled studies are currently lacking.

Other interventions with a specific focus on early parent–child interaction and communication include the Hanen 'More than Words' programme (Pepper & Weitzman, 2004). This has been shown to result in increased vocabulary and communication skills and a reduction in behavioural problems in the children involved (McConachie et al., 2005), and parents report improved coping skills and a reduction in stress. Several other programmes are based on similar principles to 'More than Words': i.e. having a focus on shared attention and parental sensitivity to the child's communicative attempts, with the goal of enhancing communicative exchanges to promote communication understanding and social engagement. A small-scale randomized trial of the Child's Talk programme (Aldred et al., 2004) found that, compared to treatment-as-usual controls, parents in the experimental group showed improvements in synchrony; their children showed decreases in autism severity and increases in initiations, reciprocal social interaction and vocabulary (see also Drew et al., 2002). A much larger RCT, based on the Child's Talk programme, (Green et al., 2010) involving 152 children with core autism aged 2 to 4 years, confirmed the significant improvements in parent synchrony and child initiations although there was no impact on overall autism severity. The Responsive Prelinguistic Milieu Teaching (RPMT) model (Yoder & Stone, 2006a, 2006b) also focuses on helping parents to learn to follow the child's lead, on increasing motivation to communicate, and using social games to provide natural reinforcement. RPMT has been shown to have positive effects on joint attention, turn-taking and child initiations. The Early Bird Programme (NAS, 2009) is designed specifically to support parents in the period between diagnosis and transition to nursery or school. There are no published studies on the impact of Early Bird on children's development but parents involved in the programme report less stress, and more positive perceptions of their child post intervention (Shields, 2001).

Programmes to enhance social-emotional skills

There is an increasing number of interventions designed to improve other fundamental deficits associated with ASD, notably those related to imagination, and social and emotional understanding. Most rely on case control or case series designs, although a few randomized controlled trials are beginning to appear.

Joint attention and symbolic play
Deficits in these areas are among the earliest signs of developmental abnormality shown by young children with ASD. The Relationship Development Intervention (RDI; Gutstein, 2001) focuses specifically on difficulties in forming social and emotional relationships, but despite considerable publicity there is no empirical evidence of effectiveness. In contrast, two RCTs by Kasari and colleagues (Kasari et al., 2006, 2008) have demonstrated the effectiveness of short-term interventions to enhance joint attention (JA) or symbolic play (SP) in children who were already receiving EIBI. Both the JA and SP groups showed significant improvements in expressive language, but other changes were specific to the intervention received. Thus, children in the JA group made most improvement in joint attention and initiation; those in the SP group made more gains in symbolic and interactive play. At 1-year follow-up both intervention groups showed improved language and interaction skills, compared to controls (Kasari et al., 2008), in line with longitudinal studies that show developmental relations over time between joint attention and play and language in pre-school children with ASD (Charman, 2003).

Theory of mind
Interventions designed to address the impairments in 'theory of mind' that are characteristic of ASD range from group teaching programmes, books, cartoons, photographs and toy figures, to virtual reality techniques and interactive DVDs (e.g. Baron-Cohen et al., 2002; Golan & Baron-Cohen, 2006). Although the published findings are generally positive, improvements tend to be related to the particular skills taught. For example, children can be taught to pass specific tasks related to understanding beliefs or emotions but improvements rarely generalize to other, untaught domains or to other settings (Hadwin et al., 1996) Assessments of treatment 'success' also tend to rely on parental report or analogue measures, and there is little evidence that training significantly improves social functioning in real life. Moreover, the techniques used vary widely from study to study and, as sample size is generally small, it

is not possible to determine which particular types of intervention are likely to be most effective with which children.

Social skills

Strategies designed to help children with ASD improve social competence and social understanding include social skills groups, peer training, social scripts, structured joint play activities, and manualized programmes. Despite their widespread use in both clinical and educational settings, recent reviews (Rao et al., 2007; Ruble et al., 2008; Williams-White et al., 2007) conclude that empirical support for social skills training programmes is minimal, and it is evident that a far more systematic approach to research in this area is required. The only RCT of social skills training to date (Beaumont & Sofronoff, 2008) found improvements only in parental report and analogue measures. Assessments of the children themselves showed little change.

Social stories

'Social Stories' (Gray, 1995) are another popular approach designed to improve social skills and social understanding. These utilize simple, cartoon-type drawings to help even very young children with ASD understand why they have experienced specific social problems, why other people react as they do, and how behaviour might be modified in future. Although there are several positive accounts of effectiveness, group sizes tend to be very small, experimental controls are generally absent, and as with social skills training more generally, the evidence base for social stories remains limited (Kokina & Kern, 2010).

Interventions for mental health problems

Most of the best-evaluated interventions for ASD have been conducted with children aged 6 years or younger. However, mental health difficulties affect many children as they move into adolescence and it is estimated that up to a third of young people with ASD develop psychiatric disorders, mainly related to anxiety (Ghaziuddin, 2005; White et al., 2009) and attention-deficit/hyperactivity disorder (ADHD); Simonoff et al., 2008). Although the evidence base for the use of cognitive behavioural therapy (CBT) with children with ASD is improving (Sze & Wood, 2008; White et al., 2009), RCTs have shown mixed results. Thus, whereas parental reports of outcome are often positive, self-report measures of anxiety tend to show less change and evidence of improved functioning in daily life is generally lacking (Chalfant et al., 2007; Sofronoff et al., 2005; Wood et al., 2009). There are presently no systematic data available to indicate for which individuals with ASD CBT is likely to be most effective, or which CBT-based procedures are potentially most successful. There is also the question of how far techniques with a focus on cognitions can be adapted for use with individuals for whom abstraction, imagination, and social/emotional understanding are fundamentally impaired. The issue of whether *cognitive* behavioural approaches can offer more than *behavioural* approaches is one requiring more research.

Identifying which therapies work for whom?

It is becoming increasingly clear that no one intervention is *consistently* more effective than any other for children with ASD—which is hardly surprising given the heterogeneity of this condition. In consequence, recent research has begun to shift the focus from attempts to demonstrate that any one treatment is superior to all others to exploration of which interventions (or components of intervention) produce the best effects for which children, and in which domains. For example, within behavioural programmes, there is some indication that PRT may be more successful for children who are making more social initiations pre-intervention

(Koegel et al., 1999). Ingersoll et al. (2001), investigating the effects of an inclusive educational group programme for toddlers with ASD, found that those with low social avoidance at baseline made more gains than those with high social avoidance initially. In Kasari and colleagues' (2008) trial exploring the differential effects of joint attention (JA) vs symbolic play (SP) training, JA training had a greater impact on expressive language, particularly in children with the lowest levels of language pre-treatment. Yoder and Stone (2006a, 2006b) compared PECS with RPMT training and found that, although the latter significantly enhanced turn-taking, joint attention and initiation, initiations only increased in children with some joint attention skills initially. PECS training appeared to have a greater effect on requesting behaviour, but only for children with initially low levels of initiation/joint interaction and higher levels of object exploration.

It is also apparent that the effects, even of successful programmes, are often relatively circumscribed. Thus, for example, interventions to improve non-verbal communication do just that—they do not tend to have a significant impact on verbal skills or broader cognitive functioning. It is important to note, too, that until relatively recently, almost all intervention studies have presented their findings in terms of *group* or *average* improvements and this frequently obscures individual differences in response to treatment.

Pharmacological interventions

There are no medications that have a demonstrated impact on the core symptoms of ASD, although drugs may be helpful for associated problems such as aggression, self-injury, hyperactivity or sleeping problems. Seizure disorders are also relatively common, especially in individuals with ASD of lower IQ, and often require anticonvulsant medication. However, few of the medications commonly prescribed for children with ASD have been approved for use either with children or for

individuals with ASD and there are few studies investigating the side effect of medications in common use. Santosh and Baird (2001) provide a helpful and practical approach to prescribing in ASD. They point to the dangers of polypharmacy and stress the importance of a *symptom-focused* approach. Thus, certain symptoms, including hyperactivity, obsessions, rituals, inattention and tics, appear to be directly helped by medication. Some, such as aggression, anxiety, depression, impulsivity and sleep difficulties, may require a behavioural approach in conjunction with medication. Other problems, such as academic or social difficulties, are unlikely to respond to medication.

Following a number of randomized control trials, older, antipsychotic medications such as haloperidol, thioridazine and chlorpromazine are now rarely used. Low dosages of risperidone have been found to be successful in decreasing irritability, hyperactivity, aggression and self-injurious behaviour, although weight gain continues to be a significant problem (RUPP, 2005b). Other atypical antipsychotics that appear to have positive effects are olanzapine and ziprasidone (the latter is less associated with weight gain). Selective serotonin reuptake inhibitors (SSRIs) are also being increasingly used in ASD. Fluoxetine is reported as helpful in reducing compulsive and repetitive behaviours (Hollander et al., 2005) and fluvoxamine has similar effects in adults. However, this appears to be less successful, and have more serious side effects when given to children and adolescents. Sertraline, in combination with CBT, has proved effective in treating anxiety in children with ASD (Walkup et al., 2008). In a large-scale RCT, methylphenidate was found to be less effective for children with autism than with other conditions, and side effects, such as irritability, were frequent. However, in low doses, and with careful clinical monitoring, stimulants may be helpful for children with comorbid ASD and ADHD (RUPP, 2005a). Mood stabilizers such as lithium and valproic acid have been used successfully to treat affective instability, impulsivity and aggression in individuals with ASD (Hollander et al., 2001; see also van Engeland & Buitelaar, 2008 for a summary).

While acknowledging the benefits that some of these new-generation medications can bring, Santosh and Baird (2001) note that clinical trial evidence for the use of psychotropics is in its infancy and needs close monitoring. As well as careful consideration of possible side effects, they recommend caution when using long-term medication and warn that psychotropics can sometimes worsen behaviour. In particular, certain antiepileptic medications and psychotropic drugs may interact in such a way as to significantly alter the effects of both. They suggest that specialist clinics should be involved when complex medication regimes, experimental drugs or polypharmacy are necessary, or if patients show unusual side effects or are drug resistant. Multiprofessional and parent partnership is considered essential in managing the problems associated with ASD, and psychopharmacology should only be used in conjunction with environmental manipulation, educational modification and/or behavioural management strategies.

There is no evidence for the effectiveness of 'alternative' medical treatments such as secretin (a gastrointestinal peptide hormone). Despite claims of 'miraculous' effects (Horvath et al., 1998; Rimland, 1998), a comprehensive review of 13 placebo-controlled studies (involving around 600 children) failed to demonstrate any positive effects (Esch & Carr, 2004). Evidence for the effectiveness of widely used dietary and vitamin treatments for autism (e.g. 'Eye Q' supplements) is also lacking. A Cochrane Review of 18 studies of vitamin B_6 and magnesium treatments for autism (Nye & Brice, 2005) concluded that there was no evidence of effectiveness. Another Cochrane Review of gluten- and casein-free diets for children with autism (Millward et al., 2007) found only one small-scale study that met basic research criteria, and this reported only limited effects. Moreover, there is very little consideration of

the possible dangers of removing basic foodstuffs such as gluten, milk or wheat without ensuring that there is adequate compensation for any resulting dietary deficiencies. The potential risks of unnecessarily adding vitamins or other supplements also tend to be almost completely ignored.

AUTISM SPECTRUM DISORDERS ACROSS THE LIFE SPAN

The vast majority of research in the field of ASD has focused on children. Apart from drug and imaging trials, studies of adults are much more limited and the substantial funding devoted to diagnosis and intervention for pre-school children has not been paralleled by funding for adults. Even studies of school-age children are relatively few in number compared with those for pre-schoolers and there is far less systematic evaluation of interventions for adolescents and adults. There are no adequately controlled trials of educational, occupational or social interventions for adults despite the fact that most individuals with ASD live well into old age. Knowledge about trajectories of development, as individuals move from childhood into adulthood, is also relatively limited, although it is clear that long-term prognosis is closely associated with IQ level and the development of language. Outcome is generally poor for those individuals with an IQ below 70, or for those who fail to develop communicative speech by the age of 5–6 years (Lord & Bailey, 2002).

Although, as discussed below, some individuals with ASD may show an increase in problem behaviours as they grow older, in many studies tracing progress from childhood to adulthood, there is clear evidence of improvement over time. Kanner himself (1973) noted that for some individuals, particularly those who were more able, mid-adolescence was often a period of 'remarkable improvement and change' and of opportunities for learning and development. Over 40% of the individuals in a follow-up study by

Kobayashi et al. (1992) were rated as showing marked improvement, and Billstedt et al. (2005) noted that 38% of their sample had a remarkably problem-free adolescent period. Mawhood and her colleagues (2000) also found that almost one-third of the young men whom they had followed had moved from a rating of 'Poor' functioning as children to a 'Good' rating as adults. Many other studies, both retrospective and prospective, suggest that change over time is more likely to be positive rather than negative, with scores on standardized assessments such as the ADI and ADOS indicating a decline in the severity and frequency of autistic symptoms with age (Charman et al., 2005; Fecteau et al., 2003; Gilchrist et al., 2001; Howlin, 2003; Moss et al., 2008; Piven et al., 1996; Seltzer et al., 2003; Shattuck et al., 2006; Starr et al., 2003). Furthermore, the majority of follow-up studies show no indication of any decline in cognitive functioning and, if anything, verbal IQ tends to increase slightly with age (Farley et al., 2009; Howlin et al., 2004; Mawhood et al., 2000).

It is also clear that, generally, the prospects for adults with autism have improved considerably over recent decades. In the last 30 years there have been a number of systematic follow-up studies exploring trajectories from childhood to adolescence and adulthood. Some studies have involved individuals with very mixed levels of ability—from severe cognitive impairment to average or above average IQ (e.g. Ballaban-Gil et al., 1996; Billstedt et al., 2005; Cederlund et al., 2008; Eaves & Ho, 2008; Howlin et al., 2004; Larsen & Mouridsen, 1997; Lockyer & Rutter, 1969, 1970; Lotter, 1974a, 1974b; Venter et al., 1992). Other studies have focused specifically on individuals with Asperger syndrome or high-functioning autism (Engström et al., 2003; Farley et al., 2009; Mawhood et al., 2000; Rumsey et al., 1985; Szatmari et al., 1989). Findings from some of these earlier studies were far from positive. For example, in the group of 63 individuals followed up by Lockyer and Rutter (1969, 1970) over half were living in long-stay hospitals, and

educational and training opportunities were minimal (less than half had received as much as 2 years' schooling and many had never attended school at all). In contrast, a study of 68 individuals (childhood IQ-50–130) from the same diagnostic centre, three decades later (Howlin et al., 2004), found that, as adults, only a small minority were in long-stay hospital provision; 20% had obtained formal qualifications at schools, 31% were in some form of employment (although jobs were generally poorly paid); and 10% were living more or less independently. Venter et al. (1992), in a study of 58 children and adolescents, also noted a marked improvement in children's academic attainments compared with earlier follow-up reports. Thus, even amongst lower-functioning individuals, over half could read and do simple arithmetic, compared to about one-fifth in the Lockyer and Ruttter studies conducted 20 years previously.

Nevertheless, long-term follow-up studies continue to report very variable results, with some individuals achieving highly as adults, but others remaining highly dependent (Billstedt et al., 2005; Cederlund et al., 2008; Howlin et al., 2004). Although outcome is clearly correlated with IQ (few individuals with a childhood IQ < 70 live independently as adults; Howlin et al., 2004), outcome for individuals with a childhood IQ in the normal range remains unpredictable. Almost all the 14 individuals (aged from 18–39 years) described by Rumsey et al. (1985) continued to have significant problems. A similar outcome was reported by Mawhood et al. (2000) for 19 young men, all of whom had a nonverbal childhood IQ within the normal range. Only three individuals were living independently, three had jobs, and three were described as having close friendships. The majority showed continuing problems in social relationships and over two-thirds were described as having moderate to severe behavioural difficulties, associated with obsessional or ritualistic tendencies. Cederlund et al. (2008) found that outcome in individuals with Asperger syndrome (AS) was significantly better than for those with a diagnosis of autism, but even in the higher-ability AS group (mean full-scale IQ-103) only 27% were rated as having a good outcome. Szatmari et al. (1989) reported more positive findings for a group of 16 young adults (average IQ > 90): half had attended college or university (six had a degree or equivalent qualification); seven were in full-time employment; and five lived independently, although 10 were still living at home or semi-independently. A quarter of the group had dated regularly or had long-term relationships and one was married. These relatively positive findings led the authors to conclude that 'A small percentage of non-retarded autistic children … can be expected to recover to a substantial degree. It may take years to occur, and the recovery may not always be complete, but substantial improvement does occur' (p. 224). Even more positive findings are reported in a recent study by Farley et al. (2009) of 41 adults (age 22–46 years; mean IQ-89) originally diagnosed as children. Compared with previous follow-up studies of similar IQ cohorts, rates of tertiary education were higher (39%), as were rates for full-time employment (27%), friendships (52%), close sexual relationships (20%; 12% were or had been married and 7% had children of their own) and independent or semi-independent living (27%).

Difficulties in adulthood

Although as indicated above, the severity of autistic symptomatology tends to decline over the years, adults with ASD, even those who are of normal intelligence face many challenges.

Further education and employment
Although access to post-school education has improved in recent decades, and a growing number of colleges and universities now offer specialist support networks for students with ASD, these are still in the minority. Even individuals who have achieved well in the structured environment of school may struggle to cope in college or university, where their work is no longer closely monitored, attendance at lectures is often optional and when, in many cases they are also struggling to learn to live away from home and how to cope with social situations. Exams are a particular source of pressure, and many intellectually competent individuals fail to complete their college courses successfully because of a lack of adequate support.

Lack of specialist support to help individuals find work, or to keep employment once they have found a job, is also a major problem. Even amongst follow-up studies with a focus on higher-functioning individuals, fewer than 50% are reported as finding work and few studies report employment rates above 30%. Moreover, jobs tend to be unskilled and poorly paid, and are often at a much lower level than would be expected given the individual's intellectual ability. In the group of 68 individuals studied by Howlin and colleagues (2004), for example, one-third had performance IQs of 80 or above and several had university degrees or diplomas. Despite this, only eight were working independently and employment stability was poor, with many individuals experiencing lengthy periods without paid work. If anything, employment prospects tended to worsen with age and, in a subsequent follow-up of the same group, Hutton (1998) found no increase in the numbers in independent work and three previously employed individuals were no longer working. There is good evidence that specialist-supported employment can have a significant impact on an individual's ability to find and maintain employment (Howlin et al., 2004; Keel et al., 1997, Smith et al., 1995). The types of job obtained via these schemes are also much more appropriate to participants' intellectual and educational levels. Although initially expensive, because of the level of support required in the early stages, the costs of specialist employment programmes reduce as participants become able to work more independently. Earning a salary also means that individuals begin to contribute to the economy via taxes, and reliance on state benefits decreases. However, provision of autism-specific job schemes is very limited and although some adults with ASD may find work through support schemes for people with intellectual disability or other special needs, many individuals, and particularly those of average or above average intelligence, have access to little or no help.

Independent living and social relationships

Support to help individuals with ASD cope with independent or semi-independent living is also sparse and individuals of higher cognitive ability may find it even more difficult to access help than those with intellectual impairments. Most follow-up studies indicate that only a minority of adults live in their own homes (the mean figure reported is around 12%) and many remain living with their parents or in residential provision. Systematic follow-up studies also suggest that although around 20–30% of participants are reported to have close friendships, very few individuals marry or have children of their own. However, it is important to note that the cohorts involved in long-term outcome studies are not necessarily representative of the wider autism spectrum and there are many personal accounts by or about married people with autism or Asperger syndrome (see, for example, Holliday-Wiley, 2001; Lawson, 1998; Paradiž, 2002; Pyles, 2002; Slater Walker & Slater-Walker, 2002). Moreover, since ASD is largely a genetic condition, many parents of children with autism and Asperger syndrome are likely themselves to be undiagnosed individuals within the spectrum, who have clearly succeeded in maintaining close relationships and in bringing up families of their own.

Factors related to outcome

The variability in outcome amongst individuals with ASD has been noted since the earliest follow-up studies (Eisenberg, 1956; Kanner & Eisenberg, 1956). Factors that seem to be related to a better prognosis include cognitive ability (few individuals with an IQ < 70 live independently as adults) and the development of useful language by elementary school age (~6 years). The need for appropriate education has been recognized for many years (cf. Kanner, 1973; Lockyer & Rutter, 1969, 1970; Lotter, 1974a, 1974b) and Kanner (1973) noted the importance of specialist skills or interests (such as competence in mathematics, music or computing), which may allow individuals to find their own 'niche' in life, and thus enable them to be more readily integrated into society. The relationship between adult outcome and other variables is less clear. Overall severity of early symptoms (as measured by the ADI-R) does not seem to predict later outcome, although there is a negative association between prognosis and degree of language *abnormality* and/or the level of disruption caused by stereotyped and repetitive behaviours (Lord & Venter, 1992). In almost every follow-up study, outcome has been poorer for females than males, but the number of women participants has generally been very small and the differences found rarely reach *statistical* significance. The impact of family factors, socioeconomic status, or personal characteristics such as personality and temperament, has never been satisfactorily explored.

Lord and Venter (1992) have suggested that, at least among individuals of normal IQ, prognosis depends less on intellectual ability and more on external factors, such as the adequacy of support systems provided by educational, employment and social services. This view is supported by the recent findings of Farley et al. (2009). It is significant that their study was conducted in Salt Lake City, Utah, and all but three individuals belonged to the Church of Jesus Christ of Latter-Day Saints (LDS). The LDS church and community provide a highly exceptional level of support for its members, and it may have been this, rather than any other factor, that was responsible for the unusually positive outcome in this sample.

Onset of new problems
in adulthood

The transition to adulthood can be a time of upheaval and difficulties for many young people and problems are likely to be exacerbated if individuals also have intellectual or developmental disorders. Although the majority of individuals with ASD make positive progress as they move into adolescence and adulthood, a minority shows increases in behavioural disturbance and mental health problems (estimates vary from < 10% to > 50%; cf. Ballaban-Gil et al., 1996; Billstedt et al., 2005; Eaves & Ho, 2008; Hofvander et al., 2009; Kobayashi et al., 1992; Larsen & Mouridsen, 1997; Lockyer & Rutter, 1969). In some instances, too, there are reports of significant deterioration in communication and general cognitive ability (Gillberg & Steffenberg, 1987; Lockyer & Rutter, 1970).

Hutton et al. (2008) explored the onset of new psychiatric problems in a group of 135 individuals with ASD (age 21–57 years; IQ-33–133). Around one-fifth had developed mental health problems in adulthood, mainly related to affective disorders, anxiety or obsessive compulsive disorder (OCD) (in four cases accompanied by catatonia). In the majority of cases, onset occurred in the early 20s, although others developed problems in adolescence and a few in later life (age 30–40). Psychiatric and emotional difficulties were frequently related to environmental stresses, such as loss of job or move of residence. Some researchers have suggested that the risk of mental health problems in adulthood is increased in individuals who are more able, and hence more aware of their difficulties and differences, and may be more exposed to the stressors that come with independent or semi-independent functioning. There is also the possibility that psychiatric problems may be underdiagnosed in individuals with autism who have intellectual impairments, because of limited ability to describe their moods and feelings (Sturmey, 1998). However, in the Hutton et al. (2008) study, rates of psychiatric problems were similar across the IQ range.

A number of other studies have reported increased rates of anxiety or obsessional problems from adolescence onwards in individuals with ASD compared to typically developing peers (Eaves & Ho, 2008; Kim et al., 2000) and the risk of mental health problems is higher than in teenagers with conduct disorders (Green et al., 2000) or language disorders (Gillott et al., 2001). Follow-up studies, as well as clinical case reports, confirm high rates of mental health problems, and it is estimated that around 30% of adults suffer from clinical depression or anxiety-related problems (see Ghaziuddin, 2005; Howlin 2004 for reviews). In contrast, despite Kanner's assertion (1949) that 'I do not believe that there is any likelihood that early infantile autism will at any future time have to be separated from the schizophrenias' (p. 418), there is little evidence that the incidence of schizophrenia is increased. Relatively large-scale studies of adults (Billstedt et al., 2005; Cederlund et al., 2008; Ghaziuddin et al., 1998; Howlin et al., 2004; Volkmar & Cohen, 1991) have identified only very small numbers of individuals who meet full diagnostic criteria for schizophrenia. Volkmar and Cohen (1991) concluded that the frequency of schizophrenia in individuals with autism was similar to that in the general population, at around 0.6% (see also Howlin, 2004; Lainhart, 1999). Although one study, using the nationwide Danish Psychiatric Register, has suggested rates may be higher— 3.4% in individuals with a childhood diagnosis of infantile autism and 34.8% of individuals with a diagnosis of atypical autism (Mouridsen et al., 2008b, 2008c)—psychiatric diagnoses in these cohorts were not independently confirmed. There are also occasional reports of delusional disorders, unspecified psychoses (sometimes associated with epilepsy), paranoid ideation, catatonia and hallucinations (Ghaziuddin, et al., 1991; Hofvander et al., 2009; Hutton et al., 2008; Rumsey et al., 1985; Szatmari et al., 1989; Tantam, 2000; Wing & Shah, 2000). OCD has also been reported. Although it can often prove very difficult to distinguish between this condition and the ritualistic and stereotyped behaviours that are characteristic of ASD, there are a number of features that can help to inform differential diagnosis (McDougle et al., 1995; Russell et al., 2005). Nevertheless, there remain substantial difficulties in making a valid diagnosis of psychosis in people with ASD. Impoverished language, literal interpretation of questions, concrete thinking and obsessionality can all give rise to misunderstandings, leading to possible misdiagnosis, even in the case of relatively able individuals. For those individuals with little or no speech, the risks of an incorrect diagnosis (or failure to diagnose when problems do exist) are even higher.

Mortality and suicide in ASD

Recent research suggests that death rates may be higher in individuals with ASD than in the population as a whole. Two recent register-based studies, one in Denmark of 313 individuals with ASD (Mouridsen et al., 2008a) the other in California of 13,111 individuals (Shavelle et al., 2001), suggest that mortality in ASD may be twice as high as in the general population. These studies identified the presence of epilepsy as a major risk factor and, amongst individuals with more severe mental retardation, there was a threefold increase in deaths from all causes (other than cancer) compared to non-disabled controls. Death was also sometimes associated with inadequate standards of care in residential settings. In individuals with milder intellectual impairments or those of normal IQ, deaths were linked to a wide range of causes, including seizures, other neurological disorders, accidents (traffic, drowning and suffocation) and physical conditions such as asthma and pneumonia. Death due to complications arising from long-term psychotropic medication has also been reported (Ballaban-Gil et al., 1996).

Incidents of suicide, or attempted suicide, have been reported in a number of studies (e.g. Tantam, 1991; Wing, 1981; Wolff & McGuire, 1995) and anecdotal accounts of suicides appear with some frequency on the Internet.

However, although it has been suggested that suicide rates may be raised in individuals with ASD, particularly those who are of higher intellectual ability, there have been no systematic studies in this area. Nevertheless, it is likely that better understanding of, and support for, the difficulties that lead some young people to attempt suicide could avoid unnecessary loss of life.

Forensic issues

Occasional and sometimes lurid press publicity has led to suggestions that there may be an excess of violent crimes amongst people with ASD, and the media are often quick to label individuals who have committed apparently cold-blooded massacres (as in the Virginia Tech killings) as having Asperger syndrome. There are also a number of clinical case reports of individuals who have committed serious crimes, such as murder, sexual violence or assault (cf. Howlin, 2004; Allen et al., 2007). Scragg and Shah (1994) found that the prevalence of individuals with ASD in secure hospital provision for psychiatric offenders was higher than expected and concluded that there was a particular association between Asperger syndrome and violence. Another study based on the Danish Register of Criminality (Mouridsen et al., 2008d) reported that just under 1% of individuals with infantile autism, 8% of those with atypical autism, and 18% of those with Asperger syndrome had been convicted of crimes (arson was particularly high in the Asperger group). Rates of offending in an age- and social class-matched comparison group were around 18%. However, it should be noted that the cohort studied by Mouridsen et al. (2008c, 2008d) also appears to have much higher rates of pathology, generally, than found in other follow-up studies. Ghaziuddin et al. (1991) noted that rates of violent offending by people with ASD were far less than the rates of violent offending in young men in the USA of similar age. Nevertheless, there may well be more people with ASD in prisons or secure accommodation than is realized, and it is clearly important that such individuals are correctly identified and treated. Allen et al. (2007) found that the 16 individuals whom they interviewed in prison (offences included violence, threatening behaviour, sexual offences and murder) were frequently deeply confused, shocked and distressed by the whole process leading up to and including their incarceration. Generally, too, there was little understanding of their condition by police, lawyers, judges, prison staff or other inmates. On the other hand, access to support from sympathetic police or prison officers, members of the legal establishment or appointed advocates ('appropriate adults') made a significant difference to their ability to understand and cope with the situation. Indeed, for some the structured regime of the prison environment was viewed as a positive aspect: 'Yeah, I'm happy with it…not that it was intended as a therapy, but I have grown a lot in confidence since being in prison' (Allen et al., 2007: p. 755). Allen et al. (2007) also explored factors associated with offending. The most common precipitating factors were social or sexual rejection, bullying, mental health problems or problems related to disruption within the family or support networks. Social naivety, misinterpretation of social rules, lack of appreciation of outcome, impulsivity and, though to a lesser degree, obsessional behaviours, also played an important role.

Interventions for adults

As noted above, marked regression in adulthood appears to be the exception, not the rule. Nevertheless, many adults with ASD experience significant mental health problems, and prospects for independent living or finding suitable employment remain very limited. Moreover, even those who are able to find work and independent accommodation frequently live very isolated and restricted lives. Although it is evident that specific schemes to provide training or jobs or sup-

ported living environments can be effective, such schemes are few and far between and funding is frequently short term and sporadic. Provision for adults with ASD who are of normal intelligence is even more limited than for those who have associated intellectual impairments. The lack of specialist support programmes for adults is paralleled by a lack of funding for research into interventions that might help to improve outcome. There is a marked discrepancy between the amount of funding for research and specialist programmes for pre-school children and funding for older individuals. Thus, there are no well-evaluated, comprehensive programmes for adolescents with ASD, despite the fact that normal adolescence is a time of rapid neurological and social development when focused programmes could, perhaps, achieve a great deal. In adulthood, although the importance of structure, support and stability is well recognized, research into, or dedicated funding for, programmes that might better meet the needs of adults, is rarely provided.

CONCLUSION

Autism spectrum disorders persist throughout an individual's life. Although a number of different treatment programmes have been shown to be effective for young children, the types of intervention needed in early childhood (which focus mainly on behaviour and communication) may be very different to those required in adolescence or adulthood (when social, emotional and mental health problems are often of greater concern). Thus, there is a need for provision that can both monitor and meet individuals' changing needs over the years. Support should not come to an abrupt end at the age of 19, when in many countries formal schooling terminates. Whereas the importance of good liaison between families and health, educational and social services is generally recognized during childhood, there is far less support to facilitate the transition from childhood to adulthood. Although there can be no doubt that the future for most people with ASD is far less bleak than was the case 50–60 years ago, ultimately the extent to which they can succeed will depend on the support systems to which they have access. Improving access to such provision is the major challenge for the decades to come.

REFERENCES

Aldred, C., Green, J., & Adams, C. (2004) 'A new social communication intervention for children with autism: pilot randomised controlled treatment study suggesting effectiveness', *Journal of Child Psychology and Psychiatry*, 45: 1420–1430.

Ali, S. & Frederickson, N. (2006) 'Investigating the evidence base of social stories', *Educational Psychology in Practice*, 22: 355–377.

Allen, D., Peckett, H., Evans, C., Hider, A., Rees, H., Hawkins, S., & Morgan, H. (2007) 'As perger Syndrome and the criminal justice system', *Good Autism Practice*, 8: 35–42.

Baird, G., Simonoff, E., Pickles, A., Chandler, S., Loucas, T., Meldrum, D., & Charman, T. (2006) 'Prevalence of disorders of the autism spectrum in a population cohort of children in South Thames: the Special Needs and Autism Project (SNAP)', *Lancet*, 368: 210–215.

Ballaban-Gil, K., Rapin, I., Tuchman, R., & Shinnar, S. (1996) 'Longitudinal examination of the behavioral, language, and social changes in a population of adolescents and young adults with autistic disorder', *Pediatric Neurology*, 15: 217–223.

Baron-Cohen, S., Hill, J, Golan, O., & Wheelwright, S. (2002) 'Mindreading made easy', *Cambridge Medicine*, 17: 28–29.

Bauminger, N. (2002) 'The facilitation of social-emotional understanding and social interaction in high-functioning children with autism: intervention outcomes', *Journal of Autism and Developmental Disorders*, 32: 283–298.

Beaumont, R. & Sofronoff, K. (2008) 'A multi-component social skills intervention for children with Asperger syndrome: the Junior Detective Training Program', *Journal of Child Psychology and Psychiatry*, 49: 743–753.

Bernard-Opitz, V., Sriram, N., & Sapuan, S. (1999) 'Enhancing vocal limitations in children with autism using the IBM SpeechViewer', *Autism: International Journal of Research and Practice*, 3: 131–147.

Billstedt, E., Gillberg, I.C., & Gillberg, C. (2005) 'Autism after adolescence: population-based 13- to 22-year follow-up study of 120 individuals with autism diagnosed in childhood', *Journal of Autism and Developmental Disorders*, 35: 351–360.

Bondy, A.S. & Frost, L.A. (1998) 'The Picture Exchange Communication System', *Seminars in Speech and Language*, 19: 373–389.

Bosseler, A. & Massaro, D.W. (2003) 'Development and evaluation of a computer-animated tutor for vocabulary and language learning in children with autism', *Journal of Autism and Developmental Disorders*, 33: 653–672.

Butera, G. & Haywood, H.C. (1995) 'Cognitive education of young children with autism: an application of Bright Start', in E. Schopler & G. Mesibov (eds), *Learning and Cognition in Autism*. New York: Plenum Press.

Cederlund, M., Hagberg, B., Billstedt, E., Gillberg, I.C., & Gillberg, C. (2008) 'Asperger syndrome and autism: a comparative longitudinal follow-up study more than 5 years after original diagnosis', *Journal of Autism and Developmental Disorders*, 38: 72–85.

Chalfant, A., Rapee, R., & Carroll, L. (2007) 'Treating anxiety disorders in children with high functioning autism spectrum disorders: a controlled trial', *Journal of Autism and Developmental Disorders*, 37(10): 1842–1857.

Charman, T. (2003) 'Why is joint attention a pivotal skill in autism?', *Philosophical Transactions of the Royal Society, London*, 358: 315–324.

Charman, T. & Baird, G. (2002) 'Practitioner review: diagnosis of autism spectrum disorder in 2- and 3-year-old children', *Journal of Child Psychology and Psychiatry*, 43(3): 289–305.

Charman, T. & Stone, W. (2006) *Social and Communication Development in Autism Spectrum Disorders*. New York: Guilford Press.

Charman, T., Taylor, E., Drew, A., Cockerill, H., Brown, J., & Baird, G. (2005) 'Outcome at 7 years of children diagnosed with autism at age 2: predictive validity of assessments conducted at 2 and 3 years of age and pattern of symptom change over time', *Journal of Child Psychology and Psychiatry*, 46: 500–513.

Dawson, G., Rogers, S., Munson, J., Smith, M., Winter, J., Greenson, J., Donaldson, A., & Varley, J. (2010) Randomized, Controlled Trial of an Intervention for Toddlers with Autism: The Early Start Denver ModelPediatrics, 125: 17–23.

Drew, A., Baird, G., Baron-Cohen, S., Cox, A., Slonims, V., Wheelwright, S., Swettenham, J., Berry, B., &

Charman, C. (2002) 'A pilot randomised control trial of a parent training intervention for pre-school children with autism. Preliminary findings and methodological challenges', *European Child and Adolescent Psychiatry,* 11: 266–272.

Durand, V.M. & Merges, E. (2001) 'Functional communication training: a contemporary behavior analytic intervention for problem behaviors', *Focus on Autism and Other Developmental Disabilities,* 16: 110–119.

Eaves, L.C. & Ho, H.H. (2008) 'Young adult outcome of autism spectrum disorders', *Journal of Autism and Developmental Disorders,* 38(4): 739–747.

Eikeseth, S. (2009) 'Outcome of comprehensive psycho-educational interventions for young children with autism', *Research in Developmental Disabilities,* 30(1): 158–178.

Eisenberg, L. (1956) 'The autistic child in adolescence', *American Journal of Psychiatry,* 1112: 607–612.

Engström, I., Ekström, L., & Emilsson, B. (2003) 'Psychosocial functioning in a group of Swedish adults with Asperger Syndrome or high-functioning autism', *Autism,* 7: 99–110.

Esch, B.E. & Carr, J.E. (2004) 'Secretin as a treatment for autism: a review of the evidence', *Journal of Autism and Developmental Disorders,* 34(5): 543–556.

Farley, M.A., McMahon, W.M., Fombonne, E., Jenson, W.R., Miller, J., Gardner, M., Block, H., Pingree, C.B., Ritvo, E.R., Ritvo, R.A., & Coon, H. (2009) 'Twenty-year outcome for individuals with autism and average or near-average cognitive abilities', *Autism Research,* 2: 109–118.

Fecteau, S., Mottron, L., Berthiaume, C., & Burack, J.A. (2003) 'Developmental changes of autistic symptoms', *Autism,* 7(3): 255–268.

Ghaziuddin, M. (2005) *Mental Health Aspects of Autism and Asperger Syndrome.* London: Jessica Kingsley.

Ghaziuddin, M., Tsai, L.Y., & Ghaziuddin, N. (1991) 'Brief report. Violence in Asperger syndrome: A critique', *Journal of Autism and Developmental Disorders,* 21: 349–354.

Ghaziuddin, M., Weidmer-Mikhail, E., & Ghaziuddin, N. (1998) 'Comorbidity in Asperger syndrome: a preliminary report', *Journal of Intellectual Disability Research,* 42: 279–283.

Gilchrist, A., Green, J., Cox, A., Rutter, M., & Le Couteur, A. (2001) 'Development and current functioning in adolescents with Asperger syndrome: a comparative study', *Journal of Child Psychology and Psychiatry,* 42: 227–240.

Gillberg, C. & Steffenberg, S. (1987) 'Outcome and prognostic factors in infantile autism and similar conditions: a population-based study of 46 cases followed through puberty', *Journal of Autism and Developmental Disorders,* 17: 272–288.

Gillott, A., Furniss, F., & Walter, A. (2001) 'Anxiety in high-functioning children with autism', *Autism,* 5: 277–286.

Golan, O. & Baron-Cohen, S. (2006) 'Systemizing empathy: teaching adults with Asperger syndrome or high-functioning autism to recognize complex emotions using interactive multimedia', *Development and Psychopathology,* 18: 591–617.

Gray, C. (1995) *My Social Stories Book.* London: Jessica Kingsley.

Green, J., Charman, T., McConachie, H., Aldred, C., Slonims, V., Howlin, P., Le Couteur, A. et al. (2010) Parent-mediated communication-focused treatment for preschool children with autism (MRC PACT); a randomised controlled trial. The Lancet, 375, Issue 9732, 2124–2125.

Green, J., Gilchrist, A., Burton, D., & Cox, A. (2000) 'Social and psychiatric functioning in adolescents with Asperger syndrome compared with conduct disorder', *Journal of Autism and Developmental Disorders,* 30: 279–293.

Grove, N. & Walker, M. (1990) *The Makaton Vocabulary: Using Manual Signs and Graphic Symbols to Develop Interpersonal Communication.* Camberley: MVDP.

Gutstein, S. (2001) *Solving the Relationship Puzzle.* Arlington, TX: Future Horizons.

Hadwin, J., Baron-Cohen S., Howlin P., & Hill, K. (1996) 'Can we teach children with autism to understand emotions, belief or pretence?', *Development and Psychopathology,* 8: 345–365.

Handleman, J.S., Harris, S.L., Arnold, M., Gordon, R., & Cohen, M. (2006) 'The Douglass Developmental Disabilities Center: options for school-age students', in J.S. Handleman & S.L. Harris (eds), *School-Age Education Programs for Children with Autism. The In-Between Years.* Austin, TX: PRO-ED, pp. 89–113.

Hanson, E., Kalish, L.A., Bunce, E., Curtis, C., McDaniel, S., Ware, J., & Petry, J. (2007) 'Use of complementary and alternative medicine among children diagnosed with autism spectrum-disorder', *Journal of Autism and Developmental Disorders,* 37: 628–636.

Harris, S.L., Handleman, J.S., & Jennet, H.K. (2005) 'Models of education for students with autism: home, center and school-based programmes,' in F. Volkmar, R. Paul, A. Klin, & D. Cohen (eds), *Handbook of Autism and Pervasive Developmental Disorders,* 3rd edn. Hoboken, NJ: pp. 1043–1054.

Hofvander, B., Delorme, R., Chaste, P., Nyden, A., Wentz, E., Stahlberg, O., Herbrecht, E., Stopin, A., Gillberg, C., Rastam, M., & Leboyer, M. (2009) 'Psychiatric and psychosocial problems in adults with normal-intelligence autism spectrum disorders', *BioMed Central Psychiatry*, 9: 35–62.

Hollander, E., Dolgoff-Kaspar, R., Cartwright, C., Rawitt, R., & Novotny, S. (2001) 'An open trial of divalproex sodium in autism spectrum disorders', *Journal of Clinical Psychiatry*, 62: 530–534.

Hollander, E., Phillips, A., Chaplin, W., Zagursky, K., Novotny, S., Wasserman, S., & Iyengar, R. (2005) 'A placebo controlled crossover trial of liquid fluoxetine on repetitive behaviors in childhood and adolescent autism', *Neuropsychopharmacology*, 30: 582–589.

Holliday-Willey, L. (2001). *Asperger Syndrome in the Family*. London: Jessica Kingsley.

Horvath, K., Stefanotos, G., Sokolski, K.N., Wachtel, R., Nabors, L., & Tildon, T. (1998) 'Improved social and language skills after secretin administration in patients with autistic spectrum disorders', *Journal of the Association of the Academy of Minority Physicians*, 9: 9–15.

Howlin, P. (2003) 'Outcome in high-functioning adults with autism with and without early language delays: implications for the differentiation between autism and Asperger syndrome', *Journal of Autism and Developmental Disorders*, 33: 3–13.

Howlin, P. (2004) *Autism and Asperger Syndrome: Preparing for Adulthood*. London: Routledge.

Howlin, P. (2006) 'Augmentative and alternative communication systems for children with autism', in T. Charman & W. Stone (eds), *Social and Communication Development in Autism Spectrum Disorders*. New York: Guilford Press, pp. 236–266.

Howlin, P. (2008) 'Special educational provision', in M. Rutter et al. (eds), *Rutter Handbook of Child and Adolescent Psychiatry*, 5th edn. Oxford: Blackwell, pp. 1189–1206.

Howlin, P. & Rutter, M. (1987) *Treatment of Autistic Children*. London: Wiley.

Howlin, P., Goode, S., Hutton, J., & Rutter, M. (2004) 'Adult outcome for children with autism', *Journal of Child Psychology and Psychiatry*, 45(2): 212–229.

Howlin, P., Gordon, K., Pasco, G., Wade, A., & Charman, T. (2007) 'A group randomised, controlled trial of the Picture Exchange Communication System for children with autism', *Journal of Child Psychology and Psychiatry*, 48: 473–481.

Howlin, P., Magiati, I., & Charman, T. (2009) 'Systematic review of early intensive behavioral interventions for children with autism', *American Journal of Intellectual and Developmental Disability*, 114(1): 23–41.

Hutton, J. (1998) 'Cognitive decline and new problems arising in association with autism'. Doctor of Clinical Psychology thesis, Institute of Psychiatry, University of London.

Hutton, J., Goode, S., Murphy, M., Le Couteur, A., & Rutter, M. (2008) 'New-onset psychiatric disorders in individuals with autism', *Autism*, 12: 373–390.

Ingersoll, B., Schreibman L., & Stahmer, A. (2001) Brief report: Differential treatment outcomes for children with autistic spectrum disorder based on level of peer social avoidance', *Journal of Autism and Developmental Disorders*, 31: 343–349.

Jocelyn, L.J., Casiro, O.G., Beattie, D., Bow, J., & Kneisz, J. (1998) 'Treatment of children with autism: a randomized controlled trial to evaluate a caregiver-based intervention program in community day-care centers', *Journal of Developmental Behavior and Pediatrics*, 19: 26–34.

Kanner, L. (1943) 'Autistic disturbances of affective contact', *Nervous Child*, 2: 217–250.

Kanner, L. (1949) 'Problems of nosology and psychodynamics of early infantile autism', *American Journal of Orthopsychiatry*, 19: 416–426.

Kanner, L. (1973) *Childhood Psychosis: Initial Studies and New Insights*. New York: Winston/Wiley.

Kanner, L. & Eisenberg, L. (1956) 'Early infantile autism', *American Journal of Orthopsychiatry*, 26: 55–65.

Kasari, C., Freeman, S., & Paparella, T. (2006) 'Joint attention and symbolic play in young children with autism: a randomized controlled intervention study', *Journal of Child Psychology and Psychiatry*, 47: 611–620.

Kasari, C., Paparella, T., Freeman, S., & Jahromi, L.B. (2008) 'Language outcome and autism: randomized comparison of joint attention and play interventions', *Journal of Consulting and Clinical Psychology*, 76: 125–137.

Keel, J.H., Mesibov, G., & Woods, A.V. (1997) 'TEACCH-supported employment program', *Journal of Autism and Developmental Disorders*, 27: 3–10.

Kim, J.A., Szatmari, P., Bryson, S., Streiner, D.L., & Wilson, F. (2000) 'The prevalence of anxiety and mood problems among children with autism and Asperger syndrome,' *Autism: International Journal of Research and Practice*, 4: 117–132.

Kobayashi, R., Murata, T., & Yashinaga, K. (1992) 'A follow-up study of 201 children with autism in Kyushu and Yamaguchi, Japan', *Journal of Autism and Developmental Disorders*, 22: 395–411.

Koegel, R.L. & Koegel, L.K. (1995) *Teaching Children with Autism*. Baltimore: Paul H Brookes.

Koegel, L.K., Koegel, R.L., Shoshan, Y., & McNerney, E. (1999) 'Pivotal response intervention II: Preliminary long-term outcome data. *Journal of the Association for Persons with Severe Handicaps.* 24: 186–198.

Kokina, A. & Kern, L. (2010) 'Social Story interventions for students with autism spectrum disorders: a meta-analysis', *J. Autism Dev Disord*, 40(7): 812–826.

Krebs-Seida, J., Ospina, M.B., Karkhaneh, M., Hartling, L., Smith, V., & Clark, B. (2009) 'Systematic reviews of psychosocial interventions for autism: an umbrella review', *Developmental Medicine and Child Neurology*, 51: 95–104.

Lainhart, J.E. (1999) 'Psychiatric problems in individuals with autism, their parents and siblings', *International Review of Psychiatry*, 11: 278–298.

Larsen, F.W. & Mouridsen, S.E. (1997) 'The outcome in children with childhood autism and Asperger syndrome originally diagnosed as psychotic. A 30-year follow-up study of subjects hospitalized as children', *European Child and Adolescent Psychiatry*, 6: 181–190.

Lawson, W. (1998) *Life Behind Glass: A Personal Account of Autistic Spectrum Disorder.* Lismore, Australia: Southern Cross University Press.

Levy, S.E. & Hyman, S. (2008), 'Complementary and alternative medicine treatments for children with autism spectrum disorders', *Child and Adolescent Psychiatric Clinics of North America*, 17(4): 803–820.

Lockyer, L. & Rutter, M. (1969) 'A five- to fifteen-year follow-up study of infantile psychosis. III. Psychological aspects', *British Journal of Psychiatry*, 115: 865–882.

Lockyer, L. & Rutter, M. (1970) 'A five- to fifteen-year follow-up study of infantile psychosis. IV. Patterns of cognitive ability', *British Journal of Social and Clinical Psychology*, 9: 152–163.

Lord, C. & Bailey, A. (2002) 'Autism Spectrum Disorders', in M. Rutter & E. Taylor (eds), *Child and Adolescent Psychiatry*, 4th edn. Oxford: Blackwell, pp. 636–665.

Lord, C. & Venter, A. (1992) 'Outcome and follow-up studies of high functioning autistic individuals', in E. Schopler & G.B. Mesibov (eds), *High Functioning Individuals with Autism.* New York: Plenum Press, pp. 187–200.

Lord, C., Risi, S., Lambrecht, L., Cook, E.H., Leventhal, B.L., DiLavore, P.C, Pickles, A., & Rutter, M. (2000) 'The Autism Diagnostic Observation Schedule-Generic: a standard measure of social and communication deficits associated with the spectrum of autism', *Journal of Autism and Developmental Disorders,* 30: 205–223.

Lord, C., Wagner, A., Rogers, S., Szatmari, P., Aman, M., Charman, T., Dawson, G., Durand, V.M., Grossman, L., Guthrie, D., Harris, S., Kasari, C.,

Marcus, L., Murphy, S., Odom, S., Pickles, A., Scahill, L., Shaw, E., Siegel, B., Sigman, M., Stone, W., Smith, T., & Yoder, P. (2005) 'Challenges in evaluating psychosocial interventions for Autistic Spectrum Disorders', *Journal of Autism and Developmental Disorders*, 35: 695–711.

Lotter, B. (1974a) 'Factors related to outcome in autistic children', *Journal of Autism and Childhood Schizophrenia*, 4: 263–277.

Lotter, B. (1974b) 'Social adjustment and placement of autistic children in Middlesex: a follow-up study', *Journal of Autism and Childhood Schizophrenia*, 4: 11–32.

Lovaas, O.I. (1987) 'Behavioral treatment and normal educational and intellectual functioning in young autistic children', *Journal of Consulting and Clinical Psychology,* 55: 3–9.

Ma, H. (2009) 'The effectiveness of intervention on the behavior of individuals with autism: a meta-analysis using percentage of data points exceeding the median of baseline phase (PEM)', *Behavior Modification*, 33(3): 339–359.

McConachie, H., Randle, V., Hammal, D., & le Couteur, A. (2005) 'A controlled trial of a training course for parents of children with suspected autism spectrum disorder', *Journal of Paediatrics,* 147: 335–340.

McDougle, C.J., Kresch, L.E., Goodman, W.K., Naylor, S.T., Volkmar, F.R., Cohen, D.J., & Price, L.H. (1995) 'A case-controlled study of repetitive thoughts and behavior in adults with autistic disorder and obsessive-compulsive disorder', *Am J Psychiatry*, 152: 772–777.

McDougle, C.J., Kresch, L.E., & Posey, D.J. (2002) 'Repetitive thoughts and behavior in pervasive developmental disorders: treatment with serotonin reuptake inhibitors', *Journal of Autism and Developmental Disorders*, 30: 427–435.

McEachin, J.J., Smith, T., & Lovaas, O.I. (1993) 'Long-term outcome for children with autism who received early intensive behavioral treatment', *American Journal on Mental Retardation*, 4: 359–372.

Magiati, I., Charman, T., & Howlin, P. (2007) 'A two-year prospective follow-up study of community-based early intensive behavioural intervention and specialist nursery provision for children with autism spectrum disorders', *Journal of Child Psychology and Psychiatry*, 48: 803–812.

Maurice, C., Green, G., & Luce, S. (eds) (1996) *Behavioral Intervention for Young Children with Autism: A Manual for Parents and Professionals.* Austin, TX: PRO-ED.

Mawhood, L., Howlin, P., & Rutter, M. (2000) 'Autism and developmental receptive language disorder: a follow-up comparison in early adult life. I: Cognitive and language outcomes', *Journal of Child Psychology and Psychiatry*, 41: 547–559.

Mesibov, G., Shea, V., & Schopler, E. (2005) *TEACCH Approach to Autism Spectrum Disorders.* Autism Society of North Carolina.

Millward, C., Ferriter, M., Calver, S.J., & Connell-Jones, G.G. (2007) 'Gluten- and casein-free diets for autistic spectrum disorder', *Cochrane Database of Systematic Reviews* 2007, Issue 2. Art. No.: CD003498. DOI: 10.1002/14651858.CD003498.pub3.

Moore, M. & Calvert, S. (2000) 'Brief report: Vocabulary acquisition for children with autism: teacher or computer instruction', *Journal of Autism and Developmental Disorders.* 30(4): 359–362.

Moss, J., Magiati, I., Charman, T., & Howlin, P. (2008) 'Stability of the Autism Diagnostic Interview–Revised from pre-school to elementary school age in children with autism spectrum disorders', *Journal of Autism and Developmental Disorders*, 38: 1081–1091.

Mouridsen, S.E., Bronnum-Hansen, H., Rich, B., & Isager, T. (2008a) 'Mortality and causes of death in autism spectrum disorders: an update', *Autism,* 12: 403–414.

Mouridsen, S.E., Rich, B., & Isager, T. (2008b) 'Psychiatric disorders in adults diagnosed as children with atypical autism. A case control study', *Journal of Neural Transmission,* 115: 135–138.

Mouridsen, S.E., Rich, B., Isager, T., & Nedergaard, N.J. (2008c) 'Psychiatric disorders in individuals diagnosed with infantile autism as children: a case control study', *Journal of Psychiatric Practice,* 14: 5–12.

Mouridsen, S.E., Rich, B., Isager, T., & Nedergaard, N.J. (2008d) 'Pervasive developmental disorders and criminal behavior: a case control study', *International Journal of Offender Therapy and Comparative Criminology,* 52: 196–205.

NAS (National Autistic Society), London. *The Early Bird Programme.* http://www.nas.org.uk/early bird. Accessed 1 January 2009.

Nye, C. & Brice, A. (2005) 'Combined vitamin B$_6$–magnesium treatment in autism spectrum disorder', *Cochrane Database of Systematic Reviews*, Oct 19; 4: CD 003497.

Odom, S.L, Boyd, B.A., Hall, L.J., & Hume, K. (2010) 'Evaluation of comprehensive treatment models for individuals with autism spectrum disorders', *Journal of Autism and Developmental Disorders*, 40(4): 425–436.

Paradiž, V. (2002) *Elijah's Cup, A Family's Journey into the Community and Culture of High-Functioning Autism and Asperger's Syndrome.* New York: The Free Press.

Pepper, J. & Weitzman, E. (2004) *It Takes Two to Talk: A Practical Guide for Parents of Children with Language Delays.* Toronto, ON: The Hanen Centre.

Piven J., Arndt S., Bailey J., & Andreasen N. (1996) 'Regional brain enlargement in autism: a magnetic resonance imaging study', *Journal of the American Academy of Child and Adolescent Psychiatry,* 35: 530–536.

Prizant, B. & Wetherby, A. (2005) 'Critical issues in enhancing early language in children with autism spectrum disorders'. in F. Volkmar, R. Paul, A. Klin, & D. Cohen (eds), *Handbook of Autism and Pervasive Developmental Disorders,* 3rd edn. Hoboken, NJ: Wiley, pp. 925–945.

Pyles L. (2002) *Hitchhiking through Asperger Syndrome.* London: Jessica Kingsley.

Rao, P.A., Beidel, D.C., & Murray, M.J. (2007) 'Social skills interventions for children with Asperger's syndrome or high-functioning autism: a review and recommendations', *Journal of Autism and Developmental Disorders*, 38: 353–361.

Reichow, B. & Wolery, M. (2009) 'Comprehensive synthesis of early intensive behavioural interventions for young children with autism based on the UCLA Young Autism Project model', *Journal of Autism and Developmental Disorders*, 28: 25–41.

Rimland, B. (1998) 'First secretin efficacy study produces positive results! Editorial comment', *Autism Research Review International,* 15 (No 2).

Rogers, S.J. & Vismara, L.A. (2008) 'Evidence based comprehensive treatments for early autism', *Journal of Clinical Child and Adolescent Psychology*, 37: 8–38.

Rogers, S.J., Hayden, D., Hepburn, S., Charlifue-Smith, R., Hall, T., & Hayes, A. (2006) 'Teaching young nonverbal children with autism useful speech: a pilot study of the Denver Model and PROMPT interventions', *Journal of Autism and Developmental Disorders*, 36: 1007–1024.

Ruble, L., Willis, H., & McLaughlin Crabtree, V. (2008) 'Social skills group therapy for autism spectrum disorders', *Clinical Case Studies*, 7: 287–300.

Rumsey, J.M., Rapoport, J.L., & Sceery, W.R. (1985) 'Autistic children as adults: psychiatric social and behavioral outcomes', *Journal of the American Academy of Child Psychiatry*, 24: 465–473.

(RUPP) Research Units on Pediatric Psychopharmacology, (2005a) Randomized, controlled, cross over trial of methylphenidate in pervasive developmental disorders with hyperactivity', *Archives of General Psychiatry*, 62: 1026–1032.

(RUPP) Research Units on Pediatric Psychopharmacology, (2005b) Risperidone treatment of autistic disorder: longer-term benefits and blinded discontinuation after 6 months', *American Journal of Psychiatry*, 162: 1361–1369.

Russell, A., Mataix-Cols, D., Anson, M., & Murphy, D. (2005) 'Psychological treatment for obsessive-compulsive disorder in people with autism spectrum disorders: a pilot study', *Psychotherapy and Psychosomatics*, 78(1): 59–61.

Rutter, M. (1972) 'Childhood schizophrenia reconsidered', *Journal of Autism and Childhood Schizophrenia*, 2: 315–337.

Rutter, M. & Bartak, L. (1973) 'Special educational treatment of autistic children: a comparative study. II. Follow-up findings and implications for services', *Journal of Child Psychology and Psychiatry*, 14: 241–270.

Rutter, M., Le Couteur, A., & Lord, C. (2003) *Autism Diagnostic Interview revised (ADI-R)*. Los Angeles, CA: Western Psychology Services.

Santosh, P.J. & Baird, G. (2001) 'Pharmacotherapy of target symptoms in autistic spectrum disorders', *Indian Journal of Pediatrics*, 68: 427–431.

Schreibman, L. & Koegel, R.L. (2005) 'Training for parents of children with autism: pivotal responses, generalization, and individualization of interventions', in E.D. Hibbs & P.S. Jensen (eds), *Psychosocial Treatment for Child and Adolescent Disorders: Empirically Based Strategies for Clinical Practice*, 2nd edn. Washington, DC: American Psychological Association, pp. 605–631.

Scragg, P. & Shah, A. (1994) 'Prevalence of Asperger's syndrome in a secure hospital', *British Journal of Psychiatry*, 161: 679–682.

Seltzer, M., Krauss, M., Shattuck, P., Orsmond, G., Swe, A., & Lord, C. (2003) 'The symptoms of autism spectrum disorders in adolescence and adulthood', *Journal of Autism and Developmental Disorders*, 33: 565–581.

Shattuck, P., Seltzer, M., Greenberg, J., Orsmond, G., Bolt, D., Kring, S., et al. (2006) 'Change in autism symptoms and maladaptive behaviors in adolescents and adults' *Journal of Autism and Developmental Disorders*, 33: 565–581.

Shavelle, R.M, Strauss, D.J. & Pickett, J. (2001) 'Causes of death in autism', *Journal of Autism and Developmental Disorders*, 31: 569–576.

Shields, J. (2001) 'The NAS Early Bird programme: partnership with parents in early intervention', *Autism*, 5: 49–56.

Simonoff, E., Pickles, A., Charman, T., Chandler, S., Loucas, T., & Baird, G. (2008) 'Psychiatric disorders in children with autism spectrum disorders: prevalence, comorbidity, and associated factors in a population-derived sample', *Journal of the American*

Academy of Child and Adolescent Psychiatry, 47(8): 921–929.

Slater-Walker, G. & Slater-Walker, C. (2002) *An Asperger Marriage*. London. Jessica Kingsley.

Smith, M.D., Belcher, R.G., & Juhrs, P.D. (1995) *A Guide to Successful Employment for Individuals with Autism*. Baltimore. Paul H. Brookes.

Sofronoff, K., Attwood, T., & Hinton, S. (2005) 'A randomised controlled trial of a CBT intervention for anxiety in children with Asperger syndrome', *Journal of Child Psychology and Psychiatry*, 46(11): 1152–1160.

Solomon, R., Necheles, J., Ferch, C., Bruckman, D. (2007) 'Pilot study of a parent training program for young children with autism: the PLAY Project Home Consultation program', *Autism*, 7: 425–435.

Spreckley, M. & Boyd, R. (2009) 'Efficacy of applied behavioral intervention in preschool children with autism for improving cognitive, language, and adaptive behavior: a systematic review and meta-analysis', *Journal of Pediatrics*, 154(3): 338–344.

Starr, E., Szatmari, P., Bryson, S., & Zwaigenbaum, L. (2003) 'Stability and change among high-functioning children with pervasive developmental disorders: a 2-year outcome study', *Journal of Autism and Developmental Disorders*, 33: 15–22.

Sturmey, P. (1998) 'Classification and diagnosis of psychiatric disorders in persons with developmental disabilities', *Journal of Developmental and Physical Disabilities*, 10: 317–330.

Szatmari, P., Bartolucci, G., Bremner, R.S., Bond, S., & Rich, S. (1989) 'A follow-up study of high-functioning autistic children', *Journal of Autism and Developmental Disorders*, 19: 213–226.

Sze, K.M. & Wood, J.J. (2008) 'Enhancing CBT for the treatment of autism spectrum disorders and concurrent anxiety', *Behavioural and Cognitive Psychotherapy*, 36: 403–409.

Tantam, D. (1991) 'Asperger's Syndrome in adulthood', in U. Frith (ed), *Autism and Asperger Syndrome*. Cambridge: Cambridge University Press, pp. 147–183.

Tjus, T., Heimann, M., & Nelson, K.E. (2001) 'Interaction patterns between children and their teachers when using a specific multi-media and communication strategy. Observations from children with autism and mixed intellectual disabilities', *Autism: International Journal of Research and Practice*, 5: 175–187.

Tonge, B., Brereton, A., Kiomall, M., Mackinnon, A., King, N., & Rinehart, N. (2006) 'Effects on parental mental health of an education and skills training program for parents of young children with autism: a randomized controlled trial', *Journal of the*

American Academy of Child and Adolescent Psychiatry, 45: 561–569.

Tsang, S.K.M., Shek, D.T.L., Lam, L.I., Tang, F.L.Y., & Cheung, P.M.P. (2007) 'Brief report: Application of the TEACCH program on Chinese pre-school children: does culture make a difference?', *Journal of Autism and Developmental Disorders*, 37: 390–396.

van Engeland, H. & Buitelaar, J.K. (2008). 'Autism Spectrum Disorders', in M. Rutter et al. (eds), *Rutter Handbook of Child and Adolescent Psychiatry,* (5th edn.) Oxford: Blackwell, pp. 758–781.

Venter A., Lord C., & Schopler E. (1992) 'A follow-up study of high-functioning autistic children', *Journal of Child Psychology and Psychiatry*, 33: 489–507.

Volkmar, F.R. & Cohen, D.J. (1991) 'Comorbid association of autism and schizophrenia', *American Journal of Psychiatry*, 148: 1705–1707.

Walkup, J.T., Albano, A.M., Piacentini, J., Birmaher, B., Compton, S.N., Sherrill, J.T., Ginsburg, G.S., Rynn, M.A., McCracken, J., Waslick, B., Iyengar, S., March, J.S., & Kendall, P.C. (2008) 'Cognitive behavioral therapy, sertraline, or a combination in childhood anxiety', *New England Journal of Medicine*, 359: 2753–2766.

White, S.W., Oswald, D., Ollendick, T., & Scahill, L. (2009) 'Anxiety in children and adolescents with autism spectrum disorders', *Clinical Psychology Review*, 29(3): 216–229.

Wieder, S. & Greenspan, S.I. (2003) 'Climbing the symbolic ladder in the DIR Model through Floor Time/Interactive Play', *Autism,* 7: 425–435.

Williams-White, S., Keonig, K., & Scahill, L.J. (2007) 'Social skills development in children with autism spectrum disorders: a review of the intervention research', *Journal of Autism and Developmental Disorders,* 37: 1858–1868.

Wing, L. (1981) 'Asperger's syndrome: a clinical account', *Psychological Medicine*, 11: 115–129.

Wing, L. & Shah, A. (2000) 'Catatonia in autistic spectrum disorders', *British Journal of Psychiatry,* 176: 357–362.

Wolff, S. & McGuire, R.J. (1995) 'Schizoid personality in girls: a follow-up study. What are the links with Asperger's syndrome?', *Journal of Child Psychology and Psychiatry*, 36: 793–818.

Wong, H.H. & Smith, R.G. (2006) 'Patterns of complementary and alternative medical therapy use in children diagnosed with autism spectrum disorders', *Journal of Autism and Developmental Disorders*, 36: 901–909.

Wood, J., Drahota, A., Sze, K., Har, K., Chiu, A., & Langer, D. (2009) 'Cognitive behavioral therapy for anxiety in children with autism spectrum disorders: a randomized, controlled trial', *Journal of Child Psychology and Psychiatry*, 50(3): 224–234.

Yoder, P.J. & Stone, W.L. (2006a) 'Randomized comparison of two communication interventions for preschoolers with autism spectrum disorders', *Journal of Consulting and Clinical Psychology,* 74: 426–435.

Yoder, P.J. & Stone, W.L. (2006b) 'A randomized comparison of the effect of two pre-linguistic communication interventions on the acquisition of spoken communication in preschoolers with autism spectrum disorders', *Journal of Speech and Language Hearing Research,* 49: 698–711.

16

Developmental Language Disorders: Overview

Courtenay Frazier Norbury

INTRODUCTION

Language is a fundamental achievement of the human species. For most of us, learning our native language is an effortless process, one that we take for granted. However, competent language acquisition involves mastery of a number of interacting domains in at least two modalities, production and comprehension. These domains include *phonology* (speech sounds and rules for combining speech sounds to form words), *semantics* (meaning), *morphology* (prefixes and suffixes that modify meaning), and *syntax* (hierarchical rules that govern word combinations). Mastery of sounds, words, and grammar does not guarantee communication; most of what we say is at least temporarily ambiguous. For instance, sentences such as 'the fish is on the table' have multiple meanings, the intended meaning may only be clear when non-linguistic contextual factors are taken into account. *Pragmatics* refers to such use of language in context. Importantly, skilled language users are rapidly able to perceive multiple sources of information from the environment and to integrate that information with language in memory and general knowledge, in order to achieve meaning. Thus, when the enormity and complexity of the language learning task is considered, the fact that most children acquire language within a few years, with no explicit instruction and with variable input, is nothing short of miraculous.

For a substantial minority of children, however, language does not develop at a typical rate or fashion. Language impairments are common correlates of numerous developmental disorders, including autistic spectrum disorders, hearing impairment, Down syndrome and Williams syndrome. The focus of this chapter, however, is on language impairments that occur in the absence of other developmental disorders, sensory impairments or cognitive delays. These are commonly referred to as specific language impairments (SLI) in recognition of the fact that the deficits appear to be relatively circumscribed. However, there is a growing consensus that truly 'specific' language impairments are the exception rather than the rule. In reality, many children presenting in clinic and in research studies have subtle difficulties outside the language system—for example, poor motor skills (Hill, 2001)—and the boundaries between SLI and other developmental disorders are frequently blurred. For that reason the term developmental language disorder (DLD) will be used in this and the following chapter and can be assumed to include children previously described as having SLI.

BRIEF HISTORICAL PERSPECTIVE

Descriptions of children with impaired language date back to the early nineteenth century (see Leonard, 1998; Paul, 2007 for more comprehensive reviews). These descriptions highlighted striking impairments in language production and comprehension in the face of preserved cognitive ability. At the same time, advances in the study of neurology had isolated regions of the adult brain in which lesions resulted in distinctive language impairments. Throughout the early twentieth century, childhood language impairments were likened to acquired language disorders. Terms such as 'congenital aphasia' and 'developmental dysphasia' were popular and presupposed a biological, and specifically neurological, origin.

However, by the 1960s it was becoming apparent that most children with DLD did not have obvious neurological lesions that could explain their language difficulty. In fact, we now know that children with early focal brain lesions rarely have long-term deficits in language learning and they do not show the patterns of language impairment that are characteristic of DLD (Bates, 2004). A second consideration was the burgeoning interest in theoretical linguistics, in which the study of language itself was catapulted to center stage. This provided a framework for the detailed analysis of the grammatical structure of spoken language, and emphasized the notion of language as a discrete

cognitive entity. This, in turn, gave way to increased interest in 'specific language impairment'.

As the twentieth century drew to a close, rapid developments in our understanding of genetics and our ability to study brain structure and function in situ greatly enriched the field of DLD. It has become increasingly clear from family and twin studies that genetic factors exert a strong influence (Bishop, 2006b), but, it is equally clear that we are unlikely to discover a 'gene for language'. Instead, it is probable that multiple genes of small effect alter the way the brain develops in subtle but important ways, rendering the developmental path from genes to brain to behavior extremely complex and difficult to predict (Fisher, 2006). As we begin the twenty-first century, research will begin to hone in on environmental influences, including intervention, that serve as protective factors in DLD. A better understanding of the cognitive and biological correlates of DLD will support that endeavor.

DIAGNOSTIC CRITERIA AND CORE CHARACTERISTICS

Despite more than 50 years of intensive research there is still little consensus in the field regarding diagnostic criteria for DLD, largely because of substantial heterogeneity and a clinical picture that changes with age. Broadly speaking, however, language skills lag behind other cognitive abilities, and grammatical aspects of language are particularly vulnerable.

Cognitive characteristics

The term SLI implies that language skills are impaired in the context of otherwise normal cognitive development. More stringent definitions require a significant mismatch (equivalent to at least 1 standard deviation) between measures of verbal and non-verbal ability (cf. ICD-10, World Health Organization, 1996).

There is considerable controversy regarding the use of discrepancy criteria, not least because these may exclude large numbers of children from clinical services despite evident therapeutic need. A second major criticism is that different combinations of tests may give different outcomes, because many children with DLD have uneven language profiles. For example, vocabulary skills are not universally impaired in DLD, and so may be more in line with non-verbal IQ scores, while measures of morphosyntax are likely to be more severely impaired, resulting in very large discrepancies with non-verbal IQ. Moreover, the profile of language difficulty and the genetic risk factors underlying those impairments may be similar in children, regardless of verbal and non-verbal discrepancies (Bishop, 2006b; Rice et al., 2004). Finally, there is some evidence from longitudinal studies that non-verbal IQ scores may decrease over time (Botting, 2005), reducing the gap between verbal and non-verbal abilities. This is unlikely to reflect an actual loss in ability, but rather that non-verbal assessments are rarely 'pure' measures of non-verbal reasoning. In practice, children are regarded as having DLD if scores on non-verbal assessments are broadly within normal limits (usually better than −1.25 SD, or a standard score of 80 or more).

Linguistic characteristics

In clinical practice, assessment typically involves the use of several standardized tests that tap production and comprehension of a range of language behaviors. It is unclear what level of impairment on a standardized test is indicative of significant impairment, and the cut-off scores used to determine access to clinical services are largely arbitrary. For example, a score of −1 SD (equivalent to the 16th centile) on a single assessment may not be sufficient to interfere with the child's education or daily living, providing other language scores are within the normal range. However, scores of −1 SD across a range of language tests, or extremely low scores of −2 SD or greater on a single test may be cause for concern. ICD-10 (World Health Organization, 1996) criteria stipulate that language test scores must be −2 SD or greater; if more stringent diagnostic criteria are employed, fewer children will meet these criteria or qualify for clinical services.

It often seems that there is a mismatch between the language characteristics of children with DLD that are the focus of clinical attention and those that exercise the research community. Clinicians may give greater consideration to how impairments impact on daily living; they may highlight problems in narrative production over selective grammatical errors, because the narrative deficit may be a bigger obstacle to educational attainment than the more focused problem with morphology. Researchers, on the other hand, have extensively investigated specific deficits in grammar because these are of great theoretical importance to our understanding of how language may be situated in the human brain. Both groups, however, may be equally frustrated by the lack of consistent linguistic criteria for diagnosing DLD, and the fact that there is no particular pattern of language impairment that is necessary for a diagnosis of DLD. Thus, children with fairly circumscribed impairments in expressive grammar as well as children with pervasive deficits in all aspects of language comprehension will be labeled as having DLD, yet their behavioural profiles and therapeutic need might be very different.

Below is an outline of the key linguistic characteristics of DLD with respect to grammar, phonology, semantics, and pragmatics (summarized in Table 16.1). It is important to realize that language is an interactive system; deficits in one component of language may impact other areas of language development. For example, early deficits in phonological discrimination may have long-term consequences for learning words and grammatical rules (Joanisse & Seidenberg, 2003). Also, patterns of language impairment for any one child are relatively unstable

TABLE 16.1   Core Linguistic Characteristics of Developmental Language Disorder

- Delayed acquisition of first words and phrases

- Errors in speech production and poor phonological awareness, i.e. the ability to manipulate sounds of the language, particularly in the pre-school years

- Restricted vocabulary and/or problems finding the right word for known objects: for example, use of the word 'thing' for most common objects

- Errors in marking grammatical tense, specifically the omission of past-tense –ed and third-person singular –s, as well as omission of copular 'is', and errors in case assignment (e.g. 'Him run to school yesterday')

- Simplified grammatical structures and errors in complex grammar: for example, poor understanding/use of passive constructions, wh- questions, dative constructions ('the boy is giving the girl the present')

- Weak verbal short-term memory: for example, in poor repetition of words and sentences

- Difficulties understanding complex language and long stretches of discourse

- Difficulties telling a coherent narrative

- Difficulties understanding abstract and ambiguous language

Note: The number of symptoms present in any one child is variable and profile of language impairment may change over time.

over time (Conti-Ramsden & Botting, 1999; Tomblin et al., 2003).

Syntax and morphology

Deficits in grammar are hallmarks of DLD. While many grammatical deficits occur in the context of weak phonology and semantics, they may also occur in isolation (van der Lely, 2005). The most consistently reported finding is that young children with DLD omit morphosyntactic markers of tense in spontaneous speech. These errors include omission of past tense –ed, third-person singular –s, and the copular form of the verb *be* (e.g. 'I eating chocolate') (Leonard, 1998), all of which are typically acquired by the age of 5. Therefore, persistent errors in older children are a sensitive indicator of language impairment. Older children with DLD have problems producing wh- questions, may omit obligatory verb arguments ('the woman is placing on the saucepan'), and use fewer verb alternations ('the girl is opening the door' vs 'the door is opening'). These deficits in production are matched by problems in making correct grammaticality judgments and in understanding complex syntax such as passive constructions, embedded clauses (e.g. 'the boy chasing the horse is fat'), pro-

nominal reference, locatives ('the apple is on the napkin'), and datives ('give the pig the goat') (see Ebbels, 2008 for a review).

Although grammatical errors are a striking feature in DLD, children with DLD do not completely lack grammatical knowledge. Instead, they are inconsistent in their application of this knowledge, behaving as if certain grammatical rules were 'optional' (Rice et al., 1995). For example, performance on grammatical tests is typically above chance levels, suggesting that factors other than grammatical knowledge influence performance. This hypothesis is supported by the finding that grammatical errors may be induced in typically developing individuals by increasing processing demands (Hayiou-Thomas et al., 2004).

Phonology

Speech sound disorders (SSD) are frequently described in terms of a child's repertoire of available speech sounds and the consistent error patterns that a child uses in speech. An epidemiological study of 6 year olds in the United States found the prevalence of SSD to be 3.8%, with a co-occurrence of SSD and language impairments of 1.3% (Shriberg et al., 1999). Problems with speech production are likely to be more prevalent in clinically referred samples, perhaps because they are more readily identified by parents and teachers (Bishop & Hayiou-Thomas, 2008).

For the most part, phonological impairments do not have a physical basis, but instead arise from problems with phonological processing. Phonological processing encompasses a range of behaviors, including the ability to discriminate and categorize speech sounds, produce speech sounds, and meaningful phonemic contrasts, remember novel sequences of speech sounds, and manipulate the sounds of the language. Children with phonological deficits may therefore fail to recognize which sounds are important for signaling. Many of the grammatical markers of English are signaled using perceptually indistinct phonemes such as /s/ and /t/, leading some investigators to propose that early deficits in phonological processing derail learning of grammatical rules (Joanisse & Seidenberg, 2003).

Semantics

Children with DLD tend to have impoverished vocabularies throughout development, but their semantic difficulties extend beyond the number of words available to them. In general, children with DLD are slow to learn new words, have difficulty retaining new word labels, and encode fewer semantic features of newly learned items (cf. Alt et al., 2004). Children with DLD often make naming errors for words they do know: for instance, labeling 'scissors' as 'knife' or using less specific language such as 'cutting things'. As children get older, the problem may not be how many words the child knows, but what the child knows about those words. They may not realize that words can have more than one meaning: for example, that 'cold' can refer to the temperature outside, an illness or a personal quality of unfriendliness. This lack of flexible word knowledge may account for reported difficulties in understanding jokes, figurative language, and metaphorical language, all of which draw on in-depth knowledge of semantic properties of different words, and how

words relate to one another. Finally, there is some indication that learning about verbs may be a particular source of difficulty for children with DLD (Riches et al., 2005). This has implications for learning about sentence structure, because of the unique role that verbs have in determining other sentence constituents (arguments) and in signaling grammatical tense.

Pragmatics

Pragmatics is commonly associated with the notion of 'social communication', which encompasses formal pragmatic rules, social inferencing, and social interaction (Adams, 2008). In general, pragmatic skills of children with DLD are considered to be immature rather than qualitatively abnormal, as in the case of autistic spectrum disorders (ASD). In addition, although they perform more poorly than age-matched peers on various measures of social understanding, their difficulties are rarely as severe as those seen in ASD. Nevertheless, children with DLD may have difficulties understanding and applying pragmatic rules. In conversation these may include initiating and maintaining conversational topics, requesting and providing clarification, turn-taking, and matching communication style to the social context. Individuals with DLD may be impaired relative to peers in their understanding of other minds (Clegg et al., 2004) and in understanding emotion from a situational context (Spackman et al., 2006). They also have difficulties integrating language and context, resulting in difficulties generating inferences and understanding non-literal language and constructing coherent narratives (Norbury & Bishop, 2002, 2003).

A key question is whether these pragmatic deficits are a secondary consequence of impairments in structural aspects of language, or a co-occurring deficit in social cognition. Norbury et al. (2004) noted that deficits in structural aspects of language are likely to adversely affect pragmatic development and that for many children with DLD, pragmatic skills are in line with level of language ability.

However, other children appear to have disproportionate difficulties with pragmatic skills relative to other language abilities. The diagnostic status of these children with 'pragmatic language impairment' is discussed below. The important point here is that children with DLD are likely to have deficits in language pragmatics and social communication which will require support.

Social, behavioral, and emotional characteristics

There is clear evidence that children with DLD have difficulty navigating the social world, resulting in fewer friends and poorer-quality friendships throughout adolescence and into adulthood (Durkin & Conti-Ramsden, 2007). Tomblin (2008) reported that adolescents identified in the pre-school years as having DLD were also more likely than peers to have conduct problems and serious rule breaking, though absolute rates of offending were small. Not surprisingly, children with DLD were also more likely to have lower self-esteem compared to peers.

Furthermore, early studies indicated that language impairment was a strong predictor of other problems in the middle school years, with attention-deficit/hyperactivity disorder (ADHD) and emotional disorders the most common psychiatric diagnoses (Beitchman et al., 1996). Convergent evidence from child psychiatry indicates that approximately one-third of children referred for assessment of socioemotional disturbances may have previously undiagnosed language impairments (Cohen et al., 1998) and, when combined with referrals whose language impairments had already been identified, some 50% of school-aged referrals to psychiatric clinics have significant language difficulties. However, recent longitudinal studies have demonstrated that while children with DLD are at increased risk for poor mental and emotional health, absolute rates of psychiatric disorder are low (Conti-Ramsden & Botting, 2008; Snowling et al., 2006).

Although DLD places children at higher risk of long-term social and emotional difficulties, the precise nature of the relationship between language and social functioning is clearly complex. Conti-Ramsden and Botting (2008) found that scores on language measures were not associated with mental health outcomes. On the other hand, Snowling et al. (2006) indicated that the pattern of language impairment, rather than the severity of language difficulty per se, may be related to particular psychiatric diagnoses. Specifically, adolescents with deficits in expressive language were more likely to have attention deficits, whereas individuals with pervasive deficits in both receptive and expressive language had more social difficulties. Overall, consistency and persistence of language impairment, involvement of language comprehension, and lower non-verbal abilities are all associated with poorer psychiatric outcomes (Beitchman et al., 1996; Conti-Ramsden & Botting, 2008; Snowling et al., 2006; Tomblin, 2008).

EPIDEMIOLOGY

Prevalence estimates of DLD are difficult to establish, owing to the variety of diagnostic criteria employed and a clinical picture that changes over time. Furthermore, studies vary in the extent to which they explicitly include or exclude children with comorbid conditions, or subthreshold symptoms of comorbidities. Prevalence estimates therefore depend crucially on the inclusion and exclusionary criteria adopted for diagnosis.

The most frequently cited prevalence figure for specific DLD comes from an epidemiological study of 5-year-old children in Iowa (Tomblin et al., 1997). These investigators used a battery of tests that tapped three language domains (vocabulary, grammar, and narrative) in two modalities (production and comprehension), yielding five composite scores. They diagnosed DLD at school entry if at least two of the five composite scores was more than −1.25 SD (10th centile), the standard score on a non-verbal intelligence test was >87, and the child met typical exclusionary criteria. This resulted in 0.85 sensitivity (ability to identify true cases of disorder) and 0.99 specificity (ability to correctly identify unimpaired cases), yielding a prevalence estimate of 7.4%. Three points about this study are noteworthy. First, the degree of impairment required by these authors was more lenient than ICD-10 criteria (overall severity of −1.12 SD), and therefore may have included children with more transient language delays. Indeed, 46% of children identified by Tomblin et al. as having DLD at school entry did not meet diagnostic criteria for DLD a year later, suggesting these criteria identify a large number of false positives (Tomblin et al., 2003). Consequently, the prevalence of persistent DLD in older children is likely to be somewhat lower than 7%. Secondly, an intriguing finding from the Iowa study was that only 29% of children who met the research criteria for DLD had been identified by parents or practitioners as having language difficulties. This suggests that the features that lead to identification of DLD in everyday circumstances are different from those identified by standardized tests. Thirdly, the assessment battery did not include measures of phonological skill or pragmatic ability; deficits in these areas may be more likely to negatively affect educational and/or social development. Interestingly, Bishop and Hayiou-Thomas (2008) reported that in a population sample of twins with DLD, children referred for speech-language evaluation were more likely than the others to have phonological deficits. Thus, inclusion of phonological measures in diagnostic batteries may increase concordance between population and clinical samples. Equally, these data demonstrate that while children with overt speech problems are noticed by adults in their environment, subtle problems with spoken language processing may be easily missed. There have been no epidemiological studies of DLD in the UK; such a study would be worthwhile

using updated diagnostic criteria and incorporating measures of functional impairment in order to estimate the true scale of the problem for school-aged children in the UK.

Similar to other neurodevelopmental disorders, more males than females are affected by DLD, though male preponderance varies according to sampling procedures. Robinson (1991) reported a ratio of 3.8:1 in a clinical sample, while Tomblin et al. (1997) reported a much more equal gender distribution, with a male:female ratio of 1.33:1.

CAUSATION

Causal theories of DLD abound, though there is now substantial evidence that genetic factors exert a strong influence in determining risk for DLD (Bishop, 2006b). However, the precise developmental path from genes to behavior is highly complex and there is considerable work to be done before we fully understand how genes alter the course of neurodevelopment in ways that adversely and disproportionately affect language acquisition. The evidence for genetic influences on language impairment is reviewed below. In this section, I first consider possible environmental influences on language impairment and then cognitive theories of language impairment that mediate biology and behavior.

Environmental factors

Conventional wisdom posits that if only parents would turn off the television and spend more time talking to their children, we could ameliorate DLD. However, the research evidence is that language learning is remarkably robust in the face of impoverished language input and that environmental factors alone could not account for the relatively circumscribed deficits that characterize DLD (Bishop, 2006b). Nevertheless, environmental factors can have an important role in mediating the developmental course of the disorder and the impact of disorder on the child's esteem and well-being.

Family socioeconomic status (SES) has long been associated with language development, a relationship that may be mediated by maternal education, via the quantity and quality of mothers' interactions with their children (Hoff & Tian, 2005). However, other studies have found that SES (measured by income or maternal education) is not a reliable predictor of long-term language impairment (Dale et al., 2003; Rice et al., 2008). Furthermore, environments are often at least partially genetically influenced; in other words, limited education and lower incomes may reflect parental language difficulties. Therefore, DLD in the context of low SES should alert clinicians and educators to the need for careful monitoring and language support.

In a multicultural society, clinicians are frequently asked whether or not exposure to more than one language can cause language delay or exacerbate language impairment. Unfortunately, there is very limited evidence available to address these important questions. In general, the view is that exposure to two or more languages does not cause or compound DLD (Paradis et al., 2003) and families are advised to provide rich linguistic input to their children in whichever language they themselves are most comfortable.

An added complication is that few culturally appropriate assessments are available for diagnosing DLD in non-English-speaking language communities. In these instances, clinicians must take care to ascertain the child's communication abilities from the child's primary caregivers. DLD should not be diagnosed if the child is a competent communicator in his or her home language, but struggling to learn English as an additional language. Ideally, language therapy should target both languages; however, there is no systematic research comparing monolingual and bilingual language interventions.

Cognitive theories of DLD

Cognitive theories of DLD have traditionally attempted to explain why language may be selectively impaired in otherwise normal individuals. DLD represents a test case for the idea that language is an innate, domain-specific cognitive system. Under such a view, DLD results from a genetic contribution that 'plays a crucial role in determining the neural circuitry underlying specialised cognitive systems' (van der Lely, 2005). Domain-specific accounts vary but generally point to uneven language profiles in which grammar is most severely affected as evidence of selective impairment to language systems in the brain. Others have argued that a number of domain-general processes act in concert to achieve normal language acquisition, with impairments to one or more of these processes resulting in the variable linguistic profiles seen in DLD (Bates, 2004).

Candidates for domain-general theories of DLD include deficits in auditory temporal processing, limited processing capacity, or combinations of the two (reviewed in Leonard, 1998). Auditory accounts suggest that children with DLD have difficulties perceiving sounds that are presented rapidly, are of brief duration, and therefore not perceptually salient. Such deficits could lead to problems perceiving and categorizing meaningful phonemic contrasts, resulting in problems with language learning. Furthermore, many grammatical contrasts in English are signaled with unstressed phonemes of brief duration, occurring in a rapidly changing speech stream; thus, a general impairment in temporal or perceptual processing may lead to highly selective impairments in grammar (Joanisse & Seidenberg, 2003). However, research has demonstrated that auditory deficits are neither necessary nor sufficient to cause DLD. Notably, while auditory deficits are common in children with DLD, not all children are affected and some children with auditory deficits do not have any language difficulties (Bishop et al., 1999b). In addition, intervention studies have indicated that improving auditory skills does not confer improvements to other aspects of language (McArthur et al., 2008).

Leonard (1998) suggested that perceptual deficits are more detrimental to language development in the context of a system that has limited capacity to hold information in store while processing perceptually challenging input. Evidence for a limited capacity system stems from poor performance on tasks of working memory and phonological short-term memory. Assessment of working memory typically requires children to make true/false judgments about simple statements such as 'balls are round' and 'pumpkins are purple' (the processing component) and then recall the last words of each statement, 'round' and 'purple' (the capacity component). The argument is that there is a trade-off between processing and capacity, such that when processing demands increase, capacity for recall is reduced and vice versa. Deficits in phonological short-term memory are typically indexed by the ability to repeat non-sense words of increasing syllable length ('hampent' vs 'blonterstaping'). Children with DLD make few errors on two-syllable words, but performance decreases sharply with increasing syllable length, suggesting it is the memory component of the task that is particularly challenging (see Archibald & Gathercole, 2006 for review). The significance of the test relates to its role in language learning; acquiring new words depends on the ability to retain novel sound sequences in memory, learning syntax requires the child to hold sentences in memory while they are analyzed. Thus, a deficit in non-word repetition (NWR) could lead to a host of language deficits, but is more likely to result in a diagnosis of DLD when it co-occurs with other deficits in memory or language (Archibald & Gathercole, 2006; Bishop et al., 2006).

There is little doubt that children with DLD have substantial verbal memory deficits, but the direction of causation is debatable. These theories appear to take a bottom-up view of language processing but there is also evidence for top-down influences. For example, the more 'word-like' non-words are (i.e. 'trumpetine') the easier they are to remember, suggesting that existing vocabulary knowledge influences NWR abilities (Dollaghan et al., 1995). Therefore, children with poor vocabularies may be disadvantaged on tests of NWR. Also, verbal working memory tasks are essentially language tasks, making poor performance in DLD populations difficult to interpret. Recent findings of working memory deficits outside the verbal domain lend credence to the view that domain-general cognitive processes contribute to language difficulties (Bavin et al., 2005). However, a limited capacity theory would predict strong correlations between NWR deficits and deficits in vocabulary and grammar and this does not appear to be the case. Bishop et al. (2006) investigated language skills in 6-year-old twins and found little relationship between scores on NWR and vocabulary or tests of morphosyntax (producing verb inflections).

Recently, Ullman and Pierpont (2005) made a distinction between procedural memory systems, which are important for rule-based learning (such as grammar), and declarative memory systems, which underlie knowledge-based learning (such as vocabulary). They hypothesized that DLD was the result of a primary deficit in procedural memory systems, which could potentially be compensated for by reliance on relatively intact declarative systems. The appeal of this theory is that it makes explicit connections between brain and behavior, has the potential to explain deficits outside the language system that are also contingent on procedural learning (such as some motor tasks), and is developmentally more attractive in its emphasis on reorganization and compensation. Empirical investigations are needed to test the predictions of this hypothesis, but it is an exciting new direction for causal theories of DLD.

The conclusion from theoretical studies of DLD is that there is unlikely to be a single cognitive factor that can cause the variety of language profiles seen. Instead, multiple risk factors are likely to determine symptom profile and severity. Investigations that combine genetic, biological, and behavioral methodologies will greatly inform our understanding of DLD.

ASSESSMENT

Comprehensive assessment of DLD will involve parent interview, informal observation, and detailed assessment of language ability (Baird, 2008). In the first instance, a detailed case history will highlight the major concerns of parents. Parents do not always see language as the primary problem, and may be more concerned about the child's behavior or social skills, or problems with learning that may be related to underlying language difficulties. A case history provides an opportunity to document any pre-, peri- or postnatal risk factors that may affect language development (e.g. drug and alcohol misuse, illness, hearing loss) and family history of speech, language or literacy difficulties. The case history should also be used as a vehicle to elicit from parents clear examples of the child's communicative attempts, what motivates the child to communicate, how and with whom the child communicates, and what he or she does when communication fails. This information will highlight aspects of language and communication that the clinician should attempt to explore further in the course of assessment.

If the child has sufficient verbal abilities, informal observation may be supplemented by engaging the child in conversation and asking him or her to relay a favorite story or game. During these less formal tasks, a number of observations can be made. First, the practitioner will gain an impression of the child's expressive language abilities, including the length, complexity, and intelligibility of utterances. The clinician may also note the ease with which the child chooses words, how fluent the child is, and whether stories are coherent narratives with a clear structure.

Secondly, comprehension difficulties may be apparent in the child who fails to respond appropriately to the questions or comments of others, cannot follow adult directions, echoes what others say, or misinterprets key events in a story. Pragmatic skills may also be observed: for instance, the child's ability to use eye contact, facial expression, and gesture to communicate, the ways in which the child initiates and maintains conversation, requests clarification, and demonstrates recognition of listener needs. Finally, observation of behaviors outside the domain of language may also be informative. These may include the quality of the child's imaginative play, attention span, gross and fine motor skills, and social interests and interactions. This set of observations provides the clinician with a working hypothesis of the nature and severity of the child's language impairment, which can then be tested using standardized assessments.

There are a number of standardized assessments tapping all aspects of speech, language, and communication (see Bishop & Norbury 2008, for those used in the UK). Standardized assessments are necessary to determine objectively the child's current level of functioning relative to his or her peer group; it is difficult for even the most experienced clinician to gauge a child's level of comprehension accurately (Baird, 2008). However, limitations of standardized assessment should also be considered. Performance may be affected by attention, motivation, how the child feels on the day, and rapport between child and clinician. Thus, if a child succeeds on a particular test we may be confident that the child has some knowledge of the construct being tested, but if a child does poorly on a particular test, we cannot always know what factors are contributing to that low score. In addition, some language behaviors are difficult to measure in a standardized way. For example, pragmatic skills are context-dependent; creating a standardized context in which task demands are explicit may provide quite a different picture of the child's pragmatic capabilities in daily life where interactions are dynamic and the rules of engagement are largely implicit. Similarly, reliable tests of language skills in very young children or older adolescents and young adults are almost non-existent. Finally, many tests sample a wide range of language behaviors using few exemplars of individual language constructions. This can be useful in telling the clinician whether or not the child has a problem, but is less helpful in formulating an intervention plan.

Recently, there has been a move away from omnibus tests of language ability and the problems inherent in using standardized scores with arbitrary cut-offs for disorder. Instead, researchers (and to some extent clinicians) have begun to focus on 'clinical markers' of impairment. In English, these include two areas of skill: grammar and verbal memory. Conti-Ramsden et al. (2001) compared potential clinical markers, including production of third person singular –s and past tense –ed, non-word repetition, and sentence repetition, in a school-aged sample of children with DLD, and found that sentence repetition was the most efficient marker of DLD, with high levels of sensitivity (0.90) and specificity (0.85).

DIFFERENTIAL DIAGNOSIS AND COMORBID CONDITIONS

Speech, language, and communication impairments are some of the most common developmental concerns resulting in referral to child health services in the pre-school years (Baird, 2008). When a child presents with impaired language development, clinicians need to establish whether the language impairment is occurring in the context of a recognized syndrome and whether there is any identifiable causal factor contributing to the language delay.

Hearing impairment

It is logical to assume that DLD may be secondary to peripheral hearing impairments, as children with hearing difficulties would be less able to hear and therefore discriminate speech sounds, morphological endings or subtle function words that signal word boundaries or grammatical meaning in English. However, population studies of children with chronic middle ear disease (otitis media with effusion), and smaller studies of children with mild to moderate sensorineural hearing loss, have demonstrated that language is remarkably resilient to moderate hearing impairments (Feldman et al., 2003; Norbury et al., 2001). Nevertheless, any child presenting with DLD should be referred to an audiologist for a hearing assessment. Children with profound sensorineural hearing losses will almost certainly be disadvantaged in acquiring spoken English, but this does not mean they have DLD; such children may acquire language in the visual modality, such as British Sign Language.

Acquired epileptic aphasia

Acquired epileptic aphasia (AEA), also known as Landau–Kleffner syndrome, is a rare cause of severe language disorder that is often misdiagnosed because overt epileptic seizures are uncommon. In textbook cases, a child loses language skills rapidly after a period of normal development, and comprehension is usually most severely affected. Deafness may be suspected, but ruled out after a hearing test is conducted. Selective mutism may also be considered, given the child's history of verbal communication. However, in the case of AEA, there is a genuine loss of language. Whereas the language impairment may be relatively circumscribed with non-verbal cognitive abilities intact, AEA may be associated with behavioral difficulties and stereotypies that may further confuse the clinical picture (Deonna & Roulet-Perez, 2005). Thus, when a child presents with severe comprehension deficits and language regression, referral to a pediatric neurologist is warranted so that a sleep electroencephalogram (EEG) may be carried out. Deonna and Roulet-Perez (2005) suggest that pharmacological treatments may be effective, but outcome is variable and evidence is limited. Prognosis is more optimistic in children for whom onset occurs after the age of 6 years, after language has been established. However, outcomes for children with onset in the pre-school years are particularly poor, and significant language deficits may persist into adulthood. It is essential to provide these children with alternative means of communication, such as sign language, which can be used in conjunction with speech.

Selective mutism

Selective mutism is diagnosed in the child who consistently does not speak in situations where there is an expectation for speech (i.e. school) but does speak normally in other situations (i.e. home; Steinhausen et al., 2006). DSM-IV-TR (APA, 2000) further stipulates that mutism must persist for more than 1 month (not including the first month of school), and cannot be accounted for by a DLD or familiarity with the language environment.

Selective mutism is generally regarded as an anxiety disorder, rather than a variant of DLD (Steinhausen et al., 2006). However, social anxiety is rarely the only problem and language impairments are frequently present, suggesting that self-consciousness about communicative abilities plays a part in maintaining the disorder. Interventions may include language therapy, positive reinforcement for speaking, desensitization to anxiety-provoking situations, family therapy, and self-modeling techniques, in which the child listens to him- or herself speaking in situations in which he or she is usually mute (see Johnson & Wittgens, 2001). Longitudinal studies report improvements in the core symptoms over time, though rates of psychiatric disorder, especially social phobia, remain high, and prognosis is particularly poor when there is a family history of select mutism (Steinhausen et al., 2006).

Reading disorders

Skilled reading requires the marriage of two complementary skills: reading accuracy (the ability to decode single words) and reading comprehension (understanding connected text) (Hoover & Gough, 1990). Extensive research on typical reading development has demonstrated that these skills are in turn reliant on underlying language processes (see Bishop & Snowling, 2004 for a review). Decoding in alphabetic languages such as English is supported by phonological processing as the mapping of orthography (the letters of printed words) to phonology (the sounds represented by the letters) is required. Reading comprehension, on the other hand, is supported largely by non-phonological language skills such as semantics and contextual processing (Perfetti et al., 2005). Although decoding and comprehension frequently develop in concert, they may be dissociated (Bishop & Snowling, 2004).

Children who experience problems decoding printed text are frequently referred to as having 'dyslexia'. The majority of these children have phonological processing difficulties that disrupt their decoding abilities (see Snowling, 2000 for review). Deficits in other aspects of language have also been reported. For instance, McArthur et al. (2000) found that approximately 50% of children identified as having a specific reading disability also met criteria for DLD (defined as Total Language scores of 85 or less on the Clinical Evaluation of Language Fundamentals (CELF)), with a similar percentage of children with DLD achieving significantly low scores on a measure of reading accuracy.

Children who experience problems understanding text despite adequate decoding skills are commonly referred to as 'poor comprehenders.' Nation et al. (2004) reported that poor comprehenders scored within normal limits on measures of phonological processing but showed significant deficits in all other language domains, including vocabulary, grammar, verbal working memory, and higher-level discourse processing (i.e. making inferences), relative to skilled comprehenders.

There is little doubt that DLD places children at greatly increased risk for reading impairments, contributing to lower educational attainments (Catts et al., 2002). The particular profile of literacy skill will depend in part on the profile of language impairment, but comprehension deficits are particularly detrimental to reading success. For example, Botting et al. (2006) found that of children identified as having DLD at age 7, 67% with predominantly expressive language impairments and 88% with comprehension deficits had literacy impairments at age 11.

Autism spectrum disorders and pragmatic language impairment

Delays acquiring language and poor communication are key characteristics of ASD and issues surrounding overlap between DLD and ASD are hotly debated in both research and clinical practice.

Early studies comparing ASD and DLD reported considerable overlap in structural language profiles (especially vocabulary and grammar) of the two disorders, though children with ASD invariably had more severe impairments (Bartak et al., 1975). However, these studies also highlighted language behaviors that reliably differentiated the two groups. Children with ASD were less likely than peers with DLD to have impairments in speech production; recent studies have also demonstrated that articulation deficits rarely feature in ASD (Kjelgaard & Tager-Flusberg, 2001). In addition, the language profiles of children with ASD are more likely to be characterized by deviant features that would not be regarded as typical at any age. These features include repetitive use of stereotyped phrases, unusual and exaggerated intonation, pronoun reversal, idiosyncratic words, echolalia, and failure to respond to the speech of others. Furthermore, pragmatic skills are universally impaired in ASD, whereas children with DLD present with more variable pragmatic abilities.

Textbook cases of ASD and DLD are relatively easy to distinguish; the prototypical child with DLD enjoys social interactions, seeks friendships with peers, is keen to communicate, and uses gesture and other forms of non-verbal communication to get his or her message across. However, many children present with a symptom profile that does not unambiguously align with either diagnosis (Bishop & Norbury, 2002). These children have pragmatic deficits that cannot be fully accounted for by the grammatical impairments that are more characteristic of DLD, yet they do not have the full triad of impairments in severe enough form to warrant a diagnosis of autism. Differential diagnosis may be further hampered by a clinical picture that changes with time; children with unequivocal diagnoses of DLD early in development may more closely resemble individuals with ASD years later when structural language impairments resolve and the social demands of society increase (Howlin et al., 2000). Conti-Ramsden et al. (2006) applied two standard diagnostic assessments to 76 adolescents with DLD, none of whom had been regarded as having ASD at the age of 7. Although the majority of participants did not meet criteria on either measure, 3.9% of participants met criteria on both, a prevalence rate approximately three times greater than would be expected from the general population (Baird et al., 2006). A further 26% met criteria on one or other measure but not both. Similar findings are reported by Bishop and Norbury (2002) and Bishop et al. (2008). Both studies found that children were more likely to meet criteria on these measures if they had been identified as having 'pragmatic language impairment'; however, repetitive and restricted interests and behaviors were not characteristic of these children. It is still an open question as to whether this overlap represents misdiagnosis, a changing symptom profile, or 'diagnostic substitution' (Bishop et al., 2008) in which current diagnostic criteria identify more children who would not have met more stringent diagnostic criteria in the past. Bishop et al. (2008) argue that a proportion of children diagnosed with DLD have pragmatic impairments and some evidence of autistic symptomatology, but they are eager to communicate and their pragmatic deficits do not interfere with daily family life, which in the past may have precluded a diagnosis of autism.

It may be most helpful to think of pragmatic language impairment as a descriptive term rather than a diagnostic category, that can be applied to children with DLD and ASD alike (cf. Rapin & Allen, 1983). Indeed, Norbury et al. (2004) found that children with DLD who were not thought to have significant pragmatic deficits were nevertheless rated by parents and teachers as having more pragmatic difficulties than typical peers. However, their pragmatic problems were entirely in keeping with their structural language deficits, unlike children with ASD who showed disproportionate weaknesses on pragmatic items. Thus, DLD is likely to interfere with social communication to some extent, but, for children with ASD, social communication deficits are far worse than would be predicted given language ability.

In practice, diagnostic labels may reflect the practitioner's theoretical perspective or the practical implications a particular diagnostic label brings for accessing clinical and educational services. The main point is that the diagnostic boundaries between DLD and ASD are frequently blurred, and it may be more helpful to abandon categorical distinctions and instead focus on symptom dimensions, in which children vary according to the severity of impairment in language, social response, and rigidity of interests and behaviors.

CURRENT RESEARCH

Neurological and genetic correlates

Neurobiology of the DLD brain

The use of magnetic resonance imaging (MRI) to investigate neurobiological substrates of language processing in typical development is in its infancy and, not surprisingly, only a handful of investigators

have applied MRI to the study of DLD. These studies have demonstrated no gross abnormalities of the brain, though more detailed analyses have revealed subtle differences in brain structure and function. These include atypical patterns of asymmetry of language cortex (De Fosse et al., 2004; Gauger, et al., 1997), abnormalities in white matter volume (Herbert et al., 2004; Jancke et al., 2007), cortical dysplasia (abnormalities in the organization of different types of brain cell; Galaburda et al., 1985), additional gyri in frontal or temporal regions (Clark & Plante, 1998; Plante & Jackson, 1997) and unusual proportions of anatomical structures implicated in language processing (Jernigan et al., 1991; Leonard et al., 2006).

Interpretation of these findings is hampered by inconsistencies across studies. For instance, numerous investigators have reported abnormalities of the planum temporale in the superior temporal sulcus, an area known to be involved in processing speech. However, some investigators have reported this region to be smaller and more symmetrical relative to controls (Plante et al., 1991), while others report reversed asymmetry (Gauger et al., 1997). Similarly, DLD has been associated with small cerebral volume in some studies (Jancke et al., 2007; Jernigan et al., 1991), but enlarged cerebral volumes in others (Herbert et al., 2004).

Studies of brain function using functional MRI are rarer still and limited by small sample sizes and task difficulties. Hugdahl et al. (2004) investigated language processing in five Finnish family members with DLD and six age-matched peers as they listened passively to isolated vowel sounds, pseudowords and real words. The family members with DLD showed bilateral activation in the temporal lobes, including the medial temporal gyrus and the superior temporal sulcus, which was much weaker and more focal than activations seen in the comparison group. This reduced activation is believed to be associated with the difficulties individuals with DLD have in decoding the phonological structure of words and pseudowords (Friederichi,

2006). Weismer et al. (2005) investigated working memory abilities using fMRI in eight adolescents with DLD and eight individuals with normal language (NL) abilities. As found by Hugdahl et al. (2004) individuals with DLD exhibited hypoactivation in frontal and parietal regions that are implicated in memory and attention, and the inferior frontal gyrus, commonly associated with semantics and other aspects of language processing. However, the participants performed more poorly on the working memory task overall, so it is not clear whether these differences are attributable to working memory deficits specifically, or increased/decreased effort in task performance.

Despite the confusions in the literature, a number of observations can be made. First and foremost, the direction of causation is not at all clear. Do differences in brain structure or activation cause language impairment, or do these differences reflect a lifetime of processing language differently? Secondly, the relationships between brain and language in DLD are weak and probabilistic, and not specific to DLD (Herbert et al., 2004; Leonard et al., 2006). Comparisons across developmental disorders will be necessary to identify clearer relationships between disorder and brain anomaly (cf. De Fosse et al., 2004; Leonard et al., 2006). Finally, the anomalies that are associated with DLD appear to arise early in development, rather than as a result of an early acquired lesion. Bishop and Norbury (2008) suggest that this is consistent with genetic influences on brain development, leading to a brain that is wired up in a non-optimal fashion for language learning.

Genetic factors

Clinicians and researchers have known for some time that DLD tends to run in families, suggesting that genes may influence susceptibility to disorder. Such a supposition is not watertight, however, because families share environments as well as genes. Fortunately, research over the last 20 years has elucidated genetic and environmental contributions to DLD, and is beginning to isolate specific genes associated with DLD. This section briefly considers findings from behavioral genetics, which has sought to refine the DLD phenotype (the observable, measurable characteristics related to individual variations in genetic makeup) and molecular genetics, which attempts to isolate specific genes (see Bishop, 2006a; Newbury & Monaco, 2008 for respective reviews).

Twin studies have been invaluable in establishing that DLD is a highly heritable disorder. Twin studies capitalize on the fact that monozygotic (MZ) or identical twins are genetically identical, whereas dizygotic (DZ) or fraternal twins share only 50% of segregating alleles (normal genetic variations). MZ twins resemble each other with respect to DLD diagnosis more closely than do DZ twins, with heritability estimates (i.e. the proportion of variance explained by genetic relationships) of 0.50–0.75 (see Bishop, 2006b for review). One exception to this pattern was a population study of 4-year-old twins, which found negligible genetic influence on language impairment (Hayiou-Thomas et al., 2005). In this study, children were classified as having DLD on the basis of standardized tests of speech and language (cf. Tomblin et al., 1997). When referral to speech-language therapy services was used to index affected cases, heritability estimates increased substantially, suggesting that children attracting clinical attention may represent a phenotypically and etiologically distinct group (Bishop & Hayiou-Thomas, 2008).

This highlights the challenges that stem from investigating a complex and heterogeneous disorder like DLD; heritability estimates vary, depending on the precise definition of DLD used, and isolating specific genes becomes much more challenging in the midst of so much phenotypic noise. An alternative approach is to move away from studying 'DLD' and instead investigate genetic influences on underlying cognitive traits that affect language skills. Bishop (2006a) illustrates how fruitful this approach may be, using twin methodology to test different cognitive theories of DLD. Bishop et al. (1996) reported that NWR was highly heritable, a finding that has been replicated in different samples (cf. Bishop et al., 2006). Later studies explored whether NWR deficits were the result of primary deficits in auditory processing (Bishop et al., 1999a) and whether NWR deficits contributed to broader impairments in morphosyntax (Bishop et al., 2006). Findings indicated that performance on auditory processing tasks was influenced by environmental factors rather than genetic ones and though both NWR and morphosyntactic skills were highly heritable, there was little correlation between the two, suggestive of independent genetic influences. These studies have also demonstrated that the most severely affected children are ones who have multiple deficits. Thus, language may be fairly robust in the face of adversity, but accumulation of risk factors of either genetic or environmental origin may have deleterious consequences for language development.

Family and twin studies have directly informed molecular genetic studies of DLD. In 2001, researchers discovered a single-gene mutation that caused a severe speech and language disorder in members of a three-generation family (Lai et al., 2001). This caused much speculation that the gene *FOXP2* may be implicated in more common forms of DLD. This does not appear to be the case; the gene is entirely normal in most individuals with DLD (SLI Consortium, 2004) and the pattern of inheritance seen in more common forms of DLD is inconsistent with a single-gene disorder. Instead, DLD is likely to result from many genes of small effect acting in concert with environmental risk factors. Thus, recent investigations have focused on quantitative trait analyses, in which individuals are identified using quantitative measures of language ability. The SLI Consortium selected families in which one member scored −1.5 SD below the normative mean on one of three measures: non-word repetition, expressive language ability, or receptive language ability. Genome-wide screens found linkage (a correlation between an inherited stretch of DNA and a phenotypic trait) between chromosome 16q and NWR, and chromosome 19q and expressive language scores (see Newbury & Monaco, 2008 for review). These findings are only a first step in unravelling the relationships between genes and behaviors. In complex disorders, this relationship is probabilistic; even if we were able definitively to identify specific genetic variations associated with DLD, we still could not accurately predict individual phenotypes. In addition, genes do not encode specific behaviors—there is no 'gene for non-word repetition'. Instead, investigators are working to understand the downstream effects of genetic variations for the developing organism. With respect to DLD, it is most likely that normal genetic variations affect the efficiency of gene expression in the developing brain (Newbury & Monaco, 2008). How these early alterations in neural development affect the course of language development, and why language should be specifically affected, are empirical questions that will occupy researchers in this field for a long time to come.

Implications for clinical practice

In summary, current research has elucidated the biological basis of DLD as a strongly genetic disorder. It is also increasingly clear that DLD is a multifactorial disorder, with a number of genetic and environmental risk factors acting synergistically to produce the rich variation seen in DLD. At least two implications follow, with important consequences for assessment and remediation. First, isolated impairments in grammar are likely to be rare in DLD; attention to aspects of language and cognition that are reliably *associated* in DLD is as important as knowing the aspects of language and cognition that may dissociate. Secondly, although genes play a role in determining who will have DLD, this does not suggest that we are powerless to intervene. Twin studies have demonstrated that while identical twins are more similar in their language profiles, they frequently differ with regard to symptom severity and variety, suggesting that environmental influences are important in determining the developmental course and outcome of disorder. There is a clear need to test hypotheses about cognitive factors influencing DLD presentation with theoretically sound intervention studies. Nevertheless, there is unlikely to be a 'quick-fix' for resolving language impairments. For many children, DLD represents a lifelong disorder, requiring educational and social support throughout the schoolyears and into adult life.

In the following chapter, the trajectory of development of individuals with DLD is further explored. Interventions that may be effective in reducing the impact of DLD at different ages are also discussed.

REFERENCES

Adams, C. (2008) 'Intervention for children with pragmatic language impairments' in C.F. Norbury, J.B. Tomblin, & D.V. Bishop (eds), *Understanding Developmental Language Disorders*. Hove and New York: Psychology Press, pp. 189–204.

Alt, M., Plante, E., & Creusere, M. (2004) 'Semantic features in fast-mapping: performance of preschoolers with specific language impairment versus preschoolers with normal language', *Journal of Speech, Language and Hearing Research,* 47(2): 407–420.

American Psychiatric Association. (2000) *Diagnostic and statistical manual of mental disorders* (4th ed., text revision). Washington, DC: Author.

Archibald, L. & Gathercole, S. E. (2006) 'Short-term and working memory in specific language impairment', *International Journal of Language and Communication Disorders,* 41: 675–693.

Baird, G. (2008) 'Assessment and investigation of children with developmental language disorder', in C.F. Norbury, J.B. Tomblin, & D.V. Bishop (eds), *Understanding Developmental Language Disorders*. Hove and New York: Psychology Press, pp. 1–22.

Baird, G., Simonoff, E., Pickles, A., Chandler, S., Loucas, T., Meldrum, D., & Charman, T. (2006) 'Prevalence of disorders of the autism spectrum in a population cohort of children in South Thames: the Special Needs and Autism Project (SNAP)', *Lancet,* 368: 210–215.

Bartak, L., Rutter, M., & Cox, A. (1975) 'A comparative study of infantile autism and specific developmental receptive language disorder', *British Journal of Psychiatry,* 126: 127–145.

Bates, E. (2004) 'Explaining and interpreting deficits in language development across clinical groups: where do we go from here?', *Brain and Language,* 88: 248–253.

Bavin, E., Wilson, P., Maruff, P., & Sleeman, F. (2005) 'Spatio-visual memory of children with specific language impairment: evidence for generalised processing problems', *International Journal of Language and Communication Disorders,* 40: 319–332.

Beitchman, J.H., Brownlie, E.B., Inglis, J., Wild, J., Ferguson, B., & Schachter, D. (1996) 'Seven year follow-up of speech/language impaired and control children: psychiatric outcome', *Journal of Child Psychology and Psychiatry,* 37: 961–970.

Bishop, D.V. (2006a) 'Developmental cognitive genetics: how psychology can inform genetics and vice versa', *Quarterly Journal of Experimental Psychology,* 59: 1153–1168.

Bishop, D.V.M. (2006b) 'What causes Specific Language Impairment in children?', *Current Directions in Psychological Science,* 15: 217–221.

Bishop, D.V.M. & Hayiou-Thomas, M.E. (2008) 'Heritability of specific language impairment depends on diagnostic criteria', *Genes Brain and Behavior,* 7: 365–372.

Bishop, D.V.M., & Norbury, C.F. (2002) 'Exploring the borderlands of autistic disorder and specific language impairment: a study using standardised diagnostic instruments', *Journal of Child Psychology and Psychiatry,* 43: 917–929.

Bishop, D.V.M. & Norbury, C.F. (2008) 'Speech and language disorders', in M. Rutter, D.V.M. Bishop, D.S. Pine, S. Scott, J. Stevenson, E. Taylor, & A. Thapar (eds), *Rutter's Child and Adolescent Psychiatry*. Oxford: Blackwell, pp. 782–801.

Bishop, D.V.M. & Snowling, M.J. (2004) 'Developmental dyslexia and specific language impairment: same or different?', *Psychological Bulletin,* 130(6): 858–886.

Bishop, D.V.M., North, T., & Donlan, C. (1996), 'Nonword repetition as a behavioural marker for inherited language impairment: evidence from a twin study', *Journal of Child Psychology and Psychiatry,* 37: 391–405.

Bishop, D.V.M., Bishop, S.J., Bright, P., James, C., Delaney, T., & Tallal, P. (1999a) 'Different origin of auditory and phonological processing problems in children with language impairment: evidence from a twin study', *Journal of Speech, Language and Hearing Research,* 42: 155–168.

Bishop, D.V.M. , Carlyon, R.P., Deeks, J.M., & Bishop, S.J. (1999b) 'Auditory temporal processing impairment: neither necessary nor sufficient for causing language impairment in children', *Journal of Speech, Language and Hearing Research,* 42: 1295–1310.

Bishop, D.V.M., Adams, C.V., & Norbury, C.F. (2006) 'Distinct genetic influences on grammar and phonological short-term memory deficits: evidence from 6-year-old twins', *Genes, Brain and Behavior,* 5: 158–169.

Bishop, D.V.M., Whitehouse, A., Watt, H., & Line, E. (2008) 'Autism and diagnostic substitution: evidence from a study of adults with a history of developmental language disorder', *Developmental Medicine and Child Neurology,* 50: 341–345.

Botting, N. (2005) 'Non-verbal cognitive development and language impairment', *Journal of Child Psychology and Psychiatry,* 46: 317–327.

Botting, N., Simkin, Z., & Conti-Ramsden, G. (2006) 'Associated reading skills in children with a history of specific language impairment', *Reading and Writing,* 19: 77–98.

Catts, H.W., Fey, M.E., Tomblin, J.B., & Zhang, X. (2002) 'A longitudinal investigation of reading outcomes in children with language impairments', *Journal of Speech Language and Hearing Research,* 45(6): 1142–1157.

Clark, M. & Plante, E. (1998) 'Morphology of the inferior frontal gyrus in developmentally language disordered adults', *Brain and Language,* 61: 288–303.

Clegg, J., Hollis, C., Mawhood, L., & Rutter, M. (2004) 'Developmental language disorders: a follow up in later adult life. Cognitive, language and psychosocial outcomes', *Journal of Child Psychology and Psychiatry,* 46(2): 128–149.

Cohen, N., Barwick, M., Horodezky, N., Vallance, D., & Im, N. (1998) 'Language, achievement, and cognitive processing in psychiatrically disturbed children with previously identified and unsuspected language impairments', *Journal of Child Psychology and Psychiatry,* 36: 865–878.

Conti-Ramsden, G., & Botting, N. (1999) 'Classification of children with specific language impairment: longitudinal considerations', *Journal of Speech Language & Hearing Research,* 42(5): 1195–204.

Conti-Ramsden, G. & Botting, N. (2008) 'Emotional health in adolescents with and without a history of specific language impairment', *Journal of Child Psychology and Psychiatry,* 49: 516–525.

Conti-Ramsden, G., Botting, N., & Faragher, B. (2001) 'Psycholinguistic markers for specific language impairment', *Journal of Child Psychology and Psychiatry,* 42(6): 741–748.

Conti-Ramsden, G., Simkin, Z., & Botting, N. (2006) 'The prevalence of autistic spectrum disorders in adolescents with a history of specific language impairment', *Journal of Child Psychology and Psychiatry,* 47(6): 621–628.

Dale, P.S., Price, T.S., Bishop, D.V., Plomin, R. (2003) 'Outcomes of early language delay: I. Predicting persistent and transient language difficulties at 3 and 4 years', *Journal of Speech Language & Hearing Research,* 46: 544–560.

De Fosse, L., Hodge, S., Makris, N., Kennedy, D.N., Caviness, V., McGrath, L., Steele, S., Ziegler, D.A., Herbert, M.R., Frazier, J.A., Tager-Flusberg, H., & Harris, G.J. (2004) 'Language-association cortex asymmetry in autism and specific language impairment', *Annals of Neurology,* 56(6): 757–766.

Deonna, T. & Roulet-Perez, E. (2005) *'Cognitive and Behavioural Disorders of Epileptic Origin in Children.* London: MacKeith Press/Cambridge University Press.

Dollaghan, C., Biber, M.E., & Campbell, T.E. (1995) 'Lexical influences on non-word repetition', *Applied Psycholinguistics,* 16: 211–222.

Durkin, K. & Conti-Ramsden, G. (2007) 'Language, social behavior, and the quality of friendships in adolescents with and without a history of specific language impairment', *Child Development,* 78: 1441–1457.

Ebbels, S. (2008) 'Improving grammatical skill in children with SLI', in C. Norbury, J.B. Tomblin & D.V.M. Bishop (eds), *Understanding Developmental Language Disorders. Hove & New York: Psychology Press,* 149–174.

Feldman, H.M., Dollaghan, C., Campbell, T.F., Colborn, D.K., Janosky, J., & Kurs-Lasky, M. (2003) 'Parent-reported language skills in relation to otitis media during the first 3 years of life', *Journal of Speech, Language and Hearing Research,* 46: 273–287.

Fisher, S.E. (2006) 'Tangled webs: tracing the connections between genes and cognition', *Cognition,* 101: 270–297.

Friederichi, A.D. (2006) 'The neural basis of language development and its impairment', *Neuron,* 52: 941–952.

Galaburda, A.M., Sherman, G.G., Rosen, G.D., Aboitiz, F., & Geschwind, D.H. (1985) 'Developmental dyslexia: four consecutive cases with cortical anomalies', *Annals of Neurology,* 18: 222–233.

Gauger, L., Lombardino, L., & Leonard, C. (1997) 'Brain morphology in children with specific language impairment', *Journal of Speech, Language and Hearing Research,* 40: 1272–1284.

Hayiou-Thomas, M.E., Bishop, D.V., & Plunkett, K. (2004) 'Simulating SLI: general cognitive processing stressors can produce a specific linguistic profile', *Journal of Speech Language and Hearing Research,* 47(6): 1347–1362.

Hayiou-Thomas, M.E., Oliver, B., & Plomin, R. (2005) 'Genetic influences on specific versus non-specific language impairment in 4-year-old twins', *Journal of Learning Disabilities,* 38: 222–232.

Herbert, M., Ziegler, D., Makris, N., Filipek, P., Kemper, T.L., & Normandin, J.J. et al. (2004) 'Localization of white matter volume increase in autism and developmental language disorder', *Annals of Neurology,* 55: 530–540.

Hill, E.L. (2001) 'Non-specific nature of specific language impairment: a review of the literature with regard to concomitant motor impairments', *International Journal of Language and Communication Disorders,* 36: 149–171.

Hoff, E. & Tian, C. (2005) 'Socioeconomic status and cultural influences on language', *Journal of Communication Disorders,* 38: 271–278.

Hoover, W.A. & Gough, P.B. (1990) 'The simple view of reading', *Reading and Writing,* 2: 127–160.

Howlin, P., Mawhood, L., & Rutter, M. (2000). 'Autism and developmental receptive language disorder— a follow-up comparison in early adult life. II. Social, behavioural and psychiatric outcomes', *Journal of Child Psychology and Psychiatry,* 41(5): 561–578.

Hugdahl, K., Gundersen, H., Brekke, C., Thomsen, T., Rimol, L.M., Ersland, L., & Niemi, J. (2004) 'fMRI brain activation in a Finnish family with specific language impairment compared with a normal control group', *Journal of Speech, Language and Hearing Research,* 47: 162–172.

Jancke, L., Siegenthaler, T., Preis, S., & Steinmetz, H. (2007) 'Decreased white-matter density in a left-sided fronto-temporal network in children with developmental language disorder: evidence for anatomical anomalies in a motor-language network', *Brain and Language,* 102: 91–98.

Jernigan, T., Hesselink, J.R., Sowell, E.R., & Tallal, P. (1991) 'Cerebral structure on magnetic resonance imaging in language- and learning-impaired children', *Archives of Neurology,* 48: 539–545.

Joanisse, M.F. & Seidenberg, M.S. (2003) 'Phonology and syntax in specific language impairment: evidence from a connectionist model', *Brain and Language,* 86: 40–56.

Johnson, M. & Wittgens, A. (2001) *The Selective Mutism Resource Manual.* Bicester, Ox: Speechmark Publishing.

Kjelgaard, M.M., & Tager-Flusberg, H. (2001) 'An investigation of language impairment in autism: implications for genetic subgroups', *Language and Cognitive Processes,* 16(2/3): 287–308.

Lai, C.S., Fisher, S.E., Hurst, J.A., Vargha-Khadem, F., & Monaco, A.P. (2001) 'A novel forkhead-domain gene is mutated in a severe speech and language disorder', *Nature,* 413: 519–523.

Leonard, C., Eckert, M., Given, B., Berninger, V., & Eden, G. (2006) 'Individual differences in anatomy predict reading and oral language impairments in children', *Brain,* 129(12): 3329–3342.

Leonard, L.B. (1998). *Children with Specific Language Impairment.* Cambridge, MA: MIT Press.

McArthur, G.M., Hogben, J.H., Edwards, S., Heath, S.M., & Mengler, E.D. (2000) 'On the "specifics" of specific reading disability and specific language impairment', *Journal of Child Psychology and Psychiatry,* 41: 869–874.

McArthur, G.M., Ellis, D., Atkinson, C.M., & Coltheart, M. (2008) 'Auditory processing deficits in children with reading and language impairments: can they (and should they) be treated?', *Cognition,* 107(3): 946–977.

Nation, K., Clarke, P., Marshall, C.M., & Durand, M. (2004) 'Hidden language impairments in children: parallels between poor reading comprehension and specific language impairment?', *Journal of Speech, Language and Hearing Research,* 47(1): 199–211.

Norbury, C.F. & Bishop, D.V.M. (2002) 'Inferential processing and story recall in children with communication problems: a comparison of specific language impairment, pragmatic language impairment and high-functioning autism', *International Journal of Language and Communication Disorders,* 37: 227–251.

Newbury, D.F. & Monaco, A.P. (2008) 'The application of molecular genetics to the study of developmental language disorder', in C.F. Norbury, J.B. Tomblin, & D.V. Bishop (eds), *Understanding Developmental Language Disorders.* Hove and New York: Psychology Press, pp. 79–91.

Norbury, C.F., & Bishop, D.V.M. (2003) 'Narrative skills of children with communication impairments', *International Journal of Language and Communication Disorders,* 38(3): 287–313.

Norbury, C.F., Bishop, D.V.M., & Briscoe, J. (2001) 'Production of English finite verb morphology: a comparison of SLI and mild-moderate hearing impairment', *Journal of Speech, Language and Hearing Research,* 44: 165–178.

Norbury, C.F., Nash, M., Baird, G., & Bishop, D.V.M. (2004) 'Using a parental checklist to identify diagnostic groups in children with communication impairment:

a validation of the Children's Communication Checklist—2', *International Journal of Language and Communication Disorders,* 39(3): 345–364.

Paradis, M., Crago, M., Genesee, F., & Rice, M.L. (2003) 'French-English bilingual children with SLI: how do they compare with their monolingual peers?', *Journal of Speech, Language and Hearing Research,* 46: 113–127.

Paul, R. (2007) *Language Disorders from Infancy through Adolescence,* 3rd edn. St. Louis, MO: Mosby.

Perfetti, C.A., Landi, N., & Oakhill, J. (2005) 'The acquisition of reading comprehension skill', in M.J. Snowling & C. Hulme (eds), *The Science of Reading.* Oxford: Blackwell Publishing, pp. 227–247.

Plante E., Swisher L., Vance R., Rapcsak S. (1991) *MRI findings in boys with specific language impairment. Brain and Language,* 41(1):52–66.

Plante, E. & Jackson, T. (1997) 'Gyral morphology in the posterior Sylvian region in families affected by developmental language disorder', *Neuropsychology Review,* 6: 81–94.

Rapin, I. & Allen, D. (1983) 'Developmental language disorders: nosological considerations', in U. Kirk (ed.), *Neuropsychology of Language, Reading and Spelling.* New York: Academic Press.

Rice, M.L., Wexler, K., & Cleave, P.L. (1995) 'Specific language impairment as a period of extended optional infinitive', *Journal of Speech, Language and Hearing Research,* 38: 850–863.

Rice, M.L., Tomblin, J.B., Hoffman, L., Richman, W.A., & Marquis, J. (2004) 'Grammatical tense deficits in children with SLI and nonspecific language impairment: relationships with nonverbal IQ over time', *Journal of Speech, Language and Hearing Research,* 47: 816–834.

Rice, M.L., Taylor, C.L., & Zubrick, S.R. (2008) 'Language outcomes of 7-year-old children with or without a history of late language emergence at 24 months', *Journal of Speech, Language and Hearing Research,* 51: 394–407.

Riches, N., Tomasello, M., & Conti-Ramsden, G. (2005) 'Verb learning in children with SLI: frequency and spacing effects', *Journal of Speech, Language and Hearing Research,* 48: 1397–1411.

Robinson, R.J. (1991) 'Causes and associations of severe and persistent specific speech and language disorders in children', *Developmental Medicine and Child Neurology,* 33: 943–962.

Shriberg, L.D., Tomblin, J.B., & McSweeny, J.L. (1999) 'Prevalence of speech delay in 6-year-old children and comorbidity with language impairment', *Journal of Speech, Language and Hearing Research,* 42: 1461–1481.

SLI Consortium (2004) 'Highly significant linkage to the SLI1 locus in an expanded sample of individuals affected by specific language impairment', *American Journal of Human Genetics,* 74: 1225–1238.

Snowling, M. (2000) *Dyslexia,* 2nd edn. Oxford: Blackwell.

Snowling, M., Bishop, D.V., Stothard, S.E., Chipchase, B., & Kaplan, C. (2006) 'Psychosocial outcomes at 15 years of children with a preschool history of speech-language impairment' *Journal of Child Psychology and Psychiatry,* 47: 759–765.

Spackman, M.P., Fujiki, M., & Brinton, B. (2006) 'Understanding emotions in context: the effects of language impairment on children's ability to infer emotional reactions', *International Journal of Language and Communication Disorders,* 41(2): 173–188.

Steinhausen, H.C., Wachter, M., Laimbock, K., & Winkler Metzke, C. (2006) 'A long-term outcome of selective mutism in childhood', *Journal of Child Psychology and Psychiatry,* 47: 751–756.

Tomblin, J.B. (2008) 'Validating diagnostic standards for specific language impairment using adolescent outcomes', in C.F. Norbury, J.B. Tomblin, & D.V. Bishop (eds), *Understanding Developmental Language Disorders.* Hove and New York: Psychology Press, pp. 93–114.

Tomblin, J.B., Records, N.L., Buckwalter, P., Zhang, X., Smith, E., & O'Brien, M. (1997) 'Prevalence of specific language impairment in kindergarten children', *Journal of Speech, Language and Hearing Research,* 40, 1245–1260.

Tomblin, J.B., Zhang, X., Buckwalter, P., & O'Brien, M. (2003) 'The stability of primary language impairment: four years after kindergarten diagnosis', *Journal of Speech, Language and Hearing Research,* 46: 1283–1296.

Ullman, M.T., & Pierpont, E.I. (2005) 'Specific language impairment is not specific to language: the procedural deficit hypothesis'. *Cortex,* 41(3): 399–433.

van der Lely, H.K.J. (2005) 'Domain-specific cognitive systems: insight from Grammatical-SLI', *Trends in Cognitive Science,* 9: 53–59.

Weismer, S.E., Plante, E., Jones, M., & Tomblin, J.B. (2005) 'A functional magnetic resonance imaging investigation of verbal working memory in adolescents with specific language impairment', *Journal of Speech, Language and Hearing Research,* 48(2): 405–425.

World Health Organization (1996) *Multiaxial Classification of Child and Adolescent Psychiatric Disorders: The ICD-10 Classification of Mental and Behavioural Disorders in Children and Adolescents.* Cambridge, UK: Cambridge University Press.

17

Developmental Language Disorders: Lifetime Course and Strategies for Intervention

Rhea Paul & Kimberly Gilbert

Language is a fundamental means by which humans interact; consequently, any disruption in its acquisition will have negative effects on social and academic development. As a unique feature of the human mind, any disturbance in cognitive growth can affect language development. For this reason, disorders of language development typically accompany a variety of conditions, including hearing impairment, mental retardation, autism, and fetal alcohol syndrome, as well as disruptions in development that accompany environmental trauma such as abuse and neglect. In this chapter, however, we focus on disorders of language development that are relatively circumscribed.

The term *developmental language disorder* (DLD) is the label that is now generally accepted for referring to children whose language skills do not meet expectations for their age or developmental level. A basic condition of this diagnostic label is its definition by exclusion (Benton, 1959). That is, children with DLD evidence problems with language that cannot be explained by intellectual disability, hearing impairment, autism, emotional disturbance, neglect, or neurological damage. Their difficulty in the ability to produce speech and understand language appears relatively isolated, with other aspects of development proceeding in a more-or-less typical fashion. This chapter describes the developmental course of children who show delays in their language learning, and outlines the intervention methods typically applied to these conditions.

DELAYED LANGUAGE DEVELOPMENT IN LATE-TALKING TODDLERS

Developmental course

In the past 20 years, several research groups have studied the development of children who are late to begin speaking, those often referred to as 'late talkers'. Late talkers are usually identified between 18 and 30 months of age when parents become concerned about children who appear to be developing normally but fail to begin speaking or have a very small expressive vocabulary. Although a variety of criteria have been used to identify these late-talking toddlers, they usually include a vocabulary size below the 10th percentile for age; below 50 words at 24 months (Fenson et al., 2007; Rescorla & Lee, 2000). Studies following these children through the pre-school years have shown that they tend to combine words later than other children (Dale et al., 2003), have less advanced sentence structures than others their age (Dale et al., 2003; Hadley & Holt, 2006; Paul, 1996; Paul & Riback, 1993; Thal et al., 2004), and to be delayed in the development of speech sounds (Carson et al., 2003; Law et al., 2000; Paul, 1991; Rescorla & Ratner, 1996; Thal et al. 1995). They are also predominantly male, more likely than children with typical language development to have a family history of language delay, and to have been born small and early (Zubrick et al., 2007).

A few researchers have followed these children beyond the pre-school years to examine longer-term outcomes. These studies reveal that over 75% of children identified as late-talking toddlers move into the normal range for vocabulary by 3 years of age and on standardized tests of grammar and discourse skills by kindergarten (Paul, 1996; Rescorla & Lee, 2000; Rice et al., 2008; Roos & Weismer, 2008; Whitehurst & Fischel, 1994). However, even though most late talkers would not be identified as having DLD by school age, they continue to score significantly lower, as a group, than typically developing controls from similar backgrounds, particularly in the area of grammatical development (Paul, 1996; Rescorla, 2002; Rice et al., 2008; Thal, 2005). In addition, Rescorla (2005) found significant group differences in reading at ages 8 and 9, though none of the children who had been late talkers were formally diagnosed with a reading disorder.

Only a few studies have examined outcomes in adolescence in children who were late to talk as toddlers. Data from Rescorla (2005) suggest that these children continue to score within the normal range on tests of language and reading, and not to qualify for special educational services or a diagnostic label such as specific language impairment (SLI). However, they score significantly lower than peers of similar socioeconomic status and continue to demonstrate weakness in language skills, including vocabulary, grammar, verbal memory, and reading comprehension. They perform similarly to peers on reading mechanics and writing. However, to date, there are no studies that have followed these children into adulthood.

DEVELOPMENTAL LANGUAGE DISORDER: LIFE COURSE

Children who appear to have typical cognitive, motor, and social/emotional development but who show significant delays in the ability to understand and produce language at the age of 4–5 years or older are considered to have a developmental language disorder (DLD). For children with chronic mild to moderate language disorders, problems in the school years tend to be concentrated in subtle difficulties of language organization and efficiency, rather than frank errors (Rescorla, 2002, 2005). Word retrieval, or 'word finding', difficulties are common. Instead of using correct words (e.g. 'chair'), a child with DLD may substitute an incorrect word of related meaning (e.g. 'table'); or use functional descriptors (e.g. 'thing to sit on'); vague or general terms (e.g. 'thing'), or his or her own made-up jargon. Storytelling and discourse problems often persist and affect both oral and written modes of expression (Paul, 1996; Reilly et al., 2004). These children may lack the ability to elaborate and/or self-correct when needed for clarity in conversation (Graham et al., 1983; Trantham & Pedersen, 1976). There may be tangential or inappropriate responses to questions, a limited range of communicative functions (e.g. requests, imperatives, questions) expressed, difficulty maintaining and/or changing topics, and difficulty initiating interactions (Kuder, 1997). Children with DLD may sound abrupt, rude, or impolite simply because they do not have access to the full and diverse range of linguistic forms used in normal conversation to encode pragmatic nuance and make language sound appropriate to the social context. Although these children continue to show slowed growth in basic vocabulary and sentence structures through the elementary school years, the great majority do attain basic functional language skills. Still, they continue to score below typical peers in terms of vocabulary and word learning ability (Weismer & Evans, 2002), grammatical markers, particularly markers on verbs (Rice et al., 2004), sentence length (Rice et al., 2006), as well as the use of complex and elaborated sentences (Greenhalgh & Strong, 2001) at least until age 10.

Children with DLD show heightened risk for attention deficit and activity disorders (Tetnowski, 2004). Moreover, Conti-Ransden and Botting (2004) reported that over one-third of children with DLD had poor social adjustment at age 11. In fact, DLD has been found to overlap significantly with psychiatric disorders (Toppelberg & Shapiro, 2000) and findings of previously undiagnosed language problems are highly prevalent in children seen in mental health clinics. The most common comorbidities include attention-deficit/hyperactivity disorder (ADHD) anxiety disorders, depression, and conduct, oppositional, or antisocial personality disorder (Sundheim & Voeller, 2004).

There is also evidence that children with DLD have problems with certain kinds of non-verbal cognition, including figurative thinking, mental rotation, and hypothesis formation (Bavin et al., 2005; Van der Lely, 2005). Botting (2005) showed that children with DLD score, on average, 20 points lower on IQ tests at age 14 than the same children did at age 7. Although it is not known whether this observation is a result of the learning

obstacles presented by the child's language problems, or a reflection of a general representational deficit that affects both language and other forms of symbolic thinking, it seems clear that persistent language disorders place children at risk for a range of concomitant deficits.

The most common of these concomitant problems are in reading, writing, and spelling. Estimates of co-occurrence of DLD and school learning disabilities run as high as 60% (Schoenbrodt et al., 1997). Tallal (1988) and Nelson (1998) have suggested that children with DLD 'change diagnoses' when they get to the intermediate grades, not because the underlying nature of their problem changes but simply because the demands of literacy put stress on their recently acquired, less-elaborated language skills. Nation et al. (2004) found that children with reading comprehension problems, as a group, had low oral language ability, while some of these individuals had marked language impairments that had not been previously identified. This high level of comorbidity between DLD and literacy difficulties has led some writers to propose the term *language-learning disability* to describe those children with a history of delayed language development that persists to the school years and is associated with literacy disorders.

In adolescence, 60% of children who showed DLD at kindergarten continue to show significant deficits in language skills (Pence & Justice, 2008). In these children a range of difficulties has been reported, including persistence of immature language forms, frequent false starts and revisions in speech, word finding problems, difficulties with abstract meanings, inability to adapt their language appropriately for different listeners (resulting in perceptions of rudeness or aggressiveness), and difficulty in repairing conversational breakdowns (Reed, 2005). As we have seen, these deficits have consequences for success in both academic and social settings. Snowling et al. (2006) reported that there was increased risk of attention and social difficulties in 15 year olds who had language deficits at age 5. Aram et al. (1984) reported that *all* children in a group of adolescents followed since pre-school identification with language disorders required special educational services, and that one-third now had IQs below 70, although all had been in the normal range at pre-school testing. The children were rated by their parents as being less socially competent and having more behavioral problems than their peers. Despite these persistent problems, however, most children with DLD finished high school and lived independent lives (Hall & Tomblin, 1978; Snowling et al., 2001). Some went on to higher education, but Snowling et al. (2001) reported that adolescents who had DLD at age 5 were more likely to follow vocational and employment training courses in high school than to attend preparatory programs for college.

Prognosis is more guarded for children with severe DLD. Paul and Cohen (1984) defined this group as those who were not speaking in full sentences by the time they were 6. In a long-term study, these individuals with severe impairments when seen as adolescents were likely to score in the intellectually impaired range on IQ tests, even if they had scored in the normal range at the pre-school level. Given intensive intervention, all had made steady progress in language skills throughout their school years. Still, 90% of these individuals who did not have basic functional oral language by age 6 continued to score significantly below the normal range on language as well as on IQ tests by adolescence. All required intensive special education, with most in special classrooms, schools, or residential facilities. Clegg et al. (2005) followed a group of males with severe language disorders into their 30s, and compared them to their siblings with normal language. The men with histories of DLD continued to show significant language problems as adults. They had IQ scores in the normal range, although their non-verbal scores were higher than their verbal IQ. They also showed severe literacy impairments, poor social adaptation, prolonged periods of

unemployment, and a dearth of close friendships and love relationships when compared to their siblings with typical language. Self-reports showed a higher rate of schizotypal features; four of these adults had serious mental health problems, with two having developed schizophrenia. However, it is important to be aware that the group followed for this study was more severely impaired than subjects in most other studies of DLD. In fact, some may have met criteria for autism spectrum disorders (ASD), using current diagnostic formulations.

Summary: life course

Children with delayed language development in the toddler and pre-school years tend to have relatively low risk for long-term difficulty when their delays resolve before they enter kindergarten. Although they continue to score somewhat lower than peers on measures of language and literacy, they are generally not identified as having significant learning disabilities. In contrast to this pattern, children who are late to begin speaking and manifest language deficits that persist to school age are likely to show chronic deficits in language use, and are at high risk of concomitant disabilities including attention disorders, social problems, psychiatric disorders, and school learning difficulties, particularly in the areas of reading and writing. Although these children do, for the most part, complete high school, they are less likely than their peers to attend higher education. Those with severe disorders who have been followed to adulthood show significant social and vocational difficulties, and some risk for psychiatric disorders.

APPROACHES TO INTERVENTION

At this time, the principal approaches to remediation of language disorder are educational and behavioral. The primary choices to

A continuum of approaches for language intervention

↓	↓	↓
Didactic	Naturalistic	Developmental/Pragmatic
Discrete trial	Milieu teaching	Conversational recasts
Teach me language	Focused stimulation	Interactive book reading

Figure 17.1   A continuum of approaches for language intervention

be made in selecting intervention approaches concern the agent of intervention—whether a parent or paraprofessional trained to implement a particular approach by a consulting professional or a professional implementing the intervention directly—and the degree to which the approach is directed by the adult or more centered on child interests. This latter continuum, often referred to as the degree of *naturalness,* which is schematized in Figure 17.1, is generally divided into three major categories:

1) Didactic methods are based on behaviorist theory and take advantage of behavioral technologies such as massed trials, operant conditioning, shaping, prompting, and chaining. Extrinsic reinforcement (a treat, prize, or token) is used to increase the frequency of desired target behaviors. Teaching sessions using these approaches involve high levels of adult control, repetitive periods of drill and practice, precise antecedent and consequent sequences, and a passive responder role for the client. The adult directs and controls all aspects of the interaction.

2) Naturalistic approaches attempt to incorporate behaviorist principles in more natural environments using functional, pragmatically appropriate social interactions, instead of stimulus–response–reinforcement sequences. Naturalistic approaches focus on the use of 'intrinsic', rather than tangible or edible reinforcers. Intrinsic reinforces include the satisfaction of achieving a desired goal through communication (the client says, 'I want juice' and gets juice), rather than more contrived, extrinsic reinforcers such as getting a token or being told 'good talking'. Finally, and perhaps most important, naturalistic approaches attempt to get clients to initiate communication, rather than casting them always in a responder role.

3) Developmental or pragmatic approaches emphasize functional communication, rather than speech, as a goal. As such, they encourage the development of multiple aspects of communication, such as the use of gestures, gaze, affect, and vocalization, and hold these behaviors to be necessary precursors to speech production. Activities provide multiple opportunities and temptations to communicate; the adult responds to any child initiation by providing rewarding activities. Thus, the child directs the interaction and chooses the topics and materials from among a range that the adult provides. Teachers strive to create an affectively positive environment by following the child's lead, and react supportively to any behavior that can be interpreted as communicative (even if it was not intended in that way). In most developmental approaches, specific language goals—such as particular vocabulary, grammatical forms, or speech sounds—are de-emphasized; the focus is on general stimulation and enrichment that takes place in the context of what the child is attending to and interested in talking about. As such, these approaches differ from the other two in that they may not target individual language goals, but are more generally aimed at improving functional communication, by responding contingently to the child's focus of attention and providing more sophisticated models of what the child already tries to communicate.

In the following discussion of intervention for child language disorders, approaches are geared to the developmental level of the child and thus follow a sequence of developmental levels. Within each level, approaches are presented that exemplify the above three points along the continuum of naturalness. The role of direct (clinician-implemented) vs indirect (parent-implemented) intervention is also discussed.

Interventions for emerging language

Goals at this stage include the development of first words and word combinations, as well as improvement in the intelligibility of beginning speech. In some methods, preverbal communicative behaviors, such as intentional use of gestures and vocalizations, are considered prerequisites to speech and word use.

Didactic methods

A large body of research (summarized by Goldstein, 2002; Koegel et al., 2008; Paul & Sutherland, 2005; Rogers, 2006) has demonstrated that didactic approaches are an effective means of initially giving attention to and understanding language, as well as initiating speech production in preverbal children. Discrete Trial Instruction (DTI), the most basic method within the didactic approach, entails dividing the chosen skill into components and training each component individually, using highly structured, drill-like procedures. Intensive training utilizes shaping, prompting, prompt fading, and reinforcement strategies. Trials continue until the child produces the target response with minimal prompting; at which point the next step in the hierarchy of behaviors (such as correctly pointing to the named picture from among two pictures) is presented and trained. Difficulties related to generalization and passivity (Fey et al., 1995; Koegel et al., 2008), along with changes in theoretical views of language learning that emphasized the central role of social exchanges in the acquisition of language, have led to the introduction of more naturalistic methods of intervention. Still, these methods are often employed to initiate speech in children who have not yet begun talking. Although many didactic approaches use first vocal and then verbal imitation strategies as a basic component, some make use of alternative means of expressing intentions in order to teach the basic concept of a communicative exchange.

The Picture Exchange Communication System (PECS) is one example of an augmentative/alternative communication (AAC) approach. It was designed primarily for use with children with ASD who have no speech and minimal functional communication. It begins by teaching children, with the help of an adult seated behind them to guide their initial exchanges, to request a desired object by trading a representation of it for the actual object with a second adult seated across from the child. Although speech is not required during the exchange, empirical evidence suggests that spontaneous speech may increase in some children with ASD following intervention with PECS (Charlop-Christy et al., 2002). However, there are no data on its effectiveness for children with DLD.

Naturalistic methods

A strong line of treatment research on methods of language intervention in the last few decades has focused on adapting the advantages of behavioral methods to more natural communication circumstances in order to increase the spontaneity and generalization of language use. These approaches are often referred to as 'applied behavior analysis' or naturalistic behavioral approaches. Several of these approaches are outlined below.

Incidental/milieu approaches These methods are known by a variety of labels, including *incidental teaching, mand-modeling*, and *milieu teaching*. What these methods share is an emphasis on teaching in the context of ongoing everyday activities in both home and school settings, following the child's lead, and providing natural consequences for communication (Koegel et al., 2008). These approaches, which we will subsume here under the umbrella term *milieu communication training* (MCT), have one of the largest empirical evidence bases of any method of intervention designed to elicit early communication and language behaviors in young children with a variety of developmental disabilities (ASHA, 2008).

At the earliest stage of language development, these techniques are used to elicit preverbal communicative acts such as gestures and vocalization. As these become more frequent and reliable, the adult 'ups the ante', withholding the object of interest until the child produces a word approximation, then a word, and later a word combination or sentence. A key principle of all phases of this approach, however, is avoiding frustrating the child. Although adults use expectant waiting to elicit child communication behaviors, if the child does not produce the desired act within 10–15 seconds, the adult still provides what the child wants, although perhaps for a very short time, then tries again. Part of the lesson being taught by incidental approaches is that communication is an affectively rewarding activity; children will not be motivated to learn to communicate if they encounter frustration. Rather, the aim of this approach is to demonstrate to the child that using communication brings rewards more quickly than using other, maladaptive behaviors, such as crying. Moreover, the approach aims to show the child that, in interaction with other people, it is possible to obtain more enjoyable activities and more interesting objects than the child can procure on his own. In this way, the child learns that manipulating others through communication supplies highly rewarding outcomes.

Milieu approaches have been successfully implemented by both clinicians (e.g. Hancock & Kaiser, 2002) and trained parents (Culatta & Horn, 1981; Kaiser et al., 2000; Wetherby & Woods, 2006). Several investigators using this approach (Kaiser et al., 2000; Yoder & Warren, 2002) advocate for a combination of clinician and trained-parent intervention as a way to maximize its effectiveness.

Developmental/pragmatic methods

These approaches differ from naturalistic methods in that they do not rely on concepts derived from behavioral theory. Although both naturalistic and developmental approaches advocate following the child's lead, developmental approaches make less use of time delay, environmental manipulations, and the provision of reinforcement.

Instead, they rely primarily on contingent responding on the part of the adult, who follows the child's lead and attempts to provide language input contingent on the child's actions and choices. Some examples of developmental/pragmatic methods are outlined below.

It Takes Two to Talk—The Hanen Program for Parents (Manolson, 1992). This program trains parents in methods designed to improve parent–child communication by increasing the contingency of parents' language. Parents are trained by speech language pathologists, and training is conducted in a series of small-group sessions, supplemented by individual videotaped feedback sessions. Research on the method shows overall increases in interaction variables for the parents, such as increased use of child-focused strategies and language modeling (Girolametto, 1988; Tannock & Girolametto, 1992). Gains were also seen in the children's interactions in one study (Girolametto, 1988), but not within a second study (Tannock & Girolametto, 1992). Three randomized controlled studies (Girolametto et al., 1996a, 1996b, 1997, 1998) showed positive effects on the interactional styles of mothers and also demonstrated improved language outcomes for children, with larger effects for late talkers rather than children with Down syndrome.

Conversational recast intervention (Camarata & Nelson, 1992). Conversational recasts involve responding to child productions with language models that are somewhat more complex than the original utterance. Recasts can expand meaning (C: 'Doggy.' A: 'Yes, it's a brown doggy.') or form (C: 'Him go fast.' A: 'Yes, he goes fast.'). Linguistic forms that can be recast include phonemes (C: 'Wabbit!' A: 'Yes, a rabbit.'), words (C: 'I see doggy!' A: 'Yes, there's a cow. I see it, too'), grammatical morphemes (C: 'two doggy!' A: 'Yes, there are two doggies.'), or grammar (C: 'I got no cars!' A: 'Oh, you don't have any cars?'). Several studies offer support for the use of conversational recasting

(Camarata & Nelson, 1992; Camarata et al., 1994; Nelson et al., 1996). However, research suggests that recast forms must be within the child's zone of proximal development in order for the target form to be acquired (Fey & Frome Loeb, 2002). Conversational recast treatment in these studies has been delivered by clinicians; however, more general language stimulation programs that employ similar techniques have been successfully taught to parents as well (Fey, 1986).

Interventions for pre-school language

Once children have begun to combine words consistently, the focus of treatment shifts from increasing frequency of spoken language to expanding vocabulary, increasing sentence length, including more grammatical markers, and reducing the number of grammatical errors in sentences, as well as improving the intelligibility of the child's speech. Approaches to these goals also fall at various points on the continuum of naturalness.

Didactic methods

Several programs have been developed using a Skinnerian framework to teach vocabulary and sentence structure. One example is Teach Me Language (Freeman & Dakes, 1996), a comprehensive language program that provides a step-by-step guide with in-depth detail on intervention activities targeting language areas such as grammar, syntax, concepts, and advanced narrative skills. Children are expected to follow a teacher's lead and regular repetition of drills is a key feature in the program. The program was developed for children who have at least single word expressive language and some basic concept knowledge and was designed to help them make the transition from this emerging language stage to more fully developed forms of expression and functional communication. The *Verbal Behavior* program takes a similar Skinnerian approach to language learning (Partington & Sundberg, 1998; Sundberg &

Michael, 2001). Partington and colleagues have published data indicating increases in verbal production using their method (e.g. Partington et al., 1994; Sundberg & Michael, 2001; Sundberg et al., 1995). Still, little research is available on the functional effects of these programs on real-world communication, or on their consequences for adaptive communication and independence. There are as yet few data on their general, long-term effects on the child's functioning.

Naturalistic methods

Several approaches that fall near the midpoint of the continuum of naturalness have been proposed to address the language development of children functioning at the preschool level. Some examples appear below.

Focused stimulation Focused stimulation involves exposing the child to multiple exemplars of specific linguistic forms, content, or use within meaningful contexts. This is followed by the provision of an opportunity to produce a similar form in the context of a conversational interaction. For example, the clinician might engage the child in play with a farm set and comment: 'Oh, look! The cow is in the field. The horse is in the barn. The goat is in the pen. Tell me about the sheep.' Robertson and Ellis Weismer (1999) reported that this approach works well for children who can sustain joint attention. Studies of focused stimulation have demonstrated gains in vocabulary, grammar, and speech production in late talkers (Lederer, 2001), as well as in children with DLD with cognitive delays (Fey et al., 1993) and with Down syndrome (Cheseldine & McConkey, 1979; Girolametto et al., 1998). Robertson and Ellis Weismer (1999) reported that although both clinicians and parents can deliver the intervention effectively, intervention from trained professionals showed a somewhat higher level of efficacy.

Script therapy Olswang and Bain (1991) discussed script therapy as a way to reduce the cognitive load of language training by embedding it in the context of a familiar routine. Here the adult develops some routines or scripts with the child in the intervention context. After establishing the routine, the adult can omit parts of it, and wait for the child to fill in the missing slot before continuing the routine. McClannahan and Krantz (2005) have presented an elaborated curriculum for using scripts to teach grammatical structures as well as social language use. They advocate combining the use of scripts with *script-fading*; i.e. beginning with written, pictured or audio recorded scripts that children can reiterate, and eventually withdrawing more and more of this support until the child can produce the script independently.

Script therapy can also involve role-playing of familiar routines, with verbal scripts describing the familiar actions. Examples could include going to a birthday party, or eating at a fast-food restaurant. The language to accompany each step of the routine can be practiced in role-play activities. Later in the intervention, the familiar activity might be disrupted in some way, challenging the child to communicate to call attention to or repair the disruption. For example, the adult, playing the role of 'fast-food server' can ask for payment without providing food.

Developmental/pragmatic methods

Methods of language intervention for pre-schoolers that take a developmental approach are generally aimed at providing language stimulation and promoting communication, without necessarily targeting specific language form or content goals.

Learning Language and Loving It (Weitzman & Greenberg, 2002). This program is aimed at pre-school teachers, and attempts to impart contingent language strategies that promote children's social, language, and literacy development within everyday activities and conversations in early childhood settings. Methods are similar to those taught to parents in *It Takes Two to Talk* (Manolson, 1992).

Girolametto et al. (2003) have shown that pre-school and day care teachers can be taught to use these techniques within the classroom setting.

Interactive book reading Cole et al. (2006) argue that book-sharing contexts are particularly effective language-learning contexts because the book provides more opportunities for asking questions, making comments, and taking turns than occur in unsupported conversational settings. However, they emphasize that simply reading to children is not enough; the reading must be accompanied by specific interactive techniques if it is to be effective as a language therapeutic tool. They review studies (e.g. Crain-Thoreson & Dale, 1999; Hargrave & Senechal, 2000) showing that children with language disorders associated with a variety of disabilities, as well as children with limited English proficiency (Lim & Cole, 2002), benefit from interacting with adults who use specific picture book interaction methods. They also cite studies demonstrating that clinicians can teach parents, teachers, and librarians to use and disseminate these techniques (Crain-Thoreson & Dale, 1999; Huebner, 2000); however, more gains were found when parents were involved (Dale et al., 1996).

Language interventions for school-aged children

Children with a history of delayed language development during the pre-school years, as we have seen, typically develop functional spoken language but are at risk for concomitant disorders in literacy development, especially when delays persist to kindergarten age. Thus, intervention for language disorders in school-aged children will need to focus on the development of both oral and written language skills. We can examine the kinds of goals and activities usually targeted at this stage in terms of the continuum of naturalness, as we have before. Interventions at this level more rarely involve parents and are usually delivered by professionals, teachers or clinicians, or trained paraprofessionals.

Didactic methods

Many basic goals of instruction at this level are delivered in a teacher-directed manner involving drill and practice.

Basic language skills   Children who retain oral language deficits into the primary grades will often continue to receive didactic instruction in the use of word endings, sentence forms, and articulation. However, at the school-age level, attempts are made to relate newly learned language to the classroom curriculum. If a child is still learning past tense forms, drills for contrasting present and past tense may take place using elements from stories the teacher is reading in class, or from concepts being addressed in the science curriculum (*Today we water our plant, yesterday we watered our plant.*), for example.

Phonological awareness   Phonological awareness (PA), the ability to segment words into sounds and manipulate sounds in words, is essential to learning to read in an alphabetic language such as English, in which letters are used to represent sounds (Catts & Kamhi, 2005; Ehri et al., 2001; Snow et al., 1998). A wide range of studies (e.g. Bradley & Bryant, 1985; Liberman & Liberman, 1990; Mann & Liberman, 1984; Scarborough, 2003; Snowling & Nation, 1997; Stackhouse & Wells, 1997) have shown that PA is highly correlated with reading ability, and that children with a history of speech and/or language delays have delayed development of PA. Thus, PA training is often provided, either in conjunction with speech/language intervention, or in primary classroom programs aimed at preventing reading failure. A drill-play format is often used for this instruction. Students may be given a set of tokens—nickels for vowels and pennies for consonants, perhaps. The adult demonstrates segmenting a vowel-consonant word, such as

oat (/ot/), by moving the nickel as /o/ is pronounced and the penny as the /t/ is produced. The students are then instructed to follow the teacher's model and move their coins as the sounds are pronounced. When students can accomplish this kind of phonological segmentation, CVC (coat) words can be introduced. Eventually, CCV (blue), CCVC (stone), CVCC (taps), and CCVCC (blast) words can be incorporated into the activity. Many of the phonological awareness programs used in research demonstrating the efficacy of PA training on literacy (e.g. Ehri et al., 2001; Gillon, 2000) make use of this format. Several studies have provided empirical support for the effectiveness of PA instruction in improving reading and spelling skills (Gillon, 2000, 2002, 2005).

Spelling and word study   Many children with a history of language disorders struggle with writing and spelling as much as with reading. Explicit instruction in morphology, or the study of root words, prefixes, and suffixes, is often provided to assist children in both learning new words and in mastering the tricky spelling conventions of English. For example, teaching children that the words *muscle* and *muscular* share the same root can help them remember the silent *c* in *muscle* by teaching them to remind themselves of its related word, *muscular,* in which the *c* is pronounced. Explicitly linking word study to spelling has been shown to improve both word knowledge and spelling ability (Bauman et al., 2002).

Naturalistic methods

Focused stimulation and script therapy are still appropriate approaches for school-aged children who require additional instruction and practice with basic language forms. Justice and Kaderavek (2004) proposed embedded-explicit emergent literacy instruction as a naturalistic form of early literacy development. This method combines engineering opportunities within the primary school classroom for children to engage in reading and writing, such as setting up a 'post office' station—at which children can address, deliver, read, and write letters to each other—along with small amounts of didactic instruction to support the naturalistic opportunities. Their research suggests that such embedded-explicit instruction is more effective in improving early literacy skills than indirect instruction alone. Naturalistic methods can also be applied to improving oral language comprehension, which serves as an important foundation for reading comprehension. Children with reading comprehension difficulties can be given material from classroom reading selections in oral form, whether by being read to or by means of audio recordings. Instruction consists of reinforcing reading comprehension through teaching skills and strategies for oral language comprehension, and practicing these in both oral and written formats. Kamhi (2003) suggested making use of activities that involve multiple re-readings of texts the students arc using in the classroom, in order to work toward fluent reading, as well as comprehension. Re-readings may take place in the context of drama activities, in which children act out the text as it is read aloud, having a 'readers' theater' presentation in which the students take turns reading the same text aloud, as if in different moods ('Keisha can read it as if she is happy, then Hector can read it as if he is mad...'), or as choral readings for recording on tape and listening to with parents as the child reads the text along with the recording at home. Combining these kinds of fluency-enhancing activities with comprehension practice can assist struggling readers in two aspects of literacy development simultaneously.

Pragmatic approaches

These methods focus on the development of social and conversational skills, rather than on the acquisition of specific aspects of oral and written language. One such method is Reciprocal Teaching. Brown and Campione (1990) and Brown and Palinscar (1987) outlined this approach to helping students engage in self-regulated learning within the classroom setting. A 'facilitator' (teacher) first models each step of a new skill to be taught on a segment of curricular material, such as a lecture, reading selection, or mathematics or science problem. The facilitator then assigns one of the students to use the same series of steps on a related passage or problem. Each student is given a turn to act as facilitator for the group.

The 'writing lab approach' (Nelson et al., (2004) is another pragmatically-based method used with students whose language and literacy learning difficulties have a negative impact on academic achievement and social interaction. It facilitates the enhancement of complexity and appropriateness of oral and written communications as well as social interaction and self-regulation, and uses inclusive, computer-supported, classroom-based activities, with specialists working in collaboration with general education teachers. Preliminary research on this approach has shown improvement in writing and classroom participation.

CONCLUSION

A variety of methods, from highly structured and didactic to informal and child-centered, are available to address the needs of children with communication disorders. Although research on the efficacy of these methods is still in its infancy, it appears that a broad range of methods has some limited evidence of usefulness. The goals of communication intervention change with development, from focusing on increasing the frequency of intentional communication in toddlers with language delays, to expanding and refining oral language skills in pre-schoolers, to providing a strong foundation in oral language for the development of literacy at school age. For each of these phases, there is an emerging literature on evidence-based practices available to address the needs of children who struggle to acquire language.

ACKNOWLEDGMENTS

Preparation of this chapter was supported by Research Grant P01-03008 funded by the National Institute of Mental Health (NIMH); the National Institute of Deafness and Communication Disorders R01 DC07129; MidCareer Development Award K24 HD045576 funded by NIDCD; NIMH Autism Center of Excellence grant # P50 MH81756; by the STAART Center grant U54 MH66494 funded by the National Institute on Deafness and Other Communication Disorders (NIDCD), the National Institute of Environmental Health Sciences (NIEHS), the National Institute of Child Health and Human Development (NICHD), the National Institute of Neurological Disorders and Stroke (NINDS), as well as by the National Alliance for Autism Research, and the Autism Speaks Foundation.

REFERENCES

ASHA (American Speech-Language-Hearing Association) (2008) *Incidence and Prevalence of Communication Disorders and Hearing Loss in Children*. Rockville, MD: ASHA.

Aram, D., Ekelman, B., & Nation, J. (1984) 'Preschoolers with language disorders: 10 years later', *Journal of Speech and Hearing Research*, 27: 232–244.

Bauman, J., Edwards, E., Font, G., Tereshinski, C., Kameenui, E., & Olejnik, S. (2002) 'Teaching morphemic and contextual analysis to fifth-grade students', *Reading Research Quarterly*, 37: 150–176.

Bavin, E.L., Wilson, P.H., Maruff, P., & Sleeman, F. (2005) 'Spatio-visual memory of children with specific language impairment: evidence for generalized processing problems', *International Journal of Language and Communication Disorders*, 40(3): 319–332.

Benton, A. (1959) 'Aphasia in children', *Education*, 79: 408–412.

Botting, N. (2005) 'Nonverbal cognitive development and language impairment', *Journal of Child Psychology and Psychiatry, and Allied Disciplines*, 46: 317–326.

Bradley, L. & Bryant, P. (1985) *Rhyme and Reason in Reading and Spelling*. Ann Arbor, MI: University of Michigan Press.

Brown, A. & Campione, J. (1990) 'Communities of learning and thinking, or a context by any other name' in D. Kuhn (ed.), *Developmental Perspectives on Teaching and Learning Thinking Skills*. New York: Karger, pp. 108–126.

Brown, A. & Palinscar, A. (1987) 'Reciprocal teaching of comprehension strategies' in J. Day & J. Borkowski (eds), *Intelligence and Exceptionality: New Directions For Theory, Assessment, And Instructional Practice*. Norwood, NJ: Ablex, pp. 81–132.

Camarata, S. & Nelson, K. (1992) 'Treatment efficacy as a function of target selection in the remediation of child language', *Clinical Linguistics and Phonetics*, 6: 167–178.

Camarata, S., & Nelson, K., & Camarata, M. (1994) 'A comparison of conversation based to imitation procedures for training grammatical structures in specifically language impaired children', *Journal of Speech and Hearing Research*, 37: 1414–1423.

Carson, C., Klee, T., Carson, D., & Hime, L. (2003) 'Phonological profiles of 2-year-olds with delayed language development: predicting clinical outcomes at age 3', *American Journal of Speech-Language Pathology*, 12: 28–39.

Catts, H. & Kamhi, A. (2005) 'Causes of reading disabilities', in H. Catts & A. Kamhi (eds), *Language and Reading Disabilities*, 2nd edn., Boston: Allyn & Bacon, pp. 94–126.

Charlop-Christy, M.H., Carpenter, M., Le, L., Leblanc, L., & Kellet, K. (2002) 'Using the Picture Exchange Communication System with children with autism: assessment of PECS acquisition, speech, social-communication behavior, and problem behaviors', *Journal of Applied Behavior Analysis*, 35: 459–465.

Cheseldine, S. & McConkey, R. (1979) 'Parental speech to young Down's syndrome children: an intervention study', *American Journal of Mental Deficiency*, 83: 612–620.

Clegg, J., Hollis, C., Mawhood, L., & Rutter, M. (2005) 'Developmental language disorders—a follow-up in later adult life. Cognitive, language and psychosocial outcomes', *Journal of Child Psychology and Psychiatry, and Allied Disciplines*, 46: 128–149.

Cole, K., Maddox, M., & Lim, Y. (2006) 'Language is the key', in R. McCauley & M. Fey (eds), *Treatment of Language Disorders in Children*. Baltimore: Paul H. Brookes.

Conti-Ramsden, G. & Botting, N. (2004) 'Social difficulties and victimization in children with SLI at 11 years of age', Journal of Speech, Language & Hearing Research, 47(1): 145–161.

Crain-Thoreson, C. & Dale, P.S. (1999) 'Enhancing linguistic performance: parents and teachers as book reading partners for children with language delays', *Topics in Early Childhood Special Education,* 19: 28–40.

Culatta, B. & Horn, D. (1981) 'Systematic modification of parental input to train language symbols', *Language, Speech, and Hearing Services in Schools,* 12: 4–13.

Dale, P., Crain-Thoreson, C., Notari, A., & Cole, K. (1996) 'Parent-child storybooks reading as an intervention technique for young children with language delays', *Topics in Early Childhood Special Education,* 16: 213–235.

Dale, P., Price, T., Bishop, D., & Plomin, R. (2003) 'Outcomes of early language delay: I. Predicting persistent and transient language difficulties at 3 and 4 years', *Journal of Speech, Language, and Hearing Research,* 46: 544–560.

Ehri, L., Nunes, S., Stahl, S., & Willows, D. (2001) 'Systematic phonics instruction helps students learn to read: evidence from the National Reading Panel's meta-analysis', *Review of Educational Research,* 71: 393–447.

Fenson, L., Marchman, V. A., Thal, D. J., Dale, P. S., Reznick, J. S, & Bates, E. (2007) *MacArthur-Bates communicative development inventories: User's guide and technical manual* (2nd ed.) Baltimore: Paul H. Brookes Publishing Co.

Fey, M. (1986) *Language Intervention with Young Children.* San Diego, CA: College-Hill Press.

Fey, M. & Frome Loeb, D. (2002) 'An evaluation of the facilitative effects of inverted yes-no questions on the acquisition of auxiliary verbs', *Journal of Speech, Language, and Hearing Research,* 45: 160–174.

Fey, M.E., Cleave, P., Long, S., & Hughes, D. (1993) 'Two approaches to the facilitation of grammar in children with language impairment', *Journal of Speech and Hearing Research,* 36: 114–157.

Fey, M., Windsor, J., & Warren, S. (1995) *Language Intervention: Preschool through Elementary Years.* Baltimore: Panl H. Brookes.

Freeman, S., & Dakes, L. (1996) *Teach Me Language: A Language Manual for Children with Autism, Asperger's Syndrome and Related Disorders.* Langley, Canada: SKF Books.

Gillon, G. (2000) 'The efficacy of phonological awareness intervention for children with spoken language impairment', *Language, Speech, and Hearing Services in Schools,* 31: 126–141.

Gillon, G. (2002) 'Follow-up study investigating benefits of phonological awareness intervention for children with spoken language impairment', *International Journal of Language and Communication Disorders,* 37(4): 381–400.

Gillon, G. (2005) 'Facilitating phoneme awareness development in 3- and 4-year-old children with speech impairment', *Language, Speech, and Hearing Services in Schools,* 36: 308–324.

Girolametto, L. (1988)' Improving the social-conversational skills of developmentally delayed children: an intervention study', *Journal of Speech and Hearing Disorders,* 53: 156–167.

Girolametto, L., Pearce, P., & Weitzman, E. (1996a) 'The effects of focused stimulation for promoting vocabulary in children with delays: a pilot study', *Journal of Childhood Communication Development,* 17: 39–49.

Girolametto, L., Pearce, P., & Weitzman, E. (1996b) 'Interactive focused stimulation for toddlers with expressive vocabulary delays', *Journal of Speech and Hearing Research,* 39: 1274–1283.

Girolametto, L., Pearce, P., & Weitzman, E. (1997) 'Effects of lexical intervention on the phonology of late talkers', *Journal of Speech, Language, and Hearing Research,* 40: 338–348.

Girolametto, L., Weitzman, E., & Clements-Baartman, J. (1998) 'Vocabulary intervention for children with Down syndrome: parent training using focused stimulation', *Infant-Toddler Intervention,* 8: 109–125.

Girolametto, L., Weitzman, E., & Greenberg, J. (2003) 'Training day care staff to facilitate children's language', *American Journal of Speech-Language Pathology,* 12: 299–311.

Goldstein, H. (2002) 'Communication intervention for children with autism: a review of treatment efficacy', *Journal of Autism and Developmental Disorders,* 32: 373–396.

Graham, J., Bashir, A., & Stark, R. (1983) 'Communicative disorders', in M. Levine, W. Carey, & A. Crocker et al. (eds), *Developmental-Behavioral Pediatrics.* Philadelphia: W.B. Saunders, pp. 847–864.

Greenhalgh, K. & Strong, C. (2001) 'Literate language features in spoken narratives of children with typical language and children with language impairments', *Language, Speech, and Hearing Services in Schools,* 32: 114–125.

Hadley, P. & Holt, J. (2006) 'Individual differences in the onset of tense marking: a growth curve analysis', *Journal of Speech, Language, and Hearing Research,* 49: 984–1000.

Hall, P. & Tomblin, J. (1978) 'A follow-up study of children with articulation and language disorders', *Journal of Speech and Hearing Disorders,* 43: 227–241.

Hancock, T.B. & Kaiser, A.P. (2002) 'The effects of trainer-implemented enhanced milieu teaching on the social communication of children with autism', *Topics in Early Childhood Special Education,* 22: 39–54.

Hargrave, A. & Senechal, M. (2000) 'Book reading intervention with preschool children who have limited vocabularies: the benefits of regular reading and dialogic reading', *Early Childhood Research Quarterly,* 15: 75–90.

Huebner, C. (2000) 'Promoting toddlers' language development through community-based intervention', *Journal of Applied Developmental Psychology,* 21: 513–535.

Justice, L. & Kaderavek, J. (2004) 'Embedded-explicit emergent literacy intervention I: Background and description of approach', *Language, Speech, and Hearing Services in Schools,* 35: 201–211.

Kaiser, A.P., Hancock, T.B., & Nietfeld, J.P. (2000) 'The effects of parent-implemented enhanced milieu teaching on social communication of children who have autism', *Journal of Early Education and Development (special issue),* 4: 423–446.

Kamhi, A. (2003) 'The role of the SLP in improving reading fluency', *The ASHA Leader,* 5–9.

Koegel, L., Koegel, R., Fredeen, R., & Genoux, G. (2008) 'Naturalistic behavioral approaches to treatment', in K. Chawarska, A. Klin, & F. Volkmar, (eds), *Autism Spectrum Disorders in Infants and Toddlers.* New York: Guilford Press, pp. 207–242.

Kuder, J. (1997) *Teaching Students with Language and Communication Disabilities.* Boston: Allyn & Bacon.

Law, J., Boyle, J., Harris, F., Harkness, A. & Nye, C. (2000) 'Prevalence and natural history of primary speech and language delay: findings from a systematic review of the literature', *International Journal of Language and Communication Disorders,* 35: 165–188.

Lederer, S.H. (2001) 'Efficacy of parent-child language group intervention for late-talking toddlers', *Infant-Toddler Intervention,* 11: 223–235.

Liberman, I., & Liberman, A. (1990) 'Whole language vs. code emphasis: underlying assumptions and their implications for reading instruction', *Annals of Dyslexia,* 40: 51–76.

Lim, Y.S. & Cole, K.N. (2002) 'Facilitating first language development in young Korean children through parent training in picture book interactions', *Bilingual Research Journal,* 26: 367–381.

McClannahan, L., & Krantz, P. (2005) *Teaching Conversation to Children with Autism: Scripts and Script Fading.* Bethesda, Maryland: Woodbine House.

McGee., D., Morrier, M., & Daly, T. (1999) 'An incidental teaching approach to early intervention for toddlers with autism', *Journal of the Association for Persons with Severe Handicaps,* 24: 133–146.

Mann, V. & Liberman, I. (1984) 'Phonological awareness and verbal short-term memory', *Journal of Learning Disabilities,* 17: 592–598.

Manolson, A. (1992) *It Takes Two to Talk.* Toronto: The Hanen Centre.

Nation, K., Clarke, P., & Marshall, C. (2004) 'Hidden language impairments in children: parallels between poor reading comprehension and specific language impairment?', *Journal of Speech, Language, and Hearing Research,* 47: 199–211.

Nelson, K.E., Camarata, S.M., Welsh, J., Butkovsky, L., & Camarata, M. (1996) 'Effects of imitative and conversational recasting treatment on the acquisition of grammar in children with specific language impairment and younger language-normal children', *Journal of Speech and Hearing Research,* 39: 850–859.

Nelson, N. (1998) *Childhood Language Disorders in Context: Infancy through Adolescence,* 2nd edn. Columbus, OH: Merrill.

Nelson, N.W., Bahr, C.M., & Van Meter, A.M. (2004). *The Writing Lab Approach to Language Instruction and Intervention.* Baltimore: Paul H. Brookes.

Olswang, L., & Bain, B. (1991) 'Intervention issues for toddlers with specific language impairments', *Topics in Language Disorders,* 11: 69–86.

Partington, J., Sundberg, M., Newhouse, L., & Spengler-Schelley, M. (1994) 'Overcoming an autistic child's failure to acquire a tact repertoire', 27: 733–734.

Partington, J. & Sundberg, M. (1998) *Teaching Language to Children with Autism and Other Developmental Disabilities.* Danville, CA: Behavior Analyst.

Paul, R. (1991) 'Profiles of toddlers with slow expressive language development', *Topics in Language Disorders,* 11: 1–13.

Paul, R. (1996) 'Clinical implications of the natural history of slow expressive language development', *American Journal of Speech-Language Pathology,* 5: 5–21.

Paul, R., & Cohen, D. (1984) 'Outcomes of severe disorders of language acquisition', *Journal of Autism and Developmental Disorders,* 14: 405–421.

Paul, R. & Riback, M. (1993) 'Sentence structure development in late talkers'. Poster session presented at the Symposium for Research in Child Language Disorders, University of Wisconsin-Madison, 1993 and at the National Convention of the American Speech-Language and Hearing Association, Anaheim, CA.

Paul, R. & Sutherland, D. (2005) 'Enhancing early language in children with autism spectrum disorders', in F. Volkmar, R. Paul, A. Klin, & D. Cohen (eds.), *Handbook of Autism and Pervasive Developmental Disorders,* 3rd edn, Vol. 2. New York: Wiley, pp. 946–976.

Pence, K. & Justice, L. (2008) *Language Development From Theory to Practice*. Columbus, OH: Pearson.

Reed, V. (2005) *An Introduction to Children with Language Disorders,* 3rd. edn Boston: Allyn & Bacon.

Reilly, J., Losh, M., Bellugi, U., & Wulfeck, B. (2004) '''Frog, where are you?'' Narratives in children with specific language impairment, early focal brain injury, and Williams syndrome', *Brain & Language*, 88: 229–247.

Rescorla, L. (2002) 'Language and reading outcomes to age 9 in late-talking toddlers', *Journal of Speech, Language, and Hearing Research*, 45: 360–371.

Rescorla, L. (2005) 'Age 13 language and reading outcomes in late-talking toddlers', *Journal of Speech, Language, and Hearing Research*, 48: 459–472.

Rescorla, L., & Lee, E. (2000) Language impairments in young children. In T. Layton & L. Watson (Eds.), *Handbook of early language impairment in children*: Vol I. Nature (p. 1–38). New York: Delmar.

Rescorla, L. & Lee, E.C. (2000) 'Language impairments in young children', in T. Layton & L. Watson (eds), *Handbook of Early Language Impairment in Children: Vol. I: Nature.* New York: Delmar, pp. 1–38.

Rescorla, L. & Ratner, N. (1996) 'Phonetic profiles in toddlers with specific expressive language impairment', *Journal of Speech and Hearing Research, 39*: 153–166.

Rice, M., Tomblin, B., Hoffman L., Richman, W., & Marquis, J. (2004) 'Grammatical tense deficits in children with SLI and nonspecific language impairment: relationships with nonverbal IQ over time', *Journal of Speech, Language, and Hearing Research,* 47: 816–834.

Rice, M. Redmond, S., & Hoffman, L. (2006) 'Mean length of utterance in children with specific language impairment and in younger control children shows concurrent validity and stable and parallel growth trajectories', *Journal of Speech, Language, and Hearing Research,* 49: 793–808.

Rice, M., Taylor, C., & Zubrick, S. (2008) 'Language outcomes of 7-year-old children with or without a history of late language emergence at 24 months', *Journal of Speech, Language, and Hearing Research,* 51: 394–407.

Robertson, S.B. & Ellis Weismer, S. (1999) 'Effects of treatment on linguistic and social skills in toddlers with delayed language development', *Journal of Speech, Language, and Hearing Research,* 42: 1234–1248.

Rogers, S. (2006) 'Evidence-based intervention for language development in young children with autism' in T. Charman, & W. Stone, (eds), *Social and Communication Development in Autism Spectrum Disorders: Early Identification, Diagnosis, and Intervention.* New York: Guilford Press.

Rogers-Warren, A. & Warren, S. (1980) 'Mands for verbalization: facilitating the generalization of newly trained language in children', *Behavior Modification,* 4: 230–245.

Roos, E., & Ellis Weismer, S. 'Outcomes of late talking toddlers at preschool and beyond' *'Perspectives on Language and Learning Education'* 15, 119–126. Rockville, MD: American Speech-Language-Hearing Association.

Scarborough, H.S. (2003) 'Connecting early language and literacy to later reading (dis)abilities: evidence, theory, and practice', in S. Neuman & D. Dickinson (eds), *Handbook of Early Literacy Research.* New York: Guilford Press, pp. 97–110.

Schoenbrodt, L., Kumin, L., & Sloan, J. (1997) 'Learning disabilities existing concomitantly with communication disorder', *Journal of Learning Disability,* 30: 264–281.

Snow, C., Burns, S., & Griffin, P. (1998) *Preventing Reading Difficulties in Young Children.* Washington, DC: National Academy Press.

Snowling, M. & Nation, K. (1997) 'Language, phonology and learning to read', in C. Hulme & M. Snowling (eds), *Dyslexia: Biology, Cognition, and Intervention.* London: Whurr Publishers, pp. 153–166.

Snowling, M., Adams, J., Bishop, D., & Stothard, S. (2001) 'Educational attainments of school leavers with a preschool history of speech-language impairments', *International Journal of Language and Communication Disorders,* 36: 173–183.

Snowling, M., Bishop, D., Stothard, S., Chipchase, B., & Kaplan, C. (2006) 'Psychosocial outcomes at 15 years of children with preschool history of speech-language impairment', *Journal of Child Psychology & Psychiatry,* 47: 759–765.

Stackhouse, J. & Wells, B. (1997) 'How do speech and language problems affect literacy development?', in C. Hulme & M. Snowling (eds), *Dyslexia: Biology, Cognition, and Intervention.* London: Whurr Publishers, pp. 182–211.

Sundberg, M., Michael, J., Partington, J., & Sundberg, C. (1995) 'The role of automatic reinforcement in early language acquisition', *Analysis of Verbal Behavior,* 13: 21–37.

Sundberg, M. & Michael, J. (2001) 'The benefits of Skinner's analysis of verbal behavior for children with autism', *Behavior Modification,* 25: 698–724.

Sundheim, S.T. & Voeller, K.K. (2004) 'Psychiatric implications of language disorders and learning disabilities: risks and management', *Journal of Child Neurology,* 19(10): 814–826.

Tallal, P. (1988) 'Developmental language disorders', in J.F. Kavanagh & T.J. Truss, Jr. (eds), *Learning*

Disabilities: Proceedings of the National Conference. Parkton, MD: York Press, pp. 181–272.

Tannock, R. & Girolametto, L. (1992) 'Reassessing parent-focused language intervention programs' in S.F. Warren & J. Reichle (Series & Vol. eds), *Communication and Language Intervention Series: Vol. 1. Causes and Effects in Communication and Language Intervention.* Baltimore: Paul H. Brookes, pp. 49–80.

Tetnowski, J. (2004) 'Attention deficit hyperactivity disorders and concomitant communicative disorders', *Seminars in Speech and Language,* 25: 215–224.

Thal, D. (2005) *'Early detection of risk for language impairment: What are the best strategies?'.* Paper presented at the Congress on Language and Speech Disorders, Urbino, Italy.

Thal, D., Oroz, M., & McCaw, V. (1995) 'Phonological and lexical development in normal and late-talking toddlers', *Applied Psycholinguistics,* 16: 407–424.

Thal, D., Reilly, J., Seibert, L., Jeffries, R., & Fenson, J. (2004) 'Language development in children at risk for language impairment: cross-population comparisons', *Brain and Language,* 88: 167–179.

Toppelberg C.O. & Shapiro T. (2000) 'Language disorders: A 10-year research update review', *Journal of the American Academy of Child & Adolescent Psychiatry,* 39: 143–152.

Trantham, C. & Pedersen, J. (1976) *Normal Language Development: The Key to Diagnosis and Therapy for Language-Disordered Children.* Baltimore: Williams & Wilkins.

Toppelberg, C. & Shapiro, T. (2000) Language disorders : A 10-year research update review. Journal of the American Academy of child and Adolescent Psychiatry, 39, 143–152.

Van der Lely, H. (2005) 'Domain-specific cognitive systems: insight from grammatical SLI', *Trends in Cognitive Sciences,* 9: 53–59.

Warren, S.F. & Yoder, P.J. (1998) 'Facilitating the transition to intentional communication' in S.F. Warren & J. Reichle (Series eds) & A.M. Wetherby, S.F. Warren, & J., Reichle (Vol. eds), *Communication and Language Intervention Series: Vol. 7. Transitions in Prelinguistic Communication.* Baltimore: Paul H. Brookes, pp. 39–85.

Weismer, S. & Evans, J. (2002) 'The role of processing limitations in early Identification of specific language impairment', *Topics in Language Disorders,* 22(3): 15–29.

Weitzman, E. & Greenberg, J. (2002) *Learning Language and Loving it.* Tornoto: The Hanen Program.

Wetherby, A. & Woods, J. (2006) 'Early social interaction project for children with autism spectrum disorders beginning in the second year of life: a preliminary study', *Topics in Early Childhood Special Education,* 26: 67–82.

Whitehurst, G.J. & Fischel, J.E. (1994) 'Early developmental language delay: What, if anything, should a clinician do about it?', *Journal of Child Psychology and Psychiatry,* 35: 613–648.

Yoder, P.J. & Warren, S.F. (1998) 'Maternal responsivity predicts the extent to which prelinguistic intervention facilitates generalized intentional communication', *Journal of Speech, Language, and Hearing Research,* 41(5): 1207–1219.

Yoder, P.J. & Warren, S.F. (2002) 'Effects of prelinguistic milieu teaching and parent responsivity in education on dyads involving children with intellectual disabilities', *Journal of Speech, Language, and Hearing Research,* 45(6): 1158–1174.

Zubrick, S., Taylor, C., Rice, M., & Slegers, D. (2007) 'Late language emergence at 24 months: an epidemiological study of prevalence, predictors and covariates', *Journal of Speech, Language, and Hearing Research,* 50: 1562–1592.

18

Intellectual Disability: Concepts, Definitions, and Assessment

Cory Shulman, Heidi Flores, Grace Iarocci, & Jacob A. Burack

NON-SPECIFIC INTELLECTUAL DISABILITY

Intellectual disability is an odd behavioral classification in that it is based on amorphous concepts, arbitrary designations, and highly charged social values, all of which have changed often during the past century (AAMR, 2002). Despite this ambiguity, intellectual disability is relatively easily conceptualized. Across the decades and even centuries of work with persons with intellectual disabilities, the basic notion has been that there is a certain number of persons whose levels of intelligence and social competence are so low that they cannot function independently in society or that they need some intensive support to do so (e.g. AAMR, 2002; for a review see Rosen et al., 1976). Intellectual disability has often been linked to specific biological causes, and the number of individuals for whom an organic base is identified has grown considerably over the years as a result of increasingly sophisticated medical and related technologies, in addition to significant progress in understanding genetic transmissions of intellectual ability and disability. Yet, for many individuals, no specific origin is identified, and their intellectual disability is best characterized as a developmental delay arising from some combination of genetic heredity of intelligence and environmental influence (e.g. Iarocci & Petrill, in press; Zigler, 1969; Zigler & Hodapp, 1986). These individuals, who make up the bulk of the group labeled with non-specific intellectual disability, are the focus of this chapter. By the very designation of non-specific intellectual disability, we recognize the ambiguity inherent both in the grouping and in our task in defining it. However, as the number of individuals in this group decreases with the identification of previously unknown specific causes, the group is becoming increasingly homogeneous. We argue that it is primarily composed of persons whose intellectual disability is a function of some combination of familial transmission of low levels of intelligence and less than optimal environmental situations.

THE AMORPHOUS NATURE OF INTELLECTUAL DISABILITY

The amorphous nature of intellectual disability (formerly referred to as 'mental retardation') is most evident in that its definition has changed at least nine times over the past 100 years in the United States (AAMR, 2002; Matson & Boisjoli, 2009). Changes in nomenclature arise from the acquisition of knowledge regarding the causes of intellectual disability, perspectives on eventual outcomes, the significance of social competence and adaptive behaviors, policy attitudes toward individuals' roles in the community, and efforts to preserve the dignity of individuals whose intellectual functioning is slower or different than that found among people with typical intellectual development. In this chapter, the term 'intellectual disability' is used to refer to the group of individuals with significant impairments in both cognitive functioning and adaptive skills, the onset of which occurs before the age of 18 years (AAMR, 2002; Jacobson et al., 2007). Although the term 'mental retardation' continues to be used in the primary psychiatric diagnostic frameworks—e.g. the *International Classification of Diseases* (ICD) and the *Diagnostic and Statistical Manual of Mental Disorders* (DSM-IV)—like earlier terms such as 'moron' and 'feeble-minded' that were once commonly used by the scientific and medical communities, it is now associated with considerable stigma. The transition in nomenclature from mental retardation to intellectual disability reflects the historic and ongoing challenge to find a balance between the utilization of a common language about persons with intellectual disabilities for research, services, education, and policy on the one hand, and sensitivity to the profound effects of a label on individuals and their families on the other (Schalock et al., 2007).

Even as researchers and practitioners of intellectual disability discuss relevant issues—including the meaning of intelligence, the role of indices of social competence in the classification, the measures that should be used for testing, and specific criteria for a diagnosis—the pragmatic reality is that the classification of intellectual disability is usually entirely determined by a score on an IQ test. As quantitative indices of the elusive construct of intelligence, IQ tests ideally provide a measure both of the individual's intellectual ability in relation to other persons of the same age with similar backgrounds and of the rate of development of these intellectual abilities. IQ scores are typically standardized in that they are normed across a representative sample, and, thereby reflect a statistically calculated 'average' for a specific level of functioning. The developmental aspect of these IQ scores is highlighted by its formula, which involves dividing mental age (MA) by chronological age (CA) and then multiplying that number by a constant, usually 100 (for discussions, see Hodapp et al., 1990; Zigler & Hodapp, 1986). This measurement reflects rate, as in this context, chronological age represents the amount of time taken to attain the level of abilities expressed as mental age. As IQ scores tend to be relatively stable over time, scores in childhood can also be seen as an index of future levels of functioning in relation to one's peers.

The primary criterion for the designation of intellectual disability generally involves a cutoff score on a standardized IQ test that is associated with some statistical designation. This cutoff score is usually 2 standard deviations (2 SD) below the mean for the general population, indicating that the rate of the development of persons with intellectual disability is in approximately the bottom 3% of the population. However, the use of 2 SD as the cutoff point is arbitrary as is any other designation, and it has no inherent scientific significance with regard to differentiating among persons. Rather, the most meaningful aspect of the score is its numerical convenience. Clearly, persons with IQs just above and below the designated cutoff scores may not differ significantly, either statistically or pragmatically, from each other, whereas the differences among individuals within the range of either intellectual disability or of so-called typical functioning are often vast. One rationale for designating a number as the cutoff is that some criterion is needed as a standard for social policy and decisions about who should receive specialized services. Thus, the designated score offers a rough estimate of the number of persons who are eligible for some combination of additional funding, resources, services, and supports.

HISTORICAL PERSPECTIVES ON SPECIFIC AND NON-SPECIFIC CAUSES OF INTELLECTUAL DISABILITY

Early notions of the familial transmission of intellectual disability

With arbitrary designations based almost solely on cutoff criteria of one or more indicators of general notions of intellectual functioning and, in some cases, of social competence, the individuals included under the rubric of 'intellectually disabled' often seem to have little in common with one another. This heterogeneity has long been discussed by researchers and practitioners in the field. As far back as the turn of the seventeenth century, the physician Felix Platter articulated two groups of persons with intellectual disability. One group included individuals described as 'simple-minded' since infancy, and the second included individuals who were also born with physical atypicalities that pointed to underlying organic disorders. This differentiation between those born with and without deformities continued to be highlighted by later workers in the field. For example, near the end of the nineteenth century, John Langdon Hayden Down (1886) and William Wetherspoon Ireland (1877) both provided detailed early classifications in which they distinguished between intellectual

disability that was the outcome of some obvious genetic anomaly or other organic insult, and intellectual disability which appeared to be the outcome of some combination of familial genetic influences and environmental, societal, and cultural factors (for a review, see Burack, 1990). Down (1887) classified mentally deficient persons into the three etiological groups of congenital, accidental, and developmental, whereas Ireland's classification of intellectual disability included 9 of 10 categories that were associated with medical conditions linked with mental retardation, and a tenth category of 'idiocy by deprivation'. In subsequent classifications in the nineteenth and twentieth centuries, the number of genetic or organic conditions associated with neurological problems and intellectual disability grew rapidly as a result of increasingly sophisticated technologies and scientific advances. Current estimates include more than 1000 organic conditions associated with intellectual disability (Hodapp & Burack, 2006). Yet, many persons with intellectual disability, especially in the mild to moderate range, remain unclassified with regard to etiology. Whereas, some of these persons might be eventually diagnosed with a specific organic etiology, many, or most, are likely to fit into the type of classification initially described as 'simple-minded from birth' by Platter, developmental in nature by Down, and 'idiocy by deprivation' by Ireland.

Consistent with the classifications by Down and Ireland, as well as by later researchers who differentiated intellectual disability by etiology (e.g. Kephart & Strauss, 1940; Lewis, 1933; Zigler, 1967, 1969), the intellectual disability of persons with no organic etiology seems to be associated with some combination of familial-genetic and environmental factors that affect the development of intelligence and the occurrence of intellectual disability (Hodapp & Dykens, 2001; Zigler & Hodapp, 1986). These complex associations among potential factors and the development of intelligence provided the framework for rather intensive work in the mid to late twentieth century by researchers of intellectual disability, most notably Edward Zigler (1967, 1969), who advocated the use of the terms cultural-familial or familial to denote the essential contributors to the transmission of intellectual level and disability. As would be expected in the case of any hereditarily transmitted trait, the ancestors and contemporary relatives displayed similarities to the identified individual on the characteristic of interest — in this case, IQs that fell in or close to the range of intellectual disability. Thus, persons with this type of intellectual disability are characterized by IQ scores that are typically in the mild, or sometimes moderate, range, as they represent a statistically expected downward extension of the typical IQ range.

The politics of eugenics in conceptualizing intellectual disability associated with familial transmission

The claim that intelligence is hereditary was historically associated with considerable social stigma for those with intellectual disability and for their families (see Rosen et al., 1976; Siperstein et al., 2007; Zigler & Hodapp, 1986). This stigmatization was especially perpetuated by the proponents of the eugenics movement, who, in the late nineteenth century and beginning of the twentieth century, reported on supposed ancestral lines in which 'feeble-mindedness', criminality, and other forms of behavior considered to be generally immoral were linked through the generations. In one notable example, Arthur Estabrooks (1916) used the sociologist Robert Dugdale's (1877, 1910) report on the criminal history of the 'Jukes' family from upstate New York, originally intended to make a case for better social welfare and improved environments, to argue that persons from such families should not be allowed to reproduce.

The claim that allowing persons with intellectual disability to procreate was a detriment to society found its strongest voice in Henry Goddard (1912), a leader of that era's eugenics movement, who argued for the association between 'feeble-mindedness' and heredity in his influential book, *The Kallikak Family: A Study in the Heredity of Feeble-Mindedness*. In a post hoc recreation of the genetic tree of a Revolutionary War hero, Martin Kallikak Sr, Goddard contrasted between the offspring from an evidently 'feeble-minded woman' whom Kallikak met on his way home from the fighting and the offspring from Kallikak's evidently intelligent wife. Goddard claimed that of the 480 descendents from the "feeble-minded" woman, 36 were classified as illegitimate, 33 sexually immoral, 24 confirmed alcoholics, three epileptics, 82 died in infancy, three were criminal, and eight kept houses of ill fame (Goddard, 1912), while all but three of the 496 descendents from Kallikak's wife were considered normal. The latter group of descendants was described as prosperous, morally upstanding, and intellectually normal. Goddard concluded that intelligence, sanity, and morality were hereditary, and those classified as 'feeble-minded' should be prohibited from procreating in order to prevent intellectual disability and its deleterious effects on society. Since its publication, the scientific merits of Goddard's work have been questioned, and factors other than inherited feeble-mindedness, such as fetal alcohol syndrome, have been suggested as possible primary influences in the outcome of many of Kallikak's descendants (Karp et al., 1995). Furthermore, the integrity of the work was questioned, with allegations that the published photos of the Kallikaks were changed in order to make them appear more sinister (Elks, 2005). Yet, Goddard's message of hereditary transmission and intrinsic moral shortcomings of cultural-familial intellectual disability was clearly influential and resonated in the Western world through much of the first half of the twentieth century.

Despite the obviously controversial nature of their work, Goddard's and Estabrook's views on eugenics and intellectual disability (see Fernald, 1919; Lewis, 1933) attained full realization in the United States in the sterilization laws that were passed in 25 states between 1907 and 1936 and in the Supreme Court decision that ruled in support of the sterilization laws in Virginia (for a review, see Zigler & Hodapp, 1986). As Zigler and Hodapp (1986) note, the sentiment of the Supreme Court and that of much of the nation at the time was summed up by the eminent Supreme Court Justice, Oliver Wendell Holmes Jr, who wrote that "three generations of imbeciles are enough" (Buck vs Bell, 1927). The American laws and attitudes of this period were so pernicious that they are even cited by some as sources of inspiration for the sterilization and extermination practices of the Nazis toward Jews, Gypsies, homosexuals, and others (Khul, 2002).

The role of early intelligence testing in delineating hereditarily transmitted intellectual disability

The differentiation between the type of persons whose intellectual disability appeared to be a function of the heredity of low levels of intelligence and those with some type of organic insult was supported by the advent of the use of educational tests to determine cognitive abilities of children at the beginning of the twentieth century. These psychometric tests, such as the one developed by Alfred Binet and Theodore Simon (1905) to select children for special education based on their abilities, were introduced by Goddard (1912) into the United States specifically to diagnose intellectual disabilities. These tests provided some statistically standardized assessments across large populations of children. However, the expected statistical standardization was not entirely realized, as the frequency of intellectual disability did not follow the theoretical predictions based on the normal distribution curve on which IQ scores were based. Whereas the number

of persons with intellectual disability that fell within 2 or 3 SD below the mean was consistent with the approximately 2.5% expected in a normal distribution, the number that fell below 3 SD under the mean was significantly greater than the expected 0.3% (Pearson & Jaederholm, 1914; Penrose, 1970; Roberts et al., 1938). To explain these findings, two distributions of intelligence were proposed (Dingman & Tarjan, 1960), with one reflecting the low end of the normal distribution of IQ and the other a separate population with organic pathological processes that lead to more severe intellectual disability.

Individuals with no discernible cause for their intellectual disability were conceptualized as those who were simply at the low end of the normal distribution of IQ (Lewis, 1933; Pearson & Jaederholm, 1914; Penrose, 1963; Zigler, 1967). They were likely to have at least one parent with an IQ in or near the range of intellectual disability and to be indistinguishable from persons with IQs in the lower end of the typical range (Hodapp & Burack, 2006; Lewis, 1933; Zigler & Hodapp, 1986). Within a given population, scores on the early Binet intelligence tests of school children showed neither a natural split nor significant differences between the children at the lower end of the normal distribution and a group of typical school children (Pearson & Jaederholm, 1914). This point was echoed prominently by Lewis (1933), who noted that there "seems to be a close biological kinship between the subcultural defective and the main body of normal persons…" (p. 300). These types of conceptual, empirical, and statistical arguments for a unique group of persons that is inherently distinct from persons with specific organic etiologies of intellectual disability became a hallmark of the two-group approach that characterized developmental theorizing about intellectual disability and the notion of cultural-familial transmission (e.g. Dingman & Tarjan, 1960; Kephart & Strauss, 1940; Penrose, 1949; Zigler, 1967, 1969).

DEVELOPMENTAL THEORY AND CULTURAL-FAMILIAL INTELLECTUAL DISABILITY

A developmental approach to cognitive processing among persons with cultural-familial intellectual disability

The notion that persons with familially transmitted intellectual disability simply represented the lower end of the typical distribution of IQ scores was the foundation of Zigler's (1967, 1969) application of classic developmental theory to intellectual disability. In response to the so-called 'defect' or 'difference' theorists who dominated research on intellectual disabilities in the 1960s, 1970s, and 1980s with their search for a core deficit of intellectual disability regardless of etiology (for a review, see Burack, 1990). Zigler's developmental approach (Hodapp & Zigler, 1986: Zigler, 1967, 1969) was focused on persons with cultural-familial intellectual disability whom he differentiated from those with organic etiologies. Weisz and colleagues (Weiss et al., 1986; Weisz, 1990; Weisz & Yeates, 1981; Weisz & Zigler, 1979; Weisz, et al., 1982) extended the argument that these persons with cultural-familial intellectual disability simply represented a downward extension of the typical IQ range and argued that their patterns of development would be indistinguishable from those of typically developing persons, even if the rate is slower and the asymptote is lower. This developmental approach entailed two hypotheses of similarities between persons with cultural-familial intellectual disability and typically developing persons. The first hypothesis is the similar-sequence hypothesis, which reflects the basic tenet of developmental theory that the development of a specific area of cognitive functioning necessarily follows a clear, prescribed order of the attainment of abilities (Hodapp & Zigler, 1997). The second hypothesis is the similar-structure hypothesis, which refers to the relations

across areas of functioning with regard to developmental level. Whereas the similar-sequence hypothesis was initially considered to be relevant to all groups of persons with intellectual disabilities (Weisz & Zigler, 1979), the similar-structure hypothesis was specific to those with cultural-familial intellectual disability who would be expected to show the same level of performance on virtually every aspect of cognitive functioning when compared to typically developing persons at a similar general level of functioning (i.e. mental age) (Weiss et al. 1986; Weisz, 1990; Weisz & Yeates, 1981).

In a series of extensive literature reviews, Weisz and colleagues assessed the veracity of both the similar-sequence and similar-structure hypotheses for persons with intellectual disabilities. For the similar-sequence hypothesis, Weisz and Zigler (1979) found that almost all groups of persons with intellectual disabilities, including those with cultural-familial intellectual disability, showed typical Piagetian sequences of development. Although the invariance of the sequences may become less inevitable with social tasks or those that occur later in development (Hodapp & Zigler, 1997), the integrity of normative sequences seems well entrenched among persons with cultural-familial intellectual disability, as it is with virtually all other groups of persons with intellectual disability (for a discussion, see Hodapp & Burack, 2006).

The evaluation of the similar-structure hypothesis among persons with cultural-familial intellectual disability is more complicated than that of the similar-sequence hypothesis. It is based on the notion of typical interrelationships across the various domains of cognitive functioning, with the premise that development unfolds in some universally systematic hierarchic way. Although each individual's pattern of relationships across domains is unique, the variability is typically minimal and consistent within the integrity of the system. Theoretically, this organization is consistent with the conceptualization of meaningful stages that characterize different points in development, and pragmatically, it allows for the delineation of norms that characterize a population at a given age. In this framework, the developmental profile across domains should be, with only minor differences, consistent across persons at any given age. Thus, evidence for the similar-structure hypothesis among persons with cultural-familial intellectual disability is based on support of the null hypothesis — in this case, the finding of no differences in performance on a task between them and typically developing persons matched on general developmental level (i.e. MA).

The similar-structure hypothesis was formulated in direct competition to the difference theories of intellectual disability of the 1960s and 1970s in which the focus was entirely on deficits (Weiss et al., 1986; Weisz & Yeates, 1981), and highlighted the extension of the developmental approach to understanding and studying persons with cultural-familial intellectual disability. With more appropriate methodological techniques, including the utilization of matching by mental age, or developmental level, and by differentiating persons with cultural-familial intellectual disability from those with organic etiologies, the development of persons with cultural-familial disability could be understood as simply delayed rather than as different (Burack et al., 2001). In a first systematic test of the similar-structure hypothesis that entailed an extensive review of comparisons on Piagetian-type tasks, Weisz and Yeates (1981) found that it was supported in 90% of the 39 comparisons between persons with intellectual disability and typically developing persons in which appropriate matching of mental age was used and care was taken to exclude persons with any indication of organic impairments or genetic anomalies. However, in a subsequent analysis of comparisons of performance on information-processing tasks, Weiss et al. (1986) found examples of inferior performance by persons with cultural-familial intellectual disability, as compared to typically developing persons, in the specific information-processing areas

of memory, discrimination learning, and learning set, but not in others, such as concept usage and incidental learning.

Weisz et al.'s review of the similar-structure hypothesis highlights the need for two types of more fine-tuned analyses. One is the more precise study of specific areas of functioning in situations in which homogeneous groupings of persons with cultural-familial intellectual disability are compared to typically developing persons carefully matched on mental age. For example, Iarocci and Burack (1998; see also, Burack et al., 2001) challenged the commonly accepted notion that attention deficits are inherent to intellectual disability with a critical analysis of the relevant literature. They showed that the supposed evidence for the attention-deficit hypothesis was based on flawed studies that were confounded both by effects of organicity with the inclusion of persons with organic etiologies, and by the use of chronological age, rather than mental age, as the basis for matching between groups. However, no evidence for any attention deficit was found in the few studies in which the persons with intellectual disability were homogeneous with regard to cultural-familial status and the groups were matched on the basis of mental age. Weisz et al's review also highlights the need to consider potential sources of any deficits in cognitive functioning that are found among persons with cultural-familial intellectual disability as compared to typically developing persons (Mundy & Kasari, 1990). For example, the differences cited by Weiss et al. are clearly inconsistent with the similar-structure hypothesis, but their implications are diminished because the number of domains in which differences are found are limited and because of extenuating, and potentially confounding, factors in the paradigms. Weiss and colleagues (Weisz, 1990; Weiss et al., 1986) note that differences are only evident in situations in which the tasks were long and repetitive, lacked ecological validity, and in which certain motivational and personality characteristics can affect performance. This is consistent with Zigler's early conceptualization of the effects of a lifetime of experiences of failure by persons with intellectual disability. Weisz (1990) extends this notion and argues that the impaired performance of persons with intellectual disability highlights a 'helpless' style of behavior. Thus, the discrepancies in performance may have been a function of the approach to the task at hand, rather than of inherent differences in cognitive processing (Weiss et al., 1986). More recently, intellectual disability has been discussed within a multi-axial paradigm. This paradigm shift emphasizes the interface of the individual and the environment in a dynamic and developing process. Intellectual impairment is not seen as a trait, but rather as the interaction between a person with limited intellectual and adaptive abilities and the environmental demands.

The recognition of the impact of social and personality characteristics even on performance on cognitive tasks highlights the need to focus on the 'whole' individual with cultural-familial intellectual disability (Zigler, 1999) rather than simply on lower levels of intellectual functioning. In a review of studies of motivational processes among persons with intellectual disabilities, Switzky (2006) emphasized the importance of this area and lamented that 'bearing in mind all the papers written in the last 50 years in the area of intellectual disabilities, the area of individual differences in personality and motivational systems has been neglected' (p. xiii). One person who prioritized these issues was Zigler (1967, 1987) who argued that the concept of social adaptation involves behaviors that do not necessarily stem from intellectual influences, but rather from personality characteristics that are often ignored. He argued that the personality and motivational characteristics of persons with intellectual disability were affected by a lifetime of the experience of being less intelligent and successful than others. For example, Zigler and Burack (1989) specified personality traits such as over-dependency, low self-esteem,

limited mastery motivation, and an outwardly directed approach to problem solving as characteristic of persons with intellectual disability. Weisz's (1990) notion of learned helplessness extends these notions by providing a more clinically relevant framework for understanding the social and emotional development of persons with cultural-familial intellectual disability and their pervasive effects on all aspects of functioning.

Recognition of the effects of these factors is essential at all ages (Lunsky, 2006), as motivational characteristics are the best predictors of the success and integration of persons within the range of mild intellectual disability (for reviews, see McClearn et al., 1997; Zigler & Hodapp, 1986). Despite obvious limitations, many persons with mild intellectual impairment are able to hold jobs, live independently, and even start their own families (Keogh et al., 2004). In this framework, they are clearly part of a sometimes erratic continuum of variation that is shared with typically developing persons with regard to issues of intellectual and non-intellectual characteristics and markers of lifelong adaptation.

THE CULTURAL-FAMILIAL INHERITANCE OF INTELLECTUAL DISABILITY

Based on the notion that persons with cultural-familial intellectual disability represent a downward extension of the natural variation in intellectual ability, a variety of possibilities related to the interplay of the genetic transmission and environmental influences on intelligence in this population have been put forward (for reviews, see Hodapp & Zigler, 1995; Iarocci & Petrill, in press; Simonoff et al., 1998; Zigler & Hodapp, 1986). These include attempts to fine-tune the understanding of both the genetic process in transmission of intelligence and the interplay between intellectual heredity and environmental influences.

The notion of a polygenic model

Consistent with the notion that persons with cultural-familial intellectual disability meld into the typically developing population, polygenic inheritance models are highlighted in the explanations of the transmission of intellectual disability within families (for reviews, see Gottesman, 1963; Iarocci & Petrill, in press; Plomin, 1999a, 1999b, 1999c). According to this framework, many human traits are continuously distributed and are determined by a number of genes that work independently and additively to produce the particular trait whenever normal environmental conditions prevail. Thus, polygenic models are used to address the likelihood of inheritance of particular gene combinations, regardless of environmental impact (Zigler & Hodapp, 1986). Within the framework of genetic and environmental interplay in phenotypic outcome, the primary goal is to identify the polygenes that additively accumulate genetic risk and, together with environmental risk factors, increase an individual's susceptibility to familial intellectual disability.

The interplay of genetic and environmental influences

In order to better understand the impact of familial genetic and environmental influences on low cognitive ability, Richardson et al., (1985) measured the family pedigree factor on the basis of the proportion of the child's relatives who had received services for persons with intellectual disability. They used a five-point scale, ranging from stable to markedly unstable, to measure family stability and infer the degree of psychosocial adversity. Richardson et al. found that psychosocial adversity had a greater impact on IQ when in combination with genetic predisposition, as measured by family pedigree. Jointly, these factors were present in 85% of persons with mild intellectual disability,

indicating a vulnerability to a host of genetic, organic, and environmental risk factors, many of which may be subtle and difficult to detect. Richardson et al. argued against the primacy of either the genetic or environmental causes of intellectual disability, and instead focused on the interplay between them. This is consistent with the notion that intelligence emerges through the coalescence of inherited developmental structures and the organism's ongoing and active engagement with the environment (Fischer & Bullock, 1984; Thelen & Smith, 1998). In this context, intelligence is both structured and malleable, with different possible phenotypes arising from the same genotype in response to varying environmental supports (Fischer, Bullock. Rotenberg & Raya, 1993; Scarr-Salapatek, 1973). It is likened to an elastic band, for which environmental conditions may broaden or constrain inherent potential, but only within the limits of the elasticity, or integrity, of the structure (i.e. inherited familial genes).

This relationship between familial transmission and environmental influence in intellectual disability was examined in a longitudinal study of pre- and perinatal causes of intellectual disabilities by Broman et al. (1987) who sought to differentiate the developmental trajectories of persons with cultural-familial intellectual disability from those with a clear organic etiology. Broman et al. found a 12-fold increase in the frequency of intellectual disability among full siblings of children with mild intellectual disability, and significantly more affected relatives than among the siblings of children with severe intellectual disability. They concluded that mild, but not severe, intellectual disability shows a familial link with normal variation in general intelligence.

When the children were classified according to socioeconomic status (SES), Broman et al. (1987) found that the child's SES level was associated with intellectual disability at 7 years. In the lowest SES group (bottom 25%), 3.3% scored in the intellectual disability range, whereas only 1.3% and 0.3% of children from middle (50%) and high (top 25%) SES groups, respectively, scored in that range. This is consistent with other evidence that mild, non-organic, intellectual disability (IQ-60–69) is noted primarily at lower SES levels, whereas the prevalence of moderate to severe intellectual disability (IQ < 50) is generally evenly distributed across SES levels (Richardson & Koller, 1996). In Broman et al.'s study, the relationship between SES and IQ was even stronger in the African-American groups, for whom 7.8% from the lowest SES, 3.6% from the middle SES, and only 1.2% from the highest SES scored in the range of intellectual disability.

The clear link between low SES and the familial transmission of mild intellectual disability highlights the complexity of disentangling the relative contributions of genetic transmission and environmental factors in cultural-familial intellectual disability. The finding that familiality of IQ and increased risk for intellectual disability is greatest with parents of particularly low IQ (for a review, see Simonoff et al., 1998) reflects the inevitability of the transmission of intellectual disability that was of concern historically to proponents of the eugenics movement and other derisive perspectives on persons with intellectual disability. Yet, this transmission is not simply one of the familial passing of genes, but entails a complex relation between the occurrence of low IQ and the environment in which persons develop. For example, children of parents with intellectual disabilities may be more likely to be raised in environments and situations that are not optimal for development (Simonoff et al., 1998). The parents' limited abilities likely mean life in less affluent neighborhoods and with fewer resources, which is particularly detrimental to these parents who have less capacity to best utilize the available resources. This may be particularly exacerbated among minority populations who may have fewer opportunities to optimize child-rearing situations because of linguistic, cultural, or other idiosyncratic reasons. However, SES should not be confounded with racial or ethnic background, as their independent effects on cognitive ability are not clear (Helms, 1992) and the discrepancies in IQ scores are at least partly due to limitations of the measurement tools which are often culturally biased and particularly problematic when used to assess children from minority cultures (Grados-Johnson & Russo-Garcia, 1999). These qualifications in understanding the occurrence of lower IQs highlight the complexity of understanding either the unique contributions or the confluence of issues related to the genetic heredity of intelligence and environmental effects associated with cultural-familial intellectual disability.

DIAGNOSTIC CRITERIA AND ASSESSMENT

The diagnostic process, guided by the established criteria for defining intellectual disability, facilitates the identification and description of intellectual disability, and establishes an individual's eligibility for services. Through this process, both level of functioning and developmental rate are gauged, and information relevant to remediation and educational planning is provided. However, the process is not without its limitations (Charman et al., 2008). For example, a disproportionate number of minority children are diagnosed with mild intellectual disability, as intelligence tests may underestimate the abilities of minority children who often fail to meet the dominant culture's expectations concerning performance in academic settings (Hays, 2001; Mercer, 1973; Valencia & Suzuki, 2001). Because of concerns regarding the narrow focus of intelligence tests and their use as an exclusive vehicle for defining intellectual disability, the American Association of Intellectual and Developmental Disabilities (AAIDD) emphasizes the importance of adaptive behavior as well as cognitive functioning in its definition of intellectual disability (Borthwick-Duffy, 2007). In addition, other non-cognitive factors that might inhibit a child's performance on IQ tests, including the child's health history, physical impairments, motivation levels, and social milieu, must be considered when assessing intellectual abilities. Although the compilation of information from various sources and the inclusion of non-cognitive features are particularly important when service provision is dependent on ascertaining a clear diagnosis, in practice it is not always true that both intellectual and adaptive functioning are included in the criteria of intellectual impairment. In practice, many services use only an IQ score cutoff, without noting the level of adaptive functioning. The result is that people are often denied help and services simply because they have an IQ score over 70; regardless of their severe problems in other areas of functioning. The integration of information, including various areas of functioning and background variables, is essential in the assessment of cultural-familial intellectual impairment as the familial concordance and environmental variables are necessary for ruling out other explanations for decreased intellectual and adaptive functioning.

Today, traditional methods of examining cognitive and adaptive abilities are supplemented with a thorough examination of the child's developmental history, family history, and social and cultural environment. A broader picture of the child's developmental status is obtained with parent and teacher interviews and evaluations of medical and school records. For example, information about the child's physical problems, peer interactions, social skills, and emotional state can be productively used in conjunction with more formal assessment methods, despite their somewhat limited reliability and validity. Consequently, within the framework of a multifactorial model of assessment, the evaluation of intellectual disability is increasingly taking place within an interdisciplinary social developmental framework.

The emphasis is on providing a diagnosis as early as possible in order to identify a child's specific needs, to ascertain the required services, and to facilitate communication across professional disciplines and among family members. However, this process can also stigmatize the child if it creates unwarranted negative projections by professionals and parents regarding the child's potential. Thus, professionals need to be sensitive to the effects and limitations of labels, and recognize that intellectual disability is only one aspect of an individual.

A comprehensive assessment program needs to follow the individual throughout the developmental period. Current social and behavioral models are characterized by emphasis on the need for repeated assessments to evaluate the child's changing developmental status and needs, the impact of medical treatments, the appropriateness of educational placements, and the effectiveness of educational programming. This approach to assessment captures the dynamic and changing quality of development, as well as its social nature, as individuals with intellectual disability vary not only in their cognitive functioning but also in physical and emotional characteristics.

Tools for the assessment of cognitive development and adaptive behavior

The multi-disciplinary assessment approach to intellectual disability should include a battery of tests and an assortment of techniques. The correct choice of tests and the interpretations of the results comprise an essential component in establishing projected levels of ability. Most of the tools typically used in the assessment of cognitive and adaptive behavior were not developed specifically for use with individuals with intellectual disability, but have been found to be appropriate for use with this group, albeit not without limitations (for a review, see Charman et al., 2008).

Tests of cognitive development
The Bayley Scales of Infant Development — Second Edition (Bayley, 1993) is an individually administered instrument for

assessing the development of infants and very young children (aged 2 months to $3\frac{1}{2}$ years old). It is composed of the Mental, Motor, and Behavior rating scales, with subscales in each. The Mental scale is used to assess recognition memory, object permanence, shape discrimination, sustained attention, purposeful manipulation of objects, imitation (vocal/verbal, gestural), verbal comprehension, vocalization, early language skills, short-term memory, problem solving, counting, and expressive vocabulary. The Motor scale is used to assess the areas of gross and fine motor abilities in a relatively traditional manner, and the Behavior rating scale is used to rate the child's behavior and emotional status throughout the assessment. The raw scores of the Mental and Motor scales are converted to standard scores with a mean of 100 and an SD of 15, whereas the Behavior rating scores are interpreted by the use of percentile ranks. The Bayley Scales are one of the most widely used infant assessment tools and have been used with children older than $3\frac{1}{2}$ years who have significant developmental delays and cannot be evaluated using tools appropriate for their chronological ages.

The McCarthy Scales of Children's Abilities (McCarthy, 1972) are used with children between the ages of $2\frac{1}{2}$ and $8\frac{1}{2}$ years of age, and include verbal, perceptual-performance, quantitative, memory, motor, and general cognitive scales. In addition to yielding a General Cognitive Index (GCI), the McCarthy Scales provide several ability profiles, such as verbal, non-verbal reasoning, and number aptitude. The overall GCI has a mean of 100 and an SD of 16 and is an estimate of the child's ability to apply accumulated knowledge to the tasks assessed in the test. The ability profiles, which are specific to this instrument, make this a useful tool for assessing young children with intellectual disabilities. However, the GCI is not interchangeable with the IQ score rendered by standardized intellectual assessment instruments such as the Wechsler Scales,

and therefore caution should be exercised in making placement decisions based solely on the GCI in the case of children with intellectual disability.

The Differential Ability Scale (DAS: Elliot, 1990) consists of a battery of individually administered cognitive and achievement tests subdivided into three age ranges: lower pre-school ($2\frac{1}{2}$ years to 3 years 5 months); upper pre-school ($3\frac{1}{2}$ years to 5 years 11 months); and elementary school (6 years to 17 years 11 months). The cognitive battery is focused on reasoning and conceptual abilities and is interpreted as a composite score, referred to as the General Composite Ability (GCA). Verbal and non-verbal cluster standard scores and individual subtest standard scores can also be calculated. The advantages of the DAS over other instruments that are employed to assess cognitive abilities in individuals with intellectual disabilities include a built-in mechanism for assessing significantly delayed children who are older than $3\frac{1}{2}$ years. It can also provide information comparable to that provided by other similar instruments in about half the time, is well standardized, and correlates highly with other cognitive measures.

The Wechsler tests are used at different points in the life span: the Wechsler Pre-school and Primary Scale of Intelligence—Third Edition (WPPSI-III: Wechsler, 2002) is used with children ranging in age from 3 years to 7 years and 3 months; the Wechsler Scale for Children—Fourth Edition (WISC-IV: Wechsler, 2003) with children aged 6 to 16 years; and the Wechsler Adult Intelligence Scale—Fourth Edition (WAIS-IV: Wechsler, 2008) with adolescents older than 16 years and adults. Each of these tests has a mean of 100 and an SD of 15, with scaled scores with a mean of 10 and an SD of 3 for each subtest. The 12 subtests are divided into two overall domains of Verbal and Performance. The six Verbal subtests are information, similarities, arithmetic, vocabulary, comprehension, and the optional sentences; and the six Performance subtests are picture completion, geometric design, block design, mazes, object assembly, and the optional animal pegs. In all the Wechsler tests, separate IQ scores can be calculated for verbal, performance, and full-scale IQs.

The Stanford–Binet Fifth Edition (SB5: Roid, 2003) is appropriate for use with individuals ranging in age from 2 to 85+ years, and in its present revision includes 10 subtests. The test provides a full-scale IQ, a nonverbal IQ, a verbal IQ, and an Abbreviated Battery IQ. The SB5 yields scaled scores that are similar to domain scores in the Wechsler tests, but are divided differently. In addition to general intelligence, the five factors of cognitive ability in the SB5 are fluid reasoning, knowledge, quantitative reasoning, visual-spatial processing, and working memory. As in the Wechsler tests, there is a mean of 100 and an SD of 15.

The Leiter International Performance Scale-Revised (Leiter-R: Roid & Miller, 1997) is a non-verbal test of intelligence and cognitive abilities that can be administered to children from 2 years of age to adults 20 years and 11 months of age. The Leiter-R consists of nationally standardized batteries of a revision of the original Visualization and Reasoning domains for measuring IQ and the new tests of the Attention and Memory domains. Both batteries include unique growth scores that are used to measure small but essential improvement in children with significant cognitive disabilities. Because the Leiter-R is non-verbal, it is especially suitable for children and adolescents who are cognitively delayed, from lower SES backgrounds, non-verbal, non-English speakers, non-Native English speakers, have attention-deficit/hyperactivity disorder (ADHD), or are speech-, hearing- or motor-impaired. It includes 20 subtests organized into the domains of Reasoning, Visualization, Memory, and Attention.

The interpretation of results of intellectual assessments, administered according to the standardized procedures, requires the consideration of cultural, situational, and psychological factors that may influence test performance. Situational factors that may partially explain performance levels or patterns include overt behaviors, emotionality, attentiveness, distractibility, mannerisms, preferred language, and motor issues (Coolican et al., 2008; Morgenstern & Klass, 1991). Because the use of standardized testing does not always reflect the abilities of individuals raised in different cultures or in disadvantaged circumstances, three strategies have been suggested to guard against misclassifying children as suffering from mild intellectual impairment based on cultural and linguistic artifacts, aside from the necessity of testing in the child's preferred language. One strategy is to develop compensation for cultural test bias. A second strategy is to employ a more stringent cutoff score as the intellectual performance criterion. A third strategy is to apply criteria that relate to both intellectual and adaptive functioning instead of relying principally on IQ scores. In all cases, the tester must consider the limitations of interpretations based solely on such scores and be aware that genetic background, medical, psychological, and environmental factors interact to determine the degree of cognitive and adaptive disability (Borkowski et al., 2007).

Tests of adaptive functioning

Within the context of the later diagnostic systems that are oriented toward a more comprehensive assessment of the entire individual, adaptive functioning is now an integral component in the diagnosis and assessment of intellectual disability. Adaptive behavior can be conceptualized as the degree of association between behavioral performance and cultural expectations. Although intellectual and adaptive performance are related, adaptive behavior is separate and only moderately correlated with measures of intelligence and school achievement (see Cicchetti et al., 1991). For example, Terrasi and Airasian (1989) found two distinct factors of intelligence and adaptive functioning when they performed a factor analysis based on intellectual performance and adaptive behavioral scores. There is a social element at the base of adaptive functioning that dovetails with the use of skills in everyday life and the ability to function successfully within the various social frameworks with which individuals come in contact on a daily basis. Thus, adaptive functioning refers primarily to the performance of individuals as they interact with the environment.

Social competence is often incorporated into the adaptive behavior measures, and development or impairment of adaptive behavior performance is recognized as socially mediated, along with such constraints as maturation, learning, and personal independence. Social standards are applied as a basis for stipulating adaptive functioning and reflect the effectiveness with which an individual can cope with the social and personal demands of the environment (Bensberg & Irons, 1986). Proficient coping leads to experiences of success (Terrasi & Airasian, 1989), as the individual becomes more independent, as reflected in meeting personal needs and engaging in age-appropriate behavior.

The assessment of adaptive behavior is focused on the manner in which individuals function and maintain themselves independently and how well they meet the personal and social demands imposed upon them by their cultures. The most widely used instrument is the Vineland Adaptive Behavior Scales (VABS) Second Edition (Vineland-II: Sparrow et al., 2005), a recent revision of the much-used 1984 version of the VABS, which was originally developed to assess the social competence of individuals with and without disabilities (Sparrow et al., 1984). The revised version has been expanded to include the entire lifespan of individuals with intellectual and developmental disabilities, has updated norms, and can be administered in the form of a survey interview, parent/caregiver rating form, expanded interview form, or teacher rating form. As is evident from these formats, the information is collected from a respondent familiar with the behavior of the individual rather than on direct assessment. The

scores are interpreted in different domains and as an overall adaptive behavior composite, with mean standard scores of 100 and SD of 15. The domains measured by the Vineland-II are Communication (subdomains of receptive, expressive, and written); Daily Living Skills (subdomains of personal, domestic, community); Socialization (subdomains of interpersonal relationships, play and leisure time, coping skills), and for children aged 6 years or less, Motor Skills. The three primary domains correspond to the Conceptual, Practical, and Social domains of adaptive functioning that are identified by the AAIDD. There is also an optional maladaptive behavior index (subdomains of internalizing, externalizing, other), in which the behaviors are intended to relate to those that interfere with adaptive functioning

The American Association on Mental Retardation (AAMR) Adaptive Behavior Scale (ABS) has two forms which are used to address survival skills and maladaptive behaviors of individuals living in residential and community settings (ABS-RC: Nihira et al., 1993) or school-age children (ABS-S: Lambert et al., 1993). It is limited in scope, but the results of this assessment can be readily translated into objectives for intervention.

An additional method for assessing adaptive behavior is the Gunzberg Progressive Assessment Charts (Gunzberg, 1972) which record development in four areas of adaptive functioning, similar to those in the Vineland: self-help, communication, socialization, and occupation. The skills are recorded on charts which provide a visual representation of the profile, emphasizing both skills and deficit areas. Separate charts have been established for different ages and levels of functioning. The Primary Progress Assessment Chart (PPAC) is appropriate for very young children or profoundly handicapped people, while the Progress Assessment Chart 1 (PAC1) is appropriate for children 6–16 years old with a modified version (M/PAC1) for children with Down syndrome. Progress Assessment Chart 2 (PAC2) targets teenagers and older intellectually impaired people. This tool stresses ongoing evaluation and can be used to set goals for intervention.

DIFFERENTIAL DIAGNOSIS AND COMORBID CONDITIONS

The prevalence of associated psychiatric disorders is three to four times greater among persons with intellectual disability than in the general population, and the full spectrum of recognized psychiatric disorders can be found in this group (Bouras & Holt, 2004). Chart reviews reveal that psychotic disorders are overdiagnosed, while anxiety, affective, and personality disorders are under-recognized (Whitaker & Read, 2006). Consistent with the notion that persons with non-specific intellectual disability represent persons with intellectual disability at the lower end of the typical bell curve, children and adults with mild to moderate intellectual disabilities manifest profiles of psychiatric symptoms and disorders similar to those found among their typically developing peers (Chaplin, 2009). These include attention-deficit disorders, hyperactivity, conduct disorders, anxiety disorders, obsessive-compulsive disorders, affective disorders, and schizophrenia (Whitaker & Read, 2006).

SUMMARY

The term non-specific intellectual disability is difficult to characterize as it is primarily defined by what it is not. It is not any of the more than 1000 identifiable disorders associated with intellectual disability; rather, it entails intellectual disability for which there is no identifiable organic or physical origin — or, at least, none that has been identified yet. Thus, it is a classification for a group of persons that has consistently diminished for more than a century because of increasingly sophisticated medical and scientific advances that have led to the identification of different origins of intellectual disability and to more finely-tuned technology that has allowed for the identification of previously undiagnosed persons. Conversely, with the reduction in numbers, this group has become more homogeneous, with the vast majority likely to be from the group that was historically recognized as those who have inherited low intellectual ability. Thus, members of this group can be positively identified by having low IQ and one or both parents with the same characteristic. Throughout this chapter we have referred to these persons as those with cultural-familial intellectual disability and viewed their intellectual disability as the outcome of intellectual heredity and environmental influence, although issues such as cultural context, motivation, and personality must also be considered. Over the past 50 years, this group of persons with non-specific, or cultural-familial, intellectual disability has become an important link in the study of the heritability of intelligence and the effect of environment on the intellectual, social, and emotional development of all individuals.

ACKNOWLEDGMENTS

The work on this chapter was supported by a grant from the Social Sciences and Humanities Research Council of Canada to Jacob A. (Jake) Burack. The authors thank the following members of the McGill Youth Study Team (MYST) who helped in the preparation of the manuscript: Fabienne Bain, Kira Barey, Michael D'Abate, Alexandra D'Arrisso, Jacqueline Hodgson, Janice LaGiorgia, and Ariel Stee. The authors thank Tamara Fitch for editing several drafts of the manuscript. The authors thank the editors for the invitation to contribute to this important volume and for their constructive feedback on an earlier draft.

REFERENCES

AAMR (2002) *Mental Retardation: Definition, Classification, and Systems of Supports*, 10th edn. Washington, DC: American Association for Mental Retardation.

Bayley N. (1993) *Bayley Scales of Infant Development*, (2nd edn.) San Antonio, TX: Psychological Corporation.

Bensberg, G. & Irons, T. (1986) 'A comparison of the AAMD Adaptive Behavior Scale and the Vineland Adaptive Behavior Scales within a sample of persons classified as moderately and severely retarded', *Education and Training of the Mentally Retarded*, 21(3): 220–228.

Binet, A. & Simon, T. (1905) 'Application of the new methods to the diagnosis of the intellectual level among normal and subnormal children in institutions and in the primary schools', *L'annee psychologique*, 12: 245–336.

Borkowski, J.G., Carothers, S.S., Howard, K., Schatz, J., & Farris, J.R. (2007) 'Intellectual assessment and intellectual disability', in J.W. Jacobson, J.A. Mulick, & J. Rojahn (eds), *Handbook of Intellectual and Developmental Disabilities*. New York: Springer Press, pp. 261–277.

Borthwick-Duffy, S.A. (2007) 'Adaptive behavior', in J.W. Jacobson, J.A., Mulick, & J. Rojahn, (eds) *Handbook of Intellectual and Developmental Disabilities*. New York: Springer, pp. 279–293.

Bouras, N. & Holt, G. (2004) 'Mental health services for adults with learning disabilities', *British Journal of Psychiatry*, 184: 291–292.

Broman, S., Nichols, P.L., Shaughnessy, P., & Kennedy, W. (1987) *Retardation in Young Children: A Developmental Study of Cognitive Deficit*. Hillsdale, NJ: Erlbaum.

Burack, J.A. (1990) 'Differentiating mental retardation: the two group approach and beyond', in J.A. Burack, R.M. Hodapp, and E. Zigler (eds), *Issues in the Developmental Approach to Mental Retardation*. New York: Cambridge University Press, pp. 27–48.

Burack, J.A., Evans, D.W., Klaiman, C., & Iarocci, G. (2001) 'The mysterious myth of attentional deficit and other defect stories: contemporary issues in the developmental approach to mental retardation', *International Review of Research in Mental Retardation*, 24: 300–321.

Charman, T., Hood, J., & Howlin. P. (2008) 'Psychological assessment in the clinical context', in M. Rutter, D. Bishop, D. Pine, S. Scott, J.S. Stevenson, E.A. Taylor, & A. Thapar (eds), *Rutter's Child and Adolescent Psychiatry*, 5th edn. Oxford: Blackwell Scientific, pp. 299–316.

Chaplin, R. (2009) 'New research into general psychiatric services for adults with intellectual disability and mental illness', *Journal of Intellectual Disabilities Research*, 53(3): 189–199.

Cicchetti, D.V., Sparrow, S.S., & Rourke, B.P. (1991) 'Adaptive behavior profiles of psychologically disturbed and developmentally disabled children', in J.L. Matson & J.A. Mulick (eds), *Handbook of Mental Retardation*, 2nd edn. New York: Pergamon Press, pp. 222–239.

Coolican, J., Bryson, S., & Zwaigenbaum. L. (2008) 'Brief report: data on the Stanford-Binet Intelligence Scales (5th ed.) in children with autism spectrum disorder', *Journal of Autism and Developmental Disorders*, 38(1): 190–197.

Dingman, H.F. & Tarjan, G. (1960) 'Mental retardation and the normal distribution curve', *American Journal of Mental Deficiency*, 64: 991–994.

Down, J.L.H. (1886) 'Observations on an ethnic classification of idiots', *Clinical Lecture Reports, London Hospital*, 3: 259–262.

Down, J.L.H. (1887) *Mental Affections of Children and Youth*. London: J. & A. Churchill.

Dugdale, R.L. (1877) *'The Jukes': A Study in Crime, Pauperism, Disease, and Heredity*. New York and London: G.P. Putnam's Sons.

Dugdale, R.L. (1910*) 'The Jukes': A Study in Crime, Pauperism, Disease, and Heredity*, 4th edn. New York: Putnam.

Elks, B.W. (2005) *A Theory of Run-Time Verification for Safety Critical Reactive Systems*. Charlottesville, VA: University of Virginia.

Elliott, C.D. (1990) *The Differential Ability Scales. Introductory and Technical Handbook*. San Antonio, TX: Psychological Corporation.

Estabrooks, A.H. (1916) *The Jukes in 1915*. Washington: The Carnegie Institution of Washington.

Fernald, W.E. (1919) 'A state program for the care of the mentally defective', *Mental Hygiene*, 3: 566–574.

Fischer, K.W. & Bullock, D. (1984) 'Cognitive development in school-age children: conclusions and new directions', in W.A. Collins (ed.), *Development During Middle Childhood: The Years from Six to Twelve*. Washington, DC: National Academy Press, pp. 70–146.

Fischer, K. W., Bullock, D. H., Rotenberg, E. J., & Raya, P. (1993) *The dynamics of competence: How context contributes directly to skill. Development in Context*, (pp. 93–117). Hillsdale, NJ: Erlbaum.

Goddard, H.H. (1912) *The Kallikak Family: A Study in the Heredity of Feeble-Mindedness*. New York: The Macmillan Company.

Gottesman, I.I. (1963) 'Heritability of personality: a demonstration'. *Psychological Monographs,* 77(9): 1–21.

Grados-Johnson, J. & Russo-Garcia, K.A. (1999) 'Comparison of the Kaufman Brief Intelligence Test and the Wechsler Intelligence Scale for Children-Third Edition in economically disadvantaged African American youth', *Journal of Clinical Psychology,* 55(9): 1063–1071.

Gunzberg, H.C. (1972) *Progress Assessment Charts (PAC) Manual.* Birmingham: SEFA Publishing.

Hays, P.A. (2001) 'Putting culture to the test: considerations with standardized testing', in P.A. Hays (ed.), *Addressing Cultural Complexities in Practice: A Framework for Counselors and Clinicians.* Washington, DC: American Psychological Association, pp. 11–127.

Helms, J.E. (1992) 'Why is there no study of cultural equivalence in standardized cognitive-ability testing', *American Psychologist,* 47: 1083–1101.

Hodapp, R.M. & Burack, J.A. (2006) 'Mental retardation', in D. Cicchetti & D.J. Cohen (eds), *Developmental Psychopathology, Vol. 3: Risk, Disorder, and Adaptation.* New York: Wiley, pp. 235–267.

Hodapp, R.M. & Dykens, E.M. (2001) 'Strengthening behavioral research on genetic mental retardation disorders', *American Journal on Mental Retardation,* 106(1): 4–15.

Hodapp, R.M. & Zigler, E. (1986) 'Definition and classification of mental retardation—comments', *American Journal of Mental Deficiency,* 91: 117–119.

Hodapp, R.M. & Zigler, E. (1995) 'Past, present, and future issues in the developmental approach to mental retardation and developmental disabilities', in D. Cicchetti & D.J. Cohen (eds), *Developmental Psychopathology, Vol. 2: Risk, Disorder and Adaptation.* Oxford: John Wiley & Sons.

Hodapp, R.M., Burack, J.A., & Zigler, E. (1990) 'The developmental perspective in the field of mental retardation', in R.M. Hodapp, J.A. Burack, & E. Zigler (eds), *Issues in the Developmental Approach to Mental Retardation.* New York: Cambridge University Press, pp. 3–26.

Hodapp, R., & Zigler, E. (1997) 'New issues in the developmental approach to mental retardation', in W.E. MacLean (ed), *Ellis' Handbook of Mental Deficiency, Psychological Theory and Research, 3rd Edition.* New Jersey: Lawrence Earlbaum Associates, Inc.

Iarocci, G. & Burack, J.A. (1998) 'Understanding the development of persons with mental retardation: challenging the myths', in J.A. Burack, R.M. Hodapp, E. Zigler (eds), *Handbook of Mental Retardation and Development.* New York: Cambridge University Press, pp. 349–381.

Iarocci, G. & Petrill, S. (in press) 'Behavioral genetics, genomics, intelligence, and mental retardation', in J.A. Burack, R.M. Hodapp, G. Iarocci, and E. Zigler (eds), *Handbook of Intellectual Disability and Development,* 2nd edn. New York : Oxford University Press.

Ireland, W.W. (1877) *On Idiocy and Imbecility.* London: J. & A. Churchill.

Jacobson, J.W., Mulick, J.A., & Rojahn, J. (eds) (2007) *Handbook of Intellectual and Developmental Disabilities.* New York: Springer.

Karp, R.J., Quasi, Q.H., Moller K.A., Angelo, W.A., & Davis, J.M. (1995) 'Fetal alcohol syndrome', at the turn of the 20th century: an unexpected explanation of the Kallikak family', *Archives of Pediatrics & Adolescent Medicine,* 149(1): 45–48.

Keogh, B.K., Berheimer, L.P., & Guthrie, D. (2004) 'Children with developmental delays twenty years later: Where are they? How are they?' *American Journal on Mental Retardation,* 109(3): 219–230.

Kephart, N.C. & Strauss, A.A. (1940) 'A clinical factor influencing variations in IQ', *American Journal of Orthopsychiatry,* 10: 343–351.

Khul, S. (2002) *The Nazi Connection: Eugenics, American Racism, and German National Socialism.* Oxford: Oxford University Press.

Lambert, N., Nihira, K., & Leland, H. (1993) *AAMR Adaptive Behavior Scale: School (ABS– S:2).* Austin, TX: PRO-ED.

Lewis, E.O. (1933) 'Types of mental deficiency and their social significance', *Journal of Mental Science,* 79: 298–304.

Lunsky, Y. (2006) 'Individual differences in interpersonal relationships for persons with mental retardation', in H.N. Switzky (ed.), *Mental Retardation, Personality, and Motivational Systems Volume 31 in International Review of Research in Mental Retardation.* Boston, MA: Elsevier Academic Press, pp. 117–161.

McCarthy, D. (1972) *McCarthy Scales of Children's Abilities.* New York: Psychological Corporation.

McClearn, G.E., Johansson, B., Berg, S., Pedersen, N.L., Ahern, F., Petrill, S.A., & Plomin, R. (1997) 'Substantial genetic influence on cognitive abilities in twins 80 or more years old', *Science,* 276(5318): 1560–1563.

MacLean, W.M. (ed.) (1997) *Ellis' Handbook of Mental Deficiency, Psychological Theory and Research,* 3rd edn. Mahwah, NJ: Lawrence Erlbaum Associates.

Matson, J.L. & Boisjoli, J.A. (2009) 'An overview of developments in research on persons with intellectual disabilities', *Research in Developmental Disability,* 30: 587–591.

Mercer, J.R. (1973) *Labeling the Mentally Retarded: Clinical and Social Systems Perspectives in Mental Retardation.* Berkeley, CA: University of California Press.

Morgenstern, M. & Klass, E. (1991) 'Standard Intelligence tests and related assessment techniques', in J.L. Matson and J.A. Mulick (eds), *Handbook of Mental Retardation,* 2nd edn. New York: Pergamon Press. pp. 195–210.

Mundy, P. & Kasari, C. (1990) 'The similar-structure hypothesis and differential rate of development in mental retardation', in R.M. Hodapp, J.A. Burack, and E. Zigler (eds), *Issues in the Developmental Approach to Mental Retardation.* New York: Cambridge University Press, pp. 71–92.

Nihira, K., Leland, H., & Lambert, N. (1993) *AAMR Adaptive Behavior Scales, Residential and Community Edition,* 2nd edn. Austin, TX: PRO-ED.

Pearson, K. & Jaederholm, G.A. (1914) *On the Continuity of Mental Defect.* London: Dalau & Co.

Penrose, L.S. (1963) 'Measurements of likeness in relatives of trisomics', *Annals of Human Genetics,* 27(2): 183–187.

Penrose, L.S. (1949) *The Biology of Mental Defect.* London: Sidgwick and Jackson.

Penrose, L.S. (1970) 'Measurement in mental deficiency', *British Journal of Psychiatry,* 116(533): 369–375.

Plomin, R. (1999a) 'Genetic research on general cognitive ability as a model for mild mental retardation', *International Review of Psychiatry,* 11(1): 34–36.

Plomin, R. (1999b) 'Genetics and general cognitive ability', *Nature,* 402(6761 Suppl): C25–29.

Plomin, R. (1999c) 'Genetics of childhood disorders: genetics and intelligence', *Journal of the American Academy of Child and Adolescent Psychiatry,* 38(6): 786–788.

Richardson, S.A. & Koller, H. (1996) *Twenty-Two Years: Causes and Consequences of Mental Retardation.* Cambridge, MA: Harvard University Press.

Richardson, S.A., Koller, H., & Katz, M. (1985) 'Relationship of upbringing to later behavior disturbance of mildly mentally retarded young people', *American Journal of Mental Deficiency,* 90(1): 1–8.

Roberts, J.A., Norman, R.M., & Griffiths, R. (1938) 'Studies on a child population. IV. The form of the lower end of the frequency distribution of Stanford-Binet intelligence quotients with advancing age', *Annals of Eugenics,* 8: 319.

Roid, G. (2003) *Stanford-Binet Intelligence Scales: Fifth Edition.* Itasca, IL: Riverside Publishing.

Roid, G. & Miller L. (1997) *Leiter International Performance Scale-Revised.* Wood Dale, IL: Stoelting.

Rosen, M., Clark, G.R., & Kivitz, M.S. (eds) (1976) *The History of Mental Retardation: Vol. 1.* Baltimore, MD: University Park Press.

Schalock, R.L., Luckasson, R.A., Shogren, K.A., Borthwick-Duffy, S., Bradley, V., Buntinx, W.H.E., Coulter, D.L., Craig, E.M., Gomez, S.C., Lachapelle, Y., Reeve, A., Snell, M.E., Spreat, S., Tasse, M.J., Thompson, J.R., Verdugo, M.A., Wehmeyer, M.L., & Yeager, M.H., (2007) 'The renaming of mental retardation: understanding the change to the term intellectual disability', *Intellectual and Developmental Disabilities,* 45: 116–124.

Scarr-Salapetek, S. (1973) 'Unknowns in the IQ equation', in F. Rebelsky & L. Dorman (eds), *Child Development and Behavior,* 2nd edn. Oxford: Alfred A. Knopf.

Simonoff, E., Bolton, P., & Rutter, M. (1998) 'Genetic perspectives on mental retardation', in J.A. Burack & R.M. Hodapp (eds), *Handbook of Mental Retardation and Development.* New York: Cambridge University Press, pp. 41–79.

Siperstein, G.N., Norkins, J., & Mohler, A. (2007) 'Social acceptance & attitude change', in J.W. Jacobson, J.A., Mulick & J. Rojahn (eds), *Handbook of Intellectual and Developmental Disabilities.* New York: Springer, pp. 133–154.

Sparrow, S., Balla, D., & Cicchetti, D. (1984) *Vineland Adaptive Behavior Scales.* Circle Pines, MN: AGS.

Sparrow, S., Cicchetti, D., & Balla, D. (2005) *Vineland Adaptive Behavior Scales, Second Edition (Vineland-II).* Circle Pines, MN: AGS.

Switzky, H.N. (2006) *Mental Retardation, Personality, and Motivational Systems. Volume 31 in International Review of Research in Mental Retardation.* Boston, MA: Elsevier Academic Press.

Terrasi, S. & Airasian, P.W. (1989) 'The relationship between adaptive behavior and intelligence for special needs students', *Psychology in the Schools,* 26(2): 202–208.

Thelen, E. & Smith, L.B. (1998) 'Dynamic systems theories', in W. Damon and R.M. Lerner (eds), *Handbook of Child Psychology,* 5th edn. Vol. 1. New York: Wiley, pp. 563–633.

Valencia, R.R. & Suzuki, L.A. (2001) *Intelligence Testing and Minority Students: Foundations, Performance and Assessment Issues.* Thousand Oaks, CA: Sage Publications.

Wechsler, D. (2002) *Wechsler Preschool and Primary Scale of Intelligence—Third Edition.* San Antonio, TX: Psychological Corporation.

Wechsler, D. (2003) *Wechsler Intelligence Scale for Children—Fourth Edition.* San Antonio, TX: Psychological Corporation.

Wechsler, D. (2008) *WAIS-IV Manual: Wechsler Adult Intelligence Scale—Fourth Edition*. New York: Psychological Corporation.

Weiss, B., Weisz, J.R., & Bromfield, R. (1986) 'Performance of retarded and nonretarded persons on information-processing tasks: further tests of the similar structure hypothesis', *Psychological Bulletin,* 100: 157–175.

Weisz, J.R. (1990) 'Cultural-familial mental retardation: a developmental perspective on cognitive performance and "helpless" behavior', in R.M. Hodapp, J.A. Burack, & E. Zigler (eds), *Issues in the Developmental Approach to Mental Retardation*. New York: Cambridge University Press. pp. 137–168.

Weisz, J.R. & Yeates, K.O. (1981) 'Cognitive development in retarded and nonretarded persons: Piagetian tests of the similar structure hypothesis', *Psychological Bulletin,* 90(1): 153–178.

Weisz, J.R. & Zigler, E. (1979) 'Cognitive development in retarded and nonretarded persons: Piagetian tests of the similar sequence hypothesis', *Psychological Bulletin,* 86(4): 831–851.

Weisz, J.R., Yeates, K.O., & Zigler, E. (1982) 'Piagetian evidence and the developmental-difference controversy', in E. Zigler & D.A. Balla (eds), *Mental Retardation,* the Developmental-Difference Controversy. Hillsdale, NJ: Lawrence Erlbaum Associates, pp. 213–269.

Whitaker, S. & Read, S. (2006) 'The prevalence of psychiatric disorders among people with intellectual disabilities: an analysis of the literature', *Journal of Applied Research in Intellectual Disabilities,* 19(4): 330–345.

Zigler, E. (1967) 'Familial mental retardation: a continuing dilemma', *Science,* 155(3760): 292–298.

Zigler, E. (1969) 'Developmental versus difference theories of mental retardation and the problem of motivation', *American Journal of Mental Deficiency,* 73: 536–556.

Zigler, E. (1987) 'Formal school for four-year-olds? No', *American Psychologist,* 42(3): 254–260.

Zigler, E. (1999) 'The individual with mental retardation as a whole person', in E. Zigler & D. Bennett-Gates (eds), *Personality Development in Individuals with Mental Retardation*. New York: Cambridge University Press, pp. 1–16.

Zigler, E. & Burack, J.A. (1989) 'Personality development and the dually diagnosed person', *Research in Developmental Disabilities,* 10(3): 225–240.

Zigler, E. & Hodapp, R.M. (1986) *Understanding Mental Retardation*. New York: Cambridge University Press.

19

Intellectual Disability: Lifetime Course and Strategies for Intervention

Jane McCarthy & Nick Bouras

INTRODUCTION

People with non-specific intellectual disability are identified as a group with impairment of intellectual and adaptive function for which no identifiable genetic or chromosomal or environmental cause has been found. Progress in diagnosis and identification of new disorders will mean many more people with non-specific intellectual disability will receive a genetic diagnosis in the future. Therefore, this is a heterogeneous group and so the lifetime trajectories vary considerably, depending to some extent on the severity of the impairment of intellectual and social functioning.

The term intellectual disability as used in this chapter is synonymous with mental retardation, learning disability, intellectual disabilities and developmental disability. The International Classification of Diseases 10 (ICD-10) (World Health Organization (WHO),1992) and *Diagnostic and Statistical*

Manual of Mental Disorders (DSM-IV) (American Psychiatric Association (APA), 2000) are the diagnostic classification systems most often used to refer to intellectual disability. Both these classifications system use the term 'mental retardation' to refer to intellectual disability and distinguish four degrees of functioning according to level of intelligence quotient (IQ). The WHO classification uses the following categories: mild, IQ 50–70; moderate, IQ 35–49; severe, IQ 20–34; and profound, IQ <20.

This chapter focuses on lifetime trajectories from infancy to adulthood in relation to social integration and physical health, with emphasis on the mental health needs of individuals with non-specific intellectual disability. Psychological and medical interventions are reviewed and a brief overview of educational, social and occupational interventions is also undertaken. Risk factors for mental ill-health and how they impact on outcomes for the individual with intellectual disability will be highlighted. Finally, we offer a description of future challenges plus the impact of research to improve outcomes and the quality of life of people with non-specific intellectual disability.

SOCIAL INTEGRATION—CHILDHOOD TO ADULT LIFE

Prospective studies are the most informative means of understanding the developmental trajectory of behaviour and skill acquisition. These studies provide evidence on whether patterns of impairments and abilities are maintained throughout the development. Evidence to date confirms that people with mild non-specific intellectual disability have the best outcome for independent adult life (Richardson & Koller, 1996). The follow-up of a cohort of young people with intellectual disability in Scotland by Richardson and Koller (1996) found a quarter of young people have disappeared from adult services, with the remainder needing some form of extra support in adult life. Those individuals who required little or no extra support in adult life were those with mild intellectual disability to borderline intellectual functioning. Family stability was the strongest predictor and IQ the weakest predictor of outcome in adult life, suggesting that early social factors for those with mild intellectual disability are very relevant to outcome for social integration in adult life (Maughan, et al., 1999). Individuals with moderate to severe intellectual disability had greater degrees of impairment, with significant impact on their social development and integration. They were unlikely to reach self-sufficiency and independence in adult life. Individuals with severe and profound intellectual disability required high levels of support and supervision, with significantly reduced communication skills limiting their opportunities for social integration.

The opportunities for social integration through childhood are in part influenced by the educational choices available. Globally, most young people with intellectual disability use special educational facilities although more and more are using mainstream education services, depending on the extent of integration within each local area or country (WHO, 2007). The existence of segregated and inclusive education was found to be worldwide, with over 90% of countries having special schools for children with intellectual disability (WHO, 2007). In high-income countries, the availability of education as a legal requirement has only occurred in the past 30 years: for example, Education of All Handicapped Children in 1975 in the USA and the Education Act in 1981 in the UK. The intent of the legislation was to maximize opportunities for children with disabilities, including those with intellectual disability, to be educated with their peers. Following on from 1994, UNESCO has promoted the principle of inclusive education for children with special needs (UNESCO, 1994). More recent legislation in the USA is the Individuals with Disability Education Act (IDEA) in 1997 and the Improved IDEA in 2004, which ensured free and appropriate education for more than 6 million children with disabilities. The models for providing education run across a spectrum, from full inclusion within educational facilities for all children to those that are exclusively for children with intellectual disability. This education provision can include special schools, special classes in mainstream schools, support in regular classes and homebound services. Evidence accumulated over the past decade shows that inclusive education has a number of educational and social benefits for young people with intellectual disability and for their peers without disabilities (Hunt & McDonnell, 2007). The benefits to a child with disabilities are improved functioning and academic skills, plus improved social contact with their peers without disabilities. For the young person without disabilities, the benefits are significantly improved academic progress and an increased likelihood of having a peer with disabilities in their social network.

During their child and adolescent years most young people with intellectual disability live in the family home; families learn to work in partnership with schools, with many parents appreciating frequent contact with teachers. The last few years at school are more concerned with encouraging independence and the opportunities for further education and possibly some form of employment for those with mild intellectual disability. Those with severe intellectual disability will be looking at day and educational services that provide further opportunities to develop skills. Studies of young people with disabilities have found particular school- based practices are linked to positive post- school outcomes (Bambara et al., 2008). These include programmes based on the individual, active involvement of the young person and their families, inclusive educational opportunities and interagency collaboration.

The possible outcomes in adult life are one of three: independence, semi-independence, and dependence requiring a high level of support. Adaptive skills have been found to be relatively stable in adults with intellectual disability. The study of the skills of adults with intellectual disability over a 25-year period found after early adolescence that changes in skills are rare (Beadle-Brown et al., 2006). This study involved a cohort of 91 individuals, first assessed in the 1970s, and aged between 27 and 42 years when assessed 25 years later. At that time, 68% of individuals lived in the community, with 27% still living with their parents. Those individuals who had an IQ score below 50 (64%) were in the group with moderate to profound intellectual disability and 72% had some form of autistic spectrum disorder. Interestingly, for those who had been in institutionalised care, self-care skills significantly increased after the move into the community.

However, many people with intellectual disability across the world still reside in asylum-type institutions, with half of countries reporting this type of care (WHO, 2007).

Asylum-type institutions for children and adolescents are less common in low-income countries (33.3%) than in countries with an upper middle level of income. Historically, in high-income countries such as the UK, children and adolescents with intellectual disability were admitted into large 'mental handicap hospitals'. Those with severe, persistent and complex mental health problems were admitted, usually in adolescence, but a number in early childhood. Legislation over the past 30 years has changed the type of care provided for people with intellectual disability. The focus over the past decades has been on providing good educational provision and support to the families, with emphasis on the closure of the large hospital-based institutions. Beadle Brown et al. (2008) reviewed the process of the de-institutionalization in the lives of people with intellectual disability in the UK and showed that outcomes are better in the community than in institutional care. However, just moving people out of institutions into community settings does not bring about automatic improvement in the quality of life and access to effective healthcare and treatment. The level of de-institutionalization varies across countries and so the opportunities for social integration, with a steady decline in countries such as the UK, the USA, Canada, Norway and Sweden. For many countries the process is less advanced, such as in Australia and Ireland, and in other countries such as Belgium, the Netherlands, Germany, Spain and Greece, where the process has recently begun but institutional care is still dominant (European Intellectual Disability Research Network, 2003). In some countries the trend is still towards more institutional provision rather than less (Chou & Schalock, 2007).

Adults with intellectual disability want to be part of the wider society in having relationships, bringing up children and gaining employment (Department of Health, 2001). One area that is of particular relevance to services for adults with intellectual disability is parenthood (Bernard, 2007). The number of parents with intellectual disability is not easy to estimate but figures of 1–2% of families in Australia have a parent with an intellectual disability, with estimated figures of 250,000 in the UK and 1.4 million in the USA (O'Keefe & O'Hara, 2007). Intellectual impairment in itself is not an absolute bar to parenthood. Sadly, many young women with difficulties in intellectual and emotional immaturity are likely to find partners with even more problems and so put their children at risk from neglect and abuse. Problems such as these, rather than the intellectual disability, make agencies and courts question the safety of the children.

PHYSICAL HEALTH

Children with non-specific intellectual disability may suffer from a number of health problems affecting all the systems of the body: for example, respiratory problems such as lung disease associated with low birth weight (Singer et al., 1997), congenital heart disease and epilepsy. A quarter to a third of adults with intellectual disability have epilepsy commonly from childhood (McGrother et al., 2006). In addition, they may have impairment of motor and sensory development, affecting mobility, hearing and vision. Therefore, it is essential they have a multidisciplinary assessment within child health services to include physiotherapists and speech and language therapists. Children with severe intellectual disability may have feeding difficulties, requiring assessment by a speech and language therapist because of the associated risk of gastric reflux and direct aspiration into the airways with the subsequent problem of pneumonia (Morton et al., 1999). As discussed below, pneumonia is the leading cause of mortality in people with intellectual disability; therefore, children and adults with severe intellectual disability and feeding problems should be offered gastrotomy tube insertion to reduce the risk of aspiration pneumonia.

Although life expectancy is improving in people with intellectual disability (Patja,

2000), they are 58 times more likely to die before the age of 50 than the general population (Hollins et al., 1998). Respiratory disease is the leading cause of these early deaths and is linked to posture, swallowing and feeding problems. These early deaths in people with intellectual disability are significantly associated with cerebral palsy, incontinence, problems with mobility and residence in hospital (Hollins et al., 1998). One study found medium life expectancy of 74, 67 and 59 years, respectively, for individuals aged ≥ 5 years with mild, moderate and severe levels of disability and an overall medium life expectancy of 69 years (Bittles et al., 2002). The comparison medium life expectancy of the general population was 76 in males and 81 in females in the same study.

This improvement in life expectancy has caused changes in mortality patterns. Deaths from age-related conditions have shown a progressive increase, while tuberculosis and status epilepsy, formerly common causes of deaths in institutionalized populations, have declined (Carter & Jancar, 1983). Leading causes of mortality among the general population are neoplasms, ischemic heart disease and cerebrovascular diseases, but for adults with intellectual disability the leading causes are respiratory and neoplastic diseases. The rate of mortality for cardiovascular disease has been found to be one-third of the rate of the general population from a study in New York (Janicki et al., 1999). Other studies of mortality in people with intellectual disability in institutions in the Netherlands found a high mortality rate in the severely and profoundly disabled group until the age of 30 (Maaskant & Haverman, 1990). This high mortality rate was mainly determined by postnatal birth disorders. The healthiest residents were found in the 30–50 age group. When comparison was made with the Dutch general population, it was found that the overall mortality of individuals with severe intellectual disability is substantially higher for all age groups until the age of 70 years, when the mortality risks approach those for the general population.

In addition to higher mortality rate, people with intellectual disability experience high levels of morbidity, which is often unrecognized or poorly managed (O'Hara et al., 2010). This is well recognized through national reports into access to healthcare for people with intellectual disability in the UK (Healthcare for All, 2008) and other countries (Krahn et al., 2006). People with intellectual disability are found to have a higher rate of illness than the general population; 6% reported no illness compared to 37% of the general population (Welsh Office, 1995). A recent Dutch national survey of general practice found that people with intellectual disability had 1.7 times more visits to a GP (Straetmans et al., 2007). In the Dutch survey, people with intellectual disability also received four times as many repeat prescriptions. The association between poverty and intellectual disability accounts in part for these health inequalities (Emerson, 2007).

MENTAL HEALTH—CHILDHOOD TO ADULT LIFE

Compared to their more able peers, the rate of psychiatric disorder is four to five times greater in children and adolescents with intellectual disability, so giving a prevalence rate of just under 40–50% (Einfeld & Tonge, 1996; Emerson, 2007; Rutter et al., 1970). Prevalence of psychiatric disorder in children with intellectual disability has been found to vary with intellectual functioning in earlier studies (Gillberg et al., 1986; Rutter et al., 1970). A large study in Australia did not find a relationship with disorder and functioning when comparing those with mild intellectual disability to those with moderate to severe intellectual disability (Einfeld & Tonge, 1996). Those with profound intellectual disability, who tend to have physical disabilities, have lower rates of challenging behaviours such as physical aggression and disruption to the environment (Emerson et al., 2001) but others have found individuals with profound to severe intellectual disability to show more challenging behaviours such as self-injury and stereotypy behaviours (McLintock et al., 2003). Age also influences prevalence, with conduct disorder and anti-social behaviour being more prevalent among older than younger children (Einfeld & Tonge, 1996).

Studies have shown that the most common disorders in those with severe intellectual disability are the pervasive developmental disorders, which include autism, followed by conduct problems of aggression and hyperactivity disorders (Corbett, 1977; Einfeld & Tonge, 1996). Children and adolescents with mild intellectual disability, i.e. IQ above 50, present with disorders similar to those without disability, i.e. disorders of conduct, activity level and attention, anxiety, mood and psychotic disorders (Dykens, 2000). When comparing the prevalence of ICD-10-diagnosed disorders, conduct disorder, anxiety disorder, hyperkinesias and pervasive developmental disorders, the rates are significantly greater among children with intellectual disability than their non-disabled peers (Emerson, 2003). Studies of outcome of psychopathology in young people with intellectual disability indicate that problems continue into adult life (Richardson & Koller 1996; Tonge & Einfeld, 2003). The prevalence of psychopathology seems to peak at the transition period of late adolescence, falling to a lower rate in adult life (Tonge, 2007)

Hyperactivity

Symptoms of attention-deficit/hyperactive disorder (ADHD) are increased in children with mild intellectual disability compared to their non-disabled peers (Simonoff et al., 2007). However, a number of children and adolescents with severe intellectual disability are persistently overactive, impulsive and distractable with short attention span. In making the diagnosis of ADHD the clinician needs to make allowance for the developmental level of the young person, but if the overactivity is so severe as to impair educational and social activities then this requires treatment. Studies show that ADHD affects 8.7–16% of children with intellectual disability (Emerson, 2003; Stromme & Diseth, 2000), with others finding 32% of children with intellectual disability showing symptoms of ADHD (Tonge & Einfeld, 2003). No relationship to gender is found, which contrasts to more able peers, but the prevalence of ADHD symptoms does reduce from late adolescence into early adult life (Tonge & Einfeld, 2003).

Conduct disorder and behaviour problems

It has been recognized for many years that young children with conduct problems across the range of abilities are at substantial risk for antisocial behaviours in adolescence and in adult life, and are likely to have difficulties in interpersonal function and work, with an increased risk of adult psychiatric disorders (Scott, 2009). There is a robust association between poverty and social disadvantage and conduct problems in children and adolescents without intellectual disability (Farrington, 1995). A cross-sectional population-based study of children and adolescents with intellectual disability across Britain found that the most common diagnosis was conduct disorder affecting, 25% of the group (Emerson, 2003). Children living in lower- income households and children of lone parents were more likely to have a conduct disorder. Studies of children with severe intellectual disability and behavioural problems show no association with social class (Chadwick et al., 2000).

Aggressive behaviour is the most frequently reported problem behaviour for children and adults with intellectual disability (Benson & Brooks, 2008). Aggressive behaviour in young people with mild intellectual disability is a prominent problem compared to those without intellectual disability (Dekker et al., 2002). As with other adolescents, it may emerge as a pattern of a conduct disorder or secondary to other underlying psychosocial factors: for example, family bereavement or parental illness. Repeated self-injurious behaviour occurs in 10% of young people with intellectual disability in a mild form (Oliver, 1995), although a more recent study of younger children reported a rate of 4.6% (Berkson et al., 2001). Less common are more destructive acts, such as head banging, eye poking and biting of limbs.

Mood and anxiety disorders

It is difficult to diagnose depression in young people with significant communication problems. Usually changes in behaviour—e.g. loss of interest in activities, self-injurious behaviour and becoming withdrawn—or evidence of biological symptoms of depression—e.g. loss of appetite, sleep disturbance and weight loss—may indicate a mood disorder. When comparing groups of children with intellectual disability and those without, no difference has been found in rates of depressive disorders (Emerson, 2003) or anxiety symptoms (Dekker et al., 2002). In the Australian study of children with intellectual disability (Tonge & Einfeld, 2003), a prevalence rate of 9% was reported for persistent symptoms of depression and 8% for anxiety. Depressive symptoms were less prevalent in those with severe or profound intellectual disability, with a rate of 3%. The prevalence of depression for both genders and prevalence of anxiety disorders for boys did not change over the 14 years of follow-up from childhood. However, for girls, the prevalence of anxiety disorders did increase to a rate of 20% over the follow-up period.

MENTAL HEALTH—ADULT LIFE

The point prevalence of mental ill-health in a large study of adults with intellectual disability in Scotland was from 40.9% to 15.7%, depending on how diagnosis was made and which diagnostic criteria were used (Cooper et al., 2007). Clinical diagnosis and use of diagnostic criteria developed for people with intellectual disability produce the highest rate of 40.9% and 35.2%, respectively. Research diagnostic criteria developed for the general population produced lower prevalence rates of 16.6% using ICD-10-DCR criteria (WHO, 1993) and 15.7% using DSM-IV-TR diagnostic criteria (APA, 2000). The most prevalent type was problem behaviours, with a prevalence rate of 22.5%; the prevalence rate was 4.4% for psychotic disorder; 6.6% for affective disorders; 3.8% for anxiety disorders; and 0.7% for obsessive compulsive disorder. Mental ill-health was associated with a number of factors, including life events, female gender, type of support and lower ability.

Assessment and diagnosis

One of the main problems in the study of mental health needs of people with intellectual disability is the relative lack of suitable techniques for detection and diagnosis in this population. The problem of interviewing people with intellectual disability about their mental state is clearly a major obstacle. People with intellectual disability are likely to find it difficult to express their emotions verbally; as a result, many studies have relied on third-party reports for information on which to make a diagnosis (Bouras & Holt, 2010; Sturmey et al., 1991).

Assessment must include a full history of presenting problems, developmental history, family and social history. It is important to obtain information from parents, teachers for children, day centre workers and carers and this gain a picture of the behaviour in more than one environment. Examination should identify any evidence of sensory impairment or neurological problems. Investigations are not usually indicated, although all people with non-specific intellectual disability should be screened to identify a possible cause of

their disability, as genetic testing continues to advance. Neuroimaging and an electroencephalogram (EEG) are required if there is clear evidence of neurological disorder.

There are a variety of standardized assessment tools for use with children and adults with intellectual disability. These include the Developmental Behaviour Checklist which was developed for children and adolescents (Einfeld & Tonge, 1995) but now has an adult version (Mohr & Costello, 2007). Measures developed for psychiatric assessment of adults include the Psychiatric Assessment Schedule for Adults with Developmental Disabilities (PAS-ADD) (Moss et al., 1993) and Diagnostic Assessment for the Severely Handicapped (DASH) scale (Matson et al., 1991). However all the checklists and rating scales have practical, psychometric and theoretical limitations (Mohr & Costello, 2007). These assessment tools are still mainly used for research purposes rather than in routine clinical practice.

Schizophrenia and psychoses

People with mild intellectual disability who suffer from schizophrenia present with similar psychotic symptoms to those without intellectual disability (Meadows at al., 1991). The presence of cognitive impairment increases the likelihood that psychotic symptoms can present atypically and may aggravate a pre-existing behaviour disturbance (Paschos & Bouras, 2007). Psychosis is rare until late adolescence, usually presenting with auditory hallucinations, simple delusions or the emergence of odd or bizarre behaviour. The prevalence of schizophrenia in adults with intellectual disability is 2–6% across studies, compared to 1% for the general population (Clarke, 2007). The risk of schizophrenia increases gradually as IQ score falls, but the relationship between IQ scores and non-clinical psychotic symptoms is more of a non-linear one, with symptoms being associated with low IQ and less strongly with high IQ scores (Horwood et al., 2008). The diagnosis of schizophrenia or any other psychotic disorder in people with moderate to profound intellectual disability is thought not possible due to impaired communication and the individual's difficulty in describing complex subjective experiences of delusions and hallucinations (Brugha et al., 1988).

Depression and anxiety disorders

Depression occurs in people with intellectual disability and point prevalence rates of depressive episodes in adults with intellectual disability is about 4% (Deb et al., 2001) and 6.6% for affective disorders (Cooper et al., 2007). Several factors increase vulnerability to depression, including higher rates of physical illness, socioeconomic diversity and reduced life supports (Richards et al., 2001). The whole range of psychological and somatic symptoms of depression can be observed, but changes are often subtle and develop over time (Paschos & Bouras, 2007). Other mood disorders, including bipolar affective disorders (Cain et al., 2003), are also observed, including rapid-cycling bipolar disorder (Vanstraelent & Tyrer, 1999). The rates of depression in older people with intellectual disability vary from 4.8% to 6.9% (Cooper, 1997a; Lund, 1985; Patel et al., 1993). Cooper (1997b) found an older cohort of adults with intellectual disability to have higher rates of depression and anxiety than a younger cohort.

The anxiety disorders, including phobias, generalized anxiety, panic disorder, obsessive-compulsive disorder and post-traumatic stress disorder (PTSD), are all reported in people with intellectual disability (Stavrakaki & Lunsky, 2007). Children and adults do suffer from PTSD (McCarthy, 2001).Common presenting symptoms include the usual symptoms of PTSD such as re-experiencing the traumatic event and avoidance of stimuli associated with the trauma but also aggression, disruptive behaviour, self-harm, agitation,

distractibility, sleep problems and depressed mood. Abuse, sexual and physical, is the commonest aetiological factor in the onset of PTSD in adults with intellectual disability.

Dementia

As life expectancy of many people with intellectual disability has increased, so has their risk for age-related disorders. The link between Down syndrome and Alzheimer's disease has been established for many years (Oliver & Holland, 1986). Studies of prevalence of dementia in people with intellectual disability not due to Down syndrome find conflicting evidence, which is partly explained by different methodologies (Torr & Davis, 2007). In earlier population studies of people with intellectual disability, the prevalence rates of dementia were shown to be from 6% (Day, 1987) to 14% (Lund, 1985), depending on the age of the group or whether a hospital or community population, was being studied. Zigman et al. (2004), in a cross-sectional group of 126 adults with intellectual disability over the age of 65 in New York State, found no difference in the cumulative incidence to that of dementia of Alzheimer's disease in the general population. Other studies have reported prevalence rates of dementia in elderly people with intellectual disability to be higher than that in the general population (Cooper, 1997a; Styrdom et al, 2007). Cooper (1997a) found a rate of 22% in those aged ≥ 65 years, with only 3 of the 29 individuals with dementia having Down syndrome. The study by Zigman and colleagues (2004) may have been skewed towards those with Alzheimer's disease and may be missing those with vascular dementia. The current consensus is that the prevalence of dementia is considered to be higher in older people with intellectual disability when compared with an age-matched general population (Cooper & Holland, 2007). For people with intellectual disability the risk of dementia is bought forward by about 15 years.

Behaviour problems

Challenging behaviours are frequent among adults with intellectual disability and their relationship to comorbid psychopathology is complex (McCarthy et al., 2010). Prevalence rates have been reported at about 10–15% (Lowe et al., 2007). The type of behaviours typically include self-injury, physical aggression, destructive behaviours and inappropriate social behaviour such as difficult sexual behaviour. These challenging behaviours can be chronic and serious challenging behaviour can persist over a long period in the adult life of a person with intellectual disability (Totsika et al., 2008). In one study of challenging and problem behaviour in young adults with intellectual disability living in the family home, over half (59%) showed the same level of challenging behaviour across a 5-year period (Kiernan & Alborz, 1996). Individuals with persisting behaviour problems differed from those who do not present with serious behavioural problems on the basis of their younger age, increased mobility, decreased sociability and reduced living skills (Totsika et al., 2008).

There are guidelines, such as those developed by European Association for Mental Health in Intellectual Disability (Dosen et al., 2007) for assessing people with intellectual disability and behaviour problems. These guidelines follow a developmental perspective to assessment, diagnosis and treatment using a biopsychosocial approach.

Risk factors

Factors that increase the risk to psychiatric disorder and behavioural problems include genetic factors, physical illness, low IQ, trauma, bereavement, family factors and socioeconomic deprivation. People with intellectual disability have increased risk to factors such as low IQ, epilepsy, psychological adversity, and genetic disorders, compared with more able peers, so increasing the

risk for psychiatric and behavioural problems (Dykens, 2000). The most important risk factor for psychopathology at any given time is psychopathology occurring at an earlier age of onset (Tonge & Einfeld, 2003; Wallander et al., 2003).

Functioning

It is well-recognized that behaviour problems in children with intellectual disability show a strong association with the severity of disability, regardless of whether severity is defined in terms of IQ or the child's level of functional skills. Recent studies confirm this strong relationship between skills deficits and severe behavioural problems (Chadwick et al., 2000; Einfeld & Tonge, 1996). The best predictor of behaviour problems is level of functioning (Chadwick et al., 2000). The type of psychopathology varies with level of functioning. Depression, anxiety and antisocial behaviours are more common among those with a higher level of functioning (Dekker et al., 2002; Einfeld and Tonge, 1996; Richardson & Koller, 1996). Self-absorbed and autistic behaviours are more common among those with lower levels of functioning.

Family and social environment

Families of children with intellectual disability have been keenly studied since the 1960s (Dykens & Hodapp, 2001; Gath & McCarthy, 2009). Parental factors, which may be genetic in basis, may determine how the parents cope with a child with a disability. There is cross-sectional evidence pointing to an association between the psychopathology and behavioural problems in children with intellectual disability and parental stress and other minor psychiatric problems shown by parents such as depression and anxiety (Dekker & Koot, 2003; Emerson, 2003). Factors in the family environment, such as parental mental health, mother's adjustment to child, marital difficulties and child management practices, are linked to increased rates of psychiatric disorder and behaviour problems (Emerson, 2003).

Adolescents with mild intellectual disability from the British Survey of Health and Development showed a fourfold increase in the risk of affective disorder persisting well into midlife that was not accounted for by social and material disadvantage or by medical disorder (Richards et al., 2001). It seems that early social risk factors did not increase the vulnerability for adult-onset affective disorders in those with mild intellectual disability. The authors concluded that more subtle factors operate for this group, such as coping capacity and self-worth.

Life events

Outside of the field of intellectual disability, empirical research over several decades has demonstrated that negative life events have an impact on psychological functioning (Brown & Harris, 1989). Population studies have found negative life events to be associated with increased risk for psychiatric disorders in children with intellectual disability (Dekker & Koot, 2003). Richards et al. (2001) found no association with adverse life events in the past 12 months and affective disorder in adults with mild intellectual disability. Studies have found an association with recent life events occurring in the past 12 months and behaviour disorder (Owen et al., 2004). An association between traumatic life events and a range of psychopathology has been described in adults with intellectual disability (Martorell & Tsakanikos, 2008). Abuse and maltreatment must be considered in a person with intellectual disability presenting with severe behaviour problems.

INTERVENTIONS

Educational and occupational

Early intervention to pre-schoolers with disabilities, which focuses on the parent's capacity to promote the child's learning and development, have a strong evidence base for children with intellectual disability (Dunst,

2007). When practitioners support parents, and parents in turn support their children, both parents and the child have an increased sense of competence and confidence (Dunst et al., 2007).

The focus of educational outcomes for children with severe intellectual disability is on social development, self-care skills, communication skills and motor development, rather than the outcomes for typically developing children. For many years the mainstay of special education has been on behavioural interventions but the approach now is a naturalistic one that teaches skills in sequence with other skills as they would typically occur (Prett-Frontczak & Bricker, 2004). The spotlight for the future must be on the implementation of known effective educational interventions that contribute directly to improved outcomes for children with intellectual disability (Carta & Kong, 2007). This may include educational training programmes directed towards improved communication, social skills and self-help skills.

One of the key tasks for the future is to improve the knowledge and skills of practitioners across a number of agencies, including education, health and social services, on the mental health needs of people with intellectual disability. It is important to detect mental health problems before the transition into adult life, as such problems may hinder movement into a successful placement within adult services. There is an array of information and policy documents in planning transition from childhood to adult life for people with intellectual disability; however, the area is still under-researched (Barron & Hassiotis, 2008). A good practice guideline document developed in the UK (Deb et al., 2006) on transition needs for young people with mental health and challenging behaviour strongly advocates for an inter-professional and multi-agency approach, with the person with intellectual disability and their families at the centre of the planning process for transition.

Programmes aimed at development of work skills, sheltered employment and supported employment are available in the majority of countries for adults with intellectual disability (WHO, 2007). Globally, only a minority of countries provide employment opportunities for a person with intellectual disability to work alongside people without disabilities: therefore, for many adults with intellectual disability, the choice can be limited, with a heavy reliance on large, often institutional, day centres (Department of Health, 2001).

Psychological interventions

Psychological interventions are the cornerstone of management of behavioural problems in people with intellectual disability. Most behaviour, such as self-injurious behaviour, temper tantrums and aggression, can be modified through a behavioural approach (Benson & Havercamp, 2007). The overall management depends on a detailed assessment of the underlying cause of the behaviour. It is very important to consider the needs of the person, their family and the wider environment, such as school and other support services, in developing and implementing an effective treatment plan.

However, psychosocial interventions for people with intellectual disability across the spectrum of mental health problems are poorly developed (Dagnan, 2007). A number of studies have shown benefits from psychosocial intervention in areas such as supported employment and residential provisions (Perry & Felce, 2003). The evidence base for cognitive behavioural therapy is limited in people with intellectual disability. The few reported studies are of group interventions for anger and those who offend (Dagnan, 2007). Other psychological approaches include individual psychotherapy for those who have suffered traumatic events. There is evidence for improved outcome in emotional and behavioural symptoms when using psychodynamic psychotherapy for people with intellectual disability (Beail, 2003). An audit of an outpatient specialist psychotherapy service for people with intellectual disability found a significant number (up to a third) suffered trauma and abuse, being the primary reason for referral, with presentation of challenging behaviour, loss and depression being the other reasons for referral (Parkes & Hollins, 2007).

Pharmacological interventions

People with intellectual disability do experience the side effects of psychotropic medication (Deb & Fraser, 1994). Medication should not be the first or only treatment for difficult-to-manage behaviour. Optimum treatment is multimodal, with pharmacological intervention only one component of the therapeutic package for children and adults with intellectual disability (Antochi et al., 2003; Handen & Gilchrist, 2006; King, 2007). Medication should be targeted for specific conditions.

Stimulants

Stimulants such as methylphenidate are safe and effective for the treatment of hyperactivity in young people with mild to moderate intellectual disability but are less helpful in those with severe to profound intellectual disability (Aman et al., 1997). The stimulant methylphenidate has produced positive response rates from 45% to 66%, in young people with intellectual disability, with evidence of improvement in cognitive functioning (Pearson et al., 2004). There is a greater risk of side effects for children with intellectual disability such as motor tics and social withdrawal. Alternatives need to be considered when stimulants do not produce response or cannot be tolerated. The alternatives include atomoxetine and alpha antagonists such as clonidine or guanfacine, although their is current evidence little on the safety and efficacy of these drugs in children with intellectual disability.

Antipsychotics

The majority of studies on the use of antipsychotic medication in children and adults with intellectual disability tend to be open trials case reports in controlled studies with small sample size (Handen & Gilchrist, 2006).

Antipsychotic medication is used for specific behaviour symptoms as well as for the treatment of psychotic disorders. Surveys on the use of antipsychotic drugs for the treatment of challenging behaviours in people with intellectual disability have found a high use: up a third to over a half of individuals with intellectual disability living in the community are on antipsychotic medication (King, 2007). A recent review of the use of psychotropic medication for behaviour problems supports the use of some antipsychotic medication, particularly the atypical antipsychotic risperidone (Deb & Unwin, 2007). The review reported on one randomized controlled trial among adults and four on children with intellectual disability showing effectiveness of low-dose risperidone in the management of behaviour problems as compared with the placebo. Most of the studies showed adverse effects of somnolence and weight gain being associated with risperidone medication. A recent randomized controlled trial, which is rare in the field of intellectual disability, compared risperidone, haloperidol and placebo in patients with intellectual disability and concluded that the routine prescribing of antipsychotic drugs early in the management of aggressive challenging behaviour is no longer a satisfactory form of care (Tyrer et al., 2008). There was no good evidence to support the use of other psychotropic medications such as antidepressants, mood stabilizers, antianxiety drugs and opioid antagonists (Deb & Unwin, 2007).

For cases of schizophrenia, psychosis and hypomania, the atypical antipsychotic drugs are used as first-line treatment, including risperidone, olanzapine, aripiprazole and quetiapine (King, 2007). Some of these drugs do not come without side effects with weight gain and metabolic disturbance being significant problems (Hellings et al., 2001).

Antidepressants and mood stabilizers

Pharmacotherapy must be carefully considered in a person with intellectual disability and depression or anxiety disorder. Selective serotonin reuptake inhibitors (SSRIs) are the first-choice antidepressants used in adults with intellectual disability suffering from depressive and anxiety disorders. There is evidence for the use of citalopram in adults with intellectual disability and depression (King, 2007). Escitalopram and sertraline are also used due to their higher specificity and side-effect profile. SSRIs continue also to be the recommended treatment of choice over tricyclic antidepressants for children and adolescents with intellectual disability (Handen & Gilchrist, 2000). The antiseizure drugs are now widely used to treat mood disorders in adults with intellectual disability. Commonly used drugs are sodium valproate, carbamazepine and lamotrigine (Handen & Gilchrist, 2006). Dosages are the same as in the treatment of epilepsy.

Services for people with intellectual disability

Only 39% of countries have a specific national policy or programme related to intellectual disability (WHO, 2007). There are clear gaps in resources between countries with geographical locations and socioeconomic factors hindering access to services in more than half the countries in the world (WHO, 2007). Although services have improved across the world, more so in developed countries (especially in the area of education), national reports still confirm services to this group are poorly coordinated, even in countries with some of the most developed services (Healthcare for All, 2008). In many countries, services to support adults with intellectual disability in the community do not exist. For example, in some Asian countries, supported employment, sheltered employment, day service and domiciliary services are still not available to support people with intellectual disability in the community setting (Kwok & Chui, 2008).

Children and adults with intellectual disability and high rates of mental health problems experience difficulties in accessing appropriate services (Bouras & Holt, 2010; Davidson & O'Hara, 2007; McCarthy & Boyd, 2002). There is variation within countries and across countries. A recent survey of mental healthcare across Asia found that service provision varies widely (Kwok & Chui, 2008). This variation parallels the differences in economic, social and healthcare systems among the reporting countries.

FUTURE CHALLENGES AND RESEARCH

The challenges are on a global scale and require both developed and developing countries to make the needs and welfare of both children and adults with intellectual disability a higher priority, with improved access to diagnostic health facilities and evidence-based therapeutic interventions. This is more so in low-income countries (WHO, 2007)

A number of areas need to be considered for future research, including epidemiology, diagnosis and assessment, ethical issues and therapeutic interventions. Future research needs to include people with intellectual disability in research design and dissemination.

Further epidemiological evidence is required to identify risk and protective factors to improve the emotional and behavioural outcome of people with intellectual disability. Increased knowledge of the social and psychological risk factors, and how they link to outcomes, would significantly improve the lives of people with non-specific intellectual disability. Improved recognition, assessment and diagnosis of mental health problems are needed with screening/diagnostic measures being available that require minimal training so that they can be used specifically in countries with little or no expertise. Greater understanding of the aetiologies causing non-specific intellectual disability would allow for the development of individually tailored social, educational, psychological and pharmacological interventions.

Another key priority is to improve health outcomes by increasing access to healthcare so as to reduce morbidity and increase life expectancy, which will be a major challenge in low-income countries. This may be through improved training of health professionals, but also requires a more systemic change in the providers of health services to recognize the needs of people with intellectual disability as a higher priority (O'Hara et al., 2010).

Promoting evidence-based treatment for this population is essential to improve outcome. More studies are required on the effectiveness of therapeutic interventions across the range of psychiatric and behavioural problems, including psychosocial, educational and pharmacological interventions. Ethical consideration needs to be given to involving people with intellectual disability in research, especially those who lack capacity. In some countries legislation has been implemented: for example, in England the Mental Capacity Act of 2005 provides a legal framework for involving people who lack capacity in research studies.

It is only through these advances that we will be able to move forward from the current evidence on social and health trajectories to improve the outcomes over the lifetime of people with intellectual disability.

REFERENCES

Aman M.G., Kern R.A., Osborne P., Jamonily, R., & Rohan, J. (1997) 'Fenfluramine and methylphenidate in children with mental retardation and borderline IQ: clinical effects', *American Journal of Mental Retardation*, 101: 521–543.

American Psychiatric Association (2000) *Diagnostic and Statistical Manual of Mental Disorders*, 4th edn. Washington, DC: American Psychiatric Association.

Antochi, R., Stavrakaki, C. & Emery, P.C. (2003) 'Psychopharmacological treatments in persons with dual diagnosis of psychiatric disorders and developmental disabilities', *Postgraduate Medical Journal*, 79: 139–146.

Bambara, L.M., Wilson, B.A., & McKemzie, M. (2007) 'Transition and quality of life', In S.L. Odom, R.H. Horner, M.E. Snell, & J. Blacher (eds), *Handbook of Developmental Disabilities*. New York: Guilford Press.

Barron, D.A. & Hassiotis, A. (2008) 'Good practice in transition services for young people with learning disabilities: a review', *Advances in Mental Health and Learning Disabilities*, 2: 18–22.

Beadle-Brown, J., Murphy, G., & Wing, L. (2006) 'The Camberwell Cohort 25 years on: characteristics and changes in skills over time', *Journal of Applied Research in Intellectual Disabilities*, 19: 317–329.

Beadle-Brown, J., Mansell, J., & Kozma, A. (2008) 'Deinstitutionalization in intellectual disabilities', *Current Opinion in Psychiatry*, 20: 437–442.

Beail N. (2003) 'What works for people with mental retardation? Critical commentary on cognitive behavioural and psychodynamic research', *Mental Retardation*, 41: 468–472.

Benson, B. & Brooks, W.T. (2008) 'Aggressive challenging behaviour and intellectual disability', *Current Opinion in Psychiatry*, 21: 454–458.

Benson, B. & Havercamp S. (2007) 'Behavioural approaches to treatment: principles and practices' in N. Bouras & G. Holt (eds), *Psychiatric and Behavioural Disorders in Intellectual and Developmental Disabilities*. Cambridge: Cambridge University Press.

Berkson, G., Tupa, M., & Sherman, L. (2001) 'Early development of stereotyped and self-injurious behaviours: 1. Incidence', *American Journal of Mental Retardation*, 106: 539–547.

Bernard, S. (2007) 'Parents with intellectual disabilities: the assessment of parenting ability', *Advances in Mental Health and Learning Disabilities*, 1: 14–18.

Bittles, A.H., Petterson, B.A., Sullivan, S.G. et al., (2002) 'The influence of intellectual disability on life expectancy', *Journals of Gerontology*, 57A: 470–472.

Bouras, N. & Holt, G. (2007) *Psychiatric and Behavioural Disorders in Intellectual and Developmental Disabilities*', 2nd Edn. Cambridge: Cambridge University Press.

Bouras, N. & Holt, G. (2009) Mental health needs of adults with intellectual disabilities: psychopathology, services, training and research. Maudsley Monograph, Institute of Psychiatry, London.

Bouras, N. & Holt, G. (2010). Mental health services for adults with intellectual disability: strategies and solutions. Maudsley monograph', Psychology Press: East Sussex.

Brown, G.W. & Harris, T. (1989) *Life Events and Illness*. London: Unwin Hyman.

Brugha, T.S., Collacott, R., Warrington, J. et al. (1988) 'Eliciting and reliably rating delusions and hallucinations in the mildly mentally retarded' Paper presented at the 8th IASSND Congress, Dublin.

Cain, N.N., Davidson, P.W., Burhan, A.M. et al. (2003) 'Identifying bipolar disorder in individuals with intellectual disability', *Journal of Intellectual Disability Research*, 47: 31–38.

Carta, J.J. & Kong, N.Y. (2007) 'Trends and issues in interventions for preschoolers with developmental disabilities', In S.L. Odom, R.H. Horner, M.E. Snell, & J. Blacher (eds), *Handbook of Developmental Disabilities*. New York: Guilford Press.

Carter, G. & Jancar, J. (1983) 'Mortality in the mentally handicapped: a fifty year survey at Stoke Park Group of hospitals (1930–1980)', *Journal of Mental Deficiency Research*, 27: 143–156.

Chadwick, O., Pirott, N., Walker, J., Bernard, S., Taylor, E. (2000) 'Factors affecting the risk of behavioural problems in children with severe intellectual disability', *Journal of Intellectual Disability Research* 44: 108–123.

Chou, Y.C. & Schalock, R.L. (2007) 'Trends in residential policies and services for people with intellectual disabilities in Taiwan', *Journal of Intellectual Disability Research*, 51: 135–141.

Clarke, D. (2007) 'Schizophrenia spectrum disorders in people with intellectual disabilities', in N. Bouras & G. Holt (eds), *Psychiatric and Behavioural Disorders in Intellectual and Developmental Disabilities*. Cambridge: Cambridge University Press.

Cooper, S.A. (1997a) 'High prevalence of dementia amongst people with learning disabilities not attributed to Down syndrome', *Psychological Medicine*, 27: 609–616.

Cooper, S.A. (1997b) 'Psychiatry of elderly compared to younger adults with intellectual disabilities', *Journal of Applied Research in Intellectual Disabilities,* 10: 303–311.

Cooper, S.A. & Holland, A.J. (2007) 'Dementia and mental ill-health in older people with intellectual disabilities' in N. Bouras & G. Holt (eds), *Psychiatric and Behavioural Disorders in Intellectual and Developmental Disabilities*. Cambridge: Cambridge University Press.

Cooper, S.A., Smiley, E., Morrison, J., Williamson, A., & Allan, L. (2007) 'Mental ill-health in adults with intellectual disabilities: prevalence and associated factors', *British Journal of Psychiatry*, 190: 27–35.

Corbett, J. (1977) 'Population studies in mental retardation', in P. Graham (ed.), *Epidemiological Approaches in Child Psychiatry*. London: Academic Press, pp. 305–322.

Davidson, P. & O'Hara, J. (2007) 'Clinical services for people with intellectual disabilities and psychiatric or severe behaviour disorders', in N. Bouras & G. Holt (eds), *Psychiatric and Behavioural Disorders in Intellectual and Developmental Disabilities*. Cambridge: Cambridge University Press.

Day K. (1987) 'The elderly mentally handicapped in hospital: a clinical study', *Journal of Mentally Deficiency Research*, 31: 131–146.

Dagnan, D. (2007) 'Psychosocial interventions for people with intellectual disabilities and mental ill-health', *Current Opinion in Psychiatry*, 20: 456–460.

Deb, S. & Fraser, W. (1994) 'The use of psychotropic medication in people with learning disability: towards rational prescribing', *Human Psychopharmacology*, 9: 259–272.

Deb, S. & Unwin, G.L. (2007) 'Psychotropic medication for behaviour problems in people with intellectual disability: a review of the recent literature', *Current Opinion in Psychiatry*, 20: 61–66.

Deb, S., Thomas, M., & Bright, C. (2001) 'Mental disorder in adults with intellectual disability. Prevalence of psychiatric illness among a community based population aged between 16 and 64 years', *Journal of Intellectual Disability Research*, 45: 495–505.

Deb, S. Le Mesurier, N., & Bathia, N. (2006) 'Guidelines for services for young people (14–25 years) with learning difficulties/disabilities and mental health problems/challenging behaviour' Birmingham: University of Birmingham.

Dekker, M.C., Koot, H.M., van der Ende, J., & Verhulst, F.C. (2002) 'Emotional and behavioural problems in children and adolescents with and without intellectual disability', *Journal of Child Psychology and Psychiatry*, 43: 1087–1098.

Dekker, M.C. & Koot, H.M. (2003) 'DSM-IV disorders in children with borderline to moderate intellectual disability. II: child and family predictors', *Journal of the American Academy of Child and Adolescent Psychiatry*, 42(8): 923–931.

Department of Health (2001) *A New Strategy for Learning Disability for the 21st Century*. London: The Stationery Office.

Dosen, A., Gardner, W.I., Griffiths, D.M., King, R., & Lapointe, A. (2007) 'Practice guidelines and principles: assessment, diagnosis, treatment, and related support services for persons with intellectual disabilities and problem behaviours' Centre of Consultation and Expertise, Gouda, The Netherlands. www.cce.nl

Dunst, C.J. (2007) 'Early interventions for infants and toddlers with developmental disabilities', in S.L. Odom, R.H. Horner, M.E. Snell, & J. Blacher (eds).

Handbook of Developmental Disabilities. New York: Guilford Press.

Dunst, C.J., Trivette, C.M., & Hamby, D.W. (2007) 'Meta-analysis of family-centered helpgiving practices research', *Mental Retardation and Developmental Disabilities Research Reviews*, 13: 370–378.

Dykens, E. (2000) 'Annotation: psychopathology in children with intellectual disability', *Journal of Child Psychology and Psychiatry*, 41: 407–417.

Dykens, E.M. & Hodapp, R.M. (2001) 'Research in mental retardation: toward an etiologic approach', *Journal of Child Psychology and Psychiatry*, 42: 49–71.

Einfeld, S.L. & Tonge, B.J. (1995) 'The Developmental Behaviour Checklist: the development and validation of an instrument for the assessment of behavioural and emotional disturbance in children and adolescents with mental retardation', *Journal of Autism and Developmental Disorders*, 25: 81–104.

Einfeld, S.L. Tonge, B.J. (1996) 'Population prevalence of psychopathology in children and adolescents with intellectual disability: II epidemiological findings', *Journal of Intellectual Disability Research*, 40: 91– 98.

Emerson E. (2003) 'Prevalence of psychiatric disorders in children and adolescents with and without intellectual disability', *Journal of Intellectual Disability Research*, 47: 51–58.

Emerson, E. (2007) 'Poverty and people with intellectual disabilities', *Mental Retardation and Developmental Disabilities Research Reviews*, 13: 107–113.

Emerson, E., Kiernan, C., Alborz, A., et al. (2001) 'Prevalence of challenging behaviours: a total population study', *Research in Developmental Disabilities*, 22: 77–93.

European Intellectual Disability Research Network (2003) *Intellectual disability in Europe: working papers*. Canterbury: Tizard Centre, University of Kent at Canterbury.

Farrington, D.P. (1995) 'The development of offending and antisocial behaviour from childhood: key findings from the Cambridge Study in Delinquent Development', *Journal of Child Psychology and Psychiatry*, 36: 29–64.

Gath, A. & McCarthy, J. (2009) 'Families with a person with intellectual disability and their needs', In M.G Gelder, N.C Andreasen, J.J Lopez-Ibor, & J.R Geddes, *New Oxford Textbook of Psychiatry*, 2nd Edn. Oxford: Oxford University Press, pp. 1883–1886.

Gillberg, C., Perrson, E., Grufman, M., & Themner U. (1986) 'Psychiatric disorders in mildly and severely retarded urban children and adolescents: epidemiological aspects', *British Journal of Psychiatry*, 149: 68–74.

Handen, B.L. & Gilchrist, R. (2006) 'Practitioner review: Psychopharmacology in children and adolescents with mental retardation', *Journal of Child Psychology and Psychiatry*, 47: 871–882.

Healthcare for All (2008) *Report of the Independent Inquiry into Access to Healthcare for People with Learning Disabilities.* London: Aldridge Press.

Hellings, J.A., Kobayashi, T., Fujita, T., & Fujino, O. (2001) 'Weight gain in a controlled study of risperidone in children, adolescents and adults with mental retardation', *Journal of Child and Adolescent Psychopharmacology*, 11: 329–338.

Hollins S., Attard, A.T., von Fraunhofer, N., & Sedgwick, P. (1998) 'Mortality in people with learning disability: risks, causes, and death certification in London', *Developmental Medicine and Child Neurology*, 40: 50–56.

Horwood, J., Salvi, G., Thomas, K. et al. (2008) 'IQ and non-clinical psychotic symptoms in 12-year-olds: results from ALSPAC birth cohort', *British Journal of Psychiatry*, 193: 185–191.

Hunt, P. & McDonell, J. (2007) 'Inclusive education', In S.L. Odom, R.H. Horner, M.E. Snell, & J. Blacher (eds), *Handbook of Developmental Disabilities.* New York: Guilford Press.

Janicki, M.P., Dalton, A.J., Henderson, C.W., & Davidson, P.W. (1999) 'Mortality and morbidity among older adults with intellectual disability: health services considerations', *Disability and Rehabilitation*, 21: 284–294.

Kiernan, C. & Alborz, A. (1996) 'Persistence and change in challenging and problem behaviours of young adults with intellectual disability living in the family home', *Journal of Applied Research in Intellectual Disabilities*, 9: 181–193.

King, B. (2007) 'Psychopharmacology in intellectual disabilities', in N. Bouras & G. Holt (eds), *Psychiatric and Behavioural Disorders in Intellectual and Developmental Disabilities.* Cambridge: Cambridge University Press.

Krahn, G.L., Hammond, L., & Turner, A. (2006) 'A cascade of disparities: health and health care access for people with intellectual disabilities. *Mental Retardation and Developmental Disabilities Research Review*, 12: 70–82.

Kwok, H.W.M. & Chui, E.M.C. (2008) 'A survey of mental health care for adults with intellectual disabilities in Asia', *Journal of Intellectual Disability Research*, 52: 996–1002.

Lowe, K., Allen, D., Jones, E. et al. (2007) 'Challenging behaviours: prevalence and topographies', *Journal of Intellectual Disability Research*, 51: 625–636.

Lund, J. (1985) 'The prevalence of psychiatric morbidity in mentally retarded adults', *Acta Psychiatrica Scandinavica*, 72: 563–570.

Maaskant, M.A. & Haverman, M.J. (1990) 'Elderly residents in Dutch mental deficiency institutions', *Journal of Mental Deficiency Research*, 34: 475–482.

Matson, J., Gardner W. I., Coe D. A., & Sovner, R. (1991) 'A scale for evaluating emotional disorders in severely and profoundly mentally retarded persons. Development of the Diagnostic Assessment for the Severely Handicapped (DASH) Scale', *British Journal of Psychiatry*, 159: 404–409.

McCarthy, J. (2001) 'Post-traumatic stress disorder in people with learning disability', *Advances in Psychiatric Treatment*, 7: 163–169.

McCarthy J & Boyd J. (2002) 'Mental health services and young people with intellectual disability: is it time to do better?', *Journal of Intellectual Disability Research*, 46: 250–256.

McCarthy, J., Hemmings, C., Kravariti, E. et al. (2010) 'Challenging behaviour and co-morbid psychopathology in adults with intellectual disability and autism spectrum disorders', *Research in Developmental Disabilities*, 31: 362–366.

McGrother, C., Bhaumik, S., Thorp, C., Hauck, A., Branford, D., & Watson, J. (2006) 'Epilepsy in adults with intellectual disabilities: prevalence, associations and secondary implications', *Seizure*, 15: 376–386.

McLintock, K., Hall, S., & Oliver, C. (2003) 'Risk markers associated with challenging behaviours in people with intellectual disabilities: a meta-analytic study', *Journal of Intellectual Disability Research*, 47: 405–416.

Martorell, A. & Tsakanikos, E. (2008) 'Traumatic experiences and life events in people with intellectual disability', *Current Opinion in Psychiatry*, 21: 445–448.

Maughan, B., Collishaw, S., & Pickles, A. (1999) 'Mild mental retardation: psychosocial functioning in adulthood', *Psychological Medicine*, 29: 351–356.

Meadows, G., Turner, T., Campbell, L., Lewis, S.W., Reveley, M.A., & Murray, R.M. (1991) 'Assessing schizophrenia in adults with mental retardation. A comparative study', *British Journal of Psychiatry*, 158: 103–105.

Mental Capacity Act (2005) London: The Stationery Office.

Mohr, C. & Costello, H. (2007) 'Mental health and monitoring tools for people with intellectual disabilities', in N. Bouras & G. Holt (eds), *Psychiatric and Behavioural Disorders in Intellectual and Developmental Disabilities.* Cambridge: Cambridge University Press.

Morton, R.E., Wheatley, R., & Minford, J. (1999) 'Respiratory tract infections due to direct and reflux aspiration in children with severe neurodisability', *Developmental Medicine and Child Neurology*, 41: 329–334.

Moss, S.C., Patel, P., Prosser, H. et al. (1993) 'Psychiatric morbidity in older people with moderate and severe learning disability (mental retardation). Development and reliability of the patient interview (PAS-ADD), *British Journal of Psychiatry*, 163: 471–480.

O'Hara J., McCarthy, J., & Bouras, N. (2010) *Intellectual Disability and Ill health: A Review of the Evidence.* World Psychiatric Association Booklet. Cambridge: Cambridge University Press.

O'Keefe, N. & O'Hara, J. (2007) 'Mental health of parents with intellectual disabilities', *Current Opinion in Psychiatry*, 21: 463–468.

Oliver C. (1995) 'Self-injurious behaviour in children with learning disabilities—recent advances in assessment and intervention', *Journal of Child Psychology and Psychiatry*, 36: 909–927.

Oliver, C. & Holland, A.J. (1986) 'Downs syndrome and Alzheimer's disease: a review', *Psychological Medicine*, 16: 307–322.

Owen, D.M., Hastings, R.P., Noone, S.J. et al. (2004) 'Life events as correlates of problem behaviour and mental health in a residential population with developmental disabilities', *Research in Developmental Disabilities,* 25: 309–320.

Patja, K. (2000) 'Life expectancy of people with intellectual disability: a 35-year follow-up study', *Journal of Intellectual Disability Research*, 44: 590–599.

Parkes, G. & Hollins, S. (2007) 'Psychodynamic approaches to people with intellectual disabilities: individuals, groups/systems, and families', in N. Bouras & G. Holt (eds), *Psychiatric and Behavioural Disorders in Intellectual and Developmental Disabilities.* Cambridge: Cambridge University Press.

Paschos, D. & Bouras, N. (2007) 'Mental health supports in developmental disabilities', in S.L. Odom, R.H. Horner, M.E. Snell, & J. Blacher (eds), *Handbook of Developmental Disabilities.* New York: Guilford Press.

Patel, P., Goldberg, D., & Moss, S. (1993) 'Psychiatric morbidity in older people with moderate and severe learning disabilities II: The prevalence study', *British Journal of Psychiatry*, 163: 481–491.

Pearson, D., Lane, D., Santos, C., et al., (2004) 'Effects of methylphenidate treatment in children with mental retardation and ADHD: individual variation in medication response', *Journal of American Academy of Child and Adolescent Psychiatry*, 43: 686–698.

Perry, J. & Felce, D. (2003) 'Quality of life outcomes for people with intellectual disabilities living in staffed community housing services: A stratified random sample of statutory, voluntary and private agency provision', *Journal of Applied Research in Intellectual Disabilities*, 16: 11–28.

Pretti-Frontczak, K. & Bricker, D. (2004) *An Activity-Based Approach to Early Intervention,* 3rd ed. Baltimore: Brookes.

Richards, M., Maughan, B., Hardy, R. et al. (2001) 'Long-term affective disorder in people with mild learning disability', *British Journal of Psychiatry*, 179: 523–527.

Richardson, S.A. & Koeller, H. (1996) *Twenty-Two Years: Causes and Consequences of Mental Retardation.* Cambridge, MA: Harvard University Press.

Rutter, M., Tizard, J., & Whitmore, K. (1970) *Education, Health and Behaviour.* London: Longman.

Scott, S. (2009) 'Conduct disorders in childhood and adolescence', In M.G. Gelder, N.C. Andreasen, J.J. Lopez-Ibor Jr, & J.R Geddes (eds), *New Oxford Textbook of Psychiatry,* 2nd edn. Oxford: Oxford University Press, pp.1654–1663.

Simonoff, E., Pickles, A., Wood, N., Gringas, P., & Chadwick, O. (2007) 'ADHD symptoms in children with mild intellectual disability', *Journal of the American Academy of Child and Adolescent Psychiatry*, 46: 591–600.

Singer, L., Yamashita, T., Lilien, L., Collin, M., Baley, A., (1997) 'A longitudinal study of developmental outcome of infants with bronchopulmonary dysplasia and very low birth weight', *Journal of Paediatrics*, 100: 987–993.

Stavrakaki, C. & Lunsky, Y. (2007) 'Depression, anxiety and adjustment disorders in people with intellectual disabilities', In N. Bouras & G. Holt (eds), *Psychiatric and Behavioural Disorders in Intellectual and Developmental Disabilities.* Cambridge: Cambridge University Press.

Stromme, P. & Diseth, T.H. (2000) 'Prevalence of psychiatric diagnoses in children with mental retardation: data from a population-based study', *Developmental Medicine and Child Neurology*, 42: 266–270.

Styrdom, A., Livingston, G., King, M., & Hassiotis, A. (2007) 'Prevalence of dementia in intellectual disability using different diagnostic criteria', *British Journal of Psychiatry*, 191: 150–157.

Straetmans, J.M.J.A.A., van Schrojenstein Lamtman-de Valk, H.M.J., Schellevis, F.G., & Dinant, G-J. (2007) 'Health problems of people with intellectual disabilities: the impact of general practice', *British Journal of General Practice*, 57: 64–66.

Sturmey, P., Reed, J., & Corbett, J.A. (1991) 'Psychometric assessment of psychiatric disorders in people with learning disabilities (mental handicap): a review of measures', *Psychological Medicine*, 21: 134–155.

Tonge, B. (2007) 'The psychopathology of children with intellectual disabilities', in N. Bouras & G. Holt (eds), *Psychiatric and Behavioural Disorders in Intellectual and Developmental Disabilities.* Cambridge: Cambridge University Press.

Tonge, B.J. & Einfeld, S. (2003) 'Psychopathology and intellectual disability: the Australian child to adult longitudinal study', in L.M. Glidden (ed.), *International Review of Research in Mental Retardation.* San Diego, CA: Academic Press, 27: 61–91.

Torr, J. & Davis, R. (2007) 'Ageing and mental health problems in people with intellectual disability', *Current Opinion in Psychiatry*, 20: 467–471.

Totsika, V., Toogood, S., Hastings, R.P., & Lewis, S. (2008) 'Persistence of challenging behaviours in adults with intellectual disability over a period of 11 years', *Journal of Intellectual Disability Research*, 52, 446–457.

UNESCO (1994) *Salamanca Statement and Framework for Action.* World Conference on Special Needs Education: Access and Equality. Salamanca, Spain.

Vanstraelen, M. & Tyrer, S.P. (1999) 'Rapid cycling bipolar disorder in people with intellectual disability: a systematic review', *Journal of Intellectual Disability Research,* 43: 349–359.

Wallander, J.L., Dekker, M.C., & Koot, H.M. (2006) 'Risk factors for psychopathology in children with intellectual disability: a prospective longitudinal-based study', *Journal of Intellectual Disability Research*, 50: 259–268.

Welsh Office (1995) *Welsh Health Survey 1995.* Cardiff: Welsh Office.

World Health Organization (WHO) (1992) *The ICD-10 Classification of Mental and Behavioural Disorders.* Geneva: World Health Organization.

WHO (World Health Organisation) (1993) *ICD-10 Classification of Mental and Behavioural Disorders. Diagnostic Criteria for Research.* Geneva: World Health Organization.

World Health Organization (2007) *Atlas on Global Resources for Persons with Intellectual Disabilities.* Geneva: World Health Organization.

Zigman, W.B., Schupf, N., Devenny, D.A. et al. (2004) 'Incidence and prevalence of dementia in elderly adults with mental retardation without Down syndrome', *American Journal of Mental Retardation*, 109(2): 126–141.

20

The Disintegrative Disorders

Fred R. Volkmar

The two current official approaches to diagnosis—*International Classification of Diseases* (ICD-10) (WHO, 1994) and *Diagnostic and Statistical Manual of Mental Disorders,* 4th edn (DSM-IV) (APA, 1994, 2000)—recognize two conditions in which developmental deterioration is a prominent and defining central feature. These are childhood disintegrative disorder (CDD) (previously sometimes referred to as disintegrative psychosis of Heller's syndrome) and Rett disorder. In addition to these two explicitly defined conditions it also has long been recognized that in perhaps 20% of cases children with more classical autism some degree of developmental skill loss occurs. In this chapter the primary focus is on CDD and Rett disorder, although the issue of 'regressive autism' and its relationship, particularly to CDD, is discussed.

HISTORICAL PERSPECTIVES

A century ago Theodore Heller, a Viennese special educator (Heller, 1908) reported six cases in which children who had previously been normal exhibited a profound regression

in their development around ages 3–4 years. Following this regression, recovery was minimal. His first term for the condition, dementia infantilis, was succeeded by a number of other terms, of which the most frequently used was the term 'disintegrative psychosis.' However, the term 'psychosis' was used quite broadly and the children would not be thought of as exhibiting a psychotic condition as the latter term is typically used today (Volkmar, 1996). For many years debate centered on whether CDD and/or autism might be some form of schizophrenia, but the pioneering work of Kolvin (1971) and Rutter (1972) questioned this view. As cases of CDD were more carefully assessed, it became clear that the clinical features were much more like those observed in autism—e.g. in terms of impaired social interaction and communication—although the age and type of onset were distinctive (Volkmar & Rutter, 2005). Autism was first accorded official diagnostic status in DSM-III and there was some provision for a new 'later onset' form of pervasive developmental disorder (PDD); childhood-onset PDD although this was not truly analogous to Heller's diagnostic concept. Indeed, in general, in DSM-III the presumption was that most cases of what now would be termed

CDD were probably a function of some form of childhood dementia.

In contrast, the 9th edition of the *International Classification of Diseases*: (ICD-9, 1978) had disintegrative psychosis or Heller's syndrome defined on the basis of 'normal or near normal development in the first years of life, followed by a loss of social skills and of speech together with a severe disorder of emotion, behavior, and relationships.' For DSM-IV and ICD-10 a large, international field trial was undertaken, and in addition to sampling known cases of CDD others were newly identified (Volkmar & Rutter, 1995; Volkmar et al., 1994) and the condition was included in both manuals and defined in essentially the same way (see below).

In 1966, Andrea Rett (1966) reported on a series of girls with developmental difficulties suggestive of autism but who also exhibited unusual and striking hand-wringing movements. His original report suggested that the condition was associated with movement problems and deterioration as well as autistic features and hyperammonemia; the latter was a false lead for subsequent research and probably also delayed broader recognition of the condition. Hagberg and his colleagues independently observed similar cases (Hagberg et al., 1983).

Unaware of Rett's work, Bengt Hagberg was working with patients displaying similar symptoms in Sweden. In 1980, he presented a paper at the European Federation of Child Neurology Societies describing 16 girls he had observed. Later, he and a number of colleagues (Hagberg et al., 1983) published a series of cases of what they termed 'a progressive syndrome of autism, dementia, ataxia, and loss of purposeful hand use in girls.' Their work stimulated additional research which led to the official recognition of Rett disorder as an officially accepted condition placed within the overarching PDD category in both DSM-IV and ICD-10. A gene has subsequently been discovered that appears to be involved in most, if not all, cases of Rett disorder.

EPIDEMIOLOGY

CDD is clearly a relatively rare condition, with most reviews of the literature suggesting a rate of 1–2 cases in 100,000 live births (Fombonne, 2005). Given the rarity of the condition, cases generally seem sporadic within a particular family, although one case has been noted in a family with an additional child on the autism spectrum (Zwaigenbaum et al., 2000).

In Rett disorder the early work of Hagberg (1985) suggested a rate of about 1 in 12,000 to 13,000 females. A prevalence study conducted in Texas (Kozinetz et al., 1993) reported a rate of about 1 in 23,000 live births. Although relatively uncommon, the condition is an important differential diagnostic consideration in girls with progressive developmental disabilities and probably accounts for up to one-third of cases (VanAcker et al., 2005). Boys with the condition and girls with variants of it have now been identified.

The phenomenon of regression in more classical cases of autism is of interest given the potential that 'regressive' autism may overlap largely or entirely with CDD: i.e. it is the phenomenon of regression that is particularly important. Although there is a body of work on this topic, the data tend to be somewhat confusing, which reflects several issues. First it is clear that parent report of the phenomenon of regression typically suggests that 20–25% of cases in autism are reported as 'regression'. And while it is clear that the phenomenon occurs, very different approaches have been taken to defining it: e.g. is parent report sufficient? Must the regression be dramatic? What if a pattern of developmental stagnation rather than regression is noted? One study from our center (Siperstein & Volkmar, 2004) suggested that in many cases of reported 'regressive autism' the regression was not so clear, since the child had pre-existing developmental delays (also reported by the parents). In other cases the pattern was one more of developmental stagnation (e.g. one or two words develop, but then language does not 'blossom'). Clear-cut cases of regression were relatively uncommon. Given these issues, comparison of studies of 'regressive autism' are particularly difficult to interpret, with some studies finding few, if any, differences (Davidovitch et al., 2000) but in other cases regression, even at an early age, appears associated with poor outcome (Klin et al., 2004). Fortunately the advent of videotape has simplified, to some extent, the issue of documentation and the issue will probably be particularly well addressed in the series of ongoing prospective studies of siblings at risk for autism.

CAUSATION

The original impression that CDD represented a childhood dementia has not proven easy to verify—indeed, in most cases, despite careful and thorough neurological work-up, a specific biological cause is not found. On the other hand, several lines of data do suggest the relevance of neurobiological processes: e.g. electroencephalo gram (EEG) abnormalities and frank seizure disorders are relatively common (Kurita et al., 2004; Malhotra & Gupta, 1999, 2002; Mouridsen et al., 1999; Volkmar, 1992; Volkmar & Rutter, 1995; Volkmar et al., 2005). The phenomenon of regression in autism has been reported with, and without, obvious seizure disorder (Tuchman & Rapin, 1997). The frequency with which seizures are observed suggests that EEG should be part of routine medical assessment.

The early impression, e.g. in DSM-III and DSM III-R, was that CDD was always associated with a progressive neuropathological process. Clearly, regression can be associated with a host of neurological conditions (Nunn et al., 2002). However, such cases are not usually observed in CDD (Volkmar, 1997) (see Table 20.1).

Initially it appeared that Rett disorder was a condition only found in girls, which suggested an X-linked dominant pattern of inheritance in girls with the mutation being lethal in the case of males. Following the recognition of Rett disorder as a specific category of disturbance,

Table 20.1   Selected Disorders Associated with Loss of Developmental Skills*

Infections (HIV, measles, CMV)	Mitochondrial deficits (e.g. Leigh disease)
Hypothyroidism	Subacute sclerosing panencephalitis
Neurolipidosis	Metachromatic leukodystrophy
Addison–Schilder disease	Seizures
Angleman syndrome	Gangliosidoses
Lipofuscinosis	Aminoacidopathies (e.g. PKU)

CMV, cytomegalovirus; HIV, human immunodeficiency virus, PKU, phenylketonuria.

*For an exhaustive list, see Dyken, P. & Krawiecku, M. (1983), 'Neurodegenerative disorders of infancy and childhood', *Annals of Neurology*, 13: 351–364. Reprinted with permission from Volkmar, F.R., Koenig, K., & State, M. (2005) 'Childhood disintegrative disorder' in *Handbook of Autism and Pervasive Developmental Disorders*, 3rd edn, Vol. 1. Hoboken, NJ: John Wiley and Sons, p. 76.

a specific genetic connection was identified, owing to mutations in the *MeCP-2* gene (Amir et al., 1999). This gene is involved in repressing other genes and appears to be particularly important in the functioning of nerve cells, particularly mature ones, in the brain (Ballestar et al., 2005; Balmer et al., 2002) and is expressed as an X-linked dominant condition. Following the identification of this gene, various variant forms have also been identified. A substantial majority of females with classic Rett disorder express this gene or its variants (Van den Veyver & Zoghbi, 2002); the ability to identify cases with a defect in this gene has also led to the identification of a small number of males with intellectual disability as well as other cases with more autistic-like features or features suggestive of it (Ylisaukko-Oja et al., 2005). Most of the various mutations in this gene appear to be de novo ones, although in a few instances familial transmission has occurred—suggesting a potential use of screening information relative to future pregnancies. It is important to note that while the vast majority of cases exhibit the *MECP-2* defect, others do not (Chahrour et al., 2008); it is possible that future studies will identify other variants in this group of cases. One important aspect of this work is that, with the idenfication of the *MECP-2* gene, it is now possible to develop animal models of the disorder (Zoghbi, 2005). They are being used to evaluate potential treatments (Chahrour & Zoghbi, 2007; Percy, 2008). It is of note that the severity of Rett disorder has been related to the size of the deletion within the *MECP-2* gene (Neul et al., 2008). Neuropathological changes in Rett disorder include changes in neuron size, dendritic branching, and number of dendritic spines (Armstrong, 2005).

DIAGNOSTIC FEATURES AND CLINICAL CHARACTERISTICS

Following its onset, the clinical presentation of CDD is, in general, very much that of severe 'classical' autism. The onset of the condition is, however, highly distinctive. By definition, in both DSM-IV and ICD-10 the child must have the essentially normal development, with the ability to speak in sentences by age 2 years. In his 1930 review, Heller (1930) noted that the onset was between ages

3 and 5 years and, in general, this remains the peak onset period; in a 2005 review, we (Volkmar et al., 2005) noted that most reported cases, to that point, had an onset between ages 3 and 4 years. By definition, autism has its onset before age 3 years and usually in the first year or two of life. The main problem in differentiation from autism, as is discussed subsequently, relates to later-onset autism—i.e. after age 2 years. It is possible for CDD to have its onset before age 3 years. Interestingly, it is more frequently the case that later-onset autism is autism associated with higher IQ levels (presumably, thus delaying parental and healthcare provider concern) (Volkmar & Cohen, 1989). In some cases, of course, the apparent 'regressive autism' sometimes observed may represent CDD. Kurita (1988) has observed that occasional mild delay may precede the more dramatic onset of CDD. Although current criteria mandate onset after age 2 years, it is possible that some cases of very early-onset 'regressive autism' manifest the same underlying pathophysiological process involved in CDD, although differential diagnostic issues become more complex, e.g. relative to Rett disorder. Figure 20.1 provides a summary of onset in a series of cases of CDD compared to those with autism.

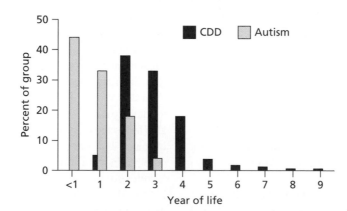

Figure 20.1   Age of onset in 160 cases with clinical diagnoses of CDD and 316 cases with clinical diagnoses of autism. Reprinted with permission from Volkmar, F.R., Koenig, K., & State, M. (2005) 'Childhood disintegrative disorder', in *Handbook of Autism and Pervasive Developmental Disorders,* 3rd edn, Vol. 1. Hoboken, NJ: John Wiley and Sons, p. 73.

In addition to the distinctive age of onset, the pattern of onset of CDD is striking. Prior to the deterioration, the same premonitory period of anxiety, agitation, or dysphasia may be observed. Onset can be relatively rapid (days to weeks) or occasionally somewhat longer (weeks to months), but loss of skills is very striking. Many case reports have noted that onset of the condition is temporally related to some stressful psychosocial or medical event (Evans-Jones & Rosenbloom, 1978; Kobayashi & Murata, 1998), although the significance of such associations remains unclear: one the one hand, the kinds of events typically observed, such as birth of a sibling or death of a grandparent, are fairly common in this age group; on the other hand, the possibility does remain that stress might play some role in syndrome pathogenesis.

A summary of clinical features in reported cases is provided in Table 20.2. In addition to loss of language, self-care skills such as toileting may be lost. The clinical presentation once CDD is established resembles that of autism, with markedly impaired social skills, limited, if any, expressive language, severe cognitive delay, and motor mannerisms. Even when some degree of speech recovery occurs, speech does not usually return to previous levels and is more typically limited to single words/phrase speech. Even for those individuals who subsequently regain speech, it does not typically return to previous levels of communicative ability. Rather, communicative abilities are more similar to those observed in autism, with a scarcity of communicative acts, limited expressive vocabulary, and markedly impaired pragmatic skills. Unusual behaviors—including stereotyped behaviors, problems with transitions and change, and non-specific overactivity—are typically observed (Malhotra & Gupta, 2002).

Table 20.2 Characteristics of Disintegrative Disorder Cases*

Variable	Cases 1908–1975 $N = 48$	Cases 1977–1995 $N = 58$	Cases 1996–2004 $N = 67$
Sex ratio (male/female)	35/12	49/9	53/14
Age at onset[†] (years)	3.42 (1.12)	3.32 (1.42)	3.21 (0.97)
Age at follow-up[†] (years)	8.67 (4.14)	10.88 (5.98)	10.25 (4.81)
Symptoms	Percent of N cases	Percent of N cases	Percent of N cases
Speech deterioration/loss	100 47	100 58	100 54
Social disturbance	100 43	98 57	100 54
Stereotypy/ resistance to change	100 38	85 54	68 54
Overactivity	100 42	77 37	59 54
Affective symptoms/anxiety	100 17	78 38	55 54
Deterioration of self-help skills	94 33	82 49	66 54

* Results based on available data.

† Standard deviation (SD) in parentheses.

Table adapted with permission from Volkmar F.R. (1992) 'Childhood disintegrative disorders: issues for DSM-IV', *Journal of Autism and Developmental Disorders.* 22: 625–642, and Volkmar, F.R., et al. 'Childhood disintegrative disorder', in *Handbook of Autism,* 2nd edn. Additional cases based on case series reported by Kurita et al., 1994; Malhotra & Gupta, 2002 and Mourdisen et al., 2000, with additional cases supplied by Christopher Gillberg and Fred Volkmar. Reprinted with permission from Volkmar, F.R., Koenig, K., State, M. (2005) 'Childhood disintegrative disorder', in *Handbook of Autism and Pervasive Developmental Disorders,* 3rd Edn, Vol. 1 Hoboken, NJ: John Wiley and Sons, p. 74.

In contrast to DSM-IV, the ICD-10 notes that a general loss of interest in the environment can be observed. Loss of self-help skills, e.g. previously acquired toilet training, is fairly frequent (Volkmar et al., 2005); in contrast, in autism, toilet skills may be late in their acquisition but are not usually dramatically lost.

In Rett disorder early development is normal but then followed by a period of slowing and then actual decline, with the onset of the characteristic hand-washing mannerisms. Head growth begins to slow and patients lose interest in their environment. The loss of social interest and deterioration in communication skills become pronounced during the pre-school years and it is during this time that there is the most potential for confusion with autism. A range of symptoms are exhibited and vary depending on the stage of the illness (VanAcker et al., 2005) (see below). EEG abnormalities and breathing problems are frequent, as are characteristic motor and orthopedic problems. Growth and feeding problems are common. Seizures frequently develop (Chahrour & Zoghbi, 2007). The identification of the *MECP-2* gene and potential variant mutations has increased interest in the potentially broader range of cases exhibiting some features suggestive of Rett disorder.

In autism associated with regression there is considerable debate about whether there are important clinical differences between the two conditions. Various problems complicate the interpretation of currently available data: e.g. definitions used for regression, reliance on parent report vs direct observations (e.g. by videotape) (Werner & Dawson, 2005). The tendency, particularly in older studies, to rely exclusively on parent report has been problematic. As noted by some researchers, several rather different patterns of 'regression' in autism are identified, of which the least frequent may be 'true' regression (as defined by clear and unequivocal loss of skills). Inclusion of language deterioration or word loss appears to be one of the

more robust diagnostic markers, but even here issues in definition arise and more stringent definitions (where differences are probably more likely to result) are found in smaller sample sizes. In one recent study, e.g. Hansen and colleagues (2008) conducted a careful study with standard measures and reported that about 15% of their sample lost both social and communication skills, with the suggestion of lower communicative abilities in cases exhibiting regression. The effect size was small, however, reflecting the small number of cases with regression. Other studies have not reported significant differences based on regression histories (Lord et al., 2004). Large sample sizes and, particularly, prospective studies may be of great interest here. With the increased focus on at-risk samples, e.g. siblings, cases where the child has been seen by researchers prior to regression are beginning to be identified (Klin et al., 2004).

ASSESSMENT, DIFFERENTIAL DIAGNOSIS, AND COMORBID CONDITIONS

Rett disorder and CDD are sometimes confused: given that regression is involved in both conditions, this is not surprising. The differential diagnosis of CDD and Rett disorder includes the other pervasive developmental disorders and other conditions. Careful history and clinical assessment are indicated. Once established, CDD shares many essential features with autism and the early course of Rett disorder, particularly in the pre-school years, may be suggestive of autism. In most cases of autism, parents do not report a clear period of normal development, although in a minority of cases a regression may be noted. Accordingly, complexities may arise if historical information is inadequate. Often, in autism, the report of truly prolonged normal development becomes questionable if a careful history is taken (Siperstein &

Volkmar, 2004). In CDD, early development should be essentially unequivocally normal, with the child able to speak in sentences prior to the onset of the condition. In rare instances, there may be confusion of CDD with other psychiatric disorders such as schizophrenia, although onset of schizophrenia before age 5 years is vanishingly rare; usually, the characteristic findings of schizophrenia on clinical examination will clarify the diagnosis.

The identification of the *MECP-2* gene mutation had led to the development of laboratory tests that may confirm the diagnosis, although false negatives are sometimes observed. Mutations in the gene can take several forms, including deletions or insertions of DNA and changes at the level of single base pairs. Case reports of individuals with features of both Rett disorder and Angelman syndrome (intellectual deficiency associated with movement problems and affective symptoms) have been noted.

Other conditions may present with loss of skills. The syndrome of acquired aphasia with epilepsy (Landau–Kleffner syndrome) is characterized by acquired aphasia in association with multifocal spike and spike/wave discharges on EEG, with an onset in childhood (Landau & Kleffner, 1998). Typically, the regression is largely confined to language, with social and non-verbal abilities relatively spared; often there can be considerable recovery (Bishop, 1985). History, EEG, clinical presentation, and course help differentiate this condition from CDD and Rett disorder. A history of language regression should always prompt careful clinical assessment and EEG since clearly this, and other, epileptic conditions may present with some degree of regression. Seizures and EEG abnormalities are, of course, also frequent in both CDD and Rett disorder but the pattern observed with Landau–Kleffner syndrome is relatively unique (Shinnar et al., 2001). Developmental deterioration, with at least some features suggestive of autism, may be observed following major CNS insult or the onset of seizure disorder, although these observations are based on a relatively small number of cases and issues of diagnosis can be problematic.

EVALUATION AND MANAGEMENT

Initial evaluation of the child with significant regression typically involves the efforts of many professionals from various disciplines, including psychology, speech-communication, medicine (psychiatry, neurology, pediatrics, and genetics) and others (occupational, physical, and respiratory therapists). There is considerable potential for duplication of effort and, accordingly, coordination is needed. Sometimes this is provided the child's primary healthcare provider but at other times one of the various professionals may need to assume this role, which, depending on the results of various evaluations and potentially even the laboratory tests, may change over time. Parents should be actively involved in the assessment process to the extent possible.

A careful developmental, medical, and family history is particularly helpful for diagnostic purposes. This should include systematic review of the pregnancy and neonatal period. Any documentation (baby books, videotapes) of early development of the child is often helpful. Dramatic developmental deterioration will usually prompt rapid and thorough evaluation for potentially inherited neurological or genetic conditions. Laboratory tests for inherited conditions will be informed by history and clinical presentation. EEG is almost routine, although the yield is variable. Computed tomography (CT) or magnetic resonance imaging (MRI) scan may also be obtained. Given advances in the diagnosis of Rett disorder, consultation with a specialist in genetics is indicated.

The goal for developmental assessments (including communication and, if relevant, motor skills) include obtaining estimates of current levels of functioning both for purposes of programming and in document subsequent response to treatment (Klin et al., 2005). Given sometimes much lower levels of cognitive or communicative ability' 'out of level' testing, e.g. via use of developmental tests or instruments designed for younger children, may be appropriate. Similarly, for the non-verbal child, assessment of non-verbal problem-solving skills may be appropriate. Autism-specific diagnostic instruments may be helpful in document levels of autistic symptomatology (Lord & Corsello, 2005). The Vineland Adaptive Behavior Scales (expanded form) (Sparrow et al., 2005) is a valuable instrument, given its ability to document current levels of adaptive ability and highlight areas for intervention. For children with Rett disorder, the efforts of occupational and physical therapists as well as respiratory therapists may be needed (VanAcker et al., 2005).

In evaluating the child with a history of regression, careful attention should be paid to current, and past development, e.g., social skills (e.g. deferential attachments, interest in parents and peers, use of gaze), communication (receptive and expressive, articulation problems, typical utterances, language levels prior to the regression, nature of language loss), and the presence of difficulties with change or unusual motor behaviors. Loss of skills should be a particular focus for inquiry. Observation of the child in various structured and less-structured settings is also often very helpful.

CURRENT RESEARCH

As noted above, the body of research on these conditions is relatively small. The great advance represented by discovery of the *MECP-2* gene has triggered a marked increase in work on Rett disorder and associated disorders and the development of an animal model and possible new treatments is particularly exciting (Zoghbi, 2005). Research on CDD and 'regressive autism' has proceeded at a slower pace that reflects

both the lack of specific etiological models and the difficulties in obtaining a sufficiently large sample. Recent attempts to deal with the latter problem, e.g. through collaborative, multi-site studies, are promising (Luyster et al., 2005).

COURSE AND PROGNOSIS

Information on course and outcome is an important factor for evaluating the validity of psychiatric conditions. In CDD, in approximately 75% of cases, the child's behavior and development deteriorate to a much lower level of functioning and remains there. On the one hand, no further deterioration occurs but subsequent developmental gains appear to be minimal (Volkmar & Cohen, 1989). In other cases, the marked developmental regression seems to be followed by a limited recovery: e.g. a child regains the capacity to speak, although usually only in a limited way (Volkmar & Cohen, 1989). Burd et al. (1998) provided data on two children with CDD, followed up after 14 years; at the time of follow-up, both were severely impaired, exhibited seizure disorder, were non-verbal, and were in residential treatment. With greater awareness of the condition, more cases are being seen at younger ages and eventual longer-term follow-up of these cases will be needed.

In general, it appears that in most (75%) of cases of CDD, behavior and development deteriorate to lower levels of functioning but then remain stable (Volkmar et al., 2005). This is different than the pattern usually seen in autism (Howlin, 2005) and different from that in progressive neurological disorders. In a comparatively small number of cases, some degree of recovery occurs: e.g. the child who has entirely lost speech regains the ability to use single words or simple word combinations (Volkmar & Cohen, 1989). In general, it appears that no further regression occurs, but recovery is minimal (Burd et al., 1998; Volkmar & Cohen, 1989). Less commonly, the course of deterioration is progressive and this is more likely if an associated progressive neuropathological process is identified (Corbett, 1987; Mouridsen et al., 1998). In one case, the author is personally aware of the child died in adolescence during a seizure. In rare instances, notable recovery is observed; sadly, this is uncommon (Volkmar et al., 2005).

In Rett disorder several distinct clinical stages of the condition have been identified (Hagberg, 2002; VanAcker et al., 2005). Onset of the condition is usually noted between 6 and 18 months, with slowed motor growth and hypotonia developing. The second phase of the condition, sometimes referred to as the rapid destructive phase, follows (ages 1–4 years), where previously acquired developmental skills are lost and the characteristic hand movements are noted. Breathing problems and ataxia/apraxia are often observed. It is during this phase that the resemblance to autism is most striking, with loss/deterioration of social and communication skills. During the plateau or 'pseudostationary' period (roughly 2–10 years) the autistic-like features become less dramatic; scoliosis and movement problems are observed and seizures may develop, although communication skills may actually improve. In the final period of late motor deterioration (ages 10+), seizures may decrease and cognitive functioning stabilize, although decreased mobility and additional motor deterioration is typical.

difficulties may be helpful, e.g. in relation to agitation and repetitive movements (Scahill & Martin, 2005). There should be a careful assessment of potential risks and benefits.

The management of Rett disorder also includes careful attention to motor and respiratory difficulties as well as surveillance for potential medical problems (seizures, possible cardiac problems including long QT syndrome) and nutritional issues (limited weight gain). A small body of work on drug treatment of behavioral difficulties exists, including use of SSRIs (selective serotonin reuptake inhibitors) and antipsychotic drugs.

Support of family members is critical, particularly since the long-term outcome of these conditions may be worse than that for autism. This support should include parents and siblings as well as extended family members (particularly when they can offer practical support for the child and family). Parents should be helped to obtain access to needed resources. Other parents may be valuable sources of support. School programs for the child should include a focus on generalization of skills to home and community settings. The families (parents, siblings, and extended family members) of patients should be supported. This includes provision of appropriate information about the condition, helping families make use of available local and other resources, and helping family members receive mutual support, e.g. through support groups.

INTERVENTION

Treatment of cases of CDD is essentially the same as for children with autism. Thus, special education and behavioral interventions should be used to encourage development, or redevelopment, of basic skills. Fostering communication at whatever level is possible is also important; this can take the form of augmentative approaches. Although there are no specific pharmacological treatments, as in autism, the use of certain agents for behavioral

CONCLUSION

As outlined in this chapter, the discovery of a specific genetic mechanism has transformed research into Rett disorder. Although CDD has been recognized for over a century, its study remains, paradoxically, much less advanced. Several different sets of issues present challenges for future research. In Rett disorder, the current focus is on development of animal models, evaluation of new treatments, and exploration of the range of variants of the condition. It is important to note that this work would not have been possible without a mechanism for explicitly 'flagging' cases of the condition. Similarly, the development of case registries and efforts to stimulate research have been amply rewarded.

For CDD and late-onset or regressive autism the lack of research reflects the considerable difficulty in assembly of reasonably large samples of cases. This is particularly unfortunate since some obvious and fundamental issues could, presumably, be resolved relatively quickly if such research were conducted. For example, the rather conflicting literature on the significance (or lack thereof) of regression in autism might be significantly advanced by large-scale studies and, indeed, a few have now been conducted. Given the rarity of CDD, multicenter studies and case registries may facilitate advancement of the research enterprise. As the *MECP-2* story in Rett disorder illustrates, having specific etiological mechanisms can produce profound changes in our understanding of disorders of these types.

REFERENCES

Amir, R.E., Van den Veyver, I.B. et al. (1999) 'Rett syndrome is caused by mutations in X-linked MeCP2, encoding methyl-CpG-binding protein 2', *Nature Genetics,* 23: 185–188.

APA (1994/2001) *Diagnostic and Statistical Manual of Mental Disorders,* 4th edn. Washington, DC: American Psychiatric Association Press; text revision 2001.

Armstrong, D.D. (2005) 'Neuropathology of Rett syndrome', *Journal of Child Neurology,* 20(9): 747–753.

Ballestar, E., Ropero, S. et al. (2005) 'The impact of MECP2 mutations in the expression patterns of Rett syndrome patients', *Human Genetics,* 116(1–2): 91–104.

Balmer, D., Arredondo, J. et al. (2002) 'MECP2 mutations in Rett syndrome adversely affect lymphocyte growth, but do not affect imprinted gene expression in blood or brain', *Human Genetics,* 110(6): 545–552.

Bishop, D.V. (1985) 'Age of onset and outcome in "acquired aphasia with convulsive disorder"

(Landau–Kleffner syndrome)', *Developmental Medicine and Child Neurology,* 27(6): 705–712.

Burd, L., Ivey, M. et al. (1998) 'Two males with childhood disintegrative disorder: a prospective 14-year outcome study', *Developmental Medicine and Child Neurology,* 40(10): 702–707.

Chahrour, M. & Zoghbi, H.Y. (2007) 'The story of Rett syndrome: from clinic to neurobiology', *Neuron,* 56(3): 422–437.

Chahrour, M., Jung, S.Y. et al. (2008) 'MeCP2, a key contributor to neurological disease, activates and represses transcription', *Science,* 320(5880): 1224–1229.

Corbett, J. (1987) 'Development, disintegration and dementia', *Journal of Mental Deficiency Research* 31(Pt 4): 349–356.

Davidovitch, M., Glick, L. et al. (2000) 'Developmental regression in autism: maternal perception', *Journal of Autism and Developmental Disorders,* 30(2): 113–119.

Evans-Jones, L.G. & Rosenbloom, L. (1978) 'Disintegrative psychosis in childhood', *Developmental Medicine and Child Neurology,* 20(4): 462–470.

Fombonne, E. (2005) 'Epidemiological studies of pervasive developmental disorders', in F.R. Volkmar, R. Paul, A. Klin, & D. Cohen (eds), *Handbook of Autism and Pervasive Developmental Disorders,* 3rd edn. Hoboken, NJ: John Wiley & Sons, pp. 42–69.

Hagberg, B. (1985) 'Rett's syndrome: prevalence and impact on progressive severe mental retardation in girls', *Acta Paediatrica Scandinavica,* 74(3): 405–408.

Hagberg, B. (2002) 'Clinical manifestations and stages of Rett syndrome', *Mental Retardation and Developmental Disabilities Research Reviews,* 8(2): 61–65.

Hagberg, B., Aicardi, J. et al. (1983) 'A progressive syndrome of autism, dementia, ataxia, and loss of purposeful hand use in girls: Rett's syndrome: report of 35 cases', *Annals of Neurology,* 14(4): 471–479.

Hansen, R.L., Ozonoff, S. et al. (2008) 'Regression in autism: prevalence and associated factors in the CHARGE Study', *Ambulatory Pediatrics,* 8(1): 25–31.

Heller, T. (1908) 'Dementia infantilis', *Zeitschrift fur die Erforschung und Behandlung des Jugenlichen Schwachsinns,* 2: 141–165.

Heller, T. (1930) 'Uber Dementia infantalis', *Zeitschrift fur Kinderforschung,* 37: 661–667.

Howlin, P. (2005) 'Outcomes in autism spectrum disorders', in F.R. Volkmar, R. Paul, A. Klin, & D. Cohen (eds), *Handbook of Autism and Pervasive Developmental Disorders,* 3rd edn. Hoboken, NJ: John Wiley and Sons, pp. 201–222.

Klin, A., Chawarska, K. et al. (2004) 'Autism in a 15-month-old child', *American Journal of Psychiatry*, 161(11): 1981–1988.

Klin, A., Saulnier, C. et al. (2005) 'Clinical evaluation in autism spectrum disorders: psychological assessment within a transdisciplinary framework', in F.R. Volkmar, R. Paul, A. Klin, & D. Cohen (eds), *Handbook of Autism and Pervasive Developmental Disorders,* 3rd edn. Hoboken, NJ: John Wiley & Sons, 2: 772–798.

Kobayashi, R. & Murata, T. (1998) 'Setback phenomenon in autism and long-term prognosis', *Acta Psychiatrica Scandinavica,* 98(4): 296–303.

Kolvin, I. (1971) 'Studies in the childhood psychoses. I. Diagnostic criteria and classification', *British Journal of Psychiatry,* 118(545): 381–384.

Kozinetz, C.A., Skender, M.L. et al. (1993) 'Epidemiology of Rett syndrome: a population-based registry', *Pediatrics,* 91(2): 445–450.

Kurita, H. (1988) 'Brief report: a case of Heller's syndrome with school refusal', *Journal of Autism and Developmental Disorders,* 18(2): 315–319.

Kurita, H., Osada, H. et al. (2004) 'External validity of childhood disintegrative disorder in comparison with autistic disorder', *Journal of Autism and Developmental Disorders,* 34(3): 355–362.

Landau, W.M. & Kleffner, F.R. (1998) 'Syndrome of acquired aphasia with convulsive disorder in children. 1957 [classical article]', *Neurology,* 51(5): 1241, 8 pages following 1241.

Lord, C., Corsello, C. (2005) 'Diagnostic instruments in autistic spectrum disorders', in F.R. Volkmar, R. Paul, A. Klin, & D. Cohen (eds), *Handbook of Autism and Pervasive Developmental Disorders,* 3rd edn. Hoboken, NJ: John Wiley & Sons, 2: 730–771.

Lord, C., Shulman, C. et al. (2004). 'Regression and word loss in autistic spectrum disorders', *Journal of Child Psychology and Psychiatry,* 45(5): 936–955.

Luyster, R., Richler, J. et al. (2005) 'Early regression in social communication in autism spectrum disorders: a CPEA study', *Developmental Neuropsychology,* 27(3): 311–336.

Malhotra, S. & Gupta, N. (1999) 'Childhood disintegrative disorder', *Journal of Autism and Developmental Disorders,* 29(6): 491–498.

Malhotra, S. & Gupta, N. (2002) 'Childhood disintegrative disorder: re-examination of the current concept', *European Child & Adolescent Psychiatry,* 11(3): 108–114.

Mouridsen, S.E., Rich, B. et al. (1998) 'Validity of childhood disintegrative psychosis. General findings of a long-term follow-up study', *British Journal of Psychiatry,* 172: 263–267.

Mouridsen, S.E., Rich, B. et al. (1999) 'Epilepsy in disintegrative psychosis and infantile autism: a long-term validation study', *Developmental Medicine and Child Neurology,* 41(2): 110–114.

Mouridsen, S.E., Rich, B. et al. (1999) "Psychiatric morbidity in disintegrative psychosis and infantile long-term follow-up study," *Psychopathology,* 32(4): 177–183.

Neul, J.L., Fang, P. et al. (2008) 'Specific mutations in methyl-CpG-binding protein 2 confer different severity in Rett syndrome [see comment]. *Neurology,* 70(16): 1313–1321.

Nunn, K., Williams, K. et al. (2002) 'The Australian Childhood Dementia Study', *European Child & Adolescent Psychiatry,* 11(2): 63–70.

Percy, A.K. (2008) 'Rett syndrome: recent research progress', *Journal of Child Neurology,* 23(5): 543–549.

Rett, A. (1966) 'Uber ein eigenartiges hirntophisces Syndroem bei hyperammonie im Kindersalter', *Wein Medizinische Wochenschrift,* 118: 723–726.

Rutter, M. (1972) 'Childhood schizophrenia reconsidered', *Journal of Autism and Childhood Schizophrenia,* 2(4): 315–337.

Scahill, L. & Martin, A. (2005) 'Psychopharmacology', in F.R. Volkmar, R. Paul, A. Klin, & D. Cohen (eds), *Handbook of Autism and Pervasive Developmental Disorders,* 3rd edn. Hoboken, NJ: John Wiley & Sons, 2: 1102–1122.

Shinnar, S., Rapin, I. et al. (2001) 'Language regression in childhood', *Pediatric Neurology,* 24(3): 183–189.

Siperstein, R. & Volkmar, F. (2004) 'Brief report: parental reporting of regression in children with pervasive developmental disorders', *Journal of Autism and Developmental Disorders,* 34(6): 731–734.

Sparrow, S.S., Cicchetti, D.V. et al. (2005) *Vineland Adaptive Behavior Scales: Second Edition (Vineland II). Survey Interview Form/Caregiver Rating Form.* Livonia, MN: Pearson.

Tuchman, R.F. & Rapin, I. (1997) 'Regression in pervasive developmental disorders: seizures and epileptiform electroencephalogram correlates', *Pediatrics,* 99(4): 560–566.

VanAcker, R., Loncola, J.A. et al. (2005) 'Rett syndrome: a pervasive developmental disorder', in F.R. Volkmar, R. Paul, A. Klin, & D. Cohen (eds), *Handbook of Autism and Pervasive Developmental Disorders,* 3rd edn. Hoboken, NJ: John Wiley & Sons, pp. 126–164.

Van den Veyver, I.B. & Zoghbi, H.Y. (2002) 'Genetic basis of Rett syndrome', *Mental Retardation and Developmental Disabilities Research Reviews,* 8(2): 82–86.

Volkmar, F.R. (1992) 'Childhood disintegrative disorder: issues for DSM-IV', *Journal of Autism and Developmental Disorders,* 22(4): 625–642.

Volkmar, F.R. (ed.) (1996) 'The disintegrative disorders: childhood disintegrative disorder and Rett's disorder', *Psychoses and Pervasive Developmental Disorders in Childhood and Adolescence.* Washington, DC: American Psychiatric Press, pp. 223–248.

Volkmar, F.R. (1997) 'Childhood disintegrative disorder', in T.A. Widiger, H.A. Pincus, R. Ross, M.B. First, & W. Davis (eds), *DSM-IV Sourcebook.* Washington, DC: American Psychiatric Association Press, 3: 35–42.

Volkmar, F.R. & Cohen, D.J. (1989) 'Disintegrative disorder or "late onset" autism', *Journal of Child Psychology and Psychiatry,* 30(5): 717–724.

Volkmar, F.R. & Rutter, M. (1995) 'Childhood disintegrative disorder: results of the DSM-IV autism field trial', *Journal of the American Academy of Child and Adolescent Psychiatry,* 34(8): 1092–1095.

Volkmar, F.R., Klin, A., Siegel, B., Szatmari, P., Lord, C., Campbell, M., Freeman, B.J., Cicchetti, D.V., Rutter, M., Kline, W., et al. (1994) 'Field trial for autistic disorder in DSM-IV', *American Journal of Psychiatry,* 151: 1361–1367.

Volkmar, F.R., Koenig, K. et al. (2005) 'Childhood disintegrative disorder', in F.R. Volkmar, R. Paul, A. Klin, & D. Cohen (eds), *Handbook of Autism and Pervasive Developmental Disorders,* 3rd edn. Hoboken, NJ: John Wiley & Sons, pp. 70–78.

Werner, E. & Dawson, G. (2005) 'Validation of the phenomenon of autistic regression using home videotapes', *Archives of General Psychiatry,* 62(8): 889–895.

World Health Organization (1994) *Diagnostic Criteria for Research.* Geneva: World Health Organization.

Ylisaukko-Oja, T., Rehnstrom, K. et al. (2005) 'MECP2 mutation analysis in patients with mental retardation', *American Journal of Medical Genetics Part A,* 132(2): 121–124.

Zwaigenbaum, L., Szatmari, P. et al. (2000) 'High functioning autism and childhood disintegrative disorder in half brothers', *Journal of Autism and Developmental Disorders,* 30(2): 121–126.

Zoghbi, H.Y. (2005) 'MeCP2 dysfunction in humans and mice', *Journal of Child Neurology,* 20(9): 736–740.

21

Epileptic Disorders

Ian Miller & Roberto Tuchman

INTRODUCTION AND HISTORICAL PERSPECTIVE

Epilepsy is a common problem in the general population, with a lifetime prevalence of 1 to 2% (McDermott et al., 2005). Epileptic disorders do not represent a single disease entity. As with many of the developmental disorders highlighted in this handbook, epilepsy is a chronic disorder with an array of etiologies and pathologies. The hallmark of epilepsy is recurrent unprovoked seizures, which are associated with cognitive, language, behavioral, and psychiatric problems in a significant proportion of children. The severity and variety of developmental impairment associated with epileptic disorders reflect focal or global, structural or functional disruption of neuronal networks.

Individuals with epileptic disorders are more likely to have developmental impairments affecting learning, social interaction, and mood than those without epilepsy (Bender et al., 2007; Camfield & Camfield, 2007a; Fastenau et al., 2008; Piccinelli et al., 2008; Prassouli et al., 2007; Salpekar & Dunn, 2007). One in four children with epilepsy are likely to have subnormal global cognitive skills (Berg et al., 2008). The con-

verse is also true: in individuals with developmental disabilities, the lifetime prevalence of epilepsy is 10–30% (Kirby et al., 1995; Murphy et al., 1995). The association between developmental disorders and epilepsy increases with the degree of mental impairment. Severe cognitive impairment and motor involvement are both associated with higher risk of epilepsy (Goulden et al., 1991; Hadjipanayis et al., 1997; Hauser et al., 1993).

The historical roots between epilepsy and developmental disorders can be traced to the 1950s when an association between infantile spasms and mental retardation was first described (Low et al., 1958). The association of metabolic disorders with epilepsy and with developmental disorders was described in the 1960s (Stemmermann, 1965), as was the relationship between genetic syndromes associated with both epilepsy and developmental impairments (Bower & Jeavons, 1967). In addition, the high prevalence of behavioral disorders and cognitive impairments in individuals with epilepsy was recognized (Hung, 1968). From a historical perspective the coexistence of epilepsy and autism was a significant observation that shifted the paradigm of thinking about developmental and behavioral disorders within a neurobiological framework (Tuchman, 1994).

In the 1970s and 1980s diagnostic criteria for epilepsy (Anon, 1989) and specific developmental disorders such as autism (Lord et al., 1989) were developed. Consistent definitions allowed for systematic collection of epidemiological data, which helped identify common risk factors for epilepsy and related developmental conditions (Tuchman & Rapin, 1997; Tuchman et al., 1991; Volkmar & Nelson, 1990).

The understanding of the relationship between developmental disorders and epilepsy from the 1990s until the present has built upon these initial classification systems with genetic and computational tools. Developmental disorders that are associated with epilepsy, such as autism, are increasingly becoming the models for how the two interact. Molecular biology has played a key role in this progress, and will remain an area of active research (Abrahams & Geschwind, 2008). An understanding of the molecular neurobiology common to epilepsy and development will foster specific treatments and methods of prevention.

EPIDEMIOLOGY

Understanding the terminology of epileptic and developmental disorders is essential for any discussion of their epidemiology.

Epilepsy, like developmental disorders, is a heterogeneous group of conditions. The term 'epilepsy' is used to refer to the occurrence of more than one unprovoked seizure. A seizure is a paroxysmal, clinically evident event associated with sustained, periodic electrical activity in the brain. A distinction exists between 'provoked seizures', which are due to an external provocation (such as fever, medication withdrawal, infection, trauma, or metabolic illness), and 'unprovoked seizures' which occur in the absence of any trigger. Studies of epilepsy in populations with developmental disorders do not

always respect the distinction between provoked and unprovoked events, or between seizures and epilepsy.

Similarly, there is a distinction between 'primary' (or idiopathic) epilepsy, which is the existence of epilepsy with no identifiable cause, and 'secondary' (or symptomatic) epilepsy, which is epilepsy due to an identifiable medical condition. Here we will focus on idiopathic epileptic disorders and their associated developmental features, as the epidemiology of symptomatic epilepsies is discussed in the respective chapters of this handbook. Nevertheless, some of this discussion may apply more broadly, because individuals with the same primary developmental disorder and similar phenotypes who have the same putative baseline for epilepsy will vary according to underlying biological factors such as cognition, age, and genotype (including polygenic and epigenetic factors).

The most widely used system of terminology, the ILAE Epilepsy Classification System (1989), is not specific to, or even very accommodating of, children with developmental disorders. Whereas there are several epilepsy syndromes that have developmental delay as a feature, there is only one category for secondary epilepsy, 'symptomatic focal epilepsy', in which the clinician is expected to identify the primary process when possible. The category for 'secondary generalized epilepsy' does not officially exist. Therefore, the ILAE system is really a classification system for *primary* epilepsy syndromes, and secondary syndromes are best referred to as the etiologic diagnosis 'with secondary epilepsy'.

The implication is that using a standardized classification system for children with heterogeneous developmental disorders is less meaningful than classification by the primary disorder. This is shown directly by a study on epilepsy and autism by Pavone et al. (2004). They compared rates of epilepsy in two groups of autistic patients: those without identified cause (primary/idiopathic), and those with a known etiology for the autism (secondary/symptomatic). Of 72 children, 7.4% of children in the idiopathic group had epilepsy, as compared to 54% in the symptomatic group.

It may be helpful to classify the seizure type (rather than the epilepsy syndrome), but even this can be difficult, and findings by authors who have studied seizure types in children with developmental disorders have been inconsistent. This may be due to the observation by Camfield et al. (2003) that recognition and classification of seizures in children is difficult, particularly for children with developmental disorders.

Of children with epilepsy, approximately 20% have mental retardation (Camfield & Camfield, 2007b). Similarly, of children with mental retardation, 20% will develop epilepsy by age 21, and the cumulative risk of developing epilepsy increases fivefold in individuals with severe mental retardation (35%) as compared to those with mild mental retardation (7%) (Airaksinen et al., 2000). A population-based registry of adults with mental retardation found the prevalence of epilepsy to be 26% and also found that these individuals had behavioral issues and a range of mental and physical problems requiring complex care (McGrother et al., 2006).

McDermott et al. (2005) looked at rates of epilepsy in patients in a primary care practice. They found prevalence rates of 1% in the general population (patients without neurological disability), as compared to 13% for cerebral palsy, 14% for Down syndrome, 25% for autism, 25% for mental retardation, and 40% for adults with both cerebral palsy and mental retardation. The population prevalence of epilepsy in specific developmental disorders is shown in Table 21.1, which provides population-based estimates of risk. For any individual patient within the population, however, the risk will be influenced by other factors as well.

Age of seizure onset is an important epidemiological variable that is related to cognitive and behavioral outcome. For example, children with autism who have a history of epilepsy at an early age probably represent a subgroup associated with more significant insults to the developing brain, which are manifested as epilepsies of early childhood such as infantile spasms (Curatolo & Cusmai, 1987; Riikonen and Amnell, 1981). From an epilepsy perspective it is estimated that approximately 6–7% of children with epilepsy whose seizure onset is in the first year of life go on to develop autism with mental

Table 21.1   Rates of Epilepsy in Selected Developmental Disorders

Developmental Disorder	Epilepsy Prevalence
Autism	With severe mental retardation rate of epilepsy is approximately 40%. Without significant mental retardation rate of epilepsy is 6% (Tuchman et al., 1991)
Angelman syndrome	Approximately 90% with epilepsy (Pelc et al., 2008)
Disintegrative disorder	Approximately 77% with epilepsy (Mouridsen et al., 1999)
Down syndrome	Approximately 8% with epilepsy (Goldberg-Stern et al., 2001)
Rett syndrome	Approximately 80% with epilepsy (Jian et al., 2007)
Fragile X syndrome	Epilepsy occurs in 10–20% of children with fragile X (Berry-Kravis, 2002)
Smith–Magenis syndrome	Epilepsy occurs in approximately 18% (Goldman et al., 2006)
Tuberous sclerosis	Reported as 80–90% with epilepsy (Holmes & Stafstrom, 2007), but likely less due to ascertainment bias
Turner syndrome	Rare instances of epilepsy (Striano et al., 2005; Vulliemoz et al., 2007)
Velocardiofacial syndrome	Rare instances of epilepsy (El Tahir et al., 2004; Roubertie et al., 2001)
Prader–Willi syndrome	Approximately 15% with epilepsy (Wang et al., 2005)

retardation (Saemundsen et al., 2007). Children with seizure onset prior to age 5 years are at highest risk for poor outcome, as the younger the age of onset of seizures, the higher the association with lower intellectual functioning (Vasconcellos et al., 2001).

ASSESSMENT AND DIFFERENTIAL DIAGNOSIS

The assessment of children with epileptic disorders should be organized and step-wise. Typically, it begins with a child who has had one or more paroxysmal events, usually stereotyped to some degree. Initially, the clinician must consider the diverse list of non-epileptic conditions which can cause paroxysmal attacks. If the clinician is satisfied that the events are epileptic, then he/she must determine if there are features which suggest that the epilepsy is a secondary problem, and that a primary disorder causing the seizures may exist. If the seizures are secondary, the goal should be to identify the primary cause as precisely as possible. If the seizures are the primary problem, then the most precise diagnosis will be the epilepsy syndrome, which is largely determined by the patient's age and seizure semiology.

Differential diagnosis of paroxysmal events

Determining that stereotyped paroxysmal events are seizures can be straightforward. Often, however, the child is unable to articulate the subjective features, the history is obtained from a person who did not witness the events, the events are infrequent, or the events have a non-specific appearance. As a result, distinguishing between epileptic seizures and non-epileptic paroxysmal events can be difficult; more so for children with overt developmental impairment (Camfield et al., 2003). A list of common etiologies of

Table 21.2   Possible Etiologies for Paroxysmal Events

Seizures

Migraine

Syncope/arrhythmia

Tics

Mirror movements

Behavior (stereotypies, response to pain, etc.)

Soothing or self-stimulation (non-sexual)

Onanism/masturbation

Metabolic derangement or crisis

Medication effect/intoxication/ingestion

Psychiatric symptoms, including non-epileptic seizures

Narcolepsy/cataplexy

Physiologic sleep movements

Choreoathetosis

Hyperreflexia/clonus

paroxysmal events is provided in Table 21.2, which illustrates the diversity of possible explanations.

The biggest clue to diagnose a paroxysmal event is the history. Along with epilepsy, migraine and syncope are the most common causes for paroxysmal events. Both have high-specificity features that aid in their distinction. Migrainous phenomena are more often prolonged than epilepsy or syncope. They often have a prodrome with positive neurological symptoms. Frequently, the prodrome is visual, and consists of bright spots, or jagged lines that are either foveal or peripheral. They are often associated with stomach upset or vomiting, are made worse by light, sound, or noise, and are relieved by sleep.

Syncope can be identified by its presyncopal features, short duration, relationship to vagal tone, and relatively prompt recovery. Presyncopal symptoms may include dysequilibrium, diaphoresis, pallor, nausea, palpitations, and blurred vision. Often, the visual change occurs early, and is described as blackening of the peripheral vision, 'as if looking through a tunnel'. The relationship with vagal tone is established by its occurrence when vagal tone changes: most often orthostatic- or Valsalva-related activities. The presence of clonic movements after loss of consciousness does not exclude syncope as a mechanism. 'Convulsive syncope' is well-described, and refers to clonic movements following a syncopal event that are non-epileptic. Electroencephalogram (EEG) testing during head-up tilt table testing shows that they are not seizures (Grubb et al., 1991). They are probably due to brainstem and spinal cord release, rather than being cortically mediated. In children where convulsive syncope is suspected, head-up tilt table testing may be helpful (Samoil et al., 1993).

Ultimately, however, even with a reliable and articulate first-person history, an ictal video EEG (vEEG) is often required. This is especially true in the population of children with developmental disabilities. Thirumalai et al. (2001) evaluated 193 children with undiagnosed paroxysmal events using VEEG, of whom 36% had developmental delay. Definitive diagnosis was successful in 67% of the children overall. Children with developmental delay were more likely ($p < 0.05$) to have events during the study, but the two groups had a similar breakdown between epileptic (52%) and non-epileptic events (41%). In addition, vEEG is often necessary during nocturnal events because the onset is not witnessed and there is physiological alteration of consciousness. Benign sleep myoclonus and sleep starts are common in the general population and occur even more frequently in children with developmental delay and epilepsy (Fusco et al., 1999). They are often associated with sleep transitions, and are associated with arousals from sleep on EEG. In children with cortical injury, the picture is further complicated by the possibility of disinhibited and exaggerated subcortical movements, and as a result, vEEG with ictal capture is frequently required.

Determination of etiology

If the paroxysmal symptoms are determined to be seizures, the clinician must determine if the epilepsy is primary or secondary, and if there is a well-circumscribed clinical syndrome that explains the child's findings. Children with epileptic disorders will segregate themselves into three categories:

- Group 1—children with epilepsy **secondary** to a systemic problem which is **identifiable** and well-circumscribed. Children with an etiological diagnosis are always in this category. Children without an etiologic diagnosis may be in this category if there are characteristic (i.e. highly specific/pathognomonic) features.
- Group 2—children with epilepsy **presumed secondary** to a systemic or neurological condition, but who have **no diagnostic features** of an identifiable primary disorder.
- Group 3—children with **isolated primary epilepsy**. If these children have overt problems with development, behavior, or cognition, then it is termed an **epileptic encephalopathy**.

Examples of children in the first group include disorders such as tuberous sclerosis complex, Aicardi syndrome, or Sturge–Weber syndrome. In these cases, there is unambiguous evidence that the child belongs to a well-circumscribed clinical cohort which will best predict their natural history, prognosis, comorbidities, and response to treatment. The more common of such syndromes (Rett syndrome, fragile X, trisomy 21, etc.) have dedicated chapters in this handbook which are more directly applicable to their constituent populations, and therefore will not be directly discussed here.

The second group is composed of children with neurological problems which predate the epilepsy, or with systemic features which are non-specific, presumably from an occult primary process. It is likely that they will gradually move into the first category as our diagnostic tools improve. Until then, specific diagnoses should be considered whenever new symptoms, problems, or findings are identified. There may also be clues on metabolic screening tests, and a broad range of diagnostic testing is sometimes pursued. Unfortunately, the rate of diagnosis is often low. Kosinovsky et al. (2005) reported a series of 132 infants with autism, 36% of whom had regression. In spite of strong evidence of a primary problem causing the epilepsy, the only helpful diagnostic test was for fragile X (and not EEG, neuroimaging, or metabolic testing).

Children with developmental delay which predates the onset of epilepsy compose a large part of the second group. For these children, the developmental delay may already have been evaluated, and epilepsy represents a new finding to narrow the differential diagnosis. The most common conditions which can explain both findings are summarized in Table 21.3.

Table 21.3 Partial Differential Diagnosis of Epilepsy with Developmental Delay

Trisomy 21

Cytomegalovirus

Lead encephalopathy

Fetal alcohol syndrome

Perinatal encephalopathy ('cerebral palsy')

Chromosome 1p36 deletion

Tuberous sclerosis

Lennox–Gastaut syndrome

Galactosemia type I

Toxoplasmosis

Angelman syndrome

Rett syndrome

MELAS syndrome

Other chromosomal disorders (particularly 22q11.2 deletions)

MCAD

Fukuyama type congenital muscular dystrophy

Lissencephaly; isolated, idiopathic

Smith–Lemli–Opitz syndrome

Cornelia de Lange syndrome

Children in the last group have problems due exclusively to the epilepsy and its effects. An etiological diagnosis may be possible (such as a particular mutation in a sodium channel gene), but is both less likely and less meaningful. Since development was normal prior to the onset of epilepsy, any developmental impairments are likely secondary, and will be determined by seizure frequency, duration, quality, and medication requirements. As a result, the most clinically meaningful classification system for both groups (those with and without encephalopathy) will be the ILAE epilepsy syndromes. For these children, the most helpful features are usually the age of onset, the seizure type, and the degree of cognitive impairment.

In any child without an etiological diagnosis, categorizing the seizure type helps to frame the diagnostic possibilities. For example, both infantile spasms and myoclonic seizures are strongly associated with a short list of etiologic diagnoses (Tables 21.4 and 21.5, respectively), and their presence should guide the diagnostic evaluation. Most seizures in children with developmental disorders of childhood onset begin focally. The challenge is that most parents have difficulty providing a history of early, subtle symptoms (which suggest focality) when subsequent spread causes much more dramatic semiology.

Table 21.4 Etiological Diagnoses Associated with Infantile Spasms

Menkes disease

Pyridoxine-dependent seizures

Folate-deficient seizures

Rett syndrome

Aicardi syndrome

Pyruvate dehydrogenase deficiency

Down syndrome

Serine/threonine kinase 9 gene mutation (severe, X-linked)

ARX (Aristaless related homeobox) gene mutation (with dystonia, X-linked phenotypes)

Kabuki syndrome

Table 21.5 Etiological Diagnoses Associated with Myoclonic Seizures

MERRF syndrome

Lafora body disease

Neuronal ceroid lipofuscinosis

Unverricht–Lundborg disease

MECP2 mutation in males

Menkes disease

Aicardi syndrome

Senile myoclonic epilepsy of Genton in adults with Down syndrome)

SPARKLE mutations

SCN1a mutation causing GEFS+ or Dravet syndrome

As a result, aura or other early subtle features are very specific for focal onset, but very insensitive. The practical implication is that children in the second category can be safely considered to have focal onset, and the children in the third group may or may not. Children in the third, ambiguous category should be strongly considered for vEEG, because the presence of focal onset has implications for treatment (such as epilepsy surgery) as well as diagnosis.

Mental and medical health issues in children with epileptic disorders

Although a seizure is the defining and most overt symptom of epilepsy, there are consistent, measurable effects in other neurological domains. Associations have been demonstrated between epilepsy and cognitive, behavioral, and psychiatric disorders (Caplan et al., 2002; Plioplys et al., 2007). Rates of depression and anxiety are higher for individuals with epilepsy than for the general population (Devinsky et al., 2005). Even though this fact has been recognized for more than 2000 years (Stevens, 1988), they are still underrecognized and undertreated in individuals with epileptic disorders. Wiegartz et al. (1999) reported that 68% of individuals

with epilepsy and a depressive disorder went untreated. This observation is consistent with that of Gilliam et al. (2004), who showed that 80% of neurologists do not routinely screen such individuals for depression.

Children with epileptic disorders are also at high risk for learning disorders. The effects on learning are obvious in a child with an epileptic encephalopathy, but even children with no subjective learning complaint should be screened. Selassie et al. (2008) identified all children with epilepsy in a geographically defined population of 15,457 children. They found that, by age 6, half had an identified associated developmental disorder; i.e. learning disability, cerebral palsy, or autism. The remaining half, however, also had higher rates of learning difficulty, associated with early-onset epilepsy and polytherapy. Measurable differences were seen in performance IQ, auditory attention, and speech-language tasks. These effects are particularly important as they relate to school aptitude. The attentional difficulty, for example, was seen with auditory tasks that would be common in a school setting, and was observed even though none of the children had attention-deficit/hyperactivity disorder (ADHD). The difficulty with speech-language tasks such as early literacy is also notable, due to its potential impact on learning to read or write. The effects on literacy seemed to stem from difficulty with phoneme blending or letter recognition due to visuospatial problems. The authors concluded that oromotor, speech, language, and neuropsychological evaluations are important for all children with epilepsy.

These results are probably affected by clinical heterogeneity as well. Focal epilepsy is network-specific, and can cause impairments based on which network is affected. This is most clearly seen in children with benign childhood epilepsy with central-temporal spikes (BCECTS), who are at particular risk of language impairment (Metz-Lutz & Filippini, 2006). Focal epilepsy also differs from forms of non-focal epilepsy, being 30% more likely to have a language disability (Parkinson, 2002).

Comprehensive neuropsychological assessment of children with epilepsy is helpful from a medical and functional standpoint. Medically, the results of neuropsychological testing can aid in seizure localization by providing indirect evidence of focal dysfunction in discrete networks. Functionally, the results can identify the child's cognitive and academic abilities relative to their peers, which helps in academic placement. It can further identify strengths and weaknesses in specific cognitive domains, which allows teachers to use the child's strengths in the classroom, and therapists to target the child's weaker areas for rehabilitation. Comprehensive testing incorporates elements of general intelligence, academic performance, motor function, language and visual skills, attention and executive function, and emotional and behavioral issues (Stanford & Miller, 2007). It is an indispensable tool to identify educational needs as children enter school, and to intervene with an educational treatment plan.

The general intelligence portion of testing provides the global baseline against which discrete cognitive skills can be compared. When there is a discrepancy, it helps flag that cognitive domain as an area of strength or weakness. In addition, most intelligence scores provide a separate score for verbal and non-verbal performance, thereby helping determine the laterality of the dysfunction. Finally, the general intelligence measure may provide information regarding processing speed, attention, and working memory. Patterns of impairment within these domains segregate with seizure type and location. Temporal foci often affect memory, frontal epilepsies often affect attention, and generalized epilepsies often affect processing speed (Stanford & Miller, 2007).

Children with epileptic disorders also have more sleep problems than the general population (Batista & Nunes, 2007), which interact with any comorbid developmental problems. The relationship between sleep and epilepsy is complex, as sleep influences epilepsy, and sleep deprivation directly facilitates both interictal epileptiform discharges and seizures (Malow, 2004).

Fortunately, recognition and treatment of sleep disorders can improve epilepsy control, daytime alertness, and health-related quality of life (HRQOL) (Malow, 2007). The type of treatment depends upon the specific sleep disorder which is present. Mild obstructive sleep apnea may be treated with weight loss or altered sleep positioning, but the mainstay of treatment is continuous positive airway pressure (CPAP) ventilation (Kakkar & Berry, 2007). For problems with sleep initiation, melatonin is an effective treatment in the setting of epilepsy. Doses starting at 3 mg and titrated as high as 9 mg were effective in a randomized double-blind crossover trial (Coppola et al., 2004). Melatonin treatment improves sleep latency, and has very little potential for adverse effects.

Several factors put individuals with epilepsy and developmental disorders at high risk for osteopenia. The process is influenced by medications, motor function, and nutrition. The risk factors for the general population, such as female gender and advanced age, also apply, but in the population with epilepsy the largest risk factor is anticonvulsant treatment (Sheth et al., 2008). The greatest risk is conferred by enzyme-inducing medications such as phenytoin, carbamazepine, and phenobarbital. Phenytoin, in particular, appears to possess special risk in this regard (Pack et al., 2008). Medications with weak carbonic anhydrase inhibiting activity or which can cause a mild metabolic acidosis (such as topiramate and zonisamide) may also increase bone turnover.

When an associated developmental disorder is sufficiently severe that weight bearing is affected, it puts the child at higher risk for fractures. Fractures associated with reduced weight bearing tend to occur in the femur during low-impact activities, such as maintenance of personal hygiene or transfers (Glick et al., 2005). Behavior can also affect bone health through its influence on food choices and nutrition. Children who receive adequate calories but have restricted dietary variety may develop nutritional rickets, as well (Noble et al., 2007). A nutritional history in all children with epileptic disorders, especially in those with developmental disorders, that compromise feeding, is necessary to ensure adequate intake of vitamin D and calcium, with supplementation when intake is low.

Medication toxicity is a common problem for children with epileptic disorders. The risk increases with polypharmacy, which is often unavoidable in children with epilepsy and severe cognitive and behavioral impairments. Medications which affect neuronal activity can have overlapping physiological effect, such as benzodiazepines and barbiturates, which can lead to inadvertent overdose. Interaction can also occur due to hepatic metabolism or displacement from protein-binding sites. The pharmacokinetics also change with age, and young children and older adults may need more or less medication than a typical adult, making overdose or toxicity more likely (Ramsay et al., 2007). The effects of anticonvulsant toxicity tend to be dose-dependent, reversible, and neurological. Symptoms such as fatigue, sleepiness, ataxia, tremor, nystagmus, diplopia, headache, nausea, and dizziness are common.

INTERVENTIONS IN EPILEPTIC DISORDERS

The goal of prophylactic epilepsy treatment is complete seizure prevention. Unfortunately, the goal is sometimes tempered by pragmatism in children with intractable epilepsy, which is overrepresented in children with comorbid developmental delay. As a result, these children often require higher doses of medication, which causes more frequent and severe adverse effects. The consequence is that the goal of seizure freedom cannot be achieved without intolerable side effects, and must be modified (Shields, 2004). The long-term goal of pharmacotherapy in children with epilepsy and other associated developmental impairments should be to minimize the need for rescue therapies and visits to the emergency department (Ramsay et al., 2007).

Pharmacotherapy in epileptic disorders has evolved from the treatment of seizures to include consideration regarding cognitive symptoms, mood, and psychiatric disorders (Devinsky, 2003). In addition to treating seizures, the psychotropic mechanism of action of several anticonvulsants is now well established and there are several reviews that attempt to place this within the context of treating children with developmental problems and epilepsy (Di Martino & Tuchman, 2001; Ettinger, 2006; Ettinger et al., 2007).

It is also important to consider the effects of anticonvulsant use on cognitive function and behavior. For example, Coppola et al. (2008) reported 29 children with mental retardation treated with add-on topiramate therapy. They noted an association with mild to moderate cognitive/behavioral worsening in about 70% of patients at 3 months. This is similar to the findings reported by Singh and White-Scott (2002), who observed 20 adults with developmental delay and epilepsy while initiating topiramate treatment. Lamotrigine is a well-tolerated anticonvulsant in patients with developmental delay and epilepsy (McKee et al., 2006). Buchanan (1995) reported a case series of 34 children, adolescents, and adults with developmental delay and resistant seizures. Seventy-four percent of the subjects had their seizures reduced by half or more, and 35% became seizure-free. Quality of life scores were higher in 65% of patients, as evidenced by improvements in alertness, mobility, speech, and independence. Use of zonisamide in patients with mental retardation shows statistically measurable but clinically non-significant reduction in efficacy as compared to individuals with epilepsy with normal cognition. Iinuma et al. (1998) studied 130 children, 60% of whom had developmental delay. Of those that completed the study, 41% of individuals had a reduction in seizure frequency by more than 50%, whereas 67% of the non-impaired children so responded. Side effects occurred in 30% of both groups.

The selection of anticonvulsants in order to treat comorbid psychiatric symptoms is often anecdotally helpful but lacks an evidence-based justification. More clinical trials are required to address the questions raised by smaller and less rigorous studies of epilepsy in children with developmental delay in order to devise 'best practice' guidelines (Garcia-Penas, 2005; Pellock, 2004).

When medications fail, the remaining options are the ketogenic diet, vagus nerve stimulator, and epilepsy surgery. Unfortunately, there are very few data regarding their efficacy that is specific to the population of children with developmental delay. Several studies have looked at the utility of the vagus nerve stimulation for autism and epilepsy, some finding benefits (Park, 2003; Warwick et al., 2007) and others finding no benefit (Danielsson et al., 2008). For the ketogenic diet and epilepsy surgery, developmental delay in the context of epilepsy is not a contraindication.

Even when treatment is effective, the HRQOL is reduced in children with developmental delay and epilepsy. The HRQOL is affected by both epilepsy and developmental delay (Sabaz et al., 2001), and their coexistence creates a substantial burden. Treatment options which can restore quality of life for this group of children are needed.

LIFETIME COURSE

Long-term descriptions of natural history are limited, and in most cases are only available for patients who are in an institutionalized setting. The available data suggest that seizure frequency decreases over time. The effect is related to medication changes, but is associated with other factors as well: it is more likely to occur when children have frequent seizures at the initial evaluation, and becomes more likely with age (Huber et al., 2007). For institutionalized children who have developmental disabilities and epilepsy, the cumulative probability of 5-year remission

by age 22 is 32% (Airaksinen et al., 2000). As with other aspects of epileptic disorders, clinical heterogeneity limits how far the conclusions can be generalized. Subpopulations can be on either side of this average, however. In Rett syndrome, for example, seizures tend to wane in severity and frequency over time (Steffenburg et al., 2001). Children with trisomy 21 and autism (McDermott et al., 2005), however, appear to be at special risk of seizure *onset* (and not just absence of remission) during adulthood. As a result, prognostic statements should be based on populations relevant to particular patients, when possible.

Late-onset epilepsy in trisomy 21, called LOMEDS (late-onset myoclonic epilepsy in Down syndrome; Li et al., 1995) has several unique features. The clinical phenotype is myoclonic jerks upon awakening and generalized tonic-clonic seizures. It occurs more often in the setting of Alzheimer's disease, which is also a special risk of the population with trisomy 21. EEG features include generalized fast spike waves, polyspikes, or polyspike waves that may or may not be associated with bilateral myoclonic seizures. Given the association between chromosome 21 and Unverricht-Lundborg disease, there may be a pathogenic relationship as well.

Severity of disability affects a patient's chances of having a late worsening of their seizures, but it is only part of the story. Twenty-year follow-up of populations with severe motor and intellectual disability show that seizures in children with more severe impairments are more likely to occur, and less likely to resolve. Nevertheless, frequent seizures stop in approximately half of such individuals.

One factor which helps to explain the residual variance in the incidence of remission is the age of seizure onset. Children with mental retardation whose seizures begin before age 2 have higher rates of uncontrolled epilepsy and cerebral palsy. In contrast, most patients with adult-onset epilepsy are well-controlled and have lower rates of cerebral palsy. In patients with later onset, discontinuation of antiepileptic medications may be possible, with up to 60% remaining seizure-frec after 2 years. Therefore, selected patients should be given a therapeutic trial off medication if they have a prolonged seizure-free period (Brodtkorb, 1994).

A separate question from whether seizures still occur later in life is whether seizure frequency influences developmental outcome. In children with mental retardation and epilepsy, the data fail to show a relationship between seizure control and degree of cognitive impairment or neurological findings (Marcus, 1993). Here again, however, heterogeneity is the rule. The role of seizures in autism is well-studied, and there is compelling evidence that seizure frequency is associated with poorer cognitive, adaptive, behavioral, and social outcomes (Hara, 2007).

The marked differences in natural history between different subgroups of children with epileptic and developmental disorders are difficult to fully reconcile. It may be that children in whom seizures worsen during adulthood may represent a qualitatively different type of pathology. Another possibility is that the effects are synaptically mediated. Plasticity during adulthood is largely a synaptic process, and the differences may be due to whether the synapses are forming when they shouldn't versus failing to form when they should.

Children with developmental disorders and epilepsy utilize the healthcare system extensively. Most admissions are for respiratory infections and seizures (Mahon & Kibirige, 2004), but epilepsy has an indirect effect on utilization as well. Even when visits directly related to epilepsy management are removed, standardized activity ratios are still 2.5. The marginal cost of epilepsy in patients who have developmental disorders amounts to approximately $150 per patient per month (Morgan et al., 2003), primarily due to costs of personnel and medications. As a result of the medical complexity of such patients, children with epilepsy and developmental disorders can benefit from evaluation by epilepsy specialty programs. When such consultation is available, including EEG, vEEG, and/or magnetic resonance imaging (MRI), when appropriate, over half improve, and a fifth can become seizure free (Arain et al., 2006).

For children with intractable epilepsy who do not remit, death due to epilepsy is sometimes seen. Although uncommon in the general epilepsy population (Tomson et al., 2005), it is a bigger risk for children with comorbid developmental delay. The risk of death for institutionalized patients with mental retardation goes up almost threefold when epilepsy is present (Hayashi et al., 2001; McKee & Bodfish, 2000). Factors associated with death include the absence of ambulation, increased seizure frequency, and polypharmacy.

Unsurprisingly, dealing with issues related to chronic illness is a significant stressor for families. Little research has focused on the purely psychosocial aspects of epileptic disorders. In general, stressors relating to children with epilepsy are not unique to epilepsy, and are similar to other chronic illnesses (Buelow et al., 2006). When concerns are solicited in an open-ended way, they fall into areas relating to the child's well-being, the transition from infancy to adulthood, and the integration of the child into the community. Explicit attention to these details during visits for epilepsy maintenance will identify ways to improve quality of life that have little to do with seizure reduction, but are no less substantial to the patient. The landscape of needs for children with developmental delay and epilepsy is very much unexplored. We need additional skills training, better information regarding quality of life and its determinants, and more knowledge about living environments (Van Blarikom et al., 2006).

CURRENT RESEARCH

Advancements in genetics and computational techniques have set the stage for profound improvements in the understanding of neurological disease at the molecular, cellular, and network level. Direct benefits to patients are already being seen, and there is potential for incredible progress in the diagnosis, prognosis, and treatment of developmental disorders.

Genetic techniques continue to have improved resolution and speed. When coupled with computerized tools to process data and automatically detect associations, it becomes possible and practical to screen for ever-smaller variations in ever-wider populations. It is already possible to identify discrete mutations, genetic syndromes, and de novo copy number variations in 10–20% of individuals with autism (Abrahams & Geschwind, 2008). As these techniques are refined, this number will continue to increase, along with our understanding of brain development as a dynamic process (neuronal proliferation, migration, organization, synapse formation, and dendritic pruning). Activity-dependent gene expression is one example of a novel pathophysiology that could hardly have been anticipated a decade ago (Morrow et al., 2008; Sutcliffe, 2008).

Similar progress has already led to direct improvements in the treatment of tuberous sclerosis complex (TSC). Initial experiments revealed that mutations in tuberous sclerosis genes (TSC1 and TSC2) limited their ability to bind to mTOR (mammalian target of rapangcin) in order to downregulate it. Since mTOR is an oncogene which allows a cell to progress through the cell cycle, failure to regulate it leads directly to the tumors which are characteristic of tuberous sclerosis. This discovery, made in 2002, was followed quickly by hypothesis, study, and then proof that an existing medication called sirolimus (or rapamycin), which inhibited mTOR, might treat the pathogenic condition in TSC. It has now been conclusively shown that sirolimus is effective for the treatment of angiomyolipoma (Bissler et al., 2008), and there is anecdotal evidence that it may be helpful for the treatment of other TSC complications (Franz et al., 2006; Koenig et al., 2008), including cognitive and behavioral effects (Ehninger et al., 2008).

Progress toward treatment has been less rapid for children with epileptic encephalopathy due to channelopathies. Identifiable mutations in the sodium and chloride channel genes account for a small fraction of all children with epilepsy, but they are often intractable with developmental consequences (Wallace et al., 1998). The SCN1a gene is the most commonly affected, and can range from isolated febrile seizures to Dravet syndrome; an intractable form of epilepsy starting in infancy. Despite the lack of treatment, identification of the gene provides an etiological diagnosis to the patient, along with the attendant improvement in prognostic information and reduced diagnostic testing which is required. Another indirect benefit is the understanding of why some children experience a temporal association between vaccines and subsequent developmental deterioration, which allows the scientific community to focus on more fruitful areas of research regarding the causation of autism, epilepsy, and developmental delay.

One such area relates to the role played by mitochondria in autism and epilepsy. Several reports have highlighted an association with mitochondrial dysfunction, with a rate between 7 and 20% in children with non-syndromic autism (Filipek et al., 2003; Fillano et al., 2002; Holtzman, 2008; Oliveira et al., 2005, 2007). Hypotheses regarding the role of mitochondria in autism are compelling, because mitochondrial disorders are common among children with epilepsy and developmental delay (Lee et al., 2008), two conditions which co-segregate with autism. They are also able to explain the variable severity in autistic disorders as a natural consequence of the threshold effect, heteroplasmy, and mitochondrial dosage (Coleman, 2005). Finally, mitochondrial senescence may help explain the epidemiological observation that adolescent- and adult-onset epilepsy occurs in individuals with autism and developmental delay, whereas improvement is more common in other populations. The connection between autism, epilepsy, and respiratory function is much less settled than the others discussed in this section, but it is an area in need of further research (Garcia-Penas, 2008).

CONCLUSION: CHALLENGES FOR THE FUTURE

The challenge for epilepsy and developmental disorders in the twenty-first century is to resolve the heterogeneous group into its constituent populations. To do this, we must identify the common pathophysiological mechanisms, as well as identify how discrete disorders feed into these pathways. Doing so will allow us to understand why they occur together, and how to intervene in a way to alter their natural course. Progress toward this goal will require incremental advancement, guided by clinical experience and observations about patients, and facilitated by continued improvements in our genetic and computational tools.

Even without novel treatments for specific diagnoses, evidence for existing treatments in specific conditions is needed (Huber & Seidel, 2006). Current studies of anticonvulsant medications lump heterogeneous populations into a single group for purposes of demonstrating efficacy. It is likely that some medications are more effective for some specific clinical conditions than others, but this cannot be shown using conventional experimental populations. Conditions with sufficient numbers of subjects exist (such as Down syndrome, fragile X syndrome, tuberous sclerosis complex, Rett syndrome, infantile spasms, and sodium channel mutations) and therefore disease-specific trials are possible and should be pursued.

The example of rapamycin to treat tuberous sclerosis shows how understanding molecular pathogenesis accelerates subsequent identification and investigation of effective treatments. It not only serves as an example of therapeutic success but also provides circumstantial support for the emerging concept of autism as a disease of dysregulated synaptic development (Rapin & Tuchman, 2008). Future advancements will broaden our understanding of neuronal health at the subcellular and network level, as well as provide a prospect for direct benefit to patients. The resulting understanding of genetic and molecular mechanisms will make rational pharmacotherapy a realistic possibility for individuals with complex developmental disorders.

REFERENCES

Abrahams, B.S. & Geschwind, D.H. (2008) 'Advances in autism genetics: on the threshold of a new neurobiology', *Nat Rev Genet,* 9: 341–355.

Airaksinen, E.M., Matilainen, R., Mononen, T., et al. (2000) 'A population-based study on epilepsy in mentally retarded children', *Epilepsia,* 41: 1214–1220.

Anon (1989) 'Proposal for revised classification of epilepsies and epileptic syndromes. Commission on Classification and Terminology of the International League Against Epilepsy', *Epilepsia,* 30(4): 389–399.

Arain, A., Shihabuddin, B., Niaz, F., et al. (2006) 'Epilepsy and the impact of an epileptology clinic for patients with mental retardation and associated disabilities in an institutional setting', *Epilepsia,* 47: 2052–2057.

Bender, H.A, Marks, B.C., Brown, E.R., Zach, L., & Zaroff, C.M. (2007) 'Neuropsychologic performance of children with epilepsy on the NEPSY', *Pediatr Neurol,* 36: 312–317.

Berg, A.T., Langfitt, J.T., Testa, F.M., et al. (2008) 'Residual cognitive effects of uncomplicated idiopathic and cryptogenic epilepsy', *Epilepsy Behav ,*13: 614–619.

Berry-Kravis, E. (2002) 'Epilepsy in fragile X syndrome', *Dev Med Child Neurol,* 44: 724–728.

Bissler, J.J, McCormack, F.X., Young, L.R., et al. (2008) 'Sirolimus for angiomyolipoma in tuberous sclerosis complex or lymphangioleiomyomatosis', *N Engl J Med,* 358: 140–151.

Bower, B.D. (1967) 'Epilepsy and television', *Dev Med Child Neurol,* 9: 504–505.

Bower et Jeavons (1967) Bower BD, Jeavons PM. The "happy puppet" syndrome. *Arch Dis Childh,* 1967; 42: 298–302.

Brodtkorb, E. (1994) 'The diversity of epilepsy in adults with severe developmental disabilities: age at seizure onset and other prognostic factors', *Seizure,* 3: 277–285.

Buchanan, N. (1995) 'The efficacy of lamotrigine on seizure control in 34 children, adolescents and young adults with intellectual and physical disability', *Seizure,* 4: 233–236.

Buelow, J.M., McNelis, A., Shore, C.P., & Austin, J.K. (2006) 'Stressors of parents of children with epilepsy and intellectual disability', *J Neurosci Nurs,* 38: 147–154.

Camfield, P. & Camfield, C. (2007a) 'Long-term prognosis for symptomatic (secondarily) generalized epilepsies: a population-based study', *Epilepsia,* 48: 1128–1132.

Camfield, C. & Camfield, P. (2007b) 'Preventable and unpreventable causes of childhood-onset epilepsy plus mental retardation', *Pediatrics,* 120: e52–55.

Camfield, C., Breau, L., & Camfield, P. (2003) 'Assessing the impact of pediatric epilepsy and concomitant behavioral, cognitive, and physical/neurologic disability: Impact of Childhood Neurologic Disability Scale', *Dev Med Child Neurol,* 45: 152–159.

Caplan, R., Guthrie, D., Komo, S., et al. (2002) 'Social communication in children with epilepsy', *J Child Psychol Psychiatry,* 43: 245–253.

Coleman, M. (2005) 'Advances in autism research', *Dev Med Child Neurol,* 47: 148.

Coppola, G., Iervolino, G., Mastrosimone, M., et al. (2004) 'Melatonin in wake-sleep disorders in children, adolescents and young adults with mental retardation with or without epilepsy: a double-blind, cross-over, placebo-controlled trial', *Brain Dev,* 26: 373–376.

Coppola, G., Verrotti, A., Resicato, G., et al. (2008) 'Topiramate in children and adolescents with epilepsy and mental retardation: a prospective study on behavior and cognitive effects', *Epilepsy Behav,* 12: 253–256.

Curatolo, P. & Cusmai, R. (1987) 'Autism and infantile spasms in children with tuberous sclerosis', *Dev Med Child Neurol,* 29: 551.

Danielsson, S., Viggedal, G., Gillberg, C., & Olsson, I. (2008) 'Lack of effects of vagus nerve stimulation on drug-resistant epilepsy in eight pediatric patients with autism spectrum disorders: a prospective 2-year follow-up study', *Epilepsy Behav,* 12: 298–304.

Devinsky, O. (2003) 'Psychiatric comorbidity in patients with epilepsy: implications for diagnosis and treatment', *Epilepsy Behav,* 4 (Suppl 4): 2–10.

Devinsky, O., Barr, W.B., Vickrey, B.G., et al. (2005) 'Changes in depression and anxiety after resective surgery for epilepsy', *Neurology,* 65: 1744–1749.

Di Martino, A. & Tuchman, R.F. (2001) 'Antiepileptic drugs: affective use in autism spectrum disorders', *Pediatr Neurol,* 25: 199–207.

Ehninger, D., Han, S., Shilyansky, C. et al. (2008) 'Reversal of learning deficits in a Tsc2+/- mouse model of tuberous sclerosis', *Nat Med,* 14: 843–848.

El Tahir, M.O., Kerr, M., & Jones, R.G. (2004) 'Two cases of generalized seizures and the Velocardiofacial syndrome—a clinically significant association?', *J Intellect Disabil, Res,* 48: 695–698.

Ettinger, A.B. (2006) 'Psychotropic effects of antiepileptic drugs', *Neurology,* 67: 1916–1925.

Ettinger, A.B., Kustra, R.P., & Hammer, A.E. (2007) 'Effect of lamotrigine on depressive symptoms in adult patients with epilepsy', *Epilepsy Behav,* 10: 148–154.

Ettinger, A.B. & Argoff C.E. 'Use of antiepileptic drugs for nonepileptic conditions: psychiatric disorders and chronic pain. Neurotherapeutics. 2007 Jan; 4(1): 75–83. Review.PMID: 17199018 [PubMed - indexed for MEDLINE].

Filipek, P.A., Juranek, J., Smith, M., et al. (2003) 'Mitochondrial dysfunction in autistic patients with 15q inverted duplication', *Ann Neurol,* 53: 801–804.

Fillano, J.J., Goldenthal, M.J., Rhodes, C.H., & Martin-Garcia, J. (2002) 'Mitochondrial dysfunction in patients with hypotonia, epilepsy, autism, and developmental delay: HEADD syndrome', *J Child Neurol,* 17: 435–439.

Franz, D.N., Leonard, J. Tudor, C., et al. (2006) 'Rapamycin causes regression of astrocytomas in tuberous sclerosis complex', *Ann Neurol,* 59: 490–498.

Fusco, L., Pachatz, C., Cusmai, R., & Vigevano, F. (1999) 'Repetitive sleep starts in neurologically impaired children: an unusual non-epileptic manifestation in otherwise epileptic subjects', *Epileptic Disord,* 1: 63–67.

Garcia-Penas, J.J. (2005) '[Antiepileptic drugs in the treatment of autistic regression syndromes]', *Rev Neurol,* 40 (Suppl 1): S173–176.

Garcia-Penas, J.J. (2008) '[Autism, epilepsy and mitochondrial disease: points of contact]', *Rev Neurol,* 46 (Suppl 1): 79–85.

Gilliam, F.G., Santos, J., Vahle, V., et al. (2004) 'Depression in epilepsy: ignoring clinical expression of neuronal network dysfunction?', *Epilepsia,* 45 (Suppl 2): 28–33.

Glick, N.R., Fischer, M.H., Heisey, D.M., Leverson, G.E., & Mann, D.C. (2005) 'Epidemiology of fractures in people with severe and profound developmental disabilities', *Osteoporos Int,* 16: 389–396.

Goldberg-Stern, H., Strawsburg, R.H., Patterson, B., et al. (2001) 'Seizure frequency and characteristics in children with Down syndrome', *Brain Dev,* 23: 375–378.

Goldman, A.M., Potocki, L., Walz, K., et al. (2006) 'Epilepsy and chromosomal rearrangements in Smith–Magenis Syndrome [del(17)(p11.2p11.2)]', *J. Child Neurol,* 21: 93–98.

Goulden, K.J., Shinnar, S., Koller, H., Katz, M., & Richardson, S.A. (1991) 'Epilepsy in children with mental retardation: a cohort study', *Fpilepsia,* 32: 690–697.

Grubb, B.P., Gerard, G., Roush, K., et al. (1991) 'Differentiation of convulsive syncope and epilepsy with head-up tilt testing', *Ann Intern Med,* 115: 871–876.

Hadjipanayis, A., Hadjichristodoulou, C., & Youroukos, S. (1997) 'Epilepsy in patients with cerebral palsy', *Dev Med Child Neurol,* 39: 659–663.

Hara, H. (2007) 'Autism and epilepsy: a retrospective follow-up study', *Brain Dev,* 29: 486–490.

Hauser, W.A., Annegers, J.F., & Kurland, L.T. (1993) 'Incidence of epilepsy and unprovoked seizures in Rochester, Minnesota: 1935–1984', *Epilepsia,* 34: 453–468.

Hayashi, Y., Hanada, K., Horiuchi, I., Morooka, M., & Yamatogi, Y. (2001) '[Epilepsy in patients with severe motor and intellectual disabilities: a long-term follow-up]', *No To Hattatsu,* 33: 416–420. [in Japanese]

Holmes, G.I. & Stafstrom, C.E. (2007) 'Tuberous sclerosis complex and epilepsy: recent developments and future challenges', *Epilepsia,* 48: 617–630.

Holtzman, D. (2008) 'Autistic spectrum disorders and mitochondrial encephalopathies', *Acta Paediatr,* 97: 859–860.

Huber, B. & Seidel, M. (2006) 'Update on treatment of epilepsy in people with intellectual disabilities', *Curr Opin Psychiatry,* 19: 492–496.

Huber, B., Hauser, I., Horstmann, V. et al. (2007) 'Long-term course of epilepsy in a large cohort of intellectually disabled patients', *Seizure,* 16: 35–42.

Hung, T.P. (1968) 'Intellectual impairment and behaviour disorder in 500 epileptic patients', *Proc Aust Assoc Neurol,* 5: 163–170.

Iinuma, K., Minami, T., Cho, K., et al. (1998) 'Long-term effects of zonisamide in the treatment of epilepsy in children with intellectual disability', *J Intellect Disabil Res,* 42: 68–73.

Jian, L., Nagarajan, L., de Klerk, N., et al. (2007) 'Seizures in Rett syndrome: an overview from a one-year calendar study', *Eur J Paediatr Neurol,* 11: 310–317.

J Learn Disabil. 2008 May -Jun; 41(3): 195 -207. doi: 10.1177/0022219408317548.

Kakkar, R.K. & Berry, R.B. (2007) 'Positive airway pressure treatment for obstructive sleep apnea', *Chest,* 132: 1057–1072.

Kirby R.S., Brewster, M.A., Canino, C.U., & Pavin, M., 'Early childhood surveillance of developmental disorders by a birth defects surveillance system: methods, prevalence comparisons, and mortality patterns', *J Dev Behav Pediatr.* 1995 Oct; 16(5): 318–26. PMID:8557831.

Koenig, S.A., Longin, E., Bell, N., Reinhard, J., & Gerstner, T. (2008) 'Vagus nerve stimulation improves severely impaired heart rate variability in a patient with Lennox-Gastaut-Syndrome', *Seizure,* 17: 469–472.

Kosinovsky, B., Hermon, S., Yoran-Hegesh, R., et al. (2005) 'The yield of laboratory investigations in children with infantile autism', *J Neural Transm,* 112: 587–596.

Lee, Y.M., Kang, H.C., Lee, J.S., et al. (2008) 'Mitochondrial respiratory chain defects: underlying etiology in various epileptic conditions', *Epilepsia,* 49: 685–690.

Li, L.M., O'Donoghue, M.F., & Sander, J.W. (1995) 'Myoclonic epilepsy of late onset in trisomy 21', *Arq Neuropsiquiatr,* 53: 792–794.

Lord, C., Rutter, M., Goode, S., et al. (1989) 'Autism diagnostic observation schedule: a standardized observation of communicative and social behavior', *J Autism Dev Disord,* 19: 185–212.

Low, N.L., Bosma, J.F., Armstrong, M.D., & Madsen, J.A. (1958) 'Infantile spasms with mental retardation. I. Clinical observations and dietary experiments', *Pediatrics,* 22: 1153–1164.

McDermott, S., Moran, R., Platt, T., et al. (2005) 'Prevalence of epilepsy in adults with mental retardation and related disabilities in primary care', *Am J Ment Retard,* 110: 48–56.

McGrother, C.W., Bhaumik, S., Thorp, C.F. et al. (2006) 'Epilepsy in adults with intellectual disabilities: prevalence, associations and service implications', *Seizure,* 15: 376–386.

McKee, J.R. & Bodfish, J.W. (2000) 'Sudden unexpected death in epilepsy in adults with mental retardation', *Am J Ment Retard,* 105: 229–235.

McKee, J.R., Sunder, T.R., Vuong, A., & Hammer, A.E. (2006) 'Adjunctive lamotrigine for refractory epilepsy in adolescents with mental retardation', *J Child Neurol,* 21: 372–379.

Mahon, M., & Kibirige, M.S. (2004) 'Patterns of admissions for children with special needs to the paediatric assessment unit', *Arch Dis Child,* 89: 165–169.

Malow, B.A. (2004) 'Sleep disorders, epilepsy, and autism', *Ment Retard Dev Disabil Res Rev,* 10: 122–125.

Malow, B.A. (2007) 'The interaction between sleep and epilepsy', *Epilepsia,* 48 (Suppl 9): 36–38.

Marcus, J.C. (1993) 'Control of epilepsy in a mentally retarded population: lack of correlation with IQ, neurological status, and electroencephalogram', *Am J Ment Retard,* 98 (Suppl): 47–51.

Metz-Lutz, M.N. & Filippini, M.(2006)'Neuropsychological findings in Rolandic epilepsy and Landau–Kleffner syndrome', *Epilepsia,* 47(Suppl 2) : 71–75.

Morgan, C.L, Baxter, H., & Kerr, M.P. (2003) 'Prevalence of epilepsy and associated health service utilization and mortality among patients with intellectual disability', *Am J Ment Retard* 108: 293–300.

Morrow, E.M., Yoo, S.Y. Flavell, S.W., et al. (2008) 'Identifying autism loci and genes by tracing recent shared ancestry', *Science,* 321: 218–223.

Mouridsen, S.E., Rich, B., & Isager, T. (1999) 'Epilepsy in disintegrative psychosis and infantile autism: a long-term validation study', *Dev Med Child Neurol,* 41: 110–114.

Murphy, C.C., Trevathan, E., & Yeargin-Allsopp, M. (1995) 'Prevalence of epilepsy and epileptic seizures in 10-year-old children: results from the Metropolitan Atlanta Developmental Disabilities Study', *Epilepsia,* 36: 866–872.

Noble, J.M., Mandel, A., & Patterson, M.C. (2007) 'Scurvy and rickets masked by chronic neurologic illness: revisiting "psychologic malnutrition"', *Pediatrics,* 119: e783–790.

Oliveira, G., Diogo, L., Grazina, M. et al. (2005) 'Mitochondrial dysfunction in autism spectrum disorders: a population-based study', *Dev Med Child Neurol,* 47: 185–189.

Oliveira, G., Ataíde, A., Marques, C. et al. (2007) 'Epidemiology of autism spectrum disorder in Portugal: prevalence, clinical characterization, and medical conditions', *Dev Med Child Neurol,* 49: 726–733.

Pack, A.M., Morrell, M.J., Randall, A., McMahon, D.J. & Shane, E. Bone health in young women with epilepsy after one year of antiepileptic drug monotherapy. Neurology. 2008 Apr 29; 70(18):1586–93. PMID: 18443309 [PubMed - indexed for MEDLINE].

Park, Y.D. (2003) 'The effects of vagus nerve stimulation therapy on patients with intractable seizures and either Landau–Kleffner syndrome or autism', *Epilepsy Behav,* 4: 286–290.

Parkinson, G.M. (2002) 'High incidence of language disorder in children with focal epilepsies', *Dev Med Child Neurol,* 44: 533–537.

Pavone, P., Incorpora, G., Fiumara, A. et al. (2004) 'Epilepsy is not a prominent feature of primary autism', *Neuropediatrics,* 35: 207–210.

Pelc, K., Boyd, S.G., Cheron, G., & Dan, B. (2008) 'Epilepsy in Angelman syndrome', *Seizure,* 17: 211–217.

Pellock, J.M. (2004) 'The challenge of neuropsychiatric issues in pediatric epilepsy', *J Child Neurol,* 19 (Suppl 1): 1–5.

Piccinelli, P., Borgatti, R., Aldini, A., et al. (2008) 'Academic performance in children with rolandic epilepsy', *Dev Med Child Neurol,* 50: 353–356.

Plioplys, S., Dunn, D.W., & Caplan, R. (2007) '10-year research update review: psychiatric problems in children with epilepsy', *J Am Acad Child Adolesc Psychiatry,* 46: 1389–1402.

Prassouli, A., Katsarou, E., Attilakos, A., & Antoniadou, I. (2007) 'Learning difficulties in children with epilepsy with idiopathic generalized epilepsy and well-controlled seizures', *Dev Med Child Neurol,* 49: 874–875.

Ramsay, R.E., Shields, W.D., & Shinnar, S. (2007) 'Special issues in the management of young children, older adults, and the developmentally disabled', *J Child Neurol,* 22: 53S–60S.

Rapin, I. & Tuchman, R.F. (2008) 'Autism: definition, neurobiology, screening, diagnosis', *Pediatr Clin North Am,* 55: 1129–1146.

Riikonen, R. & Amnell, G. (1981) 'Psychiatric disorders in children with earlier infantile spasms', *Dev Med Child Neurol,* 23: 747–760.

Roubertie, A., Semprino, M., Chaze, A.M., et al. (2001) 'Neurological presentation of three patients with 22q11 deletion (CATCH 22 syndrome)', *Brain Dev,* 23: 810–814.

Sabaz, M., Cairns, D.R., Lawson, J.A., Bleasel, A.F., & Bye, A.M. (2001) 'The health-related quality of life of children with refractory epilepsy: a comparison of those with and without intellectual disability', *Epilepsia,* 42: 621–628.

Saemundsen, E., Ludvigsson, P., Hilmarsdottir, I., & Rafnsson, V. (2007) 'Autism spectrum disorders in children with seizures in the first year of life—a population-based study', *Epilepsia,* 48: 1724–1730.

Salpekar, J.A. & Dunn, D.W. (2007) 'Psychiatric and psychosocial consequences of pediatric epilepsy', *Semin Pediatr Neurol,* 14: 181–188.

Samoil, D., Grubb, B.P., Kip, K., & Kosinski, D.J. (1993) 'Head-upright tilt table testing in children with unexplained syncope', *Pediatrics,* 92: 426–430.

Selassie, G.R., Viggedal, G., Olsson, I., & Jennische, M. (2008) 'Speech, language, and cognition in pre-school children with epilepsy', *Dev Med Child Neurol,* 50: 432–438.

Sheth, R.D., Binkley, N., & Hermann, B.P. (2008) 'Progressive bone deficit in epilepsy', *Neurology,* 70: 170–176.

Shields, W.D. (2004) 'Management of epilepsy in mentally retarded children using the newer antiepileptic drugs, vagus nerve stimulation, and surgery', *J Child Neurol,* 19 (Suppl 1): 58–64.

Singh, B.K. & White-Scott, S. (2002) 'Role of topiramate in adults with intractable epilepsy, mental retardation, and developmental disabilities', *Seizure,* 11: 47–50.

Stanford, L. & Miller, J. (2007) 'Neuropsychological evaluation in children with epilepsy', in A. Ettinger & A. Kanner (eds), *Psychiatric Issues in Epilepsy.* Philadelphia: Lippincott Williams & Wilkins, pp. 173–184.

Steffenburg, U., Hagberg, G., & Hagberg, B. (2001) 'Epilepsy in a representative series of Rett syndrome', *Acta Paediatr,* 90: 34–39.

Stemmermann, M.G. (1965) 'Metabolic errors & seizures', *Epilepsia,* 6: 16–23.

Stevens, J.R. (1988) 'Psychiatric aspects of epilepsy', *J Clin Psychiatry,* 49 (Suppl): 49–57.

Striano, S., Striano, P., Tortora, F., & Elefante, A. (2005) 'Intractable epilepsy in Turner syndrome associated with bilateral perisylvian hypoplasia: one case report', *Clin Neurol Neurosurg,* 108: 56–59.

Sutcliffe, J.S. (2008) 'Genetics. Insights into the pathogenesis of autism', *Science,* 321: 208–209.

Thirumalai, S., Abou-Khalil, B., Fakhoury, T., & Suresh, G. (2001) 'Video-EEG in the diagnosis of paroxysmal events in children with mental retardation and in children with normal intelligence', *Dev Med Child Neurol ,* 43: 731–734.

Tomson, T., Walczak, T., Sillanpaa, M., & Sander, J.W. (2005) 'Sudden unexpected death in epilepsy: a review of incidence and risk factors', *Epilepsia,* 46 (Suppl 11): 54–61.

Tuchman, R.F. (1994) 'Epilepsy, language, and behavior: clinical models in childhood', *J. Child Neurol,* 9: 95–102.

Tuchman, R.F. & Rapin, I. (1997) 'Regression in pervasive developmental disorders: seizures and epileptiform electroencephalogram correlates', *Pediatrics,* 99: 560–566.

Tuchman, R.F., Rapin, I., & Shinnar, S. (1991) 'Autistic and dysphasic children. II: Epilepsy', *Pediatrics,* 88: 1219–1225.

van Blarikom, W., Tan, I.Y., Aldenkamp, A.P., & van Gennep, A.T. (2006) 'Epilepsy, intellectual disability, and living environment: a critical review', *Epilepsy Behav,* 9: 14–18.

Vasconcellos, E., Wyllie, E., Sullivan, S. et al. (2001) 'Mental retardation in pediatric candidates for epilepsy surgery: the role of early seizure onset', *Epilepsia,* 42: 268–274.

Volkmar, F.R. & Nelson, D.S. (1990) 'Seizure disorders in autism', *J Am Acad Child Adolesc Psychiatry,* 29: 127–129.

Vulliemoz, S., Dahoun, S., & Seeck, M. (2007) 'Bilateral temporal lobe epilepsy in a patient with Turner syndrome mosaicism', *Seizure,* 16: 261–265.

Wallace, R.H., Wang, D.W., Singh, R., et al. (1998) 'Febrile seizures and generalized epilepsy associated with a mutation in the Na$^+$-channel beta1 subunit gene SCN1B', *Nat Genet,* 19: 366–370.

Wang, P.J., Hou, J.W., Sue, W.C., & Lee, W.T. (2005) 'Electroclinical characteristics of seizures-comparing Prader–Willi syndrome with Angelman syndrome', *Brain Dev,* 27: 101–107.

Warwick, T.C., Griffith, J., Reyes, B., Legesse, B., & Evans, M. (2007) 'Effects of vagus nerve stimulation in a patient with temporal lobe epilepsy and Asperger syndrome: case report and review of the literature', *Epilepsy Behav,* 10: 344–347.

Wiegartz, P., Seidenberg, M., Woodard, A., Gidal, B., & Hermann, B. (1999) 'Co-morbid psychiatric disorder in chronic epilepsy: recognition and etiology of depression', *Neurology,* 53: 3–8.

22

Tourette Syndrome

Mary M. Robertson & Andrea E. Cavanna

HISTORICAL PERSPECTIVE

Gilles de la Tourette syndrome, currently known as Tourette syndrome (TS) in the United States and much of the rest of the world, is a neurodevelopmental disorder characterized by the presence of multiple motor tics and at least one vocal/phonic tic. Originally described over a century ago, TS is increasingly recognized as a relatively common disorder, with a privileged position at the borderlands of neurology and psychiatry: both clinical and epidemiological studies suggest that associated behavioural problems are common in people with TS, and it seems likely that the investigation of the neurobiological bases of TS will shed light on the common brain mechanisms underlying movement and behaviour regulation.

The first medical description of TS was made in 1825, when Itard reported the case of a French noblewoman, the Marquise de Dampierre, suffering from multiple twitches and inappropriate utterances (Itard, 1825). Her clinical picture was then re-documented in 1885 (when she was still ticcing and cursing

as a recluse in her 80s) by Georges Edouard Albert Brutus Gilles de la Tourette, who described her in a cohort of nine patients seen at La Salpêtrière Hospital in Paris, which earned him eponymous fame, given to him by Charcot. Of note is that in his initial description Gilles de la Tourette emphasized the triad of multiple tics, coprolalia (unprovoked, inappropriate swearing), and echolalia (imitating the speech of others) (Gilles de la Tourette, 1885). The history of TS syndrome as a quintessentially Parisian condition from the School of Charcot (Figure 22.1) has been elegantly reviewed by Lees (1986). Apparently, Gilles de la Tourette's 'Maladie des Tics' was not uniformly accepted among the Salpêtrière circle: Georges Guinon immediately rejected and disputed Gilles de la Tourette's formulation and even persuaded Charcot to moderate a debate between them (Kushner, 1999). The evolution of the modern view of TS is a fascinating scientific journey, the first real breakthrough being the trial of haloperidol, a dopamine antagonist, in patients with TS (Kushner, 1999). In 1968, American psychiatrists Arthur and Elaine

Figure 22.1   Detail from Louis Brouillet, *Une Leçon Clinique à la Salpêtrière (1885)*. This painting portrays the classroom of Jean-Martin Charcot (1825–1893) with his students and visitors at the Salpêtrière in Paris. Georges Gilles de la Tourette (1857–1904) is shown seated in the foreground

Shapiro demonstrated that TS symptoms responded to haloperidol and that relief of tics involved blockade of dopamine receptors (Shapiro & Shapiro, 1968).

Pathography literature has also developed a particular interest for TS. A convincing case has been made (e.g. Pearce, 1994) that the great British lexicographer Samuel Johnson suffered from TS with multiple motor tics and a variety of vocal tics, including ejaculations of prayers and peculiar noises. According to his biographer James Boswell:

> In the intervals of articulating he made various sounds with his mouth, sometimes as if ruminating, or what is called chewing the cud, sometimes giving a half whistle, sometimes making his tongue play backwards from the roof of his mouth, as if clucking like a hen. (Boswell, 1867)

Dr Johnson apparently suffered from severe obsessive compulsive symptoms in addition to his motor and vocal tics: he felt impelled to measure his footsteps, perform complex gestures when he crossed a threshold, and

involuntarily touch specific objects. Moreover, it has been suggested that Dr Johnson exhibited specific tic-related symptoms, namely echolalia and mild self-injurious behaviours, such as hitting and rubbing his legs, and cutting his fingernails too deeply (Pearce, 1994).

There have been suggestions also that Wolfgang Amadeus Mozart could have suffered from TS; however, the evidence supporting this retrospective diagnosis is far from compelling and has recently been subject to strong criticism (Ashoori & Jankovic, 2007). Finally, it has been speculated that a few other historical figures and fictional characters could have been afflicted by TS (for a comprehensive list see Robertson & Cavanna, 2008).

EPIDEMIOLOGY

The epidemiology of TS is more complex than once thought. Until fairly recently, TS was considered to be a rare and—according to some—

psychogenically mediated disorder (Robertson, 2003a). The prevalence of TS depends, at least in part, on the definition of TS, the type of ascertainment and epidemiological study methods used (Robertson, 2008a). In dedicated specialist TS clinics, the majority of patients were known to have positive family histories of tics or TS, and large extended multiply affected TS pedigrees also indicated that many family members had undiagnosed tics or TS (Robertson & Cavanna, 2007; Robertson & Gourdie, 1990): it was therefore realized that TS was far from uncommon.

Seven early epidemiological studies had reported that TS was uncommon or even rare, for a variety of reasons. More recently, however, two pilot studies and 13 large definitive studies in mainstream school and school-age youngsters in the community, using similar multi-stage methods, and personal interviews with the individuals under investigation, have documented remarkably consistent findings, demonstrating prevalence figures for TS of between 0.4% and 3.8% for youngsters between the ages of 5 and 18 years. Robertson (2008a) compared the total number of individuals identified with TS ($n = 3\,998$ with the total of individuals studied ($n = 420{,}761$) in order to give an overall prevalence figure (0.949%, i.e. 1%) (Table 22.1). These studies had been undertaken in the following countries: China, Hong Kong, Italy, Japan, Poland, South Africa, Sweden, Taiwan, the United Kingdom, and the United States. In several countries, more than one study was undertaken.

On the other hand, the prevalence of TS in people with autistic spectrum disorders (ASD) and those in special educational settings (such as in people with learning difficulties) is much higher. In two studies embracing a total of 484 people with ASD (Baron-Cohen et al., 1999a, 1999b), the prevalence of TS was 6.0%. A recent investigation by Canitano and Vivanti (2003) included 105 children and adolescents with ASD: TS was reported to occur in as many as 11%. One can see that this is far higher than the 1% referred to in predominantly mainstream (regular) school children and adolescents. Furthermore, individuals in special educational settings for people with learning difficulties such as mental retardation and those with emotional and behavioural difficulties have an even higher prevalence of TS.

Although TS is essentially a chronic tic disorder, in the majority of cases there are other associated comorbid conditions such as obsessive compulsive disorder (OCD) and attention-deficit/hyperactivity disorder (ADHD) (Robertson, 2008a). The prevalence of TS in these individual subtypes and those individuals with or without OCD and ADHD is unknown. In addition, coprolalia (inappropriate, involuntary swearing) is uncommon, occurring in only 10–15% of all TS patients or about 30% of dedicated TS clinic patients and it usually begins at around 15 years. In a paediatric neurology clinic, the case records of 112 patients were examined and only 8% of the TS patients had coprolalia (Goldenberg et al., 1994). The prevalence of those with coprolalia may therefore be about 10% of 1%, and as such is rare. To what extent the aetiology affects the phenotype, and thus the prevalence, is still unclear (Robertson, 2008b).

Tic disorders, usually referring to motor tics, are much more common than TS, although prevalence figures differ, depending on the population studied. They have been reported to occur with a point prevalence of between 1% to 29%, depending on the study design and methods employed, the diagnostic criteria and whether or not the sample was a population sample or a referral sample (Robertson, 2008a). Recently, there have been suggestions that TS is actually increasing in prevalence. This is unlikely; however, there is certainly an increase in awareness by both lay people (Tourette Syndrome Associations and Foundations, the media, the internet) and the scientific community.

AETIOLOGY

Aetiological theories for TS currently include (1) genetic influences, (2) infections and (3) pre- and/or perinatal difficulties. Originally,

Table 22.1 Prevalence of Tourette Syndrome in Youngsters

Author	Year	Country	Age (years)	Sample Size	No. With TS	Procedure	Prevalence %
Pelser	1994	South Africa: Afrikaans	8–18	392,386	3774	Q	0.96
Kurlan et al.	1994	USA	7–14	35	3	Observation IV	3.0
Mason et al.	1998	UK	13–14	166	5	Self-report pupil Q Parent Q Teacher Q Observation by psychologist	2.9
Comings et al.	1990	USA	7–14	3034	33	Classroom observation Teacher/parent IV	1.1
Nomoto & Machiyama	1990	Japan	4–12	1218	3	Parent Q Tel call	0.5
Wong & Lau	1992	China (Hong Kong)	4–16	718	3	Multi-component scale Probing questions	0.4
Kadesjo & Gillberg	2000	Sweden	11	435	5	Clinical examination	1.1
Hornsey et al.	2001	UK	13–14	918	11	Self-report Parent Q Teacher Q IV Psycho-path Qs	0.76–1.85
Kurlan et al.	2001	USA	8.5–17.5	1255	48	IV	3.8
Khalifa & von Knorring	2003	Sweden	7–15	4479	25	Tic screening Tel IV Clinical examination	0.6
Wang & Kuo	2003	Taiwan	6–12	2000	11	Qs Examination IV	0.56

Lanzi et al.	2004	Italy	6–11	2347	16	Classroom observation (teacher) Examination	0.68
Zheng et al. Jin et al. Jin et al.	2004 2004 2005	PR China	7–16	9742	42	Q Teacher observation IVs with doctors	0.43
Scahill et al.	2006	USA	6–12	449	9	Parent interview	
Stefanoff et al.	2008	Poland	12–15	1579	10	Parent/teacher IV Children IV	0.6
Total				**420,761**	**3998**		**0.95 (1%)**

IV, interview; Q, questionnaire; Tel, telephone; Psycho-path Qs, self-report scales for depression and obsessionality.

Modified from Robertson (2008).

the aetiology of TS was considered to be psychological and indeed even psychoanalytical; however, in the 1980s and 1990s, large families were documented (see also Robertson & Cavanna, 2007), with many related people being affected by tic or obsessive compulsive symptomatology, suggesting a familial nature. No less than six family studies conducted in United States, Europe and Japan using structured interviews to collect data from probands and first-degree family members clearly demonstrated that TS and related conditions are familial (Pauls, 2003). Specifically, the American and European studies consistently suggested that the morbid risk for TS among relatives ranges between 9.8% and 15% (Pauls, 2003). After the familial nature of TS and chronic multiple tics (CMT) was documented, and twin studies implicated genetic factors in the expression of TS, it became widely accepted that TS had a significant genetic basis.

Early complex segregation analyses of data collected provided strong evidence that the mode of transmission was compatible with an autosomal dominant model (e.g. Curtis et al., 1992; Eapen et al., 1993), but subsequent segregation analyses suggested that the mode of inheritance may be more complex.

While the mode of inheritance is not simple, it is clear that TS has a significant genetic basis and that some individuals with TS, CMT and/or OCD manifest variant expressions of the same genetic susceptibility factors. The Tourette Syndrome Association International Consortium (1999), using sib-pair analysis, undertook the first genome scan in TS, and with four other genome scans and many other recent studies, the regions of interest have been shown to be on chromosomes 2, 4, 5, 7, 8, 10, 11, 13, 17, 18, 19. It was suggested that the *DRD4* and *MOA-A* genes may also confer an increased risk for developing TS (Robertson, 2005), but no significant linkage results have been obtained and replicated. More recently, Abelson et al. (2005) reported the association of TS with the gene *SLITRK*1 on chromosome 13q31.1,

but only in a small number of individuals with TS, which is the first indication of an actual gene being involved in some cases of TS. Research over the last two decades has provided considerable data to suggest that several genes play an important role in the manifestation of TS, with some possibly having a major effect; moreover, several regions of the genome have been identified as potential locations of these susceptibility genes (Keen-Kim & Freimer, 2006; Pauls, 2003). In summary, the genetics of TS is much more complicated than was previously thought, and there is almost certainly genetic as well as clinical heterogeneity. It is therefore not surprising that other aetiological suggestions are becoming increasingly documented, including infections and perinatal difficulties.

Neuroimmunological theories operating via the process of molecular mimicry have become of interest in the aetiopathogenesis of TS. Swedo et al. (1998) described a group of 50 children with OCD and tic disorders, designated as paediatric autoimmune neuropsychiatric disorders associated with streptococcal—group A beta-haemolytic streptococcal (GABHS) infections, or PANDAS. The diagnostic criteria included presence of OCD and/or a tic disorder, prepubertal symptom onset (usually acute, dramatic), association with GABHS infections, episodic course of symptom severity and association with neurological abnormalities. The relapsing, remitting course was associated with significant psychopathology, including emotional lability, separation anxiety, night-time fears, bedtime rituals, cognitive deficits, oppositional behaviours and hyperactivity.

More recently, other centres have found laboratory evidence of GABHS infections in some patients with TS and/or documented that some TS patients have increased antibasal ganglia antibodies (ABGAs). Martino et al. (2005) measured soluble adhesion molecules in TS and compared them to healthy and diseased controls. Results showed that the molecules were significantly elevated in children and adults with TS, which suggested a role of adhesion molecules and systemic inflammation in TS. Clearly, infections do not cause TS, but it may well be that individuals inherit a susceptibility to TS and to the way they react to some infections, including GABS infections. Leckman et al. (2005) reported increased levels of interleukin-12 and tumor necrosis factor-alpha in TS and OCD patients. Both of these markers were also further increased during periods of symptom exacerbation and they suggested that longitudinal studies of children with neuropsychiatric disorders should include the assessment of innate and T-cell immunity.

Leckman (2003) outlined the potential role of pre- and perinatal events in the pathogenesis of TS. Leckman's own group demonstrated that the severity of maternal life stress during pregnancy, severe nausea and/or vomiting during the first trimester are risk factors for developing tic disorders. Other studies showed that premature low-birth-weight children, as well as those with low Apgar scores and more frequent maternal prenatal visits, were associated with having TS (Leckman, 2003). Thus, the aetiology of TS is much more complex than previously recognized, with complex genetic mechanisms, some infections possibly having effects, and pre- and perinatal difficulties affecting the phenotype. Of importance also is the correct definition of the phenotype.

DIAGNOSTIC CRITERIA AND CLINICAL FEATURES

Tics

Tics are relatively brief, rapid, intermittent, purposeless, involuntary, movements (motor tics) or sounds (vocal or phonic tics) (Jankovic, 2001; Leckman, 2002; Robertson, 2000). With regard to the noises, Jankovic (1997) made the point that the term 'vocal tics' should be preferred to 'phonic tics', as all the abnormal sounds made by patients are produced by the vocal cords. Most tics are abrupt in onset and duration ('clonic tics'),

but may also be slow and sustained ('dystonic or tonic tics'). Tics may also be classified as simple (isolated, involving only one group of muscles, single or repetitive) or complex (coordinated, sequential movements that may resemble normal motor acts or gestures but which are inappropriately intense and timed and may be repetitive (stereotypic)). The expression of complex motor tics, including stereotypic behaviours, tends to be associated with comorbid behavioural problems (Cavanna et al., 2008b).

The age of onset of tic symptoms ranges from 2 to 15 years, with a mean of 7 years being commonly reported. Tics usually begin in the head and face, and blinking is one of the most common first tics, along with head nodding, and facial grimacing. Complex movements can include touching, hitting, jumping, smelling of the hands or objects, spitting, kicking, stamping, squatting, hopping and a variety of abnormalities of gait (Robertson, 2000; Staley et al., 1997). The onset of vocal/phonic tics is usually later than that of the motor tics, with a mean age of 11 years. Simple noises include sniffing, throat clearing, gulping, snorting and coughing. Other common utterances include yelping, screaming, humming, hissing, clicking and inarticulate sounds. Complex vocal tics include barking, the making of animal noises and uttering strings of words, such as colloquial emotional exclamations.

Premonitory feelings or sensory experiences commonly precede motor and phonic tics and may be either localized (around the area of the tic) or generalized (covering a wide area of the body) sensations or discomforts (Kwak et al., 2003; Leckman et al., 1993; Prado et al., 2008; Woods et al., 2005). Tics may be abrupt in onset, fast and brief (clonic tics) or may be slow and sustained (dystonic or tonic tics) (Jankovic & Stone, 1991). Dystonic tics are more likely to be associated with premonitory sensations (Jankovic, 1997; Robertson, 2000).

It is important to note that tics fluctuate in severity (wax and wane) and change character within the same person; this variability of expression may contribute to diagnostic confusion and misdiagnosis. Jankovic (1997) elegantly described the intimate phenomenology of tics, showing how most tics are semi-voluntary ('unvoluntary') or involuntary ('suppressible'). Moreover, tics and vocalizations may be suggestible and are characteristically aggravated by anxiety, stress, boredom, fatigue and excitement; on the other hand, sleep, alcohol, orgasm, fever, relaxation and concentration lead to temporary disappearance of symptoms (Jankovic, 1997; Robertson, 2000). The significance of these factors for a pathophysiological model of tics remains unclear.

Motor and phonic tics are the hallmark of TS: the generally accepted diagnostic criteria for TS include multiple motor tics and one or more vocal/phonic tics, lasting longer than 1 year (American Psychiatric Association, 2000; Tourette Syndrome Classification Study Group, 1993; World Health Organization, 1992). Of note, the DSM-IV criteria (American Psychiatric Association, 1994) have been subject to strong criticism (e.g. Freeman et al., 1995), thus leading to the revised DSM-IV-TR criteria (American Psychiatric Association, 2000), omitting the presence of significant impairment and personal distress, which is clearly not evident in non-clinic studies (e.g. epidemiological and school populations and/or family members in

genetic studies). Current diagnostic criteria for TS are summarized in Table 22.2. Finally, the majority of studies agree that TS occurs three to four times more commonly in males than in females and that it is found in all social classes. Moreover, the main clinical features of individuals with TS appear to be uniform worldwide, irrespective of the country of origin, with possibly only some minor cultural differences (Robertson, 2000; Staley et al., 1997).

Tic-related symptoms

A number of tic-related symptoms have been described as accompanying features of TS (Cavanna et al., 2009; Robertson, 2000). Coprolalia (the involuntary and inappropriate use of obscenities as a tic, which is often disguised by the patient) is uncommon, occurring in only 10–15% of sufferers in the community and about one-third of selected patients attending tertiary referral clinics (Goldenberg, 1994). Coprolalia usually has a mean age of onset of 14 years and there is some suggestion that it may be culturally determined, as only 4% have true coprolalia in Japan (Nomura & Segawa, 1982) and some countries show higher figures than in the United States or Europe (Staley et al., 1997). Copropraxia (the involuntary, inappropriate making of

Table 22.2   Published Diagnostic Criteria for Tourette Syndrome

Criterion	TSCSG (1993)	WHO (1992)	APA (2000)
Childhood onset	Y (before 21 years)	Y (before 18 years)	Y (before 18 years)
Motor tics	Y	Y	Y
Vocal tic(s)	Y	Y	Y
Duration >1 year	Y	Y	Y
Tic-free intervals	N	Y (<2 months)	Y (<3 months)
Tics not due to drugs	Y	Y	Y
Tics not due to medical conditions	Y	Y	Y
Tics witnessed by a reliable individual	Y	N	N

TSCSG, Tourette Syndrome Classification Study Group; WHO, World Health Organization; APA, American Psychiatric Association.

obscene gestures) is reported in 3–21% of TS patients. Perhaps because of the media's fascination with this feature, many doctors are still under the misapprehension that coprolalia/copropraxia must be present in order to make the diagnosis. In addition, instead of the whole swear word, many individuals say only parts of the word and disguise it, for instance by coughing (Leckman, 2002; Robertson, 2000; Singer, 2005). Overall, tic-related symptoms occur in a substantial proportion of TS clinic patients. Whereas these clinical features are not essential to make the diagnosis, their presence would strengthen the clinician's diagnostic confidence (Robertson et al., 1999).

Echophenomena (echolalia, copying what other people say; echopraxia copying what other people do) are fairly common and very characteristic, occurring in 11–44% of patients. Other important features of TS include palilalia (repeating the last word or part of sentence said by the individual) and palipraxia (repeating one's own actions). Moreover, Kurlan et al. (1996) described non-obscene socially inappropriate (NOSI) behaviours in TS which are increasingly recognized as important to social functioning, along with complex 'disinhibition behaviours' (Cohen & Leckman, 1992). Examples include inappropriate personal comments at consultation visits or a patient who was compelled to shout "bomb" while on an aeroplane. Kurlan et al. (1996) surveyed 87 adolescent and adult TS patients (mean age: 28 years) and reported NOSI behaviours such as insulting others (22%; e.g. aspersions on weight, height, intelligence, general appearance, breath or body odour, parts of the anatomy, racial or ethnic slurs), other socially inappropriate comments (5%) and socially inappropriate actions (14%). More often subjects described having an urge to carry out the NOSI behaviours (insulting others, 30%; other socially inappropriate comments, 26%; socially inappropriate actions, 22%), which they attempted to suppress. NOSI behaviours were usually directed at a family member (31%) or familiar person (36%), at home or

in a familiar setting such as work or school; less commonly, NOSI behaviours were directed at a stranger (17%) in public settings (20%). Social difficulties such as verbal arguments, school problems, fist-fights, job problems, removal from a public place and legal trouble or arrest commonly resulted. NOSI behaviours were more common in young boys and were closely related with ADHD and conduct disorder, but not obsessionality, and it was suggested that they may well represent part of a more general dysfunction of impulse control in TS (Kurlan et al., 1996).

Self-injurious behaviour (SIB), variously referred to as self-mutilation, self-injury and self-destructive behaviour, is the deliberate, non-accidental, repetitive infliction of self-harm, and has been reported in about one-third of patients with TS, although estimates vary depending on the definition of self-injury. In his original paper in 1885, Georges Gilles de la Tourette described two patients who injured themselves. A 24-year-old man had "characteristic" movements of his head and neck:

> his mouth openws wide; when it closes again one can hear the teeth of both jaws gnashing violently. Quite often his tongue is caught between them and abruptly seized and lacerated; it is moreover all covered in scars: on one occasion a piece was completely transected and detached; there is still on its under-surface a wound of one centimetre wide and fairly deep.

His fifth patient, a 14-year-old boy,

> sometimes opened and shut his mouth with some force and abruptness so that his lower lip was bitten so as to draw blood. (Gilles de la Tourette, 1885)

As mentioned, it has been speculated that British lexicographer Dr Johnson was afflicted with TS (Murray, 1979), and indeed, he exhibited mild SIBs such as hitting and rubbing his legs, and cutting his fingernails too deeply.

A variety of SIBs have been described in individuals with TS, including compulsive skin picking, self-hitting, tongue biting, head banging, body punching, poking sharp objects into the body and eyes, and foot tapping with focal shoe deterioration and interphalangeal joint injury (Cavanna et al., 2006a; Mathews et al., 2004). For reasons which are unclear, eye damage appears to be usual in TS-related SIB (Robertson et al., 1989). Recently, Cheung et al. (2007) reported several cases of SIB associated with malignant TS and comorbid OCD, which can be extremely severe and life-threatening (see also Sachdev et al., 1996). Such symptoms included, among others, a self-punching and elbow-banging tic that led to damage to the ovary and urinary incontinence; self-evisceration associated to sexual release and orgasm during the act with self-cutting and shooting, which eventually led to the patient's death.

Finally, the DSM-IV-TR classification distinguishes TS from chronic tic disorders, in which patients have either multiple motor or vocal tics (but not both) (American Psychiatric Association, 2000). Moreover, it has been suggested (Cavanna et al., 2009; Robertson, 2000, 2003b) that it may be useful to clinically subdivide TS into: (i) 'pure TS', consisting primarily and almost solely of motor and phonic tics; (ii) 'full blown TS', which includes coprophenomena, echophenomena and paliphenomena; (iii) 'TS-plus' (originally coined by Packer, 1997), in which an individual can also have ADHD, significant obsessive-compulsive symptoms or OCD, or SIB. Others presenting with severe comorbid neuropsychiatric conditions (e.g. depression, anxiety, personality disorders and other difficult and antisocial behaviours) may also be included in this group (Table 22.3).

ASSESSMENT AND DIAGNOSIS

Assessment of patients with TS requires a thorough personal and family history, as well as mental state and neurological examinations.

Table 22.3 Main Clinical Features of Pure Tourette Syndrome (TS), Full-blown TS, and TS-plus

Clinical Feature	Pure TS	Full-blown TS	TS-plus
Motor tics	+	+	+
Vocal tic(s)	+	+	+
Echophenomena	−	+/−	+/−
Paliphenomena	−	+/−	+/−
Coprophenomena	−	+/−	+/−
NOSI	−	+/−	+/−
Forced touching	−	+/−	+/−
Stuttering	−	+/−	+/−
SIB	−	−	+/−
ADHD	−	−	+/−
OCD	−	−	+/−
Depression	−	−	+/−
Mood disorders	−	−	+/−
Personality disorders	−	−	+/−

NOSI, non-obscene socially inappropriate behaviours; SIB, self-injurious behaviours; ADHD, attention-deficit/hyperactivity disorder; OCD, obsessive compulsive disorder.

In terms of clinical diagnosis, special investigations are not useful if the assessor is experienced with the syndrome. Although the exclusion of Wilson disease with serum assay of copper and caeruloplasmin is considered mandatory, in the authors' experience no patient presenting with this distinctive picture of TS has actually had Wilson disease and certainly more extensive investigation of copper handling is not necessary. Standardized schedules are mandatory for research and are useful for accurately diagnosing TS and assessing the response to medication. There are many standardized rating scales or schedules that help in the more accurate description of symptoms, including the National Hospital Interview Schedule (Robertson & Eapen, 1996), the Yale Global Tic Severity Scale (Leckman et al., 1989), the MOVES Scale (Gaffney, 1994), the Hopkins Motor and Vocal Tic Severity Scale (Walkup et al., 1992), the Tourette's Syndrome Videotaped Scale (Goetz et al., 1987) and the Diagnostic Confidence Index (Robertson et al., 1999), which specifically highlights the phenomenological characteristics of tics, including suppression, rebound, suggestibility, waxing and waning course, and premonitory urges. For implementing the majority of these scales, familiarity with TS, as well as training by an expert, is important. Many of these scales help not only an accurate diagnosis (e.g. the National Hospital Interview Schedule) but also give a likelihood of diagnosis (e.g. the Diagnostic Confidence Index), indicate severity (e.g. the Yale Global Tic Severity Scale, MOVES Scale) and can be used in research protocols (e.g. the Tourette's Syndrome Videotaped Scale).

Patients with TS rarely present with gross abnormalities at neurological examination other than tics. However, in a large group of patients with TS examined by Shapiro et al. (1978), subtle neurological deficits were found in 57%, and 20% were left-handed or ambidextrous. Most (78%) had minor motor asymmetry, and 20% had chorea or choreoathetoid movements. Other abnormalities included posturing, poor coordination, nystagmus, reflex asymmetry and unilateral Babinski reflexes. In contrast, other investigators have found minor non-specific neurological abnormalities only in a few patients (Caine et al., 1988; Erenberg et al., 1986; Lees et al., 1984; Robertson et al., 1988). Abnormalities documented have included chorea, dystonia, torticollis, dysphonia, dysdiadochokinesia, postural abnormalities, reflex asymmetry and motor incoordination.

ASSOCIATED CONDITIONS

Moreover, an investigation embracing 3500 clinic patients with TS worldwide demonstrated that, at all ages, 88% of individuals had reported comorbidity (Freeman et al., 2000). The most common was ADHD, followed by obsessive compulsive behaviour (OCB) and OCD. Anger control problems, sleep difficulties, coprolalia, and SIB only reached high levels in individuals with comorbidity. Males were more likely than females to have comorbid disorders (Freeman et al., 2000). The relationships between psychopathology and TS are complex, and range from specific OCBs (probably genetically related to TS) to ADHD (some types of which may be genetically related to TS) and depression, which is thought to be multifactorial in origin (Cavanna et al., 2009; Robertson, 2003b). The authors' suggestions as to the relationships between TS and other various heterogeneous psychopathologies are presented in Table 22.4.

Both the World Health Organization (1992), and the American Psychiatric Association (2000) criteria have dictated that TS is a unitary condition. However, recent studies using hierarchical cluster analysis (HCA) (Mathews et al., 2007; Robertson et al., 2008), principal component factor analysis (PCFA) (Alsobrook & Pauls, 2002; Eapen et al., 2004; Robertson & Cavanna, 2007; Robertson et al., 2008; Storch et al., 2004) and latent class analysis (LCA) (Grados et al., 2008) have demonstrated

Table 22.4   Suggested Relationships between Tourette Syndrome (TS) and Comorbid Neuropsychiatric Disorders

Neuropsychiatric Disorder	Relationship With TS
ADHD	Common in TS and possibly genetically linked in some cases
OCD	Generally suggested as an integral part of and genetically related to TS
Depression	Multifactorial/possibly due to comorbidity with OCD and ADHD, rather than to TS per se
Bipolar disorder	Few cases described; probably due to related comorbidity
Schizophrenia	Uncommon, the association is by chance
Personality disorders, autistic spectrum disorders, learning disability	Relationship is unknown and more research is needed

ADHD, attention–deficit/hyperactivity disorder; OCD, obsessive compulsive disorder.

Note: Only 8–12% of TS individuals in epidemiological and clinical settings have 'pure' TS with no other neuropsychiatric diagnosis.

that there may be more than one TS phenotype (Table 22.5).

This has important implications. Recently, Martino et al. (2007) showed that ABGAs may be more strongly associated with TS without ADHD than with TS plus ADHD. With regard to the psychopathology, Eapen et al. (2004) conducted a PCFA and demonstrated two factors. Thus, both the phenotype of the 'tic-part' of TS and the psychopathology of TS are not homogeneous unitary entities. It seems that there are many causes and many phenotypes within the umbrella of TS.

In summary, it appears that TS probably should no longer be considered merely a motor disorder, and, most importantly, that TS is no longer a unitary condition, as it was previously thought. Future studies will likely demonstrate further aetiological–phenotypic relationships.

Attention-deficit/hyperactivity disorder

It has been pointed out that of all the comorbid conditions, ADHD is the most commonly encountered in TS, as evidenced by a vast literature on the subject (Robertson, 2006a). ADHD and TS present with a high rate of comorbidity: as many as 60–80% of TS probands have comorbid ADHD (Khalifa & von Knorring, 2005), and the clinical spectrum of the two neurodevelopmental disorders tends to overlap. These data are suggestive of a shared, yet unknown, neurobiological basis. Robertson (2006a) has recently reviewed the relationships between TS and ADHD, particularly as far as treatment is concerned, and suggested that when a patient has TS + ADHD, the clinician should first assess which symptoms are the most problematic, and attempt to treat the target symptoms.

The precise relationship between ADHD and TS is complex and has stimulated debate for a long time. It is still controversial whether tic disorders plus ADHD reflect a separate entity and not merely two coexisting disorders (Robertson, 2006a). Moreover, in a recent clinical study (Rizzo et al., 2007), the TS-only group obtained higher scores than controls on 'delinquent behaviour', which is to some extent in contrast to previous findings. However, according to further investigations (Cavanna et al., 2008a), these behaviours

Table 22.5 Summary of Symptom Factors/Clusters Found in Tourette Syndrome

Author	Year	Country	Study Type	Tics and/or Psychopathology	Number of TS Patients	Number of Factors /Clusters	Type of Factors/clusters
Alsobrook & Pauls	2002	USA	PCFA	Both	85	4	1. Aggression 2. Tics 3. OCS 4. Tapping + absence of grunting
Storch et al.	2004	USA	PCFA	Both	76	4	1. Aggression 2. ADHD 3. OCD 4. Tics
Mathews et al.	2007	USA	HCA	Both	254 (from two genetically isolated populations)	2	1. Simple tics 2. Complex tics + OCS
Robertson & Cavanna	2007	UK	PCFA	Both	69 (from a large multiply affected TS pedigree)	3	1. Tics 2. ADHD + aggression 3. Anxiety/depression/OCS + SIB
Robertson et al.	2008	UK	HCA and PCFA	Both	410 (from a clinic cohort)	5	1. NOSI + complex vocal tics 2. Complex motor tics 3. Simple tics 4. OCS 5. Touching self
Grados et al.	2008	International	LCA	Both	952 (subjects from 222 families)		1. TS + OCS/OCB 2. TS + OCD 3. TS + OCD + ADHD 4. Minimally affected class 5. Complex motor tics + OCD
Eapen et al.	2004	UK	PCFA	Psychopathology only	91	2	1. Obsessionality 2. Anxiety/depression

TS, Tourette syndrome; PCFA, principal component factor analysis; HCA , hierarchical cluster analysis; LCA, latent class analysis; ADHD, attention-deficit/hyperactivity disorder; OCD/OCS/ OCB, obsessive compulsive disorder/symptoms/behaviours; SIB, self-injurious behaviours; NOSI, non-obscene socially inappropriate behaviours.

Modified and updated from Robertson (2008b).

could be related to TS-specific anger symptoms rather than comorbid ADHD.

In summary, ADHD symptoms are common in people with TS and it appears that they may occur in even mild TS cases which are identified in epidemiological studies. Individuals with TS-only appear to be different to those with TS + ADHD, and this clearly has major management and prognostic implications.

Obsessive compulsive disorder

Several studies have documented that the OCB encountered in TS is both clinically and statistically different to that encountered in 'pure' or 'primary' OCD (e.g. Cavanna et al., 2006b; Frankel et al., 1986; George et al., 1993; Miguel et al., 1997, 2000; Mula et al., 2008). The obsessional items reported by TS subjects apparently change with age, in that younger patients reported more items to do with impulse control, whereas older subjects endorsed items more concerned with checking, arranging and fear of contamination. Phenomenological studies comparing OCD and TS groups revealed a group of items that were preferentially endorsed by TS patients (blurting obscenities, counting compulsions, impulsions to hurt oneself) and other items eliciting high scores from OCD patients (ordering, arranging, routines, rituals, touching one's body, obsessions about people hurting each other). George et al. (1993) demonstrated that patients with TS + OCD had significantly more violent, sexual and symmetrical obsessions and more touching, blinking, counting and self-damaging compulsions, compared to patients with OCD-alone who had more obsessions concerning dirt or germs and more compulsions relating to cleaning; the subjects who had both disorders (i.e. TS + OCD) reported that their compulsions arose spontaneously, whereas the subjects with OCD-alone reported that their compulsions were frequently preceded by cognitions (George et al., 1993).

Taken together, these data indicate that TS and OCD are somehow intertwined, and that specific OCS or OCB is likely to be integral to TS (Cavanna et al., 2009; Hounie et al., 2006; Lombroso & Scahill, 2008; Robertson, 2000).

Depression

Depression has long been found in association with TS. There is now good evidence from controlled and uncontrolled studies recently reviewed by Robertson (2006b) to support the view that affective disorders are common in patients with TS, with a lifetime risk of 10%, and prevalence of between 1.8% and 8.9%. In summary, the aetiology of depression in TS is highly likely multifactorial, as in primary depressive illness, and less likely to be caused by a single aetiological factor. The precise phenomenology and natural history of depression in the context of TS deserves more research, as well as its contribution to the TS phenotype(s). Similar to OCD, the phenomenology of depressive symptoms may differ between TS patients and those with major depressive disorder. In depressed TS patients, this may help address factors of particular relevance to the aetiology of their depression and thus improve its recognition but also treatment and outcome.

NEUROBIOLOGY

The last few decades have seen the birth and maturation of neuroimaging investigations of TS, aimed at identifying the cerebral bases of the disorder and to define the neural systems that modulate or compensate for the presence of the core symptoms. The results of these investigations, combined with prior clinical and preclinical studies, have helped to generate specific hypotheses of the neural systems involved in TS.

From a phenomenological standpoint, it is important to note that simple motor tics have been demonstrated to be associated with activation in the sensorimotor cortex, while more complex tics (such as coprolalia and clear vocal tics) were shown in one study to be associated with activity in prerolandic and postrolandic language regions, insula, caudate, thalamus and cerebellum in a functional neuroanatomical study employing positron emission tomography (PET) techniques combined with time-synchronized audio- and videotaping of tics (Stern et al., 2000). These data suggest that different types of tics may indeed have different underlying biological mechanisms. In the largest TS neuroimaging study to date, Peterson et al. (2003) demonstrated that the caudate nucleus volumes were significantly smaller in children and adults with TS, while lenticular nucleus volumes were also smaller in adults with TS and in children who had comorbid OCD. Bloch et al. (2005) demonstrated that the volumes of caudate nucleus correlated significantly and inversely with severity of tics and OCD in early adulthood and it was suggested that caudate volumes could therefore predict the future severity of TS.

Overall, the basal ganglia have consistently been implicated in the pathophysiology of TS. Most radioligand studies—PET and single-photon emission computed tomography (SPECT) have demonstrated reduced metabolism or blood flow to the basal ganglia in subjects with TS relative to controls. Reduced flow and metabolism are seen most frequently in the ventral striatum and, within the striatum, most often in the left hemisphere. The radioligand studies have also implicated the basal ganglia in the pathophysiology of TS, although with less consistency than have the metabolism and blood flow studies. The lack of consistency could be due at least in part to the complexity of the systems regulating dopamine metabolism and dopamine receptor density. Therefore, the blood flow and metabolism studies, along with the radioligand findings, quite strongly implicate in TS pathophysiology the basal ganglia portions of the cortico-striato-thalamo-cortical (CSTC) circuits, especially in or around the caudate nucleus portions of the ventral striatum. The basal ganglia are conduits for information-processing streams that serve multiple and diverse functions. The ventral striatum, and particularly the ventral caudate nucleus, tends to subserve temporolimbic and orbitofrontal portions of CSTC circuitry. These regions are thought to subserve, among other things, impulse control, reward contingencies and executive functions—all of which are behavioural systems that have been hypothesized to be dysfunctional in TS-related psychopathology. The other CSTC system in which regions differ frequently between TS and healthy controls is that involving the association cortices, particularly the frontal, parietal and superior temporal regions, all of which have been consistently implicated in attentional functioning. Clearly, more investigations are needed to clarify the relationship between the cortical and basal ganglia findings and TS symptoms (Frey & Albin, 2006).

NEUROPSYCHOLOGY

The core symptoms of TS involve those systems that are central to the control of action. Thus, it is relevant to enquire about the performance on executive function tasks in patients with TS. Studies of executive function ability reveal somehow inconsistent findings. Overall, the emerging picture is that executive deficits are common among patients with TS and can in some cases be more debilitating than the tics characterizing the syndrome (Como, 2001). Specifically, in those studies that have grouped TS patients according to comorbid conditions such as ADHD or OCD, executive dysfunctions appear to be more common in TS accompanied by psychiatric disorders ('TS-plus'). However, since few studies to date have excluded TS patients with comorbid psychopathology, the question still arises if the executive dysfunctions are to be considered artefacts of comorbid conditions in TS rather than specific to TS itself.

Overall, neuropsychology studies suggest that the level of performance of TS patients is not indicative of grossly impaired neuropsychological function (Osmon & Smerz, 2005). TS individuals score in the average or above average range on intelligence tasks, and on most other measures they are close to normal means. Moreover, where impairments have been reported (especially attentional deficits), they are in most instances linked to a comorbid condition (e.g. ADHD).

However, it is important to highlight that the neuropsychology of TS is still incomplete, in part because there have been insufficient experimental studies of key psychological systems, and in part because the studies that have been carried out have tended to include a wide mix of subjects, which may mask important neuropsychological differences that may exist between subgroups. For example, some studies have lumped together both old and young patients, or those with tic-related symptoms/comorbid conditions and those without, those with an early and a late onset of TS, and even those who are receiving medication and those who are not. Arguably, such variability prevents a careful comparison of homogeneous subgroups within the disorder. It is hoped that future research in this area will adopt a more rigorous experimental approach, drawing on methods available in experimental psychology, and define patient groups more tightly, so that if subgroups do exist, these can be better understood. Such data are needed in order to gain a better insight into the neuropsychological status of TS.

LIFETIME COURSE

It was initially thought that TS was a lifelong disorder. However, Leckman et al. (1998) suggested that the prognosis was better. They showed that the onset of TS was 5.6 years, the worst severity was at 10 years and the majority of symptoms disappeared in half of the patients by the age of 18 years. A recent study assessed youngsters with TS at a tertiary referral clinic (Coffey et al., 2004). The onset of TS was 5.1 years and the mean illness duration was 5.6

years. At baseline, 88% of subjects met threshold criteria for at least mild symptoms but only 30% met criteria for impairment. At 2-year follow-up, 82% of the subjects met criteria for tic persistence (no significant difference from baseline), but only 14% met criteria for TS-associated impairment which was significant ($p < 0.04$). These results supported the notion that TS is a persistent disorder, but also suggested a dissociation between tic persistence and tic-associated dysfunction (Coffey et al., 2004). More recently, a rigorous follow-up study with blinded video-ratings of five tic domains showed that 90% of the 31 children with TS originally assessed still had tics as adults. However, the mean tic disability score reduced significantly with age, and all tic domains improved with age. The improvements in tic disability were not related to medication, as only 13% of adults received medication for tics, compared with 81% of children. The authors concluded that although tics improve with time, most adults have persistent tics (Pappert et al., 2003). More work is needed using longitudinal prospective studies to better define the course and outcome of TS (Coffey et al., 2000).

MANAGEMENT

Pharmacotherapy

Management of TS can range from education to supportive reassurance to complex pharmacological interventions, and it has been advocated that the treatment of TS should be multidisciplinary (Stern et al., 2005). First and foremost, reassurance, explanation, supportive psychotherapy and psycho-education are mandatory and, in mild cases, may be all the intervention required. For thorough reviews of the complexities of treatment of patients with TS, the reader is referred to Robertson (2000) and Singer (2005).

In many instances, medication is required for the treatment of the tics and associated psychopathologies in patients with TS (Gilbert, 2006; Robertson, 2000, 2005; Scahill ct al., 2006; Srour et al., 2008). Double-blind trials have demonstrated that typical neuroleptics such as haloperidol, pimozide, sulpiride and tiapride are all superior to placebo. Of note, the dose given for TS is much smaller than the dose given for schizophrenia or mania. However, typical neuroleptics have a number of side effects, including sedation, cognitive difficulties and dysphoria/depression, dystonia and social phobias (Robertson, 2000). Tetrabenazine, a presynaptic dopamine depletor, has also proven effective. Clonidine or guanfacine can be given for the tics, impulse control or ADHD. If these agents are used, a baseline electrocardiogram (ECG) is advisable, as is regular monitoring of pulse and blood pressure (Robertson, 2000, 2005). It has been noted that the response to individual neuroleptics is idiosyncratic (Robertson, 2005).

Recently, the newer 'atypical' antipsychotics have been demonstrated to be useful in treating patients with TS. These are becoming popular, as they have a different side-effect profile. The main side effects are weight gain and, in some individuals, a precipitation of diabetes. In patients receiving the 'atypicals' it may be worth therefore checking their fasting glucose, especially if the patients have put on weight. The 'atypicals' used successfully in treating TS patients have included risperidone, olanzapine and quetiapine (Robertson, 2005). More recently, aripiprazole has been used successfully with, to date, few side effects. Table 22.6 classifies the tic-suppressing medications according to effectiveness categories based on empirical support (Gilbert, 2006; Scahill et al., 2006).

Antidepressants, especially the selective serotonin reuptake inhibitors (SSRIs), are useful for depression and, at higher dosages, for OCD. Clomipramine (a tricyclic antidepressant) may also be useful in OCD, but

Table 22.6   Effectiveness Categories of Tic-Suppressing Medications (and Usual Dose Ranges)

Category	Medication	Dose Range (mg/day)
A (effective in two or more PCTs)	Haloperidol	1–4
	Pimozide	2–8
	Risperidone	1–3
B (effective in one PCT)	Fluphenazine	1.5–10
	Tiapride	150–500
	Ziprasidone	20–100
	Clonidine	0.1–0.3
	Guanfacine	1–3
	Pergolide	0.1–0.4
C (effective in open-label studies)	Sulpiride	200–1000
	Tetrabenazine	37.5–150
	Olanzapine	2.5–12.5
	Quetiapine	75–150
	Aripiprazole	10–20

PCT, placebo-controlled trial.

usually has more side effects than the SSRIs and it is not safe in overdose. The management of ADHD symptoms in the context of TS is more challenging and requires more caution, since in some individuals central nervous system stimulants can precipitate tics. However, converging evidence supports the use of stimulants in patients with TS and debilitating ADHD symptoms (Erenberg, 2005).

Other treatments

Although the mainstream of tic management is represented by pharmacotherapy, different kinds of psychotherapy, along with neurosurgical interventions—especially deep brain stimulation (DBS)—play a major role in the treatment of TS.

Behavioural methods may be useful alone or in combination with medications for many aspects of TS. Recently, exposure and response prevention and habit reversal training (HRT) has been demonstrated to be significantly better than supportive psychotherapy in patients with TS (Deckersbach et al., 2006; Verdellen et al., 2004; Wilhelm et al., 2003). HRT consists of awareness training, self-monitoring, relaxation training, competing response training and contingency management. Clearly for youngsters with TS these finding with HRT are encouraging as they may obviate the need for medication, with all its adverse side effects.

Less often used but successful treatments in mainly adults can be botulinum toxin injections to affected areas (e.g. vocal cords, in the presence of loud distressing vocal tics and coprolalia) (Porta et al., 2004). Finally, DBS, which entails the implantation of stimulating electrodes in the deep structures of the brain, has recently been reported as successful in a relatively small number of individuals with severe, treatment-refractory TS (Servello et al., 2008). The brain targets have included the globus pallidus pars interna, the centro-median-parafascicular nucleus of the thalamus, and, more rarely, the nucleus accumbens and the anterior limb of the internal capsule; overall rates of improvement in tic severity have ranged between 25% and 93% (Ackermans et al., 2008; Porta et al., 2009). Understandably, there is still debate internationally as to which are the correct targets (Mink, 2006; Rickards et al., 2008).

In summary, effective treatment of children and adolescents with TS is contingent on the following factors: (1) correct diagnosis and adequate understanding of the movement disorder and comorbid behavioral symptoms; (2) collaborative assessment with the family of tic-related impairment and facilitation of realistic expectations; and (3) working knowledge of the published evidence on the efficacy and tolerability profile of available treatment interventions (Gilbert, 2006).

CONCLUSION

Tourette syndrome is a neurodevelopmental disorder characterized by the presence of multiple motor tics and at least one phonic tic. Originally described over a century ago, TS is increasingly recognized as a relatively common disorder, with a privileged position at the borderlands of neurology and psychiatry: both clinical and epidemiological studies suggest that associated behavioural problems are common in people with TS, and it seems likely that the investigation of the neurobiological bases of TS will shed light on the common brain mechanisms underlying movement and behaviour regulation. TS is a lifelong condition, usually diagnosed on clinical grounds in early childhood. At present, the main aetiological theories include (1) complex genetic vulnerability, (2) autoimmune processes triggered by streptococcal infections and (3) perinatal difficulties. Comorbid neuropsychiatric disorders occur in approximately 90% of patients, with ADHD and OCD being the most common ones, along with affect and impulse dysregulation. This multifaceted clinical picture also raises the issue of whether TS should still be considered as a unitary nosological entity. Overall, TS is a chronic condition with potentially socially disabling consequences of the symptoms and associated disorders. Recent studies have shown that both tics and comorbid behavioural problems have been shown to bear a significant impact on the health-related quality of life (HRQOL) of this patient population (Cavanna et al., 2008c; Elstner et al., 2001). Research efforts are ultimately aimed at improving the HRQOL of subjects with TS and related neurodevelopmental conditions.

REFERENCES

Abelson, J.F., Kwan, K.Y., O'Roak, B.J., Baek, D.Y., Stillman, A.A., Morgan, T.M., Mathews, C.A., Pauls, D.L., Rasin, M.R., Gunel, M., Davis, N.R., Ercan-Sencicek, A.G., Guez, D.H., Spertus, J.A., Leckman, J.F., Dure, L.S., Kurlan, R., Singer, H.S., Gilbert, D.L., Farthi, A., Louvi, A., Lifton, R.P., Sestan, N., & State, M.W. (2005) 'Sequence variants in SLITRK1 are associated with Tourette's Syndrome', *Science,* 310: 317–320.

Ackermans, L., Temel, Y., & Visser-Vandewalle, V. (2008) 'Deep brain stimulation in Tourette's syndrome', *Neurotherapeutics,* 5: 339–544.

Alsobrook, J.P. & Pauls, D.L. (2002) 'A factor analysis of tic symptoms in Gilles de la Tourette syndrome', *American Journal of Psychiatry,* 159: 291–296.

American Psychiatric Association (APA) (1994) *Diagnostic and Statistical Manual of Mental Disorders,* 4th edn (DSM-IV). Washington, DC: American Psychiatric Association.

American Psychiatric Association (APA) (2000) *Diagnostic and Statistical Manual of Mental Disorders,* 4th edn, text revision (DSM-IV-tr). Washington, DC: American Psychiatric Association.

Ashoori, A. & Jankovic, J. (2007) 'Mozart's movements and behaviour: a case of Tourette's syndrome?', *Journal of Neurology, Neurosurgery and Psychiatry,* 78: 1171–1175.

Baron-Cohen, S., Mortimore, C., Moriarty, J., Izaguirre, J., & Robertson, M.M. (1999a) 'The prevalence of Gilles de la Tourette's syndrome in children and adolescents with autism', *Journal of Child Psychology and Psychiatry,* 40: 213–218.

Baron-Cohen, S., Scahill, V., Izaguirre, J., Hornsey, H., & Robertson, M.M. (1999b) 'The prevalence of Gilles de la Tourette Syndrome in children and adolescents with autism: a large scale study', *Psychological Medicine,* 29: 1151–1159.

Bloch, M.H., Leckman, J.F., Zhu, H., & Peterson, B.S. (2005) 'Caudate volumes in childhood predict symptom severity in adults with Tourette syndrome', *Neurology,* 65: 1253–1258.

Boswell, J. (1867) *The Life of Samuel Johnson.* London: George Routledge and Sons.

Caine, E.D., McBride, M.C., Chiverton, P., Bamford, K.A., Rediess, S., & Shiao, J. (1988) 'Tourette syndrome in Monroe county school children', *Neurology,* 38: 472–475.

Canitano, R. & Vivanti, G. (2007) 'Tics and Tourette Syndrome in autism spectrum disorders', *Autism,* 11: 19–28.

Cavanna, A.E., Monaco, F., Mula, M., Robertson, M.M., & Critchley, H.D. (2006a) 'Uneven focal shoe deterioration in Tourette syndrome', *Neuropsychiatric Disease and Treatment,* 2: 587–588.

Cavanna, A.E., Strigaro, G., Martino, D., Robertson, M.M., & Critchley, H.D. (2006b) 'Compulsive behaviours in Gilles de la Tourette syndrome', *Confinia Neuropsychiatrica,* 1: 37–40.

Cheung, M.Y.C., Shahed, J., & Jankovic, J. (2007) 'Malignant Tourette syndrome', *Movement Disorders,* 22: 1743–1750.

Cavanna, A.E., Cavanna, S., & Monaco, F. (2008a) 'Anger symptoms and "delinquent" behavior in Tourette syndrome with and without attention deficit hyperactivity disorder', *Brain and Development,* 30: 308.

Cavanna, A.E., Robertson, M.M., & Critchley, H.D. (2008b) 'Catatonic signs in Gilles de la Tourette syndrome', *Cognitive and Behavioral Neurology,* 21: 34–37.

Cavanna, A.E., Schrag, A., Morley, D., Orth, M., Robertson, M.M., Joyce E., Critchley, H.D., & Selai C. (2008c) 'The Gilles de la Tourette syndrome-quality of Life scale (GTS-QOL): development and validation', *Neurology,* 71: 1410–1416.

Cavanna, A.E., Servo, S., Monaco, F., & Robertson, M.M. (2009) 'More than tics: the behavioral spectrum of Gilles de la Tourette syndrome', *Journal of Neuropsychiatry and Clinical Neurosciences,* 21: 13–23.

Coffey, B.J., Biederman, J., Geller, D.A., Spencer, T., Park, K.S., Shapiro, S.J., & Garfield, S.B. (2000) 'The course of Tourette's disorder: a literature review', *Harvard Review of Psychiatry,* 8: 192–198.

Coffey, B.J., Biederman, J., Geller, D., Frazier, J., Spencer, T., Doyle, R., Gianini, L., Small, A., Frisone, D.F., Magovcevic, M., Stein, N., & Faraone, S.V.

(2004) 'Reexamining tic persistence and tic-associated impairment in Tourette's Disorder: findings from a naturalistic follow-up study', *Journal of Nervous and Mental Disease*, 192: 776–780.

Cohen, A.J. & Leckman, J.F. (1992) 'Sensory phenomena associated with Gilles de la Tourette's syndrome', *Journal of Clinical Psychiatry*, 53: 319–323.

Comings, D.E., Himes, J.A., & Comings, B.G. (1990) 'An epidemiologic study in a single school district', *Journal of Clinical Psychiatry*, 51: 463–469.

Como, P.G. (2001) 'Neuropsychological function in Tourette syndrome', *Advances in Neurology*, 85: 103–111.

Curtis, D., Robertson, M.M., & Gurling, H. (1992) 'Autosomal dominant gene transmission in a large kindred with Gilles de la Tourette syndrome', *British Journal of Psychiatry*, 160: 845–849.

Deckersbach, T., Rauch, S., Buhlmann, U., & Wilhelm, S. (2006) 'Habit reversal versus supportive psychotherapy in Tourette's disorder: a randomized controlled trial and predictors of treatment response', *Behavioral Research Therapy*, 160: 1175–1177.

Eapen, V., Pauls, D., & Robertson, M. (1993) 'Evidence for autosomal dominant transmission in Tourette's syndrome', *British Journal of Psychiatry*, 163: 593–596.

Eapen, V., Fox-Hiley, P., Banerjee, S., & Robertson, M. (2004) 'Clinical features and associated psychopathology in a Tourette syndrome cohort', *Acta Neurologica Scandinavica*, 109: 255–260.

Elstner, K., Selai, C.E., Trimble, M.R., & Robertson, M.M. (2001) 'Quality of Life (QOL) of patients with Gilles de la Tourette's syndrome', *Acta Psychiatrica Scandinavica*, 103: 52–59.

Erenberg, G. (2005) 'The relationship between Tourette syndrome, attention deficit hyperactivity disorder, and stimulant medication: a critical review', *Seminars in Pediatric Neurology*, 12: 217–221.

Erenberg, G., Cruse, R.P., & Rothner, A.D. (1986) 'Tourette syndrome: an analysis of 200 pediatric and adolescent cases', *Cleveland Clinic Quarterly*, 53: 127–131.

Frankel, M., Cummings, J.L., Robertson, M.M., Trimble, M.R., Hill, M.A., & Benson, D.F. (1986) 'Obsessions and compulsions in Gilles de la Tourette's syndrome', *Neurology*, 36: 378–382.

Freeman, R.D., Fast, D.K., & Kent, M. (1995) 'DSM-IV criteria for Tourette's', *Journal of the American Academy of Child and Adolescent Psychiatry*, 34: 400–401.

Freeman, R.D., Fast, D.K., Burd, L., Kerbeshian, J., Robertson, M.M., & Sandor, P. (2000) 'An international perspective on Tourette syndrome: selected findings from 3,500 individuals in 22 countries', *Developmental Medicine and Child Neurology*, 42: 436–447.

Frey, K.A. & Albin, R.L. (2006) 'Neuroimaging of Tourette syndrome', *Journal of Child Neurology*, 21: 672–677.

Gaffney, G.R. (1994) 'The MOVES: a self-rating scale for Tourette's syndrome', *Journal of Child Adolescent Psychopharmacology*, 4: 269–280.

George, M.S., Trimble, M.R., Ring, H.A., Sallee, F.R., & Robertson, M.M. (1993) 'Obsessions in obsessive-compulsive disorder with and without Gilles de la Tourette syndrome', *American Journal of Psychiatry*, 150: 93–97.

Gilbert, D. (2006) 'Treatment of children and adolescents with tics and Tourette Syndrome', *Journal of Child neurology*, 21: 690–700.

Gilles de la Tourette, G. (1885) 'Etude sur une affection nerveuse caracterisee par de l'incoordination motrice accompagnée d'echolalie et de coprolalie', *Archives of Neurology (Paris)* 9: 19–42,158–200.

Goetz, C.G., Tanner, C.M., Wilson, R.S., & Shannon, K.M. (1987) 'A rating scale for Gilles de la Tourette's syndrome: description, reliability, and validity data', *Neurology*, 37: 1542–1544.

Goldenberg, J.N., Brown, S.B., & Weiner, W.J. (1994) 'Coprolalia in younger patients with Gilles de la Tourette syndrome', *Movement Disorders*, 9: 622–625.

Grados, M.A., Mathews, C.A., & the Tourette Syndrome Association International Consortium for Genetics. (2008) 'Latent class analysis of Gilles de la Tourette syndrome using comorbidities: clinical and genetic implications', *Biological Psychiatry*, 64: 219–225.

Hornsey, H., Banerjee, S., Zeitlin, H., & Robertson, M.M. (2001) 'The prevalence of Tourette syndrome in 13–14-year-olds in mainstream schools', *Journal of Child Psychology and Psychiatry*, 42: 1035–1039.

Hounie, A.G., Rosario-Campos, M.C., Diniz, J.B., Shavitt, R.G., Ferrao, Y.A., Lopes, A.C., Mercadante, M.T., Busatto, G.F., & Miguel, E.C. (2006) 'Obsessive-compulsive disorder in Tourette syndrome', *Advances in Neurology*, 99: 22–38.

Itard, J.M.G. (1825) 'Memoire sur quelques fonctions involontaires des appareils de la locomotion de la préhension et de la voix', *Archives of General Medicine*, 8: 385–407.

Jankovic, J. (1997) 'Phenomenology and classification of tics', in J. Jankovic (ed.), *Neurologic Clinics*. Philadelphia: WH Saunders, pp. 267–275.

Jankovic, J. (2001) 'Tourette's syndrome', *New England Journal of Medicine*, 345: 1184–1192.

Jankovic, J. & Stone, L. (1991) 'Dystonic tics in patients with Tourette's syndrome', *Movement Disorders,* 6: 248–252.

Jin, R., Zheng, R.Y., Huang, W.W., Xu, H.Q., Shao, P., Chen, H., Zou, Y.L., Huang, H.B., Zou, C.L., & Zhou, Z.M. (2004) 'Study on the prevalence of Tourette syndrome in children and juveniles aged 7–16 years in Wenzhou area', *Zhonghua Liu Xing Bing Xue Za Zhi* 25: 131–133.

Jin, R., Zheng, R.Y., Huang, W.W., Xu, H.Q., Shao, B., Chen, H., & Feng, L. (2005) 'Epidemiological survey of Tourette syndrome in children and adolescents in Wenzhou of P.R. China', *European Journal of Epidemiology,* 20: 925–927.

Kadesjo, B. & Gillberg, C. (2000) 'Tourette's disorder: epidemiology and comorbidity in primary school children', *Journal of the American Academy of Child and Adolescent Psychiatry,* 39: 548–555.

Keen-Kim, D. & Freimer, N.B. (2006) 'Genetics and epidemiology of Tourette syndrome', *Journal of Child Neurology,* 21: 665–671.

Khalifa, N. & von Knorring, A.L. (2003) 'Prevalence of tic disorders and Tourette syndrome in a Swedish school population', *Developmental Medicine and Child Neurology,* 45: 315–319.

Khalifa, N. & von Knorring, A.L. (2005) 'Tourette syndrome and other tic disorders in a total population of children: clinical assessment and background', *Acta Paediatrica,* 94: 1608–1614.

Kurlan, R., Whitmore, D., Irvine, C., McDermott, M.P., & Como, P.G. (1994) 'Tourette's syndrome in a special education population: a pilot study involving a single school district', *Neurology,* 44: 699–702.

Kurlan, R., Daragjati, C., Como, P., McDermott, M.P., Trinidad, K.S., Roddy, S., Brower, C.A., & Robertson, M.M. (1996) 'Non-obscene complex socially inappropriate behavior in Tourette's syndrome', *Journal of Neuropsychiatry and Clinical Neurosciences,* 8: 311–317.

Kurlan, R., McDermott, M.P., Deeley, C., Como, P.G., Brower, C., Eapen, S., Andresen, E.M., & Miller, B. (2001) 'Prevalence of tics in schoolchildren and association with placement in special education', *Neurology,* 57: 1383–1388.

Kushner, H.I. (1999) *A Cursing Brain? The Histories of Tourette Syndrome.* Cambridge, MA: Harvard University Press.

Kwak, C., Dat Vuong, K., & Jankovic, J. (2003) 'Premonitory sensory phenomenon in Tourette's syndrome', *Movement Disorders,* 18: 1530–1533.

Lanzi, G., Zambrino, C.A., Termine, C., Palestra, M., Ferrari Ginevra, O., Orcesi, S., Manfredi, P., & Beghi, E. (2004) 'Prevalence of tic disorders among primary school students in the city of Pavia, Italy', *Archives of Disease in Childhood,* 89: 45–47.

Leckman, J., Riddle, M., & Harden, M. (1989) 'The Yale global tic severity scale: initial testing of a clinician-rated scale of tic severity', *Journal of the American Academy of Child and Adolescent Psychiatry,* 28: 566–573.

Leckman, J.F. (2002) Tourette's syndrome *Lancet,* 360: 1577–1586.

Leckman, J.F. (2003) 'In search of the pathophysiology of Tourette syndrome', in M.A. Bedard, Y. Agid, S. Chouinard, S. Fahn, A.D. Korezyn, & P. Lesperance (eds), *Mental and Behavioral Dysfunction in Movement Disorders,* Totowa, NJ: Humana Press.

Leckman, J.F., Walker, D.E., & Cohen, D.J. (1993) 'Premonitory urges in Tourette's syndrome', *American Journal of Psychiatry,* 150: 98–102.

Leckman, J.F., Zhang, H., Vitale, A., Lahnin, F., Lynch, K., Bondi, C., Kim, Y.S., & Peterson, B.S. (1998) 'Course of tic severity in Tourette Syndrome: the first two decades', *Pediatrics,* 102: 14–19.

Leckman, J.F., Katsovich, L., Kawikova, I., Lin, H., Zhang, H., Kronig, H., Morshed, S., Parveen, S., Grantz, H., Lombroso, P.J., & King, R.A. (2005) 'Increased serum levels of interleukin-12 and tumor necrosis factor-alpha in Tourette's syndrome', *Biological Psychiatry,* 15: 667–673.

Lees, A., Robertson, M., Trimble, M., & Murray, N. (1984) 'A clinical study of Gilles de la Tourette's syndrome in the United Kingdom', *Journal of Neurology, Neurosurgery, and Psychiatry,* 47: 1–8.

Lees, A.J. (1986) 'Georges Gilles de la Tourette: the man and his times', *Revue Neurologique (Paris),* 142: 808–816.

Lombroso, P.J. & Scahill, L. (2008) 'Tourette syndrome and obsessive-compulsive disorder', *Brain and Development,* 30: 231–237.

Martino, D., Church, A.J., Defazio, G., Dale, R.C., Quinn, N.P., Robertson, M.M., Livrea, P., Orth, M., & Giovannoni, G. (2005) 'Soluble adhesion molecole in Gilles de la Tourette's syndrome', *Journal of Neurological Sciences,* 234: 79–85.

Martino, D., Defazio, G., Church, A.J., Dale, R.C., Giovannoni, G., Robertson, M.M., & Orth, M. (2007) 'Antineuronal antibody status and phenotype analysis in Tourette's syndrome', *Movement Disorders,* 22: 1424–1429.

Mason, A., Banerjee, S., Eapen, V., Zeitlin, H., & Robertson, M.M. (1998) 'The prevalence of Tourette syndrome in a mainstream school population', *Developmental Medicine and Child Neurology,* 40: 292–296.

Mathews, C.A., Waller, J., Glidden, D.V., Lowe, T.L., Herrera, L.D., Budman, C.L., Erenberg, G., Naarden, A.,

Bruun, R.D., Freimer, N.B., & Reus, V.I. (2004) 'Self injurious behaviour in Tourette syndrome: correlates with impulsivity and impulse control', *Journal of Neurology, Neurosurgery, and Psychiatry,* 75: 1149–1155.

Mathews, C.A., Jang, K.L., Herrera, L.D., Lowe, T.L., Budman, C.L., Erenberg, G., Naarden, A., Bruun, R.D., Freimer, N.B., & Reus, V.I. (2007) 'Tic symptom profiles in subjects with Tourette Syndrome from two genetically isolated populations', *Biological Psychiatry,* 61: 292–300.

Miguel, E.C., Baer, L., Coffey, B.J., Rauch, S.L., Savage, C.R., O'Sullivan, R.L., Phillips, K., Moretti, C., Leckman, J.F., & Jenike, M.A. (1997) 'Phenomenological differences appearing with repetitive behaviours in obsessive-compulsive disorder and Gilles de la Tourette's syndrome', *British Journal of Psychiatry,* 170: 140–145.

Miguel, E.C., Rosario-Campos, M.C., Prado, H.S., do Valle, R., Rauch, S.L., Coffey, B.J., Baer, L., Savage, C.R., O'Sullivan, R.L., Jenike, M.A., & Leckman, J.F. (2000) 'Sensory phenomena in obsessive-compulsive disorder and Tourette's disorder', *Journal of Clinical Psychiatry,* 61: 150–156.

Mink, J., & the Tourette Syndrome Association Inc. (2006) 'Patient selection and assessment recommendations for deep brain stimulation in Tourette syndrome', *Movement Disorders,* 21: 1831–1838.

Mula, M., Cavanna, A.E., Critchley, H.D., Robertson, M.M., & Monaco, F. (2008) 'Phenomenology of obsessive compulsive disorder in patients with temporal lobe epilepsy and Gilles de la Tourette syndrome', *Journal of Neuropsychiatry and Clinical Neuroscience,* 20: 223–226.

Murray, T.J. (1979) 'Dr Samuel Johnson's movement disorders', *British Medical Journal,* 1: 1610–1614.

Nomoto, F. & Machiyama, Y. (1990) 'An epidemiological study of tics', *Japanese Journal of Psychiatry and Neurology,* 44: 649–655.

Nomura, Y. & Segawa, M. (1982) 'Tourette syndrome in oriental children: clinical and pathophysiological findings', *Advances in Neurology,* 35: 277–280.

Osmon, D.C. & Smerz, J.M. (2005) 'Neuropsychological evaluation in the diagnosis and treatment of Tourette's syndrome', *Behaviour Modification,* 29: 746–783.

Packer, L.E. (1997) 'Social and educational resources for patients with Tourette syndrome', *Neurology Clinics,* 15: 457–473.

Pappert, E.J., Goetz, C.J., Louis, E.D., Blasucci, L., & Leurgans, S. (2003) 'Objective assessments of longitudinal outcome in Gilles de la Tourette's syndrome', *Neurology,* 61: 936–940.

Pauls, D.L. (2003) 'An update on the genetics of Gilles de la Tourette syndrome', *Journal of Psychosomatic Research,* 55: 7–12.

Pearce, J.M. (1994) 'Doctor Samuel Johnson: 'the great convulsionary' a victim of Gilles de la Tourette's syndrome', *Journal of the Royal Society of Medicine,* 87: 396–399.

Pelser, I. (1994) 'Die Psigiese lewensvoltrekking van die kind met Tourette sindroom'. PhD dissertation, Psychology Department, University of Pretoria.

Peterson, B.S., Thomas, P., Kane, M.J., Scahill, L., Zhang, H., Bronen, R., King, R.A., Leckman, J.F., & Staib, L. (2003) 'Basal ganglia volumes in patients with Gilles de la Tourette syndrome', *Archives of General Psychiatry,* 60: 415–424.

Porta, M., Maggioni, G., Ottaviani, F., & Schindler, A. (2004) 'Treatment of phonic tics in patients with Tourette's syndrome using botulinum toxin type A', *Neurological Sciences,* 24: 420–423.

Porta, M., Sassi, M., Ali, F., Cavanna, A.E., & Servello, D. (2009) 'Neurosurgical treatment for Gilles da la Tourette syndrome: the Italian perspective', *Journal of Psychosomatic Research,* 67: 585–590.

Prado, H.S., Rosario, M.C., Lee, J., Hounie, A.G., Shavitt, R.G., & Miguel, E.C. (2008) 'Sensory phenomena in obsessive-compulsive disorder and tic disorders: a review of the literature', *CNS Spectrums,* 13: 425–432.

Rickards, H., Wood, C., & Cavanna, A.E. (2008) 'Hassler and Dieckmann's seminal paper on stereotactic thalamotomy for Gilles de la Tourette syndrome: translation and critical reappraisal', *Movement Disorders,* 23: 1966–1972.

Rizzo, R., Curatolo, P., Gulisano, M., Virzì, M., Arpino, C., & Robertson, M.M. (2007) 'Disentangling the effects of Tourette syndrome and attention deficit hyperactivity disorder on cognitive and behavioral phenotypes', *Brain and Development,* 29: 413–420.

Robertson, M.M. (2000) 'Tourette Syndrome, associated conditions and the complexities of treatment', *Brain,* 123: 425–462.

Robertson, M.M. (2003a) 'Diagnosing Tourette Syndrome: Is it a common disorder?', *Journal of Psychosomatic Research,* 55: 3–6.

Robertson, M.M. (2003b) 'The heterogeneous psychopathology of Tourette Syndrome', in: M.A. Bedard, Y. Agid, S. Chouinard, S. Fahn, A.D. Korczyn, P. Lesperance (eds), *Mental and Behavioral Dysfunction in Movement Disorders.* Totowa, NJ: Humana Press, pp. 443–466.

Robertson, M.M. (2005) 'Tourette syndrome', in D. Skuse (ed.), *Child Psychiatry IV.* The Medicine Publishing Company, Oxfordshire, UK. *Psychiatry,* 4: 92–97.

Robertson, M.M. (2006a) 'Attention deficit hyperactivity disorder, tics and Tourette's syndrome: the relationship and treatment implications', *European Child and Adolescent Psychiatry*, 15: 1–11.

Robertson, M.M. (2006b) 'Mood disorders and Gilles de la Tourette's syndrome: an update on prevalence, etiology, comorbidity, clinical associations, and implications', *Journal of Psychosomatic Research*, 61: 349–358.

Robertson, M.M. (2008a) 'The prevalence and epidemiology of Gilles de la Tourette syndrome. Part 1: the epidemiological and prevalence studies', *Journal of Psychosomatic Research*, 65: 461–472.

Robertson, M.M. (2008b) 'The prevalence of Tourette Syndrome. Part 2: Tentative explanations for differing prevalence figures in TS including the possible effects of psychopathology, aetiology, cultural differences, and differing phenotypes, *Journal of Psychosomatic Research,* 65: 473–486.

Robertson, M.M. & Cavanna, A.E. (2007) 'The Gilles de la Tourette syndrome: a principal component factor analytic study of a large pedigree', *Psychiatric Genetics,* 17: 143–152.

Robertson, M.M. & Cavanna, A.E. (2008) *Tourette Syndrome: The Facts,* 2nd edn. Oxford: Oxford University Press.

Robertson, M.M. & Eapen, V. (1996) 'The National Hospital Interview Schedule for the assessment of Gilles de la Tourette syndrome', *International Journal of Methods in Psychiatric Research,* 6: 203–226.

Robertson, M.M. & Gourdie, A. (1990) 'Familial Tourette's syndrome in a large British pedigree: associated psychopathology, severity of Tourette's and potential for linkage analysis', *British Journal of Psychiatry,* 156: 515–521.

Robertson, M.M., Trimble, M.R., & Lees, A.J. (1988) 'The psychopathology of the Gilles de la Tourette syndrome: a phenomenological analysis', *British Journal of Psychiatry,* 152: 383–390.

Robertson, M.M., Trimble, M.R., & Lees, A.J. (1989) 'Self-injurious behaviour and the Gilles de la Tourette syndrome: a clinical study and review of the literature', *Psychological Medicine,* 19: 611–625.

Robertson, M.M., Banerjee, S., Kurlan, R., Cohen, D.J., Leckman, J.F., McMahon, W., Pauls, D.L., Sandor, P., & van de Wetering, B.J. (1999) 'The Tourette Syndrome Diagnostic Confidence Index: development and clinical associations', *Neurology,* 53: 2108–2112.

Robertson, M.M., Althoff, R.R., Hafez, A., & Pauls, D.L. (2008) 'A principal components analysis of a large cohort of patients with Gilles de la Tourette syndrome', *British Journal of Psychiatry,* 193: 31–36.

Sachdev, P., Chee, K.Y., & Wilson, A. (1996) 'Tics status', *Australian and New Zealand Journal of Psychiatry,* 30: 392–396.

Scahill, L., Erenberg, G., Berlin, C.M. Jr, Budman, C., Coofey, B.J., Jankovic, J., Kiessling, L., King, R.A., Kurlan, R., Lang, A., Mink, J., Murphy, T., Zinner, S., & Walkup, J. (2006) 'Contemporary assessment and pharmacotherapy of Tourette syndrome', *NeuroRX* 3: 192–206.

Servello, D., Porta, M., Sassi, M., Brambilla, A., & Robertson, M.M. (2008) 'Deep brain stimulation in 18 patients with severe Gilles de la Tourette syndrome refractory to treatment: the surgery and stimulation', *Journal of Neurology, Neurosurgery, and Psychiatry,* 79: 136–142.

Shapiro, A.K. & Shapiro, E. (1968) 'Treatment of Gilles de la Tourette's syndrome with haloperidol', *British Journal of Psychiatry,* 114: 345–350.

Shapiro, A.K., Shapiro, E.S., Bruun, R.D., & Sweet, R.D. (1978) *Gilles de la Tourette Syndrome.* New York: Raven Press.

Singer, H.S. (2005) 'Tourette's syndrome: from behaviour to biology', *Lancet Neurology,* 4: 149–159.

Srour, M., Lespérance, P., Richer, F., & Chouinard, S. (2008) 'Psychopharmacology of tic disorders', *Journal of the Canadian Academy of Child and Adolescent Psychiatry,* 17: 150–159.

Staley, D., Wand, R., & Shady, G. (1997) 'Tourette disorder: a cross-cultural review', *Comprehensive Psychiatry,* 38: 6–16.

Stefanoff, P., Wolanczyk, T., Gawrys, A., Swirszcz, K., Stefanoff, E., Kaminska, A., Lojekowska-Bajbus, M., Mazurek, B., Majewska-Stefaniak, A., Mikulska, J., & Brynska, A. (2008) 'Prevalence of tic disorders among schoolchildren in Warsaw, Poland', *European Child and Adolescent Psychiatry,* 17: 171–178.

Stern, E., Silberswieg, D.A., Chee, K.-Y., Holmes, A., Robertson, M.M., Trimble, M., Frith, C.D., Frackowiak, R.S.J., & Dolan, R.J. (2000) 'A functional neuroanatomy of tics in Tourette syndrome', *Archives of General Psychiatry,* 57: 741–748.

Stern, J.S., Burza, S., & Robertson, M.M. (2005) 'Gilles de la Tourette's syndrome and its impact in the UK', *Postgraduate Medical Journal,* 81: 12–19.

Storch, E.A., Murphy, T.K., Geffken, G.R., Soto, O., Sajid, M., Allen, P., Roberti, J.W., Killiany, E.M., & Goodman, W.K. (2004) 'Further psychometric properties of the Tourette's Disorder Scale-Parent Rated version (TODS-PR)', *Child Psychiatry and Human Development,* 35: 107–120.

Swedo, S.E., Leonard, H.L., Garvey, M., Mittleman, B., Allen, A.J., Perlmutter, S., Lougee, L., Dow, S., Zamkoff, J., & Dubbert, B.K. (1998) 'Pediatric autoimmune neuropsychiatric disorders associated with streptococcal infections: clinical description of the first 50 cases', *American Journal of Psychiatry,* 155: 264–271.

Tourette Syndrome Association International Consortium for Genetics (1999) 'A complete genome scan in sib-pairs affected with Gilles de la Tourette Syndrome', *American Journal of Human Genetics,* 65: 1428–1436.

Tourette Syndrome Classification Study Group. (1993) 'Definitions and classification of tic disorders', *Archives of Neurology,* 50: 1013–1016.

Verdellen, C.W.J., Keijers, G.P.J., Cath, D.C., & Hoogduin, C.A.L. (2004) 'Exposure with response prevention versus habit reversal in Tourette's syndrome: a controlled study', *Behaviour Research and Therapy,* 42: 501–511.

Walkup, J.T., Rosenberg, L.A., Brown, J., & Singer, H.S. (1992) 'The validity of instruments measuring tic severity in Tourette's syndrome', *Journal of the American Academy of Child and Adolescent Psychiatry,* 31: 472–477.

Wang, H.S. & Kuo, M.F. (2003) 'Tourette's syndrome in Taiwan: an epidemiological study of tic disorders in an elementary school at Taipei County', *Brain and Development,* 25(Suppl 1): S29–31.

Wilhelm, S., Deckersbach, T., Coffey, B.J., Bohne, A., Peterson, A.L., & Baer, L. (2003) 'Habit reversal versus supportive therapy for Tourette's disorder: a randomized controlled trial', *American Journal of Psychiatry,* 160: 1175–1177.

Wong, C.K. & Lau, J.T. (1992) 'Psychiatric morbidity in a Chinese primary school in Hong Kong', *Australia and New Zealand Journal of Psychiatry,* 26: 459–466.

Woods, D.W., Piacentini, J., Himle, M.B., & Chang, S. (2005) 'Premonitory Urge for Tics Scale (PUTS): initial psychometric results and examination of the premonitory urge phenomenon in youths with Tic disorders', *Journal of Developmental and Behavioural Pediatrics* 26: 397–403.

World Health Organization (WHO) *'International Statistical Classification of Diseases and Related Health Problems:* ICD-10 (10th revision). Geneva: World Health Organization, 1992.

Zheng, R.Y., Jin, R., Xu, H.Q., Huang, W.W., Chen, H., Shao, B., Zou, Y.L., Huang, H.B., Zou, C.L., & Zhou, Z.M. (2004) 'Study on the prevalence of tic disorders in schoolchildren aged 16 years old in Wenzhou', *Zhongua Liu Xing Bing Xue Za Zhi,* 25: 745–747.

PART 4

Environmentally Induced Disorders

23

Acquired Brain Injury during Childhood

Anna Mandalis, Frank Muscara & Vicki Anderson

INTRODUCTION

Acquired brain injury (ABI) is the most common cause of disability in childhood. There is a growing body of literature investigating the impact, recovery and outcomes of ABI during childhood, although there is relatively little data in this area compared to the adult literature. The developmental context of a brain injury during childhood and adolescence increases the complexity of prognosis and recovery following the insult, due to compromised integrity of existing skills and functions, and to disruption of the natural developmental process.

An ABI can be caused by any force, disease, or event, either internal or external, which impacts on the integrity of the brain. Depending on the mechanism of injury, the damage to the brain may be focal or generalized, or both, which may alter outcomes significantly. Irrespective of cause of injury, generalized insult sustained in childhood results in similar sequelae. This chapter will focus on outcomes and interventions associated with pediatric traumatic brain injury (TBI), since the vast

majority of research has been undertaken in this area, and the information can be broadly generalized to other forms of ABI.

BRIEF HISTORICAL PERSPECTIVE

Various theories attempt to explain the nature of the recovery, and subsequent neurobehavioral development, following an insult to the developing brain. Following her research with monkeys, Margaret Kennard (1936, 1940) hypothesized that an immature brain has greater potential for recovery and functional reorganization than the adult brain, as it was thought to be relatively undifferentiated in comparison (Dennis, 2000; Kolb, 2004). In contrast, Hebb (1949) proposed that under some circumstances, brain injury early in life led to a much worse functional outcome than a similar injury later in life. This 'vulnerability' model suggests that the immature brain is more susceptible to serious and irreversible injury, especially if the trauma is generalized. This was further described by Dennis (1989), who suggested that skills which are emerging (not yet functional) or are developing (partially acquired) are at greatest risk of impairment; therefore, children are at greater risk of impairment compared to adults following a generalized injury because they have fewer consolidated skills to rely upon.

Some research suggests that both models may be relevant in describing the recovery of function (Anderson et al., 2001b; Kolb, 2004), depending on age factors, or more specifically, the neurodevelopmental stage of the individual at the time of the injury. For example, Kolb (2004) demonstrated that injury occurring during neurogenesis is generally associated with better functional outcome, as the brain can produce more neurons, hence compensating for the insult. In contrast, damage during neural migration is associated with poor outcome. With regard to generalized brain insult during the childhood and adolescent developmental period, it is now accepted that the immaturity of the cerebral cortex is unlikely to be a protective factor (Gil, 2003; Taylor & Alden, 1997). Instead, brain insult during childhood results in poorer outcomes than a similar insult sustained in adulthood, reflecting a vulnerability recovery process.

EPIDEMIOLOGY

Traumatic brain injury is the most common form of acquired brain injury, and is one of the most common causes of acquired disability in children. Approximately 765 in 100,000 children suffer a TBI each year, with 10% requiring hospitalization (Mitra et al 2007). The incidence of significant head injury defined by the presence of intracranial pathology is low, occurring at a rate of 7 in 100,000 in the population, or 1% of all presentations to Emergency (Mitra et al., 2007).

Age differences

The cause and nature of pediatric TBI varies with age. The greatest incidence of head injury

presentations to Emergency Departments occurs in the first 3–4 years of life (Crowe et al., 2009; Keenan & Bratton, 2006), whilst older adolescents have the highest hospital admission rate compared to younger children (Keenan & Bratton, 2006). Infants are more likely to suffer injury due to falls or child abuse. About 61% of non-accidental injuries (i.e. child abuse) occur in children less than 12 months of age, and are commonly associated with more severe cerebral damage, higher mortality, and a higher morbidity than accidental injuries (Holloway et al., 1994). A high-risk period for accidental injuries occurs within the pre-school stage, with the majority of injuries caused by falls and pedestrian accidents. During this developmental stage, children become increasingly mobile as their motor skills develop; however, they lack awareness of hazards in their environment (Keenan & Bratton, 2006). Older children and adolescents are more commonly victims of road traffic accidents, falls, and recreational accidents (Kraus, 1995). Since the likely causes of TBI vary greatly during the early developmental period, the nature and characteristics of the injuries, and the injury processes, also differ.

Gender differences

Overall, males are more likely than females to experience a head injury during childhood and adolescence by an approximate 60 to 40% ratio (Crowe et al., 2009; Keenan & Bratton, 2006). During the first 2 years of life there is no gender difference in the incidence of head injury (Crowe et al., 2009).

Premorbid difficulties

There is an over-representation of pre-existing ADHD within the childhood TBI population compared to the normal population. Baseline assessments have established that approximately 20% of children with TBI met diagnostic criteria for ADHD prior to their injury (Max et al., 1997a; Gerring et al.,

1998) compared to an incidence of 3–5% in the general community. This suggests that symptoms associated with ADHD such as impulsivity, hyperactivity, and inattention may place children at risk of acquiring TBI.

TBI also occurs more frequently in socially disadvantaged families (Anderson et al., 1997b; Taylor et al., 1995), with non-accidental TBI commonly associated with poverty, deprived social background, and family dysfunction (Holloway et al., 1994). Other forms of ABI, including stroke, cancer, and cerebral infections, are not so clearly linked to these premorbid risk factors.

CAUSATION

Open and closed TBI

In the context of TBI, brain insult may be caused via a number of mechanisms, and can be classified in several ways. An open or penetrating head injury typically involves penetration of the skull and the dura causing focal damage to the brain (McAllister, 1992). Penetrating injuries account for approximately 10% of all childhood TBI. In contrast, a closed head injury is defined as an insult where the skull is not penetrated, and the integrity of the meningeal layers is not compromised (Miller, 1991). A closed or non-penetrating head injury occurs as a result of a blunt trauma to the head, which can cause immediate focal damage, as well as diffuse neuronal damage, and typically produces altered or loss of consciousness (Begali, 1992). The research that will be discussed refers to closed head injury exclusively, since it is the most common form of TBI in children. In addition, the diffuse nature of closed head injury raises relevant issues to consider for other forms of generalized brain insult.

Pathophysiology of closed TBI

Closed head injury is associated with high-velocity acceleration-deceleration forces, and is commonly caused by motor vehicle accidents

(Kraus et al., 1986; Pickett et al., 2004). In such an injury, damage results from both contact and inertial forces, which cause the brain to be shaken within the skull.

Contact forces, which occur at the point of impact when the head is struck, cause a focal injury at the point of impact. 'Contre coup' injuries occur on the opposite side of the brain, as the brain rebounds and strikes up against the skull. These contact forces cause primary pathology such as lacerations, contusions, and hematomas at the point of impact (Ewing-Cobbs et al., 1998b). The temporal lobe and basal frontal regions of the brain are particularly vulnerable to such damage, regardless of the point of impact because these areas impact on the bony sphenoid wing of the skull (Adams et al.,1980).

In contrast, inertial forces generally cause more diffuse injury to the brain. They involve acceleration-deceleration forces, as well as rotational forces, which stretch and twist the brain on its axis following the impact. As a result, the long axonal fibers within the brain are stretched and torn, causing widespread axonal shearing and disconnection and subdural and subarachnoid hemorrhaging deep in the brain (Adelson & Kochanek, 1998).

In addition to the primary pathology caused by contact and inertial forces, secondary brain insult or injury can cause further pathology. Secondary insult is initiated at the time of injury but develops over time (McAllister, 1992). Haematomas, edema, and subarachnoid haemorrhage, raised intracranial hypertension and hydrocephalus, are examples of secondary insults (Adelson & Kochanek, 1998). Brain swelling and cerebral edema occurs as a result of disruption to the normal relationship between blood, brain tissue, and cerebrospinal fluid (Yeates, 2000). For instance, the obstruction of cerebrospinal fluid, and damage to blood vessels in the central nervous system, can lead to increased intracranial pressure and cerebral edema. These events can also result in hypoxic or ischemic injury, brain herniation or death (Yeates, 2000). Secondary insult can potentially be avoided or minimised with appropriate treatment (Jankowitz & Adelson, 2006). Secondary injury refers to the cascade of biochemical events in response to the primary or secondary brain insult (Yeates, 2000; Jankowitz & Adelson, 2006). These secondary processes include excitotoxicity, loss of cerebral autoregulation, inflammation, delayed cell death and breakdown of the blood brain barrier. These events result in tissue death, causing edema and ischaemic brain injury (Jankowitz & Adelson, 2006). The goals of intervention are to avoid or minimise the effect of secondary brain damage, to reduce morbidity and prevent mortality (Jankowitz & Adelson, 2006).

Pathophysiology: comparing childhood and adult TBI

The pathophysiology of TBI is similar among children (Levin et al., 1993; Mendelsohn et al., 1992) and adults (Levin et al., 1987; Levin et al., 1992), in that the prefrontal cortices are vulnerable to injury in both age groups. The fronto-temporal cortical regions (Spanos et al., 2007; Yeates et al., 2007), as well as some subcortical regions, including the hippocampus, amygdala and globus pallidus, are particularly vulnerable to the effects of brain insult in childhood (Wilde et al., 2007). Severe injury is associated with volume loss and ongoing atrophy of the brain (Wilde et al., 2006).

The pathophysiologic response to trauma, however, is considered to be influenced by the developmental status of the brain at the time of injury (Bruce, 1995). Since the anatomy, chemistry, and physiology of the child's brain continues to change throughout childhood and adolescence, insult at different ages is likely to produce different outcomes, irrespective of whether the severity of injury is similar (Bruce, 1995).

Intracranial mass lesions such as hematomas and contusions are rare in infants and toddlers (Berney et al.,1994; Sharma & Sharma, 1994) and occur more commonly in later childhood and adolescence (Berger et al.,1985). Children

with severe TBI are less likely to suffer mass lesions, and have a lower incidence of intracerebral hematomas, than adults (Luerssen et al., 1988). Children are more likely than adults to suffer secondary insults due to hypoxia or hypotension, and to develop diffuse swelling (Adelson et al., 2001). It has been argued that children are more susceptible to diffuse axonal injury than adults, due to the lack of myelination of the developing brain, weak neck muscles and a greater head-to-body size ratio to adults (Adelson & Kochanek, 1998; Zimmerman & Bilaniuk, 1994).

The developmental status of the skull has also been implicated as an important factor in distinguishing the child's and adult's response to trauma (Bruce, 1995). Infants and toddlers have a greater tendency to suffer skull fractures due to a relatively thin skull, easily deformed by a direct blow.

ASSESSMENT AND DIAGNOSIS

The assessment and classification of TBI severity is multidetermined, and takes into account a number of factors. Duration and depth of impaired consciousness and duration of post-traumatic amnesia (PTA) are all used as indices of severity of injury.

Duration and depth of coma

A severe TBI is generally defined as a loss of consciousness exceeding 24 hours. A coma between 1 and 24 hours is considered moderately severe, whereas a mild TBI is classified as any injury resulting in coma less than 1 hour. Length of coma has been found to be predictive of cognitive and behavioral outcome (Dalby & Obrzut, 1991).

The Glasgow Coma Scale (GCS) (Teasdale & Jennett, 1974) is a universally recognized measure of consciousness. The GCS assesses the ability of an individual to open their eyes, utter words, and obey commands. Scores on the GCS range from 3 to 15, where lower scores are associated with a more severe injury and the highest score of 15 indicates a normal level of consciousness. A GCS score of 3–8 indicates a severe TBI, 9–12 a moderately severe TBI and 13–15 a mild TBI. The verbal and eye responses in the original GCS have been adapted for use with children younger than 5 years of age, to accommodate for the limited communication skills of infants and young children (Adelson & Kochanek, 1998).

Post-traumatic amnesia

Post-traumatic amnesia refers to a period of disorientation, confusion, and an inability to form new day-to-day memories, and becomes apparent once the child emerges from coma. Duration of PTA is considered to be the strongest predictor of memory outcome (Fernando et al., 2002), and is also a predictor of long-term cerebral changes post injury (Wilde et al., 2006). Duration of PTA is sensitive to identifying the 15–20% of children with mild TBI who will experience persisting sequelae (Hessen et al., 2007; Thickpenny-Davis et al., 2005).

The assessment of PTA is challenging in young children, as the measurement tools must consider the capacity of the child to understand and respond to the items assessing orientation and memory. To date, there are no reliable measures of PTA for children younger than 4 years of age (Thickpenny-Davis et al., 2005). There are a range of measures of PTA adapted for use with older children, each of which has its own strengths and limitations. Examples of these include the Westmead PTA Scale (Marosszeky et al., 1993), the Children's Orientation and Amnesia Test (COAT) (Ewing-Cobbs et al., 1990) and the Starship PTA Scale (Fernando et al., 2002). These tests assess orientation and the ability to lay down new memories post injury. In addition to providing information regarding the severity of the injury, assessment of PTA informs the treating team as to whether the child requires safety and supervision supports.

Imaging considerations

Radiological investigations also assist with the classification of injury severity, providing information regarding primary and secondary brain pathology. These radiological investigations are conducted when there is evidence of impaired consciousness, skull fracture, or abnormalities on neurological assessment. Computed tomography (CT) scans are routinely used on admission to detect mass lesions and intracranial bleeds. Of note, Zimmerman and Bilaniuk (1994) report that normal CT scan results are occasionally observed even in patients with severe TBI. Magnetic resonance imaging (MRI) and single-photon emission computed tomography (SPECT) are more sensitive to detecting neurochemical alterations, ischemia, white matter abnormalities, and hemorrhagic lesions associated with diffuse axonal injury (Ashwal et al., 2006). Findings by Wilson and colleagues (1988) also indicated that MRI data has a greater power for predicting outcome following TBI. SPECT is less routinely used in children, as structural imaging through MRI provides sufficient information regarding the site and extent of the lesion. Functional imaging, however, reveals functional areas of deficit by identifying regions of the brain that have reduced cerebral blood flow (Kant, et al., 1997).

CURRENT RESEARCH

Clinical correlates of outcome

In general, poorer neuropsychological outcomes are associated with more severe injuries and greater amount of atrophy (Bigler, 2001). The presence of frontal lobe lesions, which commonly occur following TBI, places children at further disadvantage with respect to cognitive and behavioral outcomes. Levin and colleagues (2004) demonstrated that children with frontal lesions had a higher frequency of maladaptive behaviors, and were at significantly greater risk of poorer adaptive outcomes in the domains of socialization and daily living skills, compared to children with extra-frontal lesions. Volume of frontal lesion was also associated with executive dysfunction (Levin et al., 1994). The presence of bifrontal, left frontal or right frontal lesions incrementally predicts memory performance in children with TBI once severity of injury and age factors are controlled for, while extrafrontal lesion volume is not predictive of memory performance (Di Stefano et al., 2000).

Neuropsychological research

Factors contributing to outcome

Neuropsychological outcomes following pediatric TBI are influenced by a range of factors, including severity of injury, age at injury, time post-injury, as well as child and/or family and environmental factors. The *double-hazard effect* describes the interaction of more than one of these risk factors. There is an increase in the possibility of poor outcome when two or more risk factors are present, with multiple risk factors acting to compound the effect of any one factor on recovery and outcome. The majority of outcome studies of pediatric TBI have determined such an effect, whereby an interaction of factors has contributed to cognitive and behavioral outcomes, rather than a single determinant.

Severity of injury   Injury severity is a well-established predictor of outcome following TBI (Catroppa et al., 2008). Severe brain injury is commonly associated with cognitive, behavioral, academic and social difficulties, which may be long term or even permanent (Catroppa et al., 2008; Taylor et al., 2002).

Overall, children and adolescents who sustain a mild TBI have excellent outcomes (Anderson et al., 2001a), with only 15% reporting persisting sequelae. More 'complicated' mild head injury involving cerebral pathology results in poorer outcomes compared to uncomplicated injuries where there is no evidence of cerebral pathology (Hessen et al., 2008; Hessen et al., 2007, 2008; Yeates & Taylor, 2005).

Age at injury   Age and developmental stage at the time of the injury have been identified as an important predictor of outcome following TBI during childhood (Anderson & Moore, 1995; Dennis, 1989; Taylor & Alden, 1997). Consistent with Dennis' (1989) model, emerging and developing skills are the most vulnerable to impairment following brain insult, whereas established skills are less likely to be disrupted. Deficits may not become apparent until later in development when skills are expected to emerge. Injury at a younger age is associated with a higher vulnerability and greater degree of deficits and dysfunction, compared to effects of a TBI sustained in later childhood and adolescence (Anderson & Moore, 1995; Taylor & Alden, 1997). This vulnerability associated with age has been identified across many forms of ABI, including bacterial meningitis (Anderson et al., 1997a), acute disseminated encephalomyelitis (Jacobs et al., 2004), and focal brain lesions (Jacobs et al., 2007).

Time since injury   Due to the potential impact of TBI on emerging skills, it is possible for young children to appear relatively unaffected in the early stages of recovery, when they are relying on or demonstrating skills that had previously been consolidated (Anderson & Moore, 1995). Deficits become apparent when age-expected skills fail to develop.

The pattern of cognitive recovery also varies as a function of severity of injury. For children with severe TBI, the most rapid recovery occurs in the first 12 months post injury and then tends to plateau (Jaffe et al., 1995; Yeates et al., 2002). In contrast, there is minimal change in the level of cognitive skills of the mild TBI group, which tend to remain within developmentally appropriate levels (Catroppa et al., 2008; Jaffe et al., 1995). There is currently very little data describing the link between time since injury and functional outcome in other forms of ABI.

Child and family factors/reserve Dennis (2000) described the concept of reserve and resilience as predictors of outcome following pediatric ABI. Reserve refers to the factors that buffer against or further exacerbate dysfunction. These factors can include the pre-existing abilities of the child, family functioning, supports in the community, and socioeconomic status (SES). Pre-existing difficulties or low skill levels have been associated with poorer cognitive and behavioral outcomes (Anderson et al., 1997b; Yeates et al., 2005). Taylor and colleagues (2002) reported that children from disadvantaged socioeconomic backgrounds were more likely to experience poorer academic and behavioral outcomes than children with families of higher SES at 4 years post injury. Pre-injury family functioning and coping style, and pre-injury behavioral functioning are also associated with behavioral outcomes (Rivara et al., 1993). This link between environmental and demographic factors and functional outcomes is also evident in other forms of ABI, such as bacterial meningitis (Grimwood et al., 1996).

Cognitive outcomes

Intellectual outcomes There is no uniform intellectual profile following childhood TBI; however, patterns of outcome are evident according to severity of injury and age at injury. Children with severe TBI generally have poorer intellectual outcomes than children who suffer less severe injury (Anderson et al., 2000a, 2005). The mean full-scale intellectual quotient (FSIQ) of severe TBI samples is often within the 'low average to average' range, with only a small proportion meeting diagnostic criteria for mental retardation. It is commonly accepted that children with severe TBI have poorer academic, adaptive, behavioral, and social outcomes than their peers, indicating that intellectual ability is not necessarily predictive of the child's functional outcomes.

Early age at injury is associated with lower level of intellectual functioning. Children injured in pre-school years have significantly lower FSIQ scores than children injured in primary school years (Anderson et al., 1997b; 2005; 2010), and children injured in the primary school years generally have poorer intellectual outcomes than those injured during adolescence (Levin, et al., 1982).

Attention and processing speed Formal assessment of attention skills and parent ratings of attention indicate that children with severe TBI demonstrate significant attention problems many years post injury. There are, however, minimal changes, if any, detectable in the mild TBI population (Catroppa, et al., 2007; Yeates & Taylor, 2005).

Attention skills are varied and develop at different stages in childhood. The timing of neurological insult contributes to post-injury attention functioning. Selective attention skills, which develop earlier than higher-level divided attention skills, are more vulnerable to impairment in younger children.

Simple reaction time is often not impaired following TBI; however, studies show a relationship between processing speed, as measured by more complex tasks that recruit psychomotor skills, and severity of injury (Catroppa & Anderson, 1999). Children with severe TBI are slower to process information compared to the typically developing population and children who sustain mild or moderate TBI (Anderson & Pentland, 1998). Age at injury also contributes to speed of processing outcomes, with younger children performing at significantly lower levels on speeded perceptual-motor tasks than older children (Ewing-Cobbs et al., 1998b).

Memory Memory deficits are common following TBI and are particularly impaired following severe TBI (Anderson & Catroppa, 2007; Max et al., 1999). This is not surprising given that the frontal regions and medial temporal structures, which are vulnerable to damage following TBI, are respectively involved in the retrieval of information and in the storing of new information. Severe TBI can result in generalized memory dysfunction, as evidenced by poor learning, and delayed recall and recognition memory performance (Yeates et al., 1995). Memory deficits can also occur secondary to the disruption of attention and executive skills (Mandalis et al, 2007).

The pattern of memory outcome is also dependent on the interaction between severity of injury, age at injury, and time since injury. Anderson et al. (2000b) investigated the recovery of memory skills following TBI sustained at preschool age over an 18-month period. The mild TBI group tended to improve over time and at a rate faster than the control group. In contrast, the moderate and severe groups had a flatter recovery pattern, did not make age-expected gains over time, and ultimately fell behind their same-age peers. Measurable memory difficulties were not identified in the moderate to severe TBI groups until 12 months post injury. Memory skills develop throughout childhood and adolescence; therefore, it is likely that the injury disrupts acquisition of emerging or developing memory skills (Anderson et al., 2000b).

Executive Function Executive skills are mediated by the frontal lobes, a region of the brain vulnerable to damage following TBI. Executive dysfunction can also occur due to frontal system impairment, whereby damage to extrafrontal regions can disrupt connections to the frontal lobes. Executive function deficits, such as planning, problem solving, working memory, attention, cognitive flexibility, adaptive functioning, disinhibition, self-monitoring, judgment, and decision making, are common following pediatric TBI (Catroppa et al., 1999; Eslinger & Grattan, 1993; Gioia et al., 2002). Executive deficits persist into adolescence and adulthood (Mangeot et al., 2002).

Specific executive skills develop at different stages during childhood and adolescence (DeLuca & Leventer, 2008). Whereas executive deficits become apparent in adults shortly after injury, the expression of executive difficulties may not occur until the child reaches the age when the particular skill matures in typically developing children. Younger age at injury has been found to be associated with a greater degree of executive dysfunction (Garth et al., 1997; Levin et al., 1994).

Executive dysfunction may have a secondary impact upon cognitive development (Anderson & Moore, 1995), as efficient and intact executive skills at a young age are required for adaptation and new learning, and facilitate the attainment of new skills. They may also compromise the child's social functioning (Gioia et al., 2002). Recent evidence has demonstrated a relationship between executive skill level, social problem-solving skills and social outcomes (Muscara et al., 2008a; Yeates et al., 2004).

Language Whereas aphasic disorders are rare following TBI, receptive, expressive, and pragmatic language skills are vulnerable to impairment, particularly following severe TBI (Dennis, 2006). Underlying difficulties with attention, working memory and executive skills can contribute to the ability to communicate effectively and to comprehend language (Brookshire et al., 2000). Higher-level pragmatic language deficits, which are more pronounced in the severe TBI groups (Brookshire et al., 2000), contribute negatively to social outcomes (Yeates et al., 2007).

Since language skills develop rapidly in the first 2–3 years of life, TBI sustained during this time has been specifically found to result in poor expressive language outcomes (Ewing-Cobbs & Fletcher, 1987). This is not necessarily restricted to the severe TBI population, with a study by Anderson and colleagues (2001a) suggesting that children who sustained a mild head injury during the preschool years were vulnerable to poor verbal fluency outcomes at 30 months post injury. Since higher-level discourse or pragmatic language skills develop throughout childhood and adolescence, it has been suggested that language outcomes may be dependent on the age at injury; however, there is currently a lack of evidence of such a relationship.

Visuomotor and perceptual The severe TBI population is more vulnerable to visuomotor and perceptual difficulties than mild or moderate TBI groups (Jaffe et al., 1995; Thompson et al., 1994). Thompson and colleagues (1994) demonstrated that children injured early in life had significantly reduced visuospatial skills and motor performance compared to children of similar ages with less severe injuries, and compared to older children with a similar level of severity. Children with severe TBI show dramatic improvement in their speeded motor responses and non-verbal/ visuospatial abilities in the first 12 months, with a plateau in recovery following this period, leading to a failure to reach the same level of functioning as less severely injured children (Jaffe et al., 1995).

Functional Outcomes

Academic Given the dose-response relationship with cognitive outcomes, and the range of cognitive deficits that can emerge following TBI, it is not surprising that a more severe TBI is also associated with poorer academic outcomes (Ewing-Cobbs et al., 2004). Children with severe TBI are likely to require special education resources or special class placement (Ewing-Cobbs et al., 2004). In addition to injury-related factors, lower SES has also been implicated in contributing to poorer academic outcomes, with Yeates and colleagues (2002) speculating that highly resourced families may be able to provide greater stimulation and support than families with fewer resources.

The development of academic skills following TBI is dependent on the age at injury. Children who sustained their TBI prior to the commencement of formal schooling are particularly at risk of failing to develop fundamental literacy and numeracy skills. Children injured in primary or secondary school years have often established basic academic skills, as evidenced by their normal performance on standardized tests of academic functioning; however, this performance does not correlate well with actual academic performance, with a large proportion of them requiring remedial assistance or repeating a grade (Ewing-Cobbs et al.,1998a). It has therefore been suggested

that more ecologically sound tests of academic functioning, such as the ability to organize and reason with literary material, are needed to assess the child's actual academic functioning in clinical neuropsychological assessments, rather than standard IQ and achievement tests (Ewing-Cobbs et al., 1998a).

Behavioral and social A significant TBI during childhood can result in a wide range of behavioral difficulties. Behavioral problems can be associated with poor regulation of emotions and behavior. They can manifest as a disorder of control, a disorder of drive, or a combination of both. Symptoms include apathy, inertia, disinhibition, perseveration, impulsivity, aggression, and rule-breaking behavior. Risk factors include child factors, family factors, and severity of injury. Behavioral changes can occur as a direct result of the injury, as a reaction to the effects of the injury, and can also be influenced by family functioning. The relationship between behavior disturbance and family functioning has been reported as a bidirectional one, whereby a severe injury results in significant behavior disturbance and causes higher levels of injury-related burden within the family than mild or moderate TBI (Wade et al., 2006b). Similarly, children from families of low functioning are more likely to exhibit behavioral difficulties (Taylor et al., 1999).

Poor long-term social outcomes have been identified following pediatric TBI (Muscara et al., 2009; Yeates et al., 2004), with parent ratings indicating that social dysfunction is associated with severe TBI. Andrews and colleagues (1998) identified via self-report measures that children with TBI report feeling more lonely and have lower self-esteem compared to age peers, regardless of injury severity.

Yeates and colleagues (Yeates et al., 2004, 2007) identified that negative social outcomes are partly attributable to low SES, poorer family functioning and low level of family resources, as well as cognitive factors associated with the TBI, including executive functioning, pragmatic language, and social problem solving. Similarly, Muscara and colleagues (2008a) demonstrated that higher level of executive dysfunction was associated with less sophisticated social problem-solving skills, resulting in poorer social outcome.

Psychiatric The incidence of novel-onset psychiatric disturbance following childhood TBI is estimated to be between 55% and 65% (Bloom et al., 2001; Max et al., 1998a). This includes children with a premorbid psychiatric disturbance who met diagnostic criteria for a new psychiatric disorder subsequent to the TBI (Bloom et al., 2001). Children with a premorbid history of psychiatric disturbance are pre-disposed to post-injury psychopathology.

Psychiatric disorders including ADHD (Max et al., 2004; Bloom et al., 2001), anxiety and depression (Luis & Mittenberg, 2002), personality change (Max et al., 2006) and obsessive-compulsive symptoms (Grados et al., 2008), can emerge following TBI due to primary effects of the injury associated with neuronal damage, as well as secondary effects associated with the child's adjustment to the effects of the injury. The interaction of severity of injury and premorbid child and family functioning has also been found to contribute to the maintenance of psychiatric symptoms in the long term (Max et al., 1997b; Max et al., 2006).

The most frequent psychiatric disorder to develop post-childhood TBI is secondary attention-deficit hyperactivity disorder (SADHD). Estimates of long-term SADHD diagnosed between 1 and 5 years post injury range from 35% to 44% (Bloom et al., 2001; Max et al., 2004), compared to 3–5% in the non-injured population (Schachar et al., 2004). Biological factors alone do not entirely explain the onset of SADHD, as family and socioeconomic factors also influence outcome, with low SES associated with a higher risk of developing SADHD, as well as persistence of symptoms (Levin et al., 2007).

Following SADHD, mood and anxiety disorders are most prevalent (Bloom et al., 2001), with the severe TBI population at greatest risk of developing these psychiatric disorders post injury (Luis & Mittenberg, 2002; Max et al., 2001). A number of studies report that the incidence of psychiatric disorder does not substantially change in the mild TBI population (Gerring et al., 1998; Max et al., 1998a, 1998b). Low SES also places children at greater risk of developing depressive symptoms (Kirkwood et al., 2007).

The role of age at injury in psychiatric disturbance is less clear than with other outcomes, although Bloom (2001) reported that younger children are more likely to develop externalising behavioral difficulties rather than internalising disorders. Studies have failed to find a relationship with age at injury and SADHD (Max et al., 2004; Schachar et al., 2004).

IMPLICATIONS FOR CLINICAL PRACTICE

Children with severe injury, children injured earlier in life, the presence of premorbid dysfunction, and children from disadvantaged socioeconomic backgrounds are most vulnerable to poor outcomes following TBI. Consideration of these factors in the initial history taking will help to identify children and families at greatest risk of dysfunction following TBI. Severe injury will result in chronic cognitive and behavioral impairment; thus, the allocation of intensive resources for the long term is likely to be required. This review of studies has highlighted the importance of monitoring children over time as their needs may change, particularly as the gap between the child with TBI and their peers widens. With this in mind, rehabilitation services need to intervene throughout childhood and adolescence, irrespective of the age at which the child is injured. Given the strong influence of family and environmental factors, interventions targeting these factors are essential for any change to take effect in the child.

LIFETIME COURSE AND INTERVENTIONS

Lifetime trajectory

Very few longitudinal studies have been conducted which examine outcomes of childhood TBI following the transition into adulthood. The evidence to date indicates that a significant proportion of pediatric TBI survivors who suffered a moderate to severe TBI report ongoing psychological, social, cognitive, and functional difficulties in adulthood (Klonoff et al., 1993; Muscara et al., 2009). The mild TBI population are reported to show signs of good recovery in the long term (Hessen et al., 2007).

Cognitive

Post-injury deficits in executive function, attention, and learning have been found to persist into adolescence and young adulthood (Hoofien et al., 2001; Jonsson et al., 2004; Muscara et al., 2008b). Significant difficulties in these areas may be evident despite 'normal' or intact intellectual functioning (Anderson et al., 2001b), and can impact on the subsequent development of more complex social, behavioral, and educational skills throughout the adolescent developmental period.

Psychosocial quality of life

Long-standing difficulties in social functioning have also been documented, including reduced establishment and maintenance of intimate relationships, integration and participation within the community, independent living, and participation in the workforce. These social and functional difficulties can persist into adulthood (Cattelani et al.,1998; Hoofien et al., 2001; Klonoff et al., 1993; Muscara et al., 2009), and have the greatest impact on quality of life in the long term (Oddy et al., 1985).

Although less research has focused on long-term psychological outcomes, there is evidence that psychological dysfunction is a significant and debilitating consequence of pediatric TBI. These studies have identified that the TBI population has a high risk of mental illness (Cattelani et al., 1998; Hoofien et al., 2001). A recent study by Anderson et al. (2009) which investigated psychosocial outcomes in adult survivors of pediatric TBI, found that the TBI group was at least twice as likely as other individuals in their age group to have a mental health problem, even in the very long term.

Vocational

Of the few studies that have explored long-term functional, educational, and vocational outcomes, it was found that difficulties in these areas persisted into adulthood, particularly in those who had suffered a severe TBI (Hoofien et al., 2001; Klonoff et al., 1993). Anderson and colleagues (2009) found that survivors of severe TBI had lower levels of educational attainment, and many had significant employment difficulties. The mild and moderate TBI groups generally had better functional outcomes in the very long term, specifically in areas of educational attainment and employment status, although their achievement levels in these areas were lower compared to national census data.

Nybo and colleagues (2004) investigated long-term vocational and functional outcomes in adult survivors of pre-school moderate to severe TBI. In their latest follow-up, the mean age of the sample was 40 years. The majority of the group were living independently, and there was little change in vocational status since the previous follow-up at mean age of 23 years. Despite little change in vocational status, only 33% were engaged in full-time employment, and 59% were not working at all. This study suggests that the impact of pediatric TBI on vocational functioning is persistent, and can be predicted from employment status in young adulthood.

Approaches to interventions

Neuropsychological outcomes following childhood TBI have been comprehensively investigated, with the focus of research currently shifting to determining the effectiveness of interventions. The majority of intervention studies are single case study design or group studies. There are very few randomized controlled trials (RCTs), perhaps due to the challenges that make it difficult to implement this design in this group, including the heterogeneity of the TBI population, the limited valid and reliable outcome measures, developmental variations across childhood, ethical considerations in withholding treatments during critical periods, and the need for age-specific interventions (Anderson & Catroppa, 2006). For a comprehensive review of the evidence for interventions with children with TBI, refer to Catroppa & Anderson (2006) and Laatsch et al. (2007).

Psychological and psycho-educational

With increasing knowledge of the importance of family variables to behavioral and academic outcomes, many intervention studies are now focusing on enhancing the skills of the family to improve outcomes in the child with TBI.

Wade et al. (2006a) demonstrated in an RCT design, the effectiveness of on-line cognitive behavioral intervention provided to families. The Family Problem Solving (FPS) program, delivered via the Internet, aimed to develop appropriate social skills and problem-solving skills in children, and educate families about strategies to manage challenging behaviors. Control participants in this study had access to general web-based information about brain injury, but were not provided with the FPS program. The results showed that the children in the FPS group showed significant changes in their self-regulatory skills. In addition, the parents of the FPS group reported significantly lower levels of anxiety

and depressive symptoms and distress. The children who showed greatest improvement in their behavior were older, and from families of low socioeconomic backgrounds. This latter finding is particularly important given that children of low SES background are particularly vulnerable to poorer behavioral outcomes than children from higher-resourced families. There is thus the potential to enhance outcome in this disadvantaged group. In addition, web-based programs allow families who live in remote communities to access interventions.

Rehabilitation centers are moving toward family-centred practice to varying extents. The assumptions underlying this practice include the recognition that parents are experts on their child's needs, the importance of partnerships between family and service providers, and supporting the family's role in decision-making about services for their child (Rosenbaum, et al., 1998). At the practical level, the family is engaged with the therapy team in creating goals that are meaningful to the child and family, and the direct involvement of family members is supported in therapy. Braga and colleagues (2005) demonstrated in an RCT design that children who received home-based cognitive, behavioral and physical intervention from their parents for a period of 12 months had significantly improved physical and cognitive outcomes compared to children who were inpatients of a rehabilitation facility who received intervention from therapists for the same period of time. The socioeconomic background of the family did not contribute to outcomes. Although these results are promising, future studies will need to investigate whether the cognitive and physical gains have functional outcomes and whether these benefits are maintained over time.

Ponsford and colleagues (2001) revealed the significance of providing information in the acute phase to children and families. In an RCT design, Ponsford (2005) compared the neuropsychological, behavioral, adaptive and psychological outcomes of children who had received an information booklet, which detailed symptoms of mild head injury, to children who only received treatment in Emergency. At 3 months post injury, improvement on all neuropsychological, cognitive and behavioral outcomes was observed in both groups; however, the children and their families who received the information booklet reported significantly lower levels of stress than the control group, and reduced the chance of attributing the symptoms to other causes. These results have significant implications in that they have the potential to offset the secondary psychological symptoms of anxiety and distress that can occur as a reaction to the subtle changes associated with post-concussional syndrome following mild TBI (Ponsford et al., 2000).

Feeney and Ylvisaker (2002, 2008) illustrated in a series of case studies the success of positive behavioral intervention and support (PBIS), to reduce disruptive and challenging behaviors which interfere with the child's school functioning. PBIS uses positive antecedent focused procedures. The child is taught useful, effective behaviors, and parents and teachers are trained in the strategies to maintain consistency across home and school settings. In addition, environments are adapted for the individual child, and goals are created which are realistic and attainable, with the intervention conducted within context at school, to promote generalization. This approach has also been successfully used to improve challenging behaviors of children and adults with TBI in home and community settings (Ylvisaker et al., 2007).

Educational interventions

There are few high-quality studies that have examined methods to enhance academic outcomes. Savage et al. (2005) recorded a range of strategies generated from the clinical experience of the authors. Preparing the school for the child's re-entry, adequately assessing the child's strengths and limitations, and developing a unique, tailored program for the child are considered essential in supporting the child's placement at school. It is acknowledged by Savage and colleagues (2005) that the empirical evidence for the use of classroom strategies is limited. The needs of the child will change over time; therefore, this process of assessment and program development needs to be reviewed. They also recommended a system is implemented to enable long-term monitoring and reviews at key transition points (e.g. moving from primary to secondary school). Involvement of the family in this process was also advised.

The evidence for repetitive skill training to enhance cognitive function is limited; however, attentional skills appear to be the most likely to improve with this form of intervention. An RCT study that targeted cognitive and behavioral training, and involved parents or educators in conjunction with weekly feedback from a psychologist or teacher, was found to significantly enhance the selective attention and verbal working memory skills of children with various forms of ABI (van't Hooft et al., 2007). These effects were still detectable at 6 months following the completion of treatment. This result is quite remarkable given that the children were provided with this intervention at a mean of 2 years post injury. This implies that cognitive gains are possible after the first 12 months post injury, provided the child receives targeted support. Although these results are promising, the implications of these cognitive gains to functional outcomes (academic, social, behavioral) are yet to be determined.

Pharmacology

Medication as a treatment may be an option for children and families who have experienced little success from psychological intervention. Medication may reduce the intensity and frequency of symptoms, so that the child is able to engage in therapeutic interventions. However, few studies have examined the efficacy of medication to address the range of psychiatric changes that can occur following TBI. It is not sufficient to extrapolate the findings of the effectiveness of these medications to the psychiatric non-injured population, given the difference in pathophysiology and the additional deficits associated with TBI.

In a review of studies that investigated treatment outcomes of methylphenidate for SADHD, the effects of medication were modest and the effect on cognition was less apparent than for children with a primary diagnosis of ADHD (Jin & Schachar, 2004). Medication was more likely to reduce the hyperactive, impulsive symptoms than improve concentration skills and reduce cognitive fatigue. The authors concluded that the introduction of stimulant medication within months of the injury was most effective, and did not carry adverse effects.

Medication to manage emotional and behavioral disturbance following childhood TBI is reportedly under-utilized (Bates, 2006). With the potential adverse long-term psychosocial outcomes associated with behavioral disturbance, there is a need for large, multicenter RCTs to investigate the role of pharmacology following childhood TBI.

Timing of interventions

It is recommended that interventions are provided at points of transition, when it is known that the child will experience an increase in academic, behavioral, and social demands. These points in time include transitioning between pre-school, primary school, secondary school, and employment or tertiary studies. Neuropsychological assessment is recommended to determine current strengths and weaknesses, resulting in tailored interventions to manage the new environment. The multidisciplinary team assessment is also essential to ensure that all needs are being addressed, so that the environment is modified, information is provided to those working with the child, and realistic goals are developed to maximize the potential for a successful transition.

CONCLUSION

Outcome studies of pediatric TBI have identified a range of injury, child and family factors that enable clinicians to identify children and families at risk of long-term difficulties. The research has demonstrated that cognitive and behavioral deficits persist in the long term, with many adult survivors of pediatric TBI experiencing poor vocational and social outcomes. It is expected that future research will commit to investigating the efficacy of interventions, with the view to reducing morbidity associated with pediatric TBI.

REFERENCES

Adams, J.H., Graham, D.I., Scott, G., Parker, G.S., & Doyle, D. (1980) 'Brain damage in fatal non-missile head injury', *Journal of Clinical Pathology*, 33: 12: 1132–1145.

Adelson, P.D., Jenkins, L.W., Hamilton, R.L., Robichaud, P., Tran, M.P., & Kochanek, P.M. (2001) 'Histopathologic response of the immature rat to diffuse traumatic brain injury', *Journal of Neurotrauma*, 18: 967–976.

Adelson, P.D. & Kochanek, P.M. (1998) 'Head injury in children', *Journal of Child Neurology*, 13: 2–15.

Anderson, V. & Catroppa, C. (2006) 'Advances in postacute rehabilitation after childhood-acquired brain injury. A focus on cognitive, behavioral and social domains', *American Journal of Physical Medicine and Rehabilitation*, 85: 767–778.

Anderson, V. & Catroppa, C. (2007) 'Memory outcome at 5 years post childhood traumatic brain injury', *Brain Injury*, 21: 1399–1409.

Anderson, V. & Moore, C. (1995) 'Age at injury as a predictor of outcome following pediatric head injury: a longitudinal perspective', *Child Neuropsychology*, 1: 187–202.

Anderson, V. & Pentland, L. (1998) 'Residual attention deficits following childhood head injury: Implications for ongoing development', *Neuropsychological Rehabilitation*, 8: 283–300.

Anderson, V., Bond, L., Catroppa, C., Grimwood, K., Nolan, T., & Keir, E. (1997a) 'Childhood bacterial meningitis: impact of age at illness and medical complications on long-term outcome', *Journal of the International Neuropsychological Society*, 3: 147–158.

Anderson, V., Morse, S., Klug, G., Catroppa, C., Haritou, F., Rosenfeld, J. et al. (1997b) 'Predicting recovery from head injury in young children', *Journal of the International Neuropsychological Society*, 3: 568–580.

Anderson, V., Catroppa, C., Morse, S., Haritou, F., & Rosenfeld, J. (2000a) 'Recovery of intellectual ability following TBI in childhood: Impact of injury severity and age at injury', *Pediatric Neurosurgery*, 32: 282–290.

Anderson, V., Catroppa, C., Morse, S., Haritou, F., & Rosenfeld, J. (2000b) 'Recovery of memory function following traumatic brain injury in preschool children', *Brain Injury*, 8: 679–692.

Anderson, V., Catroppa, C., Morse, S., Haritou, F., & Rosenfeld, J. (2001a) 'Outcome from mild head injury in young children: a prospective study', *Journal of Clinical and Experimental Neuropsychology*, 23: 705–717.

Anderson, V., Northam, E., Hendy, J., & Wrennall, J. (2001b) *Developmental Neuropsychology. A Clinical Approach*. Philadelphia: Psychology Press.

Anderson, V., Catroppa, C., Morse, S., Haritou, F., & Rosenfeld, J. (2005) 'Functional plasticity or vulnerability following early brain injury', *Pediatrics*, 116: 1374–1382.

Anderson, V., Brown, S., Newitt, H., & Hoile, H. (2009) 'Educational, vocational, psychosocial and quality-of-life outcomes for adult survivors of childhood traumatic brain injury', *Journal of Head Trauma Rehabilitation*, 24: 303–312.

Anderson, V.A., Spencer-Smith, M., Coleman, L., Anderson, P., Williams, J., Greenham, M., Leventer, R., & Jacobs, R. (2010) 'Children's executive functions: Are they poorer after very early brain insult', *Neuropsychologia*, 48: 2041–2050.

Andrews, T.K., Rose, F.D., & Johnson, D.A (1998) 'Social and behavioral effects of traumatic brain injury in children', *Brain Injury*, 12: 133–138.

Ashwal, S., Holshouser, B.A., & Tong, K.A. (2006) 'Use of advanced neuroimaging techniques in the evaluation of pediatric traumatic brain injury', *Developmental Neuroscience*, 28: 309–326.

Bates, G. (2006) 'Medication in the treatment of behavioral sequelae of traumatic brain injury', *Developmental Medicine and Child Neurology*, 48: 697–701.

Begali, V. (1992) *Head Injury in Children and Adolescents* (2nd edition). Brandon, VT: Clinical Psychology Publishing Company.

Berger, M.S., Pitts, L.H., Lovely, M., Edwards, M.S., & Bartkowsky, H.M. (1985) 'Outcome from severe head injury in children and adolescents', *Journal of Neurosurgery*, 62 :194–198.

Berney, J., Favier, J., & Froidevaux, A. (1994) 'Pediatric head trauma: Influence of age and sex. I. Epidemiology', *Child's Nervous System*, 10: 509–516.

Bigler, E.D. (2001) 'Quantitative magnetic resonance imaging in traumatic brain injury', *Journal of Head Trauma Rehabilitation*, 16: 117–134.

Bloom, D.R., Levin, H.S., Ewing-Cobbs, L., Saunders, A., Song, J.M.A., Fletcher, J.M. et al. (2001) 'Lifetime and novel psychiatric disorders after pediatric traumatic brain injury', *Journal of the American Academy of Child and Adolescent Psychiatry*, 40: 572–579.

Braga, L., Da Paz Jr, A.C., & Ylvisaker, M. (2005) 'Direct clinician-delivered versus indirect family-supported rehabilitation of children with traumatic brain injury: a randomised controlled trial', *Brain Injury*, 19: 819–831.

Brookshire, B.L., Chapman, S.B., Song, J., & Levin, H.S. (2000) 'Cognitive and linguistic correlates of children's discourse after closed head injury: a three-year follow-up', *Journal of the International Neuropsychological Society*, 6: 741–751.

Bruce, D.A. (1995) 'Pathophysiological responses of the child's brain following trauma', in S.H. Broman & M.E. Michell (eds), *Traumatic Head Injury in Children*. New York: Oxford University Press, pp. 40–51.

Catroppa, C., Anderson, V., & Stargatt, R. (1999) 'A prospective analysis of the recovery of attention following pediatric head injury', *Journal of the International Neuropsychological Society*, 5: 48–57.

Catroppa, C., Anderson, V., Morse, S., Haritou, F., & Rosenfeld, J. (2007) 'Children's attentional skills five years post-TBI', *Journal of Pediatric Psychology*, 32: 354–369.

Catroppa, C., Anderson, V., Morse, S., Haritou, F., & Rosenfeld, J. (2008) 'Outcome and predictors of functional recovery 5 years following pediatric traumatic brain injury (TBI)', *Journal of Pediatric Psychology*, 33: 707–718.

Cattelani, R., Lombardi, F., Brianti, R., & Mazzucchi, A. (1998) 'Traumatic brain injury in childhood: intellectual, behavioral and social outcome into adulthood', *Brain Injury*, 12: 283–296.

Crowe, L., Babl, F., Anderson, V., & Catroppa, C. (2009) 'The epidemiology of paediatric head injuries: Data from a referral centre in Victoria, Australia. *Journal of Paediatrics and Child Health*, 45: 346–350.

Dalby, P.R. & Obrzut, J.E. (1991) 'Epidemiologic characteristics and sequelae of closed head-injured children and adolescents: a review', *Developmental Neuropsychology*, 7: 35–68.

DeLuca, C. & Leventer, R.D. (2008) 'Developmental trajectories of executive functions across the life span', In V.A. Anderson, R. Jacobs, & P. Anderson (eds), *Executive Functions and the Frontal Lobes: A Lifespan Perspective*. Philadelphia, US: Taylor & Francis, pp. 23–56.

Dennis, M. (1989) 'Language and the young damaged brain', in T. Boll & B. Bryant (eds), *Clinical Neuropsychology: Research, Measurement and Practice*. Washington: APA Press, pp. 203–219.

Dennis, M. (2000). *Childhood Medical Disorders and Cognitive Impairment: Biological risk, Time, Development, and Reserve*. New York: Guilford.

Dennis, M. (2006) 'Aphasia IV: acquired disorders of language in children', in M.J. Farah & T.E. Feinberg (eds), *Patient-Based Approaches to Cognitive Neuroscience* (2nd edition). Cambridge, MA: The MIT Press, pp. 229–245

Di Stefano, G., Bachevalier, J., Levin, H.S., Song, J.X., Scheibel, R.S., & Fletcher, J.M. (2000) 'Volume of focal brain lesions and hippocampal formation in relation to memory function after closed head injury in children', *Journal of Neurology, Neurosurgery, and Psychiatry,* 69: 210–216.

Eslinger, P. & Grattan, L. (1993) 'Frontal lobe and frontal-striatal substrates for different forms of human cognitive flexibility', *Neuropsychologia,* 31: 17–28.

Ewing-Cobbs, L. & Fletcher, J.M. (1987) 'Neuropsychological assessment of head injury in children', *Journal of Learning Disabilities,* 20: 526–535.

Ewing-Cobbs, L., Levin, H.S., Fletcher, J.M., Miner, M.E., & Eisenberg, H.M. (1990) 'The Children's Orientation and Amnesia Test: Relationship to severity of acute head injury and to recovery of memory', *Neurosurgery,* 27: 683–691.

Ewing-Cobbs, L., Fletcher, J.M., Levin, H.S., Iovino, I., & Miner, M.E. (1998a) 'Academic achievement and academic placement following traumatic brain injury in children and adolescents: a two year longitudinal study', *Journal of Clinical and Experimental Neuropsychology,* 20: 769–781.

Ewing-Cobbs, L., Kraner, L., Prasad, M., Canales, D.N., Louis, P.T., Fletcher, J.M. et al. (1998b) 'Neuroimaging, physical, and developmental findings after inflicted and noninflicted traumatic brain injury in young children', *Pediatrics,* 102: 300–307.

Ewing-Cobbs, L., Barnes, M., Fletcher, J.M., Levin, H.S., Swank, P.R., & Song, J. (2004) 'Modeling of longitudinal academic achievement scores after pediatric traumatic brain injury', *Developmental Neuropsychology,* 25: 107–133.

Feeney, T. & Ylvisaker, M. (2002) 'Context-sensitive behavioral supports for young children with TBI: short-term effects and long-term outcome', *Journal of Head Trauma Rehabilitation,* 18: 33–51.

Feeney, T. & Ylvisaker, M. (2008) 'Context-sensitive cognitive-behavioral supports for young children with TBI: A second replication study', *Journal of Positive Behavior Interventions,* 10: 115–128.

Fernando, K., Eaton, L., Faulkner, M., Moodley, Y., & Setchell, R. (2002) 'Development and piloting of the Starship Post-traumatic Amnesia Scale for children aged between four and six years', *Brain Impairment,* 3: 34–41.

Garth, J., Anderson, V., & Wrennall, J. (1997) 'Executive functions following moderate to severe frontal lobe injury: Impact of injury and age at injury', *Pediatric Rehabilitation,* 1: 99–108.

Gerring, J.P., Brady, K.D., Chen, A., Vasa, R., Grados, M., Bandeen-Roche, K.J. et al. (1998) 'Premorbid prevalence of ADHD and development of SADHD after closed head injury', *Journal of the American Academy of Child and Adolescent Psychiatry,* 37: 647–654.

Gil, A.M. (2003) 'Neurocognitive outcomes following pediatric brain injury: a developmental approach', *Journal of School Psychology,* 41: 337–353.

Gioia, G.A., Isquith, P.K., Kenworthy, L., & Barton, R.M. (2002) 'Profiles of everyday executive function in acquired and developmental disorders', *Child Neuropsychology,* 8: 121–137.

Grados, M.A., Vasa, R.A., Riddle, M.A., Slomine, B.S., Salorio, C., Christensen, J. et al. (2008) 'New onset obsessive-compulsive symptoms in children and adolescents with severe traumatic brain injury', *Depression and Anxiety,* 25: 398–407.

Grimwood, K., Nolan, T., Bond, L., Anderson, V., Catroppa, C., & Keir, E. (1996) 'Risk factors for adverse outcomes of bacterial meningitis', *Journal of Paediatric Child Health,* 32: 457–462.

Hebb, D.O. (1949). *The Organisation of Behavior*. New York: McGraw-Hill.

Hessen, E., Nestvold, K., & Anderson, V. (2007). 'Neuropsychological function 23 years after mild traumatic brain injury: A comparison of outcome after paediatric and adult head injuries', *Brain Injury,* 21: 963–979.

Hessen, E., Anderson, V., & Nestvold, K. (2008) 'MMPI-2 profiles 23 years after paediatric mild traumatic brain injury', *Brain Injury,* 22: 39–50.

Holloway, M., Bye, A., & Moran, K. (1994) 'Non-accidental head injury in children', *The Medical Journal of Australia,* 160: 786–789.

Hoofien, D., Gilboa, A., Vakil, E., & Donovick, P. (2001) 'Traumatic brain injury (TBI) 10 - 20 years later: A comprehensive outcome study of psychiatric symptomatology, cognitive abilities and psychosocial functioning', *Brain Injury,* 15:189–209.

Jacobs, R., Anderson, V., Neale, J., Shield, L., & Kornberg, A.J. (2004) 'Neuropsychological outcome after acute disseminated encephalomyelitis: Impact of age at illness onset', *Pediatric Neurology,* 31: 191–197.

Jacobs, R., Harvey, A.S., & Anderson, V. (2007) 'Executive function following focal frontal lobe lesions: Impact of timing of lesion on outcome', *Cortex,* 43: 792–805.

Jaffe, K.M., Polissar, N.L., Fay, G.C., & Liao, S. (1995) 'Recovery trends over three years following pediatric traumatic brain injury', *Archives of Physical Medicine and Rehabilitation,* 76: 17–26.

Jankowitz, B.T. & Adelson, P.D. (2006) 'Pediatric traumatic brain injury: past, present and future', *Developmental Neuroscience,* 28: 264–275.

Jin, C. & Schachar, R. (2004) 'Methylphenidate treatment of attention-deficit/hyperactivity disorder secondary to traumatic brain injury: a critical appraisal of treatment studies', *CNS Spectrums,* 9: 217–226.

Jonsson, C.A., Horneman, G., & Emanuelson, I. (2004) 'Neuropsychological progress during 14 years after severe traumatic brain injury in childhood and adolescence', *Brain Injury,* 18: 921–934.

Kant, R., Smith-Seemiller, L., Isaac, G., & Duffy, J. (1997) 'Tc-HMPAO SPECT in persistent post-concussion syndrome after mild head injury: comparison with MRI/CT', *Brain Injury,* 11: 115–124.

Keenan, H.T. & Bratton, S. (2006) 'Epidemiology and outcomes of pediatric traumatic brain injury', *Developmental Neuroscience,* 28: 256–263.

Kennard, M.A. (1936) 'Age and other factors in motor recovery from precentral lesions in monkeys', *American Journal of Physiology,* 115: 138–146.

Kennard, M.A. (1940) 'Relation of age to motor impairment in man and in subhuman primates', *Archives of Neurology and Psychiatry,* 44: 377–397.

Kirkwood, M.W., Yeates, K.O., Taylor, H.G., Randolph, C., McCrea, M., & Anderson, V. (2007) 'Management of pediatric mild traumatic brain injury: a neuropsychological review from injury through recovery', *The Clinical Neuropsychologist,* 22: 769–800.

Klonoff, H., Campbell, C., & Klonoff, P.S. (1993) Long-term outcome of head injuries: a 23 year follow up study of children with head injuries. *Journal of Neurology, Neurosurgery, and Psychiatry,* 56 410–415.

Kolb, B. (2004) 'Mechanisms of cortical plasticity after neuronal injury', in J. Ponsford (ed.), *Cognitive and Behavioral Rehabilitation.* New York: Guilford, pp. 30–58.

Kraus, J.F. (1995) 'Epidemiological features of brain injury in children', in S.H. Broman & M.E. Michel (eds), *Traumatic head injury in children.* New York: Oxford University Press, pp. 117–146.

Kraus, J.F., Fife, D., Cox, P., Ramstein, K., & Conroy, C. (1986) 'Incidence, severity, and external causes of pediatric brain injury', *American Journal of Diseases of Children,* 140: 687–693.

Laatsch, L., Harrington, D., Hotz, G., Marcantuono, J., Mozzoni, M.P., Walsh, V. et al. (2007) 'An evidence-based review of cognitive and behavioral rehabilitation treatment studies in children with acquired brain injury', *Journal of Head Trauma Rehabilitation,* 22: 248–256.

Levin, H.S., Benton, A.L., & Grossman, R.G. (1982) *Neurobehavioral Consequences of Closed Head Injury.* New York: Oxford University Press.

Levin, H.S., Amparco, E., Eisenberg, H.M., Williams, D., High, W., McArdle, C. et al. (1987) 'Magnetic resonance imaging and computerised tomography in relation to the neurobehavioral sequelae of mild and moderate head injuries', *Journal of Neurosurgery,* 66: 706–713.

Levin, H.S., Williams, D.H., Eisenberg, H.M., High, W., & Guinto, F.C. (1992) 'Serial MRI and neurobehavioral findings after mild to moderate closed head injury', *Journal of Neurology, Neurosurgery, and Psychiatry,* 55: 255–262.

Levin, H.S., Culhane, K.A., Mendelsohn, D., Lilly, M., Bruce, D., Fletcher, J.M. et al. (1993) 'Cognition in relation to magnetic resonance imaging in head-injured children and adolescents', *Archives of Neurology,* 50: 897–905.

Levin, H.S., Mendelsohn, D., Lilly, M.A., Fletcher, J.M., Culhane, K.A., Chapman, S.B. et al. (1994) 'Tower of London performance in relation to magnetic resonance imaging following closed head injury in children', *Neuropsychology,* 8: 171–179.

Levin, H.S., Zhang, L., Dennis, M., Ewing-Cobbs, L., Schachar, R., Jeffrey, M. et al. (2004) 'Psychosocial outcome of TBI in children with unilateral frontal lesions', *Journal of the International Neuropsychological Society,* 10: 305–316.

Levin, H.S., Hanten, G., Max, J., Li, X., Swank, P., Ewing-Cobbs, L. et al. (2007) 'Symptoms of attention-deficit/hyperactivity disorder following traumatic brain injury in children', *Journal of Developmental and Behavioral Pediatrics,* 28: 108–118.

Luerssen, T.G., Klauber, M.R., & Marshall, L.F. (1988) 'Outcome from head injury related to patient's age: a longitudinal prospective study of adult and pediatric head injury', *Journal of Neurosurgery,* 68: 409–416.

Luis, C.A. & Mittenberg, W. (2002) 'Mood and anxiety disorders following pediatric traumatic brain injury: a prospective study', *Journal of Clinical and Experimental Neuropsychology*, 24: 270–279.

McAllister, T.W. (1992) 'Neuropsychiatric sequelae of head injuries', *Psychiatric Clinics of North America*, 15(2): 395–413.

Mandalis, A., Kinsella, G., Ong, B., & Anderson, V. (2007) 'Working memory and new learning following pediatric traumatic brain injury', *Developmental Neuropsychology*, 32: 683–701.

Mangeot, S., Armstrong, K., Colvin, A.N., Yeates, K.O., & Taylor, H.G. (2002) 'Long-term executive function deficits in children with traumatic brain injuries: assessment using the Behavior Rating Inventory of Executive Function', *Child Neuropsychology*, 8: 271–284.

Marosszeky, N.E.V., Batchelor, J., Shores, E.A., Marosszeky, J.E., Klein-Boonschate, M., & Fahey, P.P. (1993) 'The performance of hospitalized, non head-injured children on the Westmead PTA Scale', *The Clinical Neuropsychologist*, 7: 85–95.

Max, J., Lindgren, S.D., Knutson, C., Pearson, C.S., Ihrig, D., & Welborn, A. (1997a) 'Child and adolescent traumatic brain injury : psychiatric findings from a paediatric outpatient speciality clinic', *Brain injury*, 11: 699–711.

Max, J., Robin, D.A., Lindgren, S.D., Smith, W.L., Sato, Y., Mattheis, P.J. et al. (1997b) 'Traumatic brain injury in children and adolescents: psychiatric disorders at two years', *Journal of the American Academy of Child and Adolescent Psychiatry*, 39: 1278–1285.

Max, J., Koele, S.L., Smith, W.J., Sato, Y., Lindgren, S., Robin, D. et al. (1998a) 'Psychiatric disorders in children and adolescents after severe traumatic brain injury: a controlled study', *Journal of the American Academy of Child and Adolescent Psychiatry*, 37: 832–840.

Max, J., Robin, D.A., Lindgren, S.D., Smith, W.L., Sato, Y., Mattheis, P.J. et al. (1998b) 'Traumatic Brain Injury in Children and Adolescents: Psychiatric Disorders at One Year', *Journal of Neuropsychiatry*, 10: 290–297.

Max, J., Roberts, M.A., Koele, S.L., Lindgren, S.D., Robin, D.A., Arndt, S. et al. (1999) 'Cognitive outcome in children and adolescents following severe traumatic brain injury: influence of psychosocial, psychiatric and injury-related variables', *Journal of the International Neuropsychological Society*, 5: 58–68.

Max, J., Robertson, B.A.M., & Lansing, A.E. (2001) 'The phenomenology of personality change due to traumatic brain injury in children and adolescents', *Journal of Neuropsychiatry*, 13: 161–170.

Max, J., Lansing, A.E., Koele, S.L., Castillo, C.S., Bokura, H., & Schachar, R. (2004) 'Attention Deficit Hyperactivity Disorder in Children and Adolescents following Traumatic Brain Injury', *Developmental Neuropsychology*, 25: 159–177.

Max, J.E., Levin, H.S., Schachar, R.J., Landis, J., Saunders, A.E., Ewing-Cobbs, L., Chapman, S.B., & Dennis, M. (2006) 'Predictors of Personality Change due to Traumatic Brain Injury in Children and Adolescents Six to Twenty Four Months After Injury', *Journal of Neuropsychiatry and Clinical Neurosciences*, 18: 21–32.

Mendelsohn, D., Levin, H.S., Bruce, D., Lilly, M., Harward, H., Culhane, K.A. et al. (1992) 'Late MRI after head injury in children: relationship to clinical features and outcome', *Childs Nervous System*, 8: 445–452.

Miller, J.D. (1991) 'Pathophysiology and management of head injury', *Neuropsychology*, 5: 235–261.

Mitra, B., Cameron, P., & Butt, W. (2007) 'Population based study of pediatric head injury', *Journal of Pediatric Child Health*, 43: 154–159.

Muscara, F., Catroppa, C., & Anderson, V. (2008a) 'Social problem solving skills as a mediator between executive function and long-term social outcome following pediatric traumatic brain injury', *Journal of Neuropsychology*, 2: 445–461.

Muscara, F., Catroppa, C., & Anderson, V. (2008b) 'The impact of injury severity on executive function 7–10 years following pediatric traumatic brain injury', *Developmental Neuropsychology*, 33: 623–636.

Muscara, F., Catroppa, C., Eren, S., & Anderson, V. (2009) 'The impact of injury severity on long-term social outcome following pediatric traumatic brain injury', *Neuropsychological Rehabilitation*, 19: 541–561.

Nybo, T., Sainio, M., & Muller, K. (2004) 'Stability of vocational outcome in adulthood after moderate to severe preschool brain injury', *Journal of the International Neuropsychological Society*, 10: 719–723.

Oddy, M., Coughlan, T., Tyerman, A., & Jenkins, D. (1985) 'Social adjustment after closed head injury: A further follow-up seven years after injury', *Journal of Neurology, Neurosurgery, and Psychiatry*, 48: 564–568.

Pickett, W., Simpson, K., & Brison, R.J. (2004) 'Rates and external causes of blunt head trauma in Ontario: Analysis and review of Ontario Trauma Registry datasets', *Chronic Diseases in Canada*, 25: 32–41.

Ponsford, J. (2005) 'Rehabilitation interventions after mild head injury', *Current Opinion in Neurology,* 18: 692–697.

Ponsford, J., Willmott, C., & Rothwell, A. (2000) 'Factors influencing outcome following mild traumatic brain injury in adults', *Journal of the International Neuropsychological Society,* 6: 568–579.

Ponsford, J., Willmott, C., Rothwell, A., Cameron, P., Ayton, G., Nelms, R. et al. (2001) 'Impact of early intervention on outcome after mild traumatic brain injury in children', *Pediatrics,* 108: 1297–1303.

Quattrocchi, K., Prasad, P., Willits, N., & Wagner, F. (1991) 'Quantification of midline shift as a predictor of poor outcome following head injury', *Surgical Neurology,* 35: 183–188.

Rivara, J.B., Jaffe, K.M., Fay, G.C., Polissar, N.L., Martin, K.M., Shurtleff, H.A. et al. (1993) 'Family functioning and injury severity as predictors of child functioning one year following traumatic brain injury', *Archives of Physical Medicine and Rehabilitation,* 74: 1047–1055.

Rosenbaum, P., King, S., Law, M., King, G., & Evans, J. (1998) 'Family-centred service: a conceptual framework and research review', *Physical and Occupational Therapy in Pediatrics,* 18: 1–20.

Savage, R.C., Depompei, R., Tyler, J., & Lash, M. (2005) 'Paediatric traumatic brain injury: a review of pertinent issues', *Pediatric Rehabilitation,* 8: 92–103.

Schachar, R., Levin, H.S., Max, J., & Purvis, K. (2004) 'Attention deficit hyperactivity disorder symptoms and response inhibition after closed head in children: do preinjury behavior and injury severity predict outcome?', *Developmental Neuropsychology,* 25: 179–198.

Sharma, M. & Sharma, A. (1994) 'Mode, presentation, CT findings and outcome of pediatric head injury', *Indian Pediatrics,* 31: 733–739.

Spanos, G.K., Wilde, E.A., Bigler, E.D., Cleavinger, H.B., Fearing, M.A., Levin, H.S. et al. (2007) 'Cerebellar atrophy after moderate-to-severe pediatric traumatic brain injury', *American Journal of Neuroradiology,* 28: 537–542.

Taylor, H.G. & Alden, J. (1997) 'Age-related differences in outcomes following childhood brain insults: An introduction and overview', *Journal of the International Neuropsychological Society,* 6: 555–567.

Taylor, H.G., Drotar, D., Wade, S.L., Yeates, K.O., Stancin, T., & Klein, S. (1995) 'Recovery from traumatic brain injury in children: the importance of the family', in S.H. Broman & M.E. Michel (eds), *Traumatic Head Injury in Children.* New York: Oxford University Press, pp. 188–218.

Taylor, H.G., Yeates, K.O., Wade, S.L., Drotar, D., Klein, S.K., & Stancin, T. (1999) 'Influences on first-year recovery from traumatic brain injury', *Neuropsychology,* 13: 76–89.

Taylor, H.G., Yeates, K.O., Wade, S.L., Drotar, D., Stancin, T., & Minich, N. (2002) 'A prospective study of short- and long-term outcomes after traumatic brain injury in children: behavior and achievement', *Neuropsychology,* 16: 15–27.

Teasdale, G. & Jennett, B. (1974) 'Assessment of coma and impaired consciousness', *Lancet,* 2: 81–84.

Thickpenny-Davis, K.L., Ogden, J.A., & Fernando, K. (2005) 'The Starship Post-Traumatic Amnesia Scale: does it predict outcome after mild to moderate traumatic brain injury in children aged 3 to 7 years?', *Brain Impairment,* 6: 101–108.

Thompson, N.M., Francis, D.J., Stuebing, K.K., Fletcher, J.M., Ewing-Cobbs, L., Miner, M.E. et al. (1994) 'Motor, visual-spatial, and somatosensory skills after closed head injury in children and adolescents: A study of change', *Neuropsychology,* 8: 333–342.

van't Hooft, I., Andersson, K., Bergman, B., Sejersen, T., von Wendt, L., & Bartfai, A. (2007) 'Sustained favourable effects of cognitive training in children with acquired brain injuries', *NeuroRehabilitation,* 22: 109–116.

Wade, S.L., Carey, J., & Wolfe, C.R. (2006a) 'An on-line family intervention to reduce parental distress following pediatric brain injury', *Journal of Consulting and Clinical Psychology,* 74: 445–454.

Wade, S.L., Taylor, H.G., Yeates, K.O., Drotar, D., Stancin, T., Minich, N.M. et al. (2006b) 'Long-term parental adaptation and family adaptation following pediatric brain injury', *Journal of Pediatric Psychology,* 31: 1072–1083.

Wilde, E.A., Bigler, E.D., Pedroza, C., & Ryser, D.K. (2006) 'Post-traumatic amnesia predicts long-term cerebral atrophy in traumatic brain injury', *Brain Injury,* 20: 695–699.

Wilde, E.A., Bigler, E.D., Hunter, J.V., Fearing, M.A., Scheibel, R.S., Newsome, M.R. et al. (2007) 'Hippocampus, amygdala, and basal ganglia morphometrics in children after moderate-to-severe traumatic brain injury', *Developmental Medicine and Child Neurology,* 49: 294–299.

Wilson, J., Wiedmann, K., Hadley, D., Condon, B., Teasdale, G., & Brooks, T. (1988) 'Early and late magnetic resonance imaging and neuropsychological outcome after head injury', *Journal of Neurology, Neurosurgery, and Psychiatry,* 51: 391–396.

Yeates, K.O. (2000). 'Closed head injury', in K.O. Yeates, M.D. Ris & H.G. Taylor (eds.) *Pediatric Neuropsychology: Research, Theory and Practice.* New York: Guilford, pp. 192–218.

Yeates, K.O. & Taylor, H.G. (2005) 'Neurobehavioral outcomes of mild head injury in children and adolescents', *Pediatric Rehabilitation,* 8: 5–16.

Yeates, K.O., Blumenstein, E., Patterson, C.M., & Delis, D.C. (1995) 'Verbal learning and memory following pediatric closed-head injury', *Journal of the International Neuropsychological Society,* 1: 78–87.

Yeates, K.O., Taylor, H.G., Wade, S.L., Drotar, D., Stancin, T., & Minich, N. (2002) 'A prospective study of short- and long-term neuropsychological outcomes after traumatic brain injury in children', *Neuropsychology,* 16: 514–523.

Yeates, K.O., Swift, E., Taylor, H.G., Wade, S.L., Drotar, D., Stancin, T. et al. (2004) 'Short- and long-term social outcomes following pediatric traumatic brain injury', *Journal of the International Neuropsychological Society,* 10: 412–426.

Yeates, K.O., Armstrong, K., Janusz, J.A., Taylor, H.G., Wade, S.L., Stancin, T. et al. (2005) Long-term attention problems in children with traumatic brain injury. *Journal of the American Academy of Child and Adolescent Psychiatry,* 44: 574–584.

Yeates, K.O., Bigler, E.D., Dennis, M., Gerhardt, C.A., Rubin, K.H., Stancin, T. et al. (2007) 'Social outcomes in childhood brain disorder: a heuristic integration of social neuroscience and developmental psychology', *Psychological Bulletin,* 133(3): 535–556.

Ylvisaker, M., Turkstra, L., Coehlo, C., Yorkston, K., Kennedy, M., Sohlberg, M.M. et al. (2007) 'Behavioral interventions for children and adults with behavior disorders after TBI: A systematic review of the evidence', *Brain Injury,* 21: 769–805.

Zimmerman, R. & Bilaniuk, L. (1994) 'Pediatric head trauma', *Pediatric Neuroradiology,* 4: 349–366.

24

Fetal Alcohol Spectrum Disorders

Kieran D. O'Malley

GENERAL OVERVIEW AND HISTORICAL PERSPECTIVE

Although it is not uncommon for substance abuse to occur during pregnancy, maternal alcohol use probably has the earliest, most debilitating, and the longest-lasting effect on the fetus (Streissguth & O'Malley, 2000). The link between maternal alcohol consumption and the effect on the fetus was initially made by the pediatrician Paul Lemoine in 1968. Working in Nantes, a wine-growing region of France, he carefully documented 127 infants with similar facial dysmorphic features whose mothers had consumed alcohol during pregnancy (Lemoine et al., 1968). A few years later, a team of researchers from the University of Washington in Seattle, USA first named the condition fetal alcohol syndrome and published their detailed clinical findings in two seminal papers (Jones & Smith, 1973; Jones et al., 1973). Thus, a new developmental disorder entered the literature which was directly related to the teratogenic effect of maternal alcohol consumption during pregnancy. The disorder combined three essential components: specific facial dysmorphology, growth delay and central nervous system effects (Streissguth, 1997).

In 1978, the term fetal alcohol effects (or FAE) was coined to describe infants and young children with clear, documented, maternal alcohol exposure, but without the classical facial dysmorphic and/or growth features associated with fetal alcohol syndrome. Later, the Institute of Medicine in the USA introduced the more clinically useful term alcohol-related neurodevelopmental disorder (ARND), which replaced the more generic FAE (Astley & Clarren, 1996). Since 1998 (O'Malley & Hagerman, 1998), fetal alcohol spectrum disorders (FASD) has been used as an umbrella term to describe the range of effects that can be caused by maternal alcohol consumption. This term is used throughout the following chapter, unless there is a need to distinguish between different alcohol-related disorders.

Epidemiology

Most recent world statistics show a range of incidence of FASD from 1.3 to 4.8 in 1000 live births, although estimates vary. For example, the prevalence of FASD has been estimated as 9.1 in 1000 live births in Seattle, USA, whereas in small aboriginal communities in Canada, rates as high as 190 in 1000 live births have been reported. Reported figures may also seriously underestimate actual rates. For example, in the UK as a whole, 90 cases were reported in 2001–02 and 128 cases in 2002–03; in Scotland, two cases were reported in 2003, and 10 in 2004. Many countries (e.g. Wales and Northern Ireland and the Republic of Ireland) collect no systematic statistics on incidence or prevalence of FASD, although clinical experience suggests that the rates are high. Thus, a large retrospective study in Dublin of 20 years of deliveries at the Coombe Women's Hospital, documented that 75–80% of Irish-born women drank alcohol during their pregnancy (Barry et al., 2007). (See also BMA, 2007; Chudley et al., 2005; Elliott, 2006; O'Malley, 2008; Sampson et al., 1997.) It is worth noting that Ireland and the UK are said to have by far the highest rates of binge drinking amongst young women in Europe and indeed in the world.

Causation

Over 35 years of animal and human research have demonstrated the consistent teratogenic effect of maternal alcohol consumption during pregnancy. It is important to emphasize that there is no safe amount of alcohol in pregnancy, and that it is the pattern of binge drinking that produces the most complex and serious effects.

Diagnostic criteria and core characteristics of FASD including dysmorphic FAS and non-dysmorphic ARND

A clear, documented history of maternal alcohol consumption in pregnancy is an essential diagnostic criterion. The amount (low, high, binge) and timing of alcohol consumption (1st, 2nd or 3rd trimester of pregnancy) are important factors, along with the mental and physical status of the mother.

Dysmorphology of FASD

The classical FAS facial features, which are essential for diagnosis, are short palpebral fissures, flattened mid face, thin upper lip, and flattened philtrum. Although these features may be present at birth, they are more commonly seen from 6 to 12 years of age. Adolescents and adults do not usually show these features, as the mid-line facial features change with age. Thus, it is important to review earlier age photographs if assessing an adolescent or adult for FAS. There is no characteristic facial dysmorphology in ARND.

Growth retardation of FASD

The essential growth retardation features required for the diagnosis of FAS are low birth weight (below 3rd percentile for height and weight); decelerating weight over time, which is not due to nutritional depletion; disproportional low weight to height; and height and weight below the 10th percentile. There are little or no growth retardation features in ARND.

Central nervous system features of FASD

The neurotoxic, teratogenic effects of prenatal alcohol exposure on the developing fetus occur during the whole of pregnancy unlike other disorders such as congenital rubella, in which the negative effects are most common during the 1st trimester. The presence of facial dysmorphology does not determine the central nervous system features.

Cognitive features

Although the majority of individuals with FASD are not intellectually impaired, around 20–25% have an IQ in the intellectual disability range (IQ < 70). Structural abnormalities in the developing hippocampus, caudate, or the corpus callosum have been implicated in many of these cognitive deficits (BMA, 2007; Hagerman, 1999; Harris, 1995; Mukherjee et al., 2006; Stratton et al., 1996). The corpus callosum abnormalities, including agenesis, have been recognized as underpinning what have been called 'disconnection disorders' and indeed FASD are considered by some researchers as the primary examples of disconnection disorders (Bookstein et al., 2001; Geschwind, 1965; Riley et al., 1995). The characteristic cognitive deficits are listed below.

Poor working memory This is probably the most disabling and most misunderstood deficit in FASD. Deficits in this area may lead individuals to be labelled as oppositional and defiant as children, or as passive aggressive as adults. Affected individuals may be accused of lying and fantasizing, when, in fact, they may be resorting to confabulation to fill in the gaps in their memory (Carmichael Olson et al. 1998; Mattson et al., 1996).

Difficulty linking cause and effect This can result in apparently thoughtless and impulsive behaviour and can also affect the impact of standard behavioural management techniques. Consequently, individuals with FASD do not respond consistently to negative or positive consequences (Massey & Massey, 2008; Streissguth, 1997).

Marked discrepancy between verbal and performance IQ Verbal IQ frequently exceeds performance IQ by 12–15 points, although the discrepancy may be 40 points or more (O'Malley, 2008).

Deficits in school academic performance This includes disorders of reading and written expression (Hagerman, 1999; Stratton et al., 1996; Streissguth, 1995; Streissguth et al., 1996). There are also specific deficits in mathematics skills, which in turn may be linked to problems in deductive reasoning and problem solving (Butterworth, 2005).

Limited capacity for abstraction This is also linked to poor problem solving. Individuals with FASD individuals can be very concrete in their thinking and take statements literally, irrespective of their IQ

(Massey & Massey, 2008; Stratton et al., 1996; Streissguth, 1997).

Alexithymia Inability to process affect or emotion.

Executive function deficits These are often associated with poor insight and impaired judgement. Individuals with FASD typically have difficulty in understanding many of the problems that they encounter in their day-to-day lives and have difficulty in developing ways to solve these problems (Rasmussen, 2005).

Behavioural problems
A number of studies link the general cognitive effects of prenatal alcohol exposure to behavioural problems in the affected person (BMA, 2007; Chudley et al., 2005; Connor et al., 2000; Massey & Massey, 2008; Steinhausen et al., 1998; Stratton et al., 1996, Streissguth, 1997; Streissguth & O'Malley, 2000). The behavioural phenotype of FASD is intricately interwoven with motor and sensory dysregulation, as well as specific cognitive and linguistic deficits (Ayers, 1979; DC 0-3R, 2005; Driscoll et al., 1991; Nanson & Hiscock, 1990; O'Malley & Nanson, 2002; O'Malley & Storoz, 2003). Indeed, the typical behavioural phenotype, which is evident from infancy, may be more accurately described as a regulatory disorder. Thus, affected children may be:

- Hypersensitive—type A (fearful/cautious) or type B (negative/defiant)
- Hyposensitive/under-responsive—either withdrawn and difficult to engage or self-absorbed
- Sensory stimulation-seeking/impulsive

These three clinical subtypes encompass the range of behavioural presentations of FASD. Maternal alcohol exposure frequently causes a disruption of the developing sensory system, leading to a lack of sensory integration and over- or under-reactivity to normal stimuli in their children. However, it is the more subtle sensory-seeking and/or impulsive infant that frequently represents the legacy of prenatal alcohol exposure.

The most commonly reported behavioural problems are listed below.

Attention-deficit/hyperactivity disorder

ADHD is often characterized by a mixture of inattention and impulsivity. Attention problems, both auditory and visual, contribute to significant learning difficulties in school, although these may sometimes be missed or minimized because of the child's normal IQ score (Coles et al., 1997; Nanson & Hiscock, 1990; Stratton et al., 1996; Streissguth, 1997).

Poor impulse control Impulsivity is organically driven and hence unpredictable. It is especially dangerous when individuals are emotionally distraught, i.e. depressed or potentially suicidal, or when under the influence of alcohol or drugs, as the prenatal damage to the brain renders it more vulnerable to toxic disinhibition effects (O'Malley, 2008).

Distractibility This can be a lifelong problem and goes 'hand-in glove' with poor organizational skills. Understandably, this effects school academic performance and later has implications for safe parenting (Connor et al., 2000; Mattson et al., 1999).

Poor organizational skills These, coupled with the executive function deficits, can lead to lifelong problems from school to adulthood, and again are a major contributor to poor parenting (Connor et al., 2000; Mattson et al., 1999).

Hyperactivity This, too, is organically driven and often requires medication if the child is to cope in the classroom or in unstructured settings (O'Malley & Nanson, 2002).

Defiant behaviours These behaviours often leading to subsequent conduct disorder

and are related to cognitive, linguistic deficits. They are compounded by prenatal alcohol-induced structural brain damage as well as exposure to domestic violence.

Communication problems

Communication problems associated with FASD may be overlooked as most affected persons have an IQ in the normal range. Although these individuals commonly possess the basic building blocks of language, i.e. grammar and syntax, their deficits lie in the areas of social cognition and social communication. Hence, young people often misread social cues and may blurt out inappropriate comments in a group setting, which serves to alienate them from their peers.

The principal deficits associated with social communication are listed below.

Deficits in higher-order receptive and expressive language These include, for example, failure to understand the 'gist' of a conversation.

Social cognition deficits This inability to understand social situations or to see the world from another's perspective is a subtle but frequently present and socially disabling feature, and deficits in 'theory of mind' are common in individuals with FASD. The social cognition deficit also creates many problems for parents, as young people may put themselves at risk in social situations without being aware of potential dangers. In particular, they may be quite unaware of others' predatory behaviour and thus be easily led into compromising situations.

Social communication deficits This inability to communicate a misunderstanding of social situations is invariably coupled with the deficit in social cognition and hence individuals tend to act inappropriately in situations that they do not fully comprehend. This can result in others labelling them as oppositional and defiant, rather than seeking for the reasons behind this distressed behaviour.

Alexithymia In this condition, an individual lacks the words to express either positive or negative emotions and so 'acts out' these feelings or emotions instead. This linguistic problem is exacerbated by cognitive deficits in processing affect or emotional information.

For general reviews related to cognition in FASD, see Aronson et al. (1997), Coggins et al. (2003, 2008), Sifneos (1973) and Sullivan (2008).

Social problems

The social problems in individuals with FASD are not related to low IQ but to a combination of organically driven impairments, i.e. severe hyperactivity, social cognition, social communication and alexithymia difficulties, and often unrecognized psychiatric problems such as mood instability or psychotic disorder.

Standard assessments indicate deficits in social functioning, which again are not associated with low IQ. Social and communication scores on the Vineland Adaptive Behavior Scales (VABS), for example, are characteristically lower than scores for Daily Living Skills. Many individuals become increasingly socially isolated in their late teens and early adulthood when they have left the relatively protective surroundings of the school and/or the home environment.

Emotional difficulties

In many ways individuals with FASD can show emotional incontinence reminiscent of traumatic brain injury. Thus, they may display uncontrollable, and context-inappropriate crying or giggling, or laughter, and this incongruity of affect can be both perplexing and disturbing for others. The prenatal alcohol exposure seems to affect the central nervous system emotional state regulation from infancy and results in rapidly changing, unpredictable mood changes. This is not a true bipolar disorder, but more of a non-specific mood/affective instability, which can prove very difficult to manage.

CURRENT RESEARCH

Neurological abnormalities of FASD

Brain structure

Initial autopsy reports of early dysmorphic FAS infant deaths showed diffuse structural brain changes due to prenatal alcohol exposure. These included microcephaly, hydrocephalus, enlarged ventricles, cerebellar hypoplasia, corpus callosum agenesis and heterotopias. More recently, imaging techniques such as computed tomography (CAT) and magnetic resonance imaging (MRI) have begun to assess brain structure abnormalities in living individuals with FASD, either dysmorphic FAS or non-dysmorphic ARND. These studies have shown, in the main, that the presence of facial dysmorphology does not correlate with the level of brain abnormality (BMA, 2007; Chudley et al., 2005; O'Malley & Hagerman, 1998; Streissguth & O'Malley, 2000). Microcephaly is typical but the corpus callosum has been demonstrated to be the area most commonly affected by prenatal alcohol exposure. The basal ganglion caudate and the hippocampus are also affected, and these structural abnormalities have been related to the working memory and executive function deficits that are characteristic of FASD.

The cerebellum may be unusually small, especially the anterior cerebellar vermis (verbal bodies I through to V) (Bookstein et al., 2001; Hagerman, 1999; Mattson et al., 1994; Riley et al., 1995; Stratton et al., 1996). Recent studies have explored the usefulness of cranial ultrasound in the developing fetus exposed to alcohol or the subsequent neonate. This research has highlighted disturbances in frontal cortex growth prenatally, and corpus callosum morphological abnormalities have been shown postnatally. The neonatal ultrasound on prenatal alcohol-exposed infants may eventually prove to be a clinically cost-effective tool in the early diagnosis and mapping of brain structural abnormalities in FASD (Bookstein et al., 2005).

Brain neurophysiology development

Neurophysiological abnormalities in individuals with prenatal alcohol exposure have long been recognized (Lemoine et al., 1968). Animal and human research studies have noted the kindling of seizures due to the effect of prenatal alcohol on the GABAergic cells of the hippocampus. This effect on the gamma-aminobutyric acid (GABA) cells lowers the seizure threshold and suggests the potential utility of GABA agents in the management of some FASD individuals. Complex partial seizures with underlying temporal lobe dysrhythmia have also been described. Studies in infants prenatally exposed to alcohol have shown more electroencephalogram (EEG) activity during rapid eye movement (REM) sleep, which then correlated with poor motor and mental development at 10 months of age (Lemoine et al., 1968).

Brain neurotransmitter development

Global deficits have been identified in most of the neurotransmitters, including dopaminergic, noradrenergic, serotonergic, GABA-ergic, cholinergic, glutaminergic and hista-minergic effects. More specific deficits in the mesolimbic D_1 nigrostriatal dopamine receptor system have been implicated as a possible aetiogical factor in the ADHD symptoms seen in children with FASD. The role of alcohol in changing the balance of the developing GABAergic (inhibitory) and glutaminergic (excitatory) neurotransmitters is being explored and it remains to be seen if this critical shift in neurotransmitter balance has a role in subsequent seizure disorders, as well as pervasive impulsivity (Hagerman, 1999; Hannigan et al., 1996; O'Malley, 2008; O'Malley & Hagerman, 1998).

Brain cellular abnormalities

Alcohol has been shown to have a direct toxic effect on developing brain cells and can cause cell death with a massive apoptotic neurodegeneration. It can also disrupt glial and astrocyte neuronal migration and maturation. Recent work has demonstrated the selective loss of complexin protein in the frontal lobe of rats prenatally exposed to alcohol. Complexin proteins are being studied in their relationship to psychiatric disorders. The effect of alcohol, interfering with cell adhesion and later cell migration and plasticity, has been studied by showing its inhibition effect on the L1 immunoglobulin molecule (Barr et al., 2005).

Soft neurological signs

Clinicians are becoming increasingly aware of particular patterns to these signs. Sensory integration disruption may be manifested in different guises. For example, individuals may show decreased sensation in the upper and lower limbs on one side of the body. This can be to deep and soft pressure as well as to vibration. Patients can also show decreased pain sensation, which may reflect central spinothalamic tract disruption. However, it is the presence of motor coordination problems that is one of the most prevalent clinical features in FASD. Individuals typically show balance and coordination problems that are consistent with cerebellar dysfunction. The coordination disorder is often associated with ADHD with severe hyperactivity and impulsivity.

Biomedical abnormalities

Studies have identified several biochemical abnormalities caused by the effects of alcohol consumption during pregnancy (Chudley et al., 2005; Dreosti, 1993; O'Malley, 2008; O'Malley & Streissguth, 2006; Stratton et al., 1996). These include mean corpuscular volume (MCV), haemoglobin acetaldehyde adduct (HbAA), gamma-glutamyl transferase (GGT), alanine aminotransferase (ALT), aspartate aminotransferase (AST), alkaline phosphatase (AP) and carbohydrate-deficient transferrin (CDT). Other studies have identified deficiencies in folic acid, vitamin B_{12}, thiamine, zinc, magnesium, choline and methionine. Meconium deficiencies have also been found and abnormalities in fatty acid ethyl esterase (FAEE) following maternal alcohol consumption are now postulated as possible biomarkers for infants at risk for either FAS and ARND (Chudley et al., 2005; Dreosti, 1993; O'Malley, 2008; O'Malley & Streissguth, 2006; Stratton et al., 1996).

Genetic correlates

Current research is beginning to analyse the possible effect of prenatal alcohol exposure on genetic transcription, gene activation and gene expression (Densmore, 2009; Haycock, 2009; Pembrey, 2002; Tchurikov, 2005). Genetic studies of alcohol dependency or alcohol craving have rarely incorporated the possible confounding effect of prenatal alcohol. However, both animal and human studies have shown that prenatal alcohol exposure stimulates alcohol craving from infancy and that prenatal alcohol exposure poses a higher risk for young adult alcohol dependence than even a family history of alcoholism (Baer et al., 1998, 2003; Bond & Di Gusto, 1976; Le Strot et al., 2008; Li, 2000; Reyes et al., 1985). Excessive prenatal alcohol intake can decrease folate, zinc, and methionine/choline in the fetus that are critical for DNA methylation. The resulting DNA hypomethylation could lead to activating genes that would normally be silent. In addition, recent animal research demonstrated that if a baby monkey is prenatally exposed to alcohol and carried the short allele of the *5-HTT* gene, it was more likely to show increased activity in the HPA (hypothalamic–pituitary–adrenal) axis than control baby monkeys not prenatally exposed to alcohol. This increased HPA axis activation has been identified in anxiety disorders (Kraemer et al., 2008). Also, recent studies suggest an association between alcohol dependence, genetic imprinting and GABA(A) receptors (Song et al., 2003). Prenatal alcohol exposure can change the balance of developing excitatory neurotransmitters (glutamate) and inhibitory neurotransmitters (GABA) and the resulting low GABA(A) in the hippocampus has been shown to be a factor kindling seizures (Bonthius et al., 2001).

Neuropsychological correlates

Since the initial scientific papers of Jones and his colleagues (Jones & Smith, 1973; Jones et al., 1973), the neuropsychological deficits in FASD have been described in a number of systematic studies (Carmichael Olson et al., 1998; Chudley et al., 2005; DC 0-3R, 2005; Kerns et al., 1997; Massey & Massey, 2008; Mukherjee et al., 2006; O'Malley, 2008; Streissguth, 1997). The cognitive and behavioural problems typically associated with prenatal alcohol exposure are noted in the sections above but infant and early childhood research also describe a mixture of motor, sensory and developmental abnormalities that is often present from birth. These include delayed sucking reflex and long latency to suck, impairments in habituation, disturbed state regulation, abnormal startle response, excessive arousal, disturbed sleep patterns, motor restlessness with hyperactive reflexes and abnormal patterns of sensory responses (i.e. over- or under-responsive to stimuli).

LIFETIME COURSE AND INTERVENTIONS

Physical problems related to FASD

Maternal alcohol consumption has many, often hidden, effects on the embryological development of most of the body organs and systems. These are collectively known as alcohol-related birth defects (ARBD) and are summarized in Table 24.1. The physical effects of the prenatal alcohol are related to the time of gestational exposure. They are equally present in individuals with FAS and

Table 24.1 Alcohol-Related Birth Defects Associated with FAS and ARND

Body Area	Alcohol-Related Birth Defect
Eye	Visual impairment
	Strabismus
	Ptosis
	Optic nerve hypoplasia
	Refractive problems secondary to small eye globes
	Tortuosity of the retinal arteries
Ear	Conductive hearing loss secondary to recurrent otitis media
	Sensory-neural hearing loss
	Central auditory processing abnormalities related to brain damage in brainstem and cortical areas that process auditory information
Teeth	Orthodontic problems
Heart	Aberrant great vessels
	Atrial septal defects
	Ventricular septal defects
	Tetralogy of Fallot
Kidney	Urethral duplications
	Hydronephrosis
	Horseshoe kidneys
	Hypoplastic kidneys
	Aplastic or dysplastic kidneys
Skeletal	Clinodactyly
	Hypoplastic nails
	Shortened fifth digits
	Radioulnar synostosis
	Klippel-Feil syndrome
	Pectus excavatum and pectus carinatum
	Hemivertebrae
	Scoliosis

ARND and the presence of facial dysmorphology does not increase the likelihood of other physical abnormalities. Physical problems are present from infancy and may present immediate health challenges (cardiac or renal), or they may present problems in later childhood or adolescence (strabismus, orthodontic problems, hearing problems).

Among the most common problems are those related to eye, ear, teeth, kidney, heart and skeletal systems (see Table 24.1). Although FASD are not neurodegenerative conditions, the physical effects of prenatal alcohol can be detrimental to general health and well-being and sometimes need medical or surgical intervention (i.e. strabismus, cardiac structural defects, or kidney structural defects; BMA, 2007; Chudley et al., 2005; Jones & Smith, 1973; Jones et al., 1973; Koren et al., 2003; Streissguth, 1997) (see Table 24.1). The biochemical effects on liver development are more subtle, but critical in the patient's response to medication, which can be very unpredictable. Thus, a patient with FASD should always have a complete medical examination, preferably by a paediatric specialist (Hagerman, 1999; Koren et al., 2003; O'Malley, 2008; Stratton et al., 1996; Streissguth, 1997).

Mental health and psychiatric problems in individuals with FASD

Comorbid psychiatric disorders are common in individuals with FASD (Dykens, 2000; Einfeld & Tonge, 1996; Emerson & Hatton, 2007; King et al., 1998; Russell, 1997). The Secondary Disabilities Study in Seattle was the first study to show the high prevalence of comorbid mental health or psychiatric problems in this group (Streissguth et al., 1996). They found that individuals with FASD almost always present with comorbid psychiatric problems, some of which, such as regulatory disorders, are present from infancy and continue throughout life. ADHD is the most common comorbid condition, occurring in 50–60% of individuals with FASD. Difficulties in communication and social understanding and, in particular, problems related to 'theory of mind' may result in some children being diagnosed with autism spectrum disorders (autism, Asperger syndrome or pervasive developmental disorder). Although such diagnoses may be more likely to lead to special education services, they inevitably mask the true prevalence of problems related to prenatal alcohol exposure. Other problems include mood instability (though not true bipolar disorder), intermittent explosive disorder, and post-traumatic stress disorder (PTSD), especially if there is domestic violence, abuse, or abandonment. Approximately 23% of individuals require admission to psychiatric hospital at some stage in their lives, and 15% require inpatient treatment for drug and alcohol problems.

Several factors contribute to the high prevalence of psychiatric or mental health problems in this group. (Emerson & Hatton, 2007; McGee, 2001; Morrison et al., 2002). First, below average IQ or specific cognitive deficits may increase an individual's vulnerability when faced with adversity. Impaired social understanding is also likely to increase anxiety and other mixed emotional feelings and may contribute to a prolonged PTSD. Furthermore, exposure to social disadvantage increases the risk of psychiatric problems and it is not uncommon for children with FASD to be born into an environment of poverty and domestic violence. FAS and ARND are transgenerational conditions and, as such, can give rise to multilayered psychiatric disorders. The mothers may have mental health disorders themselves when they are pregnant, most likely depression, and are also at risk for postpartum depression. Thus, the infant enters a world in which the birth parent may be present but emotionally absent and so unable to offer a consistent, containing environment. These are complex clinical areas that require immediate interventions for both mother and infant (Poobalon et al., 2007). There are also layers of social adversity intermingled with alcohol abuse and domestic violence. Sadly, the mothers of children who give birth to infants with FASD have frequently experienced abuse themselves as children or adolescents. It is the interplay between the identification of risk factors and protective factors, such as positive parenting skills, that is important for achieving a healthier outcome (Dixon et al., 2005; Streissguth et al., 2004). Finally, alcohol consumption is frequently coupled with maternal anxiety during pregnancy. These joint problems have been shown, both separately and together, to affect the child's developmental trajectory (Oates, 2002; O'Malley, 2008).

In summary, it is the cumulative risk to the infant born with a history of prenatal alcohol exposure that informs clinical understanding and ultimately management (Deater-Deckhard et al., 1998). Many of the problems noted above begin in infancy but it must always be recognized that these disorders stem from a critical mixture of organic brain damage due to prenatal alcohol exposure and the strengths or stressors in the rearing environment. Mukherjee et al. (2006) and O'Malley (2008) have identified a number of common, protective factors for individuals with FASD. These include receiving a diagnosis of FAS before 6 years of age; no history of physical, sexual abuse or domestic violence; access to a good-quality home environment; and living in a stable and nurturing household for most of childhood (see also Chudley et al., 2005; Koren et al., 2003; Streissguth et al., 1996, 2004). Paradoxically, the diagnosis of FASD itself can be a protective factor, as it identifies the patient as having a specific disability and makes it easier for the child and his/her family to gain access to services. The biggest current clinical challenge is to connect early diagnosis by a geneticist with paediatric, psychology and child psychiatry services. All too often, services only become involved after the development of severe behavioural problems.

Social integration

This is the area of functioning that is the most problematic for people with FASD. These individuals begin their school lives with a higher probability of disrupted school experience because of unacceptable behaviours. These behaviours are compounded by learning disability and linguistic problems, although these are often overlooked. Children with FASD are also frequently isolated and rejected by their peers (Aronson et al., 1997). Their early experience of social isolation and lack of social integration has lifelong effects. They have great difficulty finding or keeping employment, as they are typically socially inappropriate, disorganized and impulsive. Many are unable to live independently as they have many cognitive deficits that impair their basic daily living routines (i.e. inability to organize budgets, remember what groceries or clothes to buy, and when to pay bills such as rent).

Sexually inappropriate behaviours are commonly a legacy of previous early sexual or physical abuse and the continuing trauma resulting from those experiences. Individuals with FASD may also frequently blurt things out and impulsively attempt to touch other people, not because they are sexual predators but because they are unable to inhibit their actions. They may also be suffering from chronic or even acute PTSD, but the presence of alexithymia can result in inability to explain their deep-seated trauma (Sifneos, 1973; Sullivan, 2008).

Lastly, individuals with FASD frequently become involved with the law because they are out of school, impulsive, have no vocational skills and are easily led. These are the people who guard the door while their peers rob the store and they are the ones left and arrested. They are highly gullible and can admit to crimes that they have not committed. It is important that these vulnerable individuals, especially when they have left school and/or are living away from home, have some documentation that testifies to the fact that they have a learning disability. They should not give a police statement without a 3rd party present.

It is also important to be aware that, in this vulnerable, hyperactive, emotionally unstable, impulsive population, suicide risk is a cause for concern. This suicide risk is increased by a craving for alcohol that has been nurtured by a prenatal alcohol chemical sensitization of the developing brain (Baer et al., 1998, 2003; Huggins et al., 2008).

Approaches to intervention

The evidence base for most interventions used to treat individuals with FASD is weak (Chandrasena et al., 2009). Individuals with FASD present with a mixture of intellectual, learning and psychiatric difficulties that require a range of services (see Table 24.2). In adolescence or young adulthood, addictive disorder can be a tertiary problem (Barr et al., 2006; Lemay et al., 2003; NIAAA, 1999; O'Malley, 2003).

Table 24.2   Assessment for Intervention in FASD

1. Diagnostic assessment of comorbid conditions, i.e. learning/developmental disability and psychiatric disorder, with referral to a psychiatrist if probable psychiatric disorder.

2. Blood assays: FBC, LFT, T4, TSH, glucose, serum creatinine.

3. Electrocardiogram, especially if taking medication, or being prescribed medication.

4. Occupational therapy assessment, especially under 5 and early childhood. Assess for sensory integration and gross/fine motor function.

5. Intellectual assessment (WPPSI or WISC III as age appropriate). WAIS in adult to quantify if learning/developmental disability is associated with mental retardation.

6. Sleep-deprived EEG if clinical evidence of possible seizure disorder, especially if intermittent explosiveness or episodes of 'drifting off' seen as ADHD, inattention type.

7. Medical consultations as needed: e.g. neurologist, paediatrician for general health care if marked learning/developmental disability (especially for child under 5 years of age).

8. Public health referral for pregnant teenager or young adult with FASD. Connection to advocate for help with the arrival of new baby and prevent alcohol/drug usage in pregnancy (in UK health visitor or personal advisor for 'vulnerable adult').

9. Screening of FASD teenager or young adult for alcohol usage in pregnancy using Binge Alcohol Rating Criteria (BARC), Tolerance, Worry, Eye-opener, Amnesia/blackout, Cut down (TWEAK), or blood tests (GGT, haemoglobin acetaldehyde adduct).

Educational interventions

Although individuals with FASD are not generally intellectually impaired, there is typically a significant discrepancy between verbal and performance IQ, and specific learning difficulties in areas such as mathematics, reading and written language. The deficits in coordinated thinking, working memory and mathematical skills also have a negative impact on and individual's progress in school.

Many children with FASD tend to be overwhelmed by the high sensory environment of most schools and perform better in quieter, less stimulating settings. A multisensory approach utilizing the tenets of multiple intelligence (Gardner, 1993) can be helpful and on the whole these children learn more consistently in smaller classes with a special educational focus.

As FASD are still relatively 'new' conditions in places such as the UK or Ireland, these children are not commonly acknowledged as having special education needs. On the other hand, FASD are more widely recognized in the USA and Canada where there is a background of many years of practical experience. Provinces such as Alberta and British Columbia in Canada even have school FAS/ARND teaching manuals (Alberta Education, 1995; Davis, 1992; Kapp & O'Malley, 2002; Whitehorse FAS Education). With regard to specific approaches, Kalberg and Buckley (2007) emphasize the importance of predictability and structure in the educational environment, the need for visual cues, and the breaking down of tasks into smaller, more manageable components. Bonthius et al. (2006) also recommend cognitive control therapy as a means of progressively building up skills. In the USA, the Individuals with Disabilities Education Act (IDEA) provides important guidelines on how best to help these children within the classroom (Evans et al., 2004).

Psychotherapeutic interventions

Individual therapy These approaches include motor training, sensory integration and infant massage and feeding training for infants and young children with FASD. Older children can benefit from non-verbal therapies such as play therapy, art, music or drama. Such therapies can enable these brain-damaged and often traumatized children to explore ways of expressing themselves. They can also help children to find a 'language' to express their feelings, as alexithymia commonly inhibits the understanding and articulation of emotional feelings, both positive or negative (Nowicki & Duke, 1992; Sifneos, 1973; Sullivan, 2008). Non-verbal therapies can be especially valuable for children with FASD who have experienced abuse or have severe attachment disorder due to early abandonment by birth parents. Adolescents can respond to simple relationship therapy with a sound reality base. They need help with understanding how to navigate life, relationships, growing up and moving through school. Young adults need individual mentoring and guidance. They need advocates to help them deal with multiple bureaucratic systems such as social services, housing, income support, employment, vocational rehabilitation, disability or mental health funding support.

Dyadic therapies These can also be helpful. Mother/infant or mother/toddler therapy can be used to address attachment issues (fathers of course may also be involved). The Parent–Child Assistance Program started in Seattle is a good model of support for alcohol/substance abusing mothers and children under 3 years of age (Grant et al., 1999, 2008). Parent/older child or adolescent dyadic work can be helpful in addressing behavioural issues related to passive or active defiance, which is often coupled with a pervasive ADHD. Behavioural management techniques, however, can present problems, as children with FAS and ARND do not always link cause and effect. Thus, there needs to be a more creative approach to consequences, and rewards need to have real meaning in the child's world. Working memory deficits also mean that the physical consequences of behaviour need to be immediate. Time out approaches may be of little value if the child is unable to remember why attention or another reinforcer has been withdrawn. Extinction or immediate withdrawal of reinforcers may be more effective, being more concrete and more easily remembered. Adolescents with FASD are especially prone to misunderstanding social situations and misrepresenting themselves in social groups. It is imperative to help the adolescent navigate these social situations, and role playing in the context of a dyadic situation is often helpful. It can break down barriers with parents who are embarrassed and intimidated by the sometimes innocent but impulsive sexual or other inappropriate behaviours. It also offers a chance of situation-based learning (Brown, 1993; Novick-Brown, 2008; O'Malley & Streissguth, 2006).

Group therapy   There is some evidence that group work may be less successful than individual work for young people with FASD because of their social difficulties (Chandrasena et al., 2009). However, group therapy can be useful for children who have been abused, as this can offer a 'protective space' for traumatized, brain-damaged, impulsive children to explore their confused emotional feelings and deal with primary negative emotions such as anger, sadness or rage. Adolescents or young adults can benefit from a series of time-limited sessions. This type of group is reality-based and provides an opportunity for individuals to explore their feelings and life challenges in a non-threatening environment. It also has a social integration educational role. The therapeutic power of the group is greatly enhanced by the 'universality' of diagnosis and the opportunity to meet with other individuals with FASD. This can be a valuable help to self-esteem or self-worth, as individuals discover that their trials and tribulations are both unique but also shared.

Family   Different types of family therapy may be helpful:

1. Family/parent education, which helps the family understand the nature of a complex disorder such as FASD. This is particularly useful for adults who are preparing to adopt or foster an infant or young child with FASD.
2. Instrumental family therapy can be helpful for adoptive or foster families in setting and maintaining the boundaries of behaviour, as children with FASD tend to be impulsive, hyperactive and emotionally volatile, and constantly need clear, predictable rules of social behaviour. This structure is also essential in families in which there is a transgenerational history of alcohol abuse and where one or both parents and even grandparents have FASD themselves. The chaos in these families can be pervasive and needs careful handling. An advocate working with the birth mother or caring grandparent is a necessary ally. Birth families may have a tendency to 'enable' the birth mother's continued drinking, as it is not uncommon for the grandmother to step into the primary parental role. This in turn allows the birth mother to continue drinking as she does not have the responsibility of a young infant to rear.
3. Family restoration work may be needed to help the birth parents mourn the loss of their 'ideal' child and to acknowledge their own role in this condition. This work is not about apportioning blame, but about real acceptance and healing and the establishment of a new future. Family restoration work can also be invaluable in the melding of the previous birth family with the newly established foster or adoptive family and may require cross-cultural therapy for children fostered or adopted into families from very different ethnic backgrounds. The premature death of a parent due to alcohol-related causes can have a lasting effect on the child or adolescent and there is a risk of impulsive suicide attempts among adolescents who feels unwanted or excluded and/or have experienced parental abandonment or abuse (Huggins et al., 2008). Grief work is made all the more complicated because of the sometimes ambivalent attachment to the birth parent, especially the mother.

Medical intervention

The medical management of FASD consists mainly of the clarification of the diagnosis and treatment of the comorbid symptoms (Barr & Streissguth, 2001; Chudley et al., 2005; Hagerman, 1999; O'Malley, 2003, 2008; O'Malley & Streissguth, 2006;

Stratton et al., 1996; Streissguth & O'Malley, 2000) (see Tables 24.1 & 24.2).

There is no specific pharmacological treatment for FASD and medication is primarily used to address comorbid problems or to facilitate response to other modalities of treatment. The safe use of medication is a primary concern, as prenatal alcohol can affect the developing heart, kidney and liver. The organic brain damage, in concert with the early nurturing or abusive/violent environment, may combine to present ADHD, autistic, mood disorder or anxiety symptoms. All of these clinical conditions may be exaggerated or masked by the overjudicious use of high doses of multiple medications.

Although most pharmacological trials with children with FASD have been small scale and/or compromised by other methodological limitations, there are indications that some drugs may be more helpful than others (see Chandrasena et al., 2009; O'Malley & Nanson, 2002). Dextro-amphetamine has been shown to have greater efficacy than methylphenidate in treating the ADHD symptoms in FASD. However larger-scale, randomized placebo-controlled trials are needed to inform clinical practice. Mood stabilizers such as carbamazepine and valproic acid also have a clinical role, and can be effective in treating the complex seizure disorders that may occur with FASD. Liquid fluoxetine is useful for depressive features in younger children and GABA agents such as gabapentin seem to be useful if the mood instability is coupled with anxiety. Antianxiety agents such as buspirone and guanfacine have shown clinical utility and atypical antipsychotics such as risperidone, olanazepine and quetiapine have been used to control unpredictable rage attacks. In adults, naltrexone has been used with some success as a method of decreasing the alcohol craving and melatonin may be beneficial for treating sleep disorders. (see Byrne, 2007; Hagerman, 1999; O'Malley, 2008; O'Malley & Hagerman, 1998; O'Malley & Nanson, 2002; O'Malley & Storoz, 2003).

Finally, Chandrasena et al. (2009) discuss the potential use of novel interventions, including dietary supplements. For example, choline (which is essential for effective cell membranes and cholinergic transmission) has been suggested as a possible means of improving learning memory and cell function and preliminary reports indicate its effectiveness in rats exposed prenatally to alcohol (Thomas et al., 2004).

Occupational therapy

This is an essential component of therapy as sensory integration problems often occur from infancy and throughout life. Thus, children with FASD may seem to be deliberately over-reacting to situations when in fact they are truly over-responsive to certain stimuli. Problems in coordination are particularly evident in the younger years and motor training techniques are of help (Jirikowic, 2008). Recently, techniques to improve bimanual hand coordination have been proposed as a possible means of improving brain function (Roebuck-Spencer et al., 2004).

Social and occupational therapies

These are in many ways the 'orphan' services for individuals with FASD on both sides of the Atlantic and there are really no organized, social vocational rehabilitation programmes for young adults or older individuals with FASD (Royal et al., 2007); SAMHSA, 2009. This stems from a paucity of standardized, validated vocational/work experience programmes at secondary and high school level, particularly for adolescent girls with FASD. It is a challenge to find vocational rehabilitation programmes suitable for easily bored, hyperactive, impulsive and cognitively disorganized young adults (Ware et al., 2008). These individuals work best in piecemeal small segment jobs in which they are given instant rewards (i.e. paid daily). Manual jobs such as gardening, painting, bricklaying and mechanics all have a role, but to be successful will need job coaches or supervisors. Supported employment schemes specifically for individuals with

FASD do not exist in the UK but have been developed in Canada and the USA. In the USA the Substance Abuse and Mental Health Services Administration (SAMHSA, 2009) still maintains a FASD specialist department which has pioneered training in such areas as addiction counselling for clients with FASD (Substance Abuse and Mental Health Services Administration (SAMHSA), 2009).

Unfortunately, the administration of these social/vocational rehabilitation programmes falls between three disciplines: psychiatry, learning/developmental disability and occupational therapy. Until there is more reconciliation of the respective roles and responsibilities of these agencies, individuals with FASD will continue to be underserved.

CONCLUSIONS AND CHALLENGES FOR THE FUTURE

FASD, namely, FAS and ARND, remain underdiagnosed and undertreated developmental neuropsychiatric conditions that are lifelong and pervasive. They span the domains of developmental paediatrics, learning disability and psychiatry, and ideally would benefit from collaboration between these specialities in both diagnosis and management. FAS and ARND offer unique opportunities for significant remedial treatment work from occupational therapy, speech and language therapists, psychologists and vocational rehabilitation specialists (Steinhausen & Spohr, 1998; Streissguth & O'Malley, 2000).

These conditions need a transgenerational approach to treatment, which involves combining infant and adult services, and a collective will among obstetricians and geneticists to work together with paediatricians, child psychiatrists, psychologists and adult psychiatrists. The traditional divide between child and adult services does not work with generations of alcohol-abusing women and men, as there is no opportunity to intervene at a point where treatment becomes secondary prevention, or even primary prevention for the succeeding generation.

The continuing challenge of confronting "misinformation" about pregnancy is ever present. Recent research on low dose alcohol in pregnancy has tried to paint a picture that all is rosy in the garden (Kelly et al. 2009). However it is not so simple. This study and the follow-up one were based on parent report and, for whatever reason, the researchers chose to NOT examine the infants and young children exposed to low alcohol. Its value will be short lived, but in the short term it dose not do a service to the continuing delivery of alcohol affected, brain damaged infants.

There are multiple opportunities for new advances in the area of FASD. The epigenetic effects of prenatal alcohol await further scientific research. The quantification of brain abnormalities through functional MRI (FMRI) or infant brain ultrasound is ongoing and the search for reliable biomarkers is still progressing. However, scientific research into the effectiveness of different interventions remains limited. Furthermore, research into the effects of prenatal nicotine, prenatal cocaine and marijuana needs to be combined with research on the effects of prenatal alcohol. There are existing psychosocial multimodal interventions that have a role for this polysubstance abuse group, such as the Parent–Child Assistance Program (Grant et al., 2008), which can offer a model of intervention at a preconception/prenatal and neonatal level. Lastly, neurobiological interventions are ever-expanding their horizons, and animal research is beginning to show the positive effect of dietary substances such as methionine on prenatal alcohol-induced brain dysfunction (Padmanabdan et al., 2002).

REFERENCES

Alberta Education (1995) *A Teacher's Guide to Fetal Alcohol Syndrome in the Classroom* (Brochure). Edmonton, Alberta, Canada: Government of Alberta.

Aronson, M., Hagberg, B., & Gilberg, C. (1997) 'Attention deficits and autistic spectrum problems in children exposed to alcohol during gestation. A follow-up study', *Dev Med Child Neurol*, 39: 583–587.

Astley S.J. & Clarren, S.K. (1997) *Diagnostic Guide for Fetal Alcohol Syndrome and Related Conditions.* Seattle, WA: University of Washington.

Ayers, A.J. (1979) *Sensory Integration and the Child.* Los Angeles: Western Psychological Services.

Baer, J.S., Barr, H.M., Bookstein, F.L., Sampson, P.D., & Streissguth, A.P. (1998) 'Prenatal exposure and family history of alcoholism in the etiology of adolescent alcohol problems', *Journal of Studies on Alcohol,* 59: 533–543.

Baer, J.S., Sampson, P.D., Barr, H.M., Connor, P.D., & Streissguth, A.P. (2003) 'A 21-year longitudinal analysis of the effects of prenatal alcohol exposure on young adult drinking', *Arch Gen Psychiatry,* 60: l377–l385.

Barr, A.M., Hoffman, C.E., Phillips, A.G., Weinberg, J., & Honer, W.G. (2005) 'Prenatal ethanol exposure in rats deceases levels of complexin proteins in the frontal cortex', *Alcohol Clin Exp Res,* 29: 1915–1920.

Barr, H.M. & Streissguth, A.P. (2001) 'Identifying maternal self-reported alcohol use associated with fetal alcohol spectrum disorders', *Alcohol Clin Exp Res,* 25(2): 283–287.

Barr, H.M., Bookstein, F.L., O'Malley, K.D., Connor, P.D., Huggins, J.E., & Streissguth, A.P. (2006) 'Binge drinking during pregnancy as a predictor of psychiatric disorders on the structured clinic interview for DSM–IV in young adult offspring', *Am J Psychiatry,* 163: 1061–1065.

Barry, S., Kearney, A., Daly, S., Lawlor, E., McNamee, E., & Barry, J. (2007) 'Coombe Women's Hospital study of alcohol, smoking and illicit drug use, 1987–2005'. Department of Health in Children, Dublin.

BMA (2007) *Fetal Alcohol Spectrum Disorders. A Guide for Professionals.* BMA Science and Education Department and the Board of Science, UK.

Bond, N.W. & Di Gusto, E.I. (1976) 'Effects of prenatal alcohol consumption on open field behavior study of alcohol preference in rats', *Psychopharmacologia,* 46: 163.

Bonthius, D.J., Woodhouse, J., Bonthius, N.E., Taggrad, D.A., & Lothman, E.W. (2001). 'Reduced seizure control and hippocampal cell loss in rats exposed to alcohol during brain growth spurt', *Alcohol Clin Exp Res,* 25(1): 70–82.

Bonthius, D.J., Carmichael Olsen, H., & Thomas, J.D. (2006) 'A public health program for preventing fetal alcohol syndrome among women at risk in Montana', *Neurotoxicology and Teratology,* 25: 757–761.

Bookstein, F.L., Sampson, P.D., Streissguth, A.P., & Connor, P.L. (2001) 'Geometric morphometrics of corpus callosum and subcortical structures in fetal alcohol effected brain', *Tetratology,* 4: 4–32.

Bookstein, F.L., Connor, P.D., Cowell, K.D., Barr, H.M., Gleason, C.A., Sze, R.W., McBroom, J.A., &

Streissguth, A.P. (2005) 'Preliminary evidence that prenatal alcohol damage may be visible in averaged ultrasound images of the neonatal human corpus callosum', *Alcohol,* 36: 151–160.

Brown, H.J. (1993) 'Sexuality and intellectual disability: the new realism', *Current Opinion in Psychiatry,* 6: 623–628.

Butterworth, B. (2005) 'The development of arithmetic abilities', *Journal of Child Psychology and Psychiatry,* 46: 1, 3–18.

Byrne, C. (2007) 'Psychopharmacology: basics for FASD'. Paper presentation, at FASD and Mental Health: The Wisdom of Practice Conference, 10 April 2007, Vancouver, BC, Canada.

Carmichael Olson, H., Feldman, J.J., Streissguth, A.P., Sampson, P.D., & Bookstein, F.L. (1998) 'Neuropsychological deficits in adolescents with fetal alcohol syndrome: clinical findings', *Alcohol Clin Exp Res,* 22(9): 1998–2012.

Chandrasena, A.N., Mukherjee, R.A.S., & Turk, J. (2009) 'Fetal alcohol spectrum disorders: an overview of interventions for affected individuals', *Child and Adolescent Mental Health,* 14: 162–167.

Chudley, A.E., Conroy, J., Cook, J.L., Loock, C., Rosales, T., LeBlanc, N. (2005) 'Fetal alcohol spectrum disorder: Canadian guidelines for diagnosis', *CMAJ,* 172(Supple): S1–21.

Coggins, T.E., Olswang, L.B., Carmichael Olson, H., & Timler, G.R. (2003) 'On becoming socially competent communicators: the challenge for children with fetal alcohol exposure', *International Review of Research in Mental Retardation,* 27: 121–150.

Coggins, T.E., Timler, G.R., & Olswang, L.B. (2008) 'Identifying and treating social communication deficits in school-aged children with fetal alcohol spectrum disorders', in K.D. O'Malley (ed.), *ADHD and Fetal Alcohol Spectrum Disorders (FASD),* New York: Nova Science Publishers, pp. 161–179.

Coles, C.D., Platzman, K.A., Raskin-Hood, C.L., Brown, R.T., Falek, A., & Smith, I.E. (1997) 'A comparison of children affected by prenatal alcohol exposure and attention deficit, hyperactivity disorder', *Alcohol Clin Exp Res,* 21: 150–161.

Connor, P.D., Sampson, P.D., Bookstein, F.L., Barr, H.M., & Streissguth, A.P. (2000) 'Direct and indirect effects of prenatal alcohol damage on executive function,' *Developmental Neuropsychology,* 18(3): 331–354.

Davis, D. (1992) *Reaching Out—a Handbook for Parents, Teachers and Others Who Live and Work with Children Affected by Fetal Alcohol Syndrome and Fetal Alcohol Effects.* (Available from Diane Davis, PO Box 22871, Seattle, WA 9122–0871.)

DC 0–3R (2005) *Diagnostic Classification of Mental Health and Developmental Disorders of Infancy and Early Childhood,* revised edn. Washington, DC: Zero to Three Press.

Deater-Deckhard, K., Dodge, K.A., Bates, J.E., Pettit, G.S. (1998) 'Multiple risk factors in the development of externalising behaviour problems: group and individual differences', *Development and Psychopathology,* 10: 469–493.

Densmore, R. (2009) 'Genetics and alcohol'. NOFAS-UK, Fetal Alcohol Forum, Issue 2, December.

Dixon, L., Brown, K., Hamilton-Gicchritsis, C. (2005) 'Risk factors of parents abused as children: a meditational analysis of the intergenerational continuity of child maltreatment (Part 1)', *Journal of Child Psychology and Psychiatry,* 46(1): 47–57.

Dreosti, E. (1993) 'Nutritional factors underlying the expression of fetal alcohol syndrome', *Ann NY Acad Sci,* 678: 193–204.

Driscoll, C.D., Streissguth, A.P., & Riley, E.P. (1991) 'Prenatal alcohol exposure. Comparability of effects in human and animal models', *Neurotoxicol Teratol.,* 12: 231–237.

Dykens, E.M. (2000) 'Psychopathology in children with intellectual disability,' *Journal of Child Psychology and Psychiatry,* 42: 407–417.

Einfeld, S.L. & Tonge, B.J. (1996) 'Population prevalence in psychopathology in children and adolescents with intellectual disability. II. Epidemiological findings', *Journal of Intellectual Disability Research,* 40: 99–109.

Elliott, E.J., Payne, J., Haan, E. et al. (2006) 'Diagnosis of foetal alcohol syndrome and alcohol use in pregnancy: a survey of paediatrician's knowledge, attitudes and practice', *Journal of Paediatrics and Child Health,* 42: 698–703.

Emerson, E. & Hatton, C. (2007) 'Mental health of children and adolescents with intellectual disabilities in Britain', *Br J Psychiatry,* 191: 493–499.

Evans, L., Jewett, T., Powell, C., & Thompson Smith, B. (2004) 'Fetal alcohol syndrome: a parent's guide to caring for a child diagnosed with FAS'. Wake Forest University Health Sciences, 1–40.

Gardner, H. (1993) *Multiple Intelligence. The Theory in Practice.* New York: Harper Collins.

Geschwind, N. (1965) 'Disconnexion syndromes in animals and man', *Brain,* 88: 237–294, 585–644.

Grant, T.M., Ernst, C.C., & Streissguth, A.P. (1999) 'Intervention with high-risk alcohol and drug abusing mothers: 1. Administrative strategies of the Seattle model of paraprofessional advocacy', *Journal of Community Psychology,* 27: 1–18.

Grant, T., Youngblood Petersen, J., Whitney, N., & Ernst, E. (2008) 'The role of therapeutic intervention with substance abusing mothers: preventing FASD in the next generation', in K.D. O'Malley (ed.), *ADHD and Fetal Alcohol Spectrum Disorders (FASD).* New York: Nova Science Publishers, pp. 69–93.

Hagerman, R.J. (1999) *Neurodevelopmental Disorders. Diagnosis and Treatment. Fetal Alcohol Syndrome.* New York: Oxford University Press, pp. 3–59.

Hannigan, J.H. & Randall, S. (1996) 'Behavioural pharmacology in animals exposed prenatally to alcohol', in E.L. Abel (ed.), *Fetal Alcohol Syndrome. From Mechanism to Prevention.* New York: CRC Press, PP. 191–213.

Harris, J.C. (1995) 'Developmental neuropsychiatry, Volume 11, Assessment, diagnosis and treatment of developmental disorders'. Oxford University Press, Oxford, Chapter 12.1, 361–374.

Haycock, P.C. (2009) 'Fetal alcohol spectrum disorders; The epigenetic perspective', *Biology of reproduction,* 81: 607–617.

Huggins, J.E., Grant, T., O'Malley, K.D., & Streissguth, A.P. (2008) 'Suicide attempts among adults with fetal alcohol spectrum disorders: clinical considerations', *Mental Health Aspects of Developmental Disabilities,* 11(2): 33–41S.

Jirikowic, T. (2008) 'Sensory integration and sensory processing disorders', in K.D. O'Malley (ed.), *ADHD and Fetal Alcohol Spectrum Disorders (FASD).* New York: Nova Science Publishers, pp. 39–49.

Jones, K.L. & Smith, D.W. (1973) 'Recognition of the fetal alcohol syndrome in early infancy', *Lancet,* 2: 999–1101.

Jones, K.L., Smith, D.W., Ulleland, C.N., & Streissguth, A.P. (1973) 'Pattern of malformation in offspring of chronic alcoholic mothers', *Lancet,* 1: 1267–1270.

Kalberg, W.O. & Buckley, D. (2007) 'FASD: what types of intervention and rehabilitation are useful?', *Neuroscience and Biobehavioral Reviews,* 311: 278–285.

Kapp, F.M.E. & O'Malley, K.D. (2002) *Watch for the Rainbows. True Stories for Educators and Caregivers of Children with Fetal Alcohol Spectrum Disorders,* revised edition. Calgary, Canada: Frances Kapp Education, pp. 64–83.

Kelly, Y., Sacker, A., Gray, R., Kelly, J., Wolke, D., Quigley, M.A., (2009) Light drinking in pregnancy, a risk for behavioural problems and cognitive deficits at 3 years of age? International Journal of Epidemiology, 38:129–140

Kerns, K.A., Audrey, D., Mateer, C.A., & Streissguth, A.P. (1997) 'Cognitive deficits in nonretarded adults with fetal alcohol syndrome', *Journal of Learning Disabilities,* 30(6): 685–693.

King, B.H., State, M.W., Bhavik, S., Davanzo, P., & Dykens, E. (1998) 'Mental retardation: a review of the past 10 years. Part I, in *Reviews in Child & Adolescent Psychiatry, AACAP,* 126–133.

Koren, G., Nulman, I., Chudley, A.E., & Loocke, C. (2003) 'Fetal alcohol spectrum disorder', *CMAJ,* 169(11): 1181–1185.

Kraemer, G.W., Moore, C.F., Newman, T.K., Barr, C.S., & Scheider, M.L. (2008) 'Moderate level fetal alcohol exposure and serotonoin transporter gene promoter polymorphism affect neonatal temperament and limbic–hypothalamic–pituitary–adrenal axis regulation in monkeys. *Biological Psychiatry,* 63: 317–324.

Lemay, J-F., Herbert, A.R., Dewey, D.M., & Innes, A.M. (2003) 'A rational approach to the child with mental retardation for the paediatrician', *Paediat Child Health,* 8(6): 345–356.

Lemoine, P., Harousseau, H., & Borteyru, J.P. (1968) 'Les enfants de parents alcooliques: anomalies observees a propos de 127 cas', *Quest Med,* 21: 476–482.

Le Strot, Y., Ramoz, N., Schuman, G., & Gorwoud, P. (2008) 'Molecular genetics of alcohol dependence and related endotypes', *Current Genomics,* 9: 444–457.

Li, T.K. (2000) 'Pharmacogenetics of response to alcohol and genes that influence alcohol drinking', *J Stud Alcohol,* 61: 5–12.

McGee, C. (2001) *Childhood Experiences of Domestic Violence.* 2nd edn., London and Philadelphia: Jessica Kingsley.

Massey, D.S. & Massey, V.J. (2008) 'Neuropsychological profiles of children and adolescents with fetal alcohol spectrum disorder and attention deficit hyperactivity disorder', in K.D. O'Malley (ed.), *ADHD and Fetal Alcohol Spectrum Disorders (FASD),* New York: Nova Science Publishers, pp. 95–103.

Mattson, S.N., Riley, E.P., Jernigan, T.L., Garcia, A., Kaneko, W.M., Ehlers, C.L., & Jones, K.L. (1994) 'A decrease in the size of the basal ganglia following prenatal alcohol exposure. A preliminary report', *Neurotoxicol Teratol,* 16: 283–289.

Mattson, S., Riley, E., Delis, D., Stern, C., & Jones, K. (1996) 'Verbal learning and memory in children with fetal alcohol syndrome', *Alcohol Clin Exp Res,* 20: 810–816.

Mattson, S., Goodman, A., Caine, C., Delis, D., & Riley, E. (1999) 'Executive functioning in children with heavy prenatal alcohol exposure', *Alcohol Clin Exp Res,* 24: 1808–1815.

Metford, H.C. & Sharp, A.J. (2008) 'Recurrent rearrangements of chromosome 1q2.1.1 and variable pediatric subtypes', *New Engl J Med,* Oct 16th, Vol. 359, Issue 16, 1685–1699.

Morrison, P.D., Allardyce, J., & McKane, J.P. (2002) 'Fear knot. Neurobiological disruption of long term fear memory', *Br J Psychiatry,* 180: 195–197.

Mukherjee, R.A.S., Hollins, S., & Turk, J. (2006) 'Fetal alcohol spectrum disorder: an overview', *Journal of the Royal Society of Medicine,* 99: 298–302.

Nanson, J. & Hiscock, M. (1990) 'Attention deficits in children exposed to alcohol prenatally,' *Alcohol Clin Exp Res,* 14: 656–661.

NIAAA (1999) *Identification and Care of Fetal Alcohol-Exposed Children. A Guide for Primary Care Providers.* National Institute on Alcohol Abuse and Alcoholism and Office of Research on Minority Health, National Institutes of Health, Publication No. 99-4369, Rockville, MD, USA.

Novick-Brown, N. (2008) 'Sexually inappropriate behaviour in individuals with fetal alcohol spectrum disorders', in K.D. O'Malley (ed.), *ADHD and Fetal Alcohol Spectrum Disorders (FASD).* New York: Nova Science Publishers, pp. 125–161.

Nowicki, S. & Duke, M.P. (1992) *Helping the Child Who Doesn't Fit In.* Atlanta, Georgia: Peachtree Publishers.

Oates, M.R. (2002) 'Adverse effects of maternal anxiety on children: causal effect or developmental continuum?', *Br J Psychiatry,* 180: 478–470.

O'Malley, K.D. (2003) 'Youth with comorbid disorders', in A.J. Pumariega & N.C. Winters (eds), *The Handbook of Child and Adolescent Systems of Care.* San Francisco: Jossey-Bass, pp. 276–315.

O'Malley, K.D. (ed.) (2008) *ADHD and Fetal Alcohol Spectrum Disorders (FASD).* New York: Nova Science Publishers.

O'Malley, K.D. & Hagerman, R.J. (1998) 'Developing clinical practice guidelines for pharmacological interventions with alcohol-affected children'. Proceedings of a special focus session of the Interagency Co-ordinating Committee on Fetal Alcohol Syndrome. 10 and 11 September. Chevy Chase, MA. Centers for Disease Control & National Institute of Alcohol Abuse and Alcoholism (eds), pp. 145–177.

O'Malley, K.D. & Nanson, J. (2002) 'Clinical implications of a link between fetal alcohol spectrum disorder and ADHD', *Can J Psychiatry,* 47: 349–354.

O'Malley, K.D. & Storoz, L. (2003) 'Fetal alcohol spectrum disorder and ADHD: diagnostic implications and therapeutic consequences', *Expert Review of Neurotherapeutics,* 3(4): 477–489.

O'Malley, K.D. & Streissguth, A.P. (2006) 'Clinical intervention and support for children aged zero to five years with fetal alcohol spectrum disorder and their parents/caregivers, an update in Tremblay, R.E., Barr, R.G., Peters, R. deV (eds), *Encyclopedia on Early Childhood Development (online),* Montreal, Quebec: Centre for Excellence for Early Childhood Development, pp. 1–9. Available at, http://www/

excellence-earlychildhood.ca/documents/OMalley-StreissguthANGxp.pdf.

Padmanabdan, R., Ibrahim, A., & Bener, A. (2002) 'Effect of maternal methionine pre-treatment on alcohol-induced exencephaly and axial skeletal dysmorphogenesis in mouse fetuses. Drug and alcohol dependence', Vol. 65, Issue 3, 263–281.

Pembrey, M.E. (2002) 'Time to take epigenetic inheritance seriously', European Journal of Human Genetics, 10: 669–671.

Poobalan, A.S., Aucott, L.S., Ross, L., Smith, W.C.S., Helms, P.J., Williams, J.H.G. (2007) 'Effects of treating postnatal depression on mother–infant interaction and child development', Br J Psychiatry, 191: 378–386.

Rasmussen, C. (2005) Executive functioning and working memory in fetal alcohol spectrum disorder. Alcoholism: clinical and experimental research, Vol. 29, Issue 8, 1359–1367.

Reyes, E., Garcia, K.D., & Jones, B.C. (1985) 'Effects of maternal alcohol consumption on alcohol selection in rats', Alcohol, 2: 323.

Riley, E.P., Mattson, S.N., Sowell, E.R., Jerigan, T.L., Sobel, D.F., & Jones, K.L. (1995) 'Abnormalities of the corpus callosum in children prenatally exposed to alcohol', Alcohol Clin Exp Res, 19(5): 1198–1202.

Roebuck-Spencer, T.M., Mattson, S.N., Brown, W.S., & Riley, E.P. (2004) 'Bimanual coordination in alcohol-exposed children: role of the corpus callosum', Journal of the International Neuropsychology Society, 10: 536–548.

Royall, D., Lauterbach, E.C., Kaufer, D., et al. (2007) 'The cognitive correlates of functional status: a review from the Committee on Research of the American Neuropsychiatric Association', The Journal of Neuropsychiatry and Clinical Neurosciences,19: 249–265.

Russell, O. (1997) Seminars in the Psychiatry of Learning Disabilities. The Royal College of Psychiatrists. London: Gaskell.

Substance Abuse and Mental Health Services Administration (2009) Dan Dubovsky, FASD Specialist, FASD Center for Excellence, Rockville, Maryland, USA.

Sampson, P.D., Streissguth, A.P., Bookstein, F.L., Little, R.E., Clarren, S.K., Dehaene, P., & Hanson, J.W. Jr, (1997) 'Incidence of fetal alcohol syndrome and prevalence of alcohol-related neurodevelopmental disorder', Teratology, 56(6): 317–326.

Sifneos, P. (1973) 'The prevalence of "alexithymia" characteristics in psychosomatic individuals', Psychotherapy and Psychoanalysis, 22: 225–262.

Song, J., Koller, D.J., Foroud, T., et al. (2003) 'Association of GABA(A) receptors and alcohol dependence effects and the effects of genetic imprinting', Am J Med Genet B, Neuropsychiatry Genet, 117B(1): 39–45.

Steinhausen, H-C. & Spohr, H-L. (1998) 'Long-term outcome of children with fetal alcohol syndrome: psychopathology, behaviour, and intelligence', Alcoholism: Clinical and Experimental Research, 22: 334–338.

Stratton, K.R., Rowe, C.J., & Battaglia, F.C. (1996) Fetal Alcohol Syndrome: Diagnosis, Epidemiology, Prevention and Treatment in Medicine. Washington, DC: National Academy Press.

Streissguth, A.P. (1995) Fetal Alcohol Syndrome. A Guide for Families and Communities. Baltimore: Brookes Publishing.

Streissguth, A.P. & O'Malley, K.D. (2000) 'Neuropsychiatric implications and long-term consequences of fetal alcohol spectrum disorders', Seminars in Clinical Neuropsychiatry, 5: 177–190.

Streissguth, A.P., Barr, H.M., Kogan, J., & Bookstein, F.L. (1996) 'Understanding the occurrence of secondary disabilities in clients with fetal alcohol syndrome (FAS) and fetal alcohol effects (FAE)', Final Report, August, C.D.C. Grant R04.

Streissguth, A.P., Bookstein, F.L., Barr, H.M., Sampson, P.S., O'Malley, K.D., & Kogan, Young, J. (2004) 'Risk factors for adverse life outcomes in fetal alcohol, syndrome and fetal alcohol effects', Developmental and Behavioural Pediatrics, 25(4): 228–236.

Sullivan, A. (2008) 'Fetal Alcohol, Spectrum Disorders (FASD) in the adult: vulnerability, disability, or diagnosis—a psychodynamic perspective', in K.D. O'Malley (ed.), ADHD and Fetal Alcohol Spectrum Disorders (FASD). New York: Nova Science Publishers, pp. 217–247.

Tchurikov, N.A. (2005) 'Molecular mechanisms of epigenetics', Biochemistry (Moscow), 70: 406–423.

Thomas, J.D., Garrison, M., & O'Neill, T.M. (2004) 'Perinatal choline supplementation attenuates behavioural alterations associated with neonatal alcohol exposure in rats', Neurotoxicology and Teratology, 22: 703–711.

Ware, N.C., Hopper, K., Tugenberg, T., Dickey, B., & Fisher, D. (2008) 'A theory of social integration as quality of life', Psychiatric Services, 59: 27–33.

Whitehorse FAS Education FAS Teaching Manual Yukon, Canada: Whitehorse. www.whitehorsefas.com.

25

Preterm and Low Birth Weight Babies

Dieter Wolke

HISTORICAL PERSPECTIVE

The term 'premature infant' only entered the English language some 120 years ago (Wolke, 1991). Prior to the late 1800s, infants who were born before this term were referred to as 'weaklings' or 'congenitally debilitated' (Helders et al., 1989). Before the introduction of more widely available treatment of sick babies in incubators by Carl Crede in Leipzig in 1884 (Brimblecombe, 1983) and the establishment of the first premature baby unit in 1895 by Pierre Budin at the Hospital Port Royale in Paris, these 'weaklings' were allowed to 'pine away' and die (Budin, 1900). The principles of care for premature infants changed little throughout the twentieth century until the 1950s. They consisted of minimal handling, insurance of adequate feeding, control of chilling or overheating and control of access to the infants because of the risk of infections. Parents were discouraged from visiting and prohibited from sharing any care, leading to the abandonment of some of these infants (Klaus & Kennell, 1970).

Initial interest in providing special care facilities for infants can be dated to the mid-1940s in the UK (Ministry of Health, 1944). Scientific research on temperature and physiological control and the introduction of more sophisticated medical technology resulted in steep falls of neonatal mortality. Thirty years after their introduction in the USA (Silverman, 1979), it was only in 1961 that a memorandum in the UK recommended, as a national policy, the establishment of special care nurseries in the larger maternity units in Britain (Central Health Services Council, 1961). Neonatology has since become the most rapidly developing subspecialty in paediatrics. Today's special care or neonatal intensive care units (NICUs) are highly equipped and specialized and are busy working environments (Wolke, 1987). Many NICUs, after concern for the long separations the parents used to experience from their infants (Fanaroff et al., 1972), have introduced regular or open access for parents to be with their newborns and assist with the care (Latva et al., 2004). If simple gain in life years is taken as a standard, then neonatal care is the most successful discipline in medicine today (Tyson, 1995).

TERMINOLOGY AND EPIDEMIOLOGY

Unfortunately, the terms preterm and low birth weight (LBW) are often used interchangeably, particularly in studies on the long-term outcome of these infants. Preterm birth refers to a birth occurring before term, i.e. before 37 weeks' gestation (Goldenberg et al., 2008). The low cut-off (e.g. 24 or 20 weeks' gestation) that distinguishes between preterm birth or spontaneous abortion varies by location. The limit of viability is currently around 22 weeks' gestation, but survival at this gestational age is still rare (Costeloe et al., 2000; Saigal & Doyle, 2008). Most Western countries consider an infant at 25 weeks' gestation potentially viable and recommend treatment (Cuttini et al., 2000). About 5% of preterm births occur at less than 28 weeks (extreme prematurity; EP), about 15% at 28–31 weeks (severe or very preterm; VP), about 20% at 32–33 weeks (moderate prematurity, MP) and 60–70% at 34–36 weeks (near term birth; NTB) (Goldenberg et al., 2008). NTB and MP taken together are five times more frequent than very preterm or extremely preterm births, but their public health implications are, surprisingly, rarely studied (Saigal & Doyle, 2008). In the USA, the preterm delivery rate is 12–13%; in Europe and other developed countries, reported rates are generally 5–9% (Zeitlin et al., 2008). The preterm birth rate has risen in most industrialized countries, with the USA rate increasing from 9.5% in 1981 to 12.7% in 2005 (Goldenberg et al., 2008) despite the advancing knowledge of risk factors and mechanisms related to preterm labour, and the introduction of many public health and medical interventions designed to reduce preterm birth.

Low birth weight (LBW) refers to infants born at less than 2500 g birth weight and account for 7–10% of all births (Wolke, 1991). Roughly 10–15% of LBW infants or 0.9% (UK) to 1.1% (USA) of all annual live births are of very low birth weight (VLBW; < 1500 g). Extremely low birth weight (ELBW) infants are usually labelled as such if below 1000 g birth weight (Hille et al., 2001) or sometimes below 750 g or 800 g (Whitfield et al., 1997).

Appropriate for gestational age (AGA) and small for gestational age (SGA; see Table 25.1) are determined as the relationship between

Table 25.1   Abbreviations Used in Text

Abbreviation	Meaning	Definition
EP	Extremely preterm	Variable; ranging from gestation < 28 weeks or < 26 weeks
VP	Very preterm	<32 weeks' gestation
MP	Moderate preterm	32–33 weeks' gestation
NTB	Near term birth	34–36 weeks' gestation
FT	Full term	>36 weeks' gestation
LBW	Low birth weight	Birth weight < 2500 g
VLBW	Very low birth weight	Birth weight < 1500 g
ELBW	Extremely low birthweight	Birth weight < 1000 g
AGA	Appropriate for gestational age	The fetus/newborn has a weight corresponding to his gestational age (i.e. above the 10th percentile on standard weight charts)
SGA	Small for gestational age	The fetus/infant has a weight below that expected for his gestational age (i.e. below the 10th percentile on standard weight charts)

gestation and birth weight using standard population or customized birth weight growth charts (e.g. Hemming et al., 2009). SGA children are those who are born at less than the 10% percentile (e.g. Hemming et al., 2009) or less or equal to 2 standard deviations (SD) below the mean for gestational age (Lee, et al., 2003). Within the preterm population, between 16 and 40% have been found to be small for gestational age (< 10th percentile in birth weight for gestational age). There has been a renewed interest in understanding the consequences of low birth weight and SGA due to the hypothesis dubbed as the '*fetal programming*' or the '*Developmental Origins of Health and Disease*' hypothesis (DoHaD) (Barker, 1997). According to this theory, a suboptimal prenatal environment, reflected in smaller body size at birth and shorter length of gestation, may permanently alter the organ structure and function of the body and thereby increase the risk for disease in later life. More recent studies suggest, however, that not only does a small size at birth have consequences for health later in life but also the risk is further increased if physical growth in infancy and in childhood is also altered (Raikkonen & Pesonen, 2009).

Within the group of those born preterm and/or low birth weight, there are higher rates of multiple births, with as many as 25% of very preterm infants born as twins or higher-order births (Marlow et al., 2005; Wolke & Meyer, 1999). Overall, preterm birth accounts for 75% of perinatal mortality and more than half the long-term morbidity in children born (Goldenberg et al., 2008).

CAUSATION

It is important to distinguish between obstetric precursors leading to preterm birth, risk factors and causes. Three types of these obstetric precursors are distinguished:

1. Delivery for maternal or fetal indications (e.g. infection, high blood pressure), in which labour is either induced or the infant is delivered by prelabour caesarean section (approx. 30%).

2. Spontaneous preterm labour with intact membranes (approx. 45%).
3. Preterm rupture of membranes (PPROM), irrespective of whether delivery is vaginal or by caesarean section (approx. 25%) (Goldenberg et al., 2008). PPROM is the spontaneous rupture of membranes at less than 37 weeks' gestation at least 1 hour before the onset of contractions. A small proportion of women can remain undelivered for weeks or months with PPROM, but a complication is usually asymptomatic intrauterine infection.

Preterm labour is thought of as a syndrome initiated by multiple mechanisms but in most cases the causes for spontaneous preterm labour or PPROM are not known. Thus, factors associated with preterm birth, but not obviously in the causal pathway, have been sought to predict high-risk groups and preterm labour.

Looking at the trends, the rate of preterm birth has increased (see above) across the same period as similar large changes in the characteristics of populations. In the UK, USA and Canada, the relative rate of very young women (< 20 years old) and older women (> 35 years old) giving birth have increased as has the rate of obese women (Hemming et al., 2009). Furthermore, the rate of reproductive assistance—in particular, in vitro fertilization—has steadily increased, leading to a higher rate of multiple births and preterm delivery, even when compared to spontaneously conceived twins (McDonald et al., 2005; Y.A. Wang et al., 2005). While multiple gestations account for 2–3% of all infants, they carry a substantial risk of preterm birth and result in 15–20% of all preterm births. Nearly 60% of twins are born preterm due to uterine overdistension, resulting often in PPROM or contractions.

Of the maternal risk factors, ethnic group membership has been consistently defined as a risk factor. Women classified as black, Afro-Carribean or African-American in the UK or USA have a risk of preterm delivery in the range of 16–18% compared with 5–9% in white women (Goldenberg et al., 2008). Black women are also up to three times more likely to deliver extremely or very preterm compared to other racial groups (Alexander & Slay, 2002). These higher rates are found even when correcting for a range of sociodemographic or lifestyle factors. In contrast, while East Asian, Indian subcontinent or Hispanic women have low preterm birth rates, their infants are more often born at low birth weight. However, infants from the Indian subcontinent are not only more likely to be born at low birth weight but also to continue to show poorer growth in infancy (Skuse et al., 1994). Other maternal characteristics consistently related to preterm birth include low socioeconomic status and low educational attainment and single marital status (Jenkins et al., 2009).

Pregnancy history and pregnancy spacing are other relevant factors that increase the risk of preterm birth. Women with a previous preterm delivery are about 2.5 times more likely to deliver preterm at the next pregnancy (Ananth et al., 2006). This is partly explained by pregnancies occurring in close proximity. An inter-pregnancy interval of less than 6 months confers a two-fold greater risk of preterm birth and women whose first birth was preterm are far more likely to have a short interval than those who delivered a full-term infant previously (Conde-Agudelo, et al., 2006). Either increased inflammatory status associated with a previous pregnancy or depletion of maternal stores of essential vitamins, minerals or amino acids have been proposed as possible mechanisms. Similarly, prepregnancy weight and body mass are related to more preterm birth, with both very thin and obese women at increased risk (Neggers & Goldenberg, 2003). Those individuals who are very thin may suffer chronic undernutrition and pregnancy makes high demands on body resources for the growing fetus. In contrast, obese women are more likely to have infants with congenital abnormalities and more likely to develop diabetes or pre-eclampsia during pregnancy, which also promotes preterm birth.

During pregnancy, women who experience high levels of psychological or social stress are at an increased risk to deliver preterm even after adjustment for the effects of sociodemographic, medical and behavioural factors (Copper et al., 1996; Smith et al., 2007). The stressors can be subjective or objective indicators such as housing instability or severe material hardship. Clinical depression in pregnancy (found in up to 16% of women) also increases the risk of preterm birth (Orr & Miller, 1995). However, it is not clear whether depression itself leads to an altered hormone release or whether it is the associated lifestyle choices, including increased drug use, drinking of alcohol or smoking, that increase the risk of preterm birth (Zuckerman et al., 1989). Of these lifestyle factors, smoking continued during part or the whole pregnancy by 20–25% of women in the USA (Goldenberg et al., 2008) has been consistently found to increase the likelihood of preterm birth, and in particular, lower birth weight across the gestation range (El-Mohandes et al., 2009; X. Wang et al., 2002). Smoking leads to vasoconstriction and is associated with placental damage or restricted maternal–fetal blood flow as well to more frequent inflammatory response. While both heavy illegal drug use and heavy alcohol drinking during pregnancy are related to more preterm births, there is also no such evidence for low to moderate alcohol consumption (Goldenberg et al., 2008). A whole range of pregnancy complications, ranging from diabetes, thyroid and asthma to hypertension, can also lead to or indicate preterm delivery, with placental abruption and placenta praevia being the most common causes (Goldenberg et al., 2008).

In recent years, much research has focused on understanding possible common pathways and mechanisms of how diverse risk factors may lead to preterm birth. Intrauterine infection is one of the most likely and important mechanisms and microbiological studies suggest that intrauterine infection might account for 25–40% of preterm births. However, intrauterine infections are difficult to detect with conventional methods and may differ by gestation. While at 21–24 weeks' gestation most spontaneous births are associated with histological chorioamnionitis, this is only found in about 10% at 35–36 weeks (Mueller-Heubach et al., 1990). Another pathway combined with infection and other risk factors is the influence of (or interaction with) fetal and maternal genotype. Individual genome analysis may be available in the future to detect relevant genes or to identify putative gene–environment interactions. A particular interest is proteomics, i.e. the study of the global set of proteins. The proteome is the entire set of proteins encoded by the genome. Thus, identifying the proteins in the amniotic fluid of pregnant women or those who have given preterm birth may lead to the identification of biomarkers in women at risk for preterm labour (Goldenberg et al., 2008).

THE IMPACT OF PRETERM OR LOW BIRTH WEIGHT ON DEVELOPMENT

Mortality

While the rate of preterm birth has increased, the mortality of preterm infants has reduced quite dramatically over the last two decades (Doyle et al., 2000; Saigal & Doyle, 2008). Advances in regional organization of care, improvements in obstetric and neonatal care including antenatal corticosteroids, assisted ventilation, surfactant therapy and changing attitudes towards intensive care have contributed to the rise of survival in extremely preterm infants in particular < 28 weeks' gestation (Bruckner et al., 2009; Fischer et al., 2009; Saigal & Doyle, 2008). However, there are large variations in infant mortality rates for extremely preterm children between countries, geographic regions in the same country, between different hospitals and between different racial and ethnic groups. For example, variations of 29–85% survival at 25 weeks' gestation have been reported between countries and hospitals, while survival at 22 weeks varies little (0–12%) (Saigal & Doyle, 2008).

The net effect of the increasing preterm birth and survival rates is that, in particular, more extremely preterm children survive (Fawke, 2007). Biologically, prematurity means that all the organs are immature; however, the brain (Rees & Inder, 2005) and the lung (Maritz et al., 2005) have been found to be most susceptible to the consequences of preterm birth, leading to higher rates of long-term neurological and health problems. The timing of gestational insults, their severity and their nature are likely to be important factors in determining the pattern of brain injury and the extent to which it will affect the function of the individual after birth. Partly as a result, concern was raised whether the increased survival would increase major disability (Doyle et al., 1989) and early follow-up research focused on neurological problems such as cerebral palsy, blindness or mental retardation (i.e. severe disabilities; Escobar et al., 1991). Recent reviews indicate that, despite the increased survival rates, the incidence of major disabilities (moderate/severe mental retardation, neurosensory disorders, epilepsy, cerebral palsy) has remained constant (Aylward, 2002; Doyle et al., 2000; Wilson-Costello, 2007) or may even be slightly declining (Fawke, 2007). In contrast, research in the last 15 years has shown that the major problems experienced by preterm children are in their psychological development and quality of life outcomes and, as it may be these that are increasing, these have seen an increased focus of research and clinical concern (Aylward, 2002; Saigal & Tyson, 2008; Wolke, 1998). Thus, this chapter concentrates on psychological outcomes in particular. Considering the suspected effects of gestation and birth weight on the development of the brain, the major focus has been on the study of VLBW or ELBW or very preterm (<32 weeks' gestation) or extremely preterm (<28 weeks' gestation) infants (Hintz & O'Shea, 2008). In contrast, the impact of moderate or NTB on development has been somewhat neglected and only recently become an increased focus of research again (Khashu et al., 2009; van Baar et al., 2009).

Assessment of psychological development in preterm children

The psychological development of the preterm child has been considered in four main domains (Wolke, 1998):

- cognitive development (e.g. intelligence, memory, language)
- behavioural and emotional status, ranging from individual differences such as temperament to behavioural and emotional problems
- social functioning—i.e. the ability to form and maintain social relationships with adults and peers and to reflect on these relationships (e.g. autistic symptoms)
- school adaptation, integration into society and employment.

A further fifth area of enquiry is the assessment of the quality of life of ex-preterm children (Verrips et al., 2008; Zwicker & Harris, 2008).

Follow-up research designs

To provide reliable, valid, and generalizable information on the psychological developmental outcome of VLBW infants the ideal study should:

- be prospective
- be based on large populations (geographical, epidemiological, or multicentre studies)
- have few infants lost to follow-up or good documentation of the dropouts
- include full-term control groups for cohort specific comparisons
- be long term (i.e. into school age or adulthood to assess the full spectrum of abilities and behaviours)
- include differential reports of subpopulations (e.g. according to social class, SGA vs AGA, single vs multiple birth, ELBW vs VLBW)
- be conducted by independent (group-blinded) psychology researchers not involved in the neonatal care of the infants under investigation (Hille et al., 2005; Johnson et al., 2008a; Vohr, 2007; Wolke & Söhne, 1997; Wolke et al., 1994, 1995) while routine monitoring can only realistically be carried out by the neonatal units themselves (Lyon, 2007).

Until two decades ago most reports were based on single-centre studies (mostly university centres of excellence), had inadequate descriptions of study populations and those lost to follow-up, included no same aged-comparison children, ended in the pre-school years, and were often conducted by those also involved in the neonatal care of the children (Aylward et al., 1989; Escobar et al., 1991). These limitations had serious effects on the conclusions reached and usually resulted in underestimation of the true rate and prevalence of developmental deficits (Hille et al., 2005; Wolke et al., 1995). Particular emphasis in the interpretation of findings will be placed here on controlled investigations, as secular trends in shifts of cognitive and behavioural scores have been repeatedly reported (Collishaw et al., 2004; Flynn, 1987; Wolke et al., 1994).

Cognitive development

Intelligence quotients or global developmental tests

Several recent meta-analyses (Bhutta et al., 2002; Johnson, 2007; Wilson-Costello, 2007) have summarized the impact of VP or VLBW birth on general cognitive functioning in middle childhood and/or adolescence compared to full-term controls. A meta-analysis of 15 high-quality studies of cohorts born between 1975 and 1988 found mean weighted differences for individual studies ranged from 7 to 22.7 IQ points between VP/VLBW children, with an aggregated difference of 10.9 IQ points (95% CI 9.2–12.5) (Bhutta et al., 2002). The results were not systematically affected by country, age at assessment and regional vs hospital-based cohorts. Although the average IQ scores of the VLBW/ VP were usually in the normal range (+ 1 SD), the average difference in scores was a clinically significant difference of 0.73 SD lower IQ. Average scores may be deceptive, considering that between 15 and 25% of the VP/VLBW children suffer severe cognitive impairments (< −2 SD), and up to 10 times the increased risk, compared with the expected 2.3% in the rest of the population (Wolke, 1998; Wolke & Meyer, 1999).

Obstetric and neonatal care saw a range of important changes during the 1990s, including the widespread use of antenatal steroids, surfactant therapy and improved ventilatory assistance, all of which are associated with both reduced mortality and neonatal morbidity (Fanaroff et al., 2003; Rojas et al., 2009). The question has been thus whether increased survival of lower gestation infants has been matched by increased survival free of long-term cognitive impairment. The evidence from a range of studies of VP children (< 33 or < 32 weeks' gestation; Foulder-Hughes & Cooke, 2003), VLBW, extremely preterm (EP <26 weeks' gestation; Anderson & Doyle, 2008; Farooqi et al., 2006; Marlow et al., 2005) or ELBW (Anderson & Doyle, 2003; Hack et al., 2005; Mikkola et al., 2005) children continues to indicate the disadvantage in these populations. VP children continue to have an 11–13 point difference to control children while the deficit is even larger in those EP or ELBW, with differences between 9 and 24 IQ points. The rate of EP/ELBW children with IQs of < − 2SD is as high as 40% (Johnson et al., 2009a; Marlow et al., 2005) and up to 50 times more likely than in the controls.

Although a range of studies have reported on the same samples at different ages (e.g. Saigal et al., 1991, 2007), few have looked at the stability and change of general cognitive outcome over time (Breslau et al., 2006). A recent study of EP children who had been assessed at 2.5, 6 and 11 years of age showed remarkable stability of both cognitive and moderate to severe functional disability between 6 and 11 years of age (Johnson et al., 2009a). Although there is some evidence that the rate of severe neurological problems has not increased (Fawke, 2007; Wilson-Costello, 2007) or even reduced (Doyle et al., 2005) despite increased survival of extremely preterm infants, the reduction in mortality has resulted in an increase in

absolute numbers of children with cerebral palsy (Saigal & Doyle, 2008). However, no similar reduction has been found for cognitive impairment. This is disappointing (Tyson & Saigal, 2005) and indicates that, at very or extremely low gestation, brain development is substantially altered to affect overall cognitive development. Thus, survival of extremely and very preterm children is contributing to an increased number of children in the community with learning difficulties. The emerging psychometric studies into adulthood of VLBW or ELBW come to different conclusions, with some indicating continued poor cognitive outcome (USA) (Hack et al., 2002) while in others the differences are small compared to full-term controls of similar adult age (Saigal et al., 2006; see Hack, 2009 for a review). However, record linkage studies show continuous higher learning disabilities into adulthood of children born preterm (Moster et al., 2008). Furthermore, IQ differences in childhood are not just restricted to those with major neurodevelopmental problems who usually have the largest cognitive deficits. Even if children with such problems are excluded from studies, the differences remain substantial (Johnson et al., 2009a; Wolke & Meyer, 1999). Finally, few sex differences in global cognitive outcome have been observed for LBW or VLBW children (Wolke & Meyer, 1999). In contrast several studies have indicated that boys who are born extremely preterm are at up to double the risk for global cognitive impairment (Johnson, 2007; Johnson et al., 2009a; Marlow et al., 2005). It appears that the rates of brain development between 23 and 27 weeks' gestation may differ between boys and girls, with girls being relatively more mature, building a more compact brain and thus proving less vulnerable to the effects of preterm birth at this age (Vasileiadis et al., 2009).

Much less is known about the cognitive sequelae of moderately preterm or near term children born in the last two decades. The IQ differences reported for MB or NTB compared to full-term controls is small (around 2.9

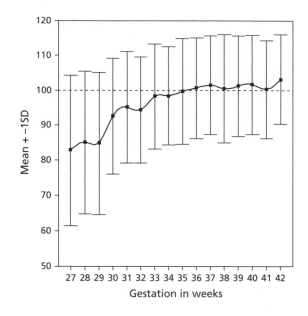

Figure 25.1   The non-linear relationship between gestation and IQ at age 4 years and 8 months in the Bavarian Longitudinal Study (*N* = 4467).

IQ points; Breslau et al., 2006; van Baar et al., 2009). The Bavarian Longitudinal Study, a population study of all children admitted to neonatal care in South Bavaria in 1985/86, investigated the relationship between gestation (27–42 weeks) and overall cognitive outcome (Wolke et al., 2001). Above 33 weeks of gestation, each loss of 1 week of gestation was associated with a loss of 0.39 IQ points. In contrast, from the breakpoint of 33 weeks' gestation, the regression function describing the relationship between gestation and IQ showed that each drop of a week gestation was associated with a reduction of 2.89 IQ points (see Figure 25.1). That is to say that the impact of each week of gestation for those born before 33 weeks on IQ was about 8 times greater than being born at or above 33 weeks' gestation. A similar non-linear relationship of birth weight and IQ with much larger impact on IQ below the breakpoint at 1500 g has also been reported (Johnson, 2007; Wolke et al., 2001). The use of these prediction functions of children born in the 1980s to those born at even lower gestation in the 1990s—i.e. at 23–25 weeks' gestation (Marlow et al.,

2005)—showed remarkable predictive accuracy and confirmed a 2.9 weekly decrement in IQ below 33 weeks' gestation (Johnson, 2007). From a public health perspective, small IQ deficits are found for the 6–9% of children born at moderate prematurity, while those 1% of births at very or extremely preterm birth show substantial impairment in global cognitive functioning.

Specific cognitive deficits and neuropsychological research

When referring to preterm children, specific language or learning difficulties are often mentioned (Wolke, 1998). Thus one question pursued in recent research is whether preterm children have problems in other functions related to cognition (e.g. language development) and, in addition, whether these are specific (i.e. not explained by general IQ). Furthermore, recent research has also focused on whether the survivors encounter more 'subtle' deficits in higher-order neurocognitive functions—the so-called executive functions (EFs) (Aarnoudse-Moens et al., 2009).

There is now increasing evidence that VP/EP children are more likely to have deficits in non-verbal reasoning and perceptual tasks compared to verbal IQ difficulties (Johnson, 2007; Mikkola et al., 2005). Furthermore, using a neurocognitive assessment battery, both in very preterm and extremely preterm children, it has been found that the preterm children have substantially more difficulties in simultaneously integrating information (e.g. pattern recognition) rather than processing sequential information (e.g. digit recall one after the other) (Marlow et al., 2005, 2007; Wolke & Meyer, 1999). Thus, non-verbal reasoning, visual-spatial skills and the ability to perceive, integrate and process stimuli simultaneously are particularly compromised by very preterm birth.

Although language development is seemingly effortless in the first years of life, it is a monumental task including many cognitive, neural and motor control systems. Specific language impairment (SLI) is found when there is a clear discrepancy between general intellectual development (e.g. performance IQ) and language scores (Rispens & van Yperen, 1997). A range of studies have reported increased language impairment in very preterm or preterm children (Jennische & Sedin, 1999; Wolke et al., 2008). However, few studies have evaluated whether these language difficulties are specific or could be explained by global cognitive deficits (Dyck et al., 2004; Wolke, 1999). Several studies in very preterm/VLBW (Aram et al., 1991; Taylor et al., 2002; Wolke & Meyer, 1999) and extremely preterm populations (Wolke et al., 2008) found little evidence that language or phonetic processing problems were due to specific deficits previously speculated to be the result of damage to (or inhibition of) normal development in specific areas of the brain (Mutch et al., 1993). Rather, findings suggest that language abilities are substantially explained by general cognitive deficits in extremely or very preterm children. In contrast, problems in speech articulation that require oral-motor skills and are often found to be impaired in very and extremely preterm children (Samara et al., in press) are not explained

by global cognitive abilities (Wolke & Meyer, 1999; Wolke et al., 2008). These are likely to be due to neonatal hypoxia–ischemia, in particular periventricular lesions and periventricular leucomalacia affecting the motor tracts in the brain (Krageloh-Mann et al., 1999).

Executive function is an umbrella term for a number of higher-order cognitive processes needed for goal-directed behaviour (Mulder et al., 2009). Important subcomponents are likely to include (but are not limited to) inhibition, working memory, planning, shifting and fluency. The aspects of verbal fluency (controlled word association tests or animal naming), working memory (e.g. digit span) and cognitive flexibility were reviewed in a recent quantitative meta-analysis that found significant differences between VP/VLBW children and controls, although the effect sizes were small to moderate: (Cohen's d) –0.36 for working memory (seven studies), –0.49 for cognitive flexibility (five studies) and –0.57 for verbal fluency (five studies) (Aarnoudse-Moens et al., 2009). (Cohen's d is the effect size index of differences in means expressed in standardized standard deviation unit.) A more detailed recent meta-analysis (Mulder et al., 2009) reviewed EF abilities according to more specific areas of functioning, including selective attention (e.g. visual search tasks), sustained attention (e.g. in continuous performance tasks), inhibition (e.g. the ability to make a movement opposite to a movement made by the examiner, such as a tapping test), semantic fluency (semantic or category tasks where the participants have to name as many items as possible in a given category), phonemic fluency (naming of as many words as possible, starting with a certain letter within a time limit), planning behaviour (tower test), shifting skills (e.g. trail making test where the participant has to connect numbers and letters in numerical and alphabetical order, switching between the two) and sorting tasks (to learn a rule, it is changed and the participant has to switch to applying the new rule; e.g. Wisconsin Card Sorting Test).

Table 25.2   Meta-Analysis Results for Executive Function and Attention Skills for Extremely Preterm (< 26 Weeks, Gestation) and Very or Moderately Preterm Children (≥26 Weeks' Gestation)

Skill	Studies N	Sample Size		Effect size M(95% CI)	χ^2	Fail-Safe N[a]
		Preterm	Term			
Selective attention	13	1196	1008	0.38 (0.21–0.54)	35.62***	363
< 26 weeks	4	351	320	0.58 (0,43–0.74)	1.82	77
≥ 26 weeks	9	845	688	0.29 (0,08–0.51)	24.58**	100
Sustained attention	9	885	802	0.45 (0.23–0.66)	30.22***	121
< 26 weeks	3	168	141	0.67 (0.31–1.03)	4.55	35
≥ 26 weeks	6	717	661	0.33 (0.13–0.54)	13.25*	33
Inhibition	8	830	740	0.25 (0,03–0.47)	26.21***	30
< 26 weeks	2	120	90	0.50 (0,10–0.89)	1.89	7
≥ 26 weeks	6	710	650	0.16 (–0.05–0.37)	14.46*	—
Semantic fluency	7	672	465	0.43 (0.28–0.59)	8.95	113
Phonemic fluency	10	1127	846	0.45 (0.30–0.60)	19.61*	219
< 26 weeks	2	108	101	0.58 (0. 30–0.86)	0.11	10
≥ 26 weeks	8	1019	745	0.43 (0.25–0.60)	16.83*	134
Planning	5	560	504	0.38 (0,08–0.68)	19.50***	67
< 26 weeks	2	228	210	0.69 (0,50–0.88)	0.53	34
≥ 26 weeks	3	332	294	0.16 (–0.10–0.42)	3.45	–
Shifting TMT-B[b]	6	458	375	0.50 (0.36–0.64)	2.75	100
Shifting sorting	6	402	429	0.10 (–0.06–0.27)	6.54	–

[a] Fail-Safe indicates the number of unpublished studies with a null result that would be necessary to overturn the statistically significant effect size to a trivial value with no statistical or practical significance. *$p < 0.05$, **$p < 0.01$, ***$p < 0.001$,

[b] TMT-B, trail making test part B.

Source: Mulder et al. (2009)

Mulder et al. (2009) found moderate (–0.5 to –0.7) standard mean differences in all areas of functioning, including selective and sustained attention, response inhibition, phonemic fluency, planning behaviour and shifting behaviour (using the trail test) in extremely preterm children (Table 25.2). The differences were smaller in children who were born very or moderately preterm ranging from not significantly different for planning, inhibition or shifting behaviour to –0.29 for selective and –0.33 for sustained attention and 0.43 for phonemic fluency

(Table 25.2). The findings thus confirm that EF is impaired in extremely preterm children but to a lesser extent in VP or MP children.

However, executive functions also draw on a range of multiple processes and are not measures of a specific skill. As a result, it is unclear whether the EF abilities are explained mainly by global cognitive impairment. Marlow and colleagues (2007) employed a range of tests of attention-executive function, evaluating the areas of planning, self-regulation, visual search accuracy, inhibition and motor persistence, comparing extremely preterm to control children. While they found significant poorer performance in the attention-executive tasks, the major problems were found in visuospatial and sensorimotor difficulties, i.e. global cognitive deficits. Similarly, Anderson and Doyle (2004) found that extremely low birthweight or very preterm children exhibited significant EF problems compared with their NBW peers in all areas assessed. The cognitive assessments revealed global impairment rather than deficits in specific executive domains.

Studies that followed up children into adulthood also found that adults who were born very preterm still showed EF impairments in tasks involving response inhibition, visual-perceptual tasks and mental flexibility, and in some studies these persisted even when adjusting for IQ, gender and age (Nosarti et al., 2007). Brain ultrasound findings or neonatal complications were unable to explain these long-lasting difficulties (Hack, 2009). Mulder et al. (2009) also reported that some executive skills are more frequent in preterm children at an early age (i.e. selective attention) but seem to disappear later. Thus, further long-term studies are needed to conclude whether these problems persist into adulthood or not.

In summary, preterm children are at an increased risk for cognitive deficits and these are quite stable across childhood into adolescence. While moderate prematurity is related to minor deficits in global cognitive functioning, language development and executive function, the deficits are substantial in very and in extremely preterm children, where boys are at even higher risk than girls. At the same time, however, there is little evidence for SLI, and many of the executive problems may be accounted for by global cognitive deficits. These global cognitive deficits pertain mainly to difficulties in simultaneous information processing, logical reasoning and visual-spatial integration. This pattern of findings suggests that the cognitive problems are more likely to result from global changes in brain development, (in size, connectivity and integration) rather than, in most cases, to

injury to specific brain areas (Marlow et al., 2005; Nosarti et al., 2008).

Behaviour and emotional problems

Early parenting and attachment

Very preterm or VLBW infants tend to be more irritable than their full-term counterparts in infancy (Medoff-Cooper, 1986). Neonatal irritability and emotionality make caretaking more challenging (Belsky, 1997) and have been linked to a predisposition for disorganization (Spangler & Grossmann, 1999). Studies also show that the interaction of mothers with their preterm infants is less adaptive and involves higher control, less responsivity and less sensitivity when compared to full-term controls (Greenberg & Crnic, 1988). In turn, these are factors that should predispose to more insecure (van Ijzendoorn et al., 1992) and possibly, more disorganized attachment (van Ijzendoorn et al., 1999) in parent–child dyads. Surprisingly, however, most studies that have investigated attachment behaviour at 12–18 months in preterm infants have found no differences in secure–insecure attachment classifications compared to full-term infants (for review, see Gutbrod & Wolke, 2004). Furthermore, a lack of association between maternal sensitivity and infant attachment classification has been found in some (Easterbrooks, 1989; Macey et al., 1987) but not other preterm studies (Goldberg et al., 1986). The majority of these however, were conducted in the 1980s and focused on small samples of larger (>32 weeks' gestation; >1500 g birth weight) infants who are at only slightly increased risk for long-term problems. A few studies have investigated attachment relationships of more recently born very preterm infants. While Mangelsdorf et al. (1996) found that more VLBW (<1250 g) infants were insecurely attached at 18 months than a full-term control group, Brisch et al. (2005) found no increased risk of insecure or disorganized attachment in a VLBW sample compared to an expected distribution. However, this latter study found that neurological delay at 14 months was significantly related to more insecure attachment. The most recent study (Wolke et al., submitted) of a large sample of very preterm and full-term control children matched for multiple birth rates and education variables found that preterm infants were just as likely to be securely attached as the full-term sample at 18 months of age. However, 32% of very preterm children compared to 17% of controls showed disorganized attachment patterns in infancy despite highly sensitive parenting. Similarly, a meta-analysis of studies on disorganized attachment (van Ijzendoorn et al., 1999) found that 35% of infants in clinical groups with neurological abnormalities were classified as disorganized compared to 15% of infants in the general population. These results challenge the primary role of the caregiver in preterm infants' attachment formation. Rather, converging evidence suggests that the underlying neurodevelopmental problems (Pipp-Siegel et al., 1999a) associated with very preterm birth are at the core of a variety of problems in the social relationships of these children.

Autism spectrum disorders

Anecdotal clinical observations have suggested an increased risk in very preterm children of autism spectrum disorders (ASD). Two recent studies that used screening instruments reported that 21–25% of very preterm infants screened positive for autistic features (Kuban et al., 2009b; Limperopoulos et al., 2008). However, the specificity of screening in infancy is confounded by the high rate of developmental delay in this population, and the prevalence of confirmed diagnoses may therefore be considerably lower later in childhood (Johnson & Marlow, 2009). Recently, three studies of school-aged outcomes have reported a 4% positive screening rate for autistic features in ELBW (<1000 g) children (Hack et al., 2009) and 1–2% prevalence of diagnosed ASD in those born with VLBW/LBW (Elgen et al., 2002; Indredavik et al., 2004). The most recent study by Johnson et al. (2010) employed both a dimensional and categorical approach to assess liability to ASD and traditional diagnostic classifications (Happe et al., 2006) to assess ASD.

The prevalence of narrowly defined autistic disorder (DSM-IV diagnosis) of 8% was found to be around 65 times higher in EP children than in community populations, and the prevalence of ASD (16% in extremely preterm children) 4–12 times higher (Williams et al., 2006). The prevalence of diagnoses was higher than in other studies of ASD in VLBW/LBW children (Elgen et al., 2002; Indredavik et al., 2004) and no high-functioning EP with Asperger syndrome were detected. Similarly, a study of linked national registry data (disability pension, health records, social security) in Norway found disability payment related to ASD to be highly increased in very and extremely preterm children (Moster et al., 2008). Compared to full-term children, those born between 28 and 30 weeks' gestation had a 7.3 times (2.7–17.6) and those born before 28 weeks' gestation a 9.7 times (1.5–36.2) increased risk. No differences were found in adults born at 31–36 weeks' gestation compared to full terms. These findings have been recently replicated in a Swedish national cohort study of autism (Buchmayer et al., 2009). Johnson et al. (2010) found that while in the general population ASD are generally considered genetic in origin, environmental factors such as obstetric complications (Gardener et al., 2009) and extreme prematurity played an important aetiologic role. The correlates of ASD symptoms and disorders, in particular the high prevalence of cognitive impairment, increased obstetric and neonatal complications (Buchmayer et al., 2009) and reduced head circumference, are consistent with autistic disorder in which there is identifiable non-genetic structural or functional brain abnormalities (Rutter et al., 1994) and suggest a different pathogenic pathway involving global impairment in brain development and cerebral connectivity.

General behaviour and emotional problems and stability/change with age

Very preterm children are at an increased risk for a range of behavioural and social problems in middle childhood (Hack et al., 2009;

Samara et al., 2008). Studies of preterm children at adolescence and early adulthood continue to report more attention/hyperactivity problems (Hack et al., 2004; Saigal et al., 2003a), difficulties in relating to peers (Dahl et al., 2006; Gardner et al., 2004; Indredavik et al., 2004) and internalizing problems including anxiety and depression (Aarnoudse-Moens et al., 2009; Saigal et al., 2003a) compared with those born at term. These emotional and behavioural problems have a considerable impact on children's daily life and pose a burden to parents and teachers (Samara et al., 2008).

Hille et al. (2001) compared the behavioural outcome across studies in four geographically defined cohorts of ELBW (≤1000 g) in the Netherlands, Germany, Canada and the USA. Using the Child Behavior Checklist (CBCL), it was found that the pattern of behavioural problems (attention problems, social problems in relationships with peers, thought problems) is universal across populations of ELBW despite marked differences in ethnic composition, health, educational and social support

services and neonatal treatment policies (see Figure 25.2).

The findings of increased attention problems have now been confirmed across a number of reviews (Aarnoudse-Moens et al., 2009; Bhutta et al., 2002; Hayes & Sharif, 2009; Johnson, 2007; Msall & Park, 2008) and recent studies of EP or VP/VLBW children (Anderson & Doyle, 2003; Samara et al., 2008) and MP children (van Baar et al., 2009; Bohnert & Breslau, 2008). General population studies report that the most frequent profile of attention-deficit/hyperactivity disorder (ADHD) is that of combined attention and hyperactivity problems or hyperactivity/impulsivity (Biederman & Faraone, 2005). In contrast, in preterm populations, there are increased attention problems in the absence of hyperactivity or impulsivity (Hack et al., 2009). Furthermore, although ADHD has been linked to the development of externalizing disorder in the general population there is a notable lack of comorbid disruptive behavioural conditions in VP/VLBW children or adults (Botting et al., 1997; Gardner et al., 2004; Hack, 2009). This suggests that

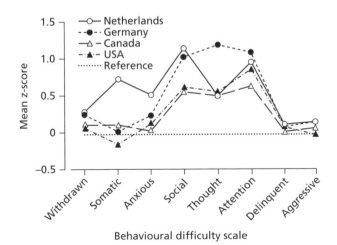

Figure 25.2   Mean *z*-scores for eight problem scales (Child Behavior Checklist; CBCL) across four cohorts of ELBW children. (Source: (Hille et al. (2001).)

the VP/VLBW child is susceptible to a 'pure' form of attentional deficit (Hack et al., 2009; Samara et al., 2008; Wolke, 1998). Neonatal white matter injuries have been found to be predictive of ADD in LBW/ELBW children (Whitaker et al., 1997), suggesting a more biologically determined form of ADHD with a neurological aetiology linked to central nervous system (CNS) injury. Indeed, studies have shown that preterm birth and medical factors are more strongly associated with ADHD than social factors (Botting et al., 1997; Johnson, 2007; Szatmari et al., 1993). Furthermore, Samara et al. (2008) showed that the attention deficits are specific and only partly accounted for by overall cognitive impairment.

Peer problems (i.e. problems in making friends and maintaining good relationships) have also been universally reported in very and extremely preterm children (Hack, 2009; Hille et al., 2001; Msall & Park, 2008; Samara et al., 2008). Social relationships in groups require the understanding of social cues, group dynamics and appropriate selection of action. However, once controlling for differences in IQ, the differences in peer problems have been found to disappear (Samara et al., 2008), which suggests that peer interactions and social skills are strongly related to overall cognitive ability, in particular, simultaneous information processing in very preterm children, and are not an additional specific problem.

There is increasing evidence that extremely, very and moderately preterm children suffer emotional problems such as anxiety more often in childhood and, in particular in adolescence, than those born at term (Aarnoudse-Moens et al., 2009; Hack, 2009; Hack et al., 2009; Saigal & Doyle, 2008; Spittle et al., 2009; van Baar et al., 2009). These emotional problems are also specific and not accounted for by general cognitive abilities (Samara et al., 2008). Again, different from the general population, the emotional problems are not comorbid with antisocial behaviours but rather related to higher shyness, lower socia-

bility, increased isolation and risk aversion (Schmidt et al., 2008), and poorer behaviour regulation (Spittle et al., 2009). Thus, preterm adolescents are less likely to engage in risky activities such as drug use, sex or anti-social activities with peers at an early age and are less likely to be in romantic relationships in early adulthood (Hack, 2009; Moster et al., 2008; Saigal & Doyle, 2008).

To summarize, increased 'pure' attention problems have been found for moderately, very and extremely preterm children and emotional problems have also been found in all preterm gestation groups but seem to be most frequent in very and extremely preterm children and adults. There is emerging evidence of highly increased ASD in very and extremely preterm populations that are related to overall cognitive impairment and neonatal complications, suggesting that the origin is not genetic but rather due to preterm birth and antenatal or perinatal complications or early extrauterine care. Finally, although preterm children are as securely attached to their mothers as those born full term, there is an increased risk of disorganized attachment. Again, early neurological problems (Pipp-Siegel et al., 1999) and early autistic features (Rutgers et al., 2004) are likely to explain the disorganized attachment despite adequate parenting in very preterm infants.

Academic problems and special schooling

Considering the cognitive, executive function and behavioural problems of preterm children it is unsurprising that preterm birth has an adverse effect on later scholastic attainment (Aarnoudse-Moens et al., 2009; D'Angio et al., 2002; Saigal et al., 2003b). The gestation-related gradient is also observed in educational outcomes, rendering EP/ELBW children more susceptible to scholastic underachievement than their lesser preterm and full-term counterparts (Breslau et al., 2006; Johnson et al., 2009b; Klebanov

Table 25.3   Parental Report of Special Education, Grade Repetition and School Difficulties in Four International Geographical Cohorts of ELBW Children in Middle Childhood: USA (New Jersey), Canada (Ontario), Germany (Bavaria) and Holland

	New Jersey		Ontario		Bavaria		Holland		
	n	%	n	%	n	%	n	%	χ^2
Special education	51/82	(62)	79/154	(51)	37/80	(39)	60/118	(51)	4,55, df = 3; P = .20
Grade repetition	16/84	(19)	31/143	(22)	23/80	(29)	40/118	(34)	7.65, df = 3; P = .05
School difficulties:									
Special education and/ or grade repetition	52/82	(63)	88/154	(57)	60/80	(68)	60/118	(51)	12.53, df = 3;P = <.01
Special education and grade repetition	13/82	(16)	22/154	(14)	0/80	(0)	20/118	(17)	14.63, df = 3; P = <.005

Source: Saigal et al., (2003b): p. 947.

& Brooks-Gunn, 1994; Saigal et al., 2000; Schneider et al., 2004; Hille et al., 1994). The marked deficits observed in standardized reading, spelling and particular mathematics scores (Aarnoudse-Moens et al., 2009; Johnson et al., 2009b; Stjernqvist & Svenningsen, 1999; Taylor et al., 2000; Wolke & Meyer, 1999) are mirrored in teacher reports of academic progress (Bowen et al., 2002; Johnson et al., 2009b; Wolke et al., 2008), and increased rates of learning difficulties are also reported for ELBW children without neurocognitive disability (Bowen et al., 2002; Grunau et al., 2002; Litt et al., 2005; Taylor et al., 2000).

The utilization of special educational needs (SEN) services is an important index of the totality of functional deficit and many studies have reported a significantly increased prevalence of special school placement and SEN provision, in particular in very preterm (Hille et al., 1994; Wolke et al., 2001) and extremely preterm children (Bowen et al., 2002; Saigal et al., 2000; Wocadlo & Rieger, 2008). A comparison across different cohorts indicated that the impact on the utilization of special educational resources is similar although differently delivered, across countries (Saigal et al., 2003a; Table 25.3). Furthermore, a recent study of children at the limits of survival (<26 weeks' gestation) indicates that over 70% of the survivors require special educational support, ranging

from special schooling to extra one-to-one help, small-group support and more specialist psychological, occupational, speech and language or outreach teacher help within mainstream schools in the UK (Johnson et al., 2009b).

Mathematics difficulties are particularly common, with the majority of studies reporting a more pronounced deficit in this domain compared with reading (Anderson & Doyle, 2003; Schneider et al., 2004). Again, in contrast to reading, significant effects of ELBW/ EP birth persist in mathematics after adjustment for IQ (Anderson & Doyle, 2003; Botting et al, 1998; Johnson et al., 2009b) and difficulties in this domain are prevalent among children with average IQ (Litt et al., 2005). Despite the preponderance of impairments, the nature and origins of mathematics difficulties in preterm children is not explained by social environmental factors but rather gestation, birth weight and early complications (Espy et al., 2009). Indeed, structural equation models have shown that neuropsychological skills may mediate the relationship between preterm birth and academic attainment (Taylor et al., 2002). Schneider et al. (2004) found that general IQ and specific difficulties in phonetic encoding and numeracy before school entry predicted academic achievement scores and schooling into early adolescence in very preterm or VLBW children. In contrast, while IQ was also important, social factors (i.e. parent's education) and specific phonetic and numeracy skills were the best predictors in full-term children. Similarly, Johnson et al. (in press) found that in EP academic underachievement was largely accounted for by general cognitive ability and specific deficits in visuo-spatial skills, phonological processing, attention and executive function. In contrast, social factors are among the strongest predictors for MP and NTB births similar to full-term children. (Breslau et al., 2006). Neuropsychological correlates of scholastic outcomes may therefore differ between EP and term children.

THE LIFETIME TRAJECTORY

The neurological, cognitive, behavioural and emotional difficulties of very and extremely preterm children are more stable over time (Bohnert & Breslau, 2008; Johnson et al., 2009a) than for larger preterm or full-term children, indicating less neurodevelopmental plasticity for VP/EP children. There are now approximately 20 studies that have followed preterm populations into late adolescence and adulthood (16–37 years of age; for a review, see Hack, 2009 and Saigal & Doyle, 2008). Neurological problems leading to disability (e.g. cerebral palsy, blindness) remain highly prevalent in preterm children, with a clear gestation-related gradient. General cognitive deficits persist in VP/VLBW or EP/ELBW even after adjusting for socioeconomic factors or excluding children with neurosensory impairment (Hack, 2009; Moster et al., 2008). Some studies in NTB/MP/LBW children report that those children from higher socioeconomic background show significant gains over time. The evidence of increased emotional problems and continuation of attention problems into adulthood is sparse and mainly based on self-report measures that require future investigations with diagnostic interviews (Hack, 2009). However, record linkage studies indicate higher disability rates and hospitalizations related to psychiatric problems in VP and EP young adults (Lindstrom et al., 2007, 2009; Moster et al., 2008). Furthermore, it has long been speculated that increased perinatal risk may be related to psychosis (Murray & Fearon, 1999), although preterm samples have so far been too small to test this hypothesis thoroughly. In addition, poorer educational attainment has also been documented for preterm adults when compared with controls. Preterm children leave school at an earlier age, are less likely to graduate from high school and are less likely to attain a university degree. However, most studies found that rates of employment do not generally differ in relation to gestation, but lower gestational age was associated with low job-related income and receiving social benefits (Lindström et al., 2007; Moster et al., 2008). Prematurely born young adults are less likely to live outside of the parental home, to start cohabiting with partners, or having started parenthood (Cooke, 2004; Hack, 2009; Moster et al., 2008) although some studies did not find this difference (Saigal et al., 2006). The differences in forming romantic relationships are most likely due to increased shyness, lower extraversion, decreased sensation seeking, decreased peer relationships and lower risk taking (smoking, alcohol use, delinquent behaviour) among preterm adults (Cooke, 2004; Hack et al., 200, 2004; Hille et al., 2004; Lindstrom et al., 2009; Saigal et al., 2006; Schmidt et al., 2008). In summary, functional differences remain in most areas into adulthood, in particular in VP and EP. However, it is important to point out that, despite the increased risk, most preterm children lead an adaptive life and are in employment.

Surprising and seemingly paradoxical findings derive from studies of the quality of life of preterm children compared to their full-term peers. Quality of life of VP and EP individuals is consistently rated as poorer in early and middle childhood (Zwicker & Harris, 2008). However, with advancing age (adolescence, early adulthood), the differences with full-term peers narrow or even disappear (Hack, 2009; Saigal & Tyson, 2008) despite the continuing more frequent functional deficits reported for VP/EP in adulthood (Saigal & Rosenbaum, 2007). This paradoxical finding may be explained by several factors. In childhood, the ratings of quality of life are made by parents and these are more closely related to the actual functioning of the child. In contrast, in adolescence and adulthood, the ratings are mostly provided by the preterm survivors themselves. The administration mode and data source has important impact on the ratings (Verrips et al., 2001). Raters usually compare to their memory of experiences and to their immediate peers rather than using a 'gold standard' anchor for their judgement (Stewart, 2009). For example, compared to other children receiving special needs support or in the same employment, the preterm adolescents/young adults consider themselves as similarly well off in terms of quality of life rather than making the comparison to all peers of the same age. Furthermore, provisions of educational and social support and cultural values related to childhood provision vary widely between countries (UNICEF, 2007) and also partly explain differences in quality of life across cohorts (Verrips et al., 2008). More research is needed that compares parents and self-ratings of quality of life and actual functional status to explain this paradoxical finding.

NEUROIMAGING

Research in the 1980s and 1990s was mainly concerned with finding relationships between early brain abnormalities (intraventricular and cystic periventricular haemorrhages or leucomalacia) assessed with ultrasound scans and developmental outcomes (Cioni et al., 1992; Whitaker et al., 1997). While severe adverse neuromotor outcomes (in particular relating to cerebral palsy) have been repeatedly found after

severe haemorrhages in the periventricular area (de Vries et al., 1998; Wood et al., 2005), much of the behavioural, cognitive and neuropsychological outcomes are not predicted by abnormal ultrasound findings in the neonatal period (Hintz & O'Shea, 2008; Krageloh-Mann et al., 1999; Wood et al., 2005). Furthermore, follow-up into adolescence indicated that even in preterm children with moderate to severe abnormalities on magnetic resonance imaging (MRI) no differences in IQ, motor clumsiness, or frequency of ADHD were detected compared to those with normal MRI scans (Cooke & Abernethy, 1999). Thus, the psychological developmental outcome in children who survive VLBW either does not or only poorly correlates with conventional markers of perinatal brain injury. In contrast, VP/VLBW may be related to global brain growth and the development of key structures in the brain (Abernethy et al., 2002).

Recent advances in neuroimaging have taken two directions: first, the development of facilities, including MRI-compatible incubators with integrated head coil, that allow for sequential scanning of the developing brain while in neonatal intensive care (Hintz & O'Shea, 2008; Kapellou et al., 2006); secondly, the routine availability of MRI to allow the study of anatomical differences and more recently, functional MRI (fMRI) studies to understand differences in brain area activation and connectivity in older ex-preterm children (Counsell et al., 2003; Hintz & O'Shea, 2008; Maalouf et al., 1999).

Findings indicate that extremely or very preterm birth confers both an insult to normal brain development and the superimposed risk of acquired brain injury. At the limits of survival (22–24 weeks' gestation), the brain consists entirely of white matter and in the following 16 weeks the grey matter expands rapidly with a dramatic increase in brain surface area by cortical folding, i.e. the surface area grows more than the volume (Hüppi et al., 1996; Kapellou et al., 2006) (see Figure 25.3). When babies are born

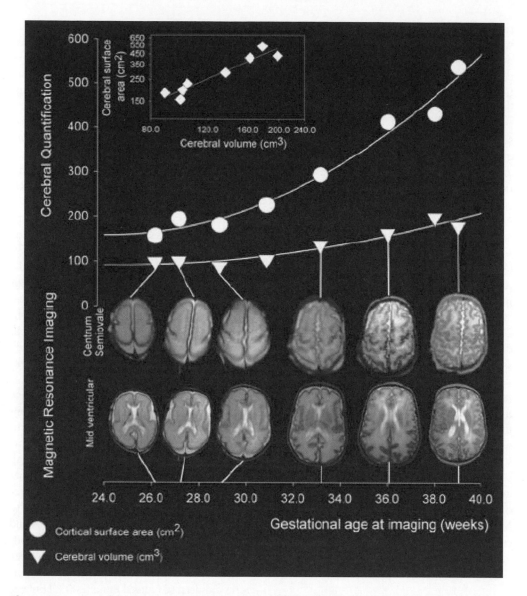

Figure 25.3   Serial magnetic resonance imaging (MRI) of brain growth of a single female normal preterm infant. When this infant was born at 25 weeks' gestational age, she weighed 710 g. The images show slices through the brain at the mid-ventricular level and at the level of the centrum semiovale from six of the eight MRI scans obtained between 26 and 39 wk gestational age; images obtained at 30 and 38 weeks are omitted for graphical clarity. Measured values for cerebral volume (triangles) and cortical surface area (circles) are related to relevant image pairs by straight lines. The insert displays a scatter plot in log-log coordinates of cortical surface area and cerebral volume (diamonds), showing a linear relationship that indicates power law scaling of cortical surface area relative to cerebral volume in this individual. Source: Kapellou et al., (2006: p. 1385).

prematurely, this pattern of growth is disrupted either due to:

- alteration in growth patterns or direct injury, e.g. to the white matter (found in 55–60% of very preterm infants) (Constable et al., 2008; Inder et al., 2005)
- injury to subplate neurons, abundant during the preterm period and which act as transition points for axonal connections to cortical and subcortical destination (Hintz & O'Shea, 2008)
- for as yet to be determined reasons

The earlier the birth, the greater the disruption is, and, in addition, boys are affected more than girls (Kapellou et al., 2006; Vasileiadis et al., 2009). This leads to building a different brain with altered grey and white matter distribution in multiple regions (indicating reorganization of cortical and subcortical structures relating to brain volume, volume distribution and connectivity) and these are still detectable in childhood and adolescence in many areas (Nagy et al., 2009; Nosarti et al., 2008; Skranes et al., 2007). Finally, the amount of disruption of brain growth before term seems to predict whether there is delayed development 2 years later (Kapellou et al., 2006).

If these findings are correct, then it may be possible to monitor brain growth after birth, in order to predict which children might need developmental support later. Furthermore, fMRI studies and tension diffuser studies are still rare but may be useful to determine differences in functional activation and connectivity between children and adults born preterm and full term and provide insights in the brain origin of the cognitive and attention deficits (Booth et al., 2005).

IMPLICATIONS FOR CLINICAL PRACTICE

First, this chapter has demonstrated a clearly defined phenotype of impairment and disability for preterm children, with a strong gradient related to the degree of prematurity (in particular below 32 weeks' gestation) and to birth weight (although to a slightly lesser extent: Gutbrod et al., 2000; Paneth, 1992; Taylor et al., 2000). Secondly, the initial costs for neonatal treatment are high and there are additional higher repeat hospitalizations, utilization of community and social services, outpatient hospital treatment and, in particular, SEN in the preterm population (Petrou, 2003; Petrou et al., 2001, 2003, 2006, 2009). Again, successively higher costs for care and treatment are found the earlier a child is born, with the highest costs reported for extremely preterm children (Petrou et al., 2006, 2009). The most costly service provision is education, with each child requiring special schooling that costs £16,443 per annum compared to £3152 for a child in a mainstream school according to 2006–2007 prices (Petrou et al., 2009). The average cost for all services were about £5658 per annum higher for EP children at 6 years of age (Petrou et al., 2006) and £2477 per annum higher for 11-year-old EP children compared to full-term control children (Petrou et al., 2009). The costs are even higher when psychiatric disorders are taken into account, with children with psychiatric problems requiring, on average, an additional £2072 to pay for services provided (Petrou et al., in press). The highest costs are found for those with severe IQ deficits (mental retardation) or autistic disorders, conditions far more frequent in VP and EP children.

Thirdly, although pre-, peri- or neonatal complications and diagnostic findings from MRI are related to later outcome, the sensitivity and specificity of prediction is generally poor (Cioni et al., 1992; Garg et al., 2009; Hintz & O'Shea, 2008; Miller et al., 2005) although substantially enhanced by the functional assessment in the second year of life of growth, motor, neurosensory, cognitive and behavioural functioning (Kuban et al., 2009b; Wolke et al., 2001).

These findings have several implications for clinical practice and public health:

1. *All preterm and low birth weight children require systematic follow-up at least in the first 2 years*

of life to identify developmental problems and initiate support for the children and parents (Johnson et al., 2008a). Follow-up is costly; however, recently screening instruments have been developed that allow highly sensitive screening of all preterm children with more intense assessment required for those with positive screens (Johnson et al., 2004, 2008b).

2. Clinicians should be aware of whether children presenting with cognitive, achievement, relationship or behavioural problems were born preterm or with low birth weight, and any assessment should enquire about prematurity and neonatal complications. The pattern of problems (e.g. pure attention problems rather than ADHD, etc.) and the causes (e.g. disorganized attachment, autism) are different and often not related to adverse parenting, and clinicians should be aware of this.

3. The most severe problems are found in EP/ELBW or VP/VLBW children (approx. 1–2% of all births). However, developmental and behavioural problems are also increased in MP/NTB and low birth weight children, who represent 6–12% of all births (van Baar et al., 2009), and close monitoring and follow-up should not be just restricted to very preterm children.

APPROACHES TO INTERVENTION

Initial reports of small-scale intervention studies for preterm children in the 1970s and 1980s suggested that early intervention, by supporting parenting and providing early educational support, could enhance the cognitive and/or behavioural development of preterm children (see Wolke, 1991). A recent meta-analysis (Spittle et al., 2008) identified 16 studies that started or continued intervention focused on parent–child interaction and infant development post-discharge. The results indicate that this type of intervention has positive impacts on the cognitive development of preterm born children during infancy and pre-school years. In contrast, no long-term effects on cognitive development persisting into the school years or any improvements in motor development were demonstrated (for key findings, see Dalen &

Offringa, 2008). However, only 6/16 studies were randomized studies that were judged to be of high quality. One study contributed nearly half of all subjects ($N = 985$) to the meta-analysis, the Infant Health and Development Study (IHDP) (McCarton et al., 1997; McCormick et al., 1993) followed by the Avon Premature Longitudinal Study (APIP) (APIP, 1998; Johnson et al., 2005), and thus strongly influenced the overall results. The IHDP was a highly intensive intervention, including home visits every week in the first year of life and every other week in the second and third year, daily centre-based day care—starting at 12 months and continuing until 36 months of age (minimum 20 hours per week)—with the addition of parent support groups. The intervention was stratified for two birth weight groups: ≤ 2000 g low low birth weight (LLBW) and 2001–2500 g high low birth weight (HLBW). At 3 years, of age, both birth weight groups showed significant improvements in cognitive scores compared to controls. While this positive impact continued in the HLBW group (approx. 4 point IQ differences), no differences were detected for the LLBW vs controls at the follow-up at 8 years (McCarton et al., 1997). The latest follow-up at 18 years of age included behaviour, cognitive, academic achievement and health outcomes (McCormick et al., 2006). Small but non-significant IQ advantages and some increased achievement scores were found for children of 2001–2500 g. In contrast, no differences or even slightly poorer performance were found for the intervention group of ≤ 2000 g (LLBW) children at 18 years of age. These findings suggest that highly intensive intervention similar to those in studies of socially disadvantaged full-term children have some positive impact for HLBW into school age but show no measurable benefits for LLBW children.

Similarly, the APIP study compared a Portage programme, parent advisor and treatment as usual group for children born < 33 weeks' gestation. Neither at 2 nor at 5 years of age was any positive effect on cognitive development found for the two intervention groups compared to controls (APIP, 1998; Johnson et al., 2005). A recent well-designed cross-over randomized controlled trial in six neonatal units in the UK confirmed that parent-centred intervention (starting in the neonatal unit with up to six post-discharge sessions for very preterm children) had no effect on cognitive or motor development of very preterm children at 2 years of age (Johnson et al., 2009c). Neither did this early, nurse-delivered, parent-focused intervention have any measurable effect on short-term infant neurobehavioural function, mother–child interaction or parenting stress (Glazebrook et al., 2007). It was thus a good idea that did not work (Platt, 2007).

Overall, the evidence suggests that early interventions have some short- to medium-term positive effects on cognitive outcome in MP and NTB infants and children. However, the interventions that have focused on VP children have found only short-term and no long-term positive effects on cognitive or behavioural development of early parent- and infant-focused interventions. This has been found whether the interventions were moderately (e.g. APIP study) or highly intensive (IHDP). It appears that VP/EP children are more likely to build a different brain when considered in conjunction with (1) the non-linear gestation effect (see Figure 25.1) at 33 weeks' gestation, (2) the higher stability of problems over time in VP/EP children (i.e. reduced neurodevelopmental plasticity), (3) the documented differences in brain development in size, cortical folding and connectivity and (4) the reduced influence of genetic factors explaining developmental differences (Koeppen-Schomerus et al., 2000). There is considerable heterogeneity in the VP/EP population, and those with 'healthy' brains are likely to take advantage of offers provided in the environment while a substantial minority of VP/EP children develop brains that are less able to benefit from environmental input as provided in interventions, i.e. these do not alter developmental trajectories.

Thus, interventions starting within hours of admission to reduce iatrogenic effects of treatment (e.g. frequent handling, high noise, and light, pain induction) (Wolke, 1987) and their adverse effects on physiological consequences (e.g. hypoxia) have been proposed (Neonatal Individualized Developmental Care and Assessment Programme, NIDCAP; Als et al., 1994) and tested in a range of usually small-sample intervention studies. However, meta-analyses have so far been inconclusive (Ohlsson, 2009), as are two very recent larger trials, one from Canada (Peters et al., 2009) and another from the Netherlands (Maguire et al., 2009) regarding their efficacy. Thus, the verdict is still out on whether the NIDCAP intervention starting within 48 hours of admission is an effective intervention.

CONCLUSION

Preterm birth, in particular, very and extremely preterm birth, is associated with an increased risk of cognitive, behavioural and psychiatric problems and/or disorders, poorer academic achievement, less salaried employment and poorer peer relationships. The burden is high for parents during the childhood period and continues for those with children with severe disorders into adulthood. Furthermore, the costs of initial neonatal care and for a range of health and educational services are high and although those born of moderate prematurity or near term have only a slightly increased risk of developmental problems (approx. doubled), these are also the largest group (in number) of children born preterm. The NTB/MP children are also the most likely to benefit from post-discharge interventions but are currently the most neglected group in terms of research and early intervention programmes.

Thus, follow-up and post-discharge interventions focused on MP/NTB infants are most likely to be beneficial and lead to a substantial reduction of long-term impairment and disability. In contrast, current psychoeducational interventions, whether in the NICU or post-discharge, have not been shown to consistently benefit VP/EP children. Rather, intervention efforts should focus on reducing the stress for the families and helping the whole family to deal with the early uncertainty of developmental problems and, for those affected, to help them cope with the increased demands they face.

A major challenge for the future is, first, primary prevention—i.e. reducing the prevalence of preterm delivery to decrease population disability (Iams et al., 2008). However, the current trends in postponing childbearing to a later age and the resulting increase of fertility treatment have led to an increase of preterm birth rates and the number of multiple births (Saigal & Doyle, 2008). Thus, increased awareness of the adverse consequences of delaying childbearing, public health approaches—i.e. reduction of smoking (El-Mohandes et al., 2009)—and the development of treatments to reduce causes of preterm birth (e.g. infections) and their adverse effect are needed. Secondly, higher-quality and new innovative intervention approaches to study secondary and tertiary prevention—in particular, those focused on VP and EP children—are required. Thirdly, there is a continuous need for longitudinal research on successive cohorts to document whether changes in obstetric or neonatal practices have a significant impact not only on mortality but also on reducing rates and, in particular, the total number of children affected by adverse long-term outcomes. Combining functional with neuroimaging techniques should provide better insight into not only the anatomical differences already reported but also the different organization and reorganization of brain function related to the described developmental problems. Fourthly, education is necessary for clinicians and educationalists to gain a better understanding that the pathways to developmental problems, ranging from autism to attachment or attention problems, are different in preterm than in full-term populations and occur despite sensitive parenting. Fifthly, despite the advances made in

documenting, detecting and predicting developmental sequelae, there is the possibility that very or extremely early birth may occur because of pre-existing problems (i.e. those infants that are late abortions). This implies that for some children, despite the best care, their developmental pathways may not be altered. Finally, although preterm birth is related to an increased risk of adverse developmental outcomes, most of the children develop adaptively and have a fulfilled and high-quality life (Hack, 2009). Many parents would not have a living child without the advances in obstetrics, neonatal medicine or nursing. Nevertheless, there remain ethical challenges of how intensive and early treatment should be initiated that governments, the public and those working in neonatal care need and have considered differently in different countries (Bioethics, 2007).

REFERENCES

Aarnoudse-Moens, C.S.H., Weisglas-Kuperus, N., van Goudoever, J.B., & Oosterlaan, J. (2009) 'Meta-analysis of neurobehavioral outcomes in very preterm and/or very low birth weight children', *Pediatrics,* 124(2): 717–728.

Abernethy, L.J., Palaniappan, M., & Cooke, R.W.I. (2002), 'Quantitative magnetic resonance imaging of the brain in survivors of very low birth weight', *Arch Dis Child,* 87(4): 279–283.

Alexander, G.R. & Slay, M. (2002) 'Prematurity at birth: trends, racial disparities, and epidemiology', *Ment Retard Dev Disabil Res Rev,* 8(4): 215–220.

Als, H., Lawhon, G., Duffy, F., McAnulty, G., Gibes-Grossman, R., & Blickman, J. (1994) 'Individualised developmental care for the very low birth weight preterm infant', *JAMA,* 272(11): 853–932.

Ananth, C.V., Getahun, D., Peltier, M.R., Salihu, H.M., & Vintzileos, A., M. (2006) 'Recurrence of spontaneous versus medically indicated preterm birth', *Am J Obstet Gynecol,* 195(3): 643–650.

Anderson, P. & Doyle, L.W. (2003) 'Neurobehavioral outcomes of school-age children born extremely low birth weight or very preterm in the 1990s', *JAMA,* 289(24): 3264–3272.

Anderson, P.J. & Doyle, L.W. (2004) 'Executive functioning in school-aged children who were born very preterm or with extremely low birth weight in the 1990s', *Pediatrics,* 114(1): 50–57.

Anderson, P.J. & Doyle, L.W. (2008) 'Cognitive and educational deficits in children born extremely preterm', *Semin Perinatol,* 32(1): 51–58.

(APIP) Avon Premature Intervention Project (1998) 'Randomised trial of parental support for families with very preterm children', *Arch Dis Child Fetal Neonatal Ed,* 79(1): 4–11.

Aram, D.M., Hack, M., Hawkins, S., Weissman, B.M., & Borawski-Clark, E. (1991) 'Very-low-birthweight children and speech and language development', *J Speech Hear Res,* 34: 1169–1179.

Aylward, G.P. (2002) 'Cognitive and neuropsychological outcomes: more than IQ scores', *Ment Retard Dev Disabil Res Rev,* 8(4): 234–240.

Aylward, G.P., Pfeiffer, S.I., Wright, A., & Verhulst, S.J. (1989) 'Outcome studies of low birth weight infants published in the last decade: a meta-analysis', *J Pediatr,* 115: 515–520.

Barker, D.J.P. (1997) 'The fetal origins of coronary heart disease', *Acta Paediat, Suppl,* 422: 78–82.

Belsky, J. (1997) 'Theory testing, effect-size evaluation, and differential susceptibility to rearing influence: the case of mothering and attachment', *Child Dev,* 64: 598–600.

Bhutta, A.T., Cleves, M.A., Casey, P.H., Cradock, M.M., & Anand, K.J. (2002) 'Cognitive and behavioral outcomes of school-aged children who were born preterm: a meta-analysis', *JAMA,* 288(6): 728–737.

Biederman, J. & Faraone, S.V. (2005) 'Attention-deficit hyperactivity disorder', *Lancet,* 366(9481): 237–248.

Bioethics, (2007) *Critical Care Decisions in Fetal and Neonatal Medicine: Ethical Issues.* London: Nuffield Council on Bioethics.

Bohnert, K.M. & Breslau, N. (2008) 'Stability of psychiatric outcomes of low birth weight: a longitudinal investigation', *Arch Gen Psychiatry,* 65(9): 1080–1086.

Booth, J.R., Burman, D.D., Meyer, J.R., Lei, Z., Trommer, B.L., Davenport, N.D., et al. (2005) 'Larger deficits in brain networks for response inhibition than for visual selective attention in attention deficit hyperactivity disorder (ADHD)', *J Child Psychol Psychiatry,* 46(1): 94–111.

Botting, N., Powls, A., Cooke, R.W.I., & Marlow, N. (1997) 'Attention deficit hyperactivity disorders and other psychiatric outcomes in very low birthweight children at 12 years', *J Child Psychol Psychiatry,* 38(8): 931–941.

Botting, N., Powls, A., Cooke, R.W.I., & Marlow, N. (1998). 'Cognitive and educational outcome of very-low-birth-weight children in early adolescence', *Developmental Medicine and Child Neurology,* 40: 652–660.

Bowen, J.R., Gibson, F.L., & Hand, P.J. (2002) 'Educational outcome at 8 years for children who were born extremely prematurely: a controlled study', *J Paediatr Child Health,* 38(5): 438–444.

Breslau, N., Dickens, W.T., Flynn, J.R., Peterson, E.L., & Lucia, V.C. (2006) 'Low birthweight and social disadvantage: tracking their relationship with children's IQ during the period of school attendance', *Intelligence,* 34: 351–362.

Brimblecombe, F.S.W. (1983) 'Evolution of special care units', in J.A. Davis, M.P.M. Richards, & N.R.C. Robertson (eds), *Parent–Baby Attachment in Premature Infants.* Beckenham: Croom Helm, (pp. 22–24).

Brisch, K.H., Bechinger, D., Betzler, S., Heinemann, H., Kachele, H., Pohlandt, F., et al. (2005) 'Attachment quality in very low-birthweight premature infants in relation to maternal attachment representations and neurological development', *Parenting,* 5(4): 311–331.

Bruckner, T.A., Saxton, K.B., Anderson, E., Goldman, S., & Gould, J.B. (2009) 'From paradox to disparity: trends in neonatal death in very low birth weight non-Hispanic black and white infants, 1989–2004', *J Pediatr,* 155(4): 482–487.

Buchmayer, S., Johansson, S., Johansson, A., Hultman, C.M., Sparen, P., & Cnattingius, S. (2009) 'Can association between preterm birth and autism be explained by maternal or neonatal morbidity?', *Pediatrics,* 124(5): e817–825.

Budin, P. (1900). *Le Nourisson* (English translation by W.J. Maloney, The Nursling. London: Caxton, Trans.). Paris: Octave Dion.

Central Health Services Council (1961). *Report of the Subcommittee on the Prevention of Prematurity and the Care of Premature Infants.* London: HMSO.

Cioni, G., Bartalena, L., Biagioni, E., Boldrini, A., & Canapicchi, R. (1992) 'Neuroimaging and functional outcome of neonatal leukomacia', *Behav Brain Res,* 49: 7–19.

Collishaw, S., Maughan, B., Goodman, R., & Pickles, A. (2004) 'Time trends in adolescent mental health', *J Child Psychol Psychiatry,* 45(8): 1350–1362.

Conde-Agudelo, A., Rosas-Bermudez, A., & Kafury-Goeta, A.C. (2006) 'Birth spacing and risk of adverse perinatal outcomes: a meta-analysis', *JAMA,* 295(15): 1809–1823.

Constable, R.T., Ment, L.R., Vohr, B.R., Kesler, S.R., Fulbright, R.K., Lacadie, C., et al. (2008) 'Prematurely born children demonstrate white matter microstructural differences at 12 years of age, relative to term control subjects: an investigation of group and gender effects', *Pediatrics,* 121(2): 306–316.

Cooke, R.W. & Abernethy, L.J. (1999) 'Cranial magnetic resonance imaging and school performance in very low birth weight infants in adolescence', *Arch Dis Child Fetal Neonatal Ed,* 81(2): F116–121.

Cooke, R.W.I. (2004) 'Health, lifestyle, and quality of life for young adults born very preterm', *Arch Dis Child,* 89(3): 201–206.

Copper, R.L., Goldenberg, R.L., Das, A., Elder, N., Swain, M., Norman, G., et al. (1996) 'The preterm prediction study: Maternal stress is associated with spontaneous preterm birth at less than thirty-five weeks' gestation', *Am J Obstet Gynecol,* 175(5): 1286–1292.

Costeloe, K., Hennessy, E., Gibson, A.T., Marlow, N., Wilkinson, A.R., & EPIcure Study Group. (2000) 'The EPIcure Study: outcomes to discharge from hospital for infants born at the threshold of viability', *Pediatrics,* 106(4): 659–671.

Counsell, S.J., Allsop, J.M., Harrison, M.C., Larkman, D.J., Kennea, N.L., Kapellou, O., et al. (2003) 'Diffusion-weighted imaging of the brain in preterm infants with focal and diffuse white matter abnormality', *Pediatrics,* 112(1 Pt 1): 1–7.

Cuttini, M., Nadai, M., Kaminski, M., Hansen, G., De Leeuw, R., Lenoir, S., et al. (2000) 'End-of-life decisions in neonatal intensive care: physicians' self-reported practices in seven European countries', *Lancet,* 355: 2112–2118.

Dahl, L.B., Kaaresen, P.I., Tunby, J., Handegard, B.H., Kvernmo, S., & Ronning, J.A. (2006) 'Emotional, behavioral, social, and academic outcomes in adolescents born with very low birth weight', *Pediatrics,* 118(2): E449–E459.

Dalen, E.C.V. & Offringa, M. (2008) 'Characteristics and key findings for early developmental intervention programs post hospital discharge to prevent motor and cognitive impairments in preterm infants', *Evidence-Based Child Health: A Cochrane Review Journal,* 3(1): 213–214.

D'Angio, C.T., Sinkin, R.A., Stevens, T.P., Landfish, N.K., Merzbach, J.L., Ryan, R.M., et al. (2002). 'Longitudinal, 15-year follow-up of children born at less than 29 weeks' gestation after introduction of surfactant therapy into a region: neurologic, cognitive, and educational outcomes', *Pediatrics,* 110(6): 1094–1102.

de Vries, L.S., Rademaker, K.J., Groenendaal, F., Eken, P., van Haastert, I.C., Vandertop, W.P., et al. (1998) 'Correlation between neonatal cranial ultrasound, MRI in infancy and neurodevelopmental outcome in infants with a large intraventricular haemorrhage with or without unilateral parenchymal involvement', *Neuropediatrics,* 29(4): 180–188.

Doyle, L., Murton, J., & Kitchen, W. (1989) 'Increasing the survival of extremely-immature (24- to 28-weeks' gestation) infants—at what cost?', *Med J Aust,* 150: 558–568.

Doyle, L.W., Betheras, F.R., Ford, G.W., Davis, N.M., & Callanan, C. (2000) 'Survival, cranial ultrasound and cerebral palsy in very low birthweight infants: 1980s versus 1990s', *J Paediatr Child Health,* 36(1): 7–12.

Doyle, L.W., Anderson, P.J., & and the Victorian Infant Collaborative Study (2005) 'Improved neurosensory outcome at 8 years of age of extremely low birthweight children born in Victoria over three distinct eras', *Arch Dis Child Fetal Neonatal Ed,* 90(6): F484–488.

D'Angio, C.T., Sinkin, R.A., Stevens, T.P., Landfish, N.K., Merzbach, J.L., Ryan, R.M., et al. (2002) 'Longitudinal, 15-year follow-up of children born at less than 29 weeks' gestation after introduction of surfactant therapy into a region: neurologic, cognitive, and educational outcomes', *Pediatrics,* 110(6): 1094–1102.

Dyck, M.J., Hay, D., Anderson, M., Smith, L.M., Piek, J., & Hallmayer, J. (2004) 'Is the discrepancy criterion for defining developmental disorders valid?', *J Child Psychol Psychiatry* 45(5): 979–995.

Easterbrooks, A. (1989) 'Quality of attachment to mother and to father: effects of perinatal risk status', *Child Dev,* 60: 825–831.

Elgen, I., Sommerfelt, K., & Markestad, T. (2002) 'Population based, controlled study of behavioural problems and psychiatric disorders in low birthweight children at 11 years of age', *Arch Dis Child, Neonatal Ed,* 87(2): F128–F132.

El-Mohandes, A.A.E., Kiely, M., Gantz, M.G., Blake, S.M., & El-Khorazaty, M.N. (2009) 'Prediction of birth weight by cotinine levels during pregnancy in a population of black smokers', *Pediatrics,* 124(4): e671–680.

Escobar, G.J., Littenberg, B., & Petitti, D.B. (1991) 'Outcome among surviving very low birthweight infants: a meta-analysis', *Arch Dis Child,* 66: 204–211.

Espy, K.A., Fang, H., Charak, D., Minich, N., & Taylor, H.G. (2009) 'Growth mixture modeling of academic achievement in children of varying birth weight risk', *Neuropsychology,* 23(4): 460–474.

Fanaroff, A., Kennell, J., & Klaus, M. (1972) 'Follow-up of low birth weight infants—the predictive value of maternal visiting patterns', *Pediatrics,* 49: 287–290.

Fanaroff, A.A., Hack, M., & Walsh, M.C. (2003) 'The NICHD neonatal research network: changes in practice and outcomes during the first 15 years', *Semin Perinatol,* 27(4): 281–287.

Farooqi, A., Hagglof, B., Sedin, G., Gothefors, L., & Serenius, F. (2006) 'Chronic conditions, functional limitations, and special health care needs in 10- to 12-year-old children born at 23 to 25 weeks' gestation in the 1990s: a Swedish National Prospective Follow-up Study', *Pediatrics,* 118(5): e1466–1477.

Fawke, J. (2007) 'Neurological outcomes following preterm birth. *Semin Fetal Neonatal Med,* 12(5): 374–382.

Fischer, N., Steurer, M.A., Adams, M., Berger, T.M., & Swiss Neonatal Network (2009) 'Survival rates of extremely preterm infants (gestational age <26 weeks) in Switzerland: impact of the Swiss guidelines for the care of infants born at the limit of viability', *Arch Dis Child Fetal Neonatal Ed,* 94(6): F407–413.

Flynn, J.R. (1987) 'Massive IQ gains in 14 nations: what IQ tests really measure', *Psychol Bull,* 101(2): 171–191.

Foulder-Hughes, L.A. & Cooke, R.W. (2003) 'Motor, cognitive, and behavioural disorders in children born very preterm', *Dev Med Child Neurol,* 45(2): 97–103.

Gardener, H., Spiegelman, D., & Buka, S.L. (2009) 'Prenatal risk factors for autism: comprehensive meta-analysis', *Br J Psychiatry,* 195(1): 7–14.

Gardner, F., Johnson, A., Yudkin, P., Bowler, U., Hockley, C., Mutch, L., et al. (2004) 'Behavioral and emotional adjustment of teenagers in mainstream school who were born before 29 weeks' gestation', *Pediatrics,* 114(3): 676–682.

Garg, P., Abdel-Latif, M.E., Bolisetty, S., Bajuk, B., Vincent, T., & Lui, K. (2009) 'Perinatal characteristics and outcome of preterm singleton, twin and triplet Infants in NSW and The Act, Australia', *Arch. Dis. Child. Fetal Neonatal Ed.*, published online first 10 August. adc.2009.157701.

Glazebrook, C., Marlow, N., Israel, C., Croudace, T., Johnson, S., White, I.R., et al. (2007) 'Randomised trial of a parenting intervention during neonatal intensive care', *Arch Dis Child Fetal Neonatal Ed,* 92(6): F438–443.

Goldberg, S., Perrotta, M., Minde, K., & Corter, C. (1986) 'Maternal behavior and attachment in low birthweight twins and singletons', *Child Dev,* 57: 34–46.

Goldenberg, R.L., Culhane, J.F., Iams, J.D., & Romero, R. (2008) 'Epidemiology and causes of preterm birth', *Lancet,* 371(9606): 75–84.

Greenberg, M.T. & Crnic, K.A. (1988) 'Longitudinal predictors of developmental status and social interaction in premature and full-term infants at age two', *Child Dev,* 59: 554–570.

Grunau, R.E., Whitfield, M.F., & Davis, C. (2002) 'Pattern of learning disabilities in children with extremely low birth weight and broadly average intelligence', *Arch Pediatr Adolesc Med,* 156(6): 615–620.

Gutbrod, T. & Wolke, D. (2004) 'Attachment formation in very premature infants—a new generation', in M. Noecker-Ribaupierre (ed.), *Music Therapy for Premature and Newborn Infants.* Gilsum: Barcelona Publishers, pp. 33–49.

Gutbrod, T., Wolke, D., Soehne, B., & Riegel, K. (2000) 'The effects of gestation and birthweight on the growth and development of very low birthweight small for gestational age infants: a matched group comparison', *Arch Dis Child Fetal Neonatal Edn,* 82(3): F208–F214.

Hack, M., Flannery, D.J., Schluchter, M., Cartar, L., Borawski, E., & Klein, N. (2002) 'Outcomes in young adulthood for very-low-birth-weight infants', *N Engl J Med,* 346(3): 149–157.

Hack, M., Youngstrom, E.A., Cartar, L., Schluchter, M., Taylor, H.G., Flannery, D., et al. (2004) 'Behavioral outcomes and evidence of psychopathology among very low birth weight infants at age 20 years', *Pediatrics,* 114(4): 932–940.

Hack, M., Taylor, H.G., Drotar, D., Schluchter, M., Cartar, L., Andreias, L., et al. (2005) 'Chronic conditions, functional limitations, and special health care needs of school-aged children born with extremely low-birth-weight in the 1990s', *JAMA,* 294(3): 318–325.

Hack, M., Taylor, H.G., Schluchter, M., Andreias, L., Drotar, D., & Klein, N. (2009) 'Behavioral outcomes of extremely low birth weight children at age 8 years', *J Dev Behav Pediatr,* 30(2): 122–130.

Hack, M.M. (2009) 'Adult outcomes of preterm children', *J Dev Behav Pediatr,* 30(5): 460–470.

Happe, F., Ronald, A., & Plomin, R. (2006) 'Time to give up on a single explanation for autism', *Nat Neurosci,* 9(10): 1218–1220.

Hayes, B. & Sharif, F. (2009) 'Behavioural and emotional outcome of very low birth weight infants—a literature review', *J Matern Fetal Neonatal Med,* 22(10): 849–856.

Helders, P.J.M., Cats, B. P., & Debast, S. (1989) 'Effects of a tactile stimulation/range-finding programme on the development of VLBW-neonates during the first year of life', *Child Care Health Deve,* 15: 369–379.

Hemming, K., Hutton, J.L., & Bonellie, S. (2009) 'A comparison of customized and population-based birth-weight standards: the influence of gestational age', *Eur J Obstet Gynecol Reprod Biol,* 146(1): 41–45.

Hille, E.T., den Ouden, A.L., Bauer, L., van den Oudenrijn, C., Brand, R., & Verloove-Vanhorick, S.P. (1994) 'School performance at nine years of age in very premature and very low birth weight infants: perinatal risk factors and predictors at five years of age', *J Pediat,* 125(3): 426–434.

Hille, E.T.M., den Ouden, A.L., Saigal, S., Wolke, D., Lambert, M., Whitaker, A., et al. (2001) 'Behavioural problems in children who weigh 1000 g or less at birth in four countries', *Lancet,* 357(9269): 1641–1643.

Hille, E.T.M., Elbertse, L., Gravenhorst, J.B., Brand, R., Verloove-Vanhorick, S.P., Dutch POPS-19 Collaborative Group (2005) 'Nonresponse bias in a follow-up study of 19-year-old adolescents born as preterm infants', *Pediatrics,* 116(5): e662–666.

Hintz, S.R. & O'Shea, M. (2008) 'Neuroimaging and neurodevelopmental outcomes in preterm infants', *Semin Perinatol,* 32(1): 11–19.

Hüppi, P., Schuknecht, B., Boesch, C., Bossi, E., Felblinger, J., Fusch, C., et al. (1996). 'Structural and neurobehavioral delay in postnatal brain development of preterm infants', *Pediatr Res,* 39(5): 895–901.

Iams, J.D., Romero, R., Culhane, J.F., & Goldenberg, R.L. (2008) 'Primary, secondary, and tertiary interventions to reduce the morbidity and mortality of preterm birth', *Lancet,* 371(9607): 164–175.

Inder, T.E., Warfield, S.K., Wang, H., Huppi, P.S., & Volpe, J.J. (2005) 'Abnormal cerebral structure is present at term in premature infants', *Pediatrics,* 115(2): 286–294.

Indredavik, M.S., Vik, T., Heyerdahl, S., Kulseng, S., Fayers, P., & Brubakk, A.M. (2004) 'Psychiatric symptoms and disorders in adolescents with low birth weight', *Arch Dis Child,* Fetal Neonatal Edn, 89(5): F445–F450.

Jenkins, J., Gardner, E., McCall, E., Casson, K., & Dolk, H. (2009) 'Socioeconomic inequalities in neonatal intensive care admission rates', *Arch Dis Child Fetal Neonatal Ed,* 94(6): F423–428.

Jennische, M. & Sedin, G. (1999) 'Speech and language skills in children who required neonatal intensive care: evaluation at 6.5 y of age based on interviews with parents', *Acta Paediatr,* 88(9): 975–982.

Johnson, S. (2007) 'Cognitive and behavioural outcomes following very preterm birth', *Semin Fetal Neonatal Med,* 12(5): 363–373.

Johnson, S. & Marlow, N. (2009) 'Positive screening results on the modified checklist for autism in toddlers: implications for very preterm populations', *J Pediatr,* 154(4): 478–480.

Johnson, S., Marlow, N., Wolke, D., Davidson, L., Marston, L., O'Hare, A., et al. (2004) 'Validation of a parent report measure of cognitive development in very preterm infants', *Dev Med Child Neurol,* 46(6): 389–397.

Johnson, S., Ring, W., Anderson, P., & Marlow, N. (2005) 'Randomised trial of parental support for families with very preterm children: outcome at 5 years', *Arch Dis Child* 90(9): 909–915.

Johnson, S., Wolke, D., & Marlow, N. (2008a) 'Outcome monitoring in preterm populations—measures and methods', *Zeitschrift fuer Psychologie—J Psychol,* 216(3): 135–146.

Johnson, S., Wolke, D., & Marlow, N. (2008b) 'Developmental assessment of preterm infants at 2 years: validity of parent reports', *Dev Med Child Neurol,* 50(1): 58–62.

Johnson, S., Fawke, J., Hennessy, E., Rowell, V., Thomas, S., Wolke, D., et al. (2009a) 'Neurodevelopmental disability through 11 years of age in children born before 26 weeks of gestation', *Pediatrics,* 124(2): e249–257.

Johnson, S., Hennessy, E.M., Smith, R.M., Trikic, R., Wolke, D., & Marlow, N. (2009b) 'Academic attainment and special educational needs in extremely preterm children at 11 years of age: the EPICure Study', *Arch Dis Child Fetal Neonatal Ed,* 94: F283–F289.

Johnson, S., Whitelaw, A., Glazebrook, C., Israel, C., Turner, R., White, I.R., et al. (2009c) 'Randomized trial of a parenting intervention for very preterm infants: outcome at 2 years', *J Pediatr,* 155(4): 488–494.

Johnson, S., Hollis, C., Kochhar, P., Hennessy, E., Wolke, D., & Marlow, N. (2010) 'Autism spectrum disorders in extremely preterm children', *Pediat,* 156: 525–531.

Johnson, S., Wolke, D., Hennessy, E., & Marlow, N. (in press) 'Educational outcomes in extremely preterm children: neuropsychological correlates and predictors of attainment', *Dev Neuropsychol.*

Kapellou, O., Counsell, S.J., Kennea, N., Dyet, L., Saeed, N., Stark, J., et al. (2006). 'Abnormal cortical development after premature birth shown by altered allometric scaling of brain growth', *PLoS Med,* 3(8): e265.

Khashu, M., Narayanan, M., Bhargava, S., & Osiovich, H. (2009) 'Perinatal outcomes associated with preterm birth at 33 to 36 weeks' gestation: a population-based cohort study', *Pediatrics,* 123(1): 109–113.

Klaus, M. & Kennell, J. (1970) 'Mothers separated from their newborn infants', *Pediatr Clin North Am,* 17: 1015–1037.

Klebanov, P. K., & Brooks-Gunn, J. (1994). 'School achievement and failure in very low birth weight children', *Journal of Developmental and Behavioral Pediatrics*, 15(4): 248–257.

Koeppen-Schomerus, G., Eley, T.C., Wolke, D., Gringras, P., & Plomin, R. (2000) 'The interaction of prematurity with genetic and environmental influences on cognitive development in twins', *J Pediatr*, 137(4): 527–533.

Krageloh-Mann, I., Toft, P., Lunding, J., Andresen, J., Pryds, O., & Lou, H.C. (1999) 'Brain lesions in preterms: origin, consequences and compensation', *Acta Paediatr*, 88(8): 897–908.

Kuban, K.C.K., Allred, E.N., O'Shea, T.M., Paneth, N., Westra, S., Miller, C., et al. (2009a) 'Developmental correlates of head circumference at birth and two years in a cohort of extremely low gestational age newborns', *J Pediatr*, 155(3): 344–349.

Kuban, K.C.K., O'Shea, T.M., Allred, E.N., Tager-Flusberg, H., Goldstein, D.J., & Leviton, A. (2009b) 'Positive screening on the Modified Checklist for Autism in Toddlers (M-CHAT) in extremely low gestational age newborns', *J Pediatr*, 154(4): 535–540.

Klebanov, P.K. & Brooks-Gunn, J. (1994) 'School achievement and failure in very low birth weight children', *Journal of Developmental and Behavioral Pediatrics*, 15(4): 248–257.

Kuban, K.C.K., Allred, E.N., O'Shea, T.M., Paneth, N., Westra, S., Miller, C., et al. (2009) 'Developmental correlates of head circumference at birth and two years in a cohort of extremely low gestational age newborns', *The Journal of Pediatrics*, 155(3): 344–349.e343.

Latva, R., Lehtonen, L., Salmelin, R.K., & Tamminen, T. (2004) 'Visiting less than every day: a marker for later behavioral problems in Finnish preterm infants', *Arch Pediatr Adolesc Med*, 158(12): 1153–1157.

Lee, P.A., Kendig, J.W., & Kerrigan, J.R. (2003) 'Persistent short stature, other potential outcomes, and the effect of growth hormone treatment in children who are born small for gestational age', *Pediatrics*, 112(1): 150–162.

Limperopoulos, C., Bassan, H., Sullivan, N.R., Soul, J.S., Robertson, R.L., Jr, Moore, M., et al. (2008) 'Positive screening for autism in ex-preterm infants: prevalence and risk factors', *Pediatrics*, 121(4): 758–765.

Lindstrom, K., Winbladh, B., Haglund, B., & Hjern, A. (2007) 'Preterm infants as young adults: a Swedish national cohort study', *Pediatrics*, 120(1): 70–77.

Lindstrom, K., Lindblad, F., & Hjern, A. (2009) 'Psychiatric morbidity in adolescents and young adults born preterm: a Swedish national cohort study', *Pediatrics*, 123(1): e47–53.

Litt, J., Taylor, H.G., Klein, N., & Hack, M. (2005) 'Learning disabilities in children with very low birth-weight: prevalence, neuropsychological correlates, and educational interventions', *J Learn Disabil*, 38(2): 130–141.

Lyon, A. (2007) 'How should we report neonatal outcomes?', *Semin Fetal Neonatal Med*, 12(5): 332–336.

Maalouf, E.F., Duggan, P.J., Rutherford, M.A., Cousell, S.J., Fletcher, A.M., Battin, M., et al. (1999) 'Magnetic resonance imaging of the brain in a cohort of extremely preterm infants', *J Pediatr*, 135: 351–357.

McCarton, C.M., Brooks-Gunn, J., Wallace, I.F., Bauer, C.R., Bennett, F.C., Bernabaum, J.C., et al. (1997) 'Results at 8 years of early intervention for low-birth-weight premature infants—The Infant Health and Development Program', *JAMA*, 277(2): 126–132.

McCormick, M.C., McCarton, C., Tonascia, J., & Brooks-Gunn, J. (1993) 'Early educational intervention for very low birth weight infants: results from the Infant Health and Development Program. *J Pediatr*, 123: 527–533.

McCormick, M.C., Brooks-Gunn, J., Buka, S.L., Goldman, J., Yu, J., Salganik, M., et al. (2006) 'Early intervention in low birth weight premature infants: results at 18 years of age for the Infant Health and Development Program', *Pediatrics*, 117(3): 771–780.

McDonald, S., Murphy, K., Beyene, J., & Ohlsson, A. (2005) 'Perinatal outcomes of in vitro fertilization twins: a systematic review and meta-analyses', *Am J Obstetr Gynecol*, 193(1): 141–152.

Macey, T.J., Harmon, R.J., & Easterbrooks, M.A. (1987) 'Impact of premature birth on the development of the infant in the family', *J Consult Clin Psychol*, 55(6): 846–852.

Maguire, C.M., Walther, F.J., Sprij, A.J., Le Cessie, S., Wit, J.M., Veen, S., et al. (2009) 'Effects of individualized developmental care in a randomized trial of preterm infants <32 weeks', *Pediatrics*, 124(4): 1021–1030.

Mangelsdorf, S.C., McHale, J.L., Plunkett, J.W., Dedrick, C.F., Berlin, M., Meisels, S.J., et al. (1996) 'Attachment security in very low birth weight infants', *Dev Psychol*, 32(5): 914–920.

Maritz, G.S., Morley, C.J., & Harding, R. (2005) 'Early developmental origins of impaired lung structure and function', *Early Hum Dev*, 81(9): 763–771.

Marlow, N., Wolke, D., Bracewell, M.A., Samara, M., & Grp, E.P.S. (2005) 'Neurologic and developmental disability at six years of age after extremely preterm birth', *N Eng J Med*, 352(1): 9–19.

Marlow, N., Hennessy, E.M., Bracewell, M.A., Wolke, D., & Grp, E.P.S. (2007) 'Motor and executive function at 6 years of age after extremely preterm birth', *Pediatrics*, 120: 793–804.

Medoff-Cooper, B. (1986) 'Temperament in very low birth weight infants', *Nurs Res*, 35(3): 139–143.

Mikkola, K., Ritari, N., Tommiska, V., Salokorpi, T., Lehtonen, L., Tammela, O., et al. (2005) 'Neurodevelopmental outcome at 5 years of age of a national cohort of extremely low birth weight infants who were born in 1996–1997', 116(6): 1391–1400.

Miller, Ferriero, Leonard, Piecuch, Glidden, Partridge, et al. (2005) 'early brain injury in premature newborns detected with magnetic resonance imaging is associated with adverse early neurodevelopmental outcome', *The Journal of Pediatrics*, 147(5): 609–616.

Ministry of Health (1944) *Care of Premature Infants (Circular 20/44)*. London: Ministry of Health.

Moster, D., Lie, R.T., & Markestad, T. (2008) 'Long-term medical and social consequences of preterm birth', *N Engl J Med*, 359(3): 262–273.

Msall, M.E., & Park, J.J. (2008) 'The spectrum of behavioral outcomes after extreme prematurity: regulatory, attention, social, and adaptive dimensions', *Semin Perinatol*, 32(1): 42–50.

Mueller-Heubach, E., Rubinstein, D.N., & Schwarz, S.S. (1990) 'Histologic chorioamnionitis and preterm delivery in different patient populations', *Obstet Gynecol*, 75(4): 622–626.

Mulder, H., Pitchford, N.J., Hagger, M.S., & Marlow, N. (2009) 'Development of executive function and attention in preterm children: a systematic review', *Dev Neuropsychol*, 34(4): 393–421.

Murray, R.M., & Fearon, P. (1999) 'The developmental "risk factor" model of schizophrenia', *J Psychiatr Res*, 33(6): 497–499.

Mutch, L., Leyland, A., & McGee, A. (1993) 'Patterns of neuropsychological function in a low-birthweight population', *Dev Med Child Neurol*, 35: 943–956.

Nagy, Z., Ashburner, J., Andersson, J., Jbabdi, S., Draganski, B., Skare, S., et al. (2009) 'Structural correlates of preterm birth in the adolescent brain', *Pediatrics*, 124(5): e964–972.

Neggers, Y. & Goldenberg, R.L. (2003) 'Some thoughts on body mass index, micronutrient intakes and pregnancy outcome', *J Nutr*, 133(5): 1737S–1740.

Nosarti, C., Giouroukou, E., Micali, N., Rifkin, L., Morris, R.G., & Murray, R.M. (2007) 'Impaired executive functioning in young adults born very preterm', *J Int Neuropsychol Soc*, 13(4): 571–581.

Nosarti, C., Giouroukou, E., Healy, E., Rifkin, L., Walshe, M., Reichenberg, A., et al. (2008) 'Grey and white matter distribution in very preterm adolescents mediates neurodevelopmental outcome', *Brain*, 131(1): 205–217.

Ohlsson, A. (2009) 'NIDCAP: new controversial evidence for its effectiveness', *Pediatrics*, 124(4): 1213–1215.

Orr, S.T. & Miller, C.A. (1995) 'Maternal depressive symptoms and the risk of poor pregnancy outcome: review of the literature and preliminary findings', *Epidemiol Rev*, 17(1): 165–171.

Paneth, N. (1992) 'Tiny babies—enormous costs', *Birth*, 19(3): 154–155.

Peters, K.L., Rosychuk, R.J., Hendson, L., Cote, J.J., McPherson, C., & Tyebkhan, J.M. (2009) 'Improvement of short- and long-term outcomes for very low birth weight infants: Edmonton NIDCAP trial', *Pediatrics*, 124(4): 1009–1020.

Petrou, S. (2003) 'Economic consequences of preterm birth and low birthweight', *BJOG*, 110(20): 17–23.

Petrou, S., Sach, T., & Davidson, L. (2001) 'The long-term costs of preterm birth and low birth weight: results of a systematic review', *Child Care Health Dev*, 27(2): 97–115.

Petrou, S., Mehta, Z., Hockley, C., Cook-Mozaffari, P., Henderson, J., & Goldacre, M. (2003) 'The impact of preterm birth on hospital inpatient admissions and costs during the first 5 years of life', *Pediatrics*, 112(6): 1290–1297.

Petrou, S., Henderson, J., Bracewell, M., Hockley, C., Wolke, D., & Marlow, N. (2006) 'Pushing the boundaries of viability: the economic impact of extreme preterm birth', *Early Hum Dev*, 82(2): 77–84.

Petrou, S., Abangma, G., Johnson, S., Wolke, D., & Marlow, N. (2009) 'Costs and Health Utilities Associated with Extremely Preterm Birth: Evidence from the EPICure Study', *Value in Health*, 12(8): 1124–1134.

Petrou, S., Johnson, S., Wolke, D., Hollis, C., Kochhar, P., & Marlow, N. (in press). 'Economic costs and preference-based health-related quality of life outcomes associated with childhood psychiatric disorders', *British Journal of Psychiatry*.

Petrou, S., Johnson, S., Wolke, D., Hollis, C., Kochhar, P., & Marlow, N. (in press) 'Economic costs and preference-based health-related quality of life outcomes associated with childhood psychiatric disorders', *British Journal of Psychiatry*.

Pipp-Siegel, S., Siegel, C.H., & Dean, J. (1999), 'Neurological aspects of the disorganized/disorientated attachment classification system: differentiating quality of the attachment relationship from neurological impairment', in J.I. Vondra & D. Barnett (eds), *Atypical Attachment in Infancy and Early Childhood among Children at Developmental Risk*. Monographs of the Society for Research in Child Development, Serial No. 258, Vol. 64, No. 3.

Platt, M.P.W. (2007) 'A good idea that doesn't work the Parent Baby Interaction Programme', *Arch Dis Child Fetal Neonatal Ed*, 92(6): F427–428.

Raikkonen, K. & Pesonen, A.K. (2009) 'Early life origins of psychological development and mental health', *Scand J Psychol*, 50(6): 583–591.

Rees, S., & Inder, T. (2005) 'Fetal and neonatal origins of altered brain development', *Early Hum Dev,* 81(9): 753–761.

Rispens, J. & van Yperen, T.A. (1997) 'How specific are "specific developmental disorder"? The relevance of the concept of specific developmental disorders for the classification of childhood developmental disorders', *J Child Psychol Psychiatry*, 38: 351–363.

Rojas, M.A., Lozano, J.M., Rojas, M.X., Laughon, M., Bose, C.L., Rondon, M.A., et al. (2009) 'Very early surfactant without mandatory ventilation in premature infants treated with early continuous positive airway pressure: a randomized, controlled trial', *Pediatrics,* 123(1): 137–142.

Rutgers, A.H., Bakermans-Kranenburg, M.J., Van Ijzendoorn, M.H., & van Berckelaer-Onnes, I.A. (2004) 'Autism and attachment: a meta-analytic review', *J Child Psychol Psychiatry,* 45(6): 1123–1134.

Rutter, M., Bailey, A., Bolton, P., & Lecouteur, A. (1994) 'Autism and known medical conditions— myth and substance', *J Child Psychol Psychiatry,* 35(2): 311–322.

Saigal, S. & Doyle, L.W. (2008) 'An overview of mortality and sequelae of preterm birth from infancy to adulthood', *Lancet,* 371(9608): 261–269.

Saigal, S. & Rosenbaum, P. (2007) 'What matters in the long term: reflections on the context of adult outcomes versus detailed measures in childhood', *Semin Fetal Neonatal Med,* 12(5): 415–422.

Saigal, S. & Tyson, J. (2008) 'Measurement of quality of life of survivors of neonatal intensive care: critique and implications', *Semin Perinatol,* 32(1): 59–66.

Saigal, S., Szatmarl, P., Rosenbaum, P., Campbell, D., & King, S. (1991) 'Cognitive abilities and school performance of extremely low birth weight children and matched term control children at age 8 years: a regional study', *J Pediatr*, 118: 751–760.

Saigal, S., Hoult, L.A., Streiner, D.L., Stoskoph, B.L., & Rosenbaum, P.L. (2000) 'School difficulties at adolescence in a regional cohort of children who were extremely low birthweight', *J Pediatr,* 105(2): 325–331.

Saigal, S., denOuden, L., Wolke, D., Hoult, L., Paneth, N., Streiner, D.L., et al. (2003b), 'School-age outcomes in children who were extremely low birth weight from four international population-based cohorts', *Pediatrics,* 112(4): 943–950.

Saigal, S., Pinelli, J., Hoult, L., Kim, M., & Boyle, M. (2003a) 'Psychopathology and social competencies of adolescents who were extremely low birth weight', *Pediatrics,* 111(5): 969–975.

Saigal, S., Stoskopf, B., Streiner, D., Boyle, M., Pinelli, J., Paneth, N., et al. (2006) 'Transition of extremely low-birth-weight infants from adolescence to young adulthood: comparison with normal birth-weight controls', *JAMA,* 295(6): 667–675.

Saigal, S., Stoskopf, B., Boyle, M., Paneth, N., Pinelli, J., Streiner, D., et al. (2007) 'Comparison of current health, functional limitations, and health care use of young adults who were born with extremely low birth weight and normal birth weight', *Pediatrics,* 119: E562–E573.

Samara, M., Marlow, N., Wolke, D., EPICure Study Group (2008) 'Pervasive behavior problems at 6 years of age in a total-population sample of children born at ≤ 25 weeks of gestation', *Pediatrics,* 122(3): 562–573.

Samara, M., Johnson, S., Lamberts, K., Marlow, N., & Wolke, D. (2010). 'Eating problems at age 6 years in a whole population sample of extremely preterm children', *Developmental Medicine & Child Neurology,* 52(2): e16–e22.

Schmidt, L.A., Miskovic, V., Boyle, M.H., & Saigal, S. (2008) 'Shyness and timidity in young adults who were born at extremely low birth weight', *Pediatrics,* 122(1): e181–187.

Schneider, W., Wolke, D., Schlagmüller, M., & Meyer, R. (2004) 'Pathways to school achievement in very preterm and full term children', *Eur J Psychol Educ,* 19(4): 385–406.

Silverman, W.A. (1979) 'Incubator-baby side shows', *Pediatrics,* 64(2): 127–141.

Skranes, J., Vangberg, T.R., Kulseng, S., Indredavik, M.S., Evensen, K.A.I., Martinussen, M., et al. (2007) 'Clinical findings and white matter abnormalities seen on diffusion tensor imaging in adolescents with very low birth weight', *Brain,* 130(3): 654–666.

Skuse, D.H., Wolke, D., & Reilly, S. (1994) 'Socioeconomic disadvantage and ethnic influences upon infant growth in inner London', in A. Prader & R. Rappaport (eds), *Clinical Issues in Growth Disorders: Evaluation, Diagnosis and Therapy.* Tel Aviv: Freund Publishing House, pp. 57–70.

Smith, L.K., Draper, E.S., Manktelow, B.N., Dorling, J.S., & Field, D.J. (2007) 'Socioeconomic inequalities in very preterm birth rates', *Arch Dis Child Fetal Neonatal Ed,* 92(1): F11–14.

Spangler, G. & Grossmann, K. (1999) 'Individual and physiological correlates of attachment disorganization in infancy', in J. Solomon & C. George (eds), *Attachment Disorganization.* New York: Guilford Press, pp. 95–124.

Spittle, A.J., Orton, J., Doyle, L.W., & Boyd, R. (2008) 'Early developmental intervention programs post hospital discharge to prevent motor and cognitive impairments in preterm infants', *Evidence-Based Child Health: A Cochrane Review Journal,* 3(1): 145–206.

Spittle, A.J., Treyvaud, K., Doyle, L.W., Roberts, G., Lee, K.J., Inder, T.E., et al. (2009) 'Early emergence of behavior and social-emotional problems in very pre-term infants', *J Am Acad Child Adolesc Psychiatry,* 48(9): 909–918.

Stewart, N. (2009) 'Decision by sampling: the role of the decision environment in risky choice', *Q J Exp Psychol,* 62: 1041–1062.

Stjernqvist, K., & Svenningsen, N.W. (1999) 'Ten year follow up of children born before 29 gestational weeks: health, cognitive development, behaviour and school achievement', *Acta Paediatr,* 88: 557–562.

Szatmari, P., Saigal, S., Rosenbaum, P., & Campbell, D. (1993) 'Psychopathology and adaptive functioning among extremely low birthweight children at eight years of age', *Dev Psychopathol,* 5: 345–357.

Taylor, H.G., Klein, N., & Hack, M. (2000) 'School-age consequences of birth weight less than 750 g: a review and update', *Dev Neuropsychol,* 17(3): 289–321.

Taylor, H.G., Burant, C.J., Holding, P.A., Klein, N., & Hack, M. (2002) 'Sources of variability in sequelae of very low birth weight', *Child Neuropsychol,* 8(3): 163–178.

Tyson, J. (1995) 'Evidence-based ethics and the care of premature infants', *Future Child,* 5(1): 197–213.

Tyson, J.E., & Saigal, S. (2005) 'Outcomes for extremely low-birth-weight infants: disappointing news', *JAMA,* 294(3): 371–373.

UNICEF (2007) Innocenti Report Card 7. 'Child poverty in perspective: an overview of child well-being in rich countries'. The most comprehensive assessment to date of the lives and well-being of children and adolescents in the economically advanced nations. (No. 7). Geneva: UNICEF.

van Baar, A.L., Vermaas, J., Knots, E., de Kleine, M.J.K., & Soons, P. (2009) 'Functioning at school age of moderately preterm children born at 32 to 36 weeks' gestational age', *Pediatrics,* 124(1): 251–257.

van Ijzendoorn, M.H., Goldberg, S., Kroonenberg, P.M., & Frenkel, O.J. (1992) 'The relative effects of mater-nal and child problems on the quality of attachment: a meta-analysis of attachment in clinical samples', *Child Deve,* 63: 840–858.

van Ijzendoorn, M.H., Schuengel, C., & Bakermans-Kranenburg, M.J. (1999) 'Disorganised attachment in early childhood: meta-analysis of precursors, con-comitants, and sequelae', *Dev Psychopathol,* 11: 225–249.

Vasileiadis, G.T., Thompson, R.T., Han, V.K.M., & Gelman, N. (2009) 'Females follow a more "com-pact" early human brain development model than males. A case-control study of preterm neonates', *Pediatr Res,* 66(5): 551–555.

Verrips, E., Vogels, T., Saigal, S., Wolke, D., Meyer, R., Hoult, L., et al. (2008) 'Health-related quality of life for extremely low birth weight adolescents in Canada, Germany, and the Netherlands,' *Pediatrics,* 122(3): 556–561.

Verrips, G.H.W., Stuifbergen, M.C., den Ouden, A.L., Bonsel, G.J., Gemke, R.J., Paneth, N., et al. (2001) 'Measuring health status using the Health Utilities Index: agreement between raters and between modalities of administration', *J Clin Epidemiol,* 54(5): 475–481.

Vohr, B.R. (2007) 'How should we report early child-hood outcomes of very low birth weight infants?', *Semin Fetal Neonatal Med,* 12(5): 355–362.

Wang, X., Zuckerman, B., Pearson, C., Kaufman, G., Chen, C., Wang, G., et al. (2002) 'Maternal cigarette smoking, metabolic gene polymorphism, and infant birth weight', *JAMA,* 287(2): 195–202.

Wang, Y.A., Sullivan, E.A., Black, D., Dean, J., Bryant, J., & Chapman, M. (2005) 'Preterm birth and low birth weight after assisted reproductive technology-related pregnancy in Australia between 1996 and 2000', *Fertil Steril,* 83(6): 1650–1658.

Whitaker, A.H., Van Rossem, R., Feldman, J.F., Schonfeld, I.S., Pinto-Martin, J.A., Torre, C., et al. (1997) 'Psychiatric outcomes in low-birth-weight children at age 6 years: relation to neonatal cranial ultrasound abnormalities', *Arch Gen Psychiatry,* 54: 847–856.

Whitfield, M.F., Eckstein Grunau, R.V., & Holsti, L. (1997) 'Extremely premature (<800g) schoolchil-dren: multiple area of hidden disability', *Arch Dis Child,* 77: 85–90.

Williams, J.G., Brayne, C.E., & Higgins, J.P. (2006) 'Systematic review of prevalence studies of autism spectrum disorders', *Arch Dis Child,* 91: 8–15.

Wilson-Costello, D. (2007) 'Is there evidence that long-term outcomes have improved with intensive care?', *Semin Fetal Neonatal Med,* 12(5): 344–354.

Wocadlo, C. & Rieger, I. (2008) 'Motor impairment and low achievement in very preterm children at eight years of age', *Early Hum Dev,* 84(11): 769–776.

Wolke, D. (1987) 'Environmental neonatology (Annotation)', *Archives Dis Child,* 62: 987–988.

Wolke, D. (1991) 'Annotation: supporting the develop-ment of low birthweight infants', *J Child Psychol Psychiatry,* 32(5): 723–741.

Wolke, D. (1998) 'The psychological development of prematurely born children', *Arch Dis Child,* 78: 567–570.

Wolke, D. (1999) 'Language problems in neonatal at risk children: towards an understanding of developmental mechanisms', *Acta Paediatr,* 88: 488–490.

Wolke, D. & Meyer, R. (1999) 'Cognitive status, language attainment and pre-reading skills of 6-year-old very preterm children and their peers: the Bavarian Longitudinal Study', *Dev Med Child Neurol,* 41: 94–109.

Wolke, D. & Söhne, B. (1997) 'Wenn der Schein trügt: Zur kritischen Interpretation von Entwicklungsstudien. Teil 1: Studienplan, Stichprobenbeschreibung, Probandenverluste und Kontrolgruppen', *Monatsschrift fur Kinderheilkunde,* 145: 444–456.

Wolke, D., Ratschinski, G., Ohrt, B., & Riegel, K. (1994) 'The cognitive outcome of very preterm infants may be poorer than often reported: an empirical investigation of how methodological issues make a big difference', *Eur J Pediatr,* 153: 906–915.

Wolke, D., Söhne, B., Ohrt, B., & Riegel, K. (1995) 'Follow-up of preterm children: important to document dropouts', *Lancet,* 345 (8947): 447.

Wolke, D., Schulz, J., & Meyer, R. (2001a) 'Entwicklungslangzeitfolgen bei ehemaligen, sehr unreifen Frühgeborenen', *Monatsschrift für Kinderheilkunde, (Suppl 1)* 149: S53–S61.

Wolke, D., Samara, M., Bracewell, M., & Marlow, N. (2008) 'Specific language difficulties and school achievement in children born at 25 weeks of gestation or less', *J Pediatr,* 152(2): 256–262.

Wolke, D., Golonka, S., & Gutbrod, T. (submitted) 'Infant characteristics outweigh maternal characteristics in predicting very preterm infants' attachment status at 18 months of age',

Wood, N.S., Costeloe, K., Gibson, A.T., Hennessy, E.M., Marlow, N., & Wilkinson, A.R. (2005) 'The EPICure study: associations and antecedents of neurological and developmental disability at 30 months of age following extremely preterm birth', *Arch Dis Child Fetal Neonatal Ed,* 90(2): F134–140.

Zeitlin, J., Draper, E.S., Kollee, L., Milligan, D., Boerch, K., Agostino, R., et al. (2008) 'Differences in rates and short-term outcome of live births before 32 weeks of gestation in Europe in 2003: results from the MOSAIC cohort', *Pediatrics,* 121(4): e936–944.

Zuckerman, B., Amaro, H., Bauchner, H., & Cabral, H. (1989) 'Depressive symptoms during pregnancy; relationship to poor health behaviors', *Am J Obstet Gynecol,* 160: 1107–1111.

Zwicker, J.G. & Harris, S.R. (2008) 'Quality of life of formerly preterm and very low birthweight infants from preschool age to adulthood: a systematic review', *Pediatrics,* 121: e366–e376.

26

Extreme Deprivation

Michael Rutter & Camilla Azis-Clauson

In contrast to other chapters in this handbook, we face a problem in defining the topic. Thus, what is meant by 'extreme deprivation', and what is meant by syndromes due to such deprivation? In neither case, does the research literature, or indeed the clinical literature, help very much. As the title of the handbook refers to 'developmental disorders', we have mainly focused on research that involves longitudinal data providing evidence on within-individual changes over time. We have assumed that the term 'deprivation' implies the consequences of a lack of relevant experiences, rather than the much broader topic of acute and chronic stresses and adversity. Accordingly, we have excluded from our remit any discussion of syndromes associated with sexual or physical abuse and we have excluded responses to acute stresses whether of an ordinary kind or of an extreme and unusual variety, as incorporated within the concept of post-traumatic stress disorders. We have also assumed that 'deprivation' is meant to refer to deprivation of psychosocial experiences and not malnutrition. We do consider some studies of malnutrition, because any discussion of psychosocial deprivation needs to pay careful attention to the possibility that the sequelae derive from

nutritional lack rather than experiential lack. However, that aside, we do not review the extensive literature on malnourishment. Particularly in recent years there has been a growing literature, and a series of meta-analyses, of inter-country adoption. We make brief reference to these but do not discuss them in detail. That is because inter-country adoption involves a quite heterogeneous range of experiences, many of which cannot sensibly be regarded as involving extreme deprivation. Also, the evidence largely derives from cross-sectional data of one kind or another.

BACKGROUND

What this means is that, of necessity, we have had to turn to just three bodies of research.

First, there is the very small number of individual children rescued after being reared in extremely depriving and impoverished conditions: for example, seclusion and prolonged confinement under extreme physical restraint. Skuse (1984) provided an excellent summary of the evidence on this group about a quarter of a century ago. At the time of the children's discovery and rescue, certain behavioural features were almost ubiquitous: motor retardation, absent or very rudimentary vocal and symbolic language, grossly retarded perceptuo-motor skills, paucity of emotional expression, lack of attachment behaviour, and social withdrawal. Of the nine children considered in detail by Skuse (1984), six children made remarkable progress to achieve functioning in the normal range for language and cognition (although the evidence on social functioning was much more limited). By contrast, three of the nine children showed substantial deficits that persisted over many years. This was most fully documented in the detailed case study of Genie (Curtiss, 1977; see also Rymer, 1993). The findings, however, were not sufficient to allow any conclusions on any kind of pattern or syndrome that might persist long after the children were placed in a normal rearing environment.

Secondly, there is Tizard's small but well-studied sample of children who spent most of their pre-school years in a residential nursery, which provided the best of the early investigations on the outcomes following an institutional rearing. At 2 years, there was clinging and diffuse attachments; at 4 years, attention-seeking and indiscriminately friendly behaviour; and at 8 years, several years after adoption, despite generally good functioning, half the children showed unusual peer relationships (Hodges & Tizard, 1989a, 1989b; Tizard & Hodges, 1978). This half showed at least four out of the following five features:

- adult-oriented relationships
- difficulty in peer relationships
- lacking a special friend
- not turning to peers for emotional support
- lack of selectivity in choosing friends

This pattern was found in only 4% of controls. The importance of these findings is that they referred to children reared in generally well-functioning institutions (apart from the huge turnover in caregivers). Moreover, the children did not show an intellectual disability. This raises the question of which sequelae derive from institutional care and which from global deprivation within institutions.

Since the 1980s, there have been only a handful of other studies, none of which adds greatly to the earlier conclusions. There is also a rather larger literature on groups of children who have suffered gross neglect (Smith & Fong, 2004). We briefly note findings on neglect, but the differentiation between the effects of neglect and the effects of abuse is problematic in many instances. That is evident, for example, in the follow-up studies of severely abused/neglected children showing growth failure (Money et al., 1983a, 1983b). We note the follow-up of children adopted after severe early privation (Colombo et al., 1992; Lien et al., 1977; Winick et al., 1975), but do not discuss them because the findings do not make a clear distinction between the effects of psychosocial deprivation and the effects of malnutrition. Moreover, the samples studied were mainly very small, the relevant data were very sparse and the follow-up was mostly incomplete. The studies are mostly limited, however, by the fact that there are no published data on children's social functioning after severe early privation.

Thirdly, there is the early literature on the later outcome of children who spent part of their life being reared in institutions (see Rutter, 1981, 1991), but conclusions were much constrained by the fact that children had often been admitted to institutions at an age when admission could have been prompted by an awareness of handicap or problematic development. Equally, conclusions were further constrained by the fact that whether the children left the institutions for adoption, or returned to biological families, could have been influenced by their functioning at that time. Accordingly, we do not review that literature. Instead, we focus on the more recent studies of children admitted to institutions in early life in circumstances where adoption or return to families was most unusual.

KEY STUDIES OF SEVERE DEPRIVATION

In considering the epidemiology of syndromes associated with severe deprivation, we have assumed that the focus should be on possible syndromes that persist *after* the deprivation comes to an end (this usually arises as a result of adoption). Accordingly, we place emphasis on studies that provide longitudinal data with an extended follow-up and, because of the focus on possible 'syndromes', we pay most attention to investigations with wide-ranging, multimodal assessments involving direct contact. We note the extent to which the sampling is representative, and without major attrition, relying especially on studies without substantial sampling limitations.

Here we briefly summarize the major studies reviewed.

The British Columbia Canadian study

(Ames, 1997; Chisholm et al., 1995; MaClean, 2003)
This comprised a follow-up of 48 children who had spent 8–53 months in a Romanian institution, 29 children who were adopted before the age of 4 months but who would have gone to an orphanage were it not for early adoption and 46 Canadian-born never-institutionalized children. The sample was not strictly representative but probably it was not subject to systematic biases. Detailed interviews were held with adoptive parents, an attachment Q-sort was undertaken, a modified Ainsworth Strange Situation Procedure (SSP) was used, there was IQ testing, completion of the Child Behavior Checklist (CBCL) and a parenting stress index. Assessments were made at 11-month post-adoption, 3 years later, and again at 9½ years.

The Dutch study of Romanian adoptees

(Hoksbergen et al., 2003, 2004, 2005)

Out of a total of 96 children from Romania adopted into Dutch families between 1990 and 1997, 80 agreed to take part in the study. The children had a mean age of 2 years 10 months upon arrival in the Netherlands. Seventy-four of the families (with 83 children) were extensively interviewed and 72 of these were re-interviewed 2 years later. The assessments included a Dutch autism scale, a semi-structured questionnaire interview, the CBCL, and the Nijmegen Questionnaire for the Upbringing Situation (NQUS).

The English and Romanian Adoptees (ERA)

(Rutter & ERA team, 1998; Rutter & Sonuga-Barke, 2010; Rutter et al., 2001, 2009)
Out of a total group of 165 Romanian adoptees (randomly selected from within cases legally processed by British authorities), there were 144 reared in very depriving institutions, 21 who were severely deprived in family settings, and 52 within-UK adoptees who were placed before the age of 6 months and who had not experienced institutional care. All were seen at 6, 11 and 15 years of age (also at 4 years for the youngest children), with a combination of standardized interviews, observations, and questionnaires, plus a modified SSP, and psychometric assessments. The young peoples' results in the national examinations were obtained at 17–18 years of age, and at 18–20 years there was an assessment of 27 participants with possible deprivation-specific patterns using the Autism Diagnostic Interview-Revised (ADI-R) and the Autism Diagnostic Observation Schedule (ADOS). In addition, a small subgroup of 14 Romanian adoptees from institutions participated in a pilot magnetic resonance imaging (MRI) study.

The Ontario study of Romanian adoptees

(Goldberg, 1997; Marcovitch et al., 1997)

The sample was recruited from a survey of 150 parents adopting from Romania. Eighty-five families expressed interest and 56, who were in commuting distance of the hospital, participated. Thirty-seven children had spent less than 6 months in institutional care (a mean of 27 months). The assessment included a modified version of the SSP, a psychometric assessment, and the CBCL. Although this was not a longitudinal study, it is included here because the assessment included the SSP and cognitive testing.

The Bucharest Early Intervention Project (BEIP)

(Bos et al., 2009; Nelson et al., 2007; Smyke et al., 2010; Zeanah et al., 2003, 2005)
This was a randomized controlled trial (RCT) of foster care in Romania ($n = 68$) vs 'as usual' institutional care ($n = 68$), but it also included a comparison with 72 non-institutionalized children attending paediatric clinics. The broad range of individual assessments included the SSP, a behavioural questionnaire, an observational measure of the caregiving environments, the Bayley Infant Development Scales and the Wechsler Preschool IQ Scales (WPPSI-R), a computerized version of the Cambridge Neuropsychological Test and Automated Battery (CANTAB), electroencephalography (EEG), event-related potentials (ERPs) in response to pictures of emotions and video-taped emotion tasks. Assessments were undertaken at 30, 42 and 52 months following recruitment at 6–31 months.

The St Petersburg–USA study

(Groark et al., 2005; St Petersburg–USA Orphanage Research Team, 2008)
This study was quite different in that it was primarily concerned with institutional change rather than individual development but it is included here because the findings from the former have implications for the latter. A quasi-experimental design was employed

with two interventions and a control condition. The three institutions chosen were selected because they were among the best in the city and showed a willingness to cooperate with the research procedures. The assessments of children included physical growth, a functional abilities index, the Battelle Developmental Inventory (BDI), a modified free play–separation–reunion procedure, an observational parent–child early relational assessment (PCERA), and a rating of infant affect (IAM). Both cross-sectional and longitudinal analyses were undertaken at baseline, after 4–9 months of institutional intervention and at 9+ months.

Minnesota study of inter-country adoptions

(Bruce et al., 2009; Gunnar et al., 2007; Tarullo et al., 2007)
The Minnesota registry of inter-country adoptions has records on 3270 children adopted from outside the USA between 1990 and 1998 who were aged between 4 and 18 at the time of a survey in 2001. Current addresses were obtained for 2969 and parental questionnaires were completed for 1948. The studies based on the registry have the limitation of being based on a volunteer sample from a diverse mixture of countries and without longitudinal data. Nevertheless, they are included here because subsamples were seen individually for a 2½-hour laboratory assessment. One hundred and twenty children aged 6–7 years were assessed, comparing: 40 adopted following institutional rearing; 40 following family-based foster care (both groups having been adopted prior to age 36 months); and 40 non-adopted volunteers. The assessment comprised an observation of the interaction with an unfamiliar adult, a semi-structured parental interview as used in the ERA study, a retrospective report of pre-adoption experiences, two subtests of the WISC, three computerized tasks to assess the children's basic emotion abilities, two computerized tasks to assess inhibitory

control and two delay of gratification tasks also to assess inhibitory control. The same groups were also used to assess false belief and emotion understanding.

The Dutch Registry study of international adoptees

(Tieman et al., 2005, 2006; van der Vegt, 2009a, 2009b; Verhulst & Versluis-den Bieman, 1995; Verhulst et al., 1990)

Like the Minnesota study, this study has the limitation of being based on a register of inter-country adoptees from a diverse mixture of countries. Information on pre-adoption experiences was obtained from a retrospective questionnaire. The only measure of the young people's behaviour was the CBCL, but a computerized version of the Composite International Diagnostic Interview (CIDI) was used for the adult follow-up. Nevertheless, the study is included here because it included longitudinal data extending into adult life. The initial sample consisted of children legally adopted in the Netherlands from other countries between 1972 and 1975. Of the 3309 parents who could be reached, 2148 participated at baseline (but only 1984 with information on early adversities), 1417 participated at time 2 (when aged 12–15 years) and 1023 at time 3 (when adult).

The Greek prospective study of adoptees from one institution (Metera)

(Vorria et al., 2003, 2006)

The only study to investigate the links between attachment behaviours in institutions and postadoption attachment was undertaken by Vorria et al. (2003). The sample was composed of children initially cared for in the Greek Metera Babies Centre and then adopted from that institution at a mean age of 20 months (range 11–41 months). The comparison group consisted of similar-aged children attending a day centre in the

same city (Athens). The children were followed-up at a mean age of 50 months, some 28 months after adoption. The initial measures included the Early Childhood Environment Rating Scale (ECERS), the SSP, Bayley Scales of Infant Cognitive Development and Colorado Children's Temperament Inventory (CCTI) and the follow-up used similar measures except that attachment was assessed using an attachment Q-Sort. Cognitive level was measured using the McCarthy Scales and the British Picture Vocabulary Scale (BPVS). In addition, height and weight were measured, a puppet scenario was used to assess children's understanding of language and the Strengths and Difficulties Scales (SDQ) was used to assess emotional and behavioural difficulties.

CONCEPT OF EXTREME DEPRIVATION SYNDROME

Before considering epidemiology, we need to consider the concept of a severe deprivation syndrome. This cannot be equated with all the psychopathology found in children experiencing institutional deprivation because not all of it will have been caused by the deprivation. It requires both comparison with other groups and criteria by which to assess the specificity of the patterns found. The only study to make this a central focus was the ERA study (Rutter & Sonuga-Barke, 2010; Rutter et al., 2009). Seven operational criteria were imposed: first, presence at age 6 years or earlier; second, a pattern that was clearly distinctive and different from common emotional and behavioural disturbances; third, that the pattern was much more common in children whose institutional deprivation lasted to when the children were aged 6 months or older; fourth, that the deprivation-specific-pattern (DSP) must be rare in groups of children who had not experienced institutional deprivation; fifth, that the postulated DSP should persist to age 11 and should continue to have a strong association with institutional deprivation; sixth, that the pattern must be accompanied by substantial functional impairment; and, finally, that the postulated DSP should be a consequence of psychosocial deprivation even when it was not accompanied by subnutrition.

The findings at age 11 years suggested that four patterns might fulfil these criteria: quasi-autism (Rutter et al., 1999, 2007b); disinhibited attachment (Rutter et al., 2007a); cognitive impairment (Beckett et al., 2006); and inattention/overactivity (Kreppner et al., 2001; Sonuga-Barke & Rubia, 2008; Stevens et al., 2008). Quasi-autism was also reported by Hoksbergen et al. (2005) in 16% of Romanian adoptees from institutions. Possibly, the designation might have applied to Genie who suffered extreme pervasive deprivation in her own home (Curtiss, 1977), but otherwise it has not been reported in children from less depriving institutions or in those suffering abuse or neglect. Disinhibited attachment has been reported in all the studies of children adopted from depriving institutions that have used measures to assess its presence. These include the two Canadian studies (Chisholm, 1998; MacLean, 2003; Marcovitch et al., 1997); the Minnesota study (Bruce et al., 2009); the Greek study (Vorria et al., 2003) and the BEIP study (Smyke et al., 2010; Zeanah et al., 2005). Ghera et al. (2009), in the same BEIP study, showed that the children who received foster care showed higher levels of attention and positive affect compared to children who remained in the institution. The main query is that this is a pattern that seems to be associated with institutional rearing that is not globally depriving other than in the multiplicity of rotating caregivers (see, for example, Tizard & Rees, 1974). By contrast, as also shown by the Tizard study (Hodges & Tizard 1989a), significant cognitive impairment is not a usual consequence of non-depriving institutional rearing. It is, on the other hand, a very common consequence of institutional deprivation as shown by all the relevant studies (e.g. Behen et al., 2008; Morison & Ellwood, 2000; Morison et al., 1995; Nelson et al., 2007;

Vorria et al., 2003). Inattention/overactivity has been less systematically assessed but it has been noted in several studies of children adopted following institutional deprivation (Chisholm, 1998; Gunnar et al., 2007; MacLean, 2003; Miller et al., 2009).

It would have been helpful if there was something distinctive about these four patterns when they resulted from institutional deprivation as compared with their occurrence in other circumstances but, unfortunately, that did not prove to be the case—at least not to an extent that was applicable at the individual diagnostic level. Quasi-autism is particularly characterized by intense circumscribed interests and a lack of social reciprocity; it differs from 'ordinary' autism, primarily, in terms of a greater degree of social approach, a greater communicative flexibility and a tendency for the autistic features to reduce in intensity by the age of 6 years. Disinhibited attachment is characterized by a limited awareness of social boundaries and social cues, by physical and social intrusiveness, a tendency to go off with strangers and by little social anxiety. Unlike the occurrence of these features in other circumstances, it shows a marked persistence up to age 11 years. Cognitive impairments may be either general or specific, but they do not form a single recognizable pattern. Inattention/overactivity looks similar to attention-deficit hyperactivity/disorder (ADHD) in many respects but probably it is more influenced by the social situation.

These findings provide the basis for a case that the four features might be part of a severe deprivation 'syndrome' but further questions have to be addressed. To begin with, all the research has shown that, although there is overlap among the four patterns, most children who have experienced institutional deprivation do not show all four. Accordingly, there have to be further criteria to specify what is needed to constitute a syndrome. The ERA team noted that quasi-autism and disinhibited attachment were the two patterns that were most specifically related to institutional deprivation. Accordingly, with respect to cognitive impairment and inattention/overactivity, these were included in the postulated syndrome only if they were accompanied by at least one of the two 'core' features of quasi-autism and disinhibited attachment. The need for some requirement of this kind was that both cognitive impairment and inattention/overactivity are quite common in children who have never experienced institutional deprivation.

A key issue from the outset was whether the institutional sequelae applied when the institutional deprivation was restricted to early infancy. The Canadian studies showed no measurable effects below the age of 4 months and the ERA study found the same with a cut-off of 6 months. Accordingly, it may be concluded that for the syndrome to be present, institutional deprivation usually has to last to at least the age of 6 months.

A further issue concerns the need to check that the sequelae truly derive from the institutional deprivation and not from some other risk feature. Exposure to high maternal alcohol during the pregnancy constitutes the most prevalent pre-institution factor and most of the studies have taken care to exclude children where this was likely to be the case. With respect to the period of institutional care, the key non-psychosocial hazard is subnutrition. The ERA study was the only one to test this possibility systematically (Sonuga-Barke et al., 2008), but their findings showed that the four features mentioned above were present even in children who did not show evidence of subnutrition (at least, not as indexed by body weight).

The ERA study was again the only one to test the extent to which these four features taken together constituted a cohesive syndrome. The question was tackled in several different ways, including the overlap among the four as compared with the overlap with other emotional conduct disturbances, whether the overlap when the young people were older increased over that found when younger and whether the association with institutional deprivation persisted to at least age 15 years. Although none of these tests established a coherent syndrome, all suggested that the commonality among the four features was sufficiently strong to indicate the likelihood of a meaningful syndrome.

One final question regarding all four features was where the cut-off should be made. In other words, did the institutional deprivation lead to milder varieties of the same qualitative kind? The evidence suggested that it did but that, in setting possible diagnostic criteria, a conservative approach (i.e. a high cut-off) was probably safest. We return to this issue in considering epidemiology.

DIAGNOSTIC CRITERIA

The relevant clinical picture is as already noted: namely, an admixture of quasi-autistic features—disinhibited attachment, specific or general cognitive impairment and inattention/overactivity—in which the mixture includes at least one of the first two of these patterns. The assumption is that the syndrome is one that persists long after the extreme deprivation comes to an end, and which is associated with functional impairment. It follows that the diagnosis is possible only after a detailed clinical assessment using measures that tap the four key features. The ERA study used the ADI-R (Rutter et al., 2003b) and the ADOS (Lord et al., 2001) to assess autistic features, but the Social Communication Questionnaire (SCQ, Rutter et al., 2003a) which covers similar ground, would be a reasonable alternative.

Disinhibited attachment

Disinhibited attachment requires the use of an appropriate parental interview plus observational measures of interaction with strangers (see, e.g., Bruce et al., 2009; Rutter & Sonuga-Barke, 2010; Rutter et al., 2007a; Zeanah et al., 2005). It might be thought that the Ainsworth Strange Situation Procedure, as the 'gold standard' measure of security/insecurity, would be appropriate, but it is not. The concept of disinhibited attachment is of impaired development of selective attachments and not of insecurity in well-established attachments (Rutter, Kreppner & Sonuga-Barke, 2009a; Rutter, Beckett, Castle, et al., 2009b; Kreppner, Rutter, Marvin, O'Connor & Sonuga-Barke, 2010). Moreover, all studies that have examined the matter have found weak agreement between SSP ratings and measures of disinhibited attachment (Chisholm et al., 1995; Marcovitch et al., 1997; O'Connor & Zeanah, 2003; Rutter et al., 2009a&b; Smyke et al., 2010; Zeanah et al., 2005). The concept of reactive attachment disorder (American Psychiatric Association, 1994) is unhelpful because the inhibited variety functions quite differently from the disinhibited variety (Chisholm et al., 1995; O'Connor & Zeanah, 2003; Marcovitch et al., 1997; Rutter et al., 2009a&b; Smyke et al., 2010; Zeanah et al., 2005).

Cognitive impairment

Cognitive impairment obviously requires some age-appropriate psychometric test. It would be helpful if a specific cognitive pattern was diagnostic but, unfortunately, it is not (see section below on cognitive functions). The assessment of inattention/overactivity requires both a suitable parental interview and appropriate observational measures (see Taylor & Sonuga-Barke, 2008, for discussion).

It is important to rule out the possibility of a fetal alcohol syndrome (FAS)—see Chapter 24 for more details—as this could give rise to at least some of the features. The congenital stigmata found in the full FAS are diagnostic, and standardized photo measures are available (Astley et al., 2002). However, it is known that FAS operates as a spectrum in which milder varieties do not necessarily show the stigmata and there are no generally accepted ways of making the FAS spectrum diagnosis (see Gray et al., 2009).

Obviously, a history of severe deprivation is essential. This is straightforward when the child was adopted from a severely depriving institution, such as those in Romania, but it is less straightforward when the institution was in some other country such as China or Russia (see Selman, 2009) where the institutions share many of the characteristics of those in Romania but usually without the same degree of profound deprivation.

Nevertheless, there are two cross-sectional studies that suggest there may be some commonalities. Sloutsky (1997) compared 52 children aged 20–88 months living in two orphanages in Moscow with similar-aged children living with their own families. The orphanage children had a mean IQ of 86, some 21 points below the mean of 107 for the comparison group. The orphanage children were also significantly worse in identifying emotions. These differences are much less than those found in Romania (see causative factors section below) but the big difference in sampling was that most Romanian children were admitted in early infancy, whereas in the Russian sample the mean age at admission was 27 months.

Judge (2003) studied a volunteer sample of 124 children adopted from Eastern Europe. The children had been adopted at a mean age of 20 months (range 4–57 months) and had been in their adoptive homes for some 6 months at the time of study. At the time of adoption about half the children had heights or weights below the 5th percentile and, as assessed through a retrospective questionnaire, 60% were delayed in one or more areas of development. After 6 months, only 24% had no delays in development. Delays were more common in children adopted when older but the initial weight/height was unrelated to the developmental delays after 6 months, despite the association between duration of institutional care and initial height and weight.

The history is most problematic when based only on retrospective parental judgements. In our view, these are not satisfactory. It is not so much that they rely on retrospection but rather that the retrospection is from a time point when the child's outcome is known (thus introducing the possibility of bias), and that in many instances the adoptive parents will have had very little contemporaneous opportunity to observe pre-adoption rearing conditions.

EPIDEMIOLOGY

The incidence of syndromes attributable to extreme deprivation needs to be considered in two rather different ways. First, what is the incidence of deprivation-specific syndromes in individuals known to have suffered profound institutional deprivation prior to adoption? The ERA study is the only one with systematic data on this point. The findings showed that, of children adopted from Romanian institutions, at least half showed a deprivation-specific syndrome when the deprivation lasted until the children were aged at least 6 months. Because other studies did not assess the relevant range of four features, no comparable figure for incidence is possible but it is clear from the findings on disinhibited attachment and on cognitive impairment that the incidence is likely to be in the same general range. Viewed in population terms, this translates to over 6000 children worldwide adopted from Romania (in the great majority of cases from institutions) (Selman, 2009). The numbers adopted in the UK from institutions with profound deprivation are much lower, in line with the much lower overall rate of inter-country adoptions. Because information is not available on the institutional conditions in the sending countries, no overall incidence rate of children in the UK experiencing extreme institutional deprivation is possible.

The next question is whether comparable syndromes arise in children exposed to better-quality institutional rearing. The Hodges and Tizard (1989b) findings showed that, in a rather small sample, about half of those adopted from residential nurseries showed unusual peer relationships of a kind associated with disinhibited attachment. However,

although not systematically assessed, quasi-autistic features were not reported and intellectual levels were only very slightly reduced. We can only conclude that there are too few data to allow any firm conclusions.

Even less is known about the patterns found in children exposed to neglect or abuse in family settings (Jones, 2008; Smith & Fong, 2004). The findings certainly indicate a high rate of attachment disorders, of cognitive impairment and of hyperactivity, but autistic-like features have not been noted. Both the research literature and clinical experience suggest that there are some (but only some) elements that appear similar to those found in extreme institutional deprivation. No overall conclusions on incidence are possible and the main message is the urgent need for systematic research comparing the outcomes following different forms of depriving or abusive experiences.

CAUSATIVE FACTORS

Numerous observers have documented the appalling conditions in Romanian institutions (see e.g. Ames, 1990; Castle et al., 1999). Children were largely confined to their cots (or beds with sides up), placed in crowded conditions with 30 or so to a room, few staff and very little caregiver and child interaction or talk, few if any toys or playthings, feeding of gruel by a propped-up bottle with a large-holed teat, and washing by being hosed down with cold water. Moreover, studies comparing children in institutions with those in the community have consistently shown that the former show more cognitive impairments and behavioural problems (see e.g., Kaler & Freeman, 1994; Nelson et al., 2007; St Petersburg–USA Orphanage Research Team, 2008). This has also been found with children reared in somewhat better institutions (e.g. Roy & Rutter, 2005; Roy et al., 2004; Vorria et al., 2003). A meta-analysis (van Ijzendoorn et al., 2008) concluded that children being reared in an institution had a mean IQ of 84, some 20 points below those being reared in foster families. However, a very diverse range of studies was included in the meta-analysis, including many children admitted beyond infancy. The mean IQ of 84 was far higher than that found in Romanian institutions. Causation cannot necessarily be inferred because of both prenatal damage or genetic disadvantage and major postnatal health problems (Johnson et al., 1992), as well as queries about possible selective biases with respect to admissions to institutions.

There are two key tests of the causative inference: (1) the effects of improving institutional conditions, and (2) the effects of leaving institutional care to enter adoptive or foster families. The former is best represented by the St Petersburg–USA orphanage study (2008) where the two experimental conditions resulted in a gain of 27–45 developmental quotient points. The latter is best represented by the Bucharest Early Intervention Project (BEIP, Nelson et al., 2007) which showed that placement in foster homes (as part of an RCT) resulted in cognitive gains and improvements in attachment functioning (Smyke et al., 2010). The ERA study (Beckett et al., 2006) similarly showed a major cognitive catch-up following adoption at age over 6 months—from a mean DQ of 43 at the time of leaving institutional care to a mean IQ of 85 at age 11. The Greek study (dealing with a much less deprived institution) similarly showed post-adoption cognitive gains (Vorria et al., 2003, 2006) from a mean Bayley Score of 93 to a McCarthy IQ of 100. It may be concluded, therefore, that the initial impairments and problems of children at the time of leaving institutional care were truly caused by the experience of institutional deprivation.

All longitudinal studies, however, have also shown that the dramatic catch-ups during the first 2 years or so after adoption are often incomplete. Both cognitive deficits and behavioural problems of an unusual kind have been found in about half the children who experienced profound institutional deprivation (see section above on concept of extreme deprivation syndrome). Testing the causal inference with respect to these enduring impairments needs to be accomplished by determining whether the impairments are consistently associated with institutional deprivation and are *not* associated with variations in the qualities of the adoptive homes. The ERA study (Rutter & Sonuga-Barke, 2010) showed that the association between institutional care lasting to at least the age of 6 months and the postulated deprivation-specific features was as strong at the age of 15 years as it had been at 11 and 6 years of age. This strongly pointed to the validity of a causal influence. Nevertheless, it was necessary to go on to check that the findings were not an artefact of either parental selection of children or the occurrence of subnutrition. Both these further tests supported the causal inference. The enduring deficits applied to children with nutrition levels (as indexed by body weight) in the normal range. The conclusion is that it was psychosocial deprivation that had the deleterious effects on outcome at 15 years. Other studies have similarly shown differences between the early and late adoption of institution-reared children in Romania. The British Columbia study (MacLean, 2003) found at age 9½ years that, as compared with non-adopted Canadian children who had a mean IQ of 89, those adopted after 2 years had a mean IQ of 71. It should be noted, however, that unlike the ERA study (Rutter & Sonuga-Barke, 2010) there was said to be a significant effect of the adoptive home environment on IQ (Morison & Elwood, 2000; Morison et al., 1995). The meaning, however, of this claim is called in doubt by the fact that the home environment was assessed at follow-up, leaving the strong possibility that the association reflected the effect of the child on the home, rather than the other way round. It would be highly desirable to go on to specify *which* aspect of psychosocial deprivation did the damage, but no study provides adequate information on this point.

One further question is whether the behavioural problems are simply a function of cognitive impairment. The evidence overall indicates that they are not (MacLean, 2003; Rutter & Sonuga-Barke, 2010). Because of both prior theorizing and the findings of enduring effects of institutional deprivation, commentators have sometimes assumed that there is a sensitive period beyond which normal psychological development is unlikely. However, as Ames and Chisholm (2001) pointed out, the sensitive period postulate requires comparison with the effects of extreme deprivation at other ages and few such data are available. Wolkind (1974) found that indiscriminate friendliness was mainly found in institutional children admitted under the age of 2 years and was rare in those admitted when older, but his findings were confined to the children's behaviour in the institution and not post-adoption.

Sensitive periods

The sensitive period suggestion needs to be considered with respect to two different findings. First, can the extreme deprivation behavioural pattern arise in children admitted to institutions after the age of, say, 2 or 3 years? No satisfactory study provides an answer, and there would be the need to check on possible selective influences. It is noteworthy that descriptive studies have not reported autistic-like features in children admitted to institutions when older, and disinhibited attachment has also not been prominent. As both are early-appearing features, it may well be that they would not be found (other than rarely) in children admitted to an institution when older, following normal rearing in a family for the first few years. It is less self-evident that the same would apply to either cognitive impairment or inattention/overactivity.

The sensitive period possibility also needs to be considered in relation to the observation that children adopted when young rarely show deprivation-specific features (as found in all the longitudinal studies although the age cut-off has varied between 4 months and 2 years). The query is whether this sparing is a function

of the age when institutional deprivation ceases or, rather, the overall duration of the deprivation? Thus, for example, would there be a similar sparing in the case of children admitted to institutions at, say, age 1 or 2 years (i.e. within the other postulated sensory period) but then with adoption following after just 6 months? No data address this point. Whereas it is clear that the extreme deprivation pattern is a feature of institutional deprivation in early life, it is not known whether this reflects a sensory period as ordinarily understood.

Natural experiments

One of the major advantages of the adoptions from Romania following the fall of Ceaucescu's regime is that it constituted a true 'natural experiment' (Rutter et al., 2007b). It did so because:

- adoption constituted a major discontinuity from the institutional care in rearing conditions
- the timing of the transition could be accurately timed
- the children had been admitted into institutions in infancy (so largely obviating concerns regarding the impact of pre-institutional care)
- prior to the fall of the regime, few (if any) children had been adopted or returned to their biological families (so reducing the possibilities of selective bias)

Nevertheless, a range of further checks were needed to test the natural experiment assumptions. The only study to do this systematically was the ERA study (Rutter & Sonuga-Barke, 2010), but their findings provided strong support for the causation inference, particularly when combined with the strength of a design that used representative sampling and focused on within-individual change over time, as well as between-group comparisons, and with a long-term follow-up that involved very little attrition.

Heterogeneity in response

All of the studies have shown a marked heterogeneity in children's responses to institutional deprivation—indicating that the effects have to be viewed as probabilistic rather than determinative. So far there are only a few leads on the factors that account for resilience in the face of profound deprivation (see Rutter & Sonuga-Barke, 2010). Genetic influences appear to play some role, and the presence of even minimal language appears to be a protective factor in relation to cognitive, but not social, adverse outcomes. Variations in the qualities of the adoptive home had little impact in the ERA study but the British Columbia study showed some effects.

COGNITIVE FUNCTIONS

On the basis of a meta-analysis of cross-sectional data of a heterogeneous group of studies of inter-country adoption, van Ijzendoorn and Juffer (2006) concluded that, following adoption, there was a complete catch-up in IQ but that scholastic achievement tended to lag behind. Longitudinal findings contradict both claims insofar as they are applied to children who have experienced extreme institutional deprivation.

Moreover, reporting a volunteer sample of 54 institutional adoptees from Eastern Europe, whose global intellectual functioning was within normal limits, Behen et al. (2008) found that, using a broad range of specific cognitive tests, 46% showed impairment in at least one domain. Because there was no comparison group, it remains unknown whether this rate was greater than general population norms. Nevertheless, there was a significant association between specific impairments and duration of institutional care. Of those with under 6 months of institutional care, 25% showed impairment on at least one test; of these with 13–20 months, care, 53% showed impairment, and of those with more than 3 years' institutional care, 88% showed impairment. The meaning of these figures, however, is put in doubt by the fact that they are based on an enlarged sample of 85 that included 31 children with a global intellectual

impairment. It is notable that, although there were multiple domains of specific patterns, they did not constitute a particular pattern.

Specific issues regarding cognition

In turning to the findings from longitudinal studies, we focus on these key questions: Are there persisting cognitive deficits? Do they follow a consistent pattern? And does scholastic achievement function differently from general cognitive level? Pollak et al. (2010), having excluded children with photographic evidence of the foetal alcohol syndrome (FAS) or an IQ below 78, used the Minnesota and Wisconsin international adoption registry to study volunteer samples of 40 early (below 8 months) adopted children (mainly following family foster care) and a post-institutional (PI) group of 48 adopted after the age of 12 months (a mean of 23 months, with a range from 12 to 78 months) and 44 controls reared by their biological parents. Neuropsychological functioning was assessed on the CANTAB and the NEPSY (a developmental neuropsychological assessment) battery. Between-group differences were found for tests of memory, attention and learning. Findings showed that the PI children were impaired on visual memory tests but not on auditory memory. The finding is provocative but needs replication.

Bos et al. (2009) used the BEIP RCT sample (Nelson et al., 2007) to study memory and executive functioning, using the CANTAB. Impairments on memory and executive functions were found for the institutional group. Comparisons showed no beneficial effects following foster care. The implication is that cognitive impairments following institutional deprivation tend to persist.

Tarullo et al. (2007), using the Minnesota register of volunteers compared 40 children from a diverse range of countries (China, and then Russia, contributing the most) who experienced institutional care (IC), 40 adopted after foster care (FC) (almost all from Korea) and 40 birth children (BC). Among the IC children, 43% failed both trials of a (theory of mind-ToM) false belief task, as compared with 30% of the FC children and 15% of the BC group. This difference held even after taking verbal skills into account. The groups were generally similar, however, on their emotional identification (using a computerized task with Ekman faces).

The ERA study (Beckett et al., 2006: Rutter & Sonuga-Barke, 2010) employed less extensive neuropsychological testing but provided the most systematic investigation relevant to the three questions posed above. Along with all the longitudinal studies, the findings showed that there were significant (albeit small) cognitive deficits that persisted to age 15 years. There had been substantial cognitive catch-up earlier, and at 15 years (as at younger ages) there was also considerable heterogeneity, with some individuals achieving superior scores. It should be added that these findings apply to children reared in profoundly depriving Romanian institutions and not to inter-country adoptees generally, or even those reared in institutions with somewhat better conditions.

The ERA study findings also showed that all cognitive skills tended to be impaired. These included tests of ToM and executive planning as well as standard IQ tests. Also, the institution-reared individuals did not show a rate of verbal–performance discrepancies that exceeded those in the comparison group. At an individual level, there were certainly some children with marked discrepancies, but these were not consistent in direction, and the rate in the comparison group was also quite high (as would be expected from the standardization data for the WISC test). Scholastic achievement showed an overall impairment in the institution-reared group but, when this was examined using a regression equation prediction using the general cognitive score at age 6, the achievements did not differ from those predicted on the basis of IQ. This is at variance with what was reported on a meta-analysis of cross-sectional data (van Ijzendoorn et al., 2008). The findings constitute a reminder of the problems of estimating within-individual change in the absence of longitudinal data.

EMOTIONAL AND BEHAVIOURAL DISTURBANCES

The parental CBCL has been used in many studies, mostly cross-sectional postal surveys of volunteer samples from a mixture of countries where there was institutional care. As Gunnar et al. (2007) commented, this is not an ideal approach. There is a need to employ more fine-grained and objective measures of behaviour, to use representative rather than volunteer samples and, especially, to employ longitudinal designs. Nevertheless, Gunnar et al.'s(2007) use of the Minnesota register represents one of the best of the CBCL investigations. The findings highlighted the lack of differences between post-institutional (PI) children and a comparison (CO) group on either emotional disturbances or disruptive behaviour (with scores in the clinical range). By contrast, PI did differ on attention, thought and social problems when the children were at least 2 years of age at adoption. The findings from the Dutch study (Hoksbergen et al., 2003, 2004) were similar but also showed that, as assessed on a questionnaire, 20% of the Romanian adoptees had post-traumatic stress disorder (PTSD) features.

The ERA study used longitudinal data to test whether such emotional and behavioural problems, as did occur, arose on the basis of prior deprivation-specific patterns (DSP) (quasi-autism, disinhibited attachment, inattention/overactivity and cognitive impairment). The findings showed that they did. Accordingly, the co-occurrence is best regarded as part of DSP and not as comorbidity.

BIOLOGICAL EFFECTS OF EXTREME DEPRIVATION

The ERA study (Rutter & Sonuga-Barke, 2010; Sonuga-Barke et al., 2008) was the first to show that psychosocial deprivation in the absence of subnutrition was associated with a marked reduction in head size once the deprivation lasted at least 6 months. This pattern was different from that found when there was subnutrition, when the reduction in head size was found before 6 months as part of a more general impairment in body growth. Other research has shown head size is strongly related to brain size (because it is brain size the primarily drives head growth).

Cross-sectional data (van Ijzendoorn et al., 2007) implied that the catch-up in head growth lagged behind that in height and weight, and that was confirmed in the ERA longitudinal data. There was still continuing catch-up in head growth between 11 and 15 years but, even at 15, the head circumference of institution-reared Romanian adoptees was significantly, and substantially, smaller than that in the comparison group.

Previous research had shown that international adoptees tended to reach puberty unusually early, with consequent short final height (Mason et al., 2000; Posner, 2006; Tuvemo & Proos, 1993; Tuvemo et al.,1999; Virdis et al., 1998). The findings are clearer for girls than for boys. These earlier studies did not explicitly focus on those experiencing institutional deprivation, but the ERA study data showed that the early puberty was particularly associated with such deprivation. The findings also showed that the early catch-up in height and weight seen at 6 and 11 years was followed by a reduced final height at 15. The findings suggested that this was probably a result of the earlier puberty which led to the usual growth spurt seen in puberty but, because the puberty was early, it was followed by an earlier curtailing of further growth.

Brain imaging

A pilot MRI study within ERA showed that the association similarly applied within the Romanian adoptees (Spearman's $\rho = 0.62$). It might be assumed that the impaired brain growth (as indexed by head size) would play a major role in mediating psychological sequelae. In the event, partial mediation was found but it was very partial—perhaps because overall brain size constitutes a very crude index of relevant neural functioning.

The MRI study also showed that institutional children had greater amygdala volumes but there were no differences in hippocampal volume or corpus callosum mid-sagittal area. The findings suggest the likely importance of the amygdala in response to institutional deprivation, but a much larger study is required to examine the matter further. The need for this is underlined by only partially consistent findings in both humans (Tottenham et al., 2010) and animals (Spinelli et al., 2009).

An early brain imaging study of 10 children with an average age of 8 years, using positron emission tomography (PET), showed significantly reduced brain metabolism in select regions of the prefrontal cortex and various other regions associated with higher cognitive functions (Chugani et al., 2001). The sample was a convenient one, the numbers were small, and because PET uses a radioactive isotope, it is doubtful whether, as children were the subjects, the investigation would have received ethical approval in the UK. In any case, the meaning of the findings remains uncertain because of the lack of information on psychological correlates. More recently, the same research group (Eluvathingal et al., 2006) found that white matter connectivity was diminished in the uncinate fasciculus region of the brain; again, the meaning of these findings for psychological functioning remains unknown.

The BEIP study (Marshall et al., 2004, 2008; Moulson et al., 2009a, 2009b; Nelson, 2007; Parker & Nelson, 2005a, 2005b) used both EEG and ERP to assess cortical activity. The EEG findings showed a lower level of cortical activity in the institutionalized children and the ERP findings showed reduced responses to pictures of faces and of facial emotions (although institutional deprivation did not impair the discrimination of emotions). Foster care provision had a modest effect in improving the cortical function but, surprisingly, there was no variation according to the children's age when foster care commenced. In the most recent study it was found that institutionalized children showed pervasive cortical hypoarousal in response to faces of caregivers and strangers and that this deficit was ameliorated in the foster care group by 42 months of age (Moulson et al., 2009a, 2009b). There was also notable similarity between neural processing of familiar and unfamiliar faces between all the groups of children.

HPA axis

There is a large human and animal literature on the effects of stress and adversity on the hypothalamic–pituitary–adrenal (HPA) axis and its neuroactive peptides and hormones (see Gunnar & Fisher, 2006; Gunnar & Vazquez, 2006; Levine, 2005; Loman & Gunnar, 2010; Marshall & Kenny, 2009). There are many complexities in the functioning of the HPA system (see Joëls & Baram, 2009) and it would be a highly misleading oversimplification to reduce it to just cortisol levels. Nevertheless, the great majority of human studies have been solely concerned with measuring cortisol; ordinarily, there is a marked diurnal variation, with levels at a peak shortly after waking and then gradually reducing as the day proceeds. Also, there is a sharp rise after any marked stress. An early study of children living in a depriving institution (Carlson & Earls, 1997) showed that they tended to have an anomalous pattern, with low morning cortisol and a rather flat diurnal pattern. Accordingly, it came to be assumed that chronic stress may result in *hypocortisolism* (Fries et al., 2005; Gunnar & Vazquez, 2006). On the other hand, marked stress can result in *hypercortisolism* and *hyperresponsivity* to stress, with consequent damaging effects on neural function.

Several key issues emerge from a rather contradictory literature. First, it cannot be assumed that the effects of neglect and of abuse are the same (see e.g. Bruce et al., 2009). Possibly, neglect is most likely to lead to hypocortisolism. Second, responsivity to stress may vary with what is relevant to the individual child. Thus, in a study of institution-reared adoptees, Fries et al. (2008) found that post-institutionalized children had a prolonged elevation in cortisol following interactions with the mother but not with a stranger. Third, there is uncertainty over the extent to which the anomalous cortisol patterns persist after institutional deprivation comes to an end. van der Vegt et al. (2009a) reported that they did persist, whereas Kertes et al. (2008) found that they did not. Both studies relied on adoptive parent reports, of uncertain reliability, on the degree of deprivation. Fourth, there are age-related differences in the effects of acute and chronic stress on the brain (see, e.g., Lupien et al., 2009). Fifth, although there is no doubt that HPA axis effects *could* mediate adverse psychological outcomes following institutional deprivation, it is not known whether they do.

LIFETIME COURSE AND INTERVENTIONS

Only the Dutch questionnaire study (Tieman et al., 2006; van der Vegt et al., 2009a, 2009b) and the much more extensive and detailed ERA study (Rutter & Sonuga-Barke, 2010) have data on adult outcome. The Dutch study suffers from substantial attrition and reliance on a retrospective report from adoptive parents with respect to deprivation but, like the ERA study, it showed that, as judged by the CBCL, the association between problem-level scores and institutional deprivation remained strong over two decades. Nevertheless, the enduring deprivation effect did not necessarily mean that there were no changes for the better. Thus, the overall level of psychopathology tended to fall during the 1920s (van der Vegt et al., 2009b) and social and educational functioning was generally quite good (Tieman et al., 2006).

The ERA study (Rutter & Sonuga-Barke, 2010) found that the effects of institutional deprivation (as judged by the difference from the comparison group) were as great at 15 years of age as they had been at 6 and 11 years. Moreover, the deprivation-specific features not only persisted to age 15 but also were associated with substantial service usage. Despite this, the general tendency was one of gradual improvement over the years accompanied, in a substantial proportion of cases, by notable achievements and successes.

The implication would seem to be that there ought to be an opportunity for preventive and therapeutic interventions (Rutter et al., 2009). The major gains all round following adoption clearly indicate that coming out of a depriving institution in order to be reared in generally well-functioning families brings huge benefits (see Juffer & van Ijzendoorn, 2009; Rutter & Sonuga-Barke, 2010). These gains are greatest if the adoption is early rather than late, but even later adoptions bring worthwhile developmental gains. The BEIP study (Nelson et al., 2007) showed that there were similar (although lesser) benefits from foster care. Even when children remain in institutions, improvements in conditions bring major gains for the children, as shown by the St Petersburg–USA Orphanage Research Team (2008) study, confirming earlier less satisfactory studies (Bakermans-Kranenburg et al., 2008). Nevertheless, questions remain on the extent to which the gains include good intimate social functioning (Rutter, 2008a).

Future challenges

Three major challenges remain.

1. What should be done to improve institutional care when its use is necessary? There are serious concerns, even in industrialized nations, arising from too frequent examples of abuse and neglect (see Utting, 1991). A major part of the problem lies in the tendency to still have a task-based, rather than individual-based, approach to care in institutions. The St Petersburg study showed that this need not be the case. In addition, the situation is aggravated by the low salaries provided for care staff. Childcare is simply not seen as being important enough to warrant good pay and conditions.

2. There is the challenge of phasing out a reliance on institutional care to deal with parenting problems in countries (such as in Eastern Europe) that have had such a reliance (Rutter et al., 2009). To resolve this requires political and economic solutions but these have to be accompanied by a realization among policymakers that there are effective alternatives to institutionalization.

3. There are the challenges in providing effective interventions to foster the social development of children adopted from depriving institutions. Because a key element in the sequelae of institutional deprivation seems to be disinhibited attachment, it might be thought that some form of 'attachment therapy' might constitute the answer. Unfortunately, some of these therapies appear not to derive from the usually understood tenets of attachment theory and a few, such as some varieties of 'holding therapy', carry real risks and have occasionally led to deaths (Barrett, 2006; O'Connor & Zeanah, 2003). Nevertheless, there are intervention approaches focusing on caregiver–child interactions for which there is some evidence of benefit (see Berlin et al., 2008; Fisher et al., 2006; Rutter, 2008b).

CONCLUSION

Studies of children adopted after experiencing profound institutional deprivation have produced many findings that have opened up new areas of science, as well as having important clinical and policy implications. The demonstration of enduring effects lasting at least a decade after adoption show that the usual assumption that environmental effects tend to be transient is wrong in this case. This raises the question of what changes in the organism underpin this remarkably persistent effect. Researchers need to consider how environments 'get under the skin'. The possibilities are diverse—including epigenetic effects (see Meaney, 2010), biological programming and a range of mental mechanisms. Up to now this has been a largely uncharted territory and it is crucial that psychosocial researchers take on the biological challenges. A further issue concerns the findings of the continued head (and presumably) brain growth even up to age 15. What neural processes are responsible? More detailed, and varied, brain imaging research is needed to find out.

One very surprising finding has been the unusual nature of the deprivation-specific features. Very few of the studies used methods that allowed these to be detected and it should be a priority to seek to confirm (or disconfirm) the ERA findings regarding these features. Much of the literature focuses exclusively on attachment disorders and it is evident that a rethink is needed on their nature. All the evidence indicates that institutional deprivation does *not* particularly result in attachment insecurity; rather, it give rise to disinhibited attachment. Also the BEIP study clearly indicates that this has a different meaning from the inhibited variety of reactive attachment disorder. The ERA findings suggested a degree of coherence in the combination of four features, but quite what holds them together remains uncertain. What is clear, however, is that despite initial assumptions to the contrary, institutional deprivation is not particularly associated with an increase in emotional and behavioural disturbances that are independent of prior deprivation-specific features. This means that the widespread reliance on broad-based questionnaires such as the CBCL is unsatisfactory. Numerous findings also indicate that there are considerable problems in relying on cross-sectional data in order to study developmental trajectories.

The longer-term follow-up studies are striking in showing the major gains that often accompanied the persisting effects of institutional deprivation. What mechanisms accounted for these gains? Do they reflect ongoing neural changes of a protective kind? If so, what are those changes? Or do they reflect psychological or mental/behavioural coping mechanisms of some kind? If so, what are they? Most of the research has focused on risk factors and it is equally important to focus on factors that serve to foster positive adaptive outcomes.

A major priority concerns a better elucidation of the nature of extreme deprivation. How do the effects of institutional care of a better quality differ from those associated with profoundly depriving institutions? What are the commonalities and differences between the sequelae of institutional deprivation and abuse or neglect in family settings? Is there a true sensitive period for either the protection in the first 6 months or the effects thereafter? If there is a sensitive period, when does it begin and end and what influences are there on such limits? Comparative human studies are needed but so to are animal models designed to answer these questions.

Finally, there needs to be systematic research designed to foster normal development in children adopted after experiencing institutional deprivation. Much of the evidence to date stems from work with foster children: Do the findings apply equally to children who have suffered institutional deprivation? Most of the treatments used to date focus on parent–child relationships: Should they also focus on the social cognition deficits?

The concept of an extreme deprivation pattern is relatively new, but already it has given rise to many important findings, and has thrown up crucial scientific and clinical challenges.

REFERENCES

American Psychiatric Association (1994) *Diagnostic and Statistical Manual of Mental Disorders*, 4th edn. Washington, DC: American Psychiatric Association.

Ames, E.W. (1990) 'Spitz revisited: A trip to Romanian Orphanages', *Canadian Psychological Association Section Newsletter*, 9: 8–11.

Ames, E.W. (1997) 'The development of Romanian orphanage children adopted into Canada', Final Report to Human Resources Development, Simon Frasier University, Burnaby, Canada.

Ames, E.W. & Chisholm, K. (2001) 'Social and emotional development in children adopted from institutions', in D.B. Bailey, Jr, J.T. Bruer, F.J. Symons, & J.W. Lilchtman (eds), *Critical Thinking about Critical Periods*. Baltimore, MD: Brookes, pp. 129–148.

Astley, S.J., Stachowiak, J., Clarren, S.K., & Clausen, C. (2002) 'Application of the fetal alcohol syndrome facial photographic screening tool in a foster care population', *Journal of Pediatrics,* 141: 712–717.

Bakermans-Kranenburg, M.J., van Ijzendoorn, M.H., & Juffer, F. (2008) 'Earlier is better: a meta-analysis of 70 years of intervention improving cognitive development in institutionalized children', *Monographs of the Society for Research in Child Development,* 73: 279–293.

Barrett, H. (2006) *Attachment and the Perils of Parenting.* London: National Family and Parenting Institute.

Beckett, C., Maughan, B., Rutter, M., Castle, J., Colvert, E., Groothues, C., Kreppner, J., Stevens, S.E., O'Connor, T.G., & Sonuga-Barke, E.J. (2006) 'Do the effects of early severe deprivation on cognition persist into early adolescence? Findings from the English and Romanian Adoptees study', *Child Development,* 77: 696–711.

Behen, M.E., Helder, E., Rothermel, R., Solomon, K., & Chugani, H.T. (2008) 'Incidence of specific absolute neurocognitive impairment in globally intact children with histories of early severe deprivation', *Child Neuropsychology,* 14: 453–469.

Berlin, L., Zeanah, C.H., & Lieberman, A.F., (2008) 'Prevention and intervention programs for supporting early attachment security', in J., Cassidy, & P.R., Shaver, (eds), *Handbook of Attachment: Theory, Research and Clinical Applications,* 2nd edn. New York: Guilford Press, pp. 745–761.

Bos, K., Fox, N., Zeanah, C.H., & Nelson, C.A. (2009) 'Effects of early psychosocial deprivation on the development of memory and executive function', *Frontiers of Behavioral Neuroscience,* 3: 16 (EPub Sep 1).

Bruce, J., Tarulllo, A.R., & Gunnar, M.R. (2009) 'Disinhibited social behavior among internationally adopted children', *Development and Psychopathology,* 21: 157–171.

Carlson, M. & Earls, F. (1997) 'Psychological and neuroendocrinological consequences of early social deprivation in institutionalized children in Romania', *Annals of New York Academy of Sciences,* 807: 419–428.

Castle, J., Groothues, C., Bredenkamp, D., Beckett, C., O'Connor, T., & Rutter, M. (1999) 'ERA Study Team. Effects of qualities of early institutional care on cognitive attainment', *American Journal of Orthopsychiatry,* 69: 424–437.

Chisholm, K. (1998) 'A three year follow-up of attachment and indiscriminate friendliness in children adopted from Romanian orphanages', *Child Development,* 69: 1092–1106.

Chisholm, K., Carter, M.C., Ames, E.W., & Morison, S.J. (1995) 'Attachment security and indiscriminately friendly behaviour in children adopted from Romanian orphanages', *Development and Psychopathology,* 7: 283–294.

Chugani, H.T., Behen, M.E., Buzik, O., Juhasz, C., Nagy, F., & Chugani, D.C. (2001) 'Local brain functional activity following early deprivation: a study of post-institutionalized Romanian orphans', *NeuroImage,* 14: 1290–1301.

Colombo, M., de la Parra, A., & Lopez, I. (1992) 'Intellectual and physical outcome of children undernourished in early life is influenced by later environmental conditions', *Developmental Medicine and Child Neurology,* 34: 611–622.

Curtiss, S. (1977) *Genie: A Psycholinguistic Study of a Modern-Day 'wild child'.* Boston: Academic Press.

Eluvathingal, T.J., Chugani, H.T., Behen, M.E., Juhász, C., Muzik, O., Maqbool, M., Chugani, D.C., & Makki, M. (2006) 'Abnormal brain connectivity in children after early severe socioemotional deprivation: a diffusion tensor imaging study', *Pediatrics,* 117: 2093–2100.

Fisher, P., Gunnar, M.R., Dozier, M., Bruce, J., & Pears, K. (2006) 'Effects of therapeutic interventions for foster children on behaviour problems, caregiver attachment, and stress regulatory neural systems', *Annals of New York Academy of Science,* 1094: 215–225.

Fries, E., Hesse, J., Hellhammer, J., & Hellhammer, D. (2005) 'A new view on hypocortisolism', *Psychoneuroendocrinology,* 30: 1010–1016.

Fries, A.B., Shirtcliff, E.A., & Pollak, S.D. (2008) 'Neuroendocrine dysregulation following early social deprivation in children', *Developmental Psychobiology,* 50: 588–599.

Ghera, M.M., Marshall, P.J., Fox, N.A., Zeanah, C.H., Nelson, C.A., Smyke, A.T., & Guthrie, D. (2009) 'The effects of foster care intervention on socially deprived institutionalized children's attention and positive affect: results from the BEIP study', *Journal of Child Psychology and Psychiatry,* 50: 246–253.

Goldberg, R. (1997) 'Adopting Romanian children: making choices, taking risks', *Marriage and Family Review,* 25: 79–98.

Gray, R., Mukherjee, R.A.S., & Rutter, M. (2009) 'Alcohol consumption during pregnancy and its effects on neurodevelopment: what is known and what remains uncertain', *Addiction,* 140: 1270–1273.

Groark, C.J., Muhamderahmov, R.J., Palmov, O.I., Nikiforova, N.V., & McCall, R.B. (2005) 'Improvements in early care in Russian orphanages and their relationship to observed behaviors', *Infant Mental Health Journal,* 26: 96–109.

Gunnar, M.R. & Fisher, P. (2006) 'Bringing basic research on early experience and stress neurobiology to bear on preventive interventions for neglected and maltreated children', *Development and Psychopathology*, 18: 651–677.

Gunnar M. & Vazquez, D.M. (2006) 'Stress neurobiology and developmental psychopathology', in D. Cicchetti & D. Cohen (eds), *Developmental Psychopathology: Developmental Neuroscience*, 2nd edn, Vol. 2. New York: Wiley, pp. 533–577.

Gunnar, M.R., van Dulmen, J.H.M., & International Adoption Project Team (2007) 'Behavior problems in postinstitutionalized internationally adopted children', *Development and Psychopathology*, 19: 129–148.

Hodges, J. & Tizard, B. (1989a) 'IQ and behavioral adjustment of ex-institutional adolescents', *Journal of Child Psychology and Psychiatry, and Allied Disciplines*, 30: 53–75.

Hodges, J. & Tizard, B. (1989b) 'Social and family relationships of ex-institutional adolescents', *Journal of Child Psychology and Psychiatry*, 30: 77–97.

Hoksbergen, R.A.C., ter Laak, J., van Dijkum, C., Sijk, S., Rijk, K., & Stoutjesdijk, F. (2003) 'Posttraumatic stress disorder in adopted children from Romania', *American Journal of Orthopsychiatry*, 73: 255–265.

Hoksbergen, R., Rijk, K., van Dijkum, C., & ter Laak, J. (2004) 'Adoption of Romanian children in the Netherlands: behavior problems and parenting burden of upbringing of adoptive parents', *Developmental and Behavioral Pediatrics*, 25: 175–180.

Hoksbergen, R., ter Laak, J., Rijk, K., van Dijkum, C., & Stoutjesdijk, F. (2005) 'Post-institutional autistic syndrome in Romanian adoptees', *Journal of Autism and Developmental Disorders*, 35: 615–623.

Joëls, M. & Baram, T.Z. (2009) 'The neuro-symphony of stress', *Nature Reviews Neuroscience*, 10: 459–466.

Johnson, D.E., Miller, L., Iverson, S., Thomas, W., Franchino, B., Dole, K., Kiernan, M., Georgieff, M.K., & Hostetter, M.K. (1992) 'The health of children adopted from Romania', 268: 3446–3451.

Jones, D.P.H. (2008) 'Child maltreatment', in D. Bishop, D. Pine, M. Rutter, S. Scott, J. Stevenson, E. Taylor, & A. Thapar (eds), *Rutter's Child and Adolescent Psychiatry*, 5th edn. Oxford: Blackwell, pp. 421–439.

Judge, S. (2003) 'Developmental recovery and deficit in children adopted from Eastern European orphanages', *Child Psychiatry and Human Development*, 34: 49–62.

Juffer, F. & Van Ijzendoorn, M.H. (2009) 'International adoption comes of age: development of international adoptees from a longitudinal and meta-analytical perspective', in G.M. Wrobel & E. Neil (eds), *International Advances for Adoption Research for Practice*. London: John Wiley & Sons, pp. 169–192.

Kaler, S.R. & Freeman, B.J. (1994) 'Analysis of environmental deprivation: cognitive and social development in Romanian orphans', *Journal of Child Psychology and Psychiatry*, 35: 769–781.

Kertes, D.A., Gunnar, M.R., Madsen, N.J., & Long, J. (2008) 'Early deprivation and home basal cortisol levels: a study of internationally-adopted children', *Developmental Psychopathology*, 20: 473–491.

Kreppner, J.M., O'Connor, T.G., Rutter, M., & ERA Study Team (2001) 'Can inattention/overactivity be an institutional deprivation syndrome?', *Journal of Abnormal Child Psychology*, 29: 513–528.

Kreppner, J., Rutter, M., Marvin, R., O'Connor, T.G., & Sonuga-Barke, E. (2010) 'Assessing the concept of the insecure-other category in the Marvin scheme: changes between 4 and 6 years in the English and Romanian adoptee study', *Social Development*, ePub Jan.

Levine, S. (2005) 'Developmental determinants of sensitivity and resistance to stress', *Psychoneuroendocrinology*, 30: 939–946.

Lien, N.M., Meyer, K.K., & Winick, M. (1977) 'Early malnutrition and "late" adoption: a study of their effects on development of Korean orphans adopted into American families', *American Journal of Clinical Nutrition*, 30: 1734–1739.

Loman, M.M. & Gunnar, M.R. (2010) 'Early experience and the development of stress reactivity and regulation in children', *Neuroscience and Biobehavioral Reviews*, 34: 867–876.

Lord, C., Rutter, M., DiLavore, P.C., & Risi, S. (2001) *Autism Diagnostic Observation Schedule (ADOS Manual)*. Los Angeles, CA: Western Psychological Services.

Lupien, S.J., McEwen, B.S., Gunnar, M.R., & Heim, C. (2009) 'Effects of stress throughout the lifespan on the brain, behaviour and cognition', *Nature Review, Neuroscience*, 10: 434–445.

MacLean, K. (2003) 'The impact of institutionalization on child development', *Development and Psychopathology*, 15: 853–884.

Marcovitch, S., Goldberg, S., Gold, A., Washington, J., Wasson, C., Krekewich, K., & Handley-Derry, M. (1997) 'Determinants of behavioural problems in Romanian children adopted in Ontario', *International Journal of Behavioral Development*, 20: 17–31.

Marshall P.J. & Kenny, J.W. (2009) 'Biological perspectives on the effects of early psychosocial experience', *Developmental Review*, 29: 96–119.

Marshall, P.J., Fox, N.A., & BEIP Core Group (2004) 'A comparison of the electroencephalogram between institutionalized and community children in Romania', *Journal of Cognitive Neuroscience,* 16M: 1327–1338.

Marshall, P.J., Reeb, B.C., Fox, N.A., Nelson, C.A., & Zeanah, C.H. (2008) 'Effects of early intervention on EEG power and coherence in previously institutionalized children in Romania', *Development and Psychopathology,* 20: 861–880.

Mason, P., Narad, C., Jester, T., & Parks, J. (2000) 'A survey of growth and development in the internationally adopted child', *Pediatric Research,* 47. 209A.

Meaney, M. (2010) 'Epigenetics and the biological definition of gene x environment interactions', *Child Development,* 81: 41–79.

Miller, L., Chan, W., Tirella, L., & Perrin, E. (2009) 'Outcomes of children adopted from Eastern Europe', *International Journal of Behavioral Development,* 33: 289–298.

Money, J., Annecillo, C., & Kelly, J.F. (1983a) 'Growth of intelligence: failure and catch-up associated respectively with abuse and rescue in the syndrome of abuse dwarfism', *Psychoneuroendocrinology,* 8: 309–319.

Money, J., Annecillo, C., & Kelley, J.F. (1983b) 'Abuse-dwarfism syndrome: after rescue, statural and intellectual catch-up growth correlate', *Journal of Clinical Child Psychology,* 12: 279–283.

Morison, S.J. & Ellwood, A.L. (2000) 'Resiliency in the aftermath of deprivation: a second look at the development of Romanian orphanage children', *Merrill–Palmer Quarterly,* 46: 717–737.

Morison, S.J., Ames, E.W., & Chisholm, K. (1995) 'The development of children adopted from Romanian orphanages', *Merrill–Palmer Quarterly,* 41: 717–737.

Moulson, M.C., Fox, N.A., Westerlund, A., Zeanah, C.H., & Nelson, C.A. (2009a). 'The effects of early experience on face recognition: an event-related potential study of institutionalized children in Romania', *Child Development,* 80: 1039–1056.

Moulson, M., Fox, N.A., Zeanah, C.H., & Nelson, C.A. (2009b) 'Early adverse experiences and the neurobiology of facial emotion processing', *Developmental Psychology,* 45: 17–30.

Nelson, C.A. (2007) 'A neurobiological perspective on early human deprivation', *Child Development Perspectives,* 1: 13–18.

Nelson, C.A., Zeanah, C.H., Fox, N.A., Marshall, P.J., Smyke, A.T., & Guthrie, D. (2007) 'Cognitive recovery in socially deprived young children: the Bucharest Early Intervention Project', *Science,* 318: 1937–1940.

O'Connor, T.G. & Zeanah, C. (2003) 'Attachment disorders: assessment strategies and treatment approaches', *Attachment and Human Development,* 5: 223–244.

Parker, S.W., Nelson, C.A., & BEIP Core Group (2005a) 'The impact of early institutional rearing on the ability to discriminate facial expressions of emotion: an event-related potential study', *Child Development,* 76: 54–72.

Parker, S.W., Nelson, C.A., & BEIP Core Group (2005b) 'An event-related potential study of the impact of institutional rearing on face recognition', *Development and Psychopathology,* 17: 621–639.

Pollak, S.D., Nelson, C.A., Achlaak, M., Roeber, B., Wewerka, S., Wiik, K., Frenn, K., Loman, M., & Gunnar, M. (2010) 'Neurodevelopmental effects of early deprivation in postinstitutionalized children', *Child Development,* 81: 224–236.

Posner, R.B. (2006) 'Early menarche: a review of research on trends in timing, racial differences, etiology and psychosocial consequences', *Sex Roles,* 54: 315–322.

Roy, P.J. & Rutter, M. (2005) 'Institutional care: associations between inattention and early reading performance', *Journal of Child Psychology and Psychiatry,* 47: 480–487.

Roy, P., Rutter, M., & Pickles, A. (2004) 'Institutional care: associations between overactivity and lack of selectivity in social relationships', *Journal of Child Psychology & Psychiatry,* 48: 17–30.

Rutter, M. (1981) 'Psychological sequelae of brain damage in childhood', *American Journal of Psychiatry,* 138: 1533–1544.

Rutter, M. (1991) 'A fresh look at "maternal deprivation"', in P. Bateson (ed.) *The Development and Integration of Behaviour.* Cambridge: Cambridge University Press, pp. 331–374.

Rutter, M. (2008a) 'Institutional effects on children: design issues and substantive findings. In: The effects of early social-emotional and relationship experience on the development of young orphanage children', *Monographs of the Society for Research and Child Development,* 73: 271–278.

Rutter, M. (2008b) 'Implications of attachment theory and research for child care policies', in J. Cassidy & P.R., Shaver (eds) *Handbook of Attachment: Theory, Research and Clinical Applications.* New York: Guilford Press, pp. 958–974.

Rutter, M. & ERA Study Team. (1998) 'Developmental catch-up, and deficit, following adoption after severe global early privation', *Journal of Child Psychology and Psychiatry, and Allied Disciplines,* 39: 465–476.

Rutter, M. & Sonuga-Barke, E.J. (eds) (2010) 'Deprivation-specific psychological patterns: effects of institutional deprivation. The English and Romanian Adoptees Study Team', *Monographs of the Society for Research in Child Development.* Serial no. 295, Vol. 75, No. 1.

Rutter, M., Andersen-Wood, L., Beckett, C., Bredenkamp, D., Castle, J., Groothues, C., Kreppner, J.M., Keaveney, L., Lord, C., O'Connor, T.G., & ERA Study Team (1999) 'Quasi-autistic patterns following severe early global privation', *Journal of Child Psychology and Psychiatry*, 40: 537–549.

Rutter, M.L., Kreppner, J.M., O'Connor, T.G., & English and Romanian Adoptees (ERA) Study Team (2001) 'Specificity and heterogeneity in children's responses to profound institutional privation', *British Journal of Psychiatry*, 179: 97–103.

Rutter, M., Bailey, A., & Lord, C. (2003a). *The Social Communication Questionnaire (SCQ).* Los Angeles, CA: Western Psychological Services.

Rutter, M., Le Couteur, A., & Lord, C. (2003b). *Autism Diagnostic Interview revised (ADI-R).* Los Angeles, CA: Western Psychological Services.

Rutter, M., Colvert, E., Kreppner, J.M., Beckett, C., Castle, J., Groothues, C., Hawkins, A., O'Connor, T.G., Stevens, S.E., & Sonuga-Barke, E.J. (2007a) 'Early adolescent outcomes for institutionally-deprived and non-deprived adoptees. I: disinhibited attachment', *Journal of Child Psychology and Psychiatry*, 48: 17–30.

Rutter, M., Kreppner, J.M., Croft, C., Murin, M., Colvert, E., Beckett, C., Castle, J., & Sonuga-Barke, E.J. (2007b) 'Early adolescent outcomes for institutionally deprived and non-deprived adoptees. III: Quasi-autism', *Journal of Child Psychology and Psychiatry*, 48: 17–30.

Rutter, M., Kreppner, J., & Sonuga-Barke, E. (2009a) 'Emanuel Miller Lecture: Attachment insecurity, disinhibited attachment, and attachment disorders: where do research findings leave the concepts?', *Journal of Child Psychology and Psychiatry*, 50: 529–543.

Rutter, M., Beckett, C., Castle, J., Kreppner, J., Stevens, S., & Sonuga-Barke, E.J. (2009b) *Policy and Practice Implications from the English and Romanian Adoptees (ERA) Study: Forty Five Key Questions.* London: BAAF.

Rymer, R. (1993) *Genie: Escape from a Silent Childhood.* London: Michael Joseph.

Selman, P. (2009) 'From Bucharest to Beijing; changes in countries sending children for international adoption 1990 to 2006', in G. Wrobel & E. Neill (eds), *International Advances in Adoption Research*, Chichester: John Wiley, pp. 41–69.

Skuse, D. (1984) 'Extreme deprivation in early childhood—II. Theoretical issues and a comparative review', *Journal of Child Psychology and Psychiatry*, 25: 543–572.

Sloutsky, V.M. (1997) 'Institutional care and developmental outcomes of 6- and-7-year-old children: a contextual perspective', *International Journal of Behavioral Development*, 20: 131–151.

Smith, M.G. & Fong, R. (2004) *The Children of Neglect: When No One Cares.* New York: Brunner-Routledge.

Smyke, A.T., Zeanah, C.H., Nathan, M.D., Fox, A., Nelson, C.A., & Guthrie, D. (2010) 'Placement in foster care enhances quality of attachment among young institutionalized children', *Child Development*, 81: 212–223.

Sonuga-Barke, E.J. & Rubia, K. (2008) 'Inattentive/overactive children with histories of profound institutional deprivation compared with standard ADHD cases: a brief report', *Child: Care, Health and Development*, 34: 596–602.

Sonuga-Barke, E.J., Beckett, C., Kreppner, J., Castle, J., Colvert, E., Stevens, S., Hawkins, A., & Rutter, M. (2008) 'Is sub-nutrition necessary for a poor outcome following early institutional deprivation?', *Developmental Medicine and Child Neurology*, 50: 664–671.

Spinelli, S., Chefer, S., Suomi, S.J., Higley, J.D., Barr, C.S., & Stein, E. (2009) 'Early-life stress induces long-term morphologic changes in primate brain', *Archives of General Psychiatry*, 66: 658–665.

Stevens, S.E., Sonuga-Barke, E.J., Kreppner, J.M., Beckett, C., Castle, J., Colvert, E., Groothues, C., Hawkins, A., & Rutter, M. (2008) 'Inattention/overactivity following early severe institutional deprivation: presentation and associations in early adolescence', *Journal of Abnormal Child Psychology*, 36: 385–398.

St. Petersburg–USA Orphanage Research Team (2008) 'The effects of early social-emotional and relationship experience on the development of young orphanage children', *Monographs of the Society for Research in Child Development*, 73: 1–262, 294–5.

Tarullo, A.R., Bruce, J., & Gunnar, M.R. (2007) 'False belief and emotion understanding in post-institutionalized children', *Social Development*, 16: 57–78.

Taylor, E. & Sonuga-Barke, E.J. (2008) 'Disorders of attention and activity', in M. Rutter, D. Bishop, D. Pine, S. Scott, J. Stevenson, E. Taylor & A. Thapar (eds), *Rutter's Child and Adolescent Psychiatry*, 5th edn. Oxford: Blackwell, pp. 521–542.

Tieman, W., Van der Ende, J., & Verhulst, F.C. (2005) 'Psychiatric disorders in young adult intercountry adoptees: an epidemiological study', *American Journal of Psychiatry*, 162: 592–598.

Tieman, W., Van der Ende, J., & Verhulst, F.C. (2006) 'Social functioning in young adult intercountry adoptees compared to nonadoptees', *Social Psychiatry and Psychiatric Epidemiology*, 41: 68–74.

Tizard, B. & Hodges, J. (1978) 'The effect of institutional rearing on the development of 8-year-old children', *Journal of Child Psychology and Psychiatry*, 19: 99–118.

Tizard, B. & Rees, J. (1974) 'A comparison of the effects of adoption, restoration to the natural mother, and continued institutionalization on the cognitive development of four-year-old children', *Child Development*, 45: 92–99.

Tottenham, N., Hare, T., Quinn, B., McCarry, T., Nurse, M., Gilhooly, T., et al. (2010) 'Prolonged institutional rearing is associated with atypically larger amygdala volume and difficulties in emotion regulation', *Developmental Science*, 13: 46–61.

Tuvemo, T. & Proos, L.A. (1993) 'Girls adopted from developing countries: a group at risk of early pubertal development and short final height. Implications for health surveillance and treatment', *Annals of Medicine*, 25: 217–219.

Tuvemo, T., Gustafsson, J., & Proos, L.A. (1999) 'Growth hormone treatment during suppression of early puberty in adopted girls', *Acta Paediatrica*, 88: 928–932.

Utting, W. (1991) *Children in the Public Care: A Review of Residential Child Care*. London: HMSO.

van der Vegt, E.J., Tieman, W., van der Ende, J., Ferdinand, R.F., Verhulst, F.C., & Tiemeier, H. (2009a) 'Impact of early childhood adversities on adult psychiatric disorders: a study of international adoptees', *Social Psychiatry and Psychiatric Epidemiology*, 44: 724–731.

van der Vegt, E.J., van der Ende, J., Ferdinand, R.F., Verhulst, F.C., & Tiemeier, H. (2009b) 'Early childhood adversities and trajectories of psychiatric problems in adoptees: evidence for long lasting effects', *Journal of Abnormal Child Psychology*, 37: 239–249.

Van Ijzendoorn, M.H. & Juffer, F. (2006) 'The Emmanuel Miller Memorial Lecture 2006. Adoption as intervention. Meta-analytic evidence for massive catch-up and plasticity in physical, socio-emotional, and cognitive development', *Journal of Child Psychology and Psychiatry*, 47: 1228–1245.

Van Ijzendoorn, M.H., Bakermans-Kranenburg, M.J., & Juffer, F. (2007) 'Plasticity of growth in height, weight and head circumference: meta-analytic evidence of massive catch-up after international adoption', *Journal of Developmental and Behavioral Pediatrics*, 28: 334–343.

Van Ijzendoorn, M.H., Lujik, M.P., & Juffer, F. (2008) 'IQ of children growing up in children's homes: a meta-analysis on IQ delays in orphanages', *Merrill–Palmer Quarterly*, 54: 341–366.

Verhulst, F.C. & Versluis-den Bieman, H.J. (1995) 'Developmental course of problem behaviors in adolescent adoptees', *Journal of the American Academy of Child & Adolescent Psychiatry*, 34: 151–159.

Verhulst, F.C., Althaus, M., & Versluis-den Bieman, H.J. (1990) 'Problem behavior in international adoptees: I. An epidemiological study', *Journal of the American Academy of Child and Adolescent Psychiatry*, 29: 94–103.

Virdis, R., Street, M.E., Zampolli, M., Radetti, G., Pezzini, B., Benelli, M., Ghizzoni, L., & Volta, C. (1998) 'Precocious puberty in girls adopted from developing countries', *Archives of Disease in Childhood*, 78: 152–154.

Vorria, P., Papaligoura, Z., Dunn, J., van Ijzendoorn, M.H., Steele, H., Kontopoulou, A., & Sarafidou, Y. (2003) 'Early experiences and attachment relationship of Greek infants raised in residential group care', *Journal of Child Psychology and Psychiatry*, 44: 1208–1220.

Vorria, P., Papaligoura, Z., Sarafidou, J., Kopakaki, M., Dunn, J., van Ijzendoorn, M.H., & Kontopoulou, A. (2006) 'The development of adopted children after institutional care: a follow-up study', *Journal of Child Psychology and Psychiatry*, 47: 1246–1253.

Winick, M., Meyer, K.K., & Harris, R.C. (1975) 'Malnutrition and environmental enrichment by early adoption: development of adopted Korean children differing greatly in early nutritional status is examined', *Science*, 190: 1173–1175.

Wolkind, S. (1974) 'The components of "affectionless psychopathy" in institutionalized children', *Journal of Child Psychology and Psychiatry*, 15: 215–220.

Zeanah, C.H., Nelson, C.A., Fox, N.A., Smyke, A.T., Marshall, P., Parker, S., & Koga, S. (2003) 'Effects of institutionalization on brain and behavioural development: the Bucharest Early Intervention Project', *Development and Psychopathology*, 15: 885–907.

Zeanah, C.H., Smyke, A.T., Koga, S., Carlson, E., & BEIP Core Group (2005) 'Attachment in institutionalized and community children in Romania', *Child Development*, 76: 1015–1028.

Author Index

Subject Index